A DICTIONARY OF THE OJIBWAY LANGUAGE

A DICTIONARY OF THE OJIBWAY LANGUAGE

Frederic Baraga

With a New Foreword by
John D. Nichols

BOREALIS

MINNESOTA HISTORICAL SOCIETY PRESS • ST. PAUL

Borealis Books are high-quality paperback reprints of books chosen by the Minnesota Historical Society Press for their importance as enduring historical sources and their value as enjoyable accounts of life in the Upper Midwest.

Cover: front, Minnesota Historical Society Collections; back, Smithsonian Institution (Frances Densmore)

∞ The paper used in this publication meets the minimum requirements for the American National Standard for Information Sciences –Permanence for Printed Library Materials, ANSI Z39.48–1984.

This book is bound in Otabind, a process providing a detached, flexible spine that allows the opened book to lie flat during use.

MINNESOTA HISTORICAL SOCIETY PRESS, St. Paul 55102

First published as *A Dictionary of the Otchipwe Language* by Beauchemin & Valois, Montreal, 1878, 1880

International Standard Book Number 0-87351-281-2
Manufactured in the United States of America
10 9 8 7 6 5 4 3 2

Library of Congress Cataloging-in-Publication Data

Baraga, Friedrich, 1797–1868.
[Dictionary of the Otchipwe language]
A dictionary of the Ojibway language / Frederic Baraga : with a new foreword by John D. Nichols.
p. cm. – (Borealis books)
Originally published under title: A dictionary of the Otchipwe language. Montreal : Beauchemin & Valois, 1878.
ISBN 0-87351-281-2 (alk. paper)
1. Ojibwa language–Dictionaries–English. 2. English language–Dictionaries–Ojibwa. I. Nichols, John (John D.) II. Title.
PM853.B28 1992
497'.3–dc20 92-28915

FOREWORD TO THE REPRINT EDITION

Bishop Baraga's *Dictionary of the Otchipwe Language* of 1853 and the companion *Theoretical and Practical Grammar of the Otchipwe Language* of 1850 are enduring monuments of missionary linguistics. Of the hundreds of dictionaries and grammars of the North American languages that European missionaries made as tools in their campaign to supplant indigenous beliefs, few have proven as useful and durable as Baraga's. Language teachers across the Upper Midwest and Eastern and Central Canada, whether they speak Algonquin, Chippewa, Ojibway, Ottawa, or Saulteaux, continue to find the dictionary a useful reference, one which reminds them and community elders of old words, rarely heard today or totally lost. Tattered copies of the original editions are rare books, and even recent reprints have become eagerly sought after treasures. Academic linguists continue to cite the dictionary in comparative and historical studies of languages and find it indispensable in retrieving ancient words from living speakers. This reprint of the posthumous revised edition of 1878–80 will extend the useful life of the dictionary into another century.

The "Otchipwe" language of this dictionary is generally known today as Ojibway (often spelled Ojibwa or Ojibwe),* with the names Algonquin, Chippewa, Ottawa or Odawa, and Saulteaux used as local names in English. Its speakers call themselves *Anishinaabe* and the language *Anishinaabemowin.* It is genetically related to about twenty-five other languages in the Algonquian language family, one of forty to fifty

*The spelling *Ojibwe* is that of the most widely used contemporary writing system for the language; the spelling *Ojibway* is preferred by the Minnesota Historical Society Press.

separate families of languages and isolated single languages spoken in aboriginal North America. One of the most widespread of North American languages, it is spoken today in the United States in Michigan, Minnesota, North Dakota, and Wisconsin and in Canada in Manitoba, Ontario, Saskatchewan, and Quebec. In numbers of speakers, it is perhaps the fourth largest; recent estimates, almost certainly too high, give around fifty thousand speakers. In the United States and Southern Canada, it is spoken mainly by people of middle age and older; in some communities only the elderly are fluent. In much of Canada, it is often spoken by Anishinaabe of all ages and still learned by children as a mother tongue. While some communities use writing, radio, and television as media for the language, and most Anishinaabe communities see that the language is taught in their schools or community centers, its survival – like that of all other indigenous languages – is threatened by the immigrant languages English and French.

Ojibway is not a single language, spoken in a common form across its range, but a chain of connected dialects or local varieties. Each local variety differs from adjacent ones in details of sounds, words, and grammar. For example, the word for 'table', given as *adopowin* (*adoopowin*) in this dictionary, can also be heard in different places as *adoopowinaak, doopwin, wiisiniwaagan, wiisiniiwinaak, achigan,* or *achiganaatig.* Speakers of one local variety can be generally understood by speakers of the adjacent dialects, but the small differences pile up across distances so that people from one place may have a great deal of difficulty understanding or communicating with people from somewhere distant.

The main dialects represented in the dictionary are those that were spoken 150 years ago on the south shore of Lake Superior. However, nearly all the basic patterns of the words and the meaningful building blocks in them are the same across the whole language and, as a comparison of the words of this dictionary with several contemporary dialects has shown, have changed little since Baraga's time. Individual words have been left behind as ways of life have changed; few today will use *agwingweon* (*agwiingwe'on*) 'cradleboard bow' or *nandobani* (*nandobani*) 'goes on a war party'. Some words have changed or added meanings; for example, *odâbân* (*odaabaan*) 'sled, sleigh' now has the added meaning of 'car'. The extensive derivational and compounding mechanisms of the language have come into play to form new words for a wide range of modern activities and objects from 'wear lipstick' to 'computer'. Of course, the preinvasion language had already been adapted to European customs and technology as the dictionary entries for 'Christian', 'gun', 'rail-road', and 'violin' indicate. English too has changed, and translations in the dictionary such as "bodkin" and "apothecary" or spellings such as "warf" and "musketo" may puzzle some. All languages also change slowly and imperceptibly in the sounds they use. The contemporary Ottawa-Odawa dialect provides an example of sound change in Ojibway. A process called syncope has shortened words by dropping out certain short vowels: Baraga's Ottawa word *assiponigan* 'scissors' is now pronounced without the first and third vowels as *ssipnigan* (*sipnigan*).

Frederic Baraga was born in 1797 in Slovenia, then part of Austria. From a well-to-do family, he studied law at the University of Vienna and in 1821 entered a seminary. Two years later he was ordained a Roman Catholic priest. After some years serving parishes in his homeland, he left for America to enter the frontier missions. In early 1831 he stopped off in Cincinnati to improve his English and begin the study of Ottawa, the language of Arbre Croche (now Harbor Springs, Michigan), an occasional mission location since the seventeenth century that had been selected as Baraga's first station. He studied with William Maccatebinessi, an Ottawa preparing for the priesthood. At the end of May 1831 he arrived at Arbre Croche. Initially he performed his duties in French and used an interpreter but quickly acquired functional Ottawa. Within a year he had revised a predecessor's Ottawa catechism and prayers and seen to their publication in Detroit.

In the summer of 1835 he transferred his work to LaPointe on Madeleine Island in Lake Superior. Here Baraga shifted dialects from Ottawa to the closely related Ojibway and revised his Ottawa books into Ojibway, arranging for their first publication in Paris while on a European trip in 1836–37. From LaPointe, Baraga traveled to communities in Michigan, Minnesota, Ontario, and Wisconsin. L'Anse became his headquarters in 1843, and then ten years later he moved to Sault Ste. Marie when he was appointed the first bishop for Upper Michigan. He died in Marquette in 1868.

Baraga's linguistic work with Ojibway followed the course set by the Recollet and Jesuit missionaries to New France. He was armed with a classical education and thus knowledgeable about grammar as a scholarly discipline. He was multilingual, having in addition to the French and Latin of his predecessors his native Slovenian, as well as English, German, and Italian. He was schooled in the target language before entering the field and was familiar with a missionary grammatical and orthographic tradition for Algonquian languages. Although few of the earlier grammars and dictionaries had been published, manuscript copies were widely circulated among missionaries. On arrival at his first station, he was immersed in the Anishinaabe language environment and aided by an interpreter. He wrote down words and phrases in notebooks, a practice begun when he was in Cincinnati. These notebooks were later incorporated into the dictionary and grammar. The first translations of liturgical and devotional literature into Ottawa were followed by a primer, Bible extracts, a life of Christ, and a collection of sermons in both Ottawa and Ojibway versions.

The manuscript of the dictionary took final form in 1852 when Baraga transcribed the words from his notebooks. In March 1853, he bundled it up and rode to Detroit to seek publication but nearly lost it when his sleigh went through the ice near Green Bay. Disappointed by the printers in Detroit, who lacked the necessary equipment, he had to travel on to Cincinnati, where he worked until July correcting the proofs.

This reprint is of the second edition of the dictionary, which was published at Montreal in two parts in 1878 and 1880 and edited by Albert Lacombe, who had been a missionary to the Western Cree. He switched the order of the parts, thus placing Baraga's original introduction at the beginning of the second part, introduced Cree words into some entries for English words in the first part, and added a section on the native origins of place names and tribal names. He also revised Baraga's orthography (but failed to improve it) and changed some spellings to conform to Manitoba Saulteaux pronunciation. Baraga's grammatical codes survived only on the first few pages of the second part.

The writing system used in the dictionary was revised by Lacombe from Baraga's modification of an older one. Baraga's system of accents, partly indicating vowel length, stress, and nasalization, was reduced to the use of a circumflex for vowel length, used regularly only over *a*. The following table compares this dictionary system with a widely used contemporary orthography, devised by C. E. Fiero and based on an analysis of Ojibway sounds by the linguist Leonard Bloomfield.

Table

Fiero Orthography	Baraga-Lacombe Orthography
a	a
aa	â, a
b	b-, p-, b
ch	tch
d	d-, t-, d
e	e [occasionally with varying accents]
g	g-, k-, g
' [glottal stop]	[not written]
i	i
ii	i
j	dj
k	k
m	m
n	n
o	o
oo	o, ô
p	p
s	ss
sh	sh
t	t
w	w
y	i
z	s
zh	j

The most important difference between the two orthographies is not that words are spelled using different letters, although that is the most obvious one. The older system represents the sounds of Ojibway impressionistically, as filtered through European ears, while the newer one represents the basic sounds of Ojibway that actually function within the language to distinguish one word from another.

Ojibway has seven main vowels: short *a*, short *i*, and short *o*, three long vowels (which actually take longer to say) paired with the short ones, and an unpaired long vowel *e*. The Baraga-Lacombe orthography regularly distinguishes only one of the long vowels from its paired short vowel; a circumflex is often placed over the long vowel *â* while the short vowel is usually left unmarked. The other long vowels paired with short vowels are nearly always unmarked, but the unpaired long *e* is often given with an accent. In the Fiero orthography the long vowels are distinguished from the paired short vowels by being written double: *a* and *aa*, *i* and *ii*, *o* and *oo;* the unpaired *e* is left unmarked. The difference between the short and long vowels is fundamental to the language, signaling differences in meaning as shown in the following examples, written first in the dictionary orthography and then in the Fiero orthography: 'during the summer'–'in water' *(nibing/niibing)*–*(nibing/nibiing)*; 'he/she works'–'he/she hires' *(anoki/anokii)*–*(anoki/anookii)*.

The Ojibway consonants have always given Europeans trouble. For each place of articulation (the lips, the alveolar ridge behind the teeth, and the soft palate) there are two different stop consonants: a *weak* consonant, often accompanied by the vibration of the vocal chords called voicing, and a *strong* consonant, never accompanied by voicing. Europeans tend to associate the voiced variants of the first kind of stop consonants with their voiced consonants (written b, d, g, etc.) and the voiceless variants of the first kind and all of the second kind with their unvoiced consonants (written p, t, k, etc.). The situation is similar for the sibilant consonants. The actual stop consonants and sibilant consonants of Ojibway and the European languages do not match up one to one. Baraga, following a long tradition of missionary linguists, wrote as if the speakers of Ojibway were mixing up their own language:

> There are some consonants which the Indians don't pronounce distinctly and uniformly. They very often confound the letters B and P, D and T, G and K. It is often impossible to ascertain, by the pronunciation of an Indian, whether the word begins with a B or P, with a D or T, with a G or K (Pt. II, vii).

The problem lies not in the pronunciation of the Anishinaabe but in the perception and analysis of the sounds by the speakers of European languages. The only serious effect of this on the dictionary is in the way the initial consonants of words are written. At the beginning of Ojibway words (but not contemporary Ottawa-Odawa words), the only stop or sibilant consonants permitted are the weak ones. Since Europeans pay attention to the optional voicing of the weak consonants, they have difficulty writing them consistently, sometimes writing them one way and sometimes writing them another way. Baraga solved the problem by placing some of the words beginning with weak consonants in the sections beginning with the voiced letters *b-*, *d-*, *g-* and others in the section beginning with the voiceless letters *p-*, *t-*, and *k-*. The division is essentially an arbitrary one.

Baraga humbly introduced his dictionary by acknowledging that "it is yet very defective and imperfect." Some 150 years later it is not only a classic, but still the largest Ojibway dictionary and the most useful over the range of dialects. The main motivation for the writing of such dictionaries was to help newly arrived missionaries learn the language, as indicated by the bold subtitle of the first edition, "For the Use of Missionaries." But Baraga was a scholar as well as a missionary; he realized that language reflects the experiences of its speakers through time and was fascinated by the complex inner workings of the language. He offered his linguistic works to students of Indian history and "to the Philologist, to whom it affords pleasure and acquirement, to compare the grammatical systems of different languages." That the Anishinaabe themselves would find the dictionary important was perhaps unseen by him.

JOHN D. NICHOLS

Department of Native Studies
University of Manitoba
Winnipeg

Bibliography

References and suggestions for further reading about Algonquian and other North American languages

Goddard, Ives. "Algonkian Languages." In *International Encyclopedia of Linguistics*, edited by William Bright, 1:44–48. New York: Oxford University Press, 1992.

Pentland, David H., and H. Christoph Wolfart. *Bibliography of Algonquian Linguistics*. Winnipeg: University of Manitoba Press, 1982. Essential for locating books about Ojibway and updated in the quarterly *Algonquian and Iroquoian Linguistics*.

Pilling, James Constantine. *Bibliography of the Algonquian Languages*. Smithsonian Institution, Bureau of American Ethnology Bulletin no. 13. Washington, 1891. Lists all the early books in and about Ojibway, including those of Baraga.

Rhodes, Richard, and Evelyn M. Todd. "Subarctic Algonquian Languages." In *Handbook of North American Indians*, edited by William C. Sturtevant, 6:52–66. Washington: Smithsonian Institution Press, 1981.

Rood, David S. "North American Languages." In *International Encyclopedia of Linguistics*, edited by William Bright, 3:110–15. New York: Oxford University Press, 1992.

About Bishop Baraga and Missionary Linguistics

Baraga, Frederic. *The Diary of Bishop Frederic Baraga: First Bishop of Marquette, Michigan*. Edited by Regis M. Walling and N. Daniel Rupp. Translated by Joseph Gregorich and Paul Prud'homme. Detroit: Wayne State University Press, 1990. Diary of 1852–63, published with excellent introductory material, including a brief biography by Regis Walling, and a bibliography.

Čuješ, Rudolf P. *Ninidjanissidog Saiagiinagog: Contributions of the Slovenes to the Sociocultural Development of the Canadian Indians*. Antigonish, Nova Scotia: St. Francis Xavier University Press, 1968.

Hanzeli, Victor Egon. *Missionary Linguistics in New France: A Study of Seventeenth- and Eighteenth-Century Descriptions of American Indian Languages.* The Hague: Mouton, 1969.

Verwyst, Chrysostomus. *Life and Labors of Rt. Rev. Frederic Baraga, First Bishop of Marquette, Mich.* Milwaukee: M. H. Wiltzius, 1900.

Editions of Baraga's Dictionary and Grammar

Baraga, Frederic. *A Dictionary of the Otchipwe Language, Explained in English.* Cincinnati: Joseph A. Hermann, 1853. Reprint, Ann Arbor, Mich.: University Microfilms, n.d.

——. *A Dictionary of the Otchipwe Language, Explained in English . . . A New Edition by a Missionary of the Oblates.* [Edited by Albert Lacombe.] Montreal: Beauchemin & Valois, 1878 (Pt. I), 1880 (Pt. II). Reprint, Minneapolis: Ross and Haines, 1966, 1973; St. Paul: Minnesota Historical Society Press, Borealis Books, 1992.

——. *A Theoretical and Practical Grammar of the Otchipwe Language.* Detroit: Jabez Fox, 1850. Reprint, Ann Arbor, Mich.: University Microfilms, n.d.

——. *A Theoretical and Practical Grammar of the Otchipwe Language . . . A Second Edition by a Missionary of the Oblates.* [Edited by Albert Lacombe.] Montreal: Beauchemin & Valois, 1878.

A DICTIONARY

OF THE

OTCHIPWE LANGUAGE,

EXPLAINED IN ENGLISH.

PART I.

ENGLISH-OTCHIPWE.

By R. R. BISHOP BARAGA.

A NEW EDITION, BY A MISSIONARY OF THE OBLATES.

Let foreign nations of their language boast,
And, proud, with skilful pen, man's fate record ;
I like the tongue, which speak our men, our coast,
Who cannot dress it well, want wit not word.

MONTREAL:
BEAUCHEMIN & VALOIS, Publishers,
256 and 258, St. Paul Street.

1878

NOTICE.

The reader must not expect to find all the words of the English language in this first Part of the Otchipwe Dictionary, but, of course, only such as can be given in Otchipwe. There are thousands of technical expressions and scientific words in English (and in every other civilized language), for which the uncultivated and unlearned Indian languages have no terms.

Many English words are abbreviated in the different articles in this Part, which, however, will be easily understood by the *first* word of the article. For instance, in the article "Abolish", you will find, "I ab. it"; which means, I abolish it.—And so on respectively.

REMARKS

ON THE NEW EDITION OF THE ENGLISH OTCHIPWE DICTIONARY.

1° Wherever there is a circumflex accent on *â* or any other vowel, this letter is pronounced very long and with a certain emphasis ; v. g. *osâgiân,* he loves him ; *âmô,* a bee. When the vowels are not accompanied by this sign, they are regarded as short ; v. g. *sagaigan,* a nail.

2° The indian words placed between parenthesis ( ) are the Cree words corresponding to the Otchipwe expressions. The Cree verbs are always indicated by the 3rd. person singular of the Indicative mood, while in the Otchipwe they are known by the 1st. person singular ; v. g , Otch., *nind ina,* I tell him ; Cree : *itew,* he tells him. This last idiom does not use the sign of the pronoun o, in the 3rd person ; it is included in the verb or rather in its termination.

3° The idea of putting a certain number of Cree words to correspond with Otchipwe sayings, is 1st. to familiarize the people of Manitoba and of the North-West with some expressions which, although Cree by themselves, are employed, nevertheless, by those talking the Otchipwe in this country ; in the second place, to show to philologists some of the comparative differences existing between the roots of those two sister languages.

In fact, there are no Indian dialects which present more simitude than the Otchipwe or Sauteux and the Cree which are spoken by the Indians and the Half-breeds of the Province of Manitoba. The Otchipwe language, which is nothing else, (with but few variations,) than the Algonquin,forms one of the daughters of the great Algic family, whose harangues were heard, in olden times, on the borders of the St. Lawrence and Mississipi rivers, on the shores of lake Superior, and even as far as the immense plains of the Red River. The names of rivers, of lakes and of diverse places in Otchipwe or Cree, are still in use to attest, in future times, the existence of these languages and reclaim their rights to first possession. Obliged to disappear before the white man, the haughty savage will compel his invader to preserve these first denominations, at the risk, however, of seeing them disfigured. The Dominion of Canada in adjoining to her possessions the new territories, is anxious to give them Indian names, wishing undoubtedly, by this attention, to spare the sensitive feelings of *her brother*.

As regards the relations existing between the Otchipwe and Cree, we know beforehand that we shall please indianalogists, by placing under their notice, the different resemblances and' disparities which characterize the two idioms. It is difficult to demonstrate the precise time in which one has been derived from the other and has had its proper autonomy ; for, all the ancient Missionaries and the travellers in the North-West speak, in their writings, of the Otchipwe or Sauteux, and of the Crees or Kinistineaux.

Negation.— In Otchipwe, the negation is indicated by *kawin*, before the verb with the ending *ssi;* while in Cree we simply place *namawiya* or *nama*, as the negative sign before the verb, without changing the latter ; v. g. Otch. *nin sâgia*, I love him ; neg. *kawin nin sâgiâssi*, I don't love him ; Cree : *ni sâkihaw*, neg. *namawiya ni sâkihaw*. For the participle, we say : Otch. *wiyâbamâd*, neg. *wiyâbamâssik*, he, not seeing him ; Cree, *wiyâbamât*, neg. *eka wiyâbamât*.

In these two dialects the roots are almost always the same.

1° In Otch. : Whenever (with very few exceptions) two consonants follow each other ; usually, the first is changed into *s*, for the Cree word, and *vice versa*.

Otchipwe.		Cree.
(*) *akki*	earth	*askïy*
akkik	kettle	*askik*
ikkwe	woman	*iskwew*
sakka-on	cane-stick	*saskahun*
wiskwi	bladder	*wikkwëy*
nappâtch	the wrong way	*naspâtsh*

2° When the Otchipwe word begins by *O*, this letter is sometimes changed into *Wa* in Cree; v. g. *Onishka,* he rises up; in Cree, *Waniskaw; Ottawa, Watawa.*

3° *Na, No,* in Otchipwe, is sometimes changed into *ya, yo,* in Cree; v. g. *notin,* wind, *yotin; onâgan,* plate, *oyâgan; onagima,* he is judged so much, *oyakimaw.*

4° For the orthography of the Cree-words, we have thought proper to follow the Cree dictionaries; v. g. *U,* as the french *ou* or the Italian *u; y,* when two syllables follow each other, as in the sounds of *ya, ye, yi, yo.*

(*) Although there is, usually, only one consonant in the Otchipwe Dictionary, we here employ two because the sound of the double consonant undoubtedly exists in the pronunciation.

Some Rules for the formation of the Imperative mood of a certain number of Verbs.

All the verbs terminated, at the first person of the indic. in	Form the imperative	ex:				
âna, àna	in j	nind	awokkana,	awakkaj		
		nin	nagana	nagaj		
êna	n	nind	ajena,	ajen		
ina, îna	n	nin	webina,	webin		
		nim	pakitîna,	pakitin		
ina, îna	j	nind	ijiwina,	ijiwij		
		nim	pîna,	pij		
ôna	j	nind	anôna,	anoj		
ona	n	nin	dibakona,	dibakon		
ahân, ahige, ahwa	ah	nind	ijinijahwa,	ijinaj	*passif*	ogo
ehan, ehige, ehwa	eh	nim	bakkitehwa,	bakkiteh	*passif*	ogo
ihân, ihige, ihwa	ih	nin	jijobihwa,	jijobih	*passif*	ogo
ohân, ohige, ohwa	oh					
assa, essa, issa, ossa	shi	nind	assa,	ashi		
		nin	nissa,	nishi		
		nin	gossa,	goshi		
awa	aw	nin	dotawa	dotaw		
awa	aw	nin	windamawa	windamaw		

kawa		kaw	nim	pindikeheskawa,	pindikeheskaw *passif*	kago
ama		m	nin	wâbama,	wâbam	
ema			nind	inapinema,	inapinem	
ima			nin	kikenima,	kikenim	
oma			nin	ganzoma,	ganzom	
am		n	nin	gaskendam,	gaskendan	
a	to the 3d pers. sing.	n	nin	mâdja,	mâdjan	
e			nim	pimusse,	pimussen	
i			nim	pasikwi,	pasikwin	
o			nim	pimipato,	pimipaton	
ân		an	nin	kikendân,	kikendân	
ên		en	nind	atawen,	atawên	
in		in	nin	midjin,	midjin	
ôn		on	nin	sâkiton,	sâkiton	
ânan		an	nind	ijânan,	ijan	
enan		en	nind	atawagênan,	atawagên	
inan		in	nind	anokkinan	anokkin	
onan		on	nind	appênimonan,	appênimon	
aha		ah	nin	kitimaha,	kitimah	
eha		eh	nin	nipeha,	nipeh	
iha		ih	nim	pimâdjiha,	pimâdjih	
oha		oh	nin	moha,	moh	
jwa		j	nin	manijwa,	manij	
swa		s	nin	pâsswa,	pâss	
with some few exceptions v. g.			nin	kiskijwa	kiskijwi	
			nin	tchâkiswa	tchâkiswi &c.	
			nim	minopwa	minop	

A

A, an, *bejig.* (Peyak).

Abandon; I abandon, I give up, *nind anawendjige, nind anijitam.* I abandon him, (her, it) *nin nagana, nin webina, nind iniwea; nin nagadan, nin webinan, nind iniwean.* I abandon myself, *nind iniweidis.* I abandon it, (a habit,) *nin boniton.* (Ni nakataw).

Abandoned, (in s. in.) S. Rejected.

Abase, (in. s. in.) S. Lower.

Abhor, (hate); I abhor him, (her, it), *nin gagwânissagenima; nin gagwânissagendan.*

Abide; I abide in him or with him. S. Enter into him.

Ability, *wawingesiwin.* (Mitoniwin).

Abject. S. Low, (mean.)

Able, (skilful;) I am able, *nin wawinges.* (Ni mitonin).

Able; I am able to do it, *nin gashkiton.*

Abolish; I ab. it, *nind angoton, nind angoshkan.* I abolish it for him, or s. th. relating to him, *nind angotamawa.*

Abolished; it is ab., *angoshkamagad, angotchigade.*

Abominable, (in s. in.) S. Hateful.

Abominable; I am (it is) abom., *nin gagwânissagendagos, nin gagwanissagis; gagwânissagendagwad, gagwânissagad.*

Abort; *gih nissi,* or, *gih nissishin.* (Nipahikosissew).

Abortive fruit of the womb, *mashkijan.*

Abound; it abounds, (there is much of it,) *mishinad, bataínad.* (Mitchetin).

About, (almost,) *géga.*

Above, *pagidji; ishpiming.*

Abridgment of s. th., *eji-takwag.*

Abscess with matter, *mini.* I have an abscess, *nin miniw.* Matter or pus is running out out of an abscess or ulcer, *miniwan.* My abscess bursts, *nin pashkiminishka.*

Abscond; I abscond, *nin kas; nin kakis.*

Absent; I am (it is) absent so long, *nind inênd; inendomagad.* I am absent for so many days, *nin dassogwanend.* I am ab., *kawin nind abissi.* I am ab. for a night, *nikanend.* I am ab. two days, three days, etc., *nin nijogwanend, nin nissogwanend,* etc. I am ab. from home, *nin ondamishka.* I am ab. for such a reason, *nind ondend.*

Absolutely, *âpitchi, pâkatch.*

Absolution. S. Blotting out.

Absolve. S. Blot out.

Abstain; I abstain, *nin mindjiminidis.* I abst. from it; (I don't eat it, (*in., an.*) *nin gonwâpon; nin gonwâponan*

Abstemious person, (never drinking wine,) *menikwessig jominabo.*

Absterge. S. Wipe.

Abstinence, *gonwâpowin.*

Absurd; it is absurd, *gagibadad.*

Absurdity, *gagibadisiwin.*

Abundance, *débisiwin.*

Abuse, bad use, *matchi aiowin.* I make a bad use of it, abuse it, (*in., an.*) *nin matchiaion; nin matchiawa.*

Abuse, (treat ill;) I abuse him, (her, it,) *nind âbindjia; nind âbindjiton.* I abuse with words, *nind âbinsonge.* I abuse him (her, it) with words, *nind abinsoma; nind âbinsondan.*

Abuse, abusive words, (in. s. in.) S. Insult.

Abyss, *gondakamigissan.* There is an abyss, *gondakamigissemagad.*

Accept. Accepted. S. Take, (accept.) Taken.

Accident; frightful accident, *gagwânissagakamig ejiwebak.*

Accompany; I accompany, *nin widjiiwe.* It accompanies, *widjiiwemagad.* I acc. him., *nin widjiwa.* We acc. each other, *nin widjindimin.* I acc. him a little distance through politeness, *nin midjissikawa.* I acc. him going about, *nin babawidjiwa.* We acc. each other going about, *nin babawidjindimin.*

Accompaniment, *widjiiwewin; widjindiwin; babawidjindiwin.*

Accomplish; I acc., *nin gijita.* I make him accomplish s. th., *nin gijitaa.* I make myself acc. s. th., *nin gijitaidis, nin gijitas*

Accroach; I acc., *nind adjigwadjige.* I acc. him, (her, it,) *nind adjigwana; nind adjigwadan.*

Accumulate. S. Gather.

Accusation (causing condemnation,) *batangewin.*

Accuse; I accuse, *nin batange; nind anaminge.* I accuse him, (and cause by it his condemnation, or a penalty, etc.) *nin batama.* I am in a habit of accusing, *nin batangeshk.*

Accuse; I acc. him (her, it) in *thoughts* of some fault, *nind anâmenima; nind anâmendan.* I acc. him, (her, it) in *words* of some fault, *nind anâmima; nind anâmendan.* I acc. him *falsely*, *nin binishima, nin mamijima.* I acc. him (her) of an unlawful intercourse with a person of the other sex, *nind agwadamawa ikwewan,* (*nind agwadamawa ininiwan.*)

Accuse, (impute;) I acc. him of it, (impute it to him,) *nind apagadjissitawa, nind apagadjissitamawa.*

Accuser, *baiatangeshkid; baiatanged.*

Accustomed; I am acc., *nin nagadis, nin nogadêndam.* The state or disposition of being acc., *magadèndamowin.* I am acc. to him, (her, it,) *nin nagadenima; nin nagadêndân.* I feel acc. to s. th., *nin nagadénindis.* I endeavor to get acc. to s. th., *nin nagadjiidis.* I am acc. to do it, to make it, *nin nagadjiton.*

Acid. S. Sour.

Acorn, *mitigomin.*

Acquire, (in s. in.) S. Gain. Earn. Procure.

Acquire for food; I acq. it for food, (*an., in.*) *nin nodjia; nin nodjiton.*

Acquisition, *gashkitchigewin.*

Across a river, etc., I carry or convey him (her, it) across a river, etc., *nind ajawaona, nind ajawaa; nind ajawaodon, nind ajawaan.* I am (it is) carried or conveyed across, *nind ajawaodjigas; ajawaodjigade.*

Act; I act, *nind ijitchige, nind anoki.* I act by mistake, *nin wanitchige.* I act foolishly, *nin gagibadjige.* I act right, exactly, *nin nissitâdodam.* I act so..., *nind ijitwa, nind inanoki.* I act strangely, curiously, *nin namandâwitchige.* I act well, *nin minotwa, nin minotchige.* I act wickedly, *nin matchitwa, nin matchitchige.* I act with patience, *nin minwadjito.* I act wrongly, *nin mânâdjitchige, nin manjitchige.* We act (or work) together, *nin mâmawitchigemin.*

Action, acting, *dodamowin, ijitchigewin.* Strange acting or manners, *mamandâwitchigewin, mamandâwitchigan.* Impure action, *bishigwadodamowin, bishigwadj-dodamowin.* I commit an impure action, *nin bishigwadodam, nin bishigwadjdodam.*

Active; I am active, (diligent), *nin nitâ-anoki.* (Nitta-atuskew).

Actually, *nongum.*

Add; I add, I put more, (*in. an.*) *nawatch nibiwa nind aton; nawatch nibiwa nind assa.* I add to it, *nind aniketon, nin gikissiton.*

Added; there is s. th. added to it, *aniketchigade.*

Addition, *aniketchigan.* There is an addition made, *aniketchigade.*

Address; I address him, (her, it.) *nin ganona; nin ganodân.*

Administration. Administrator. S. Stewarship. Steward.

Admirable; I am (it is) adm., *nin mamakadendagos; mamakadendagwad.*

Admirably, *mamakâdakamig.*

Admiration, *mamakadendamowin.*

Admire; I admire, *nin mamakâdendam, nin mamakâdenim.* I make him admire, *nin mamakâdendamia, nin mamakâdenimoa.* I admire him, (her it,) *nin mamakâdenima; nin mamakâdendân.*

Admirer, *maiamaâdendang.*

Admit; I admit him, *nind odapina*

Adopt; I ad. him, (her it,) *nin wangoma; nin wangondan.*

Adopted father, mother, child, son, daughter; the same as, god-father, god-mother, god-child, god-son, god-daughter; which see respectively.

Adorn. Adorned, (in s. in.) S. Ornament. Ornamented.

Adorn, (also, paint;) I adorn, *nin wawejinge.* I adorn him, (her, it,) *nin wawejia; nin wawejiton.* I adorn myself for him, (her,) *nin wawejinodawa.*

Adorned, (also, painted;) I am (it is) ad., *nin waweginigas; wawejinigade.*

Adore; I ad. him, *nind anamietawa, nin manadjia, nin gwanwadjia*.
Adorer of God, *enamietawad Kije-Maniton.*
Adorer of idols, *enamietawad masininin.*
Adult; I am adult, *nin gijig, nin nitawig, nin nitawigiigo.*
Adulterer, *bishigwadjinini, ketchibisigwadisid inini, kekenimad bekanisididjin ikwewan.*
Adulteress, *bishigwadjikwe, ketchibishigwadisid ikwe, kekenimad bekanisinidjin ininiwan.*
Adultery, *bishigwadisiwin, kitchi bishigwadisiwin.*
Advance; in advance, *kija, nigan.*
Adversary. S. Enemy.
Adversity. S. Suffering.
Afar off, *wassa.*
Affection, *sagiiwewin.*
Affirm; I affirm, *e nind ikit,* (I say yes.)
Afflict; I afflict him, *nin kashkendamia, nin kotagia.* I afflict him with words, *nind inâpinema.*
Afflicted; I am aff., *nin kashkendam, nin mamidawendam, nin gissadendam.*
Afflicted. Afflicting. Affliction. —S. Sad. Sadness.
Affliction, *mamiaawendamowin, gibendamowin, gissadendamowin, kashkendamowin.*
Affliction; (in. s. in.) S. Suffering.
Afford; I can afford it, *nin gashkiton; nin debisse.*
Affront, *bissongewin*
Afraid, (in. s. in.) S. Fear.
Afraid; I am afraid, *nind agoski.* I am af. about him, *nind agoskana.* I am afraid for myself, *nind agoskanidis.* I make him afraid by my words, *nin gotâsoma.*
Afternoon, *gi-ishkwa-nawakweg.*
After three days, *kitche awasswabang.*
After to-morrow, *awasswabang, ajawi-wabang.*
Afterwards, *nâgatch, pânima, pama.*
Again, *minawa, andj, minawa andj; biskab; nassab, neiab.*
Age; I am of age, or, I am of such an age, *nind apitis.* I am at the age of discretion, *nin bisiskadis.*
Aged, *kitchi;* aged person, *kitchi anishinabe.* I am an aged person, *nin kitchi anishinabew.*
Agent, *ogima.*—S. Indian agent. Mining Agent.
Agitate; I agitate it, (liquid,) *nin mamadâgamissidon.*
Agitated; it is ag. by the wind, (liquid,) *mamadâgamisse.* It is ag. by the wind, (a reed, etc.) *mamâdassin.*
Aggress; I aggress, *nin mâdjita.*
Aggression, *madjitawin.*
Aggressor, *maiadjitad.*
Agree; we agree together, *nin bejigwendamin, nin minowidjindimin.* It agrees together, *widjindimagad.*
Agreeable, I am (it is) ag., *nin minwendagos, nind onijish; minwendawad, onijishin.*
Agreeableness, *minwendagosiwin.*
Agreeably, *minwendagwakamig.*
Agriculture, *kitigewin.*
Agriculturer, *kitigewinini.*
Aground; I run aground paddling, *nin tchékisse.* I run ag. sailing, *nin tchékash.*

Aha! ah! *âtaiâ! tiwe!—Niâ! ningé! ningô!*
Ahead, *nigân.*
Aim, of an archer, *bimôdjigan.*
Aim, of a gun, *kikinawâdjitchigan.*
Aim, at, (with a gun, etc.) I aim at s. th., *nin jigwêiabandjige, nin pashkingwen.* I aim at him, (her, it,) *nin jigwêiabâma; nin jigwêiabandan.*
Air; in the air, *ishpiming; gijigong.*
Air-bladder of a fish, *opikwadj,* (its air-bladder.)
Alabaster, *wâbâssin,* (white stone.)
Alabaster-box, *wabassini-makak.*
Alarm, *amanissowin, gotâdjiwin.*
Alarm. S. Intimidate.
Alarmed; I am al., *nin migoshkadjiaia.* I am al. by s. th. I heard, *nind amaniss.* It alarms me, *nin migoshkadji-aiawigon.*
Alder-forest, *wadôpiki.*
Alder-Point, *Nédôpikan.* At, to or from Alder-Point, *Nedôpikang.*
Alder-tree, *wadôp.* There are alder-trees, *wadôpika.* Place where there are alder-trees, *wadôpikang.*
Algonquin Indian, *Odishkwagami.*
Algonquin squaw, *odishkwagâmikwe.*
Alight; I alight upon him, *nin bônindawa.* The bird alights, *bôni bineshi.*
Alive, *gigibimadis.* I am alive, *nin bimadis.* It is alive, *bimadad, bimadisimagad.*
All, *kakina, misi, misi gego, kakina gego.* All of it, (*in., an.*) *endassing; endashid.* All of us, *endashiiang.*
All, (in compositions,) *kabé–.*
Alliance, *widokodadiwin.*
Allied. S. Associated.
All kinds, *anôtch, wiiagi.*
Allow; I allow it to him, *nin mina.*
Allow, (in. s. in.) S. Permit.
All Saints day, *kakina ketchitwawendagosidjig gijigong ebidjig o gijigadomiwa.*
All Souls day, *tchibaigijig.*
All is spent, all spent, (*an., in.*) *tchagisse; tchagissemagad.*
Allure. Allurement.—S. Entice. Enticing.
Almighty, *misi gego netawitod.*
Almost, *gega.*
Alms; I give alms, *nin jajawendjige, ketimagisid nin mina gego.*
Almsgiving, *jajawendjigewin.*
Alone, *nijike.* I am alone, *nin nijikewis, nin bejig.* I am alone in a canoe, *nin bejigôkam, nin nijikeôkam.* I am alone in a house, *nin nijikêwab.* I am alone, I have no more a wife; I have no more a husband, *nin bishigowis.*
Already, *jaigwa, jigwa, ajigwa; aji, jaie, jajaie.*
Also, *gaie.*
Altar, *anamessike-adopowin, anamessikan. Pagidinige-adopowin, pagidjige-adopowin.*—S. Sacrificing-altar.
Altar-cloth, *anamessike-adopowinigin.*
Alter. S. Change.
Altercation. S. Quarrel.
Altered; I am (it is) alt., *nind andjigas, nin andjitchigâs; andjigade, andjitchigade.*

Alternately, *memeshkwat.*
Although, *ano, missawa.*
Alum, *jiwabik, mikwaming eji-nagwag mashkiki, waiabish-kisigwag mashkiki.*
Always, *môjag, apine, kâginig, papagwash.*
Always the same, *mi apine.*
Am; I am, *nind aw, nind aia.* I am with him, *nin widjiaiawa.* I am in a certain place, *nin dajike, nin danis.* I am so, *nind ijiwebis.* I use to be so, *win nita-ijiwebis, nin waké-ijiwebis.*
Amability. S. Amiableness.
Ambition, *askwanisiwin.*
Ambitious; I am amb., *nind askwanis.* (Akawâtamowin).
Ambush, lying in ambush, *akan-dowin.* I lie in ambush, *nind akando.* I lie in ambush for him, *nind akkamawa.* (N't as-kamâwaw).
Amen, *mi ge-ing.*
American, *Kitchimokoman,*(Big-Knife).
American boy, *Kitchimokoma-nens.*
American girl, *Kitchimokoma-nikwens.*
American woman, *Kitchimo-komanikwe.*
Amiable; I am amiable, *nin minwendagos, nin sagiigos.*
Amiableness, *minwendagosiwin, sagiigosiwin.*
Amicability, *kijadisiwin, kijewa-disiwin.*
Amicable; I am amicable, *nin kijadis, nin kijewadis.*
Amidst, among, *mêgwaii.*
Ammunition, (powder and shot,) *pashkisigewin.*
Among, amongst, *megwe.* I am somowhere amongst others, *nin dagoaia.* It is somewhere amongst other things, *dagoaia-magad.* I am sitting some-where among others, *nin dag-wab.* I count him (her, it) among others, *nin dagogima; nin dagogindan.* I count my-self amongst others, *nin dago-gonidis.* I die amongst others, *nin dagoné.* I name him (her, it) among other words I pro-nounce, *nin dagowina; nin dagowindan.* I put him (her, it) somewhere among other objects, *nin dagossa; nin da-goton.* I stand somewhere amongst others, *nin dagoga-baw.* I swallow it amongst other objects, (*an., in.*) *nin da-gôgona; nin dagôgondan.*
Amuse. Amusement, (in. s. in.) S. Noisy amusement.
Ancester, *kitisim.*
Anchor, *bonakadjigan.* I cast anchor, *nin bonakadjige.* I lift the anchor, *nin wikwakwaan bonakadjigan.*
Anchor; I anchor it, (*in., an.*) *nin bonakadon; nin bonakana.*
Ancient, *getê.*
And, *gaie; achi; dash.* (Mina).
Andiron, *agwitchikijeigan.*
Anew, *minawa, minawa andj, nêiab.* (Kittwam).
Angel, *Anjeni.* I am an Angel, *nind Anjeniw.* (Okijiko).
Angelica-root, *wike.*
Anger, (rancour,) *nishkendjige-win, nishkadisiwin, bitchina-wesiwin.* I keep anger a long time, I am rancorous, *nin nishkeninge, nin nishkendjige.* I use to keep anger a long time, *nin nishkendjigeshk.* Bad ha-

bit of keeping anger, *nishkendjigeshkiwin.* I keep anger or rancour towards him, (her, it,) *nin nishkenima ; nin nishkendan.* We keep anger towards each other, *nin nishkenindimin.* Mutual anger or rancour, *nishkenindiwin.* Anger in the heart, *nishkideewin.* I hear him with anger, *nin nishkadisitawa.* We hear each other with anger, *nin nishkadisitadimin.* I provoke him to anger, *nin nanishkadjia.* We provoke each other to anger, *nin nanishkadjiidimin.*

Angry ; I begin to be angry, *nin madjigidas.* I am an., *nin nishkadis, nin bitchinawes, nind iniwes* I come here an., *nin bidjigidas.* I get an. on account of.., *nind ondjigidas.* I am too an., *nind osamigidas.* I go out an., *nin sagidjigidas.* I use to be an., *nin nishkadisishk.* I look an., *nin nishkadjingwe, nin nishkadjingweshka.* I am an. being sick, *nin nishkine.* I make people an., *nin nishkiiwe.* I make him an., *nin nishkia, nin bitchinawea, iniwesia.* I make him an. holding him, *nin nishkina.* I make him an. with my words, *nin bitchinawema, nin nishkima.* We make each other an. with our words, *nin nishkindimin.* My heart is angry, *nin nishkidee.*

Animal, *awessi.* Small animal, *manitoweish.* Wicked dangerous animal, *matchi aiaâwish.* (Pijiskiw).

Animate ; I animate, *nin gagânsonge.* I an. him, *nin gagânsoma.*

Ankle-bone, *pikoganân, pikwakoganân.*

Annoy. Annoying. Annoyance, (in. s. in.) S. Trouble. Troublesome. Troublesomeness.

Annihilate ; I an. it, (*an., in.*) *nind apitchi banadjia ; nind apitchi banadjiton.*

Anniversary ; I come (it comes) to the anniversary, *nin tibishka ; tibishkamagad.*

Announce ; I an., *nin windamage, nin kikendamiiwe, nin kikendamodjiwe.* I an. him s. th., *nin windamawa.* I an. it, *nin windamagen.*

Announcing, *windamagewin.*

Annunciation of the B. V. Mary, *Kitchitwa Marie od anamikagowin.*

Anodyne drops for tooth-ache, *wibida-mashkiki.*

Anoint ; I anoint him, (her, it,) *nin nomina ; nin nominan.* I anoint his head, (grease it,) *nin namâkona.* Grease to anoint the head, *namâkwiwin.* I anoint (or grease) my head, *nin namâkonidis.* (Ni tominaw).

Anon, *naningotinong, naningotinongin.*

Another ; I am another person, *nin bakânis.* Another one, *bekanisid.* It is another thing, *bekânad.* Another thing, *bekanak.* I am of another nation, *nin bakânwaiagis.* It is of another sort, *bakânwaiagad.* I take another route, *nin bakê, nin bakêwis.* (Pitus awiyak).

Answer, *nakwêtamowin.* I give him an answer, *nin nakwêta-*

wa. I give bad disrespectful answers, *nind ajidewe, nind ajidewidam.* I give him bad answers, *nind ajidema.*—(S. Gainsay).

Answer ; I answer, *nin nakwetage, nin nakwêtam.* I answer him, *nin nakwêtawa.*

Ant, *enigô.*

Anticipation ; by anticipation, *kija, nigan.*

Antipathy. S. Hatred.

Ant's hill, *enigowigamig,* (ant's house.)

Anvil, *ashotataigan.*

Anxious ; I am an. about him, *nind agoskana.* I am an. about myself, *nin agoskanidis.*

Apart, *opimeaii, maiên.*

Ape, *nandomakomeshî.*

Ape ; I ape him, imitate him, *nind ainawa.* (N't ayisinawaw).

Apostate, *waiêbinang od anamiewin.*

Apostatize ; I ap., *nin webinan, nind anamiewin.*

Apostle, *Jesus o kikinoamaganan.*

Apostume, *mini.*

Apothecary, *mashkikikêwinini.* Female apothecary, *mashkikikêwikwe.*

Apothecary's art or trade, *mashkikikêwin.*

Apothecary's laboratory, *mashkikikewigamig.*

Apothecary's shop, *mashkikiwigamig.*

Apparition. S. Vision.

Appear ; I appear, *nin nâgwi, nin nâgos.* It appears, *nâgwad.* I appear so...., *nind ijinagwi.* I make myself appear, (in a vision,) *nin nâgwiidis.* I appear (it appears) changed, different, *nind andjinagos ; andjinagwad.* (N't ijinakusin).

Appear, (in. s. in.) S. Visible.

Appearance, *nâgosiwin.* I have (it has) an astonishing app., marvellous app., *nin mamandâwinagos ; mamandâwinagwad.* I have (it has) a beautiful app., *nin onijishabaminagos ; onijishabaminagwad.* I have (it has) a changed app., *nind andjinagos; andjinagwad.* I give him (her, it) a changed or another app., *nind andjinagosia, nind andjinagwia ; nind andjinagwiton.* I take another app., *nind andjinagwi, nind andjinagwiidis.* I have (it has) a clean app., *nin bininagos ; bininagwad.* I have a curious ridiculous app., *nin goshkonâgos.* I have a fine-looking app., *nind ojiiawes, nin mikawâdis.* I have (it has) a fine app., *nin minwabaminagos ; minwabaminagwad.* I have (it has) a frightful app., *nin gagwânissaginagos, nin gotâsinagos; gagwânissagimagwad, gotâsinagwad.* I cause him (her, it) to have a frightful app., *nin gotâsinagwia ; nin gotâsinagwiton.* I have a roguish app., *nin mamandêssadendagos.* I have a sickly app., *nind âkosinagos.* I have (it has) such an app., *nind ijinagos ; ijinagwad.* I give to myself such an app., *nind ijinagwiidis.* I have (it has) an ugly app., *nin manabaminagos, nin maninagos, nin manjiiawes ; manabaminagwad, maninagwad.**

* NOTE. To form the respective substantives corresponding to the verbs of

Appease ; I appease, *nin gâgisonge*. I appease him, *nin gagisoma, nin gagidjia, nind odjitchia ; nin wangawima ; nin wangawina*. I app. him for somebody, *nin gâgisondamawa*. I app. myself, *nin gâgisondis*.

Appeased ; I am app., *nind anissendam, nin wanakiwendam*. The waves are app., *anwaweiashka*.

Appellation, *ijinikasowin*.

Apple, *mishimin*. Dry apples, *batêmishiminag*.

Apple-peel, *mishimini-okonass*.

Apple-tree, *mishiminatig*.

Appoint ; I appoint him, *nind onakona*. I appoint him to s. th., *nind inakona*. (N't kiskimaw).

Appointment, *onakonigewin, inakonigewin*.

Appreciate ; I app. him, (her, it,) *nind apitenima ; nind apitendan*. (N't ispiteyimaw).

Apprehend ; I app. *nin segendam*.

Apprehend danger. S. Fear.

Apprehension, *segendamowin*. (Astâsiwin).

Apprentice, *kikinoamagan, kikinoamawind*.

Approach ; I app., *nin nasikage*. I app. him, (her, it,) *nin nâsikawa, nin bêshodjia, nin bêshosikawa ; nin nâsikan, nin bêshodjiton, nin bêshosikan*. We app. each other, *nin nâsikodadimin, nin beshosikodadimin*.

---

this article, you have only to annex *iwin* to the *animate* verb, and you have the substantive. As, *Nin mamandawinagos ; mamandawinagosiwin*, astonishing appearance.

Appropriate ; I app. s. th. to me, *nin dibendamonidis*. (Ni tibeyittamâsun.)

Approve ; I app. him, *nin wawinawea*. I approve of it, *nin minwabandan*.

Approve, (in s. in.) S. Permit.

April, *bebokwedagiming-gisiss*.

Apron, *inapisowin*. (Ayekiwipisim.)

Archangel, *Kitchi Anjeni*.

Archbishop, *Naganisid Kitchimekatewikwanaie*.

Archer ; I am a good archer, *nin wawinâke*. I am a poor archer, *nin mamanâke*.

Ardent liquor, *ishkotewabo*.

Ark, *Noe o nabikwan*.

Ark of the covenant, *Gaiat-ijitwawini-makak*.

Arm, *onikama*. The right arm, *kitchinik, okitchinikama*. The left arm, *namândjinik, onamândjinikama*. My, thy, his arm, *ninik, kinik, onik*. I have arms, *nind onika*. I have a dead arm, *nin nibôwinike*. I have hairy arms, *nin mishinike, nin memishinike*. I have large arms, *nin mamânginike*. I have a long arm, *nin ginônike ;* I have long arms, *nin gagânonike*. One of my arms is longer than the other, *nin nabanêginonike*. I have only one arm, *nin nabanênike*. I have a short arm, *nin takonike ;* I have short arms, *nin tatakonike*. One of my arms is shorter than the other, *nin nabanêtakonike*. I have a small arm, *nind agassinike ;* I have small arms, *nin babiwinike*. I have a stiff arm, *nin tchibatakanike*. I have strong arms, *nin mashkawinike.*—I have convulsions in my arm, *nin tchitchibinikeshka.* I have pain in my arm, *nin dêwinike.* I have a scar on my arm, *nind odjishinike.* I have spasms or cramps in my arm, *nind otchinikepinig.* I have my arm stretched out in a certain manner, *nind ijiniken.* I stretch out my arm, *nin jibiniken ; nin passaginiken.* I stretch out my arms, *nin jinginike.* I stretch my arm out towards him, *nin jibiniketawa ;* I stretch out his arm, *nin passaginikena.*—I break my arm, *nin bokonikeshin.* My arm is broken, *nin bokonike.* I dislocate my arm, falling, *nin kotigonikeshin.* My arm is dislocated, *nin kotigoniketa.* I dislocate my arm, *nin gidiskakonikeshin, nin bimiskonikeshin.* My arm is dislocated, *nin gidiskakoniketa, nin bimiskoniketa.*I draw back my arm, *nind odjiniken.* I feel his arm, *nin godjinikena.* I hold or carry under my arm s. th., *nin sinsiningwandjige.* I hold or carry him (her, it) under my arm, *nin sinsiningwâma ; nin sinsiningwandan.* I lift up my arm, *nind ombiniken.* I make him move his arm, *nin nanginikeshkawa.* I put my whole arm in, *nin nikinisse.* I rub his arm with medicine, *nin sinigonikebina.* I show forth my arm, *nin saginiken.* I stretch out my arm, *nin dajôniken.* I have my arm stretched out, *nin dajônikeshin.* I sit with down-hanging arms, *nin jinginikeb.* I walk with down-hanging arms, *nin jinginikeosse.* My arm is stretched and hanging down, *nin jibinikegodjin.* My arms are stretched and hanging down, *nin jinginikegodjin.* I take him by the arm, *nin saginikena.* I tire his arm, *nind aiekonikewina, nind ishkinikewina.* It tires my arm, *nind aiekonikewinigon, nind ishkinikewinigon.*—My arms are cold, *nin takinike.* My arm is cut off, *nin kishkinike.* I cut off his arms, *nin kishkinikejwa.* My arm is pierced, *nin jibanikejigas.* My arm shakes, *nin nininginike.* My arm is swollen, *nin bâginike.* My arm is much tired, *nind apitchinikeb.* My arms are warm, *nin kijonike.* My arm is wounded, *nin mâkinike.*—The other arm, *nabanênik, âgawinik.* (Nabatenisk).

Armed ; I am armed, *nind âshwi.* I am well armed and dangerous, *nind akôtewagis.* (Nimâskwew).

Armpit; my, thy, his armpit, *niningwi, kiningwi, oningwi.*

Arms of a warrior, armor, *ashwiwin.* (Nimâskwewin).

Around, *giwitaii.*

Arrange; I arrange, *nind inakonige, nin dibowe.* I arr. it in a certain manner, *nind inakonan.* I arr. him, (her, it,) *nin dibowana; nin dibowadan.* I arr. it right, *nin gwaiakoton.* I arr. it well, put it up well, (*an., in.*) *nin naakona ; nin naakonan, nin naakossidon.* (Ni nahastasun).

Arrange, (mend;) I arr. it (*an., in.*) *nin nanâina ; nin nanâiton.* (Ni nahinaw).
Arranged ; it is arr., *inakonigade, naakonigade.*
Arrest. Arrested, (in s. in.) S. Seize. Seized. (Ni takusinin).
Arrive ; I arrive, *nind odishiwe, nind oditaowe.* I arr. by land, *nin dagwishin.* I arr. by water, *nin mijaga, nin mijagamekwajiwe, nind oditaowe.* It arrives, *dagwishinomagad.* I arr. in the night, by land, *nin nibâoditaowe, nin bi-nibaam.* I arr. in the night, by water, *nin nibâmijaga.* I arr. at halfway, *nind abitosse.* It arrives at halfway, *abitossemagad.* I arr. to the shore, walking on the ice, *nind agwaiadagak, nin mijagak.* I arr. at the summit of a mountain, *nin pagamamadjiwe, nin gijamadjiwe.* I arr. sailing, *nin pagamash.* It arrives by the wind, *pagamassin.* I arr. running, *nin pagamibato.* I arr. here in passing by, *nin bimidagwishin.* I arr. in due time, *nin gêssikage.* I arr. to him (her, it) in due time, *nin gêssikawa ; nin gêssikân.* I arr. to him in good time, *nin gessikona.* I arr. too late, *nin mêdassikage.* I arr. too late to him, (her, it) *nin mêdassikawa ; nin mêdassikan.* I arr. to him (her, it) in the night, *nin nibâoditawa ; nin nibâoditan.* I arr. to the moment of seeing him, (her, it,) *nind odissabama ; nind odissabandan.* I arr. at home, *nin pagamadis.* I make him arr. somewhere, *nin dagwishima.* I arr. somewhere, *nin pagamishka, nin pagamisse.* It arrives, (happens), *pagami-aiamagad, pagamishkamagad, pagamissemagad.* The time arrives, *kabessemagad.* It arrives, (a certain time) *odjitchisse.* It arrives again, *tibishkosse.*
Arrogant ; I am arr., *nin gotamigwenim.*
Arrogant. Arrogance. S. Proud. Pride.
Arrow, *mitigwanwi.* (Atus).
Arrow-head, arrow-point, *nabowewanwi.*
Arrow made of wood, *pikwak.* (Webisis).
Arrow with an iron head or point, *assâwan.* Long arrow, *ginwakwanwi.*
Arse, (buttocks,) *miskwassab.*
Artery, *kitchi m iskweiab.*
Artful ; I am artful, cunning, *nin gagaiênis.*
Artfulness, *gagaiênisiwin.*
Ascend ; I ascend a mountain or hill in a certain way, *nind inamâdjiwe.* I ascend a mountain, *nind amâdjiwe, nind ojidadjiwe, nind ojidakiwe.* I ascend a mountain or hill running, *nind amâdjiwebato.* I ascend a mountain carrying s. th. on my shoulder, *nind amâdjiwenige.*
Ascension-day, *api Jesus gijigond ejad.*
As far as, *binish.*
Ashamed ; I am ash., *nind agatch, nin mênissendam.* I am ash. before him, *nin agatchitawa.* I am ash. of him (in thoughts,) *nind agatenima, nin mênissenima.* I am ash.

of myself, or before myself, *nin agatenindis, nin menissenindis.* I am ash. of it, *nind agatchitan, nin mênissendân.* I am ash. of it (in thoughts,) *nind agatendan, nin mênissendân.* I make him ash., *nind agatchia, nin mênishea.* I make him ash. with my words, *nind agâsoma, nin mênishima.* It makes me ashamed, *nind agatchiigon, nind agasomigon, nin menishimigon.* (Ni nepewisin).

Ash-colored ; it is ash-colored, (stuff. *in., an.*) *jipingwegad ; jipingwegisi.* It is ash-col., (*in., an.*) *jipingwande, jipingwadile ; jipingwadisso, jipingwasso.* I dye ash-colored, *nin jipingwasige.* I dye it ash-col., (*in., an.*) *nin jipingwadissan, nin jipingwansan ; nin jipingwadisswa, nin jipingwanswa.*

Ashes, *pingwi ; pangwi.* On ashes, *mitchipingwi.* The upper white part of ashes, *jigwapingwane.* Ashes are put on me, *nin pingwiwinigo.* I put ashes upon him, *nin pingwiwina.* I throw ashes on me, *nin pingwaodis.* I throw ashes upon him, *nin pingwawa.* I have ashes on my face, *nin jipingwingwe.* I slide and fall in ashes, *nind odadjipingwesse.* (Pihkko).

Ash-tree, *agimak.* Another kind of ash-tree, *gawâkomij.* Another kind, *papagimak.* Another kind again, *wissagak.*

Ash-Wednesday, *pingwi-gijigad.*

Aside, *opimêaii, atchitchaii, bakêaii, maiên.* I step aside, *nin bakêgabaw.* I step aside for him, (I go out of his way,) *nin bakêgabawitawa.*

As it were, *nindigo.*

Ask ; I ask, *nin nandotamage, nin nandotam.* I ask him for s. th., *nin nandotamawa.*

Ask ; I ask a question or questions, *nin gagwedwe.* I ask him a question, *nin gagwedjima.* We ask each other questions, *nin gagwedjindimin.*

Ask alms. S. Beg.

Ask for s. th. to eat. I ask for s. th. to eat, *nin pagwishiiwe.* I ask him (her, it) for s. th. to eat, *nin pagwishia ; nin pagwishiton.* I am in a habit of asking to eat, *pagwishiiweshk.*

Asking, *nandôtamowin, nandotamagewin.* Asking for s. th. to eat, *pagwishiiwewin.* Habit of asking for s. th. to eat, *pagwishiiweshkiwin.*

Ask with hope ; I ask with hope, *nin pagossendam, nin pagossenim, nin pagossendjige.* I ask him, *nin pagossenima.* I ask for it, *nin pagossendan.*

Asking with hope, *pagossendamowin.* I am (it is) worth asking, *nin pagossendagos ; pagossendagwad.*

Asleep, *pawengwai.* I fall asleep, *nin bishkongwash.* I am asleep, *nin niba.*

As much, as many, *tibishko minik.* (Tatto).

Aspen-tree, *asâdi.* Another kind of aspen-tree, *manasâdi.*

Asperse. Aspersion.—S. Sprinkle. Sprinkling.

Ass, *memangishe ; mengishkatai.*

Assemble. Assembly.—S. Meet together. Meeting.
Assiduous working, *nila-anokiwin*. (Nitta-atuskew).
Assist ; I assist him, *nin 'widokawa, nin widjiwa, nin nijokawa, nin nijokamawa*. We assist each other, *nin widokodadimin, nin widjindimin*.
Assist, (in. s. in.) S. Help.
Assistant, *wadokasod*.
Associate, *widjiwagan*.
Associate. S. Company.
Associated ; we are associated, *nin widokodadimin*.
Association, *widokodadiwin*.—S. Company.
Assumption of the B. V. Mary, *api kitchitwa Marie gijigong ejad*.
Asterisk, *anangons*.
Astonish ; I ast. him, *nin mâmakâdendamoa*.
Astonished ; I am ast., *nin mâmakâdendam*.
Astonishing, *mamakadakamig*. It is ast., *mamakadendagwad*. I do astonishing things, *nin mâmandadodam*. Astonishing doing, *mamandadodamowin*.
Astonishment, *mamakadendamowin*.
Astray. S. Go astray.
Astronomer, *anangon kekenimad*.
At, *tchig', tchigaii*.
At all events, at any rate, *potch*. (Eyiwek. Missawâtch).
At first, *waiêshkat*.
At last, at length, *gêgapi, ishkwâtch*.
At once, *sêsika, gêsika*.
Attached ; I am attached to him, (her, it,) *nin sagia, nin maminawenima ; nin sagiton, nin maminawendan*.
Attack, (in s. in.) S. Insult.
Attack. Attacker.—S. Aggress. Aggression. Aggressor.
Attendant, *oshkabewiss*.
Attention, *babamendamowin, aiangwâmendamowin, angwamendamowin*. I pay attention, *nind aiangwamendam, nind angwamendan, nin babamendam, nin babamindam*. I pay attention to him, (her, it,) *nind aiangwamenima, nind angwamenima, nin babamenima, nin babamima ; nind aiangwamendan, nind angwamendan, nin babamendan, nin babamindan*. We turn our attention to one another, *nin babamenindimin, nin babamendamâdimin*. I turn my attention to myself, *nind aiangwamenindis, nin babamenindis*. I pay att. to s. th. relating to him, *nin babamendamawa*. Attention is paid to me, *nin babamendagos*. Att. is paid to it, *babamendagwad*.
At that time, *iwapi*. (Ekuspi).
At the top, *ishpiming*.
Attract ; I attract him, *nin wikobina*. It attracts me, *nin wikobinigon, nin wikoshka, nin wikonawis*.
Attract, (in. s. in.) S. Tempt.
Auction, *bibâgatandiwin*. I sell at auction, *nin bibâgatawe*.
Audacious ; I am audacious, *nin songidee*. Audacious person, *swangideed*.
Audacity, *songideewin*.
Auger, *biminigan, kitchi biminigan*.
Augment. S. Increase.
Augur, *onwatchigewinini*.
Augur ; I augur, *nind onwat-*

chige. I augur of him, *nind onwatawa.*
Auguration, *onwatchigewin.*
August, *min gisiss.*
Aunt, (father's sister) my, thy, his aunt, *ninsigoss, kisigoss, osigossan.*
Aunt, (mother's sister,) my, thy, his aunt, *ninoshe, kinoshe, onoshêian.*
Authority, (power,) *gashkiewisiwin.* I have authority, *nin gashkiewis.*—S. Power.
Avarice, *sasâgisiwin.*
Avaricious ; I am av., *nin sasâgis.* Avaricious person, *sesagisid.*
Avenge ; I avenge a bad doing on him, (I render him evil for evil,) *nind ajêdibaamawa.* I avenge it, *nind ajêdibaan.*
Avidity. S. Coveteousness.
Avoid, (in. s. in.) S. Fly.
Avowal, sincere avowal, *gwaiak dibadjimowin, gwaiakwadjimowin.*—I make a sincere avowal, *nin gwaiakwadjim.*
Await ; I await him, (her, it,) *nin bia ; nin bilon.*
Awake ; I awake, *nin goshkos, nind amâdjisse, nin amâsika.* I awake starting up, *nin goshkongwash.* I awake perfectly, *nind abisingwash.*— I awake him, *nind amâdjia, nind amâdina, nind goshkosia.* I awake him by pulling or pushing, *nin amâdjiwebina.* I awake him by making noise, *nind amadwewêwa.*
Aware ; I am aware of it, *nin kikendan.*
Away, *atchitchaii ; awâss.*
Awful ; it is awful, *gotamigwendagwad.*
Awkward. Awkwardness. — S. Stupid. Stupidity.
Awkward situation, *sanagisiwin.* I am in an awkward difficult situation, *nin sanagis.* I put him in an awkward situation, I cause him trouble, *ni sanagisia.* (Ayimisiw).
Awl, *migôss.* (Oskâtjîk).
Axe, *wagâkwad.* Small axe, *wagâkwadons.* Old bad axe, *wagâkwadosh.* (Tchikahigan).
Ay, ay ! *o !*

B

Babe, baby, *oshki-abinodji.* (Awasis).

Bachelor, *wadigessig inini.*

Back, *opikwanâma, pikwan.* My, thy, his back, *nin pikwan, ki pikwan, o pikwan.* I fall on my back, *nind âjigidjisse.* I have pain in the back, *ni dêwipikwan.* My back is cold, *nin takipikwan.* I have a sharp back, *nind oshaiawigan.* (Otâk).

Back again, *nêiab.* I come back again, *nin bi-giwe,* or, *neiab nin biija.*

Back and forward, *ajaok.* (Kekwesk).

Backbasket, or anything to carry s. th. in it, *awadjiwanagan.*

Backbite; I backbite, *nin pagwanonge, nin dajinge.* I backbite him, (her, it,) *nin pagwanoma, nin dajima; nin pagwanondan, nin dajindan.* We backbite one another, *nin pagwanondimin, nin dajindimin.*

Backbiting, *pagwanondiwin, dajindiwin.*

Backbone, *tatagâgwan, nawâwigan.*

Back of the hand, *pikwanenindj.* I strike him with the back of my hand, *nin pikwanênindjitawa.*

Backslider, *ejêssed.* I slide back, *nind ajêsse.*

Backsliding, *ajêssewin.*

Backwards; I draw (move) back wards, *nind ajêta.* I fall backwards, (on my back,) *nind âjigidjisse.* It falls backwards, *âjigidjissemagad.* I am driven backwards by the wind, *nind ajêiash.* It is driven b. by the wind, *ajêiassin.* I move him (her, it) backwards, *nind ajêbina; nind ajêbinan, nind ajêbidon.* I move backwards, sitting, *nind ajêb.* I run backwards, *nind ajêbato.* I walk backwards, *nind ajêosse.*

Bad, *matchi.* It is bad, *mânâdad.* I am (it is) bad or disagreeable, (considered such,) *nin mânêndagos; mânêndagwad.* I think he (she, it) is bad, *nin mânâdenima; nin mânâdendan.*

Bad being, *matchi aiaawish.*

Badger, *missakakwidjish.*

Bad language, offensive words; I use bad language in a certain manner, *nind inâpinewidam.* I use bad l. towards him, (her, it,) *nind inâpinema; nind inâpinendan.*

Bad language, wicked speaking, *matchigijwewin,. mânâdwe-*

win, mânâgidonowin, mânâsitagosiwin. I use bad wicked l., *nin mânâdwe, nin mânâgidon, nin mânâsitagos.*

Bad life, *matchi bimadisiwin.* I live a bad life, *nin matchi bimadis.*

Bad luck, *massagwadisiwin.* I cause him bad luck, *nin massagwia.*

Badly, *mâmanj, têbinak.*

Bad-mouth, *matchi odon.*

Badness, *matchi ijiwebisiwin.*

Bad River, *Mashki-sibi.*

Bag, *mashkimod, pindâgan.* Bad old bag, *mashkimodash.* Small bag, *mashkimodens.* So many bags full, *dassôshkin.* One bag full, *ningotôshkin.* Two bags full, etc., *nijôshkin,* etc. I put in a bag, *nin pindaganiwe.* I put in a bag, (*in., an.*) *nin pindaganiwen ; nin pindaganiwenan.* I make a bag or bags, *nin mashkimodake.* It is sewed up in the shape of a bag, *mashkimodêgwade.* Stuff for bags, *mashkimodêwegin.*

Bait (in a trap), *midjimikandjigan.*

Bait ; I bait a trap, *nin midjimikandân dassonagan.*

Bake. S. Cook.

Bake, (in. s. in.) S. Stew.

Bake bread ; I bake bread, *nin pakwêjiganike.*

Bake in hot ashes ; I bake in h. a., *nin ningwaabwe.* I bake it in h. a., (*in., an.*) *nin ningwaabwen ; nin ningwaabwenan.*

Bake-house, bakery, *pakwêjiganikewigamig.*

Baker, *pakwejiganikewinini, pekwejiganiked.*

Baking, bread-baking, *pakwejiganikewin.*

Baking-oven, *pakwejiganikan.*

Balance. S. Scale.

Bald ; I am bald, *nin papashkwâkondibe.* Bald person, *pepashkwâkondibed.* I am half bald, *nin jishigaanikwe, nin wapagakindibe.*

Baldness, *papashkwâkondibewin*

Ball, *nimiidiwin.* I give a ball, *nin nimiiwe.*

Ball. S. Musket-ball. Playing-ball.

Ballast, *sidogawishkodjigan.*

Ballast ; I ballast it, *nin sidogawishkodon.*

Ballasted ; it is ball., *sidogawishkode.*

Ball of thread, *pikodjan.* I wind it up on a ball, *nin pikodjanoadon.*

Ball-play, *pagaadowewin,* —S. Crosier.

Ball-room, *nimiidiwigamig,* (dance-house.)

Balsam, *papashkigiw ; nominigan.*

Bandage of a wound, *sinsobisowin.*

Bank, (sand-bank.) S. Shoals.

Banner, *kikinawadjion, kikinawadjiwin, kikiweon.*

Bans of marriage ; I publish his bans, *nin bibagima anamiewigamigong.* I publish bans of marriage, *nin bibagimag wawidigendidjig.* Publication of bans, *bibagiwin.*

Baptism, *sigaandadiwin.*—S. Private baptism.

Baptism *given, sigaandagewin.*

Baptism *received, sigaandagowin, sigaandasowin.*

Baptize ; I baptize, *nin sigaan-*

dage. I bap. him, *nin siga-andawa.*
Baptized ; I am bap., *nin siga-andas, nin sigaandjigas.*
Bar, S. Shut up.
Barber, *gashkibasowinini.*
Barber-shop, *gashkibasowiga-mig.*
Barber's trade or occupation, *gashkibasowin.*
Bare-armed ; I am b. a., *nin jâshâgininike.*
Barefoot ; I am b., *nin jâshâgi-niside.*
Bare hands ; I have b. h., *nin jâshâginininidji.*
Bare-headed ; I am b. h., *nin jâshâginindibe.*
Bare-legged ; I am b. l., *nin jâshâginigade.*
Barge, *mitigo-tchiman, nabagit-chiman.*
Bark ; the dog barks, *migi animosh.* The dog barks at him, (her, it,) *animosh o mi-ginan ; ô migidan.* (Mikisi-mow).
Bark, *wigwass ; onagek.* I take off the bark from trees, *nin babagwaajigwe.* I take it off, (bark, *in., an.*) *nin tchigana-gêkwaan ; nin tchiganagek-wawa.* The bark cannot be taken off, *pakwani mitig.* I eat the interior bark, *nin nôsk-was.* (Wayakesk-waskway).
Bark-canoe, *wigwass-tchiman.* (Waskwayosi).
Bark for smoking, *apâkosigan.* I mix my tobacco with bark, *nind apâkosige.* (Aspâskusâ-wew).
Barking, *migiwin.* (Mikisimo-win).
Bark-shelter, *agwanapakwaso-win.* I put myself under a bark-shelter, *nind agwana-pakwas.*
Barley, *manomin wesowawang.* (Iskwesissak).
Barn, (thrashing-floor,) *apagan-daigewigamig.*
Bar of a canoe, *bimidassa, pin-dassa.*
Barrel, *mâkak, makâkossag ; wawiiendagan.* Under a bar-rel, *anamimakak.* So many barrels full, *dassossag.* One barrel full, *ningotossag.* Two barrels full, etc., *nijossag,* etc. I make a barrel or barrels, *nin makakoke.*
Barrel-bottom, barrel-head, *gash-kissagaigan.* I put the bottom or the head to a barrel, or box, *nin gashkissagaan makak.*
Barrel-staff, *makakossagwatig.*
Barrow carried on the shoulder, *biminiganak.*
Base. S. Bad.
Base-viol, *kitchi-najabiigan, ki-tchi-kitotchigan.*
Bashful ; I am bashful, *nind agatchishk, nind agatchiwa-dis, nind agatchiwis.* I am bashful in speaking, *nind aga-som, nind agatchim, nind agatchitagos.* (Nepewisiw).
Bashfulness, *agatchishkiwin.*
Basin of water, *waiânag.* There is a basin of water, *wânama-gad, wanashkobiamagad.*
Basis, *ashotchissitchigan.*
Basket, *agôkobinagan, watabi-makak.* I make baskets, *nind akôkobinaganike, nin watabi-makakoke.*
Bassfish, *ashigan ; manashigan.*
Basswood, *wigob, wigobimij.* Bark of basswood, *wigob.*

Bastard, *giminidjagan.* I give birth to a bastard, *nin gimin-idji.*
Bastard-loon, *ashimang.*
Bat, *papakwânadji.*
Bath, bathing-house, *pagisowi-gamig.*
Bathe ; I bathe, *nin pagis.* (Pâkâsimow).
Bathing, *pagisowin.*
Bathing-tub, *pagisowimakak.*
Battle. S. Fight.
Bay, *wikwed.* In a bay, from or to a bay, *wikwedong.* There is a bay, *wikweia.* I walk around a bay, *nin giwitaiaja-game.* I go in a canoe around a bay, *nin giwitaam.* (Wasaw).
Bayonet, *nabadjashkaigan, ni-mashkaigan.*
Be ; I am, *nind aia.* I am so..., *nind ijiwebis.* It is, *âwan.* It is so..., *ijiwebad.* It was, *iban.* I am (it is) thought to be in such a place, *nin danendagos ; danandagwad.* There is, *dago, dagômagad, aiamagad, ate, atemagad.*
Beach ; on the beach, *agaming.* Along the beach, *jijodew ; titibew.* I walk on the beach, *nin jijodewe ; nin titibewe.* I coast, (near the beach or shore,) *nin jijodewaam ; nin titibewaam.* There is a fine even beach, *anatamanga.*
Beadle, *genawendang ishkwan-dem anamiewigamigong.*
Beads, (rosary,) *anamieminag.*
Beak ; its beak, (of a bird,) *okoj.* It has a long beak, *ginikoje.* It has a short beak, *takokoje.*
Beam, *agwawanak ; bimidaa-gan.*
Bean, *miskodissimin.*
Bear, *makwâ.* Young bear, *ma-kôns.* Male bear, *nabek.* Skin of a male bear, *nabêkwaian.* Female bear, *nojek.* Skin of a female bear, *nojêkwaian.* I hunt bears, *nin nandawâkwe.*
Beard, *mishidonagan.* I have a beard around the mouth, *nin mishidon.* I have a b. around the chin, *nin mishida-mikan.* I have a b. on the cheeks, (whiskers,) *nin mam-ishanowe.* I have a b. on the throat, *nin mishigondagan.*— I have no beard, *nin pashko-don.* I pull my beard out, *nin pashkodonebinidis.* I pull his b. out, *nin pashkodonebina.*
Bear-meat, *makôwiiass.*
Bear's bone, *makôgan.*
Bear's claw, *makogânj.*
Bear's croup, *makojîgan.*
Bear's den or hole, *makwâj.*
Bear's head, *makoshtigwan.*
Bear-skin, *makowaian, mak-waian.* A small bear-skin, *makwaianens.*
Bear-snowshoe, *makwassagim.*
Bear's potato, *makopin.*
Bear's tree, *makwatig.*
Beast, *awessî.*
Beat, (in s. in.) S. Surpass.
Beat ; the sea beats against s. th., (the waves beat,) *apagad-ashka.* The waves beat against my canoe, *nind apagadjiwe-baog.* It is beating against s. th., *apagadjissemagad.* The waves are beating against s. th., *apagadashkawag tigowag.*
Beaten ; I am (it is) beaten, *nin pakitêigas ; pakitêigade.*
Beautiful, *gwanâtch.* I am (it is) beautiful, *nin gwanâtchiw, nind onijish, nin bishigenda-*

gos; *gwanatchiwan, onijishin, bishigendagwad.*
Beauty, *gwanâtchiwin, onijishiwin, bishigendagosiwin.*
Beaver, *amik.* Young beaver, *amikons.* Young beaver under two years, *awenishê.* Young beaver between two and three years, *abôiawe.* Young beaver of three years, *bakêmik, patamik.* Male beaver, *nabémik.* Female beaver, *nojêmik.* Female beaver bearing young ones, *andjîmik.* I hunt beavers, *nin nandomikwe, nin nodamikwe.* I live like a beaver, *nind amikwagis.*
Beaver-duck, *amikoshib.*
Beaver-fur, *amikobiwai.*
Beaver Island, in Lake Michigan, *Amikogenda.*
Beaver's bone, *amikôgan.*
Beaver's dam, *okwanim.*
Beaver's hole, (not lodge,) *amikwaj.*
Beaver's kidney, *wijina.*
Beaver-skin, *abiminikwai.*
Beaver's lodge, *amikwish.*
Beaver's tail, *amikosow, amikwano.*
Because, *ondji, wendji–, sa.*
Beckon; I beckon, *nind aininige.* I beckon him, *nind aininamawa.*
Beckon, (in. s. in.) S. Nod.
Bed, *nibagan.* Under the bed, *anâmibagan.* I go to bed, *nin gawishim.* Any thing used as a bed to lie upon, *apishimon.*
Bed-bug, *minâgodjissi, ogowessi, maiajimagosid manitons,* (the stinking insect.)
Bed-fellow, *wibêmagan.*
Bedsheet, *nibâganigin.*
Bedstead, *nibâganatig, nibâganak.*
Bee, *amo.*
Beech-nut, *ajawêmin.*
Beech-tree, *ajawêmij.*
Beef, *pijikiwiwiiass.*
Beer, *jingobabo, kitchi jingobabo.* Beer made of fir-branches, *jingobabo.*
Beet, beetroot, *miskokâdak, miskotchiss,* (*miskwatchiss.*)
Before, *nond*; *bwa, tchi bwa, bwa mashi.* (Mayowes).
Before, beforehand, *kija*; *naiâg; nigan.*
Before all, *nakawê.*
Before, (formerly,) *gaiat.*
Before me, *enassamiiân*; *enassamabiiân*; *enassamigabawiiân*; *enassamishinân.*
Before my eyes, in my face, *enassamishkinjigweiân.*
Before something, *enassamimagak*; *enassamissing.*
Beg; I beg for s. th. to eat, weeping, *nin mokonem.* I beg him for s. th. to eat, weeping, *nin mokonemotâwa.*
Beg, (mendicate;) I beg, *nin nandotamage.* I am in a bad habit of begging, *nin nandotamageshk.* I beg him for s. th., *nin nandotamawa.* I beg him for help, *nin nanândoma.* I beg for it, (*in., an.*) *nin nandotan, nin nandotamagen*; *nin nandotamagenan.*
Beg, (in. s. in.) S. Ask with hope.
Beggar, *nendotamaged, bebânandotamaged.*
Beggary, begging, *nandotamagewin*; *nandotamageshkiwin.*
Beg for s. th., (in. s. in.) S. Ask for s. th. to eat.

Begging for s. th.—S. Asking for s. th. to eat.

Begin; I begin, *nin madjita.* I begin some work, *nin madjikan.* It begins, *madjissemagad, madjissin; madjikamigad.*

Beginning, *madjitawin; madjikamowin.* In the beginning, *madjitang; waieshkat.*

Behave; I behave, *nind ijiwebis, nin bimadis, nind inadis.* I behave so.... *nind ijiwebis.* I behave otherwise, *nind and. jijiwebis, nind andji-bimadis.* I beh. decently, chastely, *nin binadis.* I beh. impurely, *nin winadis, nin bishigwadj-ijiwebis, nin gagibadis.* I beh. badly, *nin matchi ijiwebis.* I beh. well, *nin mino ijiwebis.* I beh. too badly, *nind osamitchige.* I make him beh. so, or be so, *nind ijiwebisia.*

Behavior, *ijiwebisiwin bimadisiwin, inadissiwin.* Good beh., *mino ijiwebisiwin.* Bad behavior, *matchi ijiwebisiwin.* Changed beh., *andji-bimadisiwin, andjijiwebisiwin.* I change my beh., *nind andji-bimadis, nind andjijiwebis.* Decent chaste beh., *binadisiwin.* Impure beh., *bishigwadjijiwebisiwin, winadisiwin, gagibadisiwin.*

Behind, *ajawaii, agawaii.* Behind the lodge or house, *awâssigamig,agawigamig.* Behind the island, *agawiminiss.* Behind the others, *ishkweiang, ishwêaii.*

Behold! *bina! nashké!*

Being, *aiaa.* Young being, *aiaans.* Great being, *kitchi aiaa.* Wicked being, *aiaawish, matchi aiaawish.*

Be it so, *mi ge-ing; apeingi.* (Pitane).

Belch; I belch, *nin mêgandji; nin babisibi.*

Belfrey, *kitotagan agodeg.*

Belie; I belie him, *nin giwanima.*

Belief, *debweiendamowin.*

Believe; I bel., *nin debwetam, nin debweiendam.* I believe in him, *nin debweienima.* I bel. him, *nin debwetawa.* I bel. it, *nin debwetân.*

Believer, *daiebwetang, gagikwewin daiebwetang.*

Bell, *kitotagan; tewessekaigan.* Small glcbular bell, *jinawaodjigan.*

Bellow; the ox or cow bellows, *masitagosi pijiki.*

Bellows, *bôdadjishkotawan.*

Belly, *omissadama, missad.* My, thy, his belly, *nimissad, kimissad, omissad.* I have pain in the belly, *nind akoshkade.* I have a big fat belly, *nin pikodji, nin pikonagiji.* I have a large belly, *nin mangimissade, nin manginagiji, nin mangidji.* I have a red belly, *nin miskwashkade.* My belly is swollen up, *nin bodadjishka.* I put it in my belly, or I have it in my belly, (*in., an.*) *nin wadendan; nin wadenima.*

Belly of an animal, *môdji.*

Below, *tabashish, nissaii, nissâki, nissâdjiwan.*

Belt, (girdle,) *kitchipisowin.* (Pakwâttehun).

Woolen belt, *miskogad.* Wool

for belts, *mishkogadeiab*. I make a belt, *nin miskogadike*.

Bemoan. S. Weep over.... Weeping over...

Bench, *apabiwin, tessabiwin*.

Bend, (bow;) I bend, *nin wâginige*. I bend it, (*in*., *an*.) *nin wâginan, nin jawâginan, nin saweshkan; nin wâgina, nin jawâgina, nin sawêshkawa*. I bend it towards me, *nin bidaginan*. It bends, *jashawabissemagad*.

Bend, (fold); I bend it, (*in*., *an*.) *nin biskinan; nin biskina*. I bend my arm, *nin biskiniken*.

Bend; I bend or incline myself, *nin naweta*.

Beneath, (under,) *a n â m a i i, anâming*.

Beneficence, *jawêndjigewin, jajawêndjigewin, nitâ-jawendjigewin*.

Beneficent; I am ben., *nin jajawêndjige, nin nitâ-jawendjige*.

Beneficial. S. Useful.

Benefit, *mino dodamowin, jawendjigewin*. I bestow a benefit, *nin jawendjige*. I bestow benefits, *nin jajawendjige*.

Benefit; I benefit him, *nin jawenima, nin mino dodawa*. I benefit myself, *nin jawenindis, nin mino dodas*. The act of benefitting, *jawendjigewin, jajawandjigewin*.

Benevolence, *kijadisiwin, kijewadisiwin*.

Benevolent; I am ben., *nin kijadis, nin kijewadis*.

Benighted; I am ben., *nin nondêtibishka*.

Benighted, (ignorant;) I am ben., *nin tibikadis*.

Benignity. S. Benevolence.

Bent, (bowed;) I am (it is) bent, *nin wagishka; wagishkamagad*.

Bent, (folded;) it is bent, *biskamagad, biskigishka, biskinigade*.

Bent backwards; I am bent b. *nin jashagita*.

Bent forwards; I am bent f., *nin wagenis*. I am bent by old age, *nin wagigika*. (Wâkisiw wâkikkaw).

Benumbed; I am ben., *nin gikimanis*. My arm is ben., *nin gikimaninike*. My foot is ben., my feet are ben., *nin gikimaniside, nin babisigisidewadj*. My hand is ben., my hands are ben., *nin gikimaninindji, nin babisigimindjiwadj*. My leg is ben., *nin gikimanigâde*.

Berry; a kind of red berry, *winissimin*.

Bet, *atâdiwin*. (Attâtuwin).

Bet; I bet, *nind atâge*. I bet it. (*in*., *an*.) *nind âtagen, nind aton; nind atagenan, nind atawâ*. (Atamew).

Bête-grise Bay. *Pagidawewin*. At, to or from Bête-grise Bay, *Pagidawewining*.

Betray; I bet. him, *nin pagidina*. (Misimew).

Better; a little better, *babénag*.

Between, *nawaii, nassawaii*. (Tastawicth).

Bewail; I bew. him, (her, it,) *nin mawima, nind ondadémonan; nin mawindan, nind ondadémon*.

Bewail. Bewailing.—S. Weep over...Weeping over...

Bewilder; I bew. him, *nin giwashkweiendamia*. I am be-

wildered, *nin giwashkweiendam.*
Beyond, *awâss wedi.*
Bible, *Kije-Manito o masinaigan.* I swear on the Bible, *Kije-Manito o masinaigan nind odjindan.*
Bid ; I bid him go home, or back, *nin giwénajâwa.*
Bier, *tchibai-oniganatig.*
Big, *kitchi.* I am big, *nin mindid.* It is big, *mitchamagad.*
Bigamist, *najokwewid.* I am a bigamist, *nin nijokwew.*
Bilberry. S. Whertleberry.
Bile, *osâwâbân.*
Bilious ; I am bilious, *nind osâwâbi.*
Bill, *masinaigans.*
Bill, (beak ;) its bill, (of a bird,) *okoj.*
Bill of divorce, *webinidiwi-masinaigan,webinidiwi-ojibiigan.*
Billow, (wave,) *tigow.*
Bind ; I bind, *nin sagibidjige, nin mindjimapidjige.* I bind him, (her, it,) *nin sagibina, nin mindjimapina ; nin sagibidon, nin mindjimapidon.* I bind him, fetter him, *nin mamandjigwapina.* I bind him, (her, it) well, *nind aindapina, nin wawenapina ; nin aindapidon, nin wawenapidon.* I bind or tie well his pack, *nin wawenapidamawa wiwaj.* I bind it in the middle, (*in.*, *an.*) *nind abitotchipidon ; nind abitotchipina.* I bind it again or otherwise, (*in.*, *an.*) *nind andapidon ; nind andapina.* I bind them together, (*in.*, *an.*) *nind ansapinadonan ; nind ansapinag.* (Takkopitew).
Bind, (in. s. in.) S. Tie.
Bind ; I bind or fetter his hands, his feet. S. Hand. Foot.
Birch-bark, *wigwass.* Birch-bark for a lodge, *wigwassapakwei.* I look for birch-bark, *nin nandokwam.* I am taking off birch-bark, *nin wigwassike.* (Waskwäy).
Birch-bark box,*wigwassi-makak*
Birch-bark canoe, *wigwass-tchimân.* (Waskwäy-osi).
Birch-bark dish, *wigwass-onâgan.*
Birch-bark lodge, *wigwassiwigamig.*
Birch-tree, *wigwass.* There are birch-trees, *wigwassika.* In a place where there are birch-trees, *wigwassikang.* The birch-trees are white, *wassakodewan wigwassan.* (Wayakesk).
Bird ; a *small* bird, *binéshi ;* a *large* bird, *binéssi.* Young little bird, *panadjâ.* A kind of bird, *pashkandamo.* The bird flies quick,*kijisse bineshi.* The bird flies low, *tabassisse bineshi.* The bird has his wings closed, *nabwangeshka bineshi.* The bird is naked, has no feathers, *pashkosi, papashkosi bineshi.* The bird carries s. th. in his beak, *nimaige bineshi.* The bird starts, *pasigwao bineshi.* (Piyesis).
Bird ; a kind of black bird, *segibanwanishi.* A kind of blue bird, *ojawane.* A kind of gray bird, *okanisse.* A kind of white bird, *odamaweshi.*
Birth, *ondadisiwin, nigiwin.* I give birth, *nind ondadisike, nin nigiawass.* I give him (her, it) birth, *nind ondadisia,*

nin nigia; nind ondadisiton, nin nigiton. I give birth to a child for him or to him, *nin nigitawa.* Premature abortive birth, *nishiwin.* (Nittâwikiw).

Birth; I give birth, (in. s. in.) S. delivered.

Birthday, *nigiwini-gijigad, ondadisiwini-gijigad.*

Birth-giving, *nigiawassowin, ondadisikewin.*

Biscuit, (sea-bread,) *anâkona.*

Biscuit, (small cake,) *pakwéjigans.*

Bishop, *Kitchi-mekatewikwanaie* (Kitchi-ayami-hewiyiniw).

Bitch, *nojessim, gishkishé, animosh.* The bitch is to have young ones, *andjissimo animosh.* (Kiskânak kiskisis).

Bite; I bite, *nin takwange.* I am in a habit of biting, *nin takwangeshk.*—I bite him, (her, it,) *nin takwama; nin takwandân.* 1 bite him much, cruelly, *nind abindama.* (Takkwamew).

Bite off; I bite off, *nin pakwendjige.* I bite off a piece of it, (*an., in.*) *nin pakwema; nin pakwendân.*

Bitter; it is bitter, (*in., an.*,) *wissagan, wissaga; wissagisi.* It is bitter, (liquid,) *wissagâgami.* It is bitter, (leaf,) *wissagibag.*

Bittern, (bird,) *moshkaossi, ganawabimogisissweshi.*

Bitterness, *wissagisiwin.*

Black, *makate*–...(Kaskitewaw). I am black, *nin makatéwis, nin makatéwiwe.* It is black, (*in., an.*) *makatéwa; makatéwisi.* It is black: Metal, (*in., an.*) *makatéwabikad; makatéwabikisi.* Thread, (*in., an.*,) *makatewabigad; makatewabigisi.* Liquid, *makatewagami.*

Black; I dye black, *nin makatewadissige, nin makatewansige.* I dye it black, (*in., an.*,) *nin makatewadissân, nin makatewansân; nin makatewadisswa, nin makatewanswa.*

Black; I paint it black, (*in., an.*,) *nin makatekodon; nin makatekona.* — It is painted black: Metal, (*in., an.*,) *makatewabikinigâde; makatewabikinigâso.* Wood, (*in., an.*,) *makatewakonigâde, makatewissaginigâde; makatewakonigâso, makatewissaginigâso.*

Blackbird, a kind of blackbird, *makateianak.*

Black cloth, *makatewegin.* (Kaskitewegin).

Black dog, *makatewassim.* (Kaskitewastim).

Black duck, *makateshib.* (Kaskiteshib).

Blacken; I blacken, *nin makatéwitchige.* I blacken him, (her, it,) *nin makatéwishkawa, nin makatewishima; nin makatéwishkân, nin makatéwissiton, nin makatewiton.* (Kaskitewinam).

Blacken, (in. s. in.) S. I paint it black.

Blackfoot Indian, *Ayâtchinini.*

Black-foot woman, *Ayâtchininikwe.*

Blacking, (especially for boots or shoes,) *makatewitchigan, mitigwakisini-makatewitchigan.*

Black-lead for polishing stoves with, *apissabik, wassikwadewaigan, wassikwabikaigan.*

Black River, *Makatewagami, Makatewagamiwisibi.*

Black serpent, *makateginebig.*

Blacksmith, *awishtoia.* I am a blacksmith, *nind awishtoiaw.* (Oyahisuw).

Blacksmith's shop, *awishtoia-wigamig.* (Oyahisuwikamik).

Blacksmith's trade, *awishtoia-wiwin.*

Bladder, S. Urine-bladder.

Blame; I blame him, (her, it,) *nind ânwenima; nind ânwendan.*

Blanket, *wâboiân.* My, thy, his blanket; *nikonass, kikonass, okonass.* I tie up high my blanket, *nin takwambis.* I tie my blanket under my chin, *nin sagânikamambis.* (Wâboweyân akkup).

Blanket moccasin, *wâboiakisin.* I wear blanket-moccasins, *nin wâboiakisine.*

Blaspheme; I blas., *nin batagijwe, nin matchigijwe, nind inâpinewinam.* I blas. him, (her, it,) *nind inâpinema; nin inâpinendân.* (Wiyakimow).

Blaspheming, *bata-gijwewin, inâpidewin.* (Wiyakimowin).

Blaze; I make the fire blaze, *nin biskakonendjige, nin biskakoneton* or *nin biskakonean ishkote.* The fire blazes, *mishwakone, biskakone* or *biskane ishkote.* The fire blazes up high, *namatâkone ishkote.* The fire blazes up by the wind, *biskaneiassin ishkote.* (Wasaskutew).

Blaze on a tree, *wassâkwaigan, wawabijagakwaigan, kikinawadakwaigan.*

Blaze trees; I blaze trees, *nin wassakwaige; nin kikinawadakwaige.* The trees are blazed, *kikinawadakwaigade.*

Bleach; I bleach it, *nin wâbishkigiton.* (Wâpâsam).

Blearedness, *tchissigawisibingwewin.*

Blear-eyed; I am bl., *nin tchissigawisibingwe.* (Pasakâbiw).

Bleed; I bleed, (let blood,) *nin bâskikweige.* I bleed him, *nin bâshkikwêwa.*—Bleeding, the act of bleeding somebody, *baskikweigewin.*

Bleed; I bleed, (shed blood,) *nin miskwiw.* I make him bleed, *nin miskwiwia.*—I bleed at the nose, *nin gibitân.* I bleed at the nose by a fall, *nin gibitaneshin.* I make him bleed at the nose by a blow, *nin gibitaneganâma.* (Mikkowiw).

Bless; I bless him, (her, it,) *nind anamietawa; nind anamietan.* I bless it, (*in,, an.*) *nin sigaandan; nin sigaandawa.* (Saweyimew).

Blessed; it is blessed, (*in., an.*) *sigaandjigâde; sigaandjigâso.*

Blessed water, *anamiewâbo.*

Blind; I am blind, *nin gagibingwe.* I make him blind, I blind him, *nin gagibingwea.* (Nama wâbiw).

Blindfold; I bl. him, *nind agwingwebina, nin gagibingwebina.*

Blindfolded; I am bl., *nind agwingwebis, nin gagibingwebis.*

Blindness, *gagibingwewin.*

Blind person, *gegibingwed.*

Blink; I blink with the eyes, *nin papâssangwab, nin passangaanab, nin papâssangaanab.*

Blister. S. Visicatory.
Blister; I have a blister; *nind abishkwebigis.* I have a blister on my hand, *nind abishkwebiginindjishin.* I have a blister on my foot, *nind abishkwebigisideshin.*
Block, *kotawân.*
Block; in a block, *mâmawi.* (Mikko ni mik).
Blood, *miskwi.* Coagulated blood, *wadô.* (Let blood. S. Bleed.) My blood is coming out, *nin sâgiskwagis.* I stain him, (her, it) with blood, *nin miskwiwia; nin miskwiwiton.*
Bloody, (stained with blood;) I am, (it is) bloody, *nin miskwiw; miskwiwan.* I strike him bloody, *nin miskwiwaganâma.*
Bloody flux, *miskwabiwin.* I have the bloody flux, *nin miskwabi.* (S. Dysentery.—S. Issue of blood.)
Bloom, blossom, *wâbigon.*
Blot out; I blot out, *nin gassiamage.* I blot it out, *nin gassian.* I blot it out to him, (forgive him,) *nin gassiamawa.* We blot out to each other, (pardon each other,) *nin gassiamadimin.*—I blot out a writing, *nin gassibian.* I blot him out, strike out his name, *nin gassibiwa.*
Blotted out; it is blotted out, *gassiigade.* It becomes blotted out, *gassiikamagad.*
Blotting out, *gassiamagewin, gassiamadiwin.*
Blow; I blow, *nin bodâdjige.* I blow him, (her, it,) *nin bodânâ, nin bodâdan.* I blow a sick person, *nin babwedana,* (*nin babodana.*) I blow the fire with bellows, *nin bodâdjishkotawe.*— It blows, (it is windy,) *nodin; animad.*
Blue. S. Sky-blue.
Blunder. S. Mistake.
Blunt; it is blunt, *ajiwa, âjiwassin, ajiiabikissin.*
Bluntish; it is bl., *pangi ajiiabikissin.*
Blush; I blush, *nin miskwingwesse.*
Board; I go on board, *nin bos.* I put him, (her, it) on board, *nin bosia; nin bositon.* It is on board, (*in., an.*) *bositchigâde; bositchigâso.*
Board (plank,) *nabagissag.* Small board, *nabagissagons.* I make it of boards, *nabagissagokadan.* It is made of boards, *nabagissagokade.* Hut or house made of boards only, *nabagissagowigamig.* — The board is narrow, *agassadesi nabagissag.* The board is wide, *mangadesi nabagissag.* Under a board, *anâmissag.* In the middle of a board, *nâwissag.*
Boarding, *ashangewin, ashandiwin; wissiniwin.*
Boarding-house, *ashangewigamig.*
Boarding-master, *ashangewinini.*
Boarding-mistress, *ashangekwe.*
Board-road. S. Plank-road.
Boast; I boast of..., *nin mamikwas, nin nawijim.* (Mamiyâkâtjimow).
Boaster, S. Braggart.
Boasting, *mamikwasowin.*
Boat, *miligo-tchimân.* (Mistik'osi).

Boat-builder, boat-maker, *tchamâniked, tchimânikewinini.*
Bodkin, *migoss.*
Body, *wiiawima.* My, thy, his body, *niiaw, kiiaw, wiiaw.* I have a body, *nind owiiaw.* I have it in my body, (in me,) *nind owiiawinodan.*— In the side of the body, *opiména.* I make him lie on his side, *nind opiméshima.* I have convulsions in my body, *nin tchitchibishka.*
Body ; in a body, *mâmawi.*
Bog, *wâbashkiki.*
Boil ; I boil s. th., *nind onsekwe.* I boil it, (*in., an.*) *nind onsân ; nind onswa.* It boils, *ondémagad.* The kettle boils, *onso akik.*
Boiling water, *wéndeg-nibi.*
Bois-blanc Island, *Wigobiminiss.*
Bomb, *bimoshkodawân.*
Bombasin, *gaskigin.*
Bond, *takobinigowin.*
Bone, *okanima.* My, thy, his bone, *nikân, kikân, okân.* (Oskan). A bone comes out of my body, *nin sagiganeshin.* A certain bone in the leg, *nitchishibodagan.* I have pain in the bones, *nin dewigan.*— I have large bones, *nin mamangigan.* I have small bones, *nin biwigan,* or, *nin babiwigane.* I have strong bones, *nin mashkawigane, nin songigane.*
Bonnet, *wiwakwân.* (Astotin).
Book, *masinaigan.* A small book, *masinaigans.* I open a book, (or letter,) *nin pakiginan masinaigan.* I close a book slightly, *nin patabinan masinaigan.* I close it briskly, *nin patabiwebinan,* or, *nin patakowebinan.*
Book-case, *masinaigani-tessabân.*
Boot, *mitigwakisin.*
Bore ; I bore him, (her, it) through, *nin jabopagwanéwa ; nin jabopagwaneân.* (Pakunehwew).
Bore, (in. s. in.) S. Pierce.
Born ; I am, (it is) born, *nin nig, nind ondadis ; nigimagad, ondadisimagad.*
Born again. S. Reborn.
Born with ; I am born with it, *nin giginig.* (Kikinittâwikiw).
Borrow ; I borrow, *nind atawange.* I borrow of him, *nind atawama.* I borrow it, (*in., an.*) *nind atawangen ; nind atawangenan.* I am in a habit of borrowing, *nind âtawangeshk.* Bad habit of borrowing, *atawangeshkiwin.* (Nandâttâmow).
Borrowed ; any thing borrowed, *awiigowin.*
Borrowing ; anything borrowed, *awiigowin.*
Borrowing, *atawangewin.* (Awihâsuwin).
Bosom, *pindomowin.* I put it in my bosom, (*in.. an.*) *nin pinomon ; nin pinomonan.* (Pimoyuw).
Boss, *nâganisid, ogima.*
Boss in a copper-mine, *miskwabikokeogima.*
Both, (in compositions,) *etawa.., etawi...*
Both, *naienj, néienj, nij.* On both sides, *etawaii.* Both sides of the body, *etawina.*
Bother ; I bother him, *nin migoshkadjia.* It bothers me, *nin migoshkadjiigon.*

Bottle, *omodai.* Little bottle or vial, *omodens.* (Moteyâbisk).
Bottom ; I bottom a barrel, *nin gibidiean makak.*
Bought ; I am, (it is) bought, *nin gishpinadjigas ; gishpinadjigade.* A bought object, *gishpinadâgan.* It is a bought object, *gishpinadaganiwan.*
Bound ; I am bound, or fettered, *nin mamandjigwapis, nin mamandjigwapidjigas, nin mindjimapis, nin mindjimapikaigas, nin mindjimapidjigas.* It is bound, *mindjimapide, mindjimapidjigade.* (Takkupisuw).
Bounty. S. Benevolence.
Bow, *mitigwab* Bow over the Indian cradle, *agwingweon.* (Atchâbïy).
Bow, Bowed, (in. s. in.) S. Bend. Bent.
Bow down ; I bow down, *nin jagashkita.* I bow down before him, (her, it,) *nin jagashkitawa; nin jagashkitan.* (Wâkinew).
Bowels, *onagij.* I exonerate the bowels, *nin misi.* I exonerate the bowels in my bed, *nin mitingwam.* I have pains in the bowels, *nind akoshkade.* Pain in the bowels, *akoshkadewin.* (Kisiwaskatewin).
Bowl, *onâgans.*
Bowman. S. Archer.
Bowsprit, *niganâkwaigan.*
Bow-string, *atchâb.*
Box, *makak.* Small box, *makakons.* Wooden box, *makakossag.*
Boy, *kwiwisens.* I am a boy, *nin kwiwisensiw.* The first-born boy of a family, *madjikiwiss.* I am the first-born boy of the family, *nin madjikiwissiw.* (Nâbesis).
Bracelet or ring around the wrist, *anân ;* around the arm, *kitchiwebison.* (Atchan).
Brag ; I brag of myself, *nin mamikwas.*—S. Praise, (flatter.)
Braggart, bragger, *mamadâgowinini, memikmasod.* I am a braggart, *nin mamikwas.*
Bragging, *mamikwasowin.*
Brain ; my, thy, his brain, *ninindib, kinindib, winindib.* (Wiyitip).
Brainpan. S. Skull.
Branch, *wâdikwan, odikwan.* There are branches, *bigwebimagad.* The tree has branches, *bigwebimagisi mitig.* I cut off branches, *nin majidikwanaige, nin tchigandaweige.* I cut off the branches of a tree, *nin majidikwanêwa mitig, nin tchigandawewa mitig.* The tree has large branches, *mamangidikwanagisi mitig.* (Musâwâtikwanew).
Brand, *keshkakideg.*
Brandy, *ishkotewâbo, meshkawagamig ishkotewâbo,* (strong fire-water.)
Brass, *osawâbik.*
Brass-wire, *osawâbikons.*
Brass-wire collar, *osawâbikonabikawâgan.*
Brave ; I am brave, *nin songidee.* Brave courageous person, *swangideed.* (Nâbekkâsow).
Brave, Bravery.— S. Courageous. Courage.
Brave. Brave warrior.—S. Hero.
Bravery, *songideewin.*
Brawl. Brawling.—S. Quarrel. Quarreling.

Brazenfaced. S. Shameless person.

Brazier, *akikokewinini.*

Brazier's trade, work, business, *akikokewin.*

Breach ; there are breaches, *tatawakwissin.*

Bread, *pakwéjigan.* Unleavened bread, *wembissitchigâs o s s i g pakwejigan.* Leavened bread, *wembissitchigâsod pakwejigan.* (S. Leavened).

Breadth ; one breadth, (of stuff or cloth,) *b ej i g o s h k.* T w o breadths, etc., *nijoshk,* etc. So many breadths, *dassoshk.*

Break ; I break it, (*in. an.*) *nin bigoshkân, nin bigwaan ; nin bigoshkawa, nin bigwawa.* (Pikunew pikupitew). I break it to pieces, (*in., an.*) *nin bigonân ; nin bigona.* I break it by letting it fall down, (*in., an.*) *nin bigwissidon ; nin bigwishima.* It breaks falling down, (*in., an.*) *bigwissin,* (*bigossin ;*) *bigwishin,* (*bigoshin,*) *bigwenishin.* I break it in two, (*in., an.*) *nin bokobidon ; nin bokobina.* I break it to small pieces, (*in., an.*) *nin bissaan ; nin bissawa.* I break it to small pieces in my hand, (*in., an.,*) *nin bissibidon ; nin bissibina.* I break it, (a dish, *in.*; a watch, *an.*) *nin pâssaan ; nin passawa.* I break it to pieces by striking, (*in., an.*) *nin bissaganandân ; nin bissaganâma.* I break some *long* object, (*in., an.*) *nin bokossidon, nin bokoshkan ; nin bokoshima, nin bokoshkawa.* It breaks, *bokotchishka, bokwasika.*—I break a bone, *nin bokwaigane.* I break branches on the road, *nin bôkonige.* I break my canoe, *nin bigoneshin, nin bokoshin nin tchimân.* I break a commandment, *nin bigobidon ganasongewin.* I break a field, *nin bigwakamigaan kitigan.* I break my nose falling, *nin bissagidjaneshin.* I break the point of s. th., *nin bokokojenân.* The tree breaks, *biskibagishka mitig.* Sticks break under the feet, *bokwemagad.*

Break (in s. in.) S. Tear.

Break down ; I break down, (I am ruined,) *nind angoshka, nin bigoshka.* It breaks down, (it is ruined,) *angoshkamagad, angomagad, bigoshkamagad.* I break it down, *nin bigobidon, nin nissakobidon.* I break it down by striking, (*in., an.*) *nin bigoganandân ; nin bigoganâma.*

Breakfast, *kigijeb-wissiniwin.* I take my breakfast, *nin kigijebwissin.* (Kikijebamitjisuwin).

Break off; I break it off, (*in., an.*) *nin bokoshkobinân, nin bokwanwissidon ; nin bokoshkobina, nin bokwanwishima.* I break off a piece, (*in., an.*) *nin pakwebidon ; nin pakwebina.* I break off a piece of wood, (*in., an.*) *nin pakwégaan ; nin pakwégawa.* I break it off by small pieces, (*in., an.*) *nin pigishkibidon ; nin pigishkibina.* It breaks off, (falls off,) *pakweshkamagad.* (P a k k w e p itew).

Break open ; I break it open, *nin nassidiéan.* It breaks open, *nassidiéssin, nassidiéshka.*

Break, (split ;) I break it, *nin*

passikan, *nin passiton.* It breaks, *passikamagad.*
Break through ; I break through s. th. with my foot, *nin bokisse.* I break through the ground, *nin bokakamigisse.*
Break to pieces ; I break it to pieces, (*in.*, *an.*) *nin passibidon ; nin passibina.* It breaks to pieces falling from a height, (*in.*, *an.*) *pigishkissin ; pigishkishin.*
Breakers. S. Shoals.
Breast, *okakiganama, kakigan.* My, thy, his breast, *nin kakigan, ki kakigan, o kakigan.* (Wâskigan). I have pain in my breast, *nin dêwakigan.* I have hair on the breast, *nin mishakigan.* I warm my breast, *nin kijakigânes.* I cover my breast, *nin kashkakiganeodis.* I uncover my breast, *nin mijishakiganebinidis, nin mijishakiganenidis.* My breast is uncovered, *nin mijishakiganeshin, nin mitakiganeshin.* My breast is uncovered indecently, *nin nibadâkigan.* I uncover his, (her) breast, *nin mijishakiganebina, nin mijishakiganena.*
Breast, woman's breast, *totosh.*
Breast-pin, *kashkakiganeon.*
Breast-plate, *essimig.* Breast-plate of silver, *joniiawessimig.* Breast-plate of porcelain, *migissiiessimig.*
Breath, *nêssewin, pagidanâmowin.* My breath is short, *nin takwanam.* My breath smells bad, *nin manjiwagwanam.* (Yeyewin).
Breathe ; I breathe, *nin nesse, nin pagidanam.* I breathe forth, *nin nassanam.* I breathe into him, *nin nessenodawa.* I breathe otherwise, *nind andanam.* I breathe deeply, *nin jôganam.* I breathe interruptedly, *nin kishkanam.* I br. by long intervals, *nin jajibanam.* I br. with difficulty, *nind akwanam, nind ishkanam, nind aiekwanam.* I can be long without breathing, *nin jibanam.* I br. my last, *nind ishkwanam.* (Yeyew yeyekâmow).
Breechcloth, *ansiân.*
Breeches, *gibodeiégwasson.*
Brick, *miskwâbiganowassin.*
Bride, *wa-widiged ikwe.*
Bridegroom, *wa-widiged inini.*
Bridge, *ajogan.* There is a bridge made, *ajoganikade.* I make a bridge, *nind ajoganike.* I walk over a bridge, *nind ajoge.*
Bridle, *sagidonebidjigan.* The horse has a bridle on, *sagidonebidjigâso bebejigoganji.* (Tâpitonepitchigan).
Brigand, *makandwewinini.*
Bright ; I make it bright, *nin washkeiabikishkan.*
Bright, (in. s. in.) S. Shine. Shining.
Brightness, *wasseiâsiwin.*
Brim ; I brim it, (*in.*, *an.*) *nin nassabashkinadon ; nin nassabashkinaa.*
Brimstone, *osâwi-makate.*
Brine, *jiwitaganabo.*
Bring ; I bring, *nin bidass.* I bring him, (her, it,) *nin bina, nin bidoma ; nin bidon, nin bidondan.* I bring him s. th., *nin bidawa, nin bidamawa.* I bring him, (her, it) to some place, *nin dagwishima ; nin*

dagwissilon. I bring him,(her, it) ashore on my back, from a canoe or boat, *nind agwaô-ma ; nind agwaôndan.* (Pesiwew petaw).

Bring back ; I bring him (her, it) back again, *nin bi-giwewina, neiab nin bina ; nin bi-gewiwidon, neiab nin bidon.* (Kiwittahew).

Bring down ; I bring him (her, it) down, *nin bi-nissiwina ; nin bi-nissiwidon.*

Bring forth, (in. s. in.) S. Birth. —S. Yield fruit.

Bring in ; I bring him (her, it) in, *nin pindigana ; nin pindigadon.* I bring in wood, *nin pindigenisse.* (Pesiwew).

Bring to light ; I bring him (her, it) to light, *nin mokawa, nin mokina ; nin mokaan, nin mô-kinan.*

Bring up ; I bring him (her, it) up, *nind ikwegia, nin nitawegia ; nind ikwegiton, nin nitawigiton.*

Bring with ; I bring with me, *nin bigigis.* I bring him (her, it) with me, *nin bi-gigisinan ; nin bi-gigisin.* I cause him to bring along with him s. th., *nin bi-gigisia.* It brings along with it, *bi-gigisimagad.* (Kikiwisiw).

Brittle ; it is brittle, (*in., an.*) *kâpan, kapadad ; kapisi, kapadisi.* (Kâspisiw).

Broad, (in. s. in.) S. Wide.

Broad axe, *tchigigaigan.*

Broil ; I broil it, (*in., an.*) *nin bansan ; nin banswa.*(Pâswew).

Broken ; it is broken, *bigoshka, makishka, bigobidjigade.* It is broken to pieces, (*in., an.*) *bissaigade ; bissaigaso.* It is broken to pieces by s. th. that fell on it, (*in., an.*) *bissikode ; bissikoso.* The ground or soil is broken up, *bigwakamigaigade.* Something is broken in my body, *nin bokodjishka.* (Pikupayiw).

Broken. S. Infirm.

Broken branch on the road, *bokonigan.*

Brook, *sibiwishé.*

Broom, *tchigataigan, tchishataigan.* (Webahigan).

Broomstick, *tchigataiganak, tchigataiganâtig.*

Broth, *nabôb, wiiâssabo.* (Mitjimâbüy).

Brother, my, thy, her brother, *nin awema, kid awema, od aweman.* My, thy, his *older* brother, *nissaie, kissaie, ossaieian* My, thy, his *younger* brother, *nishime, kishime, oshimeian.* We are brothers, *nind oshimeindimin.* (N'istês ostesa).

Brother-in-law ; my, thy, his brother-in-law, *nita, kita, witan.* My, thy, her brother-in-law, *ninim, kinim, winimon.* (N'ista).

Brother or friend ; my, thy, his brother, (friend,) *nidjikiwé, kidjikiwé, widjikiwéian ; or, nikâniss, kikaniss, wikanissan.* He is my brother, (friend,) *nind owidjikiwéima, nind owikanissima.* We are brothers, (friends,) *nind owidjikiweindimin, nind owikanissindimin.* (N'itjiwa otjiwama).

Broth-pot with legs, *okâdakik.*

Brought ; it is brought here, (*in., an.*) *bidjigâde ; bidjigâso.*

It is brought somewhere, (*in.*, *an.*) *dagwissitchigâde* ; *dagwissitchigâso*.
Brought in ; I am brought in, *nin pindiganigo*. He (she, it) is brought in, *pindigana* ; *pindigade, pindigadjigade*.
Brought up ; I am brought up, *nin nitawigiigo, nin nitawig*.
Brow. S. Forehead.
Brown ; I am brown, *nin sigwaningwewadj*.
Browse, *kibins onimik*.
Browse ; it browses, (a beast,) *onimikoke, gishkâkwandjige*. (Mâmattwettawew).
Bruise, *jashagoshkosowin, dassosowin*.
Bruise ; I bruise him, (her, it,) *nin banasikawa* ; *nin banasikan*.
Bruised ; I am bruised by s. th. that fell upon me, *nin jashagoshkos*.
Brush, clothes-brush, *binawéigan*.
Brush ; I brush clothes, *nin binawéige*.
Brush, painting-brush, *bijijobiigan*.
Bucket, for fetching water, *nadobân, nimibagan*.
Buckle, *adabikissidjigan*.
Buckler, *pakâkwaan*.
Bud, *onimik, wanimik*.—S. Germ.
Buffalo, *mashkodé-pijiki*. (Maskutewimustus).
Buffalo-robe, *pijikiwegin*. (Mustusweyân).
Buffet ; I buffet him, *nin passanowéwa, nin nabagaskinindjitawa*.
Buffoon, *wembâjisid*. I play the buffoon, *nind ombâjis, nin babapinwe*.
Buffoonery, *ombajisiwin, babapinwewin*.
Bugbear, *gagawetadjitchigan*.
Bugle, *bodâdjigan*.
Build, I build a lodge, *nind ojige*. I build a house, *nin wâkaige*.
Builder, *ojigewinini, wâkaigewinini*.
Building, *ojigewin, wâkaigewin*.
Bulky ; I am, (it is) bulky, *nin mindid; mitchâ*. (Misikitiw).
Bull, *nabé-pijiki*.
Bullet, *anwi*. (Mousassinïy).
Bullet-mould, *anwikadjigan*.
Bundle, of hay or some other *in.* obj., *takobideg*.
Bundle, of shingles or some other *an.* obj., *takobisowag*.
Bundle or packet of fur, *mikindagan*.
Buoy to a net, *okandigan*. Another kind of buoy, *okandikan bikodjikosod*. (Ayâpâttik).
Buoy. S. Sea-mark.
Burbot, *awâssi, awâssissi*.
Burial, *pagigendamowin*.
Burn, *tchagisowin*. (Kisisowin).
Burn ; I burn, *nin tchâgis*. I burn and weep, *ni sessessakis*. It burns, *tchâgide*. I burn s. th., *nin tchâgisige*. I burn him, (her, it), *nin tchagiswa* ; *nin tchagisan*. I burn myself, *nin agwâbikis*. (Kisisow). I burn him, *nind agwâbikiswa*. I burn (it burns) in a certain place, *nin danakis, danakide*. (Pasitew). I burn entirely, to coal, *nind akakanakis*. It burns to coal, *akakanakide, akakanakate*. I burn him, (her, it) to coal, *nind akakanakiswa, nind akakanakisan*. I burn (or make)

coal, *nind akakajeke.*—I burn (it burns) all up, *nin kashkakis, nin tchâgakis, kashkakide, tchâgakide.* I cease (it ceases) burning, *nind ishkwaiakis, ishkwaiakide.* It burns through, *kishkakide, bigode.* I burn it through, (*in., an.*) *ni kishkakisan, kishkakiswa.*—I burn it for fuel, (*in., an.*) *nin bodawen, nin bodawenan.*—I burn s. th. to make a good odor, *nin minomagwekisige.* I burn s. th. on metal (*in., an.*) to make a good odor, *nin minomagwabikisan, nin minomagwabikiswa.* (Kisiswew).

Burn up; I burn (it burns) up entirely, *nin tchâgakis, tchâgakide.* I burn him, (her, it) up entirely, *nin tchagakiswa, nin tchagakisan.* I burn up all my fuel, *nin tchagakisama.*

Burnt; it is burnt in a certain manner, *inidemagad.* It is too much burnt, *osamakidemagad.*

Burnt forest, *wissakode.* There is a burnt forest, *wissakodewan.* (Wipuskaw).

Burnt-sacrifice, *tchâgisige-pagidinigewin.*

Burst; I burst it, *nin tâtoshkan.* It bursts, *pâshkikamagad.* It bursts by freezing, *pashkakwadin, passadin.* It bursts by heat, *pâshkide.* I make burst (berries,) *nin pashkiminassige.* I make them burst, (berries, *in., an.,*) *pashkiminassanan; nin pashkiminasswag.*

Burst asunder; I burst (it bursts) asunder, *nin nanawisse; nanawissemagad.* (Pâskitew).

Bury; I bury him, *nin pagidenima.* I bury him (her, it) under s. th., *nin ningwawa, nin ningwaakana; nin ningwaan, nin ningwaakadan.* (Nahinew).

Burying-place, *ningwaakan, tchibégamig.* (Kikwâhâskâw).

Bush, *kibinsan.* In the bushes, *anibishikang.* (Nipisikubâk).

Bushel, *dibaigan, dibaiminan.*

Business; *anokiwin, inanokiwin.* Troublesome difficult business, *animakamigisiwin.* I have a difficult business, *nind animakamigis.* (Atuskewin).

Bustle; I bustle about, *nin babâijita.*

Busy; I am busy, *nind ondamita, nind ondamis, nind ondamakamigis, nind akamigis.* I am busy at s. th., *nind ondamitchige.* I am busy at my child, (children,) *nind ondamonje.* I am no more busy, *nind ishkwakamigis.* (Otamiyuw).

But, *dash,* (after the word), *anisha dash.* (Maka).

Butcher, *nitagewinini.* (Nipahipijiskiwew).

Butcher. S. Kill animals.

Butchering, *nitagewin.*

Butter, *totoshâbo-bimide, osâwabimide.* I butter bread, *nin jijowa pakwejigan.* The bread is buttered, *jijoigaso pakwejigan.*

Butterfly, *memêngwa.* (Kâmâmak).

Buttocks, *miskwassab.* I have large buttocks, *nin pikwakossagidiie.* (Oppwâm).

Button, *boto.* I button myself up, *nin gîbwandjakwaodis.* (Aniskamân).

Buy ; I buy, *nin gishpinage, nin gishpinadjige.* I buy him, (her, it,) *nin gishpinana ; nin gîshpînadon.* I buy for myself, *nin gishpinamadis.* I buy him (her, it) for myself, *nin gishpinamadisonan ; nin gishpinamadison.* I buy it for him, *nin gishpinadawa, nin gishpinadamawa.* (Otâwew)..

Buzz ; it buzzes, *gaskwemagad.*

Buzzing fly, *kitchi âmo.*

By-and-by, *nâgatch, pitchinag, gomâpi, pama, panima.* (Tcheskwa).

By heart, *pagwana.*

By little and little, *pepangi ; gegapi.* (Ayâpisis).

By meat, *apândjigan.*

By no means, *kawin bâpish, kawêssa.* (Namawâtch).

By the side of...., *opiméaii.*

C

Cabbage, *kitchi anibish.* (Otehepok).
Cable, *kitchi biminakwân.*
Cake, *pakwejigans.*
Calash, *titibidabân, babamibaigo-titibidabân.*
Calendar, *gijigado-masinaigan.* (Akinokkwekijikasinahigan).
Calf, *pijikins.* (Mustusus).
Calf of the leg ; the calf of my, thy, his leg ; *ninân, kinân, onânan.* (Otâsiskitân).
Calico, *kitagigin.* Calico for curtains, *agobidjiganigin.*
Call, *nandomigosiwin.*
Call ; I call, *nin nandwewem.* I call for him, (her, it,) *nin nandwewema ; nin nandwewendan.*
Call loud ; I call loud, *nin bibag.* I call him (her, it) loud, *nin bibagima ; nin bîbagindan.* It calls me, *nin bibagimigon.* (Tepwâtew).
Call, (name ;) I call him, (her, it,) *nind ijinikana, nind ina, nin wina ; nind ijinikadân, nind îdân; nin windan.* I call myself so...., *nind ijinikanidis, nin winidis.*
Call, (summon, invite ;) I call, *nin nandonge, nin nandondjige.* I call him, *nin nandoma.* I call them together, *nin mawandonandomag.* I call by firing guns, *nin nandwéwesige.*
Call upon ; I call upon his name, *nin wawina.*

Called ; I am called in a certain manner, *nind ijinikanigos.* I am (it is) called so...., *nind ijinikas, nin wins, nind ijiwins ; ijinikade, ijiwinde.*
Called, (summoned, invited ;) I am called, *nin nandomigo, nin nandomigos,nin nandondjigas*
Calling, *bibagiwin.*
Calm ; I calm myself, *nind anissendam.*
Calm ; it is calm, *anwâtin ; dogissin.* The water is calm like a mirror, *wâssikogamissin.* It is calm after a heavy sea, *ishkwaiagamîsse.* (Ayowâstin).
Calumet of red stone, *miskwassinopwâgan.*
Calumniate ; I cal., *nin dajinge.* I calumniate him, (her,it,) *nin dajima, nin modjimotawa ; nin tajindan.* We cal. each other, *nin dajindimin.* (Ayimomew).
Calumniation, calumny, *dajindiwin.*
Calumniator, *dejingeshkid.* I am a calumniator, *nin dajingeshk.*
Calumnious ; I am cal., *nin dajingeshk.* (Matchi-ayimwew).
Calvary, *wijiganikan.*
Camel, *pekwawigang, megwawigang awessi.*
Camp, *gabêshiwin, nibewin.*
Camp ; I camp, *nin gabêsh.* I camp from distance to distance, *nin bimodegos.*

Camphor, *gwedasseg.*
Camping, *gabéshiwin.* Camping from distance to distance, *bimodegosiwin.*
Can; I can, *nin gashkiton.* I can do nothing with him, (her, it,) *nin bwanawia; nin bwanawiton.*
Canada, *Monia.* In, from or to Canada, *Moniang.*
Canadian, *moniâwinini, wemitigoji.*
Canadian woman, *moniâkwe, wemitigojikwe.*
Canal, *sibikadjigan.* I dig or make a canal, *nin sibikadjige.* There is a canal made, *sibikâde.*
Cancer, *manadapinewin emowemagak.* I have a cancer, *nind amôg.*
Cancerous; I am can., *nind amôg.*
Candle, *wassakwanendjigan.*
Candlestick of metal, *wassakwanendjiganabik.*
Candlestick of wood, *wassakwanendjiganatig.*
Cane, (walking stick,) *sakaon.* I use it as a cane, *nin sakaon.*
Cane-sugar, *sibwagani-sisibâkwat.*
Cannibal, eater of human flesh, *windigo; windigokwe.*
Cannot; I cannot, *nin bwanâwi, kawin nin gashkitossin.* I cannot make it, or get it, *nin bwanawiton.*
Canon, *kitchi-pâshkisigan.*
Canon-ball, *kitchi-pashkisigan anwi.*
Canoe, *tchimân.* (Osi). A small canoe, *tchimanens.* A bad old canoe, *tchimânish.* So many canoes, *dassonag.* Two canoes, three canoes, etc., *nijonag, nissonag,* etc. I have a large canoe, *nin mangôn.* I have a small canoe, *nind agasson.*—The canoe is high, *ishponagad tchimân;* it is low, *tabassônagad.* The canoe is large, *mangônagad tchiman;* it is small, *agassônagad.* The canoe is long, *ginônagad tchiman;* it is short, *takônagad.* The canoe is sure, (not dangerous,) *kitagwinde tchiman;* it is not sure, (it is rolling,) *gokokwamagad.*—In the canoe, *pindonag.* I am alone in a canoe, *nin bejigokam, nin nijikeokam.* We are two, three, etc., in a canoe, *nin nijôkamin, nin nissôkamin,* etc. We are so many in a canoe, *dassôkamin.*—In the foremost part of a canoe, *wanakodjaonag, nitamonagong;* in the stern, *odakaning.*—Under the canoe, *anâmonag.* On this side of the canoe, *ondassônag;* on the other side, *awassônag.* —I carry a canoe to the water, *nin madâdon tchimân,* or, *nin madâssidon.* I push my canoe from the shore, *nin niminaweshka.* The canoe goes out into the lake, *niminaweshkamagad tchiman.* I have nothing in my canoe, *nin pijishigonagaam.* My canoe breaks, *kishkissin nin tchimân.* I mend my canoe, *nin wawejaaton nin tchimân.*
Canoe-bark, *tchimanijig.* (Waskwây-osi).
Canoe-maker, *tchamaniked, tchimanikewinini.* I make a canoe, *nin tchimanike.* (Astoyuw).

Canoe-making, *tchimanikewin.*
Canoe-measure, *dibaonon.*
Canoe-model, *wanades h k o dj i-gan.*
Canvass, (sail-cloth,) *ningassi-mononigin.*
Cap, *wiwakwân, nebâgag wiwak-wân.* Cap made of cloth, *ma-nitoweginowiwakwân.* (Asto-tin).
Capable. S. Able.
Cape. S. Point of land.
Capricious; I am cap., *nin ba-shigwadis.*
Captive, *awokân.* I am a cap-tive, (in Indian captivity,) *nind awokâniw.*
Capsize; I cap., (in a canoe, boat, etc.), *nin gonabishka.* I cap. in a rapid, *nin gonababog.* I capsize (upset) him, (her, it,) *nin gawina; nin gawinan.*— S. Overthrow.
Capuchin, *wiwakwân.*
Carabine, *bemîdekadeg pâshki-sigan.*
Carbonized; it is car., *akaka-nakide, akakanate.* I am car., *nind akakanadis.*
Carcass, *jigoshigan.*
Card-playing, *atâdiwin, atage-win.*
Card. S. Playing-card.
Care; I care, *nin babamendam.* I care for him, (her, it,) *nin babamenima, nin sabenima; nin babamendan, nin saben-dan.* I don't care for him, *nind ajidema.* I care for my-self, *nin babamenindis.* — I take care of somebody, *nin bamiiwe.* I take care of him, (her, it,) *nin bamia; nin ba-miton.* I take care of myself, *nin bamiidis, nin bamikoda-dis.* I am taken care of, *nin babamendjigas.* It is taken care of, *babamendjigade.* —I take well care, *nind ang-wâmis, nind aiangwâmis.* I take well care of it, *nind aiangwâmendan, nind aiang-waminan, nind angwamendan, nind angwaminan.*—I take care of it, (*in., an.*) in order to conserve it long, *nin manad-jiton; nin manâdjia.*—I have too much care, *nind osamen-dam.* Too much care, *osa-mendamowin.* I take care of sick persons, *nin gatiniwe.* I take care of him in his sick-ness, *nin gatina.* (Pisiskeyi-mew).
Care, (in. s. in.) S. Take care.
Careful, (orderly;) I am careful, *nin insagâkamis.* (Pisiskeyit-tam).
Carefulness, (good order,) *sagâ-kamisiwin.*
Careless; I am careless, *kawin nin sagâkamisissi.*
Carelessly, *mamanj.*
Carnage, *nissidiwin.* (Metchihi-tuwin).
Carp, (fish,) *namébin.* Large carp, *papagessi.*
Carp-bone, *namebinigan.*
Carpet for a floor, *apishimoni-gin.* (Anâskewin).
Carp-River, *Namebinî-sibi.*
Carpenter, *wakaigewinini, ojige-winini.*
Carpenter, (in. s. in.) S. Joiner.
Carpentry, *wakaîgewin, ojige-win.* I work carpentry, (build houses,) *nin wakaige.*
Carriage. S. Cart.
Carried away; I am, (it is) car-ried away, *nin madjidjigas,*

nin madjiwidjigas ; madjidjigade, madjiwidjigade.
Carrot, *osawâkadakons.*
Carry ; I carry (or convey) him, (her, it,) *nind ijiwina ; nind ijiwidon.* I carry it to him, *nind ijiwidawa, nind ijiwidamawa.* I carry s. th. in a basket, *nind awadjiwane.* I carry it for him, *nind awadjiwanawa, nin bimiwîdawa, nin babimiwidawa.* We carry it for each other, *nin babimiwidadimin.* I carry it elsewhere, (*in., an.*) *nin bakéwîdon ; nin bakêwina.* I carry it to him, *nin madjidawa, nin madjiwidawa, nin madjiwidamawa.* I carry it on s. th. (*in., an.*), *nin nimaan ; nin nimaa.* I carry (or convey) him, (her, it) further than I ought, *nind answewina ; nind answewidon.* I carry in a canoe, *nind âwadagâodass.*
Carry away ; I carry him (her, it) away, *nin madjîna, nin madjiwina, nin b i m i w i n a ; nin madjidon, nin madjiwidon, nin bimiwidon.* (Sipwettahew). I carry myself away, *nin madjiwinidis.* I carry him (her, it) away in a canoe or boat, *nin madjiôna ; nin madjiôdon.* I carry him (her, it) away on my back, *nin madjiôma, nin madôma ; nin madjiondan, nin madondan.* I c a n n o t carry him (her, it) away, *nin bwawina ; nin bwawidon.*
Carry back again ; I c a r r y (lead or convey) him, (her, it) back again, *nin giwewina ; nin giwewidon.*
Carry down ; I carry him (her, it) down, *nin nissandawaa ; nin nissandawaton.*
Carry in ; I carry him (her, it) in, *nin pindigana ; nin pindigadon.*
Carry in or on a carriage or sled or sleigh ; I carry in a carriage, *nind âwadass, nind âwadjidabi.* (Otâbew). I carry it in or on a carriage, etc., (*in., an.*) *nind âwadon ; nind âwana.* I carry stones, *nind âwadassini.* I carry wood, *nind âwadanisse.* I carry for myself, *nind âwadjiwanadis.* I carry for somebody, *nin âwadjiwanage.* I carry for him, *nind âwadjiwanawa.*—Carrying in or on a carriage, etc., *awadjidabiwin, odabiwin.* (Otâbâtew).
Carry in or on one's self ; I carry in or on me, *nin gigishkage.* I carry him (her, it) in me or on me, *nin gigishkawa ; nin gigishkan.* (Pimoyuw kikiskawew).
Carry in the mouth ; I carry in my mouth, *nin nimandjige.* I carry him (her, it) in my mouth, *nin nimama ; nin nimandan.* (Takkwamew).
Carry on the back ; I carry a pack or load on my back, *nin bimiwane, nin bimôndan.* (Nayatchikew). I make him carry a load on his back, *nin bimiwanea, nin bimondaa.* I carry somebody on my back, (a child,) *nin bimomâwass.* (Nayew nayawasuw). I carry him (her, it) on my back, *nin bimôma ; nin bimôndan.*—I carry a heavy pack, *nin kosigowâne.* I can hardly carry my load, *nin bwawane.* I can hardly

carry him, (her, it,) *nin bwaôma; nin bwaôndan.* (Kawiskosow). I carry too heavy a load on my back, *nind osâmiwan.* I carry it all at once, *nin débiwane.* I can carry the whole of it, *nin gashkiwane.* I can carry him (her, it) on my back, *nin gashkôma; nin gashkôndân.* I carry a load in advance, *nin bidjitass.*

Carry on the shoulder; I carry on my shoulder, *nin biminige.* I carry him (her, it) on my shoulder, *nin biminigana, nin onigana; nin biminigadan, nind onigadan.* I make him carry s. th. on his shoulder, *nin biminigadamoa, nind onigadamoa.*

Carry out; I carry him (her, it) out of doors, *nin sagisia, nin sagidina, nin sagidjîwina; nin sagisiton, nin sagidinan, nin sagidjiwidon.* (Wayawittahew).

Cart, *odabân, titibisse-odabân, titibidaban.* I make carts, I am a cartwright; *nind odabanike, nin titibidabanike.*

Cartilage, *kakâwandjigan.*

Cartman, *wedabiâd bebejigoganjin.*

Cartwright, *titibidabanikewinini, odabanikewinini, wedabaniked.*

Cartwright's business or trade, *odabanikewin, titibidabanikewin.*

Carve; I carve, *nin masinikodjige.* I carve it, (*in., an.*) *nin masinikodân; nin masinikona.*

Carved; it is carved (*in., an.*), *masinikode, masinitchigade; masinikoso, masinitchîgaso.*

Carved image, (statue,) *masinikodjigan.*

Carver, *masinikodjigewinini.*

Carver's chisel, *masinikodjigan.*

Carving, *masinikodjigewin.*

Cascade, cataract; there is a cascade, a cataract, *kakâbika, kakâbikawan.* In a place where there is a cataract, to or from such a place, *kakâbikang, kakabikawang.* (Pâwistik).

Case, *pîndanonikadjigan.* I put it in a case or cover, (*in., an.*) *nin pindaodon; nin pindaona.* It is in a case, (*in., an.*) *pindaode; pindaoso.*

Case for arrows, *pindanwân.* (Pittatwân).

Casern, *jimaganishi-wakaigan.*

Cash, *gwaiak joniia.*

Cask, *makakossag.*

Cassock, *mekatewikwanaîe o babisikawagan.*

Cast; I cast, *nind apagijiwe.* I cast him (her, it) somewhere, *nind apagina; nind apagiton, nind apagitan.*—S. Throw

Cast, (in. s. in.) S. Mould. Moulded.

Casting-house, *ningikosigewigamig.*

Cast iron, *sagaigadeg biwâbik.*

Castor-oil, *bimide-jabosigan.*

Cast off. S. Throw away.

Castrate; I castrate him, *nin pakwejwa, nin kishkijwa.* (Maniswew).

Castrated; I am cast., *nin kishkijigas.*

Castration, *pakwejodiwin, kishkijigasowin.*

Cat, *gajagens, minons.* Male cat, *nabé-gajagens.* Female cat, *ikwe-gajagens.*

Catamenia. S. Monthly flowings.
Cataract. S. Cascade.
Catarrh, *agig, agigokawin.*
Catch; I catch him (her, it) with my hand, *nin debibinâ; nin debibinan.* I catch him (her, it) with my hand hastily, *nin nawâdina; nin nawâdinan.* I catch it for him, *nin nawadinamawa.*
Catch, (crush;) I catch his hand (or finger) between the door, *nin tagwakonindjiwa.* M y hand or finger is catched, *nin tagwakonindjishkos.*
Catch fish; I catch so many fishes in my net, *nin dassôbina.*
Catch in a net; I catch in a net, (or nets,) *nin pindaan.* I catch him (her, it) in a net, *nin pindaana; nin pindaadon.* I catch myself (or I am caught) in a net, *nin pindaas.* (Nakwâtew).
Catch in the air; I catch it, (*in., an.*), *nakwêbidon; nin nakwêbina.*
Catch with a hook; I catch with a hook, *nind adjigwadjige.* I catch him (her, it) with a hook, *nind adjigwana; nind adjigwadan.* It catches, *adabikissin.*
Catechumen, *wa-sigaandosod.*
Catechism, *Kateshim.*
Catholic, *katolik.*
Catholic Christian, *katolik enamiad.*
Catholic religion, *katolik enamiewin.*
Cause; I cause it to him, (her, it,) *nin dodawa, nind inikawa, nin mina; nin dodan, nind inikan.* I cause it to myself, *nin dodas, nin minidis.* It causes me s. th., *nind inikagon.*
Cause of anger or condemnation, *ondenindiwin.*
Cause to one's self. S. Deserve.
Cave. S. Cavern.
Cavern; there is a cavern in a rock, *wimbabikamagad.* There is a cavern in a mountain, *wanadinamagad.*
Cease; I cease, *nind anwata, nin bisanab.* I cease working, *nin bonita.* I cease speaking, *nin bonwewidam.* It ceases, *bisanabimagad, anwatamagad*
Cease, *boni–*, (in compostions.) I cease to be thirsty, *nin boninibâgwe*, etc.
Cedar. S. Cedar-tree.
Cedar-bag, cedar-sack, *gijikashkimod.*
Cedar-bark, *wanagek, onagek.* I take off cedar-bark, *nin gashkaanagekwe.* The cedar-bark can be taken off, *pakweshka wanagek.* (Pakkwaniw).
Cedar-branch, *gijikândag.* I break and gather cedar-branches, *nin manâjide.*
Cedar-forest, cedar-swamp, *gijikiki.*
Cedar-tree, *gijik.* Young small cedar, *gijikens.* (Mânsikiska).
Cedar-wood, *gijik.*
Cede, (deliver); I cede him, (her, it,) *nin pagidenima; nin pagidendan.* I cede it to him, *nin pagidinamâwa.*
Celebrated. Celebrity.—S. Renown. Renowned.
Cellar, (under the floor of a house,) *anamissag-wânikân.*
Cemetery, *tchibegamig.*
Cense. S. Incense.

Censer, *pakwenessatchigan, minomagwabikisigan.*
Censure; I censure him, *nin dajima.* We censure one another, *nin dajindimin.* (Atâweyittamâwew).
Census, *agindjigadewin.* (Akimiwewin).
Cent, copper-cent, *jomânike, miskwâbikons, osâwâbikons.*
Centre; in the centre, *nawaii.* It is the centre, *nawaiiwan, nassawaiiwan, nissawaiiwan.*
Certain, *gwaiak.* A certain, *bejig.* (Peyak).
Certainly, *abidêkamig, geget, angwamass, gwaiak.* Yes, certainly, *e nange ka, aningwana.* (Tâpwe-ketchina).
Certificate, *debwewini-masinaigan.*
Cerumen. S. Ear-wax.
Chagrin. S. Sadness.
Chair, *apâbiwin.* I take chair, *nin namadab.*
Chalice, *anamie-minikwâtchigan.*
Chalk, *wâbishkibejibiigan, wâbishkibeshaigan.*
Chambermaid, *anokitâgekwe, bamitâgekwe.*
Chance, *jâwendâgosiwin, minwâbamewisiwin.* I have a good chance, *nin jawendagos, nin minwabamewis.* (Papewewin).
Chandler, *wassâkwanendjiganikewinini.* I am a chandler, (I make candles,) *nin wassakwanendjiganike.*
Change; I change it, (*in.*, *an.*) *nind andjiton; nind andjia.* I change (or alter) s. th. for him, *nind andjitawa, nind ândjitamawa.*—I change my clothes, *nind andjikwanaie.* I change my life, my conduct, *nind andji-bimâdis, nind andjijiwebis.* I change my lodge, *nind andjîge.* I change my mind often, *nind aiajawendam, nin binâiendam, nin binasssawagendam.* I change my name, *nind andjinikanidis.* I change his (her, its) name, *nind andjinikana; nind andjinîkadan.* I change my shoes, *nind andakisine.* I change a writing, *nind andjibian.* (Meskutchi-pimâtisiw meskutaskisinew, etc.).
Change, exchange; I change it, (for some other object, *in.*, *an.*) *nin meshkwatonan; nin meshkwatona.* I change it to him, *nin meshkwatonamawa.*
Changed; I am (it is) changed, *nin andjiaia; andjigade, andjitchigade.* Changed life or conduct, *andji-bimadisiwîn.* Changed name, *andjinikasowin, andjiwinsowin.* I have (it has) a changed name, *nind andjinikas; andjinikade.* Changed writing, *andjibiigan.* (Meskutcikâtew).
Change, exchanged; it is changed into..., *meshwatosse.*
Changed, strange; I am (it is) changed, strange, *nin maiagendagos; maiagendagwad.* I find him (her, it) changed, *nin maiagenima; nin maiagendân.* I find myself changed, *nin maiagenindis.* I look (it looks) changed, strange, *nin maiaginagos; maiaginagwad.* I see him (her, it) changed, *nin maîaginawa; nin maiaginan.* (Mâmaskâtjinâkusiw).

Changing; it is changing fur, (an animal,) *andawe.* (Pinawew).
Changing-house, change-house, *andjikwanaiewigamig.*
Changing of mind, inconstancy, *aiajawendamowin.*
Channel, *inâonan.* Channel between islands, *jibatig.*
Chap, *oshkinawe.*
Chapel, *anamiewigamig, anamiewigamigons.*
Chapped. S. Cracked.
Charcoal, *akakanje.* I burn (or make) charcoal, *nind akakanjek.* Place where they burn charcoal, *akakanjekân.*
Charcoal-man, *akakanjekewinini.*
Charcoal-man's business or trade, *akakanjekewin.*
Charitable; I am ch., *nin kijâdis, nin kijewâdis, nin nitajawendjige.* I am ch. to him, *nin kijewâdisitawa.* We are ch. to each other, *nin kijewadisitadimin.*
Charitable heart, *jawendamideewin.* I have a ch. heart, *nin jawendamidee.*
Charitable person, *kejewâdisid, netajawendjiged.*
Charity, *kijewâdisiwin, kijâdisiwin, jawendjigewin, jajawendjigewin, jawenindiwin, jajawenindiwin.* I practise charity, *nin jajawendjige, nin jajaweninge, ketimâgisid nin jawenima.* We do charity to each other, *nin jawenindimin, nin jajawenindimin.* I ask him charity, *nin kitimâgimotawa.*
Charity of heart, heartfelt charity, *jawendamideewin.*
Chaste; I am chaste, *nin binis, nin binidee, nin nibwaka.* (Kanâtisiw).
Chastely; I behave ch., *nin binâdis.* (Kanâtji-pimâtisiw).
Chastise; I chastise, *nin bashanjeige.* I ch. him, *nin bashanjêwa.* (Pasastehwew).
Chastised; I am ch., *nin bashanjeigas.*
Chastisement, *bashanjeigewin; bashanjeogowin.*
Chastity, *binâdisiwin, binisiwin.* (Kanâtji-pimâtisiwin).
Chasuble, *anamessike-agwiwin.*
Chatter; I chatter, I speak too much, *nind osamidon.*
Chatter; I chatter with the teeth, *nin madweiabideshin, nin madweiabideshimon, nin papagabidewadj.*
Cheap; I am (it is) cheap, *nin wendis, nin wenipanis, wendad, wenipanad.* I think it is cheap, (*an., in.*) *nin wenipanenima; nin wenipanendan.* I sell cheap, *nin wendwe, nin wendis.* Wettakisuw, wettakimew).
Cheat; I cheat, *nin waiêjinge.* I use to cheat, *nin waiejingeshk.* I cheat him, (her, it,) *nin waiêjima; nin waiêjindan.*— S. Deceive.
Cheated; I am ch., *nin nanbânis.*
Cheated, (in. s. in.) S. Deceived.
Cheater, *weîejinged, weîejingeshkid.*
Cheating, *waiêjingewin, waiêjingeshkiwin.*
Cheek, *onowama.* (Manâwäy n'anâwäy, wanâwaya). My, thy, his cheek, *nînow, kînôw, onowan.* The right cheek, *okitchinowama, kitchinow.* The left cheek, *onamandjinowama, na-*

mandjinow. My cheeks are red, *nin miskwanowe.* I paint my cheeks red, *nind osânamani.* My ch. are swollen, *nin baganowe.* I have dirty ch., *nin wiiagishkanowe.* I have hollow ch., *nin gwawabanowe.* I have large ch., *nin mamângiganowe.* The other cheek, *nabanénow.*

Cherry, *okwêmin.* (Takkwahemin).

Cherry-tree, *okwêmij.* (Takkwaheminâttik).

Chest, *makak.* (Mâskigan).

Chesnut, *kitchi jawemin.*

Chew; I chew, *nin jashagwandjige.* (Mâmâkwatchiken). I chew it, (*in., an.*) *nin jashagwandan; nin jashagwama.* I chew pitch, *nin jashagwamigiwe.* (Misimiskiwew).

Chewed object, (*in. & an.*) *jashagwanendjigan.*

Chicken, *panadjâ pakaakwens.*

Chief, *ogima.* Second chief, *anikêogima.* I am a chief, *nind ogimaw, nind ogimakaniw, nind ogimakandage, nind ogimâkandawe, nind ogimâkandamage.* I make him a chief, *nind ogimawia.* (Okimâkkâtew). I am chief over him, (her, it,) *nind ogimakandawa, nind ogimakandan.* I live or act like a chief, *nind ogimâwadis.*

Chief, (in. s. in.) S. Superior.

Chief's hat, (crown,) *ogimâwiwâkwân.* (Okimâwastotin).

Chief's lodge or house, (palace,) *ogimawigamig.*

Chief's wife, *ogimâkwe.* I am the chief's wife, or a female chief, *nind ogimâkwew.* I make her a female chief, *nind ogimâkwewia.*

Chieftain. S. Chief.

Chieftainship, *ogimâwiwin, nigânisiwin.*

Child, *abinodji, onidjânissima.* (Awâsis). My, thy, his child, *ninidjâniss, kinidjâniss, onidjânissan.* Adopted child, *nidjânissikawin.* Like a child, *abinodjiing.* I am a child, *nind abinodjiiw.* I play the child, *nind abinodjiikas.* I am with child, *nind adjik, nind aiawa abinodji, nin gigishkawa abinodji.* I have a child from..., *nind ondônje.* I have only one child, *nin bejigonje.* I have many children, *nin bissagonje, nin niskonje.* I have a child (or children), *nind onidjâniss.* I have no children (or a few children), *nin manêonje.* I have two children, three children, etc., *nin nijônje, nin nissonje, etc.* All the children of a family, *ningotônjan.* I am child to somebody, *nind onidjânissimigo.* I am his (her) child, *nind onidjânissimig.* I have him, (her, it) for a child, *nin onidjânissinan; nind onidjânissindan.*

Child; like one's own child, *wenidjanissingin.*

Childhood, *abinodjiiwin.*

Childish; I am ch., *abinodjiing nind ijiwebis.*

Childishness, *abinodji-ijiwebisiwin.*

Chimney, *bodâwân.* I make a chimney, *nin bodawânike.* (Kutawânâbisk).

Chimney-sweeper, *pewindeiged, pawindeigewinini.* I am a

chimney-sweeper, I sweep chimneys, *nin pawindeige.*

Chin ; my, thy, his chin, *nindamikan, kidamikan, odamikan.* (Mikwâskunew).

Chinaware. S. Porcelain.

Chine. S. Backbone.

Chip, *biwigaigan.* I make chips, *nin biwigaige.*

Chippewa Indian, *Otchipwe.* I am a Chippewa Indian, *nind otchipwem.*

Chippewa language, *otchipwemowin.* I speak the Chippewa language, *nind otchipwem.* I translate it in the Ch. language, *nind otchipwewissiton.* It is translated in the Ch. language, *otchipwewissitchigâde.* It is in Chippewa, *otchipwewissin.*

Chippewa squaw, *otchipwekwe.*

Chippewa writing, *otchipwewibiigan.* I write in Chippewa, *nind otchipwewibiige.*

Chisel, *pagwanêgaigan, panibigaigan.* Hollow chisel, *tchigaêmikwan.* Hollow chisel to make incisions in maple-trees, *negwakwani-biwâbik.*

Chocolate, *miskwâbo.* I make (or cook) chocolate, *nin miskwaboke.*

Choice, *onâbandomowin, wawenâbandamowin.* (Nawasowâbamowin).

Choke, (eating or drinking ;) I choke him, (her, it,) *nin pakwenishkona ; nin pakwenishkodon.* I choke myself, *nin pakwenishkonidis.* It chokes me ; *nin pakwenishkagon.* (Atohuw-atohuhew).

Choke, (suffocate ;) I choke him with a rope, *nin kashkabiginamawa.* I choke myself with a rope, *nin kashkabiginamas.* (Kippwâtâmow).

Choke, (in. s. in) S. Hang. Strangle.

Choked, (eating or drinking ;) I am ch., *nin pakwenishkag, nin pakwenibi.*

Choleric. S. Passionate.

Choose ; I choose, *nind onâbandjige, nin wawenâbandjige.* I choose him, (her, it,) *nind onâbama, nin wawenâbama ; nind onabandan, nin wawenabandan.* (Nawasowâbamow).

Chop ; I chop wood, *nin manisse, nin kishkigaige.* (Nikuttew). I chop green wood, *nind ashkatigoke* I chop dry wood, *nin mishiwâtigoke* I chop into small sticks, *nin bissigaige, nin biwigaisse* I chop into chips, *nin biwigaisse.* I chop it into chips, *nin biwigaan.*—I chop for people, *nin manissâge.* I chop for him, *nin manissawa.* I chop for myself, *nin manissâs.*

Chopper, *menissed.* Somebody's chopper, *manissâgan.*

Chopping, *manissewin*

Chosen ; I am (it is) chosen, *nind onabandjigas, nin wawenabandjigas ; onabandjigade, wawenabandjigade.*

Chosen object, *onâbandgigan, wawenabandjigan.*

Church, *anamiewigamig.*

Church-banner, *anamiê-kikinawadjion.*

Church-organ, *kitchi-pipigwan.* (Kitotchigan).

Church-steeple, *kitotâgan agodeg.*

Church-tithes. S. Tithes.

Christen. S. Baptize.
Christian, *enamiad.* I am a Christian, *nind anamia.* I am no Ch., *kawin nind anamiassi.* I become a Ch., *nind odapinan anamiewin.* I am a good strong Ch., *nin songanamia.* A good strong Ch., *swanganamiad.*
Christianity, Christian religion, *anamiewin.*
Christmas, *Niba-anamiêgijigad.*
Cigar, *tetibibaginigasod assema.*
Cinnamon, *miskwanagek, meskwanagekosid wanagek.*
Cipher, *agindassowin, agindassobiigan.* (Akittâsuwin).
Cipher; I cipher, *nind agindass, nind agindassobiige, agindassowinan nind ojibiianan.*
Ciphering, *agindassobiigewin.*
Circumcise; I cir. him, *nin pakwejwa.*
Circumcised; I am cir., *nin pakwejog, nin kikinawâdji, nin kikinawâdendâgos.*
Circumcision, *pakwejodiwin; kikinawâdjion, kikinawâdendâgosiwin.*
Cite. S. Call.
City, *odena, kitchi odena.* There is a city, *odenâwan.*
Clandestinely. S. Secretly.
Clap; I clap my hands together, *nin pâpassinindjiodis.* (Pâpaditchitchehamaw).
Claw; its claw, *oshkanjin.* Claw of a cow or ox, *pijikiwiganj.*– S. Hoof. (Pijiskiwaskasiy).
Clay, *wâbigan.* White clay, *wâbabigan.* Red clay, *meiswâbigan, osaman.* I put clay on, I plaster with clay, *nin wâbigaige.* (Wâbatonisk).
Clay-bank; there is a clay-bank, *kishkabânonikaga.*
Clay-plastering, *wâbigaigewin.*
Clean; I am (it is) clean, *nin binis, binad.* (Kanâtisiw). It is clean: a board, *binissagisi;* a floor, *binissâga;* a house or room, *binate;* a liquid, *binagami;* stuff, *in., binigad;* stuff, *an., binigisi*—I clean him, (her, it,) *nin binia; nin biniton.* I clean it, (a board,) *nin binissagia.* I clean it, (a floor,) *nin binissagiton.* I clean s. th. for him, *nin binitawa, nin binitamawa.* (Kanâtjihew).
Clean or dress fish; I clean fish, *nin pakajawe.* I clean a fish, *nin pakajwa gigo.*
Clean, (in. s. in.) S. Wipe.
Cleanness, cleanliness, *binisiwin.* (Kanâtisiwin).
Cleanness of heart, *binideewin.* I have a clean heart, *nin binidee.* (Kanâtjitehewin).
Cleanse; I cleanse him, (her, it,) *nin binia; nin biniton.*
Cleanse, (in. s. in.) S. Wash clean.
Cleansed; I am (it is) cleansed, *nin biniigos; biniigâde.*
Cleansed by fire; I am (it is) cl. by fire, *nin gassiiakis; gassiiakide.*
Clear; it is clear, (in the woods,) *jibeiâmagad, jishigaâkwaigade.* I clear land, *nin majiige, nin majiiakonige.* The act of clearing land, *majiigewin, majiiakonigewin.* (Musawâtahikewin. Tawakahikewin).
Clearing, *majiigan, majiiakonigan.* There is a clearing, *papashkwamagad, papashkwakamiga.* There is a clearing

made, *majiigâde, papashkwaigâde*. I make a clearing, *nin majiige, nin papashkogaige*. A clearing is seen through the woods, *babawasse, jajibawassakweia*. (Sipeyaw).
Cleaver, *passigaigan*.
Cleave, (split;) I cleave, *nin passigaige*.—S. Split.
Cleave, (stick;) I cleave to s. th., *nind agoke*. It cleaves to s. th., *agogin, agokemagad*.
Clemency, *minwadendamowin, kijewâdisiwin, kijâdisiwin*. (Yospisiwin).
Clement; I am cl., *nin kijewâdis, nin kijâdis, nin minwadendam*. (Yospisiw).
Clerk, *ojibiigewinini, wejibiiged*.
Clerk's office, *ojibiigewigamig*.
Cliff, clift, *ajibik*. There is a cliff, *ajibikoka, kishkabika*.
Climb up; I climb up on a tree, etc., *nind akwandawe*. (Ketchikusiw).
Cloak, *kitchi babisikawâgan*.
Clock, *dibaigisisswân*. I make clocks, *nin dibaigisisswânike*. (Pisimokkàn).
Clock-manufactory, *dibaigisisswânikewin*.
Clock-manufacturer, *dibaigisisswânikewinini*.
Clog, *mitigo-makisin*. (Mistikoskisin).
Close by, *tchig', tchigaii*.— S. Near.
Closet; there is a closet made, *pikissanagokâde*. In the closet, *pikissanagong*.
Cloth, *manitowegin*. Black cloth, *bosmakatewegin*. (Kaskitewegin). Red cloth, *miskwegin*.
Clothe; I clothe him, (her, it,) *nin bisikona, nind agwia; nin bisikonan, nind agwiton*. I clothe myself, *nind agwiidis*. We clothe one another, *nind agwiidimin*. (Akwanahwew).
Clothe, (in. s. in.) S. Dress.
Clothes, *agwiwin, madindagan*. I put my clothes on, *nin bisikwanaie, nin wawepis*. (Pustayonissew). I put him his clothes on, *nin bisikona, nin wawepina*. I change clothes, *nind andjikwanaie*. I have double clothes on, *nin bitokwanaie*. I have many clothes, *nin madindass*. I give him clothes, *nind agwia, nin madindamawa, nin madimona*.
Clothing, *madindagan, bisikagan, agwiwin*. The giving or receiving of clothing, *agwiidiwin*. I give him clothing, *nin agwia*.
Clothing-store, *madindagani-wigamig*.
Cloud, *anakwad*. (Waskow). Black cloud, (mourning cloud,) *nitâganakwad*. Dark cloud, or, there is a dark cloud, *pashagishkanakwad*. There are small curled clouds, *gitchiganakwad*. The clouds are red, *miskwânakwad*. (Clouds from the north, west, etc. S. North. West, etc.)
Cloudy; it is cloudy, *anakwad, ningwakwad*. (Iyekwaskwan)
Clove, *sagâigans menomagwak*.
Clover, *nessobagak*.
Clyster. S. Injection.
Clyster-pipe, *pindabawâdjigan, siginamâdiwin*.
Coach. S. Cart.
Coachman. S. Cartman.
Coal, *akakanje*. (Kaskaskasew).

I burn (or make) coal, *nind akakanjeke*. Place where coal is burnt, *akakanjekân*. I burn him (her, it) to coal, *nind akakanakiswa; nind akakanakisan*. I am (it is) burnt to coal, or, I burnt (it burns) to coal, *nind akakanakis; akakanakide, akakanate*.—There are coals, *akakanjeka, akakanjewan*. I gather burning coals together, *nin mawandokije*.

Coal-house, *akakanjewigamig*.

Coal, red-hot coals, *miskokinje*.

Coal. S. Pit-coal.

Coarse; it is coarse, thin, light, (stuff,) (*in., an.*) *babigwêtagad; babigwetagisi*.

Coast; I coast, *nin bimâjaam, nin jijodewaam, nin tchigewaam*. (Sisoneskam).

Coat, *babisikawâgan, bisikawâgan*. (Miskutâkäy).

Coat of cloth, *manitowegino-babisikawâgan*.

Cobweb, *assabikeshiwassab*.

Cock, *pakaakwe, nabê-pakaakwe*.—Cock's crest, *pakaakwe o patakibinweon*.

Cock of a gun, *obwâmens*.

Cock; I cock a gun, *nind ajigîdabikinan pâshkisigan*.

Coffee, *makate-mashkikiwâbo*. I make coffee, *nin makate-mashkikiwâboke*.

Coffee-house, *makate-mashkikiwâbokewigamig*.

Coffee-mill, *bissibodjigans*.

Coffer, *makak*.

Coffin, *tchibai-makak*.

Cohabit; I cohabit, *nin widige*. I cohabit with her, (him,) *nin widigema*. We cohabit, *nin wedigendimin*. (Wikittuwok).

Cohabitant, *widigemâgan*. (Wikimâgan).

Cohabitation, *widigendiwin, widigewin*.

Colander, *jâbwajigawitchigan*.

Cold, bad cold, *agig, agigokawin*. I have a bad cold, *nind agigoka*.

Cold, *gikâdjiwin*.

Cold; it is cold, *kissina*. It is cold by the wind, *takâssin*. It is cold (in a building), *takate*. It is a cold night, *kissintibîkad*.—I am cold, I feel cold, *nin gikadj, nin bingedj, nin takênis*. (Kawatchiw). I am very cold, *nin niningadj*. I am cold, my body is cold, *nin takis*. I soon feel cold, *nin nitâ-gikadj, nin wakêwadj*. I can endure much cold, *nin jibadj*.—I catch cold, I become cold, *nin takash*. I make him catch cold, *nin takashima*. My hands are cold, *nin gikadjinindjiwadj*. My feet are cold, *nin gikadjisidewadj*. My ears are cold, *nin gikadjitawagewadj*. I weep from cold, *nin mokawadj*.—It is cold, (liquid,) *takâgami*. It is cold, (metal, *in., an.*) *takâbibikad; takâbikisi*.

Colic, *akoshkâdewin*. I have colics, *nind akoshkâde*. (Kisiwaskatew).

Collar, *nabikawâgan, nabikâgan*.

Collar-bone, clavicule, *bimidakiganan*.

Collar of a coat, etc., *apikweiawegwasson*.

Collect. Collected.—S. Gather. Gathered.

Collectively, *mâmawi.*
Colored ; I am colored, a colored person, *nin makatêwis, nin makatêwiwe.*
Colored person, *mekatewisid, mekatewiwed, makatewiiass.* (Kaskitewiyâs).
Color of ripeness ; it has the color of r., (*in., an.*) *gijande; gijanso.*
Colt, *bebejigoganjins ; manijins.* (Piponâskus).
Comb, *binâkwan.* Large dressing comb, *pashkâbide-bînâkwan, nassaigan.*—Comb for horses, *nasîkwéigan.*
Comb; I comb myself, *nin nasikwê.* I comb him, *nin nasikwêwa.*
Combat. S. Fight.
Come down ; I come down, *nin binissandawe.* I come down on a rope, *nin nissabigita.* I come down flying, *nin bi-nanjisse.* (Nittakusiw).
Come forth ; I come forth, *nin moki, nin mokas.* It comes forth, *mokissemagad, mokishkamagad.* I come forth by the current of a river, *nin mokabog.* (Mahaboyuw). I come forth, (out of the water,) *nin mokibi, nin moshkam.* I come (it comes) forth to the surface of the water, *nin mekigîsse ; mokigissemagad.* I come (it comes) forth to the surface of the water, and *float,* (*floats,*) *nin moshkaagwindjin ; moshkaagwinde.* —The water comes forth, *mokidjiwan nibi.* It comes forth, *sagigin.*
Come from ; I come from..., *nind ondji, nind ondjiba, nind ondadis.* It comes from..., *ondjimagad, ondjibamagad, ondadad, ondjissin, onsikamagad.*
Come here ; come here, *ondâss, ondâshân.* (Astam). I come here, *nin bi-ija ; nin bidjija.* I come here for some reason, *nin bi-inîka, nin bi-onsika.* I come here weeping, crying, *nin bidadem.* I come here speaking, talking, *nin bidwewidam.* I come to tell s. th., *nin bidâdjim, nin bidâdjimotage.* I come to tell it, *nin bidâdjimotan.* I come to tell him, *nin bidâdjimotawa.* I come here to trouble him, *nin bi-mîgoshkâsikawa.*—I come with snow-shoes, or on snow-shoes, *nin bidagimosse.* I come here running, *nin bidjibato.* I come here dragging s. th., *nin bidjidâbi.* It comes sliding, *bidjibide.*
Come in ; I come in, *nin pindige.* It comes in, *pindigemagad.* I come in to him, *nin pindigawa.* I come (or go) into him, (her, it,) *nin pindigeshkawa; nin pindigeshkan.* It comes in me, *nin pindigeshkâgon.* I come in (or go in) in a canoe or boat, *nin pindjidawaam.*
Come out ; I come out, *nin bisagaam.* It comes out, *bi-sagaamomagad, bi-sagidjissemagad.* I come out of the water, *nind agwata, nind agwabita.*
Come to..., I come to him, (her, it,) *nin bi-nasikawa, nin biodissa ; nin bi-nasikan, nin bi-oditan.* I don't come to him, (her, it,) *nin nondêshkawa ; nin nondêshkan.* It comes

to me, *nind odissigon, nind odissikagon, nind odjissikagon.* It does not come to me, *nin nondeshkagon.*—I come to the shore, *nind agwaam.* (Kapaw). I come to the shore out of the water, *nind agwaiadagas.* It comes to the shore by the wind, *agwaiâssin.*—I let it come to him from hand to hand, *nind anikênamâwa.*

Come upon ; I come upon him, *nin pagidjinotawa, nin pagamishkawa.* It comes upon me, *nin pagamishkagon.* It comes to pass, *pagamishkamagad.*—I come upon him and make him fall, *nind apagasikawa.* It comes upon me and makes me fall, *nind apagasikagon.*

Come with. S. Bring with.

Comer, *biwide.* (Okiyutew).

Comfort ; I comfort, *nin sengideeshkage, nin songideeshkawe.* I comfort him, *nin songideeshkawa.*

Comfortable life, *mino aiâwin.*

Comforter, *swangideeshkawed.*

Coming; I am coming here, *nin bidassamosse.* I am (it is) coming on, *nind apisika ; apisikamagad.* I am coming on the ice, *nin bidadagak.* I am coming here in a canoe or boat, *nin bidassamishka.* I am (it is) coming with the wind, *nin bidash ; bidâssin.* The wind is coming, *bidanimad.*

Command ; I command him s. th. urgently, *nin pâpijima.* I com. it urgently, *nin pâpījindan.* (Sikkimew).

Command, (in. s. in.) S. Reign.

Commander, *nigânossewinini.*

Commandment, *ganâsongewin.*

I make commandments, *nin ganâsonge.* (Itasowew).

Commence. Commencement.—S. Begin. Beginning.

Commerce, *atandiwin, atâwewin.*

Commission, (word sent,) *mitchitwewin.* I give or send a commission, *nin mitchitwe.* I give or send him a commission, *nin mitchitchima.* I give or send a com. for it, (*in.*, *an.*) *nin mitchitwen ; nin mitchitwenan.* (Itwehiwewin).

Commit ; I commit, *nin dodam.* I make him commit some action, *nin dodamoa.*

Commit ; I commit or intrust s. th. to his care, *nin ganawendaa, nin ganawendamona.*

Common ; in common, *mâmawi.*

Common-hall. S. Judgment-house.

Communicant, *wedapinang jâwendâgosiwin.* (Eyamihesaskamut).

Communicate ; I com. it, *nin windamâgen.* I com. it to him, *nin windamâwa.*

Communication, *windamâgewin.*

Communion, *Jâwendâgosiwin.* I take communion, *nin jâwendagos, nind odapinan Jâwendâgosiwin.* (Ayamihe-saskamowin).

Communion of Saints, *ketchitwâwendâgosidjig o widokodawiniwa, anamiê-widokôdâdiwin.* We are in the Communion of Saints, *nind anamiê-widokodâdimin.* (Ayamihestamâkewok o kanâtâtchâkwewok).

Companion, *widjiwagan, widjindinowâgan.*

Company, *anikominodewiwin.* (Witjettuwin). There is a company, *anikominodemagad.* We form a company, *nind anikominodewimin.*—I keep company with him, *nin widjiwa, nin widokawa.*—I keep comp. with him in religious respect, *nind anamie-widokawa.*

Company, (in. s. in.) S. Keep company.—S. Help.

Compared to... S. Esteemed equal.

Comparison, *awêtchigan.* I make a comparison, *nind awêtchige.*

Compass, *wawiiebiigan.*

Compass ; it compasses me, *nin giwitashkagon.*

Compassed. S. Enclosed.

Compassion, *kitimâgeningewin, kitimâgendjigewin, kitimâgenindiwin, jâwendjigewin, kijewâdisiwin.* I have comp. on him, (her, it,) *nin kitimâgenima, nin jâwenima ; nin kitimâgendan, nin jâwendan.*— I excite comp. with my words, *nind inigatagos, nin kitimâgitagos.*

Compassionate ; I am comp., *nin kitimâgendjige, nin jâwendjige, nin kijewâdis.*

Complaint, *gagimidonowin.*

Complaisant ; I am comp., *nin minwêwis.*

Compliments, *anamikâgewin ; anamikâgowin.* I give him my comp., *nind anamikawa.* We give or send comp. to each other, *nind anamikodâdimin.*

Compliments, (in. s. in.) S. Nod with the head.

Comport ; I comport myself in a certain manner, *nind ijiwebis.*

Comportment, *ijiwebisiwin.*

Compotation, *widjibindiwin.*— S. Drink together.

Compotator, *widjibimagan.*

Comprehend ; I comp. it, *nin nissitotân.*

Comprehend, (in. s. in.) S. Understand.

Comprehensible ; it is comp., *nissitotâgwad.*

Compress. S. Press together.

Comrade, *widjiwâgan.*

Comrade ; my comrade, *nidji ; nidjikiwê, nidjikiwesi.*

Conceal. S. Hide.

Conceive ; I conceive it, *nin nissitotân.*

Conceive, (in. s. in.) S. Understand.

Conclude. S. Consolidate.

Concord, *bejigwendamowin.*

Concord, (in. s. in.) S. Peace.

Concubinage, *anisha widigendiwin, matchi widigendiwin.* (Pisikwâtchi-wikittuwin). We live together in concubinage, *anisha nin widigendimin.*

Concubine ; I am a con., *anisha nin widigema inini.* I keep a con., *anisha nin widigema igwe.*

Concupiscence, *missawenimowin.* I look at her (him) with conc., *nin missawiganawâbama.* (Pisikwâtchi-mustawinawew).

Condemn ; I condemn him, *nin banâdjia, nin banâsoma, nin mamijima.* I condemn myself, *nin banâdjiidis.* I condemn him to death, *nin niboma, nin naniboma.* (Oyasuwâtew).

Conduct, *ijiwebisiwin, bimâdisiwin.* Decent chaste conduct, *binâdisiwin.* (Itâtisiwin). Changed conduct, *andjiwebisiwin, andjibimadisiwin.* Wise prudent conduct, *nibwaka-ijiwebisiwiu.* Indecent unchaste conduct, *gagibâdisiwin.* My cond. is shameful, is considered shameful, *nind agatendagos.*

Conduct, (in. s. in.) S. Behave. Behavior.

Conduct; I conduct him, *nin bimiwina.*

Conduct away. S. Lead away.

Conduct in; I cond. him in, *nin pindigana.*

Conduct out; I cond. him out, *nin sagidjiwina.*

Conduct. Conductor.—S. Guide.

Conduct. S. Oversee.

Confect, *pashkiminassigan.*

Confect; I confect, *nin pashkiminassige.* I confect them, (berries, *in., an.*) *nin pashkiminassanan; nin pashkiminasswag.*

Confectionery articles, *sisibâkwatonsan.*

Confess, declare; I confess sincerely, *nin gwaiakwâdjim.* (Kwayaskâtjimow).

Confess sins; I confess my sins, *nin webinige.* (Ayamihewâtjimisuw).

Confession, *webinigewin.*

Confidence. S. Trust.

Confidence, (in. s. in.) S. Ask with hope.

Confirm. S. Consolidate.

Confirm; I confirm, *nin migiwen Songideeshkâgewin.* I confirm him, *nin mina Songideeshkâgewin.*

Confirmation, *Songideeshkâgewin.* I give Conf., *nin migiwen Songideeshkâgewin.* I receive Conf., *nin minigo Songideeshkâgewin.*

Confirmed; I am conf., *nin giminigo Songideeshkâgewin.*

Confirmed, ratified; it is conf., *songitchigâde.*

Cenfronted; we are conf. together, *nin assamâbandimin.*

Conscience; I have bitter remorses of conscience, *nind inigâwagendam.*

Consent, *minwendamowin.* (Naskomowin).

Consent; I consent, I am willing, *nin minwendam.* (Naskomow).

Consent to do. S. Promise.

Conservation, *ganâwendamowin.*

Conserve; I conserve him, (her, it,) *nin ganâwenima; nin ganâwendan.* I conserve to me, *nin ganâwendamas.* I conserve it to me, (*in., an.*) *nin ganâwendamason; nin ganâwendamasonan.*—I conserve or put up provisions, *nind atwab.* (Astwaw).

Conserve, (in. s. in.) S. Live, I make live.

Consider. Consideration. — S. Reflect. Reflection.

Consider. Considered.—*Remark.* In regard to the expressions: I am considered to be so and so, or to be this or that, we remark here that these expressions are to be found under their respective *substantives, verbs* or *adjectives.*—For instance, I am considered superior, or to be a superior, *nin nigânendagos.* You will find it under "Superior."—It is considered shameful, *aga-*

tendâgwad. You will find this under "Shameful."—Etc.
Consolator, *aiabisiwinged.*
Consolation, *abisindiwin.*
Console; I console, *nind abisiwinge, nin gâgisonge, nin songideeshkage, nin songideeshkawe.* I console him, *nind abisiwima, nin songideeshkawa, nin gâgisoma, nin minodeea, nin gagânoma.* (Kâkitjihew). I console myself, *nin gâgisondis.*
Consoler, *swangideeshkawed, gaiâgisonged, aiâbisiwinged.*
Consolidate; I cons. it, *nin songiton, nind aindjissiton.*
Consoling, consolation, *abisiudiwin.*
Constable, *takoniwewinini, tekoniwed.*
Constancy, *songendamowin, bejigwendamowin.* (Sokkâtisiwin).
Constant; I am constant, *nin songendam, nin bejigwendam.*
Constant at work; I am con., *nin minwêwis.* (Sokkeyimow).
Constantly, *mojag, apine, bejigwanong.* (Sakamo).
Constipated; I am con., *nin mamidawitchi.*—S. Costive.
Constipation. S. Costiveness.
Constitution, *inakonigewin.*
Construct, (in. s. in.) S. Make. Build.
Constructed; it is con. (*in., an.*) *ijitchigâde, gijitchigâde; ijitchigaso, gijitchigaso.*
Consume, (in. s. in.) S. Eat up.
Consume. S. Spend all.
Consumption, *miniwapinewin.* I have the consumption, *nin miniwapine.*
Contain, (hold;) it contains, *débashkine, débibi.* It does not contain much, (*in., an.*) *nâwadab; nâwadisi.* It cannot contain all, *nonashkinemagad, nojibadjigemagad.* I cannot make it contain all, (I cannot put all in,) *nin nojibadjige.*
Contemn. S. Despise.
Contemplate. Contemplation, (in. s. in.)—S. Reflect. Reflection.
Content, *minwendamowin.* (Miweyittamowin).
Content; I content him, *nin debia; nin minwendamia.*
Contented; I am con., *nin minwendam, nin minawas, nin dêbagenim, nin dêbenim, nin dêbendam, nin dêbis, nin naêndam.* I make him contended, *nin minwendamia, nin maminwendamia, nin minwendaa, nin minonawea, nin minawasia, nin naêndamia.* I make it contented, *nin minwendamiton, nin naêndamiton.* We make each other contented, *nin maminwendamiidimin,* etc. (Miweyittam).
Contentedness, *dêbinimowin, minwendamowin.*
Contention. S. Dispute.
Continent; it is the continent, *kitakamiga.* On the continent, *kitakamigang.*
Continually, *kaginig, apine, bejigwanong, mojag.*
Continue; I continue long, *nin ginwatchita.*
Contract; I contract it, *nin sindabiginan.*
Contradict; I contradict, *nind ajidewe, nind ajidewidam, nind agonwetam, nind agonwetage.* I contradict in

thoughts, *nind ajidêendam, nin agonwêiendam*. I contradict him, *nind agonwetawa, nind ajidema*. I contradict him in thoughts, *nind ajidenima*. I cont. it, *nind agonwetân*. We cont. each other, *nind agonwetâdimin, nind ajidendimin*. I cont. myself, *nind ogonwetadis*. I am in the habit of contradicting, *nind agonwetageshk*. Bad habit of contradicting, *agonwetageshkiwin*. (Anwettam).

Contradicter, *neta-agonwetang*.

Contradiction, *agonwetamowin, ajidewidamowin, agonwetadiwin*. Cont. in thoughts, *agonwêiendamowin, ajidêendamowin*.

Contribute. Contribution.—S. Give. Gift.

Contrite; I am contrite, *nind anwenindis*. (Kesinâteyimisiw).

Contrition, *anwenindisowin*.

Conversation, *ganonidiwin, gaganonidiwin*.

Converse; I conv., *nin gâgigit*. I con. with him, *nin gaganona, nin widjidonama*. We con. together, *nin gagânonidimin*.

Conversion, *anwenindisowin, andjibimâdisiwin, andjijiwebisiwin*.

Convert, *wedapinang anamiewin*.

Convert; I convert myself, *nind anwenindis, nind andjiton, nind ijiwebisiwin; nind odâpinan anamiewin*. I convert him, *nin gashkia tchi andjijiwebisid; nin gashkia tchi anamiad*.

Converted; I am con., *nind andjibimâdis, nind andjijiwebis; nind anamia*.

Convey; I convey him (her, it) on or in a carriage, *nind odâbana; nind odâbadan*. I convey him (her, it) in a canoe or boat from the lake to the shore, *nind agwaona; nind agwaodon*. I convey him (her, it) in a canoe or boat over a river or bay, *nind ajawaa, nind ajawaona; nind ajawaan, nind ajawaodon*.

Convey back; I convey him (her, it) back, *nind ajêwina; nind ajêwidon*. I convey him (her, it) back again in a canoe or boat, *nin giweona; nind giweodon*.

Convey in; I convey him (her, it) in, *nin pindigana; nin pindigadon*.

Convey, (in. s. in.) S. Carry. Carry away. Conduct.

Conveyance in a carriage, *awadjidâbiwin*.

Conviction, *abêidiwin*. I give testimony to conviction, *nin batange*. Testimony to conviction, *batangewin*.

Convince; I convince him, *nind abea*. (Tâpwemew).

Convoke; I conv., *nin nandonge*. I con. them, *nin nandomag*.

Convulsion, *tchitchibishkawin*. —S. Spasms.

Cook, *tchibâkwewinini; tchibâkweikwe; tchabakwed*. (Opiminawasuw).

Cook; I cook, *nin tchibâkwe, nin gisisekwe*. I cook for him, *nin tchibakwawa, nin gisisama, nin gisidebona*. I cook for myself, *nin tchibâk-*

was. I cook it, (*in., an.*) *nin gisisan; nin gisiswa.* I cook it tender, (*in., an.*) *nin nokisan; nin nokiswa.* (Piminawatew).
Cooked; it is cooked, (*in., an.*) *gijide; gisiso.* It is cooked in a certain manner, *inidemagad.* It is well cooked, well done, (*in., an.*) *minodemagad; minoso.* It is cooked tender, (*in., an.*) *nokide; nokiso.*
Cookery, cooking, *tchibâkwewin, gisisekwewin.*
Cook-house, kitchen, *tchibâkwewigamig.* (Piminawasuwikamik).
Cook-maid, *tchibâkweikwe.*
Cook-stove, cooking-stove, *tchibâkwe-kijâbikisigan.*
Cool; it is cool or cold, *takissin.* It is cool, *takaiamagad.* It is cool, (liquid,) *takâgami.*
Cool; I cool, *nin takissidjige.* I cool him, (her, it), *nin takishima; nin takissidon.*
Cool, (by wetting;) I cool him, (her, it,) *nin takâbâwana; nin takâbâwadan.* I cool it, pouring cold water in, *nin takâgamishhodon, takibâdon.*
Cool, (in. s. in.) S. Cold.
Cooper, *makakokewinini.* I am a cooper, (I make barrels,) *nin makakoke.*
Cooper's business, trade, work, *makakokewin.*
Cooper-shop, *makakokewigamig.*
Copper, *miskwâbik, osâwâbik.*
Copper-mine, *miskwâbikokân, biwâbikokân.* I work in a copper-mine, *nin miskwâbikoke, nin biwâbikoke.* Miner in a copper-mine, *miskwâbikokewinini, biwâbikokewinini.*
Copper-mining business, *miskwâbikokewin.*
Copper-mining Agent or Superintendent, *miskwâbikoké-ogima.*
Copper-cent, *jomânike, miskwâbikons, osâwâbikons.*
Copy, *nassâbiigan, nabibiigan, andjibiigan.*
Copy, (in. s. in.) S. Writing.
Copy, (transcribe;) I copy, *nin nassâbiige, nin nabibiige, nind andjibiige.* I copy it, *nin nassâbian, nin nabibian, nind andjibian.*
Copy, (imitate;) I copy it, *nin kikinowâbandan, nassâb nind ojiton.*
Copying, *nassâbiigewin, nabibiigewin, andjibiigewin.*
Cord of wood, *atawissan.* (Asastatchigan).
Cord. S. Rope.
Core of a corn-ear, *okanâk.*
Cork, *wajashkwedo, kitchi wajashkwedo.*
Cork-screw, *gitaigan.*
Cork-stopper, *wajashkwedo-gibakwaigan.*
Cormorant, *kâgâgishib,* (raven-duck).
Corn. S. Indian corn.
Corn-ear, (of Indian corn,) *nisakosi.* The corn-ear bursts at the fire, *pâshkingweso nisakosi.*
Cornel-tree, *mânan.*
Corner; there is a corner, *wâwikweia.* In a corner of the room, *wikwessagag.* In a corner of the earth, *wikwekamigag aki.*
Corner-stone, *waiekwaiâbiki-assin, wikweiabikissitchigan, maiawaiekwaiabikissi assin,*

netamabikishing assin. Chief corner-stone, *nigâniwikweia-bikissitchigan.*
Corn-meal, *bissibodjigan.*
Corn-soup, corn-mash.—S. Indian corn-soup.
Corn-stalk, *sibwâgan.* Sprout of the corn-stalk, *sibwâgans.*
Costive; I am costive, *nin gibissagaje.*
Costiveness, *gibissagajewin.*
Costly. S. High.
Corpse, *tchibai.*
Corpus Christi day, *wâbigonigijigad.*
Correct, *gwaiak.*
Correct; I correct it, *nin gwaiakoton, nin nanaiton.* I correct a writing, *nin nanâibiige;* I correct it, *nin nanâibian.*
Corrected writing, *nanâibiigan.*
Correct. Correcting, (in. s. in.) S. Repair. Repairing.
Corrupt; I corrupt him, *nin matchi ijiwebisia, nin banâdjia, nin gagibâsoma.* (Misiwanâtjihew).
Corrupted; it is corrupted, (liquid,) *ajagamissin.* It is corr., (*in.,an.*) *pigishkanad; pigishkanani.* (Pikiskatin).
Cotton, *papagiwaiân, papagiwaiânigin.*
Cotton bag, made of cotton, *papagiwaiâneshkimod.*
Cough, *ossossodamowin.* (Ostustutamowin).
Cough; I cough, *nind ossossodam.*
Council, *gigitowin.* (Mawâtjihituwin).
Council-house, *gigitowigamig.*
Counsel; I counsel him, *nin gagansoma.* (Kakeskimew).
Count; I count, *nind agindass.* I mistake in counting, *nin wanagindass.* I mistake in counting it, (*in., an.*) *nin wanagindan; nin wanagima.* I count him, (her, it,) *nind agima; nind agindan.*
Counted; I am (it is) counted, *nind agindjigas; agindjigâde.*
Countenance; I have a smiling countenance, *nin babapingwe.*
Counting, *agindjigâdewin.*
Country, *aki.*
Countryman, *wid jidakiwemagan.*
Couple; so many couple, *dasswewan.*
Couple. S. Pair.
Courage, *songideewin, mangotassiwin, mangideewin.*
Courageous; I am cour., *nin songidee, nin mangotass, nin mangidee.* I make him cour., *nin songideea, nin mangideea.*
Courageous man, *mangotassiwinini, swangideed inini.* (Nâbekkâsuw).
Courageous person, *swangideed, mengotassid.*
Court, *dibakonidiwin.*
Cousin, (he-cousin;) my, thy, his cousin, *ninimoshe, kinimoshe, winimosheian;* or, *nitawiss, kitawiss, witawissan.*
Cousin, (she-cousin;) my, thy, her cousin, *nindangoshe, kidangoshe, odangosheian.*
Cover; cover of a kettle, etc., *dibabowêigan, padagwaboêigan, gibabikaigan, gibakwaigan, gibaboêigan.* Cover of a powder-pan, *agwanakokweigan.*
Cover; I cover him (her, it) with s. th., *nin padagwana-*

wa; nin padagwanaan. I cover him (her, it) with my body, *nin padagwanishkawa; nin padogwanishkan.* It covers me, *nin padagwanishkagon.* I cover him, (her, it,) with some articles of clothing, *nind agwajêwa, nind agwanâwa; nind agwanaan.*—I cover myself, *nin naagwaji, nind agwaje.* I cover my head, *nind agwanikweodis.* I cover my breast, *nind agwaiakiganeodis.*

Cover, (roof;) I cover, *nind apakodjige.* I cover it, (a lodge or house,) *nind apakodon.* (Apakkwew).

Cover with bark; I cover, *nin ningwanapakwe.* I cover it, *nin ningwanapakwadan.*

Covered; I am (it is) covered with s. th., *nin padagwanaigas; padagwanaigâde.* I am (it is) covered, *nind agwanaigas; agwanaigâde.*—All is covered with it, *misiweshkamâgad.*

Covered, (roofed;) it is covered, *apakode, apakodjigâde.*

Covet; I covet, *nin missawendam, nin missawendjige, nin missawinage.* I covet him, (her, it,) *nin missawenima, nin missawinawa; nin missawêndan, nin missawinan.* I covet s. th. belonging to him, (*in., an.*) *nin missawendamawa; nin missawinamawa.* (Mustawinawew).

Covetous; I am covetous. S. Covet.

Covetous desire, *missiwendamowin.* I look at him (her, it) with a covetous desire, *nin missawiganawâbama; nin missawiganawâbandan.*

Covetousness, *missawendjigewin, missawenindiwin, missawendamowin.*

Cow, *pijiki, ikwê-pijiki.* (Onitjâniw). The cow is to have a calf, *and jiso pijiki.* The cow has a calf untimely, abortively, *nishi pijiki.* The cow has a calf, *onidjânissi pijiki.*

Coward, *jaiâgodeed.* I am a coward, *nin jâgodee.*

Cowardice, *jâgodeewin.*

Cow-hide, *pijikigewin.*

Cow-pox, *mamakisiwin.* I inoculate with the cow-pox, *nin mamakisiiwe.* I inoculate him with the cow-pox, *nin mamakisia.* I am inoculated with the cow-pox, *nin mamakisiigo.*—Inoculating, inoculation, *mamakisiiwewin.*

Cow-pox inoculator, *memakissiiwed, mamakisiiwewinini.*

Crab. S. Craw-fish.

Crack; I crack or craunch, *nin madwendjige.* I crack or craunch it, (*in., an.*) *nin madwendân; nin madwema.* I make crack my fingers, *nin madwêganenindjibinidis.* The joints of my limbs crack, *nin madwêganeshka.* It cracks, *madweshka, mamadweshka.* The ice cracks, *madwêkwadin.*

Crack, (split;) *gipisiwin, gâgipisiwin.* There is a crack or split in a piece of wood, *tawissaga.*

Cracked; my feet, my hand, my legs, etc., are cracked.—S. Foot. Hand. Leg, etc.

Cracked through; it is cr. thr.,

(metal,) *tawâbikad.* It is cr. th., (rock,) *tawâbikamagad.*
Cracker, *anâkonans pakwejigans.*
Crackle; the fire crackles, *pakine* or *papakine ishkote.*
Cradle, *tchitchibakonagan.* Indian cradle, *tikinâgan.* (Wewebisun).
Crafty. S. Artful.
Cramps. S. Spasms.
Cranberry, *mashkigimin.* There are cran., *mashkigiminika.* Place where there are cran., *mashkigiminikan.* I gather cran., *nin mashkigiminike.*
Cranberry-River, *Mashkigiminikaniwi-sibi.*
Crane, *adjidjâd.* (Otchitchâk).
Crane-potato, *adjidjakopin.*
Crank, *kijibawebinigan.* I turn a crank, *nin kijibawebinige.*
Crank, (in. s. in.) S. Handle.
Crape, *nitagewaiân.*
Craunch. S. Crack.
Craw-fish, *ajageshi.*
Crawl. S. Creep.
Crazy, I am crazy, *nind agawadis, nin giwânadis.* (Namawiya wayeskamisiw).
Cream; I take off the cream, *nin bimaan.*
Creator, *misi gego ga-gijitod.*
Credit; I give credit to people, *nin masinamâgos.* I take on credit, *nin masinaige.* I collect my credits, (my active debts,) *nin nandoshkamage.* I ask him to pay his credit, (his debt,) *nin nandoshkamâwa.* I try to get my credits paid, *nin nandoshkas.*
Creditor, *mesinaamagosid, mesinaamawind.*
Credulous superstitious person, *anotch gego daiebwetang.*
Cree Indian, *Kinishtino.* (Nehiyaw.)
Creek, *sibi.*
Creep; I creep, *nin bimode, nin babâinode.* I creep about, *nin babâmode.* I creep out, *nin sâgidode.*
Cree squaw, *kinishtinokwe.* (Nehiyàwiskwew).
Crepusculous; it is crep., *tebikabaminâgwad.*
Crevice; there is a crevice in the ice, *tâshkikwad, passikwad.*
Cribble. S. Sieve.
Cricket, *papâkine.*
Crime, *batadowin, batâjitwawin, matchi dodamowin.* I commit a crime, *nin batâdodam, nin matchi dodam.* (Pâstâhuwin).
Cripple; I am a cripple, *nin mâkis.* I make him a cripple by striking him, *nin mâkinana.*
Cripple, (unable to walk,) *bémossessig, memândjigosid.*
Crooked knife, *wâgikomân, jashagashkâdekomân.*
Crooked root, *wagitckibik.*
Crop. S. Harvest.
Crop or craw of a bird, *omodai.* This bird has a large crop, *mangomodaie aw bineshi.*
Crosier, (Bishop's staff,) *Kitchimekatewikwanaie o sakaon.*
Crosier, (Indian crosier,) *pagaadowân, pagaadowanak.* I play with crosier and ball, *nin pagaadowe.* The play itself, *pagaadowewin.*
Cross, *tchibaiâtig, ajideiâtig;*

anamiewâtig. I make the sign of the cross upon myself, (I bless myself,) *nin tchibaiatigonige.* I make the sign of the cross upon him or over him, *nin tchibaiatigonamâwa.* (Ayamihewâttikonamâwew).

Cross-bill, cross-beak, (bird,) *ajidêkoneshi.*

Cross, (peevish); I am cross, wicked, *nin mishidee,* (I have a hairy heart.)

Cross-saw. S. Log-saw.

Cross-stick in the snow-shoe, *okwik.*

Cross, (traverse;) I cross a river, in a canoe or boat, *nind âjawa, nind âjawaam, niminam.* I cross him (convey him) over a river, etc., *nind ajawaa.* I cross it, (a river, etc.) *nind âjawaan.* I cross a river swimming, *nind âjawadaga.* I cross it walking on the ice, *nind ajawadagak, nind ajawagak.* I cross it walking over a bridge, *nind ajoge.* I cross it walking over a tree or log, *nind ajawandawe, nind ajo gêiandawe.*—I cross or convey people over a river in a canoe or boat, *nind ajawaodjige.* I get myself crossed over a river, *nind ajawaonigos.* I cross over sailing, *nind ajawash.*—It crosses, *ajidesse.*

Croup; my, thy, his croup, *nijigan, kijigan, ojigan.*

Croup-bone; my, thy, his croup-bone, *nijiganigan, kijiganigan, ojiganigan.*

Crow, *andek.* Young crow, *andekons.* (Ahâsiw).

Crow; the cock crows, *masitagosi pakaakwe.*

Crowd; we crowd too much, *nin nonîshkodadimin.*

Crowded; we are crowded, *nin moshkinemin.*

Crown, *ogimâwiwakwân, kitchiogima wiwâkwân.*

Crown; I crown him, (her,) *nind ogimâwia; nind ogimâkwewia.*

Crown of the head, *ṅawisigokwândib, maiaoshtigwân.*

Crucible. S. Melting-pot.

Cruel. Cruelty. S. Wickedness of heart.

Crumb, *biwandjigan.*

Crumb; I crumb it, (*in., an.,*) *nin gapinan; nin gapina.*

Crumble; I crumble it, (*in.,an.*) *nin biwidon, nin bissibidon; nin biwina, nin bissibina.* The bread crumbles, *biwishka pakwejigan.* The bread crumbles into small pieces, *biwisse pakwejigan.*

Crush; I crush (or bruise) him, (her, it,) *nin banasikawa; nin banasikan.* I crush him, putting myself upon him, *nin badagoshkawa.* I crush it, *nin badagoshkan.* I crush it to small pieces, to powder, (*in., an.*) *nin bissaan; nin bissâwa.* I crush his head, *nin jigoshtigwaneshka.* I crush it with my hand, (*in., an.*) *nin jishigonindjandan; nin jishigonindjima.* I crush it with my foot, (*in., an.*) *nin jishigosidandan; nin jishigosidama.* I crush it with my foot or body, (*in., an.,*) *nin jajagoshkan; nin jajagoshkawa.*

Crutch, *gwashkwandaon.*

Cry; I cry, *nin masitâgos.* I cry loud, *nind aiâjikwe.* I cry

out, *nin bibag*. I cry selling, (at an auction,) *nin bibâgatawe*. (Tepwew).
Cry, (in. s. in.) S. Weep.
Crying sale, (auction,) *bibâgatandiwin*.
Cubit, *biminik, biskinikenowin, ekodôskwaning*. One cubit, *ningobiminik*. Two, three cubits, etc., *nijobiminik, nissobiminik*, etc.
Cucumber, *eshkandaming*.
Cudgel, *pagamâgan*.
Cudgel, (round stick, not split,) *misâtig*.
Cue, (tuft of hair,) *segibanwân*. I wear a cue, *nin segibanwa*.
Cuff; I cuff him, *nin pikwakonindjitawa*.
Cumin, *memwe*.
Cunning. S. Artful. Artfulness.
Cup, *onâgans, anibishâbo-onâgans*.
Cupboard, *téssâbân*. I put it in a cupboard, (*in., an.*) *nin tessâbâdan; nin tessâbana*.
Cup-shot; I am cup-shot, *nin giwashkwebi*.
Cure; I cure, *nin nôdjimoiwe*. It cures, *nodjimoiwemagad*. I cure him, *nin nodjimoa*. I cure for him or to him, *nin nôdjimotawa*. (Iyinikkahew).
Cured; I am cured, *nin nôdjim, nin nanândawis*. (Iyiniwiw).
Curing, *nodjimoiwewin*.
Curiosity, (inquisitiveness;) bad curiosity, *mamakasabangeshkiwin, mamakasinamowin*. I use to look on with too much curiosity, *nin mamakasabangeshk*.
Curious! *ashinangwana!* (Mamaskâtch)!
Curious, *mamakadakamig, makadjaii*. I am (it is) curious, (astonishing,) *nin mamakâdendâgos, nin mamakâdis, mamakadendagwad, mamakâdad*. I find him (her, it) curious, (astonishing,) *nin mamakadenima; nin mamakadendân*. (Anakatchây).
Cūrious, (in. s. in.) S. Droll.
Curiously, *wawiiaj*.
Curl. Curled, (in. s. in.) S. Twist. Twisted.
Curled hair; I have curled hair, *nin babisigindibe*. (Titipiweyâniskwew).
Curlew, *patashkanje*.
Currant-berry, *mishidjimin*.
Currant-shrub, *mishidjiminagawanj*.
Current; the current of a river is heard, *madwêdjiwan*. There is a strong foaming current, *wâssidjiwan*. The current carries me away, *nin webabog*. The current of a river comes out of the woods and falls in the lake, *sâgidawidjiwan*.
Currycomb, *nasikwêigan, bebejigoganji-nasikwêigan*.
Curse; I curse, *nin matchi-inapinendjige*. I curse him, (her, it,) *nin matchi-inapinema; nin matchi-inapinendan*.
Curtain, *agobidjigan*. Calico for curtains, *agobidjiganigin*.
Curtain, as a partition, *gibagodjigan*. I hang up a partition-curtain, *nin gibagodjige*.
Cushion, *apikweshimon*.
Custom, *nagadisiwin*.—S. Accustomed.
Cut; I cut him, (her, it,) *nin kishkijwa, nin biwikona, nin kishkâwa; nin kishkijan, nin biwikodan, nin kishkaan*. I

cut myself, *nin kijaodis, nin kishkijodis.* I cut it with a knife, *nin kishkikodan.* I cut it with the teeth, *nin kishkandan.* I cut it with a scythe, *nin kishkashkijan.* I cut grass, *nin kishkashkossiwe.* I cut his skin, *nin kishkajéwa.* It cuts, *ginashkad.*—I cut it to make it smaller, (*in., an.*) *nind agassikodan; nind agassikona.* I cut it with difficulty, *nin gashkaan.*—I am (it is) cut, *nin kishkijigas; kishkijigâde.* I am (it is) cut by accident, *nin kijaigas; kijaigâde.* I am cut to the bone, *nin mitchiganeshin* It is cut, (metal,) *kishkâbikad.*

Cut, (a coat, etc.) I cut, *nind onijige.* I cut it, *nind onijan.*

Cut accidentally; I cut him, (her, it,) *nin pitijwa; nin pitijan.* I cut myself, *nin pitijodis.*

Cut down; I cut down a tree, *nin gawawa mitig, nin kishkigawa mitig.* I cut down trees, *nin gawaisse, nin gawakwaige, nin gawaakwandjige.* I cut down a birch-tree to get the bark, *nin gawaijigwe.* The tree is cut down, *gawaigâso mitig.* Many trees cut down, *gawaakwandjigan.* Many trees are cut down, *gawaakwandjigâde.*

Cut long; I cut it long, (*in., an.*) *nin ginwakwaan; nin ginwakwâwa.*

Cut off; I cut off what is spoiled, (*in., an.*) *nin gagigikodan; nin gagigikona, nin gagigijwa.* I cut off a piece or pieces, *nin pakwêjige.* I cut off a piece from it, (*in., an.*) *nin pakwejan; nin pakwejwa.*—I cut it off with an *axe,* (*in., an.*) *nin webigaan; nin webigawa.* I cut it off with a *knife,* (*in., an.*) *nin webijan, nin webikonan, nin tchigapidan; nin webijwa, nin webikona, nin tchigapijwa.* I cut it off, (*in., an.*) *nin kishkigaan, nin kishkigadan; nin kishkigana.*—I cut his tongue off, *nin kishkidenaniwejwa.* My tongue is cut off, *nin kishkidenaniwe.* I cut his nose off, *nin kishkidjanejwa.* My nose is cut off, *nin kishkidjane.* I cut my nails off, *nin kishkiganjisodis.*

Cut off hand, foot, leg. S. Hand. Foot. Leg.

Cut pointed; I cut it pointed, (*in., an.*) *nin patchishkijan, nin patchishkibodon; nin patchishkijwa, nin patchishkibona.* I cut it pointed with an *axe,* (*in., an.*) *nin patchishkigaan; nin patchishkigawa.* I cut it pointed with a *knife,* (*in., an.*) *nin patchishkikodan; nin patchishkikona.* It is cut pointed, (stuff, *in., an.*) *patchishkigad; patchishkigisi.* It is cut pointed, (wood, *in., an.*) *patchishkigad patchishkigisi.*

Cutler, *mokomânikewinini.* I am a cutler, (I make knives,) *nin mokomânike.*

Cutler's shop, *mokomânikewigamig.*

Cutlery, cutler's work or trade, *mokomânikewin.*

Cypress-tree, *okikandag.* (Sitta).

D

Dagger, *ajaweshkson.* (Takkatchigan).

Daily, every day, *endasso-gijigak.*

Dainty; I am fond of dainties, *nin maminâdjib.* Fondness of dainties, *maminâdjibowin.* I feed myself daintily, *nin maminoponidis.*

Dairy, *totoshâbowigamig.*

Dam, *okwanim, gibagawaigan.* I make a dam, *nind okwanimike, nin gibagawaige.* There is a dam made, *okwanimikâde, gibagawaigâde.* (Oskutim).

Damage, *banâdjitâssowin, banâdjitchigewin.* I suffer damage, *nin banâdjitass.* I make damage, *nin banâdjitchige.* I make damage to people, *nin banâdjitage.* I make or cause him damage, *nin banadjitawa, nind agawadjia.* I cause damage to myself, *nin banâdjitas, nind agawadjiidis.* (Misiwanâtjittawin).

Damage; I damage it, (*in., an.*) *nin mijiton, nind enapinadon; nin mijia, nind enapinana.* (Misiwanâtjihew).

Damage, (in. s. in.) S. Injure. Defile.

Damaged; it is dam., (*in., an.*) *banâdjitchigâde; banâdjitchigaso.*

Damaging, *banâdjitchigewin.*

Damnation, *banâdjiiwewin, banâdisiwin.* I cause his damnation, *nin banâdjia.* I cause my own damnation, *nin banâdjiidis.* It causes damnation, *banâdjiiwemagad.*

Damp; it is damp, *nissabawemagad.* It is much damp, *nibiwan, tipamagad.* It is a little damp, *awissamagad.*—S. Moistened. (Miyimawaw).

D a n c e, *nimiwin, nimiidiwin.* Dance with a scalp, *gamâdjiwin.* (Nimihituwin).

Dance; I dance, *nin nim.* I make him dance, *nin nimia.* I dance with her, (him,) *nin widjishimotawa.* We dance together, *nin nimiidimin.* I make people dance, (I give a ball,) *nin nimiiwe.* I dance for him, *nin n i m i t a w a.* I dance with a scalp in my hand, *nin gamâdj.* I come to him dancing with a scalp ,*nin g a m â d j i n o t a w a.* I dance around s. th., *nin giwitashim.* I dance like a lame person, *nin tatchigashim.*

Dancer, *nâmid, netâ-nimid, nâmishkid.*

Dancing, (ball,) *nimiidiwin, nimiiding.* I am too much in a habit of dancing, *nin nimishk.* Habit of dancing, *nimishkiwin.*

Dancing-house, *nimiidiwigamig.*

Dandruff-comb, *sagwabide-binâkwan, binaidikomân.*

Danger, *nanisânisiwin.* Eminent danger, dangerous thing, *bâpinisiwagan.* I am in danger, *nin nanisânis.* I put him (her, it) in danger, *nin nanisânia; nin nanisâniton.* I put myself in danger, *nin nanisâniidis.* I am in danger of perishing, *nin bajine, nin babanadis.* I put him in danger of perishing, *nin bajinana.*

Dangerous; it is dangerous, (*in.*, *an.*) *nanisanad; nanisanisi.* I am (it is) considered dang., *nin nanisanendâgos, nin nisaiendâgos; nanisanendâgwad, nisaiendâgwad.* I consider him (her, it) dang., *nin nanisanenima; nin nanisânendan.* I am dang. by my speaking, *nin nanisanitagos.* I think there is s. th. dangerous, *nin nanisânendam.* I look (it looks) dang., *nin nanisâninâgos; nanisâningâwad.*

Dangerously, *babanadj.*

Dare; I dare not, *nin jâgwenim.* (Nama sâkweyimow).

Daring; I am daring, *nin songidee.*

Dark; it is dark, *pashagishka, kashkitibikad.*

Dark-blue; it is dark-blue or livid, *âpissin, âpissamagad.* I have a dark-blue eye, *nind âpissab.* I have a dark-blue spot, *nind âpissabawe.* My skin is dark-blue, *nind apissage.* I have a dark-blue face, *nind apissingwe.* I am of a dark-blue color, *nind âpissis.* It is dark-blue, (metal,) *âpissabikishka.*

Dark-colored, *makatê-...*

Darkness; there is darkness, *pashagishkibikad, kashkitibikad, pashagishkinamowin.* I am in darkness, *nin pashagishkinam.* (Wanitibikkisiw).

Dash, (in. s. in.) S. Knock.

Daughter, *odânissima.* My, thy, his daughter, *nindâniss, kidâniss, odânissan.* His adult daughter, *odânan.* I have a daughter, *nind odâniss.* I have her for a daughter, *nind odânissinan, nind odânissima.* I am a daughter, *nind odânissimigo.* I am his daughter, *nind odânissimig.*

Daughter-in-law; my, thy, his daughter-in-law, *nissim, kissim, ossimin.* The daughter-in-law in a family, *naânganikwe.* I am daughter-in-law in a family, *nin naânganab, nind ojinindam.* (Witimwa).

Dawn; it begins to dawn, *bidâban.*

Day, *gijig, gijigad.* So many days, *dassogwan.* Two days, *nijogijig, nijogwan*, etc. It is so many days, *dassogwanagad.* It is two days, *nijogijigad, nijogwanagad*, etc. I am so many days old, *nin dassogwanagis.* I am two days old, *nin nijogwanagis*, etc. I am two days absent, *nin nijogwawanend*, etc.—Good day! *bojo!* I bid him good day, *nin bojoa.*

Daylight; it is daylight, *wâban.* Before daylight, *tchi bwa wabang.* It is broad daylight, *pagakâban.*

Day of judgment, *dibakonigegijigad.*

Day of resurrection, *âbitchibawinigijigad.* (Apisisinokijikaw).

Dazzled ; I am daz., *nin jiwas, nin pashagishkinam.* I am daz. by it, I cannot look at it, *nin sassâbis.*

Dead ; he is dead, *nibo, gi-nibo.* (Nipiw).

Dead person, *tchibai, nebod, ganibod.*

Dead person's bone, *tchibaigan.*

Dead smell ; *nibasomagosiwin.* I smell like a dead person, *nin nibasomagos.*

Deaf; I am deaf, *nin gagibishe.* I feign to be deaf, *nin gagibishekâs.* (Kâkepittew).

Deafness, *gagibishewin.*

Deaf person, *gegibished.*

Deal ; I deal, *nind atâwe.*

Dealer, *atâwewinini.*

Dealt with ; I am not easy to be dealt with, *nin sanagis.* (Ayimisiw). I think he is not easy to be dealt with, *nin sanagenima.* (Ayimeyimew).

Dear, (of a high price ;) it is dear, (*in., an.*) *sanagad, sanagaginde, mamissaginde ; sanagisi, sanagaginso, mamissaginso.* (Sokkakittew).

Death, *nibowin.* Sudden death, *sesika-nibowin, kakaminewin, kaiakamisiwin.*

Death from hunger, *gawanandamowin.* (Kâwakkatosowin).

Death-whoop, *bibâgotamowin.* I raise the death-whoop, *nin bibagotam.*(Kâmâtchiwaham).

Debate ; we debate with each other, *nin aiajindendimin.*

Debauch ; I debauch him, *nin gagibasoma.* (Matchi-sikkimew).

Debt, *masinaigan, masinaigewin.* I make debts, *nin masinaige.* Making debts, *masinaigewin.*

Debtor, *mesinaiged.*

Decamp ; I decamp, *nin gos.* (Pitchiw).

Decamping, decampment, *gosiwin.* (Pitchiwin).

Decant ; I decant it, *nin sikobiginan.*

Decay ; it decays, *anawissemagad, angomagad.* It decays, (clothing,) *gawanad.* It decays, (flower, herb,) *nibwashkissin.*

Decease, *nibowin.*

Deceased. S. Dead person.

Deceit, *waiêjingewin.*

Deceive ; I deceive, *nin waiêjinge.* I deceive him, (her, it,) *nin waiêjima ; nin waiêjindan.* I deceive with my speaking, *nin waiejitâgos.* I use to deceive, *nin nitâ-waiêjinge, nin waiejingeshk.* I deceive myself, *nin waiejindis.* (Wayesimew).

Deceiver, *weiêjinged, weiêjingeshkid.*

Deceiving, *waiêjingewin.* Habit of deceiving, *waiêjingeshkiwin.*

Deceiving ; I am dec., I look better than I am, *nind agawinagos.* It is dec., *agawinagwad.*

December, *manitogisissons.* (Pawatchakinasis).

Decent behavior, *binâdisiwin.* I behave decently, *nin binâdis.*

Decent narration, *binâdjimowin.* I tell decently, *nin binâdjim.*

Decide. S. Resolve.

Declare. S. Explain.

Decline ; the sun is on his decline, *giwêiassam gisiss.* (Otâkwäsan). The winter is on

its decline, *giwêbibon*. The summer is on its decline, *giwênibin*.
Decoration. S. Ornament.
Decorticate; I dec. cedar-trees, *nin gashkaanagekwe*.
Decrepit; I am dec., *nin kitchi gika*. (Kâwikikkaw).
Decry. Decried.—S. Defame. Defamed.
Deed, (action,) *dodamowin*.
Deed, (writing, document,) *débwêwini-masinaigan*.
Deep; I deep him (her, it) a little in water, *nin tangagwindjima; nin tangagwindjiton*.
Deep; it is deep, (water,) *dimi, dimitigweia, ginwindima, takwindima*.—It is deep, *bosika*. I make it deep, *nin bosikiton*. It is made deep, *bosikitchigâde*. So deep in the ground, *epitakamig*.
Deep, (hollow;) it is deep, *wânamagad*.
Deer, *wâwashkeshi*. Young spotted deer, *kitagâkons*.
Deer-meet, *wawashkeshiwiwiiass*.
Deer-bone, *wâwashkeshiwigan*.
Deer-skin, *wâwashkeshiwegin*.
Deer's tail, *wâwashkeshiwano*.
Deer-trail, *omonsom*.
Defamation, *matchi-wawindjigâdewin*.
Defame; I defame him, (her, it,) *nin mâtchi-wina, nin matchi-wawina; nin matchi-windan, nin matchi-wawindan*. (Matchi-ayimomew).
Defame, (in. s. in.) S. Tell bad reports.
Defamed; I am (it is) defamed, *nin matchi-wawindjigas; matchi-wawindjigâde*.
Defend; I defend him, *nin nâdamâwa*.
Defend, (resist;) I def. myself, *nin nanâkwi*. I def. myself against him, (her, it,) *nin nanâkona; nin nanâkonan*. Self-defence, *nanâkwiwin*. (Naskwaw).
Deficient; I am def., *nin nôndes*. (Nottepayiw).
Deficient, (in. s. in.) S. Unprofitable.
Deficiently, *nondâss*.
Defile; I defile him, (her, it,) *nin winia, nin wiiagia, nin wiaagishkawa; nin winiton, nin wiiagiton, nin wiiagishkan*. It defiles me, *nin winiigon, nin wiiagiigon, nin wiiagishkakon*. I defile myself, *nin wiiagiidis*.
Defraud. Defrauder.—S. Deceive. Deceiver.
Defunct. S. Dead. Dead person.
Dejected. S. Sad.
Delay; I delay, (in words,) *pânima, nind ikit mojag*. I delay, (in thoughts,) *pânima nind inendam mojag*. (Tcheskwa itwew).
Deliberate. Deliberation.—S. Reflect. Reflection.
Delicacy, (weakness of constitution,) *gâgidisiwin*.
Delicate, (weak of constitution;) I am del., *nin gâgidis, nin neshangadis, nin nokis*.—I am del. in my eating, *nin nokiwe*.
Delicate. Delicious.—S. Taste, good taste.
Delight. S. Joy. Joyful.
Delightful; it is del., *modjigendagwad, minwendagwad*.—S. Joyful.
Deliver, (give;) I deliver, *nin*

pagidinamage. I deliver him, (her, it,) *nin pagidina; nin pagidinan.* I deliver it to him, *nin pagidinamawa.*

Deliver, (untie, save, etc.) I deliver him, *nind âbiskona.* (Abikkunew). I deliver him from s. th., *nind ikonawa, nind ikonamâwa, nin midagwenamawa.*

Delivered, (of a child ;) I am del., *nin nigiâwass, nind ondadisike.* I am del. of a boy, *nin kwiwisensike, nind ininionje.* I am del. of a girl, *nind ikwesensike, nind ikwêonje.* I am del. of twins, *nin nijodeike.* I am often del., *nin nitâonje.* I am del. before my time, *nin nondê-nigiawass.* (Nittâwikihawasuw).

Delivery. S. Birth.

Deluge, *aki gi-moshkaang.* (Ka iskipek).

Delve, *wânikân.* (Wâtikkân).

Delve ; I delve, *nin wânike.* (Wâtikkew).

Delver, *waianiked.*

Den, *waj.* (Wâti).

Depart ; I dep. from him, *nin bakêwina.* I dep. from it, *nin bakêwinan.* (Paskewiyew).

Deplore. Deploration.—S. Weep over... Weeping over...

Depth ; in the depth, (in deep water,) *midjindin, anâmindim.*

Deride ; I deride him, (her, it,) *nin bâpia, nin bâpinodawa; nin bapiton, nin bapinodân.*

Derision, *bapinodagewin, bapinodamowin.*

Derision. S. Sing mocking.

Descend ; I desc. a hill or mountain, *nin nissâkiwe, nin nissadjiwe.* At the foot of a hill or mountain, *nissâki.*

Descend ; I descend upon him, *nin bonindawa.*

Descend, (go down ;) I desc., *nin nissandawe.* I descend a step, *nin nissâtakoki.*

Descent ; there is a steep descent of a mountain, *anibédina.*

Describe ; I describe him, (her, it,) *nind ojibiwa ; nind ojibian.*

Described ; I am (it is) desc., *nind ojibiigas, ojibiigâde.*

Desert ; in the desert, *pagwâdakawig, pagwâdj, megwékamig.* There is a desert, *pagwadakamigawan.*

Desert ; I desert, *nin gimi.* I make him desert, *nin gimia.*

Deserter, *gâmid ga-gimid.*

Deserted ; it is deserted, *nitagendagwad.*

Desertion, *gimiwin.*

Deserve ; I des., *nin wikwatchitâs, nin wikwatchitamas.* I des. it, *nin wikwatchitamâson.*

Deserving, desert, *wikwatchitamasowin.*

Desirable ; I am (it is) des., *nin nandawendâgos, nin pagossendâgos ; nandawendagwad, pagossendagwad.*

Desire, *nandawendamowin, nandawendjigewin.*

Desire ; I desire, *nin nandawendam, nin nandawendjige, nin nandawendass.* I desire him, (her, it,) *nin nandawenima; nin nandawendan.*—It desires, *nandawendamomagad*—I desire strongly, *nin kijigendam.* I des. him (her, it) strongly, *nin kijigenima ; nin kijigendan.*

Desired ; I am (it is) des., *nin*

nandawendjigas, nin nandawendâgos; nandawendjigâde, nandawendâgwad.

Desist; I desist from him, (her, it,) *nin nogenima, nin pagedina; nin nogendan, nin pagidinan.* (Ponimew).

Desist. S. Let alone.

Desolate; it becomes desolate, *angomagad.*

Desolate, (lonesome;) it is des., *nitagendagwad.*

Desolation, *banâdjitchigewin.*

Despair, *anawendjigewin.* (Iyimowin).

Despair; I despair, *nin banâdendam,* (iyimow), *nind anâwendam, nind anwendam, nind anâwendjige, nind anâwabandjige.* I despair of him, (her, it,) *nin banâdenima; nin banadéndân.* I desp. of myself, *nin banâdenindis.*—I desp. of him by his appearance, *nind anâwâbama.* I desp. of it by its app., *nind anâwâbandan.* I am (it is) despaired of by the app., *nind anâwâbaminagos; anawâbaminagwad.*—I desp. of him by his voice, *nin babanasitawa.* I am desp. of by my voice, *nin babanasitâgos.*

Despatch, (send;) I despatch him, *nind ininajâwa.*

Despicable, despisable; I am (it is) desp., *nind agatendâgos, nin tabassendagos; agatendagwad, tabassendagwad.* (Piweyittâkwan).

Despise; I despise, *nin kopâdjiiwe, nind abinsonge, nin kopâsonge, nin nishiwanasonge.* I des. him (her, it) in thoughts, *nin tabassenima; nin tabassendân.* I despise myself, *nin tabassenindis, nin tabassenim.*—I despise him (her, it) with words, *nin kopâsoma, nind abinsoma, nin nishiwanasoma; nin kopâsondan, nind abinsondan, nin nishiwanasondan.* I despise myself, *nin kopâsondis, nind abinsondis, nin nishiwanasondis.*

Destine; I destine him (her, it) to s. th., *nind inenima; nind inendan.* I dest. myself, *nind inenindis.* (Itakimew).

Destined; I am (it is) destined, *nind inendâgos; inendâgwad.*

Destroy; I destroy, *nin banâdjiiwe, nin kopâdjiiwe, nin banâdjitchige.* I destroy him, (her, it) *nind angoa, nind angoshkawa, nin kopâdjia, nin apitchi banâdjia; nind angoan, nind angoshkan, nin kopâdjiton, nind apitchi banâdjiton.*—I destroy the dam of a beaver, *nin banaige.* (Metchihew).

Destroy, (in. s. in.) S. Kill.

Destroyed; I am (it is) des., *nin banâdjitchigas; banâdjitchigâde.*

Destruction, *banâdjiiwewin, banâdjitchigewin.*

Destruction, (death.) (Metchinewin). I wish his (her, its) destruction, *nin nibôma; nin nibôndan.* We wish each other's dest., *nin nibôndimin.*

Detect. Detected.— S. Find. Found.

Determine; I det. it, *nin wawénadan.* (Kiseyittam).

Determine. Determination.—S. Resolve. Resolution.

Determined; it is det., *wawenâdjigâde*.

Detest; I detest him, (her, it,) *nin jingenima; nin jingendan*. (Pakwâtew).

Detour, *giwedéonan*. (Wâwimâttewin).

Detraction, *dajindiwin, matchi dajindiwin, dajingeshkiwin*.

Detractor, *dejingeshkid*.

Detroit, *Wawiiatan*. At, from or to Detroit, *Wawiiatanong*.

Devastation, *banâdjitchigewin*.

Devil, *matchi manito, manisiwinissi, matchi aiaawish, wanisid manito*.

Devoted; I am dev. to him, (her, it,) *nind angwamikawa; nind angwamikan*.

Devotion, *songanamiâwin*. (Ayamihewâtisiwin).

Devour; I devour him,)bite him much,) *nind abîndama*. (Pikwamew).

Devout. S. Religious.

Dew; there is dew on the ground, *mindôkad*. (Akosipeyaw).

Diarrhœa, *jabokawisiwin*. I have the diar., *nin jabokawis*.

Dictionary, *ikkitowini masinaigan*.

Die; I die, *nin nib*. It dies, (perishes,) *nibomagad*. It dies from heat, (*in., an.*) *nibode; nibodeso*. I die suddenly, *nin kakamîne, nin kaiakamis*. I die in a certain place, *nin dapine*. I make him die in a certain place, *nin dapinea*. I die on account of...., *nind ondjine*. I die for somebody, *nin nibotage*. I die for him, *nin nibotawa*. I die of hungry, *nin gawanândam*. We die all away, *nin tchaginemin*. I remain while the others die, *nind ishkone*.—I wish he would die, *nin niboma, nin naniboma*. I wish he would die, (in thoughts, *nin nibôwenima*.

Die with....; I die with...., *nin gigine, nin giginib*. I die with him, *nin widjiniboma, nin giginenan*. I die with it, *nin giginen*.

Differently, in a different manner, *bebikinong, bakân*. In different directions, in diff. places, *bepakân*. (Pitus).

Difficult; I am (it is) diff., *nin sanagis; sanagad*. (Ayimisiw).

Difficulty; I have difficulties, *nin sanagis*. I cause him diff., *nin sanagisia*. (Ayimihew).

Difficulty in thoughts, *sanagendamowin*. I have thoughts of diff., I am troubled, *nin sanagendam*. (Ayimeyittamowin).

Difficulty of temperament, *sanagisiwin*. I am of a difficult temperament, *nin sanagis*. (Ayimisiwin).

Difformed; I am (it is) difformed, *nin manâdis; manâdad*. (Mayâtisiw).

Difformed; (in. s. in.) S. Ugly.

Difformity, *manâdisiwin*.

Dig; I dig, *nin wânike*. I dig a deep hole in the ground, *nin dimiianike, nin ginwanike, nin ishpânike*. It is dug deep, *dimiianikade, ginwanikade, ishpânikâde*. (Wâtikkew).

Dig out; I dig out potatoes, *nin monâapini*. I dig out medical roots, *nin monâashkikiwe*.

Dig up, (in. s. in.) S. Bring to light.

Digest; I digest it well, *nin mi-*

nokâgon. I cannot digest it, *nin mănikâgon*.

Diligent; I am dil. at work, *nin nitâanoki, nin pajigwadis*. (Kakâyâwisiw).

Dilute; I dilute it (*in., an.*), *nin ningabawadon; nin ningabawana*.

Dim; I have dim eyes, *nin bigisawab, nin bigisawinam*.

Diminish; I diminish it, *nin pangiwagiton*.

Dinner, *nawakwe-wissiniwin*. I take my dinner, *nin nawakwe-wissin*.

Disorder; it is in disorder, *biwissin*. I put it in dis., *nin biwissidon*.

Dip in; I dip him (her, it) in water, *nin gôgina, nin tchekagamina, nin tchekagwindjima; nin gôginan, nin tchekagaminan, nin tchekagwindjiton*. I dip him (her, it) in s. th., *nin gindâbigina; nin gindâbiginan*.—I dip my hand in the same vessel with him, *nin widjigwabaamawa*.

Dipped; it is dipped in s. th., (*in., an.*) *gindabiginigâde; gindabiginigâso*.

Dirt, *ajishki* (mud); *wanak*. I am in dirt, I live in dirt, *nin winab*. Dirt, (excrement,) *mo*.

Dirtiness, *winisiwin*.

Dirty; I am dirty, *nin winis; nin mowidjiw, nin mowidjiwis*. It is dirty, *winad*. I think he (she, it) is dirty, impure, *nin winenima; nin winendan*. It is dirty, (liquid,) *winâgami*. It is dirty, (wood,) (*in., an.*) *winissaga; winissagisi*. — I make dirty somebody, *nin winishkâge, nin winiiwe*. I make him (her, it) dirty, *nin winia, nin winishkawa; nin winiton, nin winishkan*. I make myself dirty, *nin winîidis*. It makes me dirty, *nin winiigon, nin winishkagon*, I am (it is) made dirty, *nin winitchigas; winitchigâde*. — I make things dirty, *nin winitchige*. It makes dirty, *winitomagad*. (Wiyipisiw wiyipaw).

Dirty, (muddy;) it is dirty, *ajishkiwika*.

Dirty house or lodge, *momigamig*.

Dirty story, *winâdjimowin*. I tell a dirty story, *nin winâdjim*.

Disagreeable; I am (it is) dis., *nin sanagis; sanagad*. I am (it is) considered disagreeable, *nin jingendâgos, nin manendagos, nin sanagendagos; jingendâgwad, manendagwad, sanagendagwad*.—My speaking is dis., *nin jingitagos*. Its sound is dis., *jingitagwad*. (Nayattâwisiw).

Disappear; I dis., *nind angwanagos, nin boninagos, nin nawinagos*. I dis. under the water, *nin nikibishin, nin nikagwindjin*. He (she, it) disappears to me, *nind angwâbama; nind angwâbandan*. (Wanâbamew). It dis., *angwanagwad, boninagwad*.

Disappeared! gone! *weniban*. (Aweniban, aspin).

Discern; I discern, *nin maminowâb, nin nissitawâb*. I discern him, (her, it,) *nin maminonâbama, nin nissitawâbama; nin maminowâbandan, nin nissitawâbandan*.

Disciple, *kikinoamagan.*
Discontented ; I am dis., *kawin nin minwendansi.* I am dis. in my mind, *nin mânendam.* I have discontented thoughts towards him, (her, it,) *nin mânenima ; nin mânendân.*
Discontinuance, *anijitamowin, anawendjigewin.* (Pomewin).
Discontinue ; I dis., *nind anijitam.* (Ponittaw).
Discourage ; I disc. him, *nind anishima, nin jâgwenimoa.* (Iyimohew).
Discouraged ; I am disc., *nin jâgwenim.* (Iyimow).
Discourse, *gigitowin.* Prudent wise discourse, *nibwâkatogosiwin.* Foolish imprudent discourse, *gagibasitâgosiwin.* (Pikiskwewin).
Discover ; I begin to discover (to discern) a certain point of land, *nin sâgewessidon.*
Discover. Discovered, (in. s. in.) S. Find. Found. Invent. Invented.
Discoverer, (inventor,) *mekawashitod*
Discredit. S. Defame.
Discreet ; I am discreet, *nin nibwâka.* (Iyinisiw).
Disease, *akosiwin ; inapinewin.*
Disembarrass ; I dis. him from s. th., *nin midâgwenamawa.*
Disentangle. S. Unravel.
Disguise ; I dis. myself, *nin wani.* (Wayesihuw).
Disgust, *jigadendamowin.*
Disgusted ; I am dis., *nin jigadendam.*—S. Tired of...
Dish, *onâgan.* A little dish, *onagans.* Earthen dish, *wâbigan onâgan.* I make dishes, *nind onâganike.* The making of dishes, *onâganikewin.* I wash or rinse dishes, *nin kisibiginâgane.* I wipe dishes, *nin kisiinâgane.*
Dish-clout, *kisiinâganân, gâssiigan.*
Dishful ; a dishful, *ningotonâgan.*
Dish-game, *pagéssewin.* I play the dish-game, *nin pagésse.*
Dish-maker, *onâganikewinini, wenâganiked.* I am a dish-maker, *nind onâganike.*
Dishonor ; I dishonor him, (her, it,) *nind agatchia, nind agasoma ; nind agatchiton, nind agasondan.* (Nepewihew).
Dishonorable ; my conduct is dis., *nind agatendagos.* It is dis., *agatendagwad.*
Dish-water, *kisibiginâganâbo.*
Dislocate. Dislocated.—I dislocate my arm, leg, etc. My arm, leg, etc. is dislocated. S. Arm. Leg, etc.
Dislocated ; I have some limb dislocated, *nin kotigota, nin kotigoshka.*
Dislocation (of limbs in the body,) *kotigoshkâwin.*
Disobedience, *agonwetamowin.*
Disobedient ; I am dis., *nin agonwetam, nin nita-agonwêtam.* Disobedient person, *aiagonwetang, neta-agonwetang.*
Disobey ; I disobey, *nind agonwetam, nin gagansitam, nin ajidenge.* I use to disobey, *nin nita-agonwêtam, nin ajidengeshk.* I disobey him, *nind agonwetawa, nin gagansitawa.* (Sasibittawew).
Disperse ; I disperse, *biwiwebinige.* I dis. it, (*in., an.*) *nin biwiwebinan, nin bewissidon ;*

nin biwiwebina, nin biwishima. (Sawetisahwew).
Disperse. Dispersed, (in. s. in.) S. Scatter about. Scattered about.
Dispersed; it is dis., (*in., an.*) *biwissin, biwiwebinigâde; biwishima, biwiwebinigaso.*
Dispersedly, *tchétchatchiban.*
Displeasure. S. Discontent.
Dispose; I dispose of him, (her, it,) *nind atâwenan, nin migiwenan; nind atâwen, nin migiwen.*
Disposed; I am well disp., *nin minoijiwebis.* I am evil disp., *nin matchi ijiwebis.*
Disposition of mind, *ijiwebisiwin.* Good disp. *mino ijiwebisiwin.* Bad disp. *matchi ijiwebisiwin.*
Dispute, *agonwetâdiwin, aiagindendiwin.* (Kikikittowin).
Dispute; I dispute, *nin gikâwidam; nind ajidewidam, nind ajidewe.* (Kikkâwitam).
Dispute; we dispute with one another, *nind agonwetâdimin, nind aiajindendimin.*
Dispute, (in. s. in.) Quarrel.
Disquiet; I am disquiet, *nin wanishkwes.*
Disquietness, *wanishkwesiwin.*
Disrespectful answer, *ajidewidamowin.* I give him disrespectful answer, *nind ajidema.*
Dissatisfied; I am diss., *kawin nin minwendansi, nin mindawe.* I look diss., *nin mindawewînâgos.* (Mittawew).
Dissemble; I dissemble sickness, *nind âkosikas.*
Dissention, (confusion;) there is diss., *nishiwanadakamig.* (Ayâsitemowin).
Dissipate, I dissipate, *nin banâdjitchige..* I diss. it, (*in., an.*) *nin banâdjiton, nin nishiwanâdjiton, nin banadjia nin nishiwanâdjia.*
Dissuade; I diss. him from s. th., *nind anijitamoa.* (Pomemew).
Dissuade, (in. s. in.) S. Discourage.
Distance; from dist. to dist., *aiapi.* It is of such a distance, *apitchâmagad.* The distance of a place, *epitchâg.*
Distant, far, *wâssa.* It is distant, *wassawâd, apîtcha, pitcha.* (Wâyo).
Distil; I distil, (I make ardent liquor,) *nind ishkotewâboke.*
Distiller, *ishkotewâbokewinini.*
Distillery, *ishkotewâbokewigamig.*
Distort. S. Dislocate.
Distracted; I am dist. in my thoughts, *nind ondamendam.* I am dist. in listening, *nin bebishkwendam.* I am dist. in listening to him, *nin babishkotawa.* I am dist. in listening to a sermon, *nin babishkotan gagikwewin.* (Wanweyittam).
Distrain, etc.—S. Seize, etc.
Distress, *animisiwin.*—S. Suffering. (Wâwâneyittamowin).
Distribute, *nin mâdaoki.* I dist. it, (*in., an.*) *nin mâdaoken; nin mâdaokenan.* I dist. it among them, *nin mâdaonamawag.* We dist. it amongst us, *nin madaonidimin.* (Mâtinawew).
Distribute, (in. s. in.) S. Divide.
Distribution, *mâdaokiwin, mâdaonidiwin, nenawitagewin.*

Disturb; I disturb him in his speaking; *nin wanishkwea.* I disturb him in his sleep, *nin niskasoma.* I dist. it, *nin wanishkweton.*

Disturbance, (in. s. in.) S. Riot. Trouble.

Ditch, *passânikan, passânikaigan.* I dig a ditch, *nin passânike, nin passânikaige.* I make a ditch through it, *nin passânikadan.* There is a ditch made, *passânikade, passânikaigâde.*—I dig a ditch around him, (her, it,) *nin giwitaianikana; nin giwitaianikadan.*

Dive; I dive, *nin gogi.*

Diver, *gogiwinini.* I am a good diver, *nin jibânâbawe.*

Divers, *anôtch.* (Nanântok).

Divide; I divide amongst people, *nin nenawitâge.* I divide it, (*in., an.*), *nin nenawinan; nin nenawina.* I divide it to him, *nin nenawinamawa, nin nenawitawa.* I divide it to them or amongst them, *nin nenawitawag.* We divide it amongst us, *nin nenawinamadiwin.*—I divide myself, *nin nenawiidis, nin nenawinidis.* It divides itself, *nenawiidisomagad, nenawinidisomagad.*

Divide, (in. s. in.) S. Distribute. S. Open.

Divided; I am (it is) divided, *nin nenawinigâs; nenâwinigâde.*—I am div. in my thoughts, *nin bakânenim.* I am div. against myself, *nin bakânenindis.* It is div. against itself, *bakânenindisomagad.*

Divinity, divine nature, *Kije-Manitowiwin.*

Division, (in. s. in.) S. Distribution.

Divorce, *bakeshkodâdiwin, webinidiwin.* We make a divorce, *nin bakeshkodâdimin, nin webinidimin.*

Dizzy. Dizziness.— S. Giddy. Giddiness.

Do; I do, *nin dodam, nind ijitchige, nin dodâge.* It does, *dodagemagad, ijitchigemagad.* I make him do s. th., *nin dodamoa.* I do him s. th., *nin dodawa.* It does me s. th., *nin dodâgon.* We do s. th. to one another, *nin dodâdimin.*—I do s. th. by mistake, *nin wanidodam, nin pitchi-dodam.* I don't dare do it, *nin manâdodam.* I do s. th. in such a place, *nin danakamigis.* I do s. th. often, *nin wakédodam, nin nitâ-dodam.* I do it instead of him, *nin nabishkamawa.* I do (or say) what is not my business, *nin wawiiagis.* (Wâwiyatisiw).

Doctor, *mashkikiwinini, nanandawiiwewinini, nenandawiiwed.*

Doctor; I doctor, (I give medicines,) *nin nanandawiiwe.* I doctor him, *nin nanândawia, nin nanandawitwa.*

Doctored; I am doc., *nin nanândawiigos.* Doctored person, *nanândawitchigan.*

Doctoring, a doctor's art, science, business, *nanândawiiwewin, nanândawitwâwin.*

Document, (deed,) *debwewinimasinaigan.* Any writing, *ojibiigan.*

Do evil; I do evil, *nin matchi dodam, nin matchitwa.* I do

him evil, *nin matchi dodawa.* We do evil to each other, *nin matchi dodâdimin.* Mutual evil doing, *matchi dodâdiwin.*

Dog, *animosh, onim, animokadji.* I am a dog, *nind animoshiw.* My, thy, his dog, *nindai, kidai, odaian.* French dog, *jonjo, jonjowassim.* Male dog, *nâbêssim.* Female dog, (bitch,) *nojéssim.* Young dog, *oshkassim.* This dog is a good pointer, a good sporting dog, *mikwâdisi aw animosh.* I call a dog whistling, *nin wikwikwassimwe.* The dog wags his tail, *wewebanoweni animosh.* (Atim, n'tem, otema wewebâyowew).

Dog-train, dog-sled, *nabâgadâbânâk.*

Doing, *dodamowin, ijitchigewin.* Doing by mistake, *wanidodamowin, pitchi-dodamowin.*

Domination, *dibendjigéwin.*

Done! *apine!* (Aspin).

Done; it is done or placed, *gijitchigâde, gijikigâde, gijissitchigâde.*

Done. S. Cooked.

Don't, *kego.* (Ekawiya).

Door, *ishkwandem.* I make a door or doors, *nind ishkwandemike.* There is a door, *ishkwandemiwan.* There is a large door, *mangishkwandeia.* There is a small door, *agassishkwandeia.* I fix the door, *nin naishkwandenan.* Near the door, *tchigishkwand.*

Dormitory, *nibéwin.*

Dotted. S. Spotted.

Double-barreled gun, *najoshkak pâshkisigan.* It is a double-barreled gun, *nijoshkad pâshkisigan.* (Nejomok-pâskisigan).

Doubt, *giwadenkamowin.* (Wâwâneyittamowin)

Doubt; I doubt, *nin giwadendam.* I doubt whether I am able to do it or not, *nind anawenim.* (Wâwâneyittam).

Doubtful; it is doubtful, *giwadendâgwad.*

Doubtless, *gwaiak, geget, e nangé ka.* (Miyâmaw).

Dough; I make up flour into dough, *nin misiwetchishkiwagina pakwejigan, nin misiwedina pakwejigan.*

Dove, (domestic pigeon,) *wâbomimi.*

Down, (soft, underfeather,) *misségwanan.*

Down, *nissâii, mitchâii.*—Down, (respecting rivers,) *nissâdjiwan.*

Down-hanging; I have down-hanging lips, *nin âbodjidon.*

Down the stream; I go down the stream in a canoe or boat, *nin nissâbon, nin bimâbon.* I go down over a rapid, *nin nishibon.* I take him down the stream in a canoe or boat, *nin nishibona.* (Mâmik-mâmitâk).

Doze; I doze, *nind asingwam.*

Dozen, *midâsswi ashi nij.* (Mitâtat nijosâb).

Drag; I drag myself about, *nin babamode, nin babainode.* I drag s. th. with great difficulty, *nin animidâbi.*

Drag, (in. s. in) S. Draw.

Drag-net, *agwabinâgan.* S. Draw-net.

Dragon-fly, *obodashkwanishi.*

Drag out; I drag him (her, it,)

out, *nin sagisidâbâna; nin sagisidâbâdan.*

Drain-shop, *minikwéwigamig, siginigéwigamig.*

Dram-shop keeper, *siginigéwinini.*

Draught-board, *gândinigan, joshkonigan.* I draw on a draught-board, *nin gandinige, nin joshkonige.*

Draught of air; there is a dr. of air, *jâbodéiassin.*

Draught-ox, *odâbi-pîjiki.*

Draw; I draw, *nind odâbi.* I make him draw, *nind odâbia.* I draw him, (her, it,) *nind odâbâna; nind odâbâdan.* I draw a load, *nind awadjidâbi.* I make him draw a load, *nind awadjidâbia.* I cannot draw him, (her, it,) *nin bwawibina; nin bwâwibidon* I have drawn all of it, (*in.*, *an.*) *nin tchagidâbâdan; nin tchagidâbana.* — I draw back or aside, sitting, *nind ikwâb.* (Otâbew).

Draw. Drawing.—S. Paint. Painting.

Draw along; I draw or drag him, (her, it) along, *nin bimidâbâna; nin bimidâbâdan.*

Draw away; I draw or drag away, *nin mâdjidâbi.* I draw or drag him (her, it) away, *nin mâdjidâbâna; nin mâdjidâbâdan.* (Sipwetâbâtew).

Drawers, *bitawigibodeiegwâsson.*

Drawing, *odâbiwin.* (Otâbewin).

Drawing-knife, *mokodjigan, kitchiwâgikomân.*

Draw in the mouth. S. Suck.

Draw liquid; I draw, *nin gwâbaam.* I draw it, (liquid,) *nin gwâbaan, nin gwâbandan.* I draw water, *nin gwâbaige.* I draw water out of a fountain, *nin gwâbaibi.* I draw broth, etc., *nin gwäbaabowe.* I draw a fish out of the water, *nin gwâbâwa gigo.* (Akwânew).

Draw-net, large draw-net, *tchimaâgan.* I am fishing with a draw-net, *nin tchimaa.*

Draw out; I draw it out, (*in.*, *an.*) *nin gitaan, nin gitinan, nin gitchigobidon, nin gissigobidon, nin gitchigwâkonan, nin gissigwâkonan, nin nanikibidon; nin gitawa, nin gitina, nin gitchigobina, nin gissigobina, nin gitchigwâkona, nin gissigwakona, nin nanikibina.* I draw it out for him, *nin gitchibitawa, nin gitchigobidamawa.* (Pikhkohew, wikkwatinam). I draw it out with the teeth, *nin wikwandan.* I try to draw him out s. th. with the teeth, *nin wikwatchiwikwandamawa.*—I draw it out of a vessel, (*in.*, *an.*) *nind agwâbian, nind agwâbiwa.* I draw him (her, it) out of a kettle, etc., *nind agwâwa; nind agwaan.*—I draw out the threads of it, *nind abibidon.*

Draw over; I draw s. th. over a string, *nin nâjabiige.* I draw it over a string or cord, *nin nâjabian.* (I play on the violin, *nin nâjabiige.*—S. Violin, *najabiigan.*)

Draw to...; I draw to me, *nin wikobidjige.* I draw him (her, it) to me, *nin wikobina; nin wikobidon.* I am (it is) drawn to..., *nin wikobidjigas; wikobidgigâde.*

Draw up ; I draw him (her, it) up on a rope, *nind ikwâbigina, nin wikwâbigina, nin wikwâbigibina ; nind ikwâbiginan, nin wikwabiginan, nin wikwâbigibinan.*

Dread ; I dread him, (respect him,) *nin goshima.* I dread it, (respect it,) *nin gossitan.* I dread him (her, it) in thoughts, *nin gotanenima ; nin gotânendân.* (Kustonâmew).

Dread. Dreaded, (in. s. in.) S. Fear. Feared.

Dreaded ; I am (it is) dreaded, considered dreadful, *nin gotânendagos ; gotanendagwad.* (Kustâtikusiw).

Dreadful. S. Frightful.

Dream, *inâbandamowin, inâbanjigan, bawâdjigan.* — Bad dream, *mânâsabandamowin.* I have a bad dream, *nin mânâsâbandam.* Beautiful dream, *wejibâbandjigan, wejibâbandamowin.* I have a beautiful dr., *nin wejibabandjige, nin wejibâbandam.*—Good dream, *minwabandamowin.* I have a good dream, *nin minwabanjige nin minwabandam.* — Impure dream, *bishigwasabandamowin.* I have an impure dream, *nin bishigwasabandam.* Ominous unlucky dream, *âpawewin.* I have an ominous unlucky dream, *nind âpawe.*— Painful dream, *kotagâbandamowin.* I have a painful dream, *nin kotagâbandam.* (Pawâtamowin, pawâgan).

Dream ; I dream, *nind inâbandam, nind inâbandjige, nin bawadjige.* I dream often, *nin nitâ-inâbandam, nin nitâ-bawâdjige.* (Pawâtam, itâbattam). I dream of him, (her, it,) *nind inâbama, nin bawâna ; nind inabandan, nin bawâdan.*

Dreamer, *enâbandang, bewâdjiged.* Great dreamer, *netâinâbandang, netâ-bawâdjiged.*

Dreaming. S. Dream.

Dregs ; there are dregs, *jigossemagad.*

Drenched ; I am dr. with rain, *nin bosâbawe.* I am (it is) dr. through, *nin jâbwâbawe ; jabwâbawemagad.*

Dress, *agwiwin.* I have a new dress on, *nind oshkikwanaie, nind oshkigwaje.* (Miskutâkäy).

Dress ; I dress myself, *nin bisikwanaie, nin bisikonidis, nind agwiidis.* I dress him (her, it) *nin bisikona, nind agwia ; nin bisikonan, nin agwiton.* (Pustayonisew). I dress myself in a certain manner, *nind ijikwanaie.* I dress it (or clothe it) in a certain manner, *nind ijikwanaieton.* I dress like..., *nind iji, nind ijikwanaie.* It dresses (is dressed) like..., *ijiomagad, ijikwanaiemagad.*—I dress elegantly, *nin wâweji, nin wâwejikwanaie* (Wâwesiw). I dress him elegantly, *nin wâwejia.* I dress gloriously, *nin bishigendagwi.* I dress in black, *nin makatewîkwanaîe.* I dress in green, *nind ojawashkwanaie.* I dress in red, *nin miskwakwanaie.* I dress in white, *nin wâbikwanaie, nin wâbishkikwanaie.* I dress vainly, splendidly, *nin sasé-*

gakwanaie. I dress warmly, *nin kijôpis.* (Kisosuw).
Dress a wound; I dress his wound, tie it up, *nin sinsobina.* My wound is dressed, *nin sinsobis.* The dressing of a wound, *sinsobisowin.* (Akkupisuwin).
Dress. S. Tan.
Dressed; I am dressed. S. I dress.
Dressed; poorly dressed. S. Naked.
Dressed. S. Tanned.
Dried fish, *bâtégigô, naméteg.*
Dried meat, *bâtéwiiass.* (Kâkkêwok).
Drink, *minikwewin.* It is drink, *minikwewiniwan.*
Drink; I drink, *nin minikwe, nin minikwâdjige.* I drink in such a place, *nin dajibi.* I drink in diff. places, *nin babâijibi.* I drink it, *nin minikwen.* I drink it, (spend it for drinking,) (*in., an.*) *nin minikwâdan; nin minikwâna.*
Drink. S. Give to drink.
Drink all; I drink it all up, *nind iskandan, nind iskapidan, nin sikapidan.* (Kitaw).
Drink-house, drinking-house, *minikwewigamig, siginigewigamig.*
Drinking, *minikwewin.* Bad habit of drinking, habitual drinking, *minikweshkiwin.* I am in a bad habit of drinking, *nin minikweshk.*
Drinking-vessel, *minikwâdjigan.*
Drink together; I drink together with him, *nin widjiminikwema, nin widjibima.* We drink together, *nin widjibindimin.*
Driven by the waves; I am (it is) driven by the waves, *nin babamiwebaog; babamiwebaan.* I am (it is) driven away by the waves, *nin bimiwebaog; bimiwebaan.* (Webâpokow).
Driven by the wind; I am (it is) dr. about by the w., *nin babamâsh; babamâssin.* I am (it is) dr. aside by the w., *nin bimidash; bimidâssin.* I am (it is) dr. backwards by the w., *nind ajéiash; ajéiâssin.* I am (it is) dr. by the w. to the shore, *nind agwaiash; agwaîâssin.* (Webâssin).
Drive off; I drive him off, (away,) *nind ikonajâwa, nin mâdjinajikawa.* (Iyekatetisahwew).
Driver. S. Cartman.
Droll; I droll, *nin babâpinis.* (Wâwiyatwesk).
Droll, (curious, comical;) I am (it is) droll, considered droll, *nin wawiiadendâgos; wawiiadendâgwad.* I find him (her, it) droll, *nin wawiiadenima; nin wawiiadendan.* I find or think myself droll, *nin wawiiadenindis.*
Droll. Drollery, (in. s. in.) S. Buffoonery.
Drollery, *babapinwewin, wawiiajitâgosiwin.* I am telling drolleries, *nin babapinwe, nin wawiiagitâgos.*
Drop, *pangigag.* (Pakkikawiwin).
Drop; it drops, *pangiga.* (Pakkipestin).
Drop, (let fall;) I drop it, (*in., an.*) *nin bâninan; nin bânina.* —S. Fall, let fall down.
Dropsy, *missidjiwin.* I have

the dropsy, *nin missidji.* (Mistatayeppinewin).
Drought; where is a dr., *bibinekamate.*
Drown; I drown him, *nin gibwanâbawana.* (Nistâbâwâyew).
Drowned; I am dr., *nin gibwanâmabawe, nin nissâbawe.* (Nistâbâwew).
Drowsy. Drowsiness.—S. Sleepy. Sleepiness.
Drum, *teweigan, mitigwakik.* (Mistikwaskik.)
Drum; I drum, *nin teweige.* (Pakahamaw).
Drummer, *taiéwéiged, tewéigewinini.*
Drum-stick, *pagaakokwân.*
Drunk; I am drunk, *nin giwashkwebi.* (Kiiskwebew).
Drunkard, *menikweshkid.* Confirmed habitual drunkard, *gawashkwebishkid, netâ-giwashkwebid.* I am a habitual drunkard, *nin nita-giwashkwebi, nin giwashkwebishk.* I make him a perfect drunkard, *nin giwashkwebishkia.*
Drunken person, *gawashkwebid.*
Drunkenness, *minikweshkiwin, giwashkwebiwin.* Habitual drunkenness, *giwashkwebishkiwin.* (Kiiskwebewin).
Dry; I dry myself, I become dry, *nin bâss.* I dry it, (*in., an.*) *nin bâssan; nin bâsswa.* I dry meat, etc., *nin bâssama.*
Dry; I am (it is) dry, *nin btenjos, nin bâss; bengwan, bâtte.* The ground is dry, *bengwâkamiga, bibinékamate.* It is dry, (the water dried up,) *iskâtemagad, iskabimagad.* It dries and dies, *nibôbate.* (Dry-meat, kakkiwok).
Dry. S. Thirsty.
Drying, *bâssamâwin.*
Dry in smoke; I dry s. th. in smoke, *nin mawakadosama, nin gaskisige.* I dry it in smoke, (*in., an.*) *nin gaskisan; nin gaskiswa.* (Kaskâbaswew).
Duck, *jishib.* A large kind of duck, *ininishib.* Another kind of wild duck, *ansig.* Another kind, *jingibiss.* Duck with a long neck, *ginogweiaweshib.* Another kind of duck, *kinishtinokweshib.* Another kind, *siamo.* Another kind again, *wakéiawishib.* A kind of autumn duck, *pikwakoshib.* A very fat duck, *pakojishib.* —I hunt ducks, *nin nandoshibe, nin nodjishibe.*
Dug; it is dug deep, *ginwanikâde, dimiianikâde, ishpânikâde.*
Dug. S. Woman's breast.
Dull; it is dull, blunt, *ajâssin, ajiwassin, ajiiabikissin.* I am dull at work, *nin babégikâdis, nin babédjinawis.*
Dull (in. s. in.) S. Stupid.
Dullness at work, *babégikadisiwin, babédjinawisiwin.*
Dung, *pigikiwimo.* (Mustusomëy).
Duplicate, *anbjibiigan.*— S. Copy.
Durable; I am dur,, of a strong constitution, *nin jibinawis.* It is durable, (*in. an.*) *songan; songisi.* It is dur., (wood,) *jibigissin.* It is dur., metal,) *jibabikissin.* (Siban, sibinew).
During, *megwa, apitch.*
Dusky; I am dusky, *nin makatéwis.*
Dust, *wiiagassiiân.* The white

dust on the head of a person, *akinikwan.* (Pikkowakkaw). The dust is raised by the wind, *pingwêombassin.* The dust falls on s. th., *binakamigishka.* I wipe the dust off, *nin binawian.* I shake the dust off from it, (*in. an.*) *nin baweginan ; nin bawegina.*
Dusty ; I make it dusty, *nin binakamigishkan.*
Dwell ; I dwell, *nin da, nind ab.* I dwell in him, (her, it,) *nind abitawa; nind abitan.*
Dwelling. S. Habitation.
Dye, (color,) *onansigan, adissigan.*
Dye, (color ;) I dye, *nin onansige, nind adissige.* I dye ash-colored, black, etc. S. Ash-colored, Black, etc.
Dyed ; it is dyed, (*in.,an.*) *aditte ; adisso.* It is dyed so..., (*in., an.,*) *inande ; inanso.* It is dyed green, red, etc. S. Green. Red, etc.
Dying ; I am dying, *nin giwine, nin nib, nin bâbanadis.* (Atinipiw).
Dyeing, (coloring,) *adissigewin, onansigewin.*
Dyer, *edissiged, adissigewinini, onansigewinini.*
Dyer's business or trade, *adissigewin, onansigewin.*
Dyer's shop, dye-house, *adissigewigamig, onansigewigamig.*
Dye-stuff, *adissigan, onansigan.*
Dysentery, *jâbondeshkawin.* I I have the dys., *nin jâbondeshka.* (Sâbosow.)
Dysury, *gibijigiwineshkawin.* I have the dysury, *nin gibijigiwinerhka.*

E

Eagle, *migisi.* Young eagle, *migisins.* Another kind of eagle, *wâbijakwe.* Black eagle, *missansi.* (Kiyiw).

Eagle's claw, *migisiwiganj.*

Eagle-fighter, *migisananissi, pipigiwis.*

Eagle-Harbor, *Migisiwiwikwed.* At Eagle-Harbor, from or to Eagle-Harbor, *Migisiwiwikwedong.*

Eagle-River, *Migisiwisibi.* At, from or to Eagle-River, *Migisiwisibing.*

Ear, *otawâgâma.* My, thy, his ear, *nitawag, kitawag, otawag.* (N'ittawokäy, k'ittawokäy, ottawokäy). I have ears, *nind otawâga.* I have large ears, *nin mamangitawage.* I have a long ear, *ninginotawage;* I have long ears,*nin gaganotawage.*I have a small ear, *nin agâssitawage;* I have small ears, *nin babiwitawage.* I have ugly ears,*nin mâmanjitawage.* My ear is cold, (my ears are cold,) *nin takitawage, nin tatakitawage.* My ear is cut off, *nin kishkitawage.* I cut off his ear, *nin kishkitawagejwa.* I strike off his ear, *nin kishkitawageganama.* My ear is frozen, (my ears are frozen,) *nin mashkawadjitawagewadj.* My ear is stopped, *nin gibitawage;* my ears are stopped, (I am deaf,) *nin gagibitawage.* (Kipittew). I stop my ear, *nin gibitawageodis;* I stop my ears, *nin gagibitawageodis, nin gagibishebinidis.* I stop his ear, *nin gibitawagêwa;* I stop his ears, *nin gagibitawagéwa, nin gagibishebina.* My ear is swollen, *nin bagitawage.*—I have only one ear, *nin nabanétawage.* The other ear, or only one ear, *nabanétawag.* I pull his ear, *nin wikotawagebina, nin jibitawagebina.* (Tewittâwokew).

Ear-hanging. S. Ear-ring.

Earn; I earn, *nin dashkitchige.* I earn to myself, or for myself, *nin gashkitas, nin gashkîtamâs, nin gashkitamâdis, nin wikwatchitas, nin wikwatchitamâdis.*—I earn it, (*in., an.*) *nin gashkitchigen, nin gashkiton; nin gashkitchigenan, nin gashkia.* I earn it to myself, (*in., an.*) *nin gashkitamâson; nin wikwatchitamâson; nin gashkitamâsonan, nin wikwatchitamâsonan.* I earn it for him, *nin gashkitawa, nin gashkitamâwa.* (Kispinatew.)

Earn, (in. s. in.) S. Gain. Procure.

Earned; it is earned, (*in. an.*) *gashkitchigâde; gashkia.*

Earning, *gashkitchigewin, wik-*

watchitamâsowin.
Earnings, *gashkitchigan.*
Ear of fish, *otetêgwan.*
Ear of Indian corn, *nisâkosi.*
Ear-ring, *nabishebison.* (Tabittebisun.).
Earth, *akki.* On earth, *akking, ogidakamig.* (Askïy). Under the earth, (Atâmaskamik). The opposite side of the earth, *ajawakamig.* I am earth, *nind akkiw.* It is earth, or there is earth, *akkiwan.* The earth quakes, or shakes, *niningikamigishka akki; gwingwan, tchingwan, tchingwakamiga.*
Earthen dish or plate, *wâbiganonâgan.* (Ajiskiwoyâgan). I make earthen dishes and plates, *nin wâbigan-onaganike.* A man that makes earthen dishes and plates, a potter, *wâbigan-onaganikewinini.*
Earth-house, (under ground,) *akkiwigamig.*
Earthquake; there is an earthquake, *niningakamigishka aki, niningishkamagad akki.*
Ear-wax, *mowidjitawâgan.*
Easily, *wenipaj, wenipanaj.*
East, *wâban, wendjimokaang.* In the east, from or to the east, *wâbanong.*
East-cloud, *wâbanakwad.*
Easter, *Pak.* Easter-Sunday, *Pakgijigad* or *Apitchipâwikijigat.*
East-rain, *wabanibisca.*
East-star, (morning-star,) *wâbanang.*
East-wind, *wâbaninodin.*
Easy; it is easy, *wenipanad.* I think s. th. is easy, *nin wénipanendam.* I think it is easy, *nin wenipanendan,*
Eat; I eat, *nin wissin.* (Mitjisuw). I eat it, (*in*, *an.*) *nin midjin; nind amwa.* (Mowew). I eat with him, *nin widôpama.* I eat (or fare) so..., *nind inandjige, nind indanandjige.* I eat good things, *nind minwandjige.* I begin to eat, *nin madandjige.* I eat before I start, *nin nawadji.* I eat as long as..., *nind apitandjige.* I eat it raw, (*in.*, *an.*) *nind ashkandan; nind ashkama.* I eat secretly, (in a stealthy manner,) *nin gimodandjige.* (Kimipuw). I eat slowly, *nin babéjikadandjige, nin bedjissin.* I eat fast and much, *nin gâjage.* I eat s. th. with some other thing, *nind apândjige, nin dagwandjige.* I eat it (*in.*, *an.*) with some other thing as a by-meat, *nind apândjigen, nin dagwandjigen, nin dagwandân; nind apândjigenan, nin dagwandjigenan, nin dagwama.* I look for s. th. to eat, *nin nandawissin.* I go somewhere to get s. th. to eat, (or to drink,) *nin nadabowe.* I eat sufficiently, *nin debissin.* I make him eat sufficiently, *nin debissinia.*—I give to eat, *nind ashange.* I give him (her, it) to eat, *nind ashama; nind ashandan.*
Eat up, (consume;) I eat up, *nin gidawe.* I eat it all up, (*in.*, *an.*) *nin gidan; nin gidamwa.* I eat all up, s. th. belonging to him, *nin gidamâwa.* It eats me up, *nin gidamogon.*

Eatable root; a small eatable root, *watapin.*
Eatables, (provisions,) *midjim.*
Eating, *wissiniwin* (Mitjisuwin).
Eating-house, *wissiniwigamig, ashangewigamig.*
Ebb, ebbing tide; it is the ebbing tide, *odaskimagad nibi.*
Echo. S. Resound.
Eclipsed; the sun (or moon) is eclipsed, there is an eclipse, *gisiss nibo.* (Wanitibiskipayiw pisim.)
Edification, *mino kikinowâbamigowin.*
Edify; I edify, *nin mino kikinowâbandaiwe.* I edify him, *nin mino kikinowâbamig.* He edifies me, *nin mino kibinowâbama*
Edge of a tool, *gânag, ganamagak.* It has such an edge, (or such teeth,) *inabidéiamagad.*
Eel, *bimisi.*
Efface. Effaced. S. Blot out. Blotted out.
Effect; it makes a good effect, (medicine, etc.) *minoshkagemagad.* It makes a good effect in me, *nin minokâgon;* it makes a bad effect, *nin manikâgon.*
Effect; I effect it, *nin gashkiton.* I cannot effect it, *nin bwânawiton.* I eff. little, *nind inwâs.* It eff. little, *inwâsomagad.* I eff. nothing (with my working,) *nind anamewis, nind ashkonawis.* It effects nothing, *anawewisimagad.*
Effort; I make efforts, *nin mashkawis, nin wikwatchito.* (Kutchiw).
Egg, *wânan.* Small egg, *wawanons.* Bad spoiled egg, *wananosh.* Hen's egg, *pakaakwawanan.* (Wâwi).
Eight, *nishwâsswi.* We are eight of us, *nin nishwâtchimin.* There are eight *in.* obj., *nishwatchinon.* (Ayenânew).
Eight, *nishwâsso...,* in compositions; which see in the First Part.
Eight every time, eight each or to each, *nenishwâsswi.*
Eighth, *eko-nishwâtching.* The eighth time, *nishwâtching.*
Eighthly, *eko-nishwâtching.*
Eight hundred every time, eight hundred each or to each, *nenishwâsswak.*
Eight thousand, *nishwâtching midâswak.*
Eight times, *nishwâtching.*
Eight times every time, eight times each or to each, *newishwâtching.*
Eighty, *nishwâssimidana.* We are eighty, *nin nishwâssimidanawemin.* There are eighty *in.* obj., *nishwâssimidanawewan.*
Eighty every time, eighty each or to each, *nenishwâssimidana.*
Eighty hundred, *nishwâssimidanak.* We are eighty hundred of us, *nin nishwâssimidanakosimin.* There are eighty hundred *in.* obj., *nishwâssimidanakwadon.*
Eking piece, *aniketchigan.* There is an eking piece, *aniketchigâde.*
Elapsed. S. Passed, (Past.)
Elbow, *biminik, biskinikenowin, oskwan.* I lean on my elbows, *nind odoskwanishin.* I strike him with the elbow, *nind odoskwanâwa.*

Elder-tree, elder-shrub, *papashkisiganak, pipigwewanashk, wimbissagashk.*
Election. S. Choice.
Elephant, *ketchi awessi.*
Elevated; I am elevated, *nin kitchitwâwis.*
Eleven, *midâsswi ashi bejig.* (Mitâtat peyak osâb.)
Elk. S. Moose.
Elm or elm-tree, *anib.* Another kind of elm-tree, *ojâshigob.* (Atchâpâsk).
Elm-bark, *anibiwanagek.* Sack of elm-bark, *wanimod.*
Elm-forest, elm-grove, *anibiki.*
Elm-River, *Anibinsiwi-sibi.*
Eloquent; I am el., *nin nitâwê.*
Elsewhere, *ningotchi, bakân.*
Emaciated; I am em., *nin jâshâgwabewis.*
Emancipate; I em. him, *nin pagidina tchi dibenindisod.*
Embark; I embark, *nin bos.* I emb. with somebody, *nind adawâawi.* I emb. him, (her, it,) *nin bosia; nin bositon.* I em. with him, *nin adawaama.* (Tchimew). I bid him embark, *nin bosinajâwa.* I em. him by force, *nin boswebina.* I am embarked by force, *nin boswebinigâs.*
Embarkation, *bosiwin.*
Embarrass; I emb. him with my words, *nin wâwânima.* I emb. him by my requests, *nin wâwânimotawa.*
Embarrassed; I am emb. in my thoughts, *nin wâwânendam.* I cause him to be emb. in his thoughts, *nin wâwânendamia.*
Embellish; I em. him, (her, it,) *nind onijishia, nin sasegaa; nind onijishiton, nin sasegaton.*
Embellishment. S. Ornament.
Embezzle. Embezzlement. Embezzler.—S. Cheat. Cheating. Cheater.
Embrace. S. Hug.
Embroider; I embroider or ornament, *nin niskagwaige.* I embroider, making flowers, etc., *nin masinigwadam.* I embroider it, (*in*, *an.*) *nin masinigwâdân; nin masinigwana.* I emb. with porcupine-quills, *nin bimig, nind onâgaskwawaie.* I emb. with small glass-beads, *nin masiniminensike, nin niskiminesike.* I embr. or ornament it with small glass-beads, (*in.*, *an.*) *nin niskiminensikâdan; nin niskiminensikâna.*
Embroidered; it is embr. or ornamented, *niskagwaigâde, niskamagad.* It is emb. with flowers, etc., (*in.*, *an.*) *masinigwâde; masinigwâso.* It is embr. with small glass-beads, (*in.*, *an.*) *masiniminensigâde, niskiminensikâde; masiniminensikana, niskiminensikana.*
Embroidery; fine emb. with porcupine-quills, *onagaskwawai.*
Emerge; I emerge, *nin moshkaagwindjisse.* It emerges, *moshkaagwindjissemagad.*
Emetic, *jashigagowesigan.* (Pâkomosigan).
Eminently, *âpitchi.* (Nâspitch).
Emmet, *enigo.* (Eyik).
Emperor, *kitchi-ogima.*
Empire, *ogimâwiwin.*
Employ; I employ him, *nin anona.* I empl. him (her, it) in a certain manner, *nind inawêmikana; nind inawêmikadan.* (Atotew).

Employed ; employed person, *anonâgan, anonam, enonind, onotâgan.* Employed (used) thing, *aiowin anokasowin.* I am employed, *nind anonigo.* I am empl. in a certain manner, *nind inawémikas.*
Employer, *enôkid.*
Emplo yment, *anonigosiwin, anonidiwin.*
Empress, *kitchi ogimâkwe.*
Empty, (without a load,) *pijishig.*
Enable ; I enable him, *nind inenima.*
E n c a m p. Encampment. S- Camp.
Encampment, *nibewin.* (Kapesiwin).
Enclose. S. Fence in.
Enclosure, *atchikinigan, giwitakinigan.*—S. Fence. (Wâskânigan).
Encourage ; I enc., *nin gagansonge.* I enc. him, *nin gagansoma.* (Akamimew).
Encourage, (console ;) I enc., *nind abisiwinge.* I enc. him, *nind abisiwima, nin gagânoma.* (Kâkitjimew).
Encourage to do evil ; I enc. him to do evil, *nind ashia, nind ashiwima.* (Matchi-sikkimew).
Encouraging, *gagânsondiwin, gagansongewin, abisiwingewin ; ashiidiwin.*
Encumber ; I enc., *nin niskikage.* I encumber him, (her, it,) *nin niskia, nin niskikawa; nin niskikan.* It enc. me, *nin niskikâgon.*
Encumber, (in. s. in.) S. Obstruct.
End, *waiêkwa.*— (Wanaskutch). (In compositions.) There is an end, *waiekwaiamagad.* At the end, *waiêkwaiaii.* It is considered the end of it, *waiekwaiendagwad.* I think it is the end of it, *nin waiekwaiendan.* I go to the end of it, *nin kabeshkan.* I arrive at the end, *nin waiekwashkan.* I bring it to an end, *nin waiekwassiton, nin waiekwaton.* It comes to an end, *waiekwassemagad.*—It is the end of the world, *waiekwaakkiwan, ishkwa-akkiwan, boni-akkiwan*— (Kisipaskamik). The end of an action or work, *ishkwakamigisiwin, ishkwatâwin ; anwâtawin.*
Endeavor ; I endeavor, *nin wikwatchi, nin wikwatchito, nin wikwatchiton, nind aiangwamendam, nind aiangwamis.* I end. in vain to have it, *nind agawadan.* I end. (or work) in vain, *nind ânawewis.* I end. without much effect, *nind inwas.*—I e n d. t o g e t; (i n thoughts,) *nin wikwatendam.* I end. to get him, (her, it,) *nin wikwatenima ; nin wikwatendan.* (Kutchi, v. g. kutchinakamuw ; he endeavors to sing ; akâwittam.)
Endeavor, (in. s. in.) S. Try.
Endless, *weiekwaiassinog.*
Endure ; I can endure much cold, *nin jibadj.* I can end. much hunger, *nin jibanandami.* I can end. much smoke, *nin jibanamoss.* (Sibeyittam).
Enemy, *jangendjiged.* I am enemy, *nin jingendjige.* (Pakwâtâgan.)
Engage ; I engage in a service, *nind anonigos.*

Engagement, *anonigosiwin.*
England, Great Britain and Ireland, *Jâganashiwakki.* In, from or to England, *Jâganashiwakking.*
English; it is English, (Akayâssimowin), (written or printed in English,) *jâganashiwissin, jâganishimomagad.* I translate it in Eng., *nin jaganashiwissiton.* It is translated in Eng., *jâganashiwissitchigâde.*
English boy, or a little Englishman, *jâganashins.*
English girl, *jâganashikwens.*
English language, *jâganashimowin.* I speak English, *nin jaganashim.* It speaks Engl., (it is in Eng.,) *jaganashimomagad.*
Englishman, *Jâganash.* (Akayâssiw).
English minister, *Jâganashimekatewikwanaie.*
English religion, (Church of England,) *Jâganashi-anamiewin.* I profess the Eng. religion, *nin jâganashi-anamia.*
Englishwoman, *jâganashikwe.*
English writing, *jâganashiwibiigan.* I write in Eng., *nin jâganashiwibiige.*
Engrave; I engrave, *nin masinibiige.*
Engraved; I am (it is) engr., *nin masinâs, nin masinibiigâs; masinâde, masinibiigâde.*
Engraving, *masinibiigewin; masinibiigan, masinitchigan.*
Enkindle; I enk. it, *nin biskakondan.*
Enlargen. S. Widen.
Enlighten; I enl. him, *nin wâsséiabia, nin wâssenamawa.* I enl. his mind, *nin wâsséiendamia, nin wâssakwanendamawa.*
Enmity. S. Hatred.
Enormity. S. Horror.
Enormous. S. Frightful.
Enough, *mi minik, mi iw.* (Ekuyigok). There is enough of it, (*in., an.*) *débissémagad; debisse.* (Tepipayiw). I have enough, *nin débis.* I think I have enough, or, I think it is enough, *nin débênim, nin debendam, nin dêbagenim.* I talk enough, *nin dêbânagidon.* I drank enough, *nin débibi;* I ate enough, *nin dêbissin.*— We are just enough, *nin minodashimin.* There is just enough of it, *minodassin.*
Enraged person, very angry, *ketchi nishkâdisid.* I am enraged, very angry, *nin kitchi nishkâdis.* (Osâmiyawesiw).
Enslave; I ens. him, *nind awakâna.* It enslaves me, *nind awakanigon.* I ens. myself, *nind awakanidis.*
Entangled; I am ent. in a cord, *nin biswabigishin.*
Enter, (go in;) I enter somewhere, *nin pindige.* (Pittukew). It enters, *pindigemagad.* I enter into him, *nin pindigawa, nin pindigeshkawa, nin pindjinaweshkawa, nin pindjineshkawa.* It enters into me, *nin pindigeshkâgon, nin pindjinaweshkâgon, nin pindjineshkagon.*
Enter, (take in or bring in;) I enter him, (her, it,) *nin pindigana; nin pindigadon.*
Entice; I entice, *nin wikwasonge.* I ent. him; *nin wik-*

wasoma. We ent. each other, *nin wikwasondimin.* (Ayakukkâsuw).
Enticing, *wikwasongewin, wikwasondiwin.*
Entire. S. Whole.
Entirely, *kakina wâwinge, âpitchi.* (Misiwe).
Entreat. Entreaty.—S. Entice. Enticing.—S. Bequest.
Envelop. S. Wrap up.
Envy, *kijâwenindiwin, kijâwendjigewin gagawenindiwin, gagawendjigewin.* (Isawânakeyimowin).
Envy; I envy, I am envious, *nin gagawendjige, nin kijâwendjige.* I envy him, (her, it,) *nin kijâwenima, nin gagawenima; nin kijâwendan, nin gagawendan.* (Otteyittam).
Epaulet, *niskitenimanganedjigan.*
Epidemy, *mejikâgemagak inapinewin.*
Epiphany, *Ogimâ-gijigad.*
Equal; I equal him, *nin tibishkokawa, nind adima.*
Equally, *tibishko tetibishko, tâbishkotch, nassab.*
Equivalent, *tibishko.* It is eq. (*in., an.*), *tibishko apitendagwad; tibishko apitendagosi.* (Ispiteyittâkwan).
Erect; I erect him, (her, it,) *nin maiawakona, nin maiawishima, nin maiawina; nin maîawakonan, nin maiawissiton, nin maiawinan.* I erect myself, *nin maiawita, nin maiawishka, nin maiawishin, nin passagita.* He erects himself, *namatchigabawi,* (a beast.) It erects itself, *maiawishkamagad.*—I erect it, (*in., an.*) *nin patakidon; nin patakina.* (Tchimayew).
Erected; I am (it is) erected by the wind, *nin maiâwash; maiawassin.* It is erected, (*in., an.*) *maiawissin, maiawissitchigâde; maiawissitchigâso.*
Erected, (in. s. in.) S. Stand up.
Errand, *ininajaogowin.* (Itisahamâtuwin).
Erysipelas. S. Herpes.
Escape, *ojimowin.* (Paspiwin).
Escape; I escape, *nind ojim, nin giiwe, nin gidiskiiwe, nin jabwi, nin jabwiiwe, nin gidiskiidis.* I escape out of his hands, *nin gia, nin gidiskia.* I make him escape, *nind ojimoa, nin jabwia.* (Paspiw, tabasiw).
Escaped; a person esc. from a massacre, *ishkwatâgan, ishkwatchigan.*
Especially, *memindage, memdage, wâwij.*
Esquimau Indian, *Eshkibod,* (raw-eater.)
Essay. S. Try. Endeavor.
Essential. S. Foremost.
Establish; I est. it, *nind ojissiton, nind aindjissiton.*
Established; it is est., *aindjissitchigâde.*
Esteem; I esteem, *nind apitendam.* I esteem or respect him, (her, it,) *nind apitenima, nin gokwadenima; nind apitendan, nin gokwadendan.* I esteem myself, *nind apitenim, nind apitenindis, nin gokwadenim, nin gokwadenindis.* I esteem myself as high as him, *nind apitenimonan.* —I est. him (her, it) in a certain manner, *nind inassagadenima;*

nind inassagadêndân. I est. him (her, it) little, *nin bewenima; nin bewendan.* (Ispiteyimew, kisteyimew).
Esteem, (in s. in.) S. Respect. High esteem.
Esteem little. Esteemed little, (in. s. in.) S. Insignificant.
Esteemed; I am (it is) esteemed in a certain manner, *nind inassagadendâgos; inassagadendâgwad.* (Kiskeyittâkusiw).
Esteemed, (in. s. in.) S. Respectable. Highly esteemed.
Esteemed equal; I am (it is) est. equal to..., *nin tibishkowendâgos; tibishkowendagwad.*
Estimate. S. Value.
Eternal, *Kaiagige-bimâdisid.*
Eternal, *weiekwaiassinog, kâgige, kâgini.* Life eternal, *kâgige bimâdisiwin.* Eternal welfare, eternal salvation, *kâgige jawendagosiwin, kâgige mino aiâwin.* Eternal misery, eternal damnation, *kâgige kotagitowin, kâgige banâdjiidisowin.*
Eternally, *kâjigékamig,kâginig, kâgini.*
Eternity, *kâgige bimâdisiwin.*
Eucharist; the holy Eucharist, *kitchitwa Eukaristiwin.* I receive the holy Eucharist, *nind odapinan kitchitwa Eukaristiwin.*
Eunuch. S. Castrated.
Europe, *Kitchi agâming, Agâming kitchigami.*
Evangely. S. Gospel.
Evaporate; it evap., *anississin, anissassin.* (Mestâbattew).
Even; it is even, (bark, etc.) *onashkwéiamagad.* It is even, (wood, *in., an.*) *ojissaga; ojissagisi.* It is even, flat, (metal, *in., an.*) *onabikamagad, onabikad; onabikisi.*
Even if..., *missawa; missawa gaie.* (Appo).
Evening, *onâgosh, onâgwish.* It is evening, *onâgoshi, onâgwishi.* Evening is approaching, towards evening, *ani-onâgoshi, eni-onâgoshig.* (Otâkwâsaw, otâkusin).
Evening meal, *onâgoshi-wissiniwin.* (Otâkusiwimitjisuwin).
Evening-prayer, *onâgoshi-anamiang, onâgoshi-anamiewin.*
Event; good event, *mino inakamigad.* Sad event, *matchi inakamigad.* (Ikkin).
Ever; ever since, *apine.* For ever, *apine, kaginig.* (Aspin).
Everlasting, *kâgige.*
Every day, *endasso-gijigak.* (Tattwawikijikâki).
Every night, *endasso-tibikak.* (Tattwawitibiskâki).
Every second day, *nenassawigijig, nenijogijig, nenijogwan.*
Every time, *dassing.* (Tattwaw).
Everywhere, *misi misiwe.* There is of it everywhere, *misiweshkamagad.* Everywhere on earth, *misi enigokwag akik, misâkkamig.*
Evil, *maianadak,matchi aiiwish.* My evil (in sickness) increases when I speak, *nin gidjim, nin gidowe.*
Evil, *matchi.* It is evil; *manadad, matchi ijiwebad.*
Evil spirit, *matchi manito, matchi aiaawish.*
Eviscerate. S. Gut.
Exact, exactly, *gwaiâk, nissitâ, wâwinge.* I arrange it exactly, *nin wâwingeton.*

Exact; I am exact, *nin wâwinges.*
Exact, (in. s. in.) S. Severe.
Exactness, *wâwingesiwin.* I act with exactness, *nin wâwinges, nin wâwingetchige.*
Exaggerate; I ex., *osâm nibiwa nind ani-ikkit, osâm nibiwa nin dibâdjim.*
Exalt; I exalt him, *nind ishpenima, nind ishpia, nin kitchitwawia, nin kitchitwawendagosia.* I exalt it, *nind ishpendan, nin kitchitwawendan, nin kitchitwawiton.* I exalt myself, *nind ishpenindis, nind ishpenim, nin kitchitwawenindis, nin hitchitwawenim.* (Mâmitjimew).
Examen of conscience, *nanagatawenindisowin.* I examine my cons., *nin nanagatawenindis.* (Mâmitoneyimisuwin).
Examine; I examine him, (her, it,) *nin gôdji-kikenima; nin godji-kikendan.* (Nânâgatâwâbamew).
Examine, (in. s. in.) S. Try. Seek.
Example, *kikinowâbamigowin, kikinowâbandaiwewin, kikinowâbandjigan.*—Good example, *mino kikinowâbamigowin, mino kikinowâbandaiwewin.* I give a good ex., *nin mino kikinowâbandaiwe.* I give him a good ex., *nin mino kikinowâbamig.* He gives me a good ex., *nin mino kikinowâbama.* —Bad example, *matchi kikinowâbamigowin, matchi kikinowâbandaiwewin.* I give a bad ex., *nin matchi kikinowâbandaiwe.* I give him a bad ex., *nin matchi kikinowâbamig.* He gives me a bad ex., *nin matchi kikinowâbama.*
Example, imitate example; I imitate his ex., *nin kikinowâbama.* He imitates my ex., *nin kikinowâbamig.* I give an example, *nin kikinowâbandaiwe.* I regulate my mind after his ex., *nin kikinawenima.*
Exceedingly, excessively, *âpitchi.* (Nâspitchi).
Excel. S. Surpass.
Excellent, *kitchi onijishin.*
Exchange. S. Change.
Excite; I excite or push him to s. th., *nind ashia, nind inashia.* (Sikkimew).
Excite, (in. s. in.) S. Provoke to anger.
Excitement. S. Trouble, (noise.) S. Stir up.
Excrement, *mo.* (Omëy).
Excuse; I ask excuse for not being able to do s. th., *nin jagwenimotagos.* (Kâkitokkâsuw).
Execution, (hanging,) *agojiwewin, agonidiwin.* (Akosiwewin).
Executioner, (hangman,) *agojiwewinini, agonidiwinini.*
Exhale, it exhales, *anississin, anissassin.*
Exhausted; I am ex., *nind âpitchi aiekos, nind akwiwi.* (Nestuw).
Exhort; I exhort, *nind aiangwamige, nind angwamige, nind aiangwamitagos, nind angwamitagos, nin gagansonge, nin gagikwe, nin ganojiwe.* I exhort him, *nin gagikima.* I exh. him to do s. th., *nin gagânsoma.* We

exh. each other, *nin gagikindimin, nin gagansondimin.* I exhort myself, *nin gagikindis.*
Exhortation, *aiangwamitagosiwin, gagansongewin, gagikindiwin, gagikwewin.*
Exist; I exist, *nind aiâ.* (Ittaw).
Existence, *aiâwin.* (Ittâwin).
Exonerate; I exonerate the bowels, *nin misi.*
Exorbitant. S. Extravagant.
Expand. S. Extend.
Expect; I expect, *nind akawab.* I exp. him, (her, it,) *nind akawâbama; nind akawâbandan.*
Expedition, (haste,) *dadâtabiwin.*
Expeditious; I am ex., *nin dadâtabi, nin gwashkwes.* — S. Quick.
Expeditious working, *gwashkwesiwin, dadâtabiwin.*
Experience; I know it by exp., (I tried it,) *nin gotamandan, nin gotamandjiton.* I experienced it, *nin kikendan.* (Nakatchittaw).
Experiment. S. Trial.
Expire; I expire, *nin nib, nind ishkwa bimâdis.*—S. Finish. (Iskwâtâmow).
Explain; I explain it to him, *weweni nin windamawa.* (Gwayaskomew).
Expose; I expose myself, *nind iniwêidis.* (Iyiwehuw).
Expose to the sight of people.—S. Lay open.
Expressly, *mijisha, p â k a t c h.* (Meyâkwâm.)
Extend; I extend it, (*in., an.*) *nin jibadaan, nin jibadawa.* I ext. it by pulling, (*in., an.*) *nin jibabigibidon; nin jibabijibina.* It extends, *jibabishkamagad.*
Extensive, *kitchi.* It is extensive, *mitchâmagad.*
Extent; its extent, *ekwag.*
Exterminate. S. Spend all.
Externally, on the outside, *agwatchaii.* (Wayawitimâyik).
Extinguish; I extinguish, *nind atêige.* I ex. it, *nind âtêan.* (Astaweham).
Extinguisher, *atêigan.*
Extravagancy, *osâmisiwin.*
Extravagant; I am ext., *nind osâmis.* (Kiiskwew.) Extravagant spending, *tchaginigeshkiwin.*
Extremely, *âpitchi.*
Extremity, (end, summit,) *wânakowin.*
Extreme-Unction, *Anamie-nominidiwin.*
Eye, *oshkinjigoma.* (M'iskijik). The right eye, *kitchishkinjig, okitchishkinjigoma.* The left eye, *namandjishkinjig, onamandjishkinjigoma.* My, thy, his eye, *nishkinjig, kishkinjig, oshkinjig.*—I have eyes, *nind oshkinjig.* I have dim eyes, *nin tibikinam.* I have good eyes, *nin naâb.* I have hollow eyes, *nin wawinikab.* I have large eyes, *nin mamangishkinjigwe.* (Mâmakkâbiw). I have only one eye, *nin nabanêshkinjigwe.* The other eye, or one eye only, *nabanêshkinjig.* I have small eyes, *nind agassishkinjigwe, nind babiwishkinjigwe.* I have sore eyes, *nind oshkinjigones, nin sassakingwe, nind ashkashkanagingwe.* I have weak eyes, *nin biswab, nin bigisa-*

wab, nin bigisawinam.— My eyes are filled with tears, *nin moshkinêsibingwe.* My eyes are open, *nin pâkakab.* I open my eyes, *nin p a k a t a w a b.* (Tokkâbiw). I open his eyes, *nin wâbia.* My eyes are spoiled by smoke, *nin pâshkabis.* My eye is swollen, *nin bâgigoshkinjigwe.* My eyes are tired, *nind ishkatawab, nin pagissab.*—I burst one of my eyes, *nin pâshkâbidjin.* (Pâskâbiw). I cover his eyes with s. th., *nin titibingwebina.* I cover my eyes with s. th., *nin titibingwebis.* I feel a burning pain in my eyes, *nin sassakab.* I feel a burning pain in my eyes from smoke, *nin sassakisibingweiâbas.* I hurt my eye falling, *nin gidjâbishin.* I keep my eyes shut, *nin passangwab.* (Passakwâbiw.) I look with one eye only, *nin pashkingwen.* I look with almost closed eyes, *nin toskab, nin toskâbandjige.* I look with almost closed eyes at him, (her, it,) *nin toskâbama; nin toskâbandan.* I have a mote in my eye, *nin binsin.* (Pisinin). I pluck my eye out, *nin gidjâbaodis.* I pluck his eye out, *nin gidjâbawa.* I rub his eyes with some medicine, *nin sinigoshkinjigwena.* My eyes shut against my will, *nin passangwabishka.*—It is made like an eye, *oshkinjigokâde.*

Eye-apple, apple of the eye, *makatewagamishkinjigwan.*

Eyebrow, *mâma.* My, thy, his eyebrow, *nimâma, kimâma, omâman.* My eyebrows are bristled up, *nin niskimâmawe.* (Misâbiwinân).

Eyelid; the under part of the eyelid, *sibingwai.* The hair of the eyelid, *mishâbiwinân.* (Misâbiwinân).

F

Fable, *adisokan.* (Atayokkan). I tell a fable or fables, *nind adisoke.*

Fabulous giant, *windigo.*

Fabulous giantess, *windigokwe.*

Face; my, thy, his face, *nishkinjig, kishkinjig, oshkinjig;* (Mikkwâgan, n'ikkwâgan, oskwâgan) or, *nindengwai, kidengwai, odengwai.*—I have an angry face, *nin nishkâdjingwe, nin nishkâdjingweshka.* I have a black face, *nin makatewingwe.* I have a clean face, *nin biningwe.* I have a dark-blue face, *nind apissingwe.* I have a dirty face, *nin winingwe, nin mowingwe, nin mowidjiwingwe.* I have a fat full face, *nin wininwingwe.* I have a greased face, *nin nomingwe.* I grease his face, *nin nomingwena.* I grease my face, *nin nomingwenindis.* Greasing the face, or grease for the face, *nomingwewin.* I have a large face, *nin mangadangwe.* I have a lean face, *nin pakakadwengwe.* I have a face like..., *nind inadengwe.* I have a long face, *nin ginwingwe.* I have pimples or pustules on my face, *nin mossewingwe, nin babigwingwe.* I have a scar in my face, *nin odjishingwe.* I have a small face, *nind agassadengwe.* (Timikkwew). I have a strange or changed face, *nin miagishkinjigwe.* I have a wrinkled face, *nind osigingwe.*—My face is cracked, *nen gijingwe.* My face is frozen, *nin mashkawadjingwewadj.* My face is marked with sadness, *nin naninawingwe.* I mark my face with sadness, *nin naninawingwêidis.* My face is marked with the small pox, *nin mamakingwe.* My face is pale, *nin wâbishkingwe, nin wâbidewadengwe.* (Wâbinewisiw). My face is red, *nin miskwingwe.* My face is shining, radiant, *nin wassêingwe, nin wassingwes.* My face is swollen, *nin bagingwe.* My face is uncovered, *nin pakingwe.* I uncover my face, *nin pakingwenidis.* I bruise my face, *nin jashingwingwêwa.* I disfigure my face, *nin manadjingwêidis.* I disfigure his face, *nin manadjingwéwa.* I paint my face, *nin waweji.* I paint my face black, *nin makateke; nin makatekonidis.* I rub his face with medicine, etc., *nin sinigwingwebina.* I rub my face, *nin sinigwingwebinidis.* I wash my face, *nin kisibigingwe.* (Kâssikkwew). I wipe my face, *nin kisingwe.* I wrap up my face in s. th., *nin titibingwebis.* I wrap up his face, *nin titibingwebina.*

Fade; it fades; *anoshka.* It fades in washing, *kisiâbâwe.* —S. Whitish.

Fail; it fails, it gives no profit, *anawewisimagad.*

Faint; I faint, *nin wanimikaw, nin wanendama.* I faint and have a vision, *nin nikâbandam.* (Wanikiskisiw).

Fainting, *wanimikâwiwin.*

Fair, *gwanâtch.* I am fair, *nin gwanâtchiw, nind onijish, nin mikawadis.* It is fair, *gwanâtchiwan, onijishin, sasêgamagad.* I am (it is) considered fair, *nin bishigendagos; bishigendagwad.* I think it is fair, (*in., an.*) *nin sasegawêndân; nin sasegawenima.*

Fairness, *gwanâtchiwin, onijishiwin, bishigendagosiwin.*

Faith, *debweiendamowin.* I have faith, *nin debweiendam.* (Ayamiewitâpwewokeyittamowin).

Fall, *tagwâgi.* In fall, *tagwâgig.* —Last fall, *tagwâgong.* The fall before last, *awâss-tagwâgong.* I spend the fall in such a place, *nin tagwâgish.* I spend the fall with him, *nin widjitagwâgishima.*

Fall; I fall, *nin pangishin.* (Pakissin). It falls, *pangissin.* I fall, *nin gawisse, nin webagodjin.* It falls, *gawanad, gawissemagad.* I fall (it falls) somewhere, *nind apangishin; apangissin.* I fall (it falls) in a certain manner, *nind ijisse,* (Ispayiw), *ijissemagad.* I fall being drunk, *nin gâwibi.* I fall hard, *nin pakiteshin, nin wissagishin, nin tchigwakamigishin, nind apitchishin.* It falls hard, *tchigwakamigisin.* I make him fall, *nin pakitêshima.* I make it fall, *nin pangissiton.* I make him (her, it) fall, *nin gâwishkawa; nin gawishkan, nin gâwiton.* I make it fall to the ground, (*in., an.*) *nin webissiton; nin webishima.* I make it fall from its place, (*in., an.*) *nin binishkan; nin binishkawa.* I fall often, *nin nitâ-pangishin, nin wakêpangishin.* I fall on him, *nind ashosikawa.* I fall on my back, *nind atawasse.* I fall on my face, *nin tchingidjisse, nind atchitchingwesse, nind animikosse.* I fall on my feet, *nin nibawakisse.* I fall (it falls) by the wind, *nin gawâsh; gawâssin.* It will fall, *gawishkamagad.*

Fall, let fall; I let him (her, it) fall, *nind apitchishima, nin banina, nin pangishima; nin baninan, nin pangissiton.* I let fire fall, *nin binanjenan ishkote, nin gwashkwanjenan ishkote.*

Fall down; I fall (it falls) down, *nin nisakoshka; nissakoshkamagad.* I let him (her, it) fall down, *nin nissakoshkawa; nin nissakoshkan.* I fall down headlong, *nind atchitakisse.* I fall down before him, *nin gawitawa, nin gawitamawa.*

Fall in; I fall in, *nin pindjisse, nin gindjidasse.* It falls in, *pindjissemagad.* I fall (it falls) in a hole, *nin bodakwesse; bodakwesseemagad.* I let it fall in, (*in., an.*) *nin bodâkwen;*

nin bodâkwenan. I fall (it falls) in the water, *nin bakobisse, nin gôgisse ; bakobissemagad, gogissemagad.* (Pakastawepayiw). I fall (it falls) in the water out of a canoe or boat, *nin gidônagisse ; gidônagissemagad.*—I fall and hurt myself, *nin bawênishin.* I fall stumbling, *nin bisogeshin.* I fall through, *nin jabosse, nin jabwi, nin jabwiiwe.* It falls through, *jabossemagad.* (In the fire, Matchustepayiw).

Fallacious ; I am fall (I look better than I am,) *nind agwawinagos.* It is fall., *agwawinagwad.*

Falsehood. S. Lie.

False prophet, *geginawishkid niganâdjimowinini.*

Fame. Famous.—S. Renown. Renowned.

Family, *inodewisiwin.* (Kistotew). One family, *ningotôde.* (Peyakoskân). Two, three families, etc., *nijôde, nissôde,* etc. We are two, three, four families, etc., *nin nijodewisimin, nin nissodewisimin, nin niôdewisimin,* etc.—My whole family, *endashiiân, enigokodewisiiân, enigokwiniiân, enodewisiiân.* My family is so large..., *nind inigokodewis, nind inigokwin, nind inodewis.* I move with my whole family, *nin kigodewishka.* I come with my whole family, *nin dassoka, nin bi-dassoka.*

Family-mark, *odem.* I have him (her, it) for my family mark, *nind odôdeminan.* (N.B. *odem,* or, *otem* means only his parents, relations. In Cree *ototema,* his relation.)

Family way ; I am in a f. w., *nind aiâwa abinodji, nin gigishkawa abinodji.* (Ayâwew awâsissa).

Famine, *bakadéwin.* There is a famine in a country or place, *bakadêwinagad, bakadêkamigad, bakadêwiniwan.* (Nottekatewin.)

Fan, *wewésséigan,wewêssêowin.*

Fan ; I fan, *nin wewessêige.* I fan him, *nin wewessêwa.* I fan myself, *nin wewessêidis.* (Yoyowehamaw).

Far, *wâssa, wâssawekamig.* (Wâyo). It is far, *wâssawad, wâssa, pitcha.* It is considered or thought far, *wâssawendagwad.* I think it is far, I find it far, *nin wâssawêndân.* I find distances far, *nin wâssawendam.*

Far from each other, *wâwâssa.*

Far yet, but not very far, *nagêwâssa.* It is far, but not very far, *nagêwâssawad.*

Fare ; I fare (or eat) so, *nind inandjige.* I fare well, *nin minwandjige.*

Farewell-visit, *anamikâgewin.* I make my farewell-visit, *nin bianamikage nakawe.*

Farm, *aki.*

Farm ; I farm, *nin kitige.* (Nittâwikitchikew).

Farmer, *kitigewinini.*

Farming, *kitigewin.*

Fart, farting, *bogidiwin.* (Pwekitowin).

Fart ; I fart, *nin bogid, nin nessediie.*

Fast, *giigwishimowin.* (Iyewanisihisuwin).

Fast ; I fast, *nin giigwishim, nin pagidandjige, nin bakade, nin bakadêidis.* I fast one day, *nin ningotogwane.* I fast two, three, four days, etc., *nin nijogwane, nin nissogwane, nin niogwane,* etc.; I make him fast, *nin giigwiskimoa, nin bakadêa.*

Fast, fast-day, *giigwishimo wi gijigad.* (Iyewanisihisuwikijikaw).

Fasten; I fasten it to the end of s. th. (*in., an.*) *nin nâbaan; nin nabawa.* I fasten it to the end of a stick, (*in., an.*) *nin nabakwaan; nin nabakwâwa.* I fasten it to the end of s. th. so as to be able to take it off again, *nin nabadjashkaan.*

Fasten with a hook; I fasten it hooking it, *nind adabikaan.* I fasten with a small hook, *nind adjibidjige.* I fasten it, *nind adjibidon.*

Fasting, *giigwishimowin, pagidandjigewin.*

Fat, *winin, bimide.*

Fat; I am fat, *nin winin.* (Wiyinow).

Father, *oôssima, weôssimind.* (Weyottâwimit). I am father, *nind oôssimigo.* My, thy, his father, *noss, koss, ossan.* (N'ottâwïy, k'ottâwïy, ottâwiya). I have a father, *nind oôss.* He is my father, *nind oôssima, nind oôssinan.* — I have the same father with him, *nin widjoôssema.* We have all the same father, *nin widjoôssendimin.* Like one's own father, *weôssingin.*

Father, papa, *nôsse, bâba, dêde.* (N'otta).

Father-in-law; my, thy, his father-in-law, *ninsiniss, kisiniss, osinissan.*

Father or mother of my son-in-law or daughter-in-law, *nindindawa.*

Fathom; one fathom, *ningotonik.*—Two, three fathoms, etc., *nijonik, nissonik,* etc. So many fathoms, *dassonik.*—I measure by the fathom, *nin dibinikandjige.* I measure it by the f., (*in., an.*) *nin dibinikandan; nin dibinikâma.*

Fatigue. S. Tiredness. Tire.

Fatigued. S. Tired.

Fatten; I fatten him, *nin wininoa.*

Fattened; I am f., *nin wininodjigas.*

Fault, *matchi dodamowin, batadowin, indowin.* I commit a fault, *nin matchi dodam, nin bata-dodam.* I find fault with him, (her, it), *nind anwenima; nind anwendan.* I lay the fault of it upon him, *nin bimondaa.* (Pateyittamowin).

Fawn, yet dotted, *kitagakons.*

Fear, *segisiwin, gotâdjiwin, gossidiwin, segendamowin, gossitawendamowin, ashwamanissowin.* I tremble with fear, *nin niningisegis.* I am in fear of the enemy, *nind ashwâmaniss.* (Astâsiw).

Fear; I fear, *nin sêgis, nin gotâdj, nind agoski, nind atchinis, nin goshiwe, nin segendam.* I fear him (her, it,) *nin gossa; nin gotan.* It fears me, *nin gossigon.* I fear him (her, it) in thoughts, *nin gossitawe nima; nin gossitawendan.* We fear one another, *nin gossidimin.* I fear for him, or in re-

gard to him, *nin gossitawa, nin gossitamawa, nin gotamawa.*—I fear death, *nin manenawenim.*
Fear; I fear, I dare not, *nin jâgwenim.* I make him fear, *nin jâgwenimoa.* I fear myself, *nin jâgwenindis.*
Fear, (mistrust,) *nisaiendamowin.*
Fear; I fear, I mistrust, *nin nisaiendam.* I fear him, (her, it,) *nin nisaienima; nin nisaiêndân.* (Moyeyittam.)
Feared; I am feared, *nin gossitâganes, nin gotâdjiganes.* I am (it is) to be feared, *nin gotamigwendâgos; gotamigwendâgwad.*
Feared; I am (it is) feared, mistrusted, *nin nisaiendâgos; nisaiendâgwad.*
Fearful, (dreadful;) I am (it is) fearful, *nin segendâgos; segendâgwad.* (Kakwâyakeyittâkusiw.)
Fearful. S. Timid. Timorous.
Fearless; I am f., *nin songidee.*
Fearlessness, *songideewin.*
Feast, *wikongewin, wikondiwin.* I make a feast, or invite to a feast, *nin wikonge.* I invite him, *nin wikoma.* We make a feast or feasts, *nin wikondimin.*—Indian religious feast, *magoshewin.* I make an Ind. rel. feast, *nin magoshe.*
Feast; we feast together, *nin wikondimin.* I feast with him, *nin widjiwikongema.*
Feast-coat, feast-garment, *wikondiwini-bâbisikwâgan, wikondiwiniagwiwin.*
Feast of the dead, *tchibekanakewin.* I make a feast of the dead, *nin tchibekanake.*
Feather, *migwan.* Feather of a small bird, *bineshiwigwan.*—Large feather, *kitchigwânân;* small soft feather, (down,) *missegwanân.* (Mestaniwipiweyân.)
Feather-bed, *migwani-nibâgan, migwan-apishimowin.*
Feather-cushion, *migwan-apikwéshimowin.*
February, *namebini-gisiss.* (Mikisiwipisim.)
Feeble; I am feeble, *nin bwânawito.* S. Weak. (Niyâmisiw.)
Feed, (give to eat;) I feed, *nind ashange.* I feed him, (her, it,) *nind ashama; nind ashandân.* I feed myself, *nind ashandis.*
Feel; I feel, *nin gagwêdinige.* I feel him, (her, it,) *nin gagwedina; nin gagwedinan.* I feel him, (her, it,) on me, about me, in me, *nin mojia; nin mojiton.*
Feelings; I hurt his feelings, *nin kashkendamia.* He hurts my f., *nin kashkendamiig.*—I have bad feelings (anger) against him for such a reason, *nind ondenima.* We have bad f. towards one another for a certain reason, *nind ondenindimin.* (Nayettâwihew.)
Feign; I feign to be a child, *nind abinodjiikas.* I f. to be sick, *nind âkosikas.*
Fellow-citizen, *widjidakiwemâgan, wishdanakiwemâgan.*
Fellow-laborer, *widjanokimâgan.*
Fellow-liver, (neighbor;) my, thy, his fellow-liver, *nidjibimâdisi, kidji-bimâdisi, widji-bimâdisin.*

Fellow-man; my, thy, his fellow-man, *nidj'anishinâbe, kidj'anishinâbe, widj'anishinâben.* (N'itjâyisiyiniw.)
Fellow-summerer, *widjinibishimâgan.*
Fellow-winterer, *widjibibonishimâgan.*
Fell trees. S. Cut down trees.
Female, (woman,) *ikwê* (pronounce as if there were two *k*), *akwê.* (Iskwew.)
Female bear, Female beaver, &c.—S. Bear, Beaver, &c.
Female being, *ikwê-aiaa.*
Female of animals, quadrupeds, *nojé, nojê-aiaa, ikwê-aiaa, onidjâni.*
Female of birds, *nojêsse.*
Female of deer, of the deer-kind, *nojês.*
Female of fish, *nojêmeg.*
Female's skin, *nojêwaiân, onidjâniwaiân.*
Female's skin of the largest quadrupeds, *nojêwegin.* (Misiweyegin.)
Fence, *mitchikan, mitchikanakobidjigan.* I make a fence, *nin mitchikanakobidjige.*
Fence; I fence it all round, *nin giwita-mitchikanakobidon.* I fence in, *nin wakaiakossitchige.* I fence him, (her, it,) in, *nin mitchikanakobina, nin wâkâkina, nind atchikina; nin mitchikanakobidon, nin wâkakinan, nind atchikinan.*
Fenced in; it is fenced in, *wâkaiakossitchigâde.*
Fence-rail, *mitchikanâtig, mitchikanakobidjiganâtig.* (Menigan.)
Fern, *anâganashk.*
Ferret, *seniba kepagigisid.*
Ferry-boat, *ajawaodjigan, ajawaosowâgan.*
Ferryman, *ajawaodjigewinini.*
Fertile; the field is fertile, *nitâwigin kitigan.*
Festival, *kitchitwâgijigad.*
Fetch; I fetch him, (her, it,) *nin nâna; nin nâdin.* I come to fetch him, (her, it,) *nin binâna; nin bi-nâdin.* (Nâtew.) I fetch, carrying on my back, *nin nâdjiwane, nin nâdondam.* I fetch him, (her, it,) on my back, *nin nâdoma; nin nâdondan.* I fetch s. th. in a canoe or boat, *nin nâdaodass.* I fetch him, (her, it,) in a canoe or boat, *nin nâdawa; nin nâdaan.* I fetch a canoe, *nin nâdon;* I fetch, dragging, *nin nâdjidâbi.* I fetch him, (her, it,) dragging or drawing, *nin nâdjidabana; nin nadjidabadan.* I fetch fire, *nin nâdishkotawe.* I fetch hay, or reed for mats, *nin nadashkossiwe.* I fetch liquor, (in a canoe or boat,) *nin nâdjibiam.* I fetch liquor, (walking,) *nin nâdibishkam.* I fetch (or collect) the maple-sap, *nin nâdjibi, nind âwasibi.* I fetch a net or nets, *nin nâdassabi.* (Nâtayapew.) I fetch what is owed me, *nin nâdasinaigane.* I fetch what he owes me, *nin nadasinaiganawa.* I fetch water, *nin nâdobi.* I fetch wood, *nin nâdinisse.* I fetch wood in a canoe or boat, *nin nâdaisse.* I fetch wood in a canoe or boat, sailing, *nin nâdaisseiash.* I fetch a trap or traps, (or I go to visit my traps,) *nin nâdassonâgane.* (Nâtjiwanihiganew.)

Fetter. Fettered.—S. Bind. Bound.

Fetters, *mamandjigwapidjigan.*

Fever, *kijisowin.* I have the fever, *nin kijis.*

Fever with heat, *kijisowapinewin.* I have the fever with great heat, *nin kijisowapine.*

Few, a few, *bebejig, pangi.* (Apisis tchikawâsis.) We are a few of us, *nin pangiwagisimin, nin pangiwissimin, nind agassinomin* or *nind agassinimin, nin manêinomin* or *nin manêinimin.* There are a few. *in.* obj., *pangiwagadon.*

Fickle-minded ; I am f., *nin nôkidee.*

Field, *kitigan.* New field, *oshkâkaan.* I make a new field, *nind oshkâkanigaige.* There is a new field made, *oshkakanigaigâde.*

Field-house, *kitiganiwigamig.*

Field-mouse, *nenapatchinikessi.*

Fiend, *jangendjiged.*

Fife, *pipigwan.*

Fifer, *pipigwewinini.*

Fifth ; the fifth, *eko-nânâning.* The fifth time, *nâning.* (Niyânanwaw.)

Fifthly, *eko-nânâning.*

Fifty, *nânimidana.* We are fifty of us, *nin nânimidanawemin.* There are fifty *in.* obj., *nânimidanawewan.*

Fifty every time, fifty each or to each, *nênanimidana.*

Fifty hundred, or five thousand, *nânimidanâk.* We are five thousand in number, *nin nanimidanakosimin.* There are five thousand *in.* obj., *nanimidanakwadon.*

Fig, *kitchi-jomin.*

Fight, *migâdiwin ; migasowin.* (Notikewin.)

Fight ; I fight, *nin migas.* It fights, *migadimagad.* (Notikewin.) We fight together, *nin migadimin.* I fight him, (her, it,) *nin migana; nin migadan.* I fight (or beat) my wife, *nin migakikwewe.* I fight myself, *nin miganidis.* I am in a bad habit of fighting, *nin migasoshk.* Bad habit of fighting, *migasoshkiwin.* (Notinituwin.)

Fight, (for joke,) *mamigasowin.*

Fight, (for joke ;) I fight or wrestle, *nin mamigas.* I fight him, for play, *nin mamigana.* I am too much in a habit of fighting, for play, *nin mamigasoshk.*

Fighter, *migasowinini.*

Fighting-ship, (war-vessel,) *migadinâbikwân.*

Fighting-time, (time of war,) *migadinaniwan.* (Nandopayiwin.)

Fig-tree, *kitchijominâtig, kitchijominâgawanj.*

Figure, *agindassowin, agindassobiigan.* (Akittâsowin.)

Figure. S. Form.

File, *sissibodjigan, biwâbiko-sissibodjigan.* (Kiskiman.)

File ; I file, *nin sissibodjige.* I file it, (*in., an.*) *nin sissibodon ; nin sissibona.* (Kinipuyew.)

Filedust, filings, *biwâbiko-biwibodjigan.*

Fill ; I fill it, (*in., an.*) with *dry* things, *nin moshkinadon ; nin moshkinaa.* (Sâkaskinattaw.) I fill it for him, *nin moshkinadawa, nin moshkinadamâwa.* I fill it (*in., an.*) with some *liquid, nin moshkinêbadon; nin moshkinêbana.* I fill up vessels, *nin moshkâbowe.* I fill it up with another vessel, (*in., an.*) *nin moshkâbowadan; nin moshkâbowana.*—I fill it with a heap, not overflowing, (*in., an.*) *nin gwashkwashkinadon; nin gwashkwashkinaa.* I fill it to overflow, (*in., an.*) *nin bâjidebadon; nin bâjidebana.* I fill him with s. th., *nin moshkineshkawa.* It fills me, *nin moshkineshkâgon.* (Sâkaskineskâkuw.)

Filled; I am filled with s. th., *nin moshkine.* It is filled, *moshkine, moshkinebi.* (Sâkaskinew.) It is filled with smoke, *moshkineâbate.* I am filled with it, (penetrated,) *nin bosakagon.* I am filled with liquor, *nin debibi.* It is filled up with a heap, *gwashkwashkinemagad.*

Fillip, *passakonandjigan.*

Fillip; I fillip, *nin passakonandjige.* I fillip him, *nin passakonandawa.* (Mikkamew.)

Filly, *bebejigoganjins, ikwê-bebejigoganjins.* (Piponâskus.)

Filtering-vessel, *jabwâjigawitchigan.*

Filth. Filthy.—S. Dirt. Dirty.

Filth of the head, *winashâgandibân.*

Fin of a fish; its fin, *onindjigan.*

Finally, *gêgapi, ishkwâtch.* (Piyis, or iskweyâtch.)

Find; I find, *nin mikâge.* I find him, (her, it,) *nin mikawa; nin mikan.* I find s. th., for him, *nin mikamawa.* I find to myself, *nin mikamas, nin mikamadis.* I find him, (her, it,) to myself or for myself, *nin mikamâsonan, nin mikamadisonan; nin mikamâson, nin mikamâdison.* I find him, (her, it,) by feeling or groping, *nin mikodjina; nin mikodjinan.* I find him, (her, it,) among other objects, *nin mikona; nin mikonan.*

Findling, *mikâgan.* I am a findling, *nin mikaganiw.*

Fine, *gwanâtch.* I am (it is) fine, *nind onijish, nin gwanâtchiw; onijishin, gwanâtchiwan.* I make him, (her, it,) fine, *nind onijishia; nind onijishiton.* I have (it has) a fine appearance, *nind onijishabaminagos; onijishabaminagwad.* (Miyosiw-miywâsin.)

Fine; it is fine, (thread, *in., an.*) *agâssabigad; agâssabigisi.* It is fine, (stuff, *in., an.*) *bissâtagad; bissâtagisi.* (Pipakâsin.)

Fine looking child, *mikawadjabinodji.*

Fine looking man, *mikawadjinini, sasega-inini.*

Fine looking woman, *mikawadjikwe, sasega-ikwe.*

Finger, *onindjima, nibinakwanínindj.* My, thy, his finger, *ninindj, kinindj, onindj.* The small finger, *iskwênindj.* I stretch out my fingers, *nin naniskakonindjin.* — I have long fingers, *nin gaganonindji;* fig. I am a thief. I have crooked fingers, *nin wâginindji;* fig. I am a thief.

Finger-nail. S. Nail.

Finger-ring, *titibinindjipison.*

Finish; I finish, *nind ishkwâta, nind anwata.* It finishes, *ishkwassin, anwatamagad.* I finish it, (*an.*, *in.*) *nin dê-gijia ; nin dê-gijiton ; nin waiekwassiton, nin waiekwaton.*—It finishes, *angomagad, angoshkamagad.* (Kijittaw.)

Finish, (doing or placing s. th.) I finish, *nin gijissitchige, nin gijiton, nin gijita.* I make him finish, *nin gijitaa.* I make myself finish, *nin gijitaidis, nin gijitas.* (Poyuw.)

Finished ; it is f., *gijissitchigâde, gijitchigâde.*

Finishing, *ishkwatâwin, anwatâwin.*

Fire, *ishkote, ashkote.* I make fire, *nind ishkoteke, nin bodawe.* (Kutawew.) I have no fire, *nind anissab.* The fire goes out, *âtemagad ishkote, niwanje ishkote.* My fire goes out, or is gone, *nind âtawe.* (Astawew.) I make a large fire, *nin kijîkinjawe.* The fire blazes up, *biskakone, ishkote, namatâkone.* I catch (it catches) fire, *nin nawadis, nin sakis ; nawadide, sakide.* In the midst of a fire, *nawishkote.* The fire crackles, *papakinemagad ishkote.* The fire makes noise, *bidikwakone ishkote.*— I set fire, *nin sakaige, nin sakaowe.* I set fire to him, (her, it,) *nin sakawa; nin sakaan.* Fire is set to it, *sakaigade.* The act of setting fire, *sakaigewin.* Fire in the prairie, *pasitew.*

Fire; I fire a gun, *nin pâshkisige, nin madwesige.* I fire guns, *nin papâshkisige.*

Firebrand, *keshkakideg.*

Firebrand for pitching a canoe, *pigikewanissag.*

Fire-place, *bodawân.* (Kutawân.)

Fire-poker, *naikinjêigan, nanaikinjêigan, nanaikinjêiganak, tchitchikinjêigan.* I stir or repair the fire with a poker, *nin naikinjeige, nin nanaikinjeige, nin tchitchikinjeige ; nin naikinjean,* or *nin nanaikinjean ishkote, nin tchitchikinjean ishkote.*

Fire-steel, *ishkotekân.* (Piwâbisk-appit, or Sikattâgan.)

Fire-steel River, *Nibegomowinisibi.*

Fire-vessel, (steamboat,) *ishkotênâbikwân.*

Firing-day, (the fourth of July,) *madwesige-gijigad, papâshkisige-gijigad.*

Firing guns, *madwesigewin.*

Firm, (strong ;) it is firm, (*in.*, *an.*) *songan; songisi.* (Sokkan, kisiw.)

Firmament, *gijig.*

Firmly, *songan.* (Sokki.)

First, *nakawe, nitam.* (Nikân.) The first, *nitam, netamissing.* It is the first, *nitamissin.* I consider him, (her, it,) the first, *nin nitamenima ; nin nitamendan.* I am (it is) considered the first, *nin nitamendâgos ; nitamendâgwad.* I am the first after him, *nind akawishkawa.*

First, (new,) *oshki.*

First-birth, *sasikisiwin.*

First-born ; the first-born, *netaminigid, sesikisid.* I am the first-born, *nin nitaminig, nin sasikis.* The first-born child, *nitamonjân.*—First-born boy, First-born girl.—S. Boy. Girl.

Fir-tree, *ininandag.* Any kind of fir-tree, *jingob.* A branch of a fir-tree, *jingobakon*. Little fir-branch, or cedar-branch, *jingobins*. — Shelter or hut made of fir-branches, *jingobigan*. I made a shelter of fir-branches, or I am under such a shelter, *nin jingobige*. (Napaka-sitta.)

Firy; it is firy, *ishkotewad*.

Fish, *gigo*. (Kinosew.) A kind of small fish, *nigidji*. Dried fish, *namêteg*. (Namestak.) Dried smoked fish, *gaskidê-gigô*. I dry and smoke fish, *nin gaskidê-gigôike*. There is plenty of fish, *gigôika*. The fish leaps up, *gogaam-gigô*. —The fish is soft, *jigosi gigo*. The fish looks whitish, *wâbamêgoshin gigô*. The fish has many bones, *sagiganagisi gigô*. I catch a very large fish, *nin kagabadjibina*. I caught so many fishes. When the fish spawns, (Amiw.)

Fish-bladder, *pikwadj*.

Fish-bone, *gigowigan*.

Fisher, (animal,) *otchig; akâkwidjish*.

Fisher, (bird,) *okishkimanisse*.

Fisher-line with many hooks, *pagidâbân*. I set a line with hooks, *nin pagidâbi*. I haul out a fisher-line, *nin nâdaabi*.

Fisherman, *gagoiked, gigoikewinini, pegidawad, pagidawewinini*. (Notjikinusewew.)

Fisher's buoy. S. Buoy.

Fishery, fishing, *gigoikêwin*. (Notjikinusewewin.)

Fish-hawk, *mitchigigwane*.

Fish-hook, *migiskan*.

Fish-hook line, *migiskanêiâb*.

Fishing; I am fishing, *nin gigoike*. (Notjikinusewew.) I am fi. with a drag-net or draw-net, *gigôiag nind agwabinag*. I am fishing with a hook, *nin wewebanâbi*. (Kwâskwepitchikew.) I am fi. with a hook in the night, *nin nibâwewebanâbi*. I am fi. with a hook in a canoe or boat, *nind agomôwewebanâbi*. Fishing in the night with a light, (Wâswaw.)

Fishing-ground, *pagidâwewin*.

Fishing-implement, *wewebanâbân, wewebanabâgan*.

Fishing-line with a hook, *odadjigokan*. I am fishing with a hook, *nind odadjígoke; nin wewebanâbi*.

Fishing-rod or stick, *wewebanâbanak*.

Fishnet, *assâb*. A small net, *assâbins*. An old useless net, *assâbish*. (Ayapiy.)

Fish-oil, *gigo-bimide*. (Kinusewipimiy.)

Fish-scale, *wanagaai*.

Fish-store, *gigowigamig*.

Fissure; there is a fissure in a rock, *tâshkabikishka, passâbika*.

Fist, *pikwakonindj*. I strike him with the fist, *nin pikwakonindjitawa*.

Fit; it fits well, *minokamagad*. It fits me well, *nin minokâgon, nin debishkan*. It fits well in, *minoshkine*. (Miyopayiw.)

Fitchat, fitchew, *jikâg*.

Five, *nâno...*, in compositions; which see in the Second Part.

Five, *nânan*. We are five, *nin nânanimin*. There are five *in*. obj., *nânaninon*. (Niyânan.)

Five every time, five each or to each, *nenanan*.

Five hundred, *nânwâk*. (Niyânanwamitâtatomitano.)
Five hundred every time, five hundred each or to each, *nenanwâk*.
Five thousand, *nâning midâsswak, nanimidanak*. We are five thousand in number, *nin nanimidanakosimin*. There are five th. *in*. obj., *nanimidanakwadon*. (Niyânanwakitchimitâtatomitano.)
Five times, *naning*. (Niyânanwaw.)
Five times every time, five times each or to each, *nenâning*.
Fix; I fix it right, *nin gwaiakoton*. I fix it in a certain manner, *nind ijissiton*.
Fix, (in s. in.) S. Repair.
Flabby; I am flabby, *nin jagos*.
Flag. S. Banner.
Flageolet, *pipigwan*.
Flag-staff, *kikiweonâtig*.
Flail, *apagandaigan, apagandaiganak, gitchiminaigan*.
Flail or stick, to knock out wild rice, *bawâigan, bawaiganak*.
Flambeau. S. Torch.
Flame, the flame is ascending high, *sasâgakwane*. There is a blue flame, *ojâwanashkwakone*. (Kwâkkutew.)
Flame. S. Blaze.
Flank, (side of the body;) my, thy, his flank, *ninbimêbigwadai, kibimêbigwadai, obimêbigwadaian*. (Nabateyaw.)
Flannel, *wâbigin*. Yellow flannel, *osâwâbigin*. Red flannel, *miskwâbigin*.
Flask, flagon, *omodai*.
Flat; it is flat, (*in., an.*) *nabaga; nabagisi*. It is flat, (metal, *in., an.*) *nabagâbikad, tessâbikad; nabagâbikisi, tessâbikisi*.
Flat grass or herb, *nabagashk*.
Flat hand, *nabagâskinindj, têssinindj, nagâkinindjân*. I strike him with the flat hand, *nin nabagâskinindjitawa*.
Flat hat or cap, *têssiwakwân*.
Flat-head Indian, *Nebagindibe*.
Flat-iron, *joshkwâigaigan*.
Flat pipe-stem, *nabagakokidj*.
Flat stone, *tessâbik, nabagâbik*.
Flatten; I flatten it, (*in., an.*) *nin tessiton, nin nabagadaan; nin tessia, nin nabagadâwa*.
Flatten with an iron; I flatten, *nin joshkwaigaige*. I flatten it, (*in., an.*) *nin joshkwaigaan; nin joshkwaigâwa*.
Flatter. Flattery, (in s. in.) S. Praise.
Flattery, *wawijindiwin*. (Ayâkukkâsuwin.)
Flat tobacco, *nebagibagisid assema*.
Flavor. S. Taste, good taste.
Flay; I flay, *nin pakonige*. I flay him, *nin pakona, nin bishagibina, nin bishagigijwa*.
Flea, *pabig*. I have fleas, *nin pabigos*. (Pîpikus.)
Flea-herb, *animikibag*.
Flee; I flee, *nind ojim*. (Tabasiw.) I make him flee, or I save him by flight, *nind ojimoa*. (Ni tabasihaw.)
Flesh, *wiiâss, wiiâssima*. My, thy, his flesh, *niiass, kiiass, wiiass*. I have flesh, *nind owiiass*. I am flesh, *nin wiiassiw*. As one is flesh, *ejiwiiassing*. I make myself flesh, *nin wiiassiwiidis*.—I take the flesh off, *nin gitchiganejân*

wiiass. I take off his flesh, *nin gitchiganejwa.*

Fleshy part of the leg, of my, thy, his leg, *ninâsid, kinâsid, onâsid.*

Flexible, I become fl. again, *nin jejawishka.* My leg become fl. again, *nin jejawigadeshka.* —It is flexible, *sibiskagad.* (Sesâwiw.)

Flight, *ojimowin.* (Tabasiwin.)

Flight, (of birds,) *bimissewin.*

Flint, *biwânag.* (Tchakisahigan.)

Flittermouse, *papakwanadji.*

Float; I float, I am on the surface of the water, *nind agôm.* I float, being partly in the water, *n i n d agwindjin.* It floats, being partly in the water, *agwinde.* I float (it floats) down with the current, *nin bimâbog; bimâtan.* (Pimâpotew.)

Float about; I float (it floats) about, *nin tetebaagwindjin; tetebaagwinde.*

Float, for a net, *agwindjônagan.* (Ayapâttik.)

Flood, *nikibiwin, moshkaang.* There is a flood, *moshkaan, nikibimagad.* (Iskipewin.)

Flood, flowing tide; it is the fl. tide, *moshkâgami nibi.*

Floodwood, *angwâssag.* There is floodwood, *angwâssagoka.* In a place where there is much floodwood, *angwâssagokang.*

Floor; there is a floor, *apishimonikâde.* (Anâskânittak.) I make a floor, *nind apishimonike.* I make a floor in it, *nind apishimonikâdan.*-Under the floor, *anâmissag.* On the floor, *mitchissag.* In the middle of the fl., *nâwissag.* The fl. is dirty, *winissaga.* I wash the fl., *nin kisibigissaginige.* The fl. is wet, *nibiwissaga.* The fl. is clean, *binissaga.*

Floor-board in a house, *apishimonak, apishimon.*

Floor-branch in a lodge, *apishimon.* (Anâskewin.)

Floor-carpet, *apishimonigin.*

Floor-mat, *anâkan.*

Flour, *pakwejigan, bassisid pakwejigan.*

Flour-bag, *pakwejiganiwaj.*

Flour-mill, *bissibodjigan.* (Piniputjigan.)

Flour-pap, *pakwejiganâbo.*

Flower, *wâbigon.* A kind of yellow flower, *okitebagewassakwane.* Another kind, *monawingwabigon.* The fruit of it, *monawing.*--I make flowers, *nin wâbigonike.* Woman that makes fl., *wâbigonikewikwe.*

Flowings; I am in my monthly flowings, *agwatching nind aia, agwatching nin bodawe.* (Iskwewâkkusiw.)

Flute, *pipigwan.* I play on the flute, *nin pipigwe.*

Flute-player, *pipigwêwinini, pepigwed.*

Flute-playing, *pipigwewin.*

Flute-reed, elder-shrub, *pipigwêwanashk.*

Fly, *odji.* Small fly, *ojins* (Otjew.)

Fly; I fly, *nin bimisse.* It flies about, (a bird,) *babâmisse.* (Papâmiyaw.) It flies around, s. th., *giwitasse.* It fl. from..., *ondjisse.* It flies hither, *bidjisse.* It flies round, *bijibasse.* —It flies off, (something,) *mâdjibide.* It fl. from..., *ondjibide.* It flies hither, *bidjibide.*

Fly down, (in s. in.) S. Slide down.

Fly in ; it flies in, (a bird,) *pindigesse*. It flies in, (something,) *pindjibide*.

Flying, *bimissewin*.

Flying squirrel, *jagâshkandawe*.

Fly for safety ; I fly, *nind ojim*. (Tabasiw.) I fly from him, (her, it,) *nind ojima, nind ojimotawa ; nind ojindan, nind ojimotan*. I make him fly, *nind ojimoa*. I fly to him, (her, it,) *nin nâdjinijiwa ; nin nâdjinijindan*. I fly to some place, *nind ininijim*.

Fly out; it flies out, (a bird,) *sajidjisse*. It flies out, (something,) *sagidjibide*.

Fly up ; I fly up in the air, *nind ombisse*. It flies up, *ombibide*. (Oppahuw.)

Foam, *bitê*. My mouth is full of foam, *nin bitêwidon*. (Pistewatâmow.) My mouth is full of foam from anger, *nin bitêwidonegidas*.

Foam ; I foam at my mouth in running, *nin bitêwanam*. (Pistew.)

Fog, *awân*. (Kaskawan.) The fog is falling, *binawân*. The fog disappears, *pâkawân*.

Foggy ; it is foggy, *awân*. (Kaskawakkamik.

Fold ; I fold, *nin biskitenige*. I fold it, *nin biskitenan*. I fold it, (stuff *in., an.*) *nin nabwêginan ; nin nabwêgina*.

Folded ; it is folded, *biskinigâde, biskissin*.

Folks, *bemâdisidjig*.

Follow ; I follow, *nin nôpinaki*. I follow him, (her, it,) *nin nôpinana, nind ishkwêkawa ; nin nôpinadan, nind ishkwêkan*. I follow it, (*in., an.*) *nin nagatwaodon ; nin nagatwâwa*. I follow his track, *nin bimaana, nin mâdaana, nin nosswaana*. I follow a road or trail, *nin bimaadon mikana, nin mâdaadon mikana, nin nosswaadon mikana*. I follow a certain trail, *nind inamodjige*. (Mâtahew, mittimew.)

Follow in succession ; I follow in suc., *nind anikeshkâge*. I follow him, *nind anikeshkawa*. It follows, *anikessin*.

Fond ; I am fond of it, *nin nitâwandân*.

Fond of..., (in s. in.) S. Attached to...

Fond du Lac, *Waiekwâkitchigami*.

Fond du Lac, *Nagâdjiwan*. At, to or from Fond du Lac, *Nagâdjiwanang*.

Food, *midjim*. It is food, *midjimiwan*. I gather or collect food, (provisions,) *nin naênim*. I collect it for food, (*in., an.*) *nin naênimon ; nin naênimonan*.

Fool, *gawanadisid, gegibâdisid*. I am a fool, *nin giwanadis, nin gagibâdis*.

Foolish ; I am foolish, *nin gagibâdis, nin bisinâdis, nind agawadis*. It is foolish, *gagibâdad*. I make him foolish, *nin gagibâdisia, nin gagibâsoma*.

Foolishly ; I act or behave foolishly, *nin gagibâdjige*.

Foolishness, *gagibâdisiwin, agawadisiwin, gagibâdjigewin, bisinâdisiwin*.

Foolish noise, *kiwanisiwin*. I

make noise foolishly, *nin kiwanis.*

Foolish person, *gegibâdisid.*

Foot, *osidama.* My, thy, his foot, *nisid, kisid, osid.* The right foot, *kitchisid, okitchisidama.* The left foot, *namandjisid, onamandjisidama.* —I have feet, *nind osid.* I have clean feet, *nin biniside.* I have convulsions in my foot or feet, *nin tchitchibisideshka.* I have cramps in my foot or feet, *nind otchisidepinig.* I have a dead foot, *nin nibowiside.* I have dirty feet, *nin winiside.* I have hairy feet, *nin mishiside, nin memishiside.* I have large feet, *nin mamângiside.* I have a long foot, *nin ginoside.* I have long feet, *nin gagânoside.* One of my feet is longer than the other, *nin nabanêginoside.* I have only one foot, *nin nabanêside.* I have pain in my foot, *nin dewiside.* I have a scar on my foot, *nind odjishiside.* I have a short foot, *nin takoside.* I have short feet, *nin tatakoside.* One of my feet is shorter than the other, *nin nabanêtakoside.* I have a small foot, *nind agassiside.* I have small feet, *nin babiwiside.*—My foot is bloody, *nin miskwiwiside.* My feet are bound, *nin mamândjigosidebis.* I bind or fetter his feet, *nin mamandjigosidebina, nin mamândjigwapisidebina.* My foot is bruised, *nin jashâgosideshkos.* I bruise my foot, *nin tatagosideodis.* My feet are cold, *nin takiside, nin tatakiside.* My feet are cold being wet, *nin takwakisideiâbâwe.* My feet are benumbed with cold, *nin takwakisidewadj.* My feet are cracked, *nin gipiside, nin gagipiside.* My foot is cut off, *nin kishkiside.* I cut off my foot, *nin kishkisideodis.* I cut off his foot, *nin kishkisidejwa.* My foot is dislocated, *nin kotigosiketa.* I dislocate my foot, *nin kotigosideshin, nin gidiskakosideshin, nin bimiskosideshin.* My foot is frozen, *nin mashkawadjisidewadj.* My foot is pierced, *nin jibanisidejigas.* My foot is swollen, *nin bâgiside.* My foot is stiff, *nin tchibatakoside.* My foot is tender, or my feet are tender, *nin nôkiside.* My feet are warm, *nin kijôside.* My feet are wet, *nin nibiwiside.* My foot is wounded, *nin mâkiside.*—At my feet, *ejisidebiiân.* I burn my foot, *nin badagosides.* I hurt my foot, *nin nangisideshin.* I hurt my foot walking, *nin bitâkosideshin, nin pakwesideshin.* I lift up my foot, *nind ombisiden.* The other foot, *ajawisid, nabanêsid.* I press his foot, *nin magosidena.* I put my foot on s. th. sitting, *nind agwitchisideshimon.* In put my foot in..., *nin pindjisideshin.* I slide or fall in with one foot, *nin pindjisidesse.* I rub his foot or feet with some medicine, *nin sinigosidebina.* I sprain his foot by pulling, *nin pâkisidebina.* I have it sticking in my foot, it sticks in my foot, *nin patakisidedjin.* I thrust it in my foot, *nin pata-*

kisideodis. I thrust it in his foot, *nin patakisidewa.* I wash my feet, *nin kisibigiside.* I wash his feet, *nin kisibigisidena.* I wipe my feet, *nin kisiside.* I wipe his feet, *nin kisisidewa.*—The extremity of the foot, *wanâkosid.*—At the foot of a hill or mountain, *nissâki.* (Nittâmatin.)

Foot, (12 inches,) one foot, *ningotosid.* Two, three, four feet, etc., *nijosid, nissosid, niosid,* etc. So many feet, *dassosid.*

Foot-bath ; I take a warm foot-bath, *nind abakamass.* I give him a warm f., *nind abakamasswa.*

Footboard of the Indian cradle, *atchisidebison.*

Footing ; I have a good footing, *nin minôkami.* I have a bad footing, *nin mânikami.*

Footman, *bamitâgan, bamitagewinini.*

Foot-rag, *ajigan.*

Footsteps ; I make small footsteps, *nind agâssikam, nin babiwishkam.*—S. Track.

Footstool, *agwitchisideshimonowin, apisidebiwin.*

For, (because,) *sa.* (Tchikema.)

Forbear ; I forbear with him, *nin ganabitawa, nin babimiwidawa.*—We forbear with one another, *nin ganabitadimin, nin babimiwidadimin.*

Forbear, Forbearance, (in s. in.) S. Patient. Patience.

Forbid ; I forbid, *nin ginaamâge.* I forbid him, (her, it,) *nin ginaamawa ; nin ginaamadan, nin ginaamawadan.* I forbid it to myself, *nin ginaamadis.* —It forbids, *ginaamagemagad.* (Kitâhamâkew.)

Forbiddance, *ginaamagewin, ginaamadiwin.*

Forbidden ; anything forbidden, *ginaamagowin.* I am forbidden, *nin ginaamago.* It is forbidden, *ginaamagemagad.*

Forbidder, *genaamaged.*

Force. S. Power.

Ford ; I ford a river, *nin takamadasi.* (Mustâtakaw.)

Foreboding. S. Augur. Auguration.

Forefinger, (showing-finger,) *inôinindj.* (Itwahikewitchitchiy.)

Forehead, *katigwân.* (Miskâttik.)

Foreigner, stranger, *maiâginini.* —Foreign woman, *maiâgikwe.* I am a foreigner, (man or woman,) *nin maiâgis, nin maiâlawis.* (Pitusisiw.)

Foreman, *nagânisid.*

Foremost, *nigânenagwakamig.* I am foremost, *nin nigânis.* I am (it is) foremost, considered foremost, *nin nigânendagos, nin nitamendagos, nin maiawendagos ; nigânendagwad, nitamendagwad, maiawendagwad.* I consider him, (her, it,) foremost, *nin nigânenima ; nin niganendan.*—I am foremost (traveling by water,) *nin nigânâ.*—The foremost *in.* object, *nêtamissing.*

Forerunner, *naganishkad.*

Forepart ; in the forepart, *nigân.*

Forenoon ; a forenoon, or half a day, *ningo-nawakwe.* In the forenoon, *tchi bwa nawakweg.*

Forest, *mitigwaki.* (Sakaw.) There is a forest, ***bimâkwa.*** In the middle of a forest, *nawakwa.* I walk on the border of a forest, *nin jijodâkwaam* — Near the forest, *tchigâkwa.* The forest is far, *wassaakwakwa.* The forest has a white appearance, *wâbakwamagad.* The forest is low, *tabassâkwa.* The forest is thick, *gibâkwa, sagwandaga.* Indian from the thick forests, *Sagwandagawinini.* Burnt forest. S. Burnt. (Sakâwiyiniw.)

Foretell; I foretell, *nin nigânâdjim.*

Foretell. Foreteller. Foretelling, (in. s. in.) Augur. Auguration.

Foreteller, *nigânâdjimowinini.*

Foretelling, *nigânâdjimowin.*

Foretelling woman, *nigânâdjimowikwe.*

Forget; I forget, *nin wanêndam, nin bônêndam.* I forget him, (her, it,) *nin wanenima, nin bonenima; nin wanêndân, nin bonendân.* I forget myself, *nin waennindis, nin bonenindis.* I forget s. th. relating to him, *nin wanendamawa, nin bonendamawa.* We forget our mutual offences, *nin bonenindimin.* (Wani-kiskisiw.)

Forgetful; I am forgetful, *nin nitâ-wanendam.*

Forgetfulness, *manêndamowin, nitâ-wanendamowin.*

Forgetting, *wanêndamowin, bônendamowin.*

Forget to take; I forget to take, *nin wanike.* I forget to take him, (her, it,) *nin wanikenan; nin waniken.*

Forgive; I forgive, *nin bonigidetâge, nin bônendam.* I forgive it, *nin bônendân, nin wêbinân.* I forgive him, *nin bônigidetawa, nin wêbinamawa, nin wanêndamawa, nin bônendamawa, nind odjimenima.* We for. each other, *nin bônijidetadimin, nin webinamadimin, nin bônenindimin.* (Pakiteyittamâkew.)

Forgiven; I am for., *nin bonigidetagos, nin gâssiamâgo.* It is for., *bonendjigâde, webinigâde, gâssiigâde.*

Forgiven, (in. s. in.) S. Rejected. Thrown away.

Forgiveness, *bonendamowin, bonigidetagewin, bonigidetagowin, gâssiamâgewin, gassiamagowin.* Mutual forgiveness, *bonenindiwin, bonigidêtadiwin, wêbinamadiwin.*

Forgotten; I am (it is) forgotten, as well as forg., *nin wanendagos; wanendagwad.* I am (it is) quite forgotten, *nin wanendjigas; wanendjigâde.*

Fork, *nassawabideigan, patakashkaigan,* hay-fork. (Tchistahepuwin.)

Fork, table-fork, *patakâigan.* I pick up with a fork, *nin patakaige.* I pick it up, (*in., an.*) *nin patakaan; nin patakâwa.*

Form, *ijinâgosiwin.*

Form; I form it, (*in., an.*) *nin masidinan; nin masidina.* I form it for him, *nin masidinamawa.*

Formed; I am (it is) formed, *nind ojig; ojigin.*

Former, *getê*—.

Formerly, *gaiât, mêwija.* (Oskatch—kayâs.)

Formidable. S. Feared.

Fornication, *bishigwâdisiwin, gagibâdisiwin.*

Fornicator, *bishigwâdjinini, gagibâdjinini.*
Fornicatress, *bishigwâdjikwe, gagibâdjikwe.*
Forsake; I forsake him, (her, it) *nin nagana; nin nagadan.*
Forsake. Forsaken, (in. s. in.) S. Throw away. Thrown away.
Fort, fortress, *wâkaigan, akobimwân.* In the fort, *pindjwâkaigan.* Out of the fort, *agwatchiwâkaigan.* (A s w â-huwin.)
For the sake of..., *ondji.*
Forthwith, *wewib, pabige, kejidin.* (Semâk.)
Fortify; I fortify him, (her, it,) *nin sôngisia, nin mashkawisia; nin songiton, nin mashkawiton.*
Fortify the heart or mind; I for., *nin songideeshkage.* I fortify him, *nin songideeshkawa, nin mashkawendamia.*
Fortitude of the heart, *songideewin.* I give him fortitude, *nin songideeshkawa.* Giving fortitude of the heart, *songideeshkâgewin.*
Fortnight, *nijo-anamiegijigad.*
Fortunate; I am for., *nin jawendagos.* (Papewew.)
Fortune. S. Riches.
Fort William, *Gamanêtigweiag,* or *Kamanêtigweiag.*
Forty, *nimidana.* We are forty, *nin nimidanawemin.* There are forty *in.* objects, *nimidanawêwan.* There are forty pairs, *nimidanawêwân.*
Forty every time, forty each or to each, *nenimidana.*
Forty hundred, or four thousand, *nimidanak.* We are four thousand of us, *nin nimidanakosimin.* There are 4000 *in.* objects, *nimidanakwadon.*
Found; I am (it is) found, *nin mikas, nin mikadjigas; mikâde, mikadjigâde.* Found thing, *mikâgan.* It is a found thing, *mikâganiwan.*
Foundation, *ashotchissitchigan.*
Foundation of a house, *onâkamigissitchigan.*
Foundation-stone, *ashotchissitchiganâbik, ashotabikissitchigan.*
Founded; it is well founded, *mindjimossitchigâde.*
Founder. Foundry.—S. Smelter. Smelting-house.
Fountain. S. Spring.
Four, *nio...,* in compositions; which see in the Second Part.
Four, *niwin.* We are four, *nin niwimin.* There are four *in.* objects, *niwinon.* (Newo.)
Four every time, four each or to each, *neniwin.*
Four hundred, *niwak.* We are four hundred in number, *nin niwakosimin.* There are 400 *in.* objects, *niwakwadon.* Four hundred pairs, *niwakwêwân.*
Four hundred every time, 400 each or to each, *neniwak.*
Fourth; the fourth, *eko-niwing.* The fourth time, or four times, *niwing.*
Fourthly, *eko-niwing.*
Fourth of July, *pâshkisige-gijigad, papâshkisige-gijigad, madwesige-gijigad.*
Four times, *niwing.* (Newaw.)
Four times every time, four times each or to each, *neniwing.*
Fox, *wâgosh.* (Makkesis.) Young fox, *wâgoshens.*

Fragment, *bokwaii*.
Frame-house, *wâkaigan, mitigo-wâkaigan*.
France, *Wemitigojiwaki*. In France, to or from France, *Wemitigojiwaking*.
Frankincense, *minomâgwakisigan*. I burn frankincense, I incense, *nin minomâgwakisige*. —S. Perfume.
Fraud. S. Cheat. Cheating.
Free; I am free, *nin dibênindis*. (Tibeyimisuw.)
Freedom, *dibenindisowin*.
Freeze; I freeze to death, *nin gawâdj, nin mashkawâdj*. (Nipâhatchiw.) I begin to feel that a part of my body is freezing, *nin mikawadj*.—It freezes over, *gashkadin, gibadin*.
Freezing, *mashkawadjiwin, gawadjiwin*.
Freezing-moon, (November,) *gashkadini-gisiss*.
French; I speak French, *nin wemitigojim*.
French book or letter, *wemitigojimasinaigan*.
French boy, or a little Frenchman, *Wemitigojins*.
French church, *wemitigoji-anamiewigamig*.
French girl, *wemitigojikwens*.
French language, *wemitigojimowin*.
Frenchman, *Wemitigoji*.
French priest, (Catholic priest,) *wemitigoji-mekatewikwanaie*.
French religion, (Catholic religion,) *wemitigoji-anamiewin*.
Frenchwoman, *wemitigojikwe*.
French writing, *wemitigojiwibiigan*. I write in French, *nin wemitigojiwibiige*. It is written (or printed) in French, *wemitigojiwissin*. I translate it into French, *nin wemitigojiwissiton*. It is translated in French, *wemitigojiwissitchigâde*.
Frequent; I freq. bad women, *nin nodikwewe, nin nodjikwewe*.
Frequent. S. Keep company.
Frequently, *naningim, niningim, sasâgwana*. (Kâkiyipa.)
Fresh, *oshki-*.
Fret; I fret him, *nin nishkia*. It frets me, *nin nishkiigon*.—S. Angry.
Friend; my friend, (or brother) *nikâniss, nidjikiwê*. Thy friend, *kikâniss, kidjikiwé*. His friend, *wikanissan, widjikiwêian*. I am his friend, (or he is my friend,) *nin mino-inawema*. I am its friend, *nin mino-inawendan*. (Otjiwâma, or, Witchâsa).
Friendship, *inawendiwin, mino-inawendiwin, sâgiidiwin*. (Miyo-witjettuwin).
Fright, *amânissowin, gotâdjiwin, kitchi segisiwin*.
Frighten; I fr. him, *nin sêgia, nin sêgima, nind âmawa*.
Frighten, (startle;) I frighten it, (an animal,) *nind oshawa, nind oshakawa, nin nanamâa*.
Frightened; I am fr., *nin segendam, nin migoshkadji-aia*. I am fr. by s. th. I heard, *nin amaniss*. I look frightened, *nin seginagos*. (Amatisuw).
Frightened animal, *nanamâdjigan*
Frightful; I am (it is) frightful, *nin gotâmigos; gotâmigwad*.

—S. Horrible. (Kakwâyakeyittâkwan).

Frightful or enormous number or quantity. (Anakatchäy). There is a fr. number of us, *nin gagwânissaginomin*, or, *nin gagwânissaginimin*. There is a fr. quantity of it, *gagwânissaginad*.

Frivolous ; I am fr., *nin bisinadis, nin gagibâdis*. I make him friv., *nin bisinâdjia*.—S. Disquiet.

Frivolousness, *bisinâdisiwin, gagibâdisiwin*.

Frock for men, *babisikawâgan*.

Frock for women, *gôdass*. I wear a long frock, *nin ginwambis*.

Frog, *omakaki*. A kind of green frog, *jashagawashkogissi*. Another kind of frog, *passekanak*. A small kind of frog, *pikonekwe*. (Ayekis).

Frost ; there is glazed frost (or rime) on the ground, *gaskwewemagad*.

Frower, *tâshkigaigan*.

Frozen ; I am frozen, *nin mashkawadj*. It is frozen hard, *mashkawadin*. It is frozen over, *gashkadin, gibadin*. It is frozen thick, *kipagadin*.

Frugal ; I am frugal, *pepangi nin wissin*.

Fruit; different kinds of fruit, *wiiagiminan*.

Fruit of the tree, *maniwâng mitig*.

Fruit-tree, *maniwid mitig*.

Fry ; I fry, *nin sâssakokwe*. I fry it, (*in., an.*) *nin sâssakokwadan ; nin sâssakokwana*.

Frying-pan, *sâssakokwâdjigan, abwêwin*. Frying-pan with a short handle, *abwêwinens*.

Fuel, wood, *missan*. (Mitta). I have no fuel, *nind âtawe*. (Astawew).

Full ; it is full in a certain manner, *inashkine*. (Sâkaskinew).

Full. S: Filled.

Fulfil ; I fulfil it, *nin tibishkossiton*. I fulfil a promise, *nin tibissaton, nin tibissiton*.

Fulfilled ; it is fulfilled, *tibishkossitchigâde*.

Fully, *wâwinge, âpitchi*.

Funeral. S. Burial.

Funnel, *pinsibâdjigan*. I am pouring through a funnel, *nin pinsibâdjige*. I pour it through a funnel, *nin pinsibâdan*.

Fur, (hair of animals,) *biwai*. Its fur, *obiwai*. (Attäy). It has no fur or hair, *pashkwâdikwebigisi*. This animal has a black fur, *bosmakâtewawe aw awessi*. It has a fine fur, *bissibiwaie*. It has a good fur, *minwawe*. It has a long fur, *gagânobiwaie, ishpawe*. It has a short fur, *titissawe*. It has a thick and profitable fur, *bissagwawe*.

Fur, given as payment to a furtrader, *atawâgan*. (Attäy ; two, —nijwattäy).

Furnish, I furnish to people, *nind ondinamâge*. I fur. it to him, *nind ondinamâwa*. I fur. to myself, *nind ondinamâdis, nind minidis*. I furnish it to myself, (*in., an.*) *nind ondinamadison, nin minidison ; nind ondinamadisonan, nin minidisonan*.

Further, or farther, *awâss*.

Further there, *awâss wedi*.

G

Gaiety. S. Gayness.

Gain; I gain it, (*in. an.,*) *nin gashkiton; nin gashkia.* I gain nothing, *nind agawis, nind agawishka, nind agawita, nind anawewis.* I gain, (in a play,) *nin pakinage, nin mijagado.* (Paskiyâkew).

Gain; I gain, (endeavoring,) *nin wikwatchi.* I gain it, (*in., an.*) *nin wikwatchiton; nin wikwatchia.* I gain to myself, *nin wikwatchitas, nin wikwatchitamas.* I gain it to myself, (*in., an.*) *nin wikwatchitason, nin wikwatchitamason; nin wikwatchitasônan, nin wikwatchitamâsonan.*

Gain, (in. s. in.) S. Earn.

Gained; it is gained, (*in., an.*) *gashkitchigâde; gashkitchigâso.* Gained object, *gashkitchigan.*

Gaining, *gashkitchigewin.*

Gain over. S. Prevail.

Gainsay; I gainsay, *nind ajidewidam, nind ajidewe, nind ajidenge, nin gagânsitam, nin nakwetâge, nin nakwetan.* I use to gainsay, *nind ajidengeshk, nin nakwetangeshk, nind agonwetangeshk.*—I gainsay him, *nind ajidema, nin gagansitawa, nin nakwetawa, nind agonwetawa.* I gainsay in thoughts, *nind ajidéiendam, nind agonwêiendam.* I gainsay against it, *nin gagansitân.* (Anwettam, or, Naskwewojimow).

Gainsayer, *aiagonwetang.*

Gainsaying, *agonwetamowin.*

Gait, walking, *bimossewin.*

Galilean; *Galilêwinini.*

Gall, *winsop.*

Gallon, *minikwâdjigan.*

Gallows, *agonidiwi-mitig.*

Gamble; I gamble, *nin atâge, nin nitâ atage, nin matchi-atage.* (Pakessew).

Gambler, *netâ-ataged, etageshkid.*

Gambling, *atâdiwin. atageshkiwin, matchi-atâdiwin.*

Gambling-house, *atâdiwigamig.*

Game, (interested game,) *atâdiwin.* (Pakessewin.)

Game; I game, *nind atâge.*

Garden, *kitigan, kitiganens.* (Nittâwikitchigan).

Garden-house, *kitiganiwigamig.*

Garden-River, *Kitiganisibi.*

Gard-house, *akandowigamig.*

Garlic, *jigagawanj.*

Garment, *agwiwin.*

Garter, *kashkibidassebison.* (Seskipisun).

Gather; I gather together, *nin mawandinige, nin mawandonige, nin mawandjitchige.* I gather it together, (*in., an.*) *nin mawandjiton, nin mawandinan, nin mawandonan,, nin mawandjissiton; nin ma-*

wandjia, nin mawandina, nin mawandona. I gather people together, *nin mawansomag.*—I gather for somebody, *nin mawandjitamage.* I gather it for him, *nin mawandjitamawa.* I gather for myself, *nin mawandjitamas, nin mawandjitamadis, nin mawandjitass.* I gather together sewing, *nin mawandogwass.* I gather them together sewing, *nin mawandogwadan, nin mawandogwadanan.*—I gather burning coals together, *nin mawandokige.*—I gather hay, *nin mawandoshkan.*—It gathers together, *mawandossemagad.*

Gather berries ; I gather berries, *nin mawins.* I gather berries and eat them, *nin gâpon.* (Mominew). I gather them, (*in., an.*) *nin gâponan ; nin gâponag.*

Gathered ; we are gath. together in a great number, *nin mâmâwinimin, nin mâmâwinomin.*

Gathered object, *mawandjigan.*

Gatherer, *mawandjitchigewinini.*

Gauze, *jibawasséigin.*

Gay ; I am gay, *nin bâpinenim, nin jomiwadis.* I make him gay, *nin bâpinenimoa, nin jomiwadisia.* I am gay, in liquor, *nin minobi, nin jôwendam.*

Gay, (in. s. in.) S. Joyful.

Gayness, gayety, *bâpinenimowin.* Gayety in half drunkenness, *jowendamowin.*

Gaze ; I gaze at s. th. with surprise, *nin mamakâsabange.* I gaze at him (her, it) with astonishment, *nin mamakasâbama, nin mamakâsinawa ; nin mamakasâbandan, nin mamakâsinan.*

Gazed ; any object gazed at, *mamakâsabandjigan.*

Geld. S. Castrate.

General, *kitchi jimâganishiogima.*

Generally, *mâmawi.* (Mâna).

Gentile. S. Pagan.

Gentle ; it is gentle, (a horse, etc.) *wângawisi, wawangawisi.* (Watjekkamikisiw).

Gentle, (in. s. in.) S. Mild.

Gentleness, *bekâdisiwin, minodeewin.* (Peyattikowisiwin)

Gently, *béka.* (Peyattik).

Genuflection, *otchitchingwanitâwin.*

Geometer, *dibaakiwinini.*

Geometry, *dibaakiwin.*

Germ, (bud,) *saganwi.*

German, *animâ.* I speak German, *nind animâm.*

German language, *animamowin.*

German woman, *animâkwe.*

Germinate; it germinates, (*in., an.*) *saganwimagad ; saganwi.* I make it germ., (*in., an.*) *nin saganwissiton ; nin saganwia.*

Get ; I am getting worse, (in my sickness,) *nind abindis, nind abindjine.*

Get from.... ; I get s. th. from.., *nind ondinige, nind ondis.* I get him (her, it) from..., *nind ondina ; nind ondinan.*

Get lost. S. Go astray.

Get ready. S. Prepare.

Ghost, *manito ; tchibai.*

Giant, *missâbe, kitchi inini.* Fabulous giant, *windigo.*

Giantess, *kitchi ikwe.* Fabulous giantess, *windigokwe.*

Giant's bird, *windigobineshi.*

Giant's "tripes de roche," *windigowakon.*
Giddiness, *giwashkwewin.*
Giddy ; I am giddy, *nin giwashkwe ;* I am giddy from drinking, *nin giwashkwebi.* I am g. from heat, *nin giwashkwes.* I am g. by smelling, *nin giwashkwenos.* I am g. by falling, *nin giwashkweshin.* I am made giddy by s. th. falling upon me, *nin giwashkwekos.* (Kiiskwebeyâtisiw).
Gift, *minigowin, minigosiwin, migiwewin, minidiwin, pagidinigan.*
Gild ; I gild it, (*in.. an.*) *nind osâwa-joniiakadan ; nind osâwa-joniiakana.*
Gilt ; it is gilt, (*in., an.*) *osâwa-joniiakâde ; osâwa-joniiakâso.*
Gimblet, *biminigans.*
Ginger-bread, *washkobitchigâsod pakwejigan.*
Gird ; I gird myself, *nin kitchipis.* I gird myself strongly, *nin sindapis.* (Pakwâttehuw). I gird up high my blanket, *nin takwambis, nind ishpantakwebis.* I gird him, (her, it,) *nind aiasswapina ; nind aiasswapidon.*—S. Girdle.
Girdle, *kitchipison.*—S. Belt. (Pakwâttehun).
Girdle ; I girdle myself otherwise, or with another belt, *nind andapis.*
Girl ; little girl, *ikwesens.* I am a little girl, *nind ikwesensiw.* Grown up girl, *oshkinigikwe, gijikwe.* I am a grown up girl, adult, *nind oshkinigikwew, nin gijikwew.*—The first-born girl of a family, *madjikikweiwiss.* I am the first-born girl of the family, *nin madjikikwewissiw.*
Girt ; I am not well girt, *nin mânapis.*
Girth, *assotchibidjigan.*
Give ; I give, *nin migiwe.* (Mekiw). I give him, *nin mina.* (Miyew). I give to myself, *nin minidis.* We give to each other, *nin minidimin.* I give him, (her, it,) *nin bidina ; nin bidinan.* I give him (her, it) to him, *nin bidinamawa.*—I give to all, *nin débaoki.* I give also to him, *nin dêbaona.* I have not enough to give to all, *nin nondêoki.* I have not enough to give to him, *nin nondêona.*—I don't like to give soon, *nin nômagewis.*
Give, (in. s. in.) S. Present.—S. Sacrifice.
Give away. I give away, *nin migiwe.* I give him (her, it) away, *nin migiwenan, nin pagidina, nin pagidenîma ; nin migiwen, nin pagitinan, nin pagidendan.* I give it to him, *nin pagidendamawa, nin pagidinamawa.* I give it away for him, *nin migiwetawa, nin migiwetamawa.*—I am too much in a habit of giving away, *nin migiweshk.* Habit of giving away, *migiweshkiwin.*
Give back ; I give back, *nêiâb nin migiwe.* I give him (her, it) back again, *nêiâb nin migiwenan, nind ajêna ; nêiâb nin migiwen, nind ajênan.* I give him back again s. th., *nêiâb nin mina, nind ajênamawa.*
Given ; I am given s. th., *nin minigos.* I am given s. th. by

divine goodness, *nin minigowis*. It is given away, (*in.*, *an.*) *pagidinigâde; pagidinigâso.*

Give to drink; I give to drink, *nin minaiwe.* I am in a bad habit of giving to drink, *nin minaiweshk.* I give him to drink, *nin minaa.* I give (or procure) to drink to myself, *nin minaidis.* We give each other to drink, *nin minaidimin.* The act of giving to drink to each other, or to several, *minaidiwin.* The bad habit of giving to drink, *minaiweshkiwin.*

Give up; I give up, *nind anijitan, nind anawendjige, nind anwendam.* I give him up, *nind inawea, nin bonia.* I give it up, *nin boniton.*—I give myself up to somebody, *nin pingidenindis.*

Given up; it is given up, *bonitchigâde, webinigâde.*

Giving, *migiwewin, pagidendamowin.*

Giving up, *anijitamowin, anawendjigewin, anwendamowin.*

Glad; I am glad, *nin minwendam, nin bâpinenim, nin nâendam, nind onanigwendam, nin modjigendam.* (Ataminaw). I am very glad, *nind osâmenim.* I am glad to have escaped the danger of perishing, *nin bajinêwagendam.* I make him glad, *nin minwendamia, nin naéndamia, nin bâpinênimoa.*

Glad and thankful; I am glad and th., *nin mikonaweiendam.* I make him glad, (by some good service,) *nin mikonawea.* I am gl. and th. he has it, *nin mikonaweienima.* (Nanâskumow).

Gland; my, thy, his gland, *ninishk, kinishk, onishkwan.*

Glanders; the horse has glanders, *agigoka bebejigoganji.*

Glass; drinking-glass, *minikwâdjigan;* window-glass, *wâssetchiganâbik.*

Glass-bead, *manitôminens.*

Glide; I glide in the water, *nin bakobisse, nin gogisse.* It glides away, *madjibide.* (Soskupayiw).

Globe, *aki*, or, *akki.* (Askïy).

Globulous or globular; it is globulous, (*in.*, *an.*) *bikominagad, babikominagad; bikominagisi, babikominagisi.* (Wâwiyeyaw). Two, three, four, etc., globular objects, *nijominag, nisiminag, niominag,* etc. So many globular objects, *dassominag.*

Glorification, *kitchitwâwendâgosiwin, bishigendagosiwin.*

Glorify; I glorify him, (her, it,) *nin kitchitwâwina, nin minowawina, nin bishigendagwia, nin kitchitwawenima, nin bishigenima; nin kitchitwawindan, nin mino-windan, nin bishigendagwiton, nin kitchitwawendan, nin bishigendan.* I glorify myself, *nin kitchitwawiidis, nin kitchitwawenindis.* (Mâmitjimew.)

Glorify, (in. s. in.) S. Exalt.

Glorious; I am (it is) glorious, *nin kitchitwâwendâgos, nin bishigendâgos; kitchitwawendagwad, bishigendagwad.* I make him glor., *nin kitchitwawia, nin kitchitwawendago-*

sia, nin bishigendagwia. (Mâmiteyittâkusiw.)

Glory, *kitchitwâwin, kitchitwâwisiwin, kitchitwawendagosiwin, bishigendagosiwin, ishpendagosiwin.*

Glove, *mindjikawan.* (Yiyikastis).

Gow-worm, *wawatessi.*

Glue, *namêkwan.* I make glue, *nin namêkwanike.* (Pasakwahigan).

Glue-boiler, *namekwanikeweni-ni.*

Glutton, *nebâdisid.* I am a glutton, *nin nibâdis.*

Gluttonous; I am gl., *nin nibâdis.* (Kajakew).

Gluttony, *nibâdisiwin.*

Gnash; I gnash, *nin kakitchishkabiden.* I gnash and show the teeth, *nin niiabiden.* I gnash with anger, *nin niskabiden.* I gnash at him, *nin niskâbidetawa.* (Kâkitchikâpitew).

Gnaw; I gnaw, *nin jishigwandjige.* I gnaw it, (*in., an.*) *nin jishigwandan ; nin jishigwama.*

Go; I go, *nind ijâ.* (Ituttew). It goes, *ijâmagad.* I go somewhere by land, *nin bimosse;* by water, *nin bimishka ;* sailing, *nin bimâsh.* I go further and further, *nin miwi.*— It goes so....., *ijissin.* It goes in a certain direction, *inikamagad.* (Ispayiw).

Go about; I go about, *nin babaija, nin baba-inika.* I go about in a canoe or boat, *nin babamishka;* near the shore, *nin babamajaam ;* sailing, *nin babamâsh.* I am going about, roving, *nin binâs, nin binâiadis, nin binashka.* (Papa-ituttew).

Go along; I go along, *nind anibimosse.* I go along in a canoe, *nind ani-bimishka* or, *nind animishka.* I go along on the ice, *nind animâdagak.* And so forth, prefixing *ani-* to the verbs. (Atimuttew).

Go astray; I go (it goes) astray, *nin wanishin ; wanissin.* I cause him to go astray, *nin wanishima.* I cause myself to go astray, *nin wanishindis.* (Iyekâttew).

Go asunder. S. Open.

Go away; I go (it goes) away, *nin mâdja; mâdjamagad.* (Sipwettew). I go away in a canoe or boat, *nin mâdji.* I go away (out of the way,) *nind ikoga.* (Opime-ituttew). I go away, talking, *nind animwewidam, nind animweweto.*

Go from; I go from one person to another, *nin nibiteshkawag,* or, *nin bimi-nibiteshkawag.* I go from one house to another, *nin nibiteshkanan,* or, *nin bimi-nibiteshkanan wâkaiganan.* (Ottuttew).

Go in; I go (it goes) in, *nin pindige; pindigemagad.* I go in frequently, *nin pâpindige.* I go in to him, or in him, *nin pindigawa ;* I go frequently in to him, or in him, *nin papindigawa.* I go in him, (her, it,) *nin pindigeshkawa, nin pindjinaweshkawa ; nin pindigeshkan, nin pindjinaweshkan.*—I go in the woods, *nin jekakwaam.* I go in the water, *nin bakobi.* I make him go in the water, *nin bakobininajâwa.* (Pakkubew).

Go on; I go (it goes) on, *nind animâdja, nin mâdjishka; ani mâdjamagad, mâdjishkamagad.* I make it go on, (*in., an.*) *nin mâdjishkan; nin madjishkawa.* I go straight upon him, (her, it,) *nin maiawishkawa; nin maiawishkan.* —I go (it goes) on straight, right, *nin gwaiakosse, nin gwaiakoshka; gwaiakossemagad, gwaiakoshkamagad, gwaiakossin.*—I go (it goes) on slowly, *nin besika; besikamagad.*

Go out; I go (it goes) out, *nin sâgaam; sâgaamomagad.* (Wayawiw). I go out of him, (her, it,) *nin sâgisinotawa, sâgidjinotawa, sâgidjinaweshkawa; nin sâgisinotan, sâgidjinotan, sâgidjinaweshkan.* It goes out of me, *nin sâgisinotagon, nin sâgidjinotagon, nin sâgidjinaweshkagon.*—I go out of his heart, *nin sâgidjideeshkawa.* It goes out of my heart, *nin sâgidjideeshkagon.*

Go round; I go round, *nin waninishka, nin giwitashka.* I go round him, (her, it,) *nin giwitashkawa, nin giwitashkan.* (Wâskâttew).

Go to; I go to him, (her, it) *nind nasikawa, nind ijanan; nin nasikan, nind ijan.* I go to the end of it, *nin kabeshkan.* (Nâtew).

Go with...; I go with somebody, *nin widjiiwe.* I go with him, (or he goes with me,) *nin widjiwa.* I go with him somewhere in a canoe or boat, *nind adawaama.* I make him go with somebody, *nin widjindaa.* I make it go (or come) with me, *nin widjindân.* It goes with.... *widjindimagad.* We go with one another, *nin widjindimin.* I persuade him to go with me, *nin wijâma.* I go in with him, *nin widjipindigema.*

Goblet, *minikwâdjigan.*

GOD, *Kijê-Manito.* I am God, *Nin Kijê-Manitow.* God is One in Three, *Nisso-bejigo Kijê-Manito.*

Godchild; my, thy, his godchil, *ninidjânissikâwin, kinidjânissikâwin, onidjânissikâwinan.* He (she) is my godchild, *nind onidjânissikânan.* (N'tawâsisikkâwin).

Goddaughter; my, thy, his goddaughter, *nindânissikâwin, kidânissikâwin, odânissikâwinan.* She is my goddaughter, *nind odânissikânan.*

Godfather, *babâikawin; ossikâwin.* (Ottâwikkâwina). He is my godfather, (or adopted father,) *nind oôssikanan.*

Godhead, *Kijê-Manitowiwin.*

Godmother, *mamâikâwin, ogikâwin.* (Okkâwikkâwina). She is my godmother, (or adopted mother,) *nind ogikânan.*

Godson; my, thy, his godson, *ningwissikâwin, kigwissikâwin, ogwissikâwinan.* He is my godson, *nind ogwissikânan.* (Nikosisikkâwin).

Gold, *asâwa-joniia.*

Gone! *apine! wêniban!* (Aspin!)

Good, *minô, gwanâtch.* I am

(it is) good, *nin mino ijiwebis, nin gwanâtchiw, nind onijish, nin kijewâdis; mino ijiwebad, gwanâtchiwan, onijishin, kijewâdad.* I make him good, *nin mino ijiwebisia, nin kijewâdisia.* I make it good, *nind onijishiton.*

Good-for-nothing fellow, *ningot enâbadisissig, pagandjinini.* I am good for nothing, I can make nothing, no work, *kawin ningot nind inâbadisissi, nin pagandis.*

Good-hearted: I am g. h., *nin minodee.* (Miyotehew.)

Good luck; *jâwendâjosiwin.* I have good luck; *nin jâwendâgos.* (Papewew).

Good-nature, *minodeewin, mino ijiwebisiwin, minôininiwâgisiwin.*

Good-natured; I am g. n., *nin mino bimâdis, nin mino ijiwebis, nin minodee, nin minôininiwâgis.* (Miyowâtisiw).

Good-natured person, *menodeed, meno-binâdisid.*

Goodness of heart, *minodeewin.*

Good order; I put it in good order, (*in., an.*) *nin nanâinan; nin nanâina.*

Good person, *meno-ijiwebisid, meno-bimâdisid.* I am good, kind, *nin mino ijiwebis, nin mino bimâdis.*

Goods, (merchandise,) *anokâdjigan.* (Ayowinisa).

Good sense, *nibwâkâwin.* (Iyinisiwin).

Good temper, *mino bimâdisiwin, minoininiwâgisiwin.* I have a good temper or temperament, *nin mino bimâdis, nin minoininiwâgis.*

Good terms, *inawendiwin, mino inawendiwin.* I am on good terms with him, *nin mino-inawêma.* We are on g. t. with each other, *nin mino-inawendimin.*

Goose, *wêwe.*—S. Wild goose.

Gooseberry, *jâbomin.*

Gooseberry-bush, *jâbominagawanj.*

Gospel, (Evangely,) *minwâdjimowin.*

Got from; it is got from., (*in., an.*) *ondinigâde; ondinigâso.*

Gourd-bottle, (for Indian ceremonies,) *jishigwan, ogwissimanishigwan.*

Grace, *jâwenajigewin.* (Manitonisokkamâkewin).

Grain; it is a large grain, *mangiminagad.* It is a small grain, *agassiminagad.*

Grand, *kitchi.*

Grandchild; my, thy, his grandchild, *nojishé, kojishé, ojisheian.* (N'osissim, osissima). He is my grandchild, *nind oojisheima.*

Grandfather; my, thy, his grandfather, *nimishomiss, kimishomiss, omishomissan.* He is my grandfather, *nind omishomissima.* (Ni musom, omusoma).

Grand Island, *Kitchi-miniss.* At, to or from Grand Island, *Kitchi-minissing.*

Grand Medicine, *midêwiwin.*

Grand Medicine Indian, *midé.* I am an Indian of the G. M., *nin midêw.* I make him a member of the G. M., *nin midêwia.*

Grand Medicine lodge, *midewigamig.*

Grand Medicine squaw, *midêkwe.*
Grandmother, my, thy, his grandmother, *nôkomiss, kokomiss, okomissan.* My grandmother! *noko!* She is my grandmother, *nind ôokomissinan, nind ôôkomissima.*
Grand-Portage, *Kitchi-onigam.* (Kitchi-onikap). At, to or from Grand-Portage, *Kitchi-onigaming.*
Grand River, *Washtanong.*
Grant; I grant his petition, *nin babamitawa.* I grant it to him, *nin mina, nin pagidinamawa.*
Grape, *jomin.*
Grapple, *patakiskwaigan.* — S. Harpoon. Hook.
Grappling-hook, *adjigwadjigan, adjigwadjiganâbik.*
Grass, *mashkossiw.* There is grass, *mashkossiwika.* On the grass, *mitashkossiw.* — The grass begins to grow, *sâgashkamagad.* The grass is wet, *tipashkamagad, nibishkoba.*
Grass-hopper, *papakine, minabawidjissi, adissawaieshi.*
Grass-seed, *mashkossiwi-minikan.*
Grate, to dry venison, etc., *abwâtchigan.*
Grate, (in. s. in.) S. Scrape.
Grave, *tchibêgamig.*
Grave, (in. s. in. S. Hole in the ground.
Grave, I am grave, (considered grave,) *nin tchitanendagos.*— S. Serious.
Graver, or any thing to mark with, *beshigaigan.*
Graverod River, *Passabika-sibi.*
Graveyard, *tchibêgamig.*
Gray; it is gray, (stuff, *in., an.*) *nigigwêtagad; nigigwêtagisi.* (Sipikkusiw).
Gray age, *wâbikwewin.*
Gray-headed; I am g. h., *nin wâbikwe.* (Wâbistikwânew).
Gray-horse, *negigwetagawed bebejigoganji.* This horse is gray, *nigigwetagawe aw bebejigoganji.*
Grease, *bimidê.* (Pimïy).
Grease; I grease, *nin bimidêwinige, nin nominige.* (Tominam). I grease him, (her, it,) *nin bimidêwina, nin nomina; nin bimidêwinan, nin nominan.* I grease it, (wood, *in., an.*) *nin nomakonan; nin nomakona.* I grease it, (metal, *in., an.*) *nomâbikonan; nin nomâbikona.*
Greasy; I am (it is) greasy, *nin bimidêwis; bimidêwan.* (Pimiwiw, tomaw).
Great, *kitchi.*
Great bear, (constellation,) *otchiganang.* (Otchekatak).
Great grandchild, *anikobidjigan.*
Great grandfather; my, thy, his gr., *nind anike-nimishomiss, kid anikekimishomiss, od anike-omishomissan.*
Great grandmother; my, thy, his gr., *nind anike-nokomiss, kid anike-kokomiss, od anike-okomissan.*
Great water, (great lake,) *kitchigami.*
Green; it is green, (*in., an.*) *ojâwashkwa; ojâwashkosi.* (Askittakwaw). It is green, (ice,) *ojâwashkwasigwa.* It is green, (leaf,) *ojâwaihkwabaga.* It is green, (stuff, *in., an.*) *ojâwashkwawegad; ojawushkwa-*

wegisi.—I dye green, *nind ojâwashkwadissige, nind ojâwashkwansige.* I dye it green, (*in., an.*) *nind ojawashkwadissan, nind ojâwashkwansan; nind ojâwashkwadisswa, nind ojawashkwanswa.* It is dyed green, (*in., an.*) *ojawashkwadite, ojawashkwande ; ojawashkwadisso, ojawashkwanso,*—The grass begins to green *ojawashkwashkamagad.*

Green, (painted green ;) it is painted green, (*in., an.*) *ojawashkonigâde ; ojawashkonigaso.* It is painted green, (wood; *in., an.*) *ojawashkossaginigâde ; ojawashkossaginigâso.*

Greenbay, *Bodjwikwed.*

Green serpent, *ojâwashkwâ-ginebig.*

Gréet. S. Salute.

Greeting. S. Salutation.

Gridiron, *abwâtchiganâbik.* (Abwânâsk).

Grief, *naninawendamowin.*

Grief, (in. s. in.) S. Sadness.

Grieve ; I grieve, *nin naninawendam.* I grieve him, (with words,) *nin naninawima, nind inâpinema.*

Grieved ; I am grieved, *ninnaninawendâgos.*

Grieved. Grievous, (in. s. in.) S. Sadness.

Grill ; I grill it, (*in., an.*) *nin bansân; nin banswa.* (Pattam).

Grimaces ; I make grimaces or faces, *nin niskingwen.* (Mayikkwew).

Grind ; I grind, *nin bissibodjige.* (Piniputchikew). I grind it, (*in., an.*) *nin bissibodon ; nin bissibona.* I wear it out by grinding, (*in., an.*) *nin metchibodon ; nin metchibona.* It is worn out by grinding, (*in., an.*) *metchibode; metchiboso.*

Grinder, (large tooth,) *gitabid.* My, thy, his grinder, *nindamikanabid, kidamikanabid, odamikanabid.*

Grindmill, *bissibodjigan.* (Piniputchigan).

Grindstone, *jigwanâbik.*

Gristle, *kakawendjigan.*

Groan ; I groan, *nin masitagos, nin tchigine, nin mamâdwê.* I groan sleeping, *nin mâmadwêngwâm.*

Groaning, *mamadwêwin, masitâgosiwin.*

Grope ; I grope, *nind odjinige, nin nandodjinige.* I grope him, (her, it,) *nind odjina, nin nandodjina ; nin odjinan, nin nandodjinan.*

Grotto. S. Cavern.

Ground ; it is ground, (*in., an*) *bis s a, bissibode, bissibodjigâde ; bissisi, bissiboso, bissibodjigâso.*

Ground, (soil,) *aki, akki.* (Askïy, ajiskïy). Under ground, *anâmaking, anâkamig.* (Atâmaskamik). On the ground, (bare ground,) *mitâkamig, mitashkakamig, mitchikang.*— The ground is such...., *inakamigamagad.* The ground appears, (is bare,) *mitâkamiga.* The gr. is bad, *mânâkamiga.* The gr. cracks, or is cracked, from cold, *papassâkamigadin.* The ground cracks, or is cracked, from heat, *papassâbiganate.* The gr. is dry, *bêngwâkamiga, bi-*

binekamate. The gr. is good, *minokamiga.* (Miyokkamikaw). The gr. is hilly, rough, *piwâkamiga, papikwâkamiga.* There is a hollow in the gr., *wimbakamiga.* There is a hollow made in the ground, *wimbakamigâde.* The gr. is level, *onâkamiga, jingakamiga, tatagwa.* I make the gr. level, *nind onakamigaan.* It is made level, *onakamigâigade.* There is a low ground, *tabassakamiga, tabassadina, wanakamiga.* The gr. is made low or lowered, *tabassakamigaigâde.* There is a rising gr., *anibêkamiga.* The gr. shakes, from some cause above ground, thunder, etc., *tchingwamagad aki, tchingwâkamiga.* The gr. is very steep, *kishkakamiga.* The gr. thaws, *ningakamate, ningakamigishkamagad.* The gr. is thick, *kipagakamigamagad.* There is a trembling gr., *totôganowan.* Trembling ground, *totôgan.* The gr. is wet, *nibiwâkamiga.*—I stick it in the ground, *nin potakakamigissidon.* It is the end of the gr., *waiekwâkamiga.* (Kisipaskamik).

Grow; I grow (it grows) slowly, *nin bêdjig; bêdjigin.* (Sâkikiw, kiyipikiw). I grow (it grows) fast, *nin ginibig; ginibimagad, ginibigin.* I grow (it grows) taller, higher, *nin mâdjig; mâdjigin.* I grow (it grows) stronger, *songigi; songigin.*—It grows out of the earth, *sâgakimagad.* It grows together, *mamawigimagad.*

Grumble, (like a dog;) I grumble, *nin nikim.* I grumble at him, *nin nikimotawa.* (Nemow).

Guard; I guard him, (her, it,) *nin kijâna; nin kijâdan.* I guard a child, *nin kijâdawass.* I guard a lodge, *nin kijâdige.* I guard myself, *nind ashwi.* I guard myself against him, (her, it,) *nind ashwikawa; nind ashwikandan.* (Kanâweyittam, kanâwâpukew).

Guardian, *kijâdigêwinini.*

Guardian Angel; my, thy, his Guardian Angel, *Anjeni genawenimid, Anjeni genawenimik, Anjeniwan genawenimigodjin.*

Guess; I guess, *pagwana nind ikkit, pagwana nind ijiwindan.* I guess in thoughts, *pagwana nind inendam.*

Guessing, in a guessing manner, *pagwana.*

Guest, *wâkomind.*

Guide, *kikinowijiwed, kikinowijiwewinini.* (Okiskinottahiwew).

Guide; I guide, *nin kikinowijiwe.* I guide him, *nin kikinowina.*

Guilt, *indowin.*

Guitar, *madwêwetchigan.*

Gulf. S. Abyss.

Gull, *gaiashk.* (Kiyâsk). Young gull, *gaiashkons.* Gull's egg, *gaiashkwawan.*

Gum, *oshkaniganima.* My, thy, his gum, *nishkanigan, kishkanigan, oshkanigan.*

Gun, *pâshkisigan.* The stock of a gun, *pâshkisiganâtig.* I load a gun, *nind onashkinadon pâshkisigan.* The gun is loaded, *onashkinâde pâshkisigan.*

I cock a gun, *nind ajigidabikinan pâshkisigan.* The gun is cocked, *ajigidabikinigâde pâshkisigan.* The gun misses fire, *anwâbikissin pâshkisigan.* (Pwâwapittettin).

Gun-cap, *biwissidjigan.* I put a cap to a gun, *nin biwissidon pâshkisigan.*

Gun-smith, *pâshkisiganikewinini.* I am a gun-smith, *nin pâshkisiganike.*

Gun-smith's trade or business, *pâshkisiganikewin.*

Gun-worm, *gitaigan.*

Gut, *opikwad.*

Gut; I gut him, *nin kitchinagijina.* (Tâtotayeswew).

Gut of the moose, *ashkakwaonagij.*

H

Ha! *taia! ataiâ! tâwa! tiwe!* —*Niâ!*

Habit, *ijiwebisiwin, nagadisiwin.* Good habit, *mino ijiwebisiwin.* Bad habit, *matchi ijiwebisiwin.*—S. Accustomed. (Nanamâhuwin).

Habitation, *abiwin.* My, thy, his habitation, *endaiân, endad.* (Ni'ki, wiki).

Haft. S. Handle.

Hail, *sessêgan.*

Hail; it hails, *sessêgan, mikwaminaniwan.*

Hair, *winisissima.* (Mistakäy). My, thy, his hair, *ninisiss, kinisiss, winisiss;* plural, *nînisissan, winisissan.*—I have black hair, or my hair (head) is black, *nin makatewindibe.* I have curled hair, *nin babisigindibe.* My hair is in disorder, bristled up, *nin niskindibe.* My hair is long, *nin ginwânikwe, nin gagânwanikwe.* I have red hair, (a red head,) *nin miskwanikwe, nin miskwandibe,* (*miskondibe.*) I have short hair, *nin takwânîkwe.* My hair is white, *nin wâbikwe, nin wâbishkindibe.* My hair is yellow, flaxen, *nind osâwindibe.*—I lose my hair, *nin binânikwe.* I cut his hair, *nin môjwa.* I take him by the hair, *nin sagânikwena.*

Hair of animals. S. Fur.

Hair-powder. S. Powder.

Hairy; it is hairy, coarse, (stuff, *in., an.*) *mishaweigad; mishaweigisi, mishawesi.* (Wetisiw).

Half, *âbita.* Half each, *aiâbita.* Half a barrel, *abitawissag;* half a bottle, *âbita-omôdai.* Halfway across a river or lake, *âbitawagâm.* Halfway going up on a mountain or hill, *âbitawamadjiw.* Halfway from one place to another, *âbitawikana.*

Half a day, *ningo-nawakwe.*

Halfbreed, *aiabitâwisid.* I am a halfbreed, *nind abitâwis.* Halfbreed man, *wissâkodëwinini.* Halfbreed woman, *wissâkodêwikwe.* (Abittâwokosissân).

Half-cloth, *nebanêtagak.* (S. *Nabanêtagad.*)

Half drunk; I am h. d., *nin jôwibi.* I am joyful being h. d., *nin jowendam.*

Half drunkenness, *jowibiwin.* Gaiety or joyfulness in half drunkenness, *jowendamowin.*

Half full; it is half full, (a bag,) *âbitoshkin.*

Halibut, (fish) *manâmeg.*

Halloo! *haw! taga! hoi!* (Matte!)

Ham, *kokoshiwibwâm.* Smoked ham, *kokoshiwibwâm gakanamodeg.*

Hamlet, *odênawens.*

Hammer, *pakitêigan.*

Hammer; I hammer iron flat, *nind onadaan biwâbik.*

Hammered; the iron is hammered, *onadaigâde biwâbik.*

Hand, *onindjima.* (Mitchitji, otchitji). The whole hand, *misiwênindjân.* The right hand, *kitchinindj, okitchînindjima.* The left hand, *namandjinindj, onamandjinindjima.* The other hand, *nabanênindj, ojawinindj.* My, thy, his hand, *ninindj, kinindj, onindj.*—I have hands, *nind onindji.* I have abominable hands, *nin gagwânissaginindji.* I have clean hands, *nin bininindji.* I have convulsions in my hand or hands, *nin tchitchibinindjishka.* I have a dead hand, *nin nibowinindji.* I have dirty hands, *nin wininindji.* (Wiyipitchitchew). I have hairy hands, *nin mishinindji.* I have large hands, (or fingers,) *nin mamanginindji.* I have a long hand, *nin ginonindji.* I have long hands, *nin gaganônindji.* I have only one hand, *nin nabanênindji.* I have pain in my hand or hands, *nin dêwinindji.* I have a scar on my hand, *nind odjishinindji.* I have a short hand, *nin takonindji.* I have a small hand, *nînd agassinindji.* I have small hands, *nin babiwinindji.* I have spasms or cramps in my hand, *nind otchinindjipinig.* I have strong hands, *nin mashkawinindji.*— My hands are benumbed with cold, *nin tahwakinindjmadj.* My hands are bloody, *nin miskwiwinindji.* My hands are bound, *nin mamandjigonindjibis.* I bind or fetter his hands, *nin mamandjigwapinindjibana.* My hands are cold, *nin takinindji.* My hands are cracked, *nin gipinindji, nin gagipinindji.* My hand (or finger,) is cut off, *nin kishkinindji.* I cut off his hand, (or finger,) *nin kishkinindjiodis.* My hand (or finger) is dislocated, *nin gidiskakonindjishin, nin bimiskonindjishin.* I dislocate my hand by falling, *nin kotigonindjishin.* My hand is dislocated by falling, *nin kotigonindjita.* I dislocate or sprain his hand by pulling, *nin pakibinindjibina.* My hand is frozen, *nin mashkawadjinindjiwadj.* My hand is pierced, *nin jibanindjijigas.* My hand shakes, *nin niningininindji.* My hand is stiff, *nin tchibatakonindji.* My hand is swollen, *nin baginindji.* My hands are tender, *nin nôkinindji.* My hands are warm, *nin kijônindji.* My hand is wounded, *nin mâkinindji.*—I bruise my hand, *nin tatagonindjiodis.* I bruise my hand by striking, *nin jashagonindjiganandis.* My hand is bruised by s. th. that fell on it, *nin jashagonindjishkos.* I close my hand, *nin patagwakonindjin.* I hurt my hand (or finger,) *nin kishkinindjishin.* I join both hands together, *nin nijonindjin.* I keep my hands under the arms, *nin kashkaodjinikeb.* I lay my hand or hands on him, *nind ijinind-*

jitawa. I open my hand, *nin passaginindjin.* I open his hand, *nin passaginindjina.* I open my hand flat, *nin téssinindjin.* I press his hand, *nin magonindjina.* I put my hand (or finger) in, *nin pindjinindjissin.* I reach my hand out towards him, (I shake hands with him,) *nin saginindjina.* I rub his hand with medicine, *nin sinigonindjibina.* I stretch out my hand, (or finger,) *nin jibinindjin.* I stretch my hand flat towards him or over him, *nin têssinindjitawa.* I thrust s. th. in my hand, *nin patakinindjiodis.* I thrust s. th. in his hand, *nin patakinindjiwa.* It sticks (it is thrust) in my hand, *nin patakinindjishin.* I wash my hands, *nin kisibiginindji.* I wipe my hands, *nin kisinindji.*

Hand-barrow, *oniganâtig, tessakonigan, nimâkonigan.* I carry on a hand-barrow, (or pole,) *nin nimâkonige.* I carry him (her, it) on a hand-barrow, *nin nimâkona ; nin nimâkonan.*

Handful ; a handful, *ningotobanênindj.* Twice, three times, four times, a handful, *nijobanênindj, nissobanênindji, niobanênindj.* So many times a handful, *dassobanênindj.*—Both hands full, *ningotobênikan.* Twice, three times, both hands full, *nijobônikan, nissobônikan.* So many times both hands full, *dassobônikan.*

Handkerchief, *moshwe.* (Tâbiskâgan).

Handle, haft, *nabâkossidjigan.* I put a handle, haft or crank to it, *nin nabâkossidon, nin onâkossidon.*

Handle to an axe or hoe, *osidakwâtig, nabâkossidjigan.* (Mitjiminigan, or, âttik at the end of the word : v. g. *tchikahiganâttik,* handle to an axe).

Handle to a kettle, pot, etc., *sagabiginigan.*

Handle to a spear, *anitiiak, anitiiâtig.*

Hand-saw, *kishkibodjigan, tâshkibodjigan.*

Handsome, *gwanâtch.* I am (it is) handsome, *nin gwanâtchiw, nind onijish; gwanâichiwan, onijishin.*

Hang ; I hang, or I am up somewhere, *nind agodjin.* It hangs or it is up somewhere, *agode.* It does not hang well, *wewebâgode.* I hang him (her, it) up, or put him (her, it) up somewhere, *nind agôna ; nind agôdon.* I hang it or put it up for him, *nind agonamawa.* I hang him s. th. around the neck, *nin nâbikona.* I hang s. th. on my neck belonging to him, *nin nâbikamawa.*—I hang up a net, *nind agônassab.*—I hang spread out, *gibagode.* It hangs so..., *inagode.*

Hang, (execute ;) I hang persons, *nind agôjiwe, nin gibinêwebijiwe.* I hang him, *nind agôna, nin gibinêwebina.* I hang myself, *nind agonidis, nin gibinêwebinidis.* (Oppâpekipitew.)

Hanging up persons, *agojiwewin, agônidiwin, gibinêwebijiwewin.*

Hangman, *agojiwewinini, agonidiwinini, gibinéwebijiwewinini, gebinêwebijiwed.*

Hang up; I hang s. th. up to let the water drop out, (*in.,an.*) *nin sikobiginan; nin sikobigina.*
Hank. S. Skein.
Happen ; it happens, *pagamiaiamagad.* It happens to me, *nin pagamishkagon.* (Ikkin).
Happiness, *jâwendagosiwin, débisiwin, minwendamowin.*
Happy, *ningotawassidag.*
Happy ; I am happy, *nin jâwendagos, nin débis, nin minwendam.* I make him happy, *nin jâwendagosia, nin débia.* I make it happy, *nin débiton.*
Happy, (in. s. in.) S. Joyful. Glad.
Harangue, *animitâgosiwin.* I make a harangue, *nind animitâgos.*—S. Speech.
Haranguer, *netâ-gigitod, netaanimitâgosid.*
Harangue to obtain charity, *kitimâganimitâgosiwin.* I make a harangue in order to obtain charity, *nin kitimâganimitâgos.*
Harbor, *âgomowin.* I am in a harbor, *nind agom.* We are in a harbor with a vessel, *nind agomomin.* (Kapâwin).
Hard, it is hard, *mashkawissin.* It is hard and dry from heat, *mashkawâkadode.* It is hard or strong, (wood,) *mashkawakwad.*
Hard, (in. s. in) S. Strong.
Hard, painful ; it is hard, *kotâgendâgwad.* — S. Difficult. (Ayimeyittâkwan).
Harden ; I harden or temper it, *nin mashkawâbikisan.*
Hardened sinner, *aianwenindisossig.*
Hardly, *agâwa.*
Hardy ; I am hardy, *nin jibinawis.*
Hare, *missâbos.* (Mistâbus).
Harlot, *pagândjikwe, gagibâdjikwe.*
Harmony. S. Peace.
Harness, *ônapisowin.* (Otâbâneyâbïy(.
Harness ; I harness him, *nind ônapina.*
Harnessed ; I am harnessed, *nind ônâpis.*
Harp, *madwewetchigan.*
Harpoon, *patakibidjigan.*
Harpoon ; I harpoon, *nin patakibidjige.* I harpoon him, (her, it,) *nin patakibina ; nin patakibidon.*
Harrow, *bissakamigibodjigan, binâkwan, kitchi binâwan, binakwaigan, bigobidjigan.* (Ayipitchigan).
Harrow ; I harrow, *nin bissakamigibodjige, nin binâkwaige.*
Hardship, *kotâgitowin, kotâgiwin.* I endure hardship, *nin kotâgito, nin kotâgiw.*
Hart's horn, *omashkosweshkan.*
Harvest, harvesting, *mamâwin, kishkashkijigewin, pàshkkâshkijigewin.* (Mawâtchitchikewin).
Harvest ; I harvest, *nin mama, nin kishkâshkijige, nin pashkâshkijige.*
Harvester, *kishkashkijigewinini, pâshkâshkijigewinini.*
Harvesting woman, *kishkâshkijigewikwe, pashkâshkijigewikwe.*
Haste, *wewibisiwin, wewibitâwin, wewibendamowin, dadâtabiwin.* (Kiyipiwin). I make haste, *nîn wewebis.* I make h.

working, *nin wewebita.* (Papâsihew). I make h. to return home, *nin wewibendam.* I make haste, (in working, eating, speaking, etc.) *nin dadâtabi, nia pajigwadis.* I intend to make haste, *nin pajigwadendam.*—I make haste in carrying s. th., *nin wewibinige.* I make haste going somewhere, *nin wewibishka.* — It makes haste, *dadâtabimagad.*

Hasten. S. I make haste.

Hat, *wiwakwân.* (Astotin). I put my hat on, *nin bidjiwakwâne* I take off my hat, *nin gitchiwakwâne.*

Hatch ; she hatches, (hen, bird,) *padagwâwagishkam.* (Astinepiw).

Hatched ; the young chicken or bird is hatched out, *pashhaweo panadjâ.*

Hatchet, *wagâkwadons.* (Tchikahiganis).

Hate ; I hate, *nin jingendjige.* I hate habitually, *nin jingendjigeshk.* I hate him, (her, it,) *nin jingenima ; nin jingendân.* (Pakwâtew). I hate some object relating to him, (*an.,in.*) *nin jingênamima; nin jingéndamâwa.* I hate myself, *nin jingenindis.* We hate each other, *nin jingenindimin.*—I hate to hear him, (her, it,) *nin jingitawa, nin mâniiawa ; nin jingitan, nin mânitan.* (Mayittawew),

Hate, (in. s. in.) S. Abhor.

Hated ; it is hated, (*in., an.*) *jingendjigâde ; jingendjigâso.* My speaking is hated, *nin jingitagos.* Its sound is hated, *jingitagwad.*

Hateful ; I am (it is) hateful, considered hateful, *nin jingenâdgos ; jingendagwnd.*The state of being hateful, hatefulness, *jingendâgosiwin.* (Pakwâtikusiw).

Hateful, (in. s. in.) S. Horrible.

Hatred, *jingendamowin, jingendjigewin.* Habitual hatred, *jingendjigeshkiwin.* Mutual hatred, *jingenindiwin.* (Pakwâsiwewin).

Haughtiness. Haughty.—S. Pride. Proud.

Haul ; I haul on the beach a canoe or boat, *nind agwassidon tchimân.*

Haul, (in. s. in.) S. Draw.

Havannah sugar, *sibwâganisisibâkwat.*

Have ; I have him, (her, it,) *nind aiâwa ; nind aiân.* I have him with me, *nin widwidjaiawa.*

Hawen. S. Harbor.

Hawk, *gibwânasi.* (Kekkek).

Hay, *moshkossiwan, mijashkon.* (Maskusïy). I make hay, *nin mashkossike, nin manashkossiwe.*

Hay-fork, *patakashkaigaa.*

Hay-loft, hay-shed, *mashkossiwigamig.*

Hay-making, *mashkossikewin.*

Hazelnut, *pagân, pagânens.* The hazelnut begins to ripen, *pagânens winiwi.*

Hazelnut-shrub or hazel, *pagânimij, ogebwamij.*

He, *win.* (Wiya). He–, in he-bear, he-cat, etc. S. Male

Head, *oshtigwânima.* My, thy, his head, *nishtiбwân, kishtigwân, oihtigwân.* I have such a head, *nind indibe.* I have a flat head, *nin nabagindibe.* I have a large head, *nin mangishtigwâne, nin mangindibe.* I have a scar on my head, *nind adjishindibe.* I have a small head, *nind agassindibe.* My head only is out of s. th., *nin sagikwen.* My head is out of the water, *nin sagikwegom.* My head is swollen, *nin bâgiwdibe.* My head is wrapped up in s. th., or, I wrap my head up in s. th., or cover it, *nin wiwakwenindibis, nin wewindibebis.* I wrap up his head, or cover it with s. th., *nin wiwakwêwa.* I crush his head, *nin jashagondibewa.* I hold up straight my head, *nin gaiakokwen.* I incline my head backwards, *nind ajagidikwen.* I incline my head forwards, *nin nawagikwen.* I incline my head on one side, *nind anibékwen.* I keep my head stiff, *nin mashkawikwen.* I make a certain motion with my head, *nind imikwen.* I make my head perspire, *nin sassâbikwe.* I make his head perspire, *nin sassâbikona.* I move my head, *nin mamâdikwen.* I stretch my head through a window to see s. th., *nin tapikwen.* I tear his head off, *nin kishkigwebina.* I tie up my head, *nin sinsokwebis.* I tie up his head, *nin sinsokwebina.* I tie s. th. around my head, *nin bassikwebis.* I tie or put s. th. around his head, *nin bassikwebina.* Any thing tied around the head, *bassikwebison.* I turn my head round, *nin gwehikwen.* I wag my head to signify, no! *nin wewébikwen.* I wag my head to him, *nin wewébikwetawa.* I wash my head, *nin kisibigindibe.* I wash his head, *nin kisibigindibena.*

Head-ache, *déwikwewin.* I have head-ache, *nin dewikwe, nind akosin nishtigwân.* (Tchistikwânew). I have head-ache from too much heat, *nin dewikweiass.*

Headstrong ; I am h., *nin mashhawindibe.*

Head-wind ; there is head-wind, contrary wind, *ondjishkawaanigwad.* I have head-wind, *nind ondjishkawaam.* (Nahimiskam).

Heal ; my wound heals, *nin gige.* I heal his wound or wounds, *nin gégea.*

Heal. Healing, (in. s. in.) S. Cure. Curing

Health, *ganandawisiwin, mino aiâwin, mino bimâdisiwin.* I am in good health, *nin ganândawis, nin mino aia, nin mino bimâdis.* Poor health, *nitâakosiwin.* I have a poor health, *nin nitâ akos.*

Heap, (pile;) the whole heap, *enigokwissing.* I put them in a heap, (*in., an.*) *nin okwissitonan ; nind okwishimag.* They are together in a heap, (*in., an.*) *okwissinon ; okwishinog.* There is a high heap, (*in., an.*) *ishpissin ; ishpishin.* There are heaps of driven snow, *ishpadjibiwan.* (Papestin).

Hear ; I don't like to hear. S. I hate to hear.

Hear ; I hear, *nin nondam, nin n o n d a g e, nin nondamass.* (Pettawew). I hear him, (her, it), *nin nondawa ; nin nondân.* I hear myself, *nin nondas, nin nondadis.* I hear for myself, *nin nondamas.*—I hear him with anger, *nin nishkakadisitawa.* We hear each other with anger, *nin nishkadisitadimin.* I hear him speak angry, *nin nishkâsitawa.* I cannot hear him, *nin nawitawa.* I hear him coming hither speaking, *nin bidwewetawa.* I hear him (her, it) here, *nin débitawa ; nin débitan.* I go round to hear what is said, *nin nanândoshkite, nin babananândoshkite.* I am in a bad habit of going round to hear what is said, *nin nanândoshkiteshk.* I endeavor to hear what is said, *nin nandotage.* I endeavor to hear what he says, *nin nandotawa.* I stand still in different places to hear what they say, *nin nanândoshkitegabaw.* I let him hear or make him hear, *nin nondamona.* I hear him with the impression that he is telling a lie or lies, *nin ginawishkitawa.* I hear it with the impression that it is a lie, *niu ginawishkitan.* I h e a r him, (her, it) out of some place, *nind onsitawa ; nind onsitan.* I hear him with pity, *nin kitimâgitawa.* I hear him plainly, *nin pagakitawa.* I hear him, (her, it) right or correctly, *nin gwaiakotawa ; n i n gwaiakotan.* I hear what is said, *nind initam.* I hear people say so..., *nind initage.* I hear him say so..., *nind initawa.* I hear him in a stealthy manner, *nin gimitawa ; nin gimositawa.* I hear him speak stupidly, *nin kopasitawa.* I h e a r him tell wonderful things, I hear him with astonishment, *nin mamakâsitawa.*

Hear, (in. s. in.) S. Listen to....

Heard ; I am (it is) heard, *nin nondâgos, nin nondadjigas, nin nondjigas ; nondâgwad, nondadjigâde, nondjigâde.* It is heard, it is reported, *nondagwaniwan.* A n y t h i n g heard, *nondamowin.*—I c a n (it can) be heard, *nin débitâgos ; débitagwad.* Its sound is heard at such a place, *débwewessin.* I make m y s e l f heard from a certain distance, *nin débwewidam.* I am heard coming on, *nin bidweweshin.* I am heard coming hither running, *nin bidwéwebato.* I am heard coming h i t h e r speaking, *nin bidwéwetâgos.* I am heard passing by, *nin bimweweshin.* I am h e a r d making noise in passing by, *nin bimwewe.* I am heard talking in passing by, *nin bimwewedam.* I am (it is) heard from some place, *nin madwéweshin ; madwéwessin.* I am heard making noise in some place, *nin madwéta.* I am heard in a certain place, *nin donwéwe.* I am (it is) heard out of a certain place, *nind onsitâgos ; onsitâgwad.* I am (it is) heard falling, *nin madwéshin ; madwéssin.* I am (it is) heard falling to the ground, *nin madwékamigishin; madwékamigissin.* I am (it is) heard falling on the floor, *nin madwéssagishin ; madwéssagissin.* I am heard with pity, with compassion, *nin kitimâgitâgos.* I am heard with pleasure, *nin minotâgos.* I am heard with displeasure, *nin jingitâgos.* I am heard right or correctly, *nin gwaiakôtâgos.* I am heard so... *nind initagos.* I am heard telling wonderful things, *nin mamakasitagos.* The rapids of a river are heard, *gidwêwedjiwan.*

Hearing, *nondamowin.* Any thing I hear, *nin nondamowin.* My hearings, *nin nondamowinan.* (Pettamowin).

Hearken; I hearken, *nin nandotâge, nin pisindam, nin pisindage, nin nandamasitam.* I hearken in order to hear what he shall say, *nin nandotawa, nin nandamasitawa.*

Heart, *odéima.* (Miteh). My, thy, his heart, *nindé, kidé, odé.* In the heart, *anâmide.* I have a heart, *nind odé.* (N'otehin). I have such a heart, or, my heart is so..., *nind déé,* or, *nin iji déé.* I have a clean heart, *nin binidéé.* (Kanâtjitehew). I have an unclean heart, *nin winidéé.* I have a large heart, *nin mangidéé.* I have a small heart, *nind agassidéé.* I make his heart so..., *nin dééa,* or, *nind iji déea.* I make his heart large, *nin mangidéea.* I make his heart strong, *nin songidééshkâge, nin sonkidééshkawa.* I make his heart strong, *nin songidéea ; nin songidééshkawa.* I make his heart hard, or strong, *nin mashkawidééa, nin mashkawidééshkawa.* I have a strong heart, *nin songidéé.* I have a strong heart, or, I have a hard and stubborn heart, *nin mashkawidéé.* Strength or fortitude of heart, *songidééwin.* Giving strength of heart, *songidééshkâgewin.* I have the same heart with him, *nin widjidééma.* I have spasms or cramps at the heart, *nind otchidéépinig.* I feel pain in my heart, *nin dewidêé.* I have a good heart, *nin minodéé.* I have a wicked heart, *nin matchidéé.*—My heart is affected in a certain manner, *nin dééshka.* My heart is afflicted, is sorrowful, *nin wassitawidéé.* Affliction of heart, *wassitawidééwin.* My heart is angry, *nin nishkidéé.* Anger in the heart, *nishkidééwin.* My heart beats much, *nin wikwingodéé.* My heart beats violently, *nin sességidéé.* Violent beating of the heart, *sességidééwin.* My heart is cool, *nin takidéé.* I cool my heart, *nin takidééiabawanidis.* I cool his heart, *nin takidééiabawana.* My heart is in peace, *nin wanakiwidéé.* Peace of heart, *wanakiwidééwin.* My heart is so large..., *nind inigokodéé.* From all my heart, *enigokodkeiân.* My heart is tired of sorrow and grief, *nind ishkidéé.* My heart is troubled, alarmed, *nin mi-*

goshkâdjidéé. Trouble of heart, *migoshkâdjidééwin*. My heart is weak, fickle, *nin nokidéé*. Fickleness of mind, *nokidééwin*.—I come in his heart, *nin pindjidééshkawa*. It comes in my heart, *nin gindjidééshkâgon*.

Heat; there is heat, *kijâte, kijide*. The heat comes in, *pindigéiâte*.

Heathen, *enamiassig*.

Heaven, *gigig, wakwi*. In heaven, from or to heaven, *gijigong; wakwing*.

Heavy, (difficult;) it is heavy to me, it comes heavy upon me, *nind âkoshkâgon*. (Ayimeyittam).

Heavy, ponderous; I am (it is) heavy, *nin kosigwan; kosigwan*. I make him, (her, it) heavy, *nin kosigwania; nin kosigwaniton*. I find him (her, it) heavy, *nin kosigwanenima; nin kosigwanendan*.

Heavy object; to keep s. th. down, *mindjimishkodjigan*. I put a heavy object on s. th. to keep it down, *nin minjimishkodjige*. I put a heavy object on him, (her, it,) *nin mindjimishkona; nin mindjimishkodon*.

Hectic; I am hectic, *nin jigwakâdos, nin miniwapine, nin takwamig*.

Hedge, *mitchikan*.

Heel, *odondanama*. My, thy, his heel, *nindondan, kidondan, odandan*. I sit on my heels, *nin pitigwessab*. (N'akkwan, wakkwan).

Heifer, *gibanâkosh*.

Height; it is of a certain hight, *apitamagad*. The hight of s. th., or as it is high, *eshpâg, epitissing*.

Heighten S. High.

Helas! *tiwé! ataiâ.—Niâ!* (éé! hey! mâneka!)

Hell, *anâmakamig*. (Kitchi-iskutew).

Helm, *odâkan*.

Helmet, *agôshtigwanson*.

Help, *widokâgewin*. Mutual help, *widokodadiwin*. (Otchikkamâwewin).

Help; I help, *nin widokage, nin widokas*. I help him, *nin widokawa, widokamawa*. We help each other, *nin widokodadimin, nin widokamadimin*. I help or assist his mind, (his thoughts,) *nin widokawenima*. (Nisokkamâkew).

Helper, *wâdokaged, wâdokasod*.

Hem; I hem, *nin titibigwass*. I hem it, (*in., an.*) *nin titibigwadan; nin titibigwana*.

Hemlock, *kagagiwanj*. (Wâbanowask).

Hemlock-forest, *kagag iwanjtki*.

Hemlock-tea, *kagagiwanjiwâbo*.

Hemmed; it is hemmed, (*in., an.*) *titibigwâde; titibigwâso*.

Hen, *pakaakwe, ikwé-pakaakwe*.

Hen-house, hen roost, *pakaakwéwigamig*.

Hen's egg, *pakaakwewawan, pakaakwawawan*.

Hermit, *nejiké-bimâdisid pagwâdakamig*.

Herb, *mashkossiw*. Amongts herbs, *megweshkossiw*. The herb is bent, beaten or trodden down, *saweshkissin mashbossiw*. The herb is wet, *nibiwashka*. The herb is whitish, *wabashkad mashkossiw*.—

Aromatic herb, *wingashk.* Herb on the bottom of rivers, *ansisiw.*
Herb, (in s. in.) S. Grass.
Herb of Venus, *agoshkowewashk*
Herdsman, *genâwenimad pijikiwan.*
Here, *omâ, mangiji ajonda.* (Ota).
Here! here it is, *ow!*
Hero, *minissinô, minissinôwinini, ogitchida.* I am a hero, *nin minissinowedis, nin minissinow, nin minissinowininiw, nind ogitchidaw.*
Herpes, *onamâninesiwin.* I have the herpes, *nind onamanines.*
Herring, *okéwiss.*
Herring-net, *okéwissab.*
Hey! hear! *ish! isht! hishi!*
Hiccough or hickup, *onwâwewin.* I have the hiccough, I hiccough, *nind onwawe.*
Hide, *awéssiwaiân.*
Hide; I hide him, (her, it,) *nin kâna; nin kâdon.* I hide to him s. th., *nin kâdawa.* I hide myself, *nin kakis, nin kasoidis.* I hide myself, *nin kas, nin kakis, nin kasoidis.* I hide myself before him, *nin kasotawa.*
Hidden; I am hidden, *nin kas.* It is hidden, *kâdjigâde, gimodad.* It is hidden to me, *nin kasontagon.*
Hidden thing, mystery, *kaiadjigadeg, gimodisiwin.* It is a mystery, *kâdjigâde.*—In a hidden or stealthy manner, *gimodj.*
High, (dear, costly;) it is high, (*in., an.*) *sanagad, sanagaginde; sanagisi, sanagaginso.* (Sokkakisow TTEW).
High, on high, *ishpiming.* It is high, *ishpamagad.* It is high: A book, *ishpansika;* a canoe, *ishponagad;* a forest, *ishpakweiamagad;* a hill or mountain, *ishpadina;* a mat, *ishpashkad;* metal, *in., ishpâbika;* metal, *an., ishpâbikisi;* a rock, *ishpâbika.*
Higher than large; it is higher than large, *namadamagad.*
High esteem, *ishpendagosiwin.*
Highly esteemed; I am highly esteemed, *nind ishpendâgos.* I cause him to be highly est., *nind ishpendâgosia.*
Hill; there is a very steep hill, *kishkadina.* On a hill, or on the hill, *ogidâki.* I ascend a hill, *nind ogidâkiwe.* I run up on a hill, *nind ogidâkiwebato.* I descend a hill, *nin nissâkiwe.* I descend a hill running, *nin nissâkiwebato.*
Hill; I hill. S. Hoe.
Hilly; it is hilly, *pîkwadina, pâpikwadina, pâpikwakamiga*
Hind, *nojes.* (Wâwaskesiw).
Hinder; I hinder him, *nin nagaa, nin nagâna.* I hinder myself, *nin nagaidis, nin nagânidis.* I hinder or stop fighters, *nanâginiwe.* I hinder him, *nin nanâgina.* I hinder him to do s. th., or to go somewhere, *nind ondjia.* I hinder somebody, *nind ondjiiwe.*
Hinder, (in. s. in.) S. Forbid.
Hindered; I am hindered by rain, *nin ginâbowe.* I am h. by the wind to sail, *nin nagâiash.* I am h. by a river in my voyage, *nind adagamagishin sibi.*—The water is hindered, *nagâdjiwan.*

Hinder to sleep; I hinder people to sleep, *nind opâwe.* I h. him to sleep, *nind opâma.*—(Waspâwemew).
Hip, *onoganama.* My, thy, his hip, *ninogan, kinogan, onogan.* (Otogan). The bone of my, thy, his hip, *nintchishibodagan, kitchishibodagan, otchishibodagan.* My hip is dislocated, *nin gidiskakonoganeshka.*
Hire; I hire people, *nind anonige.* I hire him, *nind anona.* (Atotew, masinahikehew).
Hired; I am hired, *nind anonigo.*
Hired person, hireling, *anônagan, anôtâgan, anônam, anokitâgan, bamitâgan.*
Hisser, (a kind of serpent,) *newe.*
Hit; I hit him (her, it) throwing, *nin mikwâwa; nin mikwaan.*
Hit accidentally; I hit him (her, it) accidentally, *nin pisikawa; nin pisikan.*
Hither, *omâ, omâ nakakeia.* (Astamité).
Hoarfrost; there is hoarfrost: On the grass, *nigigwashkadin;* on the ground, *nigigwakamigadin, wâbikadin, wâbikamidadin;* on the ice, *migwanangewadin;* on the trees, *nigigwanakad, nigigwanakadin.*
Hoarse; I am hoarse, *nin gibiskwe.* (Paskikuttaganew).
Hoarseness, *gibiskwewin.*
Hoe, *bimidjiwagâkwad, pigongweigan.*—S. Plough.
Hoe; I hoe or hill, *nin ningwatchaige.* I hill it, (*in., an.*) *nin ningwatchaan; nin ningwatchâwa.*
Hog, *kokosh.*
Hogslard, *kokoshi-bimide, nengag bimide.*
Hogsmeat, *kokoshiwi-wiiâss.*
Hog's snout, *kokoshiwishkinj*
Hoist the sail; I hoist the sail, *nind ombâkobidjige.*
Hoist up. S. Lift up.
Hold; in the hold of the vessel, *pindônag nâbikwaning.*
Hold; I hold him, (her, it,) *nin mindjimina, nin takona; nin mindjiminan, nin takonan.* I hold myself, (refrain,) *nin mindjiminidis* I hold him (her, it) well, *nind aindina; nind aindinan.* I hold him (her, it) strongly, *nin mashkawimindjimina; nin mashkawimindjiminan.* I take hold of him, (her, it,) *nin mashkawina; nin mashkawinan.* I hold a child, *nin takonâwass.* —I hold him (her, it) up, *nind ashidakwawa; ning ashidakwaan.* I hold him under me, *nin mindjimishkawa.* It holds me under, *nin mindjimishkâgon.* It holds, *mindjimissin, minjimossin.*—I hold the rudder, I steer, *nind adikweam.* (Takkwaham).
Hold, (in. s. in) S. Seize.
Hold, (contain;) it holds, *debashkine; débibi.* I cannot hold all, *ishkwashkinemagad; ishkwabimagad.*
Hold on! *béka!* (Peyattik).
Hole; there is a hole, *pagwaneiamagad, jibamagad.* There is a hole in a rock, *pagwanéiabika.* I make a hole or holes, *nin pagwaneige, nin pagwanégaige, nin panibigaige, nin pagwanébitchige, nin twaige.*

I make a hole in it or through it, (*in.*, *an.*) *nin pagwanéan, nin panibigaan, nin twâan; nin pagwanéwa, nin panibibigâwa, nin twâwa.* I burn a hole in it, (*in.*, *an.*) *nin pagwanéiakisan; nin pagwanéiakiswa.* There is a hole burnt in it, (*in.*, *an.*) *pagwanéiakide; pagwanéiakiso.* I wear a hole in it, (*in.*, *an.*) *nin pagwanessidon, nin pagwaneshkan; nin pagwaneshkawa.* There is a hole worn in it, it has a hole, *pagwanessin, pagwaneshka.*

Hole in the ground, *wânikan.* I dig a hole, *nin wânike* There is a hole dug in the ground, *wânikâde* (Wâtikâtew).

Hole of a beaver, *amikwaj.*

Hole of any animal, (its abode or den,) *waj.* (Wâti).

Hole of a serpent, *ginibigwaj.*

Holocaust, *tchâgisige-pagidinigewin.*

Holy, *kitchiwa.* I am (it is) holy, *nin kitchitwâwendagos, kitchitwâwendagwad.* I make him, (her, it) holy, *nin kitchitwâwia; nin kitchitwâwiton.*

Holyday, *kitchitwâgijigad.*

Holy Ghost, *Wenijishid-Manito.*

Holy water, *anamiewâbo.*

Home; I am at home, *nind ab.* I go home, *nin giwe.* My, thy, his home, *endaiân, endâian, endad.* (Niki, wiki).

Homesick; I am h., *nin kashkendam.*

Homesickness, *kashkendamowin.*

Hone, *jigwanâbik.*

Honesty, honest life, *gwaiakobimâdisiwin.* I lead an honest and just life, *nin gwaiakobimâdis, jaiaw nin bimâdis.*

Honey, *amô-sisibâkwat*

Honey-bird, *nonokasse.*

Honor, *kitchitwâwisiwin, kitchitwâwendagosiwin, minadenindiwin.*

Honor; I honor, *nin minâdendam*, etc. (Kisteyimew). I honor him, (her, it,) *nin manâdenima. nin kitchitwâwenima, nin manâdjienima, nin gwanwadjia; nin minâdendân, nin kitchitwâwendan, nin bishigendan, nin manâdjiton, nin manâdjiendan, nin gwanwadjiton.* I honor myself, *nin kitchitwâwenindis, nin minâdenim.* We honor each other, *nin minâdenindimin, nin kitchitwâwenindimin, nin manâdjiidimin.*

Honor. Honored, (in. s. in.) S. High esteem. Highly esteemed.

Honorable, *kitchitwa.* I am (it is) honorable, *nin kitchitwâwendâgos; kitchitwâwendagwad.* I cause him to be honored, *nin kitchitwâwisia, nin kitchitwawendagosia.*

Hood, *wiwâkwan.* (Astotin).

Hoodman's blind, *gagibingwebisowin, nandôdjiindiwin.* We play hoodman's blind, *nin gagibingwebisomin, nin nandodjindimin.*

Hoof; its hoof, *oshkanjin.*—*Bebejigoganji*, horse, that is, one-hoofed animal.—S. Claw. (Oskasiya).

Hook; a small hook, *adjibidjigan.* Iron hook for catching sturgeon, *adjigwâdjigan, adjigwâdjiganâbik, patakibidjigan.*

Hook; I hook up, *nind adjigwâdjige, nin patakibidjige.* I hook him, (her, it,) *nind adjigwâna, nin patakibina; nind adjigwadan, nin patakibidon.* I hook it, *nind adâbikaan, nind adâbikissidon.* It hooks, it catches, *adâbikissin.*

Hoop, barrel-hoop, etc., *takobidjigan, makakossag-takobidjigan.*

Hooping-cough, *kitchi ossossodamowin.*

Hope; I hope in him, *nin pagossenima, nind apénimonan.* S. Ask with hope.

Horizontally; I put it horizontally, *nin gwaiakossidon.*

Horn, *éshkan, êskanigan.* It has horn, *odeshkani.* It has only one horn, *ningoteshkani.* It has two horns, *nijodeshkani.* It has crooked horns, *wâgiwine.*

Horn, *bodâdjigan, madwewetchigan.*

Horned owl, *wewendjigano.*

Horrible; I am (it is) horrible, *nin gagwânissagis, nin gagwânissagendâgos, nin gotamigos, nin gotamigwendâgos, gagwânissagâd, gagwânissagendagwad, gotâmigwad, gotâmigwendagwad.*—It is horrible, (painful,) *aiimad.*

Horribly, *gagwânissâgakamig, gagwânissagendagwakamig.*

Horror, *kitchi segisiwin, gagwânissagendogosiwin.*

Horse, *bebejigoganji.* (Mistatim).

Horseback; I am on horseback, *nin têssab, bebejigoganji nin bimomig.*

Horse-comb, curry-comb, *bebejigoganji-binâkwan, bebejigoganji-binâkweigan, bebejigoganji-nasikweigan.*

Horse- dung, *bebejigoganjiwimo.*

Horse-fly, *misisâk.*

Horse-hair, (the mane of a horse,) *bebejigoganji-winisissan.*

Horse-harness, *bebejigoganjionapisowin.*

Horseman, *bebamomigod bebejigoganjin.*

Horse-shoe, *oshkanjikâdjigan.*

Horse-stable, *bebejigoganjiwigamig.*

Horse-tail, *bebejigoganjiosow, bebejigoganjiwano.* (Osüy).

Horsetail, (plant,) *kisibanashk.*

Hospitable; I am hosp., *nin kijewâdis, nin mino dodawag bebamâdisidjig.*

Hospital, *akosiwigamig.*

Hospitality, *kijewâdisiwin, mino dodawind bebamâdisid.*

Host, *Ostiwin, kitchitwa Ostiwin.*

Host, (landlord,) *ashangêwinini.*

Hostess, *ashangêkwe.*

Hotel, *ashangêwigamig.*

Hotel-keeper; *ashangêwinini.*

Hot weather, very hot weather, *wissagâtewin.* It is very hot, *wissagâte.* It is hot, warm, *kijâte.*

House, *wâkaigan, wigiwâm.* In the house, *pindigamig.* One house, *ningotogamig.* Two, three, four houses, etc., *nijogamig, nissogamig, niogamig,* etc. On the top of the house, *ogidigamig.*

Household, (family,) *inodewisiwin.* I have such a household, *nind inodewis.* One

household, *ningotôde.* Two, three households, etc., *nijôde, nissôde,* etc.
House of commerce or trade, trading-house, *atâwéwigamig.*
How? *anin? wegonen? tani? tanish?* (Kekway? tâneki?)
Howl; I howl, *nin won, nin wâwon.*
Howling, *wonowin, wâwonowin.*
How much? how many? *anin minik?* (Tândatto).
How often? *anin dassing?* (Tândattwaw).
Hug; I hug him, embrace him, *nin kishkigwena.*
Hull; I hull corn, *nin gitchikwanaiesige nin gitchikwanaieswag mandâminag.*
Hulled corn, *gitchikwanaiesiganag.*
Humane; I am humane, *nin kijewâdis, nin mino bimâdis.*
Humanity, human nature, *anishinâbewiwin.* (Ayisiyiniwiwin).
Humble; I am humble, I have humble thoughts of myself, *nin tabassenim, nin tabassenindis, nind agassenim.* (Piweyimisuw).
Humble-bee, *ano, kitchi amo.*
Humble submission, *tabassipagidenindisowin.* (Piweyimisuwin.)
Humbly; I humbly submit myself, *nin tabassipagidenindis.* I humbly submit him, (her, it,) *nin tabassipagidina, nin tabassipagidenima; nin tabassipagidinan, nin tabassipagigendan.*
Humiliation. S. Humility.
Humility, *tabassenindisowin, tabassenimowin, agassenimowin.*
Humor. S. Temper. Temperament.
Humpback, *magwawigan, pikwowigan, bokwawigan.* (Pitikopiskwanew).
Humpbacked or hunchbacked; I am h., *nin magwawigan, nin pikwawigan, nin bokwawigan, nin bokwawigneshka.*
Hundred, *ningotwâk.* (Mitâtattomitano). We are a hundred of us, *nin ningotwakosimin.* There are a hundred *in.* objects, *ningotwakwadon.*
We are so many hundred of us, *nin dasswakosimin.* There are so many hundred *in.* objects, *dasswakwadon.* So many hundred, *dasswâk.* (Tattwaw mitâtatto mitano).
Hundred each or to each, *neningotwâk.*
Hundred times, *ningotwâk dassing.*
Hunger, *bakadéwin.* (Nottekatewin). There is hunger, a famine, *bakadéwiniwan, bakadéwinagad, bakadékamigad.* I die of hunger, *nin gawanândam.* Death from hunger, *gawanândamowin.* I can endure much hunger, *nin jibanândam.*
Hunger; I hunger, *nin bakadé.* I hunger after it, *nin bakadenodan.*
Hungry; I am hungry, *nin bakade.* I make him hungry, *nin bakadéa.* I make myself hungry, *nin bakadéidis.*
Hung up; it is hung up, (*in., an.*) *agodemagad; agodjin.* It

hung up, to let the water drop out of it, (*in.*, *an.*) *sikobigagode; sikobigagodjin.*
Hunt; I hunt, I am hunting, *nin giosse, nin nandawendjige.* I hunt with a bow and arrows, *nin nandobimwa.* (Mâtjitotawew, mâtjîw).
Hunter, huntsman, *gaossed, nendawendjiged.* Good hunter, *nitagewinini.* (O n'taminahuw).
Hunting, *giossewin, nandawêndjigewin.* (Mâtjîwin).
Hunting district, *giossewin.*
Hurrah! *haw!*
Hurry, *wewibisiwin.*—S. Haste. (Kakweyahuwin).
Hurry; I hurry him, *nin wewebia.* (Nanikkimew). I hurry myself, *nin wewebiidis.* I hurry him away, *nin madjinajikawa.*—I am in a hurry, *nin nâgâwagendam.* (Nanikkisiw).
Hurt; I hurt, *nind akwendamoiwe.* I hurt him, *nind akwendamia.* I hurt him by striking, *nind akwendamaganâma.* I hurt him, falling upon him, *nin gijikawa, nin nisâkoshkawa.* I hurt him touching his wound, *nin gidjibina.*— I hurt myself, *nin batas, nin bataidis.* I hurt myself by carrying, *nin gijikos.* I hurt myself falling, *nin pagamakosse.* I hurt myself by lifting up s. th., *nin tchakiwi, nin kitchakiwi.* I hurt or strike myself frightfully, *nin gagwânissakishkonidis.*— I hurt my eye. S. Eye.
Hurt, (in. s. in.) S. Bruise. Injure.
Husbandman, *kitigewinini.*
Husbandry, *kitigewin.*
Husk, *jigoshdâdjigan.*
Hymn, *nagamon, anamie-nagamon.*
Hymn-book, *nagamô-masinaigan.*
Hypocrisy, *anamiêkâsowin.*
Hypocrite, *enamiêkâsod.* I am a hypocrite, *nin anamiêkas.* (Kakayehisiw).
Hurtful; any hurtful bad thing, (*in.*, *an.*) *matchi-aiiwish; matchi-aiaawish.*
Hurting of one's self, *batasiwin.*
Husband, *onobemina, wâdiged inini, widigemagan, wigimâgan, widjiwâgan.* My, thy, her husband, (unpolitely,) *nin nâbem, ki nâbem, o nâbeman;* (politely) *nin widigemâgan,* etc.

I

I, *nin, nind.* (Ni, N', Niya.)

Ice, *mikwam,* There is ice, *mikwamika.* (Miswamïy). I am coming on the ice, *nin bidâdagak.* (Pimiskuttew.) I make a hole in the ice, *nin twâige, nin twâwa mikwam.* I make a hole in the ice to have water, *nin twaâibi.* Hole in the ice for water, *twâibân.* I break through the ice, walking on it, *nin twâshin.* I walk on the ice, *nin bimâdagak.* I walk on the ice in water, *nin twatwaskobiginam.* The ice breaks off, (the water appears again,) *jâgigamiwan.* The ice of a river goes off, *bimiwébidjiwan sibi.* (Mâtchistan.) The ice is floating down the stream, *mikwam bimâbogo.* There are holes in the ice, *pagwané-jagigamiwan.* The ice is hollow, *wimbagodjin mikwam.* The ice splits or opens, *tâshkikwadin.*

Ice-bank, *gagénigwaan.* There are ice banks, *gagénigwaanaka.*

Ice-cutter, *éshkan.* (Enskâgan.) I make a hole with an ice-cutter, *nin twâige.*

Ice-house, ice-pit, *mikwamiwigamig.*

Icicle, *mikwam, mikwamins.*

Idol, *masinini.* I adore or worship idols, *nin manitoke.* I adore him, (her, it, an idol,) *nin manitokenan; nin manitoken.*

Idolator, idolatress, *masininin menitoked.*

Idolatry, *manitokewin, matchimanitokewin.* I practise idolatry, *nin manitoke.*

I don't know, (in s. in.) is expressed by *gwinawi-;* and sometimes by *endogwen.* (Wiskowin).

If, *kishpin.*

Ignorance, *gagibâdisiwin, pagwanâwisiwin.*

Ignorant; I am ig., *nin gagibadis, nin pagwanawis, nin pagwanawadis, kawin gego nin kikendansin.* I am ignorant, (benighted,) *nin tibikâdis.*

Ignorant person, *pegwanawisid, gego kekendansig, tebikâdisid.*

Ill, *matchi.* It is ill, evil, *manâdad, matchi ijiwebad.*

Ill. Illness, (in s. in.) S. Sick. Sickness.

Illegitimate child. S. Bastard.

Ill humor, ill temper, (difficult temperament,) *sanagisiwin, manjininiwagisiwin, matchi bimâdisiwin, matchi ijiwebisiwin.* (Nayettâwisiwin)

Ill tempered ; I am ill-tempered, *nin sanagis, nin manjininiwagis, nin matchi bimâdis.*

Illusion, *waiéjindisowin*

Image, *masinitchigan.* (Naspasinahigan). I make images,

nin masinitchiganike. Maker of images, *masinitchiganikewinini.* The making of images, *masinitchiganikewin.*

Imagination, *anisha inendamowin.*

Imagine ; I imagine, *anisha nind inendam.*

Imbecile, I am im., *nin gagibâdis, nind kopâdis.*

Imbecility, *gagibâdisiwin, kopâdisiwin.*

Imitate; I im., *nin kikinowâbange.* I imitate him, *nin kikinowâbama.* I im. it, (copy it,) *nin kikinowâbandan.* (Ayisinawew.)

Immediately, *pabige.* (Semâk.) S. Quickly.

Immolate. Immolation.—S. Sacrifice.

Impatience, *bitchinâwesiwin, mamidawendamowin.*

Impatient; I am im., *nin bitchinâwes, nind iniwes, nin mamidawendam.* (Kisiweyittam)

Impenitent; I am im., *kawin nind anwenindisossi.*

Impenitent heart; my, thy, his impenitent heart, *nindé kidé, odé aianwenindisomagassinog.* (Nama-kesinateyittam.)

Impenitent person, *aianwenin, disossig.*

Imperfect, (bad ;) I am (it is) imperfect, *nin waiawanendâgos, kawin gwaiak nind ijiwebisissi ; waiawanendagwad, kawin gwaiak ijiwebassinon.*

Importune; I imp. him, *nin migoshkadjia.* I importune him with my words, *nin migoshkâsoma.*—S. Troublesome.

Importunity. S. Troublesomeness.

I impose ; I impose upon him, *nin mina.* I impose upon myself, *nin minidis.*

Impose, (deceive ;) I impose upon him, *nin waiéjima, nin giwanima, nin gaginawishkima.*

Impostor. Imposture.—S. Cheater. Cheat.

Impotent ; I am imp., *nin nanâpogis.*—S. Weak. (Pwâtâwihuw.)

Imprint ; I imprint it with fire, *nin masinakisan.*

Imprinted ; I am (it is) imp. on s. th., *nin masinibiigas ; masinibiigâde.*

Imprison ; I imprison him, *nin gibâkwâwa.*

Imprisoned ; I am imp., *nin gibâkwaigas.* (Kippahikâsuw.)

Improve. Improvement.—S. Repair. Repairing.

Imprudent ; I am (it is) imprudent, *nin bisinâdis, nin gagibâdis ; bisinadad, gagibâdad.*

Impudency, *gagibâdisiwin, agatchissiwin.*

Impudent ; I am impudent, *nin gagibâdis, kâwin nind agatch issi.*

Impudent, impudent person, *egatchissig.* — S. Shameless person.

Impure ; I am (it is) impure, *nin winis, nin winâdis, nin bishigwâdis, nin gagibâdis, winad, winadad, bishigwâdad, gagibâdad.*—I think he, (she, it) is impure, *nin winenima ; nin winendan.*

Impure fire, *winéwishkote.* There is an impure fire, *winewishkotewan.*

Impurity, *bishigwâdisiwin, bishigwadj-ijiwebisiwin, gagibâ-*

disiwin, winâdisiwin, winisiwin.—I commit impurity. S. I am impure.—I make him (her) commit imp., *nin bishigwâdjia, nin gagibadisia.*
Impurity of heart, *winidéëwin.* I have an impure heart, *nin winidéé.*
Impute; I impute to him, *nind apagadjissitawa, nind apagadjissitamawa, nin bimondaa.* (Atâmimew.)
In, *pindig, pindj'*... I am in, *nind ab, pindig, nind aia.* I am (it is) in s. th., *nin pins; pinde.* (Pittukamik.)
Incapable; I am incapable, *nin bwanâwito, kawin nin gashkitossin.* (Pwâtâwittaw.)
Incapacity, *bwanâwitowin.*
Incarnate; I inc. myself, *nin wiiassiwiidis, nind anishinâbewiidis.* (Owiyâwihisuw.)
Incarnation, *wiiassiwiidisowin, anishinâbewiidisowin.*
In case..., *kishpin.*
Incendiary, *sekaowed, sekaiged, sakaigéwinini.* I am an incendiary, *nin sakaowe, nin sakaige.*
Incendiary's work, *sakaigewin*
Incense, *minomagwakisigan.* I burn incense, *nin minomagwakisige.*
Incense; I incense, *nin minomagwabikisige, nin pakwenessatchige.* I incense him, (her, it,) *nin pakwenéssatawa ; nin pakwenessaton.*
Incensory, *minomagwabikisigan, pakwenessatchigan.*
Incessantly. S. Always.
Inch; one inch, *ningoloniudj.* Two, three inches, etc., *nijonindj, nissonindj,* etc. So many inches, *dassonindj.* (Peyakonitch.)
Incision, in a maple-tree, *ojigaigan.* A fresh incision, *oshkigaigan.* I make incisions in maple-trees, *nind ojigaige.* I make large incisions, *nin mangigaige.* There is a large incision, *mangigaigâde.* I make small incisions, *nin babiwigaige.* There are small incisions, *babiwigaigâde.* The incision is whitish, *wâbigad ojigaigan.*
Incite; I incite, *nin gagansonge.* (Oppwemew). I incite him, *nin gagânsoma, nin gândjia, nind ombia, nind ombima, nind ashia, nind ashiwina.* (Sikkimew).
Inciting, *gagansondiwin.* (Sikkimiwewin).
Incline; I incline my head on one side, *nind anibekwen.*— S. Head.
Incline, (in s. in.) S. Bow down.
Inclined; it is inclined in such a manner, *inagode.* (Skiw, v. g. —to drink, minikkweskiw.)
Inclined, (in s. in.) S. Bent forward.
Inconstancy, *aiâjawendamowin.*
Inconstant; I am inc., *nind aiâjawendam.* (Mâmeskuteyittam).
Inconvenient; it is inc., *sanagad.*
Incorporated; it is incorp. to me, *nind owiiâwinodan.*
Incorruptible, *neta-pigishkanassinog.*
Increase; I increase it, *nin mishinaton, nin mishinoton.* I increase it to him, *nin mishinotamawa.* We increase in

population, *nin nitâwigimin, nin nitâwigiidimin.*

Incredulity, *agonweiendamowin, agonwêtamowin.* (Anwettamowin).

Incredulous ; I am inc., *nind âgonwéiendam, nind âgonwetam, nind agonwetage, nin nitâ-agonwetam.*

Incredulous person, *aiâgonwéiendang, netâ-agonwetang, daiebwetansig.*

Incur ; I incur it, *nind onditamâdison, nin wikwatchitamâdison.*

Indecent. S. Impure. Dirty.

Indeed, in truth, *geget.* (Tâpwe).

Indent ; I indent it, (*in., an.*) *nin kiichigijan ; nin kitchigijwa.*

Indented ; it is ind., (*in., an.*) *kitchigijigâde ; kitchigijigâso.*

Independence, *dibénindisowin.*

Independent; I am independent, *nin dibénindis.*

Indian, *anishinâbe.* (Ayisiyiniw). Bad Indian, *anishinâbewish.* I am an Indian, *nind anishinâbew.* I play the Indian, *nind anishinâbekas.* I live like an Indian, *nind anishinâbe-bimâdis, anishinâbeng nind ijibimâdis.* A strange Indian, *maiâganishi- nâbe, maiatâwanishinâbe.* A kind of strange Indian, *mishi nimakinago.*

Indian Agent, *anishinâbe-ogima.*

Indian character, *anishinâbewâdisiwin* I have the Indian character, *nind anishinâbewâdis.*

Indian corn, *mandâmin, mandâminag.* I produce Indian corn, *nin mandâminike.* I stamp Indian corn, *nin tagwawag mandâminag.* Indian corn-soup or corn-mash, *mandâminâbo, tagwaanâbo.* I make corn-soup, *nin mandâminâboke, nin tagwaanâboke.*

Indian corn field, *mandâminikitigan.*

Indian corn bag, *mandâminiwaj.*

Indian corn store-house, *mandâminiwigamig.*

Indian country, *anishinâbewaki.* I live in the Indian country, *nind anishinâbeki.* (Iyiniwaskïy).

Indian cradle, *tikinagan.* I make a cradle, *nin tikinaganike.* (Wewebisuwin).

Indian dancing, *anishinâbewishimowin.* I dance after the Indian fashion, *nind anishinâbewishim.*

Indian fashion, Indian mode of living, *anishinâbewidjigewin.* I live or act after the Indian fashion, *nind anishinâbewidjige.* (Iyiniwittwâwin).

Indian from the back woods, *sagwândagawinini.* (Sakâwiyiniw).

Indian language, *anishinâbemowin.* I speak the Indian language, *nind anishinâbem.* It speaks Indian, (it is written in the Ind. lang.,) *anishinâbemomagad.* It is Indian, (it is written in the Ind. lang.,) *anishinâbewissin.* I translate it in the Ind. lang., *nind anishinâbewissiton.*

Indian life, *anishinâbe-bimâdisiwin.*

Indian name, *anishinâbewinikâsowin.* I have (it has) an Indian name, *nind anishinâbewinikas ; anishinâbewini-*

kâde. I give him, (her, it) an Indian name, *nind anishinâbewinikana ; nind anishinâbewinikadan.*

Indian not belonging to the Grand Medicine, *sagima, sagimawinini.* I don't belong to the Gr. M., *nin sagimaw.*

Indian of the Grand Medicine, *midê.* I am an Indian of the Gr. M., *nin midéw.*

Indian ornament ; a kind of Ind. or., *magisi.*

Indian religion, *anishinâbe-ijitwâwin.*

Indian song, *anishinâbe-nagamon.* I sing an Indian song, *nind anishinâbe-nagam.*

Indian tea ; a kind of tea, *winissibag.* Another kind, *winisikensibag.* (Maskekowipokwa).

Indian to whom a woman is given to marry her, (*nolens, volens,*) *wawikawind.*

Indian woman, *anishinâbekwe.* I am an Indian woman, *nind anishinâbekwew.*

Indian writer, a man that writes in Indian, *anishinâbewibiigewinini.*

Indian writing, *anishinâbewibiigan.* I write in Indian, *nind anishinâbewibiige.* The act of writing in Indian, *anishinâbewibiigewin.*

India rubber, *gâssibiigan.*

Indicate ; I indicate, *nin windamage, nin kikinoamage.* I ind. him s. th., *nin windamawa weweni, nin kikinoamawa.*

Indigence, *kitimâgisiwin.*

Indigent. S. Poor.

Indisposed, (a little sick ;) I am indisposed, *pangi nind âkos, nin mânamandji, nin sibiskâdis.*

Indisposition, *mânamandjiowin, sibiskâdisiwin.*

Indolent, Indolence.—S. Lazy. Laziness.

Indulgence, *webinâmagowini-jâwendâgosiwin.*

Industrious ; I am ind., *nin nitâ-anoki, nin minwanoki, nin kijijawis, nin minwéwis, nin mikos, nin gashkiichige.*

Industrious man, gaining or earning much by his labor, *gashkitchigewinini.*

Industrious person, *netâ-anokid, kijijawisid.* (Mamiyow).

Industry, *nita-anokiwin, kijijawisiwin, minwéwisiwin.*

Infancy, *abinodjiiwin.*

Infant, *oshki-abinodji, tekobisod abinodji.*

Infect ; I infect a place with sickness, *âkosiwin nin bidon, âkosiwin nin bi-migiwen.*

Infidel, *enamiâssig, daiebwetamsig anamiewin.*

Infirm, (sick, weak ;) I am infirm, *nind âkos, nin nita-âkos, nin nanipinis.* (Nanekkâtisiw.)

Infirmary, *âkosiwigamig.*

Infirmity, *âkosiwin, nita-âkosiwin, nanipinisimin, inapinewin ; batasiwin.*

Inflame ; I inflame it, (kindle it,) *nin biskanendan.* (Saskisam).

Inflexible. S. Brittle.

Inform ; I inform, *nin windamage, nin kikioamage.* I inform him, *nin windamawa, nin kikinoamawa.*

Inform. Information.—S. Inquire. Inquiry.

Information, *windamâgewin, windamâwewisiwin.*

Informed; I am inf., *nin windamâgo, nin windamawewis.*
Inhabit; I inhabit it, dwell in it, *nind abitân.*
Inhabitant, *ebitang, bemiged.*
Injection, (clyster,) *pindabawâdjigan, siginamadiwin.* I receive an injection, *nin pindabawânigo, nin siginamâgo.* I give an inj., *nin pindabawadjige, nin siginamage.* I give him an inj., *nin pindabawana, nin siginamawa.*
Injure; I injure, *nin mijiiwe.* I injure him, (her, it,) *nin mijia, nind inigaa, nind enapinana; nin mijiton, nind inigaton, nind enapinadon.* I injure myself, *nind inigas, nind inigaidis.* It injures me, *nind inigaigon.* (Koppâtjimew).
Injure, (in s. in.) S. Defile.
Injury. S. Insult.
Ink, *ojibiiganâbo.* (Masinahiganâbüy).
Inland, (in the woods,) *nopiming, migwékamig.* I go in the inland, (in the woods, in the interior,) *nin gopi.* I go in the inland, on a river in a canoe, *nin gopaam.* The road or trail leads in the woods, *gopamo mikana.* (Notjimik).
Inland, (in. s. in.) S. Woods.
Inland lake, *sâgaigan.* The inland lake is large, *mangigama sâgaigan.*
Inn. Inn-keeper.—S. Hotel. Hotel-keeper.
Innocence, *benisiwin.*
Innocent; I am innocent, *nin binis.*
Inoculate; I in. with the cow-pox, *nind atagen mamâkisiwin, nin mamakisiiwe.* I in. him with the cow-pox, *nind atawa mamâkisiwin, nin mamâkisia.*—S. Cow-pox.
Inoculator, *etaged mamâkisiwin.*—S. Cow-pox inoculator.
In order to..., *tchi, tchi wi-.*
Inquire; I inquire, *nin gagwédwe.*
Inquiry, *gagwedwewin.*
In regard to..., *ondji.*
Insane; I am ins., *nin giwanâdis.* I am ins. by intervals, *nin giwanâdapine.* (Kiiskwappinew).
Insaneness, *giwanâdisiwin.* Insaneness by intervals, *giwadapinewin.*
Insect, *manitons.* A kind of poisonous insect, *omiskossi.*
Inside, *pindig, pindjii, pindj'..., pindjina.* Towards the inside, *pindig inakakeia.* (Pitchâyîk).
Insignificant; I am (it is) insignificant, considered ins., *nin nagikawendâgos, nind agassendâgos; nagikawendagwad.* I think he, (she, it) is insignificant, *nin nagikawenima, nind agassenima; nin nagikawendan, nin agassindam.* I think myself ins., *nin nagikawenindis, nind agasseníndis.*—I make him ins., *nin nagikawendagosia, nind agassendagosia.*
Insipid; it is insipid, (*in., an.*) *binissipogwad; binissigogosi.* (Nama nissitospokwan).
Insipidity, insipidness, *binissigosiwin.*
Instantly, *sesika.* (Semâk).
Instead of..., *meshkwat.* (Meskutch, kekutch).
Instigate; I instigate, *nin gagânsonge.*—S. Incite. (Sikkimew).

Instigation, *gagansondiwin.*
Instinct, *awessi-ainendamowin.*
Instruct; I instruct, *nin kikinoamâge.* I inst. him, *nin kikinoamawa.*
Instruction. S. Teaching.
Instruction, religious inst., *gagikwewin, anamie-gagikwewin.* (Ayamihe-kakeskwewin).
Instrument, (tool,) *anokasowin.* (Abatchitjigan).
Insult, *bissongewin, mawinéigewin.*
Insult; I insult, *nin mawinêige, nin bissonge, nin bissitâgos.* I insult him, (her, it,) *nin mawinéwa, nin mawineshkawa, nin bissoma; nin mawinean, nin mawineshkan, nin bissondan.* I insult him and make him weep, *nin sessessima.* It insults me, *nin mawineshkagon.*—S. Insulting language.
Insult, (in. s. in.) S. Mock.
Insult by signs with the hand, *nimiskangewin, nimiskandjigewin, nimiskandiwin.*
Insult; I insult by signs with the hand, *nin nimiskange, nin nimiskandjige.* I insult him, (her, it) by signs, *nin nimiskama; nin nimiskandan.* We insult each other, *nin nimiskandimin.* (Nimikkamew.)
Insulted; I am ins., *nin mawineogo, nin bissamigo, nin bissitawa.*
Insulter, *neta-bissonged, neta-nimiskanged.*
Insulting. S. Insult.
Insulting language, *bissitâgosiwin, bissongewin.* I use insulting language, *nin bissitam.* I hear him using insulting language, *nin bissitawa.*
Insupportable; I am ins., *nin sanagis.*
Intellect, intelligence, *nibwâkâwin.*
Intelligent; I am intelligent, *nin nibwâka.* I make him int., *nin nibwâkaa.*
Intelligent man, *nibwâkawinini.*
Intelligible; it is int., *nissitotagwad.*
Intemperance in eating, *nibâdisiwin;* in drinking, *minikweshkiwin, giwâskwebishkiwin.* (Kasakewin, kiiskwebewin).
Intemperate; I am in. in eating, *nin nibâdis.* I am intemperate in drinking, *nin minikweshk, nin giwashkwebishk.* (Kiiskwebeskiw).
Intend; I intend, *nin inendam.* I intend to do s. th., I am preparing, *nind apitchi.* (Ispisiw).
Intention, *inendamowin.*
Intercede; I intercede for somebody, *nin gaganodamage.* I int. for him, *nin gaganodamawa.* (Pikiskwestamâwew).
Intercession, *gaganodamâgewin.*
Intercessor, *geganodamâgad.*
Interior. S. Inland.
Interiorly, *pindjina, pindjaii.*
Interpret; I interpret, *nind ânikanotage.* I interpret him, (her, it,) *nind ânikanotawa; nind ânikanotan.* (Itwestamâkew).
Interpretation, *ânikanotagewin.*
Interpreted; I am (it is) interpreted, *nind ânikanotago; anikanotabjigâde.*
Interpreter, *aianikanotâged, ânikanotagewinini.* Female interpreter, *ânikanotagekwe.* (Itwestamâkewiyiniw).

Intersect ; it intersects, *ajidesse.*
Interval ; the interval between two lodges or houses, *ajawigamig, nissawigamig.*
Intice ; I intice, *nin gagwedibeninge, nin gagwedibendjige.*—S. Tempt.
Inticer. S. Tempter.
Intimidate ; I int., *nin segiiwe.* I int. him, *nin segia, nin segima.* I try to intimidate, *nin gagwêsegiiwe.* I try to int. him, *nin gagwêsegia, nin gagwêsegina.*
Intoxicate ; I int. myself, I got drunk, *nin giwashkwebi.* I int. him, I make him drunk, *nin giwashkwebia.*—It intoxicates, (it is intoxicating,) *giwashkwebimagad, giwashkwebishkagemagad.* It intoxicates me, *nin giwashkwekishkâgon.*
Intoxicated ; I am int., *nin giwashkwebi.* (Kawibew).
Intoxication, *giwashkwebiwin.*
Intractable ; I am int., *nin sanagis.* I find him intr., *nin sanagenima.*
Intractableness, *sonagisewin.* (Ayimisiwin).
Intrepid. Intrepidity.—S. Courageous. Courage.
Intrust. S. Commit.
Inundation. S. Flood.
Inured. S. Accustomed.
Inurement, *nagadisiwin,*
Invent ; I invent it, or discover it, *nin mikawashiton.* (Miskweyittam).
Invented ; it is invented, *mikawedjigâde.*
Invention, *mikawashitowin.*
Inventor, *mekawashitod, gamikawashitod.*
Invisible ; I am (it is) invisible, *kawin nin wâbaminagosissi, kawin wâbaminagwassinon.* Invisible *an.* being, *waiamaminagasissig.* Invisible *in.* object, *waiâbaminagwassinog.*
Invitation, *wigongewin, wikondiwin.* (Wisâmew).
Invite ; I invite to a meal, *nin wikonge.* I invite him, *nin wikoma.*
Invite, (in. s. in.) S. Call.
Inwardly. S. Inside.
Inwardly, in the body, *anâmina.* (Atâmiyâk).
Ire. S. Anger.
Ireland, *Jâganâshiwaki.* (England.)
Irish boy, *jâganâshins,* (English boy.)
Irish girl, *jâganâshikwens,* (English girl.)
Irishman, *jâganâsh,* (Englishman.)
Irishwoman, *jâganâshikwe,* (Englishwoman.)
Iron, *biwâbik.* A piece or fragment of iron, *bokwâbik.* I work or produce iron, *nin biwâbikohe.* Place where they produce iron, *piwâbikokan.*—S. Cast iron. Wrought iron.
Iron ; I iron, *nin joshkwaigaige.* I iron it, (*in., an.*) *nin joshkwêgaan ; nin joshkwêgâwa.*
Iron boat, *biwâbiko-tchimân.*
Iron chain, or iron fetters, *biwâbiko-sagabiginigan, biwâbiko·sagibidjigan, biwâbikotakobidjigan.*
Ironed ; it is ironed, (*in., an.*) *joshkwaigaigâde ; joshkwaikaigaso.*
Iron-mine, *biwâbikokân,* (properly,) I work in a iron-mine, *nin biwabikoke,* (properly.)

Iron-Mountain, *Biwâbiko-wadjiw.*
Iron pot, *biwâbikwâkik.*
Iron-River, *Biwâbiko-sibi.*
Iron-road, (rail road,) *biwâbikomikana.*
Iron vessel, *biwâbiko-nâbikwân.*
Iroquoi Indian, *Nâdowé.*
Iroquoi language, *nâdowêmowin.* I speak the Iroquoi language, *nin nâdowêm.*
Iroquoi squaw, *nâdowékwe.*
Irrational; I am irr., *nin gagibâdis.* It is irr., *gagibâdad.*
Irritate; I irritate him, *nin nishkia.* (Kisiwahew). S. Angry. Provoke to anger.
Island, isle, *miniss.* The end of the island, *waiekwaminiss.* (Ministik).
Islander, *minissing endanakid, minissing endaji-bimâdisid.*
Island in a current, *minitigodjiwan, meminitigodjiwang.*
Island in a river, *minitig.*
Isle Royal, *Minông.*
Issue of blood, *miskwiwapinewin.* I have an issue of blood, *miskwiwapine.*
Itch, itching, *gijibisiwin, gijibojewin.* I feel itchings, *nin gijibis.* (Kiyakisiwin). I feel itchings: On my arm, *nin gijibinike;* in my ears, *nin gijibitawage, nin ginagitawage;* on my foot or feet, *nin gijibiside;* on my hand, *nin gijibinindji;* on my head, *nin gijibindibe, nin gijibishtigwâne, nin ginagishtigwane;* on my leg, *nin gijibigâde;* on my skin, *nin gijibaje.*
Itchy; I am itchy, *nin gijibaje.* (Kiyakisiw).
Ivy, *wâbijéshiwatchâb.*

J

Jacket, *bâbisikawâgan.*
Jack-knife, *biskabikikomân.* I shut a jack-knife, *nin biskâbikinan mokomân.* (Pikikkumân).
Jagg. Jagged.—S. Indent. Indented.
Jail, *gibakwaodiwigamig.* (Kippahikâsowikamik).
Jailer, *genawenimad gebakwaigâsonidjin.*
January, *manitogisis.* (Kisêpisim).
Jar. S. Jug.
Jaundice, *osâwinesiwin.* I have the jaundice, *nind osâwines.*
Jaw, *odamikanama.* My, thy, his jaw, *nindamikân, kidamikân, odamikân.* My jaw is swollen, *nin bâgashkamige.*
Jawbone, *odâmikiganima.* My, thy, his jawbone, *nindamikigan, kidamikigan, odamikigan.* I have bare jawbones, *nin mitaskkanige.*
Jay, *pikwakokweweshi.*
Jealous; I am jealous, *nin gâwe, nin gagawendjige, nin bimimassige.* I am jea. in thoughts, *nin gâwendam.* I am jealous in thoughts towards her, (him,) *nin gâwenima, nin gagâwenima.* I am too jealous, or in a habit of being jealous, *nin gâwesk, nin gagâwendjigeshk.* I am jealous for him, *nin aâwetawa, nin gawetamawa.* We are jealous towards one another, *nin gâwindimin, nin gagâwenindimin.*
Jealousy, *gâwewin, gagâwendjigewin, gâwindiwin, gagâwenindiwin.* Habitual jealousy, *gâweshkiwin, gagâwendjigeshkiwin.*
Jeopardy, *nanisânisiwin.* — S. Danger.
Jest. S. Buffoon. Buffoonery.
Jester, *bebâpinisid, bebâpinwed.* Great jester, *netâ-babâpinisid.* —S. Buffoon. (Wâwiyatweskiwin.)
Jew, *Judawinini.*
Jewess, *Judawikwe.*
Jingle; it jingles, *madweiâbikissin.*
Join; I join it together, *nin mâmâwiton.* It joins together, *mâmâwissin.*
Joiner, (carpenter,) *mokodâssowinini.*
Joiner's shop, *mokodâssowigamig.*
Joiner's trade or work, *mokodâssowin.*
Joke; I am telling jokes, I joke, *nin babâpinwe, nin babâpinis, nin maiêssandwas, nin wâwiiagitâgos.*
Joker. S. Jester.
Jokery, *babâpinwewin, babapinesiwin, wawiiajiiâgosiwin.*
Joy, joyfulness, *minawânigosiwin, minawanigwendamowin,*

minawasiwin, onanigosiwin, onanigwendamowin, bapinenimowin, bapinendamowin, jamiwadisiwin, modjigisiwin, modjigendamowin. There is joy, *minawanigwad.* Joyfulness in half drunkenness, *jowendamowin.* Joyfulness in drunkenness, *minawanigobiwin, modjigibiwin.* (Miyawâtamowin).

Joyful; I am joyful, *nin minawanigos, nin minawanigwendam, nin minawas, nind onanigos, nind onanigwendam, nin bapinenim, nin bapinendam, nin jomiwâdis, nin modjigis, nin modjigendam.* I am joyful being half drunk, *nin jowêndam.* I am joyful in drunkenness, *nin minawanigobi, nin modjigibi.* I am joyful in my heart, *nin modjigidee.*

Judea, *Judêing.*

Judge, *dibakonigewinini, dibakoniwewinini, debakoniged.* (Wiyasuwew.)

Judge; I judge, *nin dibakonige, nin dibakoniwe.* I judge him, *nin dibâkona, nin dipâgima, nind onagima.* I judge him in thoughts, *nind onênima.* It judge it in thoughts, *nind onendân.* (Wiyasuwatew).

Judged; I am (it is) judged, *nin dibâkonigâs ; dibakonigâde.*

Judgment, *dibabonigewin, dibakonigowin, dibakoniwewin, dibakonidiwin.*

Judgment-day, (day of divine judgment,) *dibakonige-gijigad.*

Judgment-house, *dibakonigewigamig, dibakonidiwigamig.*

Judgment-seat, *dibakoniwewiniapabiwin.*

Jug, *omodai, wâbigan-omodai.*

Juggler, *tchessakid, tchissakiwinini.*

Juggler's lodge, *tchissakan.*

Jugglery, *tchissakiwin.* I practice jugglery, *nin tchissaki.*

Jugglery in regard to sickness, *kosâbandamowin.* I practice jugglery for a sick person, *nin kosâbandam.* I practice jug. on him or for him, *nin kosâbama.*

July, *miskwimini-gisiss, madwesigegisiss, papâshkisige-gisiss* (Opaskuwipisim).

Jump. S. Leap.

June, *odeimini-gisiss.* (Opâskâwehupisim).

Juniper-berry, *okâwanjimin.*

Juniper-bush, *okâwanj.*

Jury, *dibowewin.* I serve on a jury, *nin dibowe.*

Juryman, *dibowewinini.*

Just, *mémwetch, nâita.* (Mwetchi).

Just; I am just, *nin gwaiakobimâdis, gwaiak nind ijiwebis.*

Just, justly, *gwaiak ; jaiaw.*

Justice, (virtue,) *gwaiako-bimâdisiwin, gwaiak ijiwebisiwin ; jaikwinâdisiwin.*

Justice, (law,) *dibakonigewin.*

Justice of the peacc. S. Judge.

Just, so, *tibishko.* (Mwetchi ekusi).

K

Kalendar. S. Calender.
Keg, *makagôns, makakossagons.*
Keep; I keep him, (her, it,) *nind mindjimina, nin mindjimishkawa; nin mindjiminan.* I keep him, (her, it) slightly, *nin sagina; nin saginan.* It keeps me, *nin mindjimishkagon.* I keep myself back, *nin mindjiminidis.* I keep myself from him, *nin midagwetawa.*
Keep, (in. s. in.) S. Conserve. Reserve.
Keep company; I keep com., *nin wissoke.* I keep company with him, (her, it,) *nin wissokawa; nin wissokan.*
Keep, (contain; it keeps much, (*in., an.*) *bissâgwan; bissâgosi.*
Keep in memory; I keep in m., *nin mindjimendam.* I keep him, (her, it) in memory, *nin mindjimenima; nin mindjimendân.* I keep myself in m., (I think on myself,) *nin mindjimenindis.* (Mittimeyittam).
Kept, (in. s. in.) S. Conserved. Reserved.
Kernel, (stone,) *opikominân.*
Kettle, *akik.* I make kettles, *nind akikoke.* The kettle is too small, *naawadisi akik.*
Kettle-hook, or kettle-hanger, *agodakikwân.*
Kettle-maker, kettle-manufacturer, *akikokewinini.*
Kettle-manufactory, *akikokewin.*
Key, *abâbikaigan.* I make keys, *nind abâbikaiganike.* (Abikkokahigan).
Kick; I kick, *nin tângishkige, nin tângishkage.* I kick him, (her, it,) *nin tângishkawa, nin tatângishkawa; nin tângishkan, nin tatângishkan.*
Kicked; I am (it is) kicked, *nin tangishkigas; tângishkigâde.*
Kidney; my, thy, his kidney, *nindôdikossiw, kidodikossiw, ododikossiwan.* (Otittikusiw).
Kill; I kill, *nin nishiwe, nin nitage.* I use to kill, *nin nishiweshk.* (Nipattâkew). It kills, *nishiwemagad.* I kill him, (her, it) *nin nissâ, nin niwanawa; nin niton.* I seek an opportunity to kill him, *nin nândânissa.* I kill him in a certain manner, *nind inâpinana.* I kill him for such a reason, or on account of...., *nind ondjinana.* (Nipahew).
Kill animals; I kill for people, *nin nitamâge.* (Nipattamawew). I kill it for him, *nin nitamawa.* I kill for myself, *nin nitamas, nin nitamadis.*
Killed person, *nitâgan.*
Killer of animals, *nitagéwinini.*
Killer of persons, murderer, *neshiwed, neshiweshkid.* (Onipattâkesk).

Killing, *nishiwewin, nissidiwin; nitagewin.*

Kind; only objects of one and the same kind are lying there, (*in., an.*) *mojagissinon; mojagishinog.* We are of so many kinds, *nin dasswaiagisimin.* It is of so many kinds, *dasswaiagad.* We are (it is) of two, three kinds, etc., *nin nijwaiagisimin, nin nisswaiagisimin; nijwaiagad, nisswaiagad,* etc.

Kind; I am kind, *nin kijâdis, nin kijewâdis, nin mino bimâdis.*

Kindle; I kindle it, *nin sakaan.* —S. Blaze.

Kindle-wood, *mishiwâtig, biskakonendjigan.*

Kindness, *kijâdisiwin, kijewâdisiwin, mino bimâdisiwin.*

Kindred, *inawendiwin.*

King, *ogima, kitchi-ogima.* I am a king, *nind ogimaw.* I make him a king, *nind ogimâwia.* I live or act like a king, *nind ogimâwâdis.*

Kingdom, *ogimâwiwin.*

Kingfisher, (bird,) *ogishkimanissi.*

Kinsman, kinswoman, *inawemâgan, inawendagan.*

Kiss, kissing, *odjindiwin.*

Kiss; I kiss, *nind odjindam.* I kiss him, (her, it,) *nind odjima; nind odjindân.* I kiss s. th., relating to him, *nind odjindamâwa.* We kiss each other, *nind odjindimin.* Kissing each other, *odjindiwin.*—

Kissing-day, *odjindiwini - gijigad.* (New-year's day, (Otshettuwikijikaw).

Kitchen, *tchibâkwewigamig.* — (Piminawasuwikamik).

Kite, *gibwânasi; mishikekek.*

Kite, made of paper, *babamassitchigan.*

Knead; I knead, *nin onadinige.* I knead it, (*in., an.,*) *nind ojitchishkiwaginan; nind ojitchishkiwagina.* I knead bread, *nind onadina pakwejigan.*

Knee, *ogidigwama.* My, thy, his knee, *ningidig, kigidig, ogidigwan.*

Kneel; I kneel, I am kneeling, *nind otchitchingwanab, nind otchitchingwanigabaw.* I kneel before him, (her, it,) *nind otchitchingwanigabawitawa; nind otchitchingwanigabawitam.*

Kneel down; I kneel down, *nind otchitchingwanita.* I kneel down before him, (her, it,) *nin otchitchingwanitawa; nind otchitchingwanitam.* I fall down on my knees, *nind otchitchingwanisse.*

Knife, *môkomân.* Small knife, (penknife,) *mokomânens.* I make knives, *nin mokomânike.*—S. Cutler.

Knife-sheath, *pindikomân.*

Knife with two edges, *etawikomân.*

Knit; I knit socks or stockings, *nind ajiganike.* I knit stockings, *nind akôkomidâssike, nin misatigomidâssike.*

Knitting, *akokomidâssikewin.*

Knob on a tree, *pikwakwad.*

Knock; I knock, *nin pakiteige.* I knock with s. th., *nin pagakwaige.* I knock him with my shoulders, *nin pakiteshkawa.* I knock him, (her, it) down, *nin pakiteoshima; nin pakiteossidon.* (Pakamahwew).

Knock against ; I knock against him, *nin bitâkoshkawa.* I knock against it, *nin bitâkoshkan.* It knocks against me, *nin bitâkoshkagon.*—I knock my foot against s. th., *nin bitâkosideshin ;* my forehead, *nin bitâkokwatigweshin ;* my hand, *nin bitâkonindjishin ;* my head, *nin bitâkondibeshin ;* my knee, *nin bitâkogidigweshin.*

Knock at a door ; I knock, *nin pâpagakwaige.* I knock at a door, *nin pâpagakwaan ishkwandem, nin pâpagaan ishkwandem.*

Knocked out ; the head and the bottom of a barrel are knocked out, *jâbondeia makakossag.*—I knock the head and the bottom of a barrel out, *nin jâbondean makakossag.*

Knocking, *pakiteigewin, pagakwaigewin.*

Know ; I know, *nin kikendjige, nind inâmandjige.* I know him, (her, it,) *nin kikenima, nind inâmama, nin nissitawinawa ; nin kikendân, nind inamandan, nin nissitawinan.* I know myself, *nin kikenendis.*—I try to know him, (her, it,) *nin nandakikenima ; nin nandakikendân.* I want to know him, (her, it,) *nin wikikenima ; nin wi-kikendân.*- I make him know, *nin kikendamoa, nin kikendamona.*— I know plainly, surely, *nin pakakendam, nin bisiskendjige.* I know him, (her, it,) plainly, *nin pakakenima, nin bisiskenima ; nin pakakendan, nin bisiskendan.*—I know, (I am learned,) *nin kikendâss.*— I don't know, *endogwen.* I don't know what, *wegotogwen.* I don't know who, *awegwen.* I don't know why, *wegotogwen wendji-...*

Knowledge, (science,) *kikendâssowin.* I possess kn., *nin kikendâss.*

Knowledge of s. th., *kikendamowin.* Perfect kn., *bisiskendamowin, bisiskendjigewin.*

Known ; I am (it is) known, *nin kikendâgos, nin kikendjigas ; kikendagwad, kikendjigâde.*— I make known, *nin kikendamiiwe, nin kikendamodjiwe.* I make it known, (*in., an.*,) *nin kikendamiiwen, nin kikendamodjiwen ; nin kikendamiiwenan, nin kikendamodjiwenan.*—I look, (it looks, known, *nin nissitawinâgos ; nissitawinâgwad.*

L

Labor, *anokiwin, kitchi anokiwin, kotagiwin.*—Labor of a woman in giving birth to a child, *nigiawassowin.* (Atuskewin, nittâwikihawasow).
Labor ; I labor, toil, *nind anoki, nin kitchi anoki, nin kotagiw.* (Atuskew).
Labor, (in s. in.) S. Serve.
Laborer, *anokiwinini, enokid, enonind.*
Labrador, *mashkigobag.*
Lace, *niskitchigan, wibidekadjigan.* I ornament with lace, *nin niskitchige, nin wibidekadjige.*—I lace or fill snowshoes, *nind ashkime.* Lacing snowshoes, *askkimewin.*
Laced ; it is laced, ornamented with lace, *niskitchigâde, wibidekâde.*
Lad, *oshkinawe, weshkinigid.*
Ladder, *akwândawâgan.* I ascend a ladder, *nind akwandâwe.* I ascend a ladder running, *nind akwandawebato.* I descend a ladder, *nin nissandâwe.* (Ketchikusiwinâttik).
Laid ; two are laid together, (*an. in.,*) *nijossitchikâsowag ; nijossitchigadewan.*
Lake ; large lake, *kitchigami.* Small lake, inland-lake, *sâgaigan.* The lake looks dark, (by the wind,) *makatewigami.* In the middle of a lake, (or other water), *nâwagâm.* (Tâwâkâm.) Along the great lake, *tchigikitchigami.*—I come to the lake from the woods, *nin madâbi.* (Matâwisiw). It comes to the lake, *madâbimagad.* I come to the lake from camp to camp, *nin madâbigos.* I go down to the lake by water, *nin madâbon.*—I carry or convey him, (her, it) to the lake, *nin madâbina ; nin madâbidon.* I slide (it slides) down to the lake, *nin madâbisse ; madâbissemagad.* At the end of a lake, *waiékwagâm.*
Lake Superior, *Otchipwe-kitchi gami,* (the sea of the Chippewas.)
Lamb, *manishtanishens.*
Lame ; I am lame, *nin mamândjigos, nind adjâosse.* I am lame in one leg, *nin tatchigâde.* I am lame in the back, *nin bokwawiganeta.* I lame myself, *nin batas.* (Watchiskaw).
Lame, (in. s. in.) S. Cripple.
Lame person, unable to walk, *bemossessig, memandjigosid.*
Lament ; I lament, *nin gagidowe, nin naninawitâgos.* (Mawikkâsiwewin).
Lament. L a m e n t a t i o n.—S. Weep over... Weeping over....
Lamp, *wassakwanendjigan.*
Lamp-oil, *wassakwanendjigan-bimide.*

Lance, *jimâgan.*
Lancer, (soldier,) *jimâganish.*
Lancet for bleeding, *baskikweigan.*
Land, *aki.*—S. Ground, (soil.)—(Askïy).
Land; I land, *nin gabâ,* I land it, (*in., an.*) *nind agwassiton; nind agwashima.* It is landed, put ashore; (*in., an.*) *agwassitchigâde; agwassitchigâso.*
Landing, landing-place, *gabêwin.*
Landlady, *ashangekwe.*
Landlord, *ashangewinini.*
Language, *inwewin.* (Itowewin). Foreign language, *maiagwewin, pakân inwewin.* I speak a foreign language, *nin maiagwe, nin maiagitâgos, pakân nin inwê.* I make him speak a foreign language, *nin maiagwea.* Difficult language, *sanagwewin.* I speak a different language, *nin sanagwe.*—I try to speak the language of the people with whom I live, *nin nandaniinawe.*
Language. S. Bad language.
L'Anse, *Wikwed.* At L'Anse, to or from L'Anse, *Wikwedong.*
Lantern, *wâssakwanendjigan.*
Lapointe, *Moningwanekan.* At Lapointe, to or from Lapointe, *Moningwanêkaning.*
Lapwing, (bird,) *moningwane.*
L'Arbre-croche, *Wâganakisi.*
Lard. S. Hogslard.
Larder, *atâssowin.*
Large, *kitchi.*
Large; I am (it is) large, big, *nin mindid; mitcha.* (Mishikitiw,misaw). I am very large, *nin kagabadis, nin mamadokis.* I am a large big person, *nin mangiiawes.*—It is large, *mangishkamagad.* It is large: Clothing material, *mangasika; metal, in., mitchâbikad; metal, an., mitchâbikisi; stuff, in., mitchigad; stuff, an. mitchigisi; wood, in., mitchâkwad; wood, an., mitchâkosi.*—I am so large, *nind inigin.* It is so large, *inigokwissin, inigokwamagad.* It so large: Metal, *in., inigokwâbikad;* metal, *an., inigokwâbikisi;* stuff, *in., inigokwâbigad;* stuff, *an., inigokwabigisi.* I appear (it appears) so large, *nind inigokwabaminâgos; inigokwabaminâgwad.*—I catch a very large fish, *nin kagabadjibina.*—I make it large, *nin mitchâton.* Large lake, *kitchigami.* At the end of a large lake, *waiëkwakitchigami.*
Lark, *kikibikomeshi.*
Lascivious. S. Libertine.
Lasciviousness. S. Licentiousness.
Lash, *bashanjêigan.* (Pasastehigan).
Lashing, *bashanjêigewin.*
Last; I am the last, *nind ishkwaiadjiw.* I am (it is) considered the last, *nind ishkweidâgos; ishkweiendâgwad.* I live in the last lodge or house, *nind ishkwege.* The last lodge or house, *ishkwegamig.* It comes to me in the last place, (I receive it in the last,) *nind ishwekâgon.* The last or youngest child in a family, *ishkwetchâgan.* It is the last object, *ishkwessin.* The last object, *eshkwessing.* The last

time, *ishkwâtch*. For the last time, *ganâpine*. At last, *gegapi, ishkwâtch*. (Iskweyâtch).

Latch of a door, *pakakonigan*.

Late, the late. S. Deceased.

Late, *wika*. I come late, *wika nin dagwishin*. (Nama mayo).

Late ; it is late, (in the forenoon,) *ishpi-gijigad*. It is not late, (in the afternoon,) *ishpi-gijigad*. It is late in the night, *ishpi-tibikad*. (Akwa-kijikaw, etc.)

Late, (in the beginning of the evening,) *âpitchi onâgoshig*.

Lately, *nomaia, anomaia*. (Anotchikke).

Later, by-and-by *ponima, nâgatch, panima nâgatch*. — (Tcheskwa).

Lath, *gijikens*.

Lath ; I lath, *gijikensag nind agwakwawag*.

Laudanum, opium, *nibewâbo*.

Laugh ; I laugh, *nin bâp*. I laugh with him, *nin bâbâpijima*. I am in a habit of laughing, or I laugh too much, *nin bâpishk*. I laugh with tears in my eyes, *nin gigisibingwêbâp*.

Laugh at ; I laugh at him malignantly, *nin gandj-bapia*. I laugh at him, (her, it,) mockingly, *nin bapinôdawa ; nin bapinodan*. I laugh at him, (her, it) friendly, *nin bâpia ; nin bâpiton*.

Laughter, *bâpiwin*. I burst into laughter, *nin pashkap, nin nanissap*. I expose it to laughter, (*in., an.*) *nin bapitamowiniken ; nin bapitamowinikenan*.

Launch ; I launch him, (her, it) in the water, *nin bakobina ; nin bakobinan*. I launch a vessel, *nin madâssidon nâbikwân, nin niminawenan*. (Pakastaweham).

Launderer. Laundress. Laundry. — S. Washer. Washerwoman, Wash-house.

Law, *dibakonigewin, inakonigewin, onakonigewin*. (Wiyasuwewin). I make laws, *nind onakonige*. I make a law for him, *nind onakonamawa*. I try to make good laws, *nin nandâonakonige*.

Lawgiver, *onakonigewinini, inakonigewinini*.

Lawgiving, *onakokigewin, inakonigewin*.

Lay ; I lay or put two objects together, (*an., in.*) *nin nijoshimag ; nin nijossitonan*. I lay s. th. on him to carry, *nin bimondaa, nind ombondaa*. I lay it badly, *nin manjissiton, nin mânossiton*. I lay him down, (especially to sleep,) *nin jingishima, nin gawishima*. I lay him down on some hard object, *nin mitâkoshima*. I lay him, (her, it) down otherwise or somewhere else, *nind andjishima ; nind andjissiton*. I lay him, (her, it) down on the side, *opimêshima ; nind opimêssidon*.—I lay my head on s. th. lying down, *nind apikweshin*. I lay my head on it, (*in., an.*) *nind apikweshimon ; nind apikweshimonan*.

Lay-baptism, *kikiweiâbâwadjigewin*. I receive lay-baptism, *nin kikiweiâbâwas*. I give lay-baptism, *nin kikiweiâbâwadjige, nin- kikinâwadabawad-*

jige. I give him lay-baptism, *nin kikiweiâbâwana, nin kikinawadabawana.* (Kiskinowâbâwayew).

Lay eggs; she lays eggs, *bônam.* (Owâwiw).

Lay on; I lay it on thick, (*in., an.*) *nin kipagissiton; nin kipagishima.*

Lay open; I lay it open, (*in., an.*) *nin mijishaton, nin mijishawissiton; nin mijishassa, nin mijishawishima.* I lay it open before him, *nin mijishawissitamawa.* It lays open, or it is laid open, *mijiskawissin, mijishawissitchigâde.*

Laziness, *kitimiwin, kitimishkiwin, tâtagâdisiwin, tatagadjiwin.*

Lazy; I am lazy, *nin kitim, nin kitimishk, nin tâtagâdis.* I look lazy, *nin kitiminâgos.*

Lazy person, *ketimishkid, taiatagadisid, enokissig.*

Lead, *ashkikomân.* I work or produce lead, *nind ashkikomânike.*

Lead-mine, *ashkikomânikan.* I work in a lead-mine, *nind ashkikomânike.*

Lead, (plumb;) I lead or plumb a pipe, *nin sigâwa opwâgan.* I lead, I ornament with lead, *nin masinajigawitchige, nin masinikwassige.*—I lead it, (*in., an.*) *nin masinajigawiton; nin masinajigawia.*—It is leaded, (moulded,) (*in., an.*) *masinajigawitchigâde; masinajigawitchigâso.*

Lead; I take the lead, *nin nigâni, nin nigânosse.* A man that takes the lead, *nigânossewinini.* A woman that takes the lead, *nigânossekwe.*

Lead, (in s. in.) S. Guide.

Lead astray; I lead him astray, *nin wanishima.*

Lead away; I lead him away, *nin mâdjiwina.* I endeavor to lead him away, *nin wikwatchiwina.* I lead him away on a cord, *nin sâgabigina.*

Lead back; I lead him, (her, it,) back, *nind ajêwina, nin giwewina; nind ajêwinân, nin giwewidon.*

Lead in; I lead him in, *nin pindigana.* (Pittukahew.)

Lead out; I lead him out, *nin sâgisia, nin sâgidjiwina.*

Leaf, *anibish.* (Nipïy). There are leaves, (in a bush or shrub,) *anibishikang, megwébag.*—The leaves are budding, *ashkibagad.* The leaves are coming forth, *sâgibaga.* The leaves are falling off, *binâkwi.* The dry leaves make noise, *gaskibaga.* The wind moves the leaves, *gaskibagassin, goshkobagassin.* Red leaf, *miskobag.* There are red leaves, or the leaves are red, *miskobaga.* The tree has red leaves, *miskobagisi mitig.* The leaves are wet, *tipabaga.* The leaves become yellow, *watêbaga.*

Leaf for tea or medicine, *winisikensibag.*

Leak; it leaks, *ondjika.* (Otchikawiw).

Lean; I lean with my head on s. th., *nind assokweshin.* I lean on s. th., *nind asswashin, nind asswadjishimon.* (Asosimow).

Lean, (poor ;) I am lean, *nin pakakados, nind oskanis, nind oskanabewis.* I am extremely lean, *nin gawâkados, nin kashkâkados, nin pakakadwabewis.* (Sikkatchiw).

Leanness, *pakâkadosowin, kushkâkadosowin.*

Leap ; I leap or jump, *nin gwâshkwân.* I leap down, *nin nissigwashkwân.*

Learn ; I learn it, (I want to know it,) *nin wi-kikendan.* I endeavor to learn, *nin nandakikendan.*

Leather, *pashkwêgin.*

Leather-bottle, *pashkwégin-omodai.*

Leather-coat, *pashkwêgino-bâbisikawâgan.*

Leather-legging, *pashkwégino-midass.*

Leather-manufactory, *assekêwigamig.*

Leather-manufacturer, *assekéwinini.*

Leather-string for snowshoes, *ashkimaneiâb.* Narrow leather-string, *bishâganâb..*

Leave ; I leave him, (her, it,) *nin nagana, nin pakewina ; nin nagadan, nin pakewidon.* I leave him, (her, it,) flying away for safety, *nin nagadjinijima, nin nagajinijima ; nin nagadjinijindan, nin nagajinijindan.* I leave him in a stealthy manner, *nin gimodjikana.* I leave him weeping, *nin mokawiodjima.*

Leaven, *ombissitchigan, jiwissitchigan.*

Leavened ; the bread is leav., *ombissitchigâso pakwejigan.* The bread rises up, (there is leaven in,) *ombishin pakwejigan.*

Leech, *sagaskwâdjime.* There are leeches, *sagaskwâdjimeka.* (Akakkwäy).

Leech-Lake, *Ga-sagaskwadjimekag.*

Left-handed ; I am left-h., *nin namandji.*

Leg, *okâdima.* My, thy, his leg, *nikâd, kikâd, okâd.* The bone of my, thy, his leg, *nikâdigan, kikâdigan, okâdigan.* The right leg, *kitchigâd, okitchigadima.* I have large legs, *nin manangigâde.* I have a long leg, *nin ginogâde.*

Legging, *midâss.* My, thy, his legging, *nidâss, kidâss, odâss.* I have torn leggings, *nin bigodasse.* I have only one legging on, *nin nabanédasse.*

Legging-string, *sagassanojebison.*

Leg of a chair, &c., *okâdetchigan.* It has legs, *okâdetchigâde.*

Lend ; I lend, *nind awiiwe.* I lend it to him, *nind awiâ.* I lend it, (*in. an.*) *nind awiiwen ; nind awiiwenan.*

Lending, *awiiwewin.* (Awihâsuw).

Length ; my, thy, his length, *ekôsiiân, ekosiian, ekôsid.* Its length, *ekosing.* I am (it is) of such a length, *nind akôs ; akôssin, akwâ.*

Lengthen ; I lengthen it, make it long, *nin ginwâton.* I lengthen it out, *nind aniketon.* It is lengthened out, *aniketchigâde.* Lengthening string, *anikôbidjigan.*

Lent, *kitchi giigwishimowin.* (Kitchi-iyewanisihisuwin).

Leper, *wemigid, ketchi-omigid.* I am a leper, *nin kitchi omigi.*
Leprosy, *omigiwin, kitchi-omigiwin.*
Less, *nawatch pangi, nondâss.* (Astameyigok).
Lessen ; I lessen it, *nin pangiwagiton.*
Let alone ; I let him, (her, it) alone, *nin bonima, nin bonia ; nin boniton.* It is let alone, (*in., an.,*) *bonitchigâde; bonitchigâso.*
Let down ; I let him, (her, it) down on a rope, *nin nissibigina, nin bonâbigina ; nin nissâbiginan, nin bonabiginan.* I am (it is) let down, *nin nissâbiginigas, nin bonâbiginigas ; nissabiginigâde, bonâbiginigâde.*
Let go ; I let him, (her, it) go, *nin pagidina, nin pagisikawa ; nin pagidinan, nin pagisikan.* I let him, (her, it) go suddenly, *nin pagidjiwebina ; nin pagidjwebinan.*
Let me see ! *taga ! taga !* (Matte !)
Letter, *masinaigan, nindaiwemasinaigan.* Letter *sent, mâdjibiigan.* Letter *received, bidjibiigan.*
Level ; I put level, *nind aindjissiton.*—The country is level, *jingakamiga, tatagwamagad.*
Lever, *ombâkwâigan, agwakidaigan, agwidaigan.*
Lewd ; I am lewd, *nin gagibâdis, nin bishigwâdis.*
Lewdness, *gagibâdisiwin, bishigwâdisiwin.*
Liar, *geginawishkid.* I am a liar, *nin ginawhishk, nin gaginawhishk.* (Okiyâskiw).
Libertine, *pagândjinini, nwadikwewed, nwâdjiikwewed.* I am a libertine, *nin nôdikwewe, nin nôdjiikwewe, nin bishigwâdis.*
Liberty, *dibenindisowin.* I give him liberty, *nin pagidina tchi dibenindisod.*
Lick ; I lick, *nin noskwâdjige, nin noskwâdam.* I lick him, (her, it,) *nin noskwâna ; nin noskwâdan.* I lick s. th. belonging to him, *nin noskwâdamawa.* I lick and suck it, (*in., an.*) *nin sôbandan ; nin sôbama.*
Lie, *pinwâbo.*
Lie, *giwanimowin, ginawishkiwin..* I give him the lie, *nind âbea.*
Lie, tell lies ; I lie, *nin giwanim, anisha nind ikkit.* I tell him a lie, *nin giwanima.* I tell him lies, *nin gaginawishkima.* I am in a habit of telling lies, *nin ginawishk, nin gaginawishk.* I make him tell a lie, *nin ginawishkia, nin giwanimoa.* (Kiyâskiwin).
Lie ; I lie, (I am lying,) *nin jingishin.* I lie down, *nin gawishim.* (Pimisin.) I lie down further there, *nind ikwishin.* I lie down otherwise or somewhere else, *nind andjishin.* I lie (it lies) well, *nin minoshin ; minossin.* I lie wrapped up, *nin wiweginishin.* (We lie two, three, four, etc. together, *nin nij*oshimin, *nin nissoshimin, nin nioshimin,* &c. A piece of wood lies on high, *bimakwamo mitig.* It lies there, (*in., an.*) *bimakwissin ; bimakwishin.*

Life, *bimâdisiwin.* Another life, (in the next world,) *ajida bimâdisiwin*. (Kutak pimâtisiwin). Indian life, *anishinâbe-bimâdisiwin, anishinâbewidjigewin.* — Life everlasting, *kagige bimâdisiwin.* Pure life, *binâdisiwin.* Impure life, *winâdisiwin.*

Lift ; I am lifting with a lever, *nind agwakidaige, nind agwidaige.* I lift him (her, it) with a lever, *nind agwakidâwa, nind agwidâwa ; nind agwakidaan, nind agwidaan.*

Lift up ; I lift up, *nind ombakonige, ombabiginige, nind ombâkobidjige, nind ombakwaige, nind ombinige.* I lift him up, *nin pasigwindina.*

Light, *wâssêiâsiwin, wâssênamowin, wâssêia.* I am in the light, *wâsseianing nind aia, nin wâsseiadis.*

Light, (moon-shine,) it is light, *gijigâte.* (Kijikâstew).

Light ; it is light, *wasséiamagad, wâssétemagad.* I make it light, *nin wâssakwanean.* I make it light for him, *nin wâssakwanéamawa.* I make light a place by burning s. th., *nin wassakwanendjige.* I burn it for a light, *nin wâssakwanendjigen.* I make him (her, it) light, *nin wâsseshkawa ; nin wâsseshkan.*—I light, (set on fire,) *nin sakaan.* I light a pipe, *ninsakaipwâgane, nin biskanepwa.*

Light, (not heavy ;) I am (it is) light, *nin nângis ; nângan.* I find him (her, it) light, *nin nangenima ; nin nangendan.* I make it light, I lighten it, (*in., an.*) *nin nângiton ; nin nângia.* I have a light pack, *nin nângiwane.* (Yâkkasin).

Light-footed ; I am l., *nin nângiside.* Light-footed Indian, *naiângisided anishinâbe.*

Lighthouse, *wâssakwanendjigan.*

Lightning, *wâssamowin, wâssakwaam.* There are lightnings, it lightens, *wâssamowag* (*wâwâssamowag*) *animikig, wassakwaamog* (*animikig.*) Uninterrupted lightnings, *gijigassigewag* (*animikig*). (Wâsaskutepayiw).

Light-timbered ; it is light-timbered, *jigaakwa, jigaakweia,* (Sibeyâskweyaw).

Like..., like as..., *tanassag, tibishko, nindigo.*

Like, *dowa, dowan ; dino, dinowa.* (Tâbiskotch).

Like ; I like him, (her, it), *nin minwénima, nin sâgia ; nin minwendân ; nin sâgiton.*

Liken ; I liken him to somebody, *nind awea.* I liken it to something, *nin aweton.*

Likewise, *nassab, tibishko, tâbishkotch ; mipi dash, mipi dash gaie.*

Lily, *nabagashk, mashkodepinig.*

Limb, *pakesiwin.* I have small limbs, *nin babiwig.* I have large big limbs, *nin mamângig.* I have a hole (wound) in some limb, *nin pagwanes.*

Lime, *wâbâbigan.* I burn lime, *nin wâbâbiganike.*

Lime-burner, *wâbâbiganikewinini.*

Limekiln, *wâbâbiganikân.*

Linden-bark, *wigob.*

Linden-tree, *wigob, wigobimij.* (Nipisïy).

Line, *biminakwân, biminakwânens*. Line on the upper and under border of a fish net, *jinodagan*.

Line ; I line, *nin bitogwadjige*. I line it (*in., an.*), *nin bitogwadan ; nin bitogwana*.

Linen ; *assabâbiwegin*.

Lining, *bitogwadjigan, bitogwasson*.

Lion, *mishibiji*.

Lip ; my, thy, his lips, *nindon, kidon, odon*. — My lips are cracked, sore, *nin gipidon, nin gagipidon*.—On the lips only, *ogidjidon*.

Liquid ; it has the appearance of such a liquid, *inâgami*. It is a bad liquid, *mânâgami*. I find this liquid has a bad taste, *nin mânâgamipidan*. It is a good liquid, *minwâgami*. I find this liquid has a good taste, *nin minwâgamipidan*. It is a clean liquid, *binâgami*. It is a dirty l., *winâgami*. It is an excellent liquid, *wingâgami*. It is a thin liquid, *jigaagami*. I make it thin, *nin jigaâgamiton*. - Something is in a liquid state, *jogamamagad*. It is brought to a liquid state, *jogamamagad*. It is brought to a liquid state, *jogamitchigâde*. I make it liquid, (*in., an.*) *nin jogamiton ; nin jogamia*. I make pitch liquid, *nin jogamia pigiw*. The pitch is in a liquid state, *jogamisi pigiw*.

Liquor, ardent liquor, *ishkotewâbo*. I like liquor, *nin wingâgamandjige*.

Liquor-house, *minikwêwigamig, siginigéwigamig*.

Liquor-selling, *siginigewin*.

Liquor-selling license, *siginigemasinaigan*.

Listen ; I listen, *nin pisindam*. I listen with pleasure, *nin minotam*. It listens with pleasure, *minotamomagad*. I listen to him, (her, it,) *nin pisindawa ; nin pisindân*.—I listen to him (her, it) : With apprehension or danger, *nin nanisanitawa ; nin nanisanitan*. With astonishment, *nin mamakasitawa ; nin mamakasitan*. With attention, *nin nâgasotawa ; nin nâgasotan*. With displeasure, *nin jingitawa, nin migoshkasitawa ; nin jingitan, nin migoshkasitan*. With fear, *nin sêgitawa ; nin ségitân*. With pleasure, *nin minotawa ; nin minotân*. With sorrow, *nin wassitâwitawa ; nin wassitawitân*. With trouble of mind, *nin wanishkwetawa ; nin wanishkwetân*.—I listen to him with the impression that he is telling or recommending difficult things, *nin sanagitawa*. I listen to him with the impression that he talks foolishly, absurdly, *nin gagibâsitawa*. (Nandottawew).

Listen, (obey ;) I listen, *nin babâmitam*. I listen to him, *nin babâmitawa*. I listen to myself, *nin babamitas*. (Nanahittawew).

Little, a little, *pangi, naégâdam*. —(Apisis). Very little, *pangishê, agâwa*. I am of a little number, *nin naiêtawis*. There is little of it, *naiétawad, manéinad, âgassinad, pangiwagad*. There is little of it, (*an.* obj.,) *pangiwisi, pangiwagisi, naiétawisi.* We are in a little number, *nin pangiwagisimin.* — There is very little of it, (*in., an.*) *pangishéwagad ; pangishéwagisi.* We are very little of us, *nin pangishéwagisimin.*—I reduce it to little, *nin pangiwagiton.*

Little girl's Point, *Gaangwâssagokag.*

Live ; I live, *nin bimâdis.* It lives, *bimâdisimagad, bimâdad.* I live of new, *nind ajita-bimâdis.* I live in a certain place, *nin danaki.* I live in peace in a certain place, *nin wanaki.* I live in different places, *nin baba-ainda, nin babamâdis.* I live with him in the same place or country, *nin wishkanakiwema, nin widjidakiwema, nin wishdanakima.*—I live like a beaver, *nind amikwâdis.* I live like an Indian, *nind anishinâbebimâdis.* I live in the Indian country, *nind anishinâbeki.* I live in a village with others, *nin bimige.* We live together in a village, *nin bimigéidimin.* We live or dwell together, *nin mamawigemin, nin widigendimin.*

Live, make live ; I make live, *nin bimâdjiiwe.* I make him (her, it) live, *nin bimâdjia ; nin bimâdjiton.* I make myself live, *nin bimâdjiidis.* I make live to me s. th., *nin bimâdjitamas, nin bimâdjitamodis.*

Liver, *bemâdisid.* My fellow-liver, *nidji-bimâdisi.*

Liver, *okonima.* My, thy, his liver, *nikôn, kikôn, okôn.* I have a large liver, *nin mângikone.* I have a small liver, *nind agâssikone.*

Lizard, *ogikadânangwe.* Red lizard, *kwiwisens.* Another kind of lizard, *otawagameg.*

Lo ! *na ! bina ! gowengish ! nashke ! nâginin ! wegwâgi !*

Loach, (fish,) *misäi.*

Load, carried on the back, *bimiwanan.*

Load ; I load a gun, *nind onashkinadon pâshkisigan.* The gun is loaded, *onashkinâde pâshkisigan.*

Lock, *abâbikaigan*, or rather, *kashkâbikaigan.* I make locks, *nin kashkâbikaiganike.*

Lock ; I lock it, *nin kashkâbikaan.*

Locked ; it is locked, *kashkâbikaigâde.*

Locust, *adissawaieshi.* (Papakinês).

Lodge, *wigiwâm.* (Apakkwâsun). Lodge of cedar-bark, *wanagekogamig.* Lodge of birch-bark, *wigwassiwigamig.* Round lodge, *wâginogan.* I live in a round lodge, *nin wâginoge.* Pointed lodge, *nassawaogan.* I live or dwell in a pointed lodge, *nin nassawaoge.* In the lodge, *pindigamig.* In the back part of the lodge, *giskabag.* On the top of the lodge, *ogidigamig.* Between two lodges, *nassawigamig.*—I make or build a lodge, *nind ojige.* I make another lodge, *nind ândjige.* I lodge or live in the lodge, *nin da.* I live in the first lodge, *nin nitamige.* I live in the last lodge, *nind ishkwége.* We live in two, three, four lodges, etc., *nin nijogamigisimin, nin nissogamigisimin, nin niogamigisimin*, etc. Two, three lodges, etc., *nijogamig, nissogamig*, etc. So many lodges, *dassogamig*.

Lodge-mat, *apâkwei*. (Anâskasun).

Lodge-pole, *abâj*. (Apasüy)

Log, *mitig*. The end of a log, *wanakwâtig*.

Log-canoe, *mttigo-tchimân*.

Log-house, *wâkaigan, mitigowâkaigan*. I build a log-house, or live in a log-house, *nin wâkaige*.

Log for a house, *wâkaiganâtig, wâkaiganak*.

Log for a sawmill, *mitig kashkibosod, mitig ge-tâshkibosod*.

Log-saw, cross-saw, *kitchi kishkibodjigan*.

Lonesome ; I feel lonesome, *nin kashkendam, nin mamidawendam*. It is l., *kashkendâgwad*.

Long ; I am long, (tall,) *nin ginos*. I have a long (slender) body, *nin ginwâbigiiawe*. It is long, *ginwâmagad, ginonde, ginwaiakossin*. It is long : Metal, *in., ginwâbikad* ; metal, *an., ginwâbikisi* ; string, *in., ginwâbigad* ; string or thread, *an., ginwâbigisi* ; stuff, *in., ginwêgad* ; stuff, *an., ginwêgisi* ; wood, *in., ginwâkwad* ; wood, *an., ginwâkosi*.

Long, a long time, *ginwenj, kabéaii, naiânj*. Long every time, *gagânwenj*. It is long, it lasts long, *pitchâ*.—Long ago, *mêwija*. As long as..., *apitch*. (Kayâs).

Long, (wish ;) I long after him, *nin wikodenima*. I long after s. th., *nin mamidawendam*. (Kwitaweyimew).

Long-suffering, *bekadendâgosiwin*.

Long-suffering ; I am l., *nin bekadendâgos*.

Look, *inâbiwin*. (Itâbiwin).

Look ; I look (it looks) somewhere, *nind inâb ; inâbimagad*. I look at him, (her, it,) *nin ganawâbama ; nin ganawâbandan*. I look at myself, *nin ganawâbandis*.

Look for ; I look for, (especially in hunting or fishing,) *nin nandawendjige*. Looking for, *nandawendjigewin*.

Look like...; I look (it looks) like..,*nind ijinâgos;ijinâgwad*.

Look on ; I look on, *nin wâbange*.

Look out ; I look out, *nind akawâb*. I look out for him, (her, it,) *nind akawâbama ; nind akawâbandan*.

Look upwards ; I look upwards, *nin dâtagab, nin dâtaganab*.

Look with hope ; I look on with hope, *nin pagossâbange*. I look at him with hope, *nin pagossâbama*.

Looking-glass, *wâbmotchichâgwan*. (Wâbamun).

Loon, *mang*. Young loon, *mangons*. Loon's foot, *mangosid*. Loon's louse, *mangodikom*.

Loose ; I am loose, *nin pagidjiaia*. I get loose, *nind abiskota*. It gets loose, *abiskokamagad, abiskosse*. It is loose, *gêshawishka, neshangissemagad*.

Loosen ; I loosen him, (her, it,) *nind âbawa, nind âbiskona ; nind âbiskobidon*.

Loosened ; it is loosened, *âbiskobide, âbiskôbidjigâde.*
Loquacity, *osâmidonowin.*
Lord, (God,) *Debêndjiged.* Our Lord, *Debeniminang.*
Lord, (master), *debéndjiged.* I am lord or master, *nin dibendjige.*
Lose ; I lose, *nin wanitass, nin wanitage.* I lose him, (her, it,) *nin wania ; nin waniton.* I lose myself, *nin waniidis.* I lose s. th., belonghing to him, *nin wanitawa, nin wanitamawa.* I lose all, in gaming, *nin tchâginâgo.*
Lose, (drop, let fall ;) I lose it, (*in., an.*) *nin pangissiton ; nin pangishima.*
Lose, (ruin ;) I lose property, *nin banâdjitass.* I lose him, (her, it,) *nin banâdjia ; nin banâdjiton.*
Lose sight ; I lose sight, *nind angwâbandjige, banâbandjigé.* I lose sight of him, (her, it,) *nind angwâbama, nin benâbama ; nind angwabandan, nin banâbandan.* (Wanâbamew).
Lose time ; I lose my time by drinking liquor, *nind ondamibi.* I make people lose their time, *nind ondamiiwe.* I make him lose his time by talking to him, *nind ondamima.* (Otamimew).
Losing ; I am losing myself, or losing property, *nin banâdis, nin babanadis.*
Loss, losing, *banâdisiwin, banâdjitassowin, banadjiiwewin.* (Wanittâwin).
Loss, at a loss, I am at loss for..., *nin wawanis.* I am at a loss to do s. th., *nin wawanidodam.*
Lost : it is lost, (*in., an.*) *banâdad, banâdjitchigâde ; banâdisi, banâdjitchigâso.* I am (it is) considered lost, *nin banâdendâgos ; banâdendâgwad.* I consider him (her, it) lost, *nin banâdenima ; nin banâdendan.* I consider myself lost, *nin banâdenindis.*
Lot ; we cast lots, *nind atâdimin.* I cast lots for it, (*in., an.*) *nind atandikandan ; nind atandikana.*
Loud, *enigok ; epitoweng.* I speak loud, *nin kijiwe.* I call loud, *nin bibâg.*
Louse, *ikwa.* I have lice, *nind odikon.* (Otikkumiw.) I search lice, *nin nandomakome, nin nodjidikome.* I searce lice on his head, *nind nandonassa.* I crack lice, *nin pâshkidjikome.*
Love, *sâgiiwewin, sâgiidiwin.*
Love ; I love, *nin sâgiiwe.* I love him, (her, it,) *nin sâgia ; nin sâgiton.* I love him in thoughts, *nin sâgienima.* I love myself, *nin sâgiidis.* We love one another, *nin sâgiidimin.*—I am loved, *nin sâgiigos.*
Love-letter, *sâgiiwe-masinaigan.*
Love-medicine, *sâgiidi-mashkiki, sâgiiwe mashkiki, gegibâdak mashkiki.*
Lover, *saiâgiiwed.*
Low ; it is low, *tabassamagad.* It is low, (thin,) *tabassansika.*
Low, (below,) *tabashish.*
Low, (in s. in.) S. Cheap.
Low, (mean ;) I am low, *nin tabassadis.* I esteem him (her, it) low, *nin tabassenima ; nin tabassendân.* I esteem myself low, *nin tabassénim, nin ta-*

bossénindis. I am (it is) esteemed low, considered low, *nin tabassendâgos ; tabassendâgwad.*

Lower ; I lower it, put it lower, (*in., an.*) *nin tabassaton,* or *nin tabâssiton,nin tabâssinan ; nin tabâssia, nin tabâssina.* I lower myself, *nin tabâs.*—It lowers, *newishkamagad.*

Luck ; good luck, *jawendâgosiwin, minwabamewisiwin,* (papêwewin,) *onwâsiwin.* Bad luck, *massagwâdisiwin.* (Mayakusiwin).

Lucky ; I am lucky, *nin jawendagos , nin minwabamewis, nind onwas.* (Papewew). (I am unlucky, *nin massagwâdis.*) (Mayakusiw.)

Lull; I lull him to sleep,*ninnibea.*

Lunatic, *gawânadapined.* I am a lunatic, *nin giwanâdapine.*

Lungs ; my, thy, his lungs, *nipan, kipan, opan.*

Lurk ; I lurk, *nind akando.* I lurk for somebody, *nind akamawe.* I lurk for him, *nind akamawa.*

Lurking, *akamawewin.*

Lust. S. Concupiscence.

Lustre ; it has a lustre, (stuff, *in., an.*) *wâssikwegad ; wâssikwegisi.* I give it a lustre, (*in , an.*) *nin wâssikwegîton, nin wâssikwegaan ; nin wâssikwegia, nin wassikwegâwa.*

Lying down ; I am lying, *nin jingishin.* It is lying there, *jingishinomagad.* I am lying in a fatiguing way or manner, *nind ishkâkoshin.*—S. Lie.

Lying, (telling lies,) *giwanwi,* lie, *ginawishkiwin.* Lying habit, *gaginawishkiwin.* (Kiyâskiskiwin.)

Lynx, *bisîw.*

Lynx-skin, *bisîwaiân.*

M

Mackinaw or Mackinac, *Makinang, Mishinimakinang.*
Mackinaw-boat, *nabagitchimân, kitchi mitigotchimân.*
Mad ; I am mad, *nin giwanâdis.* (Kiiskwew).
Made ; it is made, (*in., an.*) *ojitchigâde, gijitchigâde, ijitchigâde, gijikikâde ; ojitchigâso, gijitchigâso, ijitchigâso, gijikigâso.*
Madness, *giwanâdisiwin.*
Magic, *mamandjitchigewin, mamandjinowin, sassagodisiwin.* I pratice magic, *nin mamandjitchige, nin mamandjin, nin sassagodis..*
Magician, *mamandjitchigewinini, mamandjinowinini, sassagodisiwinini.*
Magistrate , *dibakonigewinini.* (Wiyasuwewiyiniw).
Magnificent ; it is mag., *kitchi onijishin, bishigendagwad.*
Magpie, *apishgâgagi.* A kind of small magpie, *gwingwishi.*
Maid, *oshkinigikwe, weshkinigid ikwe.* I am a maid, *nind oshkinigikwew.* S. Virgin.
Maid, *anokitâgekwe, bamitâgekwe, banikwe.*
Majesty, *kitchitwâwisiwin.*
Make ; I make it, (*in., an.*) *nind ojiton, nin gijiton, nin gijikân ; nind ojia, nin gijia, nin gijikawa.* I can make it, I use to make it, (*in., an.*) *nin nitâwiton ; nin nitâwia.* I don't know how to make it, I make it at random, (*in., an.*) *nin pagwanawiton ; nin pagwanawia.* I make s. th. badly, negligently, *nin mamâjimâdji.* I make s. th. for somebody, *nind ojitâge, nin gijitâge.* I make it for him or to him, *nind ojissitamâwa, nind ojitawa, nind ojitamâwa, nin gijitawa, nin gijitamâwa.*
Make be ; I make him (her, it) be this or that, *nind âwia, nind awekana ; nind âwiton, nind awekadan.* I make myself be this or that, *nind âwiidis.*
Male, man, *inini, anini.* (Iyiniw, nâbew).
Male bear, male beaver, etc. S. Bear, Beaver, etc.
Male being, *nâbé-aiaa.*
Male of animals, *aiabe, nâbé,* (in compositions).
Male of birds, *nâbésse.*
Male of fish, *nâbémeg.*
Male's skin, *aiâbéwaiân, nâbéwaiân.*
Malice, malignity, *matchi ijiwebisiwin, matchi bimâdisiwin, manjininiwagisiwin.*
Malicious, malign, malignant, *matchi.* I am mal., *nin matchi ijiwebis, nin manjininiwagis.*

It is mal., *manadad, matchi ijiwebad.* I make him mal., *nin matchi ijiwebisia.*

Malicious joy, *gagândenimowin.* I have a malicious joy over his grief, etc., *nin gagândenima.* I express in words a mal. joy over his grief, etc., *nin gagandjididema.* I express a mal. joy over people's grief, etc., *nin gagandjigitage.*

Mallet, *mitigo-pakitêigan, tagwaadonênak.*

Man, (human being,) *anishinâbe.* I make myself man, *nind anishinâbewiidis.*

Man, male, *inini, anini.* I am a man, *nind ininiw.* I make myself man, *nind ininiwiidis.* —Big stout man, *missâbe.* I have a stout big body, I am a big man, *nin mitchâbêwis.*

Man that has no more a wife, *pijigwabe.* I am a man who has no more a wife, *nin pijigwabew.* (Môsâbew).

Manchester, *mashawesid senibâwegin.*

Mandate, *ganâsongewin.*

Manifest; I man. it to him, *nin missâbandaa.*

Manger, *wissiniwâgan, pijikiwiwissiniwâgan.* (Maskusiwâjiwatchigan).

Mangy, *wemigid.* I am mangy, *nind omigi.*

Manners, *ijiwebisiwin.*

Manominee Indian, *Manômini.*

Manominee squaw, *manôminikwe.*

Mansion, *abiwin.*

Many, *nibiwa, nibina.* (Mitchet.) We are many, *nin nibiwagisimin, nin batainimin, nin mishinimin, nin mishinomin.* We are many together, *nind okwinomin, nind okwinimin, nin bimiokwinomin.* We are very many, *nind osâminimin, nind osâminomin.* We are so many, *nind ijinimin, nind ijinomin, nind inigokwinimin, nind inigokwinomin.* — There are many *in.* objects, *nibiwagadon, batainadon, mishinadon.* There are very many, *osâminadon.* There are so many *in.* objects, *mi endassing.*

Maple. S. Maple-tree.

Maple-forest, *mânakiki.*

Maple-Point, *Nemânakiki.*

Maple-sap; the maple-sap runs quick, *kijiga,* or *kijigawan ininatigon.* The maple-sap runs no more, *ishkwaga.* The sugar tastes the spoiled maple-sap, *ishkwagapogwad sisibâkwat.* Last sugar made of the spoiled maple-sap, *ishkwaga-sisibâkwat.*

Maple-syrup, *jiwâgamisigan.*

Maple-sugar, *sisibâkwat, nesséiigan.* (Sisibâskwat).

Maple-sugar resembling pitch, *pigiwisigan.*

Maple-tree, *ininâtig, assanâmij.* (Sisibâskwatâttik).

Maple-wood, *ininâtigossag.*

March, *onâbani-gisiss.* (Niskipisim).

March; I march, *nin bimosse.* I march foremost, *nin nigânosse, nin maiâosse.* A man that marches foremost, *nigânossêwinini, naiaossewinini.*

Mare, *ikwé-bebejigoganji.* (Kiskisis).

Mariner, *nâbikwâninini.*

Mark, *kikinawâdjitchigan, kiki-*

nawâdjion, kikinawâdjiowin, beshibiigan, *masinibiigan*. Any thing to make marks upon, *masinaigan*.

Mark, (make marks ;) I mark, *nin kikinawâdjitchige*, *nin kikinawâdjiiwe,nin beshibiige, nin masinaige, nin masinibiige, nind ojibiige.* I mark him, (her, it,) *nin kikinawâdjia, nin beshibia, nin masinibia, nind ojibiwa ; nin kikinawâdjiton, nin beshibian, nin masinibian, nind ojibian.* — Making marks, *masinaigewin, beshibiigewin.*

Mark (for travelers), *kikâigan.* I make marks on the road, *nin kikaige.* I make marks for him on a road or trail, *nin kikitawa, nin gikaamâwa.* I tell him a mark, *nin kikinawâdjitawa.*

Marked ; I am (it is) marked, *nin kikinawadji, nin kikinawâdjitchigas, nin kikinawâdendagos* , *nin masinaigas* ; *kikinawadjitchigâde* , *kikinawadendâgwad, masinaigâde.*

Market, *atâwewin.*

Marksman, *ga-godaakwed, gwedaakwed.*

Marriage, *widigewin, widigendiwin.* (Ayamihewikittuwin). Christian marriage, Sacrament of Matrimony, *anamie-widigendiwin, anamie-nibâwiwin.* Lawful marriage for lifetime,*âpitchi-widigendiwin.* I give in marriage, *nin wiwikage.* I join him (her) in marriage, *nin widigendaa* , *nind âpitchi-widigendaa.*

Married ; I am married, *nin widige.* I am married to her, (him,) *nin widigema.* We are m. together, *nin widigendimin.* I am m. according to the rites of the church, *nind anamie-widige.* I am m. lawfully, for lifetime, *nind âpitchi-widige.* I am m. to her (him) for lifetime, *nind âpitchi-widigema.* We are m. together for lifetime, *nind âpitchi-widigendimin.*

Married state , *widigendiwin.* (Single state, *oshkinigiwin.*)

Marrow, *win.* Marrow-bone, *winigan.* (Wini).

Marry ; I marry, *nin wiwikodâdis.* I marry her, *nin wiwima, nîn wiwiman.* We marry, *nin wiwikodadiimin.*

Marry, (join parties in marriage ;) I marry him, (her,) *nin widigendaa.*

Marsh, *mashkig, wâbashkiki.*

Marsh-partridge, *mashkodésse.*

Marten, *wâbijeshi.* (Wâbistân).

Marten-skin, *wâbijéshiwaiân.*

Martyr, *anamiewin wendjinânind.*

Mask, *banishkwatagan.*

Mask ; I mask, *nin banishkwatage.*

Mason , *wâkaigewinini, assiniwâkaigewinini.*

Masonry, *wâkaigewin, assinikwâkaigewin.*

Mass, *anamessikewin.* I say mass, *nind anamessike.* I say m. for somebody, *nind anamessikage.* I say m. for him, *nind anamessikawa.* I say m. for me, *nind anamessikas.* The time of mass, *anamessikewinagad.* (Kitchitwa-pakitinâsuwin).

Massacre, *nissidimin.* (Nipahituwin).

Mass-book, *anamessike-masinaigan.*

Massive, massy ; it is massive, *mitchâmagad.*

Mass-prayer, *anamessike - anamiewin.*

Mass-vestment, *anamessike-agwiwin.*

Mast, *ningassimononâtig, ningassimononak.*

Master, *debendang, debendjiged, debeninged, nagânisid ;* I am master, *nin dibendjige, nin dibeninge, nin nigânis ; nin kikinoamâge.* I am my own master, *nin dibenindis ; nin kikinoamas, nin kikinoamadis.*

Mastery, *dibeningêwin, dibendjigewin, nigânisiwin.*

Mat, floor-mat, *anâkan.* (Lodge-mat, *apakwei.*) I make a mat, *nind anâkanike.* The making of mats, *anâkanikewin.*

Match, *ishkotens,* (little fire.) (Kutawâgan).

Match ; I match it, (*in., an.*) *nin bassikodan ; nin bassikona.*

Matching-plane, *bassikodjigan.*

May, *wâbigoni-gisiss.* (Opiniyâwewipisim).

Me, *nin, nind.* (Niya).

Meadow, *mashkossikan, manashkossiwan , mashkode.* — S. Prairie.

Mean, *matchi.* It is mean, *manadad, tabassendâgwad.*

Measles, *miskwajewin.* I have the measles, *nin miskwaje.*

Measure, *dibaigan.*

Measure ; I measure, *nin dibaige.* I m. it, (*in., an.*) *nin dibaigen ; nin dibaigenan.*

Measurement ; measuring, *dibaigewin.*

Measurer, *debaiged, dibaigewinini.*

Meat, *wîiâss.* I make meat, (procure meat,) *nin wiiâssike.* A piece of meat, *misiâ.* I cut meat into pieces, *nin misiâke.* Dried smoked meat, *gaskidê wiiâss, gaskiwiiâss, gaskiwag.* (Kâkkiwok.) I dry and smoke meat, *nin gaskidé-wiiâssike, nin gaskiossige.*

Medical-root for head-ache, *sassabikwân.*

Medicine, *mashkiki, nanândowiowin.* I make or prepare medicine , *nin mashkikike.* Liquid medicine, *mashkikiwâbo.* I prepare liquid medicine, *nin mashkikiwâboke* I give medicine, *nin nanândawiiwe.* I give him m., *nin nanândawia* I prepare m. for him to drink, *nin mashkikiwâbokawa.*

Medicine-bag, *pindjigossan.*

Meditate. S. Reflect.

Meditation, *nanagatawendamowin.* Religious meditation, *anamienanagatawindamowin .*

Meek ; I am meek, *nin bekâdis, nin kijewâdis.* I am meek, (kind, patient,) towards him, *nin nokâdisitawa, nin bekâdisitawa.* (Yospisiw).

Meekness, *bekâdisiwin, nokâdisiwin.* I treat him with meekness, *nin nokadisitawa, nin nokadisitamâwa.*

Meet ; I meet, *nin nagishkâge, nin nakweshkâge.* I meet him, (her, it,) *nin nagishkawa, nin nakweshkawa ; nin nagishkan, nin nakweshkan.* I meet him (her, it) in a canoe, *nin nagawa ; nin nagaan*. I go to meet him, *nind asikawa*. We meet each other, *nin nagishkodâdimin, nin nakweshkodâdimin*. I try to meet, *nin nandanagishkâge, nin nandanakweshkage*. I try to meet him, *nin nandanagishkâwa, nin nandanakweshkawa*.

Meeting, (on the road,) *nagishkodâdiwin, nakweshkodâdiwin*.

Meet, (assemble ;) we meet, *nin mâmawiidimin, nin mawandijidiwin*.

Meeting, (assembling,) *mâwandjiidiwin*.

Meeting-house, *mawandiwigamig*. Religious meeting-house, *gagikwêwigamig, anamiêwigamig*.

Melancholic ; I am mel., *nin goshkwawâdis, nin goshkwawâdendam*.

Melody, *inwewin*. I give a certain melody or tune to a hymn, *nind inweton*.

Melon, *eshkwandaming*.

Melt ; I melt it, (*in., an.*) *nin ningikosan ; nin ningikoswa*. It melts, (*in., an.*) *ningikode. ningide ; ningikoso, ningiso*. I melt it, (metal, *in., an*.) *nin ningabikiswa*. It melts, (metal, *in., an.*) *ningabikide ;ningabikiso*. I melt snow, *nin ningashkobissige*. (Tikkipeswew) The snow melts, *ningiso gon*.

Melt, let melt ; I let it melt in my mouth, (*in., an.*) *nin ninganendan ; nin ninganema*. (Tikkisam).

Memory, *mikwendamowin,, mikwendassowin,takwendamowin, mindjimendamowin*. (Kiskisiwin.) I keep in memory, *nin mindjimêndam, nin takwendam*. I keep him (her, it) in mem., *nin mendjimenima, nin takwenima ; nin mindjimendân, nin takwendân*. (Kiskisototawew.) I recall s. t. to his mem., *nin mikawâma, nin mikwândamawa, nin mikwéndawia*. I recall s. th. often to his mem.,*nin mamikawama, nin mamikwêndamawa , nin mamikwêndamia*. (Miskawâsomew).

Mendicant, *nendotamaged, bebanandotamaged*.

Mendicity , *nandotamagewin , baba-nandotamagewin*.

Merchandise, *anokadjigan;gishpinadagan*. (Ayowinis).

Merchant, *atâwêwinini*.

Mercy, *jawéndjigewin, jawéningewin, jawénindiwin*. (Kijewâtisiwin.) I have mercy, *nin jawendjige, nin jaweninge*. I have m. on him, (her, it,) *nin jawenima ; nin jawendân*. (Kitimâkeyimew.) I have m. on myself, *nin jawenindis*. We have m. on one another, *nin jawenindimin*. I look upon him with mercy, *nin jawendamiganawâbama*. I hear him or listen to him with m., *nin jawêndamitawa*. I speak to excite mercy on me, *nin jawendamitâgos*.

Merriment, *bapinenimowin, jomiwâdisiwin*.

Message, *ininajaogowin*. (Itisahamâtuwin.)

Messenger, *ininajawâgan, ijinajawâgan, eninajaond*.

Metal, *biwâbik*. On metal, *mitâbik*. In the midst of metal,

nâwâbik. One object of metal, *bejigwâbik.* Two, three objects of metal, *nijwâbik, nisswâbik.* So many objects of metal, *dasswâbik.*
Meteor, *tchingwan.*
Middle ; in the middle, in the midst, *nassawaii, nissawaii, nawaii.* It is the middle, the centre, *nawaiiwan, nassawaiiwan.* (Tâwâyik).
Middle-finger, *nâwinindj.* (Tâwitchitchi).
Middle part of a mocassin, ornamented, *apingwéigan.* (Asesin.)
Middling, *eniwek, gomâ minik.* (Eyiwek).
Midnight, *abitâtibikad.*
Midwife, *gatiniwekwe.* A good practical midwife, *neta-gatiniwed.* A man (physician) practising midwifery, *gatiniwewinini.*
Midwifery, *gatiniwewin.*
Milch-cow, *sâninind pijiki.* I milk a cow, *nin sinina pijiki,* (Yikinew onitjâniwa).
Mild weather ; it is mild, *âbawa, âbawamagad.*
Military Fort, *jimâganishiodena.*
Military man, soldier, *jimâganish.*
Military Officer, *jimâganishiogima, minissino-ogima.*
Milk, *totoshâbo.* I milk a cow, *nin sinina pijiki.* I milk a cow thourougly, *nin wingêsinina pijiki.*
Milk-house, *totoshâbowigamig.*
Milky Way, *tchibekana.*
Mill. S. Grindmill. Sawmill.
Miller, *bissibodjigewinini.*
Million, *midâsswâk dassing midâsswâk.*
Milliped, *baiatinogâded, wemâkwaiani.*
Mill-stone, *bissibodjiganâbik.*
Milt, *wiss.*
Milwaukie, * *Minéwag.*
Mind ; I make up my mind, *nind gijendam, nin gijenindis.* I put it in his mind, *nin mindjimissitawa, nin mindjimissitamawa.* (Mitjimeyimew).
Mind ; I mind him, (her, it,) *nin babamenima ; nin babamendan.* (Pisiskeyimew).
Minded ; I am (it is) minded, taken care of, *nin babamendjigas ; babamendjigâde.*
Mine, *nin.* (Niya).
Mine, *biwâbikokân,* (in general.) I work in a mine, *nin biwâbikoke.*
Miner, *biwâbikokêwinini,* (in general.)
Miner in a copper-mine, *miskwâbikokéwinini,* (properly.)
Miner in an iron mine, *biwâbikokéwinini,* (properly.)
Miner in a lead-mine, *ashkikomanikêwinini,* (properly.)
Mining ; I am mining, (in general,) *nin biwâbikoke.* I am mining in a copper-mine, lead-mine, etc. S. Copper-mine, Lead-mine, etc.
Mining Agent, *biwâbikoké-ogima.*
Mining business, *biwâbikokêwin.*
Minister, *gagikwewinini,* (preacher.)
Mink, *jangwêshe.* Young mink, *jangwêshens.* (Sâkwesiw, or, atchakâs).
Miracle, *mamandâdodamowin, kikinawâdjitchigan, maman-*

---

* It is for : *Minowaki,* good land.

dâwanokiwin, *mamakâdjitchigan*. I do wonderful things, I do miracles, *nin mamandâdodam, nin kikinawâdjitchige, mamandâwanoki, nin mamakâdjitchige*. Doing miracles, *mamandawanokiwin, mamakâdjitchigewin*.
Miraculous, wondrous, *mamakâdakamig*.
Mirage, *ombanitewin*. There are mirages, *ombanitemagad*.
Mire, *ajishki*. There is mire, *ajishkika*, *winidjishkiwaga*, *gwanagodjishkiwaga*. (Pasakuskiwokaw).
Mirror, *wâbmotchitchagwan*. (Wâbamun).
Miry; it is miry at the bottom, (a river,) *ajishkiwamika*.
Miscarry; I miscarry, (a woman speaking,) *nin nondêbinike*.
Misconduct, *anotch ijiwebisiwin, matchi ijiwebisiwin*.
Misdeed, *batajitwâwin*. I commit a misdeed, *nin batajiwa*. S. Crime.
Misdemeanor. S. Misconduct.
Miser, *sesâgisid*.
Miserable; I am mis., *nin kitimâgis, nin kotâgis, nin kotâgito*. S. Poor.
Misery, *kitimâgisiwin, animisiwin, kotagisiwin, kotagitowin*.
Misery-River, *Kitchisâgi*.
Miss, (to notice absence;) I miss him, (her, it,) *nin wania; nin waniton*. (Patahwew).
Miss; I miss, (I don't hit,) *nin banaige*. I miss him, (her, it,) *nin bâjia, nin banawa; nin bâjiton, nin banaan*. I miss him (her, it) *shooting, nin bishkonawa, nin medassinawa; nin bishkonan, nin medassinan*. I miss him in my snare, *nin banagwâna*. I miss him (her, it) striking, *nin mêdassaganama; nin mêdassaganandan*. I miss him in my trap, *nin banikona*. I miss him in the road, (âsiskawew,) *nind ajidekawa, nind ajideia, nind answekawa*. I miss him, traveling by water, *nind ajidewa*. (Mwesiskawew).
Missal, *anamessike-masinaigan*.
Missionary, *mekatêwikwanaie*. (Ayamihewiyiniw).
Missive. S. Letter *sent*.
Mist, *awân*. (Kaskawokkamik.)
Mistake, *pitchi-dodamowin*. I say s. th. by mistake, *nit pitchi-ikkit, nin pitchidon*. Mistake in counting, *wanagindassowin*; in doing or acting, *wanidodamowin, wanitchigewin*; in singing, *wanamowin*; in speaking, *wanigijwewin, wanowewin*; in writing, *wanibiigewin, wanibiigan*.
Mistake; I mistake, *nin wanisse, nin pitchi-dodam*. (*Pitchi-*, always alludes to mistake or accident.)
Mistake; I mistake in my calculations or thoughts, *nin pitendam*.
Mistress, *debendjiged, debendang* (*ikwe*). (Okimâskwew).
Mistrust; I mis. him, *nind ashowina*. I mis. his speaking, *nin bewitawa*. I hear a speaking with mistrust, *nin bewitan*. I am heard with mist, *nin bewitagos*. (Moyeyimew).
Misty; it is misty, *awânibissa*.
Misunderstand; I mis., *nin*

wanitam, nin wanitage. I mis. him, (her, it,) *nin wanitawa; nin wanitân.*
Misunderstood ; I am mis., *nin wanitagos.*
Mitre, *Kitchi-mekatêwikwanaie o wiwâkwân.*
Mitten, *mindjikawân.* (Astis).
Mix ; I mix, *nin kiniginige.* I mix it, (*in., an.*) *nin kiniginan, nin kinigina.* (Pimikkew).
Mix, (put in ;) I mix it with s. th., (*in., an.*) *nin dagonan ; nin dagona.*
Mixed ; we are together mixed or mixtly, *nin kinigawâbimin.* We stand together mixed, *nin kinigawigabawimin.* We live together mixed, *nin kinigawigeidimin.* The ducks swim mixed, *jishibag kinigawagomowag.* It is mixed, *kinigawissin, kinigissin.*
Mixed, (put in ;) it is mixed with s. th., *dagonigâde.*
Moccasin, * (Indian shoe,) *makisin.* I make moccasins, *nin makisinike.* The upper part of a moccasin, *agwigagan, apiganegwasson.* I have only moccasins (or shoes) on, *nin mamigoshkam.* I put a moccasin (or shoe) on, without anything in, *nin mamigoshkan makisin.*
Moccasin-string, *makisinêiâb.*
Mock ; I mock, *nin bapinodage, nin nishibapinodage, nin nanâpagansonge.* I speak in a mocking manner, *nin nanâpigigwe, nin nanâpigansitagos.* I mock him, (her, it,) *nin bapidonawa, nin nishibapinodawa, nin nanâpagansoma, nin nanâpagândjiâ ; nin bapinodan, nin nishibaginodan, nin nanâpagasondan, nin nanâpagandjiton.* I mock, repeating words, *nin nanâpidotam.* I mock him, repeating his words, *nin nanâpidotawa.*
Mocker, *neshibapinodang, nenapigijwed, nenapidotang.*
Mockery, mocking language, *nishibapinodagewin, nanâpigijwewin, nanâpidotamowin.*
Model for imitation, *kikinowabandjigan.*
Moderate ; I mod. myself, *nin dibamenim, nin mindjiminidis.*
Moderation, *dibamenimowin, mindjimininidisowin.*
Moisten ; I moisten it, (*in., an.*) *nin tipawadon, nin nissabawadon ; nin tipawana, nin nissabawana.*
Moistened ; it is moistened, (*in., an.*) *tipamagad ; tipisi.*
Molasses of cane-sugar, *sibwâganâbo, kitchi jiwâgamisigan.*
Molassês of maple-sugar, *jiwâgamisigan.*
Mole, *gagibingwekwe, kitchi-gagagibingwekwe, memôkiwido.*
Mole-hill, *memôkiwidowigamig.*
Molest ; I mol. or fatigue him, *nind aiêkwia, nind aiêkosia, nind akoshkawa, nin migoshkadjia.* It molests me, *nind akoshkâgon, nin migôshkâdjiigon.*
Molest, (in s. in.) S. Trouble.
Moment ; one momemt, *ningôpassangwâbiwin, ningo-passangaânâbiwin.* In a moment, suddenly, *sesika.* A moment,

* That word comes from the Indian word : *makisin.*

a short time, *atchina, wênibik.* (Atchiyaw).

Monday, *gi-ishkwa-anamiegijikak.*

Money, *joniia.* Money-box, *joniia-makak.* Money-purse, *joniia-mashkimodens.*

Monkey, *nandomakomeshi.*

Month, *gisiss.* (Pisim.) One month, *ningo gisiss.* I am one month old, *nin ningogisisswagis.* I am two, three months old, *nin nijogisisswagis, nin nissogisisswagis,* etc. I am so many months old, *nin dassogisiss*wagis. It is a month since, *ningogisisswagad.* It is two, three months since, *nijogisisswagad, nissogisisswagad,* etc.

Monthly, *neningogisiss,*

Monthly flowings, *winéwisiwin.* I am in my monthly fl., *nin winêwis, nin wâbandama, agwatching nind aia, âgwatching nin bodawe.* I am in m. fl. for the first time, *nind oshkisagis.*

Montreal, *Moniang.**

Montreal - River, *Gawassidji - wang.*

Moon, *gisiss, tibigisiss, tibikigisiss* The moon is in her first or last quarter, *gisis âbitâwisi.* The m. is growing, *gisiss animitchâbikisi.* The m. is on her decline, *gisiss ani bakwési.* The moon shines no more, *gisiss ishkwaiassige.* It it full moon, *gisiss wâwiiêsi.* The moon has pointed horns, *gisiss patchishkkiwine.* The m. has a circle, *gisiss winibassige.*

Moor-berry, moss-berry. S. Cranberry.

Moose, *mons.* Young moose, *monsons.*

Moose-bone, *monsôgan.*

Moose-horn, *monséshkan.*

Moose-meat, *monswiiâs.*

Moose-skin, *monswêgin.*

Morass, *wâbashkiki.*

More, *nawatch, nibiwa.* (Mitchet).

More, *minawa.*

More and more, *êshkam.* (Atjipiko).

Morning; it is morning, *kigijebâwagad.* In the m., *kigijeb.* This mor., *jêba.* Good morning! *Bo jo!* from the French word: bonjour.

Morning-star, *wâbanang.*

Morrow; to-morrow, *wâbang.* The day after to-morrow, *awâsswâbang.*

Mortar. S. Stamper.

Mortify; I mortify, *nin pigishkanan.*

Mortise; I make a mortise, *nin wimbigaige, nin pagwanéige, nin pagwanêgaige.* I make a mortisc in a piece of wood, *nin wimbigaan mitig.* I put it in a mort., (*in., an.*) *nin pindakossiton; nin pindakoshima.* It is in a mor., (*in., an.*) *pindakosse; pindakoshin.*

Moss-berry. S. Cranberry.

Moss hanging from trees, *missâbendjakon.*

Moss in swamps, *assâikamig.* (Askiya).

Moss on stones in the water, *atagib.*

Moss on trees, (eatable,) *wâkon.*

Most, *mâmawi, âpitchi.*

Mote, any little thing that falls in the eye, *bensiniwin.* I have

* The indian form is given to the French word.

a mote in my eye, something fell in my eye, *nin binsin*. (Pisiniw).

Moth, *totowêsi, kokowesi.*

Mother, *wegimind.* My, thy, his mother, *ningâ, kigâ, ogin.* (Ot. *ningashi,kingashi,ogashiwan.*) I have a mother, *nind ôgi.* I have her for a mother, *nind oginan, nind ogima.* I am a mother, *nind ogimigo.* Like one's own mother, *wegingin.* I have the same mother as he, we have both the same mother, *nin widjogima.* We have all of us the same mother, *nin widjogindimin.* I am like a mother to my younger brothers and sisters, *nind madjikikwewissikandage* I am like a mother to him or her, (my brother or sister,) *nin madjikikwewissikandamâ.*

Mother! *ninge!* (Néga).

Motherhood; my, thy, her motherhood, *ningiwin, kigiwin, ogiwin.*

Mother-in-law; my, thy, his mother-in-law, *ninsigosiss, kisigosiss, osigosissan.*

Motion; I am (it is) in motion, *nin mâdjishka; mâdjishkamagad.* I put it in motion, (*in., an.*) *nin mâdjiskan; nin mâdjishkawa.* (Waskawiw).

Mould, *sigaiganâtig.*

Mould; I mould, *nin sigaige, nin sigaâbowe.* I mould it, *nin sigaân.*—I mould balls, *nind anwike.*

Moulded; it is m., (*in., an.*) *sigaigâde; sigaigâso.* Any moulded object, *sigaigan.*

Moulded sugar-cake, *sigaigan, misiwetchigan.*

Mouldy; it is mouldy, (*in., an.*) *agwagwissin; agwagwishi.* It tastes mouldy, (*in., an.*) *agwagopogwad; agwagopogosi.*—The floor is mouldy, *agwagwissaga.* It is mouldy, (a leaf, or s. th. in leaves,) *agwagobaga.* This tobacco is mouldy, *agwagobagisi aw assêma.* (Akwâkusin).

Moulting; the bird is moulting, *pinigwane bineshi.* The animal is moulting, shedding its fur, *pinewe awessi,* or *pinaweshka.* (Pinawew).

Mountain, *wadjiw.* There is a mountain, *wadjiwan.* Near a mountain, *tchigwadjiw.* There is a group of mountains, *sagadina.* On a mountain, on the top of a m., *ogidadjiw, ogigaki.* I go up on a mountain, *nind ogidadjiwe.* I run up on a m., *nind ogidadjiwebato.* At the foot of a m., *nissâki.* On the other side of a m., *awâssadjiw, awassâki.* I pass a m., I am on the other side of the m., *nin pakidadjiwe.* A mountain, or a spot on a m., from where a place is seen, *sagadinang.* I arrive to such a spot, *nin sagadjiwe.*

Mountainous; it is moun., *papikwadina.*

Mount Olivet, *Bimidêwadjiw.*

Mourn; I mourn, *nin gagidowe.* I mourn, I am in mourning, *nin nitage.* (Sikâwihuw).

Mourner, *netaged.*

Mourner's crape, *nitagêwaiân.*

Mourner's dress, *nitageowin.*

Mournful, (lonesome); it is m., *nitagendagwad.*

Mourning, *nitagewin.*

Mouse, *wawabigonodji.* (Apakusis).
Mouse-trap, *wawabigonodji-dassônâgan.*
Mouth, *odônima.* My, thy, his mouth, *nindôn, kidôn, ôdôn.*— I have a large mouth, *nin mangidon, nin mangânagidon.* It has a large mouth, *mangidonea.* I have a small m., *nind agâssidon.* It has a small m., *agassidonea.* I have an unclean m., *nin winidon.* I have a clean m., *nin binidon.* My mouth is stopped, *nin kashkamakodoneshka.* My m. is swollen, *nin bâgidon.* I put my finger in his m., *nin pindanôna, nin pindanobina, nin pindjidonebina.* I open my mouth, *nin tâwan, nin pakidonen.* I open my m. to him, *nin pakidonetawa.* I open his m., *nin tâwanona, nin pakidonena.* Inside the mouth, *pindjidon.*
Mouthful; one mouthful, *ningotodon, ningotonendjigan.*— (Peyakokunês).
Mouth of a river, *sâgi.* At the mouth, from or to the mouth, *sâging.* The place in the lake round the mouth, *sâgida.* Here is the mouth of the river, *oma sâgidjidjiwan sibi,* or, *sâgiwan sibi.* (Sâkittawaw).
Move; I move or stir, *nin mamâdji, nin mamâdjisse, nin mâmâsika.* I move, sitting, *nin mamâdab.* I move in such a direction, sitting, *nind ijigikab.* It moves, stirs, *mamadjimagad, mamâdjissemagad, mamasikamagad.* I move him, (her, it,) *nin mamâdina, nin mamadjibina, nin mamasikawa; nin mamadinan, nin mamâdjibinan, nin mamasikan.* I move backwards, standing, *nind ajêta.* (Asettew). I move backwards, sitting, *nind ajêb.* I move (or walk) slowly, *nin bêsika.* It moves (or goes on) slowly, *bêsikamagad.*
Move, change places; I move, *nin gos.* (Pîtchiw). I make move, *nin gosia.* I move out of one house into another, *nin sâgidode.* I move away altogether, *nin mâdjidode.* I move with my whole family, *nin kigodewishka.* I move about, *nin babadanis.* I move about on earth, *nin babishagi.* I move about with him, *nin babishagishkawa.* I move to another place or country, *nind ândanaki.*
Mow; I mow, *nin kishkashkijige, nin pashkwashkijige.* I mow it, *nin kishkashkijan, nin pashkwashkijan.* I mow grass, *nin kishkashkossiwe.*
Mower, *keshkashkossiwed, kishkashkossiwewinini.*—S. Harvester.
Mowing, *kishkashkossiwewin.*— S. Harvesting.
Much, *nibiwa, nibina, âpitchi, enigok, gagabâdj, kitchi, ondjita, gwâshkawad, wanina, onina.*—As much as.., *minik.., âpitch.* As much as I can, *epitchiiân.* There is so much of it, *ijinad.* There is much of it, (*in., an.*) *batinad, batainad, nibiwagad, mishinad; batini, bataini, nibiwagisi.* There is very much of, or too much, *osawinad.* (Mistahi, âm).

Much every time, *nenibiwa*.
Much to each *nenibiwa*.
Mud, *ajishki*.
Muddy ; it is muddy, *ajishkiwika*, *nibishkitchishgiwaga*, *gwanagadjishkiwaga*. It is muddy at the buttom, (a river,) *ajishkiwamika*.
Mulatto, *makatéwiiâss*.
Mulatto-woman, *makatêwiiâssikwe*.
Mulberry, *odatagâgomin*.
Mulberry-shrub, *odatagâgominagawanj*.
Mule, *memangishe*, *kitchi memangishe*. (Sosowatim).
Murder, *nishiwewin*, *nishiweshkiwin*. (Nipattâkewin).
Murder ; I murder, commit murder, *nin nishiwe*, *nin nishiweshk*. I murder him, *nin nissâ*. (Nipahew).
Murderer, *neshiwed*, *neshiweshkid*. I am a murderer, *nin nishiwe*, *nin nishiweshk*. (Onipattâkew).
Murmur, *nenawadjimowin*, *gimidômowin*, *gagimidônowin*.
Murmur ; I murmur, *nin gimidon*, *nin gagimidon*. I mur. against him, *nin mindawa*, *nin mindamawa*.
Mushroom, *pikwadjish*, *wajashkwedo*.
Music, *madwewetchigewin*, (producing sounds.) I make music, (produce sounds,) *nin madwewetchige*.
Musician, *madwewetchigewinini*, *medwewetchiged*, *pipigwewinini*, *pepigwed*.
Musket, *pâshkisigan*, *jimâganishipâshkisigan*.
Musketeer, *jimâganish*.
Musket-ball, *anwi*. I am making or moulding or casting musket-balls, *nind anwike*.
Muskrat, or muskcat, *wajashk*. The fur of a musk., *wajashkobiwai*. The skin of a m., *wajashkwaiân*. The hole of a m., *wajashkwaj*. I hunt muskrats, *nin nodajashkwe*, *nin nodjajashkwe*.
Musketo, *sagimê*. There are musketoes, *sagimêka*.
Musketo-bar, musketo-gauze, *sagimêwaiân*.
Mustard, *wessâwag*, *degwandaming*.
Mustard-plant, *osâwanashk*.
Mustard-seed, *osâwanashkominikan*.
Mute-person, *neta-gigitossig*.
Mutton, *manishtanishiwiwiiass*.
Muzzle, . I muzzle him, *nin gibidonena*.
My, *nin*, *nind*. (Niya).
Myself, *nin*, *nin igo*, *niiaw*. (Niyatibiyawe).

N

Nag, *bebejigoganji, bebejigoganjins.*

Nail, *sagâigan.* Small nail, (shingle-nail, tack),*sagâigans.* Large nail, (spike,) *kitchi sagâigan.*

Nail; I nail, *nin sassagâkwaige.* I nail him (her, it) to s. th., *nin sassagâkwâwa, nin badakakwâwa; nin sassagakwaan, nin badakakwaan.*

Nail, (on a finger or toe,) *oshkanjima.* My, thy, his nail, *nishkânj, kishkânj, oshkanjin.* I have long nails, *nin gagânoganji.* I bruise my nail, *nin tatagoganjiodis.* I lose a nail, *nin banaganjishka.* White spot on a nail, *mindawéganjan.* I have white spots on my nails, *nin mindawéganji.* (M'iskasiy).

Nailed; I am (it is) nailed, *nin sassagâkwaigas; sassagâkwaigâde.*

Nail-maker, nail-manufacturer, *sagaiganikewinini.*

Nail-making, nail-manufactory, *sagaiganikewin.*

Naked; I am naked, *nin pingwashâgid.* I lie n., *nin pingwashagidoshin.* I sit n., *nin pingwashagidab.* I walk n., *nin pingwashagidôosse.* I put him naked, *nin pingwashagidobina.* (Moseskatew).

Nakedness, *pingwashâgidiwin.*

Name, *ijinikâsowin, anosowin.* (Winsowin, wiyowin). I have the same name as he, *nin widj'ijinikâsoma.* I have a name, *nind ijinikas.* I have several names, *nin batainonikas, nin mishinonikas.* Glorious or holy name, *kitchitwawinikâsowin.* I have (it has) a glor. holy name, *nin kitchitwawinikas, kitchitwawinikâde.* Ugly name, *manjinikâsowin.* I have (it has) an ugly name, *nin manjinikas; majinikâde.* (Bad name. S. Defame, Defamation. —Changing names. S. Change. Changed.)

Name; I name him (her, it) so.. *nind ijinikana; nind ijinikadan.* I name or mention him, (her, it,) *nin wina; nin windan.* I name him (her, it) frequently, *nin wâwina; nin wâwindan.* I name myself, *nin winidis.* I can name him, (her, it,) *nin gashkiwina; nin gashkiwindan.* (Wiyisuw).

Named; I am (it is) named so.., *nind ijinikas; ijinikâde.* I am (it is) named often, *nin wâwindjigas; wâwindjigâde, winidimagad.*

Name, Named, (in s. in.) S. Call. Called.

Namesake; my, thy, his namesake, *niiawee, kiiawee, wiiaweeian.* He is my namesake, or, I am his namesake, *nin widj'ijinikâsoma.* (Okwimensa).

Name well; I name him (her, it) well, praising, *nin mino-wâwina ; nin mino-wâwindan.*

Narration, *dibâdjimowin.* Decent narration or story, *binâdjimowin.* Indecent narration or story, *winâdjimowin.* (Atjimowin).

Narrow ; it is narrow, (small,) *agassa, agassadea.* It is narrow : cotton, linen, (sâkâwaw), *agassigad, tabashkad;* metal, stone, *in., agassadéiabikad ;* metal, stone, *an., agassadéiabikisi;* ribbon, silk, *agassadesi ;* a road, *agassademo mikana.* — I make it narrow or narrower, (*in., an.*) *nind agassadeton ; nind agassadea.*

Nasty ; I am nasty, *nin winis.* (Wiyipisiw).

Native ; I am a native of a certain place or country, *nin danaki.* I am a n. of the same country as he, *nin widjidakiwema.*

Natural ; it is natural to me, *nind owiiawinodan.*

Nausea. S. Squeamishness.

Navel, *odissima.* My, thy, his navel, *nindiss, kidiss, odis.*

Navigable ; it is navigable, (a river,) *minobiiamagad, bimishkawinagad.*

Navigation, sailing, *bimâshiwin, babamâshiwin ;* not sailing, *bimishkâwin, babamishkâwin.*

Navigator, sailor, *nâbikwâninini.*

Nazarine, *Nazarêwinini, Nazarething daji inini.*

Near, *besho.* It is near, *beshowad.* (Kisiwâk). It is considered near, *beshowendagwad.* I find it near, *nin beshowendan.* I come near him, (her, it,) *nin beshosikawa, nin beshodjia ; nin beshosikan, nin beshodjiton.* It comes near me, *nin beshosikâgon.*

Near by, *tchig', tchigâii.*

Nearly, *géga.* (Kekâtch).

Near together, *bebêsho.*

Neat. S. clean.

Neck, *okwéganama.* (M'ikweyaw). My, thy, his neck, *nikwêgan, kokwêgan, okwégan.* I have a long neck, *nin ginogweiâwe.* I have a short neck, *nin takogweiâwe.* I have a small neck, *nind agâssigweiâwe.* I have a big neck, *nin mangigweiawe.* I have a stiff neck, *nin tchibatakogweiâwe.*

Neck-handkerchief, *moshwe, nâbikagan, nâbikawâgan.* (Tâpiskâgan).

Neck-lace, *nâbikawâgan.*

Need. S. Want.

Needle, *jâbonigan.* I make needles, *nin jâboniganike.*

Needler, *jâboniganikewinini.*

Neglect; I neglect him, (her, it,) *kawin nin babamenimassi ; kawin nin babawendansin.*

Neglected ; I am (it is) negl., *kawin nin babamendjigasossi ; kawin babamendjigadessinon.*

Negligent, neglectful ; I am negl., *kawin nin sagakamisissi.* (Nama pisiskegittam).

Negligently, *mâmanj, têbinâk, kawin, wewêni.*

Negro, *makatewiiâss,* (blackflesh).

Negro woman, *makatewiiâssikwe.*

Neighbor, fellow-man; my, thy, his neighbor, *nidj'anishinâbe, kidj'anishinâbe, widj'anishinâben* ; or, *nidji-bimâdisi, kidji-bimâdisi, widji-bimâdisin.* (N'itj'ayisiyiniw).

Neighbors in a village or town, *bemigeididjig.* We are neighbors, *nin bimigeidimin.*

Neighborhood, (next house or lodge,) *kotaging.*

Neither of them, *kawin awiia nijiwad,* or, *kawin awiia endashiwad.*

Neophyte, *weshki-anamiad.*

Nephew; my, thy, his nephew, *nindojimis, kidojimiss, odojimissan* ; or, *nindojim, kidojim, odojiman.*

Nerve, (or sinew ;) *atiss, atissiwag, odatissiwagoma.* My, thy, his nerve, *nind atissiwag, kid atissiwag, odatissiwagon* ; or, *nindjitad, kidjitad, odjitad.*

Nest, *wasisswan.* The bird builds its nest, *wasisswanike bineshi.* (Watsistun).

Net, *assâb.* Small net, *assâbins.* (Ayapïy). Old bad net, *assâbish.* I make a net, *nind assâbike.* I am getting a net ready for setting, *nind oninassâbi.* I fix or prepare a net to set it, tying stones to it, *nin sasassâgibina assâb.* I set a net or nets, *nin pagidawa.* I go to my nets, or fetch my net or nets, *nin nâdassabi.* I visit my net, *nin ninikinassâbi.* I take a net out of the water, *nin maminassâbi.* The net breaks, *bokotchishka assâb.* I mend a net, *nin wapidassâbi, nin bagwaassabi, nin bagwâwa assâb.* (Misayapew). The net has large meshes, *pâshkisi assâb.* The net has small meshes, *sagôsi assâb.* (Nâtayapew).

Net-stone, *misassin.*

Netting, *assâbikewin.* (Ayapikkewin).

Netting-needle, *nâbîgwaagan.*

Nettle, *masân.*

Nettle-stalk, *masânashk.*

Never, *ka wika, kawin wika.* (Nama wikkâtch).

Nevertheless, *minotch.* (Atawiya).

New, *oshki.* It is new, (*in., an.*) *oshki-aii* or *oshki-aiiwan* ; *oshki-aiaa.* It seems new, it looks new, or like new, (*in., an.*) *oshkinagwad* ; *oshkinagosi.*—Of new, *ajida.* (Kâwi).

New object, (*in., an.*) *oshki-aii* ; *oshki-aiaa,* (young being).

News, *babamâdjimowin.* News brought to some place, *bidâdjimowin.* I send news, *nin mâdjiiadjimoiwe.* I bring news, *nin bidâdjim.*—There are news, *inakamigad.* There are frightful news, *gagwânissagakamigad,* or, *gagwânissâgakamig ejiwebak.* There are good news, *mino inakamigad.* Good news, good tidings, *minwâdjimowin.* I bring good news, *nin bi-minwâdjim.* I tell good news, *nin minwâdjim.* There are great news, *kitchi inakamigad.*

News-paper, *babamâdjimo-masînaigan.*

New Testament, *Oshki-ijitwâwin.*

New-year's day, *anamikodading, odjindiwini-gijigad.* (Otjettuwikijikaw).
Niagara Falls, *Waiânag kakabikawang.*
Niece, my, thy, his niece, *nishimiss, kishimiss, oshimissan.* My, thy, her niece, *nindôjimiss, kidojimiss, odojimissan.*
Nigh, *tchig', tchigaii.*
Nigh. S. Near.
Night, *tibik, tibikad.* Towards night, *anî-tibikad, eni-tibikak.* It is night, *tibikad.* Last night, *tibikong.* At night or by night, *tibikak, tebikâkin.* Every night, *dassing tebikâkin, endasso-tibik, endasso-tibikak.* All night, *kabétibik.*—It is the beginning of the night, *oshkitibikad.* It is late in the night, *ishpitibikad.* It is mid-night, *abita-tibikad.*—I am absent for a night, *nin nikanend.* I remain over night, *nin nikanab.* I spend the night in...., *nin kabêtibikwe.* I spent the whole night indecently, *nin wâbanimassige.* I survive the night, *nin wâbans,nin kabétibikanam.*—It is a bright night, *mijakwanitibikad.* It is a cold night, *kissintibikad.* It is a dark night, *pashagishkibikad, kashkitibikad.*
Nightingale, *gaskaskanedji.* Another kind, *sâsina.*
Nightly, every night, *endasso-tibik, endasso-tibikak.*
Nightly, in the night or at night, *tibikak, tebikâkin.*
Night-meal, *nibâwissiniwin.* I take a night-meal, *nin nibâwissin.*
Nightmare; I am oppressed by the nightmare, *nin badagonig.*
Nightpot, *jigiwinâgan.*
Night-rover, *nebâshkad.* I am night-rover, *nin nibâshka.*
Night-roving, *nibâshkâwin.*
Night-time, *nibâtibik,* (at night.)
Nimble; I am nimble, *nin wadjépi, nin wadjepadis.*
Nine, *jang, jangasswi.* (Kekamitâtat). We are nine of us, *nin jângatchimin.* There are nine *in.* objects, *jangatchinon.*
Nine, *jângasso..*, in compositions, which see in the Second Part.
Ninefold, *jangatching.* (Kekamitâtatwaw).
Nine hundred, *jângasswâk.* We are nine hundred in number, *nin jângasswâkosimin.* There are nine hundred *in.* objects, *jângasswâkwadon.* (Kekamitâtatwawmitano).
Nineteen, *midâsswi ashi jângasswi.*
Nineteenth, *midâtching ashi jângatching.*
Nine thousand, *jângatching mîdâsswak, jangassimidanak.* We are 9000 in number, *nin jangassimidanakosimin.* There are 9000 *in.* objects, *jângassimidanokwadon.*
Nine times, *jângâtching.*
Nine times each or to each, *je, jangatching.*
Ninety, *jangassimidana.* We are ninety of us, *nin jangassimidanawemin.* There are ninety *in.* objects, *jangassimidanawewan.*
Ninth; the ninth, *eko-jangatching.* The ninth time, *jangatching.*
Ninthly, *eko-jangatching.*

Nippe, *ajigan.*
Nippers, *tokwândjigans.*
Nit, *iskinâk.* I have nits, *nind iskinakom.*
No, not, *ka, kawin.* (Nama, namawiya). Not at all, *kawin bâpish, kawessa.* (Nama wâwâtch). No, that won't do, *kawessa mika.*
Noble; I am noble, *nin kitchtiwâwis.*
Nobody, *ka awiia, kawin awiia.* (Nama awiyak).
Nod; I nod, *nin watikwaige.* I nod him, or towards him, *nin watikwaamawa.*
Nod with the head; I nod, *nin nômikwen.* I nod towards him (her, it,) saluting, *nin nomikwetawa; nin nomikwetan.*
Noise, *ombigîsiwin, kiwanisiwin.* (Kiyakittawin). I make noise, *nind ombigis.* I make a foolish noise, *nin kiwanis.* I cause him to make noise, *nind ombigia.* It makes noise, *ombigwemagad.* It makes a dreadful noise, *gotamigwewemagad.* A noise comes from ..., *ondwewemagad.* — A partridge makes noise with his wings, *mâdweweo biné.*
Noised; it is noised round, *passwewessin.*
Noised, rumored; it is noised out, *wawindjigâde, baba-madodjigâde.* (Matwe-itwâniw).
Noisy amusement or play, *ombâkamigisiwin.* I begin to make noise, *nin mâdakamigis.* I amuse myself in a noisy manner, *nind ombakamigis.* I like too much noisy amusements, *nind ombakamigisishk.* Habit of indulging in noisy am., *ombakawigisishkiwin.* I amuse myself together with him, *nin widakamigisima.*
Noisy. S. Troublesome.
No more, *kawin keiâbi.* (Nama kittwàm). There is no more of it, (in., an.) *kawin gego, mi kakina, mi endassîng; kawin awiia, mi kakina, mi endashid, mi endashiwad.*
Noon, *nâwakwe.* At noon, *nâwakweg.* Always at noon, *naiawakwegin.* Every noon, *dassing naiâwakwegin.* It is noon passed, *kabikônawakwe.*
North, *giwédin.* At, from or to the north, *kiwédinang.* The clouds come from the north, *kiwedinakwad.* The rain comes from the north, *kiwedinobissa.* It thunders in the north, *kiwedinakwaamog* (*animikig*).
Northwind, *kiwédin.*
Nose, *odjângima.* My, thy, his nose, *nindjanj, kidjanj, odjanj.* (Oskiwan). The side of my, thy, his nose, *nindenigom, kidenigom, odenigâman.* — I have a crooked nose, *nin wagidjane, nin washkidjane.* I have a fetid nose, *nin miniwidjane.* I have a flat nose, *nin nabagidjane, nin kishkidjane.* I have a knob on my nose, *nin pikodjane.*
Nose-ring, *nabidenigomébison.*
Nostril, *pindjidjanj.* I have large nostrils, *nin mangidenigome.*
Not any, (*an., in.*) *ka awiia, kawin awiia; ka gego, kawin gego, kawin nîngot.* (Nama nândo).
Not before now, *pitchinag.*

(Tcheskwa).
Notch. S. Incision.
Notch; I notch it, (*in., an.*) *nin pagwanoshkan; nin pagwanoshkawa.*—S. Incision.
Notched; it is notched, *pagwanoshkamagad.*
Note, (small letter,) *masinaigans.*
Not even, *kawin ganage.* (Nama appo).
Nothing; I am (it is) nothing, worth nothing, *nin nagikawis; nagikawad.* Or, *nin nagikawendagos; nagikawendagwad.* (Piweyittâkwan).
Nothing, for nothing, *anisha; anish, wenipaj, wenipanaj, pinishi.* (Konata.)
Nothing, to nothing; I bring him (her, it) to nothing, *nin angoa, nind angoshkawa; nind angoan, nind angoton, nind angoshkan.* I am (it is) brought to nothing, *nind angoshka, nind ângotchigas; angoshkamagad, angotchigâde.* I bring it to nothing for him, *nind angotamawa.* It comes to nothing, *angomagad.*
Notice; I take notice of him, (her, it,) *nin babawenima; nin babamendan.*—I take notice of him (her, it) in going by, *nin babijâgenima; nin babijâgendân.*
Not in the least, *kawin bâpish, kawin ganage.*
Not now, *mâdji, mâdjikamig.* (Nameskwa.)
Notwithstanding, *kitwen minotch, potch, missawa.*
Not yet, *ka mashi, kawin mashi.*
Now, or now-a-days, *nongom.* (Anotch).
Now and then, *naningotinong, naningotinongin.*
Nowhere, *kawin ningotchi.* (Nama nândo).
Now only, *pitchinag.* (Tcheskwa).
Number; we are few in number; we are many... S. Few. Many.
Number; I number, *nind agindass, nind agindassobiige.*
Numbering, *agindassowin, agindassobiigewin.*
Numb. S. Benumbed.
Numbness, *gikimanisiwin.*
Numerous. S. Many.
Nun, *mékatéwikwanaieékwe.* (Ayamihewiskwew).
Nuptial. Nuptials.—S. Wedding.
Nurse, (woman taking care of sick persons,) *gatiniwekwe, genawenimad aiakosinidjin, neta-gatiniwed.*
Nut, *pakân, pakânak, pakânakomin.*
Nutmeg, *kitchi gawissakang.*
Nut-tree, *pakânakomij.*

O

O! as an interjection of wishing or exclamation, *o!*

Oak, *mitigomij*. White oak, *mishimij*. (Maskawâttik).

Oar, *ajéboian, ajéboianak*. (Abüy).

Oar-strap, *ajéboianeiab*.

Oats, *bebejigoganji manomin*.

Obedience, *babamitâgewin, babamitâmowin, naitamowin*.

Obedient; I am ob., *nin babamitam, nin babamitâge, nin naitam*.

Obedient person, *netâ-babamitang*.

Obey. S. Obedient.

Obey; I obey him, *nin babamitawa, nin naitawa*. I obey myself, I listen to myself, *nin babamitas*. I will not obey or listen, *nin jagibitam*.

Object, animate object, *aiaa;* inanimate object, *aii*.

Object; I object, *kawin nin minwendansi, nind anawéndam*. I object against him, (her, it,) *kawin nin minwenimassi, nind anawenima; kawin nin minwendansin, nind anawendân*.

Obliquely, *opimeaii*. I look obliquely, *nin bimadawab*. I sit obl., *nin bimidab*. I hold him (her, it) obl., *nin bimâdina; nin bimidinan*. I lay or put him (her, it) obl., *nin bimidjishima; nin bimidjissidon*. I lie (it lies) obl., *nin bimidjishin; bimidjissin*.

Obliterated. S. Forgotten.

Oblong; it is oblong, *jagawamagad*. It is oblong: Metal, *in., jagawabikad;* metal, *an., jagawabikisi;* stuff, *in., jagamabigad, jagawegad, namatchigad;* stuff, *an.*, or board, *jagawabigisi, jagawegisi, namatchigisi;* wood, *in., jagawigad;* wood, *an., jagawigisi*. —I make it oblong, *nin jagawaton, nin jagawissiton*. I cut it obl., (*in., an.*) *nin jagawikodan; nin jaganikodawa*.

Oblong island, *jaiagawagwindeg miniss*.

Observatory, *anangog endajiganawabamindwa*.

Observe; I observe or watch him, (her, it,) *nin nagatawâbama, nin nanagatawâbama, nin ganadenima, nin dadibabama, nind ashôwina,* (*ashwiwina;*) *nin nagatawâbandan, nin nanagatawâbandan, nin ganadendan, nin dadibabandan, nind ashôwinan,* (*ashwiwinan.*)

Observe, keep; I observe it, (a commandment, etc.), *nin ganawendân*.

Obstinacy, *washkawideewin, mashkawindibewin*.

Obstinate; I am obs., *nin mashkawidee, nin mashkawindibe*.

Obstruct; I obstruct a passage, *nin gibishkâge.* I obs. his passage or way, *nin gibishkawa.* I obstruct it, *nin gibishkan.*

Obstruct, (in. s. in.) S. Shut up.

Obtain, I obtain him, (her, it,) *nin gashkia, nin gashkiton.*

Occasionally, *naningotinong, naningotinongin.* (Miskawi.)

Occident, *épangishimog, ningâbian.* (Pakisimotâk). In, to or from the occident or west, *ningâbianong.*

Occupation, *ondamitâwin, ondamisiwin.* (Otamiyuwin).

Occupied, busy; I am occ., *nind ondamita, nind ondamis.* (Otamiyuw) I am occupied about him, (her, it,) *nin dajikawa; nin dajikan.* We are occ. at each other somewhere, *nin dajikodâdimin.* I am occ. at s. th. in a certain place, *nin dajita.* I am occupied in doing s. th., *nin apitchita.* I am occ. elsewhere, *nind ondamishka.* I am occ. in writing, *nind ondamibiige.* I feign to be occ. or busy, *nind ondamitakas.*

Occupy; I occupy him, make him busy, *nind ondamia, nind ondamisia.* I occupy people, *nind ondamiiwe.* (Otamihew).

Occupy the mind; he, (she, it) occupies my mind, my thoughts, *nind ondamenima; nind ondaméndân.* My mind is occupied by s. th., *nind ondaméndam.* (Otameyittam).

Ocean, *jiwitâgani-kitchigami.*

October, *binâkwi-gisiss.* (Kaskatinowipisim).

Odious. S. Hateful.

Odor. S. Smell.

Offend; I offend him, *nin nishkia, nin bitchinawea, nind iniwesia.* I offend him with my words, *nin nishkima, nin bitchinawema.* (Kisiwâhew).

Offended; I am off., *nin nishkiigo, nind iniwes.*

Offer. Offering, (in. s. in.) S. Sacrifice.

Offering, (vow,) *dibandowin.* Religious offering, *anamiepagidinigewin, anamie-pagidinigan.* I perform a religious off., *nin anamie-pagidinige.* (Asotamowin).

Office, *ojibiigéwigamig.*

Officer; civil officer, *ojibiigewinini; takoniwewinini.* Military officer, *jimâganishi-ogima*

Oft, often, oftentimes, *naningim, niningim, awâkam, sasagwana.* (Kâkiyipa).

Oh! *io!*

Oil, *bimide.* Sweet oil, *mitigobimide.* Holy oil or blessed oil, *ketchitwawendâgwak bimide.*

Oint. S. Grease.

Ointment, *nôminigan.* (Tominigan).

Ointment for the face, *nômingwewin.*

Ointment for the head, *namâkwiwin.*

Old; I am old, *nin kitchi anishinâbew, nin kitis.* (Kiseyiniwiw). I am very old, *nin gikâ.* I am getting old fast, *nin ginibininike.*—It is old, (*an., in*) *kitchi-aiaa; getê-aii.* (Kâwikikkaw).

Old, (ancient,) *geté-.*

Old age, *kitchi-anishinâbemiwin, kitisiwin.* Very old age, *gikâwin.*

Olden times; in olden times, *gaiat, waiéshkat.* (Kayâs).
Older, or the oldest; I am older, or the oldest, *nin sasikis.*
Oldest; the oldest or first-born, *sesikisid.*
Old Field,)Indian village,) *Getékitigan.* Indian of Old Field, *Getékitiganiwinini.*
Old man, *akiwesi.* I am an old man, *nind akiwesiiw.* (Kiseyiniw).
Old Nick, (devil,) *matchi manito, matchi aiaawish, manissiwinissi.*
Old person, *kitchi anishinâbe, gekad.* Old people, *gekâdjig.*
Old Testament, *Gaiât-ijitwâwin, Geté-ijitwâwin.*
Old woman, *mindimoié.* I am an old woman, *nin mindimiiéiw.* (Notukew).
Olive-oil, *mitigô-bimide.*
Omit; I omit it, *nind answekan.*
Omit. Omitted, (in. s. in.) S. Forget. Forgotten.
Omnipresent, *misiwe eiad.*
Omniscient, *misi gego kekendang.*
On, *ogidj', ogidjâii.* (Takkutchâyik).
On account of..., *ondji.*
Once, *âbiding, ningoting.* Once more. (Peyakwaw), *andj, minawa andj, minawa âbiding.*
Once, (absolutely,) *pâkatch.*
One, *bejig.* I am one, *nin bejig.* It is one, *bejigwan.* One by one, *bébejig.*— One object... See under the respective substantives. (Peyak).
One, *ningo* or *ningoto.*
One-eyed, *nin pâshkâb.* I make him one-eyed, *nin pâshkâbawa.*
One of the two, *bejig nijawad.* One of the three, of the four, etc., *bejig nissiwad, niwiwad,* etc.
Onion, *kitchi jigâgamanj.* (Witjekaskusïy).
Only, *eta, mi eta.* An only child, *bejigonjân.* (Piko).
Only now, *nanabem.* (Anotch piko).
Ontonagan, *Nindonagan.* At, from or to Ontonagan-River, *Nindonaganing.*
Ontonagan-River, *Nindonagânisibi.*
Open; I open it, *nin pâkakonan, nin pâkissiton, nin pâkakoshkan, nin nassâkonan, nin nissakonan.* I open it to him, *nin pâkakonamawa, nin pâkissitamawa, nin nassâkonamawa, nin nissakonamâwa.* It opens, *pâkakossin, nassakashka, pakokoshka, nassâkosse, pakissin, pakissemagad.* It is open, *pâkakonigâde, pâkissin.*—I open a barrel, *nin pâkisagaan makak.* (Yottenam).
Open, (lift up;) I open it, *nin pâkinan.* I open it to him, *nin pâkinamawa.* It opens, or it is open, *pâkissin.*
Open, (split,) the earth opens, *igadekamigishka.* The water opens, *igadeiagamishka.*
Open, (with a key;) I open it, (*in., an.*) *nind âbabikaan; nind ababikawa.* I open it to him, *nind âbabikamawa.*
Opening; there is an opening, *jeiakossin.* I make an opening, *nin jeiakossiton.* I make an op. to him, *nin jeiakonamawa.* I put my foot in an

op., *nin jegwakosidesse.*
Openly, *mijisha.* (Mosis).
Operate ; it operates well, (a medicine,) *minoshkademagad.* It op. well in me, *nin minoshkagon.*
Opinion, *inendawowin.* It is my opinion, *nind inendam.*
Opium, *nibéwabo.*
Oppose ; I oppose it, *nin mîgâdân.*
Opposite, (vis-à-vis,) *tibishko.* I arrive opposite to it, *nin tibishkokan.*
Oppress ; I oppress him, (her, it) with my body, *nin badagoshkawa; nin badagoshkan.*
Orator, *nata-gigitod.* I am an orator, *nin nita-gigit.* (Nettapikiskwet).
Or, *kêma, kéma gaié.* (Appo).
Order, *inakonigéwin.*
Order, (good order, carefulness,) *sagâkamisiwin.* I put in order, *nin sagâkinige.* I put it in order, *nin sagâkinan, nin sagâkissidon.* It is put in order, *sagâkissin.* (Nâhastâsuw).
Order, (Sacrament,) *Mekatéwikwanaiewiwin.* (Ayamihewiyiniwijihituwin).
Order ; I order some work to be done, *nind anôki.* I order it to be made, (*in., an.*) *nind anokin ; nind anokênan.* (Atuskemow).
Order, (arrange, command ;) I order, issue an order, *nind inâkonige.* (Wiyasuwew).
Orderly, in good order, *sagakatch.*
Orderly ; I am orderly, I live orderly, *nin nibwâka, gwaiak nind iji bimâdis, gwaiak nind ijiwebis.*—I am orderly, careful, I keep things in good order, *nin sagakamis.*
Orient, *wâban wendji-mokaang.* In, from or to the orient, *wâbanong.* (Sâkâstenâk).
Ornament, *sasegatchigan.* I am dressed with many ornaments, *nin sasegakwanaie.*
Ornament ; I orn., *nin sasegatchige.* I orn. him, (her, it,) *nin sasegana ; nin sasegaton.*
Ornament, (in. s. in.) S. Embroider.
Ornamented, (fair ;) I am (it is) ornamented, *nin saséga ; sasegamagad.*
Orphan, *giwâsh-abinodji.* I am an orphan, *nin giwis, nin giwashis, nin giwashito, nin naninawis.*
Other ; the other, *bejig, nabané.* —The other foot. The other hand, etc. S. Foot. Hand, etc. (Kutak).
Otherwise, *bakân, andj.* (Pitus).
Otter, *nigig, nikig.* Young otter, *nigigons.* Female otter, *nojéiakig.*
Otter-skin, *nigigwaiân.*
Ottawa Indian, *Otâwa.*
Ottawa language, *otawamowin.* I speak the Ott lang., *nind otawam.* It is written in the Ott. lang., *otawawissin, otawamomagad.* I translate it in the Ott. lang., *nind otawawissiton.*
Ottawa squaw, *otawakwe.*
Our, *ki, kid, nin, nind.* (Ki, kit, ni, n't.)
Ours, *kinawind, ninawind.* (Kiyânow, niyanân).
Out, outside, out of doors, *agwatching, agwatchaii.* (Wayawitimik).

Outgo ; I outgo, outwalk or outrun him, *nind enimishkawa.*

Outlive ; I outlive yet this day, *nin kabegijiganam.* I outlive yet this night, *kabetibikanam, nin wâbans.*

Outwardly, *agwâtchaii, ogidjina, ogidjaii.*

Over, *pâdjidji.*

Over, all is over, *ishkwakamigad.* (Ekusi kakiyaw).

Over-coat, over-all. S. Overvestment.

Overcome ; I overcome, *nin jâgôdjiiwe, nin mamânjitwa.* It overcomes, *jâgodjiiwemagad.* I overcome him, (her, it,) *nin jâgodjia, nin gashkia, nin magwia, nin mamânjia, nind aniwia, nind aniwishkawa ; nin jâgodjiton, nin gashkiton, nin magwiton, nin mamânjiton, nind aniwiton, nind aniwishkan.* I overcome in speaking, *nin jâgosonge.* I overcome him in speaking, *nin jâgosoma.*—I overcome myself, *nin jagodjiidis, nin gashkiidis.* It overcomes me, *nin mawiigon, nin jâgodjiigon, nin mamânjiigon.*—It is overcome, *gashkitchigâde, jâgodjigâde.*

Overflow ; it overflows, *sigissémagad.* It overflows boiling, *amidégamide, sigigâmîde.* The kettle overflows, *amidegamiso akik.* The river overflows, *bajidédjiwan sibi.* (Pâsitjipew).

Overflowed ; it is ov., *moshkaan, bajidebi.* I am (it is) overfl., *nin nikibi ; nikibimagad.* (Iskipew).

Overgrow ; I overgrow him, (her, it,) *nind aniwigima ; nind aniwigindan.*

Overhear ; I overhear, *nin pagwanotam, nin gimositam.* I ov. him, *nin gimitawa, nin pagwanotawa.*

Oversee ; I oversee him, *nin dibagima.*

Overseer, *naganisid.*

Overshadow ; I overshadow, *nind agawâteshkam.* I ov. him, (her, it,) *nind agawâteshkawa ; nind atawâteshkan.*

Overstrain ; I overstrain myself, *nind sindji.* I ov. him, *nind sindjia.* (Misamiw).

Overtake ; I ov. him, (her, it,) *nind adima ; nind adindan.*

Overthrow ; I overthrow, *nind ombwéwebinige, nind animikowebinige.*

Over-vestment, *pitâwajan, pitâwigwiwin, tashkanashkidieweiân.*

Owe ; I owe, *nin masinaige.* I owe him, *nin masinaamawa.*

Owl, *kokoko.* A kind of small owl, *gwengowia.* Another kind, *peshkwe.* Great horned owl, *wewendjigano.* (Hohuw).

Own ; I own it, (*in., an.*) *nin dibêndân ; nin dibénima.* (Otayân).

Owner, *debêndang.* (Wetayânit).

Ox, *pijiki.*

Oxen-driver, *wedabiad pijikiwan.*

Ox-fly, *misisâk.*

Ox-hide, *pijikiwegin.*

Oyster, *ess, ens.* Red oyster, *miskwess.*

P

Pace, *takokiwin.* (Takuskewin).
Pacific ; I am pacific, *nin bekâdis, nin bisânis.*
Pacifier, *besâniiwed.*
Pacify ; I pacify, *nin bisâniiwe.* —S. Appease.
Pack, carried on the back, *bimiwanan, wiwâjima.* (Nayatchigan). My, thy, his pack, *niwaj, kiwaj, wiwaj.* My pack is heavy, or, I carry a heavy pack, *nin kosigowane.* My pack is light, or, I carry a light pack, *nin nângiwane* I encumber him with a heavy pack, *nin niskia.* It encumbers me, carrying, *nin niskiigon.* (S. Carry on the back.)
Pack ; I pack, I carry a pack on my back, *nin bimiwane.*— S Carry on the back.
Packing, *bimiwanewin.*
Packing-strap, *apikan.* (This is also the name of a certain snake.)
Pack-thread or string, *takobidjigan.*
Paddle, *abwi.*
Paddle ; I paddle, *nin tchime.* I paddle in the foremost part of the canoe, *nin nimitamaam.* It paddles, *tchimémagad.* (Pimiskaw).
Paddler, *tchamed.* A good paddler, *netâ-tchimed.*
Padlock, *bekominagak kashkâbikaigan.*
Pagan, *enamiâssig.* Pagan Indian, *enamiâssig anishinâbe, maiâganishinâbe.* (Eka eyamihât).
Pagan sacrifice, *sâgiwitchigan, sasâgiwitchigan.* I make a pagan sac., or, I give s. th. for a sacrifice, *nin sasâgiwitchige.* I give it to him as a sacrifice, *nin sasâgiwina.* The gift received as a sacrifice, *sasâgiwinigowin.* (Webinâsuwin).
Pagan sacrificer, Indian sacrificer, *sasâgiwitchigewinini.*
Pagan sacrificing, *sasâgiwitchigewin.* I sacrifice some object, (*in., an.*) according to pagan rites, *nin sâgiwiton ; nin sâgiwia.* I sacrifice s. th. to him, *nin sâgiwitawa, nin sâgiwitamawa.*
Paid ; I am paid, *nin dibaamâgos, nin dibaamâgo.* It is paid, *dibaamagemagad.*
Pain, *kotagitowin, kotagendamowin, âkosiwin.* Much pain, *gibendamowin.* I am in pain, I have pain, *nin kotagito, nin kotagendam, nin wissagendam.* I have much pain, *nin gibendam.*–I cause or give pain, *nin kotagiiwe.* It causes pain, *kotagiiwemagad.* I give him pain, make him suffer, *nin kotagia.*—I have pain in such a part of my body, (*in., an.*) *nind âkosin ; nind âkosinan.*

—Little pain of a child, *bobo*.
Pain in the *head*, in the *leg*, etc, S. Head. Leg, etc.
Painful ; it is painful, *sanagad, ânimad*. It is painful, considered painful,*kotagendâgwad, wissagendâgwad*. I consider it p., *nin kotagendân, nin wissagendân*. It is a painful event, *kotagendagwakamigad*.
Paint, (colors,) *jijobiigan, wejinigan*.
Paint ; I paint, *nin jijobiige,nin jijinige*. I paint it, (*in* , *an*.) *nin jijobian, nin wéjinan ; nin jojokian, nin wéjina*.
Paint, (draw ;) I paint, *nin masinibiige, nin masinitchige, masinitgân nind ojibiwa*. I paint him, (her, it,) *nin wasinibiwa ; nin masinibian*.
Painted ; it is painted, (*in*., *an*.) *jijobigâde, wejinigâde; jijobigâso, wejinigâso*.
Painter, *jijobiigewinini, wejinigewînini*.
Painting, (drawing, picture, image,) *masinigiigan, masinitchigan*. The art or act of painting, *masinibiigewin, masinitchigewin*.
Pair; one pair, *ningotwéwân, ningotwewanagisiwin*. We are a pair, *nin ningotwéwagisimin*. Two, three pair, *nijwéwân, nisswéwân*, etc. So many pair, *dasswêwân*.
Palace, *ogimâwigamig*.
Palate, my, thy, his palate, *ninagask, kinagask, onagaskon*. (Mayakask).
Pale ; I am pale, *nin wâbinéwis, nin wâbinéwadengwe, nin wâbishkingwe*. I look pale, *nin wâbinagos*.
Paleness of the face, *wâbinêsiwin, wâbishkingwewin*.
Palm of the hand, *nobogaskinindj*.
Palm-Sunday, *jingobi-gijigad*.
Palpitate ; I palpitate, *nin mamâdjipagis*.
Palsy, *nibowâpinewin*. I have the palsy, *nin nibow, nin nibôwapine*. I have the palsy on one side, *nin nabanénibom*.
Pan, *abwêwin, sassakokwadjigan*. A panful, *ningot-abwéwin*.
Pan-cake, *gwékissodjigan*. I am frying pan-cakes, *nin gwékissadjige*.
Pane, *wassétchiganâbik*.
Pantry, *atâssowin*.
Pants, pantaloons, *gibodiêgwâson*.
Paper, *masinaigan*. Clean paper, (unwritten,) *banigak masinaigan*. White paper, (unwritten,) *waiâbishkag masinaigan*. Unwritten paper, *wejibiigadessinog masinaigan*.
Parable, *awétchigan, agotagosiwin, gimodowewin*. I speak or use a parable, *nind awetchige, nind agotagos, nin gimodowe*. (Akwanokijwewin).
Paradise, *wakwi, gijig*. In paradise, (in heaven,) *gijigong, wakwing*. Terrestrial paradise, *kitchi-kitigan*.
Parasite, *pagwishiiweshkid*. I am a parasite, *nin pagwishiiweshk*.
Parasitic habit, *pagwishiiweshkiwin*.
Parasol, (or umbrella,) *agawâteon*.
Parch; (burn a little,) I parch, *nin gâpisige*. I parch it, (*in*.,

an.) *nin gâpisan ; nin gapiswa.*

Pardon. S. Forgive. Forgiveness. Blot out.

Parent, *kitisi, onigiigoma.* My, thy, his parent, (father or mother,) *nin kitisim, ki kitisim, o kitisiman.* My, thy, his parents, (father *and* mother,) *ninigiigog, kinigiigog, onigiigon;* or, *nin kitisimag, ki kitisimag, o kitisiman.*

Paring, *okonass.*

Park, (enclosure,) *atchikinigan.*

Part; there is part or half of s. th., *ajiganê.* Part or half of..., *ajiganéaii.* Part or half of the earth, *ojiganêkamig aki.* (Pakki).

Particular, (difficult;) I am particular, *nin sanagis.*

Partition, *gibikinigan, pikissanâgokan, atchikinigan.* I make a partition in it, (in a house, etc.) *nin gibikinigadan, nin pikissanagokadan, nind atchikinigadan.*

Partridge, *biné.* Young par., *binêns.* I hunt part., *nin nandabinéwe.* The partridge shakes his wings, *gwigwingwao binê.* The tree on which he shakes his wings, *gwigwingwaowâtig.* (Pihyew).

Partridge-berry, *binêmin.*

Partridge-leaf, *binébag.*

Pass; I pass him, (her, it,) *nin kâbikawa; nin kâbikan.* It passes me, *nin kâbikagon.* It passes, *kâbikosse.*

Pass away; it passes away, *angomagad, angoshkamagad.*

Pass by; I pass by, *nin bimiija, nin bimosse.* I pass by in a canoe or boat, *nin bimâkwajiwe.* I pass by in a canoe or boat, singing, *nin bimâamas.* I pass by, carrying him (her, it) in a sleigh, *nin bimidabana; nin bimidabadan.* I pass by, riding, *nin bimibaigo.* I pass by, running, *nin bimibato.* I pass by, walking with snowshoes, *nin bimâgimosse.* —The road passes by, *bimamo mikana.*—I am heard passing by, *nin bimwéweshin.* I am heard making noise in passing by, *nin bimwêwe.* I am heard talking in passing by, *nin bimwéwidam.*

Passenger, traveler, *bebamâdisid.*

Passionate, (easily moved to anger.) I am passionate, *sesika nin nishkâdis, waiba nin nishkâdis, nin mishidee, nin babigodee, nin bitchinawes, nin nishkadisishk.* (Wokkewisiw).

Passionate person, *neshkâdisishkid, netâ-nishkâdisid.* (Kisiwâsiskiw).

Passionate temper or temperament, bad passion, *bitchinawesiwin, babigodeewin, nishkâdisishkiwin, matchi bimâdisiwin.* I have a passionate temperament, *nin nishkâdisishk, nin matchi bimâdis.*

Passover, *pak-wissiniwin.*

Pass over, (or miss;) I pass over him, (her, it,) *nind answekawa; nind answekan.* (Miyâskawew).

Pass through; I pass (it passes) through, *nin jâbode; jâbodemagad.* The water passes through, *jâbobi.* I succeed in passing through or over s. th., *nin gashkio.*

Paste; I paste, *nind agokiwassitchige.* I paste it, (*in., an.*) *nind agokiwassan; nind agokiwasswa.* (The same as sealing.)
Patch, (piece,) *bagwaigan.*
Patch; I patch, *nin bagwâige.* I patch it, (*in., an.*) *nin bagwaan; nin bagwâwa.*—I patch a canoe, *nin bagwaon.* I patch leggings, *nin bagwaidasse.* I patch shoes, *nin bagwaass.*
Patching, *bâgwaigewin.*
Path, *mikan, mikana.*—S. Road. (Meskanaw).
Patience, *minwadendamowin, jâjibendawowin, bekâdisiwin, bekâdendagosiwin.*—I have patience with him, *nin babimiwidawa.* We have patience with each other, *nin babimiwidadimin.* (Sibeyittamowin, yospisiwin).
Patient; I am patient, *nin minwadis, nin minwadendam, nin jajibendam, nin bekâdis, nin bekadendagos, beka nin kotagis, beka nin kotagendam.* I find him patient, *nin minwadenima, nin jâjibenima.*
Patient, (sick person,) *aiâkosid.*
Patron-Saint; he is my Patron-Saint, *nin widj'ijinikasoma aw ketchitwâwendagosid.*
Pattern for net-meshes, *bimidakonigan, bimidakonagan.*
Pattern for vestments, *tibijigan.*
Paunch, *missâd, winassag.*
Paw, *wanasid.*
Pay; I pay, *nin dibaamage.* I pay him, *nin dibaamawa, nin napanona.* I pay for it, (*in., an.*) *nin dibaan; nin dibawa.* I pay so much for it, (*in., an.*) *nind ipinean; nind ipinéwa.*
Pay debts; I pay my debts, *nin dibaan nin masinaigan, nin kijikan nin masinaigan.* I pay him in full, *nin kijikawa.* I pay all I owe, *nin kijikas.*
Payer, *debaamâged.*
Payment, *dibaâmâgewin, dibaâgowin, dibaamâdiwin.*
Peace, *bisâniiwewin, inawendîwin, mino inawendiwin, mino wîdjindiwin, wanakiwin.* (Wetaskiwin). We live in peace and harmony together, *nin mino inawendimin, nin mino widjindimin.*—I live somewhere in peace, *nin wanakî.* I make him live in peace, *nin wanakia.*
Peace of heart, *bisânideewin, wanakiwîdeewîn.* (Kiyâmitehewin.) I enjoy peace of heart, *nin bisanîdee, nin wanakiwidee.*
Pea-cock, *saséga-misisse.*
Peaceable; I am p., *nin bisânis, nin bekâdis.*
Pear, *osigwâkomin.*
Pearl, *ananidji, bikomigens, babikomigens.*—I have a pearl in my eye, *nin jiwâb.*
Pear-tree, *osigwâkominagawanj.*
Pebble, *assîn.*
Peddle; I peddle, *nin babamatawe.*
Peddler, *babamatâwewinini.*
Peddlery or peddling, *babamatâwewin.*
Peel, *okonass.*—S. Shell.
Peep; I peep in, *nin tapâb, nin tapikweshin.*—I peep out from under s. th., *nin pinsâb.*
Peevish; I am peevish, *nin babigodee, nin mishidee, nin matchi bimâdis.*
Peevishness, *mishideewin, babigodeewin.*

Peg, *sagâkwaigan, sassagâkwaigan.*
Peg ; I peg, *nin sagâkwaige, nin sassagâkwaige.*
Pen, *migwan.*
Penance, *kotagiidisowin.*
Pencil, *ojibiiganâtig.*
Penetrate ; it penetrates into s. th., *bosasse.* It penetrates in the flesh, *gondasse.*
Peninsula ; there is a peninsula, *gigawêkamiga.*
Penitent, *aianwênindisod.*
People, *bemâdisidjig.*
Pepper, *gawissagang, tipweban.*
Peppermint, *tekassîng.*
Perdition, *banâdisiwin ; banâdjiiwewin.*
Peregrination, *babâmâdisiwin.*
Perfect, perfectly, *gwaiâk, wewéni, wâwinge, âpitchi.*
Perfection, *wâwingesiwin.* I do or say s. th, to perfection, *nin wâwinges.*
Performance ; religious perf., *manitokâsowin.* I do some rel. perf., *nin manitokas.*
Perfume, *minomâgodjigan, (minomâgwadjigan,) nokwêsigan.*
Perfume ; I perfume, *nin minamagodjige, nin nokwêsige.*
Perhaps, *gonima, gonigé, géma, kéma, ganabâtch, mâkija.* (Mâskutch).
Peril, *bapinisiwâgan.*
Perish ; I perish, *nîn nib, nin nishiwanadis.* It perishes, *nibomagad, nishiwanadad.*
Permit ; I permit, (allow,) *nin ganabendjige, nin pagidinige, nin naêndam.* I permit him to do s. th., *nin pagidina, nin pagidjia, nin ganabênima, nin mina.* I permit it, *nin ganabêndân, nin naéndân.*
Perpetual, *kâgige.*
Perpetually, *kagigêkamig, kâginig, mojag, apine.*
Perseverance, *jibendamowin, jajibendawowin, pajigwadisiwin.*
Persevere ; I persevere, (at work, etc.) *nin jibendam, nin jajîbendan.*
Persist ; I persist, *nin pajigwendaw, nin pajigwâdis.* I persist upon what I say, *nin wi-debwe.* (Atji piko wi-tâpwew).
Perspiration, *abwêsowin.*
Perspire ; I perspire, *nind abwes.*
Persuade ; I persuade, *nin gagânsonge.* I persuade him, *nin gagânsoma ;* I persuade him to go with me, *nin wijâma.* (Kaskimew, sâkotchimew).
Persue ; I persue him, *nin noswanéwa.*
Perversity, *matchi ijiwébisiwin, matchi aiaâwishiwin.*
Pervert ; I pervert him, *nin matchi-ijiwebisia, nin wanishima, nin banodjia.* (Misiwanâtjihew).
Pest, pestilence, *jindâgan, kijindagan mânâdapînewin.* There is pestilence, *mânâdapinôkamigad.*
Pestle, *botâganak, botashkwanak.*
Petition, *nanândamowin, nandôtamowin.*
Petrified ; I am (it is) petrified, *nind assîniw ; assiniwan.*
Petticoat, *godass, matshîgode.* I wear a short petticoat, *nin takwâmbis.*
Pew, *apâbiwin.*
Pewter, *wâbashkikomân.*
Phantom, *tchibai.*

Pharmacy, *mashkikikewin.*
Phenomenon; it is a phen., *mamandâwinagwad.*
Phlegm, *agig, sibiskanamowin.*
Physician, *mashkikiwinini, nanândawiiwêwinini, nenândawiiwed.*
Pick; I pick a bird, *nin pashkobina binéshi.*
Pickerel, (fish,) *ogâ.* Young pickerel, *ogâns.*
Pick out; I pick them out, (*in.*, *an.*) *nin gagiginanan, nin mamiginanan ; nin gagiginag, nin mamiginag.*
Pick up; I pick up, *nin patakaige.* I pick it up with s. th. pointed, (*in.*, *an.*) *nin patakaan ; nin patâkawa.*—I pick it up and *eat* it, (*in.*, *an.*,) *nin mamajagandan; nin mamojagama.*
Picture, *masinibiigan, masinitchigan.*
Piece, *bokwaii.* A piece of any clothing material, *bokweg.* A piece of meat, fish, etc., *ningotonijigan.* Two, three pieces, *nijonijigan, nissonijigan,* etc. So many pieces, *dassonijigan.*—I make it all of one piece, *nin misiweton.* It is made all of one piece, *misiwetchigâde.*
Pierce, (bore;) I pierce, *nin pagwanéige, nin pagwanêbidjige.* I pierce it, (*in.*, *an.*) *nin pagwanéan ; nin pagwanéwa.* I pierce it with my finger, (*in.*, *an.*) *nin pagwanébidon ; nin pagwanébina.*—I pierce it with difficulty, *nin gashkaan.* —I pierce him, *nin jabwenawa, nind inishkawa.* It pierces me, *nin jabwenaogon, nind inishkagon.*—I am pierced, *nin jibajigas.*
Piety, *sôngananiawin.* (Ayamihewatisiwin.)
Pig, *kokosh.* Youngpig, *kokoshens.*
Pigeon; wild pigeons, *omimi.* Young wild pigeon, *omimins.* Domestic pigeon, dove, *wâbmimi, wâbomimi.* Young dom. pigeon, *wâbmimins.*—I hunt pigeons, *nin nândâomimi, nin nodjomimiwe.*
Pigeon-tail, *aawé.*
Pike, (fish,) *kinoje.* Another kind, *mâshkinoje.*
Pile; I put it on the top of a pile, (*in.*, *an.*) *nind agwitawissidon ; nind agwitawishima.*
Pill, pills, *mashkiki bebikominagak.*
Pillage, *makandwewin.*
Pillage; I pillage, *nin makandwe.*
Pillager, *makandwéwinini.*
Pilot, *wedaked, odâkéwinini.*
Pimple, *minins.* I have a pimple on my lip, *nin mininsiwidon.* My face is full of small pimples, *nin mosséwîngwe, nin babigwingwe.*
Pin, *oshtigwân-jâbonigan, nessegwabideon, sagâkwaon, sagâkwaonens.*
Pin; I pin it, (*in.*, *an.*) *nin sassagâkwaodon ; nin sassâgâkwaona.*
Pincers, *takwândjigans.*
Pinch; I pinch him, *nin tchissibina, nin wiskîbina.*
Pinery, *jingwakoki.*
Pine-tree, *jingwak.* Young pinetree, *jingwakens.* Dry pinetree, *mânissag.* Red pine, *pakwanagémak.* White pine *amikwândag, kawândag.*

Pinnacle, *wanakowin.*
Pint, *abitâ-omôdai ; kishkitchiag minikwâdjigan.*
Pipe, *opwâgan.* Stone-pipe, *assinîopwâgan.* Wooden-pipe, *mitigopwâgan.* A pipe full, *ningotôpwâgan.* I fill my pipe, *nind onâshkinaa nind opwâgan.* I light my pipe, *nin sakaipwâgane.*
Pipe-stem, *okidj, odamaganak, odagamanâtig.* Flat broad pipe-stem, *nabagakokidj.* (Oskitjïy).
Pipe-stone, *opwâgan-assin.*
Piss, *jigiwinâbo.*
Piss, I piss, *nin jishig.* I piss in the bed, *nin jigingwâm.* (Sikiw, sikikwâmiw). The dog pisses, *agwinoie animosh.*
Piss-pot, *jigiwinâgan.*
Pistol, *pâshkisigans.*
Pitch, *pigiw, pagin.* I make (gather) pitch, *nin pigike.*—
Pitch of the fir-tree, (balsam,) *papashkigiw.*
Pitch ; I pitch, *nin pikike.* I pitch it, (*in., an.*) *nin pigikadan ; nin pigikana.*—I pitch over, (a canoe or boat,) *nin jijokiwéige.* I pitch over my canoe, *nin jijokiwèan nin tchimân.*
Pitch-brush, *jijokiwéigan.*
Pitcher, *minikwâdjigan.* Earthen pitcher, *wâbigan-minikwâdjigan.*
Pit-coal, *akakanjéwassin, akakanjéwaki.* There is pit-coal, *okakajéwassinika.*
Pit-coal mine, *akakanjêwassinikan.*
Pit-coal miner, *akakanjéwassinikewinini.*
Pit-coal miner's work or business, *akakanjéwassinikiwin.*

Pith, *win.* (Wiyin).
Pity, *kitimâgeningewin, kitimâgendjigewin, kitimâgenindiwin.*—It is a pity, *wiiagad.*
Pity ; I pity, *nin kitimâgendam, nin kitimâgeninge, nin kitimâgendjige.* I pity him, (her, it,) *nin kitimagenima ; nin kitimagendan.* I pity myself, *nin kitimagenim, nin kiiimagenindis.* We pity each other, *nin kitimagenindimin.*
Place in a lodge or house allotted to a family, *abinass.*
Place of crossing, *nîminagan.* (Ajiwahunân).
Place where a wild animal in the woods uses to eat, *indajitagan.*
Place where s. th. is conserved or hidden, *assândjigon.* (Astatjikun).
Place ; I place it, (*in., an.,*) *nind atôn ; nind assâ.* I place it well, (*in , an.*) *nin minôssitôn ; nin minôshima.*
Placed ; it is placed, (*in., an.,*) *atchigâde ; atchigâso.*
Plague, *kotagapinewin, mânâdapiwewin, kitchi inâpinewin.*
Plague, *kotagisiwin, kotagitewin.*
Plague ; I plague people, *nin kotagiiwe, nind odjanimiiwe.*
Plain ; it is plain, intelligible, *nissitotagwad.*
Plainly, *mijisha.* (Mosis).
Plane, *joshhotchigan, gândinigan, môkodjigan.*
Plane ; I plane, *nin joshkotchige ;* I plane it, (*in., an.*) *nin joshkogaan ; nin joshkogawa.*
Plank, *kitchi nabagissag.*
Plank-road, *nabâgissago-mikana.*

Plant, *mashkossiw*. A hollow plant or herb, *wimbashk*. The plant is hollow, *wimbashkad*.
Plant; I plant, *nin kitige, nin pagidinige*. I plant it, (*in., an.*) *nin kitigadan, nin pagidinan; nin kitigana, nin pagidina*.
Planted; it is planted, *kitigâde*.
Plaster, *agobison, agobisowin*. I have a plaster on my wound, *nind agobis*. I tie a plaster on his wound, *nind agobîna*.
Plaster, *wâbigan*.
Plaster; I plaster, *nin wâbiganaige* I plaster it, *nin wâbiganaan*. I plaster with a trowel, smoothly, *nin joshkwabigonaige*.
Plastering, *wâbigonaigewin, joshkwabiganaigewin*.
Plat; I plat, *nind okadenige*. I plat it, (*in., an.*) *nind okadenan; nind okadena*. I plat it to him, *nind okadenamawa*.
Plate, *tessinâgan*. A plate full, *ningo tessinâgan*. Twice, three times a plate full, *nijo tessinâgan, nisso tessinâgan*, etc. Earthen plate, *wâbiganonâgan*.
Platted cord, *okadêiâb*.
Play, playing, *odaminowin*.
Play; I play, (like children,) *nind odamin*. I play with noise, *nin kiwanis*. I play, neglecting my duty, *nin kiwanakamigis*. (Metawew).
Play; I play, (game,) *nind atâge*. —We play together, (at cards, etc.) *nind atâdimin*. I play it, I play for it, (*in., an.*) *nind atâgen; nind atâgenan*. (Astwâkew).
Play; I play the child, *nind abinodjiikas;* I play the Indian, *nind anishinâbekas*.
Playing, (gaming,) *atâgewin, atâdiwin*.
Playing-ball or play-ball, *pikwakwad*.
Playing-card, *atâdi-masinaigan*.
Playing-house, play-house, *atâdiwigamig*.
Plaything, *odaminowâgan*. (Metawâgan).
Please; I please him, *nin minonawea, nin wawijia*. (Atamihew). As thou pleasest, *potch gaie kin*. (Appokiya). As you please, *potch gaie kinawâ*, or, *aposhkekin*.
Pleasing; I am (it is) pleasing, agreeable, *nin minwendagos, minwendagwad*.
Pleasure, *minwendamowin, bapinenimowin*. I make him pleasure with my arrival, *nin sagineshkawa*.
Plenty, *dêbisiwin*. I live in plenty, *nin dêbis*.
Plenty of...., *nibiwa*. (Mitchet, mistahi).
Plenty, plentiful, *gwâshkawad*.
Plough, *bigwakamigibidjigan, bigobidjigan, tashkikamijibidjigan, bimibodjigan, bissakamigibodjigan*. I make a plough or ploughs, *nin bigwakamigibidjiganike*.
Plough; I plough, *nin bigwakamigibidjige, nin bigobidjige, nin tashkikamigibidjige, nin bimibodjige, nin bissakamigibodjige*. I plough a field, *nin bigwakamigaan kitigan*. I plough (or break) the ground, *nin bissakamigaan aki*. I plough in a sandy ground, *nin tashkatawangibidjige*.

Plover, (bird,) *tchitchwishkiwê.* (Sesesiw).

Pluck out ; I pluck (or pull) it out, (*in., an.*) *nin mamibiton, nin mamibina.* I pluck it out, (herb, plant,) *nin jishanashkibidon, nin pashkobidon.*— I pluck him an eye out, *nin gidjabâwa.* I pluck my eye out, *nin gidjabaodis.*

Plum, *pagéssân, pagessâniminn.*

Plume of feathers, *nimashkaigan, migwangena, paiakibinweon.* I have a plume of feathers on my head, *nin nimashkaige.*

Pocket, *mashkimodêgwadjigan.*

Point of land, projecting in the lake, *neiâshi.* On the other side of a point, *ajâwew.* I go around a point in a canoe or boat, *nin giwidewa, nin giwitaam, nind awassêwaam, nikéwaam.* I cross (or traverse) a point on foot, *nin kakiwe.* The place where they traverse a point on foot, *kakiwêonan.* I traverse a point partly in a canoe, *nin kakimassato.*

Poison, *matchi mashkiki, pitchibowin.* Deadly poison, *nibowinipitchibowin.*

Poison ; I poison, *matchi mashkiki nind ashange, nin pitchibojiwe, nin matchi inapinodjige, nin matchiinopiaas.* I poison myself, *matchi mashkiki nind odapinan, nin pitchib, nin pitchibonidis.* I poison him, *matchi mashkiki nind ashama, nin pitchibona, nin matchiinapinana.*

Pole, boat-pole, to push a boat or canoe, *gaâdaktigan, gandakiiganak.* (Kwâskusowinâttik).

Pole ; I pole, (a canoe or boat,) *nin gandakiige.* (Kwâskusow).

Polecat, *jikâg.*

Pole, net-pole, to hang or spread a net on to dry, *bassassabanak.*

Polish ; I polish, (give lustre,) *nin wâssikwadjige.* I polish it, *nin wâssikwadon.*

Polish ; I polish, (make smooth), *nin joshkotchige.* I polish it, *nin joshkogaan ; nin joshkogawa.* I pol. it, (metal, *in., an.*) *nin joshkwâbikaan ; nin joshkwâbikawa.*

Pomade, *namakwiwin.* (Tomikkwewin). I put pomade on his head, *nin namâkona.*

Pond or pool, *bitobig, wajibiia.* Small pond, *bitobigons, wajibiians.* (Pittukahân).

Poodle-dog, or a dog with long hair, *pagwawed animosh, missâbassim.* (Tchimistawew, pikwâskaw).

Poor, *kitimâgakamig.* I am (it is) poor, considered poor, *nin kitimâgis, nin kitimagendagos ; kitimagad, kitimagendagwad.* I make him, (her, it) poor, *nin kitimagia ; nin kitimagiton.*

Pope, *Maiamawi-nigânisid Kitchimekatewikwanaie.*

Poplar, poplar-tree, *asâdi.* There are poplar-trees, *asâdika.* (Mitus).

Porcelain, *migiss.*

Porcelain breastplate, *migissiiessimig.*

Porcelain cup or saucer, *migissinâgans.*

Porcelain plate or dish, *migissinâgan.*

Porcelain-strap, *migissâpikan.*
Porch, *tessitchigan.* There is a porch made, *tessitchigâde.*
Porcupine, *kâg.* Young porcupine, *kâgons.* Male porcupine, *nabêiâg.* Female porcupine, *nojéiâg.* I hunt porcupines, *nin nandawâgwe.* (Kâkwa).
Porcupine Mountain. *Kâgwadjiw.*
Porcupine quill, *kâgobiwe.* (Kâwïy).
Porcupine's skin, *kâgwaiân.*
Pork, *kokosh.*
Port, *agomowin.* (Kapâwin.)
Portage, *onigam.* I carry s. th. over a portage, *nind onige.*
Portage-strap, *apikan.*
Portrait, *masinibiigasowin, masinasowin.*
Portrait; I portrait him, (her, it,) *nin masinibiwa; nin masinibian.*
Portraited; I am (it is) portraited, *nin masinibiigas, nin masinas; masinibiigâde, masinâde.*
Position; it is in a difficult position, (*in.. an.*) *bâtâssin; bâtâshin.*
Possess; I possess, I have property, *nin dan, nind indân, nin dibendass.* I possess him, (her, it,) *nin dibenima; nin dibêndan.*
Possession, *dibendassowin, daniwin.*
Post-office, *masinaiganiwigamig.*
Pot, *minikwâdjigan.*
Pot, iron pot with legs, *okâdakik.*
Potato, *opin.*
Potato-bud or germ, *pakwekotchigan.*
Potato-paring, *opini-okonass.*
Potato-sprout, *wâbidwi.*
Potentate, *kitchi-ogima.*
Pot-herb, *jigâgawanj meshkossimid.*
Pot-ladle, *anéigan.*
Potter, *wâbigan-onaganikewinini.*
Pound, *dibabishkodjigan.*
Pour; I pour it in another vessel, *nind ajawi-siginan.* I pour him s. th. in the mouth, *nin sigaanôwa.*—I pour water on s. th., *nin sigaandage, nin sigeandjige.* I pour it, *nin sigaandagen, nin sigaandjigen.* I pour it on him, (her, it,) *nin sigaandawa; nin sigaandan.*
Pour out; I pour out, *nin siginige.* I pour it out, *nin siginan.* I pour out for somebody, for people, *nin siginamage.* I poor it out for him, *nin sigînamawa.*
Pouring out, *siginigewin.*
Pout; I pout, *nin mindawê.* I am in a habit of pouting, *nin mindawishk.* I pout towards him, *nin mindawa, nin mindamawa.* I pout because I have no liquor to drink, *nin mindâwebi.*—I pout, (I hang out the lips,) *nin jibidonen.*
Pouter, *meâdawed, mendaweshkid.*
Pouting, *mindawewin.* Bad habit of pouting, *mindaweshkiwin.* Pouting for want of liquor, *mindawekiwin.*
Poverty, *kitimâgisiwin.*
Powder, *makatê.* (Kaskitê). My powder is all gone, *nin tchagakateweshin.*
Powder, (hair-powder,) *gingwaodiwin, wâbosanamân.*

Powder; I powder myself, *nin pingmaodis.* I powder him, *pingwâwa, nin pingwiwima.*—Powdering, *pingwaodimin.*

Powder-horn, *pinâakatewan.* (Pitchipikkwân). I fill my powder-horn, *nin pindakatewe.*

Powder-house, *makatewigamig.*

Power, *gashkiéwisiwin, niganisikandamowin.* I have power, (authority,) *nin gashkiewis.* I have power (authority) over him, (her, it,) *nin gashkiêwisikawa, nin niganisikandawa; nin gashkiêwisikandan, nin niganisikandan.*—I do all to my power, *nin nandagenim.*

Pox, small pox, *makakisiwin.* I have the small pox, *ning omamakie.* (Omikiw).

Practice, *ijitchigewin, ijitwâwin.*

Practise; I practise, *nind ijitchige.* I practise it, *nind ijitchigen.* I practise religion, *nind ijitwa.*

Prairie, *mashkodê.* There is a prairie, or there are prairies, *mashkodêwan.*

Prairie, large open prairie, *mishawashkode, mijiskâwashkode.*

Prairie-ox, (buffalo,) *mashkodépijiki.* (Maskutewimustus).

Prairie-wolf, *pashkwadashi.*(Mahingan).

Praise, (flattering,) *mamikwadiwin, mamikwadamowin.* Self-praise, *mamikwasowin.*

Praise, (flatter;) I praise, *nin mamikwâdam.* I praise myself, *nin mamikwas, nin mamikwadis.* We praise one another, *nin mamikwadiwin.* (Mâmitjimew).

Praise, (glorifying,) *kitchitwawinidiwin, wawijinkiwin, mino-wawinidiwin.* Self-praise, *mino-wawinidisowin.*

Praise, (glorify;) I praise him, (her, it,) *nin kitchitwawina, nin kitchitwawenima, nin wawijenima.*

Prattle, I prattle, *nind osâmidon, nind osâminowe.*

Pray, I pray, *nind anamia.* I pray for him, *nind anamiêtawa, nind anamietamawa, nin gaganodamawa.* (Ayamihâw).

Prayer, *anamiewin.* (Ayamihâwin).

Prayer-book, *anamie-masinaigan.*

Preach; I preach, *nin gagikwe.* I preach to him, (her, it,) *nin gagikima; nin gagikindân.* We preach to one another, *nin gagikindimin.*

Preaching, *gagikwemin, anamiêgagikwewin.*

Precede; I precede him, (her, it,) *nind aniwia, nind aniwishkawa; nind aniwiton, nind aniwishkan.* (Nikânuttawew).

Precedence, *nigânisiwin.*

Precept, *ganâsongewin.*

Preceptor, *kekinoamaged, kikinoamagewinini.*

Precious; I am precious, *nin kitchi âpitendagos.*

Precipitate; I precipitate some work, *osâm nin wewibita.*

Precise; I am pr., *nin wâwinges.*

Precisely, *wâwinge, gwaiak.* (Ketisk).

Precision, *wawingesiwin.* I act with precision, *nin wâwingetchige, nin wâwinges.*

Predecessor, *naganishkad.*
Prediction, *niganâdjimowin.*
Pre-eminent, *kitchi.*
Prefer; I prefer him, (her, it,) *nin bajidenima, nawatch nin minwenima ; nin bajidendan, nawatch nin minwendan.*
Pregnant, (with child;) I am pr., *nind andjik, nin gigishkage, abinodji nind aiawa, abinodji nin gigishkawa.*
Preparation, *âpitchiwin, ojitâwin, wâwejitâwin.*
Prepare, (get ready ;) I prepare, *nind ojita, nin wâwejita, nind âpitchita.* I make him prepare, *nind ojitaa, nin wâwejitan.*
Preparing ; I am pr. to do s. th., *nind âpitchi.* I am pr. for a voyage, *nind ojita.*
Present, (gift,) *migiwewin, minigowin, minidiwin.*
Present, (give ;) I present, *nin migiwe.* I present it, (*in., an.*) *nin migiwen ; nin migiwenan.* I present it to him, *nin mina.*
Present, (bring or put before somebody ;) I present it, *nind ininan.* I present it to him, *nind ininama, nind ininamawa.*—It is presented in a certain manner, (*in., an.,*) *ininigâde, ininigâso.*
Press, *sindaagan, sindakwaigan.*
Press; I press *strongly,* (in my hand,) *nin mâgobinige.* I press *slightly,* (in my hand,) *nin mâgonige.* I press it *strongly,* (*in., an.*) *nin mâgobidon, nin mâgobina.* I press it *slightly,* (*in., an.*) *nin mâgonan; nin mâgona.*
Press down ; I press down, *nin gindjigadjige, nin gindjidaige, nin mâgoshkinadjige, nind onadinige.* I press it down. (*an., in.*) *nin gindjidâwa, nin gagindjidawa, nin gindjidashima, nind onadina ; nin gindjidaan, nin gagindjidaan, nin gindjidassidon, nind onadaan.* —I press it down in a vessel, *nind assânashkinadon, nin mâgoshkinadon.*
Press in ; I press in through the crowd, *nin gindjidawi.*
Press together, (compress ;) I press in, (*in., an.*) *nin sindagaan ; nin singagwa.*
Pressed together; it is pressed together, (*in., an.*) *sindaigâde ; sindaigâso.*
Press upon ; I press upon him, (her, it,) *nin sinsikawa ; nin sinsikan.*
Pretend; I pretend to be this or that, *nind awiidis.*
Pretty, *gwanâtch.*
Pretty, *eniwek.* (Eyiwek).
Prevail ; I prevail, *nin gashkito, nin gashkiéwis.* I prevail upon him, *nin gashkia.* (Shâkohcw). I pr. upon myself, *nin gashkiidis.* I cannot pr. upon him, *nin bwama, nind agawâdamawa.*
Prevent; I prevent him, *nin ganwêwema.*
Prey-bird; a kind of prey-bird, *tchains.*
Price; I put a price on him, (her, it,) *nind onagima ; nind onagindan.* I make a price for him, *nind onagindamawa.*
Pride, *maminâdisiwin, gokwâdenindisowin, ishpênindisowin, kitchitwawenindisowin, kitênimowin.*
Priest, *mekatêwikwanaie.* I am

a priest, *nin makatéwikwanaiew.* (Ayamihewiyiniw).
Priesthood, *mekatéwikwanaiewiwin.*
Prime; I prime a gun, *nin biwissidon pâshkisigan.*
Primogeniture, *sasikisiwin, nitaminigiwin.*
Principal, *kitchi.* The principal commandment, *kitchi ganasongewin.* I am the principal person here, *nin niganendagos oma.* It is the principal thing, *niganendagwad.*
Principally, *mémindage, mémdage.* (Osâm).
Print; small print, (small type,) *bissibiigan.* Large print, *mangibiigan.*
Print; I print, *nin masinakîsige.* I print it, *nin masinakisan.*
Printed; it is printed, *masinakisigade.* It is printed in small type, *bissibiigade.* It is printed in large type, *mângibiigâde, mamângibîigâde.*
Printer, *masinakisigéwinini, mesinakisang masinaigan.*
Printing, printer's art, work or business, *masinakisigewin.*
Printing-office, *masinakisigêwigamig.*
Prisoner, *gebâkwaigâsod.* I am a prisoner, *nin gibâkwaigas.*
Prisoner of war, slave, *awakân.* I am a prisoner of war, (I am enslaved,) *nind awakaniw.*
Prize, put at stake, *atchigewin.*
Probity, *gwaiako-bimâdisiwin.*
Procession, *anamiê-bimossewin.* We walk in procession, (religious procession,) *nind anamié-bimossemin.*
Procure; I procure, *nind ondinamage.* I procure s. th. to him, *nind ondinamawa.* I proc. to myself, *nind ondinamas, nind ondinamadis.*
Prodigious, *mamakâdakamig.*
Produce; it produces, (a field,) *nigin.* It produces well, *minogin.* It produces nothing, *anawigin, anawewisimagad.* It produces spontaneously, *binishigimagad.*
Profess; I profess religion, *nind anamia, nind ijitwa.*
Profession of religion, *anamiewin, ijitwâwin.* Profession of an art or trade, *inanokiwin.*
Professor, (teacher,) *kikinoamâgewinini.*
Profit, *gashkitchigewin, âbadjitowin.*
Profit; I profit by it, *nin pagwishiton, nind âbadjiton.* I profit by it in a certain manner, *nind inabadjiton.*—It profits, it brings profit, *gashkitchigemagad.* It does not profit, it brings no profit, *anawéwisimagad.* The field yields no profit, *anawigin kitigan.*
Profitable; it is prof., *minogiwemagad, ondisin.* It is prof. to me, (*in., an.*) *nind ondisîn; nind ondisinan.*
Promise, *wâwindamagewin, wâwindamadiwin, nakôdamowin.*
Promise; I promise, *nin wâwindamage, nin nakodam.* (Asotam, asotamâwew) I promise him, *nin wâwindamawa, nin nakoma.*
Pronounce; I pronounce well, *nin minowe.* I pronounce badly, I have a defective pronunciation, *nen mânowe.*
Prop, *asswâkwaiâan, asswakai-*

ganak, sakaagan, nagaiakwaiganak.

Prop; I prop, *nind asswâkwaige, nin sakaâgadgige.* I prop it, *nind asswakwaan, nin sakaâgadân, nin sagâiakwaan.*

Proper, properly, *wendjita.* (Iyenato).

Properly, as a property, *tibinawe, tetibinawe.*

Property, *inodewisiwin, tibinawewisiwin, dibendassowin, daniwin.* My, thy, his property, (*in., an.*) *nind aiim, kid aiim, od aiim; nind aiam, kid aiaam, od aiaaman.*—I have property, *nin dan, nin dibendass.* I have such a property, *nin inodewîs.*

Prophecy, *ningânâdjimowin.*

Prophesy; I pro., *nin nigânâdjim, nigân nin dibâdjim gedijiwebak,* (I tell beforehand what shall come to pass.)

Prophet, *niganâdjimowinini, ga-nigani-dibadjimod, ga-nigani-kikendang.*

Prophetess, *niganâdjimokwe.*

Propriotor, *debendang, debendjiged, debendassod, tebinawewewisid.* I am the proprietor, *nin tibinawewis, nin dibendjige, nin dibendass.* I am the proprietor of him, (her, it,) *nin dibenima, nin tibinawesinan; nin dibendân, nin tibinawewisin.* — I make myself proprietor of s. th., *nin tibinawewiidis.*

Proprietor of a house, *wewigiwamid.* I am proprietor of a house, *nind owigiwâm.*

Prosperity, *jawendagosiwin.*

Prosperous; I am pro., *nin jawendagos.*

Prostitute, *bishîgwâdjikwe.*

Proud; I am proud, *nin maminâdis, nin gokwadenindis, nind ishpenindis, nind ishpendan niiaw, nin sasegawendan niiaw.* I think him proud, *nin kiténima.* Proud thought, proud thinking, *maminadendamowin.* I have proud thoughts, *nin maminadendam.* (Kisteyimow).

Proud person, *meminadisid, eshpenindisod, ketchitwawenindisod.*

Provided, *kishpin.*

Provisions, *midjim.* My provisions are all gone, *nin tchagaé.* I procure prov., *nin midjimike.*

Provisions for a voyage, *nawâpon.* (Nimâwin). I take prov. for a voyage, *nin nawâp.* I take it with me on my voyage to eat it, (*in., an,*) *nin nawâpon,* (nimaw) *nin nawâponan.* I give him prov. for his voyage, *nin nawapona.*—Scrip or sack to put in in prov. for a voyage, *nawapwaniwaj.*

Provision-store, *midjimiwigamig.*

Provocation; malicious provocation to anger, *gagandjinawêidiwîn.*

Provoke; I provoke him to anger, *nin mikindjîa.* (Mawinehwew). We pro. each other to anger, *nin mikindjîidimin.* —I provoke him to anger maliciously, purposely, *nin gagândjia, nin gagândjinawea, nin gagândjigidea.* We prov. each other purposely to anger, *nin gagândjiidimin.*

Prudence, *nibwâkâwin, gagitâwendamowin.*

Prudent; I am pru., *nin nibwâka, nin gagitaw, nin gagitawendam.*

Publican, *mamandjitchigewinini.*

Publication, *windamâgowin.*

Publish; I publish s. th., *nin kikendamiiwe, nin kikendamodjiwe, nin windamage.* I publish it, *nin kikendamiiwen, nin kikendamodjiwen, nin windamagen.*

Pull; I pull or haul him (her, it) forth, *nin môkibina; nin môkibidon.*

Pull down; I pull it down, (*in.*, *an.*) *nin nissibidon; nin nissibina.*

Pulled down; it is p. d., (*in.*, *an.*) *nissibîdjigâde; nissibidjigâso.*

Pulley, *ombâbiginigan.*

Pull out; I pull out, *nin mamibîdjige.* I pull it out, (*in.*, *an.*) *nin mamibidon, nin bakwakobidon; nin mamibina, nin bakwakobina.*

Pulse, *oskwéiâb, miskwéiâb.* (Pakkahan). I feel the pulse, *nin godjinike.* I feel his p., *nin godjiskweiabigian.* — The pulse is beating, *pangaan miskweiâb,* or *oskweiab.* (Pakkahokuw). My p. is beating, *nin pangaog, pangaan nind oskweiâb.* My p. beats quick, *nin kijipangaog.*

Pump, *iskaibân.*

Pump; I pump, *nind iskaibi.* I pump it out, *nind iskaibadân, nind iskaan.*

Pumpkin, *ôgwissimân.* Large pumpkin, *missabigon.* The bloom of a pumpkin, *wâssakone,* (*wâssakwane.*)

Punished; I am pun. deservedly, *nin mânâbamewis.*

Pupil, *kikinoamâgan, kikinoamâwind.*

Purgative, purge, *jâbosigan.* I take a purgative, I purge myself, *nin jâbos.* I give him a purge, *nin jâboswa.*

Purgatory, *gassiiakisowin.* The souls in purgatory, *gassiiakisowining ebidjig.* (Kâssihamâkewiskutew).

Purify; I purify him, (her, it,) *nin binia; nin biniton.* I purify him s. th., *nin binitawa, nin binitamawa.*—I purify him (her, it) by fire, *nin banakiswa; nin binâkisan.* I pur. him s. th. by fire, *nin binâkisamawa.* (Kâssihew, kanâtjihew).

Purity of heart, *binideewin.* I have a pure heart, *nin binidee.* (Kanâtjitehew).

Purpose; I purpose, *nind inendam.*—S. Resolve.

Purposely, *ôndjita, awândjish.* Like purposely, *naita.*

Purse, *joniia-mashkimodens.*

Pursue; I pursue him, (run after him,) *nin biminajikawa, nin mâdaana.* (Pimitisahwew).

Push; I push, *nin gândaige, nin gândinige, nin gagândinige.* I push him, (her, it,) *nin gândina, nin gandâwa; nin gândinan, nin gandaan.*

Pusillanimous; I am pus., *nin jâgodee.*

Pusillanimity, *jâgodeewin.*

Puss, cat, *gajagens, minons.*

Pustule, *minins.* My skin is full of small pustules, *nin pikwajeshka, nin papikwajeshka.*

Put; I put, *nind atâge.* I put him, (her, it,) *nind assa; nind aton.* It is put, *atchigâde.* I put it in a certain manner, *nind ijissiton.* I put him s. th., *nind atawa.* — I cannot put it, (*in., an.*) *nin nondéssiton; nin nondêshima.*

Put aside; I put aside with my hands, *nin midâgwenige.* I put him (her, it) aside, or out of the way, *nin midâgwena; nin midâgweaan.* I put it aside for him, *nin midagwenamawa.* I put it aside in thoughts, *nin midâgwendan.* I put myself aside, *nin midâgweta.*

Put away, (reject;) I put him (her, it) away, *nin bakêwina; nin bakéwinan.* I put it away, reject it, I refuse to take it, *nin miwitan, nin mîwiton.* I put it away for him, *nin miwitawa, nin miwitamawa.*

Put back; I put it back again, (*in., an.*) *nin nassabissiton; nin nassabishima.*

Put down; I put him (her it) down, *nin nissina; nin nissinan.* I put him, (her, it) down from my back, *nin pagidoma; nin pagidondan.* I put down a load, *nin pagidjiwane, nin pagidjinige.*

Put in; I put it in, (*in., an.*) *nin pindjissiton; nin pindjishima.* I put it in a hole or vessel, *nin bodâkwe.* I put it in a hole or vessel, (*in., an.*) *nin bodâkwen; nin bodâkwenan,* I put in my mouth s. th. to eat, *nin jakâm.* I put it in my mouth, (*in., an.*) *nin jakamon; nin jakamonan.*—I put my things in a trunk, etc., *nind onashkinadass.*

Put on; I put on, (clothing,) *nin bisikâge.* I put it on, *nin bisikân.* I put it on easily, *nin débishkan, nin géshawikan.* I put it on well, (it fits me well,) *nin minokan.* (Tebiskam). I put it on so.... (*in., an.*) *nind inikan; nind inikawa.* I put on stockings, socks or nippes, and shoes or boots, *nin bâbitchi.* I put him socks and shoes on, *nin babitchia.*

Put to; I put it to the fire in a vessel to cook, (*in., an.*) *nin gabâton; nin gabâshima.* It is put to the fire to cook, (*in., an.*) *gabâtchigâde; gabatchigâso.*

Put together; I put them together, (*in., an.*) *nin mamawissitonan; nin mamawassag.* It is put together, *mamawissitchigâde.* I put two together, (thread,) *nin nijwabiginan, nin nabwabiginan.*

Putty, *wâssétchigani-pigiw.*

Putty; I putty, *nin pigike.* I putty a window, *nin pigikadan wâssetchigan.*

Q

Quack-doctor, *geginawishkid mashkikiwinini.*

Quadruped, *naogâded.* It is a quadruped, *niogâde.*

Quarrel, *gikandiwin, gikangewin, gikawidamowin.*

Quarrel; I quarrel, *nin gikange, nin gikawîdam.* We quarrel with one another, *nin gikandimin, nind aiajindendimin.* (Kikâmew).

Quarreler, *netâ-gikawidang.* I am a quarreler, I am quarrelsome, *nin nitâ-gikawidam.*

Quarter; first or last quarter of the moon, *gisiss abitâwisi.*

Queen, *ogimâkwe, kitchi-ogimâkwe.* I am a queen, *nind ogimâkwew.* I make her a queen, *nind ogimâkwewia.*

Quench; I quench fire, *nind âtéige.* I quench it, *nind âtéan.*

Question, *gagwédwewin, gagwédjindiwin.*

Quick; I walk quick, *nin kijikâ.* (Kisiskâttew). I walk as quick as I can, *nind apisika.*

I am quick in working, etc., *nin gwashkwes.*

Quicken; I quicken my hands, *nind abakinindjiwas.* I quicken my feet, *nind abakisidis.* It quickens, *abisiwemagad.*

Quickly, *kéjidin, kékejidin, kékejidine, wéwib, ningim.* (Kiyipi or kiyipa).

Quid of tobacco, *agwanendjigan.*

Quiet; I am quiet in my thoughts, in my mind, *nin bissânendam, nin nibwâkadendam.*

Quietly, *beka, naégatch.* (Peyattik).

Quietude, *bisânabiwin, nibwâkâwin.*

Quill, *migwan.*

Quilt, *mawandôgwasson, mawandôgwassowin.*

Quit; I quit, give up, *nind anijitam, nind anawendjige.* (Nagatew). I quit a place entirely, *nind âpitchi mâdja.* I quit him, *nin bakeshkawa.* I quit it, *nin bakéwidon.*

Quiver, *pindanwan.*

R

Rabbit, *wâbos*. Young rabbit, *wâbosons*.
Rabbit's berry, *wâbôsomin*.
Rabbit-skin, *wâbôsowaian*.
Rabbit-skin coat, *wâboswékon*. I make a coat of rabbit-skin, *nin wâboswêkonike*.
Race on foot, *gagwédjikanidiwin*.
Race in canoes or boats, *gagwédjikadaowin*.
Race; I run a race on foot, *nin gagwêdjikajîwe*. I run with him, *nin gagwêdjikana*. We run a race together, *nin gagwédjikanidimin*.—I run a race in a canoe, *nin gagwédjikadaowe*. We run a race in canoes, *nin gadwédjikadaomin*.
Rackoon, *éssikan*. Young rackoon, *essîkans*.
Rackoon-skin, *essikaniwaian*.
Radish, *okâdakons*.
Raft, *babindassagan*. I make a raft, *nin babindassaganike*. (Mittot).
Rafter, *abâjiiak*.
Rage, violent anger, *kitchi nishkâdisiwin*.
Ragged; I am ragged, *nin nissiwegodjin*.
Rags, *wiiagassiiman*. (Matchikonâs).
Rail for a fence, *mitchikanâkobidjiganâtig, mitchikanâtig*.
Rail-road, *biwâbiko-mikana*.
Rail-road car, *ishkoté-odâbân*, (fire-carriage.)
Rain, *gimiwan*. Rain coming from the north, west, etc. S. North. West, etc.—I walk or travel in rain, in rainy weather, *nin gimiwanishka*. I embark or start in a canoe in rain, *nin gimiwanibos*.—I travel in a canoe or boat in rain, *nin gimiwanaam*.
Rain; it rains, *gimiwan*. It begins to rain, *mâdjibissa, papânginibissa*. It rains a little, *awanibissa*. It rains hard, *kitchi gimiwan*. The rain is heard, *madwébissa*. Showers of rain are passing by, *babamîbissa*. It rains by intervals, *tatâwibissa*. The rain is cold, *takibissa*. It rains no more, *ishkwâbissa*.
Rainbow, *nagwéiâb, odagwanibissan*. (Pisimweyâbïy).
Raindeer, *atik*. Young raindeer, *atikons*.
Rain-water, *gimiwanâbo*.
Raise; I raise him from the dead, *nin abitchibaa*. I raise myself from the dead, *nin abitchibaidis*. (Apisisimew).
Raisin, *jomin, batê-jomin, baiâteg jomin*.
Rake, *binakwân, binakwaigan, mawandâshkaigan*.
Rake; I rake, *nin pinakwaige*. I rake hay together, *nin mawandoshkaige*.
Ram, *nabê-manishtanish*.

Ramble, rambling, *babamossewin, babamadisiwin; giwaadisiwin.*

Ramble; I ramble, *nin babâmosse, nin babâmadis, nin giwaadis.*

Ramrod, *jishibanagidjigan.*

Rancid; it is rancid, (*in., an.*) *satessin, sateshin.* It looks r., (*in., an.*) *satenagwad; satenagosi.* It tastes r., (*in., an.*) *satepogwad; satepogosi.* (Sâstesiw).

Rancor, *bitchinawesiwin.* I keep rancor, *nin bitchinawes.* (Kisistâkewin).

Rancor. Rancorous.—S. Anger.

Random; at random, *pagwana.*

Rapid or rapids in a river, *bâwitig.* There is a rapid, or there are rapids, *kijidjiwan.* (Kisiskâtjiwan) The rapids are long, *ginodjiwan.* There is a strong rap. over rocks, *kakabikedjiwan.* In the middle of a r., *nawâdjiwan.* Along the rap. of a river, *tchigâdjiwan.*

Rapids of St. Mary, (Sault de Ste-Marie,) *Bawiting.*

Rasp, *mitigo-sisibodjigan.*

Rasp; I rasp wood, *mitig nin sissibodon.* I rasp a board, *nabagissag nin sissibona.*

Raspberry, *miskwimin, miskomin.* Flat raspberry, *jagashkimin.*

Raspberry bush, *miskwiminagawanj.*

Rat, *kitchi-wawabigonodji.*(Watjask).

Rather, *nindawa, nindawâtch; enabigis.*

Ratified; it is rat., *songitchigâde.*

Ratify; I ratify it, *nin songiton.*

Rattle, *jishigwan.*

Rattle; it rattles, *jinawemagad, jinawissemagad.* I make it rattle, *nin jinawiwebinan.*

Rattle-snake, *jinawe, jishigwe.* A kind of rattle-snake, *mitigojishigwe.*

Rattling in the throat, *madwégamisowin.* A rattling is heard in my throat, *nin madwêgamis.*

Raven, *kagâgi.* Raven's beak, *kagâgiwikoj.*

Ravine; there is a ravine, *passakamiga.* (Pasatchaw).

Raw; it is raw, (*in., an.*) *ashkin; ashkini.* I eat raw, *nind ashkib.* I eat it raw, (*in., an.*) *nind ashkandan; nind ashkama.*

Raw fish, (also, fresh fish, not salted,) *ashkigigo.*

Raw meat, (also fresh meat, not salted,) *ashkiwiiass.*

Razor, *gashkibâdjigan.*

Reach; I reach him (her, it,) *nin débina, nin débishkawa; nin débinan, nin débishkan.* We reach one another, *nin débishkodadimin.* I cannot reach him, (her, it,) *nin nondena, nin nâwina, nin nanâwina.*

Reach, (arrive;) I reach him, (her, it,) *nind odissa, nin oditan.*

Reached; I am reached by the water, *nin moshkaog.*

Reach forth; I reach forth after him, (her, it) *nin mawinana; nin mawinadon.*

Read; I read, *nin wâbandan masinaigan.* I can read, *nin nissitawinan masinaigan.* I

read it aloud, *nin nâbowadan.*
Reader, *waiâbandang masinaigan.*
Reap ; I reap, *nin mamâ.*
Reaping, *mamâwin.*
Reaping-hook, *kishkashkijigan.*
Reason, *nibwâkâwin, inendamowin.*
Reason, (cause,) *iw wendji-dodaming, wendji-ijiwebak.* Without reason, *anishâ, binisikâ.* (Pikonata, or, konata). For such a reason, *mi wendji-...* (Eokotchi).
Reasonable ; I am reas., *nin nibwâka.*
Reasonable man, *nibwâkawinini.*
Reasonable person, *nebwâkad.*
Reborn ; I am reborn, *nind andjinig.*
Rebound; I rebound, (it rebounds,) falling, *nin gwashkweshin, nin gwashkweiâbikisse ; gwashkwessin, gwashkweiabikissemagad.*
Receive ; I receive him, (her, it,) *nind odâpina ; nind odâpinan.* I receive a letter, *nin bidjibiamago, masinaigan nind odissigon.*
Recent, *oshki-....*
Recently, *nômaia, anômaia.* (Anotch ikke).
Reciprocally, *memeshkwat.* (Mâmeskutch).
Recognize ; I recognize people, *nin nissitawinage.* I rec. him, (her, it,) *nin nissitâwina, nin nissitâwenima ; nin nissitâwinan, nin nissitâwendân.*
Recollect ; I try to recollect him, (her, it,) *nin nandamikwenima ; nin nankamikwendan.*
Recommend ; I recommend, *nin gagikinge, nind aiangwamige, nind aiangwamitâgos.* I rec. him to do s. th., *nind angmamima, nind aiangwamima.* I rec. him s. th., (in thoughts) *nind aiangwamenima.* I rec. it to myself, *nind aiangwamenindis.* (Akamimew).
Recommendation, *aiangwamitagosiwin, gagikingewin, gagikindiwin.*
Recompense ; I rec., *nin dibaamâge.* I rec. him, *nin dibaamâwa, nin napanona.*
Reconcile ; I rec. myself with him, *nin bonigidetawa, nin bonendamawa, nin mino ganona.* We get reconciled with each other, *nin bonigidetadimin, nin mino ganonidimin.*— I reconcile him to somebody, *nind inawendaa, nin mino inawendaa.*
Recover ; I recover my senses, (after fainting,) *nind abisiwis, nind âbisishin, nind âbisiwendam.* I recover from my fear, *nin bôme.* I rec. from my sickness, *nin nodjim, nind âbisiwâdis.* I make him rec., *nin nodjimoa.* (Apisisin).
Recovering, recovery, (from sickness,) *nodjimowin.*
Red ; I am (it is) red, *nin miskos ; miskwa, miskwamagad.* It is red, painted red, (*in.*, *an.*) *miskonigâde ; miskonigâso.* It is red ; metal, *in.*, *miskwabikad ;* metal, *an.*, *miskwabikisi ;* stuff, *in.*, *miskwégad ;* stuff, *an.*, *miskwegisi ;* wood, *in.*, *miskossaginigade ;* wood, *an.*, *miskossaginigâso.*
Red-barked twig, *miskwâbimij.*
Red bird, *natchinamanessi.*

Redbreast, (bird,) *memiskendinimanganeshi.*
Red carp, (fish,) *miskwanebin.*
Red cedar, *miskwâwak.* There are red cedar, *miskwawakoka.* In a place where there are red cedars, *miskwâwakokang.*
Red clay, *miskwâbigan.*
Red cloth, *miskwégin.*
Red flannel, *miskwâbigin.*
Red-head, (a person with red hair,) *miskwândîb, meskwândibed.* I have a red head, *nin miskwândibe,* (*miskondibe.*)
Red-hot; (metal, *in., an.*)*miskwâbikide ; miskwâbikisi.* I make it red-hot, (*in., an.*) *nin miskwabikisan; nin miskwabikiswa.*
Red-hot coals, *akakanje, miskwakinje,* (*miskokinje.*)
Red Lake, *Miskwâwâkokan.*
Red liquid, *miskwâgami.*
Redoubt, *wâkaigan.*
Red River, *Miskwâgamîwi-sibi.*
Red Sea, *Miskwâgimiwi-kitchigami.*
Red-stone, *miskwassin.*
Red-stone, pipe or calumet, *miskwassin opwâgan.*
Reduce in boiling; I reduce, *nind iskigamisige.* (Ikkagamisam). I red. it, (diminish it,) by boiling, *nind iskigamisan.* Place where they reduce maple-sap, *iskigamisigan.* Woman that reduces maple-sap, *iskigamisigekwe.*
Reduced by boiling; it is red., *iskigamidemagad.*
Reducing by boiling, *iskigamisigewin.*
Reed, *obiwaiashkina ; wimbashk; assâganashk.*
Reed for mats, *apakwéshkwai, anakanashk,kitchigamiwashk.* I cut reed for mats, *nin manashkossiwe.*
Reel, *abaodjigan, titibaodjigan.*
Reflect; I reflect, *nin dibéwagendam, nin minonendam, nin mitonendam, nin nanagatawendam, nin wawenendam.*
Reflection, *nanagatawendamowin, dibéwagendamowin*
Reflection upon one's self, *nanagatawenindisowin.*
Reform ; I reform or alter it, (*in., an.*) *nind andjiton ; nind andjia.*
Refrain; I ref., *nin mindjiminidis, nin nagâidis, nin nagânidis.*
Refraining, *minidjimindisowin.*
Refuge, *ininijimowin.* I take refuge, *nind ojim, nin bi-ojim.* I take refuge to him, *nin binadjinijima, nin nâdenima.* I take ref. to some place, *nind ininijim, nind nâdjinijim, nind apâgis.* We take ref. to some place, *nind apâidimin, nin nâdjinijimomin.* (Nâtamototawew).
Refuse; I refuse to take him, (her, it,) *nin miwia, nin miwina ; nin miwiton, nin miwinan.* (Assenew).
Regeneration, *andjinigiwin.*
Regret, *kashkendamowin, aiajeiendamowin.*
Regret; I regret, *nin kashkendam,. nin mindjinawes ; nind aiajeiendam.* I regret to have lost him, (her, it,) *nin mindadenima ; nin mindadendan.* (Mitâtam).
Regretful, *mindjinawéiadakamig.* (Kesinâtakamik).
Regulation, *inâkonigewin.*

Reign; I reign, *nind ogimaw, nind ogimâkandawe, ning ogimakandange, nind ogimâkangamage.* It reigns, *ogimâkandamâgemagad.* I reign over him, (her, it,) *nind ogimâkandawa, nind agimâkandamawa; nind ogimâkandan.*

Reject; I reject, *nin wêbinige, nin pagidinge.* I reject him, (her, it, (*nin wêbina, nin pagidenima; nin wêbinan, nin pagidendan.* We reject each other, *nin wébinidimin, nin bakéidimin.*

Reject; I am (it is) rejected, *nin wébinigas, nin naninawendagos*; *webinigade, naninawendagwad.* (Assenikâtew).

Rejected person, abandoned, *wébinigan,* (*an.*)

Rejected thing, *wêbinigan,* (*in.*)

Rejoice; I rejoice, *nin bâpinenim.* (Miyâwâtam). I make him rejoice, *nin bapinenimoa.* I rejoice in thoughts, *nin bapinendam.* I make him rej. in th., *nin bapinendamoa.*

Rejoicing, *bapinenimowin, bapinendamowin, wawijendamowin.* (Miyâwâtamowin).

Rejoice with; I rej. with him, *nin widjonwatoma.*

Relapse, *ajessewin.*

Relapse, ; I rel., *nin ajêsse.* I rel. in sickness, *nind ândjine.*

Relation, relative, *inawemagan, inawendagan.* (Wâkkomâgan). He is a relation of mine, *nind inawéma.* (Wâkkomew). We are relations to each other, *nind inawendimin.* I make him a relative to somebody, *nind inawendaa.*

Relationship, *inawendiwin.*

Relax; I relax, *nind ajésse.*

Relaxation, *ajéssewin.*

Release; I release him, (her, it,) *nin pagidina, nin pagisikawa; nin pagidinan, nin pagisikan.* It releases me, *nin pagisikagon.*

Released; I am rel., *nin pagidendâgos, nin pagidjaia.*

Religion, *anamiewin ijitwâwin.* Indian religion *anishinâbeijitwâwin.* (Ayamihâwin).

Religious, (pious;) I am rel., *nin songanamin.* (Ayamihewâtisiw).

Reluctance; with rel., *kitwen.* (Kittwâm).

Remain; I remain somewhere, *nind ishkwi.* I remain, (I am left or spared,) *nind ishkwasse.* It remains, *ishkwassemagad.* —I remain around him, (her, it,) *nin wâkaikawâ; nin wâkaikan.*

Remain; I remain, I refuse to go, *nin gîdjikas.* (Kitisimow).

Remainder, *biwijigan, eshkosseg.*

Remaining; I have some of it remaining, (*in., an.*) *nind ishkwassiton; nind ishkwashima.*

Remark; I remark him, (her, it,) *nin kikinawadenima; nin kikinawadendan.* (Pisiskâbamew.)

Remarkable; it is rem., *kikinawadad.* In a remarkable manner, *kikinawâdj.* (Kiskinowâteyittâkwan).

Remedy, *mashkiki, nanândawiowin.*

Remember; I remember, *nin mikwéndass, nin mikwéndam, nin mikwéndjige.* (Kiskisiw). I rem. him, (her, it,) *nin mikwenima, nin mikawinan, nin mikwendan, nin mikawin, nin mindjiwendan.* I rem. him (her, it) well, *nin bisiskenima; nin bisiskendan.* (Kiskisototawew). I rem. him (her, it) strongly, *nin mashkawimindjimenima ; nin mashkawimindjimendan.*—I make him remember it, *nin mikwéndamia, nin mikawâma.*

Remembering, *mikwendamowin, mikwendassowin.*

Remind ; I remind him of s. th., *nin mikawama.* (Miskawasomew).

Remnant of a board, *ishkobodjigan.* Remnant after cutting a coat, etc , *ishkojigan.* I leave a remnant, *nind ishkojige.* Remnant after cutting, *ishkândjigan.* I leave a remnant, *nind ishwândjige.*

Removal, *gosiwin.*

Remove ; I remove him, (her, it,) *nind ikona ; nind ikonan.* I remove it for him, *nind ikonawa, nind ikonamawa.*

Removed ; I am (it is) rem., *nind ikonigas ; ikonigâde.*

Removed from office ; I am rem., *nin bigoshka, nind ishkwaanonigo.*

Rend ; it rends, *pâssikamagad.*

Render ; I render him a service, *nin dodawa.* I render him evil for evil, *nind ajédibaamawa maianadak.* (Abatjihew).

Rendez-vous ; I promise to come to a rendez-vous, *nin kikinge.* I promise him a rendez-vous, *nin kikima.* We promise each other a ren., *nin kikindimin.* Mutual promise of a ren., *kikindiwin.* Promise to come to a ren., *kikingewin.* (Kiskimow).

Renounce ; I renounce him, (her, it,) *nin pâgidenima ; nin pagidendan.* (Assenew).

Renown, *wâwindaganesiwin, wâwindjigâdewin.* Good renown, *mina wawindaganesiwin, mino wawindjigâdewin.*

Renowned ; I am ren., *nin wâwindaganes, nind aiadjimigowis.*

Rent ; it is rent, *kishkika.*

Renunciation, *pagidendamowin.*

Repair ; I repair, *nanâitchige, nin nanâissitchige.* I repair it, (*in., an.*) *nin nanâiton, nin nanaissiton ; nin nanâina, nin nanâishima.*

Repair ; (restore ;) I repair it, (*in., an*) *nin nôdjimoton ; nin nodjimoa.*

Repair, (sewing ;) I repair, sewing, *nin wawekwadass.* I repair it, (*in., an.*) *nin wâwekwadan ; nin wâwekwana.* (Misahwew).

Repairing, reparation, *nanâitowin, nanâissitowin.*

Repay ; I repay him, *nind ajedibaamawa, nind ajidawa.* I repay it, *nind ajêdibaan.*

Repeat ; I repeat, *nâssab nind ikkit, nâssab nin dibâdjim.* I repeat his words, *nind anikanotawa, nind inotawa, nin nabinotawa.* I repeat old sayings, *nind ajéiadjim.* (Nanâspitottawew).

Repeatedly, *naningim, sasâgwana, nâssab.* Kâkitwâm).

Repeated word, *nassab-ikkitowin.*

Repeating of old sayings, *ajéiadjimowin.*

Repent ; I repent, *nind ândwenindis, nin mindjinawes.* I

repent in thoughts, *nind anweiendam, nin mindjinaweiendam.* (Kesinâteyimisuw).

Repentance, repenting, *anwenindisowin, mindjinawesiwin.* (Kesinâteyimisuwin).

Repenting person, penitent, *aianwenindisod.*

Replace; I replace it, (*in.*, *an.*) *nin nâbissiton; nin nâbishima.* (Attastaw).

Report, *dibâdjimowin.* Report brought, *bidâdjimowin.* I bring a rep., *nin bitâdjim.* Good report, *minwâdjimowin.* I tell a good rep., *nin minwâdjim.* Bad report, *mânâdjimowin.*

Representation, *awetchigan.* I make a rep., *nind awetchige.*

Reprimand; I reprimand, *nind anweninge, nind aiawiwe.* I rep. him, *nind anwenima, nind aiâwa, nin nanibikima.*—I rep him with hard words, *nind animima.* I reprimand myself, *nind ânwenindis.* (Kitotew).

Reprimanding, *aiâwin, aiawidiwin, anwenindiwin,*

Reproach, (cold;) I rep. for such a reason, *nind onsonge.* I rep. him for a certain reason, *nind onsoma.* I reproach or scold in regard to my children, *nind onsomâwass.*—I reproach him in a certain manner, *nind inopinema.* (Ataweyittamâwew).

Reproachable; my conduct or behavior is repr., *nind ânwêndagos.* It is repr., *ânwêndagwad.* (Atâweyittâkwan).

Reprove; I reprove his conduct, *nind anwenima.* I reprove myself, *nind anwenindis.*

Repudiate; I repudiate her, (him,) *nin bakêwina, nin bakéshkawa.*

Repudiation, *bakêwidiwin, bakéshkodadiwin.*

Request, *pagoseendamowin, nandôtamowin, nanandomowin, nandotamagewin.*

Request, I request, *nin nandotam, nin nandotamage, nin pagossendam.* I request him, *nin nanâdpma, nin nandotamawa.*

Require; I require it, *nin nandotân.*

Resemblance, *inabaminagosiwin.* (Nanâspitâtuwin).

Resemble; I resemble him. *nind inama.* I resemble to..., *nind inabaminagos.* I make him, (her, it) resemble to..., *nind inabaminagwia, nind awetchigenan; nind inabaminagwiton, nind awetchigen.* (Naspitawew)..

Resembling; I am (it is) resembling..., *nâssab nind ijinâgos... nâssab ijinagwad.*

Reserve, s. *ishkonigan.*

Reserve; I reserve, *nind ishkônige.* I reserve him, (her, it,) *nind ishkona; nind ishkonan.* I res. it to him, *nind ishkonamama.* I res. it to me, *nind ishkonamas.*

Resolve; I resolve, *nin gigendam, nin gîjenindis.* I resolve firmly, *nin songendam, nin mashkawendam.* I res. it firmly, *nin songêndân.*

Resolved; I am firmly resolved, *nin webendam, nind âpitchi webendam.*

Resolvedly, *pâkatch.*

Resolution, *gijendamowin.* Firm resolution, *songendamowin, mashkawendamowin.* I make or have a firm res., *nin songendam, nin mashkawendam.* I make him take or have a firm res., *nin songendamia, nin mashkawendamia, nin mashkawima, nin songideeshkawenima.*

Resound; I make resound my voice, *nin passweweshin.* I resound, *passwewe, passwewessin.* I make it resound, *nin passweweton.* (Matwewesin).

Respect, *dabandendamowin, kitchitwawenindiwin.* (Kisteyimiwewin).

Respect; I respect him, (her, it,) *nin manâdjia, nin kitcki apitenima, nin kitchitwawenima, nin dabandenima; nin manadjiton, nin kitchi apitendân, nin kitchitwawendan, nin dabandendan.* We respect one another, *nin kitchitwawenindimin, nin manâdjiidimin.*

Respectable; I am (it is) resp., considered resp., *nin dabâdis, nin gokwadis, nin gokwadendagos, nin dabandendagos, nin gikadendagos.*

Respiration, *néssewin, pagidanamowin.* I take respiration, *nin nésse, nin pagidanam.* I have a quick resp., *nin dadâtabanam.* (Yêyêwin). I have a heavy oppressed resp., *nin gindjidanam.*

Resplendant; I am resp., *nin wâssêias.*

Rest, *anwebiwin.* Day of rest, *onwebiwini-gijigad.* (Ayowebiwin).

Rest; I rest myself, *nin ânweb* (Ayowebiw). I make him rest, *nind anwebia.* I rest or repose, lying down, *nind anweshim.*—The bird rests on..., *agosi bineshi.*

Resting-place in a portage, *pagidjiwanan.*

Resurrection, *âbitchibâwin.* Resurrection-day, *âbitchibâwinigijigad.* (Apisisin).

Return; I return, (go back again,) *nin giwe, nind ajégiwe.* I return the same day, *nin biskaki.* I return running, *nin giwibato, nin biskabato.* I think to return home, *nin giwéiendam.* I return home, with s. th. to eat, *nin giwéiabowe.* I return to my native place or country, *nin giwéki.*

Return, (repay;) *nin dibaamage, nind ajémigiwe.* I return it to him, *nind ajénamawa, nind ajêdibaamawa.*

Re-unite: we re-unite, *nêiâb nin nasikodadimin.*

Reveal; I reveal it, *nin mijishawissiton.* It is revealed, *mijishawissitchigâde.*

Revenge, *ajidawaawin, ajidawiwin.* In revenge, *ajida.*

Revenge; I revenge myself, *nind ajidawaige.* (Abehuw). I revenge myself on him, *nin ajidawaa.* I revenge myself on him in words, *nind ajidamawa.* (Naskwâhwew).

Revere; I rev. him, (her, it,) *nin manâdjia, nin kitchitwawenima; nin manâdjiton, nin kitchitwawendan.*

Revered; I am (it is) revered, *nin kitchitwâwendâgos; kitchitwawendâgwad.*

Revile; I revile, *nind inapinendam, nin bapijiwe.* I revile him, (her, it,) *nin bapijima,*

nind inapinema; nin bapijindan, nind inâpinendan. (Koppâtjihew).
Revive; I revive, (after fainting,) *nind âbisishin.* It revives, *abisisinomagad.*
Revolver of three, four, six barrels, *pâshkisigans nessoshkak, naoshkak, nengotwassoskak.*
Rhubarb, *wâbado.*
Rib, *opigeganama.* My, thy, his rib, *nipigegan, kipigegan, opigegan.*
Ribbon, riband, *senibâ.*
Rib of a canoe, etc., *wâgina.*
Rice, *wâbanomin.*
Rich; I am rich, *nin dân, nin kitchi dân, nin wânadis.* I make him rich, *nin dania, nin wânadisia.* (Weyotisiw).
Riches, *dâniwin, kitchi dâniwin, wânadisiwin.*
Rich, wealthy person, *ketchidanid.*
Ride; I ride in a carriage or sleigh, *nind odâbanigo, nin babamibaigo.* I ride on horseback, *bebejigoganji nin bimomig.* (Tettapiw).
Rider, *bemomigod bebejigoganjin, bebamomigod bebejigoganjin.*
Ridge; there is a narrow ridge of a mountain, *oshédina.*
Ridiculed; I make it ridiculed, (*in., an.*) *nin bapiiamowiniken; nid bapitamowinikenan.*
Ridiculer, *neshibapiñodang.*
Right, *gwaiak, wewêni, kitchi, âpitchi, nissitâ.* It is right, considered right, (*in., an.*) *gwaiakwendâgwad, gwaiakwendâgosi.* I consider him, (her, it) right, just, *nin gwaiakwênima; nin gwaiakwéndan.* I put it right, (horizontally,) *nin gwaiakwissidon,* (*gwaiakossidon.*)
Right, (not left,) *kitchi; debani.* —Right hand, foot, etc. S. Hand. Foot, etc.
Righteous; I am righteous, *nin nibwâka.* I am righteous before him, *nin nibwâkabandawa.*
Ring or bracelet round the wrist, *anân.*
Ring the bell; I ring, *nin madwéssitchige.* (Sisowepitchikew). I ring it, *nin madwéssiton, nin tewessekaan.* It rings, *madwessin, madwewe.* I ring or strike the bell only on one side, *nin nabané-wewéssiton.* The bell is struck only on one side, *totakwêwessin kitotâgan.* (Sisowepitaw sisoweyâgan).
Riot, *nishigiwanisiwin, ombâsondiwin.*
Riot; I riot, *nin nishigiwanis, nind ombâsonge.*
Rip; I rip it, (*in.; an.*) *nind abijan, nin gakikijan; nind abijwa, nin gakikijwa,* I rip him, *nin bagwadjina.*
Ripe; I am ripe, *nin gijig.* It is ripe, (*in., an.*) *adite, wâbide. gijigin, gijimagad, gijissin; adisso, wâbiso, gijigi.* It is very ripe, (*in., an.*) *jigwande; jigwanso.*
Ripe fruits, *editegin.*
Ripped; it is ripped, *gakikishka.*
Rise; I rise from the dead, *nind âbitchiba.*
Rise boiling; it rises, *ombigamide.* I make rise boiling, *nind ombigamisige.* I mak it rise up, *nind ombigamisan.*

Rise on high; I rise, (it rises) on high, *nind ombishka; ombishkamagad.* I rise up briskly, *nind onishkabato.*

Rise up, sitting; I rise up, *nin pasigwi.* I make him, (her, it) rise up, *nin pasigwia; nin pasigwiton.* I rise up quickly or briskly, *ninpasigwindjisse.* I rise up with him, *nin widjipasigwima.*

Rising ground; there is a rising ground, *anîbékamiga.* (Oppatchaw).

Risk; I risk, *nind iniwéidii.* (Webinuw).

River, *sibi.* The river is large or wide, *mangitigweia sibi.* The river is small or narrow, *agâssitigweia sibi.* The river is so wide, *igigotigweia sibi.* The river is dark-colored, (black,) *makatewagâmitigweia sibi.* The river divides, *bakétigweia sibi.* The river splits out in two or more branches, *ningitawitigweia sibi.* Place where a river splits, *ningitawitigweiag.* The river turns round, *giwitatigweia sibi.* The river has an entrance, *pindjidawamagad sibi.* It is the end of the river, *waiekwatigweia sibi.*

River-net, *sibiwassâb.*

Rivet; I rivet, *nin biskadaige.* I rivet it, (*in.*, *an.*) *nin biskadaan; nin biskadawa.*

Riveted; it is riveted, (*in.*, *an.*) *biskadaigâde; bishadaigâso.*

Rivet-hammer, *biskadaigan.*

Rivulet, *sibiwishê.*

Road, *mikana, mikan.* Public road, large road, *kitchi mikana.* On or in the road, *megwêkana, maiâwikana.* On this side of the road, *ondass inakékana.* On the other side of the road, *wedi inakékana.*—The road comes from..., *ondamo mikana.* The road leads to..., *inamo mikana.*—I make a road, *nin mikanake.* I make him a road, *nin mikanakawa.* I make him a road straight, *nin gwaiâkomotawa.* I make him a road so..., *nind inamotawa.* I make a road even or level, *nind onâdamoton mikana.* I repair a road, *nin nanâadamoton mikana, nin wawenadamoton mikana.* — The road is crooked, *wawashkamo mikana.* The road is even or level, *onakamigamo mikana.* The road is large or wide, *mangademo mikana.* The road is small or narrow, *agassademo mikana.*—The road splits out, *naningitawamo mikana.*

Roast; I roast, *nind abwe.* (Nawatjiw). I roast it, (*in.*, *an.*) *nind abwen; nind abwenan.* I roast Indian corn, *nind abwâmine.* I roast an ear of Indian corn, *nind agwâtigwe.*

Roasted ear of Indian corn, *abwâtigwan.*

Rob; I rob, *nin makandwê.* (Maskattwew). I rob him, *nin makamâ.* I rob it, take it by force, (*in.*, *an.*) *nin makandwen; nin makandwenan.*

Robber, *makandwéwinini.*

Robbery, robbing, *makandwêwin.*

Rock, *âjibik.* On the rock, *ogidâbik, ogidâbikang.* Under the rock, *anamâjibik.* There is a perpendicular rock, *kish*

kabika. In a place where there is a perp. rock, *kishhâbikang.* There is a steep rock, *passabika.* In a place where there is a steep rock, *passâbikang.* The rock is wet, *nibiwabikamâgad.*—I make a hollow in a rock, *nin wimbâbikaan ajibik.*
Rock ; I rock him, *nin tchitchibakona.* I rock myself, *nin wewébis.*
Rocking-chair, *wewêbisoni-apâbiwin.*
Rock island, *minissâbik.*
Rocky ; it is rocky, *ajibikoka.*
Rocky Mountains, *Assini-wadjiw.* (Stone-mountain.)
Rod ; little rod or twig, *kibins, mitigons.*
Roe, *wak.* Roe, eggs of fish, *otig, otigwag.*
Rogue, *matchi aiâwish.* I am a rogue, *nin matchi-aiaawishiw, nin mamandêssandis.*
Roll, (on rollers ;) I roll, *nin titibakossatchige.* I roll it, (*in., an.*) *nin titibakossatwadan ; nin titibakôssatwana.*—It rolls (a canoe, etc.) *aiânibesse.*
Roll about ; I roll about, lying, *nin titibita, nin titibishimon, nin gwekwenibita.*
Roll away ; I roll away s. th., *nin titibinige.* I roll him, (her, it) away, *nin titibina ; nin titibinan.* I roll it away for him, *nin titibinamawa.*
Roll down ; I roll him (her, it) down, *nin titibibina ; nin titibibinan.* I make him (her, it) roll down, *nin titibishkawa ; nin titibishkan.*
Roller, *titibakossatchigan.*
Rolling ; it is rolling, (a canoe, boat, etc.) *gakokwamagad.* It is not rolling, it is sure, *kitagwinde, songigawishkamagad.*
Roof, *apakôdjigan* (Apakkwân).
Roof ; I roof, (make a roof,) *nind apakodjige.* I roof it, *nind apakodon.*
Room ; there is room, *tâwissin, tâwishkâde, inaiemagad.* There is room enough in it, *dêbishkine.*—There is room enough for us, *nin dêbishkinemin.* I have room, (sitting,) *nin dêbab.* I make room for him to sit down, *nin tawabitawa.* I make room in stopping aside, *nin tawigabaw.* I make room for him in stopping aside, *nin tawigabawitawa.*
Room, (in a house,) *abiwin.* It is all in one room, *mishâwate.* It is made all in one room, *mishâwatchigâde.* I make it all in one room, *nin mishâwaton.*
Roost, hen-roost, *pakaakwewigamêg.*
Root, *otchibik.* It is with the root, *gigitchibikagissin.* A big root growing in the water, *akandamo.*
Root-house, *opiniwigamig, akiwigamig*
Root of fir or pine, to sew a canoe, *watab.* I fetch thin roots, to sew a canoe, *nin manadabi.*
Rope, *biminakwân.* Small rope, *biminakwânens.* I make ropes, *nin biminakwânike.*
Ropemaker, *biminakwânikewinini.*
Ropemaker's work, trade or business, *biminakwânikewin.*
Rosary, *anamiéminag.* I say

the rosary, *nind agimag anamieminag.* I make a rosary, *nind anamieminike.*

Rose, rose-flower, *ogin, oginiwâbigon.*

Rose-bush, rose-tree, *oginiminagawanj.*

Rose-colored; it is rose-colored, (*in., an.*) *oginiwâbigoning inande; oginiwâbigoning inanso.*

Rotten; I am (it is) rotten, *nin pigishkanan; pigishkanad.*

Rotten potato, *pigishkani-opin.*

Rotten wood, *pigidjissag.* It is rotten, (wood, *in., an.*) *pigidjissagad; pigidjissagisi.*

Rouge, *osânaman.* I put rouge on my cheeks, *nind osanamani.* (Wiyaman).

Round; I am (it is) round, *nin wâwiies; wâwiieia.* I cut it round, (*in., an.*) *nin wâwiiekedan; nin wâwiiekona.* I make it round, *nin wâwiieton.*

Round, (globular;) it is round, (*in., an.*) *wawiieminagad, bikominagad, babikominagad; wawiieminagisi, bikominagisi, babikominagisi*

Round, around, *giwitaii.* Round in the country, *giwitakamig.*

Route; I take another route, *nin baké, nin bakéwis.* I make a crooked route, *nin washkosse, nin washkika.*

Rove; I rove, *nin baba-danis.*

Row; we are all in a row or range, *nin nibidé-aiâmin.* We sit in a row, *nin nibidébimin.* We sleep in a row, *nin nibidegwâmin.*

Row; I row, *nin ajéboie.*

Rub; I rub with s. th., *nin jijobiige, nin sinigwaige.* I rub him, (her, it,) *nin jijobiwa, nin sinigona, nin sinigonindjama; nin jijobian, nin sinigwaan, nin sinigonindjangan.*

Rub against, it rubs, *sinigwîssin.*

Rudder, *odâkan, adikweigan.* (Takkwahamonâttik).

Ruffle, *niskanagwetchigan.*

Ruin, *banâdisiwin, banâdjiiwewin, nishiwanâdjiiwewin.*

Ruin; I ruin, *nin banâdjiiwe, nin nishiwanâdjiiwe.* I ruin him, (her, it,) *nin banâdjia, nin nishiwanadjia; nin banadjiton, nin nishiwanadjiton.*

Rum, *ishkotewâbo.*

Rumor, *babamâdjimowin.*

Rump, *miskwassab.* I have a large rump, *nin pikwakossagidiie.*

Rumple; I rumple or crush it, (stuff,) (*in., an.*) *nin mimigibidon; nin mimigibina.*

Run; I run, *nin bimibato, nind abato.* I begin to run, *nin mâdjibato.* I run slowly, *nin bédjibato.* I run fast, *nin babâpijisse, nin kijikabato, nin kijibato.* It runs fast, *kijikamagad.* It runs, (water, etc.) *bimidjiwan.* It runs this way, (water, etc.) *bidjidjiwan.* It runs fast, *kijidjiwan.* It runs on, *madjidjiwan.* It runs out, *iskidjiwan; ondjigamagad.*

Run about; I run about, *nin babâmibato.* I am made to run about, *nin babâmibaigo.*

Run after; I run after him, *nin biminajikawa.* (Pimitisahwew). I make him run after me, *nin babamibaa.* I run after persons of the other sex, *nin nishibanikam.* I run breathless after it, *nind ondanam.* We run or rush greedily after s. th., *nin gandjibaidimin.*

Run around; I run around s. th., *nin giwitabato, nin bijibato.*

Run away; I run away, *nin gimi, nind ojim.* I run away for safety, *nin gindjibaiwe, nind ojim.* I run away to great haste, *nin madjibaiwe.*

Run back; I run back again, *nin giwébato.*

Run backwards; I run b., *nind ajébato.*

Run down; I run down, *nin nissandawebato.* I run down the hill, *nin nissâkiwebato, nin gakadjiwébato.*

Run in; I run in, *nin pindigébato.* I run in the water, *nin bakobibato.*

Runner, *bemibatod.* Fast runner, *kejikabatod.*

Running, *bimibatowin.*

Run out; I run out, *nin sâgisibato.*

Run over, I fill it so that it runs over, *nin sagadashkinadon, nin sikashkinadon, nin sigibadon.* It is so full that it runs over, *sigashkine.* It runs over, *sigissemagad.*

Run together, we run together, *nin mawandôbaidimin.*

Run up; I run up stairs, *nind akwandawébato.* I run up on a mountain, *nind amâdjiwebato.*

Rush for mats, *anâkanashk, apagwêshkwai.* I cut rush for mats, *nin manashkossiwe.*

Rush; I rush to some place, *nind apâidis.* We rush to some place, *nind apâidimin.* We rush or run together, *nin mawandôbaidimin.* I rush upon somebody, *nin mawinajiwe.* I rush upon him, (her, it,) *nin mawinanadan.* I rush upon him suddenly, *nin môkitawa.*

Rush. S. Run out.

Rusty; it is rusty, *agwâgwissin.* It is rusty, (metal, *in., an.*) *agwagwabikissin, agwagwabikad; agwâgwabikishin, agwagwabikisi.*

Rut; the animal is rutting, *amanôso awessi.* The dog is rutting, *amanâssimo animosh.* (Notjihituw).

Rutabaga, *osawitchiss.*

Rye, *misimin.* (Wâbanomin).

S

Sabbath or sabbath-day, rest-day, *anwebiwinigijigad, anamiegijigad.*
Sack, bag, *mashkimod.* Sack made of linden-bark, *assigobanimod.* A sack of..., *ningotowan, ningotoshkin.*—S. Bag.
Sackcloth, *mashkimodewegin.*
Sackcloth, (mourner's or penitent's dress,) *netageowegin.*
Sack Indian, *Osagi.*
Sack language, *osagimowin.* I speak the Sack lan., *nind osagim.*
Sack squaw, *osagikwe.*
Sacrament, *Sakremâ.* (Ayamihewinanâtâwihuwin).
Sacrifice,* (act of sacrificing,) *pagidendamowin, pagidjigewin, pagidinigan.* (Webinâsuwin, pakitinâsuwin).
Sacrifice, (gift,) *pagidinigan, pagidjigan.*
Sacrifice, (vow,) *dibandowin.* (Asotâmowin).
Sacrifice; I sacrifice, *nin pagidjige, nin pagidinige.* I sacrifice to somebody, *nin pagidinamage, nin pagidendamage.* I sac. it to him, *nin pagidinamawa, nin pagidendamawa.* I sacr. him, (her, it,) *nin pagidenima ; nin pagidendan.* I sacr. myself, *nin pagidenindis.* I sacr. (or give) to myself, *nin pagidinamadis.* I sacr. him (her, it) to myself, *nin pagidinamadisonan ; nin pagidinamadison.*
Sacrificer, *pagidjigewinini, pagidinigewinini.*
Sacrificing-altar, *pagidinigéwinikan, pagidjigéwinikan.* (Pakitinâsuwinâttik).
Sacristy, *endaji-bisikwanoied mekatewikwanaie.*
Sad, *kashkendagwakamig.* I am sad, *nin kashkêndam, nin wassitawendam, nin naninawendagos, nin nibongadis.* (Kesinateyittakwan).
Saddle, *tessabiwin.* I make saddles, *nin tessabiwinike.* (Aspapiwin).
Saddler, *tessabiwinikewinini.*
Sadness, *kashkendamowin, wassitawendamowin.*
Sadness of heart, *kashkendamideewin.*
Safety; I fly to some place for safety, *nind ininijim.* I fly to him (her, it) for safety, *nin nâjinijima, nin nâdjinijima.*
Sagacity of an animal, *awessiainendamowin.*
Said ; it is said, *kiwê.* (Yâkki).
Sail, *ningâssimonon.*
Sail ; I sail, *nin bimash.* (Yâkâstimow). I sail about, *nin babâmash.* I sail to the shore, I make for the shore, *nind agwaiash.* I sail across a bay,

* NOTE. For the sacrifices of *pagan* Indians, see Pagan sacrifice, etc.

etc., *nind âjawash.* I sail with him, *nin bimiwidashima.* I sail in a certain manner, *nind inash.* I sail fast, *nin kijiiash.* I sail with a fair wind, *nin minwash.*
Sail-cloth, *ningâssimononigin.*
Sailing, *bimâshiwin.*
Sailor, *nâbikwâninini.*
Sail-pole, (mast,) *ningâssimononak, ningâssimononâtig.*
Sail-rope, *ningâssimononeiâb.*
Sail-yard, *bimidakobidjigan.*
Saint, *kitchitwa.*
Saint in heaven, *ketchitwâwendagosid gijigong ebid.*
Salmon-trout, *majamégoss, adajawameg, ajawameg.* There are salmon-trout, *majamégossika.*
Salt, *jiwitâgan,* or *siwitâgan.*
Salt; I salt, *nin jiwitâganaige.* I salt for somebody, *nin jiwitaganaamage.*
Salted; it is salted, (*in., an.*) *jiwan, jiwitaganiwan, jiwitaganaigâde; jiwisi, jiwitâganiwi, jiwitaganaigâso.* It tastes salted, (*in., an.*) *jiwitaganipogwad; jiwitaganipogoss.*
Saltfish, salted fish, *jiwitâganigigô.*
Salting, *jiwitaganaigewin.*
Saltmeat, salted meat, *jiwitaganiwiiass.*
Saltwater, *jiwitâganâbo.*
Salutation, greeting, *anamikâgewin, anamikâgowin.* Mutual salutation, *anamikodâdiwin.*
Salute; I salute or greet, *nind anamikage.* I am saluted, *nind anamikâgo.* I salute him, (her, it,) *nind anamikawa; nind anamikan.*
Salute; I salute, inclining the head, *nin gândikwêtage.* I salute him, *nin gândikwetawa.*
Salve, *jijobiigan, mashkiki.*
Same, (Peyakwan), we are considered all the same person, *nin bejigwendagosimin.* It is considered all the same thing, *bejigwendagwad.* Always in the same place, or in the same manner, *bejigwanong.* At the same time, *bekish.* (Kisik). It is all the same, *mi tibishko.*
Sanctify; I sanctify him, *nin kitchitwawendagosia, nin kitchitwawina, nin kitchitwawenima.* I sanctify it, *nin kitchitwawinan, nin kitchitwawendan.*
Sand, *négaw, mitawan.* On the sand, *mitâwang.* (Iyekaw). There is sand, *négawika, mitawanga.* Fine white sand, *pîngwi, négaw.*
Sand cherry, *négawimin, assissawemin.*
Sand cherry shrub, *négawiminagawanj, assissawéminagawanj.*
Sand-hill; there is a steep sandhill, *kishkatâwanga.*
Sand-stone, *pingwâbik.*
Sandy beach; there is a sandy beach, *mitâwanga.* There is a lake with a sandy beach, *mitâwangâgama.*
Sandy Lake, *Ga mitâwangâgamag.*
Sap, *onsiban.* (Mestan). I collect the sap of maple-trees, *nind awasibi.* The sap begins to run, *mâdjiga.* (Mestasuw, mestanawiw). The sap runs fast, *kijiga.* It runs at night, or in the night, *nibâgâ.* The sap is spoiled, *wakwaga-*

mi nibi. It runs no more, *ishkwâgâ.*
Sash, *wâssétchiganâtig.*
Satan, *matchi manito, matchi aiaâwish, manisiwinissi.*
Satisfied ; I am sat., *nin minwendam, nin débenim, nin débendam, nin débagenim.*
Satisfy ; I satisfy him, *nin minonawea, nin débia, nin debisia, nin mînwendamia.* I satisfy it, *nin dêbiton.*
Satisfying ; it is sat., *minwendâgwad.*
Saturate ; I saturate him, *nin débissinia.* I saturate myself, *nin débissin.*
Saturated ; I am sat., *nin débissin, nin gi-débissin.*
Saturday, *mariegijigad.* It is Saturday, *mariegijigad.* On Sat., *mariegijigak,* or, *wâbang wa-anamihegijigak.*
Saturity, *débissiniwin.*
Saucer, *onâgans, anîbishâbo-onâgans.*
Savage. S. Indian.
Savage life, *pagwanawisiwin, pagwanawanisiwin, anishinâbe bimâdisiwin.* I lead a savage life, *nin pagwanawis, nin pagwanawâdis.*
Save, *jeniia makak.*
Save ; save it, conserve it, (*in., an.*) *nin mâwandjiton ; nin mâwandjia.*
Save, (in. s. in.) S. Live. I make live.
Savior, *ga-nodgimoad ki tchitchâgonânin.* (Pemâtjihiwet).
Saw, *kishkibodjigan, tâshkibodjigan.*
Saw; I saw, *nin kishkibodjige, nin tâshkibodjige.* I saw it (*in., an.*), *nin kishkibodon, nin tâshkibodon ; nin kishkibona, nin tâshkibona.*
Saw-bill, (bird,) *ansig.*
Saw-dust, *biwibodjigan.*
Sawing, *kishkibodjigewin, tâshkibodjigewin.*
Sawmill, *tâshkibodjigan, tâshkigibodjigan.* Steam sawmill, *ishkoté-tâshkibodjigan.*
Sawn ; it is sawn, (*in., an.*) *kishkibode, tâshkibode ; kishkiboso, tâshkiboso.*
Sawyer, *taiâshkibodjiged, tâshkibodjigewinini*
Say ; I say, *nind ikkit.* He says, *iwa.* It says, *ikkitomagad.* I say it aloud, *nin nâbowadan.* (Itwew). I say s. th., of or to him, (her, it,) *nind ina,* (Itew), *nind idân.* I say s. th. of myself, *nind idis.* We say s. th. of each other, or to each other, *nind idimin.* I say what I ought not to say, *nin wawiiagim.*
Saying, *ikkitowin, gigitowin.*
Scab, *omigiwin.*
Scabbard, (or cover,) *pindanonikaâjigan, pindaodjigan.*
Scabbious person, *wemigid.* I am scabbious, *nind omigi.*
Scabby ; I am scabby, *nind omigi.*
Scaffold, *agôdjiwanan, agôdjiwananak, tessakwaigan.* I make a scaffold, *nind agôdjiwananakoke.*
Scald ; I scald him, (her, it,) *nin bashkobisswa, nin baskwabowasswa.*
Scale, (balance,) *dibâbishkodjigan ; tibâbadjigan.*
Scale (of a fish,) *wanagâai.*
Scale ; I scale, *nin tchigaawe.* I scale a fish, *nin tchigaana gigo.*

Scalp, Siou-scalp, *banishtigwân.*
Scalp; I scalp him, *nin manijwa; nin pakwandibejwa,* (*pabondibejwa.*)
Scandal, *matchi kikinowâbamigowin, matchi kikinowâbandaiwewin.*
Scandalize; I scand. him, *nin matchi kikinoamawa, nin matchi kikinowâbamig.* He scandalizes me, *nin matchi kikinoamag, nin matchi kikinowâbama.*
Scar, *odjishiwin.* I have a scar, *nind odjishig.*—I have a scar on the arm, hand, etc.
Scarcely, *agâwa.* (Etataw).
Scarcity, *manêsiwin.* There is scarcity of wood for fuel, *manéssaga.*
Scare; I scare him, *nin segia, nin segisia, nind oshâwa, nind oshâkawa.*
Scared; I am scared, *nin segis, nin segendam, nin nisaiendam.*
Scarification, for bleeding, *pepeshowewin.*
Scarifier, *paiêpeshowed.*
Scarify, for bleeding; I scarify, *nin pepeshowe.* I scar. him, *nind pepeshwa.* I scar. myself, *nin pepeshodis.*
Scarlet, *miskwégin, onandewegin, pagakigin.*
Scatter; I scatter, *nin biwimebinige.* I scatter it, (*in., an.*) *nin biwiwebinan, nin biniwebina.*
Scatter about; I scatter it about, (*in., an.*) *nin saswenan, nin sasweshkan; nin saswéna, nin sasweshkawa.*
Scent; I search by scent, *nin nandomandjige.*
Scholar, *kikinoamâgan, kekinoamâwind.*
School, *kikinoamâding.* I go to school, *kikinoamâding nind ija.* I come from school, *kikinoamâding nind ondjiba.* I keep school, *nin kikinoamâge.*
School-book, *kikinoamâdi-masinaigan.*
School-house, *kikinoamâdiwigamig.*
School-section, *kikinoamâdiwaki*
School-teacher, *kekinoamaged, kekimoamagewinini..* Female school-teacher, *kikinoamagekwe.*
Science, *kikendâssowin, bisiskendjigewin.* I possess science, *nin bisiskendjige, nin kikendass.*
Scissors, *mojwâgan, assiponigan, tagokomân.* (Paskwâhamâtuwin).
Scold; I scold, *nind aiâwiwe, nin nanibikiwe, ningikawidam.* I scold him, *nind aiâwa, nin nanibikima, nin nanibikiganona, nin gikama.*
Scolding, *aiâwiwin, aiâwidiwin, nanibikiwewin, nanibikindiwin.*
Scorn; I scorn, *nin bâpinodage, nin nishibapinodage.* I scorn him, (her, it,) *nin nishibâpinodawa; nin nishibopinodân.*
Scorning, *nishibapinodamowin, bapinodagewin.*
Scoundrel, *matchi-aiâawish.*
Scourge, *bashanjeigan.* (Pasastehigan).
Scourge; I scourge, *nin bashanjêige.* I scourge him, *nin bashanjêwa.*
Scourged; I am scourged, *nin bashanjêogo, nin bashanjéigas*

Scranch; I scranch it, (*in.*, *an.*) *nin gâpandan, nin gapwewendan; nin gâpama, nin gapwewema.*

Scrape; I scrape, *nin gaskaskaige.* I scrape him, (her, it,) *nin gaskaskâwa; nin gaskaskaan.*—I scrape a bark, *nin gashkakwaige.* I scrape a fish, *nin gashkamegwaige.* I scrape a skin, *nin mâdaige, nin nâjigaige.* I scrape it, (skin, *in.*, *an.*) *nin mâdaan; nin mâdâwa.*—Also, I scrape a skin or hide, *nin tchishakwaige.* I scrape it, (skin, *in.*, *an.*) *nin tchishakwaan, nin tchishakwâwa.*

Scraper, *mâdaigan, najigaigan, tchishakwaigan.*

Scratch; I scratch, *nin pasagobijiwe.* I scratch him, (her, it,) *nin pasagobina; nin pasagobidon.*

Scratch slightly; I scratch him sl., *nin tchitchigibina.* I scratch myself, *nin tchitchigi, nin tchitchigibinidis.* I scr. his head, *nin tchitchigindibebina.* I scr. my head, *nin tchitchigindibebinidis.*

Screetchowl, *kakâbishé.*

Screw, *bamiskwaigâdeg sagaigan.*

Screw; I screw, *nin bimiskwaige.*

Screw-driver, *bimiskwaigan.*

Screw-vice, *kitchi-takwandjigan.*

Scribe, *ojibiigéwinini.*

Scythe, *kishkashkijigan, pashkwashkijigan.*

Sea, *kitchigami, jiwitâgani-kitchigami,* (ocean.)

Sea; very far out in the sea or lake, *mijishâwagâm, mishâwagâm.*—The sea runs high, *mamangâshka.* The sea runs in a certain manner, *inâshkamagad.*

Sea-bread, *anakona.*

Sea-dog, *panossim.*

Seal, *askik.* The skin of a seal, *askigwaiân.*

Seal, *agokiwassitchigan, agakiwassitchiganâbik, ashidjikiwakaigan; masinihiwakaigan, masinikiwagaiganâbik.*

Seal; I seal, *nind agokiwassige, nind agokiwassitchige, nind ashidjikiwagaige; nin masinikiwagaige.* I seal it, (*in.*, *an.*) *nind agokiwassan, nin masinikiwagaan; nind agokiwasswa; nin masinikiwagâwa.*

Sealed; I am (it is) sealed, *nind agokiwassigas, nin masinikiwagaigas; agokiwassigade, agokiwassitchigade, masinikiwagaigade.*

Sealing-wax, *agokiwassigan.*

Sea-mark, *kikinnandawan.* I put up sea-marks, *nin kikinândawaige.* There are sea-marks, *kikinandawade.*

Seamstress, *gashkigwassoike.*

Search by scent; I search by s., *nind nandomandjige.*

Sea-shell, *wawiiemigan, ess.*

Season; I season, *nind apâbowe.* I season it, (*in.*, *an.*) *nind apabowadan; nind apabowana.* Any thing to season victuals with, *apabowân.*

Seasoned; it is seasoned, *apabowâde.*

Seasoning victuals, *apabowewin.*

Seat, *apawiwin, namadabiwin.* I change seats, *nind ândab.*

Secret, *gimodisiwin, kaiadjigadeg.* It is a secret, *gimodad, kâdjigâde.*

Secretly, *gimodj.*
Sedition, *ombâsondiwin.*
Seduce; I seduce him, *nin banâdjia, nin waiejima, nin wanishima, nin matchi kikinoamawa, nin matchi ijiwebisia, nin nishiwanâdjia.* I seduce him (her) to impurity, *nin gagibasoma, nin pisigwâdisia.* —I seduce (deceive) with my words, *nin waiejitagos.*
See! *wegwagi!* (Mâdjikutji).
See; I see, *nin wâb.* I see well, *nin minwâb.* I see s. th., *nin wâbandjige.* I see him, (her, it,) *nin wâbama; nin wâbandan.* I see myself, *nin wâbandis, nin wâbandamadis.* I see so far or from so far, *nind akwâb.* I see from such a distance, *nin débab.* I make him see, *nin wâbia.* I make him see it, *nin wâbandaa.* I see s. th. relating to him, *nin wâbandamawa.* I see clearly, plainly, *nin wasseiâb.* I make him see clearly, *nin wasseiabia.* I see him (her, it) well or plainly, *nin missâbama; nin wissâbandan.* I make him see it plainly, *nin missâbandaa.* I cannot see him (her, it) well, *nin bigisawinawa; nin bigisâwinan.* I see him (her, it) so..., in a certain manner, *nind ijinawa, nind inâbama; nind ijanan, nind inâbandan.* I arrive to the point or moment of seeing him, (her, it,) *nind odissâbama; nind âdissâbandan.* I see him coming this way, *nin bidâbama, nin bidisama.* I see it in going by, *nin babishagendan.*
Seed, *minikan.*
See from a distance; I see (or look) from a certain distance, *nind onsâb.* I see him (her, it) from a certain distance, *nind onsâbama; nind onsâbandân.*
Seek; I seek, *nin nandawâbange, nin nandawâbandjige, nin nandonige, nin nandonêige, nin nandôaiâ.* I seek him, (her, it,) *nin nannawâbama, nin nandonéwa; nin nandawâbandan, nin nandonêân.*
Seeking, *nandonéigewin.*
Seem; it seems to me, *nind inendam.* It seems..., *tanassag...* It seems like..., *nindigo...* (Mana piko).
Seen; I am seen, *nin wâbamigo, nin wâbandjigas.* It is seen, *wâbandjigade.* I can (it can) be seen from..., *nin débâbaminagos; débâbaminagwad.*
See-sawing, *tchatchângekoshkamâdiwin.* We play see-sawing, *nin tchatchângakoshkamadimin.*
See through; I see through it, *nin jabwâbandan.*
Seize; I seize, *nin takonige, nin takoniwe.* I seize him, (her, it,) *nin takona; nin takonan.*
Seldom, *wika, wâwika.*
Select; I select them (*an..in.*) *nin sagiginag; nin gagiginanan.*
Self, *tibinawe, tetibinawe.*
Self-command, *mindjiminidisowin.*
Self-conceit, *maminadisiwin, sasegawenindisowin.*
Self-conceited; I am self-con., *nin maminadis, nin sasegawéndân niiaw, nin sasegawenindis.*

Self-deceit, *waiėjindisowin*. I deceive myself, *nin waiėjindis*.

Self-defence, *nanâkwiwin*. I defend myself, *nin nanâkwi*.

Self-glorification, *kitchitwawenindisowin, mamikwasowin*. I glorify myself, *nin kitchitwâwenindis, nin mamikwâdis*.

Self-tormenting, *kotagiidisowin*. I torment myself, make myself suffer, *nin kotagiidis*.

Self-willed; I am self-willed, *nin bashigwadis, nin mashkawîndibe*.

Sell; I sell, *nind atâwe*. I sell him, (her, it,) *nind atâwenan; nind atâwen*. I sell him s. th., *nind âtâma*. I sell high, at high prices, *nin sanagwe, nin sanagagindass, nin mamisswe, nin mamissagindâss*. I sell cheap, *nin wendis, nin wendwe*.

Send; I send, *nin nindâiwe*. I send him s. th., *nin nindaa*. I send it, (*in., an.*) *nin nindaiwen; nin nindâiwenan*. I send him somebody, *nind ininajaamawa, nind ijinajaamawa*. I send s. th, to somebody, *nin madjidaiwe*. (Itisahwew). I send it to somebody, (*in., an.*) *nin madjidaiwen; nin madjidaiwenan*.—I send him before me, *nin niganinijâwa*. I send him somewhere, *nind ininajâwa, nind ijinajawa* I send him somewhere pressingly, *nin gandjinajawa*. I send him away, *nind ikonajâwa, nin mâdjinajawa*. I send him down, *nin nissândawenajawa*. I send him out of doors, *nin sâgidjinajawa*. (Wiyawitisahwew).

Sense, good sense, *nibwâkâwin* nonsense, *gagibâdisiwin* (Iyinisiwin).

Senses; I have my senses, *nin mikaw, nin kikendam*. (Kiskisiw). I lose my senses (fainting), *nin wanimikaw*. (Wani-kiskisiw). I lose my senses from time to time, *nin babishkwendam*. I recover my senses, *nin bisiskâdis*. I have my senses again, *nin bisiskadondam*.

Sent; I am sent away, *nin mâdjinajaigas, nind ikonajaigas*.

Sentence; I pronounce a sentence over him, *nin gijakona*.

Sentinel, *akandowinini*.

Separate; I separate from him, (her, it,) *nin bakêshkawa, nin bakėwina; nin babêshkan, nin bakêwidon*. The road separates, *bakêmo mikana*.

Separately, *bebakân*. (Pâpiskis).

Separation of persons, *webinidiwin, babeshkodadiwin, bakėidiwin*. Separation of a lake, *bakėgama*.

September, *manomini-gisiss, manominike-gisiss*. (Notjihituwipisim).

Serene; it is serene, (clear weather,) *mijakwad*. (Wâses kwan).

Serious; I am serious, *nin gikâdis*.

Sermon, *gagikwewin, anamiêgagikwewin*.

Sermon-book, *gagikwe-masinaigan*.

Serpent, *ginébig*. Young serpent, *ginébigons*. Big borned serpent, *mishiginébig*. Another kind of serpent, *nadowe*. The serpent moults, *jigota*

ginêbig. The skin of a serpent, *ginebigojagaai, ginebigowaiân*.—Serpent with legs, *okadiginebig*.
Servant, (male or female servant,) *anokitâgan, bamitâgan*.
Serve; I serve, I am in service, *nind anokitâge, nin bamitâge*. I serve him, (her, it,) *nin anokitawa, nin bamitawa, nin bamitasikawa*.
Service, *anokitâgewin, bamitâgewin, anokiwin*. I am in service, *nind anokitâge, nin bamitâge*.—He (she, it) does me services, *nind abadjia; nind abadjiton*. He (she, it) does me services in such a manner, *nind inâbadjia; nind inabadjiton*.
Serviceable object, *an*. or *in*., *âbadjitchigan*.
Set, *ningotwêwân, ningotwêwanagisimin*. Two sets, three sets, etc., *nijwéwân, nisswêwan*, etc. So many sets, *dasswêwan*.
Set apart; I set him (her, it) apart, *nin kikassa; nin kikaton* —S. Choose. (Astwaw).
Settle; I settle, *nind inakonige, nin nanâitchige*. I settle him, *nin dibowana*.—I settle my account, I pay, *nin kijikan nin masinaigan*. I settle with him, *nin kijakawa*.—I let it settle, (liquid,) *nin wakamissiton*.
Seven, *nijwâssi*. We are seven, *nin nijwâtchimin*. (Tepâkup). There are seven *in*. objects, *nijwâtchinon*.
Seven, *nijwâsso*..., in compositions, which see in the Second Part.
Seven every time, seven each or to each, *nenijwâsswi*.
Seven hundred every time, 700 each or to each, *nenijwâsswak*.
Seventh; the seventh, *eko-nijwâtching*. The seventh time, *nijwâtching*.
Seven thousand, *nijwâtching midâsswak*.
Seven times, *nijwâtching*.
Several, *anotch ânind, wiiagi*. (Atit).
Several things, *anotch gego, wawiiag gego, wiiagiaii*.
Several times, *naningotinong, eniwek naningim*. (Ayâskaw).
Severe, (strict;) I am severe, *nin sanagis*. I think he is severe, *nin sanagenima*. (Ayimisiw).
Sew; I sew, *nin gashkigwâss*. I begin to sew, *nin mâdjigwâss*. I sew well, *nin nitawigwâss*. I sew it, (*in*., *an*.) *nin gashkigwâdan; nin gashkigwâna*. I sew it for him, *nin gashkigwadamawa*. —I gather together sewing, *nin mawandogwâss*. I sew several pieces together, *nin mawandogwadanan*.—I fix or repair sewing, *nin wawekwass*. I repair it, (*in*., *an*.) *nin wawekwadan; nin wawekwana*.—I sew a canoe, *nin gashkigon*.
Sewed slightly, (stitched;) it is sewed slightly, (*in*., *an*.) *tchitchibogwâde, sassagigwâde; tchitchibogwâso, sassagigwâso*
Sewing, *gashkigwâssowin*.
Sewing-silk, *senibawâssab*.
Sewing thread, *gashkigwâssonéiâb, assabab, nâbîkwasson*.
Shadow; there is shadow, *agawâte*. I make shadow with my body, *nind agawateshkam*,

nind agawateshin. I cover him (her, it) with my shadow, *nind agawateshkan.* It covers me with his sh., *nind agawateshkagon.* It makes shadow, *agawatesse.*

Shake; I shake, (tremble,) *nin niningishka, nin niningibinig.* (Nanâmipayiw). I shake or tremble with fear, *nin niningiségis.* My heart shakes, *nin niningidee.* I shake myself sitting, *nin mimigwab.* I I shake him, (her, it,) *nin mimigowebina, nin goshkwakobina.*

Shaken; it is shaken by the wind, *niningassin, niningánashkassin.*

Shaking fever, *niningâpinewin, niningishkawapinewin.* I have the sh. f., *nin niningâpine.*

Shake off; I shake him (her, it) off, *nin bawiwebina, nin bawiwebishkawa; nin bawiwebinan, nin bawiwebishkan.* I shake off the dust from some stuff, (*in., an.*) *nin bawéginan; nin bawégina.* It is shaken off, *biwinigâde.* I shake off the dust or some other thing from my feet, *nin bawisideshimon.* I shake it off against him, *nin bawisidetawa.*

Shallow; it is a shallow, *bâgwa.* The river is shallow, *bâgwatigweia sibi.* There is a shallow place, *pitawashka.* There is a long shallow place in the lake, *jagawamika.*

Shame! *se!* (Shey!)

Shame, *agâtchiwin, menissendamowin.* (Nepewisiw). I cause shame, *nind agâtchiiwe.* It causes shame, *agatchiiwemagad.* I cause him shame, *nind agatchiâ, nind agasoma.* (Nepewimew). I bring it to shame, *nind agatchiton.*

Shameful; it is sh., it is considered sh., *agatendagwad.*

Shamefully, *agatendagwakamig, nanâpaganj.* (Nepewâkâtch).

Shameless; I am sh., *kawin nind agatchissi, kawin nin mênissendansi.*

Shameless person, *egatchissig, maiênissendansig.*

Shape, *ijinagosiwin.*

Share; I give him a large share, *nin songaona.* I take to myself a good large share, *nin songâonidis.* I give him such a share, *nind inaona.* I take to myself such a share, *nind inaonidis.*— I think he does not give me my full share, *nind anawinama.* (Otinamâwew).

Sharp; it is sharp, *ginâmagad, ginâbikad.*

Sharpen; I sharpen, *nin sissibodjige.* I sharpen it, *nin sissibodon.*

Shave; I shave, *nin gashkibâs.* I shave him, (it,) *nin gashkibâna; nin gashkibâdan.*

Shave-grass, *kisibanashk.*

Shaving, *gashkibâsowin.*

Shaving-horse, *mokodjigan tekwandjigemagak.*

Shaving-knife, razor, *gashkibâdjigan*

Shaving-man, barber, *gashkibâsowinini.*

Shaving-house, barber-shop, *gashkibâsowigamig.*

Shaving, wood-shaving, *biwekodamagan, biwikodjigan.*

Shawl, *kitchi-moshwe.*

She, *win.* (Wiya).
Shear ; I shear, *nin mojowe, nin pashkowejonge,* (*pashkwawejonge.*) I shear him, *nin mojwa.* I shear him (her, it) thoroughly, *nin pashkojwa, nin papashkojwa; nin pashkojan, nin papâshkojan.*
Shearer, *pashkwawejongewinini.*
Shears, *mojwâgan.* (Paskwahamâtuwin).
Shed at the door, *pitawigan.* There is a shed, *pitawigâde.*
Sheep, *manishtanish.* Young sheep, lamb, *manishtanishens.*
Sheepfold, *manishtanishiwigamig.*
Sheep-skin, *mânishtanishiwaiân.*
Shell, *ess.* A kind of small shell, *ojakawess.*
Shell of an egg, *wâwan onagaawang.* Shell of a tortoise or turtle, *dashwa.*
Shell ; I shell it, (*in., an.*) *nin bishagibidon, nin bishagibidjidon; nin bishagibina, nin bishagibidjina.* I shell a corn-ear, *nin yâkina nisâkosi.*
Shelter, or shade, against the wind or the sun, *tabinôon.* I make a sh., *nin tabinôige, nin tabinôonike.* There is a sh. made, *tabinôonikâde.* I am under such a shelter or shade, *nin tâbinôshimon.*—I put myself under a shelter in rainy weather, *nind agawabawas, nind agwanabawas.* I am under a shelter in rain, *nind agwanabawe, nind atchigwanânish.*
Shepherd, *manishtânishiwinini.*
Shield, *pakâkwaan ; dashwa.*
Shieft ; the wind shifted, *gwékanimad.*
Shilling, *jôniians.*
Shinbone, *okadiganama.* My, thy, his shinbone, *nikâdigan, kikâdigan, okâdigan.*
Shine, *wâsseiasiwin.*
Shine ; I shine, *nin wâsséias.* I make it shine, (*in., an.*) *nin wakeshkkaan ; nin wakeshkâwa..* It shines, *wakeshkamagad, wawakeshkamagad.*
Shiness, *awâssâsiwin.*
Shiness, (bashfulness,) *agatchishkiwin, agatchiwâdisiwin.*
Shingle, *apakôdjigan, nabagissagons.*
Shingle ; I shingle a roof, *nind apakodjige.* I shingle it, *nind apakodon.*
Shingle-nail, *sagaigans.*
Ship, *nâbikwân.* Ship of war, *migâdi-nâbikwân.*
Ship ; I ship, *nin bôsitâss.* I ship him, (her, it,) *nin bôsia ; nin bôsiton.*
Ship-captain, *nâbikwân-ogima.*
Shipped ; it is shipped, (*in., an.*) *bôsitchigâde ; bôsitchigâso.*
Shipping, *bositâssowin.*
Shipwreck ; I shipwreck, *nin bigoneshka, nin bigoneshin.*
Shirt, *papagiwaiân.*
Shiver ; I shiver, (from cold,) *nin niningadj.* Shivering with cold, *niningadjiwin.*
Shoals ; there are shoals, *minâmika.*
Shoe, *makisin.* Hard shoe, (not Indian shoe,) *mitigwakisin.* I make shoes, *nin makisinike.* I put on my shoes, etc., *nin babitchi.* I take off my shoes, etc., *nin gagitchi.* I put him

his shoes on, *nin babitchia.* I take him his shoes off, *nin gagitchia.* I change shoes, *nind andakisine.* I have shoes on, *nin gigakisine.* I have only one shoe on, *nin nabanêkisine.* I have two pair of shoes on, *nin bitokisine.*

Shoe-brush, *wâssikwadjigan, makisin-wâssikwadjigan.*

Shoe-buckle, *sagâkisinebison.*

Shoemaker, *mekisiniked, makisinikewinini.*

Shoemaker's shop, *makisinikéwigamig.*

Shoemaker's work, trade or business, *makisinikewin.*

Shoe-string, or moccasin-string, *makasinêiâb.*

Shoot, young shoot, *oshkijin, weshkiging mitigons.* It is a young shoot, *oshkigin.*

Shoot, (with a gun;) I shoot, *nin pâshkisige.* I shoot at him, (her, it,) *nin pâshkiswa; nin pâshkisan.* I shoot in the air, *nin nakwenage.* I shoot him in the air, *nin nakwenawa.* —I shoot at a mark, *nin godaakwe.*

Shoot, (with bow and arrow); I shoot, *nin bimôdjige, nind inae.* (Pimutakkwew.) I am shooting, *nin babimodwake.* I shoot at him, (her, it,) *nin bimôa; nin bimôdân.*—I shoot at a mark, *nin bimwâtigwe,* (*bimôtigwe.*)

Shooting, *pâshkisigewin, pâpâshkisigewin; bimôdjigewin.*

Shore; on the shore, (on the beach,) *agâming* Near the shore, *tchigibig, tchigagâm.* Distant from the shore, *nâwitch.* I paddle my canoe to the shore, *nin nâdagâmeam.* On the opposite shore, *agâming, âjawagâm, awâssagâm.*

Short; I am short and thick, *nin takwâbewis, nin bitikwâbewis.*

Short; I am (it is) short, *nin takos; takwâmagad.* It is short: A building, *takondemagad.*

Short, shortly, *waiba, waieba.*

Shorten; I shorten it, *nin takwaton.* I sh. it by cutting off; (*in., an*) *nin takwakwaan; nin takwakwâwa.*

Short-legged; I am sh.-l., *nin tatakogâde.* It is short-legged, *tabassigâbawi,* (it stands low.)

Short time; a short time, *atchina, wénibik.* (Kanak).

Short way, *kakam.* I take the short way, *kakam nind ija, nin kakamishka.*

Shot, *anwins, jishibanwi, jishibanwins.* My shot and balls are all gone, *nin tchâganwissin.* (Niskasinïy).

Shot; I am shot, *nin mikoshkos.*

Shot-pouch, *pindassinân, pindassinadjigan.*

Shoulder, *odinimanganima.* My, thy, his shoulder, *nindinimangan, kidinimangan, odinimangan.* Between the shoulders, *nassawidinigan.* I lay him (her, it) on my shoulders and carry him, (her, it), *nin pagidjidinimanganeona; nin pagidjidinimanganeonân.*

Shoulder-blade; my, thy, his shoulder-blade, *nindinigan, kidinigan, odinigan.* I break my sh., *nin pakisaginebinidis.* I break his sh., *nin pakisaginebina.*

Shoulder-part of an animal, *osagin.*

Shout; I shout, *nin bibâg.* I shout with joy, *nin sassâkwe.* (Sâkowew).

Shouting, *bibâgiwin.* Shouting with joy, *sassâkwewin.*

Shove; I shove him (her, it) with my arm, *nin bidjinikawa; nin bidjinikan, nin bidjinissiton.*

Shovel, *mangânibadjigan.*

Shovel; I shovel, *nin mangânibadjige.* I shovel it, (*in., an.*) *nin mangânibadan; nin manganibana.* I shovel snow, *nin mangânibi.*

Show, (let see;) I show, *nin wâbandaiwe.* I show it to him (her, it,) *nin wâbandaa; nin wabandâan.* I show it to him plainly, *nin missâbandan.* I show him, (her, it,) *nin wâbandaiwenan; nin wâbandaiwen.*

Show, (with the finger;) I show with the f., *nind inôige, nind ijinôige.* (Itwahamâwew). I show him (her, it) with the f., *nind inôa, nind ijinoa; nind inôan, nind ijinôan.* I show it to him with the finger, *nind inôamawa, nind ininama, nind ininamawa.*

Show, showing, *wâbandaiwewin, inôigewin.*

Show-bread, *wâbandaiwê-pakwejigan, wâbandaiwéwini-pakwéjigan.*

Shower; showers of rain are passing by, *babamibissa.* A shower of rain is coming, *bidibissa.*

Shown; any object shown with the finger, *inôigan.*

Shred, *ishkojigan, onijigan, biwijigan.*

Shrink; the boards shrink drying, *jijibâssagisowag nabagissagog.*

Shrub, *kibinsan.*

Shudder; I shudder suddenly, *nin masanika.*

Shutter, *wassetchiganâtig.*

Shut up; I shut him (her, it) up, *nin gibakwâwa; nin gibâkwaan.* I shut him up in a hole, *nin gibawa.* I shut it up against him, *nin gibâkwaamawa.* I shut it up, *nin gibissagaân.*

Shy; I am shy, *nind atchinis.* The animal is shy, *awassâsi awessi.*

Shy, (bashful;) I am shy or bashful, *nind agatchishk, nind agatchiwis, nind agatchimadis.* (Nepewisiw).

Sick; I am sick, *nind âkos, nin nanipinis.* It is sick, *âkosimagad, nanipinisimagâd.* I feel sick, *nin simis, nin simâdis.* I fall sick suddenly, *nin pangishkones* I look sick, *nind âkosinâgos.* I am sick in a certain manner, *nind inapine.* I am very sick, *nind osâmine, nin mâgwito, nin mamidawito.*—It makes me sick, *nin mânikagon.*

Sickle, *kishkashkijigan, pashkwashkijigan.*

Sickly, often sick; I am sickly, *nin nita-âkos, nind akosishk, nin migwanadis.* I have a sickly appearance, *nind âkosinâgos.*

Sickness, *âkosiwin, nanipinisiwin, inâpinewin, jindagan.* Beginning of a sickness, *mâ-*

dapinewin, mâdjinewin. Very great sickness, *osâmînewin.* Hard painful sickness, *sanagapinewin, kotagapinewin.*— Sickness caused by somebody, (according to Indian superstitions,) *anisbinâbewapinewin.* Bad shameful sickness, *mânâdapinewin.*—I begin to feel a sickness, *nin mâdji-âkos, nin mâdjine, nin mâdapine.* I give him a certain sickness, *nind inâpinana.*

Sick person, *aiâkosid, enapined.*

Side; I fall on my side, *nind apimosse.* On this side of a canoe, vessel, etc., *ondâssonag.* On the other side, *awassônag.*—On this side of a river, etc., *ondâssagâm.* On the other side, *awassagâm, ajawagâm, agâming.* On one side only, *nabanêgâm.* — On this side of a hill or mountain, *ondâssaki, ondâssadjiw.* On the other side, *awâssaki, awâssadjiw.*

Sieve, *jâboshkatchigan.*

Sift; I sift, *nin jâboshkatchige.* I sift it, (*an., in.*) *nin jâbossan, nin jâboshkassa; nin jabossaan, nin jaboshkaton.*

Sigh, *pagidanâmowin, ikwanâmowin.*

Sigh; I sigh, *nin pagidanam, nin passakadem, nind ansanam.* I sigh deeply, *nind ikwanam, nind manginansanam*

Sight; I lose sight, *nind angwâbandjige, nin banâbandam.* I lose sight of him, (her, it,) *nind angwâbama, nin banâbıma; nind angwabandan, nin panâbandân.*

Sign, *kikinawâdjitchigan, mamâkadjitchigan, mamakâsabandjigan.*

Sign, (subscribe); I sign, *nind ijinikâsowin nind aton,* (I put down my name;) *migwan nin tagina,* (I touch the pen.)

Silence, *bisânabiwin, ishkwawewin,* (*ishkowewin.*)

Silence; I silence him, *nin bisânabia.* I silence him, he cannot answer, *nin wâwanima.*

Silk, silk-stuff, *senibâ, senibawegin.*

Silk for sewing, *senibawâssabâb.*

Silk handkerchief, *seniba-moshwe.*

Silver, *joniia.* I work silver, *nin joniiâke.*

Silver; I silver it, *nin joniiâkadân.*

Silvered; it is sil., *joniiâkâde.*

Silver-money, *joniiag,* (silver-pieces.)

Silversmith, *joniiâkewinini.*

Silversmith's work, trade or business, *joniiâkewin.*

Sin, *batâdowin, batâsiwin, matchi dodamowin, matchi ijiwebisiwin.* — Small venial sin, *batâdowinens.* (Pâstâhuwin).

Sin; I sin, *nin batâ-ijiwebis, nin bataidis, nin batâindind, nin batas, nin matchi dodam, nin matchi ijiwebis.*—I sin in thoughts, *nin batâsinendam;* in words, *nin batâ-gijwe, nin batâwe;* in action, *nin batâdodam.*

Sinful; it is sinful, *manatad, batâ-ijiwebad.*

Sinfulness, *batâ-ijiwebisiwin, matchi bimâdisiwin.*

Sing; I sing, *nin nagam.* I prepare myself for singing, *nin nanâanam*. I sing for a proof, *nin godji-nagam*. I mistake in singing, *nin wânaam*. I sing it high, *nind ishpwêweton*. I sing it low, *nin tabasswêweton*. I sing to him, *nin nagamôtawa*.

Singer, *nagamôwinini*. Female singer, *nagamôikwe*.

Singing, the act of singing, *nagamôwin*.

Single; I am single, (not married,) *nind oshkinig, kawin nin wedigessi, nijike nind aia*. (Mônsâbew, mônsiskwew).

Single state, *oshkinigiwin*. (Married state, *widigendiwin*.)

Sing mocking; I sing to mock somebody or something, *nin nanâpagam*. I sing him (her, it), mocking, *nin nanâpagamonan; nin ninanâpagamon*.

Sink in; I sink in the ground with my foot, *bokakamigisse*. I sink in mud, *nin gagwânagwatchishkiwesse*. I sink in the snow, *nin gindâwagonesse*. I sink in snow or sand, walking, *nin nâwaam*. I sink to the bottom, *nin gosâbi, nin mijakisse*.

Sink in; it sinks in the ground, *gindâkamigishkamagad*.

Sinner, *baiatâ-ijiwebisid*.

Sioux Indian, *Bwân, Nâdowessi*.

Sioux language, *bwânimowin*. I speak the Sioux lan., *nin bwânim*.

Sioux scalp, *bwânishtigwân*, (Sioux head.) I bring a Sioux scalp, *nin bijiwe*.

Sioux squaw, *bwânikwe*.

Sip; I sip it, *nind odonendan, nind odonamonotan*.

Siren, *memegwessi*.

Sister, *awéma*. My, thy, his older sister, *nimissé, kimissê, omisséian*. My, thy, his younger sister, *nishimé, kishimé, oshimeian*.

Sister-in-law; my, thy, his sister-in-law, (a *male* speaking to a male or in regard to a male,) *nînim, kinim, winimon*; (a *female* speaking to a female or in regard to a female,) *nindângwe, kidângwe, odângweian*.

Sit; I sit, I sit down, I am sitting, *nin nâmadab, nin wawénab, nin tessab*. I make him sit down, *nin nâmadabia, nin wawénabia*. I sit upon, *nind agwidab, nin apab*. I sit on it, *nind apabin*. I sit well, comfortably, *nin minwab, nin naab*. I sit behind, in the last place, *nind ishkweb*. I sit on the bare ground, *nin mitab*. I sit broadly, *nin gêshawab*. I sit obliquely, *nin bimidab*. I sit straight up, *nin maiawab*. I sit by his side, *nin namadabitawa*. I sit with him, *nin widabima*. I sit a certain length of time, *nîn nomageb*. I sit with down-hanging arms, *nin jinginikeb*. I sit with crossed arms, *nind ajidenikeb*. I sit like a bird, *nin binéssiwab*. —We sit around, *nin giwitabimin*.

Sitting, the act of sitting, *namadabiwin*.

Sit up; I sit up at night, *nin nibab, nin nibénab*. I sit up watching a corpse, *nin nibéb*.

Six, *ningotwâsswi*. We are six

of us, *nin ningotwatchimin.* There are six *in.* objects, *ningotwâtchinon.*
Six, *ningotwâsso.*
Six every time, six each or to each, *neningotwâsswi.*
Six hundred every time, 600 each or to each, *neningotwâsswâk.*
Sixth; the sixth, *eko-ningotwâtching.* The sixth time, *ningotwâtching.*
Sixthly, *eko-ningotwâtching.*
Six thousand, *ningotwâtching midâsswâk.*
Six times, *ningotwâtching.*
Six times every time, six times each or to each, *neningotwâtching.*
Sixty, *ningotwâssimidana.* We are sixty, *nin ningotwâssimidânawemin.*
Skate, *joshkwâdaagan.*
Skate; I skate, *nin joskwâdae.*
Skein; one skein, *ningotônsibide.*
Sketch; I sketch it, *nin masinibian.*
Skilful; I am skilful, *nin wâwinges.* (Mamiyuw).
Skill, skilfulness, *wâwingesiwin.* I act with skilfulness, *nin wâwingetchige.*
Skin; my, thy, his skin, *ninjagaâi, kijagaâi, ojagaâian.* (Masakäy). My skin is black, *nin makatewaje.* My skin is red, *nin miskwaje.* My skin is white, *nin wâbishkaje.*
Skin of an animal, *awêssiwaiân.* (Pijiskiweyân). Skin of a *male* quadruped, *âiabéwaiân;* of the largest kind, *aîabêwegin.* Skin of a *female* quadruped, *nojéwaiân;* of the largest kind, *nojêwegin.*—Green skin, *ashkatai;* of the largest kind, *ashkigin.* Dry skin, *gaskatai;* of the largest kind, *gaskigin.* Skin of a quadruped without the hair, *pashkwâwejigan.*
Skull, *wijigan.* (Mistikwânigan). My, thy, his skull, *ninindibegan, kinindibegan, winindibegan;* or, *nishtigwânigegan, kishtigwânigegan, osktigwânigegan.* The skin of my, thy, his skull, *ninikwai, kinikwai, winikwai.* —There are skulls, *wijiganika.* Place where there are skulls, *wijiganikan.*
Sky, *gijig.* The sky is blue, *mîjakwad.* (Wâseskwan). The sky is red, *miskwawad.* Under the sky, (in the open air,) *mijishawakamig.*
Sky-blue; it is dyed sky-blue, (*in, an.*) *mijakwadong inânde; mijakwadong inanso.*
Slab, *jigobodjigan.*
Slaken; I slaken it, *nin nêshangiginan, nin neshangabiginan.*
Slander, *dajindiwin, matchi dajindiwin.*
Slander; I slander, *nin dajinge, nin matchi dajinge.*
Slanderer, *dejinged, matchidajinged.* Habitual slanderer, *dejingeshkid.*
Slanderous, I am slanderous, *nin dajingeshk.*
Slate; *ojibiigan-assin, ojibîiganiwassin.*
Slaughter, *nissidiwin, dapinanidiwin.*
Slave, *awakân.* I am a slave, *nind awakâniw.* Male slave, *abanini.* Female slave, *abanikwe.*

Slavery, *awakâniwin, awakânidiwin.*

Sleigh, *odâbân, odâbânak.* I make a sleigh, *nind odâbânike.*

Sleep, *nibâwin.*

Sleep ; I sleep, *nin nibâ.* I make him sleep, *nin nibea.* I sleep in the daytime, *nin gijiniba.* I fall in a profound sleep, *nin gawingwash.* I sleep profondly, *nin nissingwâm, nin bosangwâm.* I sl. much, *nin nibâshk, nin wingogane.* I sleep too much, *nin osâmingwâm, nin bingengwâm.* I sleep softly, slightly, *nin jibingwash.*

Sleepiness, *gigibingwashiwin, wingosh, wingwai.*

Sleeping, *nibâwin.* Bad habit of sleeping too much, *nibâshkiwin, wingôganewin.*

Sleeping-room, *nibêwin.*

Sleepy ; I am sleepy, *nin gigibingwash, nin passangwabishka, nin wi-niba.* I am very sleepy, *nin mendâtchingwash, nin simingwash.*

Sleeve, *nagwai.*

Slice ; slice of dried venison, *banijâwân.* Slice of cedar in the bottom of a canoe, *apissitâgan.*

Slide ; I slide on the ice, *nin bimibos.* I slide fast, *nin kijibîs.* I slide in a certain way, *nind ijisse.* It slides, *bidjinide.* The bird slides through the bird, *bidjibiso bineshi.* It slides fast, *kijibidemagad.* It slides in a certain way, *ijissémagad.*

Slide and fall ; I slide and fall, *nind ojâshishin.* I slide and fall on the ice, *nind ojâshikwishin* ; on the snow, *nind ojashagonishin* ; on a stone, *nind ojashâbikishin.*

Slide back ; I slide back, *nind ajésse.* It slides back or backwards, *ajessemagad.*

Slide down ; I slide (it slides) down, *nin nissâkosse, nin nânji, nin nânjisse, nin nishi, nissakossemagad, nanjimagad, nanjissemagad, nishimagad.* I slide down the hill, *nin joskkwâdjiwe.* I slide (it slides) in a hole, *nin bodâkwesse ; bodakwessemagad.* I slide in with my foot, *nin pindjisidesse* ; with my leg, *nin pindigâdesse.* I slide (it slides) in the water, *nin bakobisse ; bakobissemagad.*

Slightly, *sibiskadj, naegatch.* (Nisik).

Slim ; I am of a slim or slender size, *nind agassakwaiawes, nin gigaiawes.*

Sling, *passikwebodjigan.* I am throwing with a sling, *nin passikwebodjige.*

Slippery ; it is slippery, *ojâshamagad, jojâkwad, joshkwamagad.*

Slow ; I am slow at work, *nin babêgikâdis, nin babidjinawis, nin bwaawis, nind andjinawes, nin bedjiw.*—I am slow in eating, *nin babêgikadandjige, nin bédjissin.*—I am slow in my thoughts and resolutions, *nin bêdendam.*

Slowly, *beka, naegatch, sibiskatch.* I walk, navigate or travel slowly, *nîn bésika.* (Peyattik).

Slowness at work, *babêjikadisiwin, begjiwin.* Slow walking or traveling, *bésikâwin.*
Sluggard, *ketimishkid, taiâtagadisid, enokissig.* I am a sluggard, *nin kitimisk, nin tatâgadis.*
Sluggish. Sluggishnees.—S. Lazy. Laziness.
Slumber; I slumber, *nind asingwâm.*
Slut, *wanisid ikwe.*
Sluttish; I am sl., *nin winis.*
Sluttishness, *winisiwin.*
Small; I am small, *nind agâshi, nin takos.* I am very small, *nin mâskig.* I make myself small, *nind agâshiidis.* —It is small, *agâssa, agâssin, agâssinad.* It is small: A globular object, *in., agâssiminagad;* globular object, *an., agâssiminagisi;* a house or room, *agâssate;* metal, *in., agâssâbikad;* metal, *an., agâssâbikisi;* stuff, *in., agâssigad;* stuff, *an., agâssigisi.* —It is too small for me, (*in., an.*) *nin sinsikan; nin sinsikawa.* I make it small, or smaller, *nind agâssaton, nind agâssiton.*—We are small, *nin babiwijinimin.* They are small, (*in.*) *babiwawan.*
Small person, *tekôsid.*
Small-pox, *mamakisiwin.* I have the small-pox, *nind omamakis.* (Omikiw).
Smart at work. S. Zealous.
Smell, (odor,) *ijîmâgosiwin.* I make a good smell by burning s. th., *nin minâssîge.* I burn it (*in., an.*) to make a good smell, *nin minassan; nin minasswa.* I spread the smell of s. th., *nin bidjimâssige.*—I am (it is) of such a smell or odor, *nind ijimâgos; ijimâgwad.* I have (it has) the smell of ardent liquor, *nind ishkotewâboimâgos; ishkotewaboimagwad.* I hate the smell of it, (*in., an.*) *nin jingimândân; nin jingimâmâ.* I suffer from the smell of it, (*in., an.*) *nin kotagimandân; nin kotagimâmâ.*
Smell, (scent;) I smell s. th., *nin minandjige.* I smell him (her, it), *nin ninâma, nin minandawa; nin minândân.* I give him to smell s. th., *nin minandaoma, nin minâssamawa.*
Smell, (emit odor;) I smell, *nin minâgos;* it smells, *minâgwad.* I smell (it smells) well, *nin minomâgos; minomâgwad.* Something smells well to me, *nin minomandjige.* He (she, it) smells well to me, *nin minomâmâ; nin minomândân.* It smells well when burnt, (*in., an.*) *minomâte; minomâsso.*— I smell bad from perspiration, *nin wishâgomâgos.* It smells the sweat, (liquid,) *wishagwagami.*
Smelled; I am (it is) smelled, *nin bidjimâgos; bidjimâgwad.*
Smelt; I smelt, *nin ningikosige.*
Smelter, *ningikosigewinini.*
Smelting-furnace, *ningikosigan, ningabikisigan.*
Smelting-house, (foundry,) *ningikosigéwigamig.*
Smile; I smile, *nin bâp.*
Smiling, *bâpiwin.* I have a smiling countenance, *nin ba-*

bâpingwe, nin jomingwen. I show him a smiling countenance, *ninjomingwetawa.*
Smith, *awishtoia.* I am a smith, *nind awishtoiaw*
Smithshop, *awishtoiâwigamig.*
Smith's trade, *awishtoiâwiwin.*
Smoke; there is smoke, *pakwéne, paskkine.* I make smoke, *nin pashkinawe.* (Kaskâbattew). I make smoke around him, *nin gikanamoswa* The smoke ascends, *ombâbate;* comes from..., *ondâbate.* —I can endure much smoke, *nin jibanamos, nin wakéwanamos.* —It smokes, (in a lodge or house,) *gikanamode.* It smokes in my lodge or house, *gikanâmode endaiân, nin gikanâmos.*
Smoked meat, *onâssigan.* I smoke meat, *nind onâssige.*
Smoker, *ségasswâd.* Great smoker, *neta-sagasswâd.* (Opittwaw). Smoker of mixed tobacco, *epâkosiged.* Smoker of pure tobacco, *metâkosiged.*
Smoke tobacco; I smoke, *nin sagasswa.* (Pittwaw). I smoke pure tobacco, *nin mitâkosige;* I mix my tobacco, *nind apâkosige.* I have nothing to smoke, *nin manépwa* —We smoke together, (in a council,) *nin sagasswéidimin.*
Smoking, *sagasswâwin, sagasswéidiwin.* (Pittwâwin).
Smooth; I smooth with an iron, *nin joshkwaigaige.* I smooth it, iron it, (*in. an.,*) *nin joshkwégaan; nin joshkwegawa.*
Smooth, (in. s. in.) S. Polish. Polished.
Smoothed; it is smoothed with a flat iron, (*in., an.*) *joshkwâigaigâde; joshkwâigaigâso.*
Smoothing iron, *joshkwâigaigan.*
Smooth rock; there is a flat smooth rock, *joshkwânabika.*
Snail, *bimiskodissi.*
Snake, *ginébig.*
Snake Indian, *Ginebigonini.*
Snare, *nagwâgan.* I lay snares, *nin nagwânike.* (Wanihigan, tâpakwân). I lay him a snare to catch him, *nin dagodawa.* (Tâpakwewâtew). I lay him a snare or trap, *nind oniamawa.* I catch in a snare, *nin nagwâdjige.* I catch him (her, it) in a snare, *nin nagwâna; nin nagwâdan.*
Snare-string, *nagwâganéiâb.*
Sniff; I sniff, *nin nandomândjige.*
Snipe, *padashkaanji, manominikeshi.*
Snivel; I snivel, *nin sikawidjane, nin sikawiniskigome.*
Snore; I snore, *nin madwengwâm, nin madwêngwash.*
Snoring, *madwéngwâmowin, madwéngwashiwin.*
Snot, *niskigomân.* (Siniskigomân). My, thy, his snot, *niniskigomân, kiniskigomân, winiskigomânan.* I draw up my snot, *nind ikigome, nind odissaa niskigomân, nin singigawiskigome.* The snot is running from my nose, *nin sikawiniskigome;* by cold, *nin sikawiniskigomewadj.*
Snotty; I am sn., *nin siniskigomân.*
Snout; its snout, *oshkinj.* It

has a small snout, *agâssish·kinji.* It has a large snout, *mangishkinji.*

Snow, *gôn, agôn.* (Kôna, kôniwiw). On the snow, *mitâgonag.* There is snow, *gônika.* There is much snow, a deep snow, *ishpagonaga, ishpate.* The snow is soft, *jakâgonaga, nokâgonaga.* The snow is settled, hard, *assanâgonaga, kijiwâgonaga.* The snow *lowers,* melts down; *magwâgoneshin.* The snow is frozen, *gawâgonaga.* The snow is crusty, hard, *onâbanad.* The snow is falling from the trees, *missanwimagad, binânokimagad.* I am (it is) covered with snow, *nin ningwano; ningwanomagad.* I melt snow for water, *nin kijobike.* I walk in the snow without snowshoes, *nin mamitaam.*

Snow; it snows, *sôgipo.* (Mispun). It begins to snow, *mâdipo.* It snows in small flakes, *bissipo.* It snows in large flakes, *mângadepo.* The snow begins to cover the ground, *biwipo.* Soft watery snow is falling, *jakipo.* A snow-storm passes by, *bimipo.* It snows no more, *ishkwapo.* It snowed enough, *gijipo.*

Snow-bird, *wâbaningosi.*

Snow blind; I am snow-bl., *nin sassakingwe.* (Wayesâbiw).

Snow-blindness, *sassâkingwewin*

Snow-drift; there is a snow-drift, *biwan.*

Snowshoe, *agim.* (Asâm, asamikkew). I make snowshoes, *nind agimike.* I lace or fill a snowshoe, *nind ashkima agim.* I walk with snowshoes, *nind agimosse, nind odâgim.* (Kikasâmew). I am coming on snowshoes or with snowshoes, *nin bidâgimosse* The snow sticks to my snowshoes, *nin misikwasikama.*

Snowshoe-filling or lacing, *ashkimâwin.*

Snowshoe-making, *agimikewin.*

Snowshoe-ornament, *nimaigan.*

Snowshoe string, *atiman.*

Snowshoe-trail; there is an even snowshoe-trail, *onagwanaga.*

Snowshoe-walker, *netâwagimossed.* I am a good snowshoe-walker, *nin nitâwagimosse.*

Snowshoe walking, *agimossewin.*

Snow-storm; a snow-storm is coming, *bidipo.* There is a snow-storm, or drift of snow, *biwan.* The snow-storm is driven away by the wind, *mâdjipo.* A snow-storm is passing by, *bimipo.*

Snuff, *asséma, pindakwewin.* I manufacture snuff, *nind assemake.* (*Assemakewin. Assemakewinini. Assemakewigamig.*)

Snuff; I nuff, I take skuff, *nin pindakwe, nin pindakodjane.*

Snuff; I snuff the candle, *nin kishkanjékodan wâssakwanendjigan.*

Snuff-box, *asséma makak.*

Snuffers, *kishkânjékodjigan.*

So, *mi, mi sa.* (Ekusi).

Soak; it soaks, (*in., an.*) *agwinde; agwindjin.* I put it in water to soak, (*in., an.*) *nind agwindjiton; nind agwindjima.*

Soap, *kisibigaigan.* Liquid soap, *pingwi-kisibigaigan.* I make soap, *nin kisibigaiganike.*

Soap-boiler, soap-manufacturer, *kisibigaiganikewinini.*

Soap-boilery, soap-house, soap-manufactory, *kisibigaiganikewigamig.*

Soap-making, *kisibigaiganikewin.*

Soap-suds, soap-water, *kisibigaiganâbo.*

Sob; I sob, *nin nashigide.*

Sobbing, *nashigidewin.*

Sober; I am sober, (not drunk now,) *nind anissâdis; nin bagakâdis.* I am sober again (after drnnkenness,) *nind atebi.*

Sober person, *menikwessig.* (Ayeniw).

Sobriety, *anissâdisiwin, bagakadisiwin, atebiwin.*

Sock, *ajigan.*

Sodomy, *podjidiiewin.* I commit sodomy, *nin podjidiis.*

Soft; it is soft, (*in., an.*) *nokadad; nokadisi.* (Yoskaw, yoskisiw).

Soften, I soften it, (*in., an.*) *nin nokiton, nin nokibidon, nin nokigibidon; nin nokia, nin nokibina, nin nokigibina.* I soften linden bark, *nind assigobi.*

Softly, slightly, *naegatch, béka.*

Soil, *akî.*

Sojourn, *apidanisiwin.* (Wikiwin).

Sojourn; I sojourn, *nind apidanis.*

Solace; I solace, *nind absiwinge.* I solace him, *nind âbisiwima.*

Soldier, *jimâganish minissino, migasôwinini.*

Sole of the foot, *onanagâkisidama.* My, thy, his sole, *ninanagâkisid, kinanagakisid.*

Solicit; I solicit him, *nin wikwatchia, nin wikwâsoma.*

Solid; it is solid, strong, (*in., an.*) *sôngan; sôngisi.*

Some, *ânind, pangi, bébêjig.* (Atit).

Somebody, *awiia, bemâdisid.*

Something, *gégo, ningot, ningôtano.* (Kekwäy).

Somewhere, *ningôtchi.* (Nândo).

Son, *ogwissima, wegwissimind.* My, thy, his son, *ningwiss, kigwiss, ogwissan;* or, *ningwississ, kigwississ, ôgwississan.* I have a son, *nind ogwiss.* I have him for a son, he is my son, *nind ôgwissinan, nind ogwissima.* I am a son, *nind ogwissimigo.*

Song, *nagamon, nagamôwin.* Religious song, (hymn,) *anamie-nagamon, anamie-nagamowin.*

Song-book, *nagamô-masinaigan.*

Songster, *nagamôwinini.*

Songstress, *nagamôikwe.*

Son-in-law my, thy, his son-in-law, *niningwan, kiningwan, oningwanan.* (Onahâkisima). The son-in-law of a family, *naângish.* I am son-in-law in a family, *nin naângab, nind ojinindam.*

Soon, *waiba, waiêba, pitchinag, wéwib.* As soon as possible, *agawanapi.* (Kiyipi).

Soot, *winjide.*

Sooty; it is sooty, *winjidemagad.*

Sorb-berry, *makwimin.*

Sorb-tree, *makwimij.*

Sorcerer, *wabanowinini.* I am a

sorcerer, *nin wâbanow.* (Manitokkâsuw).
Sorcery, *wâbanowiwin.*
Sorrel, *jiwibag.*
Sorrow, *kashkéndamowin, gissadendamowin, wassitawendamowin, gibendamowin, kotagendamowin.* Sorrow of the heart, *kashkendamideewin.* I have much sorrow, *nin gibendam.* I cause him much sorrow, *nin gibendamia, nin gibendamishkawa.* It causes me much sorrow, *nin gibendamishkkagon.* I die of sorrow, *nin nibendam.*
Sorrowful; I am sorrowful, *nin gissadendam, nin mamidawendam.* I make him sor., *nin gissadendamia.*
Sorry; I am sorry, *nin kashkendam.* (Mitatam).
Sought; I am (it is) sought, *nin nandawâbandjigas; nandawâbandjigâde.*
Soul, *otchitchâgoma.* My, thy, his soul, *nin tchitchâg, ki tchitchâg, o tchitchâgwan.* I have a soul, *nind otchitchâg.* (Atchâk).
Sound; I let hear a certain sound, *nind inwé.* It gives a sound, *inwémagad.* It gives a hollow sound, *wimbwêwemagad.*
Sound; it sounds, *madwêssin, madwéwemagad.* I make sound s. th., *nin madwéssitchige, nin madwéwetchige.* I make it sound, *nin madwêssiton, nin madwêweton.* Any thing that sounds or gives a sound, *madwêwetchigan.* It sounds loud, *kijiwemagad.*
Soundly, *kijija.*
Soup, *nabob.* (S. Indian corn-soup). Poor soup, (not seasoned;) *ânissâbo.* I make poor soup, *nind anissâboke.*
Sour; it is sour, (*in., an.*) *jîwan, jîwamagad; jîwisi.* I make sour s. th., *nin jiwissitchige.* I make it sour, (*in., an.,*) *nin jiwiton, nin jiwissiton; nin jiwitawa, nin jiwishima, nin jiwisia.*
Source, (fountain, spring,) *mokidjiwanibig.*
Sour milk, *meshkawikwissing totoshâbobo.* The milk becomes sour, *mashkawikwissin totoshâbo.*
South, *jâwan.* In, to, or from the south, *jâwanong.* Towards the south, *jâwanong inakakeia.*—The clouds come from the south, *jâwanakwad.* The rain comes from the south, *jâwanibissa.* It thunders in the south, *jâwanaamog* (*animikig.*)
South-bird, (bird coming from the south,) *jâwanibinéshi.*
Southwind, *jâwaninodin.* The wind comes from the south, *jâwaninodin.*
Sovereign, *kitchi-ogima.*
Sovereign Pontiff. S. Pope.
Sow, *kokosh.*
Sow; I sow, *nin kitige, nin pagidinige.* I sow it, (*in., an.*) *nin kitigâdan, nin pagidinan; nin kitigâna, nin pagidina.*
Sowed; it is sowed, *kitigâde, pagidinigâde.*
Span, (measurement); onespan, *bejigwakwagan, ningotwakwoagan, ningotwakwoagan.* Two spans, three spans, etc., *nijwakwoagan, nisswakwoa-*

gan, etc.—So many spans, *dasswakwoagan*.

Spare ; I spare it, (*in.*, *an.*) *nin manâdjiton ; nin manâdjia* I spare myself, *nin manâdjiidis*.

Spark ; sparks fly off, *papakanje*. (Papaskitew).

Sparrow-hawk, *kekek*. Another kind, *pipiwige*.

Spasms, *otchipinigowin*. I have spasms, *nind otchipinig*. (Otjipitikuw).

Spattle, *gashkakokwêigan*.

Spawn, *wak*.

Spawn ; the fish is spawning, *âmi gigô*.

Speak ; I speak, *nin gigit, nin gagigit, nin gijwe, nin inwê*. (Pikiskwew, itwew). It speaks, *gigitomagad, inwemagad*. I make him speak, *nin gigitoa*. —I speak after him, *nin kikinotawa, nind ânikanotawa*. I speak angry, *nin nishkâdji-gijwe, nin nishkâdji-gigit, nin nishkâsitâgos, nin nanishkasitagos*. I speak angry to him, *nin nishkiganona, nin nishkâdjiganona, nin nishkâsoma*. I sp. evil, *nin matchi-gijwe, nin matchi ikkit*. I sp. fast. quickly, *nin dadâtabanagidon, nin dadâtabowe*. I sp. for somebody, *nin gaganodamage*. I sp. for him, *nin ganodamawa, nin gaganodamawa*. I speak the language of the people with whom I live, *nin niinawe*. I speak like a drunken person, *nin giwashkwébiwinitâgos*. I speak low, not loud, *nin gâskanas, nin bekadowe*. I speak loud, *nin kijiwe*. I speak as loud as I can, *nind apitowe*. I speak plainly, (to be easily understood,) *nin pagakowe, nin pagakitâgos, nin pagakissidon nin gigitowin*. I speak relying on him, (her, it,) *nin nanâpimonan ; nin nanapimon*.

Speaker, *neta-gigitod, netawed, gigitowinini*.

Speaking, *gigitowin, gagigitowin, gijwewin*. (Pikiskwewin, itwewin). Angry speaking, *nishkâdji gijwewin, nishkâdji-gigitowin, nishkâsitâgosiwin, nishkâdjiganonidiwin*. Foolish, frivolous or impure sp., *gagibasitâgosiwin, gagibâdji-gijwewin, gagibâdji-gigitowin*. Hidden mysterious sp., *agotâgosiwin, gimôtowewin*. Ill sp., *matchi ikkitowin, matchi, idiwin*. Impure indecent sp., *winigijwewin, wînitâgosiwin, bishigwâdji-gijwewin*. Mistake in sp., *wanowewin, wanigijwewin*. I mistake in speaking, *nin wanowe, nin wanigijwe*. Speaking of other people, *dajindiwin, dajingewin*.—Speaking of each other, or to each other, *idiwin*.

Speaking-house, council-house, *gigitowigamig*.

Spear, *anit*. Handle to a spear, *anitiiak*. (Mitchikîw).

Spear ; I spear fish, *nind akwawa*, (*akowa*) I spear him, (her, it,) *nin bashibâwa ; nin bashibaan*. I spear fish at night, *nin wâsswa*.

Speared ; I am (it is) speared, *nin bashibaigas ; bashibaigâde*.

Spearing fish at night, *wâsswewin*.

Specie, (silver-money or gold-money,) *mitâbik*.
Spectacles, *oshkinjigokâdjigan*. (Miskijikokkân).
Spectator, *waiabanged*.
Spectre, *tchibai*.
Speech, *gigitowin*, *animitâgosiwin*, *aianimitâgosiwin*. I make a speech, *nin gigit*, *nind animitâgos*, *nind aianimitagos*.
Speed, *dadatabiwin*.
Speedy ; I am speedy, *nin dadâtabi*.
Spend ; I spend all day in such a place, *nin dajigijiganam*. I spend all night in such a place, *nin dajitibikanam*.
Spend all, consume ; I spend all, *nin tchâginige*. (Mestinikew). I spend all of it, (*in.*, *an.*) *nin tchâginan* ; *nin tchâgina*. I am in the habit of spending all, *nin tchâginigèshk*. Habit of spending all, *tchâginigeshkiwin*.
Spendthrift, *tchaiaginigeshkid*, *neshiwanâdjitchiged*, *benâdjitod od aiiman*.
Sperm-oil, *kitchi-gigô bimide*.
Spider, *assabikeshi*. Spider's web, cobweb, *assabikeshiwassab*.
Spike, *kitchi-sagaigan*.
Spill ; I spill, *nin sigwebinige*. I spill it, (*in.*, *an.*) *nin sigwebinan* ; *nin sigwebina*. I spill s. th. belonging to him, or for him, *nin sigwebinamawa*.
Spilt ; it is spilt, *sigwebinigâde*.
Spin ; I spin, *nind assabâbike*, *nin gashkatêige*. It spins, *bimatéigemagad*, *gashkatéigemagad*.
Spine, *tatagâgwan*.
Spinning, *gashkatëigewin*, *bimatéigewin*, *assabâbikewin*.
Spinning-wheel, *bimatéigan*, *gashkatêigan*.
Spirit, *manito*. I am a spirit, *nin manitow*. I am considered a spirit, *nin manitowis*. Quality or character of spirit, *manitowiwin*. Unclean spirit, *wânisid manito*. Evil spirit, *matchi manito*.
Spit, *abwânak*.
Spit ; I spit him, (her, it,) *nind onakâkwawa* ; *nind onakâkwaan*.
Spit ; I spit, *nin sik*, *nin sikwadjige*. I spit it, *nin sikwâdân*. I spit upon him, *nin sikwana*. I spit in his face, *nin sikwaningwingwêwa*.
Spit-box, *sikowini-makak*, *sikwadjige-makak*.
Spite ; in spite of..., *jâgodj*, *kitwén*, *awândjish*. (Atjipiko).
Spit out ; I spit him, (her, it) out, *nin sâgidjisikwana* ; *nin sâgidjisikwadan*.
Spitter, *sekwâdjiged*.
Spitting, *sikowin*, *sikwadjigewin*.
Spittle, *sikowâgan*. The spittle is running from my mouth, *nin sikâwidon*.
Spit water ; I spit water, *nin siswandjige*. I spit water on him, *nin siswama*. I spit water in his face, *nin siswamingwena*.
Spleen, *wiss*.
Splendid ; it is splendid, *saséga*, *saségamagad*.
Splendid coat, *saséga-babisikâwâgan*.
Splendid man, *saséga-inini*.
Splendor, (brilliancy,) *wâsséiasiwin*, *wâssésiwin*.

Splinter, in the hand or foot, *gigatigwan.* I draw out a splinter, *nin gigatigwe.* I draw him a splinter out, *nin gidaâtigwawa.*

Split, in the skin, *gipisiwin, gagipisiwin.*

Split; I split wood, *nin tâshkigaige.* I split it, (*in., an.*) *nin tâshkigan*; *nin tâshkigawa.* I split wood into fine small pieces, *nin bissigaisse.* I split it into small pieces, (wood, *in., an.*) *nin bissigaan*; *nin bissigawa.* I split it with the teeth, (*in., an.*) *nin tâshkandân*; *nin tâshkama.*

Split; it splits, *tâshkigisse, tâshkikamagad.* It splits, (rock, metal,) *tâshkabikisse.* It splits in boiling, *dadodemagad.* The road splits, divides, *bakémo mikana.*

Split; it is split, *tâshkika, tâshkigishka.* It is split, (rock, metal, *in., an.*) *tâshkabikad, tâshkabikisi.*

Split in the middle; I split it, (*in., an.*) *nin tâshkinan, nin tâshkaan; nin tâshkina, nin tâshkawa.* I split it, cutting, (*in., an.*) *nin tâshkijan; nin tâshkijwa.* I split it, sawing, (*in., an.*) *nin tâshkibodon*; *nin tâshkibona.*

Split-saw, *tâshkibodjigan.* (Cross-saw, *kishkibodjigan.*)

Splitting-wedge, *tâshkigaigan.*

Split wood for fuel, *bissigaissan.*

Spoil; I spoil, *nin banâdjiiwe, nin banâdjitchige, nin mijiiwe, nin nishiwanâdjiiwe, nin nishiwanâdjitchige.* I spoil him, (her, it,) *nin banâdjia, nin mijia, nin kopadjia, nin nishiwanâdjia; nin banâdjiton, nin mijiton, nin kopâdjiton, nin nishiwanâdjiton.*

Spoiled; I am (it is) spoiled, *nin banâdjitchigas, nin nishiwânidis; banâdjitchigade, nishiwanadad.*

Spoken of; I am (it is) spoken of, *nin wawindjigas, nin dajindjigas; wawindjigade, dajindjigade.*

Sponsor at baptism, *babaikâwin, ossikâwin; mamaikâwin, ogikâwin.* I am sponsor, *nin takonawass.* I am his sponsor, *nin takona sigaandâsod,* or, *nin gi-takona gi-sigaandasod.*

Spontaneously, *binisika.* It comes (produces) spontaneously, *binishimagad.*

Spoon, *êmikwân.* A spoonful, *ningot-êmikwân.*

Spoon-bill, (bird) *jéde.*

Sportsman, *gaossed, neta-giossed.*

Spot, *kitagisiwin.*

Spot; I spot him, (her, it,) *nin kitagia*; *nin kitagiton.*

Spotted; I am (it is) spotted, *nin kitagis; kitagisimagad, babigwetagad.*

Spread ont; I spread out, *nin tessinige, nin dajweginige.* I sp. it out, (*in., an.*) *nin tessinan, nin tessiginan, nin dajweginan; nin tessina, nin tessigina, nin dajwegina.*

Spread out, (strew;) I pread out, *nin jingadenige.* I spread it out, (*in., an.*) *nin jingadenan*; *nin jingadena.* I sp. it out, throwing, *nin jingadewabaan.*

Spring, *sigwan, minôkami.* In spring, *sigwang.* Last spring

sigwanong. Next spring, *panima sigwang.* The spring before last, *awâss-sigwanong.* —I spend the spring in a certain place, *nin sigwanish.* I spend the spring with him, *nin wijisigwanishima.* (Miyoskamik).
Spring (fountain,) *mokidjiwanibig, takib.*
Spring-water, *mokidjiwano-nibi, takigami.*
Sprinkle ; I sprinkle water, *nin saswebigandaige, nin saswebigandjige.* I sprinkle him, (her, it,) *nin saswebigandawa; nin saswebigandan.*
Sprinkling, *saswebigandjigewin.*
Sprinking-pot and brush, *saswebigandjigan, saswebigandaigan, sigândjigan.*
Sprout, *onimik.*
Sprout; it sprouts, (*in.*, *an.*) *sâganwimagad, wabidwimag ; sâganwi, wabidwi.* The potato sprouts, *sâganwi opin.*
Spruce, *ininandag ; jingob.* [C. sapin.]
Spruce-beer, *jingobâbo.*
Spunge, *iskaibân.* I dry water up with a spunge, *nind iskaibi.*
Spur, *patakimodjikadjigan.*
Spy, *nendawâtod.*
Spyglass, *jibaiabandjigan.* I look through a spyglass, *nin jibaiabandjige.* I look at him (her, it) through a sp., *nin jibaiâbama ; nin jibaiabandan.*
Spy out, I spy out, *nin nandawâto, nin gimâb.* I spy him out, *nin gimâbama.* I spy it out, *nin gimâbandan, nin nandawâton.*
Squall ; there is a squall of wind, *kitchi bidanimad, pakitéianimad, gotâmigwad.*
Squall of wind, *missibissidossi;* pl.—*wag.*
Square; it is square, *jashameiamagad, kakakamagad.* It is square, (stuff, *in.*, *an.*) *kakakigad ; kakakigisi.*
Square ; I square timber, *nin tchigigaige.* I square it, (*in.*, *an.*) *nin tchigigaan ; nin tchigigawa.* (Passahikew).
Square tobacco, *ejashawebagisid assema.*
Squaring, *tchigigaigewin.*
Squaring-axe, *tchigigaigan.*
Squat ; I squat, *nin nimissab.*
Squaw, *anishinâbekwe.* I am a squaw, *nind anishinâbekwew.*
Squaw not belonging to the Grand Medicine, *sagimâkwe.*
Squaw's play, *passikawewin.* I am playing the squaw's play, *nin passikawe, nin papâssikawe.* The stick used at that play, *passikawân, passikawanak.*
Squeeze ; I squeeze, *nin bimibiginige.* I squeeze it, (*in.*, *an.*) *nin bimibiginan ; nin bimibigina.*
Squeamish ; I feel squeamish, *nin mânjidee.*
Squeamishness, *mânjideewin.*
Squint ; I squint, I am squint-eyed, *nind awassâb, nin bimadawâb, nind atchitchâb.*
Squinter, *bemâdawâbid, ewassâbid.*
Squirrel, *atchitamo, agwingoss, assânago.* Black squirrel, *missanig.* Flying squirrel, *jagashkandawe.* (Anikwatchâs).

Stab ; I stab him, *nin bajibawa, nind anoganâma, nin jibajigawa*.
Stabbed ; I am st., *nin bojibaigas, nin jibajigas.*
Stable, *pijikiwigamig.*
Staff, for a barrel, etc., *makakossagwâtig.*
Stag, *mishewe, omashkos.*
Stagger ; I stagger, *nin babinasse.* I stagger in walking, *nind aiâjagonesse, nin goshwesse, nin goshkoshkwesse.*
Stag's hide, *omashkoswegin.*
Stag's horn, *omashkosweshkan.*
Stag's tail, *omashkoswano.*
Stairs, staircase, *akwandawagan.* I go up stairs, *nind akwandawe, ishpiming nind ija, ishpimissagong nind ija.* I run up stairs, *nind akwandawebato.* (Ketsikusiwin).
Stake ; I put at stake, *nind atchige, nind atâge.* I put it at stake, (*in., an*) *nind atâgen ; nind atâgenan.*
Stalk of Indian corn, *mandâminashk.* Stalks of Indian corn standing in the field, *mandâminashkoki.*
S t a l l i o n, *nabê-bebejigoganji.* (Nâbestim).
Stammer ; I st., *nin gagibanagaskwe, nin gagibanagaskwetagos.*
Stamp ; I stamp, *nin botage.* I stamp it, (*in., an.*) *nin botâgadan ; nin botagana.* I stamp or crush Indian corn, *nin tagwâwag mandâminag.* I stamp with the foot, *nin tângishkîge.*
Stamper, stamps, *botâgan.*
Stanch ; I stanch it, *nin gibiton.*
Stand ; I stand, *nin nibaw, nin gâbaw.* I stand here and there, *nin nanibaw, nin babâ-nibaw.* I make him, (her, it) stand, *nin nibawia, nin gâbawia ; nin nibawiton, nin gâbawiton.* —We stand around him in a circle, *nin giwitagâbawitawânan, nin wakagâbawitawânan.* We st. around him in a semicircle, *nin waganagâbawitawânan.* We stand in one line, one after another, *nin nibinégâbawimin,* or, *nin nibidégâbawimin.* We stand round, *nin bimigâbawimin.* It stands high, (an animal,) *ishpigâbawi.*
Standard, *kikinowâbandjigan.*
Standing, *nibâwiwin.*
Stand up, (erected ;) it stands up, (*in., an.*) *patakidê, patakissin ; patakiso, patakishin.* I make it stand up in s. th. or on s. th, (*in., an.*) *nin patakidon ; nin patakina.*
Star, *anâng.* Small star, *anângons.* There are stars, *anangoka.* The s t a r is bright, shining, *wâssenagoshka anâng.* (Atchâkus).
Starch, *mashkawâtchigan.*
Starch ; I starch, *nin mashkwâtchige.* I starch it, *nin mashkawâton.*
Starling, (bird,) *assiginak, nadjinamanessi.*
Starry ; it is starry, *anângoka.*
Star-shaped, *anângong ijinagwad.*
Star-shoot, *anâng pangishin.*
Start ; I start, *nin mâdja.* It starts, *mâdjamagad.* (Sipwettew). I start in a canoe or boat, *nin mâdji, nin bos.* I start first, *nin niganishka.*
Start up ; I start up, (by surprise,) *nin goshkosse.*

Starve. Starvation.—S. Hunger. Hungry.
Starve; I starve to have it, *nind ondanêndân.*
Starve to death; I st. to d., *nin gawanândam.* (Nipâhâkkatusow). Death from starvation, *gawanândamowin.*
Statement, *dibâdjimowin, dibâdodamowin.* True statement, *gwaiakâdjimowin.* I make a true statement, *nin gwaiakâdjim.*
Stature, *akossiwin.*
Stay, *âpidanisiwin.*
Stay; I stay, *nind âpidanis.* I stay in different places, *nin babâ-ainda, nin babâ-danis.*
Steady; it is steady, *sôngan.*
Steal; I steal, *nin gimôd.* I steal him, (her, it,) *nin gimôdinan, nin gimôdin.* I steal it from him, *nin gimodima.* I steal all his things from him, *nin tchagimodima.*
Stealing, *gimodiwin.* Habit of stealing, *gimôdishkiwin.* I am in a habit of stealing, *nin gimôdishk.*
Steam-bath, *madôdisson.* I take a steam-bath, *nin madôdo.* Steam-bath stone, *madonewâbik.*
Steamboat, *ishkotê-nâbikwân,* (fire-vessel.)
Steam-sawmill, *ishkotê-tâshkibodjigan,* (fire-sawmill.)
Steel, *manitobiwâbik.* I make or manufacture steel, *nin manitôbiwâbikoke.*
Steel-manufactoring, *manitôbiwâbikokewin.*
Steel-manufacturer, *manitôbiwâbikiwinini.*
Steel-pen, *biwâbiko-mîgwan, ojibiiganâbik.*
Steeple. S. Church-steeple.
Steer, *nabé-pijiki.*
Steer; I steer, *nind odâke, nind âdikweam, nind âdikwêige.* I steer for a certain point, *nind inâ, nind inikwéam.* I steer it, *nind odâken* I steer it for a certain point, *nind inikwéan.* I help him in steering, *nind odâkéekawa.*
Steering, *odâkêwin.*
Steering-paddle, *odâké-abwi.*
Steersman, *wedâked, odâkéwinini.*
Step, *takokiwin.* I make short steps, *bebêsho nin takoki,* or, *besho nin tatakoki.* I make long steps, *wâwâssa nin takoki,* or, *wâssa nin tatakoki.*
Step; I step, *nin takoki.* I step aside, *nind ikogâbaw.* I step aside, (out of the road,) *nin bakêgâbaw.* I step aside to give him room to pass by, *nin bakêgâbawitawa.* I step back, *nind ajégâbaw.* I step back for him, *nin ajêgâbawitawa.* I step out of the trail in walking, *nin goshkwêtakoki, nin goshkoshkwêtakoki.*
Step-daughter; my, his step-daughter, *nindojimikwem, odojimikweman.*
Step-father; my, thy, his step-father, *nimishome, kimishome, omishoweian.*
Step-mother; my, thy, his step-mother, *ninwishe,* (*ninoshe,*) *kinwishe, onwisheian.*
Step-son; my, thy, his step-son, *nindôjim, kidôjim, odôjiman*
Stench, *manjimâgosiwin.*

Stern, *odâkan.*
Stew; I stew it, (*in., an.*) *nin gibâsan; nin gibôswa.*
Steward, *mijinawe.* I am a steward, *nin mijinawew.*
Stewardship, *mijinawewiwin*
Stewing oven, *gibôsigan, gibosiganikan.*
Stew-kettle, stew-pot, *gibôsiganâkik.*
Stick, *mitigons.* Round stick, not split, *misâtig.* I chop round stick, (not splitting them,) *nin misâtigogaisse.*— Stirring stick, *anéigan.* Walking-stick, *sakaon.*
Stick; I stick it to s. th., (*in., an.*) *nind agôkiwassan*; *nind agôkiwassa.* I stick (it stiks) to s. th., *nind agôke; agôgin.* It sticks to it by freezing, *agoskwadin.* It sticks to the ground, *agwakamigissin*, (*agokamigissin.*) It sticks to some wooden object, *agwakossin*, (*agokossin.*)
Stick in; I stick it in s. th., (*in., an.*) *nin patakissidon, nin patakidon.*
Sticky; I have sticky hands, *nin bassakonindjin.*
Stiff; it is stiff, (stuff, *in., an.*) *tchibatchigad; tchibatchigisi.*
Stiff arm, stiff leg, etc. S. Arm. Leg, etc.
Stifle; I stifle him, *nin gibwanâmoshkawa.* I stifle myself, *nin gibwanâm.*
Stifled; I am stifled by smoke, *nin gibwanâmos.* (Kipwâbasuw).
Still, *bisân, béka.* I am still, *nin bisânab, nin bisânis, bisân nind aia, béka nind aia, nin békâdis.* It is still, *bisânamagad.* It is still, (liquid,) *bisânâgami.* It is still, (in a place,) *bisânate.* (Kiyâm, kiyâmapiw).
Still, but stlil, *minoich, ânawi, potch.* (Ata, maka).
Stilt, *mitigogad.* I walk on stilts, *nin miiigogâdekas.*
Sting, (prick;) I sting him, (her, it,) *nin patakawa, nin patchishkawa; nin patakaan, nin patchishkan.*
Stinging fly, *pingosh.* Very small stinging fly, *pingoshens.*
Stink; I stink, *nin manjimâgos.* It stinks, *manjimâgwad.* Something stinks to me, *nin manjimandjige.* He, (she, it) stinks to me, *nin manjimama; nin manjimandan.* It stinks when burnt, (*in, an.*) *manjimâte; manjimâsso.*
Stir, (riot) *ombasondiwin.*—S. Stir up.
Stir or mix; I stir, *nind anéige, nin nisséige.* I stir it, *nind anéan, nin nisséan, nin waninawean, nind ombwéan.*
Stirrup, *nagasidebison, atchisidebison bimibaigong,* or, *tessabing.* (Tâbiskuskâtchigan).
Stir up; I stir up people, *nind ombâsonge.* I stir him up, *nind ombasoma, nind âshia.* We stir up one another, *nind ombâsondimin.*
Stockfish, *jigwameg.*
Stocking, *ajigan, misâtigomidass, akokomidass.* I make stockings, I knit, *nin missâtigomidassike, nind akokomidassike.*
Stolen object, *gimodiwin.*
Stomach, *missad.* (Mâskigan). The first stomach of ruminat

ing animals, *bebitossi ;* the second stomach, *ogidagimod.* —A gargling noise is heard in my stomach, *nin madwegaminagiji.*

Stone, *assin.* Small little stone, *assinins, bissâssinins.* There are stones, *assinika.* There are little stones, *assininsika, bissâssininsika.* On a stone, *mitâssin, ogidâbik, mitâssinâbik.* There is stone upon stone, *ogidabikissin.* It is made of stone, or paved with stone, *assinikâde.* There is a foundation made of stone, *assinikande.*—A flat stone, *tessâbik.* Net-stone, *assinâb.*—It looks like stone, *assining ijinâgwad.* —I am stone, (petrified,) *nind assiniw.*

Stone ; I stone, *nin babimwâssin.* I stone somebody, *nin bimwâssinaige.* I stone him, *nin bimwâssinaa.*

Stone-building, *assini-wâkaigan.*

Stone-Siou Indian, *Assinibwân.*

Stone's throw far, *eko-débiwebinind assin.*

Stool, *apabiwin.*

Stoop ; I stoop, *nin nawéta, nin jagashki.* I make him stoop, *nin jagashkia.*

Stooped ; I am stooped down, *nin jagashkishin.*

Stop! *béka!* (Tcheskwa).

Stop, (close up ;) I stop it, (*in., an.*) *nin gibaan, nin gibiton, nin gibâkwaan ; nin gibâwa, nin gibâkwâwa.* I stop s. th. with my hands, *nin gibinindjin.* I stop one of my ears, *nin gibitawâgeodis, nin gibishebinidis.* I stop my ears, *nin gagibitâwageodis, nin gagibishebinidis.* I stop one of his ears, *nin gibitawagéwa, nin gibishebina.* I stop his ears, *nin gagibitawâgêwa, nin gagibishebina.*

Stop, (dwell ;) I stop, *nin da.* Where I stop or dwell, *endaiân.* Where he stops, *endâd.*

Stop, (stand still ;) I stop, *nin nogi, nin nogigâbaw, nin nagashka, nin nagata.* I stop running, *nin nogibato.* It stops, *nôgishkamagad, nagashkamagad, nogisse.* I stop him, (her, it,) *nin nogina, nin nogishkawa ; nin nogiton, nin nagishkan.*—I stop, *nin bisânab.* It stops, *bisânabimagad.* (Nakiw, nakinew).

Stopped ; I am stopped by a river, *nind adagâmagishin sibi.* —One of my ears is stopped, *nin gibitamagi.* My ears are stopped, *nin gagibitawage.*

Stopper, *gibaigan.* I put a stopper in, *nin gibaige.*

Storch, *jashagi.*

Store, *atâwewigamig.*

Store-house, *atâssôwigamig, mâwandjitâssowigamig.*

Storekeeper, storer, *atâwéwinini.*

Store up ; I store up, *nin mâwandjitâss, nind atâss.* I store up for me, *nind atâmas, nind atâmadis.* I store it up, (*in., an.*) *nind atâsson ; nind atâssonan.* I store it up for me, (*in,, an.*) *nind atâmâson, nind atâmâdison ; nind atâmasonan, nind atâmadisonan.*

Story, in a house ; there is a story, *ishpimissagokâde.*

Story, narration, *dibâdjimowin, babamâdjimowin, bidâdjimo-*

win. (Atjimowin). Impure indecent story, *bishigwâdâdjimowin.*

Stout; I am stout, *nin songâdis, nin songis, nin mashkawis.*

Stove, *kijabikisigan.* (Piwâbiskokutawânâbisk).

Straight, *gwaiak.*

Straighten; I st., *nin gwaiakotchige.* I st. myself, (stand up,) *nin gwaiakota, nin tajwakota, nin gwaiakogabaw, nin tajwakogabaw.* I straighten it, *nin gwaiakoton, nin tajwabikinan.*

Strain; I strain, *nin jâbogawitchige.* I strain it, *nin jâbogawiton, nin jabwajigawiton.*

Strainer, *jâbogawitchigan, jâbwâjigawitchigan.*

Strait. S. Narrow.

Straiten; I straiten it, (*in.*, *an.*) *nind agâssadeton, nin wibonan; nind agâssadea, nin wibona.*

Straitened; it is str., (*in.*, *an.*) *wibwa; wibwamagad.*

Straits; there are straits between two lakes, *wabigama, waba.*

Strange! *gowengish! ashinangwana!* (Mâmaskâtch!)

Strange; I make it in a strange manner, *nin maiâgiton.* I put it in a strange manner, *nin maiâgissiton.* I find strange what I hear, *nin maiâgitan.* I find strange what he is saying, *nin maiâgitawa.* (Mâmaskâtam).

Stranger, arriver, visitor,) *biwide.* (Omânotew).

Stranger, (foreigner,) *meiâgisid.* I am a stranger, *maiâgis, nin maiatawis.* (Pitusisiw).

Strangle; I strangle you with my hands, *nin gibinéwena.*

Strap; I strap it, *nin kaskaskibissidon.*

Straw, *pakwéjiganashk.*

Straw-bed, straw-pallet, *mashkossiwi-apishimon, mashkossiwi-nibâgan.*

Strawberry, *odéimin.*

Straw-hat, *mashkossi-wiwakwân.*

Stream, *sibi.*

Strength, *mashkâwisiwin, sabadisiwin.* Strength of mind, thought, resolution, *mashkawendamowin.* — Strength of heart, *mashkawideewin, songideewin.*

Strengthen; I strengthen him, (her, it,) *nin songisia, nin mashkawisia; nin songiton, nin mashkawiton.*

Stretch; I stretch it, (*in.*, *an.*) *nin papassâbiginan; nin papassabigina.*

Stretch out; I stretch it out, (*in.*, *an.*) *nin dajwibikinan; nin dajwebikina.* I stretch it out in every direction, (*in.*, *an.*) *nin jishibigibidon; nin jishibigibina.*

Strew; I strew, *nin biwiwebinige.* I strew it, (*in.*, *an.*) *nin biwiwebinan; nin biwiwebina.*

Strike; I strike, *nin pakitêige.* I strike him, (her, it,) *nin pakitéwa,* (pakamahwew) (*nin wewepotawa*;) *nin pakitéan.* I strike myself, *nin pakitêodis.* I strike some object belonging to him, *nin pakitéoma.*— I strike him in the face, *nin bassingwéwa.* I st. him on the mouth, *nin bassidonêwa.*

Strike accidentally; I strike him, (her, it) by accident, *nin*

pitaganama, nin pitaganandan. (Pistahwew).
String, *sagibidjigan, biminâkwanens, takobidjigan.* Narrow string of leather, *bishâganâb.*
Strip, undress; I strip, *nin gisikwanaie, nin gisikwanaiebinidis.*—I strip him, *nin gisikwanaiebina..* (Ketayonisenew).
Stripping, *gisikwanaiewin.*
Strive; I strive, *nin wikwatchito, nin godjiew.* (Kutchîw).
Strong; I am strong, *nin mashkawis, nin songâdis, nin sabadis, nin songis, nin kijijawis.* It is strong, *songan, mashkawisimagad, mashkawissin, kijijawad, songin.*
Strongly, *songan, enigok, âpîtchi, kijija, epitching, kagétin, onina, wanina.* (Sokki).
Struggle; I struggle, *nin mimigapagis.*
Strumpet, *gagibâdjikwe, bishigwâdjikwe.*
Stubborn; I am st., *nin mashkawindibi,* (my head is hard.) I have a stubborn heart, *nin mashkawidee.*
Stubbornly, *awandjish.* (Atjipiko).
Stubbornness, *mashkawindibewin, mashkawideewin.*
Stuff; one object of stuff, *bejigweg.* Two, three, four objects, etc., *nijweg, nissweg, niweg,* etc. So many objects of stuff, *dassweg.* In the middle of some stuff, *naweg.*
Stuff, I stuff, *nin pindashkwe.* I stuff it, (*in., an.*) *nin pindashkwadan; nin pindashkwana.*
Stumble; I stumble, *nin bisosideshin.*
Stumbling, *bisasideshiwin.*
Stumbling-stone, *bisosideshiwinassin.*
Stump, *kishkanakad.* Little stump, *kishkanakadons.*
Stun; I tun him, *nin giwashkwéganama.*
Stupid; I am stupid, *nin gagibâdis, nin kopâdis, nin kopadendâgos.* It is stupid, *gagibadad, kopadad.* I make him stupid, *nin gagibadisia, n-n kopadisia, nin gagibasoma.* I use him, (her, it) in a stupid and ill manner, *nin kôpâdjia; nin kôpâdjiton.*
Stupidity, *gagibâdisiwin, kôpâdisîwin.*
Sturgeon, *namê.*
Styx-bridge, *kokokajogan.*
Subdue; I subdue him, (her, it,) *nin wângawia; nin wângawiton.*
Sublime; I am (it is) sublime, *nin kitchitwâwis, nin kitchitwâwendagos; kitchitwâwendâgwad.*
Succeed; I succeed, (follow,) *nin nâbishkage, nind anikeshkage, nind odâkeshkam.* I succeed him, *nin nabishkawa, nind anikeshkawa, nind odâkeshkawa.*
Succession, *nâbishkagewin, anikeshkagewin.*—In quick succession, soon one after another, *wawaiba, bebesho.*
Suck; I suck (milk,) *nin non, nin totoshike.* I suck too much, *nin nônishk.* I give suck, *nin nonâwass.* I give him suck, *nin nona.* I cease to

give him suck, *nind ishkwâ-nona.*

Suck; I suck, I draw s. th. in my mouth, *nin wikwam, nin wikwandjige.* I suck him, (her, it), *nin wikwama; nin wikwandan.* (Ototamew).

Suck, (doctoring;) I suck, *nin nibiki.* I suck him, *nin nibikana.* (Nipiskew).

Sucker, (Indian doctor,) *nibikiwinini.*

Sucker, (fish,) *namébin.*—S. Carp.

Sucking, *nibikiwin.*

Sucking-horn, *wikwandjigan.*

Suck out; I suck out the sap, *nin siwakwe.* I suck it out, (*in., an.*) *nin siwakwadan; nin siwakwana.*

Sudden, (short, shortly,) *kakâm.* (Sesikutch).

Sudden death, *sesika-nibowin, kakaminewin, kaiâkamisiwin.*

Suddenly, *sesika, gesika, tchesika; atchitchikana.*

Suffer; I suffer, *nin kotagita, nind animis, nin kotagis, nin nanêkadis.* I suffer in thoughts, *nin kotagendam, nind animendam, nin nanêkadendam.* I suffer a long time, *nin sibiskendam.* I have to suffer, *nin kotagendâgos, nind animendâgos.*—I make him, (her, it) suffer, *nin kotagia, nin kotagima, nind animisia, nind animia, nin nanêkadjia; nin kotagiton, nind animiton, nin nanekâdjiton.* I make him suffer much by striking him, *nin wissâgaganâma.*— I make myself suffer, *nin kotagiidis, nind animiidis.* I make myself suffer by it or for it, *nin nanékâdjiton*—I suffer with him, *nin widjânimisima.* (Kwatakittaw).

Suffer bitterly; I suffer b., *nin wissagendam.* I make him (her, it) suffer b., *nin wissagendamia; nin wissagendamiton.*—I suffer burning, *nin wissagines, nin wissagakis.* I make him suffer by burning him, *nin wissagakiswa.*

Suffering, *kotagitowin, animisiwin, kotagendamowin, kotagisiwin, nanékâdisiwin* Bitter suffering, *wissagendamowin.* Suffering from burning, *wissaginesiwin.* Suffering received from somebody, *kotagiigowin.*— Long suffering, *sibiskendamowin.*—It causes suffering, *kotagendagwad, kotagiiwemagad.*

Suffer, permit; I suffer it, *nin ganabendan.*

Suffice; it suffices, *dêbisse, débissêmagad.*

Sufficiency, *débisiwin.*

Sufficient; I am (it is) suf., *nin dêbisse; débissémagad.* I am (it is) not suf., *nin nondésse, nin nondeshin; nondéssemagad, nondessin.* We are in a sufficient number, *nin dé-dashimin.* It is suff., in a suff. number or quantity, *dê-dassin.*

Sugar, *sisibâkwat.* Brown sugar, *sibwâgani sisibâkwat.* I make sugar, *nin sisibâkwatoke, nind iskigamisige.*

Sugar-bush, sugar-camp, *sisibâkwatokân, iskigamisagan.*

Sugar-cane, *sibwâgan.*

Sugar-making, *sisibâkwatokewin, iskigamisigewin.*
Sugar-making woman, *iskigamisigekwe.*
Sugar-water, (maple-sap,) *sisibâkwatâbo.*
Suicide, *nessidisod, netod wiiaw.* (Nepahisut).
Sulky; I am sulky, *nin babigodee.*
Sulphur, *osâwi-makate.*
Summer, *nibin.* It is summer, *nibin, nibinakamiga.* In summer, *nibing; nâbingin.* The summer is far advanced, *ishpinibin.* After the middle of the summer, *giwênibin.* Last summer, *nibinong.* The summer before last, *awass-nibinong.* Next summer, *pânima nibing.* It is a cool summer, *takinibin.* Il is a warm summer, *kijâte.*
Summer; I summer somewhere, *nin nibinish.* It summers, *nibinishimagad.* I summer with him, I spend the summer with him somewhere, *nin widjinibinishima.*
Summering, (spending the summer-season,) *nibinishiwin.*
Summer-skin, summer-fur, *nibiniwaiân.*
Summit, *wanakowin.* There is a summit, *wanakowiwan.* It is the summit of a mountain or hill, *gakadina.* I arrive at the summit of a mountain or hill, *nin gijamâdjiwe.*
Sun, *gisiss.* (Pisim). The sun rises, *mogisse gisiss, mokaan gisiss.* (Sâkâstew). The sun comes out of the clouds, *sâgassige gisiss.* The sun shines, *wâsseiâssige,* or *sâgate gisiss.* The sun is brilliant, *wâssesi gisiss.* The sun is red, *miskwassige gisiss.* The sun has a circle, *winibassige gisiss.* The sun is darkened, *libikabaminâgosi gisiss.* The sun sets, *pangishimo gisiss.*
Sun-burnt; I am s., *nin makatewis.*
Sunday, *anamiêgijigad, anwebiwinigijigad.*
Sun-dial, *dibaigisisswân.*
Sundry, *anôtch, wiiagi.*
Sunflower, *bassitâgan, missiiâgan.*
Superficially, *mamanj, ogidjina.*
Superior, *nagânisid, nigânisim.* I am a superior, *nin nigânis.* I am considered superior, *nin nigânendagos.* I make him a superior, *nin nigânisia.*
Superiority, *nigânisiwin, ogimâwiwin.*
Supernatural warning or communication, *windamâgosiwin.* I receive a sup. warn., *nin windamâgowis.*
Supernumerary; I am sup., *nind aniwisse.* It is sup., *aniwissemagad.*
Superstitious person, *anôtch gego daiébwetang.*
Supper, *onâgoshi-wissiniwin.* (Otâkusi-mitjisuwin).
Supplant; I supplant him, make him fall, *nind oniwishtawa, nin bosogêwa, nin bidjigéwa.*
Support, (care,) *bamiiwewin, bamiidiwin.* Support of one's self, *kamiidisowin, bamikodadisowin.*
Support, (care;) I support, *nin bamiiwe.* I support him, (her, it,) *nin bamia; nin bamiton.*

I support myself, *nin bamiidis, nin bamikodadis.*

Support, (hold up;) I support him, (her, it,) *nin ashidakwawa, nind ashidakwaan.* I support him with my hands, *nind asswana, nind asswawa.*

Suppose; I suppose, *nind inendam.* I suppose to be him, *nind awenima.*

Supposing, *kishpin.*

Supposition, *inendamowin.*

Sure, to be sure, *aningwana, e nangê ka, angwâmass.* (Tchikema).

Sure; I am sure, *nin pakakêndam.* I am sure of it, *nin pakakêndân.* I make it sure, *nin wawingeton.* (Ketchinâhuw).

Surely, *abidékamig, gwaiak.* (Ketchina).

Surf; the surf is beating on a shallow place in the lake, *bagwashka.* The surf beats against the shore and returns, *tibibashka.*

Surface; on the surface, *ogidjaii, ogidjina; ogidakamig;* (under ground, *anâmakamig.*)

Surpass; I surpass, *nind iniwiiwe; nin pakinage, nind enimaowe.* I surpass him, (beat him,) *nin pakinawa, nind aniwia, nind aniwishkawa, nind enimia.* I surpass him in a canoe, *nind enimâwa.* I surpass him running or walking, *nind enimishkawa.* I sur. it, *nind aniwiton, nind aniwishkan.* (Paskiyawew).

Surprise; I surprise him, *nin goshkoa.* (Sisikutchihew). I surprise him by my coming, *nin tchissikawa.* (Wiskawahew).

Surprised; I am surprised, *nin goshkoka, nin mamakadendam.* I am sur. in thoughts, *nin goshkwendam, nin goshkonawes.* (Sisikuteyittam).

Surround; we surround him sitting, *nin giwitabitawanan;* we surround him standing, *nin giwitagabawitawanan.* It surrounds me, *nin giwitashkâgon.*

Surrounded; I am (it is) sur., *nin giwitagâbawitâgo; giwitâgâbawitchigâde.*

Survey, *dibaabiwin.*

Survey; I survey, *nin dibaaki.*

Surveyor, geometer, *dibaakiwinini.*

Survive; I survive, *nin ishkwae,* (*ishkone.*) I survive the night, *nin wâbas.* I don't survive the night, *nin nondéiabas.* I survive the winter, *nin wâbanish.* I don't survive the winter, *nin nondêiabanish.*

Suspect; I suspect, *nind anaminge.* I suspect him, (her, it,) in *thoughts, nind anâmenima; nind anâmendan.* I suspect him, (her,it) and express it in *words, anâmima; nind anâmindân.*

Suspect, (mistrust;) I suspect, *nin monedam.* I sus. him, (her, it,) *nin mônenima; nin mônendan.* (Moyeyimew).

Suspenders, used by men, *dajoiawebison;* used by squaws, *ânikaman.*

Suspicion, *anâmingewin, anamindiwin.* I have suspicion, *nind anaminge.* We have suspicion against each other, *nind anâmindimin.*

Swallow, (bird,) *jashâwanibissi.* (Mitchâskusis).

Swallow; I swallow, *nin gondjige.* I swallow him, (her, it,) *nin gonâ, nin négwama; nin gondan, nin négwandan.* I swallow a little of it to taste it. (*in., an.*) *nin gôtandan; nin gôtama.*

Swallowed; it is sw., (*in., an.*) *gondjigade; gondjigaso.*

Swamp, *wâbashkiki, mashkig.* In the middle of a swamp, *nawashkig.*

Swan, *wâbisi.* Young swan, *wâbisins.* A kind of small swan, *manâbisi.*

Swanskin, (soft flannel,) *wâbigin bebigwatagak.*

Swan's potato, *wâbisipin.*

Sward, *kokoshiwajagaai.*

Swarthy; I am swarthy, *nin makatewis.*

Swathe; I swathe him, *nin titibitchipina.*

Swathed; I am sw., *nin titibitchipis.*

Swear; I swear, *nin mashkawigijwe.* I swear by his name, *nin dagowina.* I swear by it, *nin dagowindan.* (Kitchipikiskwew).

Swearing, oath, *mashkawigijwewin.*

Sweat, *abwesowin.*

Sweat; I sweat, *nind âbwess.* I sweat working, *nind abweta.* I sweat blood, *nin miskwiâbwes.*—My feet are sweating, *nind âbwêside.* My hands are sw., *nin âbwenindji.*

Sweep; I sweep, *nin tchigataige, nin tchishataige.* I sweep it, *nin tchigataan, nin tchishataan.*

Sweet; it is sweet, (*in., an.*) *wishkobad; wishkobisi.* (Wikkitisiw, wikkasin). It is sweet, (liquid,) *wishkobagami.* It is sweet, (meat, *in., an.*) *wishkobiwagad; wishkobiwagisi, wishkobiwe.*

Sweetcake, *washkobisid pakwejigan washkobidjigasod pakwejigan,* (weet bread, sweetened bread.)

Sweet corn, *wiskobimin.*

Swell; I swell up, *nin ombaog.*

Swelling, *bâgishiwin.* The swelling ceases or abates, *niwaan.* My swelling decreases, *nin niwaog.*

Swept; it is swept, *tchigataigade, tchishataigade.*

Swim; I swim, *nin bimâdaga.* (Yâyânam). I can swim, I swim well, *nin nitâwadaga.* I swim about, *nin babâmadaga.* I swim there, *nind inâdaga.* I swim to the shore, *nind agwâiadaga.* I swim to the other side of a river, etc., *nind âjawadaga.*

Swimmer, *bemâdagad.* A good swimmer, *netâwadagad.*

Swine, *kokosh, kokoshag.*

Swineherd, *genawenimad kokoshan.*

Swing, *webison, wébisowin, wewébison.*

Swing; I swing myself, *nin wewebis.* I swing him, *nin wewebina.*

Swinging, *wewêbisowin.*

Swollen; I am swollen, *nin bâgish, nin bodashka.* (Pâkipayiw). It is swollen, *bâgissin.* My belly is swollen, *nin bodadjishka.*

Swoon, *wanimikawiwin.*

Swoon ; I swoon, faint, *nin wanimikaw, nin wanendama.* S. Faint. Fainting. (Wanikiskisiw).

Sword, *ajaweshk.* Little sword or dagger, *ajaweshkons.* (Shimâgan).

Synagogue, *mawandiwigamig, kikinoamâdiwigamig.*

Syringe, *pindabâwadjigan, siginamâdiwin.* Little syringe, *bobogidjibigaigan.*

Syringe ; I syringe him, *nin pindabâwana, nin siginamâwa.*

T

Table, *adôpowin.* On the table, *ogidj'adopowin.* Under the table, *anâmadopowin.* (Mitjisuwinâtik).
Table-cloth, *adôpowinigin.*
Tables of the Covenant, *nij tessabikon.*
Tabourer, tabrer, *teweigiwinini.*
Tack, *sagaigans.*
Tack ; the vessel tacks about, *ajawiiassin nâbikwân.*
Tail, *osow.*—It has a long tail, *ginwanowe.* It has a short tail, *takwanowe.* It has a twisted or curled tail, *titibanowe.* It has a white tail, *wabanowe.*
Tail of a bird, *wanashkid.* (Wataniy). Tail of a small bird, *bineshi-wanishkid.* Tail of a large bird, *binessi-wanashkid.*
Tail of a cow or ox, *pijikiwano.*
Tail of a fish, *ojigwan.*
Tailor, *gashkigwassowinini.*
Take ; I take, *nin mamige.* I take him, (her, it,) *nin mamâ; nin mamôn.* I take it from him, *nin mamawa.* I take more than I ought, *nin nandagenim.*—I take before another does, *nin makandoshkamage.* I take it before others do, *nin makandoshkan.* I take it before he does, *nin makandoshkawa, nin makandoshkamawa.*
Take ; I take, *nind odâpinige.* I take or accept him, (her, it,) *nind odâpina ; nind odâpinan.* I take it for me, *nind odâpinamâdis.* I take it or accept it from him, *nind odâpinamâwa.*
Take along ; I take him, (her, it) along with me, *nind ani-gigisia ; nind ani-gigisin.*
Take away ; I take him, (her, it) away, *nin mamâ, nind mâdjina, nind ikona ; nin mamôn, nin mâdjidon, nind ikonan.*
Take care ; I take care of him, (her, it,) *nin bamia, nin ganawênima ; nin bamiton, nin ganawêndân.* I take care of myself, *nin bamiidis, nin ganawenindis.*—I take too much care of him, (I spoil him,) *nin têssina, nin téssinâwa.* I take too much care of myself, *nin têssinidis.*
Take down ; I take him, (her, it) down, *nin nissendawaa, nin pinawa ; nin nissadawatan, nin pinaan.*—I take a sail down, *nin binâkobidjige, nin binâkonige.* I take the sail down, *nin binâkonan ningassimonon.*
Take, drawing or hauling ; I take it, drawing it to me, (*in., an.*) *nind odâpibinan, nind odapibidon ; nind odâpibina.*
Take from ; I take from the fire, *nind agwâshinge.* I take from the fire what I have cooked,

nind agwâisekwe. I take it from the fire, (*in., an.*) *nind agwâshima.*
Take in; I take him (her, it,) in, *nin pindigana; nin pindigadon.* I take him in my house, *nin pindigana endaiân.*
Take off; I take it off, (*in., an.*) *nin gashkaan, nin gashkâwa.* I take it off (or away) from him, *nind angotamawa.* I take off my hat, *nin gitchiwakwane.* —Take off clothes. S. Strip.
Take out; I take him (her, it) out, *nin sâgidina; nin sâgisiton.*—I take it out of a canoe, etc., (*in., an.*) *nin agwâssiton; nind agwâshima.* I take s. th. out of his hand, briskly, *nin gidiskinindjibina.* I take it, not briskly, *nin gidiskinindjina, nin gidjinindjina.* I take out of a kettle or pot s. th. to eat, *nind agwâp.*
Take up; I take up on a thing, *nin nabidôige.* I take them up on a string, (*in., an.*) *nin nabidoanan; nin nabidoag.* Needle used in taking upon a string s. th., *nabidoigan.*—I take up with a hook, *nind adjigwâdjige.* I take him (her, it) up with a hook, *nind adjigwâna; nind adjigwâdan.*
Take without permission; I take without p., *nin wâwêjikama.* I take him (her, it) without p., *nin wâwêjikamanan; nin wâwêjikaman.*
Tale, *adisôkan, dibâdjimowin.* Decent tale, *binâdjimowin.* Indecent tale, *winâdjimowin.* (Atayokkan).
Tale-teller, *adisokewinini.*
Tale-telling, *adissokewin.*
Talk; I talk, *nin gigit, nin gâgigît, nin danânagidon, nin gijwe.* (Pikiskwew, itwew).
Talkative; I am talkative, *nind osâmidon, nind osâminowe.*
Talkativeness, *asâmidonowin, osâminowewin.*
Talking, *danânagidonowin, gigitowin, gâgigitowin, gijwewin.* Talking in a certain manner, *ijigijwewin.*
Tall; I am tall, *nin ginôs,* (I am long.) I am so tall, of a certain height, *nind akôs.*
Tallow, *mashkawadji-bimide.*
Tamarack, *mashkigwâtig.*
Tamborine, tabouret, tabret, *teweigan, mitigwakig.*
Tame; I tame him, (her, it,) *nin wangawia; nin wangawiton.* I tame it, (an animal or bird,) *nind awakana, nind awakinan.* (Nakayâhew).
Tamed; it is tamed, (*in.. an.*) *wangawitchigâde; wangawitchigâso.* (Nakatchitchikâsow).
Tamed animal, *waiangawitchigâsod awessi, mindassiwagan, awakân.* I keep a tamed animal, *nin wawekinaa awessi.*
Tamed bird, *awakân.*
Tan; I tan, I am tanning *nind asséke.* I tan a skin, (*in., an.*) *nind assékadan; nind assékanâ.* (Kesinikuw, kesinew).
Tan-house, *assekêwigamig.*
Tanned; it is tanned, (*in., an.*) *assekôde; assekâso.*
Tanner, *assekêwinini.*
Tanner's trade, tannery, *assekewin.*
Tantamount, *tibishko.*
Tar, *nabikwâni pigiw,*—S. Pitch.

Target of an archer, *bimôdjigan*. I am shooting at a target, *nin godaâkwe*.

Tarry; I tarry, *wika nin degwishin, ginwewj nind inind*.

Taste, *ipogosiwin*. Good taste, *minopogosiwin*. Bad taste, *mangipogosiwin*. —I find a good taste, *nin minopidjige*. I find a good taste in it, (*in.*, *an.*) *nin minopidan; nin minopwa*. It has a good taste, (*in.*, *an.*) *minopogwad; minopogosi*.—I find a bad taste, *nin manjipidjige*. I know s. th. by the taste, *nin nissitopidjige*. I know it by the taste, (*in.*, *an.*) *nin nissitopidan; nin nissitopwa*. It has an excellent taste, (*in*, *an.*) *wingipogwad; wingipogosi*. It has a sweet taste, (*in.*, *an.*) *wishkobipogwad; wishkobipogosi*. It has a bitter taste, (*in.*, *an*) *wissagipogwad; wisagipogosi*.

Taste; I taste, *nin godgipidjige*. I taste it, try it by the taste, (*in.*, *an.*) *nin godjipidan; nin godjipwa*. I taste or eat a little of it, (*in.*, *an.*) *nin tangandan, nin gotandan; nin tangama, nin gotama*.

Taste; it tastes, it tastes so..., (*in.*, *an.*) *ipogwad; ipogosi*. It tastes salted, (*in.*, *an.*) *jiwitâganipogwad; jiwitâganipogosi*. It tastes raw, (*in.*, *an.*) *ashkipogwad; ashkipogosi*. I find it tastes raw, it tastes raw to me, (*in.*, *an*) *nind ashkipidan; nind ashkipwa*.

Tatters, *wiiâgassiiman*.

Tattlers, *wesâmidong, neshiwanâdjigijwed*. I am a tattler, *nind osâmidon, nin nishiwanâdjigijwe*.

Tavern, *siginigêwigamig, ashangéwigamig*.

Tavern-keeper, *siginigewinini, ashangéwinini*.

Tax-gatherer, *mawandjitchigewinini*.

Tea, (in leaves,) *anibish*; tea, (ready to drink,) *anibishâbo*. (Nîpiya, maskikiwâbüy).

Teach; I teach, *nin kikinoamage*. I teach him, *nin kikinoamawa*. I teach myself, *nin kikinoamadis*. We teach each other, *nin kikinoamadimin*.

Teacher. S. School-teacher.

Teaching, *kikinoamâgewin, kikinoamâgowin, kikinoamâdiwin*.

Tea-kettle, tea-pot, *anibishâboakikons, jishibakik, jishibakikons*.

Teal, (duck,) *sagatâganishib, wewibingwange*.

Tea-spoon, *emikwânens, anibishâbo-emikwânens*.

Tear, *sibingwai*. With tears, *gigisibingwai*. (Otchikawâbüiy). I shed a tear, *nin pangigawisibigwe*. I shed tears, *nin maw*. (Mâtuw). Tears come out of my eyes, *nin sasâgisibingwe*.

Tear; I tear, *nin bigobidjige*. I tear it, (*in.*, *an.*) *nin bigobidon, nin kishkibidon, nin bigashkan; nin bigobina, nin kishkibina, nin bigoshkawa*. (Yayakipitam). I cannot tear it (*in.*, *an.*) *nin bwawibidon; nin bwawibina*.—I tear his skin, *nin bigwajéma*.—It tears, rends, *kishkigisse*.

Tear or break; I tear or break it, (*in., an.*) *nin pakishkan, nin pakibidon; nin pakishkawa, nin pakibina.* (Pikupitam). I tear a net, *nin pakinassabi.* It tears (breaks,) *pakishkamagad, bigoshkamagad.*

Tear or break by rubbing; I tear (break) it, (*in.. an.*) *nin pakibodon, nin pakibona.* It tears by rubbing, (*in an.*) *pakibote; pakiboso.*

Tear to pieces; I tear it to pieces, (*in., an.*) *nin nigoshkan, nin nanânigoshkan; nin nigashkawa, nin nananigashkawa.*

Tear with the teeth; I tear it with the teeth, (*in., an.*) *nin bigwandân, nin nanâniganDân; nin bigwama, nin nanânidama.* (Pikwamew).

Tease; I tease him, *nin migoshkadjia.*

Tell; I tell, *nin dibâdjim, nin windamage, nin dibâdjimotage.* I begin to tell, *nin mâdâdjim, nin madjiiadjim.* I tell him, *nind ina, nin dibadjimotawa, nin windamawa, nin dibâdodamawa.* (Itew). We tell each other, *nind idimin, nin windamadimin.* — I tell it, *nin windamagen nin dibadodan.* I tell s. th. in a certain manner, *nind inâdjim.* I tell s. th., of him in a certain manner, *nind inâdjima.* I tell s. th. of myself in a certain manner, *nind inadjindis.* I begin to tell s. th. of him, *nin madjiiadjima.* I tell of him s. th., *nin dajima, nin dibâdjima.* I tell s. th. good of him, (her, it,) *nin minwâdjima; nin mînwâdodan.* I tell s. th. bad of him, (her, it,) *nin matchi dajima, nin manâdjima; nin matchi dajindan.* I tell bad things, bad reports, *nîn manâdjim.* I tell bad reports about people, *nin manadjimotage.* I am heard telling bad reports, I tell bad reports, *nin manâdjimotâgos.* I tell decently, *nin winâdjim.* I tell indecently, *nin winâdjim.* I come to tell s. th. painful, difficult, *nin sanagishka, nin bi-sanagishka.* I tell difficult painful things, *nin sânagitâgos.* I come to tell him painful things, *nin bi-sanagishkawa.* I tell secretly, *nin gimodâdjim.* I tell him s. th. secretly, *nin gimodâdjimotawa.* I tell the truth, *nin dêbwe.* I tell the truth of him, *nin dêbima.* I tell wonderful things, queer stories, *nin mamakâsitâgos,* (I am heard with astonishment.) I tell tales, *nind adisôke.* I tell s. th. in different places, *nin babamâdjim.* I make a mistake in telling s. th., *nin wanâdjim.*

Telescope. S. Spyglass.

Temper. Temperament. S. Good temper. Ill temper.

Temperance, *minikwessiwin.*

Temperance-pledge, *minikwessimasinaigans.*

Temperant person, *menikwessig.*

Temple, *anamiewigamig.*

Temples; I have temples, *nin bibagingine.*

Tempt; I tempt, *nin gagwêdibeninge, nin gagwêdibendjige, nin jobiige.* I tempt him, *nin gagwêdibenima, nin gagwêdjia, nin jobia, nin gatchibia.* I tempt it, *nin jobiton.* It tempts me, *nin jobiigon, nin gatchibiigon.* (Kakwetchihew, kutchihew).

Temptation, *gagwêdibêningewin, gagwêdibêndjigewin, gagwêdibenindiwin, jobiigewin.*

Tempted ; I am tempted, *nin gagwêdibenimigo, nin gagwêdibendâgos.*

Tempting object, *jobiigowîn.*

Ten, *midâsswi ; kwetch.* We are ten of us, *nin midâdatchimin.* There are ten *in.* objects, *midâdatchinon.*

Ten, *midâsso....*, in compositions. (Mitâtat).

Tenacious. S. Viscous.

Tender, (not used to hardship ;) I am tender, *nin nishangadis, nin nôkis.*—The meat is tender, *nokiwagad wiiâss.*

Tender, (in. s. in.) S. Weak, (soft.)

Tenderly ; I bring him up tenderly, softly, *nin nishangigia.*

Ten each or to each, *memidâsswi.* (Mâmitâtat).

Ten every time, *memidâtching.*

Tent, *papâgiwaianegamig.*

Tenth ; the tenth, *eko-midâtching.* The tenth time, *midâtching.*

Tenthly, *eko-midâtching.*

Ten thousand, *midâtching midâsswâk.*

Ten times, *midâtching.*

Ten times every time, *memidâtching.*

Tepid ; it is tepid, a little warm, (liquid,) *abashkobite.* I make it tepid, *nind abashkobissân, nind abagamîsân.*

Tepid water, *ebashkobiteg nibi.* (Wiyikâgamiw).

Terror. S. Horror.

Testimony to condemnation, *bâtangewin.* I give testimony to condemnation, *nin bâtange.*

Thank ; I thank, *nin migwêtchiwiiwe, migwetch nind ikkit, nin mamoiâwe.* I thank him, *nin mamoiâwama, nin migwetchiwia, migwetch nind ina.* I thank in thoughts, *nin migwetchiweninge.* I thank him in thoughts, *nin migwetchenima, migwetch nind inénima.* (Nanâskumew, winâkkoma).

Thankful ; I am thankf., I have thankful thoughts, *nin mamoiawendam, nin mâmoiawagendam.* I am thankful to him, *nin mâmoiawenima, nin mamoiawagenima.* (Nanâskumow).

Thankfulness, *mamoiawendamowin, mamoiawagendamowin.*

Thanks ! I thank you ! *migwetch ! ondjita ! wêndjita !* (Winâkkoma).

Thanksgiving, *mîgwetchiwiiwewin, mamoiâwewin.*

That, *aw, awi, ow, iw, iwi.* (Eoko).

That, *tchi, tchi, wi.* (Kitchi, or, tchi).

Thaw ; it thaws, *ningikide.*

Thaw-weather ; it is thaw-weather, *ningiskodemagad, abawa.* The thaw-weather comes during my voyage, *nin ningiskos.* (Saskan).

Thee, *ki, kiiaw.*

Theft, *gimodiwin.*

Them, these, *igiw, iniw.* (Eokonik).

Then, *iwapi*. (Ekuspi).
Thence, *ima ondji, iwidi ondji.*
There, *ima, wedi, iwidi, iwedi, iwedi nakakeia ; wadi, wadibi, ajiwi.* (Ekute).
Therefore, *mi wendji.* (Eokotchi).
These here, *mâmig, ogôw ; mamin, onôw.* (Oki).
They, *winawa.* (Wiyawaw).
Thick ; it is thick, (*in.*, *an.*) *kipagâ ; kipagisi.* It is thick : Clothing, *in.*, *kipagigad ;* clothing, *an.*, *kipagigisi ;* liquid, *kipagâgami, bassagwâgami,* or *pasagwâgami ;* metal, *in.*, *kipagâbikad ;* metal, *an.*, *kipagâbikisi ;* stuff, *in.*, *kipagâbigad ;* stuff, *an.*, *kipagâbigisi ;* thread, *in.*, *mitchâbigad ;* thread, *an.*, *mitchâbigisi.*
Thick ; I make it thick : Liquid, *nin kipagâgamiton, nin bassagwâgamiton,* or, *non pasagwâgamiton ;* metal, *in.*, *nin kipagâbikiton ;* metal, *an.*, *nin kipagâbikia.* I make thick s. th., (*in.*, *an.*) *nin kipagiton ; nin kipagia.*
Thickly, (near together,) *bebesho.* (Kâkisiwâk).
Thickness ; it is of a certain thickness or height, *apitamagad.* The thickness of s. th., *epitag.*
Thief, *gemôdishkid, gimodiwinini.* I am a thief, *nin gimôdishk ; nin gagamindji, nin wâginindji.* Abode of thieves, *gimodiwigamig.*
Thievish ; I am thievish, *nin gimodishk.*
Thievish woman, *gimodiwikwe.*
Thievishness, *gimôdishkiwin.*
Thigh, *obwâma.* My, thy, his thigh, *nibwâm, kibwâm, obwâm.*—A part of the thigh, *tchingwan.*
Thigh-bone, *tchingwanigan.*
Thimble, *gandaigwâssowin.* (Kaskikwâsunâbisk).
Thin ; it is thin, (*in.*, *an.*) *bibaga ; bibagisi.* It is thin : A board, *bibagissagisi ;* liquid, *jigaagami ;* metal, *in.*, *bibagabikad ;* metal, *an.*, *bibagâbikisi ;* stuff, *in. babagigad ;* stuff, *an.*, *bibagigisi ;* wood, *in.*, *bibagigad ;* wood, *an.*, *bibagigisi.* The floor is thin, *bibagissaga.*
Thin ; I make it thin, metal, *in.*, *nin bibagabikia.* I make it thin by cutting it, (*in.*, *an.*) *nin bibagikodan ; nin bibagikona.*
Thine, *kin.* It is thine, (*in.*, *an.*) *kin kid aiim ; kin kid aiaa.* (Kiya, kit ayân).
Thing, *aii*, or, *keko.* Great thing, *kitchi aii.* Little thing, *aiins.* Bad wicked thing, *aiiwish.* (Kekway).
Think ; I think, *nind inendam.* I think he is (it is) in..., *nin danênima, nind indanénima ; nin danéndan, nind indanéndân.* I think of him, (her, it,) *nind inénima ; nind inéndan.* I think myself..., *nind inênindis.* I think little of him, (her, it,) *nind agâssénima, nin bewênima ; nind agâssêndân, nin bewéndan.*—I think it is so..., *nin waweiendam.* I think right, *nin gwaiakwendam.* I think wisely, prudently, *nin nibwâkadendam.*
Think on ; I think on him, (her,

it.) *nin mikwénima ; nin mikwéndân.* I think always on him, (her, it,) *nin bijibenîma, nin takwenima, mojag nin mikwénima ; nin bijibendan, nin kijibendan, nin takwendan, mojag nin mikwendan.* I think firmly or strongly on him, (her, it,) also, I think he (she, it) is strong, *nin songenima, nin mashkawenima ; nin songendan, nin mashkawendan.* I think firmly on myself, or, I think myself strong, *nin mashkawenindis, nin songenindis.* I think frequently on him, (her, it,) *nin mamikawinan, naningim nin mikwenima ; nin mamikawin, naningim nin mikwendan.* I think only on him, (her, it,) *nin bejigoenima, nin bejigwenima ; nin bejigoendan, nin bejigwendan.* I think always on him (her, it) when abroad, *nin waké-mamikwenima ; nin wakê-mamikendan.* I think always on home, *nin waké-mamikaw.*

Third ; the third, *eko-nissing.* The third time, *nissing.*

Thirdly, *eko-nissing.*

Thirst, *nibâgwewin, gaskanabâgwewin.* Ardent thirst, *gishkabâgwewin.*—I suffer thirst. S. Thirsty.

Thirsty ; I am thirsty, I thirst, *nin nibâgwe, nin gaskanabagwe.* (Notteyâbâkwew). I am thirsty, dry, *nin bengwanam.* I thirst very much, I suffer thirst, *nin pakabagwe, nin gishkabâgwe.* I thirst after s. th., *nin gishkabâgwewenodan.*

Thirteen, *midâsswi ashi nisswi.* (Mitâtat nistosâb).

Thirty, *nissimidana.* We are thirty of us, *nin nissimidanawemin.* There are thirty *in.* objects, *nissimidanawewan.* (Nistomitano).

Thirty every time, thirty each or to each, *nenissimidana.*

Thirty hundred, (3000) *nissimidanâk.* We are 3000 of us, *nin nissimîdanâkosimin.* There are 3000 *in. objects, nissimidanakwadon.*

This, this here, this one, *aw, ow, mabam, waaw ; ow, mandan.* (Eoko, awâh, oma).

Thistle, *missanashk.*

This way, *ondâshime, ondâss inakakeia.* (Astamite itekke).

Thorn, *minéssagawanj.* (Okaminakasïy).

Thorn-fruit, *minéss.*

Thoroughly, *wawinge.* (Mâmïywe).

Those, those there, *igiw, agiwi ; iniw, aniw, aniwi.*

Thou, *kin, ki, kid, kiiaw.* (Kiya).

Though, *missawa, missawa gaie, ano.* (Atawiya, âta).

Thought, *inéndamowin.*—Angry thought, *nishkâdendamowin.* I have angry th., *nin nishkâdendam.* I have angry th. towards him, *nin nishkenima.* We have angry th. towards one another, *nin nishkâdemindimin.* Fair and good th., *mino inendamowin, onijishendamowin.* I have fair and good th., *nind onijiskendam, nin mino nendam.* Impure, unchaste th., *bishigwâdendamowin.* I have impure th., *nin bishiqwâdendam, nin bi-*

shigwâdj-inendam; nin gagibâdendam. Proud th., *maminadendamowin, kiténimowin.* I have proud th., *maminâdendam, nin kitchitwâwenindis, nin kitenindis, nin kiténim.* Right and just th., *gwaiakwendamowin.* I have right and just thought, *nin gwaiakwendam.* Roguish th., *mamandéssadendamowin.* I have roguish th., *nin mamandéssadendam.* Sinful evil th., *batâinendamowin, matchi inendamowin.* I have sinful wicked th., *nin batâ-inendam, nin matchi inendam.* Strong th. or resolution, *songendamowin, maskkawendamowin.* I have strong th., *nin mashkawendam, nin songendam.* I make him have strong th., *nin mashkawendamia, nin songendamia.* Stupid, foolish, absurd, imprudent th., *gagibadendamowin, gagibadj-inendamowin.* I have stupid imprudent th., *nin gagibadendam, nin gagibadj-inendam.* Wise prudent th., *nibwâkadendamowin, gagitawendamowin.* I have wise th., *nin nibwâkadendam, nin nibwâka-inendam, nin gagitawendam.* I make him have wise prudent th., *nin gagitawendamia.*

Thought; I am (it is) thought, destined, *nind inendâgos; inendâgwad.* I am (it is) thought to be in...., *nind indanendâgos; indanendâgwad.*

Thoughtless; I am thoughtless, frivolous, *nin bisînâdis.*

Thousand, *midâsswâk.* We are a thousand in number, *nin midâsswakosimin.* There are a thousand *in.* objects, *midâsswâkwadon* A thousand each, *memidâsswâk.* A thousand times, *midâsswâk dassing.* (Kitchi mitâtatomitano).

Thumb, *mitchitchinindj.*

Thunder; thunderbolt, *animiki, animikig.* (Piyesiwok).

Thunder; it thunders, *animikika, animikiwan.* It thunders with great noise, *adjanimakwaamog* (*animikig*); *pashkikwaamog* (*animikig*). It thunders low, *tabassâkwaamog* (*animikig*). (Piyiesiwok kitowok).

Thunder-cloud, *animikawanakwad.*

Thunder-storm; there is a th. *kitchi animikika.*

Thursday, *niogijigad.*

Thy, *ki, kid.*

Thyself, *kin igo, kiiaw.* (Kiyatibiyawe).

Trash; I thrash, *nind apagandaige, nin gitchiminagaige.* I thrash it off with a stick, *nin bawaân.*

Trasher, *apagandaigewinini.*

Thrashing, *apagandaigewin, gitchiminagaigewin.*

Thrashing-floor, *apagandaigewigamig.*

Thrashing woman, *apagandaigekwe.*

Thread, *assabâb.* Small thin thread, *assabâbins.* I make thread, *nind assabâbike.* Thread for sewing, *nabikwâsson.*

Thread; I thread a needle, *nin nâbidoan jabonigan.*

Threat, threatening, *gagwésegindiwin.*

Threaten ; I threaten, *nin gagwésegiwe.* I th. him, *nin gagwésegima.*

Three, *nisswi.* We are three, *nin nissimin.* There are three *in.* objects, *nissinon.* (Nisto).

Three, *nisso...*, in compositions, which see in the Second Part.

Three ; he is three, three in one, *nissi.* (Nistiw, or, nistweyakihuw).

Three days ago, *kitchi âwassonago.* (Kitchi awassotâkusik).

Three every time, three each or to each, *nenisswi.*

Three hundred every time, 300 each or to each, *nenisswâk.*

Three thousand, *nissing midâsswâk, nissimidanâk.*

Three times, *nissing.* (Nistwaw).

Three times every time, three times each or to each, *nênissing.*

Threshold, *kashkikanokan.*

Throat, *gongâgan.* (Kuttâgan). A big throat, *pikwagondagan.* —My throat is dry, *nin bengwanam.* My th. is large, *nin mangigondagan.* My th. is sore, *nin gagidjigonewe.* My th. is swollen, *nin bâgigondagan.*—I take him by the throat, *nin sagigondaganena.* I cut his throat, *nin kishkigwejwa.* I cut my own throat, *nin kishkigwejoodis.* My throat is cut, *nin kishkigwe.*—It comes in my th., *nin pindjigoneweshkagan.*

Throne, *kitchi-ogima-apabiwin, kitcki-ogima-namadabiwin.*

Throng ; we throng, *nin sinsikodadimin.*

Through, *jibaii.* (Sâbo).

Through, (through the means of...,) *ondji.*

Throw ; I throw, *nind apagitchige, nind apagijiwe.* I th. him (her, it) somewhere, *nind apagina, nind apagitan, nind apagiton.* I th. myself somewhere, *nind apagis.* I th. it to him or for him, *nind apagitawa, nind apagitamawa.* We throw s. th. to each other, *nind apagîtâdimin.* We throw ourselves together somewhere, *nind apâidimin.* I th. myself to some place, *nind apâidis.*—I th. it to such a distance, (*in., an.*) *nin débinan ; nin débina.*

Throw about ; I throw about, *nin saswéwebinige, nin biwiwebinige.* I th. it about, (*in., an.*) *nin saswéwebinan, nin biwiwebinan ; nin saswéwebina, nin biwiwebina.*

Throw aside ; I throw aside, *nind ikowebinige, nin bakêwebinige.* I th. him (her, it) aside, *nind ikowebina, nind bakêwebina ; nind ikowebinan, nin bakêwebinan.*

Throw away ; I throw away, *nin wébinige.* I th. him (her, it) away, *nin wêbina ; nin wêbinan.* I throw away s. th. relating to him, *nin wêbinamawa.* I th. him (her, it) away, pushing, *nind gândjwebina ; nin gândjiwebinan.*

Throw down ; I throw down, *nin nissiwebinige, nind apagasikage.* I throw him down, *nin webishima, nin nissibewina, nind apagasikawa, nin pakitéoshima, nin pakitêakoshima..* I th. him down, biting him, *nin gawamâ*. I throw it down, *nin nissiwebinan, nin pakiteossidon*.—It throws me down, *nin wêbishimigon, nind apagasikagon, nin pakitéoshimigon*.—The waves throw me down, *nin gawiwebaog*.

Throw in ; I throw him (her, it) in, *nin pindigewebina, nin pindjwebina ; nin pindigewebinan*. I th. him (her, it) in the water, *nin bakobiwebina ; nin bakobiwebinan*. I throw myself in the water, *nin bakobiwebinidis*. I th. him (her, it) in a canoe, etc., *nin bôswebina ; nin bôswebinan*.

Throw off; he throws off his horns, *biniwine*.

Throw out ; I throw out, *nin sâgidjiwebinige*. I th. him (her, it) out, *nin sâgidjiwebina, nin gitchiwebina ; nin sâgidjiwebinan, nin gitchiwebinan, nin sâgidjiwebishkan*. I th. him (her, it) out of the canoe, ashore, *nind agwâwebind ; nind agwâwebinan*. I throw the water out of a canoe or boat, *nin gwakwapige*. A vessel to throw the water out, *gwakwapigan*. (Kwâpahigan).

Throw stones ; I throw a stone, *nin bimwâssin*. I throw stones, *nin babimwâssin*.—S. I stone.

Throw upon ; I throw it upon him, *nind apagadjissitawa, nind apagadjissitamawa*. I throw myself upon him, *nind ashosikawa*.

Throwing away, *webinigewin*.

Thrown ; I am (it is) thrown somewhere, *nind apagitchigas ; apagitchigâde*.

Thrown about ; it is th. about, (*in., an.*) *biwiwebinigâde, saswêbinigâde ; biwiwebinigâso, saswebinigâso*.

Thrown aside ; I am (it is) thrown aside, *nind ikowebînigas ; ikowebinigâde*.

Thrown away. S. Rejected.

Thrown down ; I am (it is) thrown down, *nin wêbishimigo, nin nissiwebinigas ; nissiwebinigade*.

Thrown in ; I am (it is) th. in., *nin pindjwebinigas ; pindjwebinigâde*. I am (it is) thrown in a canoe, etc., *nin boswebinigas ; boswebinigâde*.

Thrown out ; I am (it is) th. out, *nin sâgidjiwebinigas ; sâgidjiwebinigâde*.

Thrush, (bird,) *opitchi*.

Thrust away ; I thrust him (her, it) away ; *nind ikogandina, nin gonwâwa ; nind ikogandinan, nin gongwaan*.

Thrust back ; I thrust him (her, it) back, *nind ajégandina ; nind ajêgandinan*.

Thrust in ; I thrust it in, (*in., an.*) *nin gândinan, nin pinaan nin jégonan ; nin gândina, nin pinâwa, nin jegona*. I thrust it in for him or to him, *nin pinaamawa, nin gandinamawa*. I thrust a splinter in my hand, *nin jêgonindjidjin ;* in my foot, *nin jégosidedjin ;* under my nail, *nin jégoshkanjidjin ;* in any part of my body, *nin jégossagwedjin*.

Thrust in (in. s. in.) S. Stick in. Put in. Press down.

Thrust through ; I thrust it through, (*in., an.*) *nin jâbogandinan, nin jâbwakossidon ;*

nin jâbogandina, nin jâbonenan.

Tick or tike, *esiga.*

Tickle ; I tickle, *nin ginaginiwe.* I tickle him, *nin ginagina, ginagidjina.* I tickle his ears, *nin ginagitawagebina.*

Tickling, *ginagisiwin, ginaginiwewin.*

Ticklish ; I am t., *nin ginagis, nin ginagidji.*

Tide ; it is the flowing tide, *moshkagami nibi.* It is the ebbing tide, *odaskimagad nibi.*

Tidings. S. News.

Tie, *takobinigowin.*

Tie ; I tie, *nin takobinige, nin takobidjige.* I tie him, (her, it,) *nin takobina ; nin takobidon.* I tie it to him or for him, *nin takobidawa, nin takobidamawa.* I tie him (her, it) in a certain manner, *nind inapina ; nind inapidon.* I tie a bow, *nin biskaodon, nin biswaodon ; nin biskaona, nin biswaona.* I tie it with a knot, I tie it down, (*in., an.*) *nin gashkaodon, nind apitaodon ; nin gashkaona, nind apitaona.* I tie one string to another, to lengthen it, *nind anikobidon.* I tie it in different places, (*in., an.*) *nin sassagibidon ; nin sassagibina.*

Tie tight ; I tie tight, strongly, *nin mashkawapidjige.* I tie him (her, it) tight, *nin mashkawapina ; nin mashkawapidon.*

Tie together ; I tie them together, (*an., in.*) *nin mamâwapinag ; nin mamâwapidonan.* I tie two, three, etc. together, (*an., in.*) *nin nîiobinag, nin nissôbinag ; nin nijobidonan, nin nissôbidonan,* etc. I tie so many together, (*an., in.*) *dassobinag ; nin dassôbidonan.*

Tie up ; I tie it up in s. th. (*in., an.*) *nin kashkibidon ; nin kashkibina.* I tie up my head, *nin sinsokwebis.* I tie up his head, *nin sinsokwebina.*

Till, *binish, naiânj, nanânj.* (Eyigok).

Till ; I till or cultivate the ground, *nin kitige.*

Tillage, *kitigewin.*

Time ; a certain length of time, *nômag.* All the time, *apine, kaginig.* At the time, *iwapi.* At the same time, *baietoj, békish.* (Kisik). For a time, *gomâ minik.* From time to time, *aiâpi, nâningotinong, nonassak.* Some time, *gomapi.* (Askaw).

Time ; I have no time, *nind ondamita, nind ondamis.*

Time, lose time ; I lose time by drinking, *nind ondamibi.* I make people lose time by talking to them, *nind ondamitâgos* I make him lose time by talking to him, *nind ondamima.*

Timid, (bashful ;) I am timid, *nind agatchishk, nind agatchiwadis, nind agatchiwis.* (Nepewisiw).

Timid, (easily frightened ;) I am timid, *nin gagweshis, nin goshiweshk, nin gotânis, nin gotâdjishk, nin jâgodee.*

Timidity, bashfulness, *agatchishkiwin, agatchiwâdisiwin, agatchiwisiwin.*

Timidity, fear, *goshiweshkiwin, jâgoteewin, gagwéshisiwin.*

Tin, *wâbâbik.*
Tinder, *sagatâgan.*
Tingle; it tingles in my ears, *nin bibâgishe.*
Tin-kettle, *wâbâkik, wâbâbikwakik.*
Tippler, *menikweshkid.*
Tippling, *minikwêshkiwin.*
Tippling-house, *minikwéwigamig, siginigewigamig.*
Tipsy; I am tipsy, *nin jowibi.*
Tiptoe; I stand on tiptoe, *nin tchissigabaw.*
Tire; I tire myself, *nin aiékoidis.* I tire him, *nind aiékosia, nind aiêkwia, nind akoshkawa.* I tire it, *nind aiêkositon.* It tires me, *nind akoshkâgon.*—I tire myself traveling about, *nin babâ-akoshka.*
Tired; I am tired, *nind aiékos, nind akoshkos.* I feel tired in my arms, *nind aiêkonike;* in my legs, *nind aiékogâde.* I am tired of carrying, *nind aiékwiwi, nind ishkiwi;* of lying down, *nind ishkishin;* of sitting, *nind ishkwab.* I am tired from working hard, *nind akwiwi, nin pikikiwe, nin pikikiweta.* I look tired, *nind aiékosinâgos.*
Tired, disgusted; I am tired of s. th., *nin jigadendam.* I am tired of him, (her, it,) *nin jigadenima; nin jigadendân.* I am tired of telling the same thing so often, *nin jigadânagidon.* I am tired of waiting for him, *nin jigadjibia.* I am tired of walking, *nin jigadosse.* I am tired of writing, *nin jigadjibiige.*
Tiredness, *aiékosiwin.* Tiredness, (disgust,) *jigadendamowin.*
Tithes, church-tithes, *anamiepagidinigan.* I pay my tithes to the church and clergy, *nind anamie-pagidinige.*
Title of condemnation, *ondenindiwin.*
To, *tchi, tchiwî-.*
Toad, *omakaki, babigomakaki.* A kind of very big toad, *tende.*
Tobacco, *assêma.* (Tchistema). I manufacture tobacco, *nind assemâke.* Roll of tobacco, *wijinawassema.* This tobacco is fresh, *tipabagisi aw assema.* I have no tobacco to smoke, *nin manépwa.* Want of tobacco, *manêpwâwin.*
Tobacco-box, *assema-makak.*
Tobacco-juice, *apassagokidjân.* (Pasakuskitjân).
Tobacco-manufactory, *assemakewigamig.*
Tobacco-manufacturer, *assemâkéwinini.*
Tobacco-pouch, *kishkibitâgan.*
To-day, *nongom, nongom gijigak.* (Anotch).
Toe, *kinakwanisid.* The big toe, *kitchisidân.* I walk with my toes turned inside, *nin wawâgaami.* I walk with my toes turned outside, *nin nanâpadaami, nin jajâshagaami.*
Together, *mâmawi.*
Toil; I toil, *nin kotagiw.*
Tolerably, *eniwek.*
Toll-gatherer, *mawandjitchigewinini.*
Tomahawk, *wâgâkwadons.* (Pakamâgan).
To-morrow, *wâbang.* (Wâbaki). To-morrow morning, *wâbang*

kigijeb. To-morrow night, *wâbang onâgoshig.*

Tongs, *takwândjigan.* Small tongs, (pincers,) *takwândjigans.*

Tongue, *odenaniwama, denaniw.* My tongue is cut off, *nin kishkidenaniw.* (Miteyanïy). I cut his tongue off, *nin kishkidenaniwejwa.* My tongue is swollen, *nin bâgidenaniw.* I show my tongue, *nin jibidenaniwen, nin sâgidenaniwen.* I show him the tongue, *nin sâgidenaniwetawa.*

Tool, *anokasowin.*

Too late, *babisine, osâm wika.*

Too much, *osâm, osâm nibiwa.* (Osâm mistahi.)

Tooth, *wibidama.* My, thy, his tooth, *nibid, kibid, wibid.* I begin to have teeth, my teeth begin to come forth, *nin sagâbide.* I have teeth, *nind owibida.* I lose my teeth, *nin binâbide.* I am getting other teeth, *nind ândâbide.* I pull him a tooth out, *nin bakwabidebina.* I draw it out with the teeth, *nin wikwandan.* I try to draw it out for him with the teeth, *nin wikwatchiwikwannamâwa.* I draw it out for him with the teeth, *nin wikwandamawa.*—I have bad teeth, *nin manâdâbide.* I have good teeth, *nin minwâbide.* I have even fine teeth, *nind onâbide.* I have fine small teeth, *nin bissâbide.*

Tooth-ache, *dèwâbidewin.* I have tooth-ache, *nin dêwâbide, nind âkosin nibid.*

Tooth-ache medicine, *wibidamashkiki.*

Tooth-pick, tooth-picker, *nességwâbideon.*

Tooth-pincers, *bakwâbidêbidjigan.*

Top, *wanakowin.* There is a top, *wanakowiwan.* The top of a moccasin, *agwidagan.* The top of the tree is broken, *kishkanakisi mitig.* (Takkutch, or, waskitch).

Top, (boy's play-thing,) *towéigan.* I play with a top, *nin towéige.*

Torch, *wâssewâgan.*

Torch-stick, *wâsswâganak.*

Torment; I torment, *nin kotagiiwe.* I torment him, *nin kotagia, nin kotagima.* I torment myself, *nin kotagiidis.* It torments, *kotagiiwemagad.* It torments me, *nin kotagiigon.*

Torn; it is torn, (*in.*, *an.*) *bigoshkamagad, bigobidjigâde, nigoshkamagad, kishkibidjigâde; bigoshka, bigobidjigaso, nigoshkawa, kishkibidjigaso.* It is all torn to pieces, *nananigoskkamagad, bissibidjigâde.*—I wear torn clothes, *nin bigokwanaie.*

Tornado, *missibissidossi.*

Tortoise, *mishiké.* Another kind, *tetebikinak.*—S. Turtle.

Tortoise's shell or shield, *mishikewidashwa.*

Tossed; I am tossed about in a canoe or vessel, *nin kotagiwebaog.*

Touch; I touch him, (her, it) *nin tânginа; nin tânginan.* (Sâminew). I touch myself, *nin tânginidis, nin tânginamadis.* I don't dare touch him, (her, it,) or touch indecently, *nin manâtangina, nin manâdina, nin manâdjibina ; nin manâtanginan, nin manâdinan, nin manâdjibidon.* I touch myself indecently, *nin manâdinidis.* I touch him in a stealthy manner, *nin gimiwina, gimodj nin tângina.* I touch s. th. relating to him, *nin tânginamawa.* We touch one another, *nin tanginidimin.* —I make it touch s. th., *nin tângissiton.*—It touches the bottom, *bâgwissia.*

Tough ; it is tough, (*in., an.*) *jiban ; jibisi.* It is tough or durable, *jibissin.* The wood is tough, *mashkassissogad mitig.*

Towel, *kisinindjagan.*

Town, *odêna.* It is a town, or there is a town, *odenâwan.* A large town or city, *kitchi odena.* A small town or village, *odenâwens.*

Track, (footstep,) *okâwiwin, bimikawewin.* There are tracks, *bimikawade, okawinade.* There are my tracks, *nin bimikawe.* My tracks are visible on the road, *nind okaw.* The tracks of both my feet appear, *nind ojisidekawe.* (Ayetiskiw, namettaw). There are tracks on the road or trail, *okawamo mikana.* I see the tracks on the road, *nind okawiton mikana.*—I leave large tracks behind me walking, *nin mangishkam, nin mamângishkam.* I leave small tracks behind me, *nin biwishkam, nin babiwishkam.* I lose the track, *nin wanaadjige.*—I arrive to his track, *nin midjaana.* (Mâtahew). I see his track, *nind okawia.*—The track of the pen is visible, it appears well, (that is, the ink is black,) *okawissin ojibiiganâbo.*

Trade, *anokiwin, inanokiwin.*

Trade, (commerce,) *atâwewin, atandiwin.*

Trade; I trade, *nind atâwe.* I trade with him, *nind atâwama.*

Trader, *atâwêwinini.*

Tradesman, *anokiwinini.*

Trading, (commerce,) *atâwewin, atandiwin.*

Trading-house, store, *atawêwigamig.*

Trading-license, *atâwê-masinaigan.*

Tradition, *aiânike-dibâdjimowin, ajêdibâdjimowin.* Christian Tradition, *anamie-aiânike-dibâdjimowin.* (*Aianike, ânike,* signifies the same.)

Trail, *mikanâ, mikan.* I make a trail, *nin mikanâke.* I make a trail for him, *nin mikanâkawa.* The trail comes from...., *ondamo mikana.* The trail goes to..., *inamo mikana.* The trail is narrow, *agassâdemo mikana.* The trail is wide, *mangademo mikana.* — I lose the trail, *nin wanaadon mikana.*—I can go everywhere without a trail, *nin mitâwakamige.*

Tranquillity, *bisânisiwin, bekâdisiwin, bisânabiwin, bisâniiwewin, wanakiwin.* (Kiyâmewisiwin)

Tranquillity of heart, *wanakiwidéewin.* (Kiyâmitehewin).

Transcribe; I transcribe, *nind andjibiige.* I tr. it, *nind andjibiân.*
Transcript, *andjibiigan.*
Transfiguration *andjinagwiidisowin, andjinâgosiwin.*
Transfiguration of Jesus Christ, *Jesus od andjinâgosiwin.*
Transfigure; I transfigure myself, *nind andjinâgwiidis, nind andjinâgwi.*
Transform; I transform myself, *nind âwiidis.*
Transgress; I tr. a commandment, *nin bigobidon ganasongewin,* (I break a commandment.)
Translate; I translate, (writing,) *nind anikanotabiige.* I translate it. (writing,) *nind anikanotabiân.*
Translation, (written,) *anikanotabiigan, anikanotabiigewin.*
Translator, *anikanotabiigewinini.*
Transparent, (thin;) it is transparent, *jibawasse, jibâwasséigâde, jibâte, jibawâsso.*
Transparent stuff, *jibâwasséigin.*
Trap, *dassônagan.* (Wanihigan). I set a trap, *nind ombaan dassonagan.* I set him a trap, *nind oniamawa.* I make traps in the woods, *nind oniige.* (Wanihikew). I open a trap, *nin tawanobidon dassonagan.* I go to my traps, *nin nâdassonagane.* I miss him in my trap, *nin banikona.* I avoid or escape a trap or snare, *nin banikos.*
Trap; I trap him, (I catch him in a trap,) *nin dassona.*
Trapped; I am trapped, *nin dassôs*

Travel, *babâmâdisiwin, mâdâdisiwin.* Travel by water, not sailing, *bimishkâwin;* sailing, *bimâshiwin.*
Travel; I travel, *nin babâmadis, nin madâdis.* I travel by water, not sailing, *nin bimishkâ;* sailing, *nin bimâsh.*
Traveler, *bebâmâdisid.*
Traveling axe, *babamadisi-wâgâkwad.*
Traverse, *niminâgan.*
Traverse-Island, *Niminâgamiminiss.*
Tread; I tread, *nin takoki.* I tread into dirt, *nin jijokam.* I tread hard on the floor, *nin pitigossagishkan.* I tread on his toes, *nin tagosideshkawa.* I tread upon him, (her, it,) *nin takokânâ; nin takokâdân.*
Tread out; I tread out s. th., *nin mimigoshkan, nin gitchiminagishkam.* I tread it out. (*in., an.*) *nin mimigoshkân, nin gitchiminagishkân; nin mimigoshkawa, nin gitchiminagishkawa.*
Treasure, *daniwin, kitchi daniwin, dibendassowin.* I lay up a treasure, *nind atamâdis, nin nâwandonamâs, nin nâwandonamâdis.*
Treat; I treat him, *nin dodawa.* I treat (her, it) well, *nin mino dodawa; nin mino dodan.* I treat him (her, it) ill, *nin matchi dodawa, nind âbindjia, nin nanékadjia, nin nishkinawa; nin matchi dodan, nind abindjiton, nin nanékadjiton.* I treat him too ill, *nind osâmia.*
Tree, *mitig.* Tree with the roots, *pakwânj.* The tree has roots,

otchibikawi mitig. At the top or head of a tree, *wanakong*. —The tree begins to bud, *sâganimikwi mitig*, or *sâginimikwi*. The tree is getting new leaves, *sâgibagisi mitig*. The tree has young shoots, *sâgibimagisi mitig*. The tree is in bloom, *wabigoni mitig*. The tree has branches, *wadikwani mitig*, or *sâgidikwanagisi*. The tree has many branches, *babakêdikwanagisi mitig*.— The tree is blazed, *wassakwaigaso mitig*. The tree bends by the wind, *jashawabaski mitig*. The tree is broken by the wind, *makâkosi mitig*. There are trees blown down, *wessean*. The tree cracks or splits by cold, *pâshkakwadji mitig*. The tree is crooked, *wâwashkakosi mitig*. The head or top of the tree is crooked, *wâganakisi mitig*. The tree is dry, *mishiwâtigowi mitig*. The tree is hollow, *wimbinikisi mitig*. The tree is straight, *onâkosi mitig*. The tree is whitish, *wâbâkosi mitig*. There is a number of trees standing together, *bikwâwa, minâkwa*.

Trial, *godjiewisiwin*. I make him suffer for a trial, *nin godji-kotagia, nin gagwedji-kotagia*.

Tribunal, *dibakoniwe-apabiwin, dibakoniwewini-apabiwin*.

Trifle, *wegotogwenish*. Trifles, *wiiagassiiman*.

Trigger, *nassaténigan*. I pull the trigger, *nin nassaténige*.

Trinity, *Nesso-bejigod Kije-Manito*.

Trodden upon; I am (it is) trodden upon, *nin takokadjigas; takokadjigâde*.

Troop; the beasts are together by troops, *bimawanidiwag awéssiiag*. The birds are together by troops, *bimaamog binessîwag*.

Trouble, *kashkendamowin, kotagisiwin, nishiwanadakamigisiwin*. Trouble of mind, *nishiwanadendamowin, wanishkwéiendamowin*. I am in trouble, *nin kashkendam, nin kotagis*. I am in trouble of mind, *nin nishiwanadendam*. I cause him trouble, *nin kashkendamia, nin nishiwanadendamia*. I make or cause trouble, *nin nishiwanadakamigis, nin nîshiwanadjiiwe*. I cause trouble with my words, *nin nishiwanadjigijwe*.

Trouble, noise; there is trouble and noise, *odjanimakamigad*. I cause trouble and noise, *nind odjanimakamigis*. I speak with much trouble and noise, *nind odjanîmitagos, nind odjanimwewidam*. I cause him (her, it) trouble, *nind odjanimia*.

Trouble; I trouble him, molest him, *nin migoshkâdjia*. It troubles me, *nin migoshkâdjiigon, nin migoshkâdji-aiawigon*. I trouble him asking him for s. th., *nind mânjomotawa*. I trouble or molest with my words, *nin migoshkâsitâgos*. I trouble him with my words, *nin migoshkâsoma, nin wanishkwea, nin wanishkwema, nin wiiagiskima*.

Trouble of heart, *kashkendamideewin, migoshkâdjideewin.*

Troublesome; I am tr., *nin migoshkâdis, nin wanishkwes, nind odjanimiiwe, nin migoshkâdendâgos, nin wiiagiskendâgos, nin sanagis.*

Troublesomeness, *migoshkâdisiwin, wiiagiskendagosiwin, sanagisiwin.*

Trough, *atôban, wissiniwâgan.* I make a trough, *nind atôbanike.*

Trout, *namêgoss.* There are trout, *namêgossika.* Place where there are trout, *namégossikan.*

Trout-bone, *namêgossigan.*

Trowel, *joshkwabiganaigan.* I plaster with a trowel, *nin joshkwabiganaige.*

True; it is true, considered true, *debweiendâgwad.* I am considered true, (veracious,) *nin debweiendâgos.* I think it is true, *nin debweiendân.*

Truly, *geget.* (Tâpwe).

Trumpet, *bodâdjigan, madwéwetchigan.*

Trunk, *makak, mitigo-makak.*

Trust, trusting, *apénimowin.*

Trust; I trust in him, (her, it,) *nind apenimonan; nind apenimon.* I trust in myself, *nind apenindis.* We trust in each other, *nind apenindimin.*

Truth, *débwewin* It is the truth, *debwêwinagad, debwewinimagad, debwewiniwan.* I tell the truth, *nin débwe, nin debwetagos.* I tell the truth of him, *nin débima.* I think he tells the truth, *nin debwetaienima.*

Truth-paper, (deed, certificate, etc.) *debwewini-masinaigan.*

Truth-teller, *daiebwed, daiebwetâgosid.*

Truth-telling, *debwetâgosiwin.*

Try; I try, *nin godjiew.* I try without much effect, *nind inwâs.* I try him, (her, it,) *nin godjia, nin godjiewinodawâ; nin godjiton, nin godjiewinodan.* I try it, (a coat, boot, etc.) *nin gosikan.* I try it, (a gun,) *nin gosikaton.*

Try, (examine;) *nin gagwedjiiwe.* I try him, (her, it,) *nin gagwedji-kikenima; nin gagwedji-kikéndân.* I try him by sufferings, *nin gagwedj--kotagia.*

Try to surpass; I try to surpass, *nin gagwedjenimiiwe.* I try to surpass in speaking or debating, *nin gagwéjagosonge.* He that surpasses others in speaking, *gagwêjagosongewinini.* I try to surpass him in sp., *nin gagwéjagosoma.* We try to surpass each other in sp., *nin gagwéjagosondimin.*

Tub, *makakossag.*

Tumble; I tumble, fall, *nin pakiteshin.* I make him tumble, *nin pakiteshima.* —I tumble over head, *nin abodjigwanisse, nin tchingidaabowe.*— I tumble down, *nind ondagodjin.* It tumbles down, *pikwabikisse.*

Tumbler, *minikwâdjigan.*

Turbid; it is turbid, *pakwebigad, pakwebigami.* I make it turbid, *nin pakwebigamissidon.*

Turkey, (bird,) *misisse.* Young turkey, *misissens.*

Turn; by turns, *memeshkwat.* I in my turn, *ninitam.* (Niyaskutch). Thou in thy turn, *kinitam*. He in his turn, *winitam*. We in our turn, *ninitamiwind, kinitamiwind*. You in your turn, *kinitamiwa*. They in their turn, *winitamiwa*.

Turn; I turn, (standing or sitting,) *nin gwêkita*. I turn, (lying,) *nin gwekishin*. I turn my head, *nin bimiskokwen*. I turn this way, standing, *nin bi-gwekigabaw*. I turn this way, sitting, *nin bi-gwêkâb*.—I turn him, (her, it,) *nin gwekia; nin gwêkiton*. I turn my thoughts, (change my mind,) *nin gwêkendam*.

Turn out; I turn him out, *nin sagidjiwebina*. I turn him out, beating him, *nin sagidaganâma*.

Turn over; I turn him (her, it) over, *nin gwêkina; nin gwêkishima; nin gwêkinan, nin gwêkissidon*. I turn it over for him, *nin gwékinamâwa*. I turn it over: Metal. *in., nin gwekabikissidon*; metal, *an., gwekâbikishima*; stuff, *in., nin gwekiginan*; stuff, *an., nin gwekigina*.—I turn it over, inside out, (*in., an.*) *nind abodinan; nind abodina*. I turn it over, upside down, *nind animikonan, nind animikwissidon, nind ajigidinan*.

Turn round; I turn round, *nin kijibata, nin bimiskota*. I turn round until I get giddy, *nin giwashkwedinokwe*. I turn round until I fall down, *nin kijibadinokwe*.—I turn round, I turn myself, *nin gwikita*. I turn round, flying, *nind abamisse*; running, *nind abamibato*; standing, *nind abamigabaw, nin gwékigabaw, nin bimiskogabaw*. I turn round briskly, *nin gwékipagis*. I turn round with a canoe, *nin giwegom*. I make him turn round, sitting, *nin gwekabia*. I make him turn round, standing, *nin gwekigabawia*.—I turn him round on a cord, *nin kijibidéeshkassa*. I turn it round, twisting, (*in., an.*) *nin bimiskoton, nin bimiskwissidon, nin bimiskonan; nin bimiskona*. I turn it round briskly, (*in., an.*) *nin kijibawebinan, nin bimiskowebinan; nin kijibawebina, nin bimiskowebina*.

Turn to another side; I turn, *nin gwêki*. I turn to an. s., sitting, *nin gwékâb, nind ânigwékâb*. I turn to an. s., standing, *nin gwêkigabaw, nind âni-gwékigabaw*.

Turn towards; I turn towards (or from) him, (her, it,) *nin gwekitawa; nin gwekitân*. I turn towards him, (her, it,) standing, *nin gwékigabawitawa*.

Turn; it turns over, *gwêkissin*. I turn (it turns) round, revolves, *nin bimiskota; bimiskotamagad*. It turns a little, *bimiskwamagad*.—The river turns round, *abamitigweia sibi*. The water turns round, *abimodjiwan*.

Turn, (convert;) I turned, I am converted, *nind andjibimâdis, nin anwenindis*.

Turnip, *tchiss*. Small turnip, *tchissens*. (Otisikkân).

Turnip-seed, *tchissi-minikan.*
Turnsol, *missitagan.*
Turtle, *jingademikwan, miskwadessi, bosikado ; makinâk,* or, *mikkinâk.* The shell or shield of a turtle, *dashwâ.*
Turtle-dove, *omimi.* Young turtle-dove, *omimins.*
Twelve, *midâswi ; ashi nij.* (Mitâtat nijosâb).
Twenty, *nijtana.* We are twenty of us, *nin nijtanawemin.* There are twenty *in.* objects, *nijtanawêwan.* There are twenty pair of..., *nijtanawêwan.*
Twenty every time, twenty each or to each, *nenijtana.*
Twenty hundred, *nijtanâk.* We are two thousand in number, *nin nijtanâkosimin.* There are two thousand *in.* objects, *nijtanâkwadon.*
Twice, *nijing.* (Nijwaw).
Twice every time, twice each or to each, *nenijing.*
Twilight ; it is twilight, *tibikâbaminagwad, nanitagabaminagwad, nikiwigad.* It is twilight in the morning, *bi-wâban, wâban.*
Twin, *nijôdé.* I am delivered of twins, *nin nijodéike.*
Twine, *assabâb.*
Twine for nets, *assabikéiâb.*
Twist ; I twist with a stick, *nin bimâkwaige* I twist it with a stick, (*in., an.*) *nin bimâkwaan ; nin bimâkwâwa.* I twist him, (her, it,) *nin bimina ; nin biminan.* I twist threads together, *nin jashabwabinige.* I twist tobacco, *nin bimibagina assema.* I twist it up, curl it, *nin titibâkwaan, nin babisigakwaan.* I twist it around s. th., *nin titibabissidon.*
Twisted ; it is twisted, (*in., an.*) *titibâode ; titibâoso.* The tree is twisted, *bimakosi mitig,* or *bimoskogisi.*
Twisted line of several threads, *jashabwabiginigan.* It is twisted of several threads, *jashabwabiginigâde.*
Twisted tobacco, *bimibâginigan.*
Twisted wood, *bimâkwad.* Sweet twisted wood, *manito-bimâkwad.*
Twisting-stick, *bimâkwaigan.*
Two, *nij.* We are two, *nin nijimin.* There are two *in.* objects, *nijinon, nijinomagad.*
Two, *nijo...,* in compositions, which see in the Second Part.
Two every time, two each or to each, *nenij.*
Two families, three families, etc., *nijode, nissode,* etc. We are two families, three families, etc., *nin nijodewisimin, nin nissodewisimin.*
Two hundred, *nijwâk.* We are 200 of us, *nin nijwâkosimin.* There are 200 *in.* objects, *nijwâkwadon.* There are 200 pair of...., *nijwâkwêwân.*
Two hundred every time, 200 each or to each, *nenijwâk.*
Tying, *takobinigewin, takobidjigewin.*
Tying-string, *takobidjigan.*

U

Udder of a cow, *totosh, pijikiwitotoshim.*
Ugliness, *manâdisiwin.*
Ugly; I am (it is) ugly, *nin manâdis; manâdad.*
Ulcer. S. Abcess with matter
Ultimately, *gêgapi, ishkwâtch.*
Umbrella, *agawateon, agawabasowin.*
Unable; I am unable to walk, *nind anawito.* I am unable to do it, *kawin nin gashkitossin.* (Bwâtawittaw).
Unbend; I unbend it, *nin binangwabiginan, nin neshangabiginan.*
Unbelief, *agonwéiendamowin.*
Unbeliever, *daiébwetansing, aiâgonweiendang, aiâgonwetang.*
Unchastc. Unchastity.—S. Impure. Impurity.
Uncle, (father's brother,) my, thy, his uncle, *nimishome, kimishome, omishomeian.* (N'okkumis).
Uncle, (mother's brother;) my, thy, his uncle, *nijishé, kijishê, ojisheian.* (Ni sish).
Unclean. Uncleanness.—S. Dirty. Dirt.
Unclean spirit, *wanisid manito.*
Uncock; I uncock a gun, *nin minwâbikinan pâshkisigan, nin niwatenan pâshkisigan.*
Uncover; I uncover him, *nin pakagwajena.* I uncover myself, *nin pakagwajenidis.* I uncover it, *nin pakissiton.* I uncover it to him, *nin pakissitamawa.*
Uncovered; it is unc, *pakissitchigâde.*
Undecided; I am und., *kawin nin gijendansi.*
Under, *anâmaii, anâmina, anâming.* It is under s. th., (*in.. an.*) *ashôtchissin; ashôtchishin.*
Underbrush; thick underbrush of the fir-kind, *akâwanj.* There is thick underbrush, *akâwanjika.*
Under-chief, second chief, *anikéogima.*
Underfeather of a bird, (down,) *misségwanân.*
Underhair of an animal, *missinibiwaiân.*
Underneath. S. Under.
Understand; I understand, *nin nissitôtam.* I understand so.., *nind initam.* I under. him, (her, it) *nin nissitotawa; nin nissitôtân.* I und. him only a little, *nind aiawetawa.* I und. him so. ., *nind inîtawa.* I try to understand, *nin nandanissitotam.* I try to und. him, (her, it) *nin nandanissitôwa; nin nandanissitôtân.* We understand each other, *nin nissitôtâdimin.*—I don't understand well what I hear, *nin*

bamitam. I don't und. him (her, it) well, *nin banitawa ; nin banitân,*

Understand, (conceive;) I understand it, *nin nissitâwendân.*

Understanding, *nibwâkâwin.*

Understood; I am (it is) easily understood, *nin nissitotâgos ; nissitotâgwad.* I am und. only a little, *nind aiawetâgos.*

Underwood; there is much underwood, *sasaga.*

Undoubtedly, *geget e nange ka, aningwana, abidekamig.*

Undress. Undressing.—S. Strip. Stripping.

Undulated. S. Veined,

Uneasiness, *migoshkâdjideewin.*

Uneasy; I am uneasy, *nin migoshkâdji-aiâ, nin migoshkâdjidée.* It makes me uneasy, *nin migoshkâdjiigon, nin migoshkâdji-aiawigon.*

Unfit, *matchi, ningot enâbadassinog.* It is unfit, *manâdad ; kawin ningot inâbadassinon.*

Unfold; I unfold it, (*in., an.*) *nind abiginan, nin biniskwabiginan ; nind abigina, nin biniskwabigina.*

Unfold, (in. s. in.) S. Spread out.

Unforseen, *sesikâ.*

Unfortunate. S. Unhappy.

Unglue; it unglues, *pakwasika, pakwatchikiwagishkamagad.*

Unhappiness, *kitimâgisiwin, kotagendamowin.*

Unhappy; I am unhappy, *nin kitimâgis, nin kotagendam.* I make him (her, it) unhappy, *nin kitimagia ; nin kitimagiton.* I make myself unh., *nin kitimagiidis.* I look unhappy, *nin kitimaginâgos.* It is unhappy, *ânimad.*

Unhappy, (in. s. in.) S. Injure.

Unharness; I unharness him, *nind âbawâ.*

Unicorn, *negoteshkanid.* It has only one horn, *ningoteshkani.*

Unite; I unite with him, *nind ajodenima.*

Unite, (in. s in.) S. Put together.

United States, *Kitchimokomâniwaki.*

Unleavened bread, *wembissitchigasossig pakwejigan.*

Unload; I unload a canoe, etc., *nind agwanâss.*

Unloading, *agwanâssowin.*

Unlock; I unlock it, *nind ababikaan,* I unlock it to him, *nind abâbikamawa.*

Unlocked; it is unlocked, *abâbikaigâde.*

Unlucky; I am unl., I have bad luck, *nin massagwâdis.* I am (it is) unlucky, considered unlucky, *nin massagwadendagos ; massagwadendagwad.* (Mayakusiw).

Unpleasant; it is unp., *manâdad.*—S. Disagreeable.

Unprepared. S Undecided.

Unprofitable; I am (it is) unprofitable, *nin nanawis, nin nanawâdis ; nanawad, nanawâdad.*

Unprofitably, *nanawâj.*

Unprovoked, *biwisika.*

Unravel; I unravel it, *nin nassâbiginan.*

Unrepenting person, *aianwênindisossig.*

Unstitch; I unstitch it, (*in., an.*) *nind abijan ; nind abijwa.*

Unstitch. Unstitched.—S. Rip. Ripped.

Unswadle ; I unswadle a child, *nind âbawa abinodj.*

Untie ; I untie, *nind âbiskobidjige.* I untie him, (her, it,) *nind âbawa, nind âbiskona, nind âbiskobina ; nind âbaan, nind abiskonan, nind abiskobinan.* I untie it for him, *nind âbaamawa, nind âbiskonamawa.* It unties, *âbiskosse.*

Untied ; I am (it is) untied, *nind âbaigas, nind âbiskobidjigas, nind abiskobis, nin géshawishka ; âbaigâde, abiskobidjigâde, âbiskobide,gêshawishkamagad.* I get untied, *nind âbiskota.* It gets untied, *abiskoka.*

Until, *naiânj, nanânj, binish.*

Untutored, uneducated ; I am unt., *nin pagwanâwis, nin pagwanawâdis.* Untutored wild state, *pagwanawisiwin, pagwanawâdisiwin.*

Unwell ; I am unwell, *nin mânjâia, pangi nind âkos.*

Unwind ; I unwind from a reel, *nind âbaodjige.* I unwind it, *nind âbaodon.*

Up the stream ; I go up the stream in a canoe, *nin nitaam.* I take him up the str. in a canoe, *nin nitâona.*

Up, upwards, (respecting rivers) *ogidâdjiwan.* (Natimik).

Upbraid. S. Reprimand.

Upon. S. On.

Upper floor ; there is an up. fl., *ishgimissagokâde.*

Upright, honest ; I am an upright man, *nin naininiwagis.*

Upright, straight, *gwaiak.*

Uprightness, upright life, *gwaiakôbimâdisiwin.*

Upset. S. Capsize.

Up stairs, *ishpiming, ishpimissagong.*

Up to..., *binish....*

Upwards, *ishpiming inadakeia.*

Urge ; I urge him, *nin gagânsoma.*

Urge, (in. s. in.) S. Persist.

Urine, *jigiwinâbo.*

Urine ; I urine, *nin jishig.* I urine in the bed, *nin jishingwâm.*

Urine-bladder, *jigiwin.*

Us, *kinawind, ninawind.*

Use, (habit,) *nagadisiwin.*

Use, the use of s. th., *aiowin, abadjitowin, inâbadjitowin.* I make use of him, (her, it,) *nind awa, nind anokana, nind abadjia ; nind aion, nind anokadan, nind abadjiton.* I make a good use of him, (her, it,) *nin minoiabadjia ; nin minoiabadjiton.*

Use ; I use, *nind aiodjige.* I use him, (her, it,) *nind awâ ; nind aiôn.* I use or employ him (her, it) in a certain way or manner, *nind inâbadjia, nind inânokana, nind inawemikana ; nind inabadjiton, nind inânokadan, nind inawemikadan.* I use things profitably, (*in., an.*) *nin bissâgonan ; nin bissâgona.* I use it sparingly, savingly, (*in., an.*) *nin manâdjiton, nin manâdandan, nin manégadandan, nin manêgadjiton ; nin manâdjia, nin mânadama, nin manégadama, nin manégadjia.* I use it sparingly, (clothing, *in., an.*) *nin manêgasikan; nin manégasika.*

Used ; it is used, (made use of,) (*in.*, *an.*) *aiodjigâde ; aiodjigâso.* It is used in such a manner, (*in.*, *an*) *inâbadjitchigâde ; inâbadjitchigâso.* Any thing used, *aiôwin.* The things I use, *nind aiôwinan.*

Used, (in. s. in.) S. Accustomed.

Useful ; I am (it is) useful, *nin minoiâbadis, nin gwanâtchiw, nind onijish ; minoiâbadad, gwanâtchiwan, onijishin.* I am (it is) useful in such a manner, *nind inâbadis ; inâbadad.* I am (it is) useful, considered useful, *nind inâbadendâgos ; inâbadendâgwad.* —He (she, it) is useful to me, *nind âbadjia ; nind âbadjiton.* Useful object, *âbadjitchigan, inâbadjitchigan.*

Uusefulness, *inâbadisiwin, inabadendagsiwin, gwanâtchiwin.*

Useless. S. Unprofitable.

Useless person, *ningot enâbadisissig, aianawewisid, nenawadisid.*

Useless thing, *ningot enâbadassinog.*

Use up. Used up. S. Spend all.

Using, *aiôwin ; inâbadjitowin.*

Usurp ; I usurp s. th., *nin dibendamonidis.* I usurp it, (*in.*, *an.*) *nin dibendamonidison ; nin dibendamonidisonan.*

Utility. S. Usefuluess.

Uvula, *kagagi.*

V

Vaccinate. Vaccination. Vaccinator—S. Inoculate. Inoculation. Inoculator.

Vagabond, *gawaadisid.* I am a vagabond, *nin giwaadis.*

Vagrancy, *giwaadisiwin.*

Vain; I work or endeavor in vain, I gain nothing, *nind anawewis, nind agâwis, nind agâwishka, nind agâwita.*

Vain glory, self-glory, *kitchitwawenindisowin.*

Vainly,in vain,*anishâ.*(Konata.)

Valet, *bamîtagan, bamitâgewinini, anokitâgewinini.*

Valley; there is a valley, *passadina, tawadina.*

Valley of sand; there is a v. of sand, *passatawanga.*

Valuable; I am (it is) valuable, *nin kitchi apitendâgos; kitchi apitendâgwad*

Value; I value him (her, it) so much...., *nind apitagima, nind inagima; nind apitagindon, nind inagindan.*

Value, (esteem;) I value, *nind apitendam.* I value him, (her, it,) *nind apitenima; nind apitendân.*

Valued; I am (it is) valued at... *nind inagins, nind inagindjigas; inaginde, inagindjigade.*

Van, *noshkâtchigan, noshkatchinagan.*

Van, I van, *nin noshkâtchige.* I van it, (*in., an.*) *nin noshkaton; nin noshkassa.*

Vanish, it vanishes, *angô, angô magad.*

Vanquish; I vanquish him, *nin gashkia.* I vanquish myself, *nin gashkiidis.* (Sâkohew).

Vanquish, (in. s. in.) S. Overcome.

Variegated, of various colors; it is var. (stuff, *in. an.*) *kitagigad; kitagigisi.*

Variegated stuff, of different colors, *kitagigin.*

Vast; it is vast, *mitchâmagad.*

Veil, *agwiagweon, agwingwebison.*

Vein, *oskweiâb, miskweiâb.*

Veined, veiny; it is veined, *gidjigabikad,* (stone;) *gidjigissagad,* (wood.)

Vein of the heart, *gwashkwashkwanibikê.*

Velvet,*mashawesid senibâwegin.*

Venerable; I am (it is) venerable, considered venerable, *nin kitchitwâwendâgos; kitchîtwâwendâgwad.*

Veneration, *minâdenindiwin, kitchitwâwenindiwin; kitchitwâwendagosiwin.* I hold him (her, it) in veneration, *nin kitchitwâwenima; nin kitchitwâwendân.*

Veneral disease, *manâdapine, win.* I have the ven. dis., *nin manâdapine.*

Venison, *wiiâss.* I fetch venison, (or fish,) *nin ningwaniss.* (Nakwatisow).

Vengeance, *ajidawawin*, *ajidawiwin*.
Venom. S. Poison.
Veracious; I am ver., *nin debweiendâgos*. Veracious speaking, *debwetâgosiwin*.
Verily, *geget*. (Tâpwe).
Vermifuge, *ogejagimi-mashkiki*.
Vermillion, *onaman*, *osânaman*; also, red clay.
Vermillion-Lake, *Onamani-sâgaigan*.
Version, (written,) *anikanotabiigan*. S. Translation.
Vertigo. S. Giddiness.
Very, very much, *âpitchi*, *kitchi*, *osâm*, *ondjita*.
Vespers, *onâgoshi-anamiang*.
Vessel, *nâbikwân*. Small vessel, *nâbikwânens*.
Vessel, folded birch-bark vessel, *biskitênagan*.
Vessel to draw water with, *gwâbaigan*.
Vest, *gibideebison*.
Vestige, (footstep,) *bimikawewin*. There are vestiges, *bimikawâde*. (Ayetiskiwin).
Vestment, *agwiwin*. I wrap my vestment around me, *nin titibishoweon nind agiwin*.—S. Clothes. Clothing.
Vestry. S. Sacristy.
Vex; I vex him, *nin migoshkâdjia*, *nin nishkia*. It vexes me, *nin migoshkâdjiigon*, *nin nishkiigon*.
Vexation. S. Troublesomeness.
Vice, *botadowin*, *matchi ijiwebisiwin*.
Vicious, *matchi*. I am (it is) vicious, *nin matchi ijiwebis*, *nin batâ-ijiwebis*; *matchi ijiwebad*, *manâdad*.
Victorious. S. Overcome.
Victuals, *midjim*. I produce or procure victuals, *nin midjimike*. Labor in procuring victuals, *midjimikewin*.
Vial, *omôdens*.
Vigor, *kijijâwisiwin*.
Vigorous; I am vig., *nin kijijâwis*. I am vig. in my old age, *nin jibigika*.
Vigorous, (in. s. in.) S. Strong.
Village, *odéna*. Half or part of the village, *bokodéna*. There is a village, *odénâwan*. A small village, *odenâwens*. We live together in a village, *nind odétomin*.
Villain, *matchi aiaawish*.
Vine, *jominâtig*, *jominâgawanj*.
Vinegar, *jiwâbo*.
Vinegar-tree, *bakwanâtig*, *bakwanimij*. The fruit of it, *bakwan*.
Vine-leaf, *jominibag*.
Vineyard, *jomini-kitigan*.
Vintner, vine-dresser, *jominâbokewinini*.
Violet, *apissi*.
Violet color; it is of a v. c., *apissin*.
Violin, *najabiigan*, *kitotchigan*, *kitoweiâpikoigan*. I play on the violin, *nin najabiige*, *nin kitotchige*.
Virgin, *oshkinigikwe*, *gigang*, *tessanakwe*. I am a virgin, *nind oshkinikwew*, *nin gigangow*, *nin tessanakwew*. I am in a virginal state, (a male speaking,) *nin tessanaw*. Virgin presented to the Great Spirit, *agonâkwe*.
Virtue, *mino ijiwebisiwin*.
Virtuous, *nin minoijiwebis*.
Viscous; it is vis., *sibiskân*.
Visibility, *wâbaminâgosiwin*.

Visible; I am (it is) visible, *nin wâbaminâgos ; wâbaminâgwad.* I make myself visible, *nin wâbaminâgwiidis, nin nâgwiidis.* I am (it is) visible from a certain distance, *nin débabaminâgos; dêbabaminâgwad.* It is plainly visible, *pagakissin.* I am (it is) scarcely visible yet, *nin nâwinagos ; nawinagwad.*

Visicatory, *odji-mashkiki, ombisigan, ombibisigan.*

Vision, *nâgwiidisowin, mamânsinamowin, ijinamowin.* I appear in a vision, *nin nagwiidis.* I have or see a vision, *nin mamânsinam.* I have such a vision, *nind ijinam.*

Visit, visitation, *mawadishiwewin, nibwâtchiwewin.* Habit of making visits too often, *mawadishiwéshkiwin.*

Visit; I visit, I pay a visit, *nin mawadishiwe, nin nibwâtchiwe.* I visit him, *nin mawadissâ, nin nibwâtchia.* I visit too often, *nin mawadishiwéshk.*

Visitor, (arriver,) *biwide.*

Vitriol, *wejawashkâasigwag mashkiki.*

Vivify ; I vivify or vivificate him, *nin bimâdjia.*

Vocabulary, *ikkitowini-masinaigan.*

Voice, *inwewin, bibâgiwin.* (Itwewin, itittâkusiwin.) A voice comes from..., *ondwewe.* I have such a voice, (I am heard so...,) *nind initâgos.* I have a big strong v., *nin mângigondagan, nin sôgigondagan.* I have a feeble little v., *nind agâssigondagan.* I have a bad v., *nin mângigondagan.* I have a fine clear v., *nin minowe, nind ojigondagan.* I have a weak low voice, (from hunger, fatigue, sickness,) *nind ânawitâgos.* I find his voice weak, *nind ânawitawa.*

Vomit ; I vomit, *nin jishigagowe.* I feel an inclination to vomit, *nin bijibidee.* I make him vomit, *nin jishigagowea, nin jishigagoweswa.* The matter vomited, *jishigagowan.* (Pâkomow).

Vomiting, vomition, *jishigagowewin.*

Vomitive, *jishigagowesigan.* (Pâkomosigan).

Voracious ; I am vor., *nin nibâdis.*

Voracity, *nibâdisiwin.* (Kajakew).

Vow, *dibandowin, mashkawawindamagewin.* I make a vow, *nin dibando, nin mashkawawindamage.* I fulfil a vow, *nin dibandon.* (Asotamowin).

Voyage, *babâmâdisiwin.* S. Travel. Traveler.

Vulture, *winange.*

W

Wade; I wade, *nin bimâdagasi.* I wade through a river to the opposite shore, *nind ajawagameosse.*

Wafer, *agokiwassigan.*

Wag, *bebâpinisid, bebâpinwed.*

Wager, *atâdiwin.*

Wagon, *odâbân, titibissé-odâbân, titibidâbân.* I make wagons, *nind odâbânike, nin titibidâbânike.*

Wagonmaker, *odâbânikewinini, titibidâbânikewinini.*

Wail; I wail, *nin gagidowe.*

Waistcoat S. Vest.

Waistcoat for women, *babisikawâgan.*

Wait; I lie in wait for him, *nind akâmawa.*

Wait; I wait, *nin bi.* (Pehuw.) I wait for him, (her, it,) *nin bia, nin biton.* I wait for him, in thoughts, *nin biewagenima.*

Wait, (expect, look for ;) I wait, (look for,) *nind akawâb.* I wait or look out for him, (her, it,) *nind âkawâbama; nind akawâbendan.* I wait for game in the night in a canoe, *nin nibégom.*

Waiter, *anokitâgewinini, bamitâgan, oshkâbewiss.* Female waiter, *anokitâgekwe, bamitâgan.*

Waiting for game on the water in the night, *nibëgomowin.*

Wake; I wake him, *nind amâdina.* I wake him up by pulling or pushing, *nind amadjibina.*—S. Awake.

Walk, *bimosséwin, babâmossewin.* I take a walk, *nin babâmosse.*

Walk; I walk, *nin bimosse, nin mitosse.* I walk about, *nin babâmosse.* I walk against the wind, *nind ondjishkaosse.* I walk around s. th., *nin giwitâosse.* I walk backwards, *nind ajéosse.* I w. badly, *nin manosse.* I w. well, *nin minosse, nin nitâosse.* It walks well, goes well, *minossémagad.* I walk fast, *nin kijika, nin kijiosse, nin babapijisse.* I w. as fast or quick as I can, *nind apisika, nind apitosse.* I w. slowly, *nin bésika, nin bédosse* I walk feeling my way, *nin nandôdjishkige.* I w. foremost, *nin nigâni, nin nigânosse.* I make him walk foremost, *nin nigânia.* I walk in the night, *nin nibâam, nin nibâshka.* I walk in the water, *nin bimâdagâsi.* I w. about in the water, *nin babamâdagâsi.* I walk on, *nind ani bimosse, nin mâdjâ.* I w. on the beach, *nin jijodewe, nin bimâjagame.* I w. on the ice, *nin bimâdagak.* I walk on the lake-shore, coming, *nin bimitajagame.* I

w. on the straightest road, *nin gwaiakoshka.* I w. on the summit of a hill or mountain, *nin bimâmadjiwe.* I walk out talking, *nin sâgidwewidam.* I w. over a bridge, *nind ajoge.* I w. over a log, *nin bimândawe.* I walk round, *nin bijibâosse.* I walk straight, *nin gwaiakosse.* I become unable to walk any further, *nin nôndéshin.* He becomes unable to walk any further with me, I leave him behind, *nin nôndeshima.* I am unable to walk (by hunger, fatigue,etc.), *nind ânawito.* I walk with him, *nin widossema.* I walk with down-hanging arms, *nin jinginikeosse.* I w. with my toes turned inside, *nin wawâgaami, nin jajâshagaami.* We walk in one line, *nin nibinéossemin.* We walk many together, *nind inâwanidimin.*

Walker, *bemossed ;* good walker, *netâ-bimossed, netâossed.*

Walking, *bimossewin.* Fast walking, *kijikâwin ;* slow walking, *bêsikâwin.* There is walking, *bimossewinagad.*—I remain about him in walking, *nin wâgashkawa.*

Walking-stick, *sakaon.* I use it as a walking-stick, *nin sakaon.*

Wall, around a fortress, *giwitaiabikinigan.*

Wallow. S. Roll about.

Walnut. S. Nut.

Walnut-tree, *paganâkomij, mitigwabak.*

Wampum, *migiss.*

Wampum-ornament, *migissiiessimig.*

Wampum-strap, *migissopikan.*

Wan. S. Pate.

Want, *manêsiwin.*

Want; I want, (need,) *nin manês.* I want it, (*in., an.*) *nin manésin ; nin manésinan.* I want s. th. badly, *nin wawânis.*

Wanton. Wantonness.—S. Foolish noise.

War. S. Fight. Fighting.

Warble; the bird warbles, *masitâgosi bineshi, wiiagweweto.*

War-captain, war-chief, *maiaossêwinini, nigânossêwinini.*

War-captive, *awakân.* I try to make war-captives, or, I go on a war-excursion, *nin nandôbân.*

War-club, *pagamâgan, waganakibitchigan.* War-club with a knob, *pikwakwado-pagamâgan.*

Ware. S. Merchandise.

War-eagle, *kiniw.*

Ware-house, *atâssowin, atâssowigamig.*

Warf, *niminawekinigan.* I make a warf, *nin niminawekinigani ke.* There is a wharf made, *naminawekinigâde.*

Warfare, Indian warfare, *nandôbaniwin, nandobanikandiwin.*

Warm ; I begin to feel warm, *nind abawas.* I soon feel warm, *nin wakêwakis.* I am warm, *nind abwes, nin kijis.* I am warm in a lodge or house, *nin kijôb.* I am confortably warm, *nin kijôs.* I lie warm, *nin kijôshin.*— It is warm, (the air,) *kijâbate.* It is warm weather, *kijâte, abawa.* It is warm, (in a building,) *kijide, kijote, kijôiamagade.* It is warm, (liquid,) *kijâgamide.* It is a little warm, (liquid,) *abashkobite, jigashkobite.* It is warm, (metal, *in., an.*) *kijâbikide; kijâbikisi.*—My arms are warm, *nin kijonike.* My back is w., *nin kijipikwanes.* My feet are w., *nin kijoside.* My hands are w., *nin kijonindji.* My legs are w., *nin kijogâde.*

Warm, make warm; I warm him, (her, it), *nind abiswa, nin kijiswa; nind abisan, nin kijisan.* I warm him with my body, *nin kijôkawa.* We warm each other, *nin kijôkodâdimin.* —I warm myself, *nind akis, nind awâs, nin kijisodis.* I w. myself by drinking s. th. warm, *nin kijâgamidees.* I w. myself by walking, *nin kijisosse.* I warm my back, *nind apikwanes.* I w. my breast, *nind abakiganes, nin kijakiganes.* I w. my feet, *nind abakisides, nind abisides.* I w. my hands, *nind abakinindjiwas, nind abinindjisodis.*—I make it warm, (liquid,) *nin kijagamisan.* I make it w. a little, *nind abagamisan, nind abashkobisan.*—I make warm s. th., *nin kijisige.*

Warmer, *kijisigan.*

Warn; I warn, *nin windamâge.* I warn him, *nin windamawa.*

We warn each other, *nin windamâdimin.*

Warning, *windamâgewin, windamâdiwin, windamâgawisiwin.*

Warrior, *jimâganish, minissino.* I am a warrior, *nin minissinow.*

Wart, *tchitchigom.*

War-vessel, *migadi-nâbikwân.*

Wash; I wash, *nin kisibiginige, nin kisibigaige.* I wash for him, *nin kisibigaamawa.* I wash him, (her, it,) *nin kisibigina; nin kisibiginan.* I wash myself, *nin kisibigi.*—I wash my hands, feet, etc. S. Hand. Foot, etc.

Wash clean; I wash clean, *nin gâssiâbâwe.* I wash him, (her, it) clean, *nin gâssiâbâbawana, nin gâssiâbâwadawa; nin gâssiâbâwen, nin gâssiâbâwadon.*

Wash-dish, wash-plate, *kisibiginigeonâgan.*

Wash out; I wash it out, (*in., an.*) *nin kisiabawadan; kisiabawana.*

Washed; it is washed, *kisibigaigâde, gâssiâbâwe.*

Washer, *kisibigaigewinini.*

Washer-woman, *kisibigaigêwikwe.*

Wash-house, wash-room, *kisibigaigewigamig.*

Washing, *kisibigaigewin, kisibiginigewin.*

Wash-tub, *kisibigaige-makak.*

Wasp, *âmo.*

Waste, wasting, *banâdjitchigewin, nishiwanâdjitchigewin, bapinodagewin, nishibapinodagewin.*

Waste; I waste, *nin banâdjitchige, nin nishiwanâdjitchige, nin bapinodage, nin nishibapinodage, nin nâwadinige, nin tchaginigeshk.* I waste it, (*in., an.*) *nin banâdjiton, nin nishiwanâdjiton, nin bapino-*

dan, nin nishibapinodan, nin nâwadinan ; nin banâdjia, nin nishiwanâdjia, nin bapinodawa, nin nishibapinodawa, nin nâwadina. I waste it to him, *nin nâwadinamawa, nin banâdjitawa.*

Wasted ; it is wasted, (*in., an.*) *nishiwanâgjitchigâde, binâdjitchigâde ; nishiwanâdjitchigâso, banâdjitchigâso.*

Watch, *dibaigisisswân.* I make watches, *nin dibaigisisswânike.* (Pisimokkân).

Watch ; I watch, *nind akando.* (Aswahuw.) I watch him, (her, it,) *nin dadibabama ; nin dadibabadan.* (Asweyimew.) I watch over him, (her, it,) *nin ganawenima ; nin ganawendan.*

Watch, (sit up ;) I watch, *nin nôdab, nin nibébitam.* I watch him (her, it) in the night, *nin nibébitawa ; nin nibébitân.*

Watch, (in. s. in.) S. Observe.

Watch. S. Guardian. Guard.

Watch-house, *akandôwigamig.*

Watching, *akandowin, nodabiwin, nibébitamowin.*

Watchmaker, *dibaigisisswâninikewinini.*

Watchmaking, watch-manufactory, *dibaigisisswânikewin.*

Watchman, *akandowinini.*

Water, *nibi, nibish.* There is water, *nibika.* In the water, *nibikang, nibing, newadjindim, anâmibing, anâmindim.* On the water, *ogidibig.* I look for water, *nin nândobi.* I fetch water, *nin nibinad, nin nâsibi.* I obtain my water from..., *nind ondaibi.* I cannot find water, *nin gwinobi.* I am (it is) in the water, *nind agwindjin ; agwinde.* I am (it is) partly in the water, *nin sâgibi ; sâgibimagad.* I am (it is) half in the water, *nin sâgagwindjin ; sâgagwinde.* I put him (her, it) in the water, *nind agwindjima ; nind agwindjiton.* I draw him (her, it) a little out of the water, *nin tchekibina ; nin tchekibidon.* I push it in the water, *nin niminawewebinan.* I put water in it, *nin nibikadan.* There is water in it, *nibikâde.* —The water comes under me, *nin dênimiigon nibi.* The w. comes out of a vessel, *sâgiwan nibi.* It runs out entirely, *tchâgidjiwan.* The w. drops out of s. th., *tchissigamagad nibi.* The water goes through it, *jâbobi.* The w. moves, *madâgamishka nibi.* Moved or agitated water, *madâgami.* The w. reaches me, *nin moshkaog.* The water shuts up, *gibwakamigishka.*

Water ; I water him, *nin minaa nibi.*

Water, (in. s. in.) S. Sprinkle.

Water-closet, *misiwigamigons.*

Waterfall. S. Cascade.

Watering-cart, watering-pot. S. Sprinkling-pot.

Water-pail, water-pot. S. Bucket.

Water-serpent, *omissandamo.* The skin of that serpent, *omissandamowaiân.*

Wave, *tigow.* The wawes run high, heavy sea, *mamângâshka.* The waves roar loud, *kijiwêiâshka.* The roaring of the w. is heard, *mamadwêi-*

âshka. The water runs in heavy waves, *mamangâtigodjigwan.* The waves break on a shallow place, *bagwâshka.* The w. beat against s. th., *apagadâshka.* The w. beat against my canoe and carry me away, *nind apagadjiwebaog.* The w. leap in my canoe, *nin sigaog.* The w. are white, they flourish, *wassashkamagad, pashkikawag tigowag.* The waves cease to rise, *bonâshka.* The w. are appeased, *anwaweweiâshka.*

Wax, *âmô-bimide.*

Wax-candle. S. Wax-taper.

Wax-taper, *âmô-bimide wassakwanendjigan.* Thin wax-taper, *âmobimide wassakwanendigans.*

Way, *mikana, mikan.*—S. Road.

Way-side ; by the way-side, *tchigikana, opimêkana.* On the way-side, *bakêkana.*

We, *ki, kid, nin, nind, kinawind, ninawind.*

Weak ; I am weak, *nin jâgwiw, nin jâgos, nin jâdwadis, nin bwanawito, nin ninamis, nin ninamadis, nind anawiss.* I am weak in my bones, *nind angogane, nin jotêgane.* I feel weak, *nin bimidee, nin bimideeshka.* I feel weak in walking, *nin bimideeisse, nin jotêganeosse.* I am (it is) weak, considered weak, *nin nokendâgos ; nokendâgwad.* It is weak, *jâgwiwimagad, jâgwadad, ninamad.*—It is weak : Ice, *ninamadin ;* liquid, *jâgwagami ;* metal, *in. ninamakikad ;* metal, *an., ninamabikisi ;* wood, *in., ninamakwad, ninamissagad ;* wood, *an., ninamâkos, ninamissagisi.*—I think he (she, it) is weak, *nin jâgwenima, nin ninamenima ; nin jâgwendân, nin ninamendân.*

Weak, (easily torn, stuff;) it is weak, (*in., an.*) *wakéwan ; wakêwisi.* I am (it is) weak, not durable, *nin wakéwis, nin wakêwine ; wâkéwissine.*

Weaken ; I weaken it, *nin jâgwiton.*

Weakness, *bwanâwitowin.*

Weak often ; I am (it is) often weak, *nin naninamis ; naninamad.* I am (it is) weak, considered weak, in several ways, *nin naninamendagos, naninamendagwad.* I think or find him (her, it) weak in several ways or respects, *nin naninaménima ; nin naninaméndan.*

Weak, (soft ;) I am weak, *nin nokis.* It is weak or soft, *nokan, nokamagad.* It is weak : Metal, *in., nokâbikad ;* metal, *an., nokâbikisi ;* stuff, *in., nokabigad, nokigad ;* stuff, *an., nokabigisi, nokigisi.* I make it weak or soft, (metal, *in., an.*) *nin nokâbikisan ; nin nokabikiswa.* It becomes weak or soft, *nokigissemagad.*

Wealth. S. Riches.

Wealthy. S. Rich.

Wean ; I wean a child, *nind ishkwanona abinodji.* I wean myself of a bad habit or practice, *nin wêbinan, nin boniton.*

Weapon or armor of a warrior, *ashwiwin.* (Nimâskwewin).

Wear ; I wear it, (*in., an.,*) *nind agwin, nin gigishkan, nin ma-*

dindân; nind agwinan, nin gigishkawa, nin madimâ. I wear soft clothes, *nin nogikwanaie.* I wear torn clothes, *nin bigokwanaie.*—I wear it out, (*in.*, *an.*) *nin mêsikan, nin metakwidjidon, nin metchissidon; nin mesikawa, nin metakwidjima.* I wear it out entirely,(*in.*, *an.*) *nin tchâgishkan; nin tchâgishkawa.*

Wear around the neck; I wear it on or around my neck, (*in.*, *an.*) *nin nâbikan; nin. nâbikawa.* I make him wear s. th. around his neck, *nin nâbikona.* Any thing worn around the neck, *nâbikâgan, nâbikawagan.*

Wearied. S. Tired.

Weariness. S. Tiredness. Disgust.

Weary. S. Tired.

Weasel, *jingoss.*

Weather, it is bad weather, a bad day, *niskâdad, matchi gijigad.* It is good fair w., a fine day, *mino gijigad.* It is fine clear w., sunshine, *mijakwad.* It is hot weather, *kijâte;* it is very hot, *wissagâte.*—I have a bad day, bad weather for traveling, etc., *nin matchijijiganish.* I travel in bad weather, *nin niskasika.* I think it is too bad weather, *nin niskâdendam.* I have a fine day, fair weather, for traveling, etc., *nin minogijiganish.*

Weave; I weave, *nin bimidâbiginiganike.* I weave with holes, *nind answetaginige.*

Weaver, *bimidâbiginiganikewinini.*

Wedding, *widigendiwin.* (Wikittuwin).

Wedding-feast, *widigendiwiniwikongewin, widigendiwiniwikandiwawin.*

Wedding-garment, *widigendiwini-agwiwin, widigendiwinibabisikawâgan.*

Wedding-ring, *widigendiwinititibinindjipison.*

Wednesday; it is Wed., *âbitosse;* on Wednesday, *âbitosseg;* on Wednesdays, *aiabitossegin.*

Weed, for smoking, *apâkosigan.* —Another kind of smoking weed, *sagâkominagawanj.* The berry growing on this weed, *sagâkomin.* I mix my tobacco with weed, (or bark,) *nind apâkosige.*

Weed, noxious herb, *matchi mashkossiw.*

Weed; I weed, *nin mônashkwe.* I weed a field or garden, *nin mônashkwadan kitigan, nin pashkobidon,* or, *nin pashkwakobidon kitigan.*

Week; a week, *ningo anamiegijigad.* Two, three, four weeks, etc., *nijo anamiegijigad,* etc.

Weep; I weep, *nin maw, nin katchim.* It weeps, *mawimagad.* I weep too much, *nin mawishk, nin katchimoshk.* I make weep, I cause weeping, *nin moiwe.* I make him w., *nin moa.* I w. waking up, or awaking, *nind amadadem.* I come on weeping, *nin bidadem.* I weep after him, (molest him,) *nin mokawana.* (Mawikkâtew.) I w. bitterly, *nin naninawadem.* I w. horribly, *nin gagwânissaga-*

dem. I w. much, *nin gikim*. I go to him weeping, *nind inademotawa*. I w. from cold, *nin môkawadj*. I w. from grief, *nin naninawem*. I w. from hunger, *nin bakadem, nin mokawanandam, nin mokawashkade*. I w. through joy, *nin môkawimodjigendam*. I. w. through pain or anger, *nin mokawines*. I w. by dissimulation, *nin mawikas*. I w. in drunkenness, *nin mâwibi*. I w. for some reason, *nind ondadem*. I w. in a certain manner, *nind inadem*. I w. in a certain place, *nin danadem*. I weep over him, (her, it,) *nin mâwima ; nin mâwindân*. (Mâwikkâtew.) I w. over myself, *nin mâwindis*. I weep shedding large tears, *nin mindibigâb*. I am tired of weeping, *nin pingewewem*. (Mâtuw).

Weeper, *mewishkid, kaiatchimoshkid*.

Weeping, *mâwiwin, katchimowin*. Habit of weeping often or too much, *mâwishkiwin, katchimoshkiwin*. Weeping of s. th., or for s. th., *mâwindamowin*.

Weigh ; I weigh, (I am weighing in a balance,) *nin dibabishkodjige, nin tibabadjige*. I weigh him, (her, it,) *nin dibabishkona ; nin dibabishkodon*. I weigh him (her, it) in my hand, *nin gotina ; nin gôtinan*.—I weigh (it weighs) so much, *nind apitinigos, apitinigwad*.

Weight, *kosigoskodjigan*.

Well, *ondâibân*. (Monahipân).

Well, *wéweni, gwaiak, wawinge, mino, kitchi, nissita*. I do it well, *nin wawingeikan*. I fix it well, *nin wawingeton*. (Mitoni).

Well! *ambe ! ambissa ! ambessano ! ambessino ! haw ! taga taga ! o !* (Ekwa ! Matté !)

Well ! let it be so ! *mano ! nab ! mano nab !* (Kiyâm).

Well. S. Rather.

Welfare, *mino aiâwin*. Eternal welfare, *kâgige mino aiâwin, kâgige minawanigosiwin*.

West, *ningabian, epangishimog*. In, to or from the west, *ningabianong*. Rain coming from the west, *ningabianibissa*.

West-cloud, *ningabianakwad*.

Wesiwind, *ningabiani-nodin*.

Wet ; I am (it is) wet, *nin nibiw, nin nibiwis ; nibiwan*. I get (it gets) wet, *nin nissâbawas, nin nissâbawe ; nissâbawe*. I wet it, (*in., an.*) *nin nissâbawadon ; nin nissâbawana*. (Akustimow).

Whale, *kitchi-gigô, kitchi-manameg, missameg*.

What? *wa?*

What? what is the matter? *wegonen? ânin? tani? tanish?* (Kekwäy ?)

What is the reason? *anishwin ? wegonen wendji—...?* (Tâneki?)

What time is it? *Anin epitchgijigak? Anin epitatibikak ? Anin endasso-dibaiganeg ?*

Wheat, *pakwéjiganashk ;* or rather, *pakwejiganimin*.

Wheel-barrow, *gagândini-odabanens, gandinigani-titibidabanens*.

Wheelsman, *odakéwinini*.

Wheelwright. S. Cartwright.

When ? *aniniwapi ? anapi ? tanapi ? tapi ?* (Tâispi ?)
When, *api ; megwa*. (Ispi, ekuspi).
Where ? *anindi ? aka ? tandi ?* (Tandé ?)
Whether, *kishpin*.
Which ? what ? *anin iw ?* (Tânima ?)
While, *megwa, api*. (Megwâtch).
Whip, *bashanjéigan*. (Pasastehigan).
Whip ; I whip, *nin bashanjéige*. I whip him, *nin bashanjéwa*. I am whipped, *nin bashanjéigas*. I whip myself, *nin bashanjeodis*. (Pasastehwew).
Whipping, *bashanjéigewin*.
Whip-saw, *tâshkibodjigan*.
Whirl ; I whirl round, *nin kijibata*.
Whirlpool, *akikodjiwan*. There is a wh., *wanâtan*.
Whirlwind, *missibissidossi*. There is a wh. driving the snow round, *kijibabiwan*.
Whiskers ; I have whiskers, *nin mamishanowe*.
Whiskey, *ishkotéwâbo*, (firewater).
Whisper ; I whisper, *nin gâskanas*. I wh. to him, *nin gâskanasotawa*. — We whisper to each other, *nin gâshkanasotadimin*. The wind whispers in the leaves, *madwébagassin*.
Whistle, whistling, *kwishkwishiwin*.
Whistle ; I whistle, *nin kwishkwish*. I whistle to call him, *nin kwishkwishima*. I wh. a tune, a melody, *nin kwishkwishinagam*. I wh. to call a dog, *nin kwishkwishkwassimwe*.
White ; I am (it is) white, *nin wâbishkis ; wâbishkamagad, wâbishkisigwamagad*. I make it wh., (*in., an.*) *nin wâbishkaan, nin wâbishkiton ; nin wâbishkawa, nin wâbishkia*. I make it wh., (cord, string,) *nin wâbishkabigibidon*. I make it wh. (stuff, *in., an.*) *nin wâbishkigiton ; nin wâbishkigia*.
White, painted white ; it is white or whitened, (*in., an.*) *wâbiginigâde ; wâbiginigâso*. It is painted white, (wood, *in., an.*) *wâbissaginigâde ; wâbissaginigaso*.
White clay, *wâbâbigan*. (Wâbatonisk).
White cottou, or linen, *wâbishkigin, wâbishki-papagiwaiân*.
White crane, *wâbadjidjak*.
White dog, *wâbassim*. (Wâbastim).
White duck, *wâbansig, wâbininishib*.
White teather, *wâbigwan*.
Whitefish, *atikameg*.
White goose, *wâbwewe*.
White object, or whitened object, *wâbissoyinigan*.
White of the egg, *wâbâwan, wabishkag wâwan*.
White of the eye, *wâbagamishkinjigwan*.
White paper, (not written,) *waiâbishkag masinaigan, wejibiigadessinog masinaigan*.
White person, a white, *waiâbishkiwed*. I am a white person, *nin wâbishkiwe*. The whites, white people, *waiâbishkiwedjig*.
White stone, *wâbassin*.
White turnip, *wâbishkitchiss*.
Whitewash ; I wh., *nin wâbabiganige*.

Whitewashing-brush, *wâbishkâigan.*

Whitish; it is whitish, (*in.*, *an.*) *pangi wâbishkamagad; pangi wâbishkisi.* It becomes whitish, it fades, *wâbitchiïa.* It becomes whitish in washing, *wâbitchiiâbâwe;* by the sun, *wâbitchiiate.*

Whitish liquid, *wâbishkâgami.*

Whitlow, *jingibiss.* I have a whitlow, *nind ojingibiss.*

Whit-Sunday, *Pantkot, Pantkotgijidad.*

Whiz; it whizzes through the air, *jôkamagad.*

Who? *awenen? weni? wenish?* (Awena?)

Whoever, *awegwen.*

Whole; the whole, *kakina.* The whole of it, (*in. an.*) *endassing; endashid.* (Kakiyaw, misiwe).

Whole, (entire;) it is whole, (*in.*, *an.*) *missiwéiamagad; misiwesi.* It is whole: Metal, *in.*, *misiwéiâbikad*: metal, *an.*, *misiwêiâbikisi;* stuff, *in.*, *misiwêgad;* stuff, *an.*, *misiwêgisi;* wood, *in.*, *misiwêiâkwad;* wood, *an.*, *misiwéiâkosi.* (Misiwesiw).

Whore, *bishigwâdjikwe, gagibadjikwe.*

Whore-monger, *bishigwâdjinini, gagibâdjinini.*

Whortleberry, *min.* Dry whortleberry, *batémin.* I gather whortleberries, *nin minike.*

Why? *wegonen wendji...? ânishwin.* (Tâneki?)

Why! *anish!*

Wick, *wassakwanéndjiganêiâb.*

Wicked, *matchi.* I am wicked, *nin matchi ijiwebis, nin manjininiwagis, nin batâ-ijiwebis.* It is wicked, sinful, *batâ-ijiwebad; matchi ijiwebad, manâdad.* (Mayâtjitehew). I make him wicked, *nin matchi ijiwebisia, nin nishiwanâdjia.* I think he (she, it) is wicked, *nin manadenima; nin manâdêndan.*

Wickedness, *batâ-ijiwebisiwin, matchi ijiwebisiwîn, manjininiwagisiwin, misinânisiwin.*

Wickedness of heart, *matchideewin.* I have a wicked heart, *nin matchidee.*

Wicked person, *matchi aiaâwish, misimânisiwinish.* I am a wicked person, *nin matchi aiaawishiw, nin misimânisiwinishiw.*

Wicked thing, *matchi aiiwish.* It is a wicked thing, *matchi aiiwishiwan.*

Wide; it is wide, *mangadeamagad.* I make it wide, large, (*in.*, *an.*) *nin mangadéton; nin mangadea.*

Wide, (in. s. in.) S. High.

Widen; I widen it, (*in.*, *an.*) *nawatch nin mangadeton; nawatch nin mangadea.*

Widow, *jiga, jakawid, jagawid ikwe.* I am a widow, *nin jigaw.*

Widower, *jiga, jagawig, jagawid inini.* I am a widower, *nin jigaw.*

Widowhood, *jigâwiwin.*

Width, the width of it, (*in.*, *an.*) *enigokwadessing; enigokwadeshid.*

Wife, *wadiged ikwe, wiwima, widigemâgan, wigimâgan, widjiwâgan.* I have a wife, *nin widige, nin wiw.* My, thy, his wife, *nin widigemâgan, ki widigemagan, o widigemaganan;* or, *nin mindimôiemish, ki mindimôiemish, o mindimôiemishan;* or, *niwish, kiwish, wiwishan* or *wiwan.* I have two, three, four wives, *nin nijokwew, nin nissokwew, nin niokwew.*—I give him a wife, *nin wiwikawa.* We give a wife to one another, *nin wiwikodadimin.* I give a wife to myself, *nin wiwikodâdis.*

Wig, *bisikwandjigan.*

Wild; I am wild, *nin wanishkwes.*

Wild animal, *pagwâdj-aiiaa, pagwadjawessi.*

Wild boar, *pagwâdji-kokosh.*

Wild cat, *essiban.* Skin of the wild cat, *essibaniwaiân.* Coat made of wild cat's skins, *essibaniwekon.*

Wild cherry, *bawaiminân, sissawémin.*

Wild cherry shrub, *sissawéminagawandj, bawaiminanagawanj.*

Wild cherry-tree, *winisik.*

Wild dog, *pagwâdassim.*

Wilderness, *pagwâdakamig, pagwâdj.* There is a wilderness, *pagwâdakakamigewan.*

Wild goat, *pagwâdji-manishtânish.*

Wild goose, *nika.* Another kind, *obijashkissi.*

Wild horse, *pagwâdji-bebejigoganji.*

Wild man, *pagwâdj-inini.*

Wild rice, *mânomin.* I gather wild rice, *nin mânôminike.* The gathering of wild rice, *mânôminikewin.* The month of the gathering of wild rice, *manôminike-gisiss.*

Wild rice bag, *mânôminiwaj.*

Wild small snail, *pagwâdji-bimiskodissi.*

Wild thing, *pagwâdj-aii.*

Wild tree, *pagwâdji-mitig.*

Wild turkey, *pagwâdji-mississe.*

Wild woman, *pagwâdj-ikwe.*

Will, *inendamowin, inendjigewin.* I give him a firm will, *nin songideeshkawenima.*

Will, firm will. S. Resolution, firm resolution.

Will; I will, *nind inêndam, nind inêndjige.* (Iteyittam).

Willing; I am willing, *nin minwendam.*

Willow-tree, *osissigôbimij.* (Nipisiyâttik).

Win; I win him, (her, it,) *nin gashkia; nin gashkiton.*

Wind, *nodin.* (Yotin). The wind begins to blow, *mâdanimad.* The wind is coming, *bidanimad.* A strong wind comes on, *pagamânimad.*—I have wind, *nin nodinish, nin nodinoshka.* I come (it comes) with the w., *nin bidâsh; bidâssin.* I go (it goes) away with the w., *nin mâdjiiash; mâdjiiassin.* I am (it is) carried away by the wind, *nin webâsh; webâssin.* The wind is fair, *minwânimad, nâmaanigwad.* (Nâmiwanaw). I have a fair wind, *nin mâmaam.* I am (it is) driven or carried by a fair w., *nin minwâsh; minwâssin.* There is a good fast w., *kijiiânimad.* There is a light smooth w., *tetissânimad.* There is a cold w., *takanimad.* It is cold by the wind, *takâs-*

sin.—The wind blows in a certain direction, *apagatanimad.* The wind flies round, *abamoiânimad.* The w. strikes s. th., *pakitêiâssin.* The wind ceases blowing, *bônânimad.* (Ayowâstin).--From the four winds, *niwing inakakeia wendânimak.*

Wind-bound; I am w., *nin ginissinaog.*

Windlass, *ombobiginigan.*

Window, *wâssétchigan.*

Window-frame, *wâssétchiganâtig.*

Window-glass, pane, *wâssétchiganâbik.*

Windpipe, *gondashkwei.*

Wind up; I wind up, *nin titibaodjige, nin titibinige.* I wind it up, (*in., an.*) *nin titibaodon, nin titibiginan, nind ikwabian; nin titibaona, nin titibigina, nind ikwabiwa.*

Windy; it is windy, the wind blows, *nôdin.* It is very windy, it blows continually, *nitânodin.*

Wing, *ningwigan.* I have wings, *nind oningwigana.* (Mitâttakwan).

Wine, *jominâbo.* I make or produce wine, *nin jominâboke.* Place where they make wine, *jominâbokan.* Producer of wine, wine presser, *jaminâbokêwinini.* Production of wine, *jominâbokewin.*

Wink, *watikwaigewin, ninigewin.*

Wink; I wink, *nind aininige, nin watihwaige.* I wink him, *nind aininamawa, nin watikwaamawa.*

Wink with the eyes, *tchibingwenowin.*

Wink with the eyes; I wink with the eyes, *nin tchibingwen.* I wink him with the eyes, *nin tchibingwetawa.*

Winter, *bibôn.* In winter, *bibong, bebongin.* The winter begins, *mâdjibibon.* The winter is far advanced, *ishpibibon.* After the middle of the w., *giwêbibon.* Last winter, *bibônong.* The winter before last, *awass-bibônong.* Next winter, *pânima bibong.*

Winter; I winter, *nin bibônish.* It winters, *bibonishimagad.* I winter with him, *nin widjibibonishima.* I survive the winter, *nin wâbanish.*

Wintering, *bibônishiwin.*

Winter-path, *bibon-mikana.*

Winter-quarter, place of wintering, *bibônishiwin.*

Winter-skin, winter-fur, *bibôniwaiân.*

Wipe; I wipe him, (her, it) *nin gâssiwa, nin kisiwa, nin gâssian, nin kisian.* I wipe a child, *nin kisiawass.*—I wipe dishes, *nin gâssinâgane.* I wipe his face, *nin gâssingwéwa, nin kisingwêwa.* I wipe my face, *nin gâssingweodis, nin kisingweodis.* I wipe his tears, *nin gâssinsibingwêwa.* I wipe my tears, *nin gâssinsibingwe, nin gassinsibingweodîs.* I wipe his feet, *nin gâssisidéwa.* I wipe my feet, *nin gâssiside, nin gâssisideodis.*—I wipe the dust off, *nin binawean.*—Any thing to wipe the feet on, *bawisideshimowin.*

Wipe off, (in. s. in.) Blot out.

Wire, *biwâbikons.*

Wisconsin, *Wishkons*. In, to or from Wisconsin, *Wishkonsing*.
Wisconsin River, *Wishkonsi-sibi*.
Wisdom, *nibwâkâwin*.
Wise ; I am wise, *nin nibwâkâ, nin gagitaw, nin gagitawis*. I make him wise, *nin nibwa-kaa, gagitawia*. I think myself wise, *nin nikwâkâienin-dis, nin nibwâkâienim, nin nibwâkawenim*. I am wise before him, *nin nibwâkâkan-dawa*.
Wise, (in. s. in.) S. Prudent.
Wise man, *nibwâkâwinini*.
Wish for. Wished for.—S. Desire. Desired.
Witchcraft. S. Magic.
With, in compositions, *gigi*.—(Asitji).—With the soul, *gigi-tchitchag*. With the body, *gigi-wiiaw*.
Withdraw ; I w. from him, *nind âjétawa, nin bakéwina*. I w. from it, *nin bakéwinan*.
Wither ; it withers, *nibwashkis-sin*.
Withhold ; I w. it from him, *nin mindjiminamawa*. I w. it from myself, *nind mindjiminidis*.
Within, *pindig, pindjaii, pind-jina*.
Without, out of doors, *âgwat-ching, agwatchâii*.
Without interruption, *apine, béjigwanong*.
Withstand ; I withstand him, *nind ajidena*.
Wolf, *maingan*. There are wolves, *mainganika*. Place where there are wolves, *main-ganikan*.
Wolverene, *swingwaage*. (Kik-wââkês).
Woman, *ikwê, akwé*. I am a woman, *nind ikwew, nin ak-wew*. A woman that has no more a husband, *pijigokwe*. I am a woman that has no more a husband, *nin pijigokwew*.
Woman's breast, *totôsh*. My breast, *nin totôshim*. On both sides, *nin totôshimag*.
Wonder ; I wonder, *nin mama-kâdéndam*. I wonder at him, (her, it,) *nin mamakâdenima ; nin mamakâdendan*. I make him wonder, *nin mamakaden-damoa*.
Wonderful. S. Admirably. Astonishing.
Wonderful doing, *mamandâdo-damowin, mamandawanoki-win*.
Wonderful thing, *mamakâdjid-gan, mamakâsâbandjigan*. I can do wonderful things, *nin mamandâgashkito*.
Wondrous. S. Curious.
Wood, *mitig*. I am (it is) wood, *nin mitigow ; mitigowan*. One object of wood, *bejigwâtig*. Two, three, four obj. of wood, *nijwâtig, nisswâtig, niwâtig*, etc. So many objects of wood, *dasswâtig*. There is plenty of wood, *mitigoka, wanadjissa-ga*.—Dry wood, *mishiwâtig, mishiwâtigossag*. I chop dry wood, *nin mishiwatigoke*. Green wood, *ashkâtig*. I chop green w., *nind ashkâtigoke*. There is green standing wood, *ashkâkwa*.—I cut and split wood for a canoe, *nin passâ-ige ;* for a sled, *nin passaidâ-bâne ;* for snowshoes, *nin pas-saâgime*.—A fragment of wood, *bokwâtig*. A large piece of

wood, *mangissagad.* A flat piece of wood, *nabagâtig.* Near a piece of w., *tchigâtig.* —Rotten wood shines, *wassikogidemagad.*

Woodcock, *padjâshkaaaji.*

Wooden box, *mitigô-makak, mitigowaj.*

Wooden canoe, (boat or log-canoe,) *mitigô-tchimân.*

Wooden hammer, *mitigo-pakitéigan.*

Wooden house, (log-house,) *mitigowâkâigan.*

Wooden kettle, (drum,) *mitigwakik.*

Wooden leg, *mitigogâd.* I feign to have wooden legs, *nin mitigogâdekas.*

Wooden pin. S. Peg

Wooden plate or dish, *mitigonâgan.*

Wooden shoe, *mitigo-makisin.*

Wooden spoon, *mitig-émikwân.*

Wood file, (rasp,) *mitigo-sissibodjigan.*

Wood for fuel, *missan.* A piece of wood for fuel, *mishi.* I put wood in the fire, *nin pagidinisse.* (Ponam). The quantity of wood that is put in the fire at one time, *pagidinissan.* A piece of w. whistles in the fire, *sinakode mishi.*— I fetch wood in a canoe, *nin nâdaisse.*

Wood-louse, *bwiâtinogâded.*

Wood-pecker, *méme; pakwéamo; papâsse; bigwakokweoweshi.* White wood-pecker, *wâbipapâsse.*

Woods, (forest,) *mitigwaki.* (Sakaw). In the woods, in a forest, *mitigwaking, nôpiming.* I go into the woods, *nin gopi;* I come from the woods, *nin madâbi.* I come out of the woods, of the forest, *nin sagaâkwaam, nin papakwaam.*

Wool, *manishtânishiwibiwai.*

Word, *ikkitowin.* One word, *ningotodon.* Word said to some person, *igowin.* I send word, *nin madjiiâdjimoiwe.*

World, *aki.* In the whole world, *enigokwagaki, enigogwagamigag,* (*enigokogamigag*). It is the end of the world, *waiekwaakiwan, ishkwâ-akiwan.* At the end of the world, *waiekwaakiwang.*— The world, (people,) *bemâdisidjig.*

Work, working, *anokiwin, inanokiwin.* (Atuskewin). There is work, *anokiwinagad.* I commence some work, *nin mâdjita, nin wâdakamigis.*

Work; I work, *nind anoki.* It works, *anokimagad.* I come to work, *nin bi-anoki, nin bidjanoki.* I am able to w., *nin gashkinawi.* I work in a certain manner, *nind inanoki.* I make him work, *nind anokia.* I w. with him, *nin widjanakima.* I work in vain, *nind ânawewis, nind agâwishka.* (Mayoyuw).

Work - bench, *mogodjigan.* Work-bench for the drawing-knife, *mokodjigan tekwandjigemagak.*

Working-day, workday, *anokigijigad.*

Working-house, *anokiwigamig.*

Workman, *enokid, anokiwinini.*

Work with a knife, etc., *nin môkodâss.* I work it, (*in., an.*) *nin makodan, nin mokonan; nin makona.* I work it for

him, *nin môkodawa, nin mokodamawa.*
Worm, (in the body,) *ogejagim.* I have worms, *nind ogejagim.* Worm (in the wood,) *môsse.* Worm, (on or in the ground,) *jiginâwiss.* Worm, (coming out of a fly's egg,) *okwe.*
Worm-eaten ; it is worm-eaten, (globular object, *in., an.*) *mosséminagad, mosséminagisi, mossewidji.* It is worm-eaten, (wooden obj., *in., an.*) *mossêssagad; mossêssagisi.*
Worm - medicine, vermifuge, *ogejagami-mashkiki.*
Worn out; it is worn out, *métchissin, metchitchigâde.* It is worn out by grinding, (*in., an.*) *metchibode ; metchiboso.* It is worn out, (clothing,) *metakwidin.* It is worn out, (metal, *in., an.*) *mitabikissin ; metabikiso.*
Worse ; I am getting worse, *nind ânawisse.*
Worth ; I am (it is) worth, *apitendagos ; apitendagwad.* I am (it is) worth little, *nin bewendagos ; bewendagwad.*
Worth nothing; I am (it is) worth nothing, *nin nagikawis; nagikawad.* I am (it is) worth nothing, considered worth n., *nin nagikawendagos ; nagikawendagwad.*
Worth pity. S. Poor.
Worthy. S. Respactable.
Wound, *mâkiewin, bimwâganiigowin.* My wound heals, *nin gige.* I put s. th. in his wound, *nin pindjidikibina.* I heal his wound, *nin gigea.*
Wound. S. Dress a wound.
Wound ; I wound, *nin bimwâganiige.* I wound him, *nin mâkia, nin mâkinana, nin mâkiganama, nin mamâkiganama.* I wound him in a certain manner, *nind inaganâma.* I wound him shooting, *nind anonawa, nin mijwa.* I w. him cutting, *nin kijâwa.* I wound myself cutting, I cut myself, *nin kijâodis.*
Wounded ; I am w., *nin bimwâganes.*—I am wounded in the arm, foot, etc. S. Arm. Foot, etc.
Wounded person, *bimwâgan, mijwâgan.* I am a wounded person, *nin bimwâganiw, nin mijwâganiw.*
Wound-herb, wound-root, *mijiwéwashk.*
Wounding, inflicting wounds, *bimwâganiigewin.*
Woven; it is woven, (*in., an.*) *bimidabiginiganikâde ; bimidabiginiganigâso.*
Woven work, *bimidabiginiganikan.*
Wrangle. Wrangling.—S. Quarrel. Quarreling.
Wrangler, *neta-gikawidang.* I am a wrangler, *nin nita-gigawidam.*
Wrap up; I wrap up, *nin wiwêginige, nin kashkiweginige.* I wrap him (her, it) up in s. th. *nin wiwegina, nin kashkiwegina; nin wiweginan, nin kashkiweginan.*— Any object to wrap s. th. in, *kashkiweginigan.*
Wrapped up ; I am (it is) wrapped up, *nin wiweginigas, nin kashkiweginigas ; wiweginigâde, kashkiweginigâge.* — It

is wrapped together, (*in.*, *an.*) *okwégissin ; okwégishin.*

Wrath. Wrathful.—S. Anger. Angry.

Wrath-day, day of wrath, *nishkâdjigijigad.*

Wren, *nonokasse.* Another kind, *odanamissakadoweshi.*

Wrestle ; I wrestle with him, taking him round the body, *nind ajidena.* I wrestle with him, (her, it,) *nin gagwêdjiwanodawa ; nin gagwêdjiwanodan.*

Wretle, (in. s. in.) S. Fight.

Wrinkled ; I am (it is) wrinkled, *nin babiskishin ; babiskissin.*

Wrist ; I have a strong wrist, *nin mashkawimagonige.*

Write ; I write, *nind ojibiige.* I write in a certain manner, *nind ijibiige.* I add writing, *nin gikibiige.* I wr. otherwise, *nind andjibiige.* I write it otherwise, *nind andjibian.* I write to him or of him, *nind ojibiamawa.* I write to him or of him in a certain manner, *nind ijibiamawa.* I wr. a letter, *nin mâdjibiige.* I wr. him a letter, *nin mâdjibiamawa.* He writes me a letter, (I receive a letter of him,) *nin bidjibiamag.* I write it, or I write on it, (*in.*, *an.*) *nind ojibian ; nind ojibiwa.* I wr. it or on it, in a certain manner, (*in.*, *an.*) *nind ijibian ; nind ijibiwa.* I write and correct, *nin nanâibiige.*

Writer, *wêjibiiged, ojibiigêwinini,* (writing man).

Writing, writ, *ojibiigan, ojibiigewin.* Writing in large letters, *mamangibiigan.* Writing in small letters, *bissibiigan.* Changed or altered writing, *andjibiigan.* Corrected writing, *nanâibiigan,* (corrected copy).

Writing-house, office, *ojibiigewigamig.*

Written ; I am (it is) written or described, (or painted,) *nind ojibiigas ; ojibiigâde.* In a certain manner, *nind ijibiigas ; ijibiigade.*

Wrong ; I wrong or do wrong, *nin bata-dodam.* I wrong people, *nin bata - dodage.* It wrongs, it does evil, *batadodagemagad.* I wrong him, *nin bata-dodawa.* I wrong myself, *nin bataidis, nin wawaiiadis.* It is wrong, *bataijiwebad.*

Wrong, (in. s. in.) S. Do evil. Injure.

Wrongly, in a wrong manner, *napâtch.* I put it wrongly, *nin napâtchiton.*

Wrong way ; I put it on in the wrong way, (*in.*, *an.*) *nind âbosikan ; nind âboshima.* I put a coat or blanket over me in the wrong way, *nind âbodagwaje.*

Wrought iron, *wenadaigâdeg biwâbik.*

Y

Yankee. S. American.
Yarn, *assabâb*.
Yawl-boat, *nâbikwânens*.
Yawn; I yawn, *nin nibaiâwe, nin nanibaiâwe*.
Yawning, *nibaiâwewin, nanibaiâwewin*.
Year, *bibôn, bibonagad ; kikinonowin*.
Yearly, *endasso-bibongak*.
Yellow; I am (it is) yellow, *nind osâwis ; osâwa*.
Yellow by smoke; I make s. th. yellow by smoke, *nind osâmegisige*. I make it y. by smoke, (*in.*, *an.*) *nind osâwegisan* ; *nind osawegiswa*.
Yellow cloth, (or other yellow stuff,) *osâwegin*.
Yellow metal, brass, *osâwâbik*.
Yellow, painted yellow ; it is painted y., (*in.*, *an.*) *osâwinigâde; osâwinigâso*. It is painted y., (wood, *in.*, *an.*) *osâwissaginigâde ; osâwissaginigâso*.
Yellow serpent, *osâwi-ginébig*.
Yelp. Yelping.—S. Bark. Barking.
Yes, *ê*. *Enh-enh*.
Yest. S. Leaven.
Yesterday, *pitchinâgo*. (Otâkusik). The day before yesterday, *awâssonâgo*.
Yet, *keiâbi ; minotch, potch*.
Yield ; it yields fruit, (*an.*, *in.*) *miniwi mikwigi ; miniwan, mikwigin, mikwitomagad*. I make it yield fruit, *nin mikwigiton*.—It yields no fruit, no profit, *anewewisimagad*. The field yields no fruit, *anawigin kitigan*.
Yoke, *nâbikâwâgan, nâbikâgan*. So many yoke of..., *dasswéwân*.
Yolk of an egg, *miskwâwan, miskwawandjigan; osâwagwawan, osâwâwan*.
Yonder, *iwidi, awass, wêdi*.
You, your, *ki, kid, kin ; kinawa*.
Young, *oshki*. Young child, *oshkiabinodji*. I am young, *nind oshkibimâdis, nind oshkinig*.
Young animal or bird, *oshkiaiaans*.
Young folks, *weshkinigidjig, weshkibimâdisidjig*.
Young man, *oshkinawe, weshkinigid*. I am a young man, *nind oshkinawew*.
Young shoot, *oshkigin, weshkiging mitigons*.
Young woman, *oshkinigikwe, weshkinigid*. I am a young woman, *nind oshkinigikwew*.
Yours, *kin, kinawa*.
Youth, *oshkinigiwin, oshki-bimâdisiwin*.
Youth. S. Young man.

Z

Zeal at work, *kwashkwésiwin, minwewisiwin.*

Zealous; I am zealous at work, *nin gwashkwês, nin minwêwis.* I am z. for him, in his service, *nin minwêwisikandawa, nind angwâmikawa.* I am zealous for it, *nin minwewisikandan, nind angwâmikan* (Akameyimow).

FINIS

ETYMOLOGY

of a few Indian names by which are designated certain tribes and localities, but whose true pronunciation and orthography have been disfigured by the *Whites* who did not understand these words.

We here put the word as it is written and incorrectly pronounced in the country, and afterwards, its true orthography with the etymology given by many persons competent in this matter. It should be kept in mind that all these names, which, at the present time, designate towns, rivers, lakes, etc., have been thus disfigured by voyageurs, who pronounced them according to the best of their knowledge, without giving a thought that thereby they were destroying words and rendering them incomprehensible, in spite of the reclamations of Indianologists who were anxious to preserve the true pronunciation ; but usage has prevailed, as is still the case in our days.

ABÉNAKIS, (Otchipwe), means, " land of the East." It must come from *wâban*, it is day-break, and, *aki*, or, better, *akki*, earth, whence, *wâbanakiyak*, the people from where the sun rises.

ABITIBI, (Cree), means, intermediate water, from the root, *abit*, middle, half, and *nipïy*, water, which makes *ipi*, in composition, whence *abitipi*, water at half distance. The name of this lake comes from its position at the level of the land, between Hudson's bay and the St. Lawrence.

ASAWÂBIMOSWÂN, (Cree), where hunters watch for the Elk.

ASSINIBOINES, or, ASSINIBOÂNES, (Otchipwe), means probably: Sioux of the Stones, from : *Assin*, and *bwân*, Sioux ; or perhaps better, *Assinibwân*, means : people who roast something on stones, because it appears that those Indians used to cook their meat on red-hot stones.

ACHIGAN, (Cree), from *Manashigan*, fish of this species, that the Whites have named from the word *achigan*, or rather *ajigan*, socks or wrappings for the feet.

AYABASKA, or, ATABASKA, (Cree), means : place where there is an amount of high grass here and there.

ATTIKAMÈGUES, (Cree), from *Attikamek*, white fish.

BABICHE, (Cree), means, raw-leather line, from probably : *Assababish*, which is the diminutive of *assabâb*, thread.

BATISCAN, (Cree), from : *Tabateskan*, split horn, or, hanging horn, or, perhaps from : *nabateskan*, one horn, again, *tabaseskaw*, low grass.

CACOUNA, (Cree), means : a place where there are porcupine, from *kâkwa*, a porcupine, in the Cree language, which makes *kâkwânâk*, in the midst of porcupines, whence the Whites probably found *Cacouna*.

CANADA, (Iroquois), a village of tents or huts. Some pretend that it is derived from *kanâta*, or, *kanâtan*, (Cree), some thing which is very neat and clean.

CHAWINIGAN, (Cree), from : *Shâbonigan*, instrument for boring, piercer, or, needle ; or, perhaps from : *sâwan*, or, *shâwan*, south, and, *onigan*, portage, whence, the south portage.

CHÂWANONS, from *shâwan*, or, *sâwan*, the south. *Châwanons* is at the diminutive form. The inhabitants of the southern bank of the St. Lawrence, were, in the indian age, called by that name.

CHICAGO, (Cree), from *chicâg*, or *sikâg*, a skunk, a kind of wild cat, word, which at the local term, makes : *chicâgôk*.

CHICOUTIMI, (Cree), for, *iskotimiw*, till such a place, the water is deep ; in fact, the Saguenay is deep and profound only to that place.

ESQUIMAUX, (Cree), comes from : *aski*, raw, and, *mowew*, to eat some body, whence : *askimowew*, he eates him raw, or, better, *askimow*, he eates raw.

ESCOUMINS, (Cree), from *iskomin*, from isko, till there, and, *min*, berry, that is, there are berries till such a place.

ETCHEMIN, (Otchipwe), from *iyekomin*, from, *iyeko*, sand, and, *min*, berry, or, sand-berries, so the Otchipwe indians call raspberries.

IYÂMACHICHE, (Cree), from, *iyâmajisk*, *itâmajisk*, from, *iyâm*, or, *itâm*, at the bottom, and, *ajisk*, (*ajiskïy*), mud, that is : place in the water, where there is mud at the bottom.

IYÂMASKA, (Cree), from, *itâmaskaw*, or, *iyâmaskaw*, there is grass at the bottom of the water.

ILLINOIS, (Algonq.), for, *iliniwok*, men. The Otchipwes say : *ininiwok*, the Crees, *iyiniwok*.

MOURASKA, (Cree), for, *akâmaskaw*, (or, *akâmaraskaw*, as

pronounce the Crees from the woods), there is grass, or, hay, on the other side of the water, from, *akâm*, (*akâmik*), on the other side of the water, and, *askaw*, meaning : grass, hay.

KANKAKEE, (Cree), from, *kâkâkiw*, a crow.

KÉNÉBEC, (Cree), for, *kinekik*, a snake, serpent.

KINOGAMI, (Cree), there is a long space of water, from, *kino*, long, and, *gamiw*, or, *gamaw*, lake.

KINOGAMISHISH, (Cree), narrow long lake.

KIWATIN, (Cree and Otchipwe), pronounce, *kiwétin*, the north wind, the wind going back.

MADAWASKA, (Otchipwe), for, *matawaska*, the mouth of a river, where there is grass and hay.

MANIKWAGAN, (Cree), for, *minikkwâgan*, a vessel, a vase to drink.

MACHICHE, (Cree), from, *yâmajisk*, mud on the shore.

MATAPÉDIAC, from, *matâbiskaw*, rock advancing towards the shore.

MAKINA, (Otchip.), from, *mikkina*, a turtle.

MANITOBA, (Otchip.), from, *Manitowaba*, the strait of the spirit, from, *Manito*, spirit, divine, extraordinary, and, *waba*, or, *wapa*, a strait. That lake is so called, in account of the strange things seen and heard, in the strait which joins this lake with another one, in the old times.

MASKINONGÉ, (Otchip.), the ugly fish (Jackfish), from, *mâsk*, disfigured, ugly, and, *kinongé*, fish ; or, it may be a kind of Jackfish, who has a peculiar hump on the back.

MASCOUCHE, (Cree), from, *Maskus*, a small bear.

MATÂWAN, (Cree), it opens, (a river), it arrives in a lake.

MATABITCHOUAN, pronounce, *mâtâbitjiwan*, a stream coming in.

MASKÉGONS, from *Maskégowok*, people from the swamps.

MASHKOUTENS, (Otchp.), a small prairie. Mr. J. G. Shea makes a mistake, when he says that that word means : the nation of the fire, because if it were so, we ought to say, *iskute-wininiwok*, whence, *iskutens*, a small fire.

MALÉCHITES, from, *mayisit*, or, *malisit*, the disfigured (ugly) foot.

MÉKATINA, (Cree), for : *mekwâtinâk*, among the hills.

MANITOLINE, from : *Manitowin*, the spiritism, or better, *Mani-to l'île*, half french and indian. The Otchipwes call that island : *Manitominittik*, the Island of the spirit.

MIKWAN, (Cree), from *emikkwân*, a spoon.

MILWAUKEE, (Otchip.), from, *Milo*, or, *mino*, good, and *aki*, or, *akki*, earth, land, the fine land.

MICHIGAN, (Cree), from, *mishigâm*, or, *mishigamaw*, the big lake.

MICHIMAKINA, (Otchip.), from : *misi-mikkinâk*, big turtle. Some pronounce : *Michil mikkinâk*, whence the " *Michel-makina* " of the canadian voyageurs.

MIRAMICHI, (Cree), for, *mayamisk*, ugly beaver.

MINGAN, (Cree), from, *mahingan*, a wolf.

MISSISQUOI, (Cree), it must be : *misi-iskwew*, the big woman ; from : *misi*, big, and, *iskwew*, woman.

MISSISSIPI, (Otchip.), pronounce : *misi*, or, *mishisipi*, the big, great, river.

MÉGANTIC, from, *misâttik*, the big stick, or, *megâttik*, battle-club.

MOCCASIN, (Otchip.), from : *makkisin*, shoe.

MISTASSINI, the big stone.

NATASCOUAN, pronounce : *nâtaskewân*, going to fetch mouse, or better, from : *nâtaskwân*, going to bring the bear (his flesh, when killed).

NIPISSING, (Otchip.), in a little water, or, *nîpîssing*, in the leaves.

ORÂGAN, or, OYÂGAN, (Cree), plate, vase ; (Otchip.), *onâgan*.

OTTAWA, an abbreviation of : *ottawokay*, his ear, or, *otawask*, and, *watawask*, bull-rushes, because along the river there are a great many of those bull-rushes. It appears that the indians of that country had to call themselves : *watawawininiwok*, the men of the bull-rushes.

OUIATCHOUAN, (Cree), from, *wâwiyâtjiwan*, a whirlpool, or, *wayawitjiwan*, current coming out.

PICHOUX, (Cree), from, *Pisiw*, lynx.

PEMBINA, (Cree), from, *nipimina*, watery berries, *nipïy*, water, and, *mina*, berries, for : high bush cranberries.

QUÉBEC, from *kepek*, or, *kepâk*, being shut ; *kipaw*, it is shut. The indians of the Gulf St. Lawrence yet call it *Kepek*. In fact in that place the river looks shut up by Diamand Cape, when going up, and by the Orleans island, when coming down.

RISTIGOUCHE, from, *mistikus*, (*kous*), a small stick, tree.

(*) RIMOUSKI, (Otchip.), from, *animouski*, the dogs home.

SAGUENAY, water going out, from, *sâki*, coming from, and, *nipi*, water, *sâkinipi*.

SAGAMITÉ, (Cree), from, *kisâgamitew*, it is a hot liquid. *Kisâgamitekwew*, he drinks a hot liquid.

SASKATCHEWAN, (Cree), from, *kisiskâtjiwan*, the rapid current.

SATIGAN, (Cree), from, *astatjigan*, and, *astatchikun* (*koun*), a hiding place.

SISIQUOI, (Cree), from, *sisikwan*, an indian whistle, a kind of wind-pipe, used by the conjurors.

SQUAW, (Cree), from, *iskwew*, a woman.

STADACONÉ, from, *tatakwanak*, wings.

TADOUSSAC, (Cree), from, *totosak*, plural of *tôtôs*, woman's breast, pap.

TÉMISCOUATA, it is deep everywhere, from, *timiw*, it is deep in the water, and, *iskwatâm*, without end.

TOTEM, from, *ni totem*, my parent, my relation. Some indians use that word to mean a coat of arm. Some families got for their *Totem* (*ototemiwa*), v. g. a fish, or, a bear, etc. The wolf is my *Totem*, will say some one, *mahingan ni Totem*, or, *nind otem*.

TIMISKAMING, (Otchip.), in the deep water, from, *timiw*, it is deep, and, *gami*, water, (in composition) *ng* final, is for, *in*, (the water).

TOMAHAWK, from, *otâmahuk* (*houk*), strike them, or, *otâmahwaw*, he is striken.

WABISHTONIS, from, *wâbistânis*, a small marten.

WÂSISAGAIGAN, clear water lake.

WIGWÂM, a dwelling, a tent, a lodge.

WINNIPEK, pronounce: *Winipeg*, swamps, or, better, salt water, unclean water, *winâgami*. The indians call lake *Winipeg*, the great water, the great sea, and use the same expression to speak of the salt water of the sea.

WIQUI, from, *wikkwëy*, a bladder.

(*) It is to be remembered that some bands of the Crees, inhabiting the forest, pronounce ra, re, ri, ro, instead of na, ne, ni, no, or, ya, ye, yi, yo.

A DICTIONARY

OF THE

OTCHIPWE LANGUAGE,

EXPLAINED IN ENGLISH.

PART II.

OTCHIPWE - ENGLISH.

By R. R. BISHOP BARAGA.

A NEW EDITION, BY A MISSIONARY OF THE OBLATES.

Let foreign nations of their language boast,
And, proud, with skilful pen, man's fate record;
I like the tongue, which speak our men, our coast,
Who cannot dress it well, want wit not word.

MONTREAL:
BEAUCHEMIN & VALOIS, PUBLISHERS,
256 and 258, St. Paul Street.

1880

PREFACE.

The celebrated Lexicographer JOHNSON says: "He that un-
" dertakes to compile a Dictionary, undertakes that, which,
" if it comprehends the full extent of his design, he knows him-
" self unable to perform. Yet his labors, though deficient,
" may be useful; and with the hope of this inferior praise he
" must incite his activity, and solace his weariness."

A true saying! PROBATUM EST! If anybody experienced the truth of it, I did.

What Johnson says here, is true even in regard to Dictionaries of *civilized* languages; but by far more so in regard to a Dictionary of an *Indian* language.

This is, to the best of my knowledge, the first Dictionary of the Otchipwe language ever published. The compilation of it has cost me several years of assiduous labor; and still I must acknowledge that it is yet very defective and imperfect. I consider it as next to impossible to make such a work perfect at once, in the first edition.

In order to understand this Dictionary and make a practical use of it, the OTCHIPWE GRAMMAR ought to be first studied, especially the *Formation of Substantives* and the *Formation of Verbs*; because you will find in this Dictionary only some of the *formed* substantives and verbs, as examples after which you may form others yourself, according to the Rules explained in the Grammar.

The pronunciation of the Indian words in this Dictionary is the same as explained in the First Part of the Otchipwe Grammar. Here is a short extract of those explanations.

* *a* is pronounced long or short like *a* in *father*, *and* or *hand*.
e " " like *e* in *net*.
i " " like *i* in *live*.
o " " like *o* in *bone*.
g " " like *g* in *get*.
j has the French sound, as in *jour*, *joli*, etc.

The other consonants have the English sound.

NECESSARY REMARKS FOR THE PROPER USE OF THIS DICTIONARY.

1. The verbs in this Dictionary are given in the first person singular present, (as in Greek Dictionaries,) because there is properly no *infinite mood* in Otchipwe.
2. In the significations of *active verbs animate*, ordinarily the *masculine* gender only is expressed, and the *feminine* is understood. As: *Nin wabama*, I see him.—It means also, I see her; but this is understood.
3. Verbs ending in *endan*, *endamawa*, *endagos*, etc.; may also end in *enindan*, *enindamgwa*, *enindagos*, etc., which is not always expressed in this Dictionary. F. i. *Nin jawendagos*, or, *nin jawenindagos*, I am happy. *Nokendagwad*, or, *nokenindagwad*, it is soft.
4. The unipersonal verbs ending in a vowel, have ordinarily two terminations, but the same signification in both of them. They end in a vowel, *a*, *e*, *i*, *o*, or they add the termination, *magad*. F. i. *Sogipo*, or *sogipomagad*, it snows. *Kissina*, or *kissinamagad*, it is cold.—In this Dictionary you will find the second termination expressed by a dash and *magad*; as: *Sogipo*, or-*magad*, which means, or *sogipomagad*. And in the participle you will find a dash and *magak*; as: *Swagipog*, or-*magak*, which means, or *swagipomagak*.
5. The *imperative mood* is not always expressed, because it can be easily constructed according to the Paradigms of the Conjugations in the Grammar. But where the imperative is difficult or irregular, it is ordinarily expressed in this Dictionary.
6. Many verbs that are passive in their signification, are neuter in their formation and conjugation, and therefore marked down as neuter werbs. F. i. *Nind inendagos*, I am destined. *Nin nondagos*, I am heard, etc.
7. To indicate the plural of substantives, only the letter or let-

* In some places in the Dictionary, the letter *a*, when long, is marked with the circumflex accent.

ters are expressed that are added to the singular in order to form the plural; and the dash before these letters represents the substantive. As: *Tchiss*, turnip; pl.*-an;* which means, *tchissan*. *Inini*, man; pl.*wag*, that is, *ininiwag*. *

8. There are some consonants which the Indians don't pronounce distinctly and uniformally. They very often confound the letters *B* and *P*, *D* and *T*, *G* and *K*. It is often impossible to ascertain, by the pronunciation of an Indian, whether the word begins with a *B* or *P*, with a *D* or *T*, with a *G* or *K*. For this reason please mind the short Note you will find at the beginning of each of these letters in this Dictionary. See likewise the Note at the beginning of the letters *O* and *W*.
9. In regard to the *Second Part*, I have to remark that whatever relates to a *substantive*, is to be found under that substantive. As: I have large feet, I have small feet, I have cold feet, etc. Look for all that under the substantive "Foot."
10. Mind the same in regard to *verbs*. The adjectives relating to a verb and modifying it, are to be found under that verb. As: I look angry; I look strange, etc. This all occurs under the verb "Look."
11. Sometimes the verb act. an. is followed by the termination of the inan. F. i. *Sagia* (*nind*) *tton*, that is: *nind sagitton*.

Explanation of the abbreviations used in this Dictionary.

an.	signifies	*animate,*	See Otchipwe Grammar.
in.	"	*inanimate.*	
adv.	"	adverb.	
f. i.	"	for instance.	
imp.	"	imperative.	
interj.	"	interjection.	
n. or num	"	number.	
num. v.	"	numeral verb.	
n. v.	"	neuter verb.	
p.	"	participle.	
pl.	"	plural.	
pers. v.	"	personifying verb.	
p. s.	"	participle and substantive.	
S.	"	See.	
s.	"	substantive.	
s. th.	"	something.	

* In Manitoba the Otchipwe Indians or Sauteux pronounce more *wok* than *wag*, for verbs as well for substantives.

Sometimes, when necessary to indicate the third person sing. pres. of active verbs, *animate*, the beginning of the verb is given, and then the termination, which is *n*; as: *Nin wabama*; 3 p. *o wabn*; which means, *o wabamân.*

To show the third person sing. pres. of active verbs *inanimate,* when it is not regular the beginning of the verb is marked, and three periods; v.g.: *Nin wabandân*; 3 p. *o wab...*; which means, *o wabandân.*

To indicate the *participle,* ordinarily, when it appears to be useful for the beginner, the beginning and the end of it is marked down; as: *Mashkawadin;* p. *mesh...ing;* which means, *meshkawading.*

N. B.—To save time and expenses we have thought not always to repeat the third persons neither the participle, because we suppose that persons using this Dictionary have some previous knowledge of the Grammar.

F.	signifies,	in French.
C.	"	in the Canadian dialect of the French language.
L.	"	in Latin.
Ot.	"	in Ottawa or Otawa.
Alg.	"	in Algonquin.

A

A—This first letter of the Alphabet has principally two sounds, that is one long and the other short. We know when this first letter or the syllable with A, in the beginning of a word, is long or short, according to the way the change is formed; v.g. *Nind abawa ;* here the first letter A is long, because at the participle, you have to say: *ayabawad*—*Nind agona ;* here on contrary the first A is short, because you say for the participle: *egonad ;* see the rule of the Grammar.

A—This letter is sometimes inserted in verbs which signify repetition or changing of place; as: *Bapa-aija,* he goes from one place to another; instead of *baba-ija.*— *Anotch ainapinewag,* they have different and frequent diseases; instead of *anotch inâpinewag. Anotch ainassin nabikwan; enendang sa wedaked od ainikwean ;* the vessel goes in different directions; wherever the steersman pleases he steers it.—When the verb to which *a* is prefixed, begins with an *a,* the letter *i* is inserted between the two *a ;* as: *Agwinde,* it is on the surface of the water; *aiagwinde,* it floats about. — *Atewan,* they are there, (*in.* obj.) *aiatewan,* they are scattered round.

Aawe, s. pigeon-tail, (a kind of wild duck;) pl.-*g.*

Ab, (*nind*) I am; I am in, at home; p. *ebid.*

Abamaawa, (*nind*). I unite s. th. for him or to him; p. *aiawad.*

Abaan, (*nind*) a. v. *in.* I untie it; p. *aiabaang.*

Ababikaan, (*nind*) a. v. *in.* I open it with a key, I unlock; p. *aiab..ang.*

Ababikaigade, or-*magad,* u. v. it is opened, unlocked; p. *aiab.. deg.* or-*magak.*

Ababikaigan, s. key; improperly a lock; pl.-*an.* — S. *Kashkabikaigan.*

Ababikaiganike, (*nind*) n. v. I make a key or lock, (keys or locks ;) p. *aiab..ked.*

Ababikaiganikewin, s. lock-smith's trade or business.

Ababikaiganikewinini, s. lock-smith, (key or lock maker,) pl.-*wag.*

Ababikamawa, (*nind*) a. v. *an.* I open or unlock it to him or for him; p. *aiab..wad.*

Ababikawa, (*nind*) a. v. *an.* I

open with a key some *an.* obj. p. *aiab..wad.*
Abadad, u. v. it is useful, serviceable, beneficial; p. *aia..dak.*
Abadis, (*nind*) n. v. I am useful; p. *aia..sid.*
Abadjia, (*nind*) a. v. *an.* I make use of some *an.* obj.; he does me services, is useful to me; p. *aiabadjiad.*
Abadjitchigan, s. *an.* any *an.* object that is useful; pl.-*ag.*
Abadjiton, (*nind*) a. v. *in.* I make use of it, I profit by it, it is useful to me.
Abadjitowin, s. the use of s. th., the act of using, s. th.
Abagamisan, (*nind*) a. v. *in.* I warm it a little, (liquid;) p. *eb..ang.*
Abaigade, or–*magad,* u. v. it is untied, loosened; p. *aiab..deg.* or–*magak.*
Abaigas, (*nind*) n. v. I am loosened, untied; p. *aia. sod.*
Abâj, s. lodge-pole; pl. *abajin.*
Abajiiak, s. *an.* rafter; pl. *og.*
Abakamass, (*nind*) n. v. I take a warm foot-bath (after the Indian fashion;) p. *eb..ssod.*
Abakamasswa, (*nind*) a. v. *an.* I give him a warm foot-bath; p. *eb..wad;* imp. *abakamasswi.*
Abakiganes, (*nind*) n. v. I warm my breast; p. *eb..sod.*
Abakinindjiwas, (*nind*) n. v. I quicken or warm my hands; [F. je me dégourdis les mains;] p. *eb..sod.*
Abakisides, (*nind*) n. v. I quicken or warm my feet; p. *eb..sod.*
Abamibato (*nind*) n. v. I turn round, running; p. *aiab..tod.*
Abamigabaw, (*nind*) n. v. I turn, standing; p. *aiab..wid*
Abamigabawitan, (*nind*) a. v. *in.* I turn towards it, standing; p. *aiab..dang.*
Abamigabitawa, (*nind*) a. v. *an.* I turn towards him, standing; p. *aiab..wad.*
Abamisse, (*nind*) n. v. I turn round, flying; p. *aia..ssed.*
Abamitigweia sibi, u. v. the river makes a turn; p. *aiab..iad.*
Abamodjiwan, u. v. the water turns round, (at the foot of a rapid;) p. *aiab..wang.*
Abamoianimad, u. v. the wind flies round; [F. le vent rafale;] p. *aiab..mak.*
Abanab, (*nind*) n. v. I look behind; p. *aiabanabid.*
Abanabama, (*nind*) a. v. *an.* I look at him behind me; p. *aia..mad.*
Abanabandan, (*nind*) a. v. *in.* I look at it behind me; p. *aiâ., ang.*
Abanikwe, s. female slave; maid, pl.-*g.*
Abanini, s. male slave; servant; pl.-*wag.*
Abaodjigan, s. reel; [F. dévidoir;] pl.-*an.*
Abaodjige, (*nind*) n. v. I unwind from a reel; p. *aiab.. ged.*
Abaodon, (*nind*) a. v. *in.* I unwind it from a reel; p. *aia..baodod.*
Abashkobissan, (*nind*) a. v. *in.* I warm it a little, I make it tepid, (liquid;) p. *abash..ssang.*
Abashkobite, or–*magad,* u. v. it is a little warm, tepid, (liquid;) p. *ebash..teg,* or–*magak.*

Abato, (*nind*) n. v. I run there, to some place; p. *ebatod.*

Abawa, (*nind*) a. v. *an.* I untie or loosen him, I unswaddle (a child;) I unharness (a beast;) p. *aiabawad*; imp. *abâ.*

Abawa, or-*magad.* It is warm, mild weather, soft weather, thaw-weather; p. *aiabawag,* or–*magak.*

Abawas, (*nind*). I begin to feel warm, I am no more cold; p. *aia..sod.*

Abêa, (*nind*). I give him the lie, I convince him; [F. je le démentis;] p. *aiabead.*

Abêidiwin. Conviction.

Abibidon, (*nind*). I draw out the threads of it, (stuffs;) p. *aia..dod.*

Abidêkamig. Surely, certainly, undoubtedly.

Abiding. Once.

Abigina (*nind*). I unfold some object; p. *aia..nad;* imp. *abigin.*

Abijwa, jan, (*nind*). I rip or unstitch some object; *od abijwan;* p. *aia..wad;* imp. *abijwi.*

Abiminikwai, s.*an.* beaver-skin; pl.-*ag.*

Abinass. The place in a lodge or house allotted to a family; pl.-*an.*

Abindama (*nind*). I devour him, bite him much, cruelly; p. *aiab..mad.— Animoshag o gi-abindamawan pijikinsan;* the dogs have cruelly bitten the calf.

Abindis, (*nind*).

Abindjia, (*nind*). I treat him ill, I abuse him; p. *aia..ad.*

Abindjine, (*nind*). I am getting worse (in my sickness;) p. *aia.. ned.*

Abindjiton, (*nind*). I abuse it, treat it ill; p. *aia..tod.*

Abinindjisodis, (*nind*). I warm my hands; p. *aiab..sod.*

Abinodji, s. child; pl. -*iag.*

Abinodji-ijiwebisiwin, childishness, childish behavior.

Abinodjiikas, (*nind*). I play the child, I feign to be a child; p. *eb..sod.*

Abinodjiing, like a chid, or like children; *abinodjiing nind ijiwebis,* I behave like a child, (I am childish;) *abinodjiing iji gijwe,* he speaks like a child; *abinodjiing iji mawiwag,* they weep, or cry, like children.

Abinodjiiw, (*nind*). I am a child, p. *eb..wid.*

Abinodjiiwin, infancy, childhood.

Abinsika, or–*magad.* It is ruined, spoiled; p. *aia. kag,* or–*magak.*

Abinsoma, (*nind*). I abuse him with bad words, I despise him; p. *aia..mad.*

Abinsonge, (*nind*) n. v. I abuse with bad words, I use bad abusive language, I despise.

Abipikwanes, (*nind*). I warm my back; p. *aiab..sod.*

Abis, (*nind*). I warm myself; p. *aiabisod.*

Abisan, (*nind*). I warm it; p. *aia..ang.*

Abishkwebigininindjishin, (*nind*). I have a blister on my hand, from working; p. *eb..ing.*

Abishkwebigis, (*nind*). I have a blister; p. *eb. sid.*

Abishkwebigisidebis, (*nind*). I have a blister on my foot, from walking on snow-shoes.
Abishkwebigisideshin, (*nind*). I have a blister on my foot, from walking.
Abisides, (*nind*). I warm my feet; p. *aia..sod.*
Abisingwash, (*nind*). I awake from a profound sleep; I awake perfectly; p. *aia..id*
Abisishin, (*nind*). I revive, I recover my senses, (after fainting;) p. *aia..ing.*
Abisiwadis, (*nind*) n. v. I recover, (from a sickness;) p. *aia..sid.*
Abisiwemagad. It quickens, it revives; p. *aia..gak.*
Abisiwendam, (*nind*). I recover my senses, (after fainting;) p. *aia..dang.*
Abisiwima, (*nind*). I console him, solace him, encourage him; p. *aia..mad.*
Abisiwindiwin, consolation, consoling.
Abisiwinge, (*nind*); I console, solace, encourage; p. *aia..ged.*
Abisiwis, (*nind*). I recover.
Abiskobide, or–*magad*, it is untied, loosened; p. *aia..deg*, or–*magak.*
Abiskobidjigade, or–*magad*, it is untied; p. *aia..deg*, or–*magak.*
Abiskobidon, (*nind*). I loosen it, untie it; p. *aiab..dod.*
Abiskoka, or-*magad*, it gets loose, untied, it loosens; p *aia..kag*, or-*magak.*
A*biskona*, (*nind*). I untie him, deliver him; p. *aia..nad*; imp. *abiskon.*
Abiskosse, or-*magad.* It loosens or unties; being thrown, or falling; p. *aia..sseg*, or-*magak.*
Abiskota, (*nind*). I get loose, untied; p. *aia..tad.*
Abiswa, (*nind*). I warm him; p. *ebiswad*; imp. *abiswi.*
Abita, adv. half; *aiabita*, half each.
Abitan, (*nind*). I inhabit it, I dwell or live in it, (house, lodge;) p. *ebitang.*
Abita-omodai, half a bottle, a pint.
Abitatibikad. It is midnight; p. *aiab..kak.*
Abitawa, (*nind*). I dwell in him; p. *eb..ad.*
Abitâwâgâm, adv. halfway across a river, lake, etc.
Abitawamadjiw, adv. halfway, (going up a mountain or hill.)
Abitawikana, adv. halfway, (going from one place to another.)
Abitawis, (*nind*). I am a half breed, (half white man and half Indian;) p. *aiab..sid.*
Abitawissag, adv. half a barrel.
Abitchiba, (*nind*). I rise from the dead; p. *aia..bad.*
Abitchibaa, (*nind*). I raise him from the dead; p. *aia..ad.*
Abitchibaidis, (*nind*). I raise myself from the dead; p. *aia..sod.*
Abitchibawin. Resurrection.
Abitonana, (*nind*). I kill him almost, (I kill him half;) p. *aia..nad*; imp. *abitonaj.*
Abitoshkine, or-*magad*, u. v. it is half full, (a bag or sack;) p. *aia..neg*, or-*magak.*

Abitosse, (*nind*). I arrive at halfway; p. *aia..sed.*

Abitosse, or-*magad*. It comes or arrives to the middle; p. *aia..seg*, or-*magak*. — This word is also used for Wednesday, which is the middle of the week. *Dassing aiabitosegin*, every Wednesday.

Abitotchipidon, (*nind*). I tie or bind it in the middle; p. *aia..dod.*

Abitotchipina, (*nind*). I tie or bind some *an*. object in the middle; p. *aia..nad.*

Abiwin, habitation, mansion, room; pl.-*an*.

Abo, in compositions, signifies *liquid*. It is used when the first part of the composed word ends in a *consonant;* as: *Mandâminâbo*, corn soup; (*mandamin*, Indian corn.) *Totoshabo*, milk; (*totosh*, female breast.)—But when the first part of the composed word terminates in a *vowel*, the word *wâbo* is used instead of *âbo*.—S. *Wabo.*

Abodagwaje, (*nind*). I put a blanket or coat over me in the wrong way, inside out; p. *aia..jed.*

Abodinan, na, (*nind*). I turn it over,(a coat, etc.;) p. *aia.,ang.*

Abodishima, (*nind*). I put it in the wrong way, (some objects as *moshwe*, a handkerchief;) p. *aia..ad.*

Abodjidon, (*nind*). I have down-hanging lips; p. *aia..dong.*

Abodjigwanisso, (*nind*). I tumble over head; p. *aia..sed.*

Abôiawe, young beaver between two and three years.

Aboiaweiagig, young otter between two and three years old.

Abosikan, (*nind*). I put it on in the wrong way, inside out, (a coat, shirt, etc.; p. *aia..ang.*

Abwamine, (*nind*). I roast Indian corn; p. *ebw..ned.*

Abwânak, spit, a stick with a piece of meat on one end, put near the fire to roast.

Abwatchigan, grate to dry venison or fish on it.

Abwatchiganabik, gridiron.

Abwatigwân, roasted ear of Indian corn.

Abwatigwe, (*nind*). I roast an ear (or ears) of Indian corn; p. *ebw..wed.*

Abweiabôwe, (*nind*). I sweat eating; p. *ebw. wed.*

Abwen, (*nind*). I roast it; p. *ebwed.*

Abwenan, (*nind*). I roast some obj. (a fish, etc.;) p. *ebwed.* V. Conj.)

Abwenindji, (*nind*), my hands are sweating; p. *eb ijid.*

Abwes (*nind*). I sweat, I perspire, I am warm; p. *ebwesod.*

Abweside, (*nind*); my feet are sweating; p. *eb..ded.*

Abwesowin, sweat, perspiration.

Abweta, (*nind*). I sweat (working;) p. *ebwetad.*

Abwewin, frying-pan, pl-*an*.

Abwewinens, a frying pan with a short handle.

Abwi, paddle, p-n.

Adabikaan, (*nind*). I fasten it, hook it, (a chain, etc.;) p. *ed..ang.*

Adabikissidjigan, buckle (of metal.)

Adabikissidon, (*nind*). I hook it; p. *ed..dod.*
Adabikissin, it hooks, catches, (metal;) p. *ed..sing.*
Adagamagishin sibi, (*nind*). I am stopped by a river in my voyage, hindered to continue my journey; p. *aia..ing.*
Adawaama, (*nind*). I embark with him, I go somewhere with him in a canoe or boat; p. *aia..mad.*
Adawaawi, (*nind*). I embark (with somebody;) p. *aia..wid.*
Adikweam, (*nind*). I hold the rudder, I steer; p. *aia..ang.*
Adikweigan, rudder.
Adidweige, (*nind*). I am steering; p. *aia..ged.*
Adima, (*nind*). I overtake him; *fig.* I equal him; p. *edimad.*
Adiman, snow-shoe string; p. *an.*
Adindan, (*nind*). I overtake it; p. *edindang.*
Adisokan, tale, fable.
Adisoke, (*nind*). I tell; p. *ed..hed.*
Adisokewin, tale telling.
Adisokéwinini, tale-teller.
Adissawaieshi, a kind of large grass-hopper, locust; [F. cigale.]
Adissigan, dye-stuff, anything used for dying; pl.-*an.*
Adissige, (*nind*). I dye color; p. *edissiged.*
Adissigewigamig, dyer's shop, dye-house; pl.-*an.*
Adissigewin, dyeing, business and occupation of a dyer.
Adissigewinini, dyer; pl.-*wag.*
Adisso, it is ripe; p. *edissod.* Some berries are *animate* in Otchipwe, as: *Miskwimin*, raspberry; *adissowag miskwiminag*, the raspberries are ripe, (are colored.)
Adisso, it is dyed, (some *an.* obj.) p. *edissod.*— *Weweni adisso aw moshwe*, this handkerchief is well dyed.
Adite, or-*magad*, it is ripe, (an *inanimate* berry, etc.) p. *editeg*, or-*magak.*—*Odéimin adite odéiminan aditewan*, the strawberry is ripe, the strawberries are ripe, (colored.)
Adite, or-*magad*, it is dyed, (some *in.* obj.) p. *editeg*, or-*magak. Mandan wâboiân adite*, this blanket is dyed.
Adjaosse, (*nind*). I am lame; p. *edjaossed.*
Adjibidjigan, a small hook; [F. agrafe].
Adjibidji[illegible], (*nind*). I fasten with a small hook; p *edj..ged.*
Adjibidon, (*nind*). I fasten it by means of a small hook; p. *edj..dod.*
Adjidjâk, crane; [F. grue;] pl.-*wok.*
Adjidjakopin, crane-potato, (a big eatable root, growing in the water;) pl.-*ig.*
Adjigwadan, (*nind*). I take it up or catch it with a hook, I hook it, I accroach it; *aia..dang.*
Adjigwadjigan, hook to catch or grapple with, commonly used by the Indians in catching sturgeon; pl.-*an.*
Adjigwadjiganabik, iron hook, grappling hook; pl.-*an.*
Adjigwadjige, (*nind*). I take or catch with a hook, I accroach; p. *aia..ged.*
Adjigwana, (*nind*). I take or catch him with a hook, I

hook him, I accroach him; p. *aia..nad;* imp. *adjigwaj. Namé nin gi-adjigwana,* I caught a sturgeon with a hook.

Adjima, (*nind*). I speak of him; p. *âiadjimad.*

Adjitchikessi, a kind of fish; [C. mulet;] *wag.*

Adopowin, table.

Adopowinigin, table-cloth.

Agâming, adv. on the other side of a river, lake, etc., on the opposite shore. — *Agaming kitchigami,* on the other side of the great sea. S. *Kitchi agâming.*

Agaming, adv. on the beach, on the lake shore.

Agâshi, (*nind*). I am small, little; p. *egashiid.*

Agashiidis, (*nind*). I make myself small, little; p. *eg..sod.*

Agasom, (*nind*). I am bashful in speaking; p. *eg..mod.*

Agasoma, (*nind*). I cause him shame, I make him ashamed by my words; I dishonor him; p. *eg..mad.*

Agâss, in composition signifies *small, fine, narrow.*

Agassa, or-*magad,* it is small, narrow; p. *eg..sag,* or-*magak*

Agassabigad, it is fine, (thread, string, etc.); p. *eg..gak.*

Agassabigisi, it is fine, (sewing silk;) p. *eg..sid.*

Agassabikad, it is small, (some obj. of metal;) p. *eg..kak.* -*Osâm agassabikad ababikaigan,* the key is too small.

Agassabikisi, it is small, (a stone or a piece of silver;) p. *eg..sid.*-*Agassabikisi joniians,* a shilling is small.

Agassadea, (*nind*). I make some obj. narrow or narrower, I straiten it; p. *eg..ad.*

Agassadea, or-*magad,* it is narrow; p. *eg..ag,* or -*magak.* -*Pindigeiog egassadeag ishkwandeming,* go in through the narrow gate.

Agassadeiabikad, it is narrow, (metal;) p. *eg..kak.*

Agassadeiabikisi, it is narrow, (obj. of stone or silver;) p. *eg.. sid.*

Agassademo mikana, the path or trail is narrow; p. *eg..mog.*

Agassadengwe, (*nind*). I have a small face; p. *eg..wed.*

Agassadesii nabagissag, seniba, etc., the board, the ribbon, etc., is narrow; p. *eg..sid.*

Agassadeton, (*nind*). I make it narrow, or narrower, I straiten it; p. *eg..tod.*

Agassakwaiawes, (*nind*). S. *Gigâiawes.*

Agassate, or -*magad,* it is small, (house, room;) p. *eg..teg,* or -*maguk.*

Agassaton, (*nind*). I make it small, or I make it smaller; p. *eg..tod.*

Agassendagos, (*nind*). I am considered insignificant, I am insignificant, little; p. *eg..sig*

Agassendagwad, it is considered insignificant, it is insignificant, little; p. *eg..wak.*

Agassendan, (*nind*). I considered it insignificant; p. *eg..ang.*

Agassenim, (*nind*). I have humble thoughts of myself; I am humble; p *eg..mod.* -*Abinodjiing agassenimo,* he is humble like a child; (L. humiliat se sicut parvulus.)

Agassenima, (*nind*). I think little of him, I consider him insignificant ; p. *eg..mad.*

Agassenimôwin, humble thoughts, humiliation, humility.

Agassidee, (*nind*). I have a small heart ; p. *eg..ed.*

Agassidjane, (*nind*). I have a small nose ; p. *eg..ned.*

Agassidon, (*nind*). I have a small mouth ; p. *eg..dong.*

Agassidonea, or–*magad*, it has a small mouth, a small opening, (a bottle, etc.) p. *eg..ag*, or *–magak.*

Agassîgad, it is small, or narrow, (cotton, linen, etc.) p. *eg..gak –Agassigad adopowinigin*, the table-cloth is small.

Agassigade, (*nind*). I have a small leg ; p. *eg..ded*

Agassigisi moshwe, the handkerchief is small ; p. *eg..sid.*

Agassigondagan, (*nind*). I have a feeble voice, (properly, I have a small throat) ; p. *eg..gang.*

Agassikam, (*nind*). S. *Babiwishkam.*

Agassikodan, (*nind*). I make it smaller by cutting it ; p. *eg..dang.*

Agassikona, (*nind*). I make some obj. smaller by cutting ; p. *eg..nad.*

Agassigweiawe, (*nind*). I have a small neck ; *eg..wed.*

Agassiminagad, it is small, (some globular obj.) p *eg...gak. –Kitchi agassiminagadon onow anwin*, these musket-balls are very small.

Agassiminagisi aw opin, this potato is small ; p. *eg..sid.*

Agassin, it is small ; p. *egassing.*

Agassinad, there is little of it, it is small ; p. *eg..nak.*

Agassindibe, (*nind*). I have a small head ; p. *eg..bed.*

Agâssinike, (*nind*). I have a small arm ; p. *eg..ked.*

Agassinimin, (*nind*) or *nind agassinomin*, we are a few in number, our number is small ; p. *egassinidjig*, or *egassinodjig.*

Agassinindji, (*nind*). I have a small hand ; p. *eg..id.*

Agassishkinji, he (she, it) has a small snout, (animal ;) p. *eg..jid.*

Agassishkinjigwe, (*nind*). I have a small eye ; p. *eg..wed.*

Agassishwandeia, or *–magad*, there is a small door, or narrow door ; p. *eg..ag* or-*magak.*

Agassiside, (*nind*). I have a small foot ; p. *eg..ded.*

Agassitawage, (*nind*). I have a small ear ; p. *eg..ged.*

Agassiton, (*nind*). S. *Agassaton.*

Agasson, (*nind*). I have a small canoe ; p. *egassonod.*

Agassonagad. It is small, (canoe, boat, etc.) p. *eg..gak.*

Agatch, (*nind*). I am ashamed ; p. *egatchid.*

Agatchia, (*nind*). I cause him shame, I make him ashamed, I dishonor him ; p. *eg..ad.*

Agatchiiwe, (*nind*). I cause shame (to somebody ;) p. *eg..wed.*

Agatchiiwemagad. It causes or brings shame ; p. *eg..gak.*

Agatchim, (*nind.*) S. *Agasom.*

Agatchishk, (*nind*). I am bashful, shy, timid ; p. *eg..kid.*

Agatchishkiwin. Bashfulness, timidity, shyness.
Agatchitagos, (nind). I am ashamed of speaking, unwilling to speak before people; p. *eg..sid.*
Agatchitan, (nind). I am ashamed of it; p. *eg..ang.*
Agatchitawa, (nind). I am ashamed before him; p. *eg..wad.*
Agatchiton, (nind). I bring it to shame, I dishonor it; p. *eg..tod.*
Agatchiwadis, (nind). Agatchishk.
Agatchiwadissiwin S. *Agatchishkiwin.*
Agatchiwin. Shame.
Agatchiwis, (nind). S. *Agatchishk.*
Agatendagos, (nind). My conduct is shameful, considered shameful, dishonorable, despisable; p. *eg..sid.*
Agatendagwad. It is shameful, it is considered shameful, despisable; p. *eg..wak.*
Agatendaywakamig, adv. shamefully.
Agatendan, (nind). I am ashamed of it; p. *eg..dang.*
Agatenima, (nind). I am ashamed of him (in my thoughts;) p. *eg..mad.*
Agatenindis. I am ashamed before myself; p. *eg..sod.*
Agawa. Hardly, scarcely; very little.
Agawabawas, (nind). I put myself under a shelter, in rainy weather; p. *eg..sod.*
Agawabawasowin. Shelter against rain; umbrella.
Agawadamawa, (nind). I cannot obtain it from him, although I endeavor, I cannot prevail upon him to give it to me; p. *eg..wad.*
Agawadan, (nind). I cannot have it, although I wish and endeavor; p. *eg..dang.*
Agawâdis, (nind). I am crazy, foolish; p. *aia..sid.*
Agawâdjia, (nind). I cause or make him damage; p. *eg..ad.*
Agawâdjiidis, (nind). I make damage to myself by drinking; p. *eg. sod.*
Agawaii, adv. behind.
Agawanapi, adv. soon, as soon as possible.
Agawa nin pangaog, my pulse beats slowly. S. *Pangaog.*
Agawate, or *magad,* there is shadow; p. *eg..teg,* or-*magak.*
Agawateon, parasol; umbrella; pl.—*an.*
Agawateshimon, (nind). I am in the shadow; p. *eg..nod.*
Agawateshin, (nind). I make shadow with my body; p. *eg..ing.*
Agawateshkagon, (nind). It covers me with its shadow; p. *eg..god.*
Agawateshkam, (nind). I make shadow (with my body,) I overshadow; p. *eg..kang.*
Agawateshkan, (nind). I cover it with my shadow, I overshadow it; p. *eg..kang.*
Agawateshkawa, (nind) or *nind agawateshkamawa.* I cover him with my shadow, I overshadow him; I am in his light, I cover his light; p. *eg..wad.*
Agawatesse bineshi. The bird

throws its shadow, (flying by;) p. *eg..sed.*
Agawatesse or-*magad.* It makes shadow, (a cloud etc.; p. *eg.. seg*, or-*magak.*
Agawatessin anakwad. The cloud throws its shadow; p. *eg..sing.*—S. *Agawatesse*, or-*magad.*
Agawigamig, adv. behind the island, under the cover of the island.
Agawinagos, (*nind*). I look better, or appear better, than I am, I am fallacious, deceiving; p. *eg..sid.*
Agawinogwad. It is deceiving, fallacious, it looks better than it is; p. *eg..wak.*
Agawis, (*nind*). I gain nothing, I make nothing by what I am doing; p. *egawisid.*
Agawishka, (*nind*). S. *Agawita.*
Agawita, (*nind*). I work in vain, gaining nothing; p. *eg..tad.*
Agig. Bad cold, catarrh; phlegm.
Agigoka, (*nind*). I have a bad cold; [F. j'ai le rhume;] p. *eg..kad.*
Agigoka aw bebejigoganji. This horse has glanders; [F. ce cheval a la gourme.]
Agigokawin. Bad cold, indisposition from catching cold.
Agim. Snow-shoe; pl.-*ag.*
Agimâ, (*nind*). I count him, I put him in the number; p. *egimad.*
Agimak. Ash-tree; pl.-*wag.*
Agimike, (*nind*). I make snow-shoes; p. *aia..ked.*
Agimikewin. The art of making snow-shoes.
Agim nind ashkima. I lace or fill a snow-shoe; p. *eshkimad.*
Agimosse, (*nind*). I walk with snow-shoes; p. *aia..sed*,
Agindan, (*nind*). I count it; p. *eg..ang.*
Agindass, (*nind*). I cipher, I number, I count; p. *eg..sod.*
Agindâssobiigan. Cipher, figure; pl. *an.*
Agindassobiige, (*nind*). I cipher, I number, I write figures; p. *eg..ged.*
Agindassobiigewin. Ciphering, numbering.
Agindassowin. Cipher; numbering.
Agindassowinan nind ojibianan. S. *Agindassobiige.*
Agindjigade, or-*magad.* It is counted; p. *eg..deg*, or-*magak.*
Agindjigadewin. Counting, census
Agindjigas, (*nind*). I am counted; p. *eg..sod.*
Agobidjigan. Curtain; pl. -*an.*
Agobidjiganigin. Calico for curtains.
Agobina, (*nind*). I tie some remedy or a plaster on his wound; p. *eg..nad*; imp. *agobij.*
Agobis, (*nind*). I have a plaster on my wound; p. *egobisod.*
Agobison, or *agobisowin*, (or *agwobison, agwobisowin*). Remedy tied on a wound, pl s-ter; pl. -*an.*
Agodakikwan. Kettle-hook, kettle-hanger; pl. -*an.*
Agôde, or-*magad.* It is hung up, it hangs; it is up somewhere; p. *egodeg*, or-*magak.*
Agodjin, (*nind*). I am hanging;

I am up somewhere; p. *egodjing.*
Agodjiwanân. Scaffold, to put something on it; pl. *-an.*
Agodjiwanak. S. *Agodjiwanan.*
Agodjiwananakoke, (*n i n d*). I make a scaffold; p. *eg..ked.*
Agodon, (*nind*). I hang it up; I put it up somewhere; p. *egodod.*
Agogin. It sticks or cleaves to....; p. *egoging.*
Agogwadan, (*nind*). I sew it to s. th.; p. *eg..dang.*
Agogwâdjigan. A kind of narrow lace; [F. tavelle.]
Agogwana, (*nind*). I sew some object to s. th.; p. *eg..nad.*
Agogwass, (*nind*). I am sewing one object to another; p. *eg..sod.*
Agojiwe, (*nind*). I am hanging up persons.
Agojiwewin. S. *Agonidiwin.*
Agojiwewinini. S. *Agonidiwinini.*
Agoke, (*nind*). I stick or cleave to s. th.; p. *egoked.*
Agoke, or *-magad.* It sticks or cleaves to s. th.; p. *egokeg,* or*-magak.*
Agokiwassa, (*nind*). I seal him; I stick some obj. to s. th.; p. *eg..sad.*
Agokiwassan, (*nind*). I seal it; I stick it to s. th.; p. *eg..ang.* —*Agokiwassan ow masinaigan,* seal this letter.
Agokiwassigan. Any thing that cleaves or sticks to, sealing wax, wafer; paste.
Agokiwassigas, (*n i n d*). I am sealed; p. *eg..sod.*
Agokiwassitchigade, or*-magad.* It is sealed; pasted; p. *eg..deg,* or *magak.*
Agokiwassitchigan, or *agokiwassitchiganabik.* S e a l, a plain seal without any engraving or figures or letters. S. *Masinikiwagaigan.*
Agokiwassitchige, (*nind*). I seal; I paste; p. *eg..ged.*
Agokiwasswa, (*nind*). I seal him, I seal some obj.; p. *eg..wad.*
Assinin o gi-agokiwasswawan. They sealed the stone.
Agom, (*nind*). I am on the surface of the water, (in a canoe or boat;) I float; p. *egomod.*
Agomowewebanabi, (*nind*). I am fishing with a line and hook in a canoe or boat: p. *eg..bid.*
Agomowin. Harbor, port, haven; pl.*-an.*
Agon, Aganika, Ot. S. *Gon, Gonika.*
Agona, (*nind*). I hang him up, I hang up some obj.; I put it up somewhere, or on s. th.; p. *egonad;* imp. *agôj.*
Agonakwe. A virgin whom the pagan Indians place on an elevated scaffold and present to the Great Spirit, in order to obtain a prosperous success in war.
Agonamawa, (*nind*). I hang or lay it upon him; p. *eg..wad.*
Agonassâb, (*nind*). I hang or spread a net on a pole to dry; p. *eg..bid.*
Agonidis, (*nind*). I hang myself; p. *eg..sed.*
Agonidiwi-mitig. Gallows; pl. *-on.*
Agonidiwin. Hanging, hang-

man's work, execution of a criminal.

Agonidiwinini. Hangman, executioner; pl.-*wag*.

Agonweiendam, (*nind*). I don't believe what is said, I contradict in thoughts, I am incredulous; p. *aia..dang*.

Agonweiendamowin Unbelief, thought or thoughts contrary to what is said, contradiction in thoughts, incredulity.

Agonwetadimin, (*nind*). We contradict each other, we dispute, argue; p. *aiag..didjig*.

Agonwetadiwin. Dispute, contradiction.

Agonwetadis, (*nind*). I contradict myself; p. *aia..disod*.

Agonwetage, (*nind*). S. *Agonwetam*.

Agonwetageshk, (*nind*). I use to contradict, to gainsay, to disobey; p. *aia..kid*.

Agonwetageshkiwin. Bad habit of gainsaying, of disobeying.

Agonwetagewin. S. *Agonwetamowin*.

Agonwetam, (*nind*). I contradict, I gainsay; I disobey; I deny; I am incredulous; p. *aia..tang*.

Agonwetamowin. Contradiction, gainsaying; disobedience.

Agonwetan, (*nind*). I contradict it, I don't believe it; p. *aia..ang*.–*Nind agonwetan iw bitâdgimowin*, I contradict that news, I don't believe it.

Agonwetawa, (*nind*). I contradict him, I gainsay him; I disobey him; p. *aia..wad*.

Agoshkowewashk. Herb of Venus.

Agoshtigwaweon. Helmet; pl. *an*.

Agosi bineshi. The bird is resting on....; p. *egosid*.

Agoskana, (*nind*). I am afraid and anxious about him, (he is in a dangerous situation); p. *eg..nad*.

Agoskanidis, (*nind*). I am afraid, anxious, (about some misfortune or accident happening to me); p. *eg..sod*.

Agoski, (*nind*). I fear, I am afraid; p. *egoskid*.

Agoskwadin. It sticks to it by freezing; [G. angefroren;] p. *eg..ding*.

Agossitchigade, or-*magad*. There is s. th. hidden behind some object; p. *aiag..deg*, or-*magak*.

Agossiton, (*nind*). I put it before s. th. to hide it; p. *aia..tod*.

Agotagos, (*nind*). I speak in a hidden, mysterious manner; I use a parable; p. *aia..sid*.

Agotagosiwin. Hidden, mysterious speaking, parable; pl. *-an*.

Agwaadon, (*nind*). I draw it out of the water; p. *eg..dod*.

Agwaam, (*nind*). I come close to the shore, (in a canoe or boat, not landing); p. *egwaang*.

Agwaan, (*nind*). I sew it on; p. *eg..ang*.

Agwâbian, (*nind*) or *nind agwâbigaan*. I draw it (liquid) out of a kettle or other vessel; p. *eg..ang*.

Agwâbikide, or-*magad*. It is burnt, (something that was cooked in a kettle,); p. *eg..deg*, or-*magak*.

Agwâbikidewipogisi. Some object has the taste of being burnt; p. *eg..sid.*

Agwâbikidewipogwad. It has the taste of being burnt; p. *eg..wak.*

Agwâbikis, (*nind*). I burn myself taking in my hand a hot object of metal or stone; p. *eg..sod.*

Agwâbikisekwe, (*nind*). I burn what I am cooking; p. *eg..wed.*

Agwabikiso pakwejigan. The bread is burnt; p. *eg..sod.*

Agwâbikiswa, (*nind*). I burn him with some hot obj. of metal or stone; p. *eg..wad,* imp. *agwabikiswi.*

Agwabina, (*nind*). I draw him out of the water, (a fish, etc.) p. *eg..nad.*

Agwabinagan. Drag-net; [F. seine;] pl. *-ag.*

Agwabita, (*nind*). I come out of the water; p. *eg..tad.*

Agwabiwa, (*nind*) I draw some object out of a vessel; p. *eg..wad.*

*Agwâdamawa,ikwewan,*or(*ininiwan,*) (*nind*). I accuse him, (her) of an unlawful intercourse with a person of the other sex; p. *eg..wad.*

Agwadashi, a kind of fish, bull-pout; [C. petit crapet;] pl. *-wag.*

Agwagobaga, or-*magad.* It is mouldy, (a leaf, or something that is in leaves;) p. *eg..gag,* or-*magak.*

Agwagobagisi aw asséma. That tobacco is mouldy; p *eg..sid.*

Agwagòpogosi. It has a mouldy taste, taste of mouldiness, (some object); p. *eg..sid.*

Agwagopogwad. It tastes mouldy, (*in.* obj.); p. *eg..wak.*

Agwagwabikad, (pr. *agwagobikad*). It is rusty, (metal); p. *eg..kak.*

Agwagwâbikishin, (pron. *agwagobikishin*). It is rusty; (*an.* obj. metal); p. *eg..ing.*

Agwagwâbikisi, (pron. *agwagobikisi*). It is rusty, (*an.* obj., metal,) p. *eg..sid.*

Agwagwabikissin, (pr. *agwagobikissin*). It is rusty, (metal); p *eg..sing.*

Agwagwissaga, or-*magad,*(pron. *agwagôssaga*). The floor is mouldy, (or other objects of wood;) p. *eg..gag,* or-*magak.*

Agwagwishi, (pron. *agwagoshi.*) It is mouldy, (some *an.* obj.); p. *eg..id.*–*Pakwejigan agwagwishi, agwagwishiwag gaie, opinig;* the bread is mouldy, and the potatoes are mouldy also.

Agwagwissin, (pron. *agwagossin*). It is mouldy; also, it is rusty; p. *eg..sing.*

Agwaiadaga, (*nind*). I swim to the shore; p. *eg..gad.*

Agwaiadagak, (*nind*). I arrive to the shore, walking on the ice; p. *eg..kod.*

Agwaiadagas, (*nind*). I come to the shore out of the water; p. *eg..sid.*

Agwaiakiganeodis, (*nind*). I cover my breast; p. *eg..sod.*

Agwaiash, (*nind*). I make for the shore, I sail to the shore; p. *eg..shid.*

Agwaiâssin. It comes to the shore, it is driven towards the shore by the wind; p. *eg..sing.*

Agwaigade, or-*magad*. It is sewed to s. th.; p. *eg..deg*, or-*magak*.
Agwaigaso. It is sewed to s. th., (*an.* obj.) p. *eg..sod*.
Agwaige, (*nind*). I am sewing s. th. to s. th.; p. *eg..g..d*.
Agwaisekwe, (*nind*). I take from the fire what I have cooked; p. *eg..wed*.
Agwaje, (*nind*). I cover myself, (with a blanket, etc); p. *eg..jed*.
Agwajêwa, (*nind*). I cover him, (with a blanket, etc.); p. *eg..wad*; imp. *agwajé*.
Agwakamigissin. It sticks to the ground; p. *eg..sing*.
Agwakidaan, (*nind*). I lift it up with a lever; p. *eg..ang*.
Agwakidaigan. Lever; pl.-*an*.
Agwakidaige, (*nind*). I am lifting s. th. with a lever; p. *eg..ged*.
Agwakidawa, (*nind*). I lift up some obj. with a lever; p. *eg..wad*; imp. *agwakidâ*.
Agwâkossin. It sticks to some wooden object; p. *eg..sing*.
Agwakwâwa, (*nind*). S. *Sassagakwâwa*.
Agwanaan, (*nind*). I cover it; p. *eg..ang*.
Agwânabawas, (*nind*). I put myself under a shelter, in rain; p. *eg..sod*.
Agwânabawe, (*nind*). I am under a shelter in rain; p. *eg..wed*.
Agwanaigade, or-*magad*. It is covered; p. *eg..deg*, or-*magak*.
Agwanaigas, (*nind*). I am covered; p. *eg..sod*.
Agwanakokwêigan. Cover of the powder-pan of a gun; [F. Batteries;] pl.-*an*.
Agwanapakwas, (*nind*). I put myself under a bark-shelter, in rain; p. *eg..sod*.
Agwanapakwasowin. Bark-shelter, in rainy weather; pl.-*an*.
Agwânâss, (*nind*). I unload a canoe, boat, etc.; p. *eg..sod*.
Agwanassowin. Unloading.
Agwanawa, (*nind*). I cover him; I clothe or dress him; p. *eg..wad*; imp. *agwanâ*.
Agwanema, (*nind*). I put in my mouth some obj.; p. *eg..mad*. —*Assema nind agwanema*, I take tobacco in my mouth.
Agwanendan, (*nind*). I put it in my mouth; p. *eg..ang*.
Agwanendjigan. Chew of tobacco; [F. chique.]
Agwanendjige, (*nind*). I put or take in my mouth; p. *eg..ged*.
Agwanikweodis, (*nind*). I cover my head, (with a blanket, handkerchief, etc.); p. *eg..sod*.
Agwanikwêwa, (*nind*). I cover his head with a handkerchief, etc.; p. *eg..wad*; imp. *agwanikwé*.
Agwaôdon, (*nind*). I convey it to the shore from the lake, (a canoe, a log, etc.); p. *eg..dod*.
Agwaôma, (*nind*). I bring him ashore from a canoe or boat, on my back; p. *eg.mad*.
Agwaôna, (*nind*). I convey some obj. to the shore from the lake; p. *eg..nad*; imp. *agwaoj*.
Agwaôndân, (*nind*). I bring it ashore from a canoe or boat, on my back; p. *eg..dang*.
Agwâp, (*nind*). I take out of a

kettle or pot something to eat; p. *egwapod.*

Agwâpidon, (*nind*). I tie or bind it on s. th.; p. *eg..dod.*

Agwâpina, (*nind*). I tie or bind some obj. on s. th.; p. *eg..nad;* imp. *agwapij.*

Agwâshima, (*nind*). I take him from the fire; (a person, or any other obj.) also, I take him out of a canoe, etc.; p. *eg..mad.*

Agwâshinge, (*nind*(. I take from the fire; p. *eg..ged.*

Agwâsdidon tchimân (*nind*). I haul on the beach a canoe or boat; p. *eg..dod.*

Agwâssitchigade, or-*magad.* It is taken out of a canoe, boat, etc., it is put ashore, landed; p. *eg..deg,* or-*magak.*

Agwâssiton, (*nind*). I take it out of a canoe, vessel, etc., I land it; p. *eg..tod.* The same verb is also used for: "I take it from the fire," (*in.* obj.)

Agwâta, (*nind*). I come out of the water; p. *egwâtad.*

Agwâtchaii, adv. Outwardly, on the outside, externally.

Agwâtching, adv. Outside, out of doors, without, out.

Agwatching nakakeia, adv. From without; on the outside.

Agwatching nind aia, or, *agwatching nin bodawe,* (a squaw speaking,) I am in my monthly flowings.

Agwatchiwakaigan. Out of the fort. S. *Pindjwakaigan.*

Agwawa, (*nind*). I draw him out of a vessel, kettle, etc.; p. *agwawad;* imp. *agwa.*

Agwawânak, s. *an.* Beam, under the upper floor of a house; pl.—*og.*

Agwawebina, (*nind*). I throw him out of the water, (a fish, etc.,) also, I throw him ashore out of a canoe, etc.; p. *eg..nad;* imp. *agwawebin.*

Agwawebinan, (*nind*). I throw it out of the water, or out of a canoe or boat, ashore; p. *eg..ang.*

Agwia, (*nind*). I clothe him, I give him clothes already made, or clothing materials; p. *egwiad.*

Agwidaan. Agwidaigan. Agwidaige. Agwidawa.—S. *Agwakidaan. Agwakidaigan. Agwakidaige. Agwakidawa.*

Agwidab, (*nind*). I sit upon; p. *eg..bid.*

Agwidagan. The upper part or top of an Indian moccasin; pl. —*an.*

Agwiidimin, (*nind*). We clothe each other; p. *eg..didjig.*

Agwiiding. Receiving clothes, (present or payment in clothes, received by many together.)

Agwiidis, (*nind*). I clothe myself, I provide for my own clothing; p. *eg..sod.*

Agwiidiwin. The giving or receiving of clothes or clothing materials, as a present or payment

Agwin, (*nind*). I have it on, I wear it, (a vestment;) p. *egwid.*

Agwinan, (*nind*). I wear it, (*an.* obj.); p. *egwid.* v. Conj.—*Aw ikwe kitchi moshwen od agwinan,* that woman wears a large shawl.

Agwinde, or-*magad*. It soaks, it is in the water, or floating on the water; p. *eg..deg*, or *magak*.

Agwiadjima, (*nind*). I put him (her, it) in the water, (any *an*. obj.) I put some *an*. obj. in the water to soak; p. *eg..mad*.

Agwindjin, (*nind*). I am in the water, (sitting or lying in the water;) also, I float, being partly in the water; p. *eg..ing*.

Agwindjiton, (*nind*). I put it in the water, I put it in the water to soak; p. *eg..tod*.

Agwindjônagan. Float for a net; pl.-*an*.

Agwingoss. A kind of small squirrel; [C. suisse;] pl.-*ag*.

Agwingwebina, (*nind*). I blindfold him; p. *eg..nad*.

Agwingwebis, (*nind*). I am blindfolded; p. *eg..sod*.

Agwingweon. Bow over the Indian cradle; pl.-*an*.

Agwingweon, or *agwingwebison*. Veil; pl.-*an*.

Agwinoie animosh. The dog is pissing.

Agwitawishima, (*nind*). S. *Agwitoshima*.

Agwiiawissidon, (*nind*). I put it on a pile, I pile it up; p. *aia..dod*.

Agwitchikijeigan. Andiron; pl. *an*.

Agwitchisideshimon, (*nind*). I put my feet on s. th., sitting; p. *eg..nod*.

Agwitchisideshimonowin. Foot stool; pl.-*an*.

Agwitoiabikishin. It is piled up, (silver or stone); p. *eg..ing*.

Agwitoiabikissin. It is piled up, (metal), *in*.) p. *eg..sing*.

Agwiton, (*nind*). I clothe it; p. *egwitod*.—*Debendjiged apitchi weweni od agwitonan wabigonin kitiganing;* the Lord splendidly clotheth the flowers of the field.

Agwitoshimag, (*nind*). I pile up some objects; p. *eg..mad*.

Agwitoshinog. They are piled up, (*an*. obj.) p. *eg..shingig*.—*Kitcki nibiwa nabagissagog agwitoshinog oma;* great many boards are piled up here.

Agwitossidonan, (*nind*). I pile them up, (*in*. objects;) p. *eg..tod*.

Agwitossinon. They are piled up, (*in*. objects;) p. *eg..ssingin*.

Agwitowane, (*nind*). I put s. th. more to what, I carry on my back; p. *eg..ned*.

Agwiwin. Any vestment, clothes, clothing; pl.-*an*.

Aia, (*nind*). I am, I exist; p. *eiad*.

Aiaâ, *an*. being, any *an*. object; pl. *aiaag*.—*Kitchi aiaa*, a great, large, big being, (used both of persons and animals.) *Kitchi aiaag*, grown persons; also, great noble folks.

Aiaans, young being, (human or other being, or *an*. obj.); pl. *aiaansag*.

Aiaawish, bad wicked being; pl.-*ag*.

Aiaâ. This word is also used when one endeavors to recollect the name of a person, (or any other *an*. object.) When you ask an Indian: *Awenen ga-ikitod iw?* Who said that? —If he does not remember immediately the name of the person who said it, he will say: *Aiaa sa gi-ikito, aiaa....* (In order to gain time to recollect the name.)

Aiâbe. The male of animals, (quadrupeds,) not of birds; pl.-*g.*

Aiabêwaiân. The skin of a male quadruped; pl.-*ag.*

Aiabêwegin. Skin of a male quadruped of the largest kind, as moose, buffalo, etc.; pl.-*on.*

Aiabisiwinged. Consolator, consoling, comforting person; pl.-*jig.*

Aiâbita, half each.—*Aiabita ki gad -aiamin iw, nidji;* my friend, we shall have each half of that.

Aiabitawisid. A half-breed man or woman; pl.-*jig.*

Aiâdjimigowis, (*nind*). S. *Wawnidaganes.*

Aiâgonwetang. Gainsayer, incredulous person, disobedient person; pl.-*jig.*

Aiâjagonesse, (*nind*). I stagger, in walking; p. *eiaj..sed.*

Aiâjawendam, (*nind*). I change my mind often, I am inconstant; p. *eiaj..ang.*

Aiajawendamowin. Changing of mind, of thoughts, inconstancy.

Aiajeiendam, (*nind*). I regret; p. *eiaj..ang.*

Aiajikwe, (*nind*). I cry loud; p, *aiaiajikwed.*

Aiâjigidaami, (*nind*). S. *lajashagaami.*

Aiajindendimin, (*nind*). We debate, dispute, quarrel with each other; p. *eiaj..didjig.*

Aiâjindendiwin. Disputé, contention.

Aiâkosid. Sick person, patient; pl.-*jig.*

Aiâmagad. There is, it is; p. *eiamagak.*

Aiân, (*nind*). I have it; p. *eiad.*

Aiandj. The change of *Andj.*

Aiangwamendam, (*nind*). I endeavor; I pay attention; p. *eian..ang.*

Aiangwamendan, (*nind*). I direct my care and attention to it; *eian..ang.*

Aiangwamenima, (*nind*). I recommend him s. th. in thoughts; p. *eian..mad.*

Aiangwamenindis, (*nind*). I recommend it to myself; p. *eian..sod.*

Aiangwamige, (*nind*). I exhort, recommend; p. *eian..ged.*

Aiangwamima, (*nind*). I recommend him to do s. th., or to behave in a certain manner; p. *eia..mad.*

Aiangwaminan, (*nind*). I take well care of it, I pay attention to it; p. *eian..ang.*

Aiangwamis, (*nind*). I take care, I endeavor; p. *aian..sid.*

Aiangwamitagos, (*nind*). I am heard recommending s, th., I recommend, exhort; p. *eian.. sid.*

Aiangwamitagosiwin. Recommendation, exhortation.

Aianibesse, (*nind*). I lean now on one side and then on the other; p. *eia..sed.*

Aianibesse, or-*magad.* It is leaning or rolling from one sîde to the other, (a canoe, boat, etc.) p. *eian..seg,* or-*magak.*

Aianikanotaged. One who repeats the speaking of another, an interpreter, (man or woman;) pl.-*jig.*
Aianike. S. *Anike.*
Aianike-anamie-dibâdjimowin. Ancient religious tradition, tradition of the Christian Church; pl.-*an.*
Aianike-dibâdjimowin. Tradition, (ancient and repeated saying;) pl.-*an.*
Aianimitagos, (*nin*). I make a speech or harangue of some length; p. *aiai..sid.*
Aiânimitagosiwin. Speech or harangue of some length; pl.-*an.*
Aiano. The change of *Ano*–.
Aianwenindisod. A repenting person, a penitent; pl.-*jig.*
Aianwenindisossig. An unrepenting person, impenitent, hardened sinner; pl.-*og.*
Aiapi, adv. From time to time; from distance to distance.
Aiasswapidon, (*nind*). Freq. I gird it often; p. *eias..dod.*
Aiasswapina, (*nind*). Freq. I gird him often; p. *eias..nad.* imp. *aiâ..pij.*
Aiâwa (*nind*). I have him, I have or got some *an.* obj.; also, I scold him, reprimand him, upbraid him; p. *eiawad.*
Aiawetagos, (*nind*). I make myself understood a little, some words; I am understood only a few words; p. *eiawetagosid.*
Aiawetawa, (*nind*). I understand him a little, some words, (he speaks a strange language;) p. *eia..wad.*
Aiawigon, (*nind*). It scolds me, upbraids me; p. *eiawigod.*—*Nin kitchi aiawigon ki masinaigan;* thy letter scolds me much.
Aiawiidimin, (*nind*). We scold one another, we reprimand each other; p. *eia..didjig.*
Aiawiidiwin. Scolding, reprimanding. (of several persons.)
Aiâwin. Existence; *mino aiâwin,* comfortable existence, welfare; *kagige mino aiâwin,* eternal welfare. *Matchi aiâwin,* miserable existence, misery, *kagige matchi aiawin,* eternal misery.
Aiâwin. Scolding, reprimand.
Aiâwiwe, (*nind*). I am scolding, reprimanding; p. *eia..wed.*
Aidimin, (*nind*). S. *Idimin.*
Aiêkogade, (*nind*). I am tired in my legs; p. *eiek..deg.*
Aiekoidis, (*nind*). I tire myself, I cause to myself fatigue; p. *eie..sod.*
Aiekonike, (*nind*). I feel tired in my arm or arms; p. *eie..ked.*
Aiekonikewina, (*nind*). I tire his arm or arms; p. *eie..nad.*
Aiekonikewinigon, (*nind*). It tires my arm or arms; p. *eie..god.*
Aiekonindji, (*nind*). I feel fatigue in my hand or hands p. *eie..id.*
Aiekos, (*nind*). I am tired, fatigued p. *eiekosid.*
Aiekosia, (*nind*). I tire him; I molest him; p. *eie..ad.*
Aiêkositon, (*nind*). I tire it; p. *eie..tod.*—*Nind aiekositon niiaw anokiiân;* I tire my body, myself,) working.
Aiekosiwin. Fatigue, weariness.

Aiaekwanam, (*nind*). I breathe with difficulty; p. *eiek..mod.*

Aiekwia, (*nind*). I molest him, fatigue him; p. *eie..ad.*

Aiekwiwi, (*nind*). I am tired of carrying or packing on my back; p. *eie..wid.*

Aii. Thing, any *in.* object; pl. *aiin.–Anotch aiin*, sundry things.

Aiins. Little thing; pl.-*an.*

Aiiwish, bad contemptible thing; pl.-*an.*

Aii. This word is also employed as a help to recollect the name of some *inanimate* obj. So when you ask: *Wegonen iw?* What is that ?–the person asked (if he does not immediately recollect the name of the thing,) will say: *Aii sa....* (This gives him some seconds of time to recollect the name of the object.) –When one wants to gain time to recollect the name of a *place*, he will say: *Aiing sa....*

Ainabingwam, (*nind*). I sleep with open eyes; *ein..ang.*

Ainadjindis, (*nind*). S. *Inadjindis.*

Ainawa, (*nind*). I ape or imitate him; [F. je le contrefait;] p. *einawad.*

Aindapidon, (*nind*). I bind it well; p. *ein..dod.*

Aindapina, (*nind*). I bind him well; p. *ein..nad.*

Aindina, (*nind*). I hold him well; p. *eindinad.*

Aindinan, (*nind*). I hold it well; p. *ein..ang.*

Aindjissitchigade, or –*magad.* It is put firmly; level; it is established; p. *ein..teg*, or –*magak.*

Aindjissiton, (*nind*). I settle it, I establish it, I confirm it, conclude it, consolidate it, I put it level, right p. *ein..tod.*

Aininamawa, (*nind*). I beckon him, wink him; p. *ein..wad.*

Aininike, (*nind*). I beckon with my hand, (arm;) I wink; p. *ein..ked.*

Aiodjigade, or-*magad.* It is used, made use of; p. *eio..deg*, or-*magak.*

Aiodjige, (*nind*). I make use; p. *eio..ged.*

Aion, (*nind*). I make use of it, I use it; p. *eiod.*

Aiowin. The use of s. th., using.

Aiowin. Any thing used or employed; pl.-*an.*

Aiowin. Any obj. used or employed; pl.-*ag.*

Ajâgamissin. It spoils, corrupts, it is corrupted, (liquid);) p. *eja..sing.*

Ajageshi. Crab, crawfish; pl. -*iag.*

Ajagidikwen, (*nind*). I throw my head backwards; p. *aiaj..nid.*

Ajaok, adv. Back and forwards, from one side to the other, from one to the other.—*Ajaok ijawog*, they go back and forwards, from one side to the other; they come and go.

Ajâssin. S. *Ajiwassin. Ajiiabikissin.*

Ajaw, ajawi. In compositions, signifies *crossing* or *traversing* to the opposite side or shore of a river, bay, lake. It alludes also to the other side or opposite side of anything.

(Examples in some of the following words.)

Ajawa, (*nind*). I cross a river, bay, etc., in a canoe, boat, etc.; p. *aiajawaod.*

Ajawaa, (*nind*). I cross him or convey him in a canoe or boat over a river, etc.; p. *aia..ad.*

Ajawaam, (*nind*). S. *Ajawa.*

Ajawaan, (*nind*). I cross or convey it in a canoe, etc., (over a river etc.;) p. *aia..ang.*

Ajawadaga, (*nind*). I cross a river etc., swimming, I swim to the opposite shore; p. *aiaj..gad.*

Ajawâdagak, (*nind*) or, *nind ajawagak.* I cross on the ice a lake, a river, etc.; p. *aiaj..kod.*

Ajawagâm, adv. On the other side of a river, lake, etc.; on the opposite shore.

Ajawagameosse, (*nind*). I wade through a river to the opposite shore; p. *aiaj..sed.*

Ajawaii, adv. Behind.

Ajawakamig, adv. On the opposite side of the earth.

Ajawandawe, (*nind*). I cross or pass over a river on a tree or log; p. *aîaj..wed.*

Ajawaodjigade, or-*magad.* It is carried or conveyed across a river. etc., in a canoe or boat; p. *aiaj..deg*, or-*magak.*

Bi-ajawaodjigade. It is brought over from the opposite shore in a canoe or boat.

Ajawaodjigan. Flat-bottomed ferry-boat; pl.-*an.*

Ajawaodjigas, (*nind*). I am carried or conveyed across a river, etc., in a canoe or boat; p. *aiaj...sod.*

Ajawaodjige, (*nind*). I cross or convey people over a river, etc., in a boat, etc.; p. *aiaj..ged.*

Ajawaodjigewinini. Ferryman; [F. traversier;] pl.-*wag.*

Ajawaodon, (*nind*). I convey or carry it across a river, lake, etc., in a canoe, boat, etc.; p. *aiaj..dod.*

Nin bi-âjawaodon. I bring it to the shore, to this side of a river, lake, etc., in a canoe, etc.

Ajawaôna, (*nind*). S. *Ajawaa.*

Ajawaonigos, (*nind*). I get myself crossed over a river, bay, etc., I employ somebody to take me over; p. *aiaj..sid.*

Ajawaosowagon. Ajawaodjigan.

Ajawash, (*nind*). I cross sailing, I sail across a river, bay, etc.; p. *aiajawashid.*

Ajawémij. Beach-tree; pl.-*ig.*

Ajawémin. Beach-nut; pl.-*an.*

Ajaweshk. Sword; pl.-*on*

Ajaweshkons, dim. dagger; pl.-*an.*

Ajawew, adv. On the other side of a point, or behind a point, (in a lake.)

Ajawïgamig, adv. The space or interval between two houses or lodges.

Ajâwigâd. The other leg, the leg on the other side.)—There is always a possessive pronoun before this word; as: *Nind ajawigâd*, my other leg; *kid ajawigâd*, thy other leg, etc.

Ajawi-gwashkwan, (*nind*) I jump or leap to the opposite side of s. th.; p. *aiaj..nid.*

Ajawiiâssin nâbikwân. The ves-

sel tacks about; p. *aiaj..ing.*
Ajawinik. The other arm.—This and the two following words are always preceded by a possessive pronoun.
Ajawinindj. The other hand.
Ajawisid. The other foot, (the opposite foot.)
Ajawi-siginân, (*nind*). I pour it in another vessel; p. *aiaj..ang.*
Ajawi-wâbang, adv. The day after to-morrow.—The same as: *awasswâbang.*
Aje, or *waje,* at the end of verbs, alludes to the *human skin;* as: *Nin makatewaje,* I have a black skin. *Nin gijibaje,* I feel itchings on my skin; etc.
Ajé, in composition, signifies *going back* or *backwards;* [F. à reculons.] (Examples in some of the following words.)
Ajéb, (*nind*). I move backwards, sitting; p. *ejebid.*
Ajébato, (*nind*). I run backwards; p. *ejebatod.*
Ajebidon, (*nind*). I move it backwards; p. *ej..dod.*
Ajebina, (*nind*) I move him backwards, (any *an* obj.); p. *ej..nad; imp. ajebij.*
Ajebinan, (*nind*). S. *Ajebidon.*
Ajeboian. Oar; [F. rame;] pl.-*an.*
Ajeboianak, pl.-*on.* S. *Ajeboian.*
Ajeboianeiâb. Oar—strap; pl.-*in.*
Ajéboie, (*nind*). I row in a canoe or boat; p. *ejeboied.*
Ajédibaamawa, (*nind*). I pay him back; also I avenge on him a bad doing, I render him evil for evil; p. *aiaj..wad.*
Ajebibaan, (*nind*). I pay it back; I avenge it; p. *aiaj..ang.*
Ajégabaw, (*nind*). I step back; p. *ej..wid.*
Ajégandina, (*nind*). I thrust or push him back; p. *ej..nad;* imp. *ajegandin.*
Ajêgandinan, (*nind*). I thrust or push it back; p. *ej..ang.*
Ajêgiwe, (*nind.* I go back again, I return; [F. je retourne sur mes pas;] p. *ejegiwed.*
Ajéiâdjim, (*nind*). I repeat old sayings, old news, etc.; p. *ej..mod.*
Ajêiâdjimowin. Repeating old sayings, old traditions; pl.-*an.*
Ajéiash, (*nind*). I am driven backwards or back again by the wind; p. *ej..wid.*
Ajêiâssin. It is driven backwards or back again by the wind; p. *ej..sing.*
Ajêna, (*nind*). I give back again some *an.* obj., I return it; p. *ejenad.*
Ajénamawa, (*nind*). I give him back s. th., I return it to him; p. *ej..wad.*
Ajénan, (*nind*). I give it back again, I return it; p. *ejenang.*
Ajéosse, (*nind*). I walk backwards; [F. je marche à reculons;] p. *ejeossed.*
Ajésse, (*nind*). I slide back; I relax; I relapse; p. *ejessed.*
Ajesse, or-*magad.* It slides or goes back or backwards; p. *ejesseg,* or-*magak.*
Ajesséwin. Backsliding; relaxation; relapse.
Ajeta, (*nind*). I move backwards, draw back; p. *ejetad.*

Ajétakoki, (*nind*). I make a step backwards; p. *ej..kid.*
Ajétan, (*nind*). I draw back from it; p. *ejetang.*
Ajetawa, (*nind*). I withdraw from him, I draw back from him; p. *ej..wad.*
Ajewidon, (*nind*). I lead or convey it back; p. *ajewidod.*
Ajewina, (*nind*). I lead or convey him back; p. *ej..nad.*
Aji, adv. *Ot.* S. *Jaigwa.*
Ajibik. Rock, cliff; pl.-*on.*
Ajibikoka. It is rocky, there are rocks; p. *aiaj..kag.*
Ajida, adv. of new; in revenge.
Ajida-bimadis, (*nind*). I live of new, I live another life; p. *aiaj..sid.*
Ajida-bimadisiwin. Another life (in another world.)
Ajida-dodamowin. Revenge, vengeance.
Ajidawaa, (*nind*). I repay him (evil for evil,) I revenge myself on him; p. *aiaj..ad.*
Ajidawaawin. Vengeance, revenge.
Ajidawaige, (*nind*). I take revenge; p. *aiaj..ged.*
Ajidawama, (*nind*). I revenge myself on him in *words*; p. *aiaj..mad.*
Ajidawiwin. S. *Ajidawaâwin.*
Ajideendam, (*nind*) or *nind ajideenindam.* I contradict or gainsay in thoughts; p. *aiag..dang.*
Ajideia, (*nind*). S. *Ajidekawa.*
Ajidéiâtig. Cross; pl.-*og.* *
Ajidekawa, (*nind*). I miss him (in the road,) I don't meet him, he comes one way and I go another; p. *aiaj..wad.*
Ajidekoneshi. Cross-bill, cross-beak, (bird;) pl.-*iag.*
Ajidema, (*nind*). I gainsay him, I give him cross disrespectful answers; p. *aiaj..mad.*
Ajidena, (*nind*). I withstand him around the body, in wrestling; p. *aiaj..nad.*
Ajidenge, (*nind*). I gainsay, I give bad answers; p. *aia..ged.*
Ajidengeshk, (*nind*). I use to give bad answers, to gainsay; p. *aia..kid.*
Ajidenikeb, (*nind*). I am sitting with crossed arms; p. *aiaj..bid.*
Ajidenima, (*nind*). I contradict him in thoughts; I don't care for him; p. *aiaj..mad.*
Ajidesse, or-*magad.* It crosses or intersects, (a line or road intersecting another;) p. *aiaj..seg*, or-*magak.*
Ajidewa, (*nind*). I miss him, (traveling by water, in a canoe, boat, etc.) he comes one way and I go another; p. *aiaj..wad*; imp. *ajidé.*
Ajidewe, (*nind*). I gainsay, give bad answers; p. *aia..wed.*
Ajidewîdam, (*nind*). I gainsay, contradict, dispute; I give disrespectful answers; p. *aiaj.ang.*
Ajidewidamowin. Gainsaying, disrespectful answer; pl.-*an.*
Ajigan. Foot-rag, (nippe); sock, stocking; pl.-*an.*
Ajigané, or-*magad.* There is half or part of something; p. *ej..neg*, or-*magak.*
Ajiganeaii, adv. Half or part of...

* It is the expression used for the Cross of our Lord. The wood made in the shape of a cross.

Ajiganékamig aki, one half or part of the earth.
Ajiganike, (*nind*). I knit socks or stockings; p. *ej..ked.*
Ajigidabikinan pâshkisigan, (*nind*). I cock a gun; p. *aiaj..ang.*
Ajigidinan,, (*nind*). I turn it over, (a dish, a plate, etc.) p. *aia..ang.*
Ajigidji-pangishin, (*nind*). S. *Ajigidjisse.*
Ajigidji-pangissin. S. *Ajigidjissemagad.*
Ajigidjisse, (*nind*). I fall backwards, I fall on my back; p. *aiaj..sed.*
Ajigidjisse, or-*magad*. It falls backwards; p. *aiaj..seg*, or-*magak.*
Ajigwa, adv. S. *Jaigwa.*
Ajiiâbikissin. It is dull, blunt, it does not cut well, (steel-tool;) p. *ej..sing.*
Ajishki. Mud, mire, dirt.
Ajishkiwamika, or-*magad*. It is miry at the bottom, (a river, etc.) p. *ej..kag*, or-*magak.*
Ajishkiwika, or-*magad*. It is muddy, miry; p. *eg..kag*, or-*magak.*
Ajiwa, or-*magad*. It is dull, blunt, it does not cut; p. *ejiwag*, or-*magak.*
Ajiwassin. S. *Ajiiabikissin.*
Ajiwi, adv. *Ot*. S. *Iwidi.*
Ajodenima, (*nind*). I unite with him; p. *ej..mad.*
Ajogan. Bridge; wharf; pl.-*an.*
Ajoganikade, or-*magad*. There is a bridge made; a wharf; p. *aiaj..deg*, or-*magak.*
Ajoganike, (*nind*). I make a bridge; a wharf; p. *aiaj..ked.*
Ajoge, (*nind*). I cross a river walking on a bridge, I walk over a bridge; p. *aiajoged.*
Ajogêiandawe, (*nind*). S. *Ajawandawe.*
Ajonda, adv. *Ot*. S. *Oma.*
Ak, as end-syllable of substantives, signifies *handle*, or a *piece of wood* for a certain use; as: *Tchigataiganak*, broom-stick, (*tchigataigan*, broom.) *Anitiiak*, handle of a spear, (*anit*, spear.) *Wâkaiganak*, a log for a house, *wâkaigan*, house.) — Instead of *ak*, they sometimes use *âtig*. S. *Âtig.*
Aka? adv. Where?
Akakanakide, or-*magad*. It burns to coal, it is burnt to coal, it is carbonized; p. *ek..deg*, or-*magak.*
Akakanakis, (*nind*). I burn to coal, entirely; p. *ek..sod.*
Akakanakisan, (*nind*). I burn it to coal; p. *ek.. sang.*
Akakanakiswa, (*nind*). I burn some *an*. obj. to coal; p. *ek..wad*; imp. *ak..swi.*
Akakanate, or-*magad*. It is converted into coal; p. *ek..teg*, or-*magak.*
Akakanje. Coal, charcoal; also, red-hot coals.
Akakanjebwe, (*nind*). I am roasting s. th. on red-hot coals; p. *ek..wed.*
Akakanjebwen, (*nind*). I roast it on red-hot coals; p. *ek..wed.*
Akakanjebwenan, (*nind*). I roast some *an*. obj. on red-hot coals; p. *ek..wed*. (V. Conj.)
Akakanjeka, or-*magad*. There are coals; there are red-hot coals p. *ek..kag*, or-*magak.*
Akakanjekan. Place where

they burn (or make) charcoal; pl.-*an*.

Akakanjeke, (*nind*). I make (burn) charcoal; p. *ek..ked*.

Akakanjekewin. Charcoal-man's trade and business.

Akakanjekewinini. Charcoal-man; pl.-*wag*.

Akakanjewan. S. *Akakanjeka*.

Akakanjéwassin, or *akakanjêwaki*. Coal, pit-coal; [F. charbon de terre, houille.]

Akakanjewassinik, or-*magad*. There is a pit-coal, there is a pit-coal mine; p. *ek..kag*, or-*magak*.

Akakanjéwassinikan. Pit-coal mine.

Akakanjéwassinikéwinini. A miner in a pit-coal mine; pl.-*wag*.

Akakanjewigamig. Coal-house; pl.-*on*.

Akakwidjish. Fisher, (animal;) pl.-*ag*.

Akakwitoshimag, (*nind*). S. *Agwitoshimag*.

Akakwitoshinog. S. *Awitoshinog*.

Akakwitossidonan, (*nind*). S. *Agwitossidonan*.

Akakwitossinon. S. *Agwitossinon*.

Akamawa (*nind*). I lurk, I lie in wait for him, in ambush; p. *ek..wad*.

Akamawewin. Lurking.

Akamigis, (*nind*). *Alg*. S. *Ondamis*, or *Ondamita*.

Akandamo. A kind of big root growing in the water; pl.-*g*.

Akando, (*nind*). I watch; I lurk, I lie in ambush; p. *ekandod*.

Akândowigamig. Watch-house, guard-house; pl.-*on*.

Akandowin. Watching; lying in ambush.

Akandowinini, watchman, sentinel; pl.-*wag*.

Akawâb, (*nind*). I look out, I wait for...; p *ek..bid*.

Akawâbama, (*nind*). I look out for him, I expect him; p. *ek..mad*.

Akawâbandan, (*nind*). I look out for it, I expect it; p. *ek..ang*.

Akâwanj. Low thick underbush of the fir-kind; [C. Buis;] pl.-*ig*.

Akâwanjika, or-*magad*. There is underbush of the fir-kind, (somewhere in the woods;) p. *ek..kag*, or-*mayak*.

Akawishkawa, (*nind*). I am the first after him; p. *ek..wad*.

Aki. Earth, the globe, the world; country; farm; soil, ground.

Aking, on earth. *Akikang*, in the earth, in the ground.

Aki gi-moshkaang, deluge.

Akik. Kettle; pl.-*og*. Probably derived from *aki*, as the ancient Aborigines made their kettles of earth.—*Akikons*, a small kettle. *Akikosh*, a bad old kettle.

Akikodjiwan. There is a violent and dangerous whirlpool; p. *ek..wang*.

Akikoke, (*nind*). I make kettles; p. *ek..ked*.

Akikokewin. Brazier's trade and occupation, kettle manufactory.

Akikokewinini. Brazier, kettle manufacturer; pl.-*wag*.

Akinikwan. White dust on the head.
Akiw, (*nind*). I am earth; p. *ekiwid.*
Akiwan. It is earth, there is earth; p. *ekiwang.*
Akiwesi. Old man; pl.-*iag.*
Akiwesiiw, (*nind*). I am an old man; p. *ek..wid.*
Akiwigamig. Earth-house, habitation under ground; also, root-house; pl.-*on.*
Ako, (in the change *eko.*) This word is never used alone; it is always prefixed to a verb, and signifies, *as long as, since, ago.*—*Ged-akobimâdisiiân,* as long as I shall live. *Eko- dagwishineg,* since your arrival.
Akobimwan. S. *Wâkaigan.*
Akôgib, the name of a lake in Upper Michigan. *Akôgibing,* at, in, from or to that lake.
Akôkobinagan. Ot. A platted vessel, basket; pl.-*an.*
Akôkobinaganike, (*nind*). I plat or make a basket or baskets; p. *ek..ked.*
Akôkomidâss. Stocking; pl.-*an.* —*Akôko* alludes to platting; *midass* signifies a legging.
Akôkomidassike, (*nind*). I knit stockings; p. *ek..ked.*
Akôkomidassikewin. Knitting; [F. tricotage.]
Akôs, (*nind*). I am of a certain height, so tall; p. *eko..sid.*—*Ekosiian nind ukos,* I am as tall as thou. *Ekosiiân akôsi,* he is as tall as I.
Akos, (*nind*). I am sick, infirm; p. *aiakosid.*
Akoshkade, (*nind*). I have pain in the bowels, colic; p. *aiak.. ded.*
Akoshkadewin. Pain in the bowels, colic.
Akoshkagon, (*nind*). It comes hard upon me, it is heavy to me, it tires me, molests me; p. *ek..god.*
Akoshkawa, (*nind*). I tire him, (he carrying me;) I molest him; p. *aiak..wad.*
Akoshkos, (*nind*). I am tired, (carrying a load or pack;) p. *aiak..sod.*
Akosishk, (*nind*). I am sickly, always sick; p. *aia..kid.*
Akosikas, (*nind*). I feign to be sick, I dissemble sickness; p. *aia..sod.*
Akosin, (*nind*). I have pain (in some part of my body;) p. *aiakosid. Nishtigwân nind âkosin,* I have headache, (pain in my head.) *Nibidan nind âkosinan,* I have toothache, (pain in my teeth.)
Akosinagos, (*nind*). I look sick, I have a sickly appearance; p. *aia..sid.*
Akosinagosiwin, sickly appearance.
Akosinan, (*nind*). I have pain (in some part of my body;) p. *aiakosid.* [V. Conj.] *Nin totoshim nind akosinan,* I have pain in my breast, (on one side,) [a female speaking.] *Nin totoshimag nind akosinag,* I have pain in my breast, (on both sides.)
Akosiwigamig. Hospital, infirmary; pl.-*on.*
Akosiwin. The height of a person, his stature.—*Mi mandan nind âkosiwin,* this is my height, my stature.

Akosiwin. Sickness, infirmity, disease; pl.*-an.*
Akosiwin nin bidon, or *âkosiwin nin bi-migiwe,* I infect a place, I bring a sickness to a place.
Akossin. It is of a certain length; p. *ekossing.—Pagwana nin kikendân iw nagamon ekossing,* I know by heart that whole hymn, (as long as it is.)
Akotewagis, (*nind*). I am well armed and dangerous; p. *aia.. sid.*
Akwâ, or*-magad.* It is of such a length; p. *ekwag,* or*-magak.* —*Mi ekwag nin wâkaigan; nawatch na akwâ endaian?* My house is so long; is thine longer?
Akwab, (*nind*). I can see from such a distance; p. *ekwabid. Besho nind akwab,* I can see (only) from a short distance, I am shortsighted, myope. *Wassa nind akwab,* I can see from a great distance, from far, I am far-sighted, long-sighted.
Akwanam, (*nind*). I breathe with fatigue, I can hardly breathe, (a sick person); p. *ek..mod.*
Akwândawagan. Ladder; stairs, staircase; pl.*-an.*
Akwandawe, (*nind*). I ascend a ladder or staircase, I go up stairs, I climb up, (on a tree, etc.); p. *ek..wed.*
Akwandawêbato, (*nind*). I ascend a ladder or staircase running. I run up stairs; p. *ek.. tod.*
Akwawa, (*nind*) (pron. *nind akowa.*) I am fishing with a spear, (on the ice); I am spearing fish; p. *ekwawad,* (pron. *ekowad.*)
Akwe. Akwew.Akwessens. Akwesensiw; (*Ot.*) S. *Ikwe. Ikwew. Ikwesens. Ikwesensiw.*
Akwendamaganama, (*nind*). I hurt him by striking; p. *aiak.. mad.*
Akwendamia, (*nind*). I hurt him, I cause him pain in some part of the body; p. *aiâ..ad.*
Akwendamoiwe, (*nind*). I hurt, p. *aia..wed.*
Akwiwi, (*nind*). I am tired, (from *working;*) I am exhausted; p. *ekwiwid.*
Amadadém, (*nind*). I weep awaking; p. *em..mod.*
Amâdina, (*nind*). I awake him, I wake him up, I rouse him from sleep; p. *em..nad.*
Amadjia, (*nind*). S. *Amadina.*
Amadjibina, (*nind*). I wake him up by pulling or pushing him; p. *em..nad*
Amadjisse, (*nind*). I awake; p. *em..sed.*
Amadjiwe, (*nind*) I ascend a mountain, I go up on a mountain; p. *aiam..wed.*
Amadjiwébato, (*nind*). I run up on a mountain; p. *aiam.. tod.*
Amadjiwebina, (*nind*). I awake him briskly, I rouse him up; p. *aiam..nad.*
Amadjiwenige, (*nind*). I go up on a mountain, or hill, carrying s. th. on my shoulder; p. *aiam..ged.*
Amadjiwewane, (*nind*). I go up on a hill or mountain, carrying a pack on my back; p. *aiam..ned.*

Amadwewewa, (*nind*). I awake him by making noise; p. *em..wad*; imp. *amadwewew*.

Amanâssimo animosh. The dog is rutting; p. *aia..mod*.

Amaniss, (*nind*). I am alarmed, frightened, by s. th. I heard; p. *emanissod*.

Amanissowin. Alarm, fright.

Amanôso awessi. The animal is rutting; p. *aiam..sod*.

Amasika, (*nind*). I awake; p. *emasikad*.

Amawa, (*nind*). I frighten him, or I frighten an animal, [F. je l'effarouche;] p. *aiamawad*.

Ambé ! ambessa ! ambessano ! ambessino ! interj. well! come! come on!

Amidegamide, or-*magad*. It overflows boiling; p. *aiam..deg*, or-*magak*.

Amidegamiso akik. The kettle overflows, (what is boiling in it overflows;) p. *aiam..sod*.

Ami gigô. The fish is spawning; p. *emid*.

Amik. Beaver; pl.-*wag*. *Amikons*, young beaver; pl.-*ag*.

Amikobiwai, *an*. Beaver fur; pl.-*ag*.

Amikogan. Beaver's bone; pl.-*an*.

Amikogenda. Beaver-Island, in Lake Michigan.

Amikoshib. Beaver-duck, (a kind of wild duck;) pl.-*ag*.

Amikosow. Beaver's tail; also *amikwano*.

Amikwagis, (*nind*). I live like a beaver; p. *em..sid*.

Amikwaj. Hole (not lodge) of a beaver; pl.-*an*.

Amikwândag, *an*. Small white tamarack tree; [C. épinette blanche;] pl.-*og*.

Amikwish. Beaver's lodge; pl.-*an*.

Amo. Bee; wasp; humble-bee; pl.-*âmog*.

Amô-bimide. Wax.

Amo-bimide-wâssakwanendjigan Wax-candle, wax-taper; pl.-*an*.

Amo - bimide - wassakwanendjigans. Thin wax-taper; [F. bougie filée.)

Amôg, (*nind*). I am cancerous, I have a cancer; p. *emogod*.

Amô-sisibâkwad. Honey.

Amwa, (*nind*). I eat some *an*. obj.; p. *emwad*; imp. *amwi*.

Anâ, (*nind*). I have s. th. sticking in my throat, (a bone, a fish-bone, etc.); 3. p.—*anaô*; p. *enâod*.

Anâganashk. Fern.

Anak. A small gray bird; pl.-*og*.

Anak, adv. At all events, however it turns out; [F. en tout cas.]

Anâkan. Mat, floor-mat; [F. natte;] pl.-*an*.

Anâkanashk. Rush for mats, (floor-mats;) pl.-*on*.

Anâkaneiâb. A little cord used in platting mats; pl.-*in*.

Anâkanike, (*nind*). I am making a mat; p. *en..ked*.

Anâkona, *an*. Sea-bread, biscuit; pl.-*g*.

Anâkonans. Crackers; pl.-*ag*.

Anakwad. Cloud; pl.-*on*.

Anakwad. It is cloudy; p. *aianakwak*.

Anâm, *anami*. In compositions, signifies *under*, *underneath*, *beneath.* (Examples in some of the following words.)

Anâmadopowin, adv. Under the table.

Anâmaii, adv. Under, beneath, underneath.

Anamâjibik, adv. Under the rock, or under a rock.

Anâmakamig. Hell, abode of the devils.

Anâmakamig, adv. Under ground.

Anâmaking, adv. Under the surface of the earth, under ground.

Anâmendan, (*nind*). I have suspicious thoughts towards s. th., I suspect or accuse it in my *thoughts* of some fault or defect; p. *en..ang.*

Anamenima, (*nind*). I suspect or accuse him in my *thoughts* of some fault, I have suspicious thoughts against him; p. *en..mad.*

Anamêssikage, (*nind*). I say mass for somebody; or better: *Lamessikage,* and so on for the root: *Lamess,* instead of *Anamess;* p. *en..ged.*

Anamêssikan. S. *Anamessike-adopowin.*

Anamessikas, (*nind*). I say mass for myself; p. *en..sod.*

Anamessikawa, (*nind*). I say mass for him; p. *en..wad.*

Anaméssike, (*nind*). I say mass; p. *en..ked.*

Anamessike adôpowin. Altar; pl.-*an.*

Anamessike-adopowinigin. Altar-cloth; pl.-*on.*

Anamessike-agwiwin. Mass-vestment, especially the chasuble; pl.-*an.*

Anamessike-masinaigan. Missal, mass-book; pl.-*an.*

Anamessikewin. Mass; pl.-*an.*

Anamessikewinagad. Mass is being said, the time of mass; p. *en..gak.*

Anamia, (*nind*). I pray; I am a Christian; p. *enamiad.* *

Anâmibagan, adv. Under the bed.

Anâmibing, adv. In the water, under the surface of the water.

Anâmide, adv. In the bottom of the heart.

Anamiê-bimossémin, (*nind*) pl. We walk in procession; p. *en..sedjig.*

Anamiê-bimosséwin. Religious procession.

Anamiê-gagikwewin. Religious sermon, preaching.

Anamégijigad. Sunday, sabbath; pl.-*on.*

Anamêgijigad. It is Sunday; p. *en..gak. Dassing enamiegijigakin,* every Sunday.

Anamiêkas, (*nind*). I am an hypocrite, feigning or dissembling religion and piety; p. *en..sod.*

Anamiêkasowin. Hypocrisy.

Anamiê-kikinawadjion. Church-banner; pl.-*an.*

Anamiê-masinaigan. Prayer-book; pl.-*an.*

Anamiêminag, *an.* pl. Rosary, beads.

Anamieminag nind agimag. I say the rosary.

Anamiêminike, (*nind*). I am making a rosary; p. *en..ked.*

---

* The root *anami* signifies every thing which belongs to religion, divine worship, etc.

Anamié-minikwâdjigan. Chalice; pl.-*an.*

Anamie-nagamon, (or *nagamowin*). Religious song, hymn; pl.-*an.*

Anamié - nanagatawendamowin. Religious meditation; pl.-*an.*

Anamié-nibawiwin. Christian marriage, Sacrament of Matrimony, or. *anamie-witikendiwin.*

Anamié-nominidiwin. Extreme-Onction.

Anamié-pagidinigan. Religious offering; church-tithes; pl.-*an.*

Anamié-pagidinige, (*nind*). I perform a religious offering; also, I pay my church-duty, or tithes, due to the church and the clergy; p. *en..ged.*

Anamie-pagidinigewin. Religious offering, the act of offering or giving in religious respect; the paying of church-tithes.

Anamié-sigaandâdiwin. Anamié-sigaandâge, etc. S. *Sigaandadiwin. Sigaandage,* etc.

Anamiétamawa, (*nind*). I pray for him; I bless him; p. *en.. wad.*

Anamiétân, (*nind*). I bless it; p. *en..tang.*

Anamiétawa, (*nind*). I pray for him, I bless him, (any *an.* obj.); also, I adore him; p. *en-wad.*

Anamiêwâbo. Holy water, blessed water.

Anamiéwâtig, an. Cross; pl.-*og. Anamiéwâtigons,* a small cross; pl.-*ag.* This word would suit better to say the holy Cross than, *tchipaiâytik* or, *asiteiâtik,* but the use of the latter have prevailed.

Anamié-widige, (*nind*). I am married according to the rules of the Church; p. *en..ged.*

Anamié - widigendiwin. Christian marriage, according to the rules and rites of the Church.

Anamié-widokawa, (*nind*). I keep society or company with him in religious respect;.p. *en..wad.*

Anamié-widokodadimin, (*nind*). We are in company together in regard to religion, we are in the Communion of Saints; p. *en..didjig.*

Anamié-widokodadiwin. Communion of Saints.

Anamiéwigamig. House of prayer, church, chapel, temple; pl.-*on.*

Anamiéwigamigons. Small church, chapel; pl.-*an.*

Anamiéwin. Prayer; religion; pl.-*an.*

Anamiêwin wendjinanind. A person killed for religion's sake, that is, a Martyr; pl.-*jig.*

Anamikage, (*nind*). I salute; I make my farewell visit; (F. je fais mes adieux;) p. *en..ged.* —*Nakawe nin bi-anamikage, tchi bwa madjaiân;* I come to make my farewell visit, before I start.

Anamikagewin. Compliments, greeting, salutation, *made.*

Anamikâgowin. Compliments, greeting, salutation, *received. Remark.* In the Annunciation of the B. Virgin we see these two salutations, one *made* (by the Angel) and the other *re-*

ceived (by the B. Virgin.) Consequently we have to say: *Anjeni od anamikagewin*, the salutation of the Angel; and: *Kitchitwa Marie od anamikagowin*, the salutation of S. Mary.—The same is the case with great many other words of this description; as: *Dibaamagewin*, and *tibaamagowin*, judgment; etc. (S. Otchipwe Grammar. Formation of Substantives.)

Anamikan, (*nind*). I salute it; p. *en..ang.—Nind anamikan anamiewigamig wâssa onsabandamân;* I salute the church when I see it from far.

Anamikawa, (*nind*). I salute him, I greet him; I give or send him my compliments, my greeting; p. *en..wad.*

Anamikodadimin, (*nind*). We salute each other; p. *en..didjig.*

Anamikôdading. When they salute each other, New year's day.

Anamikodadiwin. Mutual salutation, salutation of several to several persons.

Anâmima, (*nind*). I express in *words* my suspicion against him; I accuse him of s. th.; p. *enâmimad.*

Anâmimakak, adv. Under a barrel, box, chest, etc.

Anâmina, adv. Underneath, inwardly, in the body. — *Keiâbi anamina aiâban ningwiss, api nebonid ossibanin.* My son was yet inwardly, (in my body,) when his father died.

Anâmindan, (*nind*). I express in *words* my suspicion against it; I accuse it of some fault; p. *en..ang.*

Anâmindim, adv. In the water, in the depth.

Anâmindiwin, or *anâmingewin.* Suspicion.

Anâming, adv. Under, beneath.

Anâminge, (*nind*). I have suspicion, I suspect or accuse; p *en..ged.*

Anâmissag, adv. Under a board or under boards; under the floor.

Anâmissag-wânikan. Cellar under the floor of a house.

Anâmônag, adv. Under a canoe or boat.

Anân. Ring or bracelet worn by Indians round the wrist; pl.-*an.*

Anâng. Star; pl.-*og.*

Anangog endaji—ganawabamindwa, observatory, (place where they gaze on the stars.)

Anângoka, or-*magad.* There are stars, it is starry; p. *en..kag*, or-*magak.*

Anangon ijinagwad. It is star-shaped.

Anangon kekenimad. Astronomer; pl.-*jig.*

Anangons. Little star, asterisk; pl.-*ag.*

Anang pangishin, (a star falls,) star-shoot.

Ananidji. Pearl; pl.-*g.*

Anaosse, nind. I bring nothing coming from hunting; p. *âianaossed.*

Anapi? adv. When?

Anawabama, (*nind*). I despair of him. by his appearance, (of a sick person, etc.,); p. *aian..mad.*

Anawabaminagos, (*nind*). I am

despaired of by my appearance; p. *aian..sid.*

Anawabaminagwad. It is despaired of by its appearance; p. *aian..wak.*

Anawabandan, (*nind*). I despair of it as I see it; p. *aian..ang.*

Anawabandjige, (*nind*). S. *Anawendjige.*

Anawendagos, (*nind*). I am of little profit, I am considered unable to do this or that; p. *aia..sid.*

Anawendagwad. It is rejected, not considered useful or serviceable; p. *aia..wak.*

Anawendan, (*nind*). I object against it, I think it is unfit, I find fault with it; p. *aian..ang.*

Anawendjige, (*nind*). I abandon, quit, give up; despair; p. *aian..ged.*

Anawendjigewin. Giving up, discontinuance; despair.

Anawenim, (*nind*). I doubt whether I am able to do it or not; p. *aian..mod.*

Anawenima, (*nind*). I object against him, I think he is not able to do this or that; p. *aia..mad.*

Anawenindis. Anawénindisowin. S. *Awenindis. Anwenindisowin.*

Anawéwis, (*nind*). I can effect nothing, I work or endeavor in vain; p. *aia..sid.*

Anawewisimagad. It does not profit, it yields no profit, no fruit, it fails; p. *aia..gak.*

Anawi, adv. Yet, indeed, however, for all that.

Anamigin kitigân. The field produces no fruit; p. *aian..ing.* S. *Nigin.*

Anawinamawa, (*nind*). I find he does not give me enough, not my full share; ; p. *aia..wad.*

Anwisse, (*nind*). I am getting weaker, worse, (in a sickness or starvation,); p. *aianawissed.*

Anawisse, or-*magad.* It decays, it perishes; p. *aia..seg,* or-*magak.*

Anawitagos, (*nind*). My voice is low, weak, (from hunger, fatigue, sickness;) p. *aia..sid.*

Anawitawa, (*nind*). I find his voice weak, low; p. *aia..wad.*

Anawito, (*nind*). I am unable to walk, (from starvation, etc.); p. *aia..tod.*

And, andj. In compositions, signifies *change, alteration, reiteration.* (Examples in some of the following words.)

Andab, (*nind*). I change seats, I sit down elsewhere; p. *aiandabid.*

Andabide, (*nind*). I am getting other teeth; p. *aia..ded.*

Andaki, (*nind*). I go to live in another country or place, I move to another country or place; p. *aiandakid.*

Andakisine, (*nind*). I put other shoes on, I change shoes, or I put them on in another way; p. *aia..ned.*

Andanam, (*nind*). I breathe otherwise, my respiration changed, (a sick person;) p. *aia..mod.*

Andapidon, (*nind*). I bind or tie it again, or otherwise; p. *aian..dod.*

Andapina, (*nind*). I tie again, or otherwise, some *an.* object; p. *aian..nad.*

Andapis, (*nind*). I girdle myself otherwise; I take another girdle or belt; p. *aian..sod.*

Andawe. It is changing fur, getting new fur, new hair, (an animal;) p. *aiandawed.*

Andek. Crow; pl.-*wag. Andekons*, young crow, pl.-*ag.*

Andi? adv. S. *Tandi?*

Andj, or *minawa andj*, adv. Of new, again, once more, otherwise.

Andjia, (*nind*). I change him, I change some *an.* obj., I make it otherwise; p. *aiandjiad.*

Andjiaiâ, (*nind*). I am changed, I am otherwise than before; p. *aia..iad.*

Andjibian, (*nind*). I write it once more, I transcribe it, I copy it,; also, I write it otherwise, I change it; p. *aia..ang.*

Andjibiigan. Copy, duplicate, transcript ; altered writing; pl.-*an.*

Andjibiige, (*nind*). I copy, I transcribe; I write otherwise; p. *aia..ged.*

Andji-bimâdis, (*nind*). I live or bebave otherwise, I changed my life, my conduct, I turned; p. *aian..sid.*

Andji-bimâdisiwin. Changed life or conduct, conversion.

Andjigade, or-*magad*, or *andjitchigade*, or - *magad.* It is changed, altered, made otherwise; p. *aia..deg*, or-*magak.*

Andjigas, (*nind*) or *nind andjitchigas.* I am changed, altered; p. *aian..sod.*

Andjige, (*nind*). I change a lodge, I make it otherwise or elsewhere; p. *aian..ged.*

Andjijiwebisiwin. Changed behavior.

Andjik, (*nind*). I am with child, I am pregnant; p. *endjikod.*

Andjikwanaie, (*nind*). I change clothes; p. *aian..ied.*

Andjikwanaiewigamig. Change house, or changing house; pl.-*an.*

Andjimik. She-bearer, bearing young ones; pl.-*wag.*

Andjinagos, (*nind*). I appear different, changed; p. *âia..sid.*

Andjinagosia, (*nind*). I give him another appearance, I make him look otherwise; p. *aiad..ad.*

Andjinagosiwin. Changed appearance.

Andjinagwad. It appears different, changed; p. *aian..wak.*

Andjinagwi, (*nind*). I appear changed, I take another appearance; p. *aian..wiod.*

Andjinagwia, (*nind*). I make him appear changed, (a person, or any *an.* obj.); p. *aia..ad.*

Andjinagwiidis, (*nind*). I give to myself another appearance; I transfigure myself; p. *aia..sod.*

Andjinagwiidisowin. Transfiguration.

Aadjinagwiton, (*nind*). I give to s. th. another appearance, I make it look otherwise; p. *aian..tod.*

Andjine, (*nind*). I relapse in a deadly sickness; p. *aiandjined.*

Andjinewis, (*nind*). *Alg*. S. *Babêgikadis*.
Andjinig, (*nind*). I am born again, I am reborn, regenerated; p. *aianjinigid*.
Andjinigiwin. Regeneration.
Andjinikadan((*nind*) I give another name to it, I change its name; p. *aian..ang*.
Andjinikana, (*nind*). I change his name, I give him another name, (to a person or any *an*. obj.); p. *aian..nad*.
Andjikanidis, (*nind*). I change my name, I take another name; p. *aian..sod*.
Andjinikas, (*nind*). I have another name, I am called otherwise; p. *aian..sod*.
Andjinikasowin. Changed name.
Andjishima, (*nind*). I lay him down elsewhere, or otherwise, (a person or some other *an*. obj.); p. *aian..mad*.
Andjishin, (*nind*). I lie down elsewhere, or otherwise, I change position in lying; p. *aia..ing*.
Andjiso pijiki. The cow is to have a calf; *endjisod*.
Andjissimo animosh. The bitch is to have young ones; p. *endjissimod*.
Andjissin. It is lying elsewhere, or otherwise; p. *aian..ing*.
Andjissiton, (*nind*). I lay it elsewhere, or otherwise; p. *aian..tod*.
Andjitawa, (*nind*) or, *nind andjitamawa*. I alter or change s. th. for him or to him; p. *aia..wad*.
Andjitchigade, or-*magad*. S. *Andjigade*.
Andjiton, (*nind*). I change it, alter it, I make it otherwise, I reform it; p. *aiandjitod*.
Andjiwinsowin. S. *Andjinikasowin*.
Anêakokwan. Stick to stir with; [C. brassoir]; pl.-*an*.
Anéakokwe, (*nind*). I stir what is in the kettle; p. *en..wed*.
Anéan, (*nind*). I stir it, (s. th. in a vessel;) p. *eneang*.
Anéigan. Stick to stir with; pot-ladle; pl.-*an*.
Anéige, (*nind*). I stir s. th. in a vessel; p. *en..ed*.
Anéiskwe, (*nind*). I stir blood, boiling in a kettle; p. *én..wed.*
Ango, or *magad*. It comes to nothing, it finishes, it breaks down, it decays, it becomes desolate; it passes away, vanishes; p. *aiangog* or-*magak*.
Angoa, (*nind*). I destroy him, bring him to nothing, (a person, or some other *an*. obj.); p. *aia..ad*.
Angôgane (*nind*). I am weak in my bones; p. *en..ned*.
Angoshka, (*nind*). I break down, I am brought to nothing, I perish; p. *aia..kad*.
Angoshka, or-*magad*. It passes away, it finishes, perishes; it breaks down; it is worn out; it is abolished; it is brought to nothing; p. *aia..kag*, or-*magak*.
Angoshkan, (*nind*). I destroy it, I bring it to nothing; p. *aian..ang*.
Angoshkawa, (*nind*). I destroy

or bring to nothing some *an.* obj.; p. *aia..wad.*

Angoso gon. The snow is melting; p. *aia..sod.*

Angotamawa, (*nind*). I take off or away s. th. from him, I bring to nothing or abolish s. th. belonging to him; p. *aia..wad.*— *Debenimiian, angotamawishin ga-bi-aindiiân,* Lord, take away from me (pardon me) what I have done.

Angotchigade, or-*magad.* It is taken down, taken off; it is abolished; p. *aia..deg,* or-*magak.*

Angoton, (*nind*). I bring it to nothing; I abolish it; p. *aia..tod.*

Angwabama, (*nind*). I lose sight of him, he disappears to me; p. *en..mad.*

Angwabandan, (*nind*). I lose sight of it, it disappears to me; p. *en..ang.*

Angwabandjige, (*nind*). I am losing sight of some object; p. *en..ged.*

Angwamass, adv. Certainly, to be sure, surely.

Angwâmendam. He is full of hope. *Angwâmendân. Angwamenima. Angwamenindis. Angwamima. Angwaminan. Angwamitagos. Angwamitagosiwin.*—S. *Aiangwamendam. Aiangwamendân. Aiangwamenima,* etc.

Angwamikan, (*nind*). I am devoted to it, zealous for it; p. *aia..ang.*

Angwamikawa, (*nind*). I am devoted to him, I am zealous in his service; p. *aian..wad.*

Angwanagos, (*nind*). I disappear; p. *en..sid.*

Angwanagwad. It disappears; p. *en..wak.*

Angwâssag. A piece of alluvious wood on the beach of a lake, floodwood; pl.-*og.*

Angwâssagoka, or-*magad.* There is floodwood on the beach; p. *aian..kag* or-*magak.*

Ani; S. *Ni.*

Ani-, in compositions, signifies *in future,* henceforth. It marks *going on, approaching towards... Nin gat ani-kitimagis,* henceforth I will be poor and miserable. *Ki gat ani-bakadem,* you shall starve. (P. *eni-*)

Anib. Elm-tree; pl.-*ig.*

Anibédina, or-*magad.* There is a steep descent of a hill or mountain; p. *en..nag,* or-*magak.*

Anibégabaw, (*nind*). I lean on one side, standing; p. *en..wid.*

Anibéia, or-*magad.* It is leaning; p. *enibeiag,* or-*magak.*

Anibékamiga, or-*magad.* There is a rising ground, (inclined ground, leaning ground;) p. *en..gag,* or-*magak.*

Anibékwen, (*nind*). I incline my head on one side; p. *en..nid.*

Anibéshka, or-*magad.* It is leaning on one side; p. *en..kag,* or-*magak.*—*Tchimân anibeshka,* the canoe is leaning.

Anibésse, (*nind*). I am leaning on one side; p. *enibessed.*

Anibésse, or-*magad.* It is leaning; p. *enibesseg,* or-*magak.*

Anibéssin. S. *Anibesse.*

Anibeta, (*nind*). S. *Anibegabaw*.

Anibiki. Elm-grove, elm-forest; pl.-*n*.

Anibins. Young or small elm-tree; pl.-*ag*.

Anibinsiwi-sibi. Elm-River, Lake Superior.

Anibimin. Barberry; [F. vinette, épine-vinette, pembina]; pl.-*an*.

Anibish. Leaf of a tree or plant; also, tea in leaves; pl.-*an*.

Anibishâbo. Tea.

Anibishabo-akikons. Tea-kettle, tea-pot; pl.-*ag*.

Anibishabo-emikwanens. Tea-spoon, pl.-*an*.

Anibishabo-onagans. Cup or saucer; pl.-*an*.

Anibishika, or-*magad*. There are leaves; p. *en..kag*, or-*magak*.

Anibishikang, in the shrubs, in the bushes, among leaves.

Anibiwanagek. Bark of the elm-tree, elm-bark; pl.-*wag*.

Anidjimin. A pea; pl. *anidjiminan*, peas.

Ani-gigisia, (*nind*). I take him along with me; p. *en..ad*.

Ani-gigisin, (*nind*). I take it along with me; p. *en..ing*.

Ani-gwekab, (*nind*). I turn to another side, sitting; p. *en..bid*.

Ani-gwekigabaw, (*nind*). I turn to another side, standing; p. *en..wid*.

Anijitam, (*nind*). I abandon, I give up, I discontinue; p. *aia..ang*.

Anijitamoa, (*nind*). I make him give up s. th., I dissuade him from s. th.; p. *aia..ad*.

Anijitamowin. Discontinuance, giving up.

Anikamân. Suspenders, (for women); pl.-*an*. S. *Dajoiawebison*.

Anikanotabian, (*nind*). I translate it, writing, (a letter, a book); p. *aia..ang*.

Anikanotabiigade, or-*magad*. It is translated, in writing.

Anikanotabiigan. Translation, version, (written;) pl.-*an*.

Anikanatabiige, (*nind*). I translate, writing; p. *aia..ged*.

Anikanotabiigewinini. A man that makes a written translation or version, translator; pl.-*wag*.

Anikanotage, (*nind*). I repeat what another says, I interpret; p. *aia..ged*.

Anikanotagekwe. Female interpreter; pl.-*g*.

Anikanotagewin. Interpretation, work or occupation of of an interpreter.

Anikanotagewinini. Interpreter; pl.-*wag*.

Anikanotan, (*nind*). I interpret it, (a sermon, a letter, etc.); p. *aia..tang*.

Anikanotadjigade, or-*magad*. It is interpreted, translated, orally; p. *aia-deg*, or-*wagak*.

Anikanotawa, (*nind*). I repeat his words, I interpret him; p. *aia..wad*.

Anike, or *aiânike*. This word signifies futurity in succession; also, a continued succession from ancient times; some object, *an*. or *in*., following in succession.— *G e-n i-aianike-*

bimâdisidjig ; those who shall live in future succession, the future generations. *Od aianike-ojisheian,* his grand-children of future generations. *Nind anike-nimishomiss,* my great grand-father.

Anikêmawa, (*nind*). I let s. th. come to him from hand to hand; p. *aian..wad.*

Aniké-ogima. Second chief, underchief; pl.-*g.*

Anikeshkage, (*nind*). I succeed, I follow in succession, I am the next following; p. *aian..ged.*

Anikeshkagewin. Succeeding, succession.

Anikeshkawa, (*nind*). I follow him in succession, I succeed him; p.*aia..wad.*

Anikessin. It follows, it is next after this; p. *aia..sing.—Aianikessing odena,* the next town or village.

Aniketchigade, or-*magad.* It is lengthened out, there is an addition made, an eking piece; p. *aian..deg,* or-*magak.*

Aniketchigan. Addition, eking piece; pl.-*an.*

Anikiton, (*nind*). I lengthen it, add to it; p. *aia..tod.*

Anikôbidjigan. A string tied to another, in order to lenghten it; pl.-*an.*

Anikôbidjigan. Great grandson, or great grand-daughter, great grand-child; pl. *anikôbidjiganag,* the children of grand-children. The grandchildren of grand-children, and their great grand-children, are likewise all called *anikôbidjiganag* by their great grand-parents.

Anikobidon, (*nind*). I tie one string to another, to have a greater length; p. *aia..dod.*

Anikominode, or-*magad.* There is a company, a society; p. *aian..deg,* or-*magak.*—This word has been formed after the French word "*en communauté.*"

Anikominodewimin, (*nind*). We associate, we form a society, a company; p. *aian..widjig.*

Anikominodewiwin. Society, company, association.

Anikoton, (*nind*). S. *Aniketon.*

Anim. Abbreviated from *animosh,* dog; pl.-*og.*—This word is also used as a bad name given to a person, calling him "dog."

Animâ. A German; pl.-*iag.* —This word comes from the French "*Allemand.*"—The Indians also call a German *Detchman,* which comes from *Dutchman,* as the Germans are improperly called in some parts of this country.—I say, *improperly,* because the *Dutch* and the *Germans* are two different nations.

Animad. It blows, the wind blows, in a certain manner, or in such a direction; p. *aianimak.*

Animad. It is painful, unhappy, horrible; p. *aianimak.*

Ani-mâdagak, (*nind*). I go along on the ice; p. *en..kod.*

Animakamigad. There is trouble, difficulty; p. *aian..gak.*

Animakamigis, (*nind*). I have some difficult business; p.

aia..sid, (*Animad*, painful, difficult; *nind akamigis*, I am busy, occupied.)
Animakamigisiwin. Difficult or troublesome business.
Animakwe. German woman; pl.-*g*.
Animâm, (*nind*). I speak German; p. *en..mod*.
Animamowin. German language.
Animendam, (*nind*). I suffer in my thoughts, in my mind; p. *aia..ang*.
Animia, (*nind*). I make him suffer, I torment him; p. *aia..ad*.
Animidabi, (*nind*). I drag (s. th.) with great difficulty; p. *aia..bid*.
Animidabia, (*nind*). I make him drag or draw s. th. with great difficulty; p. *aia..ad*.
Animiidis, (*nind*). I make myself suffer; p. *aia..sod*.
Animiki. Thunder, thunderbolt; pl.-*g*.
Animikibag. Flea-herb; [C. herbe à la pucc]; pl. *on*.
Animikika, or-*magad*. It thunders. *Kitchi animika*, there is a thunderstorm; p. *en..kag*, or *magak*.
Animikiwan. S. *Animikika*.
Animikiwanakwad. Thunder-cloud, black heavy cloud; pl.-*on*.
Animikogabaw, (*nind*). I turn, standing; p. *en..wid*.
Animikogabawitan, (*nind*). I turn my back towards it, standing; p. *en..ang*.
Animikogabawitawa, (*nind*). I turn my back towards him, standing; p. *en..wad*.
Animikonan, (*nind*). I turn it over, upside down; p. *en..ang*.
Animikonigade, or-*magad*. It is turned over, upside down; p. *en..deg*, or-*magak*.
Animikosse, (*nind*). I fall to the ground on the face; p. *en..sed*.
Animikowebina, (*nind*). I overthrow some *an*. object upside down; p. *en..nad*.
Animikowebinan, (*nind*). I overthrow it upside down; p. *en..ang*.
Animikwishin, (*nind*) (pron. *nind animikoshin*,) I am lying on my belly; p. *en..ing*.
Animikwissidon, (*nind*). (Pron. *nind animikossidon*;) S. *Animikonan*.
Animikwèssin. (Pron. *animikossin*,) it lies upside down; p. *en..sing*.
Animima, (*nind*). I trouble or annoy him with my words; I reprimand him with hard words; p. *aia..mad*.
Animis, (*nind*). I suffer, I am in distress, in misery; p. *aia..sid*.
Animishka, (*nind*). I go along in a canoe, boat, etc.; p. *en..kad*.
Animisiwin. Suffering, misery, distress.
Animitagos, (*nind*). I make a speech, a harangue; also, I am troublesome with my words, I annoy with my reproaches; p. *aia..sid*.
Animitagossiwin. Speech, harangue; also, troublesome speaking, hard reproach.
Animitawa, (*nind*). It annoys

me to hear him, (speaking to me or some other person;) p. *aia..wad*.

Animiton, (*nind*). I make it suffer; p. *aia..tod*. — *Nind animiton niiaw*, I make suffer my body, (myself.) *Kid animiton ninde*, thou makest suffer my heart.

Animokadji. *Ot*. dog; pl.-*iag*.

Animosh. Dog; pl.-*ag*.

Animoshiw, (*nind*). I am a dog; p. *en..wid*.

Animweweshin, (*nind*). I am heard going on, or away; p. *en..ing*.

Animweweto, (*nind*). I go away talking; p. *en..tod*.

Animwewidam, (*nind*). S. *Animweweto*.

Anin? adv. What? how? what is the matter?

Anind, pron. some, *an*. and *in*.

Anin dassing? adv.. how often?

Anindi? adv. where?

Anin endassôbinaian? How many fishes hast thou caught in thy net?—*Nin bejigôbina, nin midassobina ashi béjig;* I caught one, two, eleven fishes.

Anin endasso-dibaiganeg? What time is it? what o'clock is it?

Anin epitatibikak? What time is it? (in the night.)

Anin epitch-gijigak? What time is it? (in the day.)

Aningwana, adv. Certainly, to be sure.

Anini, *Ot*. Man, male; pl.-*wag*.

Anin iw? adv. Which? what?

Aniniwapi? adv. When?

Anin minik? adv. How much? how many?

Ani-onagoshi, or-*magad*. Evening is approaching, it is getting late; p. *eni-onagoshig*, or-*magak*.

Anish, interj. Why, well.

Anish, adv. *Ot*. S. *Anishâ*.

Anishâ, adv. For nothing; vainly, without reason, without necessity, only for the purpose of...

Anisha dash. conj. But.

Anisha-ikitowin. Lie.

Anisha-inendamowin. Imagination.

Anisha nind ikkit. I tell lies.

Anisha nin widigema ikwe. I keep a concubine.

Anishâ nin windigendimin. We live together in concubinage. P. *anisha wadigendidjig*.

Anishâ-widigendiwin. Concubinage.

Anishima, (*nind*). I discourage him, dissuade him to do s. th. or to go somewhere, I make him give up; p. *aia..wad*.

Anishinâbe. Man, (human being, man, woman or child); (L. homo;) also, Indian; pl-*g*.

Anishinabe-bimâdis, (*nind*) or *anishinabeng nind iji bimadis*. I live like an Indian, (pagan Indian,) according to the Indian mode of living; p. *en..sid*, or *anishinabeng eji-bimadisid*.

Anishinabe-bimâdisiwin. Indian life, (pagan life,) Indian fashion or mode of living.

Anishinabe ijitwawin. Indian pagan religion.

Aniihinabekas, (*nind*). I play the Indian; p *en..sod*.

Anishinabeki, (*nind*). I live in

the Indian country, among Indians; p. *en..kid.*

Anishinabekwe, Indian woman; pl.-*g*.

Anishinabekwew, (*nind*). I am an Indian woman; p. *en..wid.*

Anishinabem, (*nind*). I speak Indian; p. *en..mod.*

Anishinabemomagad. It speaks Indian, it is written in the Indian language; p. *en..gak*

Anishinabemowin. Indian language.

Anishinabe-nagam, (*nind*). I sing an Indian song, or Indian songs; p. *en..mod.*

Anishinabe-nagamon. Indian song; pl.-*an.*

Anishinabe-ogima. Indian Agent; pl.-*g*.

Anishinabew, (*nind*). I am a human being, (man, woman or child;) also, I am an Indian; p. *en..wid.*

Anishinabewadis, (*nind*). I have the Indian character, I am like an Indian, I have feelings, principles, notions and dispositions like those of an Indian; p. *en..sid.*

Anishinabewadisiwin. Indian character.

Anishinabewaki. Indian country.

Anishinabewapine, (*nind*). I have a sickness which somebody caused me, by magical influence, (according to Indian notions and superstitions;) p. *en..ned.*

Anishinabewapinewin. Sickness caused by somebody, (according to Indian superstitions.)

Anishinabewia, (*nind*). I make him man, I make him become a human being; p. *en.. ad.*

Anishinabewibiïgan. Indian writing, a writing in the Indian language.

Anishinabewibiige, (*nind*). I write in Indian; p *en..ged.*

Anishinabewibiigewin. The act or knowledge of writing the Indian language, writing in Indian.

Anishinabewidjige, (*nind*). I do or act like an Indian, after the Indian fashion; p. *en..gid.*

Anishinabewidjigewin. Indian fashion, Indian mode of living or acting.

Anishinabewiidis, (*nind*). I make myself man; p. *en..sod.* —*Debeniminang Kije-Manito gibi-anishinabewiidiso tchi nodjimoinang;* God made himself man to save us. *Anishinabewiidisowin.* Incarnation.

Anishinabewinikadan, (*nind*). I give an Indian name to s. th. I name in Indian; p. *en.. dang.*

Anishnabewinikade, or-*magad.* It has an Indian name; p. *en.. deg*, or-*magak.*

Anishinabewinikana, (*nind*). I give him an Indian name; p- *en..nad.*

Anishinabewinikas, (*nind*). I have an Indian name; p. *en.. sod.*

Anishinabewinikasowin. Indian name; pl.-*an.*

Anishinabewish. Bad wicked Indian; pl.-*ag.*

Anishinabewishim, (*nind*). I dance after the Indian fashion; p. *en..mod.*

Anishinabewishimowin. Indian dancing.

Anishinabewissin. It is in Indian, in the Indian language, (a letter, a book, etc.); p. *en.. sing.*

Anishinabewissiton, (*nind*). I make it in Indian, I write it in the Indian language; p. *en..tod.*

Anishinabewiwin. Humanity, human nature. — *Debenimin-ang Jesus o gi-odapinan o Kije-Manitowiwining kid anishinabewiwininan;* the Lord Jesus took into his divinity our humanity.

Anishwin? adv. Why? what? what is that? what is the reason?—This word always implies a reproach.— *Anishwin kikendansiwan iw?*— What? you don't know that? *Anishwin bi-ijassiwan kikinoamading?* Why don't you come to school?

Anissab, (*nind*). I have no fire in my house or lodge; p. *en.. bid.*

Anissâbô. Any kind of soup *not seasoned.*

Anisaboke, (*nind*). I make poor thin soup without any seasoning; p. *en..ked.*

Anissâdis, (*nind*). I am sober, (not drunk now;) p. *en..sid.*

Anissadisiwin. Sobriety, the state of a person after having been drunk.

Anissate, or-*magad.* There is no fire in the house or room; p. *en..deg,* or-*magak.*

Anissendam, (*nind*). I calm myself, I am appeased, I don't care; p. *aia..ang.*

Anississin, or *ânissassin.* It evaporates, it exhales; p. *aia.. ing.*

Anit. Spear; pl. *anitin.*

Ani-tibikad. Night is approaching; p. *eni-tibikak.*

Anitiak. The handle or stick of a spear; pl.-*on.*

Aniw, aniwi. Pron. S. *Iniw.*

Aniwia, (*nind*). I precede him; I surpass him, beat him; p. *eniwiad.*

Aniwigima, (*nind*). I overgrow him; I grow faster than he; p. *en..mad.*

Aniwigindan, (*nind*). I overgrow it; p. *en..ang.*—*Nin gi-aniwigendan nind babisikawagan,* I have overgrown my coat, (it is now too small for me.)

Aniwishima, (*nind*). I put too much of it, (*an.* obj., *joniia,* silver; *séniba,* silk, etc.); p *en..mad.*

Aniwishkan, (*nind*). I precede it; I overcome, surpass, bent it; p. *en..ang.*

Aniwishkawa, (*nind*). S. *Aniwia.*

Aniwishtawa, (*nind*). S. *Bisogewa.*

Animissatchige, (*nind*). I put too much of s. th.; p. *en..ged.*

Aniwisse, (*nind*). I am supernumerary; p. *en..sed.*

Aniwisse, or-*magad.* There is too much of it, it is surabundant, supernumerary; p. *en.. seg,* or-*magak.*

Aniwissiton, (*nind*). I put too much of it; p. *en..tod.*

Aniwiton, (*nind*). I precede it, I surpass it; p. *eniwitod.*

Anjeni. Angel; pl.-*wok.*—*Kitchi Anjeni,* Archangel.
Anjenigijigad. S. *Nijogijigad.*
Anjeniw, (*nind*). I am an Angel; p. *aia..wid.*
Ano, conj. Though, although; *aiano.*
Anoganama, (*nind*). I wound him, striking; I stab him; p. *aian..mad.*
Anokâdan, (*nind*). I make use of it; p. *en..ang.*
Anokadjigan. Merchandise, goods; pl.-*an.*
Anokâna, (*nind*). I make use of some *an.* obj.; p *enokanad;* imp. *anokaj.*
Anokasowin. Tool, instrument; pl.-*an.*
Anoki, (*nind*). I work, I labor, I act, ; p. *ênokid.*
Anôki, (*nind*). I order some work, I cause s. th. to be done; p. *enôkid.*
Anokia, (*nind*). I make him work, I put him to work; p. *en..ad.*
Anokigijigad. Working-day, week-day; pl.-*on.*
Anokigijigad. It is a working-day; p. *en..gak.*
Anokimagad. It is working, it is doing work; p. *en..gak.*—*Debeniminang od ikkitowin kitchi anokimagad oma;* the word of our Lord is doing great work here.
Anôkin, (*nind*). I order it to be made; p. *enôkid.*—*O gianokin o babisikawagan,* he ordered a coat to be made for him. *Nind anokinan mitigwakisinan.* I order boots.
Anôkinan, (*nind*). I order some *an.* obj. to be made; p. *enôkid*—*Nind anokinan dibaigisisswân,* I order a watch to be made.
Kid anokinag akikog, you order kettles.
Anôkitagan. Hireling, male or female servant; pl.-*ag.*
Anokitage, (*nind*). I serve, I am in service, I work for somebody; p. *en..ged.*
Anokitagekwe, or *anokitagewikwe.* Female servant or waiter, servant girl, chambermaid; pl.-*g.*
Anokitagewin. Service, state, occupation, condition, of servants.
Anokitagewinini. Male servant or waiter, valet, footman; pl.-*wag.*
Anokitan, (*nind*). I serve it, I work for it, take care of it; p. *en..ang.*—*Weweni od anokitan anamiewigamig,* he serves well the church.
Anokitas, (*nind*). I serve myself, work for myself; p. *en..sod.*
Anokitawa, (*nind*). I serve him, I work for him; p. *en..wad.*
Anokiwigamig. Working-house; pl.-*on.*
Anokiwin. Work, labor; trade, business; pl.-*an.*
Anokiwinagad. There is work; p. *en..gak.*
Anokiwinini. Workman, laborer; tradesman; pl.-*wag.*
Anomaia, adv. S. *Nomaia.*
Anôna (*nind*). I hire or employ him, to do me some service or work; p. *enonad;* imp. *anoj.*
Anônagan. Person employed or hired for some work or service; pl.-*ag.*

Anônam ; nind anonam, my hired person, (man or woman) *nind anonamag,* my hired person ; *ot anonaman,* his hired person or persons ; etc.

Anonawa, (*nind*). I wound him (shooting;) p. *aia..wad.*

Anônige, (*nind*). I hire people; p. *en..ged.*

Anônigos, (*nind*). I engage in a service, I take an employment or service ; p. *en..sid.*

Anonigosiwin. Employment, service.

Anonindiwin. S. *Anonigosiwin.*

Anoshka, or-*magad.* It fades, changes color ; p. *aiân..kag,* or-*wagak.*

Anôsowin. Ot. S. *Ijinikasowin.*

Anôtagan. S. *Anokitagan.*

Anôtch, adv. Of different kinds, of all kinds, several, divers, sundry. In the Cree language : " to-day."

Anotch gego daiebwetang. Credulous superstitious person ; pl.-*ig.*

Anotch ijiwebisiwin. Misconduct, misdemeanor, bad habits.

Ansanam, (*nind*). I sigh ; p. *aia..mod.*

Ansapinadonan, (*nind*). I tie or bind them together, (*in.* obj.) ; p. *en..dod.*

Ansapinag, (*nind*). I bind them together, (*an.* obj.) ; p. *en..nad.*

Ansiân. Breech-cloth worn by Indians ; [F. brayais ;] pl.-*on.*

Ansig. A kind of wild duck, sawbill; [C. betsie ;] pl.-*wag.*

Ansisiw. Herb on the bottom of rivers, etc. ; pl.-*an.*

Answekan, (*nind*). I omit it, I pass it over, (by mistake;) p. *aia..ang.*

Answekawa, (*nind*). I pass him over, I miss him in the road ; p. *aia..wad.*

Answetaginan, (*nind*). I leave it out, (a thread in weaving ;) p. *aia..ang.*

Answetaginigade, or-*magad.* It is woven with holes in it ; p. *aia..deg,* or-*magak.*

Answetaginige, (*nind*). I leave threads out in weaving ; p. *aia..ged.*

Answewidon, (*nind*). I carry, or convey it further than I ought ; p. *aia..dod.*

Aanwewina, (*nind*). I carry or convey him further than I ought; p. *aia..nad ;* imp. *answewij.*

Anwâbamewis, (*nind*). S. *Ma. nâbamewis.*

Anwâbikissin pâshkisigan. The gun misses fire ; p. *aian..ing.*

Anwâkam, adv. Often.

Anwâta, (*nind*). I finish, I cease ; p. *enwatad.*

Anwatawin. The ending or finishing of a work or of an action.

Anwâtin, or *anowâtin.* It is calm, the wind does not blow ; p. *en..ing.*

Anwaweweiashka, or-*magad.* The high sea is over, the waves are appeased ; p. *en.. kag,* or-*magak.*

Anweb, (*nind*). I rest, I repose ; p. *aianwebid.*

Anwebia, (*nind*). I make him rest ; p. *aia..ad.*

Anwebiwin. Rest, repose.

Anwebiwinigijigad. Day of rest, Sabbath-day, Sunday ; pl.-*on.*

Anwebiwinigijigad. It is Sabbath, Sunday, resting-day ; p. *en..gak.*

Anwendagos, (nind). I am worthy of reproach, my behavior is reproachable; p. *aia..sid.*

Anwendam, (nind). I despair, I give up ; p. *aia..ang*

Anwendan, (nind). S. *Anawendan.*

Anwenima, (nind). I find fault with him, I reprimand him, I blame and reprove his conduct, his behavior; p. *aia.. mad.*

Anwenindis, (nind). I find fault with myself, I reprove my conduct, my doings, I reproach to myself; I repent, I am contrite; I convert myself; p. *aia..sod.*

Anwenindisowin. Reproach made to one's self; repentance, contrition ; conversion.

Anweshim, (nind). I rest or repose lying down ; p. *en.. mod.*

Anwi. Musket-ball, bullet; pl.*-n.*

Anwikadjigan. Bullet-mould; pl.*-an.*

Anwike, (nind). I am making or moulding balls or bullets; p. *en..ked.*

Anwins. Shot; pl. *anwinsan.*

Apab, (nind). I am sitting on s. th. ; p. *epabid.*

Apabin, (nind). I am sitting on it; p. *epabid*

Apabiwin. Any thing to sit on it, chair, stool, bench, pew; pl.*-an.*

Apabowâdan, (nind). I season it, (something to eat;) p. *ep.. ang.*

Apabowade, or*-magad.* It is seasoned; p. *ep..deg,* or*-magak.*

Apabowân. Any object to season victuals with.

Apabowana, (nind). I season it, (some *an.* eatable object;) p. *ep..nad.*

Apabowaso. It is seasoned, (*an.* obj.) ; p. *ep..sod.*

Apabow, (nind). I season victuals ; p. *ep..wed.*

Apabowewin. Seasoning victuals.

Apagadashka, or*-magad.* The sea beats, the waves beat, against s. th. ; p. *ep..kag,* or*-magak.*

Apagadashkawag tigowag. The waves are beating against s. th.

Apagadjisse, or*-magad.* It is beating against s. th. ; p. *ep.. seg,* or*-magak.*

Apagadjissitamawa, (nind). I throw it upon him, I lay it to his fault, I impute it to him ; I accuse him of it; p. *ep.. wad.*

Apagadjissitawa, (nind). S. *Apagadjissitamawa.*

Apagadjiwebaog, (nind). The waves beat against my canoe and carry me away ; p. *ep.. god.*

Apagândaigan, or*-apagândaiganak,* s. flail; pl.*-an.* or*-on.*

Apagândaige, (nind). I thrash ; p. *ep..ged.*

Apagandaigekwe. Thrashing woman ; pl.*-g.*

Apagandaigewigamig. Thrashing floor, barn ; pl*-on.*

Apagandaigewin. Thrashing.

Apagandaigewinini. Thrasher; pl.-*wag.*

Apagasikagon, (*nind*). It comes upon me; it throws me down; p. *ep..god.—Naningim ishkotewabo od apagasikagon,* ardent liquor (firewater) throws him often down.

Apagasikawa, (*nind*). I come down upon him; I fall upon him and make him fall, I throw him down; p. *ep..wad.*

Apagatanimad. The wind blows in a certain direction; p. *ep..mak.*

Apagijiwe, (*nind*). I throw, I cast; p. *ep..wed.*

Apagina, (*nind*). I throw or cast him somewhere; p. *epaginad;* imp. *apagij.*

Apagis, (*nind*). I throw or precipitate myself somewhere; I take refuge to some place; p. *ep..sod.*

Apagitadimin, (*nind*). We throw s. th. to each other; p. *ep..didjig.*

Apagitamawa, (*nind*), or *nind apagitawa.* I throw s. th. belonging or relating to him; I throw it to him; p. *ep..wad.*

Apagitan, (*nind*). S. *Apagiton.*

Apagitchigade, or-*magad.* It is thrown or cast somewhere; p. *ep..deg,* or-*magak.*

Apagitchigas, (*nind*). I am thrown somewhere; p. *ep..sod.*

Apagitchige, ((*nind*). I am throwing; p. *ep..ged.*

Apagiton, (*nind*), or *nind apagitan.* I throw it somewhere; p. *ep..tod,* or *ep..tang.*

Apagidimin, (*nind*). We throw ourselves together somewhere, that is, we rush to some place; also, we take refuge somewhere; p. *ep..didjig.*

Apakôde, or-*magad.* It is covered, it is roofed, (house, lodge, etc.); p. *ep..deg,* or-*magak.*

Apakodjigade, or-*magad.* There is a roof to it, it is roofed; p. *ep..deg,* or-*magak.*

Apakôdjigan. Shingle; pl.-*ag.*

Apakodjigan. Roof, the covering of a lodge or house; pl.-*an.*

Apakodjige, (*nind*). I am covering, making a roof; p. *ep..ged.*

Apakôdon, (*nind*). I am covering it, putting a roof to it; p. *ep..dod.*

Apâkosigan. Weed or bark smoked with tobacco.

Apâkosige, (*nind*). I smoke wood (or bark) with tobacco; p. *ep..ged.*

Apakweshkwai. Rush for mats; pl.-*an.*

Apakwei. Mat, lodge-mat; pl.-*ag.*

Apândjigan. By-meat, any thing eaten with some other thing.

Apândjige, (*nind*). I eat s. th. with s. th.; p. *ep..ged.*

Apândjigen, (*nind*). I eat it with s. th.; p. *ep..ged.— Nind amwa wâbos, tchiss dash nind apandjigen;* I eat a rabbit, and turnips with it.

Apândjigenan, (*nind*). I eat some *an.* object with s. th.; p. *ep..ged.— Wiâss nin midjin,* or, *kokosh nind amwa, pakwejigan dash nind apandjigenan,* or, *opinig nind apandji-*

genag, I eat meat, or, I eat pork, and I eat bread with it, or, I eat potatoes with it.

Apângishin, (*nind*). I fall somewhere; p. *ep..ing.*

Apângissin. It falls somewhere; p. *ep..ing.*

Apassagokidjan. Tobacco juice in the pipe or pipe stem.

Apawe, (*nind*). I have a bad ominous dream, (dreaming of death, etc.); p. *aiapawed.*

Apawewin. Bad dream, ominous unlucky dream; pl.-*an.*

Apêgish, or *apêdash*, adv. These two adverbs express a wish, desire or request, and correspond exactly to the Latin: *utinam.—Apegish waiba bidagwishinowad;* I wish they would soon come here; (L. utinam præsto advenirent.)

Apéingi, *Ot.* Be it so, I wish it would be so.

Apénimon, (*nind*). I rely on it, I put my confidence in it, I trust to it, or in it; p. *epenimod.—Win igo o nibwâkâwin od apenimon*, he relies on his own wisdom.

Apênimonan, (*nind*). I rely on him, I place my hope and confidence in him, I trust in him; p. *openimod.* V. Conj. *Debendjiged nind âpitchi apenimonan*, I put my whole confidence in the Lord.

Apenimowin. Reliance, confidence, trust, hope.

Apênindis, (*nind*). I rely on myself, I put confidence in myself; p. *ep..sod.*

Api, adv. When.

Apidanis, (*nind*). I sojourn, I stay in some place; p. *ep..sid.—Ga-apidanisiiân otenang nibinong, gi-nibo aw inini:* that man died during my stay in town last summer.

Apiganêgwasson. The upper part of a moccasin; (C. hausse de soulier;) pl.-*an.*

Api Jesus gijigong ejâd. Ascension-day.

Apikan. Portage-strap, packing-strap; pl.-*an.*

Apikkan. A kind of snake; pl.-*ag.*

Api kitchitwa Marie gijigong ejâd. Assumption of the B. V. Mary.

Apikweiâwegwâson. Collar of a coat, etc.; pl.-*an.*

Apikwéshim, (*nind*). I have my head resting on s. th. lying down. I lay my head on s. th. [L. reclino caput;] p. *ep..mod.*

Apikweshimon. Cushion, any thing put under the head in lying down; pl.-*an.*

Apikweshimon, (*nind*). I lay my head on it, or I put it under my head, in lying down; p. *ep..mod.*

Apikweshimonan, (*nind*). I lay my head on some *an.* object, in lying down; p. *ep..mod.* (V. Conj.)

Apine, adv. Always, ever since, incessantly, always the same, without interruption; done, gone.

Apingweigan. The middle ornamented part of a moccasin; pl.-*an.*

Apishim, (*nind*). I am lying on s. th.; p. *ep..mod.*

Apishimon. Any thing to lie down upon, bed; pl.-*an.*

Apishimon, (nind). I am lying on it ; p. *ep..mod.*
Apishimonag. The boards of a floor ; the little cedar branches on the floor of a lodge.
Apishimonak. Board for a floor ; pl.-*og.*
Apishimonan, (nind), I am lying on some *an.* obj. ; p. *ep.. mod.* (V. Conj.)
Apishimonigin. Carpet for a floor ; pl.-*on.*
Apishîmonikadân, (nind). I am making a floor (in a house or lodge) ; p. *ep..ang.*
Apishimonikade, or-*magad.* There is a floor made, (in a house or lodge) ; p. *ep..deg,* or-*magak.*
Apishimonikawa, (nind). I prepare him a place to lie down upon ; (branches, mats, etc.) ; p. *ep..wad.*
Apishimonike, (nind). I am preparing a place to lie down upon ; p. *ep..ked.*
Apishimonikodadis, (nind). I prepare to myself a place to lie down upon, (branches, mats, a bed, etc.)
Apishkagagi. Mag-pie ; pl..*wag.*
Apishkamonan onagek, (nind). I put a piece of bark under my knees in a canoe ; p. *ep.. mod.*
Apisidebiwin. Footstool ; pl.-*an.*
Apisika, (nind). I am on the way, I am coming ; p. *ep..kad.*
Apisikâ, (nind). I walk as quick as I can ; p. *ep..kad.*
Apisikâ, or-*magad.* It is coming on ; p. *ep..kag,* or-*magak.*
Apissa, or-*magad.* It is of a dark, livid, black-blue color ; p. *ep..sag,* or-*magak.*
Apissâb, (nind). I have a livid or dark-blue eye, (or eyes,) (from a fall or blow ;) p. *epissabid.*
Apissâbawe, (nind). I am dark-blue, I have a livid dark-blue spot, (or spots,) from a blow or fall ; p. *ep..wed.*
Apissâbik. Black-lead, for polishing stoves ; [C. de la mine.]
Apissabikishka, or-*magad.* It is of a dark-blue color, (obj. of metal or stone) ; p. *ep..kag,* or-*magak.*
Apissaje, (nind). My skin is dark-blue, (from a blow or fall ;) p. *ep..jed.*
Apissi. Alg. Violet ; pl.-*n.*
Apissin. It is of a violet or dark-blue color ; p. *epissing.*
Apissingwe, (nind). I have a dark-blue face, from a fall or blow ; p. *ep..wed.*
Apissis, (nind). I am of a dark-blue or livid color ; p. *ep..sid.*
Apissitagan. Thin broad long slice of cedar in the bottom of a canoe ; pl.-*ag.*
Apita, or-*magad.* It is of a certain thickness or height, it is so high ; p. *epitag,* or-*magak.* —*Anin epitag ki wâkaigan?* —*Ow sa apita.* How high is your house ?—It is so high.
Apitagima, (nind). I estimate or value him at..., I put his price at..., (*an.* obj.) ; p. *ep.. mad.*
Apitagindan, (nind). I estimate or value it at..., I put its price at..., (*in.* obj.) ; p. *ep..ang.*
Apitakamig, adv. At a certain

depth under ground, so deep under ground.

Apitandjige, (*nind*). I spend so much time in eating; I eat as long as...; p. *eg..ged.—Epitandjiged nishime, nind apitandjige gaie nin;* I spend as much time in eating as my brother does; (I eat as long as my brother.)

Apitâodon, (*nind*). I tie it down, with a knot; [F. je l'attache avec un nœud;] p. *ep..dod.*

Apitch, adv. During, as long as, all the time; as much as: (in the Change, *epitch-*.) *Gedapitch-aiaiân oma*, as long as I shall remain here. *Gaapitch-âkosid*, during his sickness, or, all the time he was sick.

Apitcha, or-*magad*. It is of such a distance, as far as..., it is distant; p. *epitchag*, or-*magak.—Anin epitchag wâkaigan? odena?* etc.—*Nissimidana sa dasso dibaigan apitcha.* How far is the house? the village? etc.—It is thirty miles distant. *Moniang epitchamagak, mi epitchag wendjibaiân;* the place where I come from, is as far as from here to Montreal.

Apitchi, (*nind*). I am preparing, I contemplate or intend to do s. th.; p. *epitchid.*

Apitchi, adv. Much, very much, very, perfectly, entirely, eminently, exceedingly, excessively, extremely, absolutely; for ever.

Apitchi banâdjia, (*nind*). I destroy or annihilate some *an.* obj.; p. *aiap..ad.*

Apitchi banadjiton, (*nind*). I destroy or annihilate it, (*in.* obj.); p. *âiab..tod.*

Apitchi giwe, (*nind*). I come back again entirely, (to remain here;) p. *aia .wed*

Apitchi kigijêb, adv. Very early in the morning.

Apitchi madja, (*nind*). I move away all together, I quit or leave the place entirely; p. *aia..ad.*

Apitchinana, (*nind*). I kill him entirely; p.*aia..nad;* imp. *apitchinaj.*

Apitchinikeb, (*nind*). My arm is so tired that I cannot stretch it out; p. *aia..bid.*

Apitchi onâgochig, adv. Late at the close of the day, in the beginning of the evening.

Apitchishima, (*nind*). I let him fall to the ground; p. *aia..mad.*

Apitchishin, (*nind*). I fall to the ground stumbling, I fall hard; p. *aia.. shing.*

Apitchita, (*nind*). I am occupied in doing s. th., I am about; p. *ep..tad.*

Apitchi-widige, (*nind*). I am married lawfully, for lifetime, (not after the Indian fashion;) p. *aiap..ged.*

Apitchi-widigema, (*nind*). I am married to her, (or to him,) in a lawful manner, permanently; p. *aiap..mad.*

Apitchi-widigendaa, (*nind*). I join him in marriage lawfully, for lifetime; p. *aiap..ad.*

Apitchi-widigendimin, (*nind*). We are married together lawfully, for lifetime; p. *aia.. didjig.*

Apitchi-widigendiwin. Lawful marriage for lifetime.
Apitchiwin. Preparation.
Apitendagos, (*nind*). I am worth, I am worthy ; *nin kitchi apitendagos,* I am precious, valuable; p. *ep..sid.*
Apitendagwad. It is worth ; *kitchi apitendagwad,* it is precious, valuable; p. *ep..wak.*
Apitêndam, (*nind*). I value or esteem ; p. *ep..dang.*
Apitendân, (*nind*). I esteem it, value it, I appreciate it; p. *ep..dang.*
Apitenim, (*nind*). S. *Apitenindis.*
Apitenima, (*nind*). I esteem or respect him; I appreciate him ; p. *ep..mad.*
Apitênimonan, (*nind*), or, *nind déapiténimonan.* I esteem myself as high as him; I put myself equal to him in my estimation ; p. *epitenimod.* (V. Conj.)
Apitenindis, (*nind*). I esteem myself; p. *ep..sod.*
Apitinigos, (*nind*). I weigh so much ; p. *ep..sid.—Gega nijwâk dasso dibâbiskkodjigan apitinigôsi;* he weighs almost two hundred pounds.
Apitinigwad. It weighs so much; p. *ep..wak.—Anin minik epitinigwak ki kitchi babisikawagan?— Midasso dibabishkodjigan sa apitinigwad.* How much weighs your cloak?— It weighs ten pounds.
Apitis, (*nind*). I am of age; I am of such an age ; p. *epitisid.—Epitisiiân apitisi,* he is of my age.
Apitosse, (*nind*). I walk as quick as I can ; p. *ep..sed.*— S. *Apisika.*
Apitowe, (*nind*). I speak as loud as..., or I speak as loud as I can; p. *ep..wed.—Epitoweng nagamoda,* let us sing loud, or as loud as we can. *Epitoweian nind apitowe,* I speak as loud as you.
Apitwewedjiwan. It sounds in such a manner, or so loud, (running water, or a waterfall;) p. *ep..wang.—Tibishko sibi ga·wabandamân pitchinâgo apitwewedjiwan, ow epitwewedjiwang* ; the river I saw yesterday has the same sound (in its course,) as this here.
Asâdi. Poplar, aspen-tree ; pl.- *asâdig.*
Asâdika, or-*magag.* There are poplar-trees ; p. *es..kag,* or- *magak.*
Asadikang. Poplar Point.
Ash, or *iash,* end-syllable in verbs, signifies *sailing,* coming with the *wind,* or agitated by it ; as: *Nin kijiiash,* I sail fast. *Babâmashi,* he is sailing about. *Nin wêbash,* I am thrown or driven by the wind.
Ashamâ, (*nind*). I give him to eat, I feed him ; I give him provisions ; p. *esh..mad.*
Ashandân, (*nind*). I feed it ; p. *esh..ang.—Nind ashandân niiaw,* I feed my body.
Ashandis, (*nind*). I feed myself ; p. *esh..sod.*
Ashange, (*nind*). I give to eat ; I keep boarders ; p. *esh..ged.*
Ashangékwe. Woman that gives to eat, that keeps boarders ; boarding-mistress, hostess, landlady ; pl.-*g.*

Ashangéwigamig. Boarding-house; hotel; inn; pl.-*on.*
Ashangewin. Giving to eat, feeding, boarding; the keeping of a boarding-house or hotel.
Ashangéwinini. A man that gives to eat, that keeps boarding-house or hotel; boarding-master; landlord; pl.-*wag.*
Ashi, conj. and, (in numbers only;)—*Midâsswi ashi nij; nijtana ashi nanan;* twelve, (ten and two;) twenty and five.
Ashia, (*nind*). I incite him, I stir him up; I encourage him, to do evil; I seduce him by my bad example; p. *aia..shiad.*
Ashidaan, (*nind*). I stick it to s. th.; p. *esh..ang.*
Ashidâkwawa, (*nind*). I hold him or support him; p. *esh..wad.*
Ashidjikiwagaigan. Anything that sticks to s. th.; also, a seal; pl.-*an.*
Ashidjikiwagaige, (*nind*). I stick s. th. to some other thing; I seal; p. *esh..ged.*
Ashigan. A kind of fish, bass-fish; [C. achigan;] pl.-*ag.*
Ashimang. Bastard-loon; pl. *wag.*
Ashinangwana! strange! curious! I don't know what to think of it.
Ashi wegwagi, adv. Although, even if.
Ashiwina, (*nind*). S. *Ashia.*
Ashk, or *ashki,* in compositions, signifies *raw, fresh, new.* (Examples in some of the following words.)
Ashka. At the end of a syllable alludes to the *waves* on a lake or sea; as: *Mamângâska,* the sea is high. *Anwaweweiâshka,* the waves are appeased. *Kijiweweiâshka,* there is a loud roaring of the sea, of the waves.
Ashkakwa, or-*magad.* There is green wood, or standing wood; p. *esh..wag,* or-*magak.*
Ashkakwa-onagij. A gut of the moose.
Ashkandân, (*nind*). I eat it raw; p. *esh..ang.*
Ashkashkânagingwe, (*nind*). I have sore eyes, (red and full of matter;) p. *esh..wed.*
Ashkatai. Green skin of an animal; pl.-*og.*
Ashkâtig. A piece of green wood; pl.-*on.*
Ashhâtigoke, (*nind*). I chop green wood; p. *esh..ked.*
Ashkendagwad. Ashkendam. Ashkendamia. Ashkendamowin; Ot. S. *Kashkendagwad. Kashkendam. Kashkendamia. Kashkendamowin.*
Ashkib, (*nind*). I eat raw; p. *eshkibod.*
Ashkibagad. The leaves (of trees and bushes) are budding; p. *esh..gak.*
Ashkigin. Green skin of a large quadruped; (moose, buffalo, etc.); pl.-*on.*
Ashkikomân. Lead.
~~*Ashkikomanikan.* Lead~~-mine; pl.-*an.*
Ashkikomanike, (*nind*). I make lead, I produce lead, I work in a lead-mine; p. *esh..ked.*
Ashkikomanikewin. Work, bu-

siness, occupation, of a miner in a lead-mine.

Ashkikomanikewinini. Miner in a lead-mine; pl.*-wag.*

Ashkima, (*nind*). S. *Agim nind ashkima.*

Ashkimanéiâb. Strings of leather for lacing snowshoes; [C. babiche;] pl.*-in.*

Ashkimé, (*nind*). I lace or fill snowshoes; p. *eshkimed.*

Askiméwin. Art, work, occupation of a person lacing or filling snowshoes.

Ashkin. It is raw; p. *eshking.* —*Ashkin mandan wiiâss,* this meat here is raw. *Ashkinon tchissan,* the turnips are raw.

Ashkin. It is raw, (*an.* obj.); p. *eshking.*—*Ashkin aw gigo,* this fish is raw. *Ashkinog ogow opinig,* these potatoes are raw. (III. Conj.)

Ashkipidan, (*nind*). It tastes raw to me, I find it tastes raw to me, I find it tastes raw; p. *esh..ang.*

Ashkipwa, (*nind*). It tastes raw to me, (*an.* obj.); p. *esh..wad;* imp. *ashkipwi.*—*Nind ashkipwa aw gigo,* I find this fish tastes raw, it tastes raw to me.

Ashkiwiiâss, ashkigigo, etc. Raw meat or fresh meat, raw fish or fresh fish (not salted,) etc.

Ashkonawis, (*nind*). *Alg.* S. *Anawewis.*

Ashkote. Ashkotekan. Ashkoteke. Ashkotewâbo. Ashkwatch; Ot. —S. *Ishkote. Ishkotekan. Ishkoteke. Ishkotowabo. Ishkwatch.*

Ashôsikawa, (*nind*). I fall upon him; I throw myself upon him; p. *esh..wad.*

Ashôtabikissitchigan. S. *Ashotchissitchiganabik.*

Ashôtaganâma, (*nind*). I strike some *an.* obj. putting it on s. th.; p. *esh..mad.*

Ashôtaganandân, (*nind*). I strike it, putting it on s. th.; p. *esh..ang.*

Ashotakâmigina, (*nind*). I keep him on the ground; p. *esh..nad.*

Ashotakamiginan, (*nind*). I keep it down on the ground; p. *esh..ang.*

Ashôtakamigishima, (*nind*). I put him down on the ground; p. *esh..mad.*

Ashotakamigissidon, (*nind*). I put it down on the ground; p. *esh..dod.*

Ashôtataigan. Anvil, or any thing to strike s. th. on it; pl.*-an.*

Ashôtataige, (*nind*). I put some object to strike s. th. on it; p. *esh..ged.*

Ashotchishwa, (*nind*). I put him underneath, under s. th.; p. *esh..wad.*

Ashotchishin, (*nind*). I am underneath; p. *esh..ing.*

Ashôtchissin. It is underneath, under s. th.; p. *esh..sing.*

Ashotchissitchigan. Foundation, basis; pl.*-an.*

Ashotchissitchiganâbik. Foundation-stone; pl.*-on.*

Ashotchissiton, (*nind*). I put it underneath, under some object; p. *esh..tod.*

Ashôwina, (*nind*). I observe him, I mistrust him; p. *esh..nad.*

Ashwâmanis, (*nind*). I am in fear of the enemy; p. *esh..sod.*
Ashwi, (*nind*). I am armed, I guard myself; p. *esh..wiod.*;
Ashwikandan, (*nind*). I guard myself against it; p. *esh..ang.*
Ashwikawa, (*nind*). I guard myself against him; p. *esh..wad.*
Ashwiwin. Arms or weapon of a warrior; pl.-*an.*
Asikawa, (*nind*). I go to meet him; p. *es..wad.*
Asingwâm, (*nind*). I slumber, I am half asleep, I doze; p. *aiasingwang.*
Askig, seal; [F. loup-marin;] pl.-*ag.*
Askigwaiân. Seal's skin; pl.-*og.*
Askwanis, (*nind*). I am ambitious; p. *aia..sid.*
Assa, (*nind*). I put or place him somewhere; p. *essad*; imp. *ashi.*
Assâb. Net, fish-net; pl.-*ig.*
Asabâb. Thread; twine; yarn.
Assabâbike, (*nind*). I make thread; I spin; p. *ess..ked.*
Assababiwegin. Linen.
Assâbike, (*nind*). I am netting, making a net; p. *ess..ked.*
Assabikêiâb. Twine for making nets.
Assâbikeshi. Spider, (net-maker;) pl.-*iog.*
Assabikeshiwossab. Spider's web, cob-web; pl.-*ig.*
Assabikewin. Netting, making nets.
Assâbins. A small net, with small meshes; pl.-*ag.*
Assâbish. An old bad net; pl.-*ag.*
Assâgaanshk. Reed; [F. roseau;] pl.-*on.*
Assâkamig. Moss, on the *ground.* S. *Atagib.*
Assamâbandimin, (*nind*). We are together face to face, we are confronted; p. *aia..didjig.*
Assana, or-*magad.* It is settled down, pressed down; [F. c'est foulé;] p. *essanag*, or-*magak.*
Assânago. Gray squirrel; pl.-*g.*
Assanâgonaga, or-*magad.* The snow is hard, settled down; p. *ess..gap*, or-*magak.*
Assanânig. *Ot.* S. *Ininatig.*
Assânasshkinadon, (*nind*). I press it down, in a vessel; p. *ess..dod.*
Assânashkine, or-*magad.* It is pressed down, in a vessel; p. *ess..neg*, or-*magak.*
Assândjig, (*nind*). I put s. th. somewhere in order to keep and conserve it, or to hide it; 3. p-o; p. *ess..god.*
Assândjigon. Place where s. th. is kept and conserved, or hidden; pl.-*an.*
Assândjigon, (*nind*). I put it somewhere to keep or hide it; p. *ess. ged.*
Assândjigonan, (*nind*). I put some *an.* obj. somewhere to keep or hide it; p. *ess..god.* (V. Conj.)
Assawân. Arrow with an iron point or head; pl.-*ag.*—S. *Pikwak.*
Assâwe. Goldfish; [C. perchaude;] pl.-*g.*
Assékadan, (*nind*). I dress it, I tan it, an *in.* skin; p. *ess..ang.*—*Pijikiwegin nind assé-*

kadan, I am tanning an ox-hide.

Assékade, or-*magad*. It is dressed or tanned, (*in.* skin ;) p. *ess..deg*, or-*magak*.

Assékana, (*nind*). I dress or tan it, an *an*. skin ; p. *ess..nad*. — *Wawashkeshiweiân nind assekana*, I am tanning a deer skin.

Assékaso. It is dressed or tanned (*an*. skin ;) p. *ess..sod*.

Asseke, (*nind*). I am dressing a skin, tanning ; p. *esse..ked*.

Assekêwigamig. Tan-house, leather manufactory ; pl.-*on*.

Assêkêwin. Tannery, tanner's trade, occupation, business.

Assékéwinini. Tanner, leather manufacturer ; pl.-*wag*.

Asséma. Tobacco ; snuff ; p. k.

Assemâke, (*nind*). I manufacture tobacco or snuff ; p. *ess..ked*.

Assemâkéwigamig. Tobacco manufactory ; pl.-*on*.

Assemakéwinini. Tobacco manufacturer ; pl.-*wag*.

Assêma-makak. Tobacco-box ; snuff-box ; pl.-*on*.

Assiginâk. Startling, (bird ;) [F. étourneau ;] pl.-*wag*.

Assigobanimod. A sack made of the inner bark of the linden-tree ; pl.-*an*.

Assigobi, (*nind*). I soften the bark of the linden-tree, by boiling it ; p. *ess..bid*.

Assin. Stone, pebble ; pl.-*ig*.

Assin. At the end of verbs, signifies *coming with* the *wind* (*in*. obj.), or being *driven* or *agitated* by the wind ; as : *Bidâssin*, it comes with the wind, it is driven this way by the wind. *Webâssin*, it is thrown or driven away by the wind. — *Goshkobagâssin*, the leaves (of a tree) are agitated by the wind.

Assinâb. Stone tied to a net to sink it ; pl.-*in*.

Assinibwân. Stone-Siou ; a kind of Siou-Indian ; pl.-*ag*.

Assinika, or-*wagad*. There are stones, it is stony, full of stones ; p. *ess..kag*, or-*magak*.

Assinikade, or-*magad*. It is made of stone ; it is paved with stones ; p. *ess..deg*, or-*magak*.

Assinikande, or-*magad*. There is a stone-foundation, (a wall under a wooden building ;) p. *ess..deg*, or-*magak*.

Assining ijinâgwad. It looks like stone, it resembles stone.

Assinins. Small little stone, especially a little stone on the beach of a lake ; pl.-*ag*.

Assininsika, or-*magad*. There are little stones, it is full of little stones, (especially on the beach of lakes ;) p. *ess..kag*, or-*magak*.

Assiniw, (*nind*). I am stone, I become stone, I am petrified ; p. *ess..wid*.—*Bejig ikwe ganibod Moniang gi-assiniwi* ; a woman who died in Canada, became stone, petrified.)

Assiniwan. It is petrified, it became stone ; p. *ess..ang*.

Aasini-wadjiw. Rocky Mountains.

Assini-wâkaigan. Stone-building ; stone-built fortress ; pl-*an*.

Assini-wâkaigewin. Masonry,

work, trade or occupation of a mason.

Assini-wâkaigewinini. Mason; pl.-*wag.*

Assiponigan. Ot. Scissors; pl.-*an.*

Assissâwêmin. Sand-cherry; [C. cerises à grappe;] pl.-*an.*

Asissawêminagawanj. Sand-cherry shrub; pl.-*ig.*

Assokweshin, (*nind*). I am leaning with my head on s. th., I lay my head on s. th.; p. *aiass..ing.*

Assotchibidjigan. Girth; or a ribbon around a hat; [F. sangle;] pl.-*an.*

Asswadab, (*nind*). I lean sitting; p. *aia..bid.*

Asswadjishimon, (*nind*). I am leaning on s. th.; p. *aiass.. nod.*

Asswakwaan, (*nind*). I support it, putting a prop, I prop it; p. *ain..ang.*

Asswakwaigade, or-*magad.* It is propped, supported; p. *aiass..deg,* or-*magak.*

Asswakwaigan, or *asswakwaiganak.* Prop, support, (made of wood;) pl.-*an,* or-*on.*

Asswakwaige, (*nind*). I am propping, supporting; p. *aiass,.ged.*

Asswana, (*nind*). (Pron. *nind assona,*) I support him with my hands; p. *aiass..wanad.*

Asswapidon, (*nind*). I gird it; p. *ess..dod.*

Asswapina, (*nind*). I gird him; p. *ess..nad;* imp. *asswapij.*

Asswashin, (*nind*) or, *nind asswishin.* I am leaning on some object; p. *aia..shing.*

Asswawa, (*nind*). I support him, I hold him upright; p. *aia..wad.*

Atadikana, (*nind*). I cast lots for some *an.* obj.; p. *et..nad;* imp. *atadikaj.*

Atadi-masinaigan. Playing-card; pl.-*ag.*

Atadimin, (*nind*). We put in together; we are gambling, playing at cards or at some other interested game; we cast lots; we are betting; p. *etâdidjig.*

Atadiwigamig. Play-house, playing-house.

Atâdiwin. Interested game; card-playing; bet, wager.

Atâge, (*nind*). I put it; I play an interested game, as card-playing for money; I bet; p. *etaged.*

Atagen, (*nind*). I put it in, I put it at stake, I play for it; I bet it, (*an.* obj.); p. *etaged.*

Atagenan, (*nind*). I put at stake some *an.* obj.; I play for it, (him, her;) I bet it, (him, her;) p. *etaged.* V. Conj.

Atagen mamakisiwin, (*nind*). I inoculate with the cow-pox. S. *Mamakisiiwe.*

Atâgewin. Card-playing, or the playing of any interested game; (considered in itself, or in regard to one person only; in regard to several persons playing together, *atâdiwin.*)

Atâgib. Green moss on *stones* on the bottom of a lake, etc.

Ataiâ! interj. aha! ha! ah!—used by men or boys only, to express joy, surprise; impatience, fear; anger, indignation.

Atâma, (*nind*). I sell him s. th. ; p. *et. mad*, or, I buy s. th. of him.
Atamadis, (*nind*). I lay or store it up for me, I am laying up a treasure; [L. thesaurizo mihi ;] p. *ed..sod.*
Atandikandan, (*nind*). I cast lots for it; p. *et..ang.*
Atândiwîn. Commerce, trade, traffic, buying and selling.
Atâss, (*nind*). I put things up, I store up; p. *etassod.*
Atâsson, (*nind*). I put it up somewhere to keep and conserve it, I store it up; p. *etassod.*
Atâssonan, (*nind*). I store up some *an*. obj.; p. *etassod.* (V. Conj.)—*Nibiwa pakwejiganan od atâssonan*, he stores up much flour.
Atassowigamig. Store-house, warehouse; pl.-*on.*
Atâssowin. Place where to put or keep s. th., larder, pantry, etc.; pl.-*an.*
Atassowinini. Storer; pl.-*wag.*
Atawâ, (*nind*). I put or set him s. th.; I bet him; p. *etawad*
Atâwâgan. Any thing given to a trader in exchange for his goods, especially fur or skins of wild animals; pl.-*an*, or-*ag.*
Atâwama, (*nind*). I borrow of him; I trade with him, buying s. th. of him, or selling him s. th.; p. *et..mad.*
Atâwa mamakisiwin, (*nind*). I inoculate him with cow-pox.
Atâwange, (*nind*). I borrow; p. *etawanged.*
Atawangen, (*nind*). I borrow it; p. *etawanged.*
Atawangenan, (*nind*). I borrow some *an*. object; p. *etawanged.*
Atawangeshk, (*nind*). I am in a habit of borrowing; p. *et.. kid.*
Atawangêshkiwin. Bad habit of borrowing always.
Atawangêwin Borrowing.
Atawâsse, (*nind*). I fall backwards, I fall on my back; p. *aiâtawassed.*
Atâwe, (*nind*). I sell, I trade, I traffic, I deal; p. *etawed.*
Atawe, (*nind*). I have no fuel, my fire goes out; p. *aiâ. tawed.*
Atâwê-masinaigan. Trading-license; pl.-*an.*
Atâwen, (*nind*). I sell it, I dispose of it; p. *etawed.*
Atâwenan, (*nind*). I sell him, (her, it,) some *an*. obj., I dispose of him, (her, it;) p. *etawed.*
Atawêwigamig. House of commerce, of trade, trading-house, store; pl.-*on.*
Atâwewin. Market, commerce, trader's business or occupation, trade, traffic.
Atâwewinini Trader, merchant, store-keeper; pl.-*wag.*
Atawissan. Cord of wood; pl. *an.*
Atchâb. Bow-string; pl.-*in.*
Atchigade, or-*magad*. It is put, placed; p. *etch..deg*, or-*magak.*
Atchige, (*nind*). I put s. th. at stake as a prize; p. *et..ged.*
Atchigewin. Putting at stake s. th., also, the prize put at stake; pl.-*an.*
Atchigwananish, (*nind*). I am

under a shelter, (in rain;) p. *etch..shid.*

Atchikina, (*nind*). I make an enclosure or a park around him, I fence him in; p. *aiat..nad.—Pijiki nin wi-otchikina*, I will fence the cow in.

Atchikinan, (*nind*). I separate it, putting a partition in; I make an enclosure; p. *aia..ang.*

Atchikinigade, or-*magad*. There is a partition; an enclosure, a park; p. *aiat..deg*, or-*magak*.

Atchikinigan. Partition or separation of rooms in a house; also, enclosure, park; pl.-*an*.

Atchina, adv. A short time. a moment.

Atchinis, (*nind*). I am shy, I fear; p. *etchinisid.*

Atchisidébison. The foot-board of the Indian cradle; pl.-*an*.

Atchisidébison bimibaigong, or, *tessabing*, stir up.

Atchitakisse, (*nind*). I fall down headlong; p. *et..sed.*

Atchitamo. Squirrel; pl.-*g*.

Atchitchab, (*nind*). S. *Awassab.*

Atchitchaii, adv. Aside, away.

Atchitchibana, adv. *Ot.* Suddenly, all at once.

Atchitchingwesse, (*nind*). I fall on my face; p. *etch..sed.*

Ate, or-*magad*. The fire or candle goes out; p. *aiateg*, or-*magak*.

Atê, or-*magad*. It is, there is; p. *eteg*, or-*magak*.

Atean, (*nind*). I quench it, extinguish it, put it out, (fire or a candle, etc.); p. *aiâ..teang.*

Atebi, (*nind*). I am sober again, (after having been drunk;) p. *aiâtebid.*

Atebiwin. Soberness, the state of not being drunk.

Ateigan. Extinguisher; pl.-*an*.

Ateige, (*nind*). I quench or extinguish, (fire, etc.;) p. *aiâteiged.*

Ateshin, (*nind*). S. *Atebi.*

Atig. At the end of some compound words, signifies *wood, tree, stick* ; pl.-*og*, or-*on*.—*Wâkaiganâtig*, a log for a log house; *nibaganâtig*, bedstead. When the first part of the composition ends in a vowel, *iatig*, or *watig*, is annexed; as: *Ajidêiâtig, anamiewâtig*, cross.

Atik. Reindeer; [F. caribou;] pl.-*wag*.

Atikons. Young reindeer; pl.-*ag*.

Atikameg. White fish; pl.-*wag*.

Atiss. Sinew, nerve; pl.-*in*.

Atissiwag. Nerve or sinew with the flesh on it; pl.-*og*.

Atôban. Trough; [F. auge;] pl.-*an*.

Atôbanike, (*nind*). I am making a trough; p. *et..ked.*

Atôn, (*nind*). I put it, I place or lay it; I bet it; p. *etod.*

Atwab, (*nind*). I put up or conserve provisions, victuals; 3. p. *o.*; p. *etwabod.*

Atwakogabaw, (*nind*). I lean against s. th., standing; p. *aiat..wid.*

Atwashima, (*nind*). I put him, (her, it,) there to lean against s. th.; p. *aiat..mad.*

Atwashimon, (*nind*). S. *Atwakogabaw.*

Atwassidon, (*nind*). I put it there to lean against s. th.; p. *aia..dod.*

Aw. (*nind*). I am; p. *aiâwid.*
Aw. Pron. that, this.
Awa, (*nind*). I make use of some *an.* object; p. *aiawad.*—*Nin wi-awa ki pijikim,* I want to make use of your ox.
Awadagaodass, (*nind*). I make several trips in a canoe or boat, fetching or carrying s. th.; p. *aiaw..sod.*
Awadass, (*nind*). I am fetching or carrying s. th. in a carriage; p. *aia..sod.*
Awadassini, (*nind*). I am carrying stones; p. *aia..nid.*
Awadinisse, (*nind.* I am fetching or carrying wood fo r fuel p. *aia..sed.*
Awadjidâbi, (*nind*). I am carrying, on a carriage or sleigh; p. *aia..bid.*
Awadjidabia, (*nind*). I make him draw a load; p. *aia..ad.*
Awadjidabiwin. Conveyance in a carriage.
Awadjiwanadis, (*nind*). I am carrying s. th., in a carriage for myself; p. *aia..sod.*
Awadjiwanagan. A thing to carry s. th. in it, back-basket; pl.-*an.*
Awndjiwanage, (*nind*). I am carrying for somebody; p. *aiaw..ged.*
Awadjiwana, (*nind*). I am carrying for him; p. *aia..wad.*
Awadjiwane, (*nind*). I am carrying s. th. in a basket, etc.; p. *aîa..ned.*
Awadon, (*nind*). I carry it or convey it on a carriage or sleigh; p. *aiâwadod.*
Awakân. Slave, enslaved prisoner of war; also, domestic or tamed animal or bird; pl.-*ag.*
Awakâna, (*nind*). I enslave him; I treat him like a slave; I tame an animal or bird, or I keep a tamed animal or bird; p. *ew..nad,*
Awakânigon, (*nind*). It makes me a slave, it enslaves me; p. *god.*—*Batadowin od awakanigon,* sin enslaves - him, (he is a slave of sin.)
Awakânindis, (*nind*). I enslave myself, I make myself the slave of somebody, or something; p. *ew..sod.*
Awâkaniw, (*n i n d*). I am a slave, a prisoner of war, a captive; p. *ew..wid.*
Awakâniwin, or *awakanidiwin.* Slavery, captivity, state and condition of a slave.
Awakinan, (*nind*). I tame it, (animal or bird,) or keep it; p. *ew..nad.*
Awân. Fog, mist.
Awân. It is foggv; p. *éwang.*
Awan. It is; p. *aiâwang.*
Awana, (*nind*). I carry some *an.* obj. on a carriage or sleigh; p. *aiâwanad*; imp. *âwaj.*
Awândjish, adv. Purposely, stubbornly, contrary to a prohibition.
Awanibissa, or-*magad.* It is misty, it rains a little; p. *ew..sag,* or-*magak.*
Awâs, (*nind*). I warm myself; p. *ewasod.*
Awasibi, (*nind*). I collect or gather the sap of maple trees in sugar-making; p. *aia..bid.*
Awass. At the end of some neuter verbs, alludes to a child

or to children; as: *Nin kijâdâwass,* I give birth to a child. *Onsomâwasso,* he (she) scolds in regard to his (her) children, because they were ill used, etc.

Awass, adv. Further, away, go away.

Awassâb, (*nind*). I am squint-eyed, I squint; [F. je louche;] p. *ew..bid.*

Awassadaki, adv. Far beyond the mountains.

Awâssagâm, adv. On the other side of a river, lake, etc. The same as *agâming.*

Awassaii, adv. Further.

Awassaki, or *awâssadjiw,* adv. Beyond the mountain, on the other side of a mountain or hill.—*Awassaki Assini-wadjiw nin gi-ijanaban,* I have been beyond the Rocky Mountains.

Awassâsi aw awessi. This animal is shy, wild; p. *ewassasid.*

Awass-bibonong, adv. The winter before last.

Awassewaam, (*nind*). I go around a point in a canoe or boat; p. *ew..ang.*

Awâssigamig, adv. Behind the house or lodge, on the other side of it.

Awâssissi. Burbot (fish;) pl.-*g* also, *awâssi;* pl.-*wag.*

Awass-nibinong, adv. The summer before last.

Awassonag, adv. On the other side of a canoe, vessel, etc.

Awassonâgo, adv. The day before yesterday.

Awass-sigwanong, adv. The spring before last.

Awass-tagwagong, adv. The fall before last.

Awasswabang, adv. The day after to-morrow.

Awass wédi, adv. Further there, yonder, beyond.

Awea, (*nind*). I liken him to somebody, or to s. th; p. *aiawead.*

Awégwen, pron. whoever, whosoever; I don't know who. *Awenen aw bêmossed wêdi ?—Awégwen.* Who is that who walks there?—I don't know who.

Awékadan, (*nind*). S. *Awiton.*

Awékana, (*nind*). S. *Awia.*

Awéma. This word is never used without a possessive pronoun. *Nind awêma,* my brother, or my sister.—A male will say, *nind awêma,* my SISTER, (whether younger or older than he;) but a female says, *nind awema,* my BROTHER, (whether younger or older than she.)

Awénen ? pron. who?

Awenima, (*nind*). I suppose to be him; p. *aiâ..wenimad.*

Awénishé. A young beaver under two years old; [C. avolat;] pl.-*iag.*

Awéssi. Animal, beast; pl.-*iag.*

Awéssi-ainendamowin. Instinct, sagacity of an animal.

Awéssiwaian. Animal's skin, hide; pl.-*ag.*

Awetchigan. Comparison; representation; parable.

Awatchige, (*nind*).. I make a representation of s. th.; I make a comparison, a parable; p. *aia..ged.*

Awetchigen, (*nind*). I make it resemble s. th.; p. *aia..ged.*
Awetchigenan, (*nind*). I make him resemble s. th. or somebody; p. *aia..ged.* (V. Conj.)
Aweton, (*nind*). I liken it to s. th.; p. *aiawetod.*
Awi–, particle signifying *to go on*, or *to go to...*, to go to same place with the intention to do s. th. there; as: *Nind ija ogidaki awi manisseiân*; I go on the hill to chop wood there. *Minawa madja awi-minikwed*; he goes again to some place to drink there.
Awi, pron. *Ot.* S. *Aw.*
Awia, (*nind*). I lend it to him; p. *ewiad.*
Awia, (*nind*). I make him be this or that; p. *aiâ..wiad.*
Awiiâ, pron. somebody, some person or some other *animate* being or object.
Awiidis, (*nind*). I make myself this or that, I say of myself to be such a one, I pretend to be this or that; I transform myself; p. *aia..sod.* —*Awenen aiawiidisoian?* What do you say of yourself, who are you? Who do you pretend to be?
Awiigowin. Anything lent to somebody, borrowed by somebody; pl.-*an*, or *ag.*—*Nin bigiwewidon nind awiigowin*; I bring back again the thing I borrowed. *Ki binag na gaie kid awiigowinag?* (*joniiag?*) Do you bring also the things lent to you? (money? silver-pieces?)
Awiiwe, (*nind*). I lend to somebody; p. *ewiiwed.*
Awiiwen, (*nind*). I lend it; p. *ewiiwed.*
Awiiwenan, (*nind*).; p. *ewiiwed.* (V. Conj.)
Awiiwewin. Lending, the act of lending s. th. to somebody.
Awishtoia. Blacksmith, smith; pl.-*g.*
Awishtoiaw, (*nind*). I am a blacksmith; p. *ew..wid.*
Awishtoiâwigamig. Blacksmith's shop, forge, smithy; pl.-*on.*
Awishtoiawiwin. Blacksmith's trade, occupation or business of a blacksmith.
Awissa, or-*magad.* It is a little damp; p. *ew..sag*, or-*magak.*
Awiton, (*nind*). I make it be this or that; p. *aiâwitod.*

B

Some words which are not found under B, *may be looked for under* P. Very often you would not perceive whether the word is sounded *b* or *p*, whereas the *b* is more accentuated by some Indian tribes, while the *p* is more by some others.

Ba–, particle, (The *Change* of *Bi–*.)

Bâba. Papa, father.

Bâba–, in compositions, signifies *going* or *moving about*, from one place to another; as: *Jesus nissô bibôn gi-babagagikwe;* Jesus preached three years in different places, (went from place to place preaching.) *Babâ-dajinge*, he (or she) speaks ill of people in different places, (he (she) goes from place to place backbiting people.) P. *Bebâ–*....

Bâba-aindâ, (*nin*). I live or stay in different places, changing often; p. *beb..dad.*

Babâ-akoshka, (*nin*). I tire or fatigue myself traveling about; p. *beb..ad.*

Babâ-danis, (*nin*). I move about, I rove, I change often my place of residence; p. *beb..sid.*

Babagwaajigwe, (*nin*). I take off the bark from a tree which I cut down; p. *beb..wed.*

Babâijibi, (*nin*). I am drinking liquor in several places; p. *beb..bid.*

Babâijita, (*nin*). I bustle about; p. *beb..tad.*

Babâikawin. Godfather; sponsor at baptism; also, my adopted father; pl.-*ag*. There is always a possessive pronoun prefixed to this word; *nin babaikawin, ki babaikawin, o babaikawinan*, etc.; my, thy, his godfather, etc.

Babâinode, (*nin*). S. *Babâmode.*

Babakedikwanagisi aw mitig. This tree has *many* branches.

Babâmadaga (*nin*). I am swimming about; p. *beb..gad.*

Babâmadagas, (*nin.*) I walk about in the water; p. *beb..sid.*

Babâmadis,(*nin*). I travel about; p. *beb..sid.*

Babâmadisi-wagâkwad. Traveling axe; pl.-*on.*

Babâmodisiwin. Voyage, travel; peregrination.

Babamâdjim, (*nin.*) I tell s. th. in different places, I go from place to place to tell it; p. *beb..med.*

Babamadjimo-masinaigan. News-paper; pl.-*an.*

Babamadjimowin. The telling of a story or news in different places ; news, story, report, rumor that is going round.

Babâmadodjigade, or-*magad.* It is noised out, rumored about; p. *beb..deg,* or-*magak.*

Babâmajaam, (*nin*). I am going about in a canoe, near the shore; p. *beb..ang.*

Babâmash, (*nin*). I am sailing about; p. *beb..shid.*

Babâmassin. It is driven about by the wind; p. *beb..sing.*

Babamassitchigan. A kite made of paper; pl.-*an.*

Babamatawe, (*nin*). I pedle, I carry goods about for sale; p. *bebamgtawed.*

Babamatawewin. Pedling, pedler's trade or occupation.

Babamatawewinini. Pedler; [F. colporteur ;] pl.-*wag.*

Babamendagos, (*nin*). They pay attention to me; p. *beb.. sid.*

Babamendagwad. Attention or care is given to it; p. *beb.. wak.*

Babamendam, (*nin*). I pay attention, I care; p. *beb..ang.*

Babaméndamadimin, (*nin*). We turn our attention to each other's actions or words, or to something belonging to one or the other; p. *beb..didjig.*

Babamendamawa, (*nin*). I pay attention to s. th. belonging to him, or relating to him; p- *beb..wad.* — *Nin babamenda. mawa nimisse od ijiwebisiwin, od agwiwin,* etc.; I pay attention to the conduct, the dress, etc., of my sister.

Babamendamowin. Attention, care.

Babamendan, (*nin*). I pay attention to it, I mind it, I care for it; p. *beb..ang.*

Babamendjigade, or-*magad.* It is minded, considered, taken care of, it is not neglected ; p. *beb..deg,* or-*magak.*

Babamendjigas, (*nin*). I am taken care of, attention is paid to me; p. *beb..sod.*

Babamenima, (*nin*). I pay attention to some person, or to any other *an.* being or object; I care for him, (her, it ;) I take notice of him, (her, it; p. *beb.. mad.*

Babâmenindis, (*nin*). I turn my attention to myself, I care for myself; p. *beb..sod.*

Babamibaa, (*nin*). I make him run after me; p. *beb..ad.*

Babâmibaigo, (*nin*).I am made to run about; I ride in a carriage, sleigh, etc. ; p. *bebamibaind.*

Babamibaigo-titidabân. Calash; pl.-*ag.*

Babâmibato, (*nin*). I run about, to and fro; p. *beb..tod.*

Babâmibissa. Showers of rain are passing by ; p. *beb..sag.*

Babamima, (*nin*). S. *Babâmenima.*

Babâmindam, (*nin*). S. *Babamendam.*

Babâmindan, (*n i n*). S. *Babamendan.*

Babâmishka, (*nin*). I am going from one place to another in a canoe, boat, etc. ; p. *beb.. kad.*

Babâmisse. It is flying about, (a bird, etc.) ; p. *beb..sea.*

Babâmitam, (*nin*). I obey, I am obedient, I listen ; p. *beb..ang.*

Babâmitamowin. Obedience.

Babâmitas, (*nin*). I obey myself, I do according to my own will ; p. *beb..sod.*

Babâmitawa, (*nin*). I obey him, I listen to him, I do what he asks, I grant his petition, his prayer ; p. *beb..wad.*

Babamiwebaan. It is driven by the waves, (in a high sea ;) p. *beb..ang.*

Babamiwebaog, (*nin*). I am drîven by the waves, (in a high sea;) p. *beb..god.*

Babamode, (*nin*). I creep about, I drag myself about ; p. *beb.. ded.*

Babamosse, (*nin*). I walk from one place to another, I walk about ; p. *bom.. sed.*

Babanadis, (*nin*). I am losing myself, losing property ; I am in danger of perishing ; I am dying ; p. *beb..sid.*

Babanadj, adv. Dangerously ; losing. — *Babanadj kid indimin,* we are in danger of perishing ; also, we are losing things.

Babâ-nanandoshkite, (*nin*). I go about to hear what is said, what they say ; I am spying them out ; p. *beb..ted.*

Baba-nanandoshkitegabaw, (*nin*). I am standing here and there, to hear what they are saying ; p. *beb..wid.*

Babâ-nandotamage, (*nin*). I beg, mendicate, ask alms ; p. *beb. ged.*

Baba-nandotamagewin. Beggary, mendicity.

Babanasitagos, (*nind*). I am despaired of, by my *speaking,* for instance a sick person by his feeble dying voice ; p. *beb.. sid.*

Babanasitawa, (*nin*). I despair of him, of his recovery, by his *voice ;* p. *beb..wad.*

Babapijima, (*nind*). I laugh with him ; p. *beb..mad.*

Babâpijisse, (*nin*). I walk or run fast ; p. *beb..sed.*

Babâ-pindige, (*nin*). I go from house to house ; p. *beb..ged.*

Babapingwe, (*nin*). I have a gay smiling countenance ; p. *beb..wed.*

Babâpinis, (*nin*). I am joking, drolling ; p. *beb..sid.*

Babâpinodage. Babâpinadagewin Babapinodân. Babâpinodawa.—S. *Bâpinodage. Bâpinogewin. Bapinodan. Bapinodawa.*

Note. The duplication of the first syllable in the above four words, and in many others, does not change their signification ; it merely denotes a repetition or reiteration of the same act. So, *nin bâpinodân,* signifies, I ridicule it ; and, *nin babâpinodân.* I ridicule it often ; etc.

Babâpinwe, (*nin*). I am telling drolleries, little jokes and tricks, to make people laugh ; p. *beb..wed.*

Babapinwewin. Drollery, jokery, buffoonry.

Babâwasse, or-*magad,* A clear

piece of land, a clearing or a lake, is seen through the woods ; [C. on voit un éclairci ;] p. *beb..seg*, or-*magak*.

Babawidjiendimin, (*nin*). We accompany each other going about, we go about together ; p. *beb..didjig*.

Babawidjiendiwin. Going about together, mutual accompaniment.

Babâwidjiwa, (*nin*). I go about with him, I accompany him to several places ; p. *beb..wad*.

Babédjinawis, (*nin*). S. *Babégikadis*.

Babégikadandjige, (*nin*). I eat slowly ; p. *beb..ged*.

Babêgikadis, (*nin*). I am slow, dull, in doing s. th. ; p. *beb.. sid*.

Babégikadisiwin. Dullness, slowness, in doing s. th.

Babénag. A little better, a little more.

Babigodee, (*nin*). I am peevish, sulky ; passionate ; p. *beb.. ed*.

Babigodeewin. Peevishness; passionate temper.

Babigômakaki. A kind of big toad ; pl.-*g*.

Babigwatagad. It is spotted or dotted ; also, it is coarse, (stuff.)

Babijagéndân, (*nin*). I notice it, I see it, in going by ; p. *beb ..ang*.

Babijâgenima, (*nin*). I notice or see him in going by ; p. *beb.. mad*.

Babikomigens. Small pearl ; pl. *babikomigensag*, small pearls worn round the neck,

Babikominagad. It is globulous or globular ; p. *beb..gak*. —*Mashkiki bebikominagak*, pills.

Babikominagisi. S. *Bikominagisi*.

Babimiwidadimin, (*nin*). We carry the load or pack of one another ; *fig*. we forbear with each other ; [L. alter alterius onera portamus ;] p. *beb.,diddjig*.

Babimiwidawa, (*nin*). I carry s. th. for him ; also, *fig*., I forbear with him, I have patience with him ; p. *beb..wad*.

Babimodakwe, (*nin*). I am shooting with bow and arrows ; p. *beb..wed*.

Babimwassin, (*nin*). I am throwing stones ; p. *beb..sing*.

Babinasse, (*nin*). I stagger ; p. *bebinassed*.

Babindassagan. Raft ; pl.-*ag*.

Babindassâganike, (*nin*). I make a raft to cross a river on it ; p. *beb..ked*.

Babishagi, (*nin*). I move about on earth ; p. *bob..gid*.—*Bebishagidjig aking*, people living on earth.

Babishagishkawa, (*nin*). I move about with him ; p. *beb..wad*.

Babishkotawa, (*nin*). I listen to him with distraction, (sleeping, or otherwise distracted ;) p. *beb..wad*.

Babishkwendam, (*nin*). I lose my senses (my recollection) from time to time, fainting ; also, I am not attentive in listening to a sermon or discourse, I am distracted ; p. *beb..ang*.

Bâbisibi, (*nin*). I belch, winds come up from my stomach; p. *baia..bid.*

Babisigakwaan, (*nin*). S. *Titibakwaan.*

Babisigindibe, (*nin*). I have curléd hair; p. *beb..bed.*

Babisiginindjiwadj, (*nin*). My hands are benumbed by cold; p. *beb..djid.*

Babisigisidewadj, (*nin*). My feet are benumbed by cold; p. *beb..djid.*

Babisikawâgan. Coat, jacket, frock for men; a kind of waistcoat worn by women.

Babisine, adv. After it was done or said, too late.— *Bâbisine nin gi-mikwendan*, I remembered too late, (when s. th. was already done or said.)

Babiskishin, (*nin*). I am wrinkled; p. *beb..ing.*

Babiskissin. It is wrinkled or shriveled; p. *beb..ing.*

Babitchi, (*nin*). I put on stockings and shoes, etc., [F. je me chausse;] p. *beb..id.*

Babitchia, (*nin*). I put him stockings and shoes on; p. *beb..ad.*

Babiwawan. They are small, (*in.* objects;) p. *bebiwagin.*

Babiwig, (*nin*). I have small limbs, (hands, feet, etc.); p. *bebiwigid.*

Babiwigade, * (*nin*). I have small legs; p. *beb..ded.*

Babiwigaige, (*nin*). I make small notches or incisions in maple-trees, (in sugar-making;) p. *beb..ged.*

*See *Note* at *Agassigad.*

Babiwijinimin, (*nin*). We are small, (*an.* objects; p. *bebiwijinidjig.*

Babiwinike, (*nin*). I have small arms; p. *beb..ked.*

Babiwinindji, (*nin*). I have small hands; p. *beb..id.*

Babiwishkam, (*nin*). I leave small footsteps or traces behind me, in walking; p. *beb..ang.*

Babiwishkinjigwe, (*nin*). I have small eyes; p. *beb..wed.*

Babiwiside, (*nin*). I have small feet; p. *beb..ded.*

Babiwitawage, (*nin*). I have small ears; p. *beb..ged.*

Babwedana, (*nin*). I blow a sick person, after the Indian fashion; p. *beb..nad.*

Badagonig, (*nin*). I am oppressed by the night-mare; p. *bêdagonind.*

Badagoshkan, (*nin*). I oppress it, or crush it, putting myself upon it; p. *bod.. ang.*

Badagoshkawa, (*nin*). I oppress him, I crush him, putting myself upon him; p. *bed.. wad.*

Badagosides, (*nin*). I burn my foot putting it on some hot object; p. *bed..sod.*

Badakakwaan, (*nin*). *Ot.* S. *Sassagakwaan.*

Badakakwâwa, (*nin*). *Ot.* S. *Sassagakwawa.*

Bag, baga, in compositions, as end-syllables or in the middle of the word, signifies *leaves* of trees or of plants; or some reference to leaves; as: *Megwêbag*, among leaves. *Sagibaga*, the leaves on the trees are coming forth. *Goshkobagassin*, the leaves tremble or shake by the wind.

Bagakâdis, (*nin*). I am not drunk, I am sober; p. *beg..sid.* S. *Anissadis.*

Bagakadisiwin. Soberness; [Ill. tresnost.]

Baganowe, (*nin*). My cheek is swollen, (or, my cheeks are swollen;) p. *baiag..wed.*

Bâgashkanige, (*nin*). My jaw is swollen, (my jaws are swollen;) p. *baia..ged.*

Bâgidênaniwe, (*nin*). My tongue is swollen; p. *baia..wed.*

Bâgidjâne, (*nin*). My nose is swollen; p. *baia..ned.*

Bâgidon, (*nin*). My mouth is swollen; p. *baia..dong.*

Bâgigade, (*nin*). My leg is swollen, (or, my legs are swollen;) p. *baia..ded.*

Bâgigonbagan, (*nin*). My throat is swollen; p. *baia..gang.*

Bâgigoshkinjigwe, (*nin*). My eye is swollen, (my eyes are swollen;) p. *baiag..wed.*

Bâgindibe, (*nin*). My head is swollen; p. *baia..bed.*

Bâgingwe, (*nin*). My face is swollen; p. *baia. wed.*

Bâginike, (*nin*). My arm is swollen, (my arms are swollen;) p. *baia..ked.*

Bâginindji, (*nin*). My hand is swollen, (my hands are swollen;) p. *baia..id.*

Bâgish, (*nin*). I am swollen; p. *baiâgishid.*

Bagishiwin. Swelling, tumor.

Bâgiside, (*nin*). My foot is swollen, (my feet are swollen;) p. *baia..ded.*

Bâgissin. It is swollen; p. *baia..gissing.*

Bâgitawage, (*nin*). My ear is swollen, (my ears are swollen;) p. *baia..ged.*

Bâgwa, or-*magad.* It is shallow, not deep, (a river, lake, etc.,) p. *baiâgwag*, or-*magak.*

Bâgwaân, (*nin*). I mend it by sowing a piece to it, I patch it; p. *begwaang.*

Bagwaâss, (*nin*). I mend shoes by sewing a piece on, I patch them; p. *beg..sod.*

Bagwâassabi, (*nin*). I mend a net; p. *beg..bid.* (The same as, *nin bagwâwa assâb.*)

Bagwadjina, (*nin*). I rip him. I take his entrails out; p. *beg..nad.*

Bagwaidâsse, (*nin*). I mend or patch leggings; (*midâss*, legging;) p. *beg .sed.*

Bagwâigan. Patch, piece: pl.. *an.*

Dagwâige, (*nin*). I am patching or mending clothes, etc.; p. *beg..ged.*

Bagwâigewin. Mending, patching.

Bagwaon, (*nin*). I mend or patch a canoe by sewing and pitching a piece of bark to it; p. *beg..waonod.*

Bagwatigweia sibi. The river is shallow; p. *baiag..iag.*

Bagwâwa, (*nin*). I mend or patch some *an.* object; p. *beg..wad*; imp. *bagwa.—Nin moshwem bigoshka, nin wi-bagwawa*; my handkerchief is torn, I will mend it, (by sewing a piece to it).

Bâgwashka, or-*magad.* The

waves break on a shallow place, the surf is beating on a shallow place; p. *baia..kag,* or-*magak.*

Bâgwissin. It touches the bottom; p. *baiâgwissing.—Osâm besho tchigibig kid ani-ijâmin, ta-bagwisin tchimân;* we go too near the shore, the canoe will touch the bottom.

Baiatâ-ijiwebisid. Sinner, transgressor; pl.-*jig.*

Baiâtangeshkid. Habitual accuser; pl.-*jig.*

Baiâteg jomin. Raisin.

Baiatinogaded. Wood-loose, milliped, (millepedes;) pl.-*jig.*

Baiétoj. At the same time, just at that time.

Bajibaigas, (*nin*). I am stabbed; I am speared; p. *bej..sod.*

Bajibâwa, (*nin*). I stab him; I spear him; p. *bej..wad;* imp. *bajibâ.*

Bajidébadon, (*nin*). I make it so full that it flows over, I fill it to overflow; p. *bej..dod.*

Bajidébi, or-*makad.* It is under water, (a piece of ground, a point, etc.,) it is overflowed; p. *bej..big,* or-*magak.*

Bajidédjiwan sibi. The river is high, it flows at full banks; p. *bej..ang.*

Bajidéndan, (*nin*) (*nima*). I prefer him; p. *bej..mad.*

Bajinana, (*nin*). I put him in danger of being killed, of perishing in some manner; p. *bej..nad;* imp. *Bajinaj.*

Bajiné, (*nin*). I come near being killed.

Bajinêwagendam, (*nin*). I am glad to be saved.

Bajiton, (*nin*). I miss it; p. *bejitod.*

Bakadé, (*nin*). I am hungry, I starve, I fast, I have nothing to eat; p. *bekaded.*

Bakadéa, (*nin*). I make him hungry; p. *bek..ad.*

Bakadeidis, .(*nin*). I make myself suffer hunger; p. *bek..sod.*

Bakadém, (*nin*). I weep or cry being hungry, I weep of hunger; p. *bekademod.*

Bakadénodan, (*nin*). I hunger after it, I long after it, I desire it ardently; p. *bek..dang.*

Bakadéwin. Hunger, famine, starvation.

Bakadêwinagad. There is famine, hunger, starvation; p. *bek..gak.*

Bakama, (*nin*). I cut through with my teeth some *an.* obj.; p. *bek..mad.*

Bakân, adv. Otherwise, differently; another thing.

Bakânad. It is another thing, it is different; p. *bekanak.*

Bakandan, (*nin*). I cut it through with my teeth; p. *bek..ang.*

Bakandjigade, or-*magad.* It is cut through with the teeth; p. *bek..deg.*

Bakânenim, (*nin*). I am divided in my thoughts, in my mind; p. *bek..mod.*

Bakânenindis, (*nin*). I am divided against myself; p. *bek.. sod.*

Bakânis, (*nin*). I am another person; p. *bek..sid.*

Bakân-ishkotawe, (*nin*). I am in my monthly flowings, (a woman.) Properly, I make my fire elsewhere, not in the lodge ; (as the pagan women use to do at the time of their monthly flowings.)

Bakânwaiagad. It is of another sort or kind; p. *kek..gak.*

Bakânwaiagis, (*nin*). I am of another nation ; p. *bek..sid.*

Baké, (*nin*). I take another route, another direction, I take another branch of the road or trail.

Bakéaii, adv. Aside.

Bakêgama. Separation of a lake, where a lake is divided in two branches by a projecting point.

Bakêidimin, (*nin*). We separate from each other, we leave each other; p. *bek..didjig.*

Bakêidiwin. Separation of persons.

Bakêkana, adv. On the wayside.

Bakémik. Young beaver of three years; pl *-wag.*

Bakêmo mikana. The road splits, separates, divides; p. *bekêmod.*

Bakêshkawa, (*nin*). I leave him, quit him, I separate from him; I repudiate her, (him ;) p. *bek.. wad.*

Bakéshkodadimin, (*nin*). We separate from each other, especially married people, we make a divorce; p. *bek..didjig.*

Baketigweia sibi. The river divides, it splits out in two branches; p. *bek..iag.*

Bakéwebina, (*nin*) (*nân*). I throw him aside, (any obj.); p. *bek..nad.*

Bakêwina, (*nin*) (*don*). I withdraw from him, depart from him, I take another road; p. *bek..nad.*

Bakéwinan, (*nin*). I depart from it, withdraw from it, I put it away; p. *bek. ang.*

Bakôbi, (*nin*). I go into the water, (to bathe or to fetch s. th., etc.) ; p. *bekobid.*

Bakôbibato, (*nin*). I run into the water; p. *bek..tod.*

Bakobigwashkwan, (*nin*). I jump or leap in the water ; p. *bek..nid.*

Bakobina, (*nin*) (*nân*). I launch or put him in the water slightly, (a person or any obj.) p. *bek..nad.*

Bakobininajawa, (*nin*). I bid him go in the water, I make him go in the water ; p. *bek.. wad ;* imp. *bakobininajâ.* — *Nindai nin wi-bakobininajawa ;* I will bid my dog go in the water, (to fetch s. th. out.)

Bakobisse, (*nin*). I fall or slide in the water; p. *bek..sed.*

Bakobisse, or-*magad.* It slides or falls in the water; p. *bek.. seg,* or-*magak.*

Bakobiwebina, (*nin*) (*nân*). I throw him in the water; p. *bek..nad.*

Bakobiwebinidis, (*nin*). I throw myself in the water; p. *bek.. sod.*

Bakwabidebina, (*nin*). I pull him a tooth out; p. *bek..nad.*

Bakwabidébidjigan. Tooth-pincers; (F. davier ;) pl.-*an.*

Bakwakobidon, (*nin*) (*bina*) I pull it out; p. *bek..dod.*

Bakwakotchibikebidon, (*nin*), or, *nin bakwâkotchibikaginan,* I pull it out with the root, I root it out; p. *bek..dod*, or, *bek..ang*.

Bakwâkotchibikebina, (*nin*), or, *nin bakwâbotchibikagina*. I pull some *an*. obj. out with the root; p. *bek..nad*.

Bakwan. Fruit of the vinegar-tree; pl.-*an*.

Bakwanâtig, or, *bakwanimij*. Vinegar-tree; (C. vinaigrier;) pl.-*on*, or, *in*.

Bamiâ, (*nin*). I take care of him, I support him, I clothe and feed him; p. *bemiad*.

Bamiidis, (*nin*). I take care of myself, I support myself; p. *bem..sod*.

Bamiidisowin. Self-support.

Bamiidiwin. Support, care, of somebody, sustenance.

Bamiiwe, (*nin*). I take care (of a person or persons,) I give support, sustenance; p. *bemiiwed*.

Bamikan, (*nin*). I have it in charge, I take care of it; p. *bemikang*.

Bamikawa, (*nin*). I have some *an*. obj. in charge, I take care of him, (her, it;) p. *bem..wad*.

Bamikodadis, (*nin*). S. *Bamiidis*.

Bamiskwaigadeg sagâigan. Screw; (that is, a turned or twisted nail)

Bamitâgan. Servant, waiter; pl.-*ag*.

Bamitâgekwe. Female servant, maid-servant, servant-girl; pl.-*g*.

Bamitâgewin. Service, state and condition of a servant.

Bamitâgewinini. Male-servant, servant; pl.-*wag*.

Bamitan, (*nin*). I serve it, I labor in it or for it; p. *bemitang*.

Bamitawa, (*nin*). I serve him, I am his servant; p. *bem..wad*.

Bamiton, (*nin*). I take care of it, I support it; p. *bemitod*.—*Weweni ki bamiton niiaw*, you take well care of my body, (of me.)

Banaân, (*nin*) I miss it, I don't hit it, (shooting or throwing at it;) p. *benaang*.

Banâbama, (*nin*). I lose sight of him; p. *ben..mad*.

Banâbandân, (*nin*). I lose sight of it; p. *ben..ang*.

Banâdad, * It is spoiled, lost; p. *benadak*.

Banâdendagos, (*nin*). I am considered lost; p. *ben..sid*.

Banadendagwad. It is considered lost; p. *ben..wak*.

Banadendam, (*nin*). I despair (of s. th. or somebody;) p. *ben..dang*.

Banadenima, (*nin*). I despair of him, I consider him lost; p. *ben..mad*.

Banâdis, (*nin*). I am losing property, losing my soul, am running into perdition and ruin; p. *benadisid*.

Banâdisiwin. Loss, ruin; perdition; damnation.

Banâdjia, (*nin*). I spoil him, I seduce, ruin, lose, destroy him; p. *ben..ad*.

Banâdjiidis, (*nin*). I lose, ruin, destroy myself, I condemn

---

* Note.—The *frequentative* of this and the following seven verbs is formed by merely doubling the first syllable; as: *Babanadad*, etc.

myself, I cause my own damnation; p. *ben..sod.*

Banadjiiwemagad. It is causing loss, destruction, ruin, damnation; p. *ben..gak.* — *Minikweshkiwin memindage banadjiiwemagad;* the bad habit of drinking (ardent liquor) is especially causing loss, destruction, etc.

Banâtchitass, (nin). I lose property, I suffer loss, damage; p. *ben..sod.*

Banatchitassowin. Loss of property, damage.

Banadjitawa, (nin) or, *nin banadjitamawa.* I spoil, lose or ruin something belonging to him, or any way relating to him; p. *ben..wad.*

Banâdjiton, (nin). I spoil it, I ruin, destroy, lose it, I dissipate it, waste it; p. *ben..tod.*

Banaganjishka, (nin). I lose a nail; p. *ben..kad.*

Banâgwana, (nin). I miss him in my snare, he avoids my snare, or escapes out of it; p. *ben..nad;* imp. *banagwaj.*

Banagwâs, (nin). I avoid or escape a snare; p. *ben..sod.*

Banasikan, (nin). I bruise it, crush it; p. *ben..ang.*

Banasikawa, (nin). I bruise or crush him; p. *ben. wad.*

Banâwa, (nin). I miss him, I don't hit him, (shooting, throwing, spearing;) p. *benawad;* imp. *banâ.*

Banigak masinaigan. Clean paper, (that is, white, not written paper.)

Banijâwân. Slice of dried smoked venison; pl.-*an.*

Banikôna, (nin). I miss him in my trap, he avoids my trap, escapes out of it; p. *ben..nad;* imp. *banikoj.*

Banikos, (nin). I avoid or escape a trap, I was almost caught in a trap; p. *benikosod.*

Banina, (nin) (nân). I let some obj. fall to the ground, I drop it, it escapes my hands; p. *beninad;* imp. *banin.*

Banîshkwatagan. Alg. mask; pl.-*an.*

Banitam, (nin). I don't understand well what I hear; p. *benitang.*

Banitân, (nin) (wa). I don't understand him well, (although I hear him talking;) p. *ben..wad.*

Bansan, (nin) (swa). I broil or grill it; p. *bensang.*

Bap, (nin). I laugh, I smile; p. *baiâpid.*

Bâpia, (nin). I laugh at him, I smile at him friendly, kindly; p. *baiâpiad.*

Bâpijima, (nin). I revile him; p. *baia..mad.*

Bapijima, (nin). I speak to him urgently, commanding him; p. *bep..mad.*

Bâpinendam, (nin). I rejoice in thoughts; p. *baia..ang.*

Bapinendamona, (nin). I make him rejoice in thoughts; p. *baia..nad.*

Bapinendamowin. Rejoicing, joyful thoughts, joy.

Bâpinenim, (nin). I rejoice, I am joyful, gay, glad; p. *baia..mod.*

Bapinenimoa, (nind). I make

him rejoice, I make him gay, glad, joyful; p. *baia..ad; imp.* *bapinenimo.*

Bapinenimowin. Joy, rejoicing, pleasure, gayness, merriment.

Bapinisiwagan. Eminent danger, peril, dangerous thing; pl.-*ag.*

Bâpinôdage, (*nin*). I scorn; I waste; p. *baia..ged.*

Bapinodagewin, or, *papinodamowin.* Scorning, derision, mockery, scoffing; wasting, spoiling.

Bâpinodan, (*nin*). I laugh at it, I ridicule it, mock it, deride it; I waste it; p. *baia..dang.*

Bâpinodawa, (*nin*). I laugh at him, I deride or ridicule him, I mock him; I waste some *an.* obj.; p. *baia..wad.*

Bâpish, or *babâpish,* adv. This word always occurs connected with an adverb of negation, *ka, kawin, kego;* and is employed to give an additional force to the negation or prohibition.—*Kawin bâpish;* no, not at all. *Kego bâpish ijâken wedi;* don't go there at all.

Bâpishk, (*nin*). I like too much to laugh, I am in a habit of laughing always; p. *baia..kid.*

Bapitamowiniken, (*nin*). I expose it to laughter, I make it ridiculed; p. *baiap..ked.*—*Ki bapitamowiniken kéd anôkiwin,* you make people laugh at your work.

Bapiiamowinikenan, (*nin*). I make some *an.* obj. ridiculed; p. *baia..ked.* (V. Conj.)

Bâpiton, (*nin*). I laugh at it, I mock, deride, ridicule it; p. *baiapitod.*

Bâpiwin. Laughing, laughter.

Bashanjeigan. Whig; scourge; lash; pl.-*an.*

Bashanjéigas, (*nind*). I am whipped, scourged; p. *besh..sod*

Bashânjéige, (*nin*). I whip, I chastise; p. *besh..ged.*

Bashanjêigewin. Chastisement, whipping, scourging, flagellation, lashing.

Bashanjéwa, (*nin*). I whip him, scourge him, chastise him; I lash him; p. *besh..wad; imp. bashanjé.*

Bashigwadis, (*nin*). I am capricious, I am self-willed; p. *besh..sid.*

Bashkobissan, (*nin*) or, *nin baskwabowassan.* I scald it, I pour boiling water on it; p. *bes..ang.*

Bashkobissodis, (*nin*) or, *nin baskwabowass.* I scald myself with boiling water; p. *bes..sod.*

Bashkobisswa, (*nin*) or, *nin baskwabowasswa.* I scald him, pouring boiling water on him, (a person or any other *an.* object;) p. *bes..wad;* imp. *bash..wi.*

Bâskikwéigan. Lancet for bleeding; pl.-*an.*

Bâskikwéige, (*nin*). I let blood, I bleed somebody; p. *baia..ged.*

Bâskikweigewin. Blood-letting, bleeding

Bâskikwéwa, (*nin*). I bleed him; p. *baia..wad;* imp. *baskikwé.*

Bâss, (*nin*). I dry, I become dry; p. *baiâssod.—Nabagissagog gi-basawag*, the boards dried, (became dry.)

Bassagwagami, or-*magad*. It is thick, (some liquid;) p. *bess ..mig*, or-*magak*. (The same as *Pasagwagami*.)

Bassakonindjin, (*nin*). I have sticky hands, (from pitch, etc.); p. *bess..nid*.

Bâssama, (*nin*). I am drying meat, or other objects; p. *baiâssamad*.

Bâssamâwin. The act of drying s. th.

Bâssan, (*nin*). I dry it; p. *baiassad*.

Bassassâbanak. Pole to hang a net on to dry, net-drying pole; pl.-*on*.

Bassikodân, (*nin*). I match it (with a matching plane;) p. *baia..ang*.

Bassikôdjigan. Matching plane; pl.-*an*.

Bâssikona, (*nin*). I match it, (*an*. obj.); p. *baia..nad; imp. bassikoj.— Nabagissagog nin bassikonag*, I am matching boards.

Bassikwêbina, (*nin*). I tie or bind s. th. round his head; p. *bess..nad*.

Bassikwebis, (*nin*). I put or tie s.th. round my head; p. *bess.. sod*.

Bassikwêbison. Any thing tied round the head; pl.-*an*.

Bassingwewa, (*nin*). I strike him in the face; p. *bess..wad*; imp. *bassingwê*.

Bâssisid pakwejigan. Flour.

Bassitâgan. Sunflower; (F. tournesol;) pl.-*ag*.

Bâssiwa, (*nin*). I dry some *an*. obj.; p. *baiass..wad*.

Bâta–. This particle, prefixed to verbs or substantives, gives them a signification which implies the idea of *sin, wrong, damage*. (Examples in some of the following words.)

Bata-dodage, (*nin*). I do wrong to people, I sin against somebody; p. *baia..ged*.

Bata-dodam, (*nin*). I do wrong, I sin, (in *action*); p. *baia.. dang*.

Batâdowin. Sin, bad action, fault, vice, transgression, crime; pl.-*an*.

Batâ-gijwe, (*nin*). I speak sinful wicked words; I blaspheme; p. *baia..wed*.

Bata-gijwewin. Sinful speaking; blaspheming.

Bata-ijiwebad. It is sinful, it is wicked, wrong; p. *baia . bak*.

Bata-ijiwebis, (*nin*). I sin, I am a sinner, I am wicked; p. *baia..sid*.

Bata-ijiwebisiwin. Sin, sinfulness, wickedness, bad sinful behavior or conduct.

Batainad. There is much of it; p. *baia..nak*.

Bata-indind, (*nin*). I sin; p. *baiatadigid*.

Bata-inendam, (*nin*). I have a sinful thought, or sinful thoughts, I sin in thoughts; p. *baia..dang*.

Batâ-inendamowin. Sinful thoughts, sinful thinking; pl.-*an*.

Bataini. There is much of it, (*an*. obj;) they are numerous; also, he has a large family.

P. *baiâtainid.*—*Batâini jonia oma,* there is too much money here. *Bataini Jâganâsh,* The English are numerous. *Bâtaini aw anishinâbe,* this Indian has a numerous family.
Bâtamâ, (*nin*). I accuse him, I give testimony against him, I condemn him by my testimony; p. *baiâtamad.*
Bâtange, (*nin*). I accuse, I give testimony to conviction, to condemnation; p. *baiâtanged.*
Bâtas, (*nin*). I hurt myself, I damage or wrong myself, I lame myself; I sin; p. *baia.. tasod.*
Bâte, or-*magad.* I is dry; p. *baiateg,* or-*magak.*
Bâtégigo. Dried fish; pl.-*iag.*
Bâtémin. A dried whortleberry; pl -*an.*
Baiémishimin. Dry apple; pl.-*ag.*
Batéwiiâss. Dried meat.
Bawaan, (*nin*). I knock it off with a stick, (wild rice;) also I trash it; p. *bewaang.*
Bawâdjigan. Dream; pl.-*an.*
Bawâdjige, (*nin*). I dream; p. *bew..ged.*
Bawâigan, or *bawaiganak.* A stick to knock out; flail; pl.-*an,* or *an.*
Bawaiminân. A kind of wild cherry; pl.-*an.*
Bawâiminanagawanj. A wild cherry-tree; pl.-*in.*
Bawâna, (*nin*). I dream of him; p. *bewânad.*
Bawégina, (*nin*) (*nân*). I strike off the dust from it; p. *bew.. nad.*— *Nin moshwem nin bawegina,* I shake off the dust from my handkerchief.
Bawisideshimonowin. Any thing to wipe the feet on; pl.-*an.*
Bâwitig, (pron. *baotig*). Rapids in a river; (F. rapide, saut.)
Bawiwebina, (*nin*) or, *nin bawiwebishkawa.* I shake him off, (any *an.* obj.); p. *bew..ad.*
Bébakân, adv. Separately, differently, in different directions, in different places.
Bebamadisid. Traveler, pas senger; pl.-*jig.*
Bebâmikaigod bebejigoganjin. One who is carried in a carriage; pl.-*godjig beb...*
Bebâmomigod bebejigoganjin. One that is carried about on the back of a horse, a rider, a horseman; pl.-*godjig.*
Bebéjig, num. Some, a few; one by one.
Bebêjigoganji. Horse, (animal with one hoof, that is, uncloven hoof;) pl.-*g.*—S. *Kanj.*
Bebejigoganji-binakwéigan, or *bebejigoganji-binikwan.* Curry-comb, horse-comb; pl.-*an.*
Bebejigoganji-manomin. Oats, (properly, horse-rice.)
Bebejigoganji-nin bimomig. The horse carries me on his back, I ride on horseback.
Bebejigoganjins. Colt, filly; pl.-*ag.*
Bebegigoganji-ônapisowin. Harness of a horse; pl.-*an.*
Bebéjigoganji-osow. Horse-tail. —S. *Osow.*
Bebejigoganjiwigamig. Stable for horses, (horse-house;) pl.-*on.*
Bebéjigoganjiwimo. Horse-dung.
Bebêjigoganji-winisissan. The

mane of a horse, (horse-hair.)

Bebésho, adv. Near together, near one another, thickly.—*Bebesho nin damia*, we live near together. *Bebesho aniatewan odenâwan;* there are villages all long at short distances from each other.

Bebikinong, adv. Differently. —*Kawin bebikinong nind inenimassig*, I don't think them different, (I don't esteem them differently, but alike, without respect of persons.)

Bebitosi. The first stomach of ruminating animals.

Bebiwijinidjig. The little ones, the small ones, (persons or other *an.* objects.) *Bebiwijinidjig abinodjiiag*, little children. *Bebiwijinidjig opinig*, small potatoes. S. *Babiwijinimin.*

Bebokwedagiming-gisiss. The month of April; (the snowshoe-breaking moon.)

Bed, bedj, in compositions, signifies *slow, slack.* (Examples in some of the following words.)

Bêdendam, (*nin*). I am slow, (in my thoughts and resolutions;) p. *baiêdendang.*

Bédendamowin. Slowliness of mind, thought, resolution.

Bédjibato, (*nin*). I run slowly; p. *baie..tod.*

Bédjig, (*nin*). I grow slowly; p. *baie..gid.*

Bédjigin. It grows slowly; p. *baie..ging.*

Bédjissin, (*nin*). I eat slowly; p. *baie..nid.*

Bedjiw, (*nin*). I am slow in my doings, works, etc.; p. *baie..wid.*

Bédosse, (*nin*). I walk slowly; p. *baie..sed.*

Bějig, num. one; a certain; the other. — *Bějig kwiwisens*, a certain boy. *Bejig kinik*, thy other arm.

Béjig, (*nin*). I am one; I am alone; p. *baiejigod.*

Bejig nijiwad. One of the two, (*an.* obj.)

Bejigoênima, (*nin*). I think only on him, I think constantly on him; p *baie..mad.*

Béjigôkam, (*nin*). I am alone in a canoe or boat; p. *baie..kang.*

Bejigominag, a, an, one.—This word alludes to a *globulous* object; as: *Bejigominag tchiss, bejigominag mishimin ;* one turnip, one apple.

Bejigonjan. An only child.

Bejigonje, (*nin*). I have only one child; p. *baie..jed.*

Bějigoshk. One breadth of cloth, of cotton, linen, etc.

Béjikwâbik, a, an, one; alluding to *metal, stone, glass ;* as: *Bejigwâbik joniia ki-minin*, I give thee a dollar. *Wâsetchiganâbik nin gi-bigwaan bejikwâbik*, I broke a window-glass.

Bejigwakwoagan. S. *Ningotwakwoagan.*

Béjigwan. It is one, one thing, the same thing.

Béjigwanong, adv. Always in the same place; always the same thing.

Bejigwâtig, a, an, one; alluding to *wood;* as: *Bejigwâtig na-*

bagissag, bejigwâtig abwi; a board, or one board, one paddle.

Béjigweg, a, an, one; alluding to stuff, a blanket, a handkerchief, etc.; as: *Bejigweg wâboiân nin giminigo, win dash bejigweg moshwen;* a blanket was given to me, and to him a handkerchief.

Bejigwendagwad. It is considered all one and the same thing; p. *baie..wak.*

Bejigwendagosimin, (*nin*). We are considered all one and the same person; p. *baie..sidjig.*

Béjigwendam, (*nin*). I have always the same thought, I am constant; p. *baie..ang.*

Bejigwendamin,(*nin*).. We think all the same thing, we are united in our thoughts and sentiments, we agree together; p. *baie..dangig.*

Bejigwendamowin. The same thought, unity and conformity of thoughts and sentiments, concord; constancy.

Béka, adv. Slowly, quietly, gently.

Bêka! interj. Stop! hold on! not so quick!

Bekâdendagos, (*nin*). I am long suffering, patient; p. *baie..sid.*

Bekâdendagosiwin. Long suffering, patience.

Bekadis, (*nin*). I am quiet, still, mild, meek, forbearing; patient in contradictions, (*without saffering;*) p. *baie..sid.*

Bekadisiwin. Tranquillity, still and quiet-behavior, mildness, meekness; patience.

Bekadowe, (*nin*). I speak low, (not loud;) p. *baie..wed.*

Beka nin kotagendam. I am patient in *sufferings,* in sickness, labor, persecution.

Békanisid. Another one.

Békish, adv. At the same time.

Békominagakkashkâbikaigan. Padlock, (round lock.)

Bémâdagad. One that swims, a swimmer; pl *-jig.*

Bêmâdawabid. One that squints, a squinter; pl.*-jig.*

Bémâdisid. One that lives, somebody; pl.*-bemadisidjig,* people, folks, the world.

Bemibatod. One that runs, a runner; pl.*-jig.*

Bémidekadeg pâshkisigan. Carabine. S. *Bimidekade.*—This signifies properly: "Greased gun."

Bemiged. One living in a house or lodge, an inhabitant; pl.*-jig.*

Bemossessig. One that does not walk, a lame person, unable to walk, a cripple; pl.*-og.*

Benâdjitod od ai-man. One that wastes his things, a spendthrift, squanderer, prodigal person; pl. *benadjitodjig od aiimiwan.*

Béngos, (*nin*). I am dry, not wet; p. *baiengosid.*

Bêngwakamiga. The ground or soil is dry; p. *baie..gag.*

Béngwan. It is dry; p. *baiengwang.*

Bêngwanam, (*nin*). My throat is dry, I am thirsty; p. *baie..mod.*

Bêshibia, (*nin*). I mark it, (*an. obj.*), I make marks or figures on it; p. *baie..ad.*

Beshigaigan. A thing to mark with, a scratch-awl, a graver, etc.; pl.-*an.*

Bésho, adv. Near, nigh, close by.

Béshodjîa, (*nin*). I draw nigh him, I approach him, I come to him; p. *baie..ad.*

Bésho nin tatoki. I make a short step; *bebésho nin takoki,* or, *besho nin tatakoki,* I make short steps in walking. —S. *Wassa nin takoki.*

Beshosikawa, (*nin*). I come near him, I approach him; p. *baie..wad.*

Bêshowad. It is near, close by; p. *baieshowak.*

Béshowendagwad. It is considered near; p. *baie..wak.*

Bésika (*nin*). I walk, navigate or travel slowly; p. *baiedsika.*

Bésikamagod. It goes or moves slowly; p. *baie..gak.*

Besikawin. Slow walking, slow traveling.

Bétchig, (*nin*). I grow very slowly; p. *baietchigid.*

Bêtchigin. It grows very slowly; p. *baie..ing.*

Bewendagos, (*nin*). I am worth little; p. *baie..sid.*

Bewenima, (*nin*) (*dan*). I think little of him, I esteem him little; p. *baie..mad.*

Béwitagos, (*nin*). They mistrust my speaking, they don't believe what they hear me say; p. *baie..sid.*

Bi, or, *pi.* This particle is prefixed to verbs or substantives, to give them the signification, of *approaching, coming on;* as: *Bi-nawakwêwissinin,*come to dinner. *Bi-nagamoiok,*come here to sing.

Bi, as end-syllable in some neuter verbs, signifies, *filled with liquor,* or otherwise *relating to liquor;* as: *Débibi,* he drank enough. *Gâwibi,* he falls being drunk. *Modjigibi,* he is gay and joyful in his intoxication; etc.

Bi, (*nin*). I wait; 3. p. *bio;* p. *baod.*

Bia, (*nin*). I wait for him, I await him; p. *bâad.*

Bibâg, (*nin*). I cry out, I shout, I call loud; p. *bebagid.*

Bibagâ, or-*magad.* It is thin; p. *bebagag,* or-*magak.*

Bibagâbikad. It is thin, (metal;) p. *beb..kak.*— *Osâm bibagabikad ow abwewin,* this frying-pan is too thin.

Bibagâbikia, (*nin*). I make it thin or thinner, I thin it, (relating to *joniia,* silver, or *assin,* stone, which are *an.*)

Bibagâbikisi aw joniia, aw assin, this piece of silver, this stone is thin.

Bibâgatandiwin. Auction, (crying sale.)

Bibâgatawe, (*nin*). I am selling at auction, (I cry selling;) p. *beb..wed.*

Bibagigad. It is thin, (wood;) p. *beb..gak.*—*Kitchi bibagigad ki tikinagan,* thy cradle is very thin.

Bibagigad. It is thin, (cloth, cotton, etc.) p. *beb..gak.* — *Osâm bibagigad mandan adopowinigin,* this table cloth is too thin.

Note. The difference between

this and the preceding word consists only in the pronunciation, which must be heard.

Bibagigisi. It is thin, (a board; or some silk-stuff;) p. *beb..sid.*

Bibajikona, (*nin*) (*an*). I make some obj. thin, (or thinner,) by cutting; p. *beb..nâd;* imp. *bibagikoj.—Bibagikoj aw nabagissagons,* cut that shingle thinner.

Bibâgima, (*nin*). I call him with a loud voice. *Nin bibâgima anamiewigamigong,* I publish his bans of marriage in the church; p. *beb..mad.*

Bibâgindân, (*nin*). I call it; p. *beb..ang.— O bibagindan nibowin,* he calls death.

Bibagingine, (*nin*). I have temples, (on both sides of the head;) p. *beb..ned.*

Bibâgishe, (*nin*). It tingles in my ears; p. *beb..ed.*

Bibagisi. It is thin, (some obj.) p. *beb..sid.*

Bibagissaga, or-*magad.* The floor is thin; p. *beb..gag,* or-*magak.*

Bibagiwin. Cry, loud calling, voice; publication of the bans of marriage in the church.

Bibâgotam, (*nin*). I raise the death-whoop, indicating the number of the enemies killed.

Bibagotamowin. Indian death-whoop.

Bibinékamate, or-*magad.* The ground is dry, there is a drought, want of rain; p. *beb..teg,* or-*magak.*

Bibinêshkine, or-*magad.* It is not pressed down; p. *beb..neg,* or-*magak.*

Bibôn. Winter; year. *Bibônong,* last winter; *minawa tchi bibong,* next winter; *bibông* or *bibongin,* in winter. *Nisso bibon, nano bibon, midâsso bibon;* three years, five years, ten years.

Bibônagad. Year; p. *bebonagak.*—This word is always preceded by a number or adverb; as: *Anin endasso-binônagak eko-aiaian oma?* How many years hast thou been here?—*Jaigwa nishwasso bibonagad eko-aiaiân iweti;* I have now been eight years there.

Bibonagis, (*nin*). This verb is only used in connexion with a number or adverb, to denote the age of a person; as: *Anin endasso-bibonagisiian?* How many years art thou old? —*Nijtana nin dasso bibonagis, nishime dash midâsso bibonagisi;* I am twenty years old, and my brother ten years.

Bibônish, (*nin*). I winter, I am in my winter-quarter; I spend the winter-season in a certain place; p. *beb..id.*

Bibonishimagad. It winters, it remains or lies somewhere over winter; p. *beb..gak.*— *Mi oma gebibonishimagak ow nabibwân;* this vessel will lie here over winter, (it will winter here.)

Bibônishiwin. Wintering; winter-quarter.

Bibôniwaiân. Winter-skin, winter-fur; pl.-*ag.*

Bibôn-mikana. Winter-path, (where they use to walk only

in the winter-season; pl.-*n*.

Bid, bidj, bidji. In compositions signifies *coming this way, approaching.* (Examples in some of the following words.)

Bidâbama, (*nin*). I see him coming this way; p. *bad..mad.*

Bidâban. It begins to dawn, the break of day; p. *badabang.*

Bidâdagak. I am coming, on the ice; p. *bad..ed.*

Bidâdem, (*nin*). I come weeping; p. *bad..mod.*

Bidâdjim, (*nin*). I come to tell s. th., I bring a news or story; p. *bad..mod.*

Bidâdjimotage, (*nin*). I come to tell people s. th.; p. *bad..ged.*

Bidâdjimotan, (*nin*). I come to tell it; p. *bad..ang.*

Bidâdjimotawa, (*nin*). I come to tell him s. th., I bring him news; p. *bad..wad.*

Bidâdjimowin. Report, news brought in; pl.-*an.*

Bidâgimosse, (*nin*). I am coming on snowshoes; p. *bad..sed.*

Bidaginan, (*nin*). I bend it towards me, (wood); p. *bad..ang.*

Bidamawa, (*nin*). I bring him s. th.; p. *bad..wad.*

Bidânimad. The wind is coming; p. *bad..mak.*

Bidâsh, (*nin*). I am coming with the wind, (sailing this way before the wind; p. *badaskid.*

Bidâss, (*nin*). I bring; p. *badassod.*

Bidâssamishka, (*nin*). I am coming this way in a canoe, boat, etc.; p. *bad..kad.*

Bidâssamosse, (*nin*). I come this way; p. *bad..sed.*

Bidâssin. It is coming here by the wind; p. *badassing.—Nabikwân bidâssin,* a vessel is coming.

Bidibissa. A shower of rain is coming; p. *ba..sag.*

Bidikwâkone, or-*magad.* The fire makes noise; p. *bed..ned.*

Bidina, (*nin*). I give him or it, (some *an.* obj.); p. *bâdinad;* imp. *bidin.*

Bidinamawa, (*nin*). I give him or it to him, into his hands; p. *bad..wad.*

Bidipo, or-*magad.* A snowstorm is coming; p. *badipog,* or-*magak.*

Bidjanoki, (*nin*) or, *bi-anoki.* I come here to work; p. *ba..kid.*

Bijibato, (*nin*). I come here running; p. *ba..tod.*

Bidjibiamago, (*nin*). I receive a letter; p. *badjibiamawind.*

Bidjibide, or-*magad.* It comes, sliding or flying, it slides; p. *bad..deg,* or-*magak.*

Bidjibiigan. Letter *received,* pl.-*an.*

Bidjibiso beneshi. The bird slides through the air p. *bad..sod.*

Bidjidabi, (*nin*). I come here, dragging s. th. after me; p. *bad..bid.*

Bidjidjiwan. It runs this way, (water, etc.) p. *bad .ang.*

Bidjigade, or-*magad.* It is brought hither; p. *bad..deg,* or-*magak.*

Bidjigéwa, (*nin*). I supplant

him with my *foot;* p. *bad..wad;* imp. *bidjigé.* S. *Bisogêwa.*

Bidjigidas, (*nin*). I come here angry; p. *bad..sod.*

Bidjija, (*nin*) or, *nin bi-ija.* I come here; p. *ba..jad.*

Bidjimagos, (*nin*). I am smelled, my odor cemes; p. *bad..sid.*

Bidjimassige, (*nin*). I spread the smell or odor of s. th.; p. *bad..ged.*

Bidjinikawa, (*nin*). I push or shove him on with my arm or arms; p. *bad..wad.*

Bidjinissiton, (*nin*). I push or shove it somewhere; p. *bad..tod.*

Bidjisse bineshi. The bird flies hither, to this place; p. *bad..jissed.*

Bidjisse, or-*magad.* It flies hither, this way; p. *badjisseg.* or-*magak.*

Bidjitass, (*nin*). I carry a load before hand to a place whither I intend to move; p. *badjitassod.*

Bidjiwakwane, (*nin*). I put on my hat; p. *badj..ned.*

Bidôma, (*nin*). I bring him on my back; p. *badomad.*

Bidon, (*nin*). I bring it; p. *bâdod.*

Bidondân, (*nin*). I bring it on my back, on my carrying-strap or portage-strap; p. *bad..ang.*

Bidwewe, in compositions, alludes to the *hearing of an approaching sound.* (Examples in some of the following words.)

Bidwewedjiwan. The running of a stream is heard, or the rapids of a stream are heard; p. *bad..wang.*

Bidweweshin, (*nin*). I am heard coming on; p. *bad..ing.*

Bidwewetagos, (*nin*). I am heard coming hither speaking; p. *bad..sid.*

Bidwewetawa, (*nin*). I hear him coming hither speaking; p. *bad..wad.*

Bidwewidam, (*nin*). I come here speaking; p. *bad..ang.*

Biewagenima, (*nin*). I wait for him, in my thoughts, I am thinking on his arrival; p. *baew..mad.*

Bi-gigis, (*nin*). I have or bring with me, (somebody or s. th.); p. *ba..gigisid.—Kawin bijishig nin bi-ijassi, nin bi-gigis sa;* I don't come alone, (or with nothing,) I bring with me, (some person, or some other obj.)

Bi-gigisia, (*nin*). I cause him to bring some *an.* obj. along with him; p. *ba-..ad.*

Bi-gigisimâgad. It comes with... it brings along with it...; p. *ba-g..gak.—Kitimiwin bi-gigisimagad kitimâgisiwin, kotâgitowingaie;* laziness brings along with it poverty and suffering.

Bi-gigisin, (*nin*). I bring it along with me, I come with it; p. *ba-gigisid.*

Bi-gigisinân, (*nin*). I have him along with me, I come along with him, (any *an.* obj.); p. *ba. gigisid* (V. Conj.)

Bigisawâb, (*nin*). I cannot see

well, I huve weak eyes, dim eyes; p. *bag..bid.*
Bigisawinan, (*nin*). I cannot see it well; p. *bag..ang.*
Bi-giwe, (*nin*). I come back again; p. *ba-giwed.*
Bigobidjigade, or-*magad*. It is torn; it is taken down, (a building, etc.); it is broken, (a commandment;) p. *bag..deg*, or-*magak*.
Bigabidjigan, or *bigobodjigan*. Any thing to tear with; also, a plough; a harrow; pl.-*an*.
Bigobidjigaso. It is torn, (*an*. obj.); p. *bag..sod.*
Bigobidjige, (*nin*). I tear; I plough; p. *bag..ged.*
Bigona, (*nin*) (*don*). I tear some obj.; p. *bag..nad;* imp. *bigobij.*
Bigodass, (*nin*). I have torn leggings; p. *bag..sed.* *
Bigode, or-*magad*, (*bigwade*). It breaks in two, burning, it burns through in the middle; p. *bagodeg*, or-*magak*.
Bigoganâma, (*nin*) (or, *nin bigwaganâma*). I break it by striking it, (*an*. obj.); p. *bag..mad.*
Bigoganândan, (*nin*) (or, *nin bigwaganandan.*) I break it by striking it, I shatter it to pieces; p. *bag..ang.*
Bigokwanaie, (*nin*). I wear torn clothes; p. *bag..ied.*
Bigona, (*nin*). I break some *an*. obj. into pieces; p. *bagonad.—Pakwejigan nin bigona, ashamagwa abinodjiiag;* I break bread into pieces to give it to the children.
Bigoneshin, (*nin*). I break my canoe; I shipwreck; p. *bag..ing.*
Bigoshin, (or, *bigwishin*). It breaks, falling to the ground, (*an*. obj.); p. *bag..ing.*
Bigoshka, (*nin*). I break down, I am broken, ruined; I am put out of power, I am removed from office; p. *bagoshkad.*
Bigoshkawa, (*nin*) (*kân*). I break him down; I break some *an*. obj.; I tear it; p. *bag..wad.—Nin gi-bigoshkawa aw tipaigisiswân gaiê nin gi bigoshkawa nin moshwem;* I broke this watch, and I tore my handkerchief.
Bigossin, (or, *bigwissin.*) It breaks falling down to the ground; p. *bag..ing.*
Bigwaan, (*nin*). I break it; p. *bagwaang.*
Bigwajêwa, (*nin*). I tear his skin, scratching him; p. *bag..wad;* imp. *bigwaje.*
Bigwakamigaan kitigân, (*nin*). I break a field or garden, I plough or hoe it; p. *bag..ang.*
Bigwakamigaigade, or-*magad*. The soil or ground is broken up, it is ploughed or hoed; p. *bag..deg*, or-*magak*.
Bigwakamigibidjigan. A thing to break up the ground with, a plough; pl.-*an*.
Bigwakamigibidjige, (*nin*). I plough; p. *bag..ged.*
Bigwakôkweoweshi. A kind of wood pecker; pl.-*iag.*
Bigwama, (*nin*) (*dân*). I tear

* *Note.* In some of the following words there ought to be *wa* or *wi*, instead of *o*, in the second syllable; but as *o* is plainly heard in pronouncing, we dot it also in writing. Very often *wa* and *wi* are pronounced like *o*.

him with the teeth; p. *bagwamad.*

Bigwawa, (*nin*). I break some *an.* obj.; p. *bag..wad;* imp. *bigwâ.*

Bigwebimagad. There are branches; p. *bag..gak.*

Bigwebimagisi mitig. The tree has branches.

Bigwékab, (*nin*). I turn this way, *sitting;* p. *ba-g..bid.*—S. *Ani-gwékab.*

Bigwekigabaw, (*nin*). I turn this way, *standing;* p. *ba-g..wid.*—S. *Ani-gwékigabaw.*

Bigwenishin. It breaks falling, (*an.* obj.); p *bag..ing.*

Bigwishima, (*nin*) (*don*) (or, *nin bigoshima*). I break it to pieces, by letting it fall down; p. *bag..mad.*

Bi-ijâ, (*nin*). I come; p. *ba..ijad.*

Bi-iji-gikab, (*nin*). I put myself nearer here, sitting; p. *ba..bid.*

Bi-inika, (*nin*). I come here for some reason; p. *ba-inikad.* —*Wegonen ha-inikaian?* Why dost thou come here? (What is the reason of thy coming?)

Bijibâ, in compositions, signifies *round, around.*

Bijibâbato, (*nin*). I run round, around s. th.; p. *bej..tod.*

Bijibâbiwan. There is a whirlwind driving round the snow; p. *bej..ang.*

Bijibâosse, (*nin*). I walk round, I describe a circle in walking; p. *bej..sod.*

Bijibâsse bineshi. The bird flies round, describes a circle.

Bijibénima, (*nin*) (*dân*). I think always on him; p. *bej..mad.*

Bijibiidee, (*nin*). *Ot.* I feel an inclination to vomit; p. *bej..ed.*

Bijiw, or *pisiw.* Lynx; pl.-*ag.*

Bijiwaiân. Lynx-skin; pl.-*ag.*

Bijiwe, (*nin*). I bring a scalp, or scalps; p. *bâjiwed.*

Bikomigens. A kind of small pearl; pl.-*ag.*

Bikominagad. It is round, of a globulous form; p. *bek..gak.*

Bikominagisi. It is round or globulous, (*an.* obj.); p. *bek..sid.*

Bikwakwa, or-*magad.* There is a number of trees standing together.

Bimaadon mikana, (*nin*). I follow a road, path, trail; p. *bem..dod.*

Bimaamâs, (*nin*). I pass by in a canoe, singing; p. *bem..sod.*

Bimaamog binessiwag. The birds are together by troops, by gangs; p. *bemaamodjig.*

Bimaan (*nin*). I take off the cream, the foam; p. *bemaang.*

Bimaana, (*nin*). I follow his track; p. *bem..nad.*

Bimâbog, (*nin*). I float down with the current of a river; 3. p o.; p. *bem..god.*

Bimâbon, (*nin*). I go downstream in a canoe or boat; 3. p. o.; p. *bem..nod.*

Bimâdad. It is living, it is alive; p. *bemadak.*—*Bemadak nibi ki ga minain.* I will give thee living water to drink.

Bimâdaga, (*nin*). I swim; p. *bem..gad.*

Bimâdagak, (*nin*). I walk on the ice; p. *bem..kod.*

Bimâdagasi, (*nin*). I walk in the water, I wade; p. *bem..sit.*

Bimadawâb, (*nin*). I look obliquely or aside, I squint; p. *bam..bid.*

Bimâdis, (*nin*). I live, I am alive; p. *bem..sid.*

Bimadisimagad. It lives; p. *bem..gak.*

Bimâdisiwin. Life. *Kagigê bimâdisiwin*, life everlasting, eternity.

Bimâdjia, (*nin*). I make him live, I give him life, I save him, I vivificate or vivify him; p. *bemadjiad.*

Bimadjiiwe, (*nin*). I give life, I save life; p. *bem..wed.*

Bimâdjiton,(*nin*). I make it live, that is, I conserve or save it from destruction; p. *bem..tod.*

Bimâgimosse, (*nin*). I pass by walking with snowshoes; p. *bem..sed.*

Bimajaam, (*nin*). S. *Jijodéwaam.* *Bimajâgam*, (*nin*). S. *Jijodéwe.* *Bimâkosi mitig.* S. *Bimoskogisi.*

Bimakwa, or-*magad.* There is a forest, woods; p. *bem..ag*, or-*magak.*—*Wassa wedi bimakwa*, the forest is far off there.

Bimâkwaan, (*nin*). I twist or squeeze it with a stick; p. *bam..ang.*

Bimâkwad. Twisted wood; pl. *on.*

Bimâkwaigan. Stick used for twisting or squeezing; pl.-*an.*

Bimâkwaige, (*nin*). I twist with a stick, I squeeze; p. *bam..ged.*

Bimâkwajiwe, (*nin*). I pass by in a canoe, or boat; p. *bem..wed.*

Bimâkwamo, or-*magad.* A piece of wood lies *on high*, (not on the ground;) p. *bem..mog*, or-*magak.*

Bimâkwamoton, (*nin*). I put a piece of wood somewhere *elevated* from the ground; p. *bem..tod.*

Bimâkwâwa, (*nin*). I squeeze some *an.* obj. with a stick; p. *bem..wad*; imp. *bimakwâ.*—*Bimakwâ aw wawashkeshiwaiân*; squeeze this deer-skin.

Bimânadjiwe, (*nin*). I walk on the summit or on the ridge of a mountain; p. *bem..wed.*

Bimamo mikana. The road passes... ; p. *bemamog.*—*Mi ima bemagog mikana*, the road passes there.

Bimandawe, (*nin*). I walk over a log elevated from the ground; p. *bem..wed.*

Bimâsh, (*nin*). I am sailing; p. *bemâshid.*

Bimâshiwin. Sailing.

Bimâtan. It floats down-stream by the current; p. *bematang.*

Bimawanidiwag awessiiag. The beasts (or animals) are together by troops, by gangs.

Bimi-. prefix giving to verbs the accessory idea of *going by*, or *passing* through a place or places. (Examples in some of the following words.)

Bimibagina assema, (*nin*). I twist tobacco; p. *bam..nad.*

Bimibâginigan,. Twisted tobacco.

Bimibaigo, (*nin*). I am made

to pass by running; I pass by riding on horseback or on a carriage; p. *bemibaind.*
Bimibato, (*nin*). I pass by, running; p. *bem..tod.*
Bimibatowin. Run.
Bimibigina, (*nin*). I squeeze it, (*an.* stuff;) p. *bam..ad.*
Bimibodjigan. Plough; pl.-*an.*
Bimibodjige, (*nin*). I plough; p. *bem..ged.*
Bimibos, (*nin*). I slide on the ice for amusement; p. *bem..sod.*
Bimidaagan. S. *Agwawanak.*
Bimidab, (*nin*). I am sitting obliquely; p. *bem..id.*
Bimadabânâ, (*nin*) (*dân*). I draw or drag him along; I pass by carrying him on a sleigh; p. *bem..nad*; imp. *bimidabaj.*
Bimidabiginiganikade, or-*magad.* It is woven; p. *bem..deg,* or-*magak.*
Bimidabiginiganikan. Any woven work; pl.-*an.*
Bimidabiginiganike, (*nin*). I weave; p. *bem..ked.*
Bimidâkigânan. Clavicule, collar-bone; pl.-*an.*
Bimidakonigan. Sail-yard; pl.-*an.*
Bimidakonigan, or, *bimidakonegan.* Pattern for the meshes in making fish-nets; pl.-*an;* (mesh-pattern.)
Bimidâsh, (*nin*). I am driven aside by the wind, (in a canoe or boat;) p. *bem..id.*
Bimidassâ. Bar of a canoe or boat; pl.-*g.*
Bimidâssin. It is driven aside by the wind; p. *bem..sing.*
Bimidé. Grease, fat, oil.
Bimidee, (*nin*) or, *bimideshka.* I feel weak and sick, (properly, my heart turns;) p. *bam..ed,* or, *bam..kad.*
Bimidé-jâbosigan. Castor-oil, as a purging medicine.
Bimidekade, or-*magad.* It is greased; p. *bem..deg,* or-*magak.*
Bimidéwadjiw. Mount Olivet.
Bimidéwan. It is greasy, full of grease; p. *bem..ang.*
Bimidëwina, (*nin*). I put grease on him, (or on any *an.* obj.) I grease him; p. *bem..nad;* imp. *bimidewin.*
Bimidéwinigas, (*nin*). I am greased; p. *bem..sod.*
Bimidéwis, (*nin*). I am greasy, I am dirty with grease; p. *bem..sid.*
Bimidina, (*nin*) (*nân*). I hold some obj. obliquely; p. *bem..nad.*
Bimidjishima, (*nin*). I put it obliquely, (*an.* obj.); p. *bem..mad.*
Bimidjishin. It is obliquely, (*an.* obj.); p. *bem..ing.*
Bimidjissin. It is or lies obliquely; p. *bem..ing.*
Bimidjiwâgakwad. Hoe, axe with an oblique or turned edge; pl.-*on.*
Bimidjiwan. It is running, (water;) p. *bem..ang*
Bimidjiwidon, (*nin*). I carry it obliquely, awry; p. *bem..dod.*
Bimig, (*nin*). I work or embroider with porcupine quills; p. *bamigid.*
Bimigabawimin, (*nin*). We are standing round, (around somebody or s. th.); p. *bémigabawidjig,* bystanders.

Bimige, (*nin*). I live with others in a village or town; p. *bemiged*. Pl. *bemigedjig*, those living in a village or town.

Bimigeidimin, (*nin*). We live together in a village or town, we are neighbors; p. *bëmigeididjig*, neighbors.

Bimigemin, (*nin*). We live in a village, (not in the woods, in the wilderness;) p. *bemigedjig*.

Bimi-ija, (*nin*). I pass by, or I come through, a place, in going to another place; p. *bemiijad*.

Bimikawade, or-*magad*. There are tracks or vestiges, footsteps; p. *bem..deg*, or-*magak*.

Bimikawe, (*nin*). There are my tracks, my footsteps, they show, (on the snow, in mud, etc.); p. *bem..wed*.

Bimikawewin. Vestige, track, footsteps; pl.-*an*.

Bimimassamawa, (*nin*). I am jealous towards him; p. *bam..wad*.

Bimimâssige, (*nin*). I am jealous; p. *bam..ged*.

Bimina, (*nin*). I twist him; p. *bâminad*.

Biminâjikawa, (*nin*). I run after him, I pursue him; p. *bém..wad*.

Biminakwân. Rope, cord; line; pl.-*an*.

Biminakwânens. Small cord, line, string; pl.-*an*

Biminakwanike, (*nin*). I make cords, ropes, etc., I am a ropemaker; p. *bem..ked*.

Biminakwânikewin. Trade, work, occupation of a ropemaker.

Biminakwânikewinini. Ropemaker; pl.-*wag*.

Biminân, (*nin*). I twist it; p. *bâminang*.

Bimi-nibiteshkanan, (*nin*). I go from one thing to another; p. *bem..dang*.—*Kakina wâkaiganan o bimi-nibiteshkanan*; he passes from one house to another.

Bimi-niteshkawag, (*nin*). I pass from one person to another, (or from any *an*. obj. to another;) p. *bem..wad*.

Biminigadamoa, (*nin*). I make him carry s. th. on his shoulder; p. *bem..ad*.

Biminigâdân, (*nin*). I carry it on my shoulder; p. *bem..ang*.

Biminigan. Auger; pl.-*an*.

Biminigânâ, (*nin*). I carry on my shoulder some *an*. object; p. *bem..nad*.

Biminigânâk. Barrow carried on the shoulder; (F. brancard;) pl.-*an*.

Biminigans. Gimblet; pl.-*an*.

Biminige, (*nin*). I carry on my shoulder; p. *bem..ged*.

Biminik. Cubit elbow. This word is always preceded by a number; as: *Nisso biminik*, three cubits; *nijtana dasso biminik*, twenty cubits.

Bimiokwinomin, (*nin*) or, *nin bimiokwinimin*. We are many together; p. *bem..nodjig*, or, *bem..nidjig*.

Bimipo, or-*magad*. The snow storm passes by; *bemipog*, or-*magak*.

Bimishkâ, (*nin*). I go to some place in a canoe, boat, etc., I travel in a canoe, etc.; p. *bem..kad*.

Bimishkâwin. Traveling by water, navigation, (not sailing.)
Bimisi. Eel; pl.-*wag.*
Bimiskodissi. Snail; pl.-*g.*
Bimikogabaw, (*nin*). S. *Gwekigabaw.*
Bimiskogadeshin, (*nin*). I distort or dislocate my leg; p. *bam..ing.*
Bimiskokwen, (*nin*). I turn my head; p. *bam..nid.*
Bimiskona, (*nin*) (*nân*). I turn it round, or twist it, (some *an.* obj.); p. *bam..nad.*
Bimiskonikeshin, (*nin*). I distort or dislocate my arm; p. *bam..ing.*
Bimiskonindjishin, (*nin*). I distort or dislocate my hand; p. *bam..ing.*
Bimiskosideshin, (*nin*). I distort or dislocate my foot; p. *bam..ing.*
Bimiskota, (*nin*). I turn round; (or any *an.* obj. that turns round or revolves;) p. *bam..tad. Weweni bimiskota jigwanâbik,* the grindstone turns well.
Bimiskoton, (*nin*). I twist or turn it round; p. *bam..tod.*
Bimiskowebina, (*nin*). I turn round briskly some *an.* obj.; p. *bam..nad.*
Bimiskwa, (*nin*), or-*mdgad.* It turns a little; p. *bam..wag,* or-*magak.*
Bimiskwaigan. Screw-driver; pl.-*an.*
Bimiskwaige, (*nin*). I am driving screw; p. *bam..ged.*
Bimiskwissidon, (*nin*). S. *Bimiskonan.*
Bimissê, (*nin*). I fly; p. *bemissed.*
Bimissêwin. Flight, flying.
Bimitajagame, (*nin*). I come here walking on the lake shore; p. *bem..med.*
Bimiwané, (*nin*). I carry a load or pack on my back, I pack with a portage-strap, or carrying-strap; p. *bem..ned.*
Bimiwanéa, (*nin*). I give him a pack to carey s. th. on his back; p. *bem..ad.*
Bimiwanân. The load or pack carried on a portage-strap, pack, burden; pl.-*an.*
Bimiwébaan. It is driven away by the waves; p. *bem..ang.*
Bimiwebaog, (*nin*). I am driven away by the waves, in a canoe, boat, etc.; p. *bem..god.*
Bimiwébash, (*nin*). I am driven away by the wind; p. *bem..id.*
Bimiwébâssin. It is driven away by ths wind; p. *bem..ing.*
Bimiwebidjiwan sibi. The ice of a river goes off entirely; p. *bem..wang.*
Bimiwidashima, (*nin*). I sail with him; p. *bem..mad.*
Bimiwidawa, (*nin*). I carry s. th. for him; p. *bem..wad.*
Bimiwidon, (*nin*). I carry it, I carry it away; p. *bem..dod*
Bimiwina, (*nin*). I carry him away, I conduct or convey him; p. *bem..nad.*
Bimôa, (*nin.* I shoot at him with an arrow; p. *bemoad;* imp. *bimo.*
Bimôdan, (*nin*). I shoot at it with an arrow; p. *bem..ang.*
Bimôde, (*nîn*). I creep, I crawl; p. *bemoded.*

Bimôdëgos, (*nin*). I camp from distance to distance, (going through the woods in winter from one place to another;) p. *bem..sid.*

Bimodégosiwin. The traveling of an Indian family from camp to camp through the woods in winter.

Bimôdjigan. Aim, mark or target of an archer; pl.-*an.*

Bimôdjige, (*nin*). I shoot with an arrow; p. *bem..ged.*

Bimôma, (*nin*). I carry him on my back; p. *bemomad.*

Bimomâwass, (*nin*). I carry somebody on my back, a child; p. *bem..sod.*

Bimôndaa, (*nin*). I give him s. th. to carry on his back, I make him carry s. th.; *fig.* I lay it to his charge, I impute it to him, I lay the fault of it upon him; p. *bem..ad.*

Bimôndam, (*nin*). I carry s. th on my back; p. *bem..ang.*

Bimôndân, (*nin*). I carry it on my back; p. *bem..ang.*

Bimoshkôdawan. Comb; pl.-*an.*

Bimoskogisi aw mitig. This tree is twisted, it cannot be split; p. *bem..sid*

Bimossé, (*nin*). I walk, I pass by; p. *bemossed.*

Bimossêwin. Walk, march.

Bimossêwinagad. There is walking; p. *bem..gak.* — *Kitchi bimossewinagad nongom, mino bimossewinagad dash*; there is much walking to-day, but there is good walking.

Bimwâgan. Wounded person; pl.-*ag.*

Bimwâganes, (*nin*). I am wounded; p. *bem..sid.*

Bimwagania, (*nin*). I wound him; p. *bem..ad.*

Bimwâganiige, (*nin*), I wound, I inflict a wound or wounds; p. *bem..ged.*

Bimwâganiigewin. Wounding, inflicting wounds.

Bimwâganiigowin. Wound; pl.-*an.*

Bimwâganiw, (*nin*). I am a wounded person, I am wounded; p. *bem..wid.*

Bimwâssin, (*nin*). I throw a stone; p. *bem..ing.*—Freq. *babimwâssin.*

Bimwassinaa, (*nin*). (Pr. *bimossinaa*. I stone him, I throw stones at him; p. *bem..ad.*

Bimwâssinaige, (*nin*). (Pr. *bimossinaige*, I throw stones at somebody, I stone people; p. *bem..ged.*

Bimwâtigwe, (*nin*). I shoot at a mark with bow and arrows; p. *bem..wed.*—S. *Godaakwe.*

Bimwéwe, (*nin*). I am heard making noise, in passing by; p. *bem..wed.*

Bimweweshin, (*nin*). I am heard passing by; p. *bem..ing.*

Bimwêwidam, (*nin*). I am heard talking, in passing by; p. *bem..ang.*

Binâ! interj. lo! behold! now!

Bina, (*nin*). I bring him with me; p. *bânad.*

Binâ. This word signifies nothing by itself, and is never used alone, but always in connexion with a number, where it signifies how many fishes have been caught in a net or several nets; as: *Anin endassobinaian?* How many fishes hast thou caught in thy net (or nets)—*Nin bejigô-binâ, nin nijobina, nin midassobina, nin midassobina ashi bejig, ashi nij*, etc., *nijtana nin dassobîna ashi nanan*, etc.; I caught one, two, ten, eleven, twelve, etc., twenty-five, etc. fishes.—These verbs are n. v., and belong to the I. Conj.

Binâbide, (*nin*). I lose my teeth; p. *ben..ded.*

Binad. It is clean, neat, pure; p. *bânak.*

Bi-nâdin, (*nin*). I come for it, I come to fetch it; p. *ba..nadid.*

Binadis, (*nin*). I behave decently, purely chastely; p. *ban..sid.*

Binadisiwin. Decent chaste conduct or behavior, purity, chastity.

Binâdjim, (*nin*). I am telling s. th. decently; p. *ban..mod.*

Binâdjimowin. Modest decent narration or tale; pl.-*an.*

Binâgami. It is clean, (water or other liquid; p. *ban..mig.*

Binagidoneshka, (*nin*). The skin of my lips comes off; p *ben..kad.*

Binagingweshka, (*nin*). The skin of my face comes off; p *ben..kad.*

Binagishka, or-*magad* The skin comes off, falls off; p. *ben..kag*, or-*magak.*

Binaiadis, (*nin*). I am always go ng about, from house to house, or traveling; p. *ben..sid.*

Binâidekomân. Fine comb, dandruff comb; pl.-*an.*

Binaiendan, (*nin*). I change my thoughts or my mind often; p. *ben..ang.*

Binaige, (*nin*). I destroy the dam of a beaver in order to catch him; p. *ben..ged.*

Binakamigishka, or-*magad.* The dust falls in s. th., or upon s. th.; p. *ben..kag*, or-*magak.*

Binakamigishkan, (*nin*). I make it dusty, I make the dust fly and fall on it; p. *ben..ang.*

Binâkisân, (*nin*). I purify it by fire, by burning it; p. *ban..ang.*

Binâkiswa, (*nin*). I purify some *an.* obj. by fire p. *ban..wad; imp. binakiswi.*

Binâkobidjige, (*nin*). I take down a sail; p. *bén..ged.*

Binâkonan ningassimonon, (*nin*). I take down the sail; p. *ben..ang...*

Binâkonige, (*nin*). S. *Binakobidjige.*

Binakwaigan. Rake, harrow; pl.-*an.*

Binâkwaige, (*nin*). I rake; I harrow; p. *ben..ged.*

Binâkwân. Comb, rake, harrow; pl.-*an.*

Binakwaninindj. Finger; pl.-*in* —*Nin binakwaninindj*, my finger; *ki binâkwaninindjin*, thy fingers, etc.

Binakwanisid. Toe; pl.-*an.*—*Nin binakwanisid, ki binakwanisid*, etc.; my toe, thy toe, etc.

Binâkwi, or-*magad* The leaves of the trees fall off, autumn, fall; p. *benakwig*, or-*magak.*

Binâkwigisiss. The moon of the falling of the leaves, the month of October.

Bi-nana, (*nin*). I come for him,

I come to fetch him, to take him away, (person or any other *an.* obj.) ; p. *bananad;* imp. *bi-naj.*

Binangwabiginan, (*nin*). S. *Neshangabiginan.*

Binânikwe, (*nin*). I loose my hair; p. *ben..wed.*

Binanjênan ishkote, (*nin*). I let fall fire; p. *ben..ang.*

Bi-nanjisse, (*nin*). I come down flying; p. *ba .sed.*

Binanoki, or-*magad.* The snow is falling from the trees; p. *ben..kig,* or-*magak.*

Binâs, (*nin*). I am always going about, I don't remain long in the same place; p. *benâsid.*

Binâssawagendam, (*nin*). I often change my plans, my thoughts, my mind; p. *ben.. ang.* S. *Binaendam.*

Binate, or-*magad.* It is clean, neat, (a house, a room, eic.) p. *banateg,* or-*magak.*

Binawân. The fog is falling; p. *ben..ang.*

Binawêân, (*uin*). I wipe the dust off; p. *ben..ang.*

Binawéigan. Brush; pl.-*an.*

Binawéige, (*nin*). I brush; p. *bən. ged.*

Biné. Partridge; pl.-*wog.*

Binébag. Partridge-leaf; pl.-*on;* } a kind of Indian tea.

Binémin. Partridge-berry; pl.-*an;* } a kind of Indian tea.

Btnéshi. A *small* bird; pl.-*iag.* S. *Binéssi.*

Binéshiwanashkid. Tail of a small bird; pl.-*in.*

Binéshiwigwan. Feather of a small bird; pl.-*ag.*

Binêssi. A large bird; pl.-*wag.*

Binéssiwab, (*nin*). I am sitting like a bird; p. *ben..bid.*

Binéssiwigwan. Feathers of a bird; pl.-*ag.*

Bingedj, (*nin*). I am cold, I feel cold; p. *bangedjid.*

Bingengwâm, (*nin*). I sleep too much; p *ban..ang.*

Bini, in compositions, signifies *clean, pure chaste.* (Examples in some of the following words.)

Binia, (*nin*). I clean him, cleanse him, purify him; p. *bâniad.*

Binidee, (*nin*). I have a clean heart, I am chaste, pure; p. *ban..ed.*

Binideewin. Cleanness of heart, chastity.

Binigad. It is clean, (cloth, stuff, paper; p. *bânigak.*

Binigisi. It is clean; p. *ban.. sid.*

Biniigos, (*nin*). I am cleansed; p. *ban..sid.*

Bininâgos, (*nin*). I have a clean appearance; p. *ban. sid.*

Biningwe, (*nin*). I have a clean face; p. *ban..wed.*

Binis, (*nin*). I am clean, neat; pure, chaste; innocent; p. *banisid.*

Binish, adv. till, until, as far as, up to, to.

Binishi, in compositions, signifies, *on my own account, myself, entirely.* (Examples in some of the following words..)

Binishi-angoshka, (*nin*). I break down entirely, I come to nothing; p. *baa..kad.*

Binishima, (*nin*). I accuse him

falsely, I calumniate him; p. *ban..mad.*

Binishkan, (*nin*). I make it fall from its place; p. *ban.. ang.*

Bsnishkawa, (*nin*). I make fall some from its plaee; p. *ban.. wad.*

Binisika, adv. Without reason, unprovoked ; spontaneously, on one's own account.—*Binisika gi-nishkadisi ;* he got angry (flew into a passion without reason, (unprovoked.) *Kawin wika binisikâ nin minigossi gego ;* he never gives me anything spontaneously, (on his own account, without being asked.)

Binisiwin. Cleanness, cleanliness; purity, chastity.

Binissagia nabagissag, (*nin*). I clean a board; p. *ban..aa.*

Binissagisi nabagissag. The board is clean ; p. *ban..sid.*

Binissagiton, (*nin*). I clean it, (a floor ;) p. *ban..tod.*

Binissipogosi. It is insipid, it has no taste, (of victuals; p. *ban..sid.*

Binitawa, (*nin*) or, *nin binitamawa*. I clean or purify it for him, I make clean s. th. belonging to him; p. *ban.. wad.*—*Debenimiian, binitawishin ninde ;* Lord, make clean my heart.

Biniton, (*nin*). I clean, cleanse or purify it; p. *banitod.*

Biniwine. He throws off his horns, (a deer, a stag, etc.) ; p. *ben..ned.*

Binsin, (*nin*). I have s. th. in my eye, a mote, s. th. fell in my eye; p, *bansined.*

Bi-sâgaam, (*nin*). I come out of some place; p. *ba-..ang.*

Bisân, adv. Quiet, still.

Bisânab, (*nin*). I am still, quiet; I stop, I cease; p. *besanabid.*

Bisânabiwin. Silence, tranquillity, quietude.

Bisanâgami. It is still, quiet, (liquid ; p. *bes..ig.*—*Bisanagami sibi*, the river is still, (it does not flow rapidly.)

Bisanendam, (*nin*. I am quiet in my thoughts, in my mind: p. *bes..ang.*

Bisânis, (*nin*). I am quiet, still, peaceable ; p. *bes..sid.*

Bisânishin, (*nin*). I am lying still and quiet; p. *bes..ing.*

Bisânisiwin. Tranquillity, still quiet behavior, peaceful disposition of mind.

Bishaganâb. Little narrow string of leather; pl.-*in.*

Bishagibina, (*nin*) (*don*) or, *nin bishagibidjibina*. I peel, pare or shell some obj; also, I flay or skin him, (her, it ;) p. *besh..nad ;* imp.—*bij.* — *Opinig nin bishagibinag ;* I pare potatoes.

Bishagigijwa, (*nin*). S. *Pakona.*

Biskagika, (*nin*). My skin comes off, (from the face or other parts |of the body, in sickness ; p. *besh..kad.*

Bishigêndagos, (*nin*). I am fair, beautiful; I am glosious, splendid ; p. *besh..sid.*

Bishigendagosiwin. Beauty, fairness; glory, splendor.

Bishigendâgwi, (*bin*). I dress splendidly, gloriously ; p. *besh..wiod.*

Bishigendagwia, (*nin*). I glorify him, I make him glorious; p. *besh..ad.*

Bishigenima, (*nin*) (*dân*). I honor him, glorify him; p. *besh..ad.*

Bishigwad, in compositions, alludes to *impuritg*, *unchastity*. (Examples in some of the following words.)

Bishigwâdad. It is impure, unchaste, licentious, indecent; p. *besh..dak.*

Bishigwadâdjim, (*nin*). I tell an impure unchaste story; p *besh-.mod.*

Bishigwâdâdjimowin. Impure story or report; pl.-*an*.

Bishigwâdendam, (*nin*). I have impure unchaste thoughts; p. *besh..ang.*

Bishigwadendamowin. Unchaste thought, impure thinking.

Bishigwâdis, (*nin*). I am unchaste, impure, licentious; p. *besh..sid.*

Bishigwadisiwin. Unchastity, impurity, licentiousness; fornication, adultery.

Bishigwadj, in compositions alludes to *unchastity*. (Examples in some of the following words.)

Bishigwadjia, (*nin*). I make him (her) commit impurity, adultery; p. *besh..ad.*

Bishigwadj-dodam, (*nin*). S. *Bishigwâdodam.*

Bishigwadj-dodamowin. S. *Bishigwadodamowin.*

Bishigwadj-gijwe, (*nin*). I speak unchastely or impurely; p. *besh. wed.*

Bishigwadj-gijwewin. Unchaste talking, unchaste impure word; pl.-*an*.

Bishigwadj-ijiwebis, (*nin*). I behave unchastely, I am unchaste, impure; p. *besh..sid.*

Bishigwadj-ijiwebisiwin. Impure behavior or conduct, unchastity, impurity.

Bishigwâdjikwe. S. *Gagibadjikwe.*

Bishkonawa, (*nin*) (*nân*). I miss him, (in shooting at;) p. *besh.. wad.*

Bishkongwash, (*nin*). I get asleep, I fall asleep; p. *besh.. shid.* (Freq. *babishkongwash.*)

Bishkwâbaminagos, (*nin*). I am lost sight of, they can see me no more; p. *besh..sid.*

Bishkwabaminagwad. It is lost sight of, it is out of sight, it can be seen no more; p. *beshk.. wak.*

Bisikagan. Clothing material, any article of clothing; pl.-*an.*

Bisikage, (*nin*). I put on, (clothing;) p *bas..ged.*

Bisikân, (*nin*). I put it on, (clothing;) p. *basikang.*

Bisikawâgan. S. *Bâbisikawâgan.*

Bisikona, (*nin*) (*nân*). I clothe him, I dress him; p. *bas..nad; imp. bisikoj.*

Bisikwanaie, (*nin*) or *nin bisikonaie.* I put on my clothes, I dress myself; p. *bas. ied.*

Bisikwandjigan. Wig; pl.-*an.*

Bisinâdis, (*nin*). I am frivolous, thoughtless, imprudent, foolish, wild; p. *bes..sid.*

Bisinâdisiwin. Frivolous and imprudent behavior, foolish

conduct, frivolousness, foolishness.

Bisinâdj, in compositions, alludes to *frivolousness, foolishness, imprudence.*

Bisinadj-gigitowin, or, *bisinadj-gijwewin*. Frivolous, imprudent, indecent speaking; pl.-*an*.

Bisinâjia, (*nin*). I make him frivolous and foolish, I seduce him to an imprudent and indecent behavior; p. *bes..ad.*

Bisiskadendam, (*nin*). I have my senses again, (after fainting;) p. *bes..dang.*

Bisiskadis, (*nin*). I recover my senses, (after fainting;) also, I am at the age of discretion; p. *bes..sid.*

Bisiskendan, (*nin*). I remember it well, I know it plainly, I have knowledge of it; p. *bes..ang.*

Bisiskenima, (*nin*). I remember him well, I know him well; p. *bes..mad.*

Biska, or-*magad*. It is bent; p. *beskag*, or-*magak*.

Biskâb, adv. Again, returning, back again.

Bikâbato, (*nin*). I return, running, I run back again; p. *bes..tod.*

Biskâbi, (*nin*). I start and come back again the same day; p. *beskâbid.*

Biskabikikomân. Jack-knife, a knife that shuts up, (not a table-knife); pl.-*an*.

Biskabikinân mokomân, (*nin*). I shut the knife; p. *bes..ang.*

Biskadâân, (*nin*). I rivet it, bend it; p. *bes..ang.*

Biskadâigade, or-*magad*. It is riveted; p. *bes..deg*, or-*magak.*

Biskadâigan. Rivet-hammer, riveting hammer; pl.-*an*.

Biskadawa, (*nin*). I rivet some obj.; p. *bes..wad;* imp. *biskadâ.*

Biskakone ishkote, or-*magad*. The fire blazes, it flames up; p. *bes..neg*, or-*magak.*

Biskakonendjigan. Kindle-wood, to make the fire flame; pl.-*an*.

Biskakonendjige, (*nin*). I make a fire flame up; p. *bes..ged.*

Biskakoneton ishkote, (*nin*). I make the fire blaze, flame up; p. *bes..tod.*

Biskane, or-*magad*. S. *Biskakone.*

Biskanean ishkote, (*nin*). S. *Biskakoneton....*

Biskaneiâssin ishkote. The fire blazes up by the wind; p. *bes..sing....*

Biskanendan, (*nin*) or, *nin biskanenindan*. I enkindle it, I inflame it; p. *bes..ang.—Biskanenindan ninde, weweni tchi sagiinân, Debanimiian!* Lord, inflame my heart, that I may love thee as I ought!

Biskanepwa, (*nin*). I light my pipe or cigar; p. *bes..wad.*

Biskaona, (*nin*) (*don*). I tie a bow, obj., a ribbon, etc.; p. *bes..nad;* imp. *biskaoj.*

Biskibagishka mitig. The tree bends and breaks; p. *bes..kad.*

Biskigishka, or-*magad*. It is bent; p. *bes..kad*, or-*magak.*

Biskina, (*nin*) (*nân*). I bend some obj.; p. *bes..nad.*

Biskinigade, or-*magad*. It is bent, folded; p. *bes..deg*, or-*magak*

Biskiniken, (*nin*). I bend my arm; p. *bes..nid.*

Biskinikenowin. Elbow, cubit; (F. coudée.) — *Ningo biskinikenowin, nisso biskinikenowin nijtana dasso biskinikenowin*, one elbow, three elbows, twenty elbows (long or high). S. *Biminik.*

Biskissin. It is folded; p. *beskissing.*

Biskitênagan. Vessel or dish of birch-bark, folded together, to receive the sap running out of maple-trees in sugar making, a small birch-bark trough; pl.-*an.*

Bisogeshin, (*nin*). I fall, stumbling over s. th.; p. *bes. ing.*

Bisogêwa, (*nin*). I supplant him; I make nim fall, (with any thing); p. *bas..wad*; imp. *bisogê.*

Bisan, or *pison.* This termination of some substantives alludes to *binding, stringing, hanging from*, etc.; as: *Nagasidebison*, stir up; *gibideebison*, waist-coat, vest; *kitchipison*, girdle, belt; etc.

Bisideshin, (*nin*). I stumble; p. *bes..ing.*

Bisosideshiwin. Stumbling.

Bisosideshiwini-assin. Stumbling stone.

Bissa. At the *end* of words, signifies the *manner of raining*; as: *Awanibissa*, it rains a little; *jawanibissa*, the rain comes from the south; *ishkwabissa*, the rain ceased; etc.

Bissa, in compositions, signifies *small, fine*, in *small little pieces.* (Examples in some of the following words.)

Bissa, or-*magad.* It is ground, reduced to fine particles; p. *bassag*, or-*magak.*

Bissaan, (*nin*). I break it into small pieces, I crush it to small pieces, to powder; p. *bassaang.*

Bissâbide, (*nin*). I have fine small teeth; p. *bass..ded.*

Bissagânâma, (*nin*). I break some obj. to pieces, by striking it; p. *boss..mad.*

Bissâgona, (*nin*) (*nân*). I make a good and profitable use of it, I lose or waste nothing of it, (*an.* obj.); p. *bass..ad*; imp. *bissagon.*

Bissâgonge, (*nin*). I use things profitably; p. *bass..ged.*

Bissâgonje, (*nin*). I have plenty of children; p. *bass..ged.*

Bissâgosi akik. The kettle is profitable, it holds much; p. *bassagosid akik.*

Bissâgwan. It is profitable; it holds much, (a bag, a vessel;) p. *bass..ang.*

Bissawa, (*nin*). I crush or break to small pieces some obj.; p. *bassawad*; imp. *bissâ.*

Bissatagad. It is fine, (stuff, clothing material;) p. *bass..gak.*

Bissatagisi. It is fine, (stuff, silk;) p. *bass..sid.*

Bissi, in compositions.

Bissibidjigad, or-*magad.* It is torn to small pieces; p. *bass..deg*, or-*magak.*

Bissibidon, (*nin*). I break it into small pieces in my hands, I crumble it; p. *bass..dod.*

Bissibiigade, or-*magad*. It is written with small letters, or printed in small type; p. *bass ..deg*, or-*magak*.
Bissibiigan. Small writing, or print.
Bissibiige, (*nin*). I write with small letters; p. *bass..ged*.
Bissibina, (*nin*). I crumble some obj., I break it into small pieces with my hands; p. *bass..nad*.—*Nin bissibina pakwejigan*, I crumble bread.
Bissibiweie. It has a fine fur; p. *bass..ied*.
Bissibode, or-*magad*. It is ground; p. *bass..deg*, or-*magak*.
Bissibodjigan. Grind-mill, flour mill; pl.-*ag*; also, corn-meal.
Bissibodjiganâbik. Mill-stone; pl.-*og*.
Bissibodjigans. Coffee-mill; pl.-*ag*.
Bissibodjige, (*nin*). I am grinding, I keep a flour-mill a going; p. *bass..ged*.
Bissibodjigewinini. Miller, keeper or proprietor of a flour-mill; pl.-*wag*.
Bissibona, (*don*) (*nin*). I grind some obj.; p. *bass..nad*; imp. *bissiboj*.
Bissiboso. It is ground; p. *bass ..sod*.
Bissigaan, (*nin*). I split it into fine small pieces, (wood); p. *bass..ang*.
Bissigaige, (*nin*). I chop wood into small sticks, (for a small stove;) p. *bass..ged*.
Bissigâiisan. Split wood for fuel; pl.-*an*.
Bissigawa, (*nin*). I split it into small pieces, (*an*. obj., *gijik*, cedar;) p. *bass..wad*; imp. *bissiga*.
Bissikode, or-*magad*. It is crushed or broken to pieces by s. th. that fell on it; p. *bass..deg* or-*magak*.
Bissikoso. It is broken to pieces by s. th. that fell on it; p. *bass..sod*.
Bissipo, or-*magad*. It snows in small flakes; p. *bassipog*, or-*magak*.
Bissisi. It is ground, (*an*. obj.); p. *bassisid*.—*Bâssisid pakwejigan*, flour.
Bisistâgos, (*nin*). I insult, I use insulting or abusive language; p. *bess..sid*.
Bissitawa, (*nin*). I am insulted by his words, I feel insulted in hearing his talking; p. *bess..wad*.
Bissomâ, (*nin*). I insult him; p. *bessomad*.
Biswâb, (*nin*). I have weak eyes, I cannot see well; p. *beswâbid*.
Biswâbigishin, (*nin*). I am entangled in a cord; p. *bes..ing*.
Biswaode, or-*magad*. It is tied with a loop; p. *bes..deg*, or-*magak*.
Biswaona, (*nin*) (*don*). I tie some obj. with a loop; p. *bes.. nad*; imp. *biswaoj*.
Bitâkogidigweshin, (*nind*). I knock or dash my knee against s. th.; p. *bet..ing*.
Bitakokwatigweshin, (*nin*). I knock my forehead against s. th.; p. *bet..ing*.
Bitakondibeshin, (*nin*). I knock or dash my head against s. th.; p. *bet..ing*.

Bitakoshin. It touches or strikes s. th.; p. *bet..ing.*

Bitakoshkawa, (*nin*) (*kan*). I strike or knock against him; p. *bet..wad.*

Bitakossideshin, (*nin*). I knock or dash my foot against s. th.; p. *bet..ing.*

Bitâkossin. It touches, strikes; p. *bet..sing.* — *Tchimân bitâkossin,* the canoe strikes (touches) the ground, a rock, etc.

Bitawigibadeiegwasson. Drawers; (F. caleçons; pl.-*an.*

Bitchinawea, (*nin*). I offend him; I make him angry; p. *bet..ad.*

Bitchinawema, (*nin*). I make him angry, or offend him, with my *words;* p. *bet..mad.*

Bitchinawes, (*nin*). I am angry, I keep anger or rancor; I am passionate, impatient; p. *bet..sid.*

Bitchinawesiwin. Anger, rancor, bad passionate temper, impatience.

Bite. Foam.

Bitewanâm, (*nin*). I foam at my mouth, running; p. *bat..mod.*

Bitewidon, (*nin*). My mouth is full of foam; p. *bat..dong.*

Bitewidonêgidas, (*nin*). My mouth is full of foam from anger; p. *bat..sod.*

Bitikwabewis, (*nin*). I am thick and short; p.-*i; bet..sid.*—S. *Takwabewis.*

Bito, in compositions, signifies *double.* (Examples in some of the following words.)

Bitobig. Pond; pl.-*on.*

Bitogwadan, (*nin*). I line it, double it, (some articles of clothing;) p. *bat..ang.*

Bitogwade, or-*magad.* It is lined, (doubled;) p. *bat..deg,* or-*magak.*

Bitogwadjigan. Lining, doubling; (F. doublure.)

Bitogwadjige, (*nin*). I am lining (some article of clothing;) p. *bat..ged.*

Bîtogwana, (*nin*). I line some obj. (silk-stuff;) p. *bat..nad;* imp. *bitogwaj.*

Bitogwasson. S. *Bitogwâdjigan.*

Bitokisine, (*nin*). I have two pair of shoes on; p. *bat..ned.*

Bitokwanaie, (*nin*). I have a double suit of clothes on; p. *bat..ied.*

Biton, (*nin*). I wait for it, I await it; p. *batod.*

Biwâbik. Iron; metal; pl. *biwâbikon,* pieces of iron, or iron tools or implements.

Biwâbiko-biwibodjigan. Filings, file-dust.

Biwâbikokan. Iron-mine, or mine; pl,-*an.*

Biwâbikoke, (*nin*). I work iron, or other metal; I am mining, working in a mine; p. *bew..ked.*

Biwâbiko-mikana. Rail-road, (iron-road;) pl.-*an.*

Biwâbikons. Wire, (small iron;) pl. *biwabikonsan,* small pieces of iron, small iron implements.

Béwâbiko-sagabiginigan, or, *biwâbiko-sagibidjigan,* or, *biwâbiko-takobidjigan.* Iron chain; iron fetters; pl.-*an.*

Biwâbiko-tchimân. Iron boat; pl.-*an.*

Biwâbikwakik. Iron pot; (C. marmite;) pl.-*og.*
Biwai. S. *Obiwai.*
Biwan. The snow is driven by the wind, snow-storm, snow-drift; p. *bâwang.*
Biwanag. Flint; pl.-*og.*
Biwândjigan. Crumb; pl.-*an.*
Biwêkodamagan. Shaving, wood shaving, (thin slice of wood pared off from a board in plaining it;) pl.-*an.*
Biwibodjigan. Saw-dust.
Biwidé. A stranger who arrives to a place, visitor, comer; pl.-*g.*
Bi-widjiwa, (*nin*). I come here with him, I accompany him hither; I bring him along with me; p. *ba..wad.*
Biwidon, (*nin*). I crumble it; p. *bawidod.*
Biwigaan, (*nin*). I cut or chop it into small pieces, into chips; p. *ba. ang.*
Biwigaigan. Small piece of wood, chip; pl.-*an.*
Biwigaigé, (*nin*). I make chips; p. *baw..ged.*
Biwigaisse, (*nin*). I am chopping wood into small pieces; p. *baw..sed.*
Biwijigan. A little piece remaining after cutting a coat or any other article of clothing, remainder, shred; (F. retaille;) pl.-*an.*
Biwikodan, (*nin*). I cut it, I take off pieces; p. *baw..ang.*
Biwikodjigan. Shaving, wood-shaving; pl.-*an.*
Biwikona, (*nin*). I cut some obj.; p. *baw..nad.*
Biwina, (*nin*). I crumble some obj.; p. *bawinad.*
Biwipo. The snow begins to cover the ground; p. *bawipog.*
Biwishima, (*nin*). I disperse it, put it in disorder, (*an.* obj.); p. *baw..mad.*
Bewishka pakwejigan. The bread breaks or crumbles; p. *baw..dag.*—S. *Biwisse.*
Biwisse pakwejigan. The bread crumbles into small pieces and falls to the ground; p. *bawissed.*
Biwissidjigan. A gun-cap, powder in the pan of a gun; (F. amorce;) pl.-*an.*
Biwissidôn, (*nin*). I disperse it, I put it in disorder; p. *baw..dod.*
Biwissidon pâshkisigan, (*nin*). I put powder in the pan of a gun, or a cap, I prime a gun; p. *baw..dod.*
Biwissin. It is dispersed, it is in disorder; among one another; p. *bawissing.*— *Kakina nind aiiman biwissinon,* all my things are in disorder.
Biwiwebina, (*nin*) (*nân*). I throw or strew it about, I scatter it, (*an.* obj.); p. *bew..nad;* imp. *biw..bin.*
Biwiwebinigade, or-*magad.* It is dispersed, strewed, scattered; p. *bew..deg,* or-*magak.*
Bobo. Little pain, little wound, (in the language of children.)
Bobogidjibigaigan. Little syringe made of wood or tin; pl.-*an.*
Bodâdân, (*nin*). I blow it; p. *bwa..ang.*
Bodâdjigan. A thing to blow in, trumpet, horn, bugle; pl.-*an.*

Bodâdjige, (*nin*). I am blowing; p. *bwa..ged.*

Bodâdjishka, (*nin*). My belly is swollen up; p. *bwa..kad.*

Bodadjishkotawân. Bellows; pl.-*an.*

Bodâdjiskkotawe, (*nin*). I blow the fire with bellows; p. *bwa.. wed.*

Bodakwe, (*nin*). I let fall in a hole or vessel; I put in a hole; p. *bwa..wed.*

Bodâkwen, (*nin*). I put it in a hole or vessel, I let it go in; p. *bwa..wed.*

Bodâkwenan, (*nin*). I put it, or let it fall, in a hole or vessel, (*an.* obj.); p. *bwa..wed.*

Bodâkwesse, (*nin*). I fall or slide in a hole; p. *bwa..sed.*

Bodânâ, (*nin*). I blow him; p. *bwadanad;* imp. *bodâj.*

Bodâshka, (*nin*). I am swollen, all my body is swollen up; p *bwa..kad.*

Bodawân. Chimney, fire-place; pl.-*an.*

Bôdawe, (*nin*). I make fire, I build a fire; p. *bwadawed.*

Bodawen. I burn it as fuel, I make fire with; p. *bwadawed.*

Bodawenan, (*nin*). I burn some obj., I put it in the fire as fuel; p. *bwadawed.*— *Bejigwâtig nabagisag nin gi-bodawenan;* I burnt up a board.

Bôgid, (*nin*). I fart; p. *bwâgidid.*

Bôgidiwin. Fart, farting.

Bojo! good day! (F. bonjour.)

Bok or *boko*, in compositions, alludes to a *half* or *part* of s. th. (Examples in some of the following words.)

Bôkakamigisse, (*nin*). I break through, or sink in the ground with my foot; p. *bwa ..sed.*

Bôkisse, (*nin*). I break through s. th. with my foot; p. *bwa.. sed*

Bôkobina, (*nin*) (*don*). I break some obj. in two; p. *bwa..nad.*

Bokodena. One half or part of the village or town.

Bokodjishka, or-*magad*. Something in my body is broken; p. *bwa..kag*, or-*magak.*

Bokogade, (*nin*). I have a broken leg; p. *bwa..ded.*

Bokogadeshin, (*nin*). I break my leg; p. *bwa..ing.*

Bokogadewa, (*nin*). I break his leg; p. *bwa..wad;* imp. *bokogadew.*

Bokokojenan, (*nin*). I break the point of s. th. (of a needle, knife, etc.); p. *bwa..ang.*

Bokonigan. A broken branch to indicate the road in the woods; pl.-*an.*

Bokonige, (*nin*). I break branches to mark the road in the woods; p. *bwa..ged.*

Bokoshkan, (*nin*). I break it, (a *long* obj.); p. *bwa..ang.*

Bokoshkawa, (*nin*). I break some *long* obj.; p. *bwa..wad.*

Bokoshkibina, (*nin*). I break it off, (*an.* obj.); p. *bwa..nad.*— *Misakosi nin bokoshkibina*, I break off an ear of Indian corn.

Bokoshkibinan, (*nin*). I break it off; p *bwa..ang.*

Bokossidon, (*nin*). I break it in two; p. *bwa..dod.*

Bokotchishka assâb. The net is breaking; p. *bwak..kad.*

Bokotchishka, or-*magad*, It

breaks; p. *bwak..kag*, or-*magak.*

Bokwâbik. A piece or fragment of iron.

Bôkwaigane, (*nin*). I break a bone; p. *bwa..ned.*

Bôkwaii. A piece, a fragment.

Bokwanwishima, (*nin*). I break it off, (*an.* obj.); p. *bwa..mad.*

Bokwanwissidon, (*nin*). I break it off, I notch it; p. *bwak..dod.*

Bokwasika, or-*magad,* (pr. *bakosika.*) It breaks, (wood;) p. *bwak..kag,* or-*magak.*

Bokwâtig. A piece of wood, a fragment of wood.

Bokwâwigan, (*nin*) or *nin bokwawiganeshka.* I am humpbacked, or hunchbacked; (F. je suis bossu); p. *bwak..ned,* or, *bwak..kad.*

Bokwâwiganeta, (*nin*). I am lame in the back; p. *bwa..tad.*

Bokwêdagiming. S. *Bebokwedagiming-gisiss.*

Bôkweg. A piece of cloth, or of any other clothing material.

Bokwemagad. Branches or little sticks on the ground break, when a person or animal goes through the woods; p. *bwa..gak.*

Bôme, (*nin*). I recover from my fear or fright; p. *bwamed.*

Bon or *boni,* in compositions, signifies *finishing, ceasing, stopping,* or the *end* of s. th. (Examples in some of the following words.)

Bonâbigina, (*nin*) (*nân*). I let him down on a rope; p. *bwa..ang.*

Bonakakjigan. The line of a net with a heavy stone to keep steady the net, to anchor it; anchor; pl.-*an.*

Bonakadjige, (*nin*). I cast anchor; p. *bwa..ged.*

Bonakana; (*nin*) (*don*). I anchor it, (a net, *assâb*;) p. *bwa..nad,* imp. *bonakaj.*

Bônam. She lays eggs, (a hen, or any other female bird;) p. *bwânang.* (II. Conj.)

Bônanimad, The wind goes down, dies away, ceases blowing; p. *bwa..mak.*

Bônâshka, or-*magad.* The sea runs down, the waves cease to rise, it becomes calm; p. *bwanashkag,* or-*magak.*

Bônêndam, (*nin*). I cease to think on s. th.; I forget; p. *bwanendang.*

Bônéndamawa, (*nin*). I forget s. th. relating to him, I forget how he behaved what he did, what he said, etc., I forgive him; p. *bwan..wad.*

Bônêndamowin. Forgetting, forgiveness, pardon.

Bônênima, (*nin*) (*dan*). I forget him, I cease to think on him, (a person or any other obj.); p. *bwan..mad.*

Bônénindiwin. Mutual pardon, forgiveness.

Bônia, (*nin*). I let him alone, I desist from him; p. *bwaniad.*

Bôni-akiwan. It is the end of the world; p. *bwani-akiwang.*

Boni bineshi. The bird alights on a branch, (or somewhere else;) p. *bewanid.* (I. Conj.)

Bônigidêtawa, (*nin*). I forgive him; p. *bwan..wad.*

Bônima, (*nin*). I let him alone, I don't speak any more to him; p. *bwanimad*.
Boninagos, (*nin*). I cease to appear, to be seen, I disappear; p. *bwa..sid*.
Boninagwad. It ceases to be seen, it disappears; p. *bwan.. wak*.
Bônindawa, (*nin*). I alight upon him, I descend upon him, come upon him; p. *bwa.. wod*.—*Wenijishid-Manito o gibonindawan Jesusan api gasigaandawimind*; the Holy Ghost descended (alighted, came,) upon Jesus, after his baptism.
Boni-nibâgwe, (*nin*). I cease to be thirsty; p. *bwa--wed*.
Bônita, (*nin*). I cease working; p. *bwânitad*.
Bônitchigade, or-*magad*. It is let alone, it is given up; p. *bwa..deg*, or-*magak*.
Bôniton, (*nin*). I cease, I let it alone, I let it be, I desist from it; I give it up, I abandon a habit, etc.; p. *bwanitod*.
Bônwewidam, (*nin*). I cease speaking; p. *bwan..ang*.
Bos, (*nin*). I embark; I go on board; p. *bwasid*.
Bos, *bosa*, in compositions, signifies *penetrating* into s. th., *filling*. (Examples in some of the following words.)
Bosabawe, (*nin*). I am drenched with rain, (penetrated to the skin;) p. *bwas..wed*.
Bosangwâm, (*nin*). I sleep profoundly, (I am filled with sleep;) p. *bwa..ang*.
Bosasse, or-*magad*. It penetrates, it goes into s. th.; p. *bwasasseg*, or-*magak*.
Bôsia, (*nin*). I make him embark. I embark or ship some obj.; p. *bwasiad*.
Bôsika, or-*magad*. It is deep; p. *bwosikag* or-*magak*.—*Bwasikag onagan*, a deep dish. *Bwasikag tessinagan*, deep plate, soup-plate.
Bosikado. A kind of large turtle; pl.-*g*.
Bosikitchigade, or-*magad*. It is made deep, it is deep; p. *bwa.. deg*, or-*magak*.
Bosikiton, (*nin*). I make it deep; p. *bwa..tod*.
Bôsinajawa, (*nin*). I send him on board a vessel, a boat, etc.; I bid him embark; p. *bwas.. wad*.
Bôsitâss, (*nin*). I am loading a canoe, boat, vessel, etc.; I am shipping; p. *bwa..sod*.
Bôsitâssowin. Loading, shipping.
Bôsiton, (*nin*). I ship it; p. *bwasitod*.
Bôsiwin. Embarkation, going on board.
Bôsmakatewawe. It has a black fur, (an animal;) p. *bwas..wed*.
Bôsmakatewegin. Black cloth.
Bôswebina, (*nin* (*nan*). I throw him in a canoe, boat, etc., (a person, or some other obj.); I embark him by force; p. *bwas..nad*.
Botâgadan, (*nin*). I stamp it; p. *bwe..ang*.
Bôtagan. Mortar, stamper; pl.-*ag*.
Botâgana, (*nin*). I stamp some

obj.; p. *bwetaganad;* imp. *botâgaj.*
Botâganâk. Pestle; pl.-*on.*
Botâge, (*nin*). I stamp, (corn, etc.); p. *bwetaged.*
Boto. Button; pl.-*iag.*
Bwa, tchi bwa; prefixes signifying, *before.*
Bwaiawis, (*nin*). I am slow at work; p. *bwaiawisid.*
Bwâma, (*nin*). I cannot prevail upon him, I cannot make him come, or go, or do s. th.; p. *bwaiâmad.*
Bwân. Siou Indian; pl.-*ag.*
Bwânawi, (*nin*). I cannot (go somewhere, or do s. th.); p. *bwaiânawiod.*
Bwânawia, (*nin*). I can do nothing with him, or with it, (*an.* obj.); he does not listen to me, not obey me; p. *bwaia..ad.*
Bwânawito, (*nin*). I cannot, I am feeble, weak; p. *bwaiânawitod.*
Bwânawiton, (*nin*). I can do nothing with it, I cannot make it, I cannot do it; I cannot get it; p. *bwaia..tod.*
Bwanawitowin. Weakness, incapacity.
Bwânim, (*nin*). I speak the Siou language; p. *bwaiânimod.*
Bwânimowin. Siou language.
Bwaôma, (*nin*) (*dan*). I can hardly carry him on my back, or it, (*an.* obj.); p. *bwaiaômad.*
Bwâwane, (*nin*). I carry a heavy burden on my back; p. *bwaiawaned.*
Bwâwibina, (*nin*) (*don*). I cannot draw him, (a person, or some other obj.); p. *bwaia..nad.*
Bwâwina, (*nin*) (*don*). I cannot sift him up, (a person, or some other obj.); p. *bwaiawinad.*
Bwâwinan, (*nin*). I cannot lift it up; p. *bwaia..ang.*

D

Some words which are not found under D, *may be looked for under* T.

D. This third letter in the Otchipwe alphabet, is the euphonical letter of the Otchipwe language, to avoid a disagreeable crowd of vowels; as: *Od aiân,* he has it; instead of, *o aian.—Kid ija,* thou goest; instead of, *ki ija.**

Da–, a particle that denotes the *conditional mode* in a verb. (See the Conj. in the Grammar.)

Da, (*nin*). I lodge, dwell, stop; p. *endâd.—Kawin kin oma ki dassi, nin, nin da oma;* thou dost not stop here, I stop here, (this is my habitation.)

Da, in compositions, denotes the *place* where some work is doing, or has been done; as: *Mi ima gadagwassoiân nissogwam;* it is here I have been sewing three days. (More commonly *daji* is used in these cases.)

Dabandad. It is respectable; p. *debandak.*

Dabandendagos, (*nin*). I am respectable, I am thought (considered) respectable; p. *deb..sid.*

Dabandendagwad. It is considered respectable, it is respectable; p. *deb..wak.*

Dabandendamowin. Respect, esteem.

Dabandenima- (*nin*) (*dân*). I respect or esteem him; p. *deb..mad.*

Dabandis, (*nin*). I am respectable, worthy, I am deserving of respect and esteem; p. *déb..sid.*

Dadâtabanagidon, (*nin*). I speak fast, quick; p. *ded..dong.*

Dadâtabanam, (*nin*). I have a quick respiration; p. *ded..mod.*

Dadâtabi, (*nin*). I hasten, I do s. th. quick, I am speedy, expeditious, in doing s. th.; p. *ded..bid.*

Dadâtabimagad. It hastens, it goes on quick, runs fast, it works fast; p. *ded..gak.*

Dabâtabiwin. Haste, expedition, speed, activity.

Dadâtabowe, (*nin*). S. *Dadatabanagidon.*

---

* In Manitoba we pronounce more: *kiit ija, kit aiân,* etc., etc.

Dadibabama, (*nin*) (*dân*). I observe him, watch him, I look upon him, to see what he is going to do or to say; p. *ded..mad.*

Dâdodemagad. It opens, splits, (in boiling;) p. *daiad..gak.*

Dâdosowag mandaminag. Corn is splitting or bursting open, (in boiling;) p. *daiâdosodjig.*

Dagô, in compositions, signifies, *amongst others*, or *amongst other things*. (Examples in some of the following words.)

Dagô, or-*magad.* There is, there is some; p. *endagog.*

Dagôaia, (*nin*). I am, amongst others; p. *degôaiad.*

Dagôdawa, (*nin*). I lay him a snare to catch him; p. *deg..wad.*

Dagogâbaw, (*nin*). I stand somewhere among others; p. *deg..wid.*

Dagogabawitawa, (*nin*). I stand with him, or near him; p. *deg..wad.*

Dagôgima, (*nin*) (*dan*). I put him in the number, I count him among others; p. *deg..mad.*

Dagôgona, (*nin*) (*dan*). I swallow some obj. among another thing; p. *deg..nad.* — *Odji nin gi dagogona gi-minikweiân nibi*; I swallowed a fly when I drank water.

Dagokonidis,* (*nin*). I put myself in the number, I count myself amongst others; p. *deg..sod.*

Dagonâ, (*nin*) (*nân*). I put some obj. among another object, and *mix* it with it; p. *degonad.*

Dagonê, (*nin*). I die among others; p. *degoned.*

Dagonigâde, or-*magad.* There is..in, it is mixed with...; p. *deg..deg*, or-*magak.*—*Sisibâkwad dagonigade*, there is sugar in. *Ka na ishkotewâbo dagonigadessinon?* Is there no ardent liquor mixed with it?

Dâgos, at the end of some neuter verbs, and *dagwad*, at the end of some unipersonal verbs, allude to being *considered* or *thought* such and such; as: *Nin jingendâgos*, I am considered hateful, or, I am hateful.—*Jingendâgwad*, it is considered hateful, or, it is hateful.

Dagôssa, (*nin*) (*ton*), or *nin dagoswa.* I put some obj. among other things, *not* mixing it; p. *degossad.* — *Nin dagossa oma nin moshwem*; I put my handkerchief here among other handkerchiefs.

Dagôwina, (*nin*). I name him amongst other words I pronounce, (I swear by him, by his name;) p. *deg..nad.*

Dagowindan, (*nin*). I name it amongst other words, (I swear by it;) p. *deg..ang.*

Dagwâb, (*nin*). I am sitting with others or amongst others; p. *degwâbid.*

Dagwadân, (*nin*). I sew it in such a place; p. *endagwa-*

---

* NOTE.—In several of these words, *dago* is sometimes pronounced *dagwa*; as: *Nin dagwakonidis*, *nin dagwaton*, *nin dagwassa*, etc. It could also be written so; but for uniformity's sake we always write it *dago*; and it is ordinarily pronounced *dago*.

dang. — *Endaian nin ga-dagwadanan kid aiiman;* I will sew thy things (clothes) in thy house.

Dagwama, (*nin*); p. *deg..ad.* S. *Apandjigenan.*

Dagwanâ, (*nin*). I sew some obj. in such a place; p. *end..nad.*

Dagwandân, (*nin*). S. *Apandjigen.*

Dagwishima, (*nin*). I make him arrive to some place, (a person, or some other obj.); p. *deg..mad.*

Dagwishin, (*nin*). I arrive by land; p. *degwishing.*—S. *Mijaga.*

Dagwisiton, (*nin*). I bring it to some place; p. *deg..tod.*

Daiebwetagosid. He that tells the truth, truth-teller; pl.-*jig.*

Daiebwetang; pl.-*ig,* believer.

Daiébwetansig. Infidel, incredulous person, unbeliever; pl.-*og.*

Daji–. This word, prefixed to a substantive or verb, denotes the *place* where some action is performing, or where a certain object comes from. P. *endaji–.*—*Kego ijâken endâjinimiiding,* don't go where they dance. *Mi oma ga-dajimigadiwad,* here is the place where they fought. *Moniâng daji-ikwe,* a woman from Montreal.

Dajibi, (*nin*). I drink in a certain place; p. *endajibid.*

Dajigijiganam, (*nin*). I spend my day in such a place; p. *endaj..mid.*—*Mi ima ga-dajigijiganamiiân pitchinâgo;* there is the place where I spent my day yesterday.

Dajikân, (*nin*). I am occupied in making such a thing, I am at it; p. *endajikang.*

Dajikawa, (*nin*). I am occupied about some obj.; p. *end..wad.*—*Mojag ki dajikawa aw bebejigoganji;* thou art always about that horse.

Dajike, (*nin*). I am in a certain place; p. *end. ked.*

Dajimâ, (*nin*). I speak of him; I censure him, I speak ill of him, I backbite him, calumniate him; p. *dejimad.*

Dajindân, (*nin*). I speak of it; I speak ill of it, calumniate it; p. *end..ang.*

Dajindimin, (*nin*). We speak of each other; we speak ill of each other, censure one another; p. *dejindidjig.*

Dajindiwin. Ill speaking, detraction, backbiting, slander, calumniation.

Dajinge, (*nin*). I speak ill of people, I slander, I calumniate. I backbite; p. *dejinged.*

Dajingeshk. I am slanderous, calumnious, I am in the habit of speaking ill of people; p. *dej..kid.*

Dajita, (*nin*). I am occupied at s. th. in a certain place; p. *endajitad.*

Dajitibikanam, (*nin*). I spend the night in such a place; p. *endaj..mid.*—*Anindi ga-dajitibikanamiian?* Where didst thou stay all night? *Nôpiming nin gidajitibikanam,* I spend the night in the woods.

Dajoiawebison. Suspenders, braces, (for males.) S. *Anikamân.*

Dajoniken, (*nin*). I stretch out my arm; p. *dej..nid.*

Dajonikeshin, (*nin*). I have my arms stretched out; p. *dej..ing.*

Dajwâbikina, (*nin*) (*nan*). I unfold or stretch out some obj. of metal; p. *dej..nad.*

Dajwegagona, (*nin*) (*don*). I spread out some obj., hanging it up; p. *dej..nad.*

Dajwegishima, (*nin*). I spread it out on the floor, on the ground, etc.; p. *dej..wad.*

Dajwêgina, (*nin*) (*nan*). I spread it, holding it in my hands; p. *dej..nad.*

Dajwégissiton, (*nin*). I spread it out on the ground, etc.; p. *dej..tod.*

Dân, (*nin*). I possess, I have property, I am rich; p. *endânid.*

Danab, (*nin*). I am sitting in a certain place; p. *endanabid.*—*Mi oma mojag endanabiiân;* I am always sitting here.

Danadem, (*nin*). I am weeping in a certain place; p. *endan..mod.*

Danâkamigis, (*nin*). I do s. th. in a certain place; I play somewhere; p. *endan..sid.*

Danaki, (*nin*). I live in a certain place; or, I am a native of a certain place or country; p. *endanakid.*

Danakis, (*nin*). I burn in a certain place; p. *end..sod.*

Danakiwin. The state of living in a place or country.

Danânagidon, (*nin*). I talk; p. *endan..ong.*

Danânagidonowin. Talking.

Danêndagos, (*nin*). I am thought or believed to be in such a place; p. *endan..sid.*—*Gijigong danendagosiwag ga-mino ijiwebisidjig aking;* those that lived a good life on earth, are believed to be in heaven.

Danénima, (*nin*). S. *Indanenima.*

Danis, (*nin*). I am in a certain place; p. *endanisid.*

Dâniss. S. *Nindâniss.*

Dânissikâwin. God-daughter; pl.-*ag.* There is always a possessive pronoun prefixed to this word; *nin dânissikâwin,* my god-daughter; *ki dânissikâwin,* thy god-daughter; *o dânissikâwinan,* his god-daughter, etc.

Dâniwin. Property, riches, treasure, all that one has or possesses.

Danwéwen, (*nin*). I make noise, I am heard, in a certain place; p. *end..wed.* — *Pindig danweweweag,* they are heard inside, (working or speaking;) heard by people that are outside, out of doors.

Danwêwidam, (*nin*). I speak, I make myself heard, in a certain place; p. *end..ang.*

Dapinanidimin, (*nin*). We are killing one another; p. *end..didjig.*

Dapinanidiwin. Slaughter or murder of several persons.

Dâpinê, (*nin*). I die in a certain place; p. *endapined.* — *Nibikang gi-dâpine,* he died in the water, (he was drowned.) *De-*

beniminang tchibâiatigong (*ajiteyâtigong*) *gidapine*, our Lord died on a cross.

Dâpinea, (*nin*). I make him die in a certain place; p. *end..ad.*

Dash, conj. But, and, too, also.

Dashimin, (*nin*). We are in a certain number, in such a number, in a certain quantity, so many persons, (or other obj..)—*Mi ga.dashiwad nind opinimag*, my potatoes were so many.

Dashwa. Shell, shield; pl.-*g*.—*Mishikéwidashwa*. The shield of a tortoise.

Dassing, adv. Every time, as often as.

Dassô, (or *dasswi*.) This word, (the interpretation-word of the Otchipwe numbers,) signifies nothing in itself; it is put between *numbers* higher than nineteen, and *substantives* denoting measure, of time or of other objects. So, f. i., they will not say: *Nijtana bibon*, twenty years, but, *nijtana dasso bibon*, etc.

Dassobanênindj. So many times a handful, (in number over nineteen.) For less than twenty, see *Nijobanênindj*. *Nissobanénindj*, etc.

Dassôbidonan, (*nin*). I tie so many together, (in number over nineteen;) p. *end..ang*. *Nissimidana nin dassobidodonan ashi nij*, I tie thirty-two together. For less than twenty, see *Nijobidonan*. *Nissôbidonan*, etc.

Dassôbina, (*nin*). I catch so many fishes in a net, or in several nets; p. *indassobinad*. This word is put after numbers higher than nineteen, to denote the number of fishes caught in a net, or in several nets; as: *Nijtana nin dassobina; nissimidana dassobina;* I caught twenty fishes in my net, (nets;) he caught thirty fishes in his net, (nets.)

Dassôbinag, (*nin*). I tie so many objects together, (in numbers over nineteen.)—For less than twenty, see *Nijôbinag*. *Nissôbinag*, etc.

Dassobonikan. So many times both hands full, (in numbers over nineteen.)—For less than twenty, see *Nijobônikan*. *Nissobônikan*, etc.

Dassogamig, so many lodges or houses, (in numbers over nineteen.) — *Nimidana dassogamig kitchi wigiwaman atewan ima endajigabeshiwad anishinabeg;* there are forty large lodges there where the Indians are encamped.—For less numbers than twenty, see *Nijogamig*. *Nissogamig*, etc.

Dassogisisswagis, (*nin*). I am so many months old, (in numbers over nineteen;) p. *endass..sid*. — *Gwaiak nijtana dassogisisswagisi aw abinodji;* this child is just twenty months old. — For numbers less than twenty, see *Nijogisisswagis*. *Nissogisisswagis*, etc.

Dassogwan. So many days.—This word is always preceded either by the adverb *ânin?* how? how much? or by a number higher than nineteen.

—*Nijtana dassogwan nin giaia wedi*, I stayed there twenty days.

Dassogwanagad. It is so many days; p. *endass..gak.*—This verb is always preceded either by the adverb *anin?* or by a number higher than nineteen. —*Jaigwa nissimidana dassogwanagad eko-mâdjad noss;* it is already thirty days since my father started.

Dassogwanagis, (*nin*). I am so many days old, (a person or any other obj.); p. *end..sid.*—This verb is always preceded either by the adverb *ânin?* or by a number higher than nineteen.—*Anin endassogwanagisid kishime?* how many days is thy little brother old? *Nijtana dassogwanagisi*, he is twenty days old.

Dassogwanénd, (*nin*). I am absent so many days, going somewhere; p. *endass..did.*—This verb is put after a number higher than nineteen, to signify the number of days of absence; as: *Gi-mâdjâwâg jéba, nissimidana dash ta-dassogwanendiwog;* they started this morning, and they will be gone (or absent) thirty days.—When the number of the days of absence is under twenty, they will say, for instance, *midâssogwan ta inendiwag; midassogwan ta-inendiwog ashi nanogwan*, etc., they will be absent fifteen days, etc.—S. *Inénd.*

Dassôkamin, (*nin*). We are so many in a canoe or boat, (when the number is over nineteen; p. *endassokangig.* —*Nijtana nin dassokamin; nijtana nin dassokamin ashi nisswi;* we are twenty in the canoe; we are twenty-three in the canoe.—For less than twenty, see *Nijokamin. Nissokamin*, etc.

Dassôka, (*nin*) or, *nin bi-dassoka.* I come with my whole family, or with my whole band; p. *endassokad.*—*Enigokwiniiân nin bi-dassoka*, I come with my whole family, or, with my whole band.

Dassôminag, so many round globular objects, (in numbers higher than nineteen.)—*Nissimidana dassominag mishiminag ashi niwin*, thirty-four apples.—For numbers under twenty, see *Nijominag. Nissominag*, etc.

Dassôna, (*nin*). I catch him in a trap, I trap him; p. *dassonad;* imp. *dassôj.*

Dassônag. So many canoes, boats, etc., (in numbers higher than nineteen.) *Nijtana dassonag tchimânan nin wâbandânan;* I see twenty canoes.—For numbers under twenty, see *Nijonag. Nissonag*, etc.

Dassônâgan. Trap; snare; pl.-*an.*

Dassonijigan. So many pieces, (of meat, fish, etc.) (in numbers over nineteen.)—*Nissimidana dassonijigan gigoian giashamawag abinadjiiag;* thirty pieces of fish were given to the children to eat.—For numbers under twenty, see *Nijonigan. Nissonigan,* etc.

Dassônik. So many fathoms, (in numbers over nineteen.)—*Nijtana dassonik ashi nanan,* twenty-five fathoms. — For numbers under twenty, see *Nijonik. Nissonik.*

Dassônindj. So many inches, (in numbers higher than nineteen.)—For numbers under twenty, see *Nijanindj. Nissonindj,* etc.

Dassôs, (*nin*) I am trapped, I am caught under something that fell upon me, (a tree, a rock, etc.) ; p. *dessôsod.*

Dassoshk. So many breadths of cloth or other stuff, (in numbers higher than nineteen.)—For numbers under twenty, see *Nijôshk. Nissôshk,* etc.

Dassôshkin. So many bags full, (in numbers over nineteen.) —*Nissimidan dassoshkin opinig ninagigishpinanag ;* I bought thirty bags full of potatoes. For numbers under twenty, see *Nijoshkin. Nissoshkin,* etc.

Dassosid. So many feet, (in numbers over nineteen.)—For numbers under twenty, see *Nijosid. Nissosid.*

Dassôsowin. Being trapped or caught ; also, the bruise or bruises caused to a person by s. th. that fell upon him.

Dassossag. So many barrels or wooden boxes full, (in numbers over nineteen.)—*Nijtana dassossag pakwejigan nind aiawa ;* I have twenty barrels of flour.—For numbers less than twenty, see *Nijossag. Nisossag,* etc.

Dasswâbik. So many objects of metal, stone, or glass, (in numbers over nineteen.) — *Nanimidana dasswâbik joniian o gi-minan ;* he gave him fifty dollars. — For numbers under twenty, see *Nijwabik. Nisswabik,* etc.

Dasswaiagad It is of so many kinds ; p. *end..gak ;* (in numbers over nineteen.) — For numbers less than twenty, see *Nijwaiagad.*

Dasswaiagisimin, (*nin*) or *nin dassoiagisimin.* We are of so many kinds ; p. *endass..sidjig ;* (in numbers over nineteen.)—*Nijtana dasswaiagisiwog igiw bineshiiag ;* those birds are of twenty different kinds.—For numbers under twenty, see *Nijwaiagisimin. Nisswaiagisimin.*

Dasswâk. So many hundreds, (in numbers over nineteen which are put before the number hundred.)—*Nijtana dasswâk,* twenty hundred ; *nissimidana dasswâk,* thirty hundred, etc.—For numbers under twenty, put before the number hundred, see *Nijwâk. Nisswâk,* etc.

Dasswâkosimin, (*nin*). We are so many hundred in number ; p. *endass..sidjig ;* (in numbers over nineteen, put before the number hundred.) — *Nissimidana nin dasswakosimin,* we are thirty hundred of us, (three thousands.)—For numbers under twenty, put before the number hundred, see *Nijwakosimin.* *Nisswakosimin*, etc.

Dasswakwoagan. So many spans, (in numbers over nineteen.)—*Nijtana dasswakwoagan senibâ ki minin;* I give thee twenty spans of ribbon. —For numbers under twenty, see *Nijwakwoagan.* *Nisswâkwoagan*, etc.

Dasswâtig. So many objects of wood, (in numbers over nineteen.)— *Nânimidana dasswâtig nabagissagon o gigishpinanan ;* he bought forty boards.—For numbers under twenty, see *Nijwâtig.* *Nisswâtig*, etc.

Dassweg. So many objects of stuff, cloth, (in numbers over nineteen.)—*Nanimidana dassweg wâboianan od aiânan aw atawewinini;* that merchant has fifty blankets.—For numbers under twenty, see *Nijweg.* *Nissweg*, etc.

Dasswéwân. So many pair, couple, yoke, sets; (in numbers higher than nineteen.) *Nijtana dasswewan pijikiwog*, twenty yoke of oxen. *Nissimidana dasswewan makisinan od aianan*, he has thirty pair of shoes.—For numbers under twenty, see *Nijwéwân.* *Nisswéwân*, etc.

Dâtagâb, (*nin*) or, *nin dâtaganâb.* I lift up my eyes, I look upwards; p. *daiat..bid.*

Dâtagikwen, (*nin*). I lift up my head and incline it backwards; p. *daiat..nid.*

Dé— ; a particle which is prefixed to verbs or numbers in order to signify, *enough, sufficiently, quite;* as: *Kawin nin dé-kikenindisossi*, I don't know myself sufficiently. *Déâpitisi*, he is old enough. *Kawin dénijtana*, not quite twenty. *Nin déakos*, I am tall enough.

Déb, débi, in compositions, signify, *sufficiently, enough.* (Examples in some of the following words.)

Debaamaged. Payer; pl.-*jig.*

Débab, (*nin*). I have room enough, (in sitting;) p. *daiébabid.*

Débâb, (*nin*). I see from such *a* distance ; p. *daiébâbid..*—*Wâssa nin débâb*, I see from far, (I am not short-sighted.)

Débâbama, (*nin*). I see him, or, I can see him, from such a distance ; p. *daie..mad.*

Débâbaminagos, (*nin*). I can be seen from... I am visible from such a distance ; p. *dâieb .sid.*

Débâbaminagwad It can be seen, or, it is visible from such a distance; p. *daieb.. wak.*

Débâbandan, (*nin*) I see it, or can see it, from such a distance ; p. *daié..ang.*

Debagenim, (*nin*). I am satisfied, contented, I think I have enough ; p. *daieb..mod.*

Débaiged. One who measures, measurer ; pl.-*jig.*

Débanagidon, (*nin*). I talk enough ; p. *daie..ong.*

Débani, adj *Ol.* right. *Nin debaninik*, my right arm; *nin debaninindj*, my right hand.

Débaôki, (*nin*). I give to all,

(in a distribution ;) p. *daie..kid.*

Débaôna, (*nin*). I give also to him, (in a distribution ;) p. *daie..nad.*

Débashkine, or-*magad.* There is room enough in it, it holds, it contains, (dry objects ;) p. *daie..neg,* or-*magak.—Nibiwa dêbashkine iw makak ;* that box contains much, (holds much.)

Debashkinemin, (*nin*). We can all go in, there is room enough for us ; pl. *daie..nedjig.—Nin debashkinemin ima anamiewigamigong ;* there is room for us all in that church.

Débendam, (*nin*). S. *Débenim.*

Debendang. Proprietor, master, mistress ; pl.-*ig.*

Debendjiged. Lord ; master, mistress ; proprietor ; pl.-*jig.*

Debênim, (*nin*) or, *nin dêbendam.* I think it is enough, I think I have enough ; I am contented, satisfied ; p. *daie..mad,* or, *daie..ang.*

Débênimowin. Contentedness.

Debeninged. S. *Debendjiged.*

Debia, (*nin*). I content him, I make him happy, satisfy him, I give him sufficiently ; p. *dâiébiad.*

Débibi, (*nin*). I drank enough, I am filled with liquor ; p. *daiébibid.*

Débibi, or-*magad.* It holds, contains, (liquid ;) p. *daiébibig,* or-*magak.—Kitchi pangi dêbibi iw omodai ;* that bottle holds (contains) very little.

Débibina, (*nin*) (*nan*). I catch him, take hold of him, with my hand, (or hands ;) p. *daie..nad.*

Débima, (*nin*). I tell the truth of him, what I tell of him, is all true ; p. *daiébimad.—Aw inini nin debimig geget ; aw dash ikwe kawin nin débimigossi.* What that man is telling of me, is true indeed ; but what that woman tells of me, is not true.

Débina, (*nin*) (*nân*). I reach him, (with my hand or otherwise ;) p. *dai..nad.*

Débipo. It snowed enough ; p. *bipog.*

Débis, (*nin*). I have enough, I am contented, I am happy ; p. *daiébisid.*

Débishkan, (*nin*). I can put it on easily, its fits me well, (an article of clothing, or a hat, a shoe, a boot ;) also, I read it ; p. *daie..ang.*

Debishkodadimin, (*nin*). We reach one another ; p. *daie..didjig.*

Débisiwin. Happiness, sufficiency, abundance, plenty.

Débissatchige, (*nin*). I put enough, I put everywhere ; p. *daie..ged.*

Débissaton, (*nin*). I put enough of it, I procure enough of it ; p. *daie..tod.—Nin wi-debissatonan mashkossiwan ;* I will procure hay enough, (for the whole winter.)

Dêbisse, (*nin*). I am sufficient, I can do it, I can afford it ; p. *daiêbissed.*

Dêbisse, or-*magad.* It is sufficient, enough, it suffices ; p. *daiébisseg,* or-*magak.*

Débissin, (*nin*). I ate sufficiently, I am saturated; p. *daie..nid.*

Dêbissiniwin. Saturity, the state of having eaten enough.

Débitagos, (*nin*). I can be heard, I speak loud enough to be heard; p. *daie..sid.*

Débitagwad. It can be heard, it sounds loud enough to be heard; p. *daie..wak.—Debitagwad oma kitotâgan*, the bell can be heard here.

Débitawa, (*nin*) (*tan*). I hear him here, (he speaks loud enough;) p. *daie..wad.—Tchigishkwand nin nibaw anamiewigamigong, anawi dash nin debitawa gegikwed;* I stand at the door in the church, but still I hear the preacher.

Debiton, (*nin*). I satisfy it, I make it contented, happy; p. *daiébitod.—Nin débiton ninde dassing meno-dodamânin;* I make my heart contented as often as I act well, (as I do good.)

Débiwane, (*nin*. I carry all at once, in one trip; p. *deie..ned.*

Débiwebina, (*nin*) (*nân*). I throw some obj. to such a distance; p. *daie..nad.*

Debwe, (*nin*). I tell the truth; p. *daiëbwed.*

Débweiéndagos, (*nin*). I am veracious; I am considered as telling the truth; p. *daie..sid.*

Débweiéndâgwad. It is true; it is considered as truth; p. *daie..wak.*

Débwéiendam, (*nin*) or, *nin débwêendam*. I believe, (in my thoughts, in my mind,) I think it is true; p. *daie..ang.*

Débwéiendamowin, or, *debweendamowin*. Belief, faith.

Débwêiendân, (*nin*) or, *nin debweendan*. I believe in it, I think it is true; p. *daie..ang.*

Débwéienima, (*nin*) or, *nin debweenima*. I believe in his existence; p. *daie..mad.*

Débwétagos, (*nin*) or, *nin debwetage*. I speak the truth, I am heard speaking the truth; p. *daie..sid.*

Debwetagosiwin. Veracious speaking, truth-telling.

Debwetaienima, (*nin*). I think he is telling the truth; p. *daie..mad.*

Débwêtam, (*nin*). I believe what I hear; (fides per auditum;) p. *daiebwetang.*

Débwetân, (*nin*). I believe it, (hearing it;) p. *daie bwetang.*

Débwêtawa, (*nin*). I believe him, I believe what he says, I obey him; p. *daie..wad.*

Dêbwewessin. Its sound is heard at this or at that place; p. *daië..sing.*

Débwewidam, (*nin*). I make myself heard from a certain distance; p. *daie..ang.*

Dêbwewin. Truth.

Dêbwewinagad. It is true, it is the truth; p. *daie..gak.*

Dêbwéwinimagad. S. *Debwewinagad.*

Débwéwini-masinaigan. Certificate, document, deed, (paper of truth;) pl.-*an.*

Débwéwiniwan. It is the truth; p. *daie..ang.*

Déé, (*nin*). My heart is...; p. *daiêed.— Nin mino-dee*, (or, *nin minodee*,) my heart is good; *nin matchi-dee*, (*mat-*

chidee,) my heart is wicked. *Mi eji-deeiân*, my heart is so.

Déêa, (*nin*). I make his heart so ; p. *daiêead*. — *Nin minodêêa ; nin matchidêêa ;* I make his heart good ; I make his heart wicked. *Eji-deêian iji deêishin*, make my heart like thy heart.

Dééshka, (*nin*) or, *nind iji deeshka*. My heart is affected in a certain manner, is filled with certain sentiments; p. *daieeshkad*. *Sesika gi-nishkadji-deeshka ;* his heart was suddenly affected with anger, (filled with anger.)

Dê-gijia, (*nin*.) I finish it, I have time enough to finish it; p. *daiê..ad*.

Dejingeshkid. Habitual slanderer, detractor, calumniator ; pl.*-jig*.

Dejinged. One who speaks ill of somebody, (without a habit of doing so,) slanderer ; pl.*-jig*.

Dénaniw. Tongue. There is always a possessive pronoun prefixed to this word ; as : *Nin dênaniw*, my tongue ; *ki dênaniw*, thy tongue, etc.

Dénimiigon, (*nin*). The water comes under me, (in a camp after a rain ;) p. *daie.god*

Déw, dêwa, dêwi, in compositions, signifies *evil, ache, pain, infirmity*. (Examples in some of the following words)

Dêwâbide, (*nin*). I have toothache ; p. *paie..ded*.

Déwâbidewin. Tooth-ache.

Déwakigan, (*nin*). I have pain in the breast ; p. *daiéwakigang*.

Déwidee, (*nin*). I feel pain in my heart, my heart is oppressed, cramped ; p. *daiêwideed*.

Dêwîgâde, (*nin*). I have pain in my leg ; p. *daié..ded*.

Dêwigane, (*nin*). I have pain in my bones ; p. *daie..ned*.

Dêwikwe, (*nin*). I have headache ; p. *daie..wed*.

Déwikweiâss, (*nin*). I have head-ache from too much heat ; p. *daie..sod*.

Déwikwewin. Head-ache.

Dêwinike, (*nin*), I have pain in my arm ; p. *daie..ked*.

Dibaaki, (*nin*). I survey, (I measure the earth ;) *debaakid*.

Dibaakiwin. Survey, surveying, geometry.

Dibaakiwinini. Surveyor, geometer ; pl.*-wag*.

Dibaamâdim,. They pay together, a payment.

Dibaamâding. When they pay together, the time of a payment.

Dibaamâdiwin. Payment *made*, or *received*, by several together.

Dibaamage, (*nin*). I pay people ; I recompense ; I return, repay ; p. *deb..ged*.

Dibaamagewin. Payment or reward *given* to somebody.

Dibaamagos, (*nin*. I receive payment, I am paid ; p. *deb..sid*.

Dibaamagowin.* Payment or reward *received* by somebody.

Dibaamawa, (*nin*). I pay him,

---

* See *Remark* in article *Anamikagowin*.

I reward or recompense him, I return him or repay him what he did to me or for me ; p. *deb..wad.*

Dibaan, (*nin*). I pay it, or for it; p. *débaang.*

Dibabishkodjigan. Balance, scale, steelyard ; also, a pound ; p.-*an.*

Dibabishkodjige, (*nin*). I weigh in a balance, I am weighing; p. *deb..ged.*

Dibabishkodon, (*nin*). I weigh it; p. *deb..dod.*

Dibabishkona, (*nin*). I weigh him, (a person, or any other obj.); p. *deb .nad.*

Dibaboweigan. Cover of a kettle; pl.-*an.*

Dibâdjim, (*nin*). I tell, I narrate, I relate; p. *deb..mod.*

Dibâdjima, (*nin*). I speak of him, I tell s. th. of him, (how he is, or what he did, etc.) ; p. *deb..mad.*

Dibâdjimotage, (*nin.*) I am telling, relating; p. *deb..ged.*

Dibâdjimotawa, (*nin*). I tell him ; p. *deb..wad.*

Dibâdjimowin. Narration, story, report; pl..*an.*

Dibâdodamawa, (*nin*). I tell him s. th.; p. *deb..wad.*

Dibâdodân, (*nin*). I tell it, I relate it ; p. *deb..ang.*

Dibâgima, (*nin*). I conduct or oversee him ; I judge him ; p. *deb..ad.*

Dibâigan. Any kind of *measure,* as, yard, bushel, acre, hour, league, mile, etc.; pl.-*an.*

Dibâige, (*nin.* I measure; p. *debaiged.*

Dibaigen, (*nin*). I measure it; p. *debaiged.*

Debaigenan, (*nin*). I measure some obj. ; p. *debaiged.* (V. Conj.)

Dibaigéwin. Measurement, measuring.

Dibaigisisswân. Watch, clock, sun-diàl ; pl.-*ag.*—*Dibaigisisswân mâdjishka, kijika, bésika, nagashka ;* the watch goes, goes fast, goes slow, stops.

Dibaigisisswanikewinini Watch-maker; pl.-*wag.*

Dibaiminan. Bushel, (measuring vessel containing a bushel ;) pl.-*an.*

Dibâkona, (*nin*). I judge him ; p. *deb..nad.*

Dibakonidiwigamig. Judgment-house, common-hall; pl.-*on.*

Dibakondiwin. Judgment, court.

Dibakonigade, or *magad.* It is judged ; p. *deb..deg,* or *magak.*

Dibagonigas, (*nin*). I undergo judgment, I am judged ; p. *deb..sod.*

Dibakônige, (*nin*). I judge; p. *dek..yed.*

Dibakonigê-gijigad. Day of judgment.

Dibakonigéwigamig. S. *Dibakonidiwigamig.*

Dibakonigêwin. Judgment, *made* or pronounced; law, justice. *Gaiat dibakonigewin,* the old law, (Old Testament.)

Dibakonigéwinini. Judge, justice of the peace, magistrate ; pl.-*wag.*

Dibakonigowin. Judgment *undergone* or received.

Dibâkoniwe, (*nin*). S. *Dibabonige,* etc.

Dibakoniwewin. S. *Dibakonigewin.*

Dibakoniwewini-apabiwin. Judgment-seat, tribunal; pl.-*an.*

Dibamenim, (*nin*). I moderate myself, put myself on a certain rule; p. *deb..mod.*

Dibando, (*nin*). I make a vow; p. *debandod.*

Dibandon, (*nin*). I fulfil a vow; p. *deb..dod.*

Dibandowin. Vow; sacrifice, offering; pl.-*an.*

Dibaonon. Measure of a canoe; pl.-*an.*

Dibawa, (*nin*). I pay for some obj.; p. *deb..wad;* imp. *dibâ.*

Dibendagos, (*nin*). I have a master; (L. sub potestate constitutus sum;) p. *deb..sid.*

Dibendamoa, (*nin*) or, *nin dibenindamoa.* I make him master of s. th.; p. *deb..ad.*

Dibendân, (*nin*). I am the proprietor of it, the master of it, I possess it; p. *debendang.*

Dibendass, (*nin*). I have property, I possess, I am proprietor; p. *deb..sod.*

Dibendassowin. Property, possession; treasure.

Dibéndjige, (*nin*). I am master, lord; p. *deb..ged.*

Dibendjigewin. Domination, mastery.

Dibênima, (*nin*). I am his master, his proprietor; I possess him, (a person, or any other obj.;) p. *deb..mad.*

Dibénindis, (*nin*). I am my own master, I am free and independent; p. *deb..sod.*

Dibénindisowin. Liberty, freedom, independence.

Dibewagendam, (*nin*). I reflect, consider; p. *deb..ang.*

Dibewagendan, (*nin*). I consider it, I reflect upon it; p. *deb..ang.*

Dibewagenim, (*nin*). I reflect upon myself; p. *deb..mod.*

Dibewagenima, (*nin*). I reflect upon him, I consider him; p. *deb..mad.*

Dibinikama, (*nin*) (*dan*). I measure some obj. by the fathom; p. *deb..mad.*

Dibowana, (*nin*). I arrange or settle him; p. *deb..mad;* imp. *dibowaj.*

Dibowé, (*nin*). I arrange, I settle, I serve on the jury; p. *debowed.*

Dibowéwin. Jury.

Dibowéwinini. Juryman; pl.-*wag.*

Dimi, or-*magad.* It is deep; (a river, a lake, etc.;) p. *demig,* or-*magak.*

Dimiianike, (*nin.*) I dig deep; p. *dem..ked.*

Diminengan. Shoulder. There is always a possessive pronoun prefixed to this word; as: *Nin diminangan,* my shoulder; *o diminangan,* his shoulder, etc.

Dimitigweia, or, *dimitigweiamagad.* The river is deep; p. *dem..iag,* or, *dem..gak.*

Dinô, dinowân. Like, equal, obj. *Ow dino,* or, *ow dinowa,* one like this here. *Ow dinowân,* several like this one. *Onow dinowân,* several objects like these here.

Dinong. In the same thing; *nassâb dinong,* always in the same thing.

Dodêdimin, (*nin*). We do to each other, we treat each other; p. *dwadadidjig.—Mojag mino dodâdiwog,* they treat each other always well. *Kego wika matchi dodâdikegan,* never do evil to one another.

Dodâdiwin. Mutual treatment.

Dodagemagad. It does; p. *end.. gak.—Kitchi matchi dodagemagad ishkotewâbo*: ardent liquor does much evil.

Dôdam, (*nin*). I do, I commit; p. *endodang.*

Dodamowin. Act, action, deed, doing; pl.-*an.*

Dodân, (*nin*). I do or cause s. th. to some obj.; p. *endodang.* —*O matchi dodan wiiaw,* he does evil to his body, (to himself.)

Dôdas, (*nin*) or, *nin dodadis.* I do it to myself, I cause it to myself, I bring it upon me; p. *end..sod.*

Dôdawa, (*nin*). I do it to him, I treat him; I cause it to him, I bring it upon him; p *end.. wad.*

Dowa. Like, equal, obj.—*Nin dowa kin dowa, win dowan;* one like myself, thyself, himself. *Nin dowag, kin dowag, nin dowan,* several like myself, thyself, himself. — *Ninawind dowa, kinawa dowa, winawa dowan;* one like ourselves, yourselves, themselves. *Ninawind dowag, kinawa dowag, winawa dowan;* several like ourselves, yourselves, themselves.

E

E. This vowel has only *one* sound in the Otchipwe language, which is the sound of the same vowel in the English word *met.*

E, or *enh!* adv. Yes. (See Otch. Grammar. Adverbs denoting *affirmation.*)

Ebashkobiteg nibi. Tepid water, a little warm.

Edissiged. One who dyes, dyer; pl.-*jig.*

Editégin. Things that are ripe, (all kinds of berries.)

Egatchissig. One who is not ashamed, a shameless, impudent person; pl.-*og.*

Eij. S. *Naiénj.*

Ejashawebagisid assema. Tobacco in square piece.

Ejessed. He that slides back, backslider; *fig.*, who gives up religion, or some other good practice; pl.-*jig.*

Ejisidebiiân. At my feet; *ejisidebiian,* at thy feet; *ejisidebid,* at his feet, etc. (I. Conj.)

Ejisidekawe, (*nind*). The tracks of both my feet appear; p. *aiéj.-wed.*

Eji..tagwag, or *eji-takwamagâk.* As it is short, the abridgment of s. th.

Eko-; The Change of *Ako,*

Eko-debiwebinind assin. A stone's throw far.

Eko-doskwaning. The length of an elbow, a cubit, (a foot and a half.)—*Nijing eko-doskwaning, midâtching eko-doskwaning, nijtana dassing eko-doskwaning;* two cubits, ten cubits, twenty cubits long.

*Eko-jangatching,*num. Ninthly; the ninth.

Eko-nananing, num. Fifthly; the fifth.—(For the rest see Otch. Grammar. Chap. V. No. 5. Ordinal Number.)

Ekôsid. As he is long, his length.

Ekossing. As it is long, its length; pl.-*in.*

Ekwag. As it is large, its extent; pl.-*in.*

Emikwân. Large wooden spoon, spoon; pl.-*an.*

Emikwânens. Tea-spoon; pl.-*an.*

Enâbandang. One who dreams, dreamer; pl.-*ig.*

Enâbadassinog. Useless, being good for nothing; pl.-*in.*

Enâbadisissig. Useless unprofitable person, or other being; pl.-*og.*

Enâbigis. S. *Nindawatch. Mano.*

Enamiad. One who prays, a Christian; pl.-*jig.*

Enamiâssig. One who does not

pray, a pagan, heathen; pl.-*og*.

Enamiekâsod. One who feigns religion, an hypocrite; pl.-*jig*.

Enamietawad Kije-Maniton, adorer of God; pl.-*jig*.

Enamietawad masininin. Adorer of idols; pl.-*jig*.

Enangê ka, adv. Yes certainly, doubtless, undoubtedly.

Enâpinadon, (*nind*). I damage or injure it; p. *aien..dod*.

Enâssamabiiân. Before me, (*sitting*;) *enâssamabiian*, before thee; *enâssamabid*, before him, etc.

Enâssamigâbawiiân. Before me, (*standing*;) *enassamigabâwiian*, before thee; *enâssamigabawid*, before him, etc.

Enâssamiiân. Before me, in my presence; *enâssamid*, before him, etc.

Enassamimagak. Before something.

Enâssamishinân. Before me, (*lying*,) *enâssamishinan*, before thee, etc.

Enâssamishhinjigweiân. Before my eyes, *enâssamishkinjigwed*, before his eyes, etc.

Enassamissing. Before something, (lying on the ground, or standing there.)

Endad. He who stays; or, where he stays, his habitation, his dwelling, his lodge, his house, his home.

Endagog. What there is.

Endaiân. My home, my dwelling, my habitation, my lodging.—*Endâian*, thy home, etc.

Endaji-. (The Change of *Daji-*.)

Endaji-bisikwanaied mekatewikwanaie, where the priest puts on his church-vestments, or sacerdotal garments, sacristy, vestry.

Endashid. Himself and all his family; or, all what there is of some obj.—*Mi endashid joniia endaiân*; that is all the money there is in my house.

Endashiiân. Myself and all my family, all those who belong to me.

Endassing. All what there is of it, the whole of it.

Endassâ-. (The Change of *Dasso*.)

Endassô-gijigak. Every day, daily.—

Endasso-tibikak. Every night, nightly.

Endogwen. I don't know.

Enigo. Ant, emmet; pl.-*g*.

Enigok, adv. Strongly, much; loud.

Enigokodeeiân. From all my heart; *enigokodeeian*, from all thy heart; *ênigokodeed*, from all his heart, etc.

Enigokodewisiiân. My whole household, my whole family; *enigokodewisid*, his whole household, etc.

Enigokossing, or, *enigokwissing*, the whole extent of it, the whole heap.

Enigokwadessing. As it is wide, the whole width of it.

Enigokwag aki. As wide as the earth is, everywhere on earth.

Enigokwagamigag, or, *enigokogamigag*, adv. In the whole world.

Enigokwiniiân, S. *Enigokodewisiiân*.

Enigowigamig. Ant's hill; pl.-*on.*

Enimâwa, (*nind*). I surpass him, (in a *canoe;*) p. *aien..wad;* imp. *enima.*

Enimaowe, (*nind*). I surpass, (paddling in a canoe, or sailing;) p. *aien..wed.*

Enimia, (*nind*). I surpass him, beat him; p. *aien..ad.*

Enimiiwe, (*nind*). I surpass; p. *aien..wed.*

Enimishkawa, (*nind*). I outgo or outrun him, I arrive before him; I surpass him walking or running; p. *aien..wad.*

Eninajaond. One who is sent, a messenger; pl.-*jig.*

E, nind ikkit. I affirm, I say yes.

Eni-onâgoshig. Towards evening.

Eni tibikak. Towards night.

Eniwek, adv. Tolerably, middling, pretty; (F. passablement.)

Enôkid. Who orders s. th. to be done, who gives work, employer; pl.-*jig.*

Enônind. One that is employed to do s. th., an employed person, hireling, mercenary; pl.-*jig.*

Epangishimog. West, occident, setting of the sun.

Epitag. As it is thick, the thickness of some obj.; pl.-*in.*

Epitagamig. So deep in the ground.—*Mi epitâkamig wâniken,* dig so deep in the ground.

Epitch. (The Change of *Apitch.*)

Epitchâg. As it is far, the distance of a place.

Epitchiiân. As much as I can; as quick as I can.

Epitching, adv. Strongly, with all force.

Epitissing. As it is high, its height.

Epitoweng. As we speak, loud.

Eshanged matchi mashkiki. One who gives poison to eat, a poisoner; pl.-*jig.*

Eshkam, adv. More and more. (Examples in some of the following articles.)

Eshkam nibiwa. More and more, increasing.

Eshkam nin pakakados. I am getting lean, poor, more and more.

Eshkam nin winin. I am getting fat more and more.

Eshkam pangi. Less and less, decreasing, (more and more little.)

Eshkan. Horn (of cattle, deer, etc.); pl.-*ag.*

Eshkan. Ice-cutter; (F. tranche;) pl.-*an.*

Eshkandaming. What is eaten raw, cucumber, melon; pl.-*in.*

Eshkânigan. S. *Eshkan.*

Eshkibod. One who eats raw, an Esquimau Indian; pl.-*jig.*

Eshkosseg, or, *eshkossemagak.* Remainder, remnant; pl.-*in.*

Eshkwessing. The last obj. in a range or row; pl.-*in.*

Eshpag. As it is high, the height of s. th; pl.-*in.*

Eshwâmanissongin. S. *Ashwâmaniss.*

Esiga. Tick, tike.

Ess, or, *ens*. Shell, oyster; pl.-*ag*.
Essiban. Wild cat, rackoon; pl.-*ag*.
Essibaniwaiân. Skin of the wild cat; pl.-*ag*.
Essibaniwekon. Coat made of wild cat's skins; pl.-*an*.
Essimig. Breast-plate, (Indian ornament;) pl.-*ag*. *Joniiâwessimig*, breast-plate made of silver; *migissiiessimig*, made of beads of porcelain or china-ware.
Eta, adv. Only.
Etaged mamakisiwin. One who puts the cox-pox, inoculator; pl. *etagedjig*.
Etawa, etawi, in compositions, signifies *both*, or *both sides*. (Examples in some of the following words.)
Etawagâm, adv. On both sides of a river, lake, bay, etc.
Etawaii, adv. On both sides.
Etawidasse, (*nind*). I have both leggings on, (on both sides, on both legs;) p. *aiet..sed*.
Etawigâd. Both legs.
Etawikomân. Knife with two edges.
Etawina. Both sides of the body.
Etawinik. Both arms.
Etawinindj. Both hands, in both hands, with both hands.
Etawisid. Both feet.
Eukaristiwin. Eucharist.

G

Some words that are not found under G, *may be looked for under* K.

Ga-, or *gad-*. This particle is used in the first and second persons of the future tense, and in the participles of the past tense. (S. the Conjug. in Otch. Gram.)

Gabâ, (*nin*). I land; p. *gebad.*

Gabâshima, (*nin*) (*ton*). I put some obj. to the fire in some vessel, to cook; p. *geb..mad.*

Gabésh, (*nin*). I camp, encamp; p. *geb..id.*

Gabéshiwin. The act of camping, camp, encampment; pl.-*an.*

Gabéwin. Landing place, landing; pl.-*an.*

Gagabâdj, adv. Much.

Gagaiênis, (*nin*). I am cunning, artful, crafty; p. *geg.. sid.*

Gagaiénisiwin. Cunning, artfulness.

Gâgandawa, * (*nin*). *an.freq.* I push him repeatedly; p. *gaiag..wad*; imp. *gaganda*

Gagandenima, (*nin*). I have a malicious joy over his grief or damage, (in thoughts;) p. *geg ..mad.*

Gagandini-odabanens. Wheelbarrow; (F. brouette;) pl.-*ag.*

Gagândjia, (*nin*) *freq.* S. *Gagandjinawea.*

Gagandjigidea, (*nin*) *freq.* S. *Gagândjinnwea.*

Gâgandjigidema, (*nin*) *freq.* I express a malicious joy over his grief or damage, I say, it is right that this or that happened to him; p. *geg..mad.*

Gagândjigitage, (*nin*) *freq* I am expressing a malicious joy over the grief or damage of somebody; p. *geg..ged.*

Gagandjinawea, (*nin*). I irritate him, I provoke or excite him to anger purposely; p. *geg..ad.*

Gagândjinaweidiwin. Malicious provocation to anger.

Gagânobiwaie, *freq.* Its fur or hair is long, (of an animal;) p. *geg..ied.*

Gagânodamage, (*nin*) *freq.* I pray or speak for somebody repeatedly, I intercede; p. *geg..ged.*

---

* Note. Most of the verbs beginning with *gaga* are *frequentative* verbs, denoting a repetition or reiteration of the same act, or alluding to more than one object. They are marked here with the syllable *freq.*

Gaganôdamagewin. Intercession.
Gaganôdamawa, (*nin*) *freq.* I pray or speak for him repeatedly, I intercede for him; p. *geg..wad.*
Gagânoma, (*nin*). I console him, I tell him to take courage; p. *geg..mad.*
Gaganôna, (*nin*). I traverse with him, I speak to him, (somewhat longer;) p. *geg..nad.*
Gagânsitam, (*nin*). I gainsay; I give bad answers; p. *geg..ang.*
Gagânsitan, (*nin*). I speak against it, I gainsay it; p. *geg..ang.*
Gagânsitawa, (*nin*). I gainsay him, disobey him; p. *geg..wad.*
Gagânsoma, (*nin*). I exhort him, I encourage, incite, persuade, urge, animate, instigate, counsel, push him, to do s. th.; p *geg..mad.*
Gagânsondiwin. Encouraging, inciting, instigation.
Gagânsonge, (*nin*). I exhort, encourage, incite, animate; p. *geg..ged.*
Gagânwabide, (*nin*) *freq.* I have long teeth; p. *geg..ded.*
Gagânwanikwe, (*nin*) *freq.* I have long hair, acrocome; p. *geg..wed.*
Gagâwendjige, (*nin*) *freq.* I am jealous frequently, I am envious; p. *geg..ged.*
Gagâwenima, (*nin*) *freq.* I am frequently jealous in regard to him, (her;) I envy him; p. *geg..mad.*
Gagâwenindiwin. Jealousy, envy.
Gagânwenj, adv. (The frequentative of *ginwenj,*) a long while every time.—*Naningim bi-ija oma gagânwenj dash iko aia;* he comes here frequently, and remains a long while every time.
Gagâweshk, (*nin*) *freq.* I am in a habit of being jealous; p. *geg..kid.*
Gagénigwaan. Ice-bank on the lake-shore; pl.-*eg.*
Gagénigwaanoka, or *–magad.* There are ice-banks on the shore; p. *geg..kag,* or-*magak.*
Gagibâdad. It is foolish, stupid, imprudent, irrational, absurd, unchaste, impudent, impure; p. *geg.dak.*
Gagibâdendam, (*nin*). I have stupid, foolish, absurd, imprudent thoughts; I have impure, unchaste thoughts; p. *geg..ang.*
Gagibadendamowin. Foolish, absurd thought, impure thought; pl.-*an.*
Gagibâdis, (*nin*). I am foolish, stupid, irrational, imprudent, imbecile, ignorant; I am frivolous, lewd, unchaste, impure; p. *geg..sid.*
Gagibâdisiwin. Foolishness, imprudence, stupidity, absurdity, imbecility, ignorance, frivolousness, impurity, impudency, disorder, lewdness.
Gagibâdgi-gijwe, (*nin*). S. *Gagibasitagos.*
Gagibâdji-gijwewin, gagibadji-gigitowin. S. *Gagibâsitagosiwin.*

Gagibâdjikwe. Unchaste impudent woman, strumpet, whore, prostitute, fornicatress, adultress; pl.-*g.*

Gagibadjinini. Unchaste impudent man, whore-monger, fornicator, adulterer; pl.-*wag.*

Gagibâdjitchige, (*nin*). I act or behave foolishly; p. *geg..ged.*

Gagibanagaskwe, (*nin*). I stammer; p. *geg..wed.*

Gagibâsitagos, (*nin*). I speak foolishly, imprudently, absurdly; I speak unchastely, indecently; p. *geg..sid.*

Gagibâsitagosiwin. Imprudent, foolish, absurd talking; frivolous, impure, indecent talking.

Gagibâsitawa, (*nin*). I listen to him with the impression that he speaks foolishly, absurdly; p. *geg..wad.*

Gagibasoma, (*nin*). I make him stupid, foolish; I debauch or corrupt him, (her) into evil impure conduct or lewdness; p. *geg..mad.*

Gagibidjane, (*nin*). My nose is slopped, obstructed, (catching cold, etc.); p. *geg..ned.*

Gagibidjanetagos, (*nin*). I speak through the nose; p. *geg..sid.*

Gagibingwé, (*nin*). My eyes are shut, I am blind; p. *geg..wed.*

Gagibingwea, (*nin*). I make him blind, I blind him; p. *geg..ad.*

Gagibingwebina, (*nin*). I blindfold him; p. *geg..nad.*

Gagibingwebis, (*nin*). I am blindfolded; p. *geg..sod.*

Gagibingwekwe. A small kind of mole, a little animal that lives and works under ground; pl.-*g.*

Gagibingwewin. Blindness.

Gagibishê, (*nin*). My ears are stopped, shut, I am deaf; p. *ged..ed.*

Gagibishebina, (*nin*). I stop him both ears, I stop up both his ears; p. *geg..nad*; imp. *ga..bij.*

Gagibishêwin. Deafness.

Gâgidis, (*nin*). I am sensible, delicate, (weak of constitution,) I easily feel pain; p. *gaia..sid.*

Gâgidisiwin. Delicacy, bodily sensibility, weakness of constitution.

Gâgidjia, (*nin*). I appease him; p. *gaia..ad.*

Gâgidjigonewe, (*nin*). My throat is sore; p. *gaia..wed.*

Gâgidowe, (*nin*). I mourn, I lament, I wail; p. *gaia..wed.*

Gagigijwa, (*nin*). I cut off what is spoiled, (*an.* obj.); p. *geg..wad.*

Gagigikodan, (*nin*). I cut off what is spoiled, (*in.* obj.); p. *geg..ang.*

Gagigikona, (*nin*). I cut off what is spoiled, (*in.* obj.); p. *geg..ad.*

Gagiginag, (*nin*). I pick them out, I select them out, I select them, (*an.* obj.); p. *geg..nad.* —*Nin gagiginag mishiminag, opinig*; I pick out apples, potatoes, (the good ones, the rotten ones, etc.)

Gagiginanan, (*nin*). I pick them out or select them, (*in.* obj.); p. *geg..ang.*—*Nin gagiginanan anindjiminan,* I pick out peas.

Gâgigit, (*nin*) *freq.* I am speaking, talking, conversing; p. *gaia..tod.*
Gagijiwishin, (*nin*). I am lying contracted; p. *geg..ing.*
Gagikima, (*nin*). I preach to him, I exhort him; p. *geg.. mad.*
Gagikindan, (*nin*). I preach to it; p. *geg..ang.*—*Nin gagikindan kiiaw*, I preach to thee, (to thy body.)
Gagikindiwin. Mutual exhortation, or exhortation given to several persons.
Gagikinge, (*nin*). I am exhorting, recommending; p. *geg.. ged.*
Gagikwe, (*nin*). I preach; p. *geg..wed.*
Gagikwê-masinaigan. Sermon-book; any book containing religious instructions; pl.-*an.*
Gagikwénodawa, (*nin*). I preach him, (I preach his doctrine;) p. *geg..wad.*
Gagikwewin. Preaching, sermon, religious exhortation, or instruction; pl.-*an.*
Gagidwewin daiebwetang. Believer; pl.-*ig.*
Gagikwéwinini. Preacher, minister; pl.-*wag.*
Gâgimidon, (*nin*) *freq.* I murmur against somebody; p. *gaia..ong.*
Gâgimidowin. Murmur, complaint, not heard by the person against whom it is made.
Gaginawishk, (*nin*). I am a liar, I am in the habit of telling lies; p. *geg..kid.*
Gaginawishkima, (*nin*) *freq.* I tell him lies; p. *geg..mad.*
Gaginawishkiwin. Habit of telling lies.
Gagindjidaan, (*nin*). I press it down, (*in.* obj.); p. *geg.. ang.*
Gagindjidowa, (*nin*). I press down some *an.* obj.; p. *geg.. wad;* imp. *gagindjidâ.*—*Pakwejigan nin gagindjidawa makakong*, I press down flour in a barrel.
Gagipigade, (*nin*) *freq.**My legs are cracked, or chapped; (F. j'ai les jambes gercées;) p. *geg..ded,*
Gagipinindji, (*nin*). My hands are cracked; p. *geg..id.*
Gagipiside, (*nin*). My feet are cracked, chapped; p. *geg.. ded.*
Gagipisiwin, or *gipisiwin.* Crack, split (in the skin); pl.-*an.*
Gâgisoma, (*nin*). I appease or pacify him, I make him mild; p. *gaia..mad.*
Gâgisondamawa, (*nin*). I appease him for somebody; p. *gaia..wad.*
Gâgisonge, (*nin*). I appease, I console; p. *gaia..ged.*
Gagitaw, (*nin*). I am prudent, wise; p. *gaia..wid.*
Gagitawendam, (*nin*). I have wise prudent thoughts; p. *gaia..dang.*
Gagitawendamia, (*nin*). I make him wise; p. *gaia..ad.*
Gagitawendamowin. Prudence, wisdom.

---

* Note. This and the following two verbs are *frequentative* verbs. The *simple* verbs are: *Gigigade*, etc.—The *freq.* verb alludes to both limb cracked, or to several cracks in one limb.

Gagitawigijwe, (*nin*). I speak prudently, wisely ; p. *gaia.. wed.*

Gagitchi, (*nin*). I take off my shoes or boots, my socks, stockings or nippes; p. *gagitchid.*

Gagitchia, (*nin*). I take off his shoes, etc. ; p. *geg..ad.*

Gagiweshka, or-*magad.* It goes back and forwards, it shakes; p. *geg..kag*, or-*magak.*

Ga-godaakwed. He who shoots (or has shot) at a mark; a marksman. S. *Godaakwe.*

Gagwanagwatchishkiwesse,(*nin*) I sink in mud, or in a swampy or boggy place; p. *geg.. sed.*

Gagwânissag.... These syllables are connected in many instances with substantives, verbs or adverbs, and imply the idea of *terrible, frightful, abominable, hideous*, etc. (Examples in some of the following words.)

Gagwânissagad. It is frightful, horrid; p. *geg..gak.*

Gagwânissagadem, (*nin*). I weep bitterly, horribly ; p. *geg..mod.*

Gagwânissâgakamig, adv. Horribly, frightfully ; *Gagwânissagakamig ejiwebak*, frightful news or accident.

Gâgwânissagendagos, (*nin*). I am frightful, formidable, horrid; hateful, abominable ; p. *geg..sid.*

Gagwânissagendân, (*nin*). I abhor it, hate it ; p. *geg..ang.*

Gagwânissagenima, (*nin*). I abhor him, hate him; p. *geg.. mad.*

Gagwânissaginad. There is an enormous or a frightful quan tity of it; p. *geg..nak.*

Gagwânissaginindji, (*nin*). I have abominable hands; p. *geg..id.*

Gagwânissaginomin, (*nin*) or, *nin gagwanissaginimin.*There is an enormous or frightful number of us; p. *geg..nedjig.*

Gagwânissagis, (*nin*). I am frightful, etc.; p. *geg..sid.*

Gagwed, or-*gagwedj*, in compositions, signifies *asking, examining, proving.* (Examples in some of the following words.)

Gagwêdakadan, (*nin*). I sound it with a sounding lead; p. *geg..ang.*

Gagwédakadjigan. Sounding lead or plummet; pl.-*an.*

Gagwêdina, (*nin*). I feel him; (F. je le tâte;) p. *geg..nad* ; imp. *gagwedin.*

Gagwêdinan, (*nin*). I feel it ; p. *geg..ang.*

Gagwêdjenimia, (*nin*) I try to surpass him; p. *geg.,ad.*

Gagwèdjia, (*nin*). I try him, I tempt him; p. *geg..ad.*

Gagwedjiiwe, (*nin*). I try; p. *geg..wed.*

Gagwedjikadaodimin, (*nin*). We run a race in canoes or boats; p. *geg..didjig.*

Gagwedjikadaowe, (*nin*). I run a race in a canoe or boat; p. *geg..wed.*

Gagwédjima, (*nin*). I ask him a question, I question him ; p. *geg..mad.*

Gagwedjindimin, (*nin*). We ask each other questions; p. *ged ..didjig.*

Gagwedjindiwin. Question,

question to several persons; pl.-*an*.

Gagwedjiwânodawa, (*nin*) (*dan*). I wrestle with him, endeavoring to surpass him; p. *geg..wad*.

Gagwêdwe, (*nin*). I ask, I inquire, I inform myself; p. *geg..wed*.

Gagwetwewin. Inquiry, question, information; pl.-*an*.

Gagwéjagosoma, (*nin*). I try to surpass him in speaking or debating; p. *geg..mad*.

Gâgwejagosonge, (*nin*). I try to surpass another in a speech; p. *geg..ged*.

Gagwejagosongewinini. A man who surpasses others in speaking or debating; pl.-*wag*.

Gagwêsegima, (*nin*) or, *nin gagwésegia*. I try to frighten him, to intimidate him, I try to make him fear, I threaten or menace him; p. *geg..ad*.

Gagweshis, (*nin*). I am timid; p. *geg..sid*.

Gagwetadjitchigan. Bug-bear; (F. épouvantail); pl.-*an*.

Gaiashk. Gull; pl.-*wog*.

Gaiashkons. A young gull; pl.-*ag*.

Gaiashkwâwan. Gull's egg; pl.-*on*.

Gaiat, adv. Before, formerly, before this time, in olden times; (L. olim.)

Gaiat-ijitwâwin. The Old Testament.

Gaiat-ijitwawini-makak. Ark of the covenant.

Gaié, conj. And, also.

Gajage, (*nin*). I eat much and fast; p. *gaiajaged*.

Gâjagens. Cat, puss; pl.-*ag*.

Gâkadina, or-*magad*. It is the summit of a hill or mountain; p. *gek..nag*, or-*magak*.

Gakadjiwebato, (*nin*). I run down hill; p. *gek..tod*.

Gakikijwa, (*nin*) (*an*). I ripe some obj.; p. *gaia..wad*; imp. *gakikijwi*.

Gakikishka, or-*magad*. It is ripped up, unstitched; p. *gaia..kag*, or *magak*.

Gakina nisakosi, (*nin*). I shell a corn-ear; p. *gaiakinad*; imp. *gâkin*.

Galiléwinini. Galilean; pl.-*wag*.

Gâmâdj, (*nin*). I am dancing with a scalp in my hands, in order to receive some presents; p. *gemadjid*.

Gamâdjinodawa, (*nin*). I come to him dancing with a scalp, to receive s. th. from him; p. *gem..wad*.

Gâmâdjiwaham-ok. He dances the scalp dance.

Gâmâdjiwin. Indian dance with a scalp.

Gâmid. Deserter; pl.-*jig*.

Ganabendan, (*nin*). I allow it, I approve, permit, suffer it; p. *gen..ang*.

Ganabendjige, (*nin*). I approve, allow, permit; p. *gen..ged*.

Ganabenima, (*nin*). I let him do, I permit him, allow him; p. *gen..mad*.

Ganabitawa, (*nin*). I have patience and forbear with him, when he offends me with his *words*; p. *gen..wad*.

Gânag, or, *gânamagak*. Sharp, pointed, the edge of a tool.—S. *Gina*.

Ganagé, adv. At least.

Ganandawis, (*nin*). I am in good health, I have no infirmity on me; p. *gen..sid.*

Ganândawisiwin. Good health.

Ganâpine, adv. For the last time.

Ganasonge, (*nin*). I make commandments, regulations; p. *gen..ged.*

Ganâsongewin. Commandment, regulation, precept, mandate; pl.-*an.*

Ganawâbama, (*nin*) (*dan*). I look at him; p. *gen..mad.*

Ganawabimogisissweshi. A bird that looks at the sun, a bittern; (F. butor); pl.-*iag.* S. *Moshkaossi.*

Ganawéndaa, (*nin*). I commit s. th. to his care, I intrust it to him; p. *gen..ad.*

Ganawendamas, (*nin*). I conserve to myself; p. *gen..sod.*

Ganawenima, (*nin*) (*dan*). I keep him, conserve him, take care of him, (person or any other obj.); p. *gen..mad.*

Gand, gandi, in compositions, signifies *pushing, thrusting, pressing.* (Examples in some of the following words.)

Gândaigan. Anything to push with; pl.-*an.*

Gândaige, (*nin*). I push, shove; p. *gaia..ged.*

Gândaigwasson. Thimble; pl.-*an.*

Gandakiigan, or *gandakiiganak.* A pole to push a canoe or boat; pl.-*an*, or-*on.*

Gandakiige, (*nin*). I pole (a canoe or boat;) p. *gaia..ged.*

Gândawa, (*nin*). I push him, shove him; p. *gaia..wad.*

Gandikwena, (*nin*). I push his head; p. *gaia..nad.*

Gandikwetawa, (*nin*). I salute him with an inclination of the head; p. *gaia..wad.*

Gândina, (*nin*) (*nân*). I push him, I thrust in some obj.; p. *gaiândinad;* imp. *gândin.*

Gândinigan. Draught-board; (F. damier;) pl.-*an.*

Gandinigani-titibidabanens. S. *Gagandini-odabanens.*

Gândinige, (*nin*). I push, I draw on a draught-board; (F. je joue aux dames;) p. *gaia..ged.*

Gandj-bapia, (*nin*). I laugh at him, mocking or despising him; p. *gaia..ad.*

Gândjia, (*nin*). I incite him, I push him to s. th.; p. *gaia..ad.*

Ga-nibod. The deceased, the defunct, the late; pl.-*jig.*

Ga-nikani-dibadjimod. He that foretold, a prophet; pl.-*jig.* *Niganadjimowinini.*

Ga-nigani-kikendang. He who knew the future, a prophet; pl.-*ig.* S. *Niganadjimowinini.*

Ga-nodjimoad ki tchitchagonanin. He who saved our souls, our Savior, our Redeemer.

Ganojiwe, (*nin*). I speak to somebody, I exhort; p. *gen..wed.*

Ganona, (*nin*). I speak to him, I address him; p. *genonad;* imp. *ganôj.*

Ganwéwema, (*nin*). I keep him back from s. th. by what I am telling him; I prevent him; p. *gen..mad.*

Gâossed. He that hunts, a

hunter, huntsman, sportsman; pl.-*jig*.

Gâpama, (*nin*) (*dan*). I scranch some obj.; p. *gaia..mad*.

Gâpina, (*nin*) (*nan*). I crush or crumb some obj. with my fingers; p. *gaiapinad;* imp. *gâpin*.

Gâpisan, (*nin*). I burn it a little, I parch it; p. *gaia..ang*. — *Nin gapisan makatémashkikiwâbo*, I burn coffee.

Gâpisige, (*nin*). I parch; p. *gaia..ged*.

Gashkaan, (*nin*). I cut or pierce it with difficulty; p. *geshkaang*.

Gashkaanagekwe, (*nin*). I am taking off cedar bark, I decorticate cedar trees; p. *gesh..wed*.

Gashkadin. It freezes over, or, it is frozen over, (a lake, a river, etc.); p. *geshkading*.

Gashkadino-gisiss. The freezing moon, the month of November.

Gashkakokwéigan. Spattle to stir sugar in sugar-making; pl.-*an*.

Gâshkakwaige, (*nin*). I scrape a bark; p. *gaia..ged*.

Gâshkamegwaige, (*nin*). I scrape a fish, I take away his slime; p. *gaia..ged*.

Gashkaode, or-*magad*. It is tied with a knot; p. *gesh..deg*, or-*magak*.

Gashkaodon, (*nin*). I tie it with a knot; p. *gesh..dod*.

Gashkaona, (*nin*). I tie some obj. with a knot; p. *gesh..nad;* imp. *gashkaoj*.

Gashkaoso. It is tied with a knot, (obj.); p. *gesh..sod*.

Gashkatêigan. Spinning wheel; pl.-*an*.

Gashkatéige, (*nin*). I twist, I spin; p. *gesh..ged*.

Gashkawa, (*nin*). I take off some obj.; p. *geshkawad;* imp. *gashkaw*.—*Nin geshkawa onagek*, I take off the bark of a cedar-tree.

Gashkia, (*nin*). I prevail on him, I win him, I overcome him, I gain him over; I earn or gain some obj.; p. *geshkiad*.

Gashkibâdan, (*nin*). I shave it; p. *gesh..ang*.

Gashkibâdjigan. Razor; pl.-*an*.

Gashkibana, (*nin*). I shave him; p. *gesh..nad;* imp. *gashkibaj*.

Gashkibâs, (*nin*). I shave; p. *gesh..sod*.

Gashkibâsowigamig. Barber-shop; pl.-*on*.

Gashkibasowin. Shaving, barber's trade, occupation, business.

Gashkibasowinini. Barber; pl.-*wag*.

Gashkiéwis, (*nin*). I have power, I am powerful, I prevail; p. *gesh..sid*.

Gashkiewisikawa, (*nin*) (*dan*). I have power over him; p. *gesh..wad*.

Gashkiewisimagad. It is powerful, it prevails; p. *gesh..gak*.

Gashkiéwisiwin. Power, authority.

Gashkigon, (*nin*). I sew a canoe; p. *gesh..nod*.

Gashkigwâdamawa, (*nin*). I sew s. th. for him or belonging to him; p. *gesh..wad*.

Gashkigwâdan, (*nin*). I sew it; p. *gesh..ang*.

Gashkigwâde, or-*magad*. It is sewed ; p. *gesh..deg*, or-*magak*.

Gashkigwâna, (*nin*). I sew some obj ; p. *gesh..nad* ; imp. *gashkigwaj*.—*Moshwe nin goshkigwana*, I sew a handkerchief or shawl.

Gashkigwâss, (*nin*). I am sewing ; p. *gesh..sod*.

Gashkigwâssoneiâb. Sewing thread.

Gashkigwassoikwe. Seamstress ; pl.-*g*.

Gashkigwâssowin. Sewing,trade and occupation of a tailor or a seamstress.

Gashkigwassowinini. Tailor ; pl.-*wag*.

Gashkiidis, (*nin*). I overcome or vanquish myself; p. *gesk..sod*.

Gashkina, (*nin*) (*nan*). I can lift him up, (a person or any other obj.) ; p. *gishkinad* ; imp. *gashkin*.

Gashkinawi, (*nin*). I am able to work ; p. *gesh..wid*.

Gashkio, (*nin*). I can go somewhere, I pass through or over s. th. ; I succeed in passing through or over s. th. ; p. *geshkiod*.

Gashkitamas, (*nin*) or, *nin gashtamadis*. I earn or procure s. th. to myself; p. *gesh..sod*.

Gashkitamason, (*nin*). I earn it, I gain it ; p. *gesh..sod*.

Gashkitamasonan, (*nin*). I earn or gain it to myself; p. *gesh..sod*. (V. Conj.)

Gashkitamawa, (*nin*) or *nin gashkitawa*. I earn or gain it for him, I procure it to him or for him ; p. *gesh..wad*.

Gashkitas, (*nin*). S. *Gashkitamas*.

Gashkitchigan. Any object, inanimate or animate, earned or obtained by labor, earnings. Pl.-*an*, or-*ag*.—*Nin bidon kabiskawagan, makisi, nan gaie, mi sa nin gashkitchiganan* ; I bring a coat and shoes ; they are my earnings. *Nij kitchi osawa-joniiag nind aiâwok ; mi sa nin gashkitchiganag* ; I have two large gold pieces ; they are my earnings.

Gaskitchigé, (*nin*). I earn, I acquire, I procure by labor ; p. *gesh..ged*.

Gashkiton, (*nin*). I can, I can do or afford it, I am able, capable ; I win it ; I overcome it ; I earn, obtain, acquire it ; p *geshkitod*.

Gashkiwane, (*nin*). I carry the whole of it ; p. *gesh..ned*.

Gashkiwegina, (*nin*) etc. S. *Kashkiwegina*, etc.

Gashkiwina, (*nin*) (*dan*). I can name him ; p. *gesh..nad*.

Gashkoma, (*nin*) (*dan*). I carry him on my back, (a person or any other obj. ; p. *gesh..mad*.

Gâskanabagwe, (*nin*). I am thirsty, I am dry ; p. *gaia..wed*.—S. *Nibâgwe*.

Gaskanabagwewin, (*nibâgwewin*,) thirst.

Gâskanas, (*nin*). I speak low, not loud ; I whisper ; p. *gaia..sod*.

Gâskanasotawa, (*nin*). I whisper to him, I speak close to his ear ; p. *gaia..wad*.

Gâskaskaan, (*nin*). I scrape, grate, rub it ; p. *gaia..ang*.

Gâskaskaige, (*nin*). I scrape, grate; p. *gaia..ged.*

Gaskaskanédji. Nightingale; pl.-*iag.*

Gaskaskâwa, (*nin*). I scrape or rub some obj.; p. *gaia..wad;* imp. *gaskaska.*

Gaskatai. A dry skin; pl.-*ag.*

Gaskibaga, or-*magad.* The leaves of a tree make noise being dry; p. *gaia..gag*, or *magak.*

Gaskibagassin. The wind moves the dry leaves of a tree; p. *gaia..sing.*

Gaskidê-gigo. Dried fish, smoked fish; pl.-*iag.*

Gaskidé-gigoike, (*nin*). I dry or smoke fish; p. *gaia..ked.*

Gaskidê-wiiâss. Half-dried or smoked meat.

Gaskidé-wiiâssike, (*nin*). I dry or smoke meat a little; p. *gaia .ked.*

Gaskigin. Dry skin of a large quadruped; pl.-*on.*

Gâskigin. Bombsin, a kind of slight woolen stuff.

Gâskiswa, (*nin*). I dry some obj. in smoke; p. *gaia..wad;* imp. *gaskiswi.*

Gâskwe, or-*magad.* It buzzes, makes a slight noise; (F. il gazouille;) p. *gaia..weg*, or-*magak.*

Gaskwéwe, or-*magad.* There is glazed frost or rime on the ground; (F. verglas;) p. *gaia ..weg*, or-*magak.*

Gâssiabawadawa, (*nin*). S. *Gassiabawana.*

Gâssiabawadon, (*nin*). I wash it clean, I clean it by washing; p. *gaia..dod.*

Gâssiabawana, (*nin*). I wash him clean, I wash away his stains; p. *gaia..nad.*

Gâssiabawe, (*nin*). I wash clean, I wash away filth, stains; I cleanse; p. *gaia..wed.*

Gâssiabawe, or-*magad.* It is washed away, it is cleansed; p. *gaia..weg*, or-*magak.*

Gâssiabawen, (*nin*). I wash it, clean, washing away its stains; p. *gaia..wed.*

Gâssiamage, (*nin*). I blot out, I efface, I pardon, I absolve, I remit; p. *gaia..ged.*

Gâssiamagéwin. Blotting out, effacing, pardon, remission, absolution.

Gâssiamawa, (*nin*). I blot him out s. th.; I absolve him; I pardon him; remit him; p. *gaia..wad.— Gassiamawishin nin matchi dodamowinan, Debenimiian!* Lord! blot out my iniquities.

Gâssian, (*nin*). I blot it out, I wipe it off; p. *gaiassiang.*

Gâssibian, (*nin*). I blot out or strike out something that is written; p. *gaia..ang.*

Gâssibiigan. India rubber.

Gâssibiwa, (*nin*). I blot out or strike out his name that is written: p. *gaia..wad.*

Gâssiiakide, or-*magad.* It is cleansed for purified by fire; p. *gaia..deg*, or-*magak.*

Gâssiiakis, (*nin*). I am purified by fire; p. *gaia..sod.*

Gâssiiakisowin. Purifying by fire; purgatory.

Gâssiigade, or-*magad.* It is blotted out, effaced; pardoned; remitted; p. *gaia..deg*, or-*magak.*

Gâssiigan. Dish-clout, or any thing to wipe with; pl.-*an.*
Gâssiika, or-*magad.* It becomes blotted out, effaced, it effaces itself; p. *gaiasiikag,* or-*magak..*
Gâssinagane, (*nin*). I wipe dishes or plates; p. *gaia..ned.*
Gâssingwéwa, (*nin*). I wipe his face; p. *gaia..wad;* imp. *gassingwé.*
Gâssinsibingwe, (*nin*). I wipe my tears; p. *gaia..wed.*
Gâssinsibingwéwa, (*nin*). I wipe his tears; p. *gaia..wad;* imp. *gas..gwé.*
Gâssisidéwa, (*nin*). I wipe his feet; p. *gaia..wad;* imp. *gassisidé.*
Gâssiwa, (*nin*). I wipe him, (any obj. ;) p. *gaiassiwad;* imp. *gâssi.*
Gâtchibia, (*nin*). I tempt him, I move him; p. *gaia..ad.*
Gâtina, (*nin*). I take care of him in his sickness; p. *gaiatinad;* imp. *gâtin.*
Gâtiniwe, (*nin*). I take care of sick persons (especially of women lying in;) p. *gaia..wed.*
Gâtiniwekwe. A woman taking care of sick persons, nurse; also, a midwife; (F. accoucheuse, sage-femme;) pl.-*g.*
Gâtiniwewinini. A man taking care of sick persons; also, a man, a physician, practising midwifery; (F. accoucheur;) pl.-*wag.*
Gawaâkwandjigan. A place where many trees are cut down; (F. abattis;) pl.-*an.*
Gawaâkwandjige, (*nin*). I cut down trees; p. *gew..ged.*
Gawadj, (*nin*). I freeze to death, I starve with cold; p. *gewadjid.*
Gawâigaso mitig. The tree is cut down; p. *gew..sod.*
Gawaijigwe, (*nin*). I cut down a birch-tree, to take the bark off, for a canoe; p. *gew..wed.*
Gawâisse, (*nin*). I am felling trees; p. *gew..sed.*
Gawâkados, (*nin*). I am extremely lean, poor; p. *gew..sod.*
Gawâkomij. A kind of ash-tree; pl.-*in.*
Gawâkowebina, (*nin*) (*binan*). I overthrow or overturn some long obj.; p. *gew..nad.*
Gawâkwaige, (*nin*). I fell trees; p. *gew..ged.*
Gâwama, (*nin*). I am jealous of him, (her;) p. *gaiâwamad.*
Gawamâ, (*nin*). I throw him down biting him; p. *gewamad.*
Gawanad. It falls, being rotten, (a stick or post that stood up;) it decays, (clothing;) p. *gewanak.*
Gawanadapined. He that is lunatic, a lunatic; pl.-*jig.*
Gawanadisid. He that is mad, a fool; pl.-*jig.*
Gawanândam, (*nin*). I starve to death, I die from hunger; p. *gew..dang.*
Gawanândamowin. Starvation, death from hunger.
Gawâsh, (*nin*). I fall by the wind, the wind throws me down; p. *gewâshid.*
Gawashkwébid. A drunken person; pl.-*jig.*
Gâwendam, (*nin*). I have jealous thoughts; p. *gaia..ang.*
Gâwenima, (*nin*). I have jeal-

ous thoughts towards him, (her;) p. *gaia..mad.*

Gâweshk, (*nin*). I am too jealous; I am in a habit of being jealous; p. *gaia..kid.*

Gawetamawa, (*nin*) or, *nin gâwetawa.* I am jealous for him, instead of him; p. *gaia..ad.*

Gâwewin. Jealousy.

Gawi, in compositions, signifies *tumbling, falling down.* (Examples in some of the following words.)

Gawia, (*nin*). S. *Gawishkawa.*

Gawibi, (*nin*). I fall down, being drunk; p. *gewibid.*

Gawigika, (*nin*). I lower and become bent by old age; p. *gew..kad.*

Gawinâ, (*nin*) (*nân*). I capsize some obj.; p. *gewinad;* imp. *gawin.*

Gawingwash, (*nin*). I fall into a profound sleep; p. *gew..id.*

Gawishim, (*nin*). I lie down, I go to bed; p. *gew..od.*

Gawishkawa, (*nin*) (*kan*). I make him fall down; p. *gew..wad;* imp. *gawiskkaw.*

Ga-wissagang. Pepper, (a thing that is bitter.)

Gawîsse, (*nin*). I fall down; p. *gewissed.*

Gawisse, or-*magad.* It falls down; p. *gewisseg*, or-*magak.* —*Akwandawagan gi-gawisse, wâkaigan ta-gawissemagad;* the ladder fell down, the house will fall down.

Gawitamawa, (*nin*) or, *nin gawitawa.* I prostrate myself before him, I fall down before him; p. *gew..wad.*

Ge–, *ged–*, particle denoting the future tense. (See the Conj. in Otch. Grammar.)

Gebakwaigasod. Prisoner; pl.-*jig.*

Gega, adv. Almost, nearly; about.

Gaganodamaged. He that speaks for somebody, or in favor of somebody, intercessor; pl.-*jig.*

Gégapi, adv. Finally, ultimately, at last, at length; by little and little.

Gêget, adv. Indeed, truly, doubtless, undoubtedly, verily, in truth, certainly.

Gegibingwed. A blind person; pl.-*jig.*

Gegibished. A deaf person; pl.-*jig.*

Gegikwed. A preacher; pl.-*jig.*

Geginawishkid. A liar; pl.-*jig.*

Geginawishkid mashkikiwinini. A lying doctor, quackdoctor; (F. charlatan.)

Geginawichkid niganâdjimowinini. A lying prophet, false prophet.

Gego, adv. Something.

Gêma, adv. S. *Kêma.*

Genawendang ishkwandem anamiewigamigong. Beadle, sexton; (F. bedeau.)

Genawenimad aiakosinidjin, nurse of a sick person; (F. infirmier, infirmière.)

Genawenimad kebakwaigasonidjin. Jailor.

Genawenimad kakoshan. Swineherd.

Genawenimad pijikiwan. Herdsman.

Genawenimid Anjeni. My guardian Angel.

Geshawâb, (*nin*). I am sitting

broadly, I occupy much room in sitting; p. *gaié..bid.*

Géshawikan, (*nin*). I put it on with ease, it is large for me, (a coat, boots, etc.); p. *gaié..ang.*

Geshawishka, or-*magad.* It is loose, untied; p. *gaié..kag,* or-*magak.*

Gésika, adv. S. *Sësika.*

Géssikan, (*nin*). I come to it before it goes away, I find it yet, arriving; I arrive at it in due time; p. *gaié..ang.*—*Nin gigessikan ishkote-nâbikwân;* I found the steamboat yet there when I arrived, (I arrived there before she started.)

Géssikawa, (*nin*). I come to him, or reach him, before he goes away or dies, I find him yet when I arrive; I arrive at it in due time; p. *gaié..wad.* —*Wewib nin mâdja wi-gessikawag aw aiakosid;* I start immediately, I wish to find yet alive that sick person. *Nin gi-gessikawa k'oss;* I found yet thy father there when I arrived.

Géssikona, (*nin*). I come to him in good time, (to give him assistance in distress, in starving, etc.); p. *ges..nad.*

Geté, adj. Old, ancient, former. This word is always followed by a substantive; as: *Gete masinaigan,* an old book. *Gete Anishinâbeg,* the ancient Indians.

Gi–, participle or prefix signifying the past tense. (S. Conj. of Otchipwe Grammar.)

Gia, (*nin*). I escape out of his hands; p. *gâad.*

Gibaan, (*nin*). I stop it; p. *gebaang.*

Gibabikaigan. Cover of a kettle; pl.-*an.* S. *Padagwaboëigan.*

Gibaboëigan. S. *Gibabikaigan.*

Gibadin. It frozes over, or, is frozen over, (lake, river, etc.); p. *gébodinq.*

Gibagawaigan. Dam, causeway; pl.-*an.*

Gibagawaige, (*nin*). I am making a dam; p. *geb..ged.*

Gibagodjigan. A curtain in a house or lodge, instead of a partition, (especially for sick persons;) pl.-*an.*

Gibagodjige, (*nin*). I am hanging up a curtain for a partition; p. *geb..ged.*

Gibâigan. Stopper, in loading a gun; pl.-*an.*

Gibakwaan, (*nin*). I shut it, I stop it, I obstruct or bar it; p. *geb..ang.*

Gibakwaigan. Stopper, cork; cover of a box, etc.; pl.-*an.*

Gibakwaodiwigamig. Prison, jail; pl.-*on.*

Gibâkwawa, (*nin*). I shut him up, I imprison him; p. *geb..wad;* imp. *gibakwa.*

Gibâmikaan sâgi. The mouth of the river is shut up, is filled with pebbles; p. *geb..ang.*

Gibatâwangaan sâgi. The mouth of the river is filled or shut up with sand; p. *geb..ang.*

Gibawa, (*nin*). I shut him up in a hole; I stop the hole of a kettle; p. *gebawad;* imp. *gibâ.*

Gibendam, (*nin*). I have much sorrow; also, I have much pain from sickness; p. *gebendang*.

Gibendamowin. Sorrow, affliction, pain.

Gibendamishkawa, (*nin*). I cause him much sorrow; p. *geb..wad*.

Gibidéebison. Waistcoat, vest; (a vestment that stops or presses the heart;) pl.-*an*.

Gibidiean makak, (*nin*). I bottom a barrel, I put the head or the bottom of a barrel in; p. *geb..ang*.

Gibidjane, (*nin*). My nose is stopped, I caught a cold; (F. je suis enrhumé ;) p. *geb..ned*.

Gibidonena, (*nin*). I stop his mouth, I muzzle him; p. *geb ..nad*.

Gibijigiwineshka, (*nin*). I have the disury, difficulty in making urine; p. *geb..kad*.

Gibijigiwineshkawin. Dysury.

Gibikinigadan, (*nin*). I make a partition in it, (in a house;) p. *geb..ang*.

Gibikinigan. Middle-wall, partition; pl.-*an*.

Gibikinige, (*nin*). I make a middle-wall or partition; p. *geb..ged*.

Gibinéwebina, (*nin*). I strangle or choke him with a cord; I hang him; p. *geb..nad*.

Gibinéwena, (*nin*). I strangle him with my hands, I suffocate him; p. *geb..nad; imp. gibinéwej*.

Gibinindjin, (*nin*). I stop s. th. with my hand; p. *geb.. nid*.

Gibishkâge, (*nin*). I am in the way or passage of somebody, I encumber or obstruct the way or passage; p. *geb..ged*.

Gibishkân, (*nin*). I encumber it, I obstruct it, (a passage, a door, etc.); p. *geb..ang*.

Gibishkawa, (*nin*). I am in his way, I obstruct his way or passage; p. *geb..ad*.

Gibiskwe, (*nin*.) I am hoarse, I cannot speak loud; p. *geb.. wed*.

Gibiskwewin. Hoarseness.

Gibissagaje, (*nin*.) I am constipated, I am costive; p. *geb..jed*.

Gibitan, (*nin*). I bleed at the nose; p. *gebitang*.

Gibitaneganama, (*nin*). I make him bleed by a blow on the nose; p. *geb..mad*.

Gibitawage, (*nin*). One of my ears is stopped; p. *geb..ged*.

Gibodeiégwâson. Pants, pantaloons, breeches; pl.-*an*.

Gibodonepina, (*nin*). I tie up his mouth; p. *geb..nad;* imp. *gibodowepij*.

Gibogwâdan, (*nin*). I sew it together; p. *geb..ang*.

Gibogwana, (*nin*). I sew some obj. together; p. *geb..nad*.

Gibôsan, (*nin*). I bake it, stew it; p. *gebosang*.

Gibôsigan, or *gibôsiganikan*. Stewing oven; pl.-*an*.

Gibosigan-akik. Stew-kettle, stew-pot; pl.-*ag*.

Giboswa, (*nin*). I bake or stew some obj.; p. *geboswad;* imp. *giboswi*.

Gibwâgamishka, or-*magad*. The water shuts up, (as in the Red Sea in the days of Moses); p. *geb..kag*, or-*magak*.

Gibwanâbawana, (*nin*). I drown him, I suffocate him in the water ; p. *geb..nad ;* imp. *waj.*

Gibwanâkosh. A heifer, or any young animal between two and four years old; pl.-*ag.*

Gibwanâm, (*nin*). I stop my breath, I stifle myself; p. *geb ..mod.*

Gibwanâmabawe, (*nin*). I am drowned; p. *geb..wed.*

Gibwanâmos, (*nin*). I am stifled by smoke ; p. *geb..sod.*

Gibwanâmoshkawa, (*nin*). I suffocate him, stifle him, strangle him; p. *geb..wad.*

Gibwânasi. Kite, hawk ; pl.-*g.*

Gidâmawa, (*nin*). I eat up s. th. belonging to him ; p. *ged.. wad.*

Gidamwa, (*nin*). I eat some obj. all up; p. *gedamwad;* imp. *gidamwi.*

Gidân, (*nin*). I eat (or drink) it all up; I consume it; p. *gedang.*

Gidânawe, (*nin*). I consume all; p. *ged..wed.*

Gidâs, as end-syllable in compositions, signifies *anger, angry;* as: *Nin mâdjigidâs,* I begin to be angry. *Nin sagidjigidâs,* I go out with anger.

Gidiskakogadeshin, (*nin*). My leg is dislocated; p. *ged..ing.*

Gidiskia, (*nin*). I escape out of his hands; also, I get him out of s. th., I make him escape, I deliver him; p. *ged.. ad.*

Gidjibina, (*nin*). I hurt him touching his wound ; p. *ged,. nad;* imp. *gidjibij.*

Gidjigâbikad. It is veined or veiny, full of veins, (a stone ;) p. *ged..kak.*

Gidjigassagad. It is veiny, undulated, (wood ;) p. *ged..gak.*

Gidjikas, (*nin*). I don't want to go, I refuse to go, I remain; p. *ged..sod.*

Gidjim, (*nin*). My evil, or my sore, increases, when I speak or cough ; p. *gadjimod.*

Gidowe, (*nin*). S. *Gidjim.*

Gigaiawes, (*nin*). I am of a slim slender size; p. *geg..sid.*

Gigakisine, (*nin*). I have stockings or socks and shoes or boots on; (F. je suis chaussé) ; p. *geg..ned.*

Gigang. Ot. virgin ; pl.-*wag.*

Gigangow, (*nin*). I am a virgin ; p. *gag..wid.*

Gigâtigwan. A splinter in the hand or foot; pl.-*an.*

Gagâtigwe, (*nin*). I draw out a splinter; p. *geg..wed.*

Gigawêgamiga, or-*magad.* There is a peninsula; p. *geg..gak,* or-*magak.*

Gige, (*nin*). My wound heals up ; p. *gâged.*

Gigea, (*nin*). I heal his wound ; p. *gagead.*

Gigi-, in compositions, signifies *with, together ;* as : *Gigi-agim gi-pindige wâkaiganing;* he came in the house with his snow-shoes on.

Gigibimâdis, adv. Alive.

Gigibingwash, (*nin*). I am sleepy, drowsy ; p. *gad..id.*

Gigibingwashiwin. Drowsiness, sleepiness.

Giginê, (*nin*). I die with... ; p. *gagined.*

Giginén, (*nin*). I die with it ;

p. *gagined.—Kaginig ta-kota-gito kitchi batadowin gagined;* he who dies with a mortal sin, will suffer eternally.

Giginénan, (nin). I die with him; p. *gagined.* (V. Conj.)

Giginib, (nin). S. *Giginé.*

Giginig, (nin). I am born with... ; p. *gag..gid.—Kakina ki gi-bi-giginigimin batado-win;* we were all born with a sin.

Gigishkage, (nin). I carry in me or on me s. th.; I am in a family way; p. *geg..ged.*

Gigishkan, (nin). I carry or wear it on me or in me, I have it in me (in my body or soul;) p. *geg..ang.*

Gigishkawa, (nin). I carry some obj. on me or in me; p. *geg..wad. — Nin gigishkawa abinodji,* I am in a family way, with child.

Gigisia, (nin). I make him have or bring some obj. with him; p. *gag..ad.*

Gigisibingwai, adv. With tears.

Gigisibingwêbâp, (nin). I laugh with tears in my eyes; p. *gag ..pid.*

Gigisimagad. It comes with.., it brings or has along with it... ; p. *gag..gak.—Kitimiwin gigisimagad kitimâgisiwin,* laziness comes with poverty.

Gigisin, (nin). I come with it, I bring or have it along with me; p. *gagisid.*

Gigisinan, (nin). I bring or have some obj. with me; p. *gagisid.* (V. Conj.)

Gigit, (nin). I speak, I talk, I make a speech, a harangue; p. *gagitod.*

Gigitchibikagissin. It is with the root, the root is to it; p. *gag..sing.*

Gigi-tchitchâg. With the soul, together with the soul, body and soul.

Gigitowin. Speaking, talking, discourse, council; pl.*-an.*

Gigi-wiiaw. Together with the body, soul and body.

Gigo. Fish; pl.*-iag.*

Gigo-bimide. Fish-oil.

Gigoiag nind agwabinag. I am fishing with a drag-net.

Gigoika, or*-magad.* There is plenty of fish; p. *gag..kag,* or*-magak.*

Gigoike, (nin). I am fishing; p. *gag..ked.*

Gigoikewin. Fishery, fishing.

Gigoikéwinini. Fisherman; pl.*-wag.*

Gigowigamig. Fish-store; pl.*-on.*

Gigowigan. Fish-bone; pl.*-an.*

Giigwishim, (nin). I fast; p. *ga..mod.*

Giigwishimo-gijigad. Fast-day; pl.*-on.*

Giigwishimo-gijigad. It is a fast-day; p. *ga..gak.*

Giigwishimowin. Fast, fasting. *Kitchi giigwishimowin,* lent.

Gi-ishkwa-anamiegijigak. After Sunday, Monday.

Gi-ishkwa-nawakweg. Afternoon, in the afternoon.

Giiwe, (nin). I escape; p. *gai-wed.*

Gijakona, (nin). I pronounce a judgment or sentence over him; p. *gaj..nad.*

Gijamadjiwe, (nin). I arrive at the summit of a mountain; p.

gaj..wed. — S. *Pagamamadjiwe.*

Gijande, or-*magad.* It has the color of ripeness, (some berry ;) p. *gajandeg,* or-*magak.*

Gijanso. It has the color of ripeness, (some berry or fruit ;) p. *gajansod.* — *Gijansowog ogow mishiminag,*these apples have the color of ripeness, they look ripe.

Gijashkobite, or-*magad.* It is a little warm, half warm, (liquid ;) p. *kaj..teg,* or-*magak.*

Gijendam, (*nin*). I determine or decide upon, I resolve, I firmly purpose; p. *gajendang.*

Gijendamowin. Resolution, determination, firm purpose.

Gijenindis, (*nin*). I resolve upon, I make up my mind ; p. *gaj..sod.*

Gijia, (*nin*). I make some obj. I finish it ; p. *gajiad.*

Gijib, in compositions, signifies *itching.* (Examples in some of the following words.)

Gijibaje, (*nin*). I feel itchings on my skin, I am itchy, mangy ; p. *gej..jed.*

Gijibajewin. Itching, itch on the skin ; (F. démangeaison.)

Gijibis, (*nin*).. It itches me, I have itchings ; p. *gejibisid.*

Gijide, or *magad.* It is cooked, done ; p. *gajidek,* or-*magak.*

Gijig. Day ; sky, firmament ; heaven.

Géjig (*nin*). I am adult ; ripe ; p. *gajigid.*

Gijigad. Day ; pl.-*on.*

Gijigad. It is day ; p. *gajigak.*

Gijigado-masinaigan. Day-paper, calendar ; pl.-*an.*

Gijigassigewog (*animikig.*) There are uninterrupted lightnings, making the night almost as light as the day.

Gijigate, or-*magad.* It is light, moon-light ; p. *gaj..ted,* or-*magak.*

Gijigatesse, or-*magad.* It shines forth suddenly ; p. *gaj..seg,* or-*magak.*

Gijigi. It is ripe, (*an.* obj.) as : *Opin gijigi, mishimin gijigi ;* the potato is ripe, the apple is ripe. P. *gajigid.*—S. *Gijig.*

Gijigin. It is ripe, (*in.* obj.) as : *Manomin gijigin, tchiss gijigin ;* the wild rice is ripe, the turnip is ripe.—P. *gajiging.*

Gijiginiba, (*nin*). I sleep in the day-time ; p. *gaj..ad.*

Gigik. Cedar, cedar-tree ; pl.-*ag.*

Gijikân, (*nin*). S. *Gijiton.*

Gijikandag. Cedar-branch ; pl.-*og.*

Gijikashkimod. Bag or sack of cedar-bark ; pl.-*an.*

Gijikawa, (*nin*). I hurt him falling upon him ; p. *gej..wad.*

Gijikens. A small cedar-tree ; a lath ; pl.-*ag.*

Gijikensag nind agwakwâwog. I lath, (I nail on little cedars.)

Gijikigade, or-*magad.* It is made, done ; p. *gaj..deg,* or-*magak.*

Gijikiki. Cedar-forest ; cedar-swamp ; pl.-*wan.*

Gijikos, (*nin*). I get hurt by carrying too heavy a load ; p. *gej..sod.*

Gijikwe. Grown girl, adult ; pl.-*g.*

Gijimagad. It is ripe; p. *gaj..gak.*
Gijipo. It snowed enough; p. *gajipog.*
Gijitamaw, (*nin*) or, *nin gijitawa.* I make it for him or to him; p. *gaj..wad.*
Gijiton, (*nin*). I make it; I finish it; p. *gajitod.*
Gijwe, (*nin*). I talk, I speak; p. *gajwed.*
Gijwewin. Speaking, talking; pl.-*an.*
Gikâ, (*nin*). I am very old; p. *gekad.*
Gikaamawa, (*nin*). I make him marks, (on a trail, etc.;) p. *gak..wad.*
Gikab. S. *Bi-iji-gikab.*
Gikâd, in compositions, signifies *grave; respectable.* (Examples in some of the following words.)
Gikâdendagos, (*nin*). I am considered respectable, grave, serious; p. *gek..sid.*
Gikâdendam, (*nin*). I have grave serious thoughts; p. *gek..ang.*
Gikâdis, (*nin*). I am grave, serious; p. *gek..sid.*
Gikâdisiwin. Grave serious comportment.
Gikadj, (*nin*). I am cold, I feel cold; p. *gakadjid.*
Gikadjinindjiwadj, (*nin*). My hands are cold; p. *gak..djid.*
Gikadjisidewadj, (*nin*). My feet are cold; p. *gak..djid.*
Gikadjitawagewadj, (*nin*). My ears are cold; p. *gak..djid.*
Gikadjiwin. Cold felt in the body from cold weather.
Gikâma, (*nin*). I scold or rebuke him; p. *gakamad.*
Gikanâmode, or-*magad.* It smokes, (in a house or lodge;) p. *gak..deg,* or-*magak.*
Gikanâmos, (*nin*). It smokes in my house, or lodge; p. *gak..sod.*
Gikanâmoswa, (*nin*). I make smoke around him, I make him be in the smoke; p. *gak..wad;* imp. *gik..swi.*
Gikandân, (*nin*). I scold it, I speak ill of it; p. *gak..ang.*—*O gikandân anamiewigamig,* he scolds the church, (speaks ill of it.)
Gikâwidam, (*nin*). I quarrel, dispute, wrangle; p. *gag..ang.*
Gikâwidamowin. Altercation, quarrel, wrangling, dispute.
Gikâwin. Very old age.
Gikim, (*nin*). I weep much; p. *gakimod.*
Gikimanis, (*nin*). I am benumbed; p. *gak..sid.*
Gikimaniside, (*nin*). My foot is benumbed; p. *gak..ded.*
Gikimanisiwin. Numbness; (F. engourdissement.)
Gikissiton, (*nin*). I add to s. th; p. *gak..tod.*
Gimâb, (*nin*). I look in a stealthy manner, unperceived; I spy out; p. *gamabid.*
Gimâbama, (*nin*) (*dan*). I look at him unperceived, in a stealthy manner, I spy him out; p. *gam..mad.*
Gimi, (*nin*). I desert, I run away, I go somewhere secretly; p. *gamid.*
Gimia, (*nin*). I make him desert; p. *gamiad.*
Gimidon, (*nin*) (*freq. nin gâgimidon.*) I murmur against

somebody, not being heard by him; p. *gamidong*.

Giminidjâgan. Illegitimate child, (got in a stealthy manner,) a child out of wedlock, bastard; pl.-*ag*.

Giminidji, (*nin*). I get a child out of wedlock, (in a stealthy manner;) I bring forth a bastard; p. *gam..id*.

Giminiwa, (*nin*). I touch him in a stealthy manner without his knowing it; p. *gam..wad*.

Gimitawa, (*nin*). I hear him secretly, in a stealthy manner, he does not know that I hear him, I overhear him; p. *gam..wad*.

Gimiwan. It rains; p. *gemiwang*.

Gimiwanaam, (*nin*). I travel in a canoe or boat in rainy weather; p. *gem..ang*,

Gimiwanâbo. Rain-water.

Gimiwanibos, (*nin*). I embark or start in a canoe or boat in rainy weather; p. *gem..sid*.

Gimiwaniton, (*nin*). I make rain, I cause rain; p. *gem..tod*.

Gimiwanosse, (*nin*) or, *nin gimiwanishka*. I walk in rainy weather; p. *gem..ed*.

Gimiwin. Desertion.

Gimôd, (*nin*). I steal, I purloin, I take away s. th. and make use of it without permission, although not with the intention of keeping it; p. *gemodid*.

Gimôdad. It is hidden, it is a secret, a mystery; p. *gemodak*.

Gimodâdjim, (*nin*). I tell s. th. secretly; p. *gem..mod*.

Gimodâdjimotawa, (*nin*). I tell him s. th. secretly; p. *gem..wad*.

Gimodandjige, (*nin*). I eat in a stealthy manner; p. *gem..ged*.

Gimôdima, (*nin*). I steal s. th. from him; I take s. th. without his knowledge and permission; p. *gem..mad*.

Gimôdin, (*nin*). I steal it; I take it without permission and make use of it; p. *gemodid*.

Gimôdinan, (*nin*) I steal some obj. or take it and make use of it without permission; p. *gimodid* (V. Conj.)

Gimôdishk, (*nin*). I am in a habit of stealing, I am thievish, I am a habitual thief; p. *gem..kid*.

Gimôdishkiwin. Habit of stealing, thievishness.

Gimodisiwin. Hidden thing, secret, mystery; pl.-*an*.

Gimodiwigamig. House, abode or den of thieves; pl.-*on*. (L. spelunca latronum.)

Gimôdiwin. Stealing; theft.

Gimodj, adv. In a stealthy manner, secretly, clandestinely, privately, in a hidden manner.

Gimôdjikana, (*nin*). I leave him in a stealthy manner, I go away from him without his knowledge; p. *gem..nad*; imp. *gimodjikaj*.

Gimôdowe, (*nin*). I speak secretly, mysteriously, in a hidden manner; also, I use a parable; p. *gem..wed*.

Gimodowewin. Secret hidden speaking; parable; pl.-*an*.

Gina, or-*magad*. It is sharp;

it is pointed, (an iron tool;) p. *ganag*, or-*magak.*

Ginaamâdan, (*nin*). I forbid it, I rebuke it; p. *gen..ang.*—*Jesus o gi-ginaamâdan nodin kitchigami gaie, mi dash ga-iji-kitchi-anwatininig* ; Jesus rebuked the winds and the sea; and there was a great calm.

Ginaamâdim. One is forbidden; (F. on est défendu.)

Ginaamagewin. Prohibition, forbiddance.

Ginaamagewin. Any thing forbidden; pl.-*an.*

Ginaamawa, (*nin*). I forbid him, I hinder him to do s. th.; p. *gen..wad.*

Ginagidji, (*nin*). I am ticklish, easily tickled ; (F. je suis chatouilleux;) p. *gen..id.*

Ginagidjina, (*nin*). I tickle him; p. *gen..nad.*

Ginagina, (*nin*). S. *Ginagidjina.*

Ginashkad. It cuts, it has a sharp edge, (a plant or herb;) p. *ganashkak.*

Ginawishk, (*nin*). S. *Gayinawishk.*

Ginawishkia, (*nin*). I make him tell a lie; p. *gen..ad.*

Ginawishkitan, (*nin*). I consider as a lie what I hear; p. *gen..ang.*

Ginawishkitawa, (*nin*). I hear him, or listen to him, with the impression that he is telling a lie, or lies; p. *gen..wad.*

Gindâbigina, (*nin*) (*nan*). I dip some obj. in s. th.; p. *gen..nad.*

Gindabiginigaso. It is dipped in s. th.; p. *gen..sod.*

Gindâiawangaan, (*nin*). I sink it in the sand ; p. *gen..ang.*

Gindâiawangawa, (*nin*). I sink some obj. in the sand; p. *gen..wad.*

Gindakamigishka, or-*magad.* It sinks in the ground ; p. *gen..kag*, or-*magak.*

Gindâshka, or-*magad.* It is loaded much, it sinks deep in the water, (a vessel, canoe, etc.); p. *gen..kag*, or-*magak.*

Gindâwagonesse, (*nin*). I sink in the snow ; p. *gen..sed.*

Gindjibaiwe, (*nin*). I run away for safety ; p. *gen..wed.*

Gindjidaan, (*nin*). I thrust it in s. th., I press it down, (something contained in a vessel;) p. *gen..ang.*

Ginjidadjige, (*nin*) or, *nin gindjidaige.* I press down ; p. *gen..ged.*

Gindjidanam, (*nin*). I have a heavy oppressed respiration ; p. *gen..mod.*

Gindjidashima, (*nin*). I thrust in, or press down, some obj. (in a vessel ;) p. *gen..mad.*

Gindjidasse, (*nin*). I fall in ; p. *gen..sed.*

Gindjidassidon, (*nin*). I thrust it in, or press it down ; p. *gen..dod.*

Gindjidâwa, (*nin*). I press down or thrust in, some obj.; p. *gen..wad.*

Gindjidawi, (*nin*). I press in, I strive to get in through the crowd; p. *gen..wid.*

Ginébig. Snake, serpent; pl.-*og.*

Ginebigojagaai. The skin of a serpent; pl.-*ag.*

Ginebigônini. Snake Indian; pl.-*wog.*

Ginëbigwaiân. S. *Ginebigojagaai.*

Ginebigwaj. Hole of a serpent or snake; pl.-*an.*

Ginibi, in compositions, signifies *fast, quick.* (Examples in some of the following words.)

Ginibi, (*nin*). I am quick or expeditious in working, in doing s. th.; p. *genibid.*

Ginikig, (*nin*). I grow up fast; p. *genibigid.*

Ginibigi, or-*magad.* It is growing fast, (tree, herb, plant;) p. *gen..gig,* or-*magak.*

Ginibininike, (*nin*). I am getting old fast; p. *gen..ked.*

Ginikaje. It has a long beak, (a bird); p. *gan..jed.*

Ginôgweiawe, (*nin*). I have a long neck; p. *gen..wed.*

Ginogweiaweshib. A kind of wild duck with a long neck; pl.-*ag.*

Ginônagad. It is long, (canoe, boat, vessel, etc.); p. *gen..gak.*

Ginonde, or-*magad.* It is long, (a house, a lodge, etc.); p. *genondeg,* or-*magak.*

Ginonike, (*nin*). I have a long arm; p. *gen..ked*

Ginonindji, (*nin*). I have a long hand; p. *gen..id.*

Ginôs, (*nin*). I am long, I am tall; p. *genosid.*

Ginôside, (*nin*). I have a long foot; p. *gen..ded.*

Ginwâ, or-*magad.* It is long; p. *genwag,* or-*magak.*

Ginwabigad. It is long, (thread, string, rope, etc.); p. *gen..gak.*

Ginwabigiiâwe, (*nin*). I have a long slender body; p. *gen..wed.*

Ginwabigisi seniba. The ribbon is long; p. *gen..sid.*

Ginwâbikad. It is long, (some object made of some metal, or of stone;) p. *gen..kak.*

Ginwabikisi assin. The stone is long; p. *gen..sid.*

Ginwâiakossin. It is long, it reaches far; p. *gen..ing.*

Ginwâkosi mitig, nabagissag. The tree, the board, is long; p. *gen..sid.*

Ginwakwaân, (*nin*). I cut it long; p. *gen..ang.*

Ginwâkwad. It is long, (wooden object;) p. *genwâkwak.*

Ginwâkwanwi. A long arrow; pl.-*n.*

Ginwâkwawa, (*nin*). I cut it long; p. *gen..wad;* imp. *ginwakwâ.*

Ginwambis, (*nin*). I wear a long frock, (woman;) p. *gen..wad;* imp. *ginwakwâ.*

Ginwanowe. It has a long tail, (a beast;) p. *gen..wed.*

Ginwâtchita, (*nin*). I continue long, I am a long while in doing s. th.; p. *gen..tad.*

Ginwâton, (*nin*). I make it long, I lengthen it; p. *genwatod.*

Ginwégad. It is long, (any clothing article or material;) p. *gen..gak.*

Ginwêgisi moshwe. The handkerchief is long; p. *gen..sid.*

Ginwénj, adv. Long, a long while.

Ginwindima. It is deep, (a river, ete.); p. *gen..mag.*

Giosse, (*nin*). I go a hunting; p. *gaossed*.

Giossewin. Hunting.

Gipidon, (*nin*). My lips are cracked, or chapped or sore; p. *gâpidong*.— The freq. is, *nig gagipidon*; p. *geg..ong*.

Gipidoneias, (*nin*). My lips are cracked or sore by too much heat; p. *gap..sod*.

Gipidonewadj, (*nin*). My lips are cracked or sore from cold; p. *gap..djid*.

Gishkâbâgwe, (*nin*). I thirst much; p. *gash..wed*.—S. *Nibagwe*.

Gishkâbâgwewin. Ardent thirst.

Gishkâbâgwênodan, (*nin*). I thirst after it, I desire it ardently; p. *gash..ang*.

Gishkâkwandjige pijiki. The ox (or cow) browses, it eats little branches or browses; p. *gesh..ged*.

Gishkishê. Bitch; pl.-*iag*. S. *Nojéssin*.

Gishpinadaganiwan. It is a thing that is bought; p. *gash . ang*.

Gishpinadagan. Ware, merchandise, any obj. that may be bought; pl.-*ag*.

Gishpinadagan. Merchandise, ware, any obj. that may be bought; pl.-*an*.

Gishpinadamadis. I buy for myself; p. *gash..sod*.

Gishpinadamadison, (*nin*). I buy it for myself or to myself; p. *gash..sod*.

Gishpinadamadisonan, (*nin*) I buy some obj. to myself; p. *gash..sod*. (V. Conj.)

Gishpinadamawa, (*nin*) or, *nin gishpinadawa*. I buy it from him; I buy it of him; p. *gash..wad*; imp. *gishpinaj*.

Gishpinadjige, (*nin*). I am buying; p. *gash..ged*.

Gishpinadon, (*nin*). I buy it, purchase it; p. *gash..dod*.

Gishpinage, (*nin*). S. *Gishpinadjige*.

Gishpinana, (*nin*). I buy some obj.; p. *gash..nad*; imp. *gishpinaj*.

Gisikan, (*nin*). I take it off, (clothing;) p. *gasikang*.

Gisikwanaie, (*nin*). I strip, I undress myself; p. *gas..ied*.

Gisikwanaiebina, (*nin*). I strip or undress him; p. *gas..nad*; imp. *gisikwanaiebij*.

Gisikwanaiebinidis, (*nin*). I undress myself; p. *gas..sod*.

Gisikwanaiewin. Undressing, stripping.

Gisisamawa, (*nin*). I cook for him; p. *gas..wad*.

Gisisan, (*nin*). I cook it, bake it; p. *gasisang*.

Gisisekwe, (*nin*). I am cooking; p. *gas..wed*.

Gisisekwewin. Cooking, cookery.

Gisiso. It is cooked or baked, (some object;) p. *gasisod*.— *Gasisod gigo*, cooked or baked fish. *Gasisod pakwejigan*, baked bread.

Gisiss. Sun, moon, month; pl. -*og*. To distinguish the moon from the sun, they call her, *tibikigisiss*, or *tibikgisiss*, night-sun.

Gisiss âbitawisi. The moon is in her first quarter, or in her last quarter; p. *aiabitawisid*.

Gisiss ani-bakwêsi. The moon is declining; p. *eni-bakwesid*.

Gisiss ani-mitchâbikisi. The moon is growing, increasing; p. *eni-mitch..sid.*

Gisiss ishkwaiassige. The moon does not shine any more, (the end of a moon or month;) p. *esh..ged.*

Gisiss nibô. The sun (or moon) dies, that is, is eclipsed, there is an eclipse; p. *nebod.*

Gîsisswagad. This word never occurs alone; it is always connected with a number, and signifies a certain period of months.—*Nisso gisisswagad jaigwa eko-dagwishinân oma;* it is already three months since I arrived here.

Gisisswagiss, (nin). This word is always connected with a number, and signifies the age of some object in months.—*Aw abinodji nano gisisswagisi;* this child is five months old.

Gisiss wâwiiesi. The moon is round, that is, it is full moon; p. *waiawiiesid.*

Gisiswa, (nin). I cook or bake some obj; p. *gasiswad;* imp. *gisiswi.*

Giskabag. In the back of a lodge.

Gissadendam, (nin). I am sorrowful; p. *gess..ang.*

Gissadendamowin. Sorrow, affliction.

Gitaân, (nin). I draw it out of something; p. *getaang.*

Gitabid. Large tooth, grinder.

Gitaigan. Gun-worm, (to draw the load out of a gun;) corkscrew; pl.*-an.*

Gitawa, (nin). I draw some obj. out of s. th.; p. *getawad;* imp. *gitaw.*

Gitchiganakwad. There are small curled clouds in the sky; (F. le ciel est pommelé;) p. *get..wak.*

Gitchiganejân wiiâss, (nin). I take off the flesh from the bones; p. *getch..ang.*

Gitchiganejwa, (nin). I take his flesh off from his bones; p. *get,.wad;* imp. *-jwi.*

Gitchigitchiganeski. A small bird that flies close to the ground; pl.*-iag.*

Gitchigobina,(nin) (don). I draw some obj. out of s. th., I pull it out; p. *get..nad.*

Gitchigwakonan, (nin). I draw it out, (obj. of wood;) p. *get..ang.*

Gitchiminagishkan, (nin). I tread it out, instead of thrashing; p. *get..ang.*

Gitchiminagaigan. Flail, or any thing to trash out grain; pl.*-an.*

Gitchiminagishkawa, (nin). I tread it out; p. *get..wad.*

Gitchiwakwane, (nin). I take my hat off; p. *gat..ned.*

Gitchiwebina, (nin) (nan). I throw out some obj.; p. *get..nad.*

Giwaadis, (nin). I ramble; I am a vagabond; p. *gawaadisid,* vagabond.

Giwaadisiwin. Rambling; vagrancy.

Giwadendagwad. It is doubtful; p. *gaw..wak.*

Giwadendam, (nin). I doubt; p. *gaw..ang.*

Giwâdendamowin. Doubt, doubtful thought; pl.*-an.*

Giwanâdapine, (nin). I am insane by intervals, I am a lunatic; p. *gâw..ned.*

Giwanadapinewin Insaneness by intervals.

Giwanâdis, (*nin*). I am insane, mad, I am a fool; p. *gaw..sid.*

Giwanadisiwin. Madness.

Giwanim, (*nin*). I tell a lie; p. *gawanimod.*

Giwanima, (*nin*). I tell him a lie, I belie him; p. *gaw..mad.*

Giwanimowin. Lying, lie, falsehood; pl.-*an.*

Giwâsh-abinodji. Orphan; pl.-*iag.*

Giwâshis, (*nin*). I am a poor orphan, I am alone, I have no relatives; p. *gaw..sid.*

Giwâshito, (*nin*). S. *Giwashis.*

Giwashkwe, (*nin*). I am giddy; p. *gaw..wed.*

Giwâshkwebi, (*nin*). I am giddy from drinking, I am drunk, intoxicated; p. *gaw..bid.*

Giwashkwebia, (*nin*). I intoxicate him; p. *gaw..ad.*

Giwashkwebishk, (*nin*). I am in a habit of getting drunk, I am a habitual drunkard; p. *gaw..kid.*

Giwashkwebishkagemagad, or, *giwashkwebimagad.* It uses to intoxicate, it intoxicates; p. *gaw..gak.*

Giwâshkwêganama, (*nin*). I stun him, I make him giddy, by striking; p. *gaw..mad.*

Giwashkweiendam, (*nin*). I have confused thoughts, I am bewildered; p. *gaw..ang.*

Giwashkweiendamia, (*nin*). I bewilder him; p. *gaw..ad.*

Giwashwékôs, (*nin*). I am made giddy, or dizzy, by some object that fell upon me; p. *gaw..sod.*

Giwashkwénos, (*nin*). I become giddy by smelling s. th.; p. *gaw..sod.*

Giwashwés, (*nin*). I become giddy from heat; p. *gaw..sod.*

Giwashkweshin, (*nin*). I am made giddy, or dizzy, by falling; p. *gaw..ing.*

Giwashkwewin. Giddiness, vertigo, dizziness.

Giwe, (*nin*). I return, I go back again, I go home; p. *gawed.*

Giwe, (*nin*). I return in a canoe or boat; p. *gaweod.*

Giwe. S. *Kiwe.*

Giwébato, (*nin*). I return running; p. *gaw..tod.*

Giwébibon. It is after the middle of the winter, the winter is on its decline, on its return from where it came; p. *gaw..ong.*

Giwédin. North, northwind.

Giwédinong, in the north, from the north, to the north.

Giwedinaamog (*animikig*). It thunders in the north.

Giwêdinakwad. The clouds come from the north; p. *gaw..wak.*

Giwedinobissa. The rain comes from the north; p. *gaw..sag.*

Giwegom, (*nin*). I turn round with a canoe or boat; p. *gaw..mod.*

Giwéiabowe, (*nin*). I return home with s. th. to eat, coming from an Indian feast; p. *gaw..wed.*

Giweiassam gisiss. Alg. The sun is on his decline, it is in the afternoon; p. *gaw..ang.*

Giwêiendam, (*nin*). I think to

return, I think on my going home again; p. *gaw..ang.*

Giweki, (*nin*). I move back again to my own country, I return to my native place; p. *gawekid.*

Giwemagad. It goes back again, it returns; p. *gaw..gak.*

Giwênajawa. I bid him go home, I send him back again; p. *gaw,.wad;* imp. *gîwenaja.*

Giwênibin. It is after the middle of the summer, the summer is on its decline, on its return; p. *gaw..ing.*

Giweona, (*nin*) (*don*). I take or convey back again some object in a canoe or boat; p. *gaw..nad;* imp. *giweoj.*

Giwewina, (*nin*) (*don*). I carry back again some object, I lead or conduct back again some object; p. *gaw..nad;* imp. *giwewij.*

Giwidêonan. Detour, (place.)

Giwidewa, (*nin*). I go around a point in a canoe or boat; p. *gassidewaod.*

Giwine, (*nin*). I am dying; p. *gawined.*

Giwis, (*nin*). I am an orphan; p. *gawisid.*

Giwita, in compositions, signifies *round, surrounding.* (Examples in some of the following words.)

Giwitaam, (*nin*). I go around a point or bay in a canoe or boat; p. *gawitaang.*

Giwetabato, (*nin*). I run around s. th.; p. *gaw..tod.*

Giwitaiabikinigan. Wall around a fortress; pl.-*an.*

Giwitaiajagame, (*nin*). I walk around a bay; p. *gaw..med.*

Giwitâianikadan, (*nin*). I dig a ditch around it; p. *gaw.. ang.*

Giwitâianikana, (*nin*). I dig a ditch around him; p. *gaw.. nad;* imp. *kaj.*

Giwetaii, adv. Round, around, all round, in the environs.

Giwitâkawig, adv. Round in the country.

Giwitakinigan. Enclosure, palisades, (of a fort, etc.); pl.-*an.*

Giwita-mitchikanagobidon,(*nin*) I fence it in all round; p. *gaw..dod.*

Giwitaosse, (*nin*). I walk around s. th.; p. *gaw..sed.*

Giwitashim, (*nin*). I dance around s. th.; p *gaw..mod.*

Giwitashka, (*nin*). I go round; (F. je fais le tour;) p. *gaw.. kad.*

Giwitasse. It flies aroudd s. th.; p. *gaw..sed.*

Giwitatigweia sibi. The river turns round (or back again) in its course; p. *gaw..iag.*

Go, or *igo,* (*go,* after a vowel; *igo,* after a consonant;) particle which conveys the idea of affirmation or assurance, or to express *just;* as: *Nongom igo,* just now. *Kinawa go ki da-ijâm,* just you ought to go.

Godaakwe, (*nin*). I shoot at a mark, at a target; p. *gwedaakwed.*

Gôdass. Frock for women; petticoat; pl.-*an.*

Gôdj-, in compositions, signifies *essay, trial, experiment.* (Examples in some of the following words.)

Gôdjia, (*nin*). I try him, I essay

or try any obj.; p. *gwedjiad.*
Godjiew, (*nin*). I strive, I try; p. *gwe..wid.*
Godjiewinodan, (*nin*). I prove it, try it; p. *gwe..ang.*
Godjiewinodawa, (*nin*). I try him; p. *gwe..wad.*
Godjiewisiwin. Experiment, proof, trial; pl.-*an.*
Godji-kikendan, (*nin*). I examine it, try it; p. *gwe..ang.*
Godji-kikenima, (*nin*). I examine him, try him; p. *gwe..mad.*
Godji-nagam, (*nin*). I sing for a proof; p. *gwe..mod.*
Godjinike, (*nin*). I feel the pulse; p. *gwe..ked.*
Godjinikena, (*nin*). I feel his arm; p. *gwe..nad.*
Godjipidan, (*nin*). I try or examine it by the taste, I taste it; p. *gwê..ang.*
Godjipwa, (*nin*). I try some obj. by the taste; p. *gwa..wad;* imp. *godjipwi.*
Godjiskweiabigina, (*nin*). I feel his pulse, (*oskweîab,* his vein;) p. *gwe..nad.*
Gôdjiton, (*nin*). I try it; p. *gwedjitod.*
Gôgaam gigo. The fish leaps up, over the surface of the water; p. *gwagaang.*
Gôgi, (*nin*). I dive; p. *gwagid.*
Gôgina. I dip him in the water; p. *gwa..ad.*
Gôginan, (*nin*). I dip it in the water; p. *gwa..ang.*
Gôgisse, (*nin*). I glide, slip or fall in the water; p. *gwagissed.*
Gokokwa, or-*magad.* It is rolling, (canoe, boat, etc.); p. *gwe..wag,* or-*magak.*
Gokwadendagos, (*nin*). I am considered worthy; respectable; p. *gwe..sid.*
Gokwadendan, (*nin*). I esteem it, respect it; p. *gwe..ang.*
Gokwadenim, (*nin*). S. *Gokwadenindis.*
Gokwadenima, (*nin*). I respect him, esteem him; p. *gwe..ad.*
Gokwadenindis, (*nin*). I esteem myself too much, I am haughty, proud; p. *gwe..sod.*
Gokwadenindisowin. Pride, haughtiness.
Gokwâdis, (*nin*). I am worthy, respectable; p. *gwe..sid.*
Gomâ, or, *goma minik,* adv. Middling.—*Nibiwana kid aianan masinaiganan ?—Goma minik.* Hast thou many books ?—Middling.
Gomâ minik, adv. For a time; (L. ad tempus).
Gomâpi, adv. Some time, by-and-by. *Gomapi nin gad-aia oma;* I will remain here for some time, (not long.) *Gomapi nin gad-aia oma;* I will remain here for some time, (not long.) *Gomapi nin gamadja;* I will start by-and-by.
Gon. Snow.
Gona, (*nin*). I swallow some obj.; p. *gwenad.*
Gonababog, (*nin*). I capsize in a rapid, (my canoe or boat oversets in the rapids of a river;) p. *gwe..god.*
Gonabishka, (*nin*). I capsize my canoe, boat, etc., is overturned, it oversets; p. *gwe..kad.*
Gondâgan. Throat; (F. gorge.)
Gondakamigissan. Gulf, abyss,

(effected by the sinking down of the ground;) pl.-*an.*

Gondakamigisse, or-*magad.* The ground sinks down, (and effects an abyss, a gulf;) p. *gwe..seg* or-*magak.*

Gondashkwei. Windpipe; (F. gosier.)

Gondasse, or-*magad.* It enters or penetrates in the flesh; p. *gwendasseg,* or-*magak.*

Gôngwawa, (*nin*). I thrust him away; p. *gwe..wad;* imp. *gongwa.*

Gonige, adv. S. *Gonima.*

Gônika, or-*magad.* There is snow; p. *gwanikag,* or-*magak.*

Gonima, adv. Perhaps, may be; or.

Gonwâpon, (*nin*). I won't eat it, I abstain from it; p. *gwe..od.*

Gonwâponan, (*nin*). I won't eat some obj. I abstain from it; p. *gwe..od.*

Gonwapowin. Abstinence.

Gopaam, (*nin*). I go into the inland, in the woods, in a canoe, on a river; p. *gwepaang.*

Gopamo mikana. The road leads into the woods; p. *gwepamog.*

Gôpasoma, (*nin*). I despise him, (with words,) I have a low idea of him, or of his abilities; p. *gwa..mad.*

Gôpasondan, (*nin*). I despise it, I contemn it; p. *gwa..ang.*

Gôpasondis, (*nin*). I despise myself; p. *gwa..sod.*

Gopi, (*nin*). I go into the woods, in the interior, inland; p. *gwepid.*

Gopiwidon, (*nin*). I carry or convey it up from the lake-shore; p. *gwe..dod.*

Gopiwina, (*nin*). I carry or convey him up from the lake-shore, from the beach; p. *gwe..nad.*

Gos, (*nin*). I move to some other place, I decamp; p. *gwe..sid.*

Gosâbi, (*nin*). I sink, I go to the bottom; p. *gwesâbid.*

Goshâ. This word cannot be given in English. It signifies that a repetition is made, or that something which is told, is known. The Indians also will use it sometimes in requesting you for something. —*Ki gi-windamoninimaban goshâ;* I had told it to you repeatedly.— *Masinaigan goshâ;* I request you for a book.

Goshima, (*nin*). I respect him, dread him; p. *gweshimad.*

Goshiwe, (*nin*). I fear; p. *gwe..wed.*

Goshiweshk, (*nin*). I am timid, timorous, fearful; p. *gwe..kid.*

Goshkoa, (*nin*). I surprise him, I make him shrink or start back; p. *gwe..ad.*

Goshkobagassin. The leaves tremble, are agitated by the wind; p. *gwe..ing.*

Goshkoka, (*nin*). I shrink or start back, I am surprised; p. *gwe..kad.*

Goshkonagos, (*nin*). I have a curious, ridiculous appearance; p. *gwe..sid.*

Goshkonawes, (*nin*). S. *Goshkwêndam.*

Goshkongwash, (*nin*). I awake starting up; (F. je me réveille en sursaut;) p. *gwe..id.*

Goshkos, (*nin*). I awake, I wake up; p. *gweshkosid*.
Goshkwakobina, (*nin*). I shake him, (any obj.); p. *gwe..nad*.
Goshkwakoshka, or-*magad*. It shakes, it trembles; p. *gwe-. kag*, or-*magak*.
Goshkwakoshkawa, (*nin*). I shake some obj.; p. *gwe..wad*.
Goshkwawâdis, (*nin*). I am melancholic, pensive; p. *gwe ..sid*.
Goshkwendam, (*nin*). I am surprised in my thoughts, in my mind; p. *gwe..ang*.
Goshkwesse, (*nin*). I stagger; p. *gwe..sed*.—Freq. *nin goshkoshkwesse*.
Goshkwĕtakoki, (*nin*). I make a step out of the trail; p. *gwesh..kid*.—The *freq*. verb of it is *nin goshkoshkwetakoki*, I miss often my trail, stepping aside, (f. i. a drunken person.)
Gosia, (*nin*). I make him move to some other place; p. *gwesiad*.
Gosikan, (*nin*). I try it whether it fits me, (a coat, a shoe, etc.); p. *gwesikang*.
Gosikaton, (*nin*). I try it, (a gun, etc.); p. *gwe..tod*.
Gosiwin. Removal, decamping, moving from one camp to another. *Ningo gosiwin*, the distance from one Indian camp to another.
Gossâ, (*nin*). I fear him, I am afraid of him; p. *gwessad*; imp. *goshi*.
Gossitawa, (*nin*) or *nin gossitamawa*. I am afraid for him; p. *gwe..wad*.
Gossitawenima, (*nin*) (*dan*). I fear him, in thoughts; p. *gwe ..mad*.
Gossiton, (*nin*). I dread it, I respect it; p. *gwëssitod*.
Gotadj, (*nin*). I fear; I apprehend danger, (especially from enemies;) p. *gwetadjid*.
Gotadjiganes, (*nin*). I am feared, dreaded, I am formidable; p. *gwe..sid*.
Gotadjishk, (*nin*). I am too easily frightened, I am too fearful; p. *gwe..kid*.
Gotadjiwin. Fear, fright, alarm, apprehension of danger, (especially from enemies.)
Gotama, (*nin*). I taste some obj., I swallow a little of it; p. *gwe..mad*.
Gotamandan, (*nin*) or, *nin gotamandjiton*. I tried it, I know it by experience; p. *gwet..ang*, or, *gwet..tod*.
Gotamawa, (*nin*). I fear s. th. belonging or relating to him, in regard to him; p. *gwetamawad*.
Gotâmigos, (*nin*). I am dreadful, frightful; p. *gwet..sid*.
Gotâmigosiwin. Dreadful power.
Gotâmigwâb, (*nin*). I gaze or look on dreadful, I have a frightful look; p. *gwe..bid*.
Gotamigwabama, (*nin*) (*dan*). I look at him frightfully; p. *gwe..mad*.
Gotâmigwad. It is frightful, dreadful; there is a great storm, a gale; p. *gwe..wak*.
Gotamigwendagos, (*nin*). I am to be feared, I am horrible, frightful, formidable; p. *gwe ..sid*.
Gotamigwendagwad. It is to be

feared, it is awful, horrible; p. *gwe..wak.*

Gotâmigwenim, (*nin*). I am arrogant, I think myself high, powerful, dreadful; p. *gwe.. môd.*

Gotâmigwewe, or-*magad.* It makes a frightful noise; p. *gwe..weg,* or-*magak.*

Gotân, (*nin*). I fear it, I am afraid of it; p. *gwétang.*

Gotandan, (*nin*). I taste it, I swallow a little of it; p. *gwe.. ang.*

Gotânenima, (*nin*). I dread him, in thoughts; p. *gwe.. mad.*

Gotânis, (*nin*). I am timid, timorous, I keep far off, by fear; p. *gwe..sid.*

Gotina, (*nin*) (*nan*). I weigh some obj. in my hand, not on a balance; (F. je le soupèse;) p. *gwe..nad.*

Gowé! gowêngish! interj. strange! lo! already!

Gwâbaabowe, (*nin*). I draw broth or soup out of a kettle; p. *gwaia..wed.*

Gwâbaâgan. Scoop-net; pl.-*an.*

Gwâbaam, (*nin*). I draw, (water, etc.); p. *gwaiabaang.*

Gwabaân, (*nin*). I draw it, (water, etc., out of s. th.); p. *gwaiabaang.*

Gwabâwa gigo, (*nin*). I draw a fish (or fishes) out of the water in a small net; (C. je puise du poisson;) p. *gwai.. wad;* imp. *gwabâ.*

Gwabaibi, (*nin*). I draw water of a fountain, a river, etc.; p. *gwai..bid.*

Gwâbâigan. Any vessel to draw water or any other liquid with; pl.-*an.*

Gwaiak, adv. and adj. Just, justly, straight, right, upright, well, certain, certainly, precisely, perfect, perfectly, exact, exactly.

Gwaiak dibâdjimowin, or, *gwaiakwâdjimowin.* True statement or report, sincere avowal.

Gwaiak joniia. Ready money, cash.

Gwaiak nin bimâdis, or, *nin gwaiakobimâdis.* I live upright, I lead a just and honest life; p. *gwe..sid.*

Gwaiak nin dibâdjim, or, *nin gwaiakwâdjim.* I make a true report, I confess or declare openly, sincerely; p. *gwe.. mod.*

Gwaiako-bimâdisiwin. Upright honest life, christian justice, probity, uprightness, honesty.

Gwaiakokwen, (*nin*). I hold my head straight up; p. *gwe..nid.*

Gwaiakomotawa, (*nin*). I make a road straight for me; p. *gwe..wad.*

Gwaiakoshka, (*nin*). I walk on the road that is straightest, on the short way; p. *gwe..kad.*

Gwaiakoshka, or-*magad.* It goes right, straight; p. *gwa..kag,* or-*magak.*

Gwaiakosse, (*nin*). I walk straight; I live or act justly and honestly; p. *gwe..sed.*

Gwaiakotawa, (*nin*) (*tân*). I hear him right, correctly; p. *gwe..wad.*

Gwaiakoton, (*nin*). I make it straight and just, I straighten it, I fix it right, arrange it; p. *gwe..tod.*

Gwaiakowe, (*nin*). I speak right; just; p. *gwe..wed.*

Gwaiakwendagwad. It is considered or known to be right and just, it is right; p. *gwe.. wak.*

Gwaiakwendam, (*nin*). I have just and right thoughts, I think right; p. *gwe..ang.*

Gwaiakwendamowin. Right and just thought; concord.

Gwaiakwendan, (*nin*). I think it is just and right; p. *gwe.. ang.*

Gwaiakwenima, (*nin*). I think or consider some object right and just; p. *gwe..mad.*

Gwâkwâpigan. Any vessel used in throwing the water out of a canoe or boat; pl.-*an.*

Gwâkwâpige, (*nin*). I throw the water out of a canoe or boat; p. *gwaia..ged.*

Gwâm. As end-syllable of some neuter verbs, relates to *sleeping;* as: *Nin tawanongwâm,* I sleep with my mouth open. *Nin bigengwâm,* I sleep too much. *Ainabingwâm,* he sleep with his eyes open, or with open eyes, etc.

Gwan, (*gon.*) This word signifies *day;* but it is never used alone; it occurs always connected with a number, or with the interpolation-word *dasso.* (S. Otch. Grammar, Cardinal numbers, Remark 4.)

Gwanagad. This verb is always connected with a number, or with *dasso;* and signifies a certain number of days; as: *Nanogwanagad jaigwa ekodagwishinân;* it is five days since I arrived.

Gwanagis, (*nin*); p. *gwanagisi.* This verb always occurs with a number, or with *dasso;* and signifies the age of an object, expressed in days; as: *Jangassogwanagisi aw abinodji;* this child is nine days old.

*Gwanagodjishkiwaga,*or-*magad.* It is muddy, miry; p. *gwaia.. gag,* or-*magak.*

Gwanâtch, adj. Fair, fine, beautiful, pretty, handsome, good, useful.

Gwanâtchiw, (*nin*). I am fair, beautiful, handsome, good, useful; p. *gwe..wid.*

Gwanâtchiwan. It is handsome, beautiful, fine, good, useful; *gwe..ang.*

Gwanâtchiwin. Beauty, fairness; usefulness.

Gwanwadjia, (*nin*). *Ot.* S. *Manadjia.*

Gwash, as end-syllable in verbs, alludes to *sleep, sleeping,* as: *Nin goshkongwash,* I awake jumping up, *Nin gigibingwash,* I am sleepy, drowsy.

Gwâshkawad, adv. Much, plentiful, plenty of...—*Gwashkawad anishinabeg,* plenty of Indians. *Gwashkawad masinaiganan,* plenty of books.

Gwâshkwandaon. Crutch; pl.-*an.*

Gwâshkwan, (*nin*). I leap, spring, jump; p. *gwaia..nid.*

Gwâshkwanjenan ishkote, (*nin*). I let fall fire to the ground; p. *gwai..ang.*

Gwâshkwanodawa, (*nin*) (*dan*). I jump on him, (a person or any other object;) p. *gwaia..wad.*

Gwâshkwashkinadon, (*nin*). I fill it with a heap, not overrunning; p. *gwaia..dod.*

Gwâshkwashkwanibiké. The vein of the heart.

Gwâshkweiâbikisse, (*nin*). I rebound, falling on metal or stone; p. *gwaia..sed.*

Gwâshkwes, (*nin*). I am zealous at work, smart at work or walking, quick; p. *gwaia..sid.*

Gwâshkwesin, (*nin*). I rebound or spring up, falling; p. *gwaia..ing.*

Gwâshkwesiwin. Zeal, smart expeditious working.

Gwâshkwessin. It rebounds falling; p. *gwaia..ing.*

Gwawabanowe, (*nin*). I have hollow cheeks; p. *gwe.-wed.*

Gwêk, or *gwéki*, in compositions, signifies *turning round, turning over*. (Examples in some of the following words.)

Gwêkab, (*nin*). I turn round, sitting; p. *gwaiékabid.*

Gwekabikishima, (*nin*) (*sidon*). I turn it over, (a stone, or silver;) p. *gwaie..mad.*

Gwêkabitawa, (*nin*). I turn round *towards* him or *from* him, sitting; p. *gwaie..wad.*

Gwékanimad. The wind comes from another direction, it turned, it shifted; p. *gwaie..mak.*

Gwékendam, (*nin*). I change my mind, my thoughts, I turn them into another direction; p. *gwaie..ang.*

Gweki, (*nin*). I turn; p. *gwaiekid.*

Gwékigâbaw, (*nin*). I turn round, standing; p. *gwaie..wid.*

Gwékigâbâwitawâ, (*nin*). I turn *towards* him or *from* him, standing; p. *gwaie..wad.*

Gwékigwadan, (*nin*). I sew it on the other side; p. *gwaie..ang.*

Gwékigwana, (*nin*). I sew some obj. on the other side; p. *gwaie..nad.*

Gwekikwen, (*nin*). I turn my head round; p. *gwaie..nid.*

Gwékina, (*nin*). I turn some obj.; p. *gwaiekinad.*

Gwékissin. It turns, it is changed into...; p. *gwaiekissing.*—*Ki minawanigosiwin ta-gwekissin tchi kashkendamowiniwang;* thy joy will be changed into mourning.

Gwêkita, (*nin*). I turn round, (sitting, standing or lying;) p. *gwaiekitad.*

Gwenâtch. S. *Gwânâtch.*

Gwendâsseg. Camphor. S. *Gondasse.*

Gwengôwia. A kind of owl; (F. sorte de chouette, (bois-pourri;) pl.-*g*.

Gwênibibidon, (*nin*). I overthrow it, (a table, etc.); p. *gwaie..dod.*

Gwênbibina, (*nin*). I overthrow some obj.; p. *gwai..nad.*

Gwetch. This word is used with *kawin*, or *kego*, to signify, not much; as: *Kawin gweteh anokissi;* he does not work much. *Kego gwetch wissokawaken aw oshkinawe;* don't keep much company with that young man.

This word may also signify,

just, properly; as: *Gwetch enenimiwanen;* what thou just wilt of me, (that I should do.)

Gwigwingwao binê. The partridge is shaking his wings, (making a hollow noise, like distant thunder;) p. *gwag.. od.*

Gwigwingwaowâtig. The tree on which the partridge is shaking his wings; pl.-*on.*

Gwinawi, in compositions, signifies *doubting, not knowing, loss.* (Examples in some of the following words.)

Gwinawi-ab, (*nin*). I don't know where to be, where to live; p. *gwan..id.*

Gwinawi-dodam, (*nin*). I don't know what to do; p. *gwan.. ang.*

Gwinawi-dodawa, (*nin*). I don't know what to do for him, or to him; p. *gwan..wad.—Nin gwinawi-dodawa aw aiakosid;* I don't know what to do for this sick person, (how to treat him.)

Gwinawi-inendam, (*nin*). I doubt, I don't know what to think, I am perplexed; p. *gwan..ang.*

Gwinawi-wabama, (*nin*). I cannot see him, cannot find him; p. *gwan..mad.*

Gwingwaage. Wolverine; (C. carcajou;) pl.-*g.*

Gwingwan. There is a trembling of the ground from a cause above ground, thunder, etc.

Gwingwishi. A kind of small magpie; pl.-*wag.*

Gwinobi, (*nin*). I cannot find water; p. *gwanobid.*

H

Haw ! interjection, halloo! hurrah! well!

Hisht! interj. Hey! hear!

Hoi! interj. Halloo!

I

I.—This vowel has always the same sound in the words of the Otchipwe language; it is invariably pronounced like *i* in the English word *pin.*

Iatig. S. *Atig.*

Iban. It was, it has been.—*Mewija iban*, it has been a long while ago.

Idâm. One says, it is said, it is called; (F. on dit, on appelle;) p. *edaming.*

Idân, (*nind*). I speak of it, I say s. th. of it; p. *edang.*—*O matchi idan ow wigiwam;* he speaks ill of that house, (or lodge.)

Idimin, (*nind*) or, *nind aidimin.* We say s. th. to each other, or of each other, we speak of one another; p. *edidjig.*

Idis, (*nind*). I say s. th. of myself; p. *edisod.*

Idiwin. Speaking of each other.—*Matchi idiwin batainad oma,* there is much ill speaking of each other in this place.

Idog. This word is employed to express uncertainty, or not knowing.—*Anin ga-ijiwebak?*—*Namândj idog.* How did it happen?—I don't know how. *Anindi k'oss?* — *Tibi idog.* Where is thy father?—I don't know.

Igadeiagamishka, or-*magad.* The water opens, it divides itself; *egad..kag,* or-*magak.*

Igadekamigishka, or-*magad.* The earth opens, divides itself; p. *eg..kag,* or-*magak.*

Igadeshka, or-*magad.* It opens, it goes asunder, it divides itself; p. *ég..kag,* or-*magak.*

Igadeshkawog nabagissagog. The boards go asunder; p. *egadeshkadjig.*

Igiw, pron. These, those, them.

Igo. S. *Go.*

Igôwin. The word or words said to somebody.—*Geget osami-*

nad nin matchi igowin; the evil words that are said to me, are too many indeed.

Ijâ, (*nind*). I go; p. *ejad.*

Ijânan, (*nind*). I go to him, I go to see or visit him; p. *ejad.* (V. Conj.)

Iji. This word has sometimes no signification, and could be omitted in the phrase. (S. Otch. Gram. Remark I., after the Rules of the *Change.*) But commonly, and especially in compositions, it signifies *as, in such a manner, in a certain way, so, like...* (Examples in some of the following words.)

Iji, (*nind*). I dress like...; p. *ejiod.—Anishinabeng nind iji; Wemitigojing ijio.* I dress like an Indian; he dresses like a Frenchman.

Ijibiamawa, (*nind*). I write to him or for him in such a manner; also, I write of him or respecting him, in a certain manner; p. *ej..wad.*

Ijibiigade, or-*magad.* It is written in a certain manner, it is marked so...; p. *ej..deg,* or-*magak.*

Ijibiigas, (*nind*). I am written in such a manner, described so...; I am painted; p. *ej..sod.*

Ijibiige, (*nind*). I write in a certain manner, I mark so...; p. *ej..ged.— Ejibiigeian sa nind ijibiige gaie nin;* I write as thou writest.

Ijigijwewin. Talking in a certain manner, jargon.

Ijigikab, (*nind*). I move in such a direction, sitting; p. *ej..id.*

Ijikwanaie, (*nind*). I dress in a certain manner; p. *ej..ied.*

Ijikwanaieton, (*nind*). I dress or clothe it in a certain manner; p. *ej..tod.—Mamakadakamig ejikwanaietod Kije-Manito wâbigonin;* it is wonderful how God clothes the flowers.

Ijimâgos, (*nind*). I am of such an odor or smell; p. *ej..sid.*

Ijimâgwad. It is of such an odor or smell; p. *ej..wak.*

Ijinad. There is so much of it; p. *ejinak.—Ki kikendan na ejinak?* Do you know how much there is of it?

Ijinâgos, (*nind*). I look like...., I have the appearance of...; p. *ej..sid.*

Ijinâgosiwin. Appearance, form, figure, shape.

Ijinâgwad. It looks like..., it has the appearance of...; p. *ej..wak.*

Ijinagwi, (*nind*). I appear so. I take such a shape; p. *ej..od. — Ginebigong gi-bi-ijnagwio matchi manito kitchi kitiganing;* the evil spirit took the shape of a serpent in paradise.

Ijinikadan, (*nind*). I call it, I name it; p. *ej..ang.*

Ijinikade, or-*magad.* It is called, named; p. *ej..deg,* or-*magak.*

Ijinikana, (*nind*). I call him, (a person, or any other obj.;) p. *ej..nad;* imp. *ijinikaj.*

Ijinikanigos, (*nind*). I am named in a certain manner; p. *ej..sod.—Mi ge-wi-ijinikanigosiiân;* I want to be named so.

Ijinikas, (*nind*). I am called, my name is...; p. *ej..sod.*

Ijinikasowin. Name, appellation; pl.-*an*.
Ijiniken, (*nind*). I have my arm stretched out; p. *ej..nid*.
Ijinimin, (*nind*), or *nind ijinomin*. We are in such a number; p. *ejinidjig*, or, *ejinodjig*.—*Missawa Israel onidjanissan ijinonid ejinak negaw kitchigaming, pangi eta ta bimâdjiawog*. Although the number of the children of Israel be as the sand of the sea, a remnant only shall be saved.
Ijinindjitawa, (*nind*). I lay my hand upon him; p. *eji..wad*.
Ijisse, (*nind*). I slide or fall somewhere, or in some manner; p. *ejissed*.
Ijissin. It goes so; p. *ejissing*.
Ijissiton, (*nind*). I put it, I arrange it, fix it, in a certain manner; p. *ej..tod*.
Ijitchigade, or-*magad*. It is made or constructed in a certain manner; p. *ej..deg*, or-*magak*.
Ijitchigaso. It is made or constructed in a certain manner; p. *ej..sod*.
Ijitchige, (*nind*). I do, I act, I practise so...; p. *ej..ged*.
Ijitchigemagad. It does so...; p. *ej..gak*.—*Geget kitchi matchi ijitchigemagad ishkotewâbo oma aking;* ardent liquor does indeed much evil on earth.
Ijitwa, (*nind*). I do or act so; also, I profess or practice religion; p. *ejitwad*.
Ijitwâwin. Practice; religion; pl.-*an*.—*Gaiat ijitwâwin*, the Old Testament; also, *Getê ijitwâwin*. *Gweiakossing ijitwâwin*, the true religion. *Oshki ijitwâwin*, the New Testament.
Ijiwêbad. It is so...; p. *ejiwebak*.
Ijiwêbis, (*nind*). I conduct myself in a certain manner, I behave so, I am so; p. *ej..sid*. —*Ningot nind ijiwebis;* I am in certain circumstances.
Ijiwebisiwin. Conduct, behavior, manners, comportment.
Ijiwidawa, (*nind*) or, *nind ijiwidamawa*. I carry it to him; p. *eji..wad*.
Ijiwin, (*nind*) (*don*). I carry, conduct or convey some obj.; p. *ej..nad;* imp. *ijiwij*.
Ijiwinde, or-*magad*. It is called or named so; p. *eji..deg*, or-*magak*.
Ikigome, (*nind*). I draw up my snot; p. *eki..med*.
Ikkit, (*nind*). I say; p. *ekkitod*.
Ikkitomagad. It says; p. *ek..gak*.
Ikkitowin. Word, saying; pl.-*an*.
Ikkitowini-masinaigan. Word-book, dictionary, vocabulary; pl.-*an*.
Iko. S. *Ko*.
Ikogâ, (*nind*). I go away, I go out of the way, aside; p. *ekogad*.
Ikogâbaw, (*nind*). I step aside, out of the way of somebody; p. *ek..wid*.
Ikonâ, (*nind*). I take him away, aside, I remove, (a person or any other obj.); p. *ekonad;* imp. *ikôn*.
Ikonajaigas, (*nin*). S. *Madjinajaigas*.
Ikonâjawa, (*nind*). I send him away, I bid him go away; I

drive him off; p. *ek..wad ;* imp. *ikonaja.*

Ikonamawa, (*nind*) or *nind ikonawa.* I put him away or aside something, I deliver him from s. th., I remove it from him; p. *ek..wad.*

Ikonan, (*nind*). I put it aside or away, I remove it, I put it out of the way; p. *ekonang.*

Ikowebina, (*nind*) (*nan*). I throw or push some obj. aside; p. *ek..nad ;* imp. *ikowebin.*

Ikwâ. Louse; pl.-*g.*

Ikwab, (*nind*). I draw back or aside, sitting; p. *ekwabid.*

Ikwabian, (*nind*). I wind it up, (f. i. an anchor, in lifting;) p. *ek..ang.*

Ikwabigina, (*nind*) (*nan*). I draw him up to me on a rope; p. *ek..nad.*

Ikwabiwa dibaigisisswân, (*nind*) I wind up a watch or clock; p. *ek..wad ;* imp. *ikwabi.*

Ikwanam, (*nind*). I sigh profoundly; p. *ek..mod.*

Ikkwê. Woman; pl.-*wag.*

Ikkwé-aiaâ. Female being, female, (of animals;) pl.-*g.*

Ikkwé-bebejigoganji. Mare; pl.-*g.*

Ikkwêonje, (*nind*). S. *Ikwesensike.*

Ikkwê-pijiki. Cow; pl.-*wag.*

Ikkwésens. Little girl; pl.-*ag.* S. *Oshkinigikwe. Gijikwe.*

Ikkweséensike, (*nind*) or *nind ikkwéke.* I give birth to a girl, I am delivered of a girl; p. *ek..ked.*

Ikkwesensiw, (*nind*). I am a little girl; p. *ek..wid.*

Ikkwéw, (*nind*). I am a woman; p. *ekweiwid.*

Ikwigia, (*nind*). I bring him up, I nourish him, feed him; p. *ek..ad.*

Ikwishin, (*nind*). I lie down a little farther there; p. *ek..ing.*

Ima, adv. There, thence.

In. In some verbs, signifies a certain *way* or *manner* in which s. th. is done or used; or the *direction* in which some person or thing is going. (Examples in some of the following words.)

Inâ, (*nind*). I tell him, I say to him; I call him, I give him a name; p. *enad ;* imp. *iji.*

Ina, (*nind*). I go there in a canoe or boat, I steer for a certain point or place; p. *enaod. Gwaiak wedi neiashiwaninig inao;* he steers directly for that point.

Inâ! interj. S. *Na!*

Inâb, (*nind*). I look somewhere, to some place, to some object; p. *enabid.*

Inâbadad. It is useful, serviceable, beneficial, good for s. th., in a certain manner; p. *en..dak.*

Inâbadagendagos, (*nind*). I am esteemed useful, I am serviceable, good for s. th.; p. *en..sid.*

Inabadagendagosiwin. Utility, usefulness.

Inâbadagendagwad. It is considered useful, good for s. th.; p. *en..wak.*

Inâbadis, (*nind*). I am useful, good for s. th.; p. *en..sid.*

Inâbadisiwin. Usefulness.

Inâbadjia, (*nind*). I make use of some obj. in such a manner, it is useful to me; p. *en..ad.*

Inâbadjitchigan. Any obj. useful or serviceable in a certain manner ; pl.-*ag* or-*an*. S. *Abadjitchigan.*

Inâbadjiton, (*nind*). I use it in a certain manner, it is useful to me in such a manner; p. *en tod.*

Inâbadjitowin. The act of using s. th. in such a manner.

Inâbama, (*nind*). I see him so, in such a manner; p. *en.. mad.*

Inâbaminagos, (*nind*). I resemble to...; I look like...; p. *en..sid.*

Inâbaminagosiwin. Resemblance.

Inâbaminagwad. It resembles to..., it looks like..., it appears in a certain manner; p. *en.. wak.*

Inâbaminagwaton, (*nind*) (pron. *inabaminagoton*;) I make it look like...; I make it resemble to...; p. *en..tod.*

Inâbandam, (*nind*). I dream, (I see s. th. in a certain manner, sleeping;) p. *en..ang.*

Inâbandamowin. Dreaming, dream; pl.-*an.*

Inâbandân, (*nind*). I see it in a certain manner; p. *en..ang.*

Inâbandjigan. Dream; pl.-*an.*

Inâbandjige, (*nind*). I dream; p. *en..ged.*

Inabidêia, or-*magad.* It has such an edge, or such teeth, (an iron tool;) p. *en..og,* or-*magak.*

Inabimagad. It looks to some point; p. *en..gak.*

Inâbiwin. Look, looking somewhere.

Inadaga, (*nind*). I take my course there, swimming; p. *én gâd.*

Inadem, (*nind*). I weep in a certain manner; p. *en..mod.*

Inademotawa, (*nind*). I go to him weeping; p. *én. wad.*

Inadengwe, (*nind*). I have a face like...; p. *en..wed.*—*Anishinabeng inadengwe nandomâkomeshi*; the monkey has a face like a person.

Inâdis, (*nin*). S. *Ijiwebis.*

Inâdisiwin. S. *Ijiwebisiwin.*

Inâdjim, (*nind*). I tell s. th. in a certain manner; p. *en..mod.*

Inâdjima, (*nind*). I tell s. th. of somebody in a certain way, I speak of him; p. *ên..mad.*

Inaé, (*nind*). I shoot off an arrow; p. *enaéd.*

Inâgami. It has the appearance or taste of such a liquid; p. *en..mig.*—*Jominabong inâgami mandan*; this has the appearance (or taste) of wine.

Inagima, (*nind*). I value him so much... I put his price at..; I destine him for s. th.; p. *en . mad.* — *Ningotwâk dasswâbik od inagiman o bebejigoganjiman*; he puts the price of his horse at a hundred dollars.

Inagode, or-*magad.* It hangs so..., it is inclined so...; p. *en..deg,* or-*magak.*—*Manadadong osâm inagode nindé,* my heart is too much inclined to evil. *Mi enagodeg nindê*; such is the inclination, propension, sentiment, of my heart.

Inakaké, inakakeia, adv. S. *Nakakeia.*

Inakamiga. The ground, soil or country, is such...; p. *en..*

gag. — *Ga-iji-windamonan sa, mi gwaiak enakamigag ejaian;* the country whither thou art going, is such as I told thee.

Inakamigad. There are news; p. *en..gak.*—*Mino inakamigad,* good news. *Matchi inakamigad,* bad news. *Kitchi inakamigad,* great news.

Inakona, (*nind*) (*nân*). I appoint him for s. th., I exercise authority over him; p. *ên..nad;* imp. *inâkon.*

Inamodjige, (*nind*). I have a certain road or trail which I follow; p. *en..ged.*

Inamô mikana, or, *inamonagad mikana.* The road or trail leads to..., goes to...; p. *enamog,* or *magak.*—*Mi oma mikana enamog odenang;* here is the road that leads to the village. *Endaiân inamo ow mikana;* this trail leads to my house.

Inamôtawa, (*nind*). I make him a road so...; p. *en..wad.*

Inânde, or-*magad.* It is dyed in a certain manner; p. *en..deg,* or-*magak.*

Inandjige, (*nind*). I eat in a certain manner, I fare so...; p. *en..ged.* — *Ketimagisidjig enandjigewad, nind enandjige;* I fare, as poor people fare.

Inanokadan, (*nind*). I use it in such a manner; p. *en..ang.*

Inanokana, (*nind*). I use some obj. in a certain manner; p. *en..nad;* imp. *kaj.*

Inanoki, (*nind*). I work in a certain manner; p. *en..kid.*

Inanokiwin. Working, work.

Inanso. Some object is dyed in a certain manner; p. *enansod.*

Inaona, (*nind*). I give him a certain share; p. *en..nad;* imp. *inaoj.*—*Enaominân nind inaona;* I give him the same share as to thee.

Inapidon, (*nind*). I tie it in a certain manner; p. *en..dod.*

Inapina, (*nin*). I tie some obj. in such a manner; p. *en..nad;* imp. *inapij.*

Inapinana, (*nind*). I kill him in a certain manner; also, I give him a certain sickness, (according to Indian superstitions;) p. *en..nad;* imp. *inapinaj.*

Inapine, (*nind*). I am sick in a certain manner, I have such a sickness; p. *en..ned.*

Inapinema, (*nind*). I grieve him, afflict him with words, I reproach him, revile him, blaspheme him, give him bad words, in a certain manner; p. *en..mad.*

Inapinêndan, (*nind*). I revile it, speak ill against it, I blaspheme it in such a manner; p. *en..ang.*

Inapinewidam, (*nind*). I revile, I blaspheme, I use bad language, in a certain manner, I use offensive words; p. *en..ang.*

Inâpinewin. Sickness, disease, malady; pl.-*an.*

Inapisowin. Apron; pl.-*an.*

Inâsh, (*nind*). I sail in a certain manner; p. *enashid.*

Inâshia, (*nind*). I excite him, or push him, to s. th.; p. *en..ad.*—*Nin mino inashia,* I excite him to good actions. *Nin matchi inashia,* I excite him to evil actions.

Inâshka, or-*magad*. The sea runs in a certain manner; p. *en..gak*, or-*magak*.—*Nongom enashkag gi-inashkamagad pitchinago api mejagawad;* yesterday, when they arrived, the sea ran as high as it does to-day.

Inashkine, or-*magad*. It is full in a certain manner; p. *en..neg*, or-*magak*.

Inate, or-*magad*. There is room; p. *ênateg*, or-*magak*.

Inawa, (*nind*). I resemble him, I am similar to him; p. *enawad*.

Inawanidimin, (*nind*). We walk together; p. *én..didjig*.

Inawéma, (*nind*). I am his relative, or, he is a relative of mine; also, I am his friend, he is my friend, I live in peace and friendship with him; p. *en..mad*.

Inawémâgan. Relative, relation, kinsman, kinswoman.—This word occurs always connected with a possessive pronoun; as: *Nind inawémâgan*, a relative of mine; *Kid inawemagan*, a relative of thine, etc. (S. Otch. Gram. Chap. I. Poss. Pron. 2. Form, *an*.)

Iwawêmikana, ((*nind*) (*dan*). I employ him in such a manner; p. *en..nad;* imp. *inawémikaj*.

Inawendaa, (*nind*). I make him a relative to somebody; also, I reconcile him with somebody; p. *en..ad*.

Inawendagan. S. *Inawemagan*.

Inawendan, (*nind*). I am its friends, I am friendly to the cause; p. *en..ang*.

Ind, (*nind*). I do, I am, I behave. (S. Otch. Gram.)

Indagitagan. The place where a wild animal uses to eat in the woods.

Indân, (*nind*). I have, I possess; p. *endanid*.—*Kawin gego nind indanissi, nin kitimagis ;* I have nothing, (I possess nothing,) I am poor.

Indanenima, (*nin*). I think he is in..., or at...; p. *en..mad*.—*Moniang nind indanenima nissaie*; I think my brother is in Montreal.

Indibe, (*nind*). I have such a head; p. *endibed*. — *Kigwiss endibed, mi ga-indibed gaie ningwissiban ;* my son that died, had just such a head as thy son.

Indowin. Fault, guilt; (L. culpa.) This word is always preceded by a possessive pronoun; as: *Nind indowin*, my fault, etc.—To give more force to the expression, they will say: *Nin nind indowin*, it is thy own fault; *win od indowin*, it is his own fault, etc.

Inénd, (*nind*). I am absent, I am so long on my voyage; p. *enendid*.— *Moniang nin gad-ija nibing nisso gisiss dash nin gad-inend;* I will go to Montreal next summer; and will be absent three months.

Inéndagos, (*nind*). I am destined, I am thought; p. *en..sid*.

Inendagwad. It is destined, it is thought; p. *en..wak*.

Inéndam, (*nind*). I think, I suppose, it is my opinion, it seems to me; I will, I purpose, I intend; p. *enendang*.

Inéndamowin. Thinking, thought, opinion, supposition; will, intention, purpose; pl.-*an*.
Inendân, (*nind*). I think of it, I have an idea of it, I destine it; p. *enendang.*
Inêndjige, (*nind*). I will; p. *en..ged.*
Inêndomagad. It is absent, it did not yet come back; p. *en gak.—Kitchi ginwenj inendomagad nabikwân;* the vessel is absent a long time.
Inénima, (*nind*). I think of him..., I have the opinion of him... ; I destine him, it is my will he should...; I enable him...; p. *en..ad.*
Inenindis, (*nind*). I think myself... ; I destine myself, I have the opinion of myself...; p. *en..sod.*
Ini. In some verbs denotes a certain *manner, extent, direction.*—S. *In.* (Examples in some of the following words.)
Inidé, or-*magad.* It is cooked, or burnt, in a certain manner; p. *enideg,* or-*magak.*
Inigaa, (*nind*). I injure or hurt him, I wrong or damage him; I make him unhappy; p. *en..ad.*
Inigas, (*nind*). I make myself unhappy, I wrong or damage myself; p. *enigasid.*
Inigatagos, (*nind*). I excite compassion with my words; p. *en..sid.*
Inigaton, (*nind*). I injure or damage it; p. *en..tod.*
Inigâwagendam, (*nind*). I have bitter remorses of conscience, my conscience troubles me; p. *en..ang.*
Inigin, (*nind*). I am so large, so big, of such a size; p. *enigi-nid.—Enigiiân inigini,* he is as large as I am, (he is of my size.)
Inigôkodee, (*nind*). My heart is so large, of such an extent; p. *en..deed.* — *Enigokodeeiân,* at the extent of my heart, (from all my heart.)
Inigokodewis, (*nind*). S. *Inigokwin.*
Inigokwa, or-*magad.* It is so large, of such an extent; p. *en..wag,* or-*magak.* — *Enigokwag ki kitigan, inigokwa gaie nin nin kitigan;* my field is as large as thine. *Enigokwag aki,* as large as the earth is, (on the whole earth.)
Inikawa, (*nind*). I cause him s. th., I make him be so ..; also, I put on so some obj.; p. *en..wad.—Nin sa nin ginikawa iw wendji-âkosid;* I have caused him the sickness he has, (I made him so sick.)—*Mi iw enikawag nin mindjikawâgan;* that is the way I put my mitten on.
Inikweam, (*nind*). I steer for a certain point; p. *enikweang.*
Inikwean, (*nind*). I steer it (canoe, boat, vessel, etc.) for a certain point, in a certain direction; p. *enikweang.*
Inikwen, (*nind*). I make a certain motion with the head; p. *enikwenid.*
Ininajaamawa, (*nind*). I send him somebody; p. *en..wad.*
Ininajaogowin. Message, errand.
Ininajawa, (*nind*). I send him

somewhere, I send him on an errand, I despatch him; p. *en..wad;* imp. *ininajâ.*

Ininajawagan. S. *Ijinajawagan.*

Ininama, (*nind*). I give or present it to him, I put it before him; also, I show it to him with the finger; p. *en..mad.*

Ininan, (*nind*). I present or put it; p. *eninang.*

Ininandag. Fir-tree, spruce; (C. sapin;) pl.-*og.*

Ininâtig. Maple-tree; pl.-*on.*

Ininatigossag. Maple-wood, a piece of maple-wood; pl.-*on.*

Inini. Man, male; (L. vir;) pl.-*wok.*

Ininijim, (*nind*). I fly to some place for safety, I take refuge somewhere; p. *en..mod.*

Ininionje, (*nind*). I give birth to a boy; p. *en..jed.*

Ininishib. Duck, (of the same species as our domestic ducks;) pl.-*ag.*

Ininiw, (*nind*). I am a man; p. *eniniwid.*

Ininiwidis, (*nind*). I make myself man; p. *en..sod.*

Inishkagon, (*nind*). It pierces me; p. *en..god.*

Inishkawa, (*nind*). I pierce him; p. *en..wad.*

Initage, (*nind*). I hear people say so...; p. *en..ged.*

Initagos, (*nind*). I am heard in a certain manner, I speak so...; I have such a voice; p. *en..sid.—Ga-iji-kikinoamagoiân mi enitagosiiân;* as I have been taught, so I speak.

Initam, (*nind*). I hear what is said, or how it is said; p. *enitang.*

Initawa, (*nind*). I hear or understand him so...; p. *en..wad.*

Iniw. Pron. those, those there.

Iniwea, (*nind*). I give him up, I abandon him, reject him; p. *en..ad.*

Iniweidis, (*nind*). I abandon myself, expose myself, I risk; p. *en..sod.*

Iniwes, (*nind*). I am offended; I am impatient, angry; p. *en..sid.*

Iniwesia, (*nind*). I offend him, I make him angry; p. *en..ad.*

Ino, or-*magad.* He is; it is, it is so. (S. Otch. Gram. Def. Verbs.)

Inoa, (*nind*). I point him out with the finger, I show him with my fore-finger; (F. je le montre au doigt;) p. *enaad.*

Inoamawa, (*nind*). I show him s. th. with my finger, I point it out to him; p. *en..wad.*

Inoan, (*nind*). I point to it, or show it with my finger; p. *enoang.*

Inodewis, (*nind*). I have such a property; also, I have such a household, my family is so large; p. *en..sid.* — *Kakina enodewiiân;* my whole property and household; my whole family.

Inodewisiwin. Property, household, family.

Inôige, (*nind*). I show with the fore-finger; p. *en..ged.*

Inôigan. A person, or any other obj., that is shown with the finger; pl.-*ag.*

Inôigan. Any obj. that is shown with the finger; pl.-*an.*

Inoiganindj. Fore-finger, (which

is used in pointing to some obj.); pl.-*in*.

Inôtawa, (*nind*). I repeat his words, I say as he says or said; p. *en..wad*.

Inwâs, (*nind*). I try, I endeavor, without much effect, I effect little; p. *enwâsod*.

Inwâsomagad. It effects little; p. *en..gak*.

Inwê, (*nind*). I speak (in a certain manner,) I speak a language; I let hear a voice or a sound; p. *en..wed*. — *Nijwâtching bebakânin inwé;* he speaks several different languages.

Inwêmagad. It speaks a language, it gives a certain sound; p. *en..gak*.—*Anin enwemagak iw masenaigan?* — *Enweiân sa inwemagad*. What language does that book speak?—It speaks the language I [speak. (In what language is it written? — It is written in my language.)

Inwêton, (*nind*). I give a cer- certain melody or tune to a hymn or song; p. *enwetod*.

Inwêwin. Language; voice; tune or melody of a hymn or melody, of a hymn or song; pl.-*an*.

Io! interj. oh! ah! (expression of pain or ache.)

Ioio, pain, (in the language of children.)

Ipinean, (*nin*). I pay it so much, I give so much for it; p. *epineang*.

Ipinewa, (*nind*). I pay so much for some object; p. *ep..wad*. —*Nijwâbik nin gi-ipinewa nin moshwem;* I paid two dollars for my shawl.

Ipogosi. It has such a taste; it tastes like..; p. *epogosid*.—*Aw gigo wiiâssing ipogosi;* that fish tastes like meat.

Ipogosiwin. The taste of s. th.

Ish! interj. Hey! hear!

Ishk. As first syllable in some verbs, signifies *tired, weary*. (Examples in some of the following words.)

Ishkab, (*nind*). I am tired of sitting; p. *eshkabid*.

Ishkakoshin, (*nind*). I am lying in a fatiguing manner, on a hard bed; p. *esh..ing*.

Ishkanam, (*nind*). I breathe with difficulty, with fatigue; p. *esh..mod*.

Ishkatawâb, (*nin*). My eyes are tired by looking for a long time at some object; p. *esh..bid*.

Ishkidee, (*nind*). My heart is tired of sorrow, fatigued with grief; p. *eshkideed*.

Ishkishin, (*nind*). I am tired of lying; p. *esh..ing*.

Ishkiwi, (*nind*). I am tired of carrying; p. *esh..wid*.

Ishkobodjigan.*A piece of board sawn off, a remnant of a board; pl.-*ag*.

Ishkojân, (*nind*). Something remains when I have done cutting a coat, etc., I leave a remnant; p. *eshkojang*.

Ishkojigan. Shred, remnant after cutting a coat, or any other article of clothing; pl.-*an*.

Ishkona, (*nind*). I return him,

NOTE. The first two syllables of this and the following words, could also be written *ishkwa*, but still pronounced *ishko*.

I spare him, I keep back or retain some obj., I don't give it away, nor use it up; p. *esh-konad.*

Ishkonamâs, (nind). I reserve it to myself; p. *esh..sod.*

Ishkonamawa, (nind). I reserve it to him, I keep it back for him; p. *esb..wad.*

Ishkonan, (nind). I spare it; I keep it back, I reserve it, I don't dispose of it; p. *esh..ang.*

Ishkonigan. Reserve; pl.*-an.*

Ishkonige, (nind.) I reserve, I keep back; p. *esh..ged.*

Ishkotê. Fire.

Ishkotékân. Fire-steel ; pl.*-ag.*

Ishkotêke, (nind). I make fire, or strike fire, (with a fire-steel and flint, or with matches ;) p. *esh..ked.*

Ishkoté-nâbikwân. Steamboat, (fire-vessel ;) pl.*-an.*

Ishkotêns. A match, (a small fire;) pl.*-an.*

Isakoté-odâbân. Railroad car, (fire-carriage ;) pl.*-ag.*

Ishkoté-tashkibodjigan. Steam saw-mill, (fire-saw ;) pl.*-ag.*

Ishkotéwâbo. Ardent liquor, whiskey, rum, brandy, (fire-water.)

Ishkotêwaboimagos, (nind). The smell of ardent liquor comes out of my mouth ; p. *esh..sid.*

Ishkotêwaboke, (nind). I make ardent liquor, I distil; p. *esh ..ked.*

Ishkotewâbokéwigamig. Distillery; pl.*-on.*

Ishkotewâbokêwinini. Distiller, (a man that makes fire-water ;) pl.*-wag.*

Ishkotéwadad. It is firy ; it resembles fire ; p. *esh..dâk.*

Ishkwâ-, gi-ishwa-, after or at the end of s. th..—This word is always connected with a substantive or verb; as *Nind ishkwa-wissin,* I have done eating. *Gi-ishkwa-kikinoamading bi-ijân endaiân ;* after school come to my house.

Ishkwa-akiwan. It is the end of the world. *Ishkwa-akiwang,* or, *gi-ishkwa-akiwang,* at the end of the world.

Ishkwabi, or*-magad.* (Pron. *ishkobi,)* it cannot go all in, the vessel cannot hold all, (liquid ;) p. *eshkwabig* or*-magak.*

Ishkwabissa. It rains no more ; p. *esh..sag.*

Ishkwaga, or*-magad.* The sap of the maphe-trees runs no more, (in sugar-making;) p. *eshkwagag,* or*-magak.*

Ishkwagâpogwad| sisibâkwat. The sugar tastes the spoiled maple-sap,(the last sugar that is made, when the sap is no more good.) ; p. *esh..wak.*

Ishkwagâ-sisibâkwat. The last sugar that is made, out of the spoiled sap.

Ishkwaiadjiw, (nind). I am the last in a row or range; p. *esh ..wid.*

Ishkwaiagamisse, or*-magad.*The water is no more agitated, it is calm, (after a storm and heavy sea;) p. *esh..seg,* or*-magak.*

Ishkwaiakis, (nind). I cease burning, I burn no more ; p. *esh..sod.*

Ishkwaiassige gisiss. The moon shines no more; p. *esh..ged.*

Ishkwakamigad. All is over; p. *esh..gak. Ga-ishkwakamigak dibaamadiwin nin gi-tagwishin.* I arrived when the payment was all over.

Ishkwakamigis, (*nind*). I am no more busy, I have finished my work; p. *esh..sid.*

Ishkwakamigisiwin. The end of an action or work.

Ishkwama, (*nind*). I leave some, after eating some of it; p. *esh mad.—Nind ishkwama kokosh opinig gaie nind ishkwamag;* I leave some pork and some potatoes, (after eating some.)

Ishkwanâm, (*nind*). I breathe my last, I expire; p. *esh..mod.*

Ishkwandân, (*nind*). I leave some, after eating some of it; p. *esh..ang.— Nind ishkwandan pangi wiiâss;* I leave a little meat, (after eating some of it.)

Ishkwândem. Door; pl.-*an.*

Ishkwandemike, (*nind*). I make a door, or doors; p. *esh..ked.*

Ishkandemiwan. There is a door; p. *esh..ang.*

Ishkwanjigan. Remnant, remainder, (after eating some of an obj.); pl.-*ag.*

Ishkwandjige, (*nind*). I leave some of what I am eating, I don't eat all up; p. *esh..ged.*

Ishkwané, (*nind*). (Pron. *ishkoné,*) I remain while the others die, I survive; p. *eshkoned.— Abinodjiiag eshkwanedjig,* the children of a family that remain yet alive, when several had died.

Ishkwâ-nona, (*nind*). I wean him, (a child,) I cease to give him suck; p. *esh..nad.*

Ishkwapo, or-*magad.* It ceases snowing, it snows no more; p. *esh..pog,* or-*magak.*

Ishkwashima, (*nind*). I have some of it remaining, after putting or laying; p. *esh..mad.*

Ishkwasse, (*nind*). (Pron. *ishkosse,*)I remain, I am left or spared; (L. superstes sum;) p. *eshkwassed,* (*eshkossed.*)

Ishkwassin. It finishes, expires, (period of time;) p. *esh..sing.*

Ishkwassiton, (*nind*). I have some of it remaining, after putting or laying; p. *esh..tod.*

Ishkwâtâ, (*nind*). I finish, (doing s. th.;) p. *eshkwatad.*

Ishkwatagan. S. *Ishkwatchigan.*

Ishkwatawin. The end of a work; the end of a period of time.

Ishkwâtch, adv. Finally, at last, at length, ultimately; the last time.

Ishkwatchigan. A person that escapes from a general massacre; pl.-*ag.*

Ishkwawe, (*nind*). (Pron. *ishkowe*), I cease speaking, I finish my discourse or speech; p. *eshkwawed.*

Ishkweâii, adv. Behind, after the others.

Iskkweb, (*nind*). I am sitting in the last place, in a row or range; p. *eshkwebid.*

Ishkwegabaw, (*nind*). I am standing in the last place, in a row or range; p. *esh..wid.*

Ishkwégamig. The last lodge or house, (in a row or range, or in a camp or village.)

Ishkwegê, (*nind*). I live in the

last lodge or house of a camp or village; p. *esh..ged.*

Ishkwêiang, adv. S. *Ishkweaii.*

Ishkweiendagos, (*nind*). I am considered the last, or one of the last; p. *esh..sid.*

Ishkwêkawa, (*nind*). I walk after him, I follow him; p. *esh..wad.*

Ishkwênindji. The small finger; pl.-*in.*

Ishkwessin. It is the last, (the last object in a row or range;) p. *esh..ing.*

Ishkwétchâgan. The last or youngest child in a family, and which *remains* the last; pl.-*ag.*

Ishkwi, (*nind*). I remain, when the others are gone; p. *eshkwid.*

Ishpâ, or-*magad.* It is high; p. *eshpâg*, or-*magak.*

Ishpâbika, or-*magad.* It is high, (a rock;) p. *esh..kag*, or-*magak.*

Ishpabikad. It is high, (obj. of metal;) p. *esh..kak.*

Ishpabikisi. It is high, (object of metal or stone;) p. *esh..sid.*

Ishpadina. It is high, (a hill or mountain;) p. *esh..nag.*

Ishpadjibiwan. There are heaps of snow, driven up by the wind; p. *esh..ang.*

Ishpâgonaga. The now is deep, there is much snow; p. *esh..gag.*

Ishpakweia, or-*magad.* There are high trees, (in a forest;) p. *esh..iag*, or-*magak.*

Ishpânike, (*nind*). I dig a deep hole in the ground; p. *esh..ked.*

Ishpânsika, or-*magad.* It is high, thick, wide, (a book, a piece of cloth, etc.); p. *esh..kag*, or-*magak.*

Ishpâshkad. It is high, wide, (a mat, clothing stuff, etc.); p. *esh..kak.*

Ishpâte. The snow is deep, (high,); p. *eshpateg.*

Ishpâton, (*nind*). I make it high; p. *eshpatod.—Od ishpâtod o wâkaigan;* he makes his house high, (he builds a high house.)

Ishpawe aw awessi. This animal has long hair or fur; p. *eshpawed.*

Ishpenim, (*nind*). I am proud, I exalt myself; p. *esh..mod.*

Ishpenima, (*nind*). I exalt him, glorify him; p. *esh..mad.*

Ishpeniadis, (*nind*). I exalt myself, I am proud; p. *esh..sod.*

Ishpenindisowin. Pride.

Ishpi, in compositions, signifies *high, late, advanced.* (Examples in some of the following words.)

Ishpia, (*nind*). I put him high, I exalt him; p. *eshpiad.*

Ishpibibon. The winter is far advanced, is high; p *eshpibibong.*

Ishpigabawi aw awessi. This animal stands high, it has long legs; p. *esh..wid.*

Ishpi-gijigad. It is late, (in the forenoon,) the sun is already high. It is not late, (in the afternoon,) the sun is yet high. P. *eshpi-gijigak.*

Ishpiming, adv. Above, on high, at the top; in the air.

Ishpiming nakakeia, adv. Upwards.

Ishpimissagokade, or-*magad.*

There is an upper floor ; also, there is a story, (in a house ;) p. *esh..deg*, or-*magak.—Nijing ishpimissagokade*, there are two stories.—*Nissing, niwing, nâning ishpimissagokade ;* there are three, four, five stories.

Ishpimissagong, adv. Up-stairs, on the upper floor.

Ishpina, (*nind*) (*nan*). I raise or lift him up; p. *esh..nad.*

Ishpinibin. The summer is high, is far advanced; p. *esh. ing.*

Ishpishinog. There is a high heap of objects; p. *eshpishingig. — Ishpishinog nobagissagog ;* there is a high heap or pile of boards.—Also in the sing. ; as : *Ishpishin joniia*, there is a high heap of money.

Ishpissin. There is a high heap, (something heaped up ;) p. *eshpissing.—Ishpissinon missan ;* there is a high heap of wood, (for fuel.)

Ishpi-tibikad. It is late in the night, (high night;) p. *esh..kak.*

Ishpônagad. It is high; or deep, (a canoe, boat, etc.); p. *esh.. gak.*

Ishpowe, (*nind*). I speak with a high thin voice; p. *eshpowed.* —S. *Tabassowe.*

Ishpwêweton, (*nind*). I sing it high; p. *esh..tod.*

Isht ! interj. Hey! hear!

Ishté ! interj. Aha! yes!

Ishkaan, (*nind*). I empty it of water; I pump it out; I make it dry; p. *eskaang.*

Iskabi, or-*magad*. The water dried up; p. *eskabig*, or-*magak.*

Iskâibadan, (*nind*). I pump the water out of it, (a vessel, etc.); p. *esk..ang.*

Iskaibân. Spunge, pump; pl.-*ag.*

Iskaibi, (*nind*). I pump water out ; I dry it up with a spunge; p. *ês..bid.*

Iskandan, (*nind*). I drink it all up; p. *esk..ang.*

Iskate, or-*magad*. It is dry, there is no water, it dried up; p. *eskateg*, or-*magak.-Sipiwan iskatewan*, there is no water (or only a little water) in the rivers.

Iskidjiwan. It runs all out, (water or any other liquid, out of a vessel ;) p. *esk..ang.*

Iskigamide, or-*magad*. It is reducing, drying up, by boiling; p. *esk..deg*, or-*magak.*

Iskigamisan, (*nind*). I reduce it, by boiling ; p. *esk..ang.*

Iskigamisigan. Place where they are reducing maple-sap to sugar, by boiling ; sugar-camp; sugar-bush ; pl.-*an.*

Iskigamisige, (*nind*). I reduce, by boiling; I reduce maple-sap to sugar, by boiling, I am making maple-sugar; p. *esk,. ged.*

Iskigamisigékwe. A woman that makes maple-sugar; pl.-*g.*

Iskigamisigewin. Art, occupation or work of sugar-makers.

Iskinâk. Nit, egg of a louse; pl.-*wag.*

Iw. Pron. that; pl.-*iniw.*

Iwa. He says.

Iwapi, adv. Then, at that time.

Iwidi, or *iwedi*, adv. There ; thence ; yonder.

Iwidi nakakeia, adv. There, that way, in that direction.

J

Jâbobi, or-*magad*. The water goes or passes through s. th.; p. *jaiabobig*, or-*magak*.

Jâbode, (*nin*). I go or pass through; p. *jaiaboded*.

Jâbode, or-*magad*. It goes or passes through; p. *jaiabodeg*, or-*magak*.

Jâbogandina, (*nin*). I push or thrust through some obj.; p. *jaia..nad*.

Jâbogandinan, (*nin*). I push or thrust through, some obj.; p. *jaia..ang*.

Jâbogawitchigan. Straining vessel; pl.-*an*.

Jâbogawitchige, (*nin*). I am straining; p. *jaia..ged*.

Jâbogamiton, (*nin*). I strain it through a linen; p. *jaia..tod*.

Jâbokawis, (*nin*). I have the diarrhœa.

Jâbomin. Gooseberry; (F. groseille;) pl.-*ag*.

Jâbominagawanj. Gooseberry-bush; pl.-*ig*.

Jâbondean makakossag, (*nin*). I knock the head and the bottom of a barrel out; p. *jaia..ang*.

Jâbondeia, or-*maged*. It is knocked hollow, (a barrel, when both the head and the bottom are knocked out;) p. *jaia..ag*, or-*magak*.

Jâbondeiassin. There is a draught of the air; p. *jaia..ing*.

Jâbondeshka, (*nin*). I have the bloody flux; the dysentery; p. *jaia..kad*.

Jâbondeshkawin. Bloody flux; dysentery.

Jâbonenan, (*nin*). S. *Jabogândina*.

Jâbonigan. Needle; pl.-*an*.

Jâboniganike, (*nin*). I make needles; p. *jaia..ked*.

Jâboniganikewinini. Needle-manufacturer, needler; pl.-*wag*.

Jabopagwanean, (*nin*). I perforate it, I bore it through; p. *jaia..ang*.

Jâbopagwanêwa, (*nin*). I perforate or bore through some obj.; p. *jaia..wad*; imp. *ja..né*.

Jâbos, (*nin*). I purge myself, I take a purging medicine, a purgative; p. *jaiabosod*.

Jâbosaa, (*nin*). I sift it; p. *jaia..ad*.

Jâboshkam, (*nin*). I pass through s. th.; p. *jaia..ang*.

jâboshkassa, (*nin*). S. *Jabosaa*

Jâboshkatchigan. Sieve, cribble; pl.-*an*.

Jâboshkatchige. I am sifting, garbling; p. *jaia..ged*.

Jâboshkaton, (*nin*). I sift it; p *jaia..tod*.

Jâbosigan. Purge, purging medicine, purgative.
Jâbosse, (*nin*). I go or fall through s. th.; p. *jaia..bossed.*
Jâbosse, or-*magad.* It falls, or slides, through s. th.; p. *jaiabosseg,* or-*magak.*
Jâboswa, (*nin*). I give him a purging medicine, I purge him; p. *jai..wad;* imp. *jâboswi.*
Jâbwabandan, (*nin*). I see through it; I search it; p. *jaia..ang.* — *Debeniminang o jakwabandanan kideinânin;* the Lord searches our hearts, (he sees through them.)
Jâbwabawe, (*nin*). I am drenched all through, to the skin, (in a heavy rain;) p. *jaia..wed.*
Jâbwabawe, or-*magad.* It is drenched through, all wet; p. *jaia..weg,* or-*magak.*
Jâbwajigawitchigan. A filtering vessel, colander, strainer; pl.-*an.*
Jâbwajigawitoa, (*nin*). I strain it; p. *jaia..tod.*
Jâbwâkossidon, (*nin*). S. *Jâbogandinan.*
Jâbwenaogon, (*nin*). It pierces me through; p. *jaia..god.*
Jâbwenâwa, (*nin*). I pierce him through, I perforate him; p. *jaia..wad;* imp. *jabwenâ.*
Jâbwi, (*nin*). I pass or fall through s. th.; I escape; p. *jaiabwid.*
Jâbwia, (*nin*). I escape from him; p. *jai..ad.*
Jâbwiiwe, (*nin*). S. *Jabwi.*
Jâganâsh. Englishman, Irishman; pl.-*ag.*
Jâganâshi-anamia, (*nin*). I pray English, that is, I profess the English religion; p. *jaia..ad.*
Jâganâshi-anamiewin. The English religion.
Jâganâshikwe. English woman; Irish woman; pl.-*g.*
Jâganâshikwens. An English or Irish girl; pl.-*ag.*
Jâganâshim, (*nin*). I speak English; p. *jaia..mod.*
Jâganashimowin. The English language.
Jâganâshiwaki. England, Great Britain and Ireland.
Jagaski, (*nin*).. I stoop (going through a low door, etc.); p. *jeg..id.*
Jakaskkia, (*nin*). I make him stoop; p. *jeg..ad.*
Jagashkimin. A kind of flat raspberry; pl.-*ag.*
Jagashkita, (*nin*). I incline myself, I bow down; p. *jeg..tad.*
Jagashkitan, (*nin*). I bow down, or incline myself, before it, I salute it; p. *jeg..ang.*
Jagashkitawa, (*nin*). I bow down before him, I salute him; p. *jeg..wad.*
Jagawa, or-*magad.* It is oblong, longer than wide; p. *jaiagawag,* or-*magak.*
Jagawabigisi. It is oblong, (stuff); p. *jaia..sid.*
Jagawabigisi nabagissag. The board is oblong, longer than wide; p. *jaia..sid.*
Jagawabikad. It is oblong, (metal;) p. *jaia..kak.*
Jagawabikisi. It is oblong, (metal;) p. *jaia..sid.*
Jagawagwinde miniss. The island is oblong; p. *jaia..deg.*
Jagawamika, or-*magad.* There is a long shallow place in the lake, where the waves break,

(F. il y a une batture longue;) p. *jaia,.kag*, or-*magak*.
Jagawaton, (*nin*). I make it oblong; p. *jaia..tod.*
Jagawégad. It is oblong, (tuff;) p. *jaia..gak.*
Jagawid. Widow, widower; pl.-*jig.*—*Jagawid inini*, widower. *Jagawid ikwe*, widow.
Jagawigad. It is oblong, (wood;) p. *gaia..gak.*
Jagawikodan, (*nin*). I cut it oblong, with a knife; p. *jaia..ang.*
Jagawikodawa, (*nin*). I cut some object oblong, with a knife; p. *jaia..wad.*
Jagawissiton, (*nin*). S. *Jagawaton.*
Jagigamiwan. The ice on a lake or river breaks off, so that the water appears again; p. *jaia..ang.*
Jagodee, (*nin*). I am a coward, a poltroon, I am timid, timorous, fearful, pusillanimous; p. *jaia..ed.*
Jagodeewin. Cowardice, timidity, pusillanimity.
Jagodj, adv. In spite of....; against the will; (F. malgré.)
Jagodjia, (*nin*). I overcome him, vanquish him; p. *jaia..ad.*
Jagodjiiwe, (*nin*). I am victorious, I vanquish, surpass, overcome; p. *jaia..wed.*
Jagodjiiwe, or-*magad*. It overcomes, it is victorious; p. *jaia..weg*, or-*magak*.
Jagodjiton, (*nin*). I overcome it, I vanquish it; p. *jaia..tod.*
Jagos, (*nin*). I am flabby, weak; p. *jaiâgosid.*
Jagosama, (*nin*). I vanquish or overcome him in disputing, arguing, pleading; p. *jaia..mad.*
Jagosonge, (*nin*). I surpass or overcome in disputing, arguing, etc.; p. *jaia..géd.*
Jagwadad. It is weak; p. *jaia..dak.*
Jagwâdis, (*nin*). I am weak; p. *jaia..sid.*
Jagwagami. It is weak, (liquid;) p. *jaia..mig.*—*Jagwagami anibishâbo menikweiang;* the tea we are drinking is weak.
Jagwendan, (*nin*). I think it is weak; p. *jaia..ang.*
Jâgwenim, (*nin*). I dare not, I fear, I have not the courage to say or do s. th.; p. *jaia..mod.*
Jâgwenima, (*nin*). I think he is weak, (not stout and strong;) p. *jaia..mad.*
Jâgwenimoa, (*nin*). I discourage him, I make him fear; p. *jaia..ad;* imp. *jâgwenimo.*
Jâgwenimotagos, (*nin*). I ask excuse for not being able to do s. th., or, that I don't dare say or do s. th.; p. *jaia..sid.*
Jâgwenindis, (*nin*). I fear myself, I am afraid of my bad disposition; p. *jaia..sod.*
Jagwiton, (*nin*). I weaken it; p. *jaia..tod.*
Jagwiw, (*nin*). I am weak, (not stout and strong;) p. *jaia..wid.*
Jagwiwimagad. It is weak, impotent; p. *jaia..gak.*
Jaiagodeed. Coward, poltroon; pl.-*jig.*
Jaiaw, adv. *Ot.* S. *Gwaiak.*
Jaiaw-inadisiwin. Ot. S. *Gwaiakobimâdisiwin.*
Jaiaw nind inâdis. Ot. S. *Gwaiak nin bimadis.*

Jaie, or *jajaie*, adv. *Ot.* S. *Mêwija*.
Jaigwa, or *jaiegwa*, adv. Already.
Jajagoshkan, (*nin*). I crush it with my foot or body; p. *jaia ..ang*.
Jajagoshkawa, (*nin*). I crush some object with my foot or body; p. *jaia..wad*.
Jajashagaami, (*nin*). I walk with my toes turned outside; p. *jej..mid*.
Jajawêndjige, (*nin*), *freq*. I practise charity, I do often works of charity, I give alms, I am beneficent; p. *jej..ged*.
Jajawendjigewin. Habitual charity, alms-giving, beneficence.
Jajawênindimin, (*nin*), *freq*. S. *Jawênindimin*.
Jajibanam, (*nin*). I breathe by long intervals, with long pauses; p. *jej..mod*.
Jajibawassakweia, or-*magad*. A clearing, or clear place, is seen through the woods; p. *jej..iag*, or-*magak*.
Jajibendam, (*nin*). I am patient at work, persevering; p. *jej.. ang*.
Jajibendamowin. Patience, perseverance.
Jajibitam, (*nin*). I will not listen or obey; p. *jej..ang*.
Jakagonaga. The snow is soft or watery, (from thaw weather;) p. *jek..gag*.
Jakam, (*nin*) or, *sakkam*. I put in my mouth something eatable; p. *jekamod*.
Jakamon, (*nin*). I put it in my mouth to eat it; p. *jékamod*. —*Nin jakamon wiiâss*, I put meat in my mouth to eat it.
Jakamonan, (*nin*). I put some obj. in my mouth to eat it; p. *jekamod*. (V. Conj.)—*Pakwejigan nin jakamonan*, I put bread in my mouth to eat it.
Jakâmona, (*nin*). I put s. th. eatable in his mouth; p. *jek.. nad*. *Anamihesakamo*, he receives the holy communion.
Jakipo, or-*magad*. Soft watery snow is falling; p. *jaia..og*, or-*magak*.
Jang, abridged from *jangasswi*, nine.
Jangassimidana. Ninety.
Jangassimidanâk. Ninety hundred, (nine thousand.)
Jangassimidanakosimin, (*nin*). We are nine thousand in number; p. *jaia..sidjig*.
Jangassimidanakwadon. There are nine thousand.
Jangassimidanawemin, (*nin*). We are ninety in number; p. *jaia ..wedjig*.
Jangassimidanawewan. There are ninety objects.
Jangasso, num. nine, (before substantives denoting MEASURE of time or of other things.)
Jangasswewan. — *Nijobidonan*, etc., always changing in English, *two* into *nine*; as: *Nijobanënindj*, twice (or two times) a handful. *Jangassobanênindj*, nine times a handful.—*Nijôbidonan*, (*nin*). I tie two together. *Jangassobidonan*, (*nin*). I tie nine together. *Nijobina*, (*nin*). I caught two fishes; and so on respectively.
Jangasswi. Nine.
Jangatchimin, (*nin*). We are nine; p. *jangatchiwog*.

Jangatching. Nine times; the ninth time.

Jangatching midasswâk. Nine thousand.

Jangatchinon. There are nine obj.

Jangendjiged. He that hates, an enemy, fiend; pl.-*iig.*

Jangwéshe. Mink; (C. foutreau;) pl.-*wag.*

Jangweshens. A young mink; pl.-*ag.*

Jashabwabiginigade, or-*magad, freq.* It is twisted together of several threads; p. *jaia..deg,* or-*magak.*

Jashabwabiginigan. Cord, string or line of several threads; pl.-*an.*

Jashabwabiginige, (*nin*). I twist several threads together in one string or cord; p. *jaia..ged.*

Jâshagashkadekoman. A kind of crooked knife; pl.-*an.*

Jashâgawashkogissi. A kind of green frog; pl.-*g.*

Jashâgi. Storch; pl.-*wog.*

Jashagidjane, (*nin*). My nose is turned up; (F. j'ai le nez retroussé;) p. *jaia..ned.*

Jâshaginigade, (*nin*). I am bare-legged, I have no leggings on; p. *jaia..ded.*

Jâshâginindibe, (*nin*). I am bare-headed; p. *jaia..bed.*

Jâshâgininike, (*nin*). I am bare-armed, my arms are naked; p. *jaia..ked.*

Jâshâginindji, (*nin*). I have bare hands, I have no mittens nor gloves on; p. *jaia..djid.*

Jâshâginiside, (*nin*). I am bare-foot; p. *jaia..ded.*

Jâshâgita, (*nin*). I am bent backwards; p. *jaia..tad.*

Jâshâgodjaneshin, (*nin*). I hurt or bruise my nose by falling; p. *jaia..ing.*

Jâshâgondibéwa, (*nin*). I crush or bruise his head; p. *jaia.. wad;* imp. *ja..dibé.*

Jâshâgonindjiganandis, (*nin*). I hurt or bruise my finger or hand, (striking with a hammer, etc.); p. *jaia..sod.*

Jâshâgonindjishkos, (*nin*). My hand (or finger) is wounded or bruised by s. th. that fell upon it, or s. th. that catches my hand or finger; p. *jaia..sod.*

Jâshâgoshkos, (*nin*). I am crushed, hurt or bruised by s. th. that fell upon me; p. *jaia.. sod.*

Jâshogashkosowin. Bruise; (F. meurtrissure.)

Jâshagosideshkos, (*nin*) My foot is bruised by s. th. that fell upon it; p. *jaia..sod.*

Jâshagwabewis, (*nin*). I am emaciated, I have nothing but the skin and the bones; (F. je suis décharné;) p. *jaia..sid.*

Jâshagwama, (*nin*). I chew some obj.; p. *jaia..mad.—Assema nin jashagwama,* I chew tobacco.

Jâshagwamigiwe, (*nin*). I am chewing pitch; p. *jaia..wed.*

Jâshagwandan, (*nin*), (*jashagondan.*) I chew it; p. *jaia..ang.*

Jâshagwandjigan. Some object that is chewed, as *pigiw,* pitch; or *assema,* tobacco, quid.—Pl. *jâshagwandjiganag.*

Jâshagwandjige (*nin*),(*jashagon-*

djige.) I chew, I ruminate; p. *jaia..ged.*

Jâshawabashi mitig. The tree bends by the wind; p. *jaia..id.*

Jâshawabisse, or-*magad.* It bends; p. *jaia..seg,* or-*magak.*

Jâshawanibissi. Swallow, (bird;) pl.-*wag.*

Jâshaweia, or-*magad.* It is square; p. *jaia..iag,* or-*magak.*

Jashingâ. This word cannot be given in English with a corresponding word. It implies reproach and disapprobation. —*Gi ija na kishime anamiewigamigong gi-anamiegijigak ?* —*Jashingâ ta-ija.* Did thy brother go to church last Sunday? O no! he is very far from going there. *Abi na ki widîgemagan ?— Jashingâ taabi.* Is thy husband at home? —O no! he is almost never at home.

Jâshingningweidis, (*nin*). I bruise my face; p. *jaia..sod.*

Jâshingwingwéwa, (*nin*). I bruise his face; p. *jaia..wad;* imp. *ja-gwé.*

Jawagina, (*nin*). I bend a young tree or a rod growing; p. *jewaginad.*

Jawâginan, (*nin*). I bent it, (wood, standing; p. *jéw..ang.*

Jâwan. South; *jâwanong,* in the south, to the south, from the south.

Jâwanaamog (*animikig*). It thunders in the south.

Jâwanakwad. The clouds come from the south; p. *jaia..wak.*

Jawanibineshi. South-bird, bird coming from the south; pl.-*iag.*

Jâwanibissa. The rain comes from the south; p. *jaia..sag.*

Jâwaninodin. Southwind.

Jâwaninodin. The wind comes from the south; p. *jaia..ing.*

Jâwanong nakakeia. Towards the south.

Jawéndagos, (*nin*). I am happy, I am lucky, prosperous, fortunate; also, I take Holy Communion; p. *jew..sid.*

Jawéndagosiwin. Happiness, good luck, prosperity, chance, also, Holy Communion.

Jawéndamidee, (*nin*). I have a charitable heart; p. *jew..ed.*

Jawendamidee. Charitable disposition of mind, heart-felt charity.

Jawéndamiganawabama, (*nin*). I look upon him with mercy; p. *jew..mad.*

Jawendamitagos, (*nin*). I make a speech, a petition or a prayer, in order to excite pity and mercy upon me; p. *jew..sid.*

Jawéndamitawa, (*nin*). I hear him with pity and mercy, I grant his petition having pity on him; p. *jew..wad.*

Jawéndân, (*nin*). I have pity on it, I do charity to it, I benefit it; p. *jewêndang.*—*Wedapinang anamiewin o jawendan wiiaw;* he that takes religion, does charity to himself, (to his body, that is, to his own person.)

Jawéndjige, (*nin*). I have mercy or pity, I practise charity, I bestow a benefit; p. *jew..ged.*

Jawéndjigewin. Mercy, pity, charity, compassion, beneficence, benefit, grace, divine grace.

Jawênima, (*nin*). I have mercy or pity on him, I do him charity, I benefit him, I have compassion with him; p. *jew..mad.*

Jawênindis, (*nin*). I have pity on myself, I benefit myself; p. *jew..sod.*

Jégokinjena, (*nin*). I put some obj. in the fire; p. *jaiég..nad.*

Jégokinjenân, (*nin*). I put it in the fire; p. *jaie..ang.*

Jégona, (*nin*). I put or thrust it in; p. *jaiê..ad.*

Jégonan, (*nin*). I put or thrust it in; p. *jaiê..ang.*

Jêgonindjidjin, (*nin*). I thrust a splinter in my hand, (not purposely;) p. *jaié..ing.*

Jêgoshkanjidjin, (*nin*). I thrust a splinter under my nail, (accidentally;) p. *jaiég..ing.*

Jêgosidedjin, (*nin*). I thrust a splinter in my foot, (unpurposely;) p. *jaié..ing.*

Jêgossagwedjin, (*nin*). I thrust a thorn in some part of my body; p. *jaié..ing.*

Jegwakosidesse, (*nin*). I put my foot in an opening, my foot slide in; p. *jaié..sed.*

Jeiakonamawa, (*nin*). I open it to him; p. *jaieiak..wad.*

Jeiakossin. It is opened, there is an opening; p. *jaieiakossing.*

Jeiakossiton, (*nin*). I leave it open; I make an opening; p. *jaieiakossitod.*

Jéjawigadeshka, (*nin*). My feet and legs become flexible and warm again; (F. mes jambes se dégourdissent;) p. *jaiej.. kad.*

Jéjawishka, (*nin*). I become flexible and warm again; (F. je me dégourdis;) p. *jaeij.. kad.*

Jéjakwaam, (*nin*). I go to the woods on a trail; p. *jaiék.. ang.*

Jesus Krist. Jesus Christ.

Jesus od andjinagosiwin. The Transfiguration of Jesus Christ.

Jesus odijinikâsowin. The Name of Jesus.

Jesus o kikinoamaganan. A disciple (or the disciples) of Jesus Christ, an Apostle, or the Apostles.

Jêwabikaan biwâbik, (*nin*). I make sound a piece of iron; p. *jaiewabikaang.*

Jiba, in compositions, signifies *through* s. th.; *durable, persevering*. (Examples in some of the following words.)

Jiba, or-*magad*. There is a hole, a gap; p. *jabag*, or-*magak.*

Jibabigibidon, (*nin*). I extend, stretch, expand it, by pulling; p. *jab..dod.*

Jibabigibina, (*nin*). I extend or stretch out some obj. by pulling; p. *jab..nab.*

Jibabikissin. It is durable, (some obj. of metal;) p. *jab.. ing.*

Jibabishka, or-*magad*. It extends, it expands; p. *jab..kag*, or-*magak.*

Jibadaân, (*nin*). I expand it; p. *jab..ang.*

Jibadawa, (*nin*). I expand some obj. (*joniia*, silver;) p. *jab.. wad*; imp. *jibadâ.*

Jibadj, (*nin*). I can endure much cold; p. *jibadjid.*

Jibaiabama, (*nin*). I see him (or look at him) through a teles-

cope, (a person, or any other object;) p. *jab..mad.*
Jibaiabandan, (*nin*). I see it (or look at it) through a telescope or spy-glass; p. *jab..ang.*
Jibaiabandjigan. Spy-glass, telescope; pl.-*an.*
Jibaiabandjige, (*nin*). I am looking through a spy-glass; p. *jab..ged.*
Jibaii, adv. Through.
Jibajigas, (*nin*). I am pierced, stabbed through; p. *jab..sod.*
Jiban. It is tough; (F. c'est coriace;) p. *jabang.*
Jibanabawe, (*nin*). I can be a long time under water, I am a good diver; p. *jab..wed.*
Jibanam, (*nin*). I can be a long time without breathing, without taking respiration; p. *jab ..mod.*
Jibanâmos, (*nin*). I can endure much smoke; p. *jab..sod.*
Jibanandam, (*nin*). I can endure much starving, I can be a long time without eating; p. *jab..ang.*
Jibanikejigas, (*nin*). I have a pierced arm, my arm is pierced through; p. *jab..sod.*
Jibanindjijigas, (*nin*). My hand is pierced through; p. *jab.. sod.*
Jibanisidejigas, (*nin*). My foot is pierced through; p. *jab.. sod.*
Jibâtig. Passage or channel for canoes or boats, between islands; pl.-*on.*
Jibawasse, or-*magad.* S. *Jibawate.*
Jibawasséigad. It is thin, transparent, (gauze or other stuff; stuff;) p. *jab..gak.*
Jibawasséigin. Any transparent stuff or texture, as gauze, etc.; pl.-*on.*
Jibawâsso. It is transparent, (stuff;) p. *jab..sod.*
Jibawate, or-*magad.* It is transparent, thin, (stuff;) p. *jab.. teg,* or-*magak.*
Jibeia, or-*magad.* It is clear (in the woods,) there is no brushwood, no underwood; p. *jabeiag,* or-*magak.*
Jibendam, (*nin*). S. *Jajibendam.*
Jibendamowin. S. *Jajibendamowin.*
Jibi, (*nin*). I stretch myself; p. *jabid.*
Jibidenaniwen, (*nin*). I show the tongue; (F. je tire la langue;) p. *jab..nid.*
Jibigaden, (*nin*). I stretch out my leg or legs; p. *jab..nid.*
Jibigika, (*nin*). I am always yet vigorous in my old age; p. *jab..kad.*
Jibigissin. It is durable, (wood;) p. *jab..ing.*
Jibinawis, (*nin*). I am hardy, my bodily constitution is durable; p. *jab..sid.*
Jibingwash, (*nin*). I sleep softly, I am easy to be awakened; p. *jab..id.*
Jibinikegodjin, (*nin*). My arm is stretched and hanging down; p. *jab..ing.*
Jibiniken, (*nin*). I stretch out my arm; p. *jab..nid.*
Jibiniketawa, (*nin*). I stretch my arm out towards him; p. *jab..wad.*
Jibinindjin, (*nin*). I stretch out my hand, or my finger; p. *jab..nid.*
Jibishin, (*nin*). I am lying

stretched out; p. *jabishing.*
Jibisi. It is tough; p. *jâbisid.* —*Jibisi wawashkeshi;* the deer is tough, (the deer-meat.)
Jibissin. It is tough; it is durable; p. *jabissing.*
Jibitawagebina, (*nin*). I pull his ear; p. *jab..nad.*
Jiga. Widower, widow; pl.-*g.*
Jigaagami. It is thin, (liquid;) p. *jag..mig.*
Jigaakwa, or-*magad,* or, *jigaakweia,* or-*magad.* The wood or forest is clear, light-timbered; p. *jag..ag,* or-*magak.*
Jigaamiton, (*nin*). I make it thin, (liquid;) p. *jag..tod.*
Jigadânagidon, (*nin*). I am tired of telling the same thing so often; p. *jeg..ong.*
Jigadêndam, (*nin*). I am disgusted or tired of s. th.; p. *jeg..ang.*
Jigadéndamowin. Disgust, weariness.
Jigadendân, (*nin*). I am disgusted with it, tired of it; p. *jeg..ang.*
Jigadénima, (*nin*). I am disgusted with him, tired of him; p. *jeg..mad.*
Jigâdjibia, (*nin*). I am disgusted, or tired, of waiting for him; p. *jeg..ad.*
Jigâdjibiige, (*nin*). I am tired of writing; p. *jeg..ged.*
Jigâdosse, (*nin*). I am tired and disgusted of walking (so long or so much;) p. *jeg..sed.*
Jigâgawanj. Garlic; (F. ail; pl. -*ig.*—*Kitchijigagawanj,* onion.
Jigâgawanj meshkossiwid. Potherb.
Jigaw, (*nin*). I am a widower; I am a widow; p. *jagawid.*
Jigawiwin. Widowhood.
Jiginâwiss. Worm, (on or in the *ground;*) pl.-*ag.* (*Mosse,* worm in the *wood. Ogejagim,* worm in the *belly.*)
Jigingwâm, (*nin*). I piss in the bed during sleep; p. *jeg..ang.*
Jigiwin. Urine-bladder; pl.-*an.* —There is always a possessive pronoun connected with this word; *Nin jigiwin, ki jigiwin, o gigiwin;* my, thy, his bladder.
Jigiwinabo. Urine.
Jigiwinagan. Piss-pot, night-pot; pl.-*an.*
Jigibodjigan. Slab of a log sawn into boards; pl.-*ag.*
Jigoshigan. The carcass of an animal; pl.-*an.*
Jigoshin oma pijiki, etc., here is the carcass of an ox, etc.; p. *jegashing.*
Jigoshkadjigan. Husk of corn or wheat ground; pl.-*ag.*
Jigoshtigwaneshka, (*nin*). I crush his head; p. *jeg..kad.*
Jigosi gigo. The fish is soft, (too tender;) p. *jegosid.*
Jigosse, or-*magad.* There are dregs; p. *jagosseg,* or-*magak.*
Jigota ginebig. The serpent moults, he changes his skin; p. *jagotad.*
Jigwa, adv. S. *Jaigwa.*
Jigwakados, (*nin*). I have the consumption, I am hectic; p. *jag..sod.*
Jigwameg. Stockfish; pl.-*wag.*
Jigwanâbik. Grindstone; hone; pl.-*og.*
Jigwande min. The whortleberry (bilberry) is very ripe; p. *jeg..deg.*

Jigwanso miskwimin. The raspberry is very ripe; p. *jeg..sod.*
Jigwapingwane. The upper white part of ashes.—*Jigwapingwaneng nin apitendagos;* I am but ashes.
Jigwéiabama, (*nin*). I aim at him, (with a gun, etc.); p. *jeg..mad.*
Jigwêiabandan, (*nin*). I aim at it, (with a gun, etc.;) p. *jeg..ang.*
Jigwéiabandjige, (*nin*). I aim at; p. *jeg..ged.*
Jijibassagisowag nabagissagog. The boards shrink drying; p. *jej..sodjig.*
Jijobian, (*nin*). I rub it with s. th.; I rub s. th. on it; I paint it over; p. *jej..ang.*
Jijobiigan. Salve, or any thing that is rubbed on s. th.; also, paint; pl.-*an.*
Jijobiige, (*nin*). I am rubbing s. th. with s. th.; p. *jej..ged.*
Jijobiwa, (*nin*). I rub him with s. th., with a salve, etc.; p. *jej..wad;* imp. *jijobi.*
Jijodakwaam, (*nin*). I walk on the border of a forest; p. *jej..ang.*
Jijodéw, adv. Along the beach, along the lake-shore.
Jijodêwaam, (*nin*). I coast in a canoe or boat, (near the beach or shore); p. *jej..ang.*
Jijodéwe, (*nin*). I walk on the beach, on the lake-shore; p. *jej..wed.*
Jijoigaso pakwejigan. The bread is buttered; p. *jej..sod.*
Jijôkam, (*nin*). I tread into dirt, (human excrement;) p. *jej..ang.*
Jijôkiweân, (*nin*). I pitch it over (a canoe or boat;) p. *jej..ang.*
Jijokiweigan. Brush to pitch with, pitch-brush; pl.-*an.*
Jijokiweige, (*nin*). I am pitching over, (a canoe or boat;) p. *jej..ged.*
Jijowa pakwejigan, (*nin*). I butter bread; p. *jejowad.*
Jikâg. Polecat, fitchat, fitchew, (a stinking little beast;) pl.-*wag.*—From this word is derived the name of the City of Chicago.—*Jikagong,* at Chicago, to or from Chicago.
Jimâgan. Lance; pl.-*an.*
Jimâganish. Soldier; pl.-*ag.*
Jimâganishi-odena. A military fort; pl.-*wan.*
Jimâganishi-ogima. A military officer; pl.-*g.*
Jimâganishi-wâkaigan. Casern, (soldier's house;) pl.-*an.*
Jinawâakokwe. It sounds, (obj. of metal;) p. *jen..wed.*—*Kitchi jinaakokwe aw akik;* that kettle has a strong sound, (when struck.)
Jinawabikibidon, (*nin*). I make iron sound, (or other metal,) by moving it; p. *jen..dod.*
Jinawâbikibina, (*nin*). I make some obj. of metal sound, by moving it, as *joniia,* silver; p. *jen..nad.*
Jinawâbikishin. S. *Sangweweshin.*
Jinawabikisse, or-*magad.* S. *Sangwewe.*
Jinawaodjigan. Small globular bell; (F. grelot;) pl.-*an.*
Jinawaodjige, (*nin*). I produce a sound with some object of metal; p. *gen..ged.*
Jinawaodon, (*nin*). I make it sound, (metal;) p. *jen..dod.*

Jinawe. Rattle-snake; pl.-*g.* S. *Jishigwe.*

Jinawe, or-*magad.* It rattles; p. *jenaweg,* or-*magak.*

Jinawisse, or-*magad.* It rolls round, (inside of some hollow object,) it rattles inside; p. *jen..seg,* or-*magak.*

Jinawîwebinan, (*nin*). I make it rattle in something; p. *jen.. ang.*

Jindâgan. Sickness, pestilence.

Jîngademikwan. A kind of turtle; pl.-*ag.*

Jingadenan, (*nin*). I spread it out, strew it; p. *jan..ang.*

Jingadena, (*nin*). I spread out or strew some obj.; p. *jang.. nad.—Opinig nin wi-jingadenag oma, tchi bassowad;* I will spread out here potatoes, that they may dry.

Jingadenige, (*nin*). I spread out, strew; p. *jan..ged.*

Jingadeshin. Some object lies spread out or strewed; p. *jan ..ing.—Joniia jingadeshin adopowining,* money is spread out on the table.

Jingadeshkine, or-*magad.* A little of s. th. is spread on the bottom of a vessel; p. *jan.. neg,* or-*magak.*

Jingadessin. It lies spread out or strewed; p. *jan..ing.*

Jingadewebaan, (*nin*). I spread it, I strew it; p. *jang..ang.—Pijikimo nin jingadewebaan kitiganing;* I strew oxen dung over the field.

Jingakamiga, or-*magad.* There is a level country, even ground, no hills; p. *jen..gag,* or-*magak.*

Jingendagos, (*nin*). I am hateful, odious, abominable; disagreeable, unpleasant; p. *jaw ..sid.*

Jingendagosiwin. The state of being hateful, abominable.

Jingendagwad. It is hateful, abominable, odious; it is disagreeable, unpleasant; p. *jan ..wak.*

Jingendamawa, (*nin*). I hate s. th. belonging or relating to him; p. *jan..wad.* — *Kawin win nin jingenimassi od ijiwebisiwin eta nin jingendamawa;* I don't hate him, I only hate his conduct.

Jingendamowin. Hatred, (towards some object.)

Jingendan, (*nin*). I hate it, I detest it; p. *jan..ang.*

Jingendjige, (*nin*). I hate, I am enemy, adversary; p. *jan..ged.*

Jingendjigeshk, (*nin*). I am in a habit of hating, of bearing hatred in my heart; p. *jan.. kid.*

Jingendjigeshkiwin. The bad habit of hating, habitual hatred.

Jingendjigewin. Hatred, (towards people,) enmity, antipathy.

Jingenima, (*nin*). I hate him, I detest him, (a person, or any other obj.); p. *jan..mad.*

Jingenindimin, (*nin*). We hate each other; p. *jan..didjig.*

Jingenindis, (*nin*). I hate myself; p. *jan..sod.*

Jingenindiwin. Mutual hatred; hatred of several persons.

Jingibiss. A kind of wild duck; (C. poule d'eau;) also, a kind of inflammation, called a whitlow; pl.-*ag.*

Jingimâma, (*nin*). I hate the smell of some obj.; p. *jan..mad.—Ninjingimama assema; o jingimaman gigoian.* I hate the smell of tobacco; he hates the smell of fish.

Jingimandan, (*nin*). I hate the smell of some obj.; p. *jan..ang.—Ki jingimandan na gigô-bimide?* Dost thou hate the smell of fish-oil?

Jinginike, (*nin*). I stretch out my arms; also, my arms hang down; p. *jen..ked.*

Jinainikeb, (*nin*). I am sitting with down hanging arms; p. *jen..bid.*

Jinginikeosse, (*nin*). I walk with down hanging arms; p. *jen..sed.*

Jingishima, (*nin*). I lay or put him down, (a person, or any other object;) p. *jen..mad.*

Jingishin, (*nin*). I am lying down; p. *jen..ing.*

Jingishinomagad. It is lying there; p. *jen..gak.*

Jingitagos, (*nin*). I am disagreeable in my speaking, they don't like to hear me, my speaking is hated; p. *jan..sid.*

Jingitagwad. It sounds disagreeable, the sound of it is hated; p. *jan..wak.*

Jingitan, (*nin*). I hate to hear it; I don't like the sound of it; p. *jangitang.*

Jingitawa, (*nin*). I don't like to hear him, I hate his speaking; p. *jan..wad.*

Jingob. Any kind of fir-tree; pl.-*ig.*

Jingobabo. Beer made of fir-branches, spruce-beer. *Kitchi jingobabo*, beer.

Jingobakon. Branch of the fir-tree; pl.-*ag.*

Jingobigan. Shelter or hut made of fir-branches or boughs; pl.-*an.*

Jingobige, (*nin*). I am making a shelter or hut of fir-boughs; also, I am under such a shelter; p. *jen..ged.*

Jingobi-gijigad. Palm-Sunday; (F. Dimanche des Rameaux.)

Jingobins. Little fir-branch or cedar-branch; pl.-*ag.*

Jingoss. Weasel; pl.-*ag.*

Jingwak. Pine, pine-tree; pl.-*wag.*

Jingwakoki. Pinery, pine-forest; pl.-*wan.*

Jingwakons. A young pine-tree; pl.-*ag.*

Jinodagan. Line on the under and upper border of a fish-net; (C. maître de rêts;) pl.-*an.*

Jipingwande, or-*magad.* It is dyed ash-colored, it is ash-colored; p. *jap..eg*, or-*magak.*

Jipingwadissan, (*nin*) or, *nin jipingwansan.* I dye it ash-colored; p. *jap..ang.*

Jipingwadisso, or *jipingwasso.* It is dyed ash-colored, it is ash-colored, (obj.); p. *jap..sod.*

Jipingwadisswa, (*nin*) or *nin jipingwanswa.* I dye it ash-colored; p. *jap..wad*; imp. *jip..wi.*

Jipingwasige, (*nin*). I dye ash-colored; p. *jap..ged.*

Jipingwégad. It is ash-colored, (stuff;) p. *jap..gak.*

Jipingwingwe, (*nin*). I have

ashes on my face; p. *jap..wed.*

Jishanashkibidon, (*nin*). I pluck it out, (herb, plant;) p. *jash.. dod.*

Jishib. Duck; pl.-*ag.*

Jishibakik. Tea-pot; pl.-*og.*

Jishibanagidjiigan. Ramrod, battering rod; pl.-*an.*

Jishibanwi. One grain of shot; pl.-*n.*

Jshibanwins. One grain of small shot; pl.-*an.*

Jishibidonen, (*nin*). I stretch out the lips; p. *jash..nid.*

Jishibigibidon, (*nin*). I expand or stretch it out in every direction; p. *jash..dod.*

Jishibigibina, (*nin*). I extend or stretch some obj. in every direction; p. *jash..nad;* imp. *jish..bij.*

Jishig, (*nin*). I piss, I urine, I make water; p. *jashigid.*

Jishigaâkwaigade, or-*magad.* It is clear, or cleared, (in the woods;) p. *jash..deg*, or-*magak.*

Jishigaanikwe, (*nin*). I am half bald; p. *jash..wed.*

Jishidagowan. The matter vomited; (L. vomitus.)

Jishigagowe, (*nin*). I vomit, I retch, puke; p. *jash..wed.*

Jishigagowea, (*nin*). I make him vomit, I give him a vomitive, an emetic medicine; p. *jash..ad.*

Jishigagowesigan. Vomitive, emetic medicine.

Jishigagoweswa, (*nin*). S. *Jishigagowea.*

Jishigagowewin. Vomition, vomiting.

Jishigimewanj. Soft maple; (C. plaine;) pl.-*in.*

Jishigonindjama, (*nin*). I crush some object in my hand; p. *jesh..mad.*

Jishigonindjandan, (*nin*). I crush it in my hand; p. *jesh.. ang.*

Jishigosidama, (*nin*). I crush it with my foot; p. *jesh..mad.*

Jishigosidandan, (*nin*). I crush it with my foot; p. *jesh..ang.*

Jishigwama, (*nin*). I gnaw some obj.; p. *jesh..mad.*

Jishigwan. A gourd-bottle with some shot in, used by pagan Indians to rattle with at their Grand Medicine ceremonies. Pl.-*an.*

Jishigwandan, (*nin*). I gnaw it; p. *jesh..ang.*

Jishigwe. Rattle-snake; pl.-*g.*

Jiwa, or-*magad.* It is sour, acid; p. *jawag*, or-*magak.*

Jiwab, (*nin*). I have a pearl on my eye; p. *jewabid.*

Jiwâbik. Alum.

Jiwâbo. Vinegar, (sour liquid.)

Jiwâgamisigan. Maple-sirop. *Kitchi jiwâgamisigan.* Molasses.

Jiwan. It is sour; it is salted; p. *jawang.*

Jiwas, (*nin*). S. *Pashagishkinam.*

Jiwibag. Sorrel.

Jiwisi. It is sour; p. *jawisid.*— *Jaigwa gi-jiwisi pakwejigan;* the flour got sour.

Jiwisia, (*nin*) or *nin jiwishima* I make sour some obj.; p. *jaw..ad.*

Jiwissitchigan. S. *Ombissitchigan.*

Jiwissitchige, (*nin*). I make sour s. th.; p. *jaw..ged.*

Jiwissiton, (*nin*). I make it sour; p. *jaw..tod.*
Jiwitâgan. Salt.
Jiwitâganaamage, (*nin*). I salt for people; p. *jaw..ged.*
Jiwitaganaamawa, (*nin*). I salt for him; p. *jaw..wad.—Jaigwa nibiwa nin jiwitaganaamawa gigoian;* I have already salted many fishes for him.
Jiwitagaan, (*nin*). I salt it, I pickle it; p. *jaw..ang.*
Jiwitâganâbo. Saltwater, brine; pickle; (F. saumure.)
Jiwitaganaigade, or-*magad.* It is salted, pickled; p. *jaw..deg*, or-*magak.*
Jiwitaganaigaso. He, (she, it) is salted, (any obj.;) p. *jaw..sod.*
Jiwitaganaige, (*nin*). I am salting, I salt; p. *jaw..ged.*
Jiwitaganaigewin. Salting; (F. salaison.)
Jiwitaganawa, (*nin*). I salt or pickle some obj.; p. *jaw..wad.*
Jiwitagani-gigo. Salt-fish, salted fish; pl.-*iag.*
Jiwitagani-kitchigami. Ocean, sea.
Jiwitaganipogosi. It tastes salted; p. *jaw..sid.*
Jiwitaganipogwad. It tastes salted; p. *jaw..wak.*
Jiwitâganiwan. It is salted; p. *jaw..ang.*
Jiwitâganiwi. It is salted; p. *jaw..wid.*
Jiwitagani-wiiâss. Salt-meat, salted meat.
Jiwitawa, (*nin*). S. *Jiwisia.*
Jiwiton, (*nin*). S. *Jiwissiton.*
Jobia, (*nin*). I tempt him, I attract him; p. *jwabiad.*
Jobiton, (*nin*). I tempt or attract it; p. *jwabitod.—Ki jobiton niiaw*, thou temptest me
Jobiige, (*nin*). I tempt; p. *jwa..ged.*
Jobiigewin. Temptation, the act of tempting, of attracting.
Jobiigon. It tempts me; p. *jwa..god.*
Jobiigowin. The object that tempts; pl.-*an.*
Jâgamamagad. It is liquid, in a liquid state; p. *jwa..gak.*
Jogamia pigiw, (*nin*). I make pitch liquid; p. *jwa..ad.*
Jogamisi pigiw. The pitch is in a liquid state; p. *jwa..sid.*
Jogamitchigade, or-*magad.* It is reduced or brought to a liquid state, (some obj.); p. *jwa..deg*, or-*magak.*
Jogamiton, (*nin*). I make it liquid; p. *jwa..tod.*
Joganâm, (*nin*). I breathe deeply, (by surprise and astonishment, or from fatigue by walking or working;) p. *jwa..mod.*
Jojakwad. It is slippery, (on the ice, or on a frozen road;) p. *jwajakwak.*
Jokamagad. It whizzes through the air; p. *jwa..gak.*
Jomânike. Copper-cent; pl..*g.*
Jomin. Grape, raisin; pl.-*an.*
Jominâbo. Wine.
Jominabokan. Place where they make wine; press-house; pl.-*an.*
Jominaboke, (*nin*). I make wine, I produce wine; p. *jwam..ked.*
Jominabokewin. The work necessary to make or produce wine, production of wine.
Jominabokewinini. Vintner, producer of wine, vine-dresser, wine-presser; pl.-*wag.*

Jominagawang. S. *Jominâtig*.
Jominâtig. Vine; pl.-*on*.
Jomingwen, (*nin*) or, *nin jojomingwen*, *freq*. I have a smiling joyous countenance; p. *jwa..nid*.
Jomingwetawa (*nin*) or *nin jojomingwetawa*, *freq*. I show him a joyous smiling countenance, I smile friendly in looking at him; p. *jwa..wad*.
Jominibag. Vine-leave; pl.-*on*.
Jomini-kitigan. Vineyard; pl.-*an*.
Jomiwadis, (*nin*) or *nin jojomiwadis*, *freq*. I am joyous, joyful, gay; p. *jwa..sid*.
Jomiwadisiwin. Joy, gaiety, merriment.
Joniia. Silver; money.
Joniikadan, (*nin*). I silver it, I plate it; p. *jwan..ang*.
Joniiakade, or-*magad*. It is silvered, plated; ornamented with silver; p. *jwan..deg*, or-*magak*.
Joniiake, (*nin*). I work in silver, I manufacture silver ware, I am a silver-smith; p. *jwa..ked*.
Joniiakewin. Manufacturing silver ware, occupation and trade of a silver-smith.
Joniiakewinini. Silver-smith; pl.-*wag*.
Joniiâ-makak. Money-box, save; pl.-*on*.
Joniia-mashkimodens. Purse; pl.-*an*.
Joniiag. Silver-money; pieces of silver.
Joniians. Shilling; pl.-*ag*.
Joniiawessimig. Breast-plate of silver, (Indian ornament;) pl.-*og*.
Jonjo. French dok; pl.-*g*. Dim. *jonjons*.
Jonjowassin; pl.-*og*. S. *Jonjo*.
Joshkogaan,* (*nin*). I polish it, (wood), I make it smooth; p. *jwa..ang*.
Joshkogawa, (*nin*). I polish or smooth some obj.; p. *jwa..wad*.
Joshkonigan. S. *Ganninigan*.
Joshkonige, (*nin*). S. *Gandinige*.
Joshkotchigade, or-*magad*. It is polished, made smooth; p. *jwa..deg*, or-*magak*.
Joshkotchigan. Smoothing plane; pl.-*an*.
Joshkotchigans. Small plane; (F. rabot;) pl.-*an*.
Joshkotchige, (*nin*). I plane, I polish, I smooth; p. *jwash..ged*.
Joshkwa, or -*magad*. It is smooth, polished, even; it is slippery; p. *jwashkwag*, or-*magak*.
Joshkwâbiganaigan. Trowel; (F. truelle;) pl.-*an*.
Joshkwâbiganaige, (*nin*). I plaster with a trowel; p. *jwa..ged*.
Joshkwabikaan, (*nin*). I polish or smooth it, (metal); p. *jwa..ang*.
Joshkwabikawa, (*nin*). I polish or smooth some obj. of metal or stone; p. *jwa..wad*.
Joshkwadaagan. Skate; pl.-*an*.
Joshkwadae, (*nin*). I skate; p. *jwa..ed*.
Joshkwadjiwe, (*nin*). I descend

---

* NOTE. The two first syllables in this and the following seven words, could also be written *joshkwa*.... But they are rather pronounced *joshka*...; and therefore we write them so.

a hill sliding, I slide downhill; p. *jwash..wed.*

Joshkwaigaigade, or-*magad.* It is ironed with a smoothing iron; p.*jwash..deg*, or-*magak.*

Joshkwaigaigan. Smoothing iron, flat iron; pl.-*an.*

Joshkwaigaige, (*nin*). I flatten, iron; p. *jwa..ged.*

Joshkwanabika, or-*magad.* There is a flat smooth broad rock; p. *jwash..kag*, or-*magak.*

Joshkwaton, (*nin*). I make it smooth; p. *jwa..tod.*

Joshkwégaan, (*nin*). I iron it; p. *jwa..ang.*

Joshkwêgawa, (*nin*). I iron some obj. (*seniba*, silk, ribbon;) p. *jwa..wad*; imp. *joshkwega.*

Joshowabide, (*nin*). My teeth are set on edge; (F. j'ai les dents agacées;) p. *jwash..ded.*

Jotégané, (*nin*). I feel a weakness in my bones; p. *jwa..ned.*

Jotêganeosse, (*nin*). I can scarcely walk, I am weak, fatigued; p. *jwa..sed.*

Jowendam, (*nin*). I am merry, joyous, being half drunk; p. *jwawendang.*

Jowendamowin. Gaiety or joyfulness in half drunkenness.

Jowibi, (*nin*). I am half drunk, I am tipsy; p. *jwawibid.*

Jowibiwin. Half drunkenness.

Judawikwe. Jewess; pl.-*g.*

Judawinini. Jew; pl.-*wag.*

Judéing. Judea, or in Judea, from or to Judea.

K

Some words which are not found under K, *may be looked for under* G.

Ka, adv. No, not.

Ka awiia. Nobody, or nothing, no, none, (speaking of obj.)—*Ka awiia joniia nind aiawassi;* I have no money.

Ka gego. Nothing, no, none, (speaking of *in.* obj.)—*Ka gego missan, ki ga-gawadjimin;* there is no wood, we will freeze

Ka mashi. Not yet.

Ka ningotchi. No where.

Ka wika. Never.

Kabê–, This word is only used in compositions, and signifies *all, the whole;* as: *Kabé-bibon,* all winter ; *kabê-nibin,* all summer; *kabe-gijig,* all day ; *kabé-tibik,* all night.

Kabêaii, adv. Long, a long time.

Kabégîjiganam, (*nin*). I outlive yet this day, (sick dying person;) p. *keb..mid.*

Kabeshkan, (*nin*). I go to the end of it, (a period of time;) p. *keb..ang.*

Kabêsse, or-*magad*. The time arrives ; p. *kebesseg*, or-*magak*.—*Nishwassogwan ga-kabesseg...* ; when the eighth day was arrived...

Kabétibikanam, (*nin*). I outlive yet this night, (a sick dying person;) p. *keb..mid.*

Kabétibikwe, (*nin*). I spend the whole night in... ; p. *keb..web.*

Kabik, in compositions, signifies *passing, coming by.* (Examples in some of the following words.)

Kabikagon, (*nin*). It goes by me, it passes me ; p. *keb..god.*

Kabikan, (*nin*). I pass it, I go farther; p. *kebikang.*

Kabikawa, (*nin*). I pass him, I go farther than he is; p. *keb.. wad.*

Kabikosse, or-*magad*. It passes; p. *keb..seg*, or-*magak*. It passes noon, (it is more than twelve o'clock,) *kabikosse nawakwe, kabikonawakwe.*

Kâd, leg. This word is always connected with a possessive pronoun ; as: *Nikâd*, my leg. *Okâdan*, his legs.—The *k* is softened into *g* in compositions; as : *Niogâde*, he has four legs. *Nin dewigâde*, I have pain in my leg. *Gi-bokogâdeshin*, he broke his leg, etc.

Kâdadjim, (*nin*). I don't tell all of it, I conceal some in my report; p. *kaia..mod.*

Kâdadjimotawa, (*nin*). I don't tell him the whole of it, I make him an incomplete report; p. *kaia..wad.*

Kâdadjimowin. Incomplete report, where some circumstances are not told ; pl.-*an*.

Kâdawa, (*nin*). or nin *kâdamawa*. I hide or conceal it to him, I hide s. th. belonging or relating to him ; I don't tell or declare him s. th. ; p. *kaiâdawad*.

Kâdjigade, or-*magad*. It is hidden, concealed, secret ; p. *kaia ..deg*, or-*magak*.

Kâdon, (*nin*). I hide it, conceal it, I keep it secret ; p. *kaiâdod*.

Kâg. Porcupine, (a kind of large hedge-hog ;) pl. *kâgwag*.—The *k* of this word is softened into *g*, in compositions ; as : *Wâbigâg*, a white porcupine.—Dim. *kâgons*, a young porcupine ; pl.-*ag*.

Kagabâdis, (*nin*). I am very large ; p. *keg..sid*.

Kagabâdjibina. I catch a very large fish in my net ; p. *keg.. nad*.

Kagâgi. Raven ; (F. corbeau ;) pl.-*wog*.

Kagâgi. Uvula ; (F. luette.) There is always a possessive pronoun prefixed to this word ; as : *Nin kagagim*, my uvula ; *ki kagagim*, thy uvula, etc. (The final *m* is the possessive termination. S. Otch. Gram. Chap. II. Possess. Term.)

Kâgâgishib. Raven-duck ; cormorant, (bird ;) pl.-*ag*.

Kagagiwanj. Hemlock ; (F. pruche ;) pl.-*ig*.

Kagagiwanjiki. Hemlock forest ; pl.-*wan*.

Kagagiwanjiwâbo. Hemlock-tea, (tea made by boiling little branches of hemlock in water.)

Kagagiwikoj. Raven's beak. (The Indians call so a kind of small iron lamp.) Pl.-*in*.

Kagétin, adv. S. *Enigok*.

Kâgige, adj. Perpetual, everlasting, eternal. This word is never used alone, it is always connected with a substantive or verb. (Examples in some of the following words.)

Kagige badadjiidisowin. Eternal damnation.

Kagige bimâdisiwin. Life everlasting, eternity.

Kagige jawendagosiwin. Eternal salvation.

Kagigékamig, adv. Perpetually, eternally, for ever and ever.

Kâgini, adj. and adv. *Ot.* S. *Kagige*. *Kaginig*.

Kâginig, adv. Always, continually, eternally.

Kâgobiwai. Porcupine-quill, (used by Indians for embroidering after the Indian fashion ;) pl.-*an*.

Kâgwadjiw. Porcupine Mountain.

Kâgwaiân. The skin of a porcupine ; pl.-*ag*.

Kaiagigê-bimadisid. The Eternal.

Kaiadjigateg. A hidden thing, secret, mystery ; pl.-*in*.

Kaiâkamis, (*nin*). S. *Kakamine*

Kaiâkamisiwin. *Kakâminewin*.

Kaka, or *kakash*. They say this word to children, to express that s. th. is bad or dirty.

Kakabika. There is a cascade, a cataract, a waterfall over a steep rock ; p. *kek..kag*.

Kakâbikang. In a place where there is a waterfall; at, to or from such a place.

Kakabikawan. S. *Kakabika.*

Kakâbikedjiwan. There is a strong rapid in a river over rocks, or a little cascade; p. *kek..ang.*

Kakâbishé. Screech-owl, (an owl whose voice is supposed by Indians to foretell misfortune or death;) pl.-*iag.*

Kakakâmagad. It is square; p. *kek..gak.*

Kakakigad. It is square, (stuff;) p. *kek..gak.*

Kakakigisi moshwe. The handkerchief is square; p. *kek..sid.*

Kakâm, adv. Sudden, short, shortening the way.

Kakamaam, (*nin*). I shorten my way, I go by the short way, (traveling in a canoe or boat;) p. *kek..ang.*

Kakamibato, (*nin*). I run by the short way; p. *kek..tod.*

Kakâmine, (*nin*). I die suddenly, or, I die after a short illness; p. *kek..ned.*

Kakâminewin. Sudden death, or, death after a short illness.

Kakâmishka, (*nin*). I take the short way; p. *kek..kad.*

Kakâm nind ija. S. *Kakamishka.*

Kakamwikwedweam, (*nin*). I go (by water) from one point straight to another, shortening my way; p. *kek..ang.*

Kakâwendjigan. Cartilage gristle.

Kâkigan. Breast. There is always a possessive pronoun prefixed to this word; as: *Nin kakigan,* my breast; *ki kakigan, o kakigan,* thy breast, his breast, etc.

Kakina, adv. and adj. All, the whole, all of it, entirely.

Kakina gego daiebwetang. He that believes all, a credulous person; pl.-*ig.*

Kakina ketchitwawendagosidjig gijigong ebidjig o gijigadomiwa. All Saints day; (F. la Toussaint.)

Kakis, (*nin*). *Ot.* S. *Kas.*

Kakitchishkabiden, (*nin*). I gnash, I grind or collide the teeth; p. *kek..nid.*

Kakiwe, (*nin*). I traverse or cross a point of land on foot; p. *kekiwed.*

Kakiweonan. A place where they traverse a point of land.

Kamig, kamiga. At the end of words, alludes to the *ground;* as: *Anamakamig,* under ground; *onakâmiga,* there is a level ground; *anibekamiga,* there is a rising ground, etc.

Kan. As end-syllable in compound words, signifies *bone.* This word is always connected with a possessive pronoun; as: *Nikan, kikan, okan, nikanan;* my bone, thy bone, his bone, my bones, etc. In composition, the *k* is changed into *g;* as: *Makôgan,* bear's bone; *amikogan,* beaver's bone; *nin jotêgan,* I feel weak in my bones.

Kâna, (*nin*). I hide him, con ceal him, (a person, or any other obj.); p. *kaiânad.*

Kanj, or *shkanj.* As end-syllable in some compound words, alludes to a *nail* of a person, (on hand or foot,) to a *hoof* of an animal or bird. But the *k* of *kanj* is softened into *g* in compositions ; as : *Makoganj*, bear's claw. *Bebejigoganji*, one-hoofed animal, horse.

Kâpadad. S. *Kâpan*.

Kâpadis. S. *Kapisi*.

Kâpan. It is inflexible, it is brittle, it cannot be bent, it breaks when bent; p. *kaiâpang*.

Kâpisi. It is inflexible, brittle, it cannot be bent; p. *kaia..sid*.

Kas, (*nin*). I am hidden, concealed ; (L. lateo ;) also, I hide myself, I abscond ; p. *kaiâsod*.

Kâs. As end-syllable in some verbs, signifies *dissimulation, feigning ;* as: *Nind anamiekâs*, I feign religion and piety. *Nind âkosikas*, I dissemble sickness.

Kashkabiginamas, (*nin*). I choke or suffocate myself with a rope ; p. *kesh..sod*.

Kashkabiginamawa, (*nin*). I choke him with a rope or cord ; p. *kesh..wad*.

Kashkâbikan, (*nin*). I lock it ; p. *kesh..ang*.

Kashkâbikaigake, or-*magad*. It is locked; p. *kesh..deg*, or-*magak*.

Kashkâbikaigan. Lock ; pl.-*an*.

Kashkâbikaigan békominagak. Padlock, (round lock ;) pl. *kash..nan bek..kin*.

Kashkâbikaiganike, (*nin*). I manufacture locks, I am a locksmith ; p. *kesh..ked*.

Kashkabikaiganikewin. Work, trade, occupation of a locksmith, lock-manufacture.

Kashkâbikaiganikewinini. Locksmith, lock-manufacturer ; pl. *wag*.

Kashkâkide, or-*magad*. It burns all up, it is consumed by fire ; p. *kesh..deg*, or-*magak*.

Kashkâkiganeodis, (*nin*). I cover my breast ; p. *kesh..sod*.

Kashkâkiganeon. Breast-pin ; pl.-*an*.

Kashkâkos, (*nin*). I burn up, I am consumed by fire ; p. *kesh ..sod*.

Kashkamakodoneshka, (*nin*). My mouth is stopped ; p. *kesh.. kad*.

Kashkaodjinikeb, (*nin*). I have my hands under my arms, (I keep the hands under the armpits;) p. *kesh..bid*.

Kashkendagwad. It is sad, afflicting, grievous, sorrowful, melancholic, lonesome ; p. *kesh..wak*.

Kashkendagwakamig, adj. Sad, sorrowful.

Kashkêndam, (*nin*). I am sad, melancholy, afflicted, sorrowful, dejected, grieved ; I am homesick, I feel lonesome ; p. *kesh..ang*.

Kashkêndamia, (*nin*). I make him sad, afflicted, I give or cause him sorrow, trouble, affliction ; I hurt his feelings ; p. *kesh..ad*.

Kashkéndamidee, (*nin*). My heart is afflicted, sad, grieved, I am sad from my heart ; p. *kesh..ed*.

Kashkendamideewin. Hearty sorrow, sorrow of the heart.

Kashkéndamitân, (*nin*). I hear it with sorrow, with sadness ; p. *kesh..ang*.

Kashkéndamitawa, (*nin*). I hear him, or listen to him, with sorrow, with sadness; p. *kesh ..wâd.*

Kashkendamowin. Sorrow, sadness, affliction, melancholy, trouble, home-sickness.

Kashkibide, or-*magad.* It is tied up in s. th.; p. *kesh..deg,* or-*magak.*

Kashkibidjigan (*kaskipitâgan.*) Any object tied up in s. th.; especially an Indian medicine tied up in a little rag or piece of leather; pl.-*an.*

Kashkibidon, (*nin*). I tie it up in a handkerchief, etc.; p. *kesh..dod.*

Kashkibina, (*nin*). I tie up some obj. in s. th.; p. *kesh..nad.*

Kashkibis, (*nin*). I am tied up in s. th.; p. *kesh..sod.*

Kashkidassebison. Garter; pl.-*an.*

Kashkikanokan. The threshold of a door; pl.-*an.*

Kashkitibikad. It is dark, darkness; p. *kesh..kak.*

Kashkiwegina, (*nin*). I wrap him up in s. th., I swath him up; p. *kesh..nad;* imp. *kash.. gin.*

Kashkiweginan, (*nin*). I wrap it up in s. th., I envelop it; p. *kesh..ang.*

Kashkiweginigan. A sheet or piece of stuff, to wrap s. th. in it; pl.-*an.*

Kâsoidis, (*nin*). I hide or conceal myself; p. *kaia..sod.*

Kâsôtagon, (*nin*). It is hidden to me; (L. latet me;) p. *kaia ..god.*

Kâsôtawa, (*nin*). I hide myself before him; p. *kaia..wad.*

Kâtchim, (*nin*). I cry, I weep; p. *kaiâtchimod.*

Kâtchimoshk, (*nin*). I cry or weep always; p. *kaia..kid.*

Kateshim. Catechism.

Katigwan. Forehead, brow. This word is always preceded by a possessive pronoun; as: *Nin katigwan, ki katigwan, o katigwan ;* my forehead, thy forehead, his forehead.

Katolik, adj. Catholic.

Katolik anamiëwin. Catholic religion.

Katolik anamiad. Catholic Christian; pl.-*jig.*

Kawândag. White spruce; pl.-*og.*

Kawéssa, adv. No, not at all, that won't do.

Kâwin, adv. S. *Ka.*

Kâwin awiia. Kawin gego, etc. S. *Ka awiia. Ka gego,* etc.

Kâwin awiia endashiwad. Neither of them.

Kâwin bâpish, adv. Not at all, by no means.

Kâwin ganagê, adv. Not in the least, not even.

Kâwin nind abissi. I am absent.

Kâwin nind agatchissi. I am shameless, impudent.

Kâwen nin gijendansi. I am undecided, unprepared.

Kâwin ningot, adv. Nothing, not any.

Kâwin nin minwendansi. I am dissatisfied, discontented.

Kâwin nin sagakamisissi. I am negligent, I am careless.

Kegijêbawagakin. In the morning; *dassing kegijebawagakin.* Every morning.

Kégo, adv. Expression of prohibition, don't; (L. noli,) or,

something, *kego nin wâbandân*, I see something; *kâwin kego*, nothing.
Keiâbi, adv. Yet. *Kawin keiabi*, no more.
Kêjidin, *kekêjidin*, *kekêjidine*, adv. Quick, quickly, immediately.
Kékek. Sparrow-hawk; pl.-*wag*.
Kekendansig gego. Ignorant person, knowing nothing; pl.-*gog gego*.
Kekinoamaged. Teacher, master, school-teacher; preceptor; pl.-*jig*.
Kekinoamawind. Scholar, pupil, apprentice; pl.-*jig*.
Kekinôwijiwed. A person that shows the way, a guide; pl.-*jig*.
Këma, *kêma gaie*, adv. Or, perhaps.
Keshkakideg. Brand, fire-brand; pl.-*in*.
Keshkashkijiged. S. *Kishkashkijigewinini*.
Ketchi-bishigwadisid. Adulterer, adulteress; pl.-*jig*.
Ketchi-danid. Rich person, wealthy person; pl.-*jig*.
Ketchi-nishkadisid. Enraged person, raging person, a person in a great passion; pl.-*jig*.
Ketchi-omigid. Leper, leprous person; pl.-*jig*.
Ketchitwawendagosid. Blessed holy person, a Saint in heaven; pl.-*jig*.
Ketimagisid nin jawenima. I do charity, I give alms.
Ketiméshkid. Sluggard, lazy person; pl.-*jig*.
Ki, pron. Thou, we, you; thy, our, your.
Kibins. Browse, little rod; pl. *kibinsan*, a shrub, a bush.
Kid, pron. The same as *ki*; (*d* is the euphonical letter before a vowel.)
Kidamikan. Thy chin.
Kidji-, or *kidj'-*. This word is only used in connection with a substantive or substantive-verb, in the second person singular, and the first and second plural. It corresponds to the English word *fellow–*, or the Latin syllable *co* or *con*, in compositions; and signifies similarity or equal quality; as: *Kidj' anokitagewinini*, a servant like thyself, thy fellow-servant; (L. conservus tuus.)
Kigâ. Thy mother.
Kigijeb, adv. In the morning, early.
Kigijébawagad. It is morning, morning-time; (F. la matinée;) p. *keg..gak*.
Kigijeb-wissin, (*nin*). I breakfast; p. *kag..nid*.
Kigijeb-wissiniwin. Breakfast.
Kigiwin. Thy motherhood, thy maternity. — *Gagangowiian ketchitwawendagosiian, kigiwin mamakadendagwad!* O blessed Virgin, thy motherhood is wonderful!
Kigodewishka, (*nin*). I move with my whole family, my whole household; p. *keg..kad*.
Kiiaw. Thy body; thou, thee, thyself.
Kija, adv. Beforehand, before, in advance, by anticipation.
Kijâbate, or-*magad*. The air is warm; p. *kej..teg*, or-*magad*.
Kijâbikide, or-*magad*. It is warm, (some obj. of metal or

stone;) p. *keb..deg*, or-*magak*.

Kijabikisi. It is warm; (obj. of metal;) p. *kej..sid*.

Kijâbikisigan. Stove, box-stove; pl.-*an*.

Kijâdan, (*nin*). I watch it, guard it; p. *kejadang*.

Kejâdâwass, (*nin*). I guard a child, (or children;) p. *kej..sod*.

Kijâdige, (*nin*). I guard the lodge, house, village, etc., I remain at home when all go away; p. *kej..ged*.

Kiiâdigêwinini. Guardian, watchman; pl.-*wag*.

Kijâdis, (*nin*). S. *Kijewâdis*.

Kijâdisiwin. S. *Kijewâdisiwin*.

Kijâgamide. It is warm, (water or any liquid;) p. *kej..deg*.

Kijâgamidees, (*nin*). I warm my heart by drinking something warm; p. *kej..sod*.

Kijâgamisan, (*nin*). I make it warm, I warm it, (water or some other liquid;) p. *kej..ang*.

Kijaigade, or-*magad*. It is cut by accident, or by mistake; p. *kej..deg*, or-*magak*.

Kijaigas, (*nin*). I am cut by accident, or by mistake; p. *kej..sod*.

Kijakiganes, (*nin*). I warm my breast; p. *kej..sod*.

Kijana, (*nin*). I guard him, I watch over him; p. *kejanad*.

Kijaodis, (*nin*). I wound myself, I cut myself; p. *kej..sod*.

Kijâte, or-*magad*. It is warm, (warm weather;) p. *kejateg*, or-*magak*.

Kijâwâ, (*nin*). I wound him, cut him, (not purposely;) p. *kejawad*; imp. *kijâ*.

Kijâwendan, (*nin*). I envy it; p. *kej..ang*.—*Nin kijawendan kiiaw; kawin nin dadodansin*, I envy thee; I ought not to do so.

Kijawendjige, (*nin*). I envy, I feel envy, I feel pain at the sight of any good quality, excellence or felicity of others; p. *kej..ged*.

Kijawendjigewin. Envy, envious disposition of mind, pain felt at the sight of some good quality or prosperity of others.

Kijawenima, (*nin*). I envy him; p. *kej..mad*.

Kijawenindiwin. Envy. S. *Kijawendjigewin*.

Kijé-Manito. God, the perfect spirit.*

Kijê-Manito o masinaigan. The book of God, the Holy Bible.

Kijê-Manito o masinaigan nind odjindan. I swear on the Bible, (I kiss the book of God.)

Kije-Manitow, (*nin*). I am God; p. *kej..wid*.

Kije-Manitowiwin. Godhead, divinity, divine nature.

Kijewâdis, (*nin*). I am good, benevolent, charitable, compassionate, humane, clement, amicable; hospitable; p. *kej..sid*.

Kijewâdisitadimin, (*nin*). We are charitable to each other; p. *kej..didjig*.

Kijewâdisitawa, (*nin*). I am charitable to him; p. *kej..wad*.

Kijewâdisiwin. Charity, benignity, bounty, goodness, kind-

---

* The root *kij* means perfect, well finished, v. g. *nin kijia*, I finish him well, I render him perfect.

ness, benevolence, clemency, amicability, hospitality, compassion.

Kiji, in compositions, signifies *fast, quick, strong.* (Examples in some of the following words.)

Kijibadinoke, (nin). I turn round until I fall down, (as children do, playing;) p. *kej.. ked.*

Kijibata, (nin). I turn round (for a while,) I whirl round; (F. je tournoie;) p. *kej..tad.*

Kijibâwebina jigwanâbik, (nin). I turn a grindstone; p. *kej.. nad.*

Kijibâwebinan, (nin). I turn it round with a crank; p. *kej.. ang.*

Kijibawebinigan. Crank; (F. manivelle;) pl.*-an.*

Kijibawebinige, (nin). I turn a crank; p. *kej..ged.*

Kijibendan, (nin). I think always on it; p. *kej..ang.*

Kijibenima, (nin). I think always on him; p. *kej..mad.*

Kijibide, or*-magad.* It goes or glides fast, quick; p. *kej..deg,* or*-magak.* — *Anind ishkotenâbikwânan geget kitchi kijibidewan;* some steamboats go very fast indeed.

Kijibideeshkassa, (nin). I hang him on a cord and turn him round, until he feels sick, (as Indians do to wicked children, for a punishment;) p. *kej..sad.*

Kijibima, (nin). I speak of him; p. *kej..mad.*

Kijibindan, (nin). I speak of it; p. *kej..ang.*

Kijide, or*-magad.* S. *Kijote.*

Kijidjiwan. It runs fast, (liquid,) there is running water; a rapid or rapids; p. *kej..ang.*

Kijiga, or*-magad.* It runs fast, (speaking of the sap running out of maple-trees in spring, in sugar-making;) p. *kejigag,* or*-magak.*

Kijibâb, (nin). I look at s. th. steadily; (F. je regarde fixement;) p. *kej..bid.*

Kijigâbama, (nin). I look at him steadily, watching him; p. *kej..mad.*

Kijigabandan, (nin). I look at it steadily; p. *kej..ang.*

Kijiganona, (nin). I speak to him loud; p. *kej..nad;* imp. *kijiganoj.*

Kijigendam, (nin). I think or desire earnestly; p. *kej..ang.*

Kijigendân, (nin). I desire it earnestly, strongly; p. *kej.. ang.*

Kijigênima,(nin). I desire strongly some body; p. *kej..mad.*

Kijiiânimad. There is a good fast wind, (that makes us sail fast;) p. *kej..mak.*

Kijiiâsh, (nin). I sail fast; p. *kej..id.*

Kijij, in compositions, signifies *strong, durable.* (Examples in some of the following words.)

Kijijâ, adv. Strongly, soundly. —*Kawin kijija nin bimâdisissi;* I don't live strongly, (I am not in good health.)

Kijijawad. It is durable, strong; p. *kej..wak.*—*Geget kijijawad kiiaw, kawin wika kid akosissi;* thy body is strong indeed, thou art never sick.

Kijijawigane, (nin). I have strength in my bones, (I am a strong man;) p. *kej..ned.*

Kijijâwis, (*nin*). I am durable, strong, vigorous, industrious, persevering in working ; p. *kej..sid.*

Kijijâwisiwin. Vigor ; industry.

Kijika, (*nin*). I go on quick, I walk fast; p. *kejikad.*

Kijikabato, (*nin*). I run fast; p. *kej..tod.*

Kijikamagad. It goes or runs fast ; p. *kej..gak.*

Kijikan nin masinaïgan, (*nin*). I pay my debt, (or my debts,) I settle my accounts ; p. *kejikang.*

Kijikas, (*nin*). I clear myself of my debts, I pay all ; p. *kej..sod.*

Kijikawa, (*nin*). I pay him my debt, I settle with him ; p. *kej..wad.*

Kijikinjawe, (*nin*). I make a large fire ; p. *kej..wed.*

Kijikos, (*nin*). I get hurt by carrying too heavy a load ; p. *kej..sod.*

Kijindagan. Contagious sickness, pest.—S. *Jindâgan.*

Kijiosse, (*nin*). S. *Kijika.*

Kijipangaog, (*nin*). My pulse beats quick ; p. *kej..god.*

Kijipikwanes, (*nin*). My back gets warmed ; p. *kej..sod.*

Kijis, (*nin*). I am warm, I feel heat in my body ; I have the fever ; p. *kejisod.*

Kijisân, (*nin*). I warm or rewarm it ; p. *kejisang.*

Kijisigan. A warmer ; (F. réchauffoir ;) pl.-*an.*

Kijisige, (*nin*). I warm or rewarm ; p. *kej..ged.*

Kijisodis, (*nin*). I warm myself, I get warmed ; p. *kej..sod.*

Kijisosse, (*nin*). I get warm by walking ; p. *kej..sed.*

Kijisowapine, (*nin*). I have the fever with great heat; p. *kej..ned.*

Kijisowapinewin. Fever with heat.

Kijisowin. Heat in the body, fever.

Kijisse bineshi. The bird flies quick ; p. *kejissed.*

Kijiswa, (*nin*). I warm or rewarm some obj.; p. *kej..wad ;* imp. *kijiswi.*

Kijiwâgonaga, or-*magad.* The snow is settled, the snow is sunk down and hard ; p. *kej..gag*, or-*magak.* The same signification as *assanagonaga.*

Kijiwe, (*nin*). I speak loud; p. *kejiwed.*

Kijiwemagad. It sounds loud, it has a strong sound ; p. *kej..gak.*

Kijiwéweiâshka, or-*magad.* There is a loud roaring of the waves, high sea ; p. *kej..kag*, or-*magak.*

Kijiwêweton, (*nin*). I make it sound loudly ; p. *kej..tod.*

Kijob, (*nin*). I am warm, (in a lodge, house, etc.); p. *kejo..bid.*

Kijobike, (*nin*). I melt snow to have water ; p. *kaj..ked.*

Kijogâde, (*nin*). My legs are warm ; p. *kaj..deg.*

Kijoia, or-*magad.* It is warm, (in a building ;) p. *kaj..ag*, or-*magak.*

Kijokawa, (*nin*). I warm him with my body, lying with him ; p. *kaj..wad.*

Kijogis, (*nin*). I dress warmly, I have warm clothes on; p. *kaj..sod.*

Kijos, (*nin*). I am warm and comfortable; p. *kajosid.*

Kijoshin, (*nin*). I lie warm; p. *kaj..ing.*

Kikaigan. Mark to guide travelers, or to point out dangerous places on the road; pl.-*an.*

Kikaige, (*nin*). I make marks on the road, (setting up branches, etc.) to direct or warn the traveler; p. *kek..ged.*

Kikassa, (*nin*). I put aside, or set apart some body; p. *kek ..ad.*

Kikaton, (*nin*). I put it aside, I set it apart; p. *kekatod.*

Kikendâgos, (*nin*). I am known; p. *kek..sid.*

Kikendamiiwe, (*nin*). I make known, I publish, announce s. th.; p. *kek..wed.*

Kikendamiiwen, (*nin*). I make it known, publish it, announce it; p. *kek..wed.*

Kikendamôa, (*nin*). I make him know s. th., I make known to him s. th.; p. *kek..ad.*

Kikendamowin. Knowledge of something.

Kikendân, (*nin*). I know it, I am aware of it, I experience it; p. *kek..ang.*

Kikendass, (*nin*). I know; I am learned, I possess science; p. *kik..sod.*

Kikendassowin. Knowledge, science; p. *kek..sod.*

Kikendjige, (*nin*). I know; p. *kek..ged.*

Kikénima, (*nin*). I know him; p. *kek..mad.*

Kikênindis, (*nin*). I know myself; p. *kek..sod.*

Kikibikomeshi. Grey lark; (C. cendrille;) pl.-*iag.*

Kikima, (*nin*). I promise him a rendez-vous, I promise him to be at such a place at such a time; p. *kekimad.*

Kikinawadabawana, (*nin*). I give him private baptism, or lay-baptism; p. *kek..nad;* imp. *kik..waj.*

Kikinawâdad. It is remarkable, it is easy to be found, to be seen, to be recognized, to be noticed; p. *kek..dak.*

Kikinawadakwaidade, or-*magad.* There are marks on the trees for the traveler to find out the trail through the wood, the trees are blazed; p. *kek..deg*, or-*magak.*

Kikinawadâkwaigan. Mark on a tree, blaze; pl.-*an.*

Kikinawadâkwaige, (*nin*). I blaze trees on a road or trail; p. *kek..ged.*

Kikinawâdendagos, (*nin*). I am marked, I am considered a mark, a sign; also, I am circumcised; p. *kek..sid.*

Kikinawadendagosiwin. The state or situation of being a mark, circumcision.

Kikinawâdendân, (*nin*). I remark it in my thoughts, (in order to recognize it afterwards;) I remark it to follow it; p. *kek..ang.*

Kikinawâkenima, (*nin*). I remark him in my thoughts to recognize him; I remark him to follow him, to imitate him; p. *kek..mad.*

Kikinawadj, adv. In a remarkable manner, easy to be found, seen, noticed.

Kikinawadji, (*nin*). I am marked; I am circumcised; p. *bek ..iod.*

Kikinawâdjia, (*nin*). I mark him, I put a mark on a person, or on any other obj.; also, I tell or indicate to him a mark or marks; I circumcise him; p. *kek..ad.*

Kikinawâdjion, or, *kikinawadjiowin*. Any mark; circumcision; banner, flag; pl.-*an*. S. *Kikiweon.*

Kikinawâdjitawa, (*nin*). I give him or tell him a certain mark, to find s. th.; p. *kek..wad.*

.*Kikinawâdjitchigan*. Mark, sign; miracle; sight or aim on a gun; pl.-*an*.

Kikinawênima, (*nin*). I regulate my mind and my thoughts after his examples; p. *kek.. mad.*

Kikindimin, (*nin*). We promise each other a rendez-vous, we promise to one another to meet in a certain place at a certain time; p. *kekindidjig.*

Kikindiwin. Mutual promise of a rendez-vons, of a meeting in a certain place at a certain time.

Kikinge, (*nin*). I promise to come to a rendez-vous, to be present; p. *kek..ged.*

Kikingewin. Promise to come to a rendez-vous.

Kikinoamadi-masinaigan. Spelling-book, school-book; pl.-*an*.

Kikinoamâdiwigamig. House of instruction, school-house; Synagogue; pl.-*on*.

Kikinoamâdiwin. Teaching, instruction given or received by several persons.—S. *Kikinoamagewin*, and *Kikinoamagowin.*

Kikinoamâgan. Scholar, pupil, disciple, apprentice; pl.-*og*.

Kikinoamage, (*nin*). I am teaching, I keep school, I instruct, I show, I indicate; p. *kek.. ged.*

Kikinoamâgekwe. Female school teacher, school-mistress; pl.-*g*.

Kikinoamâgewin. Teaching or instruction *given*.

Kikinoamagewinini. Teacher, school-teacher, school-master; pl.-*wag*.

Kikinoamâgowin. Teaching or instruction *received*.

Kikinoamawa, (*nin*). I teach, instruct, inform him, I show him, indicate him s. th.; p. *kek..wad.*

Kikinonowin. A year, twelve months; pl.-*an*.

Kikinotawa, (*nin*). I speak after him, I say what he says; p. *kek..wad.*

Kikinowâbama, (*nin*). I imitate him, I do as I see him doing, I take his example; p. *kek.. mad.*

Kikinowâbamig, (*nin*). He imitates me, I give him an example; p. *kekinowabamid*, he who imitates me.

Kidinoâbamigowin. Example *taken*, imitation.

Kikinowâdandaiwe, (*nin*). I give or show an example; p. *kek..wed.*

Kikinowâbandaiwewin. Example *given*, (good example, or scandal.)

Kikinowâbandân, (*nin*). I imitate it, I copy it, I make a similar thing as I see before me; p. *kek..ang*.

Kikinowâbandjigan. Example for imitation, model, standard; pl.-*an*.

Kikinowijiwe, (*nin*). I guide, I conduct, I lead, I show the way; p. *kek..wed*.

Kikinowijiwêwinini. Guide, conductor; pl.-*wag*.

Kikinôwina, (*nin*). I guide or conduct him, I show him the way; p. *kek..nad*; imp. *kikinowij*.

Kikitâwa, (*nin*). I put marks for him on a road or trail, to direct him; p. *kek..wad*.

Kikiweiâbawadjige, (*nin*). I give private baptism; p. *kek..ged*.

Kikiweiabawadjigewin. Private baptism, lay-baptism.

Kikiweiâbawana, (*nin*). I give him private baptism; p. *kek..nad*; imp. *kik..waj*. (The same as, *nin kikinawadabawana*.)

Kikiweiâbawas, (*nin*). I receive private baptism; p. *kek..sod*.

Kikiwêon. Flag, banner; pl.-*an*.

Kikîwêonâtig. Flag-staff; pl.-*on*.

Kin, pron. Thou, thine.

Kinawa, pron. You, yours.

Kinâwind, pron. We, ours.

Kinigawabimin, (*nin*). We are together all mixed, or different kinds; (F. nous sommes tous pêle-mêle;) p. *ken..bidjig*.

Kinigawâgomowag j i s h i b a g. The ducks are swimming mixtly, of different kinds.

Kinigawigabawimin, (*nin*). We are standing together mixed, of different kinds; p. *ken..widjig*.

Kinigawigeidimin, (*nin*). We live mixed together in the same village or town; p. *ken..didjig*.

Kinigâwissin. It is mixed, things of different kinds are together; p. *ken..ing*.

Kinigina, (*nin*). I mix some obj. with another object, (dry objects;) p. *ken..nad*.

Kiniginan, (*nin*). I mix some obj. with another object, (*dry* objects;) p. *ken..ang*.

Kiniginige, (*nin*). I am mixing together objects of different kinds; p. *ken..ged*.

Kinigissin. It is mixed together, different objects in one mass together; p. *ken..ing*. (S. *Kinigawissin*.)

Kinishtino. Cree Indian; pl.-*g*.

Kinishtïnokwe. Cree squaw; pl.-*g*.

Kinishtinokweshib. A kind of wild duck; pl.-*ag*.

Kinitam. Thou in thy turn, thou now; (F. toi à ton tour.) *Kinitam nagamon*, sing now in thy turn, (it is thy turn now to sing.)

Kinitamiwa. You in your turn, you now.—*Kinitamiwa tchimeiog, ginwenj nin gi-tchimemin ninawind*. Paddle now in your turn, we have paddled long.

Kinitamiwind. We in our turn. we now.—(The person or persons spoken to, included.) S. *Ninitamiwind*.

Kiniw. War-eagle; a kind of

eagle that remains almost all day very high in the air. The Indian warriors wear his feathers as an ornament on their heads. These feathers are rare, and not easy to be obtained. Pl. *kiniwag.*

Kinôje. Pike, (fish ;) pl.-*g.*

Kinôw. Tby cheek; pl.-*ag.*

Kipagâ, or-*magad.* It is thick; p. *kegagag,* or-*magak.*

Kipagâbigad. It is thick,strong, (some narrow stuff;) p. *kep.. gak.*

Kipagâbigisi seniba. The ribbon is thick, strong; p. *kep.. sid.*

Kipagâbikad. It is thick; (metal;) p. *kep..kak.*

Kipagâbikia, (*nin*). I make it thick, (object of metal or stone;) p. *kep..ad.*

Kipagâbikisi. It is thick, (obj. of metal or stone;) p. *kep..sid.*

Kipagâbikiton, (*nin*). I make it thick, (obj. of metal;) p. *kep.. tod.*

Kipagâdin. It is frozen thick, (thick ice;) p. *kep..ing.*

Kipagâgami. It is thick, (some liquid;) p. *kep..mig.*

Kipagâgamiton, (*nin*). I make it thick, (some liquid;) p. *kep ..tod.—Osâm o gikipagagamiton mandaminâbo;* she made the corn-soup too thick.

Kipagâkamiga, or-*magad.* There is much earth, (the good soil or ground is thick, before you come to stones or sand underneath;) p. *kep..gag,* or-*magak.*

Kipagiâ, (*nin*). I make it thick or thicker, I thicken it; p. *kep..ad.*

Kipagigad. It is thick, strong, (stuff, clothing material;) p. *kep..gak.*

Kipagigisi. It is thick, strong, (*seniba,* silk;) p. *kep..sid.*

Kipagigisi nabagissag. The board is thick; p. *kep..sid.*

Kipagishima, (*nin*). I lay it on thick, or thickly; p. *kep.. mad.—Nawatch ki da-kipagishima wâbigan;* you ought to lay your clay thicker, (in plastering a house.)

Kipagisi. It is thick, strong; p. *kep..sid.*

Kipagisiton, (*nin*). I lay or put it on thick or thickly; p. *kep ..tod.*

Kipagiton (*nin*). I make it thick, I thicken it; p. *kep.. tod.*

Kishkaan, (*nin*). I cut it; p. *kash..kang.*

Kishkâbanonikaga, or-*magad.* There is a clay-bank; (F. il y a un écore de glaise;) p. *kash ..gag,* or-*magak.*

Kishkabika, or-*magad.* There is a steep rock, a perpendicular abrupt rock or cliff; there is no beach, but a high steep rock; p. *kash..kag,* or-*magak.*

Kishkabikad. It is cut, (metal); p. *kash..kak.*

Kishkadina, or-*magad.* There is a very steep hill, very steep ascent; p. *kash..nap,* or-*magak.*

Kishkajewa, (*nin*). I cut his skin; p. *kash..wad;* imp. *kishkajê.*

Kishkâkados, (*nin*). I am extremely meager, lean, poor; p. *kash..sod.*

Kishkâkamida, or-*magad.* There is a very steep place or ground; p. *kash..gag,* or-*magak.*
Kishkâkide, or-*magak.* It breaks by burning through; p. *kash ..deg,* or-*magak.*
Kishkakisân, (*nin*). I burn it through, (I break it in two by fire;) p. *kash..sang.*
Kishkakiswa, (*nin*). I burn some obj. through, in two pieces; p. *kash..wad ;* imp. *kiskkakis.*
Kishkanakad. Stump of a tree; (F. souche;) pl.-*on.*
Kishkanakadons. Little stump; (F. chicot;) pl.-*an.*
Kishdanakisi mitig. The top of the tree is broken, by the wind; p. *kash..sod.*
Kishkanâm, (*nin*). My breathing is interrupted, is cut; p. *kash..mod.*
Kishdandan, (*nin*). I cut it with the teeth, I bite it through; p. *kash..ang.*
Kishkanjékodan wâssakwanendjigan, (*nin*). I snuff the candle; p. *kash..ang.*
Kishkanjêkodjigan. Snuffers; pl.-*an.*
Kishkashkijan, (*nin*). I cut it with a scythe or sickle, I mow it; p. *kash..ang.*
Kishkashkijigan. Scythe, sickle, reaping hook; p.-*an.*
Kishkashkijige, (*nin*). I reap, I harvest, I cut, I mow; p. *kash ..ged.*
Kishkashkijigewin. Harvest, reaping, mowing.
Kishkashkijigewinini. Harvester, reaper, mower; pl.-*wag.*
Kishkashkossiwe, (*nin*). I cut down grass, I mow; p. *kash.. wed.*
Kishkatâwanga, or-*magad.* There is a steep sand-hill, or a steep sand-bank on the beach of a lake, (F. écore de sable;) p. *kash..gag.*
Kishkibidjigaso. It is torn or rent; p. *kash..sod.*
Kishkawa, (*nin*). I cut some obj.; p. *kash..wad ;* imp. *kishkaw.*
Kishkibidon, (*nin*). I tear it, I rend it; p. *kash..dod.*
Kishkibina, (*nin*). I tear or rend some obj.; p. *kash..nad ;* imp. *kishkibij.*
Kishkibitâgan. Tobacco-pouch; pl.-*ag.*
Kishkibode, or-*magad.* It is sawn; p. *kash..deg,* or-*magak.*
Kishkibodjigan. Saw, handsaw; pl.-*an.*
Kishkibodjige, (*nin*). I saw (across, not along;) p. *kash.. ged.*—S. *Tashkibodjige.*
Kishkibodjigewin. Sawing, (across only, not along.)
Kishkibodon, (*nin*). I saw it through, (across;) p. *kash..dod.*
Kishkibona, (*nin*). I saw through some object; p. *kash..nad ;* imp. *kishkiboj.*
Kishkibos, (*nin*). I am sawn through, in two; p. *kash..sod.*
Kishkidenaniwe, (*nin*). My tongue is cut off; p. *kash.. wed.*
Kishkidenaniwejwa, (*nin*). I cut his tongue off; p. *kash..wad ;* imp. *kish..jwi.*
Kishkigaige, (*nin*). I cut; I chop wood; p. *kash..ged.*
Kishkigana, (*nin*). I cut off some obj.; p. *kash..nad.*

Kishkiganjisodis, (*nin*). I cut off my nails; p. *kash..sod.*

Kishkigawa mitig, (*nin*). I cut down a tree; p. *kash..wad.*

Kishkigwe, (*nin*). My throat is cut; p. *kash..wed.*

Kishkigwebina, (*nin*). I tear his head off; p. *kash..nad;* imp. *kish..bij.*

Kishkigwejwa, (*nin*). I cut his throat; p. *kash..wad;* imp. *kishkigwejwi.*

Kishkigwena, (*nin*). I break his neck; p. *kash..nad;* imp. *kishkigwen.*

Kishkigwewa, (*nin*). I cut his neck off, (his head,) I behead him; p. *kash..wad;* imp. *kishkigwe.*

Kishkijan, (*nin*). I cut it; p. *kash..ang.*

Kishkijigas, (*nin*). I am cut; also, I am castrated, I am a eunuch; p. *kash..sod.*

Kishkijigasowin. Castration.

Kishkijodis, (*nin*). I cut myself with a knife; p. *kash..sod.*

Kishkijwa, (*nin*). I cut him; I castrate him; p. *kash..wad;* imp. *kishkijwi.*

Kishkissin nin tchimân. My canoe breaks, (it is cut by a rock or snag;) p. *kashkissing.*

Kishkitawage, (*nin*). My ear is cut off; p. *kash..ged.*

Kishkitawageganama, (*nin*). I strike one of his ears off; p. *kash..mad.*

Kishkitawagejwa, (*nin*). I cut him an ear off; p. *kash..wad;* imp. *kish..jwi.*

Kishkitching minikwâdjigan. A pint.

Kishkowe, (*nin*). I cease speaking, weeping, etc.; p. *kashkowed.*

Kishkowea, (*nin*). I make him be still, I make him cease speaking, weeping, etc.; p. *kash..ad.*

Kishpin, conj. If, provided, in case that, whether, supposing.

Kisitabawadon, (*nin*). I wash it out, I rinse it; p. *kes..dod.*

Kisitabawana, (*nin*). I wash or rinse some obj.; p. *kes..nad;* imp. *kis..waj.*

Kisiâbâwe, or-*magad.* It fades, it loses its color, in washing; p. *kes..weg*, or-*magak.*

Kisian, (*nin*). I wipe it, I absterge it; p. *kesiang.*

Kisiâwass, (*nin*). I wipe or clean an infant; p. *kes..sod.*

Kisibakwad. There is a sound produced by the rubbing of two trees against one another, when they are agitated by the wind; p. *kes..wak.*

Kisibanashk. Shave-grass, horse-tail, (a plant for polishing;) (F. prêle;) pl.-*on.*

Kisibigaamawa, (*nin*). I wash for him, I wash his clothes; p. *kes..wad.*

Kisibigaigan. Soap.

Kisibigaiganike, (*nin*). I make soap, I manufacture soap; p. *kes..ked.*

Kisibigaiganikewigamig. Soap-house, soap-boilery, soap-manufactory; pl.-*on.*

Kisibigi, (*nin*). I wash myself; p. *kesibigid.*

Kisibigina, (*nin*). I wash him, (a person, or any other obj.); p. *kes..nad.*

Kisibiginaganâbo. Dish-water, swill; (F. rinçure de vaisselle.)

Kisibiginagane, (*nin*). I wash or rinse dishes; p. *kes..ned.*

Kisibiginan, (*nin*). I wash it; p. *kes..ang.*

Kisibigindibe, (*nin*). I wash my head; p. *kes..bed.*

Kisibigingwena, (*nin*). I wash his face; p. *kes..nad.*

Kisiinaganan. Dish-clout; (F. torchon;) pl.-*an.*

Kisiinagane, (*nin*). I wipe dishes; p. *kes..ned.*

Kisingwe, (*nin*). I wipe my face; p. *kes..od.*

Kisinindjâgan. Towel; (F. essuie-main;) pl.-*an.*

Kisinindji, (*nin*). I wipe my hands; p. *kes..id.*

Kisisidê, (*nin*). I wipe my feet; p. *kes..od.*

Kisisidêwa, (*nin*). I wipe his feet; p. *kes..wad;* imp. *kisiside.*

Kisiwa, (*nin*). I clean him, I wipe him, (a person, or any other obj.;) p. *kesiwad;* imp. *kisi.*

Kissinâ, or-*magad.* It is cold, (cold weather;) p. *kessinag,* or-*magak.*

Kissintibikad. It is a cold night; p. *kes..kak.*

Kitagakons. Young deer, a fawn yet dotted or spotted; pl.-*ag.*

Kitagia, (*nin*). I spot him, (any obj.;) p. *ket..ad.*

Kitagigad. It is of various colors, variegated, (stuff, clothing material;) p. *ket..gak.*

Kitagigin. Stuff of various colors, or variegated, calico; pl.-*on.*

Kitagigisi nin moshwen. My handkerchief is spotted, (it has spots and dots of different colors.)

Kitagisiwin, (*nin*). Spot, speck; pl.-*an.*

Kitagiton, (*nin*). I spot it; p. *ket..od.*

Kitagwinde tchimân. The canoe is sure, it is not dangerous, not rolling; p. *ket..deg.*

Kitakamiga. The continent, it is the continent; p. *két..gag.* —*Kitakamigang,* on the continent, on the main land.

Kitchakiwi, (*nin*). I hurt myself, by lifting or carrying too heavy a load; p. *katchakiwid.*

Kitchi, adj. and adv. Great, grand, large, big, extensive; pre-eminent, principal, old, aged; much, well, very; arch–(in some compositions, as: Archangel, *Kitchi Anjeni.*)—This word is always followed by a substantive, verb, adjective or adverb, and remains connected with it; it cannot be used alone.

Kitchi agaming. On the other side or shore of the great water, that is, in Europe.

Kitchi aiaa. Great being; a big, great, noble, mighty or elevated person; an old aged person; also, a large, big or old animal; pl.-*g.*

Kitchi aii. Great thing; any great, big, large, important, or old object; pl.-*n.*

Kitchi-âmo. Humble-bee; buzzing fly; pl.-*g.*

Kitchi-anibish. (Big leave,) cabbage; pl.-*an.*
Kitchi-anishinâbe. Old person, (man or woman); pl.-*g.*
Kitchi-anishinabew, (*nin*). I am an old person, (man or woman;) p. *ket..wid.*
Kitchi awassonâgo. Three days ago; (L. nudius tertius.)
Kitchi awasswâbang. After three days.
Kitchi awéssi. (Large beast,) elephant; pl.-*iag.*
Kitchi babisikawagan. Big coat, cloak, riding-coat; pl.-*an.*
Kitchi bidânimad. There comes a squall of wind; p. *ket..mak.*
Kitchi biminakwân. Big rope, cable; pl.-*an.*
Kitchi biminigan. Augar; (F. tarière;) pl.-*an.*
Kitchi binâkwân. Harrow; pl.-*an.*
Kitchi bishigwâdisiwin. Adultery.
Kitchi dan, (*nin*). I am rich, wealthy; p. *ketchi-danid.*
Kitchi-daniwin. Riches, wealth, fortune.
Kitchigâd. The right leg. — There is always a possessive pronoun prefixed to this word; as: *Nin kitchigâd,* my right leg; *ki kitchigâd,* thy right leg, etc.
Kitchi gagibingwekwe. Mole.
Kitchigami. Great water, great lake. — *Otchipwe-kitchigami,* Lake Superior. *Jiwitagani-kitchigami,* the Ocean.
Kitchigamiwashk. S. *Anâkanashk.*
Kitchi gawissagang. Nutmeg; (F. muscade.)
Kitchi-gigô. Whale; pl.-*iag.*
Kitchi-gigô bimide. Sperm-oil.
Kitchi giigwishimowin. Lent; (F. carême.)
Kitchigijân, (*nin*). I indent it, I jagg it; p. *ket..ang.*
Kitchi jawêmin. Chestnut; pl.-*an.*
Kitchi jigâgawinj. Onion; pl.-*ig.*
Kitchi jimaganishi-ogima. Great military chief, that is, a general; pl.-*g.*
Kitchi jingobabo. Beer.
Kitchi jiwâgamisigan. Molasses.
Kitchi-jomin. Fig; pl.-*ag.*
Kitchi-jominâtig, or, *kitchi-jominagawanj.* Fig-tree; pl.-*gon,* or-*jin.*
Kitchi kishkibodjigan. Log-saw, cross-saw; pl -*an.*
Kitchi manameg. Whale; *wag.*
Kitchi-mekatéwikwanaie. Bishop, (Great black-gown;) pl.-*g.* *Naganisid Kitchi-mekatewikwanaie,* Archbishop. *Maiamawi-niganisid Kitchi-mekatewikwanaie,* Pope, (the foremost Bishop.)
Kitchi-mekatewikwanaie o sakaon. Crosier, (the Bishop's staff.)
Kitchi-mekatewikwanaie o wiwakwân. Mitre, (the Bishop's hat.)
Kitchi mikana. Public road, a trodden beaten road.
Kitchi miskweiâb. Artery.
Kitchimokomân. American, (big knife;) pl.-*ag.*
Kitchimokomân-aki. The United States, (the land of the big knives.)
Kitchimokomanens. An American boy; pl.-*ag.*

Kitchimokomanikwe. An American woman; pl.-*g*.

Kitchinik. The right arm.—There is always a possessive pronoun before this word; as: *Nin kitchinik, ki kitchinik, o kitchinik;* my, thy, his right arm.

Kitchinindj. The right hand. This word is always preceded by a possessive pronoun; as: *Nin kitchinindj, o kitchinindj*, my right hand, his right hand; etc.

Kitchi nishkâdis, (*nin*). I am enraged, very angry; p. *ket..sid.*

Kitchi niskâdisiwin. Violent anger, rage, fury.

Kitchinow. The right cheek.—This word has always a possessive pronoun before it; as: *Nin kitchinow*, my right cheek; *o kitchinowan*, his right cheek, etc.

Kitchi odena. City; pl.-*wan*.

Kitchi-ogima. King, emperor, sovereign, potentate, (great chief;) pl.-*g*.

Kitchi-ogima apabiwin. Throne; pl.-*an*.

Kitchi-ogimâkwe. Queen, empress; pl.-*g*.

Kitchi-ogima o wiwakwân. Crown; pl.-*an*.

Kitchi omigiwin. Leprosy.

Kitchi-pâshkisigan. Canon, gun; pl.-*an*.

Kitchi-pâshkisigan anwi. Canonball; pl.-*n*.

Kitchi-pipigwan. Church-organ; pl.-*an*.

Kitchipis, (*nin*). I gird myself, I put a girdle or belt around my waist; p. *ket..sod.*

Kitchipison. Belt, girdle;)F. ceinture;) pl.-*ag*.

Kitchi-sagaigan. Spike; pl.-*an*.

Kitchisâgi. Misery River, Lake Superior.

Kitchi sêgisiwin. Terror, fright, horror.

Kitchishkinjig. The right eye.—This word is always connected with a possessive pronoun; as; *Nin kitchishkinjig, ki kitchishkinjig ;* my right eye, thy right eye, etc.

Kitchisid. The right foot.—This word is always preceded by a possessive pronoun; as: *Nin kitchisid*, my right foot; *ki kitchisid*, thy right foot, etc.

Kitchisidan. The big toe.—*Nin kitchisidan, o kitchisidan;* my big toe, his big toe, etc.

Kitchi-takwândjigan. Screw-vice; (F. étau ;) pl.-*an*.

Kitchitwâ. Honorable, holy, saint.

Kitchitwâgijigad. Holyday, festival; pl.-*on*.

Kitchiwâgijigad. It is a holyday; p. *ket..gak*.

Kitchitwa Marie od anamikagowin. Annunciation of the Blessed Virgin Mary.

Kitchitwâwendagos, (*nin*). I am honored, revered, I am considered venerable; I am glorious, sublime, holy; p. *ket..sid.*

Kitchitwâwendagosia, (*nin*). I make him glorious, honored, I exalt him; I sanctify him; p. *ket..ad.*

Kitchitwawendagosiwin. Honor, veneration, glory, glorification, sanctity.

Kitchitwâwéndân, (*nin*). I respect it, I honore and revere it,

I hold it in veneration, I esteem it holy, glorify it; p. *ket..ang.*

Kitchitwâwenim, (*nin*). I have proud thoughts, I exalt myself in my thoughts ; p. *ket.. mod.*

Kitchitwâwenima, (*nin*). I respect, honor, revere him, glorify him, I consider him venerable, holy ; p. *ket..mad.*

Kitchitwâwenindimin, (*nin*). We think each other worthy of honor and respect ; p. *ket.. didjig.*

Kitchitwawenindis, (*nin*). I think myself worthy of honor and glory, I exalt myself; p. *ket..sod.*

Kitchitwawenindisowin. Self-glorification, vain glory, proud thoughts.

Kitchitwâwia, (*nin*). I make him glorious, honored ; I glorify him ; p. *ket..ad.*

Kitchitwâwiidis, (*nin*). I glorify or honor myself, I seek my own glory ; p. *ket..sod.*

Kitchitwâwin. S. *Kitchitwâwisiwin.*

Kitchitwâwina, (*nin*). I glorify him with words, I praise him ; p. *ket..nad.*

Kitchitwawindan, (*nin*). I glorify and praise it with words ; p. *ket..ang.*

Kitchitwâwinikas, (*nin*). I have a glorious name; my name is holy ; p. *ket..sod.*

Kitchitwawinikasowin. Glorious name ; holy name.

Kitchitwâwis, (*nin*). I am glorious, honored, noble, elevated, exalted ; p. *ket..sid.*

Kitchitwâwisiwin. Glory, honor, majesty.

Kitchitwâwiton, (*nin*). I honor it, I glorify it, sanctify it, I make it holy ; p. *ket..tod.*

Kitchi-wâgikomân. Drawing-knife ; pl.-*an.*

Kitchi-wajashkwêdo. Cork ; (F. liége.)

Kitchi - wajashkwedo - gibâkwaigan. Cork-stopper ; pl.-*an.*

Kitchi-wawabigonodji. (Rat, (big-mouse ;) pl.-*jag.*

Kitchiwébison. Bracelet ; pl.-*ag.*

Kitênim, (*nin*). I have proud thoughts of myself; p. *ket.. mod.*

Kitenima, (*nin*). I think him proud ; p. *ket..mad.*

Kiténimowin. Pride, proud thoughts.

Kitênindis, (*nin*). I think myself higher or better than others ; p. *ket..sod.*

Kitigân. Field ; garden ; pl.-*an.*

Kitigana, (*nin*). I sow it, I plant it; p. *ketigadang.—Nibiwa mandaminag nin wi-kitiganag ;* I will plant much corn.

Kitigâniwigamig. Field-house ; garden-house; pl.-*on.*

Kitigé, (*nin*). I farm, I plant, I cultivate the ground, I till the ground ; p. *ketiged.*

Kitigêwin. Agriculture, farming, husbandry, tillage.

Kitegêwinini. Farmer, plougher, husbandman ; pl.-*wag.*

Kitim, (*nin*). I am lazy, I don't like to do s. th., or to go somewhere ; p. *ketimid.*

Kitimâgad. It is poor, miserable, pitiful, pitiable, worth pity ; p. *ket..gak.*

Kitimagakamig, adv. Miserable, pitiful, poor.
Kitimaganimitagos, (*nin*). I make a speech or harangue in order to excite pity on me, to obtain charitable assistance in my wants; p. *ket..sid.*
Kitimaganimitagosiwin. Harangue in order to obtain charity.
Kitimagendagos, (*nin*). I am poor, I am known to be poor; p. *ket..sid.*
Kitimâgendam, (*nin*). I pity, I have thoughts of compassion, of pity; p. *kit..ang.*
Kitimâgendân, (*nin*). I pity it, I think it is poor and miserable; p. *ket..ang.*
Kitimâgenima, (*nin*). I pity him, I have compassion on him, I think him poor, worth pity; p. *ket..mad.*
Kitimâgiâ, (*nin*). I make him poor and miserable, I make him unhappy, unfortunate; p. *ket..ad.*
Kitimagimotawa, *nin*). I ask him charity and assistance in my wants; p. *ket..wad.*
Kitimaginagos, (*nin*). I look poor, miserable, unhappy, indigent; p. *ket..sid.*
Kitimaginagosiwin. Poor miserable appearance.
Kitimâgis, (*nin*). I am poor, indigent, I am unhappy, unfortunate, miserable, deserving of compassion and pity; worth pity; p. *ket..sid.*
Kitimâgisiwin. Poverty, indigence; unhappiness, misery.
Kitimâgitagos, (*nin*). I am heard with pity and compassion, I speak so as to excite pity on me; p. *ket..sid.*
Kitimagitawa, (*nin*). I listen to him with pity and compassion; p. *ket..wad.*
Kitimagiton, (*nin*). I make it poor and miserable; p. *ket.. tod.*
Kitiminâgos, (*nin*). I look lazy, I have the appearance of a lazy person; p. *ket..sid.*
Kitimishk, (*nin*). I am habitually lazy, slothful, I am a sluggard; p. *ket..kid.*
Kitimishkiwin. Habitual laziness, slothfulness.
Kitimiwin. Laziness, sloth.
Kitis, (*nin*). I am old; v. *kâtisid.*
Kitisi; nin kitisim. My parent, my father or my mother, my ancestor; *o kitisiman*, his father or mother, or his ancestor, etc.—Pl. *nin kitisimag*, my parents, or my ancestors; *ki kitisiminabanig*, our forefathers, etc.
Kitotâgan. Bell; pl.-*an.*
Kitotaganagodeg. Where the bell hangs, that is, the belfry, the church-steeple, steeple.
Kitôtchigan. Violin; pl.-*an.*—*Kitchikitotchigan*, base-viol. —S. *Najâbiigan.*
Kitôtchige, (*nin*). I play on the violin; p. *ket..ged.*—S. *Najabiige.*
Kitoweiâpikaigan. Alg. S. *Najâbiigan.*
Kitwên, adv. With reluctance, notwithstanding, in spite of...; against the will; (F. malgré.)
Kiwanakamigis, (*nin*). I am always playing, or diverting myself, neglecting all other occupations; p. *kaw..sid.*

Kiwanakamigisiwin. Playing or diverting with neglect of duty.
Kiwanis, (*nin*). I make noise; I am foolish and wanton; p. *kaw..sid.*
Kiwanisiwin. Foolish noise, wantonness.
Kiwe or *giwe.* It is said, they say, I understand.
Kiwish, (not much used,) thy wife.— They commonly say: *Ki widigêmagan,* or, *ki mindimôiemish,* thy wife.
Ko, (or *iko,* after a consonant,) is a particle denoting *use* or *custom.*—*Kid ija na ko wedi?* —*Nind ija sa ko.* Dost thou use to go there?— I use to go. *Nimiwog iko,* they use to dance.
Koj, in compositions, signifies the *bill* or *beak* of a bird; as: *Kagagiwikoj,* raven's beak.
Kakokâjogan. Bridge over the Styx, (in Indian mythology,) over which must go the souls of the departed, to arrive to the land of spirits. The good souls pass easily over it and enter the happy land of spirits. The wicked souls cannot pass it: they fall in the depth beneath, and are unhappy for ever.
Kâkoko. Owl; (F. hibou;) pl.-*g.*
Kokosh. Pig, hog, swine, sow; pork; pl.-*ag.*
Kokoshens. A small pig, or a young pig, suckling pig; pl.-*ag.*
Kokoshi-bimide. Hog's lard.
Kokoshiwajagaai. Sward, (skin of bacon; (F. couenne.)
Kokoshiwibwâm gakanâmodeg. Smoked ham.
Kokôshiwi-wiiâss. Hog's meat, pork.
Kokoshiwishkinj. The snout of a hog; pl.-*in.*
Kokowesi. Moth; pl.-*g.*
Kon, nikôn. My liver; *kikon,* thy liver; *okon,* his liver, etc.
Kôpadendâgos, (*nin*). I am considered stupid, awkward, I am despised; p. *kwa..sid.*
Kôpadendâgwad. It is despicable, it is awkward, (awkward situation;) p. *kwa..wak.*
Kôpâdis, (*nin*). I am stupid, dull, awkward, clumsy; p. *kwa..sid.*
Kopâdisia, (*nin*). I make him stupid, dull; p. *kwa..ad.*
Kopâdisiwin. Stupidity, awkwardness.
Kopâdjiâ, (*nin*). I treat him ill, I despise him; I use him in a stupid manner; I spoil some obj.; p. *kwa..ad.*
Kopâdjiwe, (*nin*). I treat ill, despise, destroy; p. *kwa..wed.*
Kopadjinana, (*nin*). I kill an animal uselessly, without any profit to me; p. *kwa..nad;* imp. *kopadjinaj.*
Kopâdjiton, (*nin*). I make it or do it in a stupid and awkward manner, I spoil it, destroy it; p. *kwa..tod.*
Kopanéikwe. Servant-woman, or maid; pl.-*g.*
Kopanéwinini. Servant-man; pl.-*wag.*
Kôpasitagos, (*nin*). I speak stupidly; p. *kwa..sid.*
Kôpâsitawa, (*nin*). I hear him or listen to him with the impression that he speaks stupidly; p. *kwa..wad.*
Kôpâsoma, (*nin*). I despise him

with bad words, I treat him ill; p. *kwa..mad.*

Kôpasondân, (*nin*). I despise it with bad words; p. *kwa..ang.*

Kopasondis, (*nin*). I despise myself with words; p. *kwa.. sod.*

Kosâbama, (*nin*). I practise Indian jugglery on him, to know his sickness and the right remedy for it; p. *kwe.. mad.*

Kosâbandam, (*nin*). I practise Indian jugglery, to know the future, in regard to sick persons; p. *kwe..ang.*

Kosâbandamowin. Indian divination and jugglery in order to know the future, in regard to sicknesses and their remedies.

Kosabatchigan. The jugglery tent.

Kosigosgodjigan. The weight used on a balance to weigh with; (F. le poids d'une balance;) pl.-*an.*

Kosigowane, (*nin.*) I carry a heavy pack on my back; p. *kwe..ned.*

Kosigwan, (*nin*). I am heavy, ponderous; p. *kwesigwanid.*

Kosigwan. It is heavy, ponderous; p. *kwes..ang.*

Kosigwania, (*nin*). I make heavy some obj.; p. *kwe..ad.*

Kosigwaniton, (*nin*). I make it heavy; p. *kwe..tod.*

Kosigwendan, (*nin*). I find it heavy, I think it is heavy; p. *kwe..ang.*

Kosigwanenima, (*nin*). I find him heavy, (any obj.); p. *kwe ..mad.*

K'oss. Thy father.

Kodagâbandam, (*nin*). I have a painful dream; p. *kwe..ang.*

Kotagâbandomowin. Painful dream; pl.-*an.*

Kotagapine, (*nin*). I have a painful sickness; p. *kwe..ned.*

Kotagapinewin. Painful sickness, plague; pl.-*an.*

Kotagendagos, (*nin*). I have to suffer, I am suffering; p. *kwe ..sid.*

Kotagêndagwad. It is painful, hard, causing suffering; p. *kwe..wak.*

Kotagêndagwakamigad. There is tribulation, it is a painful event, painful accident; p. *kwe..gak.*

Kotagéndam, (*nin*). I suffer, I am in a painful trouble; p. *kwe..ang.*

Kotagendamowin. Suffering, sorrow, tribulation, affliction, pain, trouble, adversity, (especially *spiritual.*) S. *Kotagitowin.*

Kotagia, (*nin*). I make him suffer, I plague him, I give him pain and trouble, I torment him, torture him, martyrize him; p. *kwetagiad.*

Kotagimandan. I suffer from the smell of some obj.; p. *kwet..ang.*

Kotaging, adv. In the neighboring lodge or house, in the neighborhood.

Kotagis, (*nin*). I suffer, I am miserable, I am in trouble; p. *kwe..sid.*

Kotagisiwin. Suffering, trouble, misery.

Kotagita, (*nin*). I suffer, (bodily from sickness or labor;) p. *kwe..tod.*

Kotagitôn, (*nin*). I make it suffer; p. *kwe..tod.—O otagikton wiiaw*, he makes suffer his body, (himself.)

Kotagitowin. Suffering, pain, distress, (especially *bodily*.)

Kotagiw, (*nin*). I toil and labor, I endure hardship; p. *kwe..wid.*

Kotagiwebaog, (*nin*). I am tossed about in a canoe, boat, vessel, etc.; p. *kwe..ged.*

Kôtawan. A block, a large piece of wood for fuel, thrown in the back of the chimney; pl.-*ag*.

Kotigôgadeta, (*nin*). My leg is dislocated; p. *kwe..tod.*

Kotigôkishin, (*nin*). I dislocate my leg by falling; p. *kwe..ing.*

Kotigônikeshin, (*nin*). I dislocate my arm by falling; p. *kwe..ing.*

Kotigôniketa, (*nin*). My arm is dislocated; p. *kwe..tad.*

Kotigônindjishin, (*nin*). I dislocate my hand by a fall; p. *kwe..ing.*

Kotigônindjita, (*nin*). I have a dislocated hand; p. *kwe..tad.*

Kotigoshka, (*nin*), or, *nin kotigota*. I dislocate some limb of my body, I have some limb dislocated; p. *kwe..ad.*

Kotigoshkawin. Dislocation of a limb of the human body.

Kotogôsideshin, (*nin*). I dislocate my foot by a fall; p. *kwe ..ing.*

Kotigôsideta, (*nin*). My foot is dislocated; p. *kwe..tod.*

Kwaam, or *kwam*, as end-syllable in compositions alludes to a *forest;* as: *Nin sagaâkwaam*, or, *nin papakwaam*, I come out of the woods. *Tchigakwam*, near the forest.

Kwen, as end-syllable in compositions, alludes to the position of the *head;* as: *Nin nawagikwen*, I incline my head before me. *Anibekweni*, he inclines his head on one side.

Kwetch. Ten, (in common quick counting.)

Kwishkwish, (*nin*). I whistle; p. *kwa..id.*

Kwishkwishima, (*nin*). I call him whistling; p. *kwash..mad.*

Kiskkwishinagam, (*nin*). I whistle an air, a song, a melody; p. *kwa..mod.*

Kwishkwishiwin. Whistling, whistle.

Kwishkwishkwassimwe, (*nin*). I whistle after a dog, I call a dog whistling; p. *kwo..wed.*

Kwiwisens. Boy; pl.-*ag*.

Kwiwisens. Kind of lizard, red lizard; pl.-*ag*.

Kwiwisensike, (*nin*). I am delivered of a boy, I give birth to a boy; p. *kwa..ked.*

Kwiwisensiw, (*nin*). I am a boy; p. *kwaw..wid.*

M

Ma ; particle signifying a reinforcement of what is said; as : *Win ma gi-ikkito ;* he said it himself. *Ka ma win ;* no, no.

Mâbam, pron , this, this one, this here.

Mâdaadon mikana, (*nin*). S. *Bimaadon.*

Mâdaan, (*nin*). I scrape a hide or skin ; p. *maiâdaang.—Nin madaan pijikiwegin,* I scrape an ox-hide.

Mâdaana, (*nin*). I go after him, I follow him ; I pursue him ; p. *maiâ..nad.*

Madâbi, (*nin*). I come out of the woods to the lake ; p. *medâbid.*

Madâbigos, (*nin*). I come from camp to camp out of the woods to the lake ; p. *med..sid.*

Madâbimagad. It comes to the lake ; p. *med..gak.*

Madâbisse, (*nin*). I slide down to the lake ; p. *med..sed.*

Madâbisse, or-*magad.* It slides down to the lake ; p. *med..seg,* or-*magak.*

Madâbiwidon, (*nin*). I carry it to the lake shore ; p. *med..dod.*

Madâbiwina, (*nin*). I carry or convey him to the lake shore, (a person, or any other obj.) ; p. *med..nad.*

Madâbon, (*nin*). I go on a river in a canoe or boat down to the lake, to the mouth of the river ; p. *med..nod.*

Mâdâdis, (*nin*). I travel, I am on a journey ; p. *maia..sid.*

Mâdadjim, (*nin*). I begin to tell, I begin my report or narration ; p. *maiadâdjimod.*(Abridged from *madji,* beginning ; and *nin dibâdjim,* I tell.)

Madâdon, (*nin*). I carry a canoe to the water ; p. *med..nod.*

Madâgami. Troubled or agitated water.

Madâgamishka, or-*magad nibi.* The water moves, it is not still and quiet ; p. *med..kag,* or-*magak.*

Mâdaigan. Scraper ; (C. gratte, grattoir ;) pl.-*an.*

Mâdaige, (*nin*). I scrape a hide, a skin ; p. *maiadaiged.*

Mâdakamigis, (*nin*). I commence some work ; I begin to make noise ; p. *maia..sid.*

Mâdandjige, (*nin*). I begin to eat ; p. *maia..ged.*

Mâdanimad. The wind begins to blow ; p. *maia..mak.*

Mâdaoken, (*nin*). I distribute or divide it among several persons ; p. *maia..ked.*

Mâdaokenan, (*nin*). I distribute or divide some object among several persons ; p. *maia..ked.*

(V. Conj.)—*Nin madaokenan nin joniiâm;* I distribute my money among several persons.

Mâdaoki, (*nin*). I divide or distribute among several persons; p. *maia..kid.*

Mâdaokiwin. Distribution, division, repartition, dividing among several persons.

Mâdaonamawag, (*nin*). I divide it amongst them, I give some to every one of them; p. *maia ..wad.*

Mâdaonidimin, (*nin*). We divide it amongst us; p. *maia..didjig.*

Mâdaonidiwin. Distribution made by several amongst themselves, to each other.

Mâdapine, (*nin*). I begin to feel a sickness; p. *maia..ned.*

Mâdapinewin. Beginning of a sickness.

Madâssidon, (*nin*). I carry it to the water, (a canoe;) I launch it, (a vessel, etc.); p. *med.. tod.*

Mâdawa, (*nin*). I scrape a hide or skin; p. *maia..wad.*—*Nin madawa wawashkêshiwaiân*, I scrape a deer-skin, or buckskin.

Madima, (*nin*). I wear it. I clothe myself with it; p. *medimad.*

Mâdimona, (*nin*). S. *Modindamawa.*

Mâdindâgan. Clothing, clothes, clothing material.

Madindâganiwigamig. Clothing-store; pl.-*on.*

Madindamawa, (*nin*). I give him clothes, I clothe him; p. *me.. wad.*

Madindân, (*nin*). I wear it, I clothe myself with it; p. *med ..ang.*

Madindâss, (*nin*). I am rich in clothing, I have many clothes; p. *med..sod.*

Mâdipo, or-*magad.* It commences snowing, it begins to snow; p. *maiâdipog*, or-*magak.*

Mâdja, (*nin*). I start, I go away, I go on; p. *maiâdjad.*

Mâdjamagad. It goes away, it goes on; p. *maia..gak.*

Mâdji. This word, in connection with a verb, signifies *beginning*, or *going on.* (Change, *maiadji.*) *Nin mâdji-anoki*, I begin to work. *Mâdjigagikwe*, he begins to preach.—(Other examples in some of the following words.)

Mâdji, adv. S. *Mâdjikamig.*

Mâdji, (*nin*). I go away, I start in a canoe or boat; p. *maiadjiod.*

Mâdjibaiwe, (*nin*). I run away in a great haste, as quick as I can; (F. je me sauve à pleines jambes;) p. *maiâ..wed.*

Mâdjibato, (*nin*). I begin to run; p. *maia..tod.*

Mâdjibiamawa, (*nin*). I write to him, I write him a letter; p. *maia..wad.*

Mâdjibide, or-*magad.* It goes or glides away; it flies off; p. *maia..deg*, or-*magak.*

Mâdjibiigan. Missive, writing sent to somebody, letter *sent;* pl.-*an.* S. *Bidjibiigan.*

Mâdjibiige, (*nin.*) I am writing a letter to send to somebody, a missive; p. *maia..ged.*

Mâdjibissa. It begins to rain; p. *maia..sag.*

Mâdjidabâdan, (*nin*). I draw or drag it away; p. *maia..ang.*

Mâdjidabana, (*nin*). I draw or drag him away, (a person or any other obj.); p. *maia..nad.*

Mâdjidabi, (*nin*). I draw or drag away; p. *maia..bid.*

Mâdjidaiwe, (*nin*). I send s. th. to somebody; p. *maia..wed.*

Mâdjidaiwen, (*nin*). I sent it to somebody; p. *maia..wed.*

Mâdjidaiwenan, (*nin*). I send some obj. to somebody; p. *maia..wed.* (V. Conj.)

Mâdjidawa, (*nin*). I carry it to him; p. *maia..wad.*

Mâdjidjigade, or-*magad*. It is carried away; p. *maia..deg*, or-*magak.*

Mâdjidjigas, (*nin*). I am carried away, (a person, or any other obj.); p. *maia..sod.*

Mâdjidjiwan. It runs on, it runs away, (any liquid;) p. *maia..ang.*

Mâdjidode, (*nin*). I move away; p. *maiadjidokeod.*

Mâdjidon, (*nin*). I carry it away, I carry it off, I convey it away; p. *maiadjidod.*

Mâdjig, (*nin*). I grow taller; p. *maiadjigid.*

Mâdjiga, or-*magad*. The sap of maple-trees begins to run; p. *maiadjigag*, or-*magak.*

Mâdjigidas, (*nin*). I begin to be angry, I get angry; p. *maia..sod.*

Mâdjigin. It grows on; p. *maia..ing.*

Mâdjigwass, (*nin*). I begin to sew; p. *maia..sod.*

Mâdjiiâdjim, (*nin*). I carry word or news; p. *maia..mod.*

Mâdjiiâdjima, (*nin*). I tell of him, I spread his fame, or his shame; p. *maia..mad.*

Mâdjiiadjimoiwe, (*nin*). I send word or news to somebody; p. *maia..wed.*

Mâdjiiâssin. It goes away driven by the wind; p. *maiâ..ing.*—*Nâbikwân madjiiâssin*, the vessel goes away, (driven by the wind.)

Mâdjikamig, or *madji*, adv. Not now, not so much.—*Mojag gi-bimatchi-ijiwebisi, mâdjika-mig nongom ta-mino-ijiwebisi.* He always behaved badly, he will not now behave well.

Mâdjikamigad. It begins, (an action or event;) p. *maia..gak.*

Mâdjikan, (*nin*). I commence some work; p. *maia..ang.*

Mâdjikikwewiss. The first-born girl of a family.

Mâdjikikwewissikandage, (*nin*). I am like a mother to my younger brothers and sisters; p. *med..ged.*

Mâdjikikwewissikandawa ni-shime, (*nin*). I am like a mother to my younger brother, (to my younger sister;) p. *med ..wad.*

Mâdjikikwewissiw, (*nin*). I am the first-born girl of the family; p. *med..wid.*

Mâdjikiwiss. The first-born boy of a family; pl.-*ag.*—*Nin mad-jikiwissim*, my first-born son; also, my oldest brother.

Mâdjikiwissiw, (*nin*). I am the first-born boy of our family; p. *medj..wid.*

Mâdjina, (*nin*). I carry him away; p. *maiadjinad;* imp. *madjij.*

Mâdjinajaigas, (*nin*). I am sent away; p. *maia..sod.*

Mâdjinajâwa, (*nin*). I send him away; p. *maia..wad*; imp. *mâdjinajâ.*

Mâdjinajikawa, (*nin*). I send away in haste, I hurry him away; I drive him away; p. *maia..wad.*

Mâdjita, (*nin*). I begin, I commence, (a work or an action;) I attack, I aggress; p. *maiâdjitad.*

Mâdjiwidawa, (*nin*), or, *nin madjiwidamawa*. S. *Mâdjidawa.*

Mâdjiwidjigas, (*nin*). I am carried away; p. *maia..sod.*

Mâdjiwiton, (*nin*). S. *Mâdjidon.*

Mâdjiwina, (*nin*). I carry or convey him away, (any obj.); p. *maia..nad*; imp. *madjiwij.*

Mâdjiwinidis, (*nin*). I carry or convey myself away; p. *maia..sod.*

Madôdisson. Indian steam-bath; (C. suerie sauvage.)

Madôdo, (*nin*). I take a steam-bath, (in order to recover of a sickness by a violent perspiration); p. *medôdod.*

Mâdôma, (*nin*). I carry him away on my back on a packing-strap; p. *maiadomad.*

Mâdondan, (*nin*). I carry it away on my back on a portage-strap, or packing-strap; p. *maia..ang.*

Madonewâbik. Hot stone used in an Indian steam-bath to heat the water; pl.-*og.*

Madwé, in compositions, signifies *hearing* a report, a sound, a noise; as: *Kishime gi-madwé-nibo*; we hear that thy brother died. *Noss gi-madwédagwishin tibidong*; I hear my father arrived last night.

Madwêdagassin. The wind whispers in the leaves of a tree; p. *med..sing.*

Madwébissa. The rain is heard (falling on a roof, on leaves, etc.); p. *med..sag.*

Madwédjiwan. The current of a stream or river is heard; p. *med..ang.*

Madweiâbideshimon, (*nin*), (or *nin madweiâbideshin*.) I chatter with the teeth, from cold; p. *med..nod.*

Madwêma, (*nin*). I crack some obj. with the teeth, I craunch it; p. *medwémad.*

Madwêngwam, (*nin*). I snore; p. *med..ang.*

Madwéngwamowin. Snoring; (F. ronflement.)

Madwéngwash, (*nin*). S. *Madwengwam.*

Madwéshim, (*nin*). I am heard falling; p. *med..ing.*

Madwésige, (*nin*). I fire a gun; p. *med..ged.*

Madwesigé-gijigad. Gun-firing day, the day of firing guns.

Madwêssagishin, (*nin*). I am heard falling on the floor, on boards; p. *med..ing.*

Madwéssagissin. It is heard falling on boards, on the floor; p. *med..ing.*

Madwéssin. It is heard falling; it sounds, it rings; p. *med..ing.*

Madwéssiton, (*nin*). I make it sound, ring, I ring it; p. *med..tod.*

Madwéta, (*nin*), (freq. *nin ma-*

madweta.) I am heard somewhere making noise; p. *medwetad.*

Madwéwe, or-*magad.* It sounds, it rings; p. *med..weg,* or-*magak.*

Madwéweo biné. The partridge is making noise with his wings; p. *med..od.*

Madwéweshin, (*nin*). I am heard from some place; p. *med..ing.*

Madwiwessin. It is heard from some place; p. *med..ing.*

Madwéwetchigan. Any thing that produces or gives a sound or sounds; a musical instrument, trumpet, horn; harp, guitar, etc.; pl.-*an.*

Madwéwetchige, (*nin*). I make something sound; I produce sounds; I make music; p. *med..ged.*

Madwéweton, (*nin*). I make it sound; p. *med..tod.—Nin madweweton bodâdjigan,* I make a trumpet sound, a bugle, a horn.

Mâgobidon, (*nin*). I press or compress it in my hand *strongly;* p. *maia..dod.*

Mâgobina, (*nin*). I press or compress some obj. *strongly* in my hand; p. *maia..nad.*

Mâgona, (*nin*). I press some obj. in my hand *slightly;* p. *maia..nad.*

Mâgonan, (*nin*). I press it in my hand *slightly;* p. *maia..ang.*

Mâgonindjina, (*nin*). I press his hand; p. *maia..nad.*

Magoshé, (*nin*). I make an Indian feast, as a religious ceremony; p. *megoshed.*

Magoshêwin. Indian religious feast.

Magwâwigan. Hunchback.

Magwâwigan, (*nin*). I am humpbacked; p. *meg..ang.*

Mâgwia, (*nin*). I am stronger than he, I surpass him, overcome him; p. *maia..ad.*

Mâgwiigon, (*nin*). It overcomes me, surpasses me; p. *maia..god.—Nin magwiigon nind âkosiwin;* my sickness overcomes me, (it is stronger than I.)

Mâgwito, (*nin*). I am very sick, I am overcome by sickness; p. *maiâgwitod.*

Mâgwiton, (*nin*). I overcome it, surpass it; p. *maia..tod.*

Maiâdaokid. He that distributes, a distributor; pl.-*jig.*

Maiâdjitad. He that commences, aggressor, attacker; pl.-*jig.*

Maiâg, in compositions, signifies *foreign, strange, changed.*

Maiâganishinâbe. Strange Indian from another tribe; in Scriptural language, pagan, gentile; pl.-*g.*

Maiagéndagos, (*nin*). I am considered, or found, strange, changed; I am changed; p. *meiag..sid.*

Maiagénima, (*nin*). I find him changed, strange, (a person, or any other obj.); p. *mai..mad.*

Maiâgikwe. Foreign, strange woman; pl.-*g.*

Maiâginagos, (*nin*). I look changed, strange; I look like a stranger; p. *meia..sid.*

Maiâginan, (*nin*). I see it changed; p. *meia..ang.*

Maiaginawa, (*nin*). I see him changed, (any obj.); p. *meia..wad.*

Maiâginini. Foreign, strange man, foreigner; pl.-*wag.*
Maiâgis, (*nin*). I am a stranger, a foreigner; p. *meiâgisid.*
Maiâgishkinjigwe, (*nin*). I have a strange face, or a changed face; p. *meia..wed.*
Maiagissiton, (*nin*). I put it otherwise, in a strange manner; p. *meia..tod.*
Maiâgitagos, (*nin*). I am heard speaking strangely, I speak like a stranger, or with an altered voice; I speak a foreign language; p. *meia..sid.*
Maiâgitawa, (*nin*). I find, in hearing him, that his language (or his voice) is changed, strange, I hear him speaking strangely, like a stranger; p. *meia..wad.*
Maiâgiton, (*nin*). I make it in a strange manner; also, it sounds strange to me, I find strange (or changed) what I hear; p. *mei..tod.*
Maiagwê, (*nin*). My speaking is strange or changed; I speak a strange or foreign language; p. *maiagwed.*
Maiagwéa, (*nin*). I make him speak a strange or foreign language; p. *meg..ad.*
Maiâjimagosid manitons. Stinking insect, bed-bug.
Maiâmakâdendang. He who admires, admirer; pl.-*ig.*
Maiâmawi-niganisid Kitchi-mekatewikwanaie. Sovereign Pontiff, Pope, (the foremost Great Black-gown.)
Maiâoshtigwân. S. *Navîsigokwandib.*
Maiâosse, (*nin*). I march foremost, at the head ef a gang, band or company; p. *mei..sed.*
Maiâossêwinini. War-captain, war-chief, who marches at the head of his band of warriors; pl.-*wag.*
Maiatawanishinabe. Strange Indian, in particular a Siou-Indian; pl.-*g.*
Maiatawis, (*nind*). S. *Maiagis.*
Maiâwab, (*nin*). I am sitting straight up; p. *me..bid.*
Maiâwaiekwaiabikisi assin. It is a corner-stone.
Maiawakonan, (*nin*). I erect it, I make it stand up; p. *meia..ang.*
Maiawâsh, (*nin*). I am put upright, I am erected, by the wind; p. *meiawâshid.*
Maiawâssin. It is erected, or put upright, by the wind; p. *mei..ing.*
Maiâwendagos, (*nin*). I am considered the foremost; p. *meia..sid.*
Maiawendagwad. It is considered foremost; p. *meia..wak.*
Maiâwendam, (*nin*). I am foremost, I am at the head of a band; p. *meia..ang.*
Maiâwikana, adv. In or on the trail, road, street.
Maiâwina, (*nin*). I raise him up, I make him sit or stand straight up; p. *meia..nad*;
Maiâwishima, (*nin*). I erect him, I put him upright, (a person or any other obj.); p. *me..mad.*
Maiâwishka, (*nin*). I erect myself, I stand up straight; p. *meia..kad.*
Maiâwishkan,(*nin*). I go straight upon it; p. *meia..ang.*

Maiawishkawa, (*nin*). I go straight upon him; p. *meia..wad.*

Maiawissitchigasso. It is erected, put upright; p. *meia..sod.*

Maiâwissiton, (*nin*). I erect it, I put it up straight; p. *mei..tod.*

Maiâwissin. It is upright, in an upright position, erected; p. *meia..ing.*

Maiâwita, (*nin*). S. *Maiawishka.*

Maien, adv. Aside, apart; as: *Maien nind aton ow;* I put this aside.

Maiênissendansig, *neg.* He who feels no shame, a shameless person, impudent, brazen-faced; pl.-*og.* S. *Egatchissig.*

Maiêssandwas, (*nin*). I joke, I tell jokes to make people laugh; p. *meie..sod.*

Maingan. Wolf; pl.-*ag.*

Mainganika. There are wolves; p. *mein..kag.*

Mainganikan. A place where there are wolves.— *Mainganikaning kid ininajaoninim;* I send you in the midst of wolves, (in a place where there are wolves.)

Majamégoss. Salmon-trout; pl.-*ag.*

Majidikwanaige, (*nin*). I cut off branches; p. *mej..ged.*

Majidikwanêwa mitig, (*nin*). I cut off the branches of a tree; p. *mej..wad ;* imp. *majidikwané.*

Majiiâkonigan. S. *Majiigan.*

Majiiâkonige, (*nin*). S. *Majiige.*

Majiigan. Clearing, a cleared piece of land; pl.-*an.*

Makak. Box, trunk, chest, coffer, barrel, Indian sugar-box; pl.-*on.*

Makakoke, (*nin*). I make barrels (or boxes); p. *mek..bed.*

Makamâ, (*nin*). I take it from him by force, I rob him of it; p. *mekomad.*

Makandôshkamage, (*nin*). I get s. th. before another, I take s. th. before some other does; p. *mek..ged.*

Makandôshkamawa, or, *nin makandôshkawa*, (*nin*). I get it or take it before he does, (he wishes or intends to get it, but I get it before him;) p. *mek..wad.*

Makandwé, (*nin*). I take by force, I rob, I pillage; p. *mek..wed.*

Makandwin, (*nin*). I take it away by force; p. *mek..wed.*

Makandwênan, (*nin*). I take some obj. away by force; p. *mek..wed.* (V. Conj.)

Makandwêwin. Taking away by force, pillage, robbery.

Makandwéwini. Robber, pillager, brigand; pl.-*wag.*

The Indians of Sandy Lake are called *Makandwewininiwag*, from the circumstance that once they pillaged the store of their fur-trader.

Makaté. Gun-powder.

Makatê, adj. Black, dark-colored.

Makatéginebig. Black serpent; pl.-*og.*

Makatéianak. A kind of black bird; pl.-*og.*

Makatéke, (*nin*). I paint my face black; p. *mek..ked.*

Makatêkodon, (*nin*). I blacken it, paint it black; p. *mek..dod.*

Makatêkona, (*nin*). I blacken some obj., I paint it black; p. *mek..ad.*

Makatêkonidis, (*nin*). I blacken my face; p. *mek..sod.*

Makaté-mashkikiwâbo. Coffee, (black medicine.)

Makatéshib. Black duck; pl.-*ag.*

Makatêwabikinigaso. It is made black, painted black, (metal); p. *mek..sod.*

Makatêwabikisi. It is black, (silver, *joniia*; stone, *assin*; the sun, *gisiss*;) p. *mek..sid.*

Makatêwâgami. It is black; of a dark color, (some liquid;) p. *mek..mig.*— *Kitchi makatéwâgami iw jominâbo*; this wine is of a very dark color, (black.)

Makatéwagamishkinjigwan. Apple of the eye; (F. pupille de l'œil)

Makatéwagamitigweia sibi. The river is black, of a dark color; p. *mek..iag.*

Makatéwaie, (*nin*). My skin is black; p. *mek..jed.*

Makatéwiiâss. Negro, mulatto, colored man; (black flesh;) pl.-*ag.*

Makatéwiiassikwe. Negro woman; mulatto woman; colored woman; pl.-*g.*

Makatéwikwanaie, (*nin*). I dress in black, I wear black clothes; p. *mekatéwikwanaie*, the priest, he that wears black clothes.

Makatéwingwe, (*nin*). I have a black face, my face is blackened; p. *mek..wed.*

Makatêwis, (*nin*). I am black, I am of a black or dark complexion; I am colored, I am swarthy, dusky, sun-burnt; p. *mek..sid.*

Mikatéwiwe, (*nin*). I am a black person, a negro; also, I am a colored person; p. *mek..wed.*

Mâkia, (*nin*). I wound him; p. *maiâkiad.*

Mâkiewin. Wounding, wound; pl.-*an.*

Mâkiganama, (*nin*). I wound him, striking him with s. th.; p. *maia..mad.*

Mâkijâ, adv. Perhaps, may be.

Mâkikinak. A kind of turtle; pl.-*wag.*

Mâkinana, (*nin*). I wound him, I lame him, cripple him by striking him; p. *maia..nad*; imp. *mâkinaj.*

Mâkis, (*nin*). I am a cripple; p. *maiakisid.*

Makisin. Shoe, moccasin; pl.-*an.*

Makisin-agwidâgan. The upper part of a moccasin; (C. hausse de soulier); pl.-*an.*

Makisinéiâb. String of a shoe or moccasin; pl.-*ia.*

Makisiniké, (*nin*). I make shoes, boots, etc., I am a shoe-maker; p. *mek..ked.*

Makisinikéwigamig. Shoe-maker's shop; pl.*on.*

Makisinikéwin. Shoe-making, occupation, work or trade of a shoe-maker.

Makogan. Bear's bone; pl.-*an.*

Makoganj. Bear's claw; pl.-*ig.*

Makojigan. Bear's croup; pl.-*an.*

Makons, (properly *makwâns*,) a young bear; pl.-*ag.*

Makopin. Bear's potato, (an eatable root;) pl.-*ig.*
Makôshtigwân. Bear's head; pl.-*an.*
Makôweiân, (properly *makwâwaiân.*) Bear-skin; pl.-*ag.*
Makowiiâss. Bear-meat.
Makwâ. Bear; pl. *makwog.*
Makwâj. Bear's hole or den; pl.-*an.*
Makwassâgim. Bear-snowshoe, a small round snow-shoe, filled or laced with basswood bark, made in the woods in a case of necessity; pl.-*ag;* (C. patte d'ours.)
Makwâtig. Bear's tree, hollow tree where a bear winters; pl.-*on.*
Makwimij. Sorb, service-tree; (F. cormier;) pl.-*in.*
Makwimin. Sorb, service-berry, (bear's berry;) pl.-*an.*
Mâma. Mother, mamma; *o mamaian,* his mother.
Mâma, nin mâma. My eyebrow; *nin mamag,* my eyebrows; *o mâman,* his eyebrows.
Mamâ, (*nin*). I harvest, I reap; p. *memad;* imp. *mamân.*
Mamâdab, (*nin*). I stir or move, sitting; p. *mem..bid.*
Mamâdinâ, (*nin*). I move some obj.; p. *mem..nad.*
Mamâdikwen, (*nin*). I move my head; p. *mem..nid.*
Mamâdji, (*nin*). I stir, I move; p. *memadjid.*
Mamâdjibina, (*nin*). I move him; p. *mem..nad;* imp. *mamâdjibij.*
Mamâdjipagis. I palpitate, I sprawl; p. *mem..sod.*—*Gigo mamadjipagiso,* the fish palpitates.
Mamâdjisse, (*nin*). S. *Mamâdji.*
Mamadokis, (*nin*). I am extremely big, large; p. *mem..sid.*
Mamadwé, (*nin*). I groan, (especially a sick person;) p. *memadwed.*
Mamadwéiabideshimon, (*nin*). S. *Madweiabideshimon.*
Mamadwéiashka, or-*magad.* The waves are roaring, the roaring of the waves is heard; p. *mem..kag,* or-*magak.*
Mamadwengwâm, (*nin*). I groan sleeping; p. *wem..ang.*
Mamâdwewin. Groaning, groans.
Mamâikawin. God-mother, sponsor at baptism; also, my adopted mother; pl.-*ag.*—There is always a possessive pronoun prefixed to this word; as: *Nin mamaikawin,* my god-mother; *o mamâikawinan,* his god-mother, etc.
Mamâjimadji, (*nin*). I do it or make it badly, negligently, not in a proper manner; p. *mem..id.*
Mamâjitawage, (*nin*). I have ugly ears, ill-formed; p. *mem..ged.*
Mamakâdakamig, adv. Admirably, surprising, astonishing, curious, marvellous, wondrous, prodigious, miraculous.
Mamakâdendagos, (*nin*). I am admirable, I am curious; p. *maia..sid.*
Mâmakâdendagwad. It is admirable, it is astonishing, curious; p. *maia..wak.*
Mâmakadendam, (*nin*). I wonder, I admire, I am surprised, astonished; p. *maia..ang.*

Mamakadendamoa, (*nin*). I make him wonder, admire, I astonish him; p. *maia..ad.*

Mâmakadendamowin. Admiration, surprise, astonishment.

Mâmakadendân, (*nin*). I admire it, I wonder at it; I find it curious; p. *maia..ang.*

Mâmakâdenim, (*nin*). I admire; p. *maiâm..mod.*

Mâmakadenima, (*nin*). I admire him, I wonder at him; I find him curious, (a person, or any other obj.); p. *maia..mad.*

Mâmakâdis, (*nin*). I am surprising, singular, curious, strange in my conduct; p. *maiamakadisid.*

Mâmakâdjaii, adv. Wonderfully, curious, strange.

Mamakâdjitchigan. Wonderful thing, sign, miracle; pl.-*an.*

Mâmakâdjitchjige, (*nin*). I do wonderful things; I work miracles; p. *maia..ged.*

Mâmâkâdjitchjigewin. Doing wonderful things, miracles.

Mâmakâsabama, (*nin*). I gaze at him with astonishment, with curiosity; p. *maia..mad.*

Mâmakâsabandan, (*nin*). I gaze at it with astonishment, with curiosity; p. *maia..ang.*

Mâmakâsabandjigan. Any thing that is gazed at with astonishment, a wonderful thing, sign; pl.-*an.*

Mâmakâsabange, (*nin*). I look on with curiosity and surprise; p. *maia..ged.*

Mâmakasabange, (*nin*). I look on with curiosity and surprise; p. *maia..ged.*

Mâmakâsabangeshk, (*nin*). I am in a habit of looking on with too much curiosity; p. *maia..kid.*

Mamakasabangeshkiwin. Bad curiosity, inquisitiveness in looks. — The same signification has *mamakâsinamowin.*

Mamakasinan, (*nin*). S. *Mamakasabandan.*

Mamakasinawa, (*nin*). S. *Mamakasabama.*

Mâmakâs, *tagos*, (*nin*). I am telling admirable wonderful things, curious stories; p. *maia..sid.*

Mâmakâsitawa, (*nin*). I listen to him with astonishment, with admiration; p. *maia..wad.*

Mâmakiganama, (*nin*), *freq.* I wound him in several places by striking him.

Mamakingwe, (*nin*). My face is marked with the small-pox; p. *mem..wed.*

Mamakisiwin. Small-pox; (F. petite vérole, picote.)

Mamanâke, (*nin*). I am a poor archer, I cannot shoot well with a bow and arrow; p. *mem..ked.*

Mamandâ, in compositions, signifies *wonderful, astonishing; miraculous.*

Mamamdâdodam, (*nin*). I do astonishing things; I work miracles; p. *mem..ang.*

Mâmandâdodamowin. Admirable, astonishing doing; miracle; pl.-*an.*

Mamandâgashkito, (*nin*). I can do wonderful things; p. *mem..tôd.*

Mamandâgonini. Braggart,

boaster; (F. fanfaron;) pl.-*wag*.

Mamandâwinagos, (*nin*). I look extraordinary, I have an astonishing, surprising appearance; p. *mem..sid*.

Mamandâwitchigan. Curious strange action; pl.-*an*.

Mamandâwitchige, (*nin*). I have curious manners, I act strangely, curiously; p. *mem..ged*.

Mamandâwitchigewin. Curious strange custom or manners; pl.-*an*.

Mamandéssadendagos, (*nin*). I am looked upon as a rascal, I have a roguish appearance; p. *mem..sid*.

Mamangêssadendam, (*nin*). I have bad roguish thoughts and plans; p. *mem..ang*.

Mamandéssandis, (*nin*). I am a rascal, a rogue; p. *mem..sid*.

Mamândjigonindjibina, (*nin*). I bind or fetter his hands by force; p. *mem..nad*; imp. *ma..bij*.

Mamandjigos, (*nin*). I am lame, I cannot walk, or, I cannot walk well; p. *mem..sid*.

Mamândjigosidebina, (*nin*). I fetter or bind his feet by force; p. *mem..nad*; imp. *mam..bij*.

Mamândjigosidebis, (*nin*). My feet are fettered; p. *mem..sod*.

Mamândjigwapidjigan. Fetters; pl.-*an*.

Mamândjigwapidjigas, (*nin*). I am fettered; p. *mem..sod*.

Mamândjigwapina, (*nin*). I fetter him, bind him by force; p. *mem..nad*; imp. *mam..pij*.

Mamândjitchige, (*nin*). I practise magic, witchcraft; p. *mem..ged*.

Mamândjitchigewin, or *mamandjinowin*. Magic, witchcraft.

Mamândjitchigewinini, or *mamândjinowinini*. Magician; pl.-*wag*.

Mamângashka, or-*magad*. The sea runs high, there is a heavy sea; p. *mem..kag*, or-*magak*.

Mamângatigodjiwan. The water runs in heavy waves, (in rapids;) p. *mem..ang*.

Mamanj, adv. Badly, negligently, carelessly, not right, superficially.

Mamânjia, (*nin*). I overcome him, I prevail against him, I vanquish him; p. *mem..ad*.

Mamânjiigon, (*nin*). It overcomes me, vanquishes me, it prevails against me; p. *mem..god*.

Mamânjiton, (*nin*). I vanquish or overcome it, I prevail against it; p. *mem..tod*.

Mamânjitwa, (*nin*). I prevail, I overcome; p. *mem..wad*.

Mamânsinam, (*nin*). I see s. th. admirable, I have an apparition, a vision, (according to Indian jugglery;) p. *mem..ang*.

Mamânsinamowin. Apparition, vision, (trick of an Indian juggler;) pl.-*an*.

Mamâsika, (*nin*). I stir or move several times; p. *mem..kad*.

Mamasikâmagad. It moves, it stirs several times; p. *mem..gak*.

Mamâsikan, (*nin*). I move it, I agitate it; p. *mem..ang*.

Mamâsikawa, (*nin*). I move, stir or agitate some obj.; p. *mem..wad.*

Mamawâ, (*nin*). I take s. th. from him, I take s. th. that belongs to him, or relates to him; p. *memawad.*

Mamawapinag, (*nin*), (pron. *nin mamaopinag.*) I tie several objects together; p. *maia..nad.*

Mâmawapidonan, (*nin*), (pron. *nin mamaopidonan.*) I tie several objects together; p *maia..dod.*

Mamawassag, (*nin*). I put several objects together, I unite them; p. *maia..sed.* — S. *Mamawissitonan.*

Mâmawi, adv. Together, in common, generally, collectively, in a body, in a block.

Mâmawi, adv. This adverb is sometimes employed to express the superlative, corresponding to the English *most,* or *at all,;* as: *Ki mamawi gashkiewis endashiwad ininiwag oma;* thou are the most powerful of all the men in this place.

Mâmawigemin, (*nin*), (*nin mamawi-ojigemin.*) We make our dwelling together; we live together in the same lodge or house; p. *maia..gedjig.*

Mâmawigimagad. It grows together in the same field; p. *maia ..gak.*

Mâmawiidimin, (*nin*). We meet together, we assemble, we come together in one place; p. *maia..didjig.*

Mamâwin. Harvest, reaping.

Mâmawinimin, (*nin*) or, *nin mamawinomin.* We are gathered together in a great number; p. *maiamawinidjig,* or *maiamawinodjig,* multitude of people; (L. turba.)

Mâmawissin. It joins together, it fits well together; p. *maia.. ing.*

Mâmawissitchigade. It is put together; p. *maia..deg.*

Mâmawîssitonan, (*nin*). I put several objects together, I unite them; p. *maia..tod.*— S. *Mamawassag.*

Mâmawitchigemin, (*nin*). We act or work together, we are in company together for some work or business; p. *maia.. gedjig.*

Mâmawiton, (*nin*). I join it together; p. *maia..tod.*

Mamibidon, (*nin*). I pull or pluck it out; p. *mem..dod.*

Mamibina, (*nin*). I pull out some obj.; p. *mem..nad;* imp. *mamibij.*

Mamidawendam, (*nin*). I am afflicted, sorrowful; I feel lonesome; I long for s. th., I am impatient, I wish to go...; p. *mem..ang.*

Mamidawitchi, (*nin*). My belly is hard, I am constipated; p. *mem..id.*

Mamidawito, (*nin*). I am very ill, very sick; p. *mem..tod.*

Mâmig, pron. These, these here.

Mamigade, or-*magad.* It is taken away; p. *mem..deg,* or-*magak.*

Mamigana, (*nin*). I fight him or wrestle with him, for joke or play; p. *mem..ad.*

Mamigas, (*nin*). I fight or wrestle, joking or playing, (not in anger;) p. *mem..sod.*

Mamgaso. It is taken away; p. *mem..sod.*

Mamigososhk, (*nin*). I am in a bad habit, or too much in a habit, of wrestling and fighting, for play; (not in anger;) p. *mem..kid.*

Mamige, (*nin*). I take, (without naming any object;) p. *memiged.*

Mamiginag, (*nin*). S. *Gagiginag.*

Mamiginanan, (*nin*). S. *Gagiginanan.*

Mamigonindjama, (*nin*). I rub some object in my hands; p. *mem..mad.*

Mamigonindjandan, (*nin*). I rub it in my hands; p. *mem..ang.*

Mamigoshkam, (*nin*). I have only moccasins or shoes on, (no stockings, socks or nippes;) p. *mem..ang.*

Mamigoshkân makisin, (*nin*). I put a shoe or moccasin on, without any thing in; p. *mem..ang.*

Mamijima, (*nin*). I accuse him falsely; I condemn him; p. *memijimad.*

Mamijwa, (*nin*). I scalp him; p. *mem..ad;* imp. *mamijwi.*

Mamikawinan, (*nin*), freq. I think often on him, I remember him for what he did me; p. *mem..wid.* (V. Conj.)

Mamikwadam, (*nin*). I praise; p. *mem..ang.*

Mamikwadân, (*nin*). I praise it, I glorify in it; p. *mem..ang.*

Mamikwadimin, (*nin*). We praise each other; p. *mem..didjig.*

Mamikwadiwin. Praise, flattery.

Mamikwana, (*nin*). I praise him; I flatter him; p. *mem..nad.*

Mamikwas, (*nin*). I praise myself, I boast of..., I brag of myself, I am a braggart; p. *mem..sod.*

Mamikwasowin. Self-praise, boasting, bragging; (F. fanfaronnerie.)

Mamikwendamawa, (*nin*) or *nin mamikwendamia.* I put him often in remembrance of s. th., I recall it repeatedly to his memory; p. *mem..ad.*

Mamin, pron. These, these here.

Maminâdendam, (*nin*). I have proud thoughts; p. *mem..ang.*

Maminâdendamowin. Proud thought; pl.-*an.*

Maminâdis, (*nin*). I am proud, arrogant, insolent, haughty; p. *mem..sid.*

Maminâdisiwin. Pride, haughtiness, arrogance.

Maminâdjib, (*nin*). I am fond of dainties; (F. je suis friand;) p. *mem..bed.*

Maminâdjibowin. Fondness of dainties, of good nice things to eat; (F. friandise.)

Maminassobi, (*nin*). I take a net out of the water; p. *mem..bid.*

Maminâwendân, (*nin*). I am fond of it, I don't like to part with it, I am attached to it; p. *mem..ang.*

Maminawenima, (*nin*). I am attached to him, like him much, I don't like to part with him; p. *mem..mad.*

Maminobama, (*nin*). I discern some obj.; p. *mem..mad.*

Maminowabandan, (*nin*). I discern it well; p. *mem..ang.*

Maminonendam, (*nin*). I reflect, I consider, I understand; p. *mem..ang.*

Maminonendân, (*nin*). I reflect upon it, consider it; p. *mem..ang.*

Maminonenima, (*nin*). I reflect upon him, I consider him; p. *mem..ad.*

Maminoponidis, (*nin*). I feed myself daintily, I always eat good things; p. *mem..sod.*

Maminwéndamiidimin, (*nin*). We make one another contented, we comfort each other; p. *mem..didjig.*

Mamishanowe, (*nin*). I have whiskers, (beard on the cheeks.)

Mamissagindass, (*nin*). I ask a high price for s. th.; p. *mem..sod.*

Mamissaginde, or-*magad.* It is high, dear; p. *mem..deg*, or-*magak.*

Mamissaginso. It is high, dear; p. *mem..sod.*

Mamisswe, (*nin*). I sell high, at high prices; p. *memisewod.*

Mamitaam, (*nin*). I walk on the snow without snowshoes; p. *memitaang.*

Mâmoiawagendam, (*nin*). I am thankful, I have thankful thoughts; p. *maia..ang.*

Mâmoiawagendamowin, or *mamoiawendamowin.* Thankfulness, gratitude.

Mâmoiawagenima, (*nin*). I feel thankful to him; p. *maia..mad.*

Mâmoiawama, (*nin*). I thank him; p. *maiam..mad.*

Mâmoiawe, (*nin*). I thank, I give thanks; p. *maia..wed.*

Mâmoiawendam, (*nin*). S. *Mamoiawadendam.*

Mâmoiawenima, (*nin*). S. *Mamoiawagenima.*

Mâmôjagama, (*nin*) or, *nin mamojagaa*, freq. I pick some object up and swallow it down; p. *maia..mad.*

Mâmôjagandan, (*nin*) or, *nin mamojagaan*, freq. I pick it up and *eat* it, swallow it down; p. *maia..ang.*

Mâmôjagina, (*nin*), freq. I pick up some obj. and *gather* it; p. *maia..nad;* imp. *mamojagin.*

Mâmôjaginisse, (*nin*). I pick up sticks to make fire; p. *maia..sed.*

Mamôn, (*nin*). I take it; p. *memod.*

Mân, *mâna*, *mânad*, in compositions, signifies *bad*, *ugly.*

Mânab, (*nin*). I am sitting uncomfortably, badly; p. *maianabid.*

Mânâbamewis, (*nin*). I am punished deservedly; p. *maia..sid.*

Mânâbawinagos, (*nin*). I look ugly, I have an ugly appearance; p. *maia..sid.*

Mânâbaminagwad. It looks ugly; p. *maia..wak.*

Manâbisi. A kind of small swan; pl.-*wag.*

Manâdabi, (*nin*). I fetch thin roots to sew a canoe; p. *menadabid.*

Mânâdâbide, (*nin*). I have bad teeth; p. *maia..ded.*

Mânâdad. It is bad, wicked,

mean, base, evil, ill, unpleasant, unfit, ugly; p. *maiânadak.*

Manâdama, (*nin*). I use sparingly some obj.; in order to have it longer, as, flour, pork, etc.; p. *mem..mad.*

Manâdandan, (*nin*). I use it sparingly, to have it longer, as, meat, liquor, etc.; p. *men..ang.*

Mânâdapine, (*nin*), I am much sick, badly sick; also, I have a shameful sickness, the venereal disease; p. *maia..ned.*

Manâdâpinekamigad. There is pestilence, or any bad sickness; p. *maia..gak.*

Mânâdapinewin. Pestilence or any bad sickness; also, venereal disease.

Mânadapinewin emowemagak. The eating bad sickness, that is, the cancer, the cancerous disease.

Manadé, in compositions, signifies *sparingly,* a little at once; as: *Nin manadé-minikwen,* I drink it sparingly, only a little at one time, (in order to have it longer.)

Mânadendan, (*nin*). I think it is bad, wicked; p. *maia..ang.*

Mânadenima, (*nin*). I think he is bad, wicked; p. *maia..mad.*

Mânâdina, (*nin*). S. *Manâdjibina.*

Mânâdinan, (*nin*). S. *Manâdjibidon.*

Manâdinidis, (*nin*). I touch myself indecently; p. *men..sod.*

Mânâdis, (*nin*). I am ugly, difformed; p. *maia..sid.*

Mânadisiwin. Ugliness, difformity.

Manâdjia, (*nin*). I honor him, I respect, revere him; I save or spare him, (it,) I use it sparingly; I take care of him, (it;) also, I adore him; p. *menadjiad.*

Manâdjibidon, (*nin*). I don't dare touch it; p. *men..dod.*

Manâdjibina, (*nin*). I don't dare touch him, (a sick or wounded person;) also, I touch him indecently; p. *mem..ad;* imp. *manâdjibij.*

Manâdjienima, (*nin*). I honor and respect him in thoughts, I think much of him; p. *men..mad.*

Manâdjiidis, (*nin*). I take care of my body, of my health, I spare myself; p. *men..sod.*

Mânadjim, (*nin*). I relate evil reports, I tell bad things; p. *maia..mod.*

Mânadjimotage, (*nin*). I report bad things about persons, I defame; p. *maia..ged.*

Mânadjimotagos, (*nin*). I am heard relating bad reports, I make bad reports, I am defaming or calumniating; p. *maia..sid.*

Mânadjimotawa, (*nin*). I defame or calumniate him, I accuse him; p. *maia..wad.*

Mânâdjingweidis, (*nin*). I disfigure my face; p. *maia..sod.*

Manâdjingwewa, (*nin*). I disfigure his face; p. *maia..wad.*

Manâdjishin, (*nin*). S. *Nibadjishin.*

Mânâdjitchigé, (*nin*). I act wrongly; p. *maia..ged.*

Manâdjiton, (*nin*). I honor or respect it; I save or spare it, I use it sparingly, economically; I take care of it; p. *menadjitod*.

Manâdodam, (*nin*). I don't dare do s. th., I don't like to do it; p. *men..ang*.

Mânadwe, (*nin*). I speak evil, I use bad wicked language; p. *maianadwed*.

Mânâdwewin. Bad wicked speaking, bad language. (From *mânâdad*, bad; and *inwéwin*, language.)

Mânâgami. It is a bad liquid, of a bad taste, (any liquid object;) p. *maia..mig*.

Mânâgamipidan, (*nin*). I find that this liquid has a bad taste; p. *maia..ang*.

Mânâgidon, (*nin*). I speak evil words; p. *maia..ong*.

Mânâgidomowin. S. *Manadwewin*.

Manâjide, (*nin*). I break and gather little cedar-branches, to lie upon, (in a camp;) p. *menâjided*.

Mânâkamiga, or-*magad*. It is a bad piece of ground; p. *maia ..gak*, or-*magak*.

Mânakiki. Forest of maple-trees; pl.-*wan*.

Mânamandji, (*nin*). I am unwell, indisposed, a little sick; p. *maia..od*.

Mânamandjiowin. Indisposition, illness, little sickness.

Mânameg. Halibut, (fish;) (F. barbue;) pl.-*wag*.

Mânan. Cornet-tree; (C. bois dur;) pl.-*og*.

Mânapis, (*nin*). I am not well girt; p. *maia..sod*.

Mânâsabandam, (*nin*). I have a bad dream, (prognosticating a sad event or accident, according to the Indian superstition;) p. *maia..ang*.

Mânâsabandamowin. Bad dream; pl.-*an*.

Manasadi. A kind of aspen-tree; pl.-*ag*.

Manashkossiwan. Meadow; pl.-*an*.

Manashkossiwe, (*nin*). I make hay; also, I cut rush or reed for mats; p. *men..wed*.

Mânashigan. A kind of fish, bass-fish; (C. gros bossu;) pl.-*ag*.

Mânâsitagos, (*nin*). I speak evil words, I speak ill; p. *maia..sid*.

Manâsoma, (*nin*). I don't dare speak to him; p. *menasomad*.

Manâtangina, (*nin*). I fear to touch some obj. (from veneration or reverence;) p. *men ..ad*.

Manâtanginân, (*nin*). I fear to touch it, (some sacred object, etc.); p. *men..ang*.

Mandâmin. (*Ot. mindâmin*,) a grain of corn; pl. *mandâminag*, corn, Indian corn, maize, Turkey wheat.

Mandâminâbo. Corn-soup, corn-mash.

Mandâminâboke, (*nin*). I make corn-soup; p. *men..ked*.

Mandâminashk. Stalk of Indian corn; pl.-*on*.

Mandaminashkoki. Stalks of Indian corn yet standing in the field *after* harvest, (a field of empty stalks;) pl.-*wan*.

Mandâminike, (nin). I produce Indian corn ; p. *men..ked.*
Mandâmini-kitigan. Corn-field ; pl.-*an.*
Mandâminiwaj. A bag for Indian corn ; pl.-*an.*
Mandâminiwigamig. Indian corn store-house ; pl.-*on.*
Mândan, pron. This, this here.
Manê, in compositions, signifies *want, scarcity.*—In the *Otawa* dialect, *mané* rather signifies the contrary. They will say, *manê,* (or *manêmagad,*) there is much of it. *Manemi,* we are many. *Nin manêwinikas,* I have several names, etc.
Manêgadandan, (nin). I eat it sparingly, savingly, (in a case of want of provisions ;) p. *men..ang.*
Manêgadjia, (nin). I spare him ; I use sparingly some obj. ; p. *men..ad.*
Manégadjiton, (nin). I use it sparingly ; p. *men..tod.*
Manégasikan, (nin). I use it sparingly, I put it on seldom, (some article of clothing, or shoes ;) p. *men..ang.*
Manégasikawa, (nin). I use it sparingly, (obj. of clothing ;) p. *men..wad.*
Manêinad. There is little of it ; p. *meneinak.*
Manêinomin, (nin) or, *nin manêinimin.* We are a few ; p. *men..nodjig.*
Manenawenim, (nin). I fear death, I am afraid of dying ; p. *men..mod.*
Mânéndagos, (nin). I am considered bad, I am disagreeable, bad ; p. *maia..sid.*
Mânéndagwad. It is bad, disagreeable, shocking ; p. *maia ..wak.*
Mânendam, (nin). I am discontented in my mind, I have evil thoughts ; p. *maia..ang.*
Mânendamowin. Discontent, displeasure.
Mânendân, (nin). I have discontented or bad thoughts against it ; p. *maia..ang.*
Mânenima, (nin). I have bad discontented thoughts towards him or against him ; p. *maia ..mad.*
Manêonje, (nin). I have no children, or only a few children ; p. *mai..jed.*
Manépwa, (nin). I am in want of tobacco, I have nothing to smoke ; p. *men..wad.*
Manés, (nin). I want, I need ; p. *menesid.*
Manésin, (nin). I want it, I need it, I am in need of it ; p. *menesid.*
Manésinan, (nin). I want or need some object ; p. *ménesid.* (V. Conj.)
Manêsiwin. Want, need, scarcity, penury.
Manéssaga, or-*magad.* There is scarcity of wood for fuel ; p. *men..gag,* or-*magak.*
Manétigweia, or-*magad.* There is scarcity of rivers, (in a country) ; p. *men..iag,* or-*magak.*
Mâng. Loon ; (F. huard ;) pl.-*wag.* — *Mângons,* a young loon ; pl.-*ag.* — *Mângosid,* loon's foot.
Mangadea, (nin). I make it large, wide ; p. *men..ad.*—*Nin mangadea aw odâbân, nibiwa*

ko tchi bosiwad; I make this sleigh wide, in order to take many persons in.

Mangadea, or-*magad.* It is wide; p. *men..ag,* or-*magak.*

Mangademo mikana. The road is wide; p. *mengademog.*

Mangadengwe, (*nin*). I have a large face; p. *men..wed.*

Mangadépo, or-*magad.* It snows in large flakes ; p. *men..og,* or-*magak.*

Mangadéton, (*nin*). I make it large, wide ; p. *men..tod.* — *Nawatch nin mangadeton,* I enlargen it, I widen it.

Mangânagidon, (*nin*). I have a large mouth ; p. *men..ong.*

Mangânibadan, (*nin*). I shovel it; p. *men..ang.*

Mangânibadjigan. Shovel, spade; pl.-*an.*

Mangânibana, (*nin*). I shovel some obj.; p. *men..nad.*— *Wabigan nin mangânibana,* I shovel clay.

Mangânibi, (*nin*). I shovel snow ; p. *men..bid.*

Mangasika, or-*magad.* It is large, (a piece of clothing material ;) p. *men..kag,* or-*magak.*

Mangidée, (*nin*). I have a large heart, my heart is large ; I am magnanimous, courageous ; p. *mengideed.*

Mangidéea, (*nin*). I make his heart large; *fig.* I make him magnanimous, courageous ; p. *men..ad.*

Mangikone, (*nin*). I have a large liver; p. *men..ned.*

Mangiminagad. It is a large grain ; p. *men..gak.*

Mangimissade, (*nin*) or, *nin maniginagij.* I have a large belly ; p. *men..did,* or, *men.. jid.*

Manginansanam, (*nin*). I sigh profoundly, deeply ; p. *men.. mod.*

Mangindibe, (*nin*). I have a large head ; p. *men..bed.*

Mangingwe, (*nin*). I have a fat full large face ; p. *men..wed.*— S. *Mangadêngwe.*

Mangishka, or-*magad.* It is large, big ; p. *men..kak,* or-*magak.*

Mangishkam, (*nin*) or, *nin mamangishkam,* freq. I leave large tracks behind me, (walking in the snow especially ;) p. *me..ang.*

Mangishkwandeia, or-*magad.* There is a large door ; p. *men ..ag,* or-*magak.*

Mangissagad. It is a large piece of wood ; p. *men..gak.*

Mangitigweia sibi. The river is large ; p. *men..ag.*

Mangodikom. Loon's louse, (the name of a small insect that runs about on the surface of the water) ; pl.-*ag.*

Mangomodaie aw bineshi, (or *binessi*). This bird has a large craw or crop ; p. *men..ied.*

Mangôn, (*nin*). I have a large canoe ; p. *mengonod.*

Mangônagad. It is large, (canoe, boat, vessel, etc.) ; p. *men.. gak.*

Mangotâss, (*nin*). I am intrepid, brave, courageous ; p. *med.. sid.*

Mangotassiwin. Bravery, intrepidity, courage.

Mangotassiwinini. Brave, courageous man ; pl.-*wag.*

Mânijins. A young animal, a colt, etc.; any animal not over two years old; pl.-*ag.*
Mânikagon, (*nin*). It makes me sick, (what I ate or drank,) I don't digest it; p. *maia..god.* —*Nin mânikagon ga midjiian jéba;* what I ate this morning, makes me sick.—S. *Minokagon.*
Mânikami, (*nin*). I have no good solid footing, (walking or standing;) p. *maia..mid.*
Maninâg na, adv. At least.
Mâninagos, (*nin*). I look ugly; p. *maia..sid.*
Mâninagwad. It looks ugly or deformed; p. *maia..wak.*
Manishtanish. Sheep; pl.-*ag.*
Manishtânishens. Lamb; pl.-*ag.*
Manishtânishiwaiân. Sheepskin; pl.-*ag.*
Manishtânishiwibiwai. Wool.
Manishtânishiwigamig. Sheepfold; pl.-*on.*
Manishtânishiwinini. Shepherd; pl.-*wag.*
Manishtânishiwiwiiâss. Mutton.
Manishiwinish. Bad wicked person; pl.-*ag.*
Mânisiwinissi. *Ot.* Devil, the evil spirit; pl.-*iag.*
Mânissag. Dry pine tree; pl.-*og.*
Mânissâgan. A person that chops wood for somebody, somebody's chopper; pl.-*ag.* —*Nin manissâgan,* my chopper; *o manissaganan,* his chopper, etc.
Manissâge, (*nin*). I chop wood for somebody; p. *men..ged.*
Manissâs, (*nin*). I chop wood for myself; p. *men..sod.*
Manissawa, (*nin*). I chop wood for him; p. *men..ad;* imp. *manissaw.*
Manissé, (*nin*). I chop wood; p. *menissed.*
Manissewin. Chopping.
Mânitam, (*nin*). I don't like to hear, (certain words;) p. *maianitang.*
Mânitân, (*nin*). I don't like to hear it; p. *maianitâng.*
Mânitawa, (*nin*). I don't like to hear him; p. *maia..ad;* imp. *manitaw.*
Manito. Spirit, ghost; pl.-*g.* *Mino-manito,* the good spirit, *matchi-manito,* the evil spirit, the devil.
Manito-bimâkwad. Sweet twisted wood; pl.-*on.*
Manitobiwâbik. Steel.
Manitobiwâbikoke, (*nin*). I manufacture steel; p. *men..ked.*
Manitogisiss. January.
Manitogisissons. December.
Manitôkas, (*nin*). I perform some religious act; p. *men..sod.*
Manitôkâsowin. Religious performance.
Manitôke, (*nin*). I practice idolatry, I worship idols; p. *men..ked.*
Manitôken, (*nin*). I worship or adore it, (an idol;) p. *men..ked.*
Manitôkenan, (*nin*). I worship or adore him, (an idol;) p. *men..ked.* (V. Conj.)
Manitôkewin. Idolatry.
Manitôminens. Glass-bead; (F. rassade;) pl.-*ag.*
Manitôns. Little spirit; insect, worm; pl.-*ag.*

Manitow, (*nin*). I am a spirit; p. *men..wid.*

Manitowegin. Cloth, piece of cloth; pl.-*on.*

Manitôwegino - babisikawâgan. Coat of cloth; pl.-*an.*

Manitôwegino-wiwakwân. Cap of cloth; pl.-*an.*

Manitôwish. Small animal, (a marten, a weasel, etc.); pl.-*ag.*

Manitôwis, (*nin*) or, *nin mamanitôwis.* I am looked upon (or considered) as a spirit or sorcerer; p. *men..sid.*

Manitowiwin. Quality or character of spirit.

Maniwang mitig, or, *maniwid mitig.* What the tree yields, the fruit of the tree.

Maniwid mitig. A tree that yields, a fruit-tree; pl. *maniwidjig mitigog.*

Mânji,* in compositions, signifies *unwell, bad, evil.*

Mânji-aia, (*nin*) or, *nin manjâia.* I am unwell; p. *maia..ad.*

Manjidee, (*nin*). I feel unwell, squeamish, inclined to vomit; I am sea-sick; p. *maianjideed.*

Manjideewin. Inclination to vomit, squeamishness, nausea; sea-sickness.

Mânjigijwe, (*nin*). I speak indistinctly, I have an impediment in my speech; p. *maia..wed.*

Mânjigondagan, (*nin*). I have a bad voice for singing, (I am no singer;) p. *maia..ang.*

* NOTE. The letter *n* is hardly heard and often not at all, in the pronunciation of *ganji*, in all the words that begin with it.

Mânjiiawes, (*nin*). I have an ugly appearance, I am of a deformed size; p. *maia..sid.*

Mânjimâgos, (*nin*). I smell bad, I stink; p. *maia..sid.*

Mânjimagosiwin. Bad smell, stench.

Mânjimâgwad. It smells bad, it stinks; p. *maia..wak.*

Mânjimâgwanam, (*nin*). My breath smells bad; p. *maia..mod.*

Mânjimama, (*nin*). He stinks to me; p. *maia..mad.*

Mânjimandan, (*nin*). It stinks to me; p. *maia..ang.*

Mânjimandjige, (*nin*). I perceive a bad smell, s.th. smells bad; p. *maia..ged.*

Mânjimâsso assema. Tobacco smells bad, (stinks); p. *mâia..sod.*

Mânjimate, or-*magad.* It smells bad (stinks) when burnt; p. *maiân..teg*, or-*magak.*

Mânjinikade, or-*magad.* It has an ugly name; p. *mai..deg*, or-*magak.*

Mânjinikas, (*nin*). I have an ugly name, ill-sounding name; p. *maian..sod.*

Mânjinigasowin. Ugly name; pl.-*an.*

Mânjininiwagis, (*nin*). I am ill-tempered, I am wicked; p. *maia..sid.*

Mânjininiwagisiwin. Ill temper, wickedness.

Mânjipidân, (*nin*). I find a bad taste in something I am eating or drinking, I don't like the taste of it; p. *maian..ang.*

Mânjipogosi. Some obj. has a bad taste; p. *maian..sid.* —

Kitchi mânjipogosi gigô ; the fish has a very bad taste.
Mânjipogwad. It has a bad taste ; p. *maian..wak.*
Mânjipwa, (*nin*). I find a bad taste in some object I am eating, I don't like the taste of it ; p. *maia..wad ;* imp. *pwi.*
Mânjishin, (*nin*). S. *Mânoshin.*
Mânjissin. S. *Mânossin.*
Mânjissiton, (*nin*). S. *Mânossiton.*
Mânjitchige, (*nin*). I act wrongly, evil ; p. *maia..ged.*
Mânjomotawa, * (*nin*). I trouble him asking him to give me this or that ; p. *maian..wad.*
Mâno, or, *mânon,* adv. Well, that's right, no matter, let it be so.
Manômin. Wild rice.
Manômini. Manominee Indian ; pl.-*g.*
Manôminîke, (*nin*). I gather wild rice ; p. *men..ked.*
Manôminikê-gisiss. The moon of the gathering of wild rice, September. †
Manôminikêwin. The gathering of wild rice.
Manôminikeshi. Snipe ; (F. bécassine.)
Manômine wesowawang. Barley, (rice with a tail.)
Mânashin, (*nin*). I lie uncomfortably, I don't lie well ; p. *maiânoshing.*
Mânosse, (*nin*). I walk badly ; p. *maiânossed.*

* NOTE. The letter *n* is scarcely perceived in the pronunciation of this word.

† The different bands of Indians have different names for the months.

Mânassin. It is badly placed, it does not lie well ; p. *maia..ing.*
Mânossiton, (*nin*). I place or lay it badly ; p. *maia..tod.*
Mânowe, (*nin*). I pronounce badly, I have a defective indistinct pronunciation ; p. *maiânowed.*
Mariegijigad. Saturday ; pl.-*on.*
Mariegijigad. It is Saturday ; p. *Mariegijigak.*
Masân. Nettle ; pl.-*ag.*
Masânashk. Nettle-stalk ; pl.-*on.*
Masânika, (*nin*). I shudder suddenly, I shrink, by fear ; p. *mes..kad.*
Mashawêsid senibawegin. Velvet, manchester.
Mashi, adv. This adverb is never used alone, it is always connected with another adverb ; as : *Kawin mashi,* or *ka mashi,* or *mashi nange,* not yet. *Bwa mashi,* before.
Mashkâssissogad mitig. The wood is tough ; p. *mesh..gak.*
Mashkawâ, or-*magad.* It is strong, hard ; p. *mesh..wag,* or-*magak.*
Mashkawâbikad. It is strong, hard, (metal ;) p. *mesh..kak.*
Mashkawabikisan, (*nin*). I temper it, I harden it, (iron, steel ;) p. *mesh..ang.*
Mashkawabikisi. It is strong, hard, (silver ;) p. *mesh..sid.*
Mashkawadin. It freezes ; it is frozen ; p. *mesh..ing.*
Mashkawadj, (*nin*). I freeze to death ; p. *mesh..id.*
Mashkawâdji-bimide. Tallow.

Mashkawâdjidjanawadj, (*nin*). My nose is frozen; p. *mesh..djid.*

Mashkawâdjingwêwadj, (*nin*). My face is frozen; p. *mesh..id.*

Mashkawâdjinindjiwadj, (*nin*). My hand is frozen, or my hands are frozen; p. *mesh..id.*

Mashkawâdjitawagewadj, (*nin*). My ear is frozen, or, my ears are frozen; p. *mesh..id.*

Mashkawâdjiwin. Freezing, hard freezing, freezing of limbs, or freezing to death.

Maskkawâgami. It is strong, (liquid;) p. *mesh..mig.—Nin minwendân meshkawagamig anibishâbo,* I like strong tea.

Mashkawâgamiton, (*nin*). I make it strong, (liquid;) p. *mesh..tod.*

Mashkawakadode, or-*magad.* It is dry and hard, from heat; p. *mesh..deg,* or-*magak.*

Mashkawâkwad. It is strong, hard, (wood;) p. *mesh..wak.*

Mashkawâkwadji. He, (she, it,) is frozen hard and stiff, (any obj.); p. *mesh..id.—Mashkawâkwâdji aw gigo;* that fish is frozen stiff.

Mashkawâpidon, (*nin*). I tie it strongly, tight; p. *mesh..dod.*

Mashkawapina, (*nin*). I tie him tight, strongly; p. *mesh..nad.*

Mashkawapis, (*nin*). I am tied strongly, tight; p. *mesh..sod.*

Maskawatchigan. Starch.

Mashkawâton, (*nin*). I make it strong, hard, stiff; I starch it; p. *mesh..tod.*

Mashkawâwindamagewin. Vow, (strong promise;) pl.-*an.*

Mashkawéndam, (*nin*). I have a firm constant thought, a strong resolution, a strong firm will; p. *mesh..ang.*

Mashkawêndamia, (*nin*). I make him have a firm thought, I fortify his mind, his resolution, I give him a firm will; p. *mesh..ad.*

Maskawéndâmowin. Firm strong thought, resolution, will.

Mashkawéndan, (*nin*). I think it is strong; also, I think strongly on it, I keep it constantly in memory; p. *mesh..ang.*

Mashkawénima, (*nin*). I think he is strong; also, I think firmly on him; p. *mesh..mad.*

Mashkawideé, (*nin*). I have a strong heart; my heart is hard, obstinate, stubborn; p. *mesh..ed.*

Mashkawideéshkawa, (*nin*). I fortify or strengthen his heart; p. *mesh..wad.*

Mashkawideéwin. Strength of heart; obstinacy, stubborness, hardness of heart.

Mashkawigabaw, (*nin*). I stand firmly; p. *mesh..wid.*

Mashkawikwen, (*nin*). I keep my head steadfast, stiff; p. *mesh..nid.*

Mashkawikwissin totoshâbo. The milk coagulates, it becomes sour; p. *meshkawikwissing totoshâbo,* sour milk.

Mashkawima, (*nin*). I make him take a firm resolution; p. *mesh..mad.*

Mashkawimagonige, (*nin*). I have a strong wrist; p. *mesh..ged.*

Mashkawimindjimendan, (*nin*). I keep it firmly in memory, I remember it strongly ; p. *mesh...ang.*

Mashkawimindjimenima, (*nin*). I keep him strongly in memory ; p. *mesh..mad.*

Mashkawimindjimina, (*nin*). I keep or hold him strongly ; p. *mesh..nad.*

Mashkawimindjiminan, (*nin*). I keep or hold it strongly; p. *mesh..ang.*

Mashkawina, (*nin*). I take hold of him ; p. *mesh..nad.*

Mashkawinan, (*nin*). I take hold of it; p. *mesh..ang.*

Mashkawindibe, (*nin*). I am headstrong, obstinate, stubborn ; p. *mesh..bed.*

Mashkawindibewin. Obstinacy, stubbornness.

Mashkawis, (*nin*). I am strong, vigorous, powerful, robust, hard ; I employ my strength, I make efforts ; p. *mesh..sid.*

Mashkawisia, (*nin*). I make him strong, I strengthen him, I fortify him ; p. *mesh..ad.*

Mashkawisiwin. Strength, power, vigor, force.

Mashkawissin. It is strong; it is hard ; p. *mesh..ing.*

Mashkig. Swamp, marsh; pl.-*on.*

Mashkigimin. Cranberry, mossberry, moor-berry ; pl.-*an.*

Mashkigiminika. There are cranberries ; p. *mesh..kag.*

Mashkigiminikan. Place where there are cranberries.

Mashkigiminike, (*nin*). I gather cranberries ; p. *mesh..ked.*

Mashkigobag. Kind of wild tea, called by Canadians, *Labrador.*

Mashkigwâtig. Red spruce, tamarac; (C. épinette rouge;) pl.-*og.*

Mashkiki. Medicine ; pl.-*wan.*

Mashkiki bebikominigagak. Pills, (globulous medicine.) S. *Bikominagad* ; freq. *babikominagad.*

Mashkikike, (*nin*). I make or prepare medicine; p. *mesh.. ked.*

Mashkikikewigamig. Apothecary's laboratory ; pl.-*on.*

Mashkikikêwikwe. Female apothecary, (in a convent;) pl.-*g.*

Mashkikikewin. The art of preparing medicine, pharmacy. trade and occupation of an apothecary.

Mashkikikêwinini. Apothecary; pl.-*wog.*

Mashkikiwâbo. Medicine, *liquid* medicine to drink ; (F. de la tisane.)

Mashkikiwâbokawa, (*nin*). I prepare medicine for him to drink ; p. *mesh..wad.*

Mashkikiwâboke, (*nin*). I prepare medicine to drink; p. *mêsh..ked.*

Mashkikiwigamig. Apothecary's shop; pl.-*on.*

Mashkikiwinini. Physician, doctor ; pl.-*wag.*

Mashkimod. Bag, sack ; pl.-*an.* —*Mashkimodash,* an old bad bag ; *mashkimodens,* a small bag.

Mashkimodégwade, or-*magad.* It is sewed up in the shape of a bag ; p. *mesh..deg,* or-*magak.*

Mashkimodêgwâdjigan. Pocket; pl.-*an.*

Mashkimodêke, (*nin*). I make a bag or bags ; p. *mesh..ked.*

Mashkimodéwegin. Sackcloth.

Mashkinoje. A kind of pike, (fish;) pl.-*g*.
Mashkodê. Large prairie; pl.-*wan*.
Mashkodê-pijiki. Buffalo; pl.-*wog*.
Mashkodëpinibag. A kind of lily; pl.-*on*.
Mashkodësse. Marsh-partridge; (F. perdrix de savane;) pl.-*g*.
Mashkodewadad. It resembles a prairie; p. *mesh..dak*.
Mashkossikân. Place where they make hay, meadow; pl. -*an*.
Mashkossike, (*nin*). I make hay; p. *mesh..ked*.
Mashkossikewin. Hay-making.
Mashkossiw. Herb, grass; hay; pl.-*an*.
Mashkossiwi-apishimowin. Straw-bed, straw-pallet; pl.-*an*.
Mashkossiwigamig. Building for keeping hay in, hay-shed, hay-loft; pl.-*on*.
Mashkossiwika, or-*magad*. There is herb or grass; p. *mesh..kag*, or-*magak*.
Mashkossiwi-minikân. Grass-seed, timothy.
Mashkossiwi-nipâgan. S. *Mashkôssiwi-apishimowin*.
Mashkossi-wiwakwân. Straw-hat; pl.-*an*.
Masinaamagos, (*nin*). I give credit, I have debtors; p. *mes..sid*.
Masinaamawa, (*nin*). I owe him; p. *mes..wad*.
Masinade, or-*magad*. It is portraited, it is engraved; p. *mes..deg*, or-*magak*.
Masinadina, (*nin*). I make or form some object; p. *mes..nad*.
Masinadinamawa, (*nin*). I form or make it for him or to him; p. *mes..wad*.
Masinadinan, (*nin*). I form it; p. *mes..ang*.
Masinâigade, or-*magad*. It is marked, there are marks or signs on it; p. *mes..deg*, or-*magak*.
Masinâigan. A thing to make marks upon, paper; book; letter; debt; pl.-*an*.
Masinaiganag. S. *Atadimasinaiganag*.
Masinaigani-tessaban. Bookcase.
Masinaigan nin nissitawinan. I can read.
Masinaigan nin wâbandan. I read, I am reading.
Masinaigans. Little book; bill, note; pl.-*an*.
Masinaigan waiabandang. Reader; pl.-*ig*.
Masinaigas, (*nin*). I am marked, I have marks on me; p. *mes..sod*.
Masinaige, (*nin*). I make marks on s. th.; also, I make debts, I take on credit; p. *mes..ged*.
Masinaigewin. Marking, making debts, debt.
Masinajigawia, (*nin*). I ornament with lead some obj., I lead it, (a pipe, etc.); p. *mes..ad*.
Masinajigamitchigade, or-*mogad*. It is leaded, ornamented with lead; it is moulded, cast in a mould; p. *mes..deg*, or-*magak*.
Masinajigawitchigaso. It is

leaded or ornamented with lead; it is moulded; p. *mes..sod.*

Masindâjigawitchige, (*nin*). I ornament with lead, I lead; I cast in a mould; p. *mes..ged.*

Masinajigawiton, (*nin*). I ornament it with lead; I cast it in a mould; p. *mes..tod.*

Masinakisan, (*nin*). I imprint a mark upon it with fire, I burn a mark upon it.—They use this word, although improperly, also for *printing* a book, etc.; p. *mes..ang.*—*Awenen ga masinakisang ôw masinaigan?* — Who printed this book?

Masinakisige, (*nin*). I print, I am printing; p. *mes..ged.*

Masinakisigéwigamig. Printing office; pl.-*on.*

Masinakisigéwin. Printing, the art, business or trade of a printer.

Masinakisigêwinini. Printer; pl.-*wag.*

Masinas, (*nin*). I am portraited, (printed or engraved;) p. *mes..sod.*

Masinasowin. Portrait, likeness.

Masinibian, (*nin*). I draw or sketch it; I paint it; p. *mes..ang.*

Masinibiigade, or-*magad.* It is portraited, painted, engraven; p. *mes..deg*, or-*magak.*

Masinibiigade, or-*magad.* It is imprinted on s. th., or painted; p. *mes..deg*, or-*magak.*

Masinibiigan. Drawing; painting; engraving; pl.-*an.*

Masinibiigas, (*nin*). I am imprinted on s. th. I am portraited, painted, engraven; p. *mes..sod.*— *Mi oma mesinibiigasoiân;* I am portraited here, (this is my portrait.)

Masinibiigasowin. Portrait, painted or engraven.

Masinibiige, (*nin*). I make marks or signs on s. th., I draw, I paint; I engrave; p. *mes..ged.*

Masinibiigewin. The act, or the art, of drawing, painting or engraving, drawing, painting, engraving.

Masinibiwa, (*nin*). I draw his likeness, I paint him, portrait him; p. *mes..wad;* imp. *masinibi.*

Masinide, or-*magad.* It is marked by heat; p. *mes..deg*, or-*magak.*

Masinigwadam, (*nin*). I embroider with figures and flowers, (representing a painting;) p. *mes..ang.*

Masinigwâdan, (*nin*). I embroider it with figures and flowers; p. *mes..ang.*

Masinigwana, (*nin*). I embroider some obj. with flowers; p. *mes..nad.*

Masinigwaso. It is embroidered with flowers, etc.; *moshwe*, handkerchief; *seniba*, ribbon, silk.

Masinikiwagaan, (*nin*). I seal it with an engraven seal; p. *mes..ang.*

Masinikiwagaigade, or-*magad.* It is sealed with an engraven seal; p. *mes..deg*, or-*magak.*

Masinikiwagaigan, or *masinikiwagaiganâbik.* Seal with an engraving upon it; pl.-*an*, or-*on.*

Masinikodan, (*nin*). I carve it, I sculp it; p. *mes..ang*.

Masinikodjigan. Chisel with a half round edge, sculptor's chisel; (F. gouge); pl.-*an*.

Masinikodjigan. Statue, or any sculptured image or representation; pl.-*ag*.

Masinikodjige, (*nin*). I carve or sculpture; p. *mes..ged*.

Masinikodjigewin. The act, or the art, of carving or sculpturing, trade or occupation of a sculptor, or engraver.

Masinikodjigewinini. Carver, sculptor; pl.-*wag*.

Masinikona, (*nin*). I carve or sculp some obj.; p. *mes..nad*.

Masinikâso. It is carved (or sculped; p. *mes..sod*.

Masinikwassige, (*nin*). S. *Masinajigawitchige*.

Masiniminênsikade, or-*magak*. It is embroidered or ornamented with flowers or figures in small glassbeads; p. *mes..deg*, or-*magak*.

Masiniminensike, (*nin*). I embroider or ornament with small glassbeads; p. *mes..ked*.

Masinini. Carved image, idol; pl.-*g*.

Masininin menitoked. Adorer of idols, idolator, idolatress; pl.-*jig*.

Masinitchigan. Image, engraving, painting, picture; pl.-*ag*.

Masinitchigan nind ojibiwa. I paint, (I mark a picture.)

Masinitchigas, (*nin*). I am painted, carved; p. *mes..sod*.

Masinitchige, (*nin*). I make an image or images; p. *mes..ged*.

Masinitchigewin. The making of images, painting, work, trade or art of a painter.

Masinitchigéwinini. Maker of images, painter; pl.-*wag*.

Masitagos, (*nin*). I cry; I groan; p. *mes..sid*.

Masitagosi bineshi. The bird warbles; p. *mes..sid*. *Pakaakwe masitagosi*, the cock crows.

Mâskig, (*nin*). I am very small; p. *maiaskigid*. (They say this of a new-born infant.)

Mâskijan. Abortive fruit of the womb; pl.-*ag*.

Massagwadendagos, (*nin*). I am considered unlucky, I am unlucky; p. *mes..sid*.

Massagwadendagwad. It is considered unlucky, it is unlucky; p. *mes..wak*.

Massagwadis, (*nin*). I am unlucky, unhappy, I have no chance to gain or make anything; p. *mes..sid*.

Massagwadisiwin. Bad luck.

Massagwia, (*nin*). I give or cause him bad luck, (according to the Indian superstition); p. *mes..ad*.

Matchi, adj. Bad, evil, ill, wicked, malignant, malicious, mean, vicious, unfit.

Matchi-aiaâwish. Bad being, devil, satan, the evil spirit, old Nick.

Matchi-aiaâwish. A wicked person, a vilain, rascal, rogue, scoundrel; also, a wicked dangerous animal; pl.-*ag*.

Matchi-aiaâwishiw, (*nin*). I am a wicked person, etc.; p. *met..wid*.

Matchi-aiâwin. Bad unhappy situation, being badly off.

Matchi-aiiwish. Any thing evil, bad, wicked, hurtful; pl.-*ak.*
Matchi-aiiwishiwan. It is a bad wicked thing, evil, hurtful, dangerous; p. *met..ang.*
Matchi-aion, (*nin*). I make a bad use of it, I abuse it; p. *met.. od.*
Matchi-awa, (*nin*). I make a bad use of some obj.; p. *met.. wad.*
Matchi-bimâdis, (*nin*). I live badly; I am bad, wicked; I have a bad temperament; bad dispositions; p. *met..sid.*
Matchi-bimâdisiwin. Bad life; bad, ill temper, quick, irritable temper, passionate temper.
Matchidée, (*nin*). I have a wicked heart; I am cruel; p. *met ..ed.*
Matchideéwin. Wickedness of heart; cruelty.
Matchigode. Petticoat, woman's dress; pl.-*ian.*
Matchi ijiwêbad. It is bad, wicked, sinful; p. *met..bak.*
Matchi ijiwebis, (*nin*). I am wicked, bad, malicious, malign, I behave badly; I have a bad temper, bad qualities; p. *met..sid.*
Matchi ijiwebisia, (*nin*). I make him wicked, I corrupt him, seduce him; p. *met..ad.*
Matchi ijiwebisiwin. Bad conduct, bad behavior, bad habit, wickedness, badness, vice, sin, malice, malignity, perversity, ill temper, bad disposition of mind.
Matchi inakamigad. It is a bad news, a sad event; p. *met.. gak.*
Matchi-inapinadjige, (*nin*). I give poison, I poison; p. *met ..ged.*
Matchi-inapinadjigewin. Poisoning.
Matchi-inapinâna, (*nin*). I poison him; also, I give him a bad sickness; p. *met..nad;* imp. *ma..naj.*
Matchi-inapinas, (*nin*). S. *Matchi-inapinadjige.*
Matchi-inapinema, (*nin*). I curse him; p. *met..mad.*
Matchi-inapinendan, (*nin*). I curse it; p. *met..ang.*
Matchi-inapinenima, (*nin*) or, *nin matchi-inâpinea, nin matchi-inâpinana.* I give him a bad sickness, (according to Indian superstitions;) p. *met.. mad.*
Matchi inapinewin. Bad sickness; pl.-*an.*
Matchi kikinoamawa, (*nin*). I teach him bad things, I give him a bad example, I seduce him, scandalize him; p. *met.. wad.*
Matchi kikinowabama, (*nin*). I follow his bad example, he gives me a bad example, he scandalizes me; p. *met..mad.*
Matchi-kikinowabamig, (*nin*). I am imitated by him in my bad example, I give him a bad example, I scandalize him.
Matchi kikinowâbamigowin. Bad example or scandal *taken;* pl.-*an.*
Matchi kikinowâbandaiwe, (*nin*). I give a bad example, (or bad examples); p. *met..wediwewin.*
Matchi kikinowabanda. Bad

example or scandal *given;* pl.-*an.*

Matchi manito. Evil spirit, devil, satan; pl.-*g.*

Matchi manitokewin. Idolatry.

Matchi mashkiki. Evil medicine; that is, poison, venom.—*Matchi mashkiki nind ashama;* I poison him, (I give him evil medicine to eat.) *Matchi mashkiki dagonigade,* there is poison in, it is poisonous; p. *deg..deg.*

Matchi mashkiki eshanged. He that gives poison to somebody, poisoner; pl.-*jig.*

Matchi mashkossiw. Noxious herb, weed in a field or garden; pl.-*an.*

Matchi-odon. Bad-mouth, a person that uses to speak ill of others.

Matchitwa, (*nin*) or *nin matchitchige,* (from *matchi ijitchige.*) I act wickedly, I do wrong; p. *metchitwad.*

Matchi wina, (*nin*) or, *nin matchi wawina,* freq. I decry or discredit him, I defame him, I speak ill of him; p. *met..nad.*

Maw, (*nin*). I weep, I cry; p. *mewid.*

Mawâdishiwe, (*nin*). I visit, I pay a visit (or visits); p. *mew ..wed.*

Mawâdishiwéshk, (*nin*). I am always making visits, I like too much to make visits; p. *mew..kid.*

Mawadishiweshkiwin. Habit of making visits too often.

Mawadishiwewin. Visiting, visit, visitation.

Mawadissa, (*nin*). I visit him, I pay him a visit; p. *mew..ad;* imp. *mawadishi.*

Mawakodasama, (*nin*). I dry meat in smoke; p. *mew..mad.* (I. Conj.)

Mâwandina, (*nin*). I gather together or collect some obj.; p. *maia..nad.*

Mâwandinan, (*nin*). I gather it together, I collect it; p. *maia ..ang.*

Mâwandinige, (*nin*). I gather, I collect; p. *maia..ged.*

Mâwandiwidjiwa, (*nin*). I gather a collect with him; p. *maia..wad.*

Mâwandiwigamig. Meeting-house; Synagogue; pl.-*on.*

Mâwandjia, (*nin*). I gather it together, I store it up, I accumulate it; I save and keep it; p. *maia..ad.*

Mâwandjidimin, (*nin*). We come together, we meet, we assemble; p. *maia..didjig.*

Mâwandjiidiwin. Assembly, meeting.

Mâwandjissiton, (*nin*). I put it together, I gather it together, I collect it; p. *maia..tod.*

Mâwandjitamage, (*nin*). I gather or collect for somebody; p. *maia..ged.*

Mâwandjitamason, (*nin*) or, *nin mawandjitamadison.* I gather it, collect it or store it up, to myself; p. *maia..od.*

Mâwândjitamasonan, (*nin*) or *nin mawandjitamadisonan.* I gather, collect or store up some obj. for myself; p. *maia ..od.* (V. Conj.)

Mawandjitamawa, (*nin*). I gather or collect it for him or to him; p. *maia..wad.*

Mawandjitassowigamig. Storehouse; pl.-*on.*

Mawandjitchigan. Any object stored up somewhere, or gathered together; pl.-*ag.*

Mâwandjitchige, (*nin*). I gather, I collect; p. *maia..ged.*

Mâwandjitchigéwinini. A gathering man, tax-gatherer, toll-gatherer; publican; pl.-*wag.*

Mawandjiton, (*nin*). I gather it together; I save and keep it; p. *maia..tod.*

Mawandodjiwan. It runs together, or streams together, in one place, (water or any other liquid;) p. *maia..ang.*

Mâwandogwadan, (*nin*) or, *nin mâwandogwadanan.* I sew several pieces together, I gather them together sewing; p. *maia..ang.*

Mâwandogwass, (*nin*). I gather together sewing; p. *maia..sod.*

Mâwandogwasson, or, *mawandogwassowin.* Quilt, several pieces sewed together in one; pl.-*an.*

Mâwandoshkaan, (*nin*). I gather it, (hay;) p. *maia..ang.*

Mâwandoshkaigan. Rake, to gather hay with; pl.-*an.*

Mâwandoshkaige, (*nin*). I rake hay together; p. *maia..ged.*

Mâwandosse, or-*magad.* It comes together, it gathers in one place, or on one heap; p. *maia ..seg,* or-*magak.*

Mâwansomag, (*nin*). I gather people together; p. *maia.. mad.*

Mawibi, (*nin*). I weep being drunk; p. *mewibid.*

Mawikas, (*nin*), feign. I weep by dissimulation, I feign weeping; p. *mew..sod.*

Mawimâ, (*nin*). I bewail him, bemoan him, deplore him, I weep or cry over him; p. *mewimad.*

Mawimagad. It weeps; p. *mew ..gak.—Ninde mawimâgad epitch-kitchi-kashkendamân;* my heart weeps from extreme sorrow.

Mawinâdân, (*nin*). I run upon it or to it; I reach forth for it; p. *mew..ang.*

Mawinadjigawa, (*nin*). I pick up the birds he is killing, to have them myself; p. *mew.. wad.*

Mawinadjige, (*nin*). I fetch, or pick up for me, the birds he kills, (ducks, etc.;) p. *mew.. ged.*—S. *Mawinadjigawa.*

Mawinadjigenan jishib, (*nin*). I fetch or pick up the duck he killed, to have it myself; p. *mew..ged.* (V. Conj.)

Mawinadjigodadis, (*nin*). I fetch or pick up myself the birds I kill; p. *mew..sod.*

Mawinânâ, (*nin*). I run or rush upon him; I reach forth after him; p. *mew..nad;* imp. *mawinaj.*

Mawindamowin. Bewailing, deploration, bemoaning, lamentation.

Mawindân, (*nin*). I bewail it, deplore it, lament it, I weep or cry over it or for it, to have it; I weep for the loss of it; p. *mew..ang.*

Mawindis, (*nin*). I bewail or deplore myself; p. *mew..sod.*

Mawinéige, (*nin*). I insult, I

quarrel, make noise; p. *mew..ged.*

Mawinéigewin. Insult, insulting, quarreling noise.

Mawinéwa, (nin). I come upon him, I insult, quarrel, attack him; p. *mew..wad;* imp. *mawinê.*

Mawineshkâgon, (nin). It insults me, it attacks me; p. *mew..god....Nin mawineshkagon geget o masinaigan;* his letter insults me indeed.

Mawineshkan, (nin). I insult it, attack it; p. *me..ang.*

Mawineshkawa, (nin). S. *Mawinéwa.*

Mawins, (nin). I gather berries; p. *mewinsod.*

Mawishk, (nin). I weep or cry too much or too often, I am in a habit of weeping; (F. je suis braillard;) p. *mew..kid.*

Mawishkiwin. Bad habit of weeping, crying.

Mawiwin. Weeping, crying.

Médassaganama, (nin). I miss him, striking, he avoids my stroke; p. *maié..mad.*

Médassikage, (nin). I arive too late; p. *maie..ged.*

Médassikan, (nin). I arrive too late to find it yet; p. *maié..ang.*— The contrary of *Nin gêssikan,* which see.

Médassikawa, (nin). I arrive too late to find him yet, he is gone, etc.; p. *maiê..wad.*— The contrary of *Nin géssikawa.*

Médassinawa, (nin). I miss him shooting; p. *maia..wad.*

Mégandji, (nin). I belch, I eject the wind from the stomach; (F. je rote;) p. *maie..gandjid.*

Mégwa, prp., conj. While, when, during.

Mégwaii, adv. Amidst, among.

Mégwawigang awessi. The humpbacked animal, camel; pl. *mêgwawigangig awessiiag.*

Mêgwe, prp. Amongst.

Megwébag. Amongst leaves, in a bush, in a shrub.

Megwêkamig, adv. In the desert, in the interior, in the inland.

Megwêkana, adv. In the road, on the road or trail.

Megwéshkossiw, adv. Amongst herbs, in the grass or weed.

Meiagisid. A stranger, (man or woman;) pl.-*jig.*

Mejikagemagak inâpinewin. Contagious sickness, epidemy.

Mekatewagamitigweiag. A black river, of dark-colored water.

Mêkatewikwanaie, or rather, *mekatewikwanaied.* A man dressed in black, black-gown, priest, missionary; pl.-*g,* or-*jig.*

Mêkatewikwanaiêkwe. A woman dressed in black, nun, sister of a convent, religious of an Order; pl.-*g.*

Mekatewikwanaié o bapisikawâgan. The priest's coat, cassock; pl.-*an.*

Mekatewikwanaiew, (nin). I am a priest; p. *mek..wid.*

Mekatêwikwanaiewiwin. Priesthood; the Sacrament of Order.

Mekawashitod. He that invents it, inventor, discoverer; pl.-*jig.*

Mekisiniked. He that makes shoes, boots, etc., shoemaker; pl.-*jig.*

Memakisiiwed. He that inoculates with the cow-pox, inoculator, cow-pox inoculator; pl.-*jig.*

Memandjigosid. He that is lame, a lame person, cripple; pl.-*jig.*

Memangishe. Ass, mule, (long-ear;) pl.-*iag.*

Mème. Wood-pecker; pl.-*g.*

Memegwêssi. Siren, (fabulous being;) pl.-*wag.*

Meméngwa. Butterfly; pl.-*g.*

Meméshkwat, adv. By turns, one after another, alternately; reciprocally.

Mêmidasswâk. A thousand every time, a thousand each or to each.

Mêmidasswi, num. Ten every time, ten each or to each.

Mêmidâtching, num. Ten times every time, ten times each.

Memikwasod. He that boasts, braggart, boaster; pl.-*jig.*

Meminabawidjissi. *Alg.* A kind of grass-hopper; (F. cigale;) pl.-*wag.*

Meminadisid. He that is proud, proud person; pl.-*jig.*

Mémindage, or *mêmdage,* adv. Especially, principally, above all.

Meminitigodjiwang. Islands in a current.

Memiskondinimanganeshi. Red-breast, robin, (bird;) pl.-*iag.*

Memokiwido. Mole; pl.-*g.*

Memokiwidowigamig. Mole-hill, (mole's house;) pl.-*on.*

Mémwetch, adv. Just.— *Memwetch kinawa ki da-ijam;* just you ought to go, (not others.)

Mendatchingwash, (*nin*). I am very sleepy, overwhelmed with sleep; p. *maien..id.*

Mengishkkatai. *Alg.* Ass; pl.-*ag.*—S. *Memangishe.*

Menikweshkid. He that drinks too much, tippler, drunkard; pl.-*jig.*

Menikwessig. He that does not drink, sober temperate person; pl.-*og.*

Menikwessig jominâbo. Abstemious person.

Mênishea, (*nin*). I cause him shame, I make him ashamed; p. *maiênishead.*

Ménishima, (*nin*). I cause him shame with my words; p. *maie..mad.*

Mènishimigon, (*nin*). It makes me ashamed, it causes me shame; p. *maie..god.*

Mênissendam, (*nin*). I am ashamed; p. *maie..ang.*

Ménissênima, (*nin*). I am ashamed of him; p. *maie..mad.*

Mênissendamowin. Shame.

Meno-ijiwebisid. He that behaves well, good person; pl.-*jig.*

Menwe. Cumin; pl.-*g.*

Meshkawagamig ishkotewâbo. Strong fire-water, brandy.

Meshkawikwissing totoshâbo. Milk that is coagulated, sour milk.

Mêshkwat, adv. Instead, instead of....

Méshkwatona, (*nin*). I change or exchange some obj.; p. *maié..nad.*

Mèshkwatonamawa, (*nin*). I exchange it for him or to him; p. *maié..wad.*

Méshkwatonan, (*nin*). I exchange one thing for another p. *maié..ang.*

Méshkwatosse, oo-*magad.* It undergoes a change, it is changed; p. *maié...seg,* or-*magak.*

Mésikan,(*inn.*) I wear it out, (clothing,) I wear it until it is all torn to pieces; p. *mâiési-kang.*

Mésikawa, (*nin*). I wear it out, (article of clothing,as *moshwe,* handkerchief;) p. *maié..wad.*

Mésinaamawind. He to whom s. th. is owed, creditor; pl.-*jig.*

Mésinaiged. He who owes s. th., debtor; pl.-*jig.*

Mésinakisang masinaigan. He that marks paper, printer; pl.-*mesinakisangig.*

Méskwânagekesid. S. *Miskwâ-nagek.*

Métabikiso akik. The kettle is worn out, it is no more useful; p. *maié..sod.*

Métabikissin. It is worn out, used up, (metal;) p. *maie..ing.*

Métakosiged. He that smokes pure tobacco, smoker of tobacco only; pl.-*jig.*—S. *Mita-kosige.*

Mêtakwidin. It is worn out in the woods, (clothing;) p. *maie ..ing.*

Métâkwidjidon, (*nin*). I wear it out in the woods, (clothing;) p. *maié..dod.*

Métchibode, or-*magad.* It is worn out or used up by grinding; p. *maie..deg,* or-*magak.*

Metchibodon, (*nin*). I wear it out by grinding; p. *maié..dod.*

Mêtchibona, (*nin*). I wear out some obj. by grinding; p. *maie..nad;* imp. *metchiboj.*

Métchiboso. It is worn out by grinding; p. *maie..sod.*

Métchi-dodang. He who does evil, criminal, malefactor; p. -*ig.*

Métchissidon, (*nin*). I wear it out working, (clothing;) p. *maie..dod.*

Métchissin, or *metchitchigade.* It is worn out, used; p. *maie.. ing,* or *maie..deg.*—*Nin maki-sinan mêtchissinon;* my moccasins are worn out.

Mêwija, or *mêwinja,* adv. Already; long ago.

Mêwishkid. He that weeps too much, weeper, crier; (F. braillard;) pl.-*jig.*

Mi, or *mi sa.* So that is, it is, that is to say.

Mi apine. Ever since; for ever, gone for ever.

Mi minik, or, *mi iw.* That is all; enough.

Midâdatchimin, (*nin*). We are ten of us; p. *med..tchidjig.*

Midâdatchinon. There are ten.

Midâgwena, (*nin*). I put him aside or out of the way, with my hands; p. *med..nad;* imp. *midagwen.*

Midâgwenamawa, (*nin*). I put or push s. th. aside for him, I deliver him or disembarrass him from s. th.; p. *med..wad.*

Midâgwenân, (*nin*). I put it aside or out of the way, with my hands; p. *med..ang.*

Midâgwendân, (*nin*). I put it away or aside in my thoughts, in my mind, I remove it from me; p. *med..ang.*

Midâgwenige, (*nin*). I put aside with my hands; p. *med..ged.*

Midagweta, (*nin*). I put myself aside; p. *med..tad.*

Midâgwetawa, (*nin*). I keep myself from him; p. *med.. wad.*

Midâss. Legging, or my legging; pl.-*an*. *kidâss*, thy legging; *odâss*, his legging.

Midâsso, num. Ten, (before substantives denoting MEASURE of time or of other things.)

Midasswêwan. — S. *Nijobanénindj*.—*Nijobidonan*. *Nijokina*, etc., always changing in English, *two* into *ten*, as: *Nijobanénindj*, twice (two times) a handful. *Midossobanénindj*, ten times a handful. — *Nijobidonan*, (*nin*). I tie two together. *Midassobidonan*, (*nin*). I tie ten together.— And so on respectively.

Midasswak dassing midasswak. A thousand times thousand, a million.—*Nijing midasswak dassing midasswak*, twice a thousand times thousand, two millions; etc.

Midâsswi, num. Ten.

Midasswi ashi bejig, num. Eleven.

Midasswi ashi nij. A dozen, twelve. (For the rest see Grammar.)

Midâtching. Ten times.

Midatching midasswak. Ten thousand.

Midé. Indian of the Grand Medicine; pl.-*g*.

Midékwe. A squaw of the Grand Medicine; pl.-*g*.

Midéw, (*nin*). I am an Indian of the Grand Medicine, I belong to the Indian Order of Grand Medicine; p. *medewid.*

Midéwia, (*nin*). I receive him into the Grand Medicine, I make him a member of the Grand Medicine; p. *mèdêwiad.*

Midêwigamig. Long narrow lodge made of branches for the ceremonies of the Grand Medicine; pl.-*on*.

Midéwiwin. Grand Medicine, Indian Order of Grand Medicine.

Midjim. They eat it; (F. on le mange;) any eatable thing, provisions, victuals, eatables, food.

Midjimigamig. Provisions-store; (F. hangar aux vivres;) pl.-*on*.

Midjimikandân odassonagan, (*nin*). I put a bait in the trap, I bait it; p. *madj..ang.*

Midjimikandjigan. Bait; pl..*an*.

Midjimike, (*nin*). I produce or procure victuals; p. *madj.. ked.*

Midjimikewin. Labor or efforts made in producing or procuring victuals.

Midjimiwan. It is food, it is eatable, it is eaten; p. *mâdjimiwang.*

Midjin, (*nin*). I eat it; p. *madjid.*

Midjindim, adv. In the water, in the depth.

Midjissikawa, (*nin*). I conduct or accompany him a little distance, through politeness; p. *med..wad.*

Migadân, (*nin*). I fight it, I oppose it; I combat it, I am against it; p. *magadaog.*—*Nin migadan ishkotewabo*; I fight ardent liquor, I am against it.

Migâdimagak. It is fighting, opposing, it is at war against; p. *mag..gak.*

Migadîmin, (*nin*). We fight together, we scuffle; we are at war; p. *mâgâdidjig.*

Migâdi-nâbikwan. War-vessel, ship of war, man of war; pl.-*an.*

Migâdinaniwan. There is war, war-time, fighting-time; p. *mag..wang.*

Migâdiwin. Fight, battle, combat, war.

Migakikwewe, (*nin*). I fight or beat my wife; p. *mag..wed.*

Migana, (*nin*). I fight or beat him; p. *maganad.*

Miganidis, (*nin*). I fight or combat against myself, I war against myself; p. *mag..sod.*

Migâs, (*nin*). I fight, I scuffle; p. *magasod.*

Migososhk, (*nin*). I am in a bad habit of fighting, of scuffling; p. *mag..kid.*

Migâsowin. Fighting, fight.

Migâsowinini. Soldier, warrior, fighter, boxer; pl.-*wag.*

Mi ge-ing. It will be so, be it so, Amen.

Migi animosh. The dog barks, yelps; p. *megid. O migidan gego animosh,* the dog barks at some obj.; p. *megidang. O wiginan animosh,* the dog barks at some obj.; p. *meginad.*

Migisananissi. Eagle-fighter, (a small blue bird;) pl.-*g.*

Migisi. Eagle; pl.-*wag.*

Migisins. A young eagle; pl.-*ag.*

Migisiwiganj. Eagle's claw; pl. -*ig.*

Migisiwisibi. Eagle River, Lake Superior.

Migisiwiwikwed. Eagle Harbor, Lake Superior.

Migiskan. Fish-hook; pl.-*an.*

Migiskaneiâb. Fish-hook line; pl.-*in.*

Migiss. Wampum, (beads of porcelain, Indian ornament and ancient money;) porcelain, chinaware; pearl; pl.-*migissag.*

Migissapikan. Wampum-strap, a large strap richly ornamented with beads of porcelain, used in Indian messages of great importance. Pl.-*an.*

Migissiiessimig. Breastplate of beads of porcelain, (of wampum.) This is the greatest Indian ornament. Pl.-*ag.*

Migissinagan. Dish or plate of porcelain; pl.-*an.*

Migissinagans. Cup, saucer, bowl, of porcelain; pl.-*an.*

Migiwe, (*nin*). I give, I contribute, I make a present, I grant, I allow; p. *mâgiwed.*

Migiwen, (*nin*). I give it away, I make a present of it to somebody; p. *mâgiwed.*

Migiwenan, (*nin*). I give away some obj.; p. *mâgiwed.* (V. Conj.)

Migiwen Songideeshkagewin, (*nin*). I give Confirmation, I confirm; p. *mag..ed.*

Migiweshk, (*nin*). I am in a habit of giving too much away; p. *mag..kid.*

Migiwetamawa, (*nin*) or, *nin migiwetawa.* I give it for

him, to his advantage ; p. *mag..wad.*

Migiwewin. Giving, or the act of giving s. th.; gift, present, contribution, *given ;* pl.*-an.*—S. *Minigowin.—Mi sa onow nin migiwewinan ;* these are my presents (*I give away.*)

Migiwin. Barking of a dog.

Migôss. Awl, bodkin ; pl.*-an.*

Migashkâdendagos, (*nin*). I am troublesome, I am considered troublesome, annoying ; p. *meg..sig.*

Migoskkadendagwad. It is troublesome or annoying; p. *meg ..wak.*

Migoshkâdendam, (*nin*). I am troubled in my thoughts, in my mind ; p. *meg..ang.*

Migoshkâdis, (*nin*). I am troublesome, I am annoying; p. *meg..sid.*

Migoshkâdisiwin. Troublesomeness, annoyance.

Migoshkâdjia, (*nin*). I trouble him, annoy him, bother him, I molest him, importune him, vex, tease, plague him ; p. *meg..ad.*

Migoshkadji-aiâ, (*nin*). I am troubled, frightened, alarmed, I am uneasy; p. *meg..iad.*

Migoshkâdji-aiawigon, (*nin*) or, *nin migoshkadjiigon.* It troubles me, bothers me, it makes me uneasy, it alarms me; p. *meg..god.*

Migoshkâdjideé, (*nin*). My heart is troubled, alarmed; p. *meg.. ed.*

Migoshkâdjideéwin. Trouble of heart, uneasiness.

Migoshkâsikawa, (*nin*), (from *nin migoshkâdjia,* I trouble him, and *nin nâsikawa,* I come to him.) I come to trouble him, to bother him ; p. *meg.. wad.*

Migoshkâsitagos, (*nin*). I am troublesome in my speaking, I trouble and annoy with my words ; p. *meg..sod.*

Migoshkâsitawa, (*nin*). I hear him with displeasure, I am troubled and annoyed by his speaking; p. *meg..wad.*

Migoshkâsoma, (*nin*). I importune him, I trouble him, I annoy him with my words ; p. *meg..mad.*

Migwan. Feather, quill, pen ; pl.*-ag.*

Migwanâdis, (*nin*). I am sickly, I am often sick ; p. *meg..sid.*

Migwanângewadin. There is hoar frost on the *ice ;* (F. il y a du frimas sur la glace ;) p. *mag..ing.*

Migwan-apikwéshimon. Feather-cushion ; pl.*-an.*

Migwan-apishimon. Feather-bed ; pl.*-an.*

Migwetch! Thanks ! (expression of thanksgiving.)

Migwetchiwenima, (*nin*) or, *migwetch nind inenima.* I have thankful thoughts and feelings towards him, I feel thankful to him ; p. *mag.. mad.*

Migwetchiwia, (*nin*). I thank him ; p. *mag..ad.*

Migwetchiwigijigad. Thanksgiving-day.

Migwetchiwiiwewin. Thanksgiving, thanks.

Migwetch nind inâ. I thank him, I say thanks to him.

Mi iw. That's it, that is enough.

Mijâana, (*nin*). I arrive to his track, his footsteps, (in the snow or mud;) p. *mej..nad;* imp. *mijaaj.*

Mijagâ, (*nin*). I arrive by water in a canoe or boat; p. *mejagad.*—S. *Dagwishin.*

Mijâgado, (*nin*). I overcome, I gain, (in a play;) p. *méj..dod.*

Mijagâk, (*nin*). I arrive, walking on the ice; p. *mej..od.*

Mijagâmekwajiwe, (*nin*). I arrive in a canoe or boat; p. *mej..wed.*

Mijakisse, (*nin*). I fall or sink down to the bottom of a river or lake; p. *mej..sed.*

Mijakisse or-*magad*. It sinks to the bottom of a river, etc.; p. *mej..seg*, or-*magak.*

Mijakwad. It is fair clear weather, serine, the sun shines, the sky is blue; p. *mej..wak.*

Mijakwadong inande. It is dyed sky-blue, it is of a sky-blue color, azure; p. *enandeg.*

Mijakwadong inanso. It is sky-colored, faint blue; p. *enansod.*

Mijakwanitibikad. It is a bright clear night, no clouds; p. *mej ..kak.*

Mijâshk. *Ot.* Herb, hay; pl.-*on*, or-*in.*

Mijiâ, (*nin*). I spoil him, I wrong him, injure him; p. *mejiad.*

Mijiiwe, (*nin*). I spoil, I make damage; p. *mejiiwed.*

Mijinawe. Steward, administrator of a property, manager; pl.-*g.*

Mijinawew, (*nin*). I am a steward, etc.; p. *mej..wid.*

Mijinawewiwin. Stewardship, administration of a property.

Mijikâgon, (*nin*). It catches me, it reaches me; p. *mej.. god.*—*Akosiwin nin gi-mijikagon;* a sickness has reached me.

Mijikawa, (*nin*). I reach him with my foot, I give him a *little* kick. (I give him a *hard* kick, would be, *nin tangishkawa;*) p. *mej..wad.*

Mijishâ, adv. Openly, plainly, expressly.

Mijishakiganebina, (*nin*) or, *nin mijishakiganena*. I uncover his breast; p. *mej..nad;* imp. *mij..bij.*

Mijishakiganebinidis, (*nin*) or, *nin mijishakiganenidis*. I uncover my breast; p. *mej.. sod.*

Mijishakiganeshin, (*nin*) or, *nin mitakineshin*. My breast is uncovered; p. *me..ing.*

Mijishâssa, (*nin*). I expose to the sight of people some obj.; p. *mej..sad;* imp. *mijishashi.*

Mijishâton, (*nin*). I expose it to the sight, I lay it open; p. *mej..tod.*

Mijishawagam, adv. Very far out in the lake, or sea.

Mijishâwakamig, adv. Under the sky, in the open air, without a shelter.

Mijishâwashkode. Large open prairie; pl.-*wan.*

Mijishâwashkode, or-*magad*. There is a large open prairie; p. *mej..deg*, or-*magak.*

Mijishâwissin. It is open, uncovered, exposed to the sight; p. *mej..ing.*

Mijishâwissitamawa, (*nin*). I expose it to him, I lay it open before him, I reveal it to him; p. *mej..wad.*

Mijishâwissitchigade, or-*magad.* It is laid open, it is exposed to the sight of people; it is manifested, revealed, it is made known, made public; p. *mej..deg*, or-*magad.*

Mijishâmissiton, (*nin*). S. *Mijishâton.*

Mijitagos, (*nin*). I make false and injurious reports; p. *mej ..sid.*

Mijiton, (*nin*). I injure it, I spoil it, damage it; p. *mejitod.*

Mijwa, (*nin*). I wound him, shooting at him; p. *mejwad*; imp. *mijwi.*

Mijwâgan. A person wounded by a shot; pl.-*ag.*

Mijwâganiw, (*nin*). I am a wounded person, (wounded by a shot;) p. *mej..wid.*

Mijwêwashk. Medical root or herb for wounds; pl.-*on.*

Mika, adv. This word is sometimes added to *kawéssa*, in order to strengthen the negation. *Kawêssa mika*, no, no, not at all, by no means.

Mikâde, or-*makad*, or, *mikâdjigade*, or-*magad.* It is found, discovered, detected, found out, invented; p. *mek..deg*, or-*magak.*

Mikâdjigas, (*nin*). I am found, discovered; p. *mek..sod.*

Mikâge, (*nin*). I find, I find out; p. *mekaged.*

Mikâgan. Any thing found, detected; pl.-*an.*

Mikaganiw, (*nin*). I am a findling; p. *mek..wid.*

Mikâganiwan. It is a found thing; p. *mek..wang.*

Mikamâdis, (*nin*) or, *nin mikamâs.* I find to myself or for myself; p. *mek..sod.*

Mikamâdison, (*nin*) or, *nin mikamâson.* I find it for me; p. *mek..sod.*

Mikamâdisonan, (*nin*). S. *Mikamasonan.*

Mikamâson, (*nin*). I find it to myself; p. *mek..sod.*

Mikamasonan, (*nin*). I find some obj. to myself; p. *mek.. sod.* (V. Conj.)

Mikamawa, (*nin*). I find it to him; p. *mek..wad.*

Mikân, (*nin*). I find it; I discover it; p. *mekang.*

Mikana. Trail, path, road, way; pl.-*n.*

Mikana inamo. The trail or road goes to...; p. *enamog.*

Mikana ondamo. The trail or road comes from... ; p. *wendamog.*

Mikanakawa, (*nin*). I make or prepare a path or road for him; p. *mak..wad.*

Mikanâke, (*nin*). I make a road; p. *mak..ked.*

Mikas, (*nin*). I am found; p. *mekasod.*

Mikaw, (*nin*). I have my senses; I recover my senses, after fainting or swooning; p. *mekawid.*

Mikawa, (*nin*). I find him; I discover him, detect him, (a person, or any other obj.); p. *mekawâd.*

Mikawâdis, (*nin*). I am a fine looking person, I have a fine appearance; p. *mek..sid.*

Mikawadisiwin. Beauty of a person, fine appearance.
Mikawadj, (*nin*). I begin to feel that a limb or part of my body is freezing; p. *meb..id.*
Mihawadjikwe. A fine looking woman; pl.-*g.*
Mikawadjinini. A fine looking man; pl.-*wag.*
Mikawâma, (*nin*). I make him think on s. th., I make him recollect or remember s. th., I remind him of s. th.; p. *mek ..mad.*
Mikawâshiton, (*nin*). I invent it, discover it; p. *mek..tod.*
Mikawâshitowin. Invention; pl. *-an.*
Mikawin, (*nin*). I remember it; p. *mekawid.*
Mikawinan, (*nin*). I remember him; p. *mekawid.* (V. Conj.)
Mikinak; pl.-*wag.* S. *Mishikê.*
Mikindâgan. A packet or bundle of fur; (C. paquet de pelleteries;) pl.-*ag.*
Mikindjia, (*nin*). I irritate him, vex him, I provoke him to anger; p. *mak..ad.*
Mikindjige. I provoke to anger; p. *mak..ged.*
Mikodjina, (*nin*), (from *nin mikawa*, I find him, and *nind ôdjina*, I feel him or grope him.) I find him by feeling or groping in the dark; p. *mek.. nad.*
Mikôdjinan, (*nin*). I find it by feeling in the dark; p. *mek.. ang.*
Mikoma, (*nin*). I speak of him in his absence; p. *mekomad.*
Mikona, (*nin*). I find some obj. among many others; p. *mekonad.*
Mikonan, (*nin*). I find it among many other things; p. *mek.. ang.*
Mikonawea, (*nin*). I make him pleasure, I render him a service; p. *mak..ad.*
Mikonaweiendam, (*nin*). I am glad and thankful; p. *mak.. ang.*
Mikonaweienima, (*nin*). I am happy and thankful he has it; p. *mak..mad.*
Mikos, (*nin*). I am industrious; p. *makosid.*
Mikoshkos, (*nin*). I am shot, (with a gun or bow;) p. *mak.. sod.*
Mikwâdisi animosh. It is a good sporting dog, a good hound, good pointer; p. *mek.. sid.*
Mikwam. Ice.
Mikwam, or *mikwamins.* Icicle.
Mikwam bimâbogo. The ice is floating down on a river, there is a drift of ice; p. *bemâbogod.*
Mikwamika, or-*magad.* There is ice; p. *mek..kag*, or-*magak.*
Mikwaminâniwan. It hails; p. *mek..ang.*
Mikwaming ejinagwak mashkiki. Alum, (medicine that looks like ice.) S. *Jiwâbik.*
Mikwamiwigamig. Ice-house, ice-pit; pl.-*on.*
Mikwâwa, (*nin*). I hit him (with s. th. I throw at him;) p. *mak ..wad; imp. mikwa.*
Mikwéndamia, (*nin*). I make him remember s. th., I recall it to his memory; p. *mek..ad.*
Mikwéndamowin. Recollecting, remembering.
Mikwéndân, (*nin*). I remember

it, I recollect it, think on it; p. *mek..ang.*

Mikwéndass, (*nin*). I recollect, I remember; p. *mek..sod.*

Mikwendassowin. Memory.

Mikwêndjigade, or-*magad.* It is remembered; p. *mek..deg,* or-*magak.*

Mikwénima, (*nin*). I remember him, I think on him; p. *mek ..mad.*

Mikwigi mitig. The tree yields fruit; p. *makwigid.*

Mikwigin. It yields fruit; p. *mak..ing.*

Mimigibidon, (*nin*). I crush it, (stuff;) p. *mem..dod.*

Mimigibina, (*nin*). I crush it, (stuff;) p. *mem..nad.*

Mimigopagis, (*nin*). I struggle; p. *mem..sod.*

Mimigoshkam, (*nin*). I am treading out s. th.; p. *mem..ang.*

Mimigoshkan, (*nin*). I tread it out, (instead of thrashing it;) p. *mem..ang.*—*Manomin nin mimigoshkan;* I tread out wild rice.

Mimigoshkawa, (*nin*). I tread it out; p. *mem..wad.*—*Pakwejigan nin mimigoshkawa;* I tread out wheat, (instead of thrashing it.)

Mimigowebina, (*nin*). I shake him; (F. je le secoue;) p. *mem..nad;* imp. *mim..bin.*

Mimigowebînan, (*nin*). I shake it; p. *mem..ang.*

Mimigwab, (*nin*). I move and shake myself, sitting; p. *mem ..id.*

Mimigwishin, (*nin*). I move and shake myself, lying; p. *mem.. ing.*

Mi minik, adv. So much, that's all; that's enough.

Min. Wortleberry; berry; pl. *-minan.*

Mi na? Is it so? is it right? will you?

Mina, (*nin*). I give him, I make him a present; I grant him, allow him s. th.; I impose it upon him; I cause it to him; p. *mânad.*

Minaâ, (*nin*). I give him drink; I water him, (a horse, an ox, etc.); p. *mênaad.*

Minâdendam, (*nin*). I honor, I respect; p. *men..ang.*

Minâdendân, (*nin*). I honor or respect it; p. *men..ang.*

Minâdenim, (*nin*) or, *nin minâdenindis.* I honor myself, I am vain; I am proud; p. *men ..od.*

Minâdenima, (*nin*). I honor him, I respect him; p. *men..mâd.*

Minâdenindiwin. Respect, honor, veneration.

Minâgodjissi. Ped-bog; pl.-*wag.*

Minâgos, (*nin*). I smell; I emit an odor; p. *menâgosid.*

Minâgwad. It smells, it has an odor; p. *men..wak.*

Minâidimin, (*nin*). We give each other to drink; we procure drink to one another; p. *men..didjig.*

Minâiwe, (*nin*). I give to drink; I procure drink; p. *men..wed.*

Minâiweshk, (*nin*). I am in a bad habit of giving or procuring drink to others; p. *men.. kid.*

Minâma, (*nin*). I smell him, I scent him, (a person, or any other obj.); p. *menâmad.*

Minâmika, or-*magad*. There are breakers, shoals, banks, (of sand or rocks;) p. *men..kag*, or-*magak*.

Minâssige, (*nin*). I make a good odor by burning s. th.; p. *men..ged*.

Minâswa, (*nin*). I burn some obj. to make a good odor; p. *men..wad;* imp. *minaswi*.

Minawa, adv. Again, more, anew.

Minawânigobi, (*nin*). I am joyous in liquor, joyful through intoxication; p. *men..bid*.

Minawânigos, (*nin*). I am joyous, joyful, I rejoice; p. *men..sid*.

Minawânigosiwin. Joy, joyfulness, rejoicing, pleasure.

Minawânigwad. There is joy, rejoicing, pleasure; p. *men..wak*.

Minawânigwendam, (*nin*). I rejoice, I have joyful thoughts; p. *men..ang*.

Minawânigwendamowin. Joy, joyful thoughts.

Minawânigwia, (*nin*). I make him joyous, I procure him joy and pleasure; p. *men..ad*.

Minawânigwiton, (*nin*), (pron. *nin minawânigoton*.) I make it joyous, joyful; p. *men..tod*. —*Debenimiian, ki gi-minawanigwiton ninde*; Lord, thou hast made my heart joyful.

Minawâs, (*nin*). I am happy, contented, I rejoice; p. *men..sid*.

Minawâsiâ, (*nin*). I make him happy, contented, I make him rejoice; p. *men..ad*.

Minawâsima, (*nin*) or, *nin minawânigoma*. I make him joyous with my *words*, with what I am telling him; p. *men..mad*.

Minawinagos, (*nin*). I look good, benevolent, charitable; p. *men..sid*.

Mindâdendân, (*nin*). I regret to have lost it; p. *men..ang*.

Mindadenima, (*nin*). I regret to have lost some object; p. *men..mad*.

Mindamawa, (*nin*). S. *Mindawa*.

Mindassiwagan. A tamed animal; pl.-*ag*.

Mindawa, (*nin*). I pout, I am dissatisfied with him, because he does not give me what I want; I murmur against him; p. *mendawad*.

Mindawe, (*nin*). I pout, I look sullen, I will not speak; I am not satisfied with what is given to me; (F. je boude;) p. *mendawed*.

Mindawebi, (*nin*). I pout, I am cross, because I have no liquor to drink; p. *men..bid*.

Mindaweganjân. White spot on a finger-nail, (mark of pouting;) pl.-*ag*.

Mindaweganji, (*nin*). I have white spots on my nails; p. *men..id*.

Mindaweshk, (*nin*). I am in a bad habit of pouting, I am a pouter; p. *men..kid*.

Mindawewin. Pouting; (F. bouderie.)

Mindawewinagos, (*nin*). I look cross, dissatisfied; p. *men..sik*.

Mindibigab, (*nin*). I weep much, I shed large tears; p. *men..bid*.

Mindid, (*nin*). I am large, big, bulky; p. *méndidod*.

Mindimoié. Old woman; pl.-*iag*.

Mindimoiéiw, (*nin*). I am an old woman; p *men..wid*.

Mindimoiêmish. Wife. This word is always preceded by a possessive pronoun. — *Nin mindimoiémish*, my wife, (my bad old woman.)

Mindjikâwan. Mitten; glove; pl.-*ag*.

Mindjimapide, or-*magad*. It is tied or bound; p. *men..deg*, or-*magak*.

Mindjimapidon, (*nin*). I bind it; p. *men..dod*.

Mindjimapikaigas, (*nin*). I am fettered, chained; p. *men..sod*.

Mindjimapina, (*nin*). I bind him; p. *men..nad*; imp. *mindjimapij*.

Mindjimêndam, (*nin*). I keep in memory; p. *men..ang*.

Mindjimêndân, (*nin*). I keep it in memory, I don't forget it; p. *men..ang*.

Mindjimênima, (*nin*). I keep him in my memory, I don't forget him; p. *men..mad*.

Mindjimina, (*nin*). I hold him; I keep him back; p. *men..nad*.

Mindjiminamawa, (*nin*). I withhold s. th. from him; p. *men..wod*.

Mindjiminidisowin. Moderation, retraining, self-command.

Mindjimishkagon, (*nin*). It keeps me, it holds me; p. *men..god*.

Mindjimishkawa, (*nin*). I hold him under me; p. *men..wad*.

Mindjimishkodjigan. Any heavy object to keep s. th. down, not to blow off; pl.-*an*.

Mindjimishkodon, (*nin*). I put some heavy object on it, to keep it down, or to keep it steady; p. *men..dod*.

Mindjimishkona, (*nin*). I put some heavy thing on some obj., in order to keep him (her, it) down; p. *men..nad*; imp. *koj*.

Mindjinawéiadakamig, adv. It is a pity, it is regretful.

Mindjinawéiendam, (*nin*). I have sorrowful and repenting thoughts; p. *men..ang*.

Mindjinawés, (*nin*). I repent, I am sorry to have done s. th.; p. *men..sid*.

Mindjinawésiwin. Repentance, hearty sorrow for having done s. th.

Mindôkad. There is dew on the ground; p. *mendokak*.

Minéss. The fruit of the thorn-shrub; (F. cenelle;) pl.-*ag*.

Minêssagawanj. Thorn, thorn-shrub, thorn-bush; pl.-*ig*.

Min-gisiss. The moon of bilberries or whortleberries, the month of August.

Mini. Apostume, abscess, or rather the matter or pus that is in an abscess, or runs out of it.

Minik,adv. So much,as much as.

Minikân. Seed; pl.-*an*.

Minikân. Seed; pl.-*ag*.— *Minikanag ogow opinig, kawin ninwi-amwassig*; these potatoes are for seed, I will not eat them.

Minike, (*nin*). I gather whortleberries; p. *manikéd*.

Minikwâdan (*nin*). I spend it for drinking, I drink it; p. *men..ang.*
Minikwâgigan. Any drinking-vessel, pot, pitcher, glass, goblet, tumbler; pl.-*an.*
Minikwâdjigan. Gallon.—*Ningo minikwadjigan,* one gallon; *nijo, nisso, nio nano minikwadjigan;* two, three, four, five gallons, etc. — *Kishkitchiag minikwâdjigan,* a pint.
Minikwânâ, (*nin*). I spend it for drinking, I drink it; p. *men.. nad.*—*Kakina o joniiaman o gi-minikwânân;* he spent all his money for drinking, (he drank all his money.)
Minikwê, (*nin*). I drink; p. *mênikwéd.*
Minikwén, (*nin*). I drink it; p. *ménikwed.*
Minikwêshk, (*nin*). I am in a bad habit of drinking (intoxicating liquor;) p. *men..kid.*
Minikwêshkiwin. Bad habit of drinking (int. liq.), drunkenness.
Minikwéssi-masinaigans. Temperance-pledge; pl.-*an.*
Minikwéssiwin. Non-drinking, temperance.
Minikwéwigamig. Drinking-house, liquor-house, dram-shop, tippling-shop; pl.-*on.*
Minikwêwin. Drinking.
Minikwéwiniwan. It is drink; they drink it; p. *men..ang.*
Minins. Small pimple or pustule; pl.-*an.*
Mininsiwidon, (*nin*). I have a small pimple on my lip; p. *men..dong.*
Miniss. Island, islè; pl.-*an.*
Minissâbik. Rock-island; pl.-*on.*
Minissing-endanakid, or, *minissing endaji-bimadisid.* He who is a native of an island, or, he who lives on an island, islander; pl.-*jig.*
Minissino. Warrior, soldier; hero; pl.-*g.*
Minissinô-ogima. Military officer; pl.-*g.*
Minissinôw, (*nin*). I am a wnrrior; I am brave; p. *men.. wid.*
Minissinowâdis, (*nin*). I am a hero; p. *men..sid.*
Minissinôwinini. Hero; pl.-*wag.*
Minitig. An island in a river; pl.-*on.*
Minitigodjiwan. An island in a rapid or in rapids; pl.-*an.*
Miniw, (*nin*). I have an abscess with matter in, the matter runs out of my abscess; p. *meniwid.*
Miniw, (*nin*). I bring forth, I yield fruit; p. *maniwid.* — *Mitig miniwi,* the tree produces or yields fruit; *maniwid mitig,* fruit-tree.
Miniwan. Matter or pus is running out of an ulcer or abscess, it brings forth matter; p. *meniwang.*
Miniwan. It produces or yields fruit; p. *maniwang.*
Miniwâpine, (*nin*). I have the consumption, I am consumptive, phthisical; p. *men..ned.*
Miniwapinewin. Consumption, phthisis.
Miniwidjane, (*nin*). I have a fetid nose; (F. je suis punais;) p. *men..ned.*
Mino, adj. and adv. Good; well.
Mino aiâ, (*nin*). I am well, in

good health ; I am comfortable and well off; p. *méno..aiad.*

Mino aiäwin. Good health ; comfortable happy existence, easy circumstances.

Minobi, (*nin*). I am gay and feel contented, in liquor ; p. *menebid.*

Minobiia, or-*magad.* It is navigable, good for navigation, (a river ;) p. *men..ag,* or-*magak.*

Mino bimâdis, (*nin*). I live well ; I am in good health ; I am good, kind, I have a good temper, a good humor ; p. *men..sid.*

Minô bimâdisiwin. Good life ; good health ; good kind temperament, good humor.

Minôdashimin, (*nin*). We are just enough, we are in a sufficient number; p. *men..shidjig.*

Minôdassin. There is just enough of it ; *men..sing.*

Minodê, or-*magad.* It is well done, well cooked ; p. *menodeg,* or-*magak.*

Minodeê, (*nin*). I have a good heart, I am good-hearted, gentle ; p. *menodeed.*

Minodeea, (*nin*). I console him, I make him be of good courage, good heart ; p. *men..ad.*

Minodeêwin. Goodness of heart, good nature, gentleness.

Minododamowin. Good action, benefit ; pl.-*an.*

Mino gijigad. It is fair weather, it is a fine day ; p. *men..gak.*

Minogijiganish, (*nin*). I have a fine, fair weather, (for traveling ;) p. *men..id.*

Minogin. It produces well, (a field, a garden ;) p. *menoging.*

Minogiwemagad. It is profitable, producing fruit ; p. *men..gad.*

Minoiabadad. It is useful ; p. *men..dak.*

Minoiâbadis, (*nin*). I am useful, (a person, or any other obj.) ; p. *men..sid.*

Minoiâbadjia, (*nin*). I make a good use of him, he is useful to me, (a person or some other obj.) ; p. *men..ad.*

Minoiabadjiton, (*nin*). I make a good use of it, it is useful to me ; p. *men..tod.*

Minoijiwêbis, (*nin*). I am good, I behave well, I have a good conduct ; I have good qualities, I am virtuous ; p. *men..sid.*

Mino ijiwébisiwin. Good conduct, good behavior, goodness, virtue.

Mino-inawéma, (*nin*). I am on good and peaceful terms with him, I am his friend, or, he is my friend ; p. *men..mad.*

Minokami, (*nin*). I have a good footing on my trail or road, (or standing somewhere ;) p. *men..mid.*

Minokami. Ot. Spring ; (F. printemps ;) p. *men..ing. Minokamig,* in spring.

Minokamiga. There is good ground, good soil ; p. *men..gag.*

Minâkan, (*nin*). I put it well on, (clothing,) it fits me well ; p. *menokang.*

Mino-kikinowabama, (*nin*). I follow his good example, he edifies me ; p. *men..mad.*

Mino kikinowabamig, (*nin*). He imitates my good examples, I edify him, I give him a good example.

Minokikinowabamigowin. Good example *taken*, edification.

Mino kikinowabandaiwe, (*nin*). I give a good example, I edify; p. *men..wed.*

Minomâgwakisigan. Any thing that smells well when burnt, incense, frankincense.

Minomâgwakisige, (*nin*). I burn s. th. that smells well, I burn incense, I incense; p. *men.. ged.*

Minomamâ, (*nin*). He smells well to me, (any obj.); p. *men ..ad.*

Minomândân, (*nin*). It smells well to me, I like its odor; p. *men..ang.*

Minomândjige, (*nin*). I smell a good odor, s. th. smells well to me; p. *men..ged.*

Minomâsso assêma. Tobacco smells well; p. *men..sod.*

Minomâte, or-*magad.* It smells well when burnt; p. *men..teg*, or-*magak.*

Minonawea, (*nin*). I make him contented, I satisfy him, I please him; p. *men...ad.*

Minông. Isle Royal, Lake Superior.

Minôns. Cat, puss.

Minôpidan, (*nin*). I find a good taste in some thing I am eating or drinking, I relish it, I like the taste of it; p. *men.. ang.*

Minôpidjige, (*nin*). I find a good taste in victuals; p. *mea..ged.* —*Nawatch mino aia aw aiakosid, jaigwa minôpidjige;* this sick person is somewhat better, he already finds a good taste in victuals.

Minôpogosi. He (she, it) has a good taste, a fine flavor; p. *men...sid.*

Minôpogosiwin. Good taste, good fine flavor, relish.

Minôpogwad. It has a good taste, it is good, delicate, delicious, (to the palate;) p. *men.. wak.*

Minôpwa, (*nin*). I find a good taste in some obj. I am eating, I relish it, I like the taste of it; p. *menôpwad;* imp. *minopwi.*

Minoshin, (*nin*). I lie well, comfortably; p. *men..ing.*

Minoshkâgemagad. It does good, it operates well, (a medicine;) p. *men..gak.*

Minôshkine, or-*magad.* It goes well in, it fits just in, (a key in a lock, etc.); p. *men..neg*, or-*magak.*

Minoso. It is well done, well cooked, (some obj.); p. *menosod.*—S. *Minode.*

Minossê, (*nin*). I walk well, easily; p. *menossed.*

Minossé or-*magad.* It goes well, it does well, it fits well; p. *menosseg*, or-*magak.*

Minôssin. It lies well, it is well placed or put; p. *menossing.*

Minôssiton, (*nin*). I place it well; p. *men..tod.*

Minotâgos, (*nin*). I am heard with pleasure, I speak or sing agreeably, I have an agreeable voice; p. *men..sid.*

Minôtam, (*nin*). I listen with pleasure; p. *menotâng.*

Minotamômagad. It listens with pleasure; p. *meno..gak.*—*Debenimiian, nitawagan minôtamomagadon kid ikkitowi-*

nan ; Lord, my ears listen with pleasure to thy words.

Minotan, (*nin*). I listen to it with pleasure, I hear it with pleasure, I like to hear it; p. *menotang.*

Minôtawa, (*nin*). I listen him with pleasure, I like to hear him; p. *men..wad.*

Minotch, adv. Still, but still, yet, nevertheless, notwithstanding.

Minôtchige, (*nin*). I act well; p. *men..ged.*

Minotwa, (*nin*). The same as, *nin minotchige.*

Mino-wâwina, (*nin*), freq. I name him well frequently, I speak well of him; I glorify, praise, exalt him; p. *men..nad.*

Mino-wâwindan, (*nin*), freq. I name it well frequently, I speak well of it; I glorify it, praise it; p. *men..ang.*

Mino-wâwindjigade, or-*magad,* freq. It is well-named, well spoken of, it is praised, celebrated; it is renowned; p. *men..deg,* or-*magak.*

Mino-wâwindjigadewin. Good renown.

Mino-wâwindjigas, (*nin*), freq. I am well named, I am well spoken of, praised, celebrated, I have a good renown, good name.

Mino-wâwinidimin, (*nin*). We praise each other, we speak well one of another; p. *men..didjig.*

Mino-wâwinidis, (*nin*), freq. I praise myself, I speak always well of myself; p. *men..sod.*

Mino-wâwinidiwin. Mutual praise, or praise of several persons.

Mino-wâwinigon, (*nin*). It praises me; p. *men..god* — *Kid anokiwin ki mino-wâwinigon;* thy work praises thee. *Wewingesid o mino-wâwinigon od anokiwin ;* he who works well, is praised by his work.

Minowe, (*nin*). I have a fine clear voice; p. *menowed.*

Mino widjindimin, (*nin*). We live together in good peace, we agree well together, we are good friends; p. *men..didjig.*

Mino widjindiwin. Good peace and harmony, concord, friendship.

Mino widjiwa, (*nin*). I am his friend, or, he is my friend, I agree well with him, I live in peace and harmony with him; p. *men..wad.*

Mino-wina, (*nin*). *Nin mino-windan. Mino-windjigade. Nin mino-windjigas. Nin mino-winidimin. Nin mino-winidis. Nin mino-winigon.*—These are the simple verbs of the above frequentative verbs; as: *Nin mino-wawina. Nin mino-wawindan,* etc., which see.—The signification is the same in both kinds of verbs; the frequentative verb only signifies a re-iteration of the same act.

Minwâb, (*nin*) (from *mino,* well; and *nin wâb,* I see;) I see well, I have good eyes; p. *menwâbid.*

Minwab, (*nin*), (from *mino,* well; and *nind ab,* I am sitted;) I sit comfortably, I am well sitted, I sit well; p. *menwabid.*

Minwabamêwis, (*nin*). I am lucky, I have a good chance; p. *mew..sid.*

Minwabamêwisiwin. Good luck, good chance.

Minwâbaminagos, (*nin*). I look well, I am fair, beautiful, I have a fine appearance; p. *men..sid.*

Minwâbaminagwad. It looks well, it has a fine beautiful appearance; p. *men..wak.*

Minwâbandam, (*nin*). I have a good dream; p. *men..ang.*

Minwâbandamowin. A good favorable dream; pl.-*an.*

Minwâbandan, (*nin*). I find it good, well done, I approve of it; p. *men..ang.*

Minwâbide, (*nin*). I have good fair teeth; p. *men..ded.*

Minwâbikinân nin pâshkisigan, (*nin*). I uncock a gun; p. *man..ang.*

Minwâdendam, (*nin*). I am forbearing, I am of a patient disposition of mind; p. *men.. ang.*

Minwadendamôwin. Patience, forbearance, clemency.

Minwâdenima, (*nin*). I think he is patient, I find him patient; p. *men..mad.*

Minwâdis, (*nin*). I am patient, long suffering; p. *men..sid.*

Minwâdjim, (*nin*). I bring good news, good tidings; p. *menwâdjimod.*

Minwâdjima, (*nin*). I tell s. th. good of him, I make a good report on him, I praise him; p. *men..mad.*

Minwâdjimowin. A good report or narration, good news, good tidings; also, the Gospel, (Evangely, which signifies in Greek, *good tidings.*)

Minwâdjito, (*nin*). I do well my business, I act with patience and perseverance; p. *men..tod.*

Minwâdodân, (*nin*) (from *mino,* well, and *nin dibâdodân,* I tell it.) I speak well of it, I praise it; p. *men..ang.*

Minwâgami. It has a good taste, it is good, (some liquid;) p. *men..mig.* — *Minwâgami iw mashkikiwâbo;* that medicine has a good taste.

Minwâgamipidân, (*nin*). I find that this liquid has a good taste; p. *men..ang.*

Minwândjige, (*nin*). I fare well, I eat good things; p. *men.. ged.*

Minwanimad. The wind is fair; p. *men..mak.*

Minwanoki, (*nin*), (*nin mino anoki.*) I am industrious; p. *men..id.*

Minwâsh, (*nin*). I have a fair wind, I sail with a fair wind; p. *men..id.*

Minwâssin. It is driven by a fair wind; p. *men..ing.*

Minwâwe aw awessi. This animal has a fine good fur; p. *menwawed.*

Minwêndaa, (*nin*). S. *Minwéndamia.*

Minwêndagos, (*nin*). I am liked, I am considered agreeable, pleasing, amiable; p. *men.. sid.*

Minwendagosiwin. Agreeableness of a person, amability, amiableness.

Minwéndagwad. It is considered

agreeable, satisfying, pleasing, delightful; p. *men..wak.*

Minwênaâgwakamig, adv. Pleasant, agreeably.—*Geget minwendâgwakamig eji-aiaeg oma;* it is truly pleasant to see how you are situated here.

Minwêndam, (*nin*). I am contented, I am happy; I consent, I am willing; p. *men.. ang.*

Minwendamia, (*nin*). I make him contented, I satisfy him; p. *men..ad.*

Minwéndamowin. Content, pleasure, happiness; consent.

Minwéndân, (*nin*). I like it, I am happy to have it; p. *men.. ang.*

Minwênima, (*nin*). I like him, I like to have him, (a person, or any other obj.); p. *men.. mad.*

Minwéwis, (*nin*). I am zealous, faithful, constant; industrious, complaisant; p. *men.. sid.*

Minwêwisikandan, (*nin*). I do it faithfully, with zeal and patience; p. *men..ang.*

Minwêwisikandawa, (*nin*). I am zealous and faithful to him, profitable to him; p. *men.. wad.*

Minwewisiwin. Zeal at work, industry.

Misi dash, or, *mipi dash gaie*, and, also, likewise.

Misai. Loach, (fish;) pl.-*ag.*

Misâkamig, adv. Everywhere on earth.

Misassin. A large stone, to sink a net to the bottom of the lake; pl.-*in.*

Misâtig. A stick not split, round piece of wood, cudgel; (F. rondin;) pl.-*on.*

Misâtigogaisse, (*nin*). I chop round sticks, not splitting them; p. *mes..sed.*

Misâtigogwadan, (*nin*). I sew it round, in a round shape; p. *mes..ang.*

Misâtigogwade, or-*magad.* It is sewed ln a round shape; p. *mes..deg*, or-*magak.*

Misâtigomidâss. Stocking, (round legging;) pl.-*an.*

Misâtikomidassike, (*nin*). I make stockings, I knit; p. *mes..ked.*

Mishâbiwinân. The hair on the eyelid.—This word is always preceded by a possessive pronoun; *nin mishâbiwinân, ki mishabiwinân, o mishâbiwinânan*, etc.

Mishâkigan, (*nin*). I have hair on the breast; p. *mash..ang.*

Mishâwagam, adv. S. *Mijishawagam.*

Mishawashkode. S. *Mijishawashkode.*

Mishâwatchigade, or-*magad* It is made all in one room, without any partition, (a house;) p. *mesh..deg*, or-*magak.*

Mishawate, or-*magad.* It is all in one room, there is no partition in it, (in a house;) p. *mesh..teg*, or-*magak.*

Mishâwaton, (*nin*). I make it all in one room, I make no partition in it; p. *mesh..tod.*

Mishawêsi. It is hairy, (stuff;) p. *mash..sid.*—This word is also used to signify velvet.

Mishawêigad. It is coarse, hairy, (stuff); p. *mash..gak.*

Mishéwe. Stag; pl.-*g.*

Mishi. A piece of wood for fuel.
Mishibiji. Lion; pl.-*g.*
Mishidamikan, (*nin*). I have a beard around the chin; p. *mesh..ang.*
Mishidee, (*nin*). I am cross, peevish, passionate; p. *meshideed.*
Mishideewin. Peevishness.
Mishidjimin. Current-berry; (F. gadelle;) pl.-*ag.*
Mishidjiminagawanj. Currant-shrub; pl.-*ig.*
Mishidôn, (*nin*). I have a beard around the mouth; p. *me..ong.*
Mishidonâgan. Beard.
Mishigâde, (*nin*), or, *nin memishigade,* freq. I have hair on the leg or legs, (hairy leg or legs); p. *meshigaded.*
Mishiginebig. Big horned serpent; pl.-*og.*
Mishigondâgan, (*nin*). I have a beard on the throat; p. *mesh..ang.*
Mishike. A kind of large tortoise; pl.-*iag.*
Mishikékek. Kite, (bird of prey;) pl.-*wag.*
Mishikewidashwa. Tortoise's shell or shield; pl.-*g.*
Mishimij. White oak; pl.-*ig.*
Mishimin. Apple; pl.-*ag.*
Mishiminatig. Apple-tree; pl.-*og.*
Misnimini-okonass. Apple-peel; pl.-*an.*
Mishinad. There is much of it, it abounds; p. *meshinak.*
Mishinaton, (*nin*). I ingrease it; p. *mesh..tod.*
Mishinike, (*nin*) or, *nin memishinike,* freq. I have hair on the arm or arms, (hairy arm or arms;) p. *me..ked.*
Mishinimakinago; pl.-*g.*—This name is given to some strange Indians, (according to the sayings of the Otchipwes,) who arc rowing through the woods, and who are sometimes heard shooting, but never seen. And from this word, the name of the village of *Mackinac,* or *Michillimackinac,* is derived.
Mishinimin, (*nin*) or, *nin mishinomin.* We are many, in great number; p. *mesh..djig.*
Mishinindji, (*nin*) or, *nin mémishinindji,* freq. I have hair on the hand or hands, (hairy hand or hands;) p. *mesh..id.*
Mishinonikas, (*nin*). I have many names; p. *mesh..sod.*
Mishinotâmawa, (*nin*). I augment or increase it for him or to him; p. *mesh..wad.*
Mishinoton, (*nin*). S. *Mishinaton.*
Mishiside, (*nin*) or, *nin memishiside,* freq. I have hair on the foot or feet; p. *mesh..ded.*
Mishiwâtig. Piece of dry wood for fuel; kindle-wood; pl.-*on.*
Mishiwatigoke, (*nin*). I chop dry wood; p. *mesh..ked.*
Mishiwâtigossag. S. *Mishiwatig.*
Mishiwatigowi aw mitig. That tree is dead and dry; p. *mesh..wid.*
Misi, (*nin*). I exonerate the bowels; p. *mâsid.*
Misi, adj. and adv. All, everywhere.
Misiâ. A piece of meat.
Misiake, (*nin*). I cut meat into pieces; p. *mes..ked.*
Misi gego, adv. All.
Misi gegoga-gijitod. He who has made all, Creator.

Misi gego kèkandang. He who knows all, the Omniscient.

Misi gego nétawitod. He who can make all, the Almighty.

Mésikwasikama, (*nin*). The snow sticks to my snowshoes; p. *mes..mad.*

Misimânisiwin. Wickedness.

Misimânisiwinish. Wicked person; pl.-*ag.*

Misimin. Rye; pl.-*an.*

Misisâk. Horse-fly, ox-fly; pl.-*wag.*

Misisse. Turkey; pl.-*g.*—*Saséga mississé,* pea-cock. *Mississens,* young turkey; pl.-*ag.*

Misiwé, adv. Everywhere.

Misiwébian, (*nin*) (from *misiwé,* everywhere; and *nind ojibian,* I mark it or write it.) I write the paper all over, I write on every part of it; p. *mes.ang.*

Misiwébiigade, or-*magad.* It is written all over, everywhere on the piece of paper; p. *mes ..deg,* or-*magak.*

Misiwedina, (*nin*). S. *Misiwetchishkiwagina.*

Misiwé eiad. He who is everywhere, the Omnipresent.

Misiwéia, or-*magad.* It is whole, entire, all of it; p. *mes..ag,* or-*magak.*

Misiwéiabikad. It is whole or entire, (metal;) p. *mes..kak.*

Misiwêiâbikisi (*ioniia, assin*). It is entire, (obj. of silver or stone;) p. *mes..sid.*

Misiwêiâkosi. It is whole or entire, (obj. of wood;) p. *mes ..sid.*

Misiwéiâkwad. It is all entire, (wood;) p. *mes..wak.*

Misiwêgad. It is whole, entire, (obj. of stuff or paper;) p. *mes ..gak.*

Misiwêgisi. It is entire, (obj. of stuff, *moshwe, senibâ;*) p. *mes..sid.*

Misiwênindjân. The hand, (without the fingers.) *Nin misiwênindjan,* my hand; *o misiwênindjan,* his hand, etc.

Misiwéshkamagad. There is of it everywhere, all is covered with it; p. *mes..gak.*

Misiwêsi. It is whole, entire, no piece is wanting; p. *mes..sid.* —*Keiâbi misiwesi aw pakwejigan;* this loaf of bread is yet entire, (nothing has been broken off.)

Misiwetchigade, or-*magad.* It is made all of one piece, or, it is all in one piece; p. *mes..deg,* or-*magad.*

Misiwetchigan. Alg. S. *Sigaigan.*

Misiwetchishkiwagina pakwejigan, (*nin*). I work up flour into dough; p. *mes..nad.*

Misiweton, (*nin*). I make it all of one piece; p. *mes..tod.*

Misiwigamig. Water-closet; pl.-*on.*

Miskobag, * Red leaf; pl.-*on.*

Miskobaga, or-*magad.* There are red leaves on a tree, or on trees, (in the fall of the year, in autumn;) p. *mes..gag,*or-*magak.*

Mikobagisi mitig. The tree has red leaves; p. *mes..sid.*

Miskodissimin. A bean; pl.-*ag.*

* Note. In this and some others of the following words, the second syllable ought to be written *kwa,* instead of *ko,* as they are composed of *miskwa,* red. But in pronouncing the words, *o* is plainly heard; therefore we put it also in writing them.

Miskogad. Woolen girdle or cincture or belt with small glass-beeds; pl.-*ag.*
Miskogadeiâb. Wool for girdles or belts.
Miskokinje. Red-hot coals.
Miskosi, (*miskwasi.*) It is red; p. *meskosid,* (*meskwasid.*)
Miskotchiss. Red turnip, that is, beet-root; the same as *miskokâdak;* pl.-*an.*
Miskwâ, or-*magad.* It is red; p. *meskwag,* or-*magak.*
Miskwâbi, (*nin*). I have the bloody flux, the dysentery; p. *mes..bid.*
Miskwâbigan. Red clay.
Miskwâbiganowassin. Stone of red clay, that is, a brick; pl.-*ig.*
Miskwâbigin. Red flannel.
Miskwâbik. Copper, (red metal.)
Miskwâbikad. It is red, (metal, glass;) p. *mes..kak.*
Miskwâbikide, or-*magad.* It is red-hot, (metal;) p. *mes..deg,* or-*magak.*—*Kijâbikisigan miskwabikide,* the stove is red-hot.
Miskwâbikisan, (*nin*). I make it red-hot, (metal;) p. *mes..ang.*
Miskwâbikisi. It is red; also, it is red-hot; (obj. of metal or stone;) p. *mes..sid.*
Miskwakikiswa, (*nin*). I make it red-hot, (metal;) p. *mes..wad;* imp. *mis..wi.*
Miskwâbikokan. Copper-mine; pl.-*an.*
Miskwâbikoke, (*nin*). I work or produce copper; I work in a copper-mine; p. *mes..ked.*
Miskwâbikoké-ogima. Agent or superintendent of a copper-mine, boss; pl.-*g.*
Miskwâbikokewin. Copper-mining business, trade or work of a miner in a copper-mine.
Miskwâbikokêwinini. Miner in a copper-mine; pl.-*wag.*
Miskwâbikons. A cent; pl.-*ag.*
Miskwâbimij. A twig or rod with a red bark, which the Indians mix with their tobacco; pl.-*in.*
Miskwâbiwin. Bloody flux, dysentery.
Miskwâbo. Chocolate, (red liquid.)
Miskwâboke, (*nin*). I make chocolate, I cook chocolate; p. *mes..ked.*
Miskwâdéssi. A kind of small turtle; (C. tortue barrée;) pl. -*wag.*
Miskwadéssi o dashwan. The shell of this kind of turtle.
Miskwâdissan, (*nin*) or, *nin miskwânsan.* I dye it red; p. *mes..ang.*
Miskwâdissige, (*nin*) or, *nin miskwânsige.* I dye red; p. *mes..ged.*
Miskwâdisso, or, *miskwânso.* It is dyed red; p. *mes..sod.*
Miskwâdisswa, (*nin*) or, *nin miskwânswa.* I dye it red; p. *mes..wad.*
Miskwâdite, or-*magad,* or *miskwânde,* or-*magad.* It is dyed red; p. *mes..eg.*
Miskwâgami. It is red, (liquid;) p. *mes..mig.*
Miskwâgamiwi-kitchigami. Red Sea.
Miskwâgamiwi-sibi. Red River.
Miskwajê, (*nin*). I have a red skin, or my skin is red; also,

I have the measles; (F. j'ai la rougeole;) p. *mes..ged.*
Miskwajêwin. Measles.
Miskwâkone, or-*magad.* It blazes, (the fire;) p. *mes..neg,* or-*magak.*
Miskwânakwad. The clouds are red, (in the morning or evening;) p. *mes..wak.*
Miskwâkwanaie, (*nin*). I dress in red; p. *mes..ied.*
Miskwânagek. Cinamon; (*miskwâ,* red; *wanagek,* bark.)
Miskwânagêkosi. It has a red bark; p. *mes..sid.*
Miskwândib, (pron. *miskôndib.*) Red-head, a kind of serpent; pl.-*ag.*
Miskwândibe, (pron. *miskôndibe.*) Red-head, a person with red hair; (L. rufus;) pl.-*g.*
Miskwândibe, (*nin*), (pron. *nin miskôndibe.*) I have red hair, (a red head;) p. *mes..bed.*
Miskwanêbin. Red carp, (fish;) pl.-*ag.*
Miskwanikwe, (*nin*). I have red hair, (a red head;) p. *mes ..wed.*
Miskwânowe, (*nin*). I have a red cheek; p. *mes..wed.*
Miskwâshkade, (*nin*). My belly is red; p. *mes..ded.*
Miskwâssab. Arse, buttocks.
Miskwâssige gisiss. The sun is red; p. *mes..ged.*
Miskwassin. Red stone; pl.-*ig.*
Miskwassin-opwâgan. Pipe or calumet of red stone; p.-*ag.*
Miskwatchiss. S. *Miskotchiss.*
Miskwâwad. The sky is red; p. *mes..wak.*
Miskwâwak. Red cedar; pl.-*og.*
*Miskwâwakoka,*or-*magad.* There are red cedars; p. *mes..kag,* or-*magak.*
Mîskwâwakokan. Place where there are red cedars; Red Lake.
Miskwâwan, or *miskwâwandjigan.* The yolk of an egg.
Miskwêgad. It is red, (stuff;) p. *mes..gak.*
Miskwégin. Red cloth, scarlet.
Miskwégisi. It is red, (stuff;) p. *mes..sid.*
Miskwéiâb. S. *Oskwéiâb.*
Miskwéss. Red oyster; pl.-*ag.*
Miskwi. Blood.
Miskwi-abwês, (*nin*). I sweat blood; p. *mes..sod.*
Miskwimin. Raspberry; (F. framboise;) pl.-*ag.*
Miskwiminagawanj. Raspberry-bush; pl.-*ig.*
Miskwimini-gisiss. The moon of raspberries, the month of July. In Manitoba, they say, *opaskowigisiss,* the moon when the birds lose their feathers.
Miskwingwe, (*nin*). I have a red face; p. *mes..wed.*
Miskwingwésse, (*nin*). I blush with shame; p. *mes..sed.*
Miskwiw, (*nin*). I bleed, (but not at the nose;) I am stained with blood; p. *meskwiwid.* (S. *Gibitan.*)
Miskwiwaganama, (*nin*). I strike him bloody, I wound him; p. *mes..mad.*
Miskwiwan. It is bloody, stained with blood; p. *mes..ang.*
Miskwiwapine, (*nin*). I am diseased with an issue of blood; p. *mes..ned.*
Miskwiwapinewin. Issue of blood, (disease.)

Miskwiwia, (nin). I make him bleed, (not at the nose,) I shed his blood; also, I stain him with blood; p. *mes..ad.*

Miskwiwinindji, (nin). I bleed on my hand, my hand is bloody; p. *mes..id.*

Miskwiwiside, (nin). I bleed on my foot, my foot is bloody; p. *mes..ded.*

Missâbâje, (nin). My skin is hairy; p. *mes..jed.*

Missâbama, (nin). I see him plainly, (a person or some other obj.); p. *mes..mad.*

Missâbandaa, (nin). I manifest it to him, I show it to him plainly; p. *mes..ad.*

Missâbandan, (nin). I see it plainly; p. *mes..ang.*

Missâbassim. Poodle-dog; pl.-*og.*

Missâbe. Giant; also, a very big stout man; pl.-*g.*

Missâbendjakon. Long moss hanging from the branches of trees.

Missâbigon. Large pumpkin; pl.-*ag.*

Missâbos. Hare; pl.-*og.*

Missad. Belly; stomach; paunch. —This word is always preceded by a possessive pronoun, which forms only one word with its noun; as: *Nimissad,* my belly; *kimissad,* thy belly, etc.

Missâkakwidjish. Badger; (F. blaireau;) pl.-*ag.*

Missameg. Whale; pl.-*wog.*

Missan. Wood to make fire, wood for fuel.

Missanashk. Thistle; pl.-*on.*

Missanig. Black squirrel; pl.-*og.*

Missansi. Black eagle; pl.-*g.*

Missanwi, or-*magad.* The snow is falling from the branches, from the trees; p. *mes..wig,* or-*magak.*

Missawâ, conj. Though, although, even if, notwithstanding.

Missawéndamawa, (nin). I covet s. th. that belongs to him, or relates to him, I wish to have it; p. *mes..wad.*

Missawéndam, (nin). I covet, I am covetous, I wish to have s. th.; p. *mes..ang.*

Missawéndamowin. Covetousness, avidity, covetous desire to have s. th. belonging to another person.

Missawendân, (nin). I covet it, I wish to have it; p. *me..ang.*

Missawéndjige, (nin). S. *Missawéndam.*

Missawendjigewin. S. *Missawênindimin.*

Missawénima, (nin). I covet him; p. *mes..mad.*

Missawenimowin. Concupiscence.

Missawénindiwin. Covetousness. S. *Missawéndamowin.*

Missawiganawabama, (nin). I look at her (him) with concupiscence, with lust, with covetous desires; p. *mes..mad.*

Missawiganawabandân, (nin). I look at it with a covetous desire to have it; p. *mes..ang.*

Missawinage, (nin). I covet, (relative to some obj.); p. *mes ..ged.*

Missawinamawa, (nin). I covet some obj. belonging to him or relating to him; p. *mes..wad.*

Missawinan, (nin). I covet it,

I desire it inordinately ; p. *mes..ang.*

Missawinawa, (*nin*). S. *Missawenima.*

Missègwanân. Down, soft under-feather of a bird; pl.-*ag.*

Missibissidossi. Tornado, whirlwind ; squall of wind; pl.-*wag.*

Missidji, (*nin*). I have the dropsy, I am dropsical, hydropical; p. *messidjid.*

Missidjiwin. Dropsy.

Missinibiwaiân. Soft underhair of an animal; pl.-*ag.*

Missitâgan. Sunflower, turnsol ; pl.-*an.*

Mitab, (*nin*). I am sitting on the bare ground, on the snow, etc., without anything under me ; p. *metabid.*

Mitâbik, adv. On metal, on a rock or stone.

Mitâbik. Money in silver or gold, specie.

Mitâgonag, adv. On the snow.

Mitâgamig, adv. S. *Mitashkakamig.*

Mitâkamiga, or-*magad.* The ground appears, (is bare,) there is no snow on the ground ; p. *met..gag,* or-*magak.*

Mitâkoshima, (*nin*). I lay him on some hard object, nothing soft under him ; p. *met..mad.*

Mitâkoshin, (*nin*). I lie hard, on a hard bed or on some other hard object, nothing soft under me ; p. *met..ing.*

Mitâkoshkan, (*nin*). I lie or sit on it ; p. *met..ang.*

Mitâkoshkawa, (*nin*). I lie or sit on some obj.; p. *met..wad.* — *Nabagissag nin mitâkoshkawa ;* I lie on a board.

Mitâkosige, (*nin*). I smoke pure tobacco, without any admixture of bark or weed ; p. *met.. ged.* S. *Apâkosige.*

Mitânike, or-*magad.* There is no more snow on the ground, the snow is gone off ; p. *met.. tag,* or-*magak.*

Mitashkakamig, adv. On the bare ground. — *Mitashkakamig gi-niba tibikong ;* he slept on the bare ground last night, (he had nothing under him.)

Mitâshkanige, (*nin*). I have bare jawbones, I have no teeth in my jawbones ; p. *met..ged.*

Mitâshkossiw, adv. On the grass, on the herb.

Mitassin, adv. On a stone.

Mitâwan. Sand ; *mitâwang,* on the sand.

Mitâwanga, or-*magad.* There is a sandy beach, sandy shore; p. *met..gag,* or-*magak.*

Mitâwangagama. There is a lake abounding with sand, with a sandy beach ; p. *met.. mag.*

Mitchâ, or-*magad.* It is large, big, bulky, massy or massive, vast, extensive ; p. *mètchag,* or-*magak.*

Mitchâbaminâgos, (*nin*). I look large, big, bulky ; p. *met..sid.*

Mitchâbaminâgwad. It looks big, large ; p. *met..wak.*

Mitchâbewis, (*nin*). I am a big stout man ; p. *met..sid.*

Mitchâbigad. It is large, thick, strong, (thread, cord, rope ;) p. *met..gak.*

Mitchâbikad. It is large, big,

massy or massive, (metal;) p. *met..kak.*

Mitchâbikisi assin. The stone is large; p. *met..sid.*

Mitchaii, adv. Down.

Mitchâkosi kôtawân. The piece of wood, or the block, is large; p. *met..sid.*

Mitchâkwad. It is large, (wood;) p. *met..wak.*

Mitchâtan, (*nin*). I make it large, wide; p. *met..tod.*

Mitchigad. It is large, (stuff or paper;) p. *met..gak.*

Mitchiganeshin, (*nin*). I am cut to the bone, the bone appears; p. *met..ing.*

Mitchigigwane, (*mitchigane.*) Fish-hawk, (bird.)

Mitchigisi. It is large, (stuff); p. *met..sid.—Kitchi mitchigisi ki moshwem;* thy handkerchief is very large.

Mitchikan. Fence, enclosure, hedge; pl.-*an.*

Mitchikanâkobidon, (*nin*). I fence it in, (a piece of ground;) p. *met..dod.*

Mitchikanakobina, (*nin*). I make a fence around him, I fence him in; p. *met..nad.*

Mitchikanâkobidjigan. Fence; pl.-*an.*

Mitchikanâkobidjige, (*nin*). I make a fence, I work at a fence; p. *met..ged.*

Mitchikanâtig. Fence-rail.

Mitchikang, adv. On the bare ground.

Mitchipingwi, adv. On ashes.

Mitchishin, (*nin*). I am lying without any cover on me; p. *met..ing.*

Mitchissag, adv. On boards, on the floor.

Mitchissin. It lies uncovered; p. *met..ing.*

Mitchitchima, (*nin*). I send him word, I send him a commission to tell or do s. th. for me; also, I give him a commission; p. *met..mad.*

Mitchitchinindj. Thumb; pl.-*in.*

Mitchitwé, (*nin*). I send word, I give or send a commission; p. *met..wed.*

Mitchitwên, (*nin*). I give or send a commission for some obj.; p. *met..wed.*

Mitchitwénan, (*nin*). I give or send a commission for some obj.; p. *met..wed.* (V. Conj.)

Mitchitwêwin. Commission, word, sent.

Mitig. Tree, living tree; pl.-*og.*

Mitig-emikwân. Wooden spoon; pl.-*an.*

Mitig kâshkibosod, or, *mitig getâshkibosod.* Log, (sawed on both ends,) saw-mill log; pl.-*mitigog kashkibosodjig,* or, *ge-tâshkibosodjig.*

Mitig nin sissibodon. I rasp wood.

Mitigo-bimidé. Olive-oil, sweet oil.

Mitigôjishigwe. A kind of rattlesnake; pl.-*g.*

Mitigo-makak. Wooden box, trunk; pl.-*on.*

Mitigô-makisin. Wooden shoe, clog; pl.-*an.*

Mitigomij. Oak, red oak; pl.-*ag.*

Mitigômin. Fruit of the oak, acorn; pl.-*an.*

Mitig-onâgan. Wooden plate or dish; pl.-*an.*

Mitigô-pakitêigan. Wooden hammer, mallet; pl.-*an.*

Mitigô-sissibôdjigan. Rasp, (wood file;) pl.-*an.*
Mitigô-tchimân. Wooden canoe, log-canoe; boat, barge; pl.-*an.*
Mitigow, (*nin*). I am a tree; I am wood; p. *met..id.*
Mitigowaj. *Alg.* S. *Mitigô-makak.*
Mitigô-wâkaigan. Wooden house, log-house, frame-house; pl.-*an.*
Mitigowan. It is a tree; it is wood; p. *met..ang.*
Mitigwâb. Bow; pl.-*in.*
Mitigwâbak. Walnut-tree; pl.-*og.*
Mitigwaki. Forest, woods; pl.-*wan.* *Mitigwaking,* in the woods.
Mitigwakik. Wooden kettle, that is, a drum; pl.-*og.*
Mitigwakisin. Properly, wooden shoe; but it is used for, boot, shoe; pl.-*an.* (To express a wooden shoe or clog, they say, *mitigo-makisin.*)
Mitigwakisini-makatéwitchigan. Blacking for boots, shoe-blacking.
Mitigwanwi. Arrow, (*mitig,* wood; *anwi,* musket-ball;) pl.-*n.*
Mitingwâm, (*nin*). I exonerate the bowels in my bed, during sleep; p. *mat..ang.*
Mitossé, (*nin*). I walk, I go on foot somewhere; p. *metossed.*
Mi wendji-. Therefore...
Miwi, (*nin*). I go further and further; p. *mâwid.*
Miwia, (*nin*). I refuse him, I will not have him, I go from him; p. *mâwiad.*
Miwina, (*nin*). I refuse to take him; p. *mâwînad.*
Miwinan, (*nin*). I refuse to take it, I will not accept of it; p. *mâwinang.*
Miwitamawa, (*nin*). I put it away from him, I keep it at a distance from him; p. *maw..wad.*
Miwitân, (*nin*). I put it away, I reject it, refuse it, I am an enemy to it; p. *mâwitang.*
Miwitawa, (*nin*). S. *Miwitamawa.*
Mo, as end-syllable in some u. v., alludes to a *trail* or *road;* as:- *Inamo, ondamo, mangademo, agassadémo, mikana;* the trail goes there, comes from there, is large, is narrow, etc.
Mo. Dirt, excrement.
Moâ, (*nin*). I make him weep, cry; p. *mwaad.*
Môdji. The belly of an animal; pl.-*modjin.*
Môdjigêndagwad. It is joyful, delightful; p. *mwod..wak.*
Modjigéndam, (*nin*). I rejoice, I am joyous, I delight; p. *mwad..ang.*
Modjigéndamiâ, (*nin*). I make him joyous, I make him rejoice, I cause him pleasure; p. *mwa..ad.*
Modjigêndamomagad. It rejoices, it delights; p. *mwad..gak.* — *Ninde modjigéndamomagad dassing mekwénimagin Jesus;* my heart rejoices as often as I think on Jesus.
Modjigibi, (*nin*). I am joyous, in liquor; p. *mw..bid.*
Môdjigidee, (*nin*). I rejoice in

my heart, my heart is delighted; p. *mwa..deed.*

Modjigis, (*nin*). I rejoice; p. *mwadjigisid.*

Môiwe, (*nin*). I cause weeping and crying; p. *mwaiwed.*

Mojag, or *monjag*, adv. Always, continually, incessantly, constantly, perpetually.

Môjagishin. There is always that, nothing but that; p. *mwâ..ing.*–*Môjogishinog moshweg adopowining;* nothing but handkerchiefs are lying on the table.

Môjagissin. There is always that, all of the same kind; p. *mwaj..ing.*—*Mojagissinon makisinan mitchissag;* nothing but moccasins are lying on the floor.

Môjia, (*nin*). I feel him on me, in me or about me; p. *mwajiad.*

Môjiton, (*nin*). I feel it on me or in me; p. *mwajitod.*

Môjowe, (*nin*). I shear; p. *mwajowed.*

Mojwa, (*nin*). I cut his hair, I shear him; p. *mwajwad;* imp. *mojwi.*

Mojwâgan. Scissors; pl.-*an.*

Mokaam gisiss. The sun rises; p. *mwakaang.*

Môkaân, (*nin*). I dig it up, I uncover it, I bring it to light; p. *mwakaang.*

Môkabog, (*nin*). I come forth by the current of a river; p. *mwa..ged.*

Môkas, (*nin*). S. *Moki.*

Mokawa, (*nin*). I dig him up, I bring him to light, (any obj.;) p. *mwakawad.*

Mokawadj, (*nin*). I weep from cold; p. *mwa..id.*

Mokawana, (*nin*). I weep or cry after him, I molest him; p. *mw..nad;* imp. *mokawaj.*

Mokawanandan, (*nin*). I weep or cry from hunger; p. *mwa..ang.*

Môkawashkade, (*nin*). S. *Mokawanandan.*

Mokawimodjigendam, (*nin*). I weep through joy; p. *mwa..ang.*

Mokawines, (*nin*). I weep through pain, or anger; p. *mwa..sid.*

Mokawiodjima, (*nin*). I leave him weeping, I weep parting with him; p. *mwa..mad.*

Môki, (*nin*). I come forth, I make my appearance; p. *mwakid.*

Môkibi, (*nin*). I come forth out of the water; p. *mwa..bid.*

Môkibidon, (*nin*). I haul it out of s. th., I bring it forth from a hiding place; p. *mwa..dod.*

Mokibigisse, (*nin*). I come up to the surface of the water; p. *mwa..sed.*

Môkibigissemagad. It comes up to the surface of the water; p. *mwa..gak.*

Môkibina, (*nin*). I pull or haul him out of s. th., I bring him forth, (a person, or any other obj.); p. *mwa..nad.*

Môkidjiwan nibi. The water comes forth from a source or spring; p. *mwa..ang.*

Môkidjiwanibig. Spring, source, fountain; pl.-*on.*

Môkidjiwano-nibi. Spring-water.

Môkina, (*nin*). I bring forth

some obj., I show it; p. *mwakinad;* imp. *mokin.—O mokinan joniiaman;* he brings forth (he shows) his money.

Môkinan, (*nin*). I bring it forth, I show it; p. *mwa..ang.*

Môkishka, or-*magad.* It rises up, it comes forth; p. *mwa..kag,* or-*magak.*

Môkisse gisiss. The sun comes forth, the sun rises; p. *mwakissed.*—The same as, *Mokaam.*

Môkisse, or-*magad.* It comes forth, it comes out of s. th., (especially out of water;) p. *mwakisseg,* or-*magak.*

Môkitawa, (*nin*). I rush upon him suddenly, I make an unexpected assault upon him; p. *mwa..wad.*

Môkodan, (*nin*). I work it with a knife or some other cutting tool, (some wooden object;) p. *mwakodang.*

Mokodâss, (*nin*). I work wood with a knife or some other cutting tool; p. *mwakodassod.*

Mokodâssowigamig. Joiner's shop, carpenter's shop; pl.-*on.*

Mokodâssowin. Joiner's or carpenter's trade, business, work.

Mokogâssowinini. Joiner, carpenter; pl.-*wag.*

Môkodawa, (*nin*), or *nin mokodamawa.* I work some wooden object with a knife, etc., for him; p. *mwak..wad.*

Môkodjigan. Any cutting tool to work wood with, as, plane, drawing-knife, etc.; also the joiner's or carpenter's work-bench; pl.-*an.*

Môkodjigan gaiândinigadeg. A cutting tool that is pushed, that is, a plane.

Mokodjigans. Small smoothing plane; (F. rabot;) pl.-*an.*

Môkodjigan tekwandjigemagak. Work-bench that bites, that is, a bench to work with a drawing-knife on it, a shaving-horse; (F. chevalet.)

Môkomân. Knife; pl.-*an.*

Môkomânike, (*nin*). I manufacture knives, I am a cutler; p. *mwa..ked.*

Mokomanikéwigamig. Cutler's shop; pl.-*on.*

Mokomanikewin. Cutlery, cutler's business or trade.

Mokamanikêwinini. Cutler; pl. -*wag.*

Mokana, (*nin*). I work it with a knife, (*an.* obj. as, *gijik,* cedar; *nabâgissag,* board;) p. *mwakonad;* imp. *mokoj.*

Môkonan, (*nin*), S. *Mokodan.*

Mokonem, (*nin*). I beg for s. th. to eat, weeping; p. *mwa..mod.*

Mokonemotawa, (*nin*). I beg him weeping for s. th. to eat; p. *mwa..wad.*

Monâapini, (*nin*). I dig out potatoes; p. *mwa..nid.*

Mônâashkikiwe, (*nin*). I dig out medical roots; p. *mwa..wed.*

Mônashkwadan kitigân, (*nin*). I weed a field; p. *mwa..ang.*

Mônashkwe, (*nin*). I weed, I root out bad herbs; p. *mwa..wed.*

Mônawing. A kind of white berry; pl.-*wag.*

Mônawingwabigon. A kind of yellow flower; pl.-*on.*

Mônendam, (*nin*). I suspect, I imagine; p. *mwa..ang.*

Mônenima, (*nin*). I suspect him,

I mistrust him; p. *mwa..wad.*

Moniâkwe. A Canadian woman; pl.-*g.*

Môniang. Montreal; Canada. —*Moniang ondjiba,* does not always signify, he comes from the city of Montreal; it may also signify, he comes from Canada.

Moniâwinini. Canadian. This word also signifies, an awkward unhandy person, unacquainted with the works and usages of the Indian life and country. Pl.-*wag.*

Moningwané. Lapwing, (bird;) (F. pivert;) pl.-*g.*

Moningwanéka. There are lapwings; p. *mwa..kag.*

*Mons.** Moose, American elk; (F. orignal;) pl.-*og.*

Moosôgan. Moose-bone; pl.-*an.*

Monsons. A young moose; pl.-*ag.*

Monswêgin. Moose-skin; pl.-*on.*

Monsweshkan. Moose-hord; pl. -*ag.*

Monswiiâss. Moose-meat.

Môpidân, (*nin*). I find its proper taste in eating or drinking it; p. *mwa..ang.*

Mopidjige, (*nin*). I find the proper taste of victuals; p. *mwa..ged.*

Môpwa, (*nin*). I find its proper taste in eating it; p. *mwapwad;* imp. *mopwi.*

Môshkâagwinde, or-*magad.* It comes up to the surface of the water, and *floats;* p. *mw..deg,* or-*magak.*

* NOTE, The letter *n* in this word, and in the words composed with it, is almost not heard.

Moshkaâgwindjin, (*nin*). I come up to the surface of the water, and *float;* p. *mwa..ing.*

Moshkâagwindjisse, (*nin*). I come up to the surface of the water, I emerge, (alive or dead;) p. *mwash..sed.*

Moshkâagwindjisse or-*magad.* It comes up to the surface of the water, it emerges; p. *mwa..seg,* or-*magak.*

Moshkaan. It is overflowed, it is inundated, there is an inundation, a flood; p. *mwashkaang.*

Moshkabôwadan, (*nin*). I fill it up, with water, etc.; (a vessel with another vessel;) p. *mwa..ang.*

Môshkabowana, (*nin*). I fill it up, with water, etc. (a kettle with some vessel;) p. *mwash..nad;* imp. *mo..waj.*

Môshkabowe, (*nin*). I am filling up a vessel or vessels, pouring in some liquid with another vessel; p. *mwa..wed.*

Môshkâgami, or-*magad nibi.* The water rises, it is the *flowing* tide; p. *mwa..mig,* or-*magak.* — S. *Odaskimagad nibi.*

Moshkam, (*nin*). I come up again to the surface of the water, (alive;) p. *mwâshkamod.*

Moshkaossi. Bittern, (bird;) pl.-*g.*

Moshkinaâ, (*nin*). I fill it, with *dry* things, (a pipe, a kettle;) p. *mwa..ad.*

Môshkinadawa, (*nin*) or, *nin môshkinadamawa.* I fill it for him or to him; p. *mwâ..wad.* —*Debenimiian, moshkinada-*

wishin ninde ki jawendjigewin; Lord, fill my heart with thy grace.

Moshkinadon, (nin). I fill it with *dry* things; p. *mwâ..dod.*

Môshkine, (nin). I am full of s. th., filled with s. th.; p. *mwashkined.*

Môshkine, or-*magad.* It is full, it is filled up, (with *dry* things;) p. *mwâshkineg,* or-*magak.*

Môshkineabate, or-*magad.* It is filled with smoke; p. *mwâ..teg,* or-*magak.*

Moshkinêbadon, (nin). I fill it up, (a vessel, with some *liquid;*) p. *mwâ..dod.*

Môshkinébana, (nin). I fill it up, (a kettle with some *liquid;*) p. *mwa..nad;* imp. *mo..baj.*

Moshkinêbi, or-*magad.* It is full, it is filled up, (with some *liquid;*) p. *mwa..big,* or-*magak.*

Moshkinemin, (nin). We are crowded (in a house, church, etc.); p. *mwâskinedjig.*

Môshkineshkagon, (nin). It fills me, it replenishes me; p. *mwa..god.*— *Minawanigosiwin nin moshkineshkagon,* joy fills me, (I am full of joy.)

Môshkineshkawa, (nin). I fill him, I replenish him with s. th.; p. *mwâ..wad.*

Minawanigosiwin nin moshkineshkawa; I fill him with joy, I cause him much joy.

Moshkinesibingwe, (nin). My eyes are filled with tears; p. *mwa..wed.*

Môshwe. Handkerchief, both neck and pocket handkerchief; pl-*g.* *Kitchi moshwe,* shawl.

Môsse. Worm; caterpillar; pl. *mosseg.*

Môsséminâgad. It is worm-eaten, (any globular obj., as, *tchiss,* turnip; *anidjimin,* pea, etc.); p. *mwass..gak.*

Môsséminagisi. It is worm-eaten, (any globular object, as *mishimin,* apple; *opin,* potato, etc.); p. *mwass..sid.*

Môssêssagad. It is worm-eaten, (obj. of wood, as, *adôpowin,* table; *apabiwin,* chair, etc.;) p. *mwa..gak.*

Môsséssagisi. It is worm-eaten, (obj. of wood, as, *nabagîssag,* board; *gijik,* cedar, etc.); p. *mwa..sid.*

Môssewâbide, (nin). I have holes in my teeth, I have rotten teeth, (worm-eaten teeth;) p. *mwa..ded.*

Môssêwingwe, (nin). I have small pimples on my face; p. *mwa..wed.*

Mowidjitawâgan. Ear-wax, cerumen.

Môwidjiw, (nin). I am dirty, filthy; p. *mwa..wid.*

Môwidjiwaje, (nin). I have a dirty skin, my skin is filthy; p. *mwa..jed.*

Môwidjiwingwe, (nin) or, *môwingwe.* I have a dirty face; p. *mwa..wed.*

Môwigamig. A dirty lodge or house; pl.-*on.*

N

Na, or *ina;* a particle denoting interrogation. — *Ki kikendan na?*—Doest thou know it? *Ki sagi na?* — Doest thou love me?

Na? is it so? will it be so? do you hear me?

Na! ina! nashké! interj. lo! behold! hark!

Naâb, (*nin*). I have good eyes; p. *neâbid.*

Naab, (*nin*). I am well sitted, I sit comfortably; p. *néabid.*

Naagwaje, (*nin*). I cover myself, being naked; p. *nea..jêd.*

Naakona, (*nin*). I arrange it, I put it up well; p. *neâkonad.*

Naakonan, (*nin*). I arrange it or put it up well, (wooden obj.); p. *neâkonang.* (The same as, *nin naákossidon.*)

Naakossidon, (*nin*). I fix it well, arrange it; p. *neâ..dod.* — *Mitchikanakobidjigan nin naakossidon;* I arrange the fence, (I put it in good order.)

Naangab, (*nin*). I am son-in-law, or daughter-in-law, in a family, living with the family; p. *neângabid.*

Naanganikwe. The daughter-in-law in a family; pl.-*g.*

Naangish. The son-in-law in a family; pl.-*ag.*

Naawodisi akik. The kettle is too small; p. *neaw..sid.*

Nab! mano nab! interj. Well! let it be so.

Nab sa. This is an expression of contempt, or at least of little esteem, signifying: Not by far, far from being...; (F. il s'en faut qu'il soit.) *Nab sa ogima;* he is far from being a chief. *Nab sa inini;* he is no man, far from being a man.

Nâbaan, (*nin*). I fasten it or put it to the end of s. th. permanently; p. *naiâbaang.*

Nabadjashkaân, (*nin*). I fasten or put it to the end of a stick in a manner as to be able to take it off again; p. *naiâb..ang.*

Nabadjashkaigan. Bayonet; pl.-*an.*

Nabaga, or-*magad.* It is flat; p. *nebagag*, or-*magak.*

Nabagabikad. It is flat, (metal;) p. *neb..kak.*

Nabagâbikisi. It is flat, (obj. as, *assin*, stone; *joniia*, silver;) p. *neb..sid.*

Nabagadaan, (*nin*). I make it flat, I flatten it; p. *neb..ang.*

Nabâgadawa, (*nin*). I flatten some obj.; p. *neb..wad;* imp. *nobagadâ.*

Nabâgakokidj. Flat broad pipe-stem; p.-*in.*
Nabagashk. Flat broad grass or herb; lily; pl.-*on.*
Nabâgaskinindj. Flat open hand, palm. This word is always preceded by a possessive pronoun; as: *Nin nabâgaskinindj,* my flat hand; *o nabagaskinindj,* his flat hand, etc.
Nabâgaskinindjitawa, (*nin*). I strike him with the flat hand, I buffet him; p. *neb..wad.*
Nabagâtig. A flat piece of wood; pl.-on.
Nabâgidjane, (*nin*). I have a flat nose; p. *neb..ned.*
Nabâgindibe, (*nin*). I have a flat head; p. *neb..bed.*
Nabâgisi. It is flat, (obj., as, *joniia,* silver, etc.); p. *neb.. sid.*
Nabâgissag. Flat broad wood, that is, a board, or plank; pl.-*og.*
Nabâgissagokadân, (*nin*). I make it of boards; p. *neb.. ang.*
Nabâgissagokade, or-*magad.* It is made of boards; p. *neb.. deg,* or-*magok.*
Nabagissago-mikana. Plank-road; pl.-*n.*
Nabagissagons. A small board; shingle; pl.-*ag.*
Nabagissagöwigamig. A hut or house nailed together of boards; pl.-*on.*
Nabâgitchimân. Flat boat, barge; pl.-*an.*
Nabâgodabân. Dog-train, a long flat sled for dogs; pl.-*ag.*
Nabâgodabanâk; pl.-*on.* S. *Nabâgodabân.*
Nabâkossidjigan. Handle, haft, crank; pl.-*an.*
Nabâkossidon, (*nin*). I put a handle to it, I haft it, (an axe, a hammer, etc.); p. *neb..dod.*
Nabâkwaan, (*nin*). I put it or fasten it to the end of a stick; p. *neb..ang.*
Nabâkwâwa, (*nin*). I put or fasten some obj. to the end of a stick; p. *neb..wad;* imp. *nabakwâ.*
Nabané. This word is not used alone; it is always connected with a substantive, and signifies: On *one* of the two sides, on the *other* side; one of the two, the other. (Examples in some of the following words.)
Nabanédasse, (*nin*). I have only one legging on; p. *neb..sed.*
Nabanêgad. The other leg, or one leg only.—*Nin nabanêgâd, ki nabanêgâd,* etc.; my other leg, thy other leg; or, only one of my legs, only one of thy legs.
Nabanégâde, (*nin*). I have only one leg; p. *neb..ded.*
Nabanégâm, adv. On one side only, (of a river, lake or bay.)
Nabanénik. The other arm, or one arm only.— *Nin nabanénike,* my other arm, or only one of my arms; *o nabanénike,* his other arm, or only one of his arms.
Nabanênike, (*nin*). I have only one arm; p. *neb..ked.*
Nabanênindj. The other hand. —*Nin nabanénindj,* my other hand; only one of my hands. *Ki nabanênindj,* thy other hand, only one of thy hands.
Nabanénindji, (*nin*). I have only

one hand, I am one-handed; (F. je suis manchot;) p. *neb.. id.*

Nabanênow. The other cheek; only one cheek.—*Nin nabanénow*, my other cheek; only one of my cheeks. *O nabanénowan*, his other cheek; only one of his cheeks.

Nabanéshkinjig. The other eye; only one eye.—*Nin nabaneskkinjig*, my other eye; only one of my eyes, etc.

Nabanéshkinjigwe, (*nin*). I have only one eye, I am one-eyed; p. *neb..wed.*

Nâbe. Male; (L. masculus;) properly of quadrupeds. But, with the possessive termination, it is also used for *husband;* as: *Nin nâbem*, my husband; *o nâbeman*, her husband; etc. A more polite expression for husband is *widigemâgan.*

Nâbé-aiaa. Male being, male animal; pl.-*g.*

Nâbê-bebejigoganji. Stallion; pl.-*g.*

Nâbê-gâjagens. Male cat, he-cat; pl.-*ag.*

Nâbek. He-bear; pl.-*wag.*

Nâbekwaiân. The skin of a he-bear; pl.-*ag.*

Nâbé-manisktanish. Male sheep, ram; pl.-*ag.*

Nâbêmeg. Male fish; pl.-*wag.*

Nâbémik. Male beaver, he-beaver; pl.-*wag.*

Nâbê-pakaakwê. Cock; pl.-*iag.*

Nâbé-pijiki. Bull, steer; pl.-*wag.*

Nâbésse. Male bird; pl.-*g.*

Nâbésse o patakibinweon. The cock's crest.

Nâbêssim. Male dog; pl.-*og.*

Nâbéwaian. S. *Aiabéwaian.*

Nâbêwegin. S. *Aiabéwegin.*

Nâbibian, (*nin*). S. *Nâssabian.*

Nâbibiigan. S. *Nâssabiigan.*

Nâbibiige, (*nin*). S. *Nassabiige.*

Nâbidenigomêbisan. Nose-ring; pl.-*an.*

Nâbidoag, (*nin*). I take them up on a string, (glass-beads, etc.); p. *naiâbidoad.*

Nabidoanan, (*nin*). I take them up on a string; p. *naia..ang.*

Nâbidoan jâbonigan, (*nin*). I thread a needle; p. *naia..ang.*

Nabidoigan. A needle to take up with it s. th. on a string or thread; pl.-*an.*

Nâbidoige, (*nin*). I take up on a string; p. *naiâ..ged.*

Nâbigwaagan. Wooden needle for making nets, netting-needle; pl.-*an.*

Nâbikan, (*nin*). I wear it on my neck, or around my neck; p. *naiâbikang.*

Nâbikawa, (*nin*). I wear some obj. on or around my neck; p. *naiâ..wad.* — *Nin nabikawa moshwe*, I wear a handkerchief around my neck.

Nâbikawâgan, or *nâbikâgan.* Any obj. that is worn on or around the neck, collar, necklace; yoke; pl.-*an.*

Nâbikawâgan, or *nabikâgan.* Any obj. that is worn on or around the neck, neck-handkerchief, string of glass-beads or pearls, a little cross or medal, etc.; pl.-*ag.*

Nâbikona, (*nin*). I hang it around his neck; p. *naia..nad; imp. nâbikoj.*

Nâbikwân. Vessel, ship; pl.-*an.*

Nâbikwânens. The boat of a vessel, yawl-boat; (F. chaloupe;) pl.-*an.*

Nâbikwâninini. Sailor, mariner, navigator: pl.-*wag.*

Nabikwân-ogima. Captain of a vessel; pl.-*g.*

Nabikwani-pigiw. Tar.

Nabikwâsson. Sewing-thread.

Nâbinotawa, (nin). I repeat his words; p. *naiâ..wad.*

Nâbishebison. Ear-ring, ear-hanging; pl.-*an.*

Nâbishkamawa, (nin). I do it or make it in his place, instead of him; p. *naiâ..wad.*

Nâbishkawa, (nin). I take his place, his employment, his power, I am instead of him, I succeed him; p. *naiab..wad.*

Nâbissiton, (nin). I replace it, I put it in its place again; p. *naiâ..tod.*

Nabôb. Broth, soup; (F. bouillon.)

Nâbowadan, (nin). I read it aloud; p. *naia..ong.*

Nabowewanwi. The point of an arrow; pl.-*n.*

Nabwâbiginan, (nin). S. *Nijwâbiginan.*

Nabwangêshka bineshi. The bird has his wings closed; p. *neb ..kad.*

Nabwégina, (nin). I fold it, (obj. of stuff or of clothing, as, *moshwe,*handkerchief; *senibâ,* silk-stuff, ribbon;) p. *neb..nad.* —*Nabwégin ki moshwem*; fold thy neck handkerchief.

Nabwéginan, (nin). I fold it, (obj. of stuff or of clothing;) p. *neb..ang.* — *Nabwêginan adopowinigin;* fold the table-cloth.

Nâdaâbi, (nin). I haul out of the water a fisher-line with hooks, (to take the fishes that are caught on the hooks;) p. *naiâdaâbid.*

Nâdaan, (nin). I fetch it in a canoe or boat; p. *naiâdaang.*

Nâdâbowe, (nin). I go to some lodge or house to get s. th. to eat; also I fetch s. th. to drink; p. *naiâ..wed.*

Nâdagâmeam, (nin). I paddle my canoe to the shore; p. *naia..ang.*

Nâdaisse, (nin). I fetch wood for fuel in a canoe or boat; p. *naiâdaissed.*

Nâdaisséiash, (nin) (fr. *nin nâdin,* I fetch it; *nin manissé,* I chop, I make wood for fuel; *nin bimâsh,* I sail.) I fetch wood for fuel, sailing; p. *naia ..id.*

Nâdamawa, (nin). I defend him; p. *naiâ..wan.*

Nâdaodass, (nin). I go to fetch s. th., or I go for s. th., in a canoe or boat; p. *naia..sod.*

Nâdashkossiwé, (nin), (fr. *nin nâdin,* I fetch it; *mashkossiw,* grass, herb, etc.) I fetch hay, I fetch reed or rush, to make mats; p. *naiâ..wed.*

Nâdasinaiganawa, (nin). I go to him to fetch what he owes me; p. *naia..wad.*

Nâdasinaigane, (nin). I go and fetch what he owed me; p. *naia..ned.*

Nâdassabi, (nin) (*assâb,* net;) I fetch a net or nets (out of the water;) p. *naiâ..bid.*

Nâdassônagane, (nin) (*dassônagan,* trap;) I go to my traps, or, I fetch my traps; p. *naiâ..ned.*

Nâdawa, (*nin*). I fetch him, in a canoe or boat; p. *naiadawad;* imp. *nâda. Nind awi-nâdawa,* I *go* to fetch him, (in a canoe.) *Nin bi-nadawa,* I *come* to fetch him, (in a canoe.)

Nâdenima, (*nin*). I take refuge to him, (for security, for charity, for help;) p. *naia..mad.*

Nâdin, (*nin*). I fetch it; p. *naiâdid. Nind awi-nâdin,* I *go* to fetch it, I *go* for it. *Nin bi-nâdin,* I *come* to fetch it, I *come* for it.

Nâdinisse, (*nin*). I fetch wood for fuel; p. *naiadinissed.*

Nâdishkotawe, (*nin*). I fetch fire, (*ishkote,* fire;) p. *naiâ..wed.*

Nâdjibi, (*nin*). I fetch or collect the sap running from the maple-trees in a sugar-bush; p. *naia..id.*

Nâdjibiam, (*nin*). I fetch liquor, (in a canoe or boat;) p. *naiâ..ang.*

Nâdjibishkam, (*nin*). I fetch liquor, (walking;) p. *naiâ..ang.*

Nâdjidâbadan, (*nin*) (*nind odabadan,* I drag it) I fetch it, dragging it after me, I carry it on a sleigh; p. *naiâ..ang.*

Nâdjidâbana, (*nin*) (*nind odâbana,* I drag him.) I fetch him, dragging him after me, I carry him on a sleigh, (a person, or any other object;) p. *naia..nad;* imp. *nadjidabaj.*

Nâdjidâbi, (*nin*). I fetch s. th. or carry s. th. on a sleigh; p. *naia..id.*

Nâdjigabawitawa, (*nin*). I come and stand before him, I put myself before him; p. *naia..wad.*

Nâdjinamanessi. A kind of starling, (bird;) pl.-*g.*

Nâdjinijima, (*nin*). I fly to him for protection, for safety; p. *naiâ..mad.*

Nâdjinijindan, (*nin*). I fly to it or in it, for safety; p. *naia..ang.*

Nâdjiwane, (*nin*). I fetch a load, carrying it on a portage-strap; p. *naia..ned.*

Nadôbân, or *nâdobâgan.* Bucket to fetch the sap of maple-tree, or water; pl.-*an.*

Nadôbi, (*nin*). I fetch or carry water; p. *naiadôbid.*

Nâdôma, (*nin*). I fetch him, carrying him on my back, (a person, or some other obj.); p. *naiâ..mad.*

Nâdôn, (*nin*). I fetch a canoe; p. *naiâdônod.*

Nâdondam, (*nin*). I fetch, carrying on my back; p. *naia..ang.*

Nâdôndân, (*nin*). I fetch it, carrying it on my back on a portage-strap; p. *naiâ..ang.*

Nâdowe. A kind of big serpent; pl.-*g.*

Nâdowe. Iroquoi Indian; pl.-*g.*

Nâdowem, (*nin*). I speak the Iroquoi language; p. *naia..dowemod.*

Nâdowemowin. Iroquoi language.

Nâdowessi. Ot. Siou Indian; pl.-*wag.* S. *Bwân.*

Naegâdam, adv. Little, very little.

Naegâtch, adv. Slowly, quietly, softly.

Naendam, (*nin*). I am glad, happy, contented ; p. *neën-dang.*

Naéndamia, (*nin*). I please him, I make him contented, glad ; p. *neé..ad.*

Naêndamiton, (*nin*). I please it ; p.*nee..tod.—O gi naêndamiton ninde ;* he made my heart contented.

Naêndan, (*nin*). I allow it, I am willing, contented ; p. *neén-dang.*

Naênim, (*nin*). I gather or put up provisions. I keep them, conserve them ; p. *neénimod.*

Naênimon, (*nin*). I put it up for food, to eat it by and by ; p. *neénimod.*

Naënimonan, (*nin*). I put it up or collect it for food ; p. *neé-nimod.* (V. Conj.)

Nagaä, (*nin*). I hinder him to do s. th., or to go somewhere, I retard him ; p. *negaad.*

Nagaân, (*nin*). I meet it, (a canoe, boat, etc.) ; p. *negaang.*

Nagadân, (*nin*). I leave it behind ; I forsake it, abandon it ; p. *neg..ang.*

Nagadaowe, (*nin*). I leave behind people, in a canoe or boat ; I leave somebody ashore ; p. *neg..wed.*

Nagadâwa, (*nin*). I leave him behind, in a canoe or boat, I surpass him in paddling, rowing or sailing ; also, I leave him ashore, I don't embark him ; p. *neg..wad ;* imp. *na-gadâ.*

Nagadêndam, (*nin*). S. *Nagadis.*

Nagadêndamowin. The state or disposition of being inured or accustomed to s. th.

Nagadén lân, (*nin*). I am used or accustomed to it, inured to it ; p. *neg..ang.*

Nagadénima, (*nin*). I am accustomed to him, I am accustomed to see him, to hear him, to converse with him ; p. *neg ..mad.*

Nagadénindis (*nin*). I accustom myself to s. th., I feel myself accustomed or used to s. th. ; p. *neg..sod.*

Naganis, (*nin*). I am accustomed, used, inured ; p. *negadisid.*

Nagadisiwin. Inurement, use, custom, habit.

Nagadjiidis, (*nin*). I get myself accustomed, I endeavor to get used to s. th. ; p. *neg..sod.*

Nagâdjinijima, (*nin*). I leave him, flying from him for safety ; p. *neg..mad.*

Nagadjinijindân, (*nin*). I leave a place, flying from it for safety ; p. *neg..ang.*

Nagadjipidan, (*nin*). I am accustomed to the taste of it ; p. *neg..ang.*

Nagadjijwa, (*nin*). I am accustomed to the taste of some obj. ; p. *neg..wad.*

Nagâdjiton, (*nin*). I am accustomed to make it, or to do it ; p. *neg..tod.*

Nagâdjiwan. The water is hindered, it stops, it cannot flow any further ; p. *neg..ang.*

Nagâiash, (*nin*). I am hindered by a contrary wind to sail any farther ; p. *neg..id.*

Nagam, (*nin*). I sing ; p. *néga-mod.*

Nagamo-masinaigan .Song-book, hymn-book ; pl.-*an.*

Nagamôn. Song, hymn ; pl.-*an.*

Nagamôtawa, (*nin*). I sing him; I sing his glory, his praise; I sing to him; p. *neg..wad.*

Nagamôwin. Singing, the act of singing.

Naganâ, (*nin*). I leave him behind, I surpass him in a walking or running; I forsake him, abandon him; p. *neganad.*

Nagânishkad. He that starts first, predecessor; forerunner; pl.-*jig.*

Nagânisid. He that is foremost, superior, master, foreman, overseer, boss; pl.-*jig.*

Nagânisid Kitchi-mekatewikwanaie. Superior Great Blackgown, that is, Archbishop.

Nagaowê, (*nin*). I meet; p. *negaowed.*

Nagâshka, (*nin*). S. *Nagâta.*

Nagâshka, or-*magad.* S. *Nâgishka.*

Nagasedebison. A thing that stops the foot and hinders it to go farther, that is, a stirrup; (F. étrier;) pl.-*an.* (*Nagâ,* alludes to stopping; *sid,* to the foot; the termination *bison,* to a string.)

Nâgasotawa, (*nin*). I listen to him attentively, I follow his discourse with my thoughts; p. *naiâ..ad.*

Nagâta, (*nin*). I stop, I stand still; p. *negâtad.*

Nâgatawâbama, (*nin*), (*nin nanagaiawâbama,* freq.) I look upon him observing him, I watch him, consider him; p. *naiâ..mad.*

Nâgatawâbandan, (*nin*) (*nin nânagatawâbandan,* freq.) I observe, watch, consider it; p. *naiâ..ang.*

Nâgatawendam, (*nin*). S. *Nanagatawendam.* *

Nâgatch, adv. Later, afterwards, a little while after; by and by.

Nâgatwaadon mikana, (*nin*), (pron. *nin nagattôadon m...*) I follow a trail or road; p. *neg..dod.*

Nagatwawa mikwam, (*nin*) (pron. *nin nagatowa m...*) I follow the ice along a crevice; p. *neg..wad;* imp. *nagatwa.*

Nagawa, (*nin*). I meet him, in a canoe, boat, etc.; p. *negawad;* imp. *nagâ.*

Nâgawagendam, (*nin*). I am in a hurry; p. *naiâ..ang.*

Nâgéwâssa, adv. Far yet, but not very far.

Nâgewassawad. It is yet far, but not very far; p. *naiag..wak.*

Nagikawad. It is nothing, it is worth nothing; *neg..wak.*

Nagikawendagos, (*nin*). I am little esteemed, little thought of, I am insignificant, worth little; p. *neg..sid.*

Nagikawendagosia, (*nin*). I make him insignificant, I put him low, I put him down; p. *neg..ad.*

Nagikawendagwad. It is insignificant, little thought of; p. p. *neg..wak.*

Nagikawendân, (*nin*). I think little of it, I esteem it low, insignificant; p. *neg..ang.*

---

* NOTE. The *frequentative* verbs of this kind being commonly used, we will put them all under *Nanag.*

Nagikawenimâ, (*nin*). I esteem him little, I think little of him; p. *neg..mad.*
Nagikawenindis, (*nin*). I esteem myself little, I have a poor opinion of myself; p. *neg..sod.*
Nagikawis, (*nin*). I am nothing, worth nothing; p. *neg..sid.*
Naginin! interj. Lo! behold!
Nagishkâge, (*nin*). I meet; p. *neg..ged.*
Nagishkân, (*nin*). I meet it; p. *neg..ang.*
Nagishkawa, (*nin*). I meet him; p. *neg..wad.*
Nagishkodâdimin, (*nin*). We meet each other; p. *neg..did-jig.*
Nagishkodâdiwin. Meeting, (in the road, not assembly.)
Nâgos, (*nin*). I appear, I am visible; p. *naiâgosid.*
Nâgosiwin. Appearance.
Nâgwad. It appears, it shows, it is visible, it is evident; p. *naiâgwak.*
Nagwâdân, (*nin*). I catch it with a snare, or in a snare; p. *neg..ang.*
Nagwâdjige, (*nin*). I catch with a snare; p. *neg..ged.*
Nagwâgan. Snare; (F. collet;) pl.-*an.*
Nagwâganeiâb. String for a snare; pl.-*in.*
Nagwâganike, (*nin*). I make snares; I lay snares; p. *neg..ked.*
Nagwâi. Sleeve; pl.-*an.*
Nagwâna, (*nin*). I catch him with a snare, or in a snare; p. *neg..nad;* imp. *nagwaj.*
Nagwâs, (*nin*). I am caught in a snare; p. *negwâsod.—Nij wâbosog gi-nagwâsowog tibikong;* two rabbits have been caught in snares last night.
Nagwêiâb. Rainbow; pl.-*in.*
Nâgwi, (*nin*). I appear, I make my appearance; p. *naiâgwiod.*
Nâgwiidis, (*nin*). I make myself visible, I appear in a vision; p. *naiâ..sod.*
Nâgwiidisowin. Apparition, vision.
Naiâg, adv. S. *Kija.*
Naiânj, adv. Till, until; a long time.—*Kawin naiânj dagwishinsi;* he does not come a long time. *Ningwiss gi-kitchimawi naiânj ginibâd;* my son wept much until he fell asleep.
Naiénj, adj. S. *Neiénj.*
Naiétawad. There is a little of it; p. *neietawak.*
Naietawis, (*nin*). I am of a little number, that is, my family is small; p. *neie..sid.*
Naiétawisimin, (*nin*). We are a few in number; p. *neie..sid-jig.*
Naikinjean ishkote, (*nin*). I repair or stir the fire with a poker; p. *neik..ang.*
Naikinjeigan. Poker to stir the fire; pl.-*an.*
Naikinjeige, (*nin*). I stir the fire with a poker; p. *neik..ged.*
Naininiwagis, (*nin*). I am an upright man; p. *nein..sid.*
Naishkwandenan, (*nin*). I fix the door, I put it well; p. *neish..ang.*
Naissiton, (*nin*). I put it well or right; p. *nei..tod.*
Naitâ, adv. Just, like purposely.—*Naita ijiwebad;* it just happens so, (like purposely,

although not purposely.) *Naita nongom kidagwishin;* thou comest just now, (when least expected, or, when much desired, or, when least desired, etc.)

Naittam, (*nin*). I am obedient; p. *neitang.*

Naittamowin. Obedience.

Naittawa, (*nin*). I am obedient to him, I obey him; p. *nei..wad.*

Nâjabian, (*nin*). I draw it over a string or cord; p. *naiâ..ang.*

Nâjâbiigan. Violin; pl.-*an.*

Nâjabiige, (*nin*). I draw s. th. over a string; also, I play on the violin; p. *naiôj..ged.*

Nâjigaigan. Scraper; pl.-*an.*

Nâjigaige, (*nin*). I scrape a skin or hide, to make it soft; p. *naia..ged.*

Nâjinijima, (*nin*). S. *Nâdjinijima.*

Nâjinijindan, (*nin*). S. *Nâdjinijindan.*

Najoshkak pâshkisigan. Double-barreled gun.

Nâjôkwewid. A man who has two wives, a bigamist; pl.-*jid.*

Nakakégâm, or *inakakégâm,*adv. This adverb, in connection with some other adverb denoting *direction,* signifies the side of a river, bay, lake, etc.; as: *Oma nakakegâm,* on this side of the river, etc. *Wedi nakakëgâm,* on that side there. *Anindi nakakegâm?* On which side?

Nakakéia, or *inakakéia,* adv. This adverb, preceded by another adverb denoting *direction,* or by a substantive, has the signification of the English syllable *ward* or *wards,* or of *towards.* (For examples see Otchipwe Grammar, "Adverbs denoting *direction.*")

Nakawé, adv. First, before all. —*Nakawé anamiân, pânima dash gawishimon wi-nibaian;* first pray, and then lie down to sleep.

Nakodam, (*nin*). I consent to s. th., I promise to do s. th., or to go somewhere; p. *nekodang.*

Nakomâ, (*nin*). I promise him to do s. th., or to go somewhere, I consent to what he is asking me; p. *nekomad.*

Nakwébidon, (*nin*). I catch some obj. that is thrown to me; p. *nek..dod.*

Nakwébina, (*nin*). I catch some obj. that is thrown to me, or that flies by me; p. *nek..nad.*

Nakwénage, (*nin*). I shoot in the air; p. *nek..ged.*

Nakwéwana, (*nin*). I shoot him in the air, (I shoot a bird flying;) p. *nek..wad.*

Nakweshkagé, (*nin*). S. *Nagishkage.*

Nakweshkân, (*nin*). S. *Nagishkan.*

Nakwéshkawa, (*nin*). S. *Nagishkawa.*

Nakwéshkodadimin, (*nin*). S. *Nagishkodadimin.*

Nakwéshkodagiwin. S. *Nagishkodadiwin.*

Nakwetage, (*nin*). I answer, I gainsay, I give bad answers, short answers; p. *nek..ged.*

Nakwetageshk, (*nin*). I use to answer, to gainsay, to give bad answers; p. *nek..id.*

Nakwétam, (*nin*). I answer, I give an answer to a question; also, I gainsay, I answer improperly; p. *nekwetang*.

Nakwêtamowin. Answer; pl.-*an*.

Nakwétawa, (*nin*). I answer him, I give him an answer to a question; or, I answer him improperly; p. *nek..wad*.

Nâm, as end-syllable in some n. v., signifies *breathing*, or s. th. relating to it; as: *Nind ishkwanâm*, I breathe my last. *Nin jajibanâm*, I breathe by long intervals; etc.

Nâmaam, (*nin*). I have a fair wind; p. *naiâmaang*.

Namaanigwad. It is a fair wind, good for sailing; p. *naia..wak*.

Namadab, (*nin*). I sit down, I am sitting; p. *nem..bid*.

Namadabia, (*nin*). I make him sit down; p. *ném..ad*.

Namadabitawa, (*nin*). I sit down by his side, near him; p. *nem..wad*.

Namadabiwin. Sitting; a seat. —*Kitchi-ogima namadabiwin*, throne. Pl.-*an*.

Namadamagad. It is higher than large; p. *nem..gak*.

Namâkona, (*nin*). I anoint his head, I put grease, ointment or pomade on his head; p. *nem..nad*; imp. *namakoj*.

Namâkonidis, (*nin*). I anoint or grease my head; p. *nem..sod*.

Namâkwiwin. Grease to anoint the head, ointment [for the head, pomade.

Namandj, adv. Expression of doubting or not knowing.

Namândj ejiwêbadogwen. I don't know what happened; or, I don't know how it is. *Namândj api gemâdjawânen*; I don't know when I shall start.

Namandji, (*nin*). I am left-handed; p. *nemandjid*.

Namândjigâd.* The left leg.

Namândjinik. The left arm.

Namândjinindj. The left hand.

Namândjinow. The left cheek.

Namândjishkingig. The left eye.

Namândjisid. The left foot.

Namatakone, or-*magad ishkote*. The fire blazes up; p. *nem..neg*, or-*magak*.

Namatchigâbawi. He sets himself upright, he stands up, he erects himself; (F. il se mâte;) p. *nem..wid*.— *Namatchigâbawi ko makwâ*; the bear uses to erect himself, (to stand upright, like a person.)

Namatchigad. It is oblong, it is longer than broad, (stuff;) p. *nem..gak*.

Namatchigisi. It is oblong, longer than broad, as, *moshwe*, handkerchief; *senibâ*, ribbon or silk-stuff; p. *nem..sid*.

Namê. Sturgeon; pl.-*wog*.

Namébin. Carp, sucker, (fish;) pl.-*ag*.

Namebinigan. Carp-bone; pl.-*an*.

Namébini-gisiss. The moon of suckers, the month of February, and too: *migisiwigisiss*, the moon of the eagle.

Namégoss. Trout; pl.-*ag*.

Namegossigan. Trout-bone; pl. -*an*.

---

*Note. There is always a possessive pronoun prefixed to this and the following five words; as: *Nin namandjigad*; my left leg. *Kit namandjinikf*, thy left arm. *O namandjinindj*, his left hand, etc.

Namêgossika, or-*magad*. There are trout, or many trout; p. or-*magak*.
Namégossikan. Place where there are many trout.
Namégossikaning. At, to or from such a place.
Namékwan. Glue.
Namékwanike, (*nin*). I make glue; p. *nem..ked*.
Namekwanikêwinini. Glue-boiler; pl.-*wâg*.
Naméteg. Dried fish; pl.-*wog*.
Namêwib. Sturgeon Lake.
Namêwibisibi. Sturgeon River.
Namewâgan. Sturgeon-bone; pl.-*an*.
Nâmishkid. He that is in a bad habit of dancing, a habitual dancer; pl.-*jig*.
Nâmos, as end-syllable in some n. v., relates to *smoke; Nin gikanâmos*, it smokes in my house. *Nin gibwanâmos*, I am stifled with smoke. *Nin jibanâmos*, I can endure much smoke, etc.
Nâna, (*nin*). I fetch him, (a person, or any other object;) p. *naiânad; imp. naj*.
Nind awi-nâna. I *go* to fetch him, I *go* for him.
Nin binâna. I *come* to fetch him, I *come* for him.
Nanândamoton mikana, (*nin*). I repair a road; p. *nen..tod*.
Nanaanam, (*nin*). I prepare myself for singing, by coughing a little; p. *nen..mod*.
Nanabânis, (*nin*). I am caught, cheated; p. *nen..sid*.
Nânabem, adv. Just now, only now; too late.—*Nänabem ki dagwishin gi-ishkwa-anoking;* thou comest only now when the work is done.
Nânagatawabama, * (*nin*). I observe him, consider him, I watch him with my eyes; p. *naian..mad*.
Nânagatawabandân, (*nin*) or, *nin nânasondân*. I contemplate it, I consider it, observe it, watch it; p. *naiân..ang*.
Nânagatawendam, (*nin*). I reflect, meditate, consider, contemplate, deliberate; p. *naia ..ang*.
Nânagatawendamadis, (*nin*). S. *Nânagatawenindis*.
Nânagatawendamadisomagad nindé. My heart reflects or meditates upon itself; p. *naian..gak*.
Nânagatawendamowin. Meditation, contemplation, reflection, consideration, deliberation.
Nânagatawendân, (*nin*). I reflect or meditate upon it, I consider it; p. *naiâ..ang*.
Nänagatawenima, (*nin*). I reflect upon him, (upon his conduct, his manners, his qualities, etc.); p. *naiân..mad*.
Nânagatawenindis, (*nin*). I reflect upon myself, I consider myself; I examine my conscience; p. *naiân..sod*.
Nânagatawenindisowin. Reflection upon one's self; examen of conscience.
Nanâgina, (*nin*). I stop him, I hinder him; p. *nen..ad*.—*Nin*

* Note. The duplication of the first syllable in this and some other verbs here, marks the *frequentative* verb, and lludes to a repetition, or continuation of the same act.

nanâginag wâ-migâdidjig; I hinder (stop, separate) people that intend to fight.—S. *Nagâkâ,* or, *Nagââ.*

Nanâginiwe, (*nin*). I stop, hinder or separate fighters; p. *nen..wed.*

Nanâibian, (*nin*). I write it, correcting it at the same time; p. *nen..ang.*

Nanâibiigan. Corrected or mended writing, corrected copy; pl.-*an.*

Nanâibiige, (*nin*). I correct or mend writing, I am writing a corrected copy; p. *nen..ged.* (*Nin nanâiton,* I mend or correct it; *nind ojibiige,* I write.)

Nanâikiajean ishkote, (*nin*), freq. I repair the fire, I stir it up; p. *nen..ang.*

Nanâikinjeigan. Poker, commonly an iron bar to stir the fire with; pl.-*an.*

Nanâikinjeiganak. A stick or pole, (not an iron bar,) to stir the fire with, wooden poker; pl.-*on.*

Nanâina, (*nin*). I arrange or repair it, I mend, fix it, I put it in good order again; p. *nen..nad.*—*Nin gi-nanâina dibaigisisswan,* I repaired the watch.

Nanainân, (*nin*). I put it in good order; p. *nen..ang..*—*Biskiténaganan nin gi-nanainânan;* I put in good order the "birch-plates." (S.*Biskiténagan.*)

Nanâissitchigade, or-*magad.* S. *Nanâitchigade.*

Nanâissitchige, (*nin*). S. *Nanâitchige.*

Nanâissiton, (*nin*). S. *Nanâiton.*

Nanâitchigade, or-*magad.* It is repaired, arranged, mended, settled; p. *nen..deg,* or-*magak.*

Nanâitchige, (*nin*). I repair, mend, correct, settle; p. *nen..ged.*

Nanaiton, (*nin*). I repair it, I mend, correct, arrange it, I improve it, I settle it; p. *nen..tod.*

Nanâitowin. Repairing, correcting, reparation, improvement, arrangement for the better.

Nanâkona, (*nin*). I defend myself against him, I resist him, I combat him in self-defence; p. *nen..nad;* imp. *nanâkon.*

Nanâkonan, (*nin*). I defend myself against it, I combat it, I resist it; p. *nen..ang.*—*Nin nanâkonan bâtâdowin;* I combat sin.

Nanâkwi, (*nin*). I defend myself; p. *nenâkwid.*

Nanâkwiwin. Self-defence.

Nanâmâa, (*nin*). I frighten it, (a wild animal, a duck, etc.) I startle it; p. *nen..ad.*

Nanamâdjigan. Frightened animal in the woods, startled animal, duck, etc.; pl.-*ag.*

Nânan, num. Five.

Nanândawia, (*nin*). I doctor him, I give him medicines in his sickness; p. *nen..ad.*

Nanândawiigos, (*nin*). I am doctored, medicines are given to me in my sickness; p. *nen..sid.*

Nanândawiiwe, (*nin*). I doctor, I give medicines to a sick person; p. *nen..wed.*

Nanândawiiwewin. Doctoring, a doctor's business, occupation, art, science.

Nanândawiiwéwinini. Doctor, physician, a man skilful in curing diseases; pl.-*wag.*

Nanândawiowin. Medicine, remedy; *anamie nanandawiowin,* a sacrament, the holy medicine.

Nanândawis, (*nin.*) I am cured, I am made whole; p. *nen..sid.* —S. *Nôdjim.*

Nanândawitchigan. A sick person taken care of and doctored; pl.-*ag.*

Nanândawitwa, (*nin*). S. *Nanandawia.*

Nanândawitwâwin. S. *Nanândawiiwewin.*

Nanândoban, (*nin*), freq. S. *Nandoban.*

Nanândobanikandimin, (*nin*), freq. S. *Nandobanikandimin.*

Nanândobanikandiwin. S. *Nandobanidandiwin.*

Nanandodjina, (*nin*), freq. For this and other *frequentative* verbs of this kind, look under *Nandodjina,* etc., where they appear as *simple* verbs.

Nanândoma, (*nin*). I beg him, I pray, ask or request him for s. th., I implore his help and assistance; p. *nen..mad.*

Nanândomandjige, (*nin*), freq. S. *Nandomadjige.*

Nanândomowin. Petition, request, entreaty; pl.-*an.*

Nanândoshkite, (*nin*). I go from one place to another to hear what they say; p. *nen..ted.*

Nanandoshkitegabaw, (*nin*). I stand still in different places, to hear what is said; p. *nen..wid.*

Nanândoshkiteshk, (*nin*). I am in a bad habit of going round to hear what is said; p. *nen..kid.*

Nanânigama, (*nin*). I tear some *an.* obj. with the teeth; p. *nen..mad.*

Nanânigandân, (*nin*). I tear it with the teeth; p. *nen..ang.*

Nanânigoshka, or-*magad,* freq. It is all torn to pieces everywhere; p. *nen..kag,* or-*magak.* S. *Nigoshka,* etc.

Nanânigoshkân, (*nin*), freq. I tear it all to pieces, every part of it; p. *nen..ang.*

Nanânigoshkawa, (*nin*), freq. I tear some obj. all to pieces; p. *nen..wad.*

Nânanimin, (*nin*). We are five of us; p. *naiâ..djig.*

Nânaninon. There are five; p. *naia..nigin.*

Nanânj, adv. S. *Naiânj.*

Nanâpadaami, (*nin*). S. *Jajashagaami.*

Nanâpagam, (*nin*). I sing, mocking somebody or something; p. *nen..mod.*

Nanâpagamon, (*nin*). I sing it mocking, for derision; p. *nen..mod.*

Nanâpagamonan, (*nin*). I sing him, mocking, I sing his character or his qualities, for derision or contempt; p. *nen..mod.* (V. Conj.)

Nanâpagandj, adv. Shamefully, worth mocking and derision.

Nanâpagandjia, (*nin*). I insult him, I mock him; p. *nen..ad.*

Manâpagandjiton, (*nin*); p. *nen..tod.* S. *Nanapagansondan.*

Nanâpagansitagos, (*nin*). I speak insulting mocking words; I murmur; p. *nen..sid.*

Nanâpagansoma, (*nin*). I mock or insult him; I murmur against him; p. *nen..mad.*

Nanâpagansondan, (*nin*). I mock or insult it; p. *nen..ang.*

Nanâpagansonge, (*nin*). I mock, I use mocking language; I murmur; p. *nen..ged.*

Nanapidotam, (*nin*). I mock repeating words, I repeat words of somebody in a mocking manner; p. *nen..tang.*

Nanâpidotawa, (*nin*). I mock him, imitating his speaking or his voice, repeating after him; p. *nen..wad.*

Nanâpigijwe, (*nin*). I speak in a mocking manner; p. *nen..wed.*

Nanâpigijwewin. Mockery, speaking mocking words.

Nanâpima, (*nin*). I speah to him certain words, relying on s. th.; p. *nen..mad.*

Nanâpimon, (*nin*). I rely on it in speaking certain words; p. *nen..mod.*

Nanâpimonan, (*nin*). I rely on him in speaking certain words, or telling s. th.; p. *nen..mod.*

Nanapimawin. Speaking with reliance on some object.

Nanâpogis, (*nin*). I am impotent, I have no power, no authority; p. *nen..sid.*

Nanâssab, adv. S. *Aiâpi.*

Nanawad. It gives no profit, does not produce anything; p. *nen..awak.*

Nanawâdad. It is deficient, useless, unprofitable; p. *nen..dak.*

Nanawâdis, (*nin*). I am an unprofitable, useless person, I am losing my time, I gain nothing, acquire nothing, I labor in vain; p. *nen..sid.*— S. *Anawéwis.*

Nanawaj, adv. Uselessly, unprofitably, loosing time, to no purpose. — *Nanawaj nin bimâdis*, I live unprofitably, (my life is destitute of good works.)

Nanâwina, (*nin*), freq. I cannot have him, cannot reach him, (any obj.); p. *nen..ad.*

Nanâwinan, (*nin*), freq. I cannot have it, I cannot reach it; p. *nen..ang.*

Nanawis, (*nin*). S. *Nanawâdis. Anawêwis.*

Nanawisse, (*nin*). I burst asunder; p. *nen..sed.*

Nanawisse, or-*magad.* It bursts asunder, it falls to pieces; p. *nen..seg*, or-*magak.*

Nandâ, in compositions, signifies *seeking, searching, trying.*

Nandagenim, (*nin*). I take more than I ought, or more than I want; also, I do all in my power; p. *nen..mod.*

Nandâkikendan, (*nin*). I try or endeavor to know it, to learn it; p. *nen..ang.*

Nandâkikenima, (*nin*). I try to know him, I inform myself about him; p. *nen..mad.*

Nandâmasitam, (*nin*). I try to hear what is said, I listen, I hearken; p. *nen..ang.*

Nandâmasitawa, (*nin*). I hearken, to know what he shall say; p. *nen..wad.*
Nandâmikwendân, (*nin*). I try to recall it to memory, I endeavor to recollect it; (*nin mikwêndân*, I recollect it;) p. *nen..ang.*
Nandâmikwenima, (*nin*). I try to recollect him, to recall him to memory, (to recollect his name, his appearance, etc.); p. *nen..mad.*
Nandâwâbama, (*nin*). I seek him, I look for him; p. *nen..mad.*
Nandawâto, (*nin*). I am spying out; p. *nen..tod.*
Nandawâton, (*nin*). I spy it out; p. *nen..tod.*
Nandawéndagos, (*nin*). I am desirable; also, I am desired to give or to do or to say s. th.; p. *nen..sid.*
Nandawendagwad. It is desired, it is desirable; p. *nen..wak.*
Nandawendam, (*nin*). I desire; p. *nen..ang.*
Nandawéndjigewin. Looking for, seeking, (especially in hunting or fishing.)
Nandawênima, (*nin*). I desire him, I wish to have him, I require him to do s. th.; p. *nen..mad.*
Nandawissin, (*nin*). I look for s. th. to eat; p. *nen..nid.*
Nandôgia, (*nin*). I am seeking, searching.
Nandoban, (*nin*). I try to make war-captives, slaves, I go on a war-party, on a war-excursion, (according to the Indian manner of making war;) p. *nen..nid.* (*Abanini*, signifies, Indian slave.)
Nandobanikandimin, (*nin*). We are at war with each other; p. *nen..didjig.*
Nandobanikandéwin. Indian warfare.
Nandobaniwin. Endeavor to make slaves, Indian warfare.
Nandobi, (*nin*). I look for water, or for s. th. to drink; p. *nendobid.*
Nandobimwa, (*nin*). I am hunting with a bow and arrows; p. *nen..wad.*
Nandodjina, (*nin*), (*nin nanândodjina*, freq.) I seek or search him by feeling in the dark, I grope him; p. *ned..nad.*
Nandôdjinan, (*nin*), (*nin nanandodjinan*, freq.) I seek it by feeling in the dark, I grope it; p. *nen..ang.*
Nandomâ, (*nin*). I call him to me, I send him word to come to me, I invite him, I cite him, I summon him; p. *nendomad.*
Nandomâkome, (*nin*). I search lice; p. *nen..med.*
Nandomâkimeshi. Ape, monkey, (louse-searcher;) pl.*-iag.*
Nandomândjige, (*nin*), (*nin nanândomandjige*, freq.) I sniff, I search s. th. by scent, (like a dog;) p. *nen..ged.*
Nandomigos, (*nin*). I am called to go to somebody, or to go somewhere; p. *nen..sid.*
Nandomigosiwin. Call received by a person to go somewhere.
Nandomikwa, (*nin*). I am hunting beavers, or searching beavers; p. *nen..wed.*
Nandonâssa, (*nin*). I search

lice on his head; p. *nen..sad.*

Nandonêwa, (*nin*). I seek him, I look for him; p. *nen..wad;* imp. *nandoné.*

Nandôshibe, (*nin*). I am hunting ducks; p. *nen..bed.*

Nandoshkamage, (*nin*). I collect my credits, my active debts; p. *nen..ged.*

Nandoshkamawa, (*nin*). I request him to pay me what he owes me, to pay his credit; p. *nen..wad.*

Nangoshkâs,) *nin*). I try to get paid, to get my credits, (active debts;) p. *nen..sod.*

Nandôtage, (*nin*) or, *nin nandôtam.* I listen, I hearken, endeavoring to hear what they say; p. *nen..ged,* or, *nendôtang.*

Nandotam, (*nin*). I ask, I request, I petition; p. *nendotang.*

Nandotamâge, (*nin*). I beg, I mendicate, ask alms: p. *nen ..ged.*

Nandotamâgen, (*nin*). I beg for it; p. *nen..ged.*

Nandotamâgenan,(*nin*). I beg for some obj; p. *nen..ged.* (V. Conj.)*Pakwejigan nin bi-nandotamagenan;* I come to beg for some bread, (or flour.)

Nandotamâgeshk, (*nin*). I am in a bad habit of begging; p. *nen..kid.*

Nandotamagewin. Begging, beggary, mendicity.

Nandotamawa, (*nin*). I ask him for s. th., I beg him, I request him; p. *nen..wad.*

Nandôtamowin. Asking, petition, request for s. th,

Nandôtan, (*nin*). I beg for it; I require it; p. *nen..ang.*

Nandotawa, (*nin*). I listen, I hearken, endeavoring to hear what he is saying; p. *nen.. wad.*

Nandwêwem, (*nin*). I am calling without seeing the person, I call; p. *nen..mod.*

Nandwéwema, (*nin*). I call him; I call for some obj. to have it; p. *gen..mâd.*

Nandwéwendan, (*nin*). I call for it, to have it back again; p. *nen..ang.*

Nandwewesige, (*nin*). I call by firing guns; p. *nen..ged.*

Nanékadendam, (*nin*). I suffer in my thoughts, in my mind; p. *nen..dang.*

Nanêkâdis, (*nin*). I suffer; p. *nen..nid.*

Nanékâdisiwin. Suffering.

Nanékâdjia, (*nin*). I make him suffer, I treat him ill; p. *nen ..ad.*

Nanêkadjion, (*nin*) or, *nin nanékâdjiton.* I make myself suffer by it, using it sparingly, in order to have it longer, (provisions or liquid;) p. *nen ..od.*

Nângan. It is light, not heavy; p. *naiângang.*

Nânge, adv. This word is used to express the *contrary* of the verb which it follows; as: *Nin kikenân nânge;* I don't know it, *Ki nibwakâ nânge;* thou art not wise. *Dêbwe nânge;* he is not telling the truth. (It is a kind of irony.)

Nângendan, (*nin*). I think it is light, not heavy; p. *naia..ang.*

Nângenima, (*nin*). I think he is light, (any obj.); p. *naia..mad.*
Nângia, (*nin*). I make light some obj., I lighten it; p. *naiângiad.*
Nângidee, (*nin*). My heart is light, contented, happy; p. *naiâ..ed.*
Nânginikeshkawa, (*nin*). I make him move his arm; p. *naia..wad.*
Nângis, (*nin*). I am light; p. *naiângisid.*
Nângiside, (*nin*). I am light-footed; p. *naiâ..ded.*
Nângisideshin, (*nin*). I hurt my foot, (knocking against s. th. in my way;) p. *naiâ..ing.*
Nângiton, (*nin*). I make it light, I lighten it; p. *naiângitod.*
Nângiwane, (*nin*). I have a light load or pack on my back; p. *naiâ..ned.*
Nângwana, adv. So, thus, then. (It is used in an interrogative manner and placed always immediately after the verb.) —*Wi madjawag nângwana?* So they will go away? *Ginibo nangwana?* He is then dead?
Nanibaiawe, (*nin*) or, *nin nanânibaiawe*, freq. I yawn or gape, (being sleepy;) p. *naiâ..wed.*
Nânibaiawewin. Yawning.
Nânibaw, (*nin*), freq. I stand here and there, in different places successively; p. *naiâ..wid.*
Nanibikiganona, (*nin*). I speak to him in a scolding manner; (*nin ganona*, I speak to him;) p. *nen..nad.*
Nanibikima, (*nin*). I scold him, I rebuke, upbraid, reprimand him; p. *nen..mad.*
Nanibikindân, (*nin*). I scold or rebuke it; p. *nen..ang.*—*Naningim nin nanibikindan ninde, iji matchi-ijiwebak;* I rebuke often my heart, because it is so wicked.
Naninawendagos, (*nin*). I am rejected, abandoned, grieved; p. *nen..sid.*
Naninawendagwad. It is rejected, abandoned, sad; p. *nen..wak.*
Naninawendam, (*nin*). I am sad, afflicted in my mind, I am sorrowful, I mourn, I grieve; p. *nen..ang.*
Naninawendamowin. Sadness, affliction, mourning, grief.
Nanigawima, (*nin*). I grieve him with *words;* p. *nen..mad.*
Naninawingwe, (*nin*). My face is marked with grief, I have a sad countenance; p. *nen..wed.*
Naninawingweidis, (*nin*). I mark my face with sadness; p. *nen..sod.*
Naninawis, (*nin*). I am an orphan; p. *nen..sid.*
Naninawitagos, (*nin*). I lament, I express grief, sadness, affliction; p. *nen..sid.*
Nâning, num. Five times; the fifth time; in five manners or ways.
Naningim, adv. Often, often times, frequently.
Naningotinong, or *naningotinongin*, adv. Sometimes, occasionally, now and then, anon.

Naningitawamo mikana. The trail or road splits in several directions, there are several branches of the road; p. *non ..mog.*

Nanipinis, (nin). I am weak, infirm, sick, broken by sickness; p. *nen..sid.*

Nanipinisimagad ninde. My heart is weak, infirm, sick; p. *nen..gâk.*

Nanipinisiwin. Weakness, infirmity, sickness.

Nanisanad. It is dangerous, perilous; p. *nenisanak.*

Nanisanendagos, (nin). I am considered dangerous; I am dangerous; p. *nen..sid.*

Nanisanendagwad. It is considered dangerous, it is dangerous, perilous; p. *nen..wak.*

Nanisanendam, (nin). I think there is danger; p. *nen..ang.*

Nanisanendan, (nin). I consider it dangerous; p. *o nan...*

Nanisanenima, (nin). I consider him dangerous, I think he is dangerous; p. *nen..mad.*

Nanisania, (nin). I put him in danger; p. *nen..ad.*

Nanisaniidis, (nin). I put myself in danger, in jeopardy; p. *nen..sod.*

Nanisaninagos, (nin). I look dangerous; p. *nen..sid.*

Nanisaninagwad. It looks dangerous; p. *nen..wak.*

Nanisanis, (nin). I am dangerous; also, I am in danger, in peril; p. *nen..sid.*

Nanisanisiwin. Danger, peril, jeopardy.

Nanisanilagos, (nin). I am dangerous by my speaking; p. *nen..sid.*

Nanisanitawa, (nin). I hear him with apprehension of danger, I listen to him with the impression that there is danger in his speaking; p. *nen.. wad.*

Nanisaniton, (nin). I put it in danger, I expose it to danger; p. *nen..tod.*

Nanitagabaminagwad. It is twilight; p. *nen..wak.*

Nânji, (nin). S. *Nanjisse.*

Nanji, or-*magad.* S. *Nanjisse,* or-*magad.*

Nanjisse, (nin). I slide down; I fly down; I descend, (sliding or flying;) p. *naiânjissed.*

Nanjisse, or-*magad.* It slides or flies down, it descends; p. *naiânjisseg,* or-*magak.*

Nâno, num. five, (before substantives denoting MEASURE, of time or other things.)

Nanwewan.—S. *Nijobanénindj. Nijôbidonan. Nijobina,* etc., always changing in English, *two* into *five*; as: *Nijobanénindj,* twice (or two times) a handful. *Nanobonénindj,* five times a handful.—*Nijôbidonan, (nin),* I tie two together. *Nanôbidonan, (nin),* I catch two fishes. *Nanôbina, (nin),* I catch five fishes; and so on respectively.

Nâogâded. He that has four legs, a four-legged animal, quadruped; pl.-*jig.*

Napanôna, (nin). I pay him, I recompense him; p. *nep..nad;* imp. *napanoj.*

Napâtch, adv. Wrongly, not in right order, not in the right place.

Napâtchiton, (nin). I put it

wrongly, not in the right place; p. *nep..tod.*

Nashigide, (*nin*). I sob; (F. je sanglote;) p. *nesh..ded.*

Nashkê ! interj. Lo! see! hark!

Nâsibi, (*nin*). I fetch water; p. *naiâsibid.*

Nâsikage, (*nin*). I approach, I go to..., or come to...; p. *naiâ..ged.*

Nasikan, (*nin*). I go to it, I approach it; p. *naiâsikang.*

Nasikawa, (*nin*). I go to him, I approach him, (a person, or any other obj.;) p. *naia..ad.*

Nind awi-nasikawa. I go to him.

Nin bi-nasikawa. I come to him.

Nâsikodadimin, (*nin*). We go to each other, we come together; we re-unite; p. *naiâ..didjig.*

Nasikwê, (*nin*). I comb my head; p. *nesikweod.*

Nasikwéigan. Currycomb, for currying horses; pl.-*an.*

Nasikwéwa, (*nin*). I comb him; p. *nes..wad;* imp. *nasikwé.*

Nâssab, adv. Equally, likewise, the same again.

Nâssabashkinaa, (*nin*). I brim it, I fill it up even, I fill it up to the brim, (some vessel, as, *akik*, kettle;) p. *naias..ad.*

Nâssabaskkinadôn, (*nin*). I fill it up to the brim, I brim it; p. *naias..dod.*

Nâssab ejinagosid, nassab ejinagwak. Similar, resembling.

Nâssabian, (*nin*). I copy it, I transcribe it; p. *naia..ang.* (*Nâssab*, equally; *nind ojibian*, I write it.)

Nâssâbiginan, (*nin*). I unravel it, disentangle it, (thread, etc.); p. *ness..ang.*

Nâssabiigan. Copy, duplicate; pl.-*an.*

Nâssabiige, (*nin*). I copy, I transcribe; p. *naia..ged.*

Nâssabiigewin. Copying, the act of transcribing a writing.

Nâssab-ikkitowin. An often repeated word; pl.-*an.*

Nâssabishima, (*nin*). I put it back in its place; p. *naia..mad.*

Nâssabissiton, (*nin*). I put it back in its place; p. *naia..tod.*

Nâssab nin dibâdjim. I repeat, (the same narration, the same report, the same speech.)

Nâssab nind ikkit. I repeat, (the same word or the same sentence.)

Nassâigan. Dressing comb; pl. -*an*

Nassâkonamawa, (*nin*). I open it to him or for him, I open s. th. belonging to him; p. *ness..wad.*

Nassâkonan, (*nin*). I open it; p. *nes..ang.*

Nassâkoshka, or -*magad.* It opens, it bursts open; p. *nes..kag*, or -*magak.*

Nassâkosse, or-*magad.* It opens, it is thrown open; p. *nes..seg*, or -*magak.*

Nassanâm, (*nin*). I breathe forth, I breathe out; p. *nes..mod.*

Nassatênigan. Trigger, (which when pulled, looses the cock of the gun;) pl.-*an.*

Nassaténige, (*nin*). I pull the trigger; p. *ness..ged.*

Nassawabide, (*nin*). I have forked teeth; p. *naia..ded.*

Nassawabideigan. Fork; pl.-*an.*

Nassawaii, adv. In the middle, in the midst.
Nassâwaiiwan. S. *Nissawaiiwan*.
Nassawâogan. A pointed Indian lodge; pl.-*an*.
Nassawange, (*nin*). I make a pointed lodge, or, I live in a pointed lodge; p. *ness..ged*.
Nassawidinigan. The place between the shoulders or the shoulderblades.
Nassawigamig, adv. Between two lodges or houses.
Nassidiêan, (*nin*). I stave it, I break it open, (a barrel, a box, etc.); p. *nes..ang*.
Nassidiêshka, or *-magad*. It opens, it breaks open, (a barrel, etc.); p. *nes..kag*, or *-magak*.
Nassidiêssin makak The barrel opens, falls into pieces; p. *nes..sing*.
Nâtamawa, (*nin*). I defend him; p. *naiâ..wad*.
Natchinamanessi. A kind of red birds; pl.-*wag*.
Nâw, *nâwa*, *nawi*, in compositions, signifies *in the middle*, *in the midst of*... (Examples in some of the following words.)
Nawaam, (*nin*). I sink in the snow, or in the sand, or in a marsh or swamp, walking on it; p. *naiwaang*.
Nâwâbik, adv. In the midst of an object of metal.
Nâwadad. It does not keep or contain much, (a vessel;) p. *naiâwadak*.
Nawâdide, or *-magad*. It catches fire, it begins to burn; p. *new..dég*, or *-magak*.
Nawadina, (*nin*). I catch him with my hand, I take hold of him with haste; p. *néw..nad*.
Nawadina, (*nin*). I waste it; p. *naiâ..nad*.
Nawadinamawa, (*nin*). I catch it for him, I catch s. th. with my hand belonging to him or relating to him; p. *new..wad*.
Nâwadinamawa, (*nin*). I waste s. th. belonging or relating to him; p. *naiâ..wad*.
Nawâdinan, (*nin*). I catch it with my hand, I take hold of it hastily; p. *new..ang*.
Nawâdis, (*nin*). I catch fire, that is, my clothes catch fire, begin to burn; p. *new..sod*.
Nâwadisi akik. The kettle does not keep or contain much; p. *naiâ..sid*.
Nawadj, (*nin*). I am eating, before I start; p. *new..id*.
Nâwadjiwan, adv. In the midst of a rapid, (in a river.)
Nâwâgam, adv. In the middle of a lake, of a bay, of a river, etc.
Nawagikwen, (*nin*). I incline my head before me; p. *new..nid*.
Nâwaii, adv. In the middle, in the centre, between.
Nâwaiiwan. It is the middle, the centre; p. *naia..ang*.
Nâwakwa, adv. In the midst of a forest.
Nawakwe, or *-magad*, (pron. *naokwe*.) It is mid-day or noon; p. *naiawakweg*, or *-magak*. *Bwa nawakweg*, or, *tchi bwa nawakweg*, before noon, or in the forenoon.
Gi-ishwa-nawakweg, afternoon, or in the afternoon.

Nawakwe-wissin, (*nin*). I take my dinner, I dine; p. *naia.. id*.

Nawakwe-wissiniwin. Meal at noon, dinner.

Nawâp, (*nin*). I take provisions for a voyage; p. *newâpod*.

Nawâpon, (*nin*). I take it with me, to eat it on my voyage; p. *newâpod*.— *Wiâss nin nawapon*; I take meat along with me, to eat it on my voyage.

Nawapona, (*nin*). I give him provisions for his voyage; p. *new..nad*; imp. *nawapoj*.

Nawaponan, (*nin*). I take some obj. with me, to eat it on my voyage; p. *newapog*. (V. Conj.)—*Kokosh nin nawaponan*; I take pork with me, to eat it on my voyage.

Nawapwân. Provisions taken for a voyage; pl.-*an*.

Nawapwaniwaj. A scrip to put provisions in for a voyage; pl.-*an*.

Nâwashkig, adv. In the middle of a swamp.

Nâwashkodé, adv. In the middle of a meadow.

Nawatch, adv. More. *Nawatch nibiwa*, more. *Nawatch pangi*, less.

Nawatch nibiwa nind assa. I add him.

Namatch nibiwa nind aton. I add it.

Nawatch nin minwendan. I prefer it.

Nawatch nin minwenima. I prefer him, her, it.

Nawawigan. Chine, backbone, spine.

Nâweg, adv. In the middle of a blanket, of a piece of clothing; of any stuff.

Nawêkide, or -*magad*. It leans; p. *new..deg*, or -*magak*.

Nawêkiso mitig. The tree leans on one side; p. *dew..sod*.

Nawéta, (*nin*). I stoop; I bend or incline myself; p. *newetad*.

Nâwina, (*nin*). I cannot reach him, he is out of my reach; p. *naiawinad*.

Nâwinagos, (*nin*). I am scarcely visible yet, I am almost out of sight; p. *naia..sid*.

Nâwinagwad. It is scarcely visible yet; p. *naia..wak*.

Nâwinan, (*nin*). I cannot reach it, it is out of my reach; p. *naia..ang*.

Nâwinindj. Middle-finger; pl.-*in*.

Nâwishkote, adv. In the middle of a fire, or in the midst of fire.

Nawisigokwandib. Crown of the head.

Nâwissag, adv. In the middle of a board, in the midst of a floor.

Nâwitam, (*nin*). I am out of hearing, out of the reach of the human voice, I cannot hear anybody; p. *naiawitang*.

Nâwitawa, (*nin*). I cannot hear him, he is too far; p. *naia.. ag*.

Nâwitch, adv. Out on a lake, etc., distant from the shore; also, far in the inland, in the interior, in the back-woods.

Nazarêwinini. Nazarene, a man from Nazareth; pl. -*wag*.

Nebagog wiwakwân. **A** flat hat, that is a cap.

Nebagibagisid assema. Flat tobacco; (*nabagisi*, it is flat, *bag*, alluding to a leaf.)

Nebagindibe, (properly, *Nebagindibed.*) Flat-head Indians; pl.-*g*.

Nebanétagak. Stuff that it cloth-like on one side only, half-cloth.—S. *Nabanétagad.*

Nébod. Dead person, deceased; pl.-*jig*.

Nêbodjig nind ondji Lamessike. I say a Requiem mass.

Negaw. Fine sand on the beach of lakes and rivers.

Négigwétagawed bebejigoganji. A gray horse.

Négwâb, (*nin*). I look from under a cover; also, I look sidewards; p. *naiêgwâbid.*—The *freq.* of it is *Nin nenegwâb.*

Negwakwan, or *negwakwatchigan.* A piece of wood put in the incision of a maple-tree.

Negwâkwani-biwâbik. Hollow chisel to make incisions in maple-trees; pl.-*on.*

Nêgwama, (*nin*). I swallow some obj.; p. *naiê..ad.*

Nêgwandan, (*nin*). I swallow it down; p. *naiê..ang.*

Néiâb, adv. Again, back again, once more, anew.—In connection with a verb it corresponds to the syllable *re* in some English verbs; as: *Nin kitigadan*, I plant it; *neiâb nin kitigadan*, I replant it.—*Nind onijishiton*, I adorn it; *neiâb nind onijishiton*, I re-adorn it, etc.

Neiâshi. Point of land projecting into a sea or a lake, promontory, cape; pl.-*wan.*

Neiâshins. A little point of land projecting in a lake or river; pl.-*an.*

Neiâshiwan. There is a point of land, a cape; p. *neieiâshiwang.*

Neiênj, or *naiénj*, adj. Both.

Nejike-bimâdisid pagwadakamig. He that lives alone in a desert, an hermit.

Nenândawiiwed. He that gives medicines to the sick, physician, doctor; pl.-*jig.*

Nenâssawijijig, adv. Every second day.

Nênawinamawa, (*nin*). I divide it to him or for him, in two parts; p. *naien..wad.*

Nenawadjimowin. Murmur.

Nenawina, (*nin*). I divide some obj. in two; p. *naien..nad;* imp. *nenawij.*

Nênawinamadimin, (*nin*). We divide it amongst us; p. *naien..didjig.*

Nénawinan, (*nin*) or *nin nenawiton.* I divide it in two; p. *naie..ang.*

Nenawitagewin. Distribution.

Nênâwitawa, (*nin*). I divide it or distribute it for him or to him; p. *naie..wad.*

Nênâwitawag, (*nin*). I divide or distribute it amongst them; p. *naien..wad.*

Nenegwâb, (*nin*), freq. I look aside; p. *naie..bid.*

Nêngag bimide. Melted-grease, that is, hogslard; (F. saindoux.)

Nengoteshkanid. He that has only one horn, a unicorn; pl. -*jig.*

Nenibikiwed. He that scolds, scolder; pl.-*jig.*

Néníj, num. Two every time; two each or to each.

Nenijing, num. Twice every time; twice each or to each.

Nenijogwan, or *nenijogijig.* Every second day.

Nenijtana, num. Twenty every time; twenty each or to each.

Nenijwâk, num. Two hundred every time; two hundred each or to each.

Neningo. This word always occurs prefixed to a substantive signifying MEASURE, (of time or other things;) and it means, one each, or one to each, or once in such a time; as: *Neningo makak pakwêjiganan o gigishpinanawan;* they bought a barrel of flour each. *Neningo dibaigan manitowegin o gi-minan;* he gave a yard of cloth to each. *Neningo gisiss bi-ija oma;* he comes here once a month.

Neningotwassimidana, num. Sixty every time; sixty each or to each.

Neningotwâsswâk, num. Six hundred every time; six hundred each or to each.

Neningotwâsswi, num. Six every time; six each or to each.

Nénisswi, num. Three every time; three each or to each.

Neniwâk, num. Four hundred every time; four hundred each or to each.

Neniwin, num. Four every time; four each or to each.

Nes, as end-syllable in some neuter verbs, marks *disease, pain, soreness;* as: *Nind oshkinjigones,* I have sore eyes. *Nind onamanines,* I have the herpes or erysipelas.

Neshangabiginan, (*nin*). I unbend it, I loosen it, I slacken it; (a string or cord;) p. *naies ..ang.*

Neshangadis, (*nin*). I am delicate, weak, (especially in walking;) p. *naie..sid.*

Neshangiginan, (*nin*). I slacken it, loosen it, (it is too much spread out;) p. *naié..ang.*

Neshangisse, or *-magad.* It is weak; it is loose; p. *naie.. seg,* or*-magak.*

Neshibâpinodang. He that mocks, mocker, ridiculer; pl.-*ig.*

Néshibâpinodawad awiia. He that mocks somebody, mocker or ridiculer of some person; pl.-*jig.*

Nésse, (*nin*). I breathe, I take respiration; p. *naiéssed.*

Nessediie, (*nin*). S. *Bogid.*

Nessegwâbideon. Toothpick or toothpicker; pin; pl.-*an.*

Néssênodawa, (*nin*). I breathe into him or upon him; p. *naies..wad.*

Nésséwin. Breath, respiration.

Nessobagak. A plant that has three leaves, clover.

Nesso-bejigod Kijé-Manito. God who is three in one, the Blessed Trinity.

Netâ-agonwetang. He that uses to gainsay, gainsayer, contradictor; also, incredulous person; disobedient person; pl.-*ig.*

Netâ-anokid. He that uses to

work, industrious person; pl. *-jig.*

Newâdjindim, adv. In the water, (not on the bottom, but floating under the surface of the water.) (C. entre deux eaux.)

Néwe. Hisser, a kind of serpent; pl.*-g.*

Néwishka, or*-magad.* It lowers, falls; p. *naiew..kag,* or *-magak.*

Ni or *ani.* This particle gives to a verb the accessory signification of departure, of going on; as: *Gi-ni-giwewag,* they returned home. *Gi ni-madja,* he is gone away.

Niâ! interj. exclamation used only by females, signifying, aha! ha! alas! ah!

Nib, (*nin*). I die, I perish, I expire, I depart this life; p. *nébod.*

Nibâ, (*nin*). I sleep, I am asleep; also, I sleep elsewhere, (not at home;) (F. je découche;) p. *nebad.*

Nibaam, (*nin*). I walk at night, in the night time; p. *nâbaang.* —*Nin bi-nibaam,* I arrive in the night.

Nibâ-anamiegijigad. Christmas.

Nibâb, (*nin*). S. *Nibénab.*

Nibadâkigan, (*nin*). My breast is uncovered indecently; p. *neb..ang.*

Nibâdis, (*nin*). I am gluttonous; intemperant (in eating;) voracious; p. *néb..sid.*

Nibâdisiwin. Gluttony, voracity, intemperance.

Nibâdjishin, (*nin*). I am lying in an indecent posture; p. *neb..ing.*

Nibâga, or*-magad.* The sap of the maple-trees is running in the night-time; p. *nebagag,* or*-magak.*

Nibâgan. Bed; pl.*-an.*

Nibâganak, or *nibâganâtig.* Bedstead; pl.*-on.*

Nibâganigin. Bedsheet; pl.*-on.*

Nibâgwe, (*nin*). I thirst, I am thirsty, I am dry; p. *neb..wed.*

Nibâgwewin. Thirst.

Nibâshka, (*nin*). I walk about in the night, I rove in the night, I am a night-rover; p. *neb..kad.*

Nibâtibik, adv. At night, in the night, in the time of sleep, night-time.

Nibaw, (*nin*). I stand, I am standing up; p. *nâbawid.*

Nibawia, *nin*). I make him stand up, I put up some obj. and make it stand; p. *nab..ad.*

Nibâwin. Sleeping, sleep.

Nibâwissin, (*nin*). I eat in the night; p. *neb..id.*

Nibâwissiniwin. Night-meal, eating in the night to keep off sleep; (F. réveillon.)

Nibawiton, (*nin*). I put it up to stand, I make it stand; p. *nab..tod.*

Nibawiwin, Standing, the standing position. — *Anamié-nibawiwin,* Christian marriage ceremony performed by a priest, Sacrament of matrimony. (It is called, *Anamie nibawiwin,* because the parties come forth and stand before the priest who performs the Rites of Matrimony.) It is called too, *anamihe widigendihiwewin*, or, *witigendiwin*.

Nibea, (*nin*). I make him sleep, I lull him to sleep, (a child ;) p. *nebead*.

Nibêb, (*nin*). I sit up at night watching a corpse ; p. *nebebid*.

Nibébitam, (*nin*). I watch in the night, I sit up at night ; p. *neb..tang*.

Nibébitân, (*nin*). I watch it in the night, (a corpse ;) p. *neb..ang*.

Nibébitawa, (*nin*). I watch him in the night, (a sick person, etc.) ; p. *neb..wad*.

Nibêgom, (*nin*). I wait for game in the night on the water in a canoe ; p. *nebegomod*.

Nibêgomowin. Waiting for game in the night on the water.

Nibénab, (*nin*). I sit up at night, I don't go to bed ; p. *neb..bid*.

Nibewâbo. Laudanum, opium.

Nibêwin. Camp, encampment, place where travelers sleep in the woods ; place or apartment where people sleep, dormitory, sleeping-room ; pl.-*an*.

Nibi. Water.

Nibid. My tooth ; pl. *nibidan*. —*Nibid nind âkosin*, I have toothache.

Nibidash. My bad rotten tooth ; pl.-*an*.

Nibide, in compositions, alludes to a *row,line* or *range*. (Examples in some of the following words.)

Nibide-aiâmin, (*nin*). We are all.in a row ; pl. *nabide-aiadjig*

Nibidbimin, (*nin*). We are sitting in a row or line ; p. *nab..djig*.

Nibidengwâmin, (*nin*). We are sleeping or lying in a row ; p. *nab..djig*.

Nibika, or-*magad*. There is water ; p. *nebikag*, or-*magak*.

Nibikadan, (*nin*). I put some water in, (in wine or some other liquid ;) p. *neb..ang*.

Nibikana, (*nin*). I suck him, (sick person, according to the Indian fashion ;) (C. je le suce ;) p. *neb..ad ;* imp. *nibikaj*.

Nibikang, or *nibing*. In the water.

Nibiki, (*nin*). I suck, (doctoring a sick person after the Indian fashion ;) p. *nebikid*.

Nibikiwin. Sucking, (a kind of Indian doctoring.)

Nibikiwinini. Sucker, (a man that sucks a sick person after the Indian fashion ;) pl.-*wog*.

Nibin. Summer. — *Nibing*, in summer. *Nibinong*, last summer. *Panimanibing*, next summer.

Nibin. It is summer ; p. *nabing*.

Nibina, adv. *Ot*. S. *Nibiwa*.

Nibinâd, (*nin*). I fetch water ; p. *nebinadid*.

Nibinakamiga, or-*magad*. It is summer, the summer-season ; p. *nab...gag*, or-*magak*.

Nibine, in compositions, alludes to a *line* or *row*. It has the same signification as *Nibide*. (Examples in some of the following words.)

Nibinébimin, (*nin*). We are sitting in a straight line or row ; p. *nab..djig*.

Nibinégabawimin, (*nin*). We are standing in a line, one after another ; p. *nab..djig*.

Nibinéossemin, (*nin*). We are walking in a line, one after another; p. *nab..djig.*

Nibinish, (*nin*). I spend or pass the summer in a certain place; I summer; p. *nab..id.—Wassa nin wi-nibinish;* I intend to spend the summer far away.

Nibinishimagad. It passes the summer, or remains all summer, in a certain place; p. *nab..gak.*

Nibinishiwin. The spending of the summer-season in a certain place, the summering.

Nibiniwaiân. Summer-skin or summer-fur of an animal; pl. *-ag.*

Nibiteshkan, (*nin*). I go from one place to another, I walk the whole length of a town, etc.; p. *nab..ang.—O nibiteshkanan wâkkaiganan;* he goes from house to house.

Nibiwa, adv. and adj. Much; many, plenty of...

Nibiwagisimin, (*nin*). We are many; p. *nab..djig.*

Nibiwakamiga, or-*magad.* The ground is wet; p. *neb..gak*, or-*magak.*

Nibiwan. It is wet, damp; p. *nebiwang.*

Nibiwashka, or-*magad.* The herb is wet; p. *neb..kag*, or-*magak.*

Nibiwis, (*nin*). I am wet; p. *neb..sid.*

Nibiwiside, (*nin*). My feet are wet; p. *neb..ded.*

Niboma, (*nin*). I wish he would die, expressing it in words; also, I condemn him to death; p. *nebomad.*

Nibômagad. It dies, it perishes; p. *neb..gak.—Nij nâbikwânan gi-nibomagadon;* two vessels perished.

Nibôndan, (*nin*). I condemn it, I wish its destruction; p. *neb ..ang.*

Nibôndimin, (*nin*). We wish destruction and death to one another; p. *nebondidjig.*

Nibongâdis, (*nin*). I am sad and afflicted; p. *neb..sid.*

Nibotâge, (*nin*). I die for somebody; p. *neb..ged.*

Nibôtawa, (*nin*). I die for him; p. *neb..wad.*

Nibow, (*nin*). I am sick of the palsy; (F. je suis paralytique;) p. *nebowid.*

Nibôwapine, (*nin*). S. *Nibow.*

Nibôwapinewin. Palsy.

Nibowenima, (*nin*). I wish him death in my thoughts, (without expressing it in words;) I condemn him to death, in my thoughts; p. *neb..mad.*

Nibôwigâde, (*nin*). I have a dead leg, by palsy; p. *neb.. ded.*

Nibôwima, (*nin*). I kill or destroy some obj.; p. *neb..mad.*

Nibôwin. Death, decease.

Nibôwindan, (*nin*). I kill it, destroy it, suppress it; p. *neb ..ang.*

Nibowini-pitchibowin. Deadly poison.

Nibwâka, (*nin*). I am wise, I am intelligent, reasonable, prudent, discreet, righteous, orderly, chaste, quiet; p. *nebwakad.*

Nibwâkâa, (*nin*). I make him wise, intelligent, prudent, etc.; p. *neb..ad.*

Nibwâkâdendam, (*nin*). I think

wisely, I have wise prudent thoughts; p. *neb..ang.*

Nibwakâdendamowin. Wise thinking, wise thought; pl.-*an.*

Nibwâkâwin. Wisdom, understanding, intelligence, prudence, good sense, intellect, reason.

Nibwâkâwinini. A wise, intelligent, prudent man; a righteous, honest man; pl.-*wog.*

Nibwâm. My thigh; pl.-*an.*

Nibwâshkissin. It withers, decays; p. *neb..ing.*

Nibwâtchiwe, (nin). I pay a visit or visits; p. *neb..wed.* S. *Mawadishiwe.*

Nibwâtchia, (nin). I visit him, I pay him a visit; p. *neb..ad.* S. *Mawadissa.*

Nibwéndam, (nin). I die of sorrow; p. *neb..ang.*

Nidj' or *nidji.* As I, like myself, my fellow–. *Nidj'ikwe,* a woman like myself. *Nidj'anokitagewinini,* my fellow-servant. *Nidji-kwiwisensag,* my fellow-boys.

Nidj' anishinâbe. My fellow-man, my neighbour; (F. mon prochain;) pl.-*g.*

Nidji, (a man or boy speaking to a man or boy.) My comrade, my friend, my equal.

Nidji-bimâdisi. My fellow-liver, my neighbour; pl.-*g.*

Nidjikiwé. My brother; my comrade; pl.-*iag.*—This word signifies, my brother, without regard to the age, whether older or younger than I am. (S. *Nissaie. Nishime.*) Only a male may say, *nidjikiwe,* my brother. A female would say, *nind awema.*

Nidjikiwesi. My friend, my comrade; pl.-*iag.* — Only a male speaking to a male or of a male, will say so. A female will say, *nindangwe.*

Nig, (nin). I am born, I come into the world; p. *nâgid.*

Nigân, adv. Ahead, before, in advance, in the forepart, beforehand.

Niganâ, (nin). I am foremost, (traveling in a canoe or boat;) p. *naganaod.*

Niganâdjim, (nin). I foretel, I prophesy or prophetize; (*nigân,* before; *nin dibâdjim,* I tell;) p. *nag..mod.*

Nigânab, (nin). I am sitting foremost, in a range or row; p. *nagânabid.*

Niganâdjimowikwe. Prophetess; pl.-*g.*

Naganâdjimowin. Foretelling, prediction, prophecy; pl.-*an.*

Niganâdjimowinini. Foreteller, prophet; pl.-*wog.*

Naganâkwaigan. Bowsprit; pl. -*an.*

Niganendâgos, (nin). I am considered a superior, I am a superior, the foremost, the first or one of the first, (in a good or bad sense;) p. *nag..sid.*

Nigânendagwad. It is the principal thing, the chief matter, it is essential, it is foremost, (in a good or bad sense;) p. *nag..wak.*

Niganendagwakamig, adv. Essentially, foremost, (considered foremost.)

Niganendân, (nin). I consider

it foremost, I think it is the principal thing, or one of the principal things, (in a good or bad sense;) p. *nag..ang.*

Nigânenimu, (*nin*). I think he is the first, or one of the first, the foremost, (in a good or bad sense;) p. *nag..mad.*

Nigâni, (*nin*). I walk foremost, I take the lead, I precede; p. *naganid.*

Nigania, (*nin*). I make him walk foremost, I make him a superior, I cause him to be the first or one of the first; p. *naganiad.*

Nigânibato, (*nin*). I run ahead, I run before another; p. *nag..tod.*

Niganinijâwa, (*nin*). I send him before me; p. *nag..wad*; imp. *niganinijâ.*

Niganis, (*nin*). I am foremost, I am the first, or one of the first, I am a superior, a chief; p. *nag..sid.*

Niganishka, (*nin*). I start first, I start before the others do; p. *nag..kad.*

Niganisikandamowin. Superiority, chieftainship, dignity or power of a superior or chief.

Niganisikandân, (*nin*). I have power over it, I am at the head of it, I exercise authority and jurisdiction over it; p. *nag..ang.*

Niganisikandawa, (*nin*). I am his superior, his chief, I have power or jurisdiction over him; p. *nag..wad.*

Nigânisim. One is superior, chief; p. *naganising.*

Nigânisim. Superior, chief; pl.-*ag.*—This word is always preceded by a possessive pronoun; as: *Nin niganisim*, my superior; *ki niganisim*, thy superior, etc.

Nigânisiwin. Precedence, superiority, chieftainship.

Nigâni - wikweiâbikissitchigan. The chief corner-stone; pl.-*an.*

Nigânosse, (*nin*) (from *nigân*, foremost; *nin bimosse*, I walk;) I walk or march foremost; p. *nag..sed.*

Niganossekwe. A woman that walks foremost, that takes the lead; pl.-*g.*

Niganossewinini. A man that walks or marches foremost at the head of a company; commander, warchief; pl.-*wog.*

Nigia, (*nin*). I give him birth, I bring him forth; p. *nâgiad.*

Nigiâwass, (*nin*). I am giving birth to a child; p. *nag..sod.*

Nigiâwassowin. Childbirth, delivery, labor.

Nigidji. A kind of fish; pl.-*iag.*

Nigig. Otter; pl.-*wog.*

Nigigons. Young otter; pl.-*ag.*

Nigigwaiân. Otter-skin; pl.-*ag.*

Nigigwakamigadin. There is hoar-frost on the *ground*; p. *neg..ding.*

Nigigwanakad, or *nigigwanakadin.* There is hoar-frost on the *trees*; p. *neg..kak*, or *neg..ding.*

Nigigwashkadin. There is hoar-frost on the *grass*, or on herbs and plants; p. *neg..ing.*

Nigigwêtagad. It is gray, of a gray color, (cloth, stuff;) p. *neg..gak.*

Nigigwetagawe bebejigoganji. The horse is gray.

Nigigwitagisi. It is of a gray color, (stuff); p. *neg..sid.*
Nigimagad. It is born, that is, it comes into existence ; p. *nag..gak.*
Nigin kitigan. The field produces fruit ; p. *naging.*
Nigitâg, (*nin*). He is born to me.—*Krist ki gi-nigitagowa ;* Christ is born unto you.
Nigitawa, (*nin*). I give birth to a child for him or to him ; p. *nag..wad.*—*Nancy o gi-nigitawan o wikigemaganan ogwissini,* (or *ogwissiniwan;*) Nancy has born a son to her husband.
Nijiton, (*nin*). I give it birth, I bring it forth; p. *nagitod.*—*Batadowin o nigiton nibowin ;* sin brings forth death. (L. peccatum generat mortem.)
Nigiwin. Birth. *Andj-nigiwin,* second birth, regeneration.
Nigiwini-gijigad. Birthday.
Nigoshka, or-*magad.* It is torn much; torn to pieces, (stuff, clothing, etc.;) p. *nag..kag,* or-*magak.*
Nigoshkân, (*nin*). I tear it to pieces; p. *nag..ang.*
Nigoshkawa, (*nin*). I tear it to pieces; p. *nag..wad.*
Niiabiden, (*nin*). I gnash and show the teeth ; p. *naiab..denid.*
Niiâss. My flesh.
Niiaw. My body ; myself.
Niiawee. My namesake. *Kiiawee,* thy namesake, *wiiaweeian,* his namesake.
Niinawe, (*nin*). I speak the language of the people with whom I live; p. *nainawed.*
Nij, num. Two.
Nijagaâi. My skin. *Kijâgaai,* thy skin. *Ojagaâian,* his skin.
Nijigan. My croup.—*Kijigan,* thy croup. *Ojigan,* his croup.
Nijiganigan. My croup bone. — This and the preceding word, have always a possessive pronoun before them, which forms one word with its noun.
Nijiké, adj. Alone.
Nijikéokam, (*nin*). I am alone in a canoe ; p. *nej..ang.*
Nijikêwab, (*nin*). I am alone, (in a room, in a house, in a lodge ;) p. *nej..bid.*
Nijikêwis; (*nin*). I am alone, (wherever ;) p. *nej..sid.*
Nijimin, (*nin*), num. We are two ; p. *najidjig.*
Nijing, num. Twice.
Nijinomagad. There are two things ; p. *naj..gak.*
Nijinon, num. There are two.
Nijishé. My uncle, my *mother's* brother ; pl.-*iag.*—*Kijishé,* thy uncle; *ojishéian,* his uncle.—S. *Nimishome.*
Nijo, num. Two, before substantives denoting MEASURE, of time or other things ; as : *Nijo dibaigan gi-ishkwa-nawakwe ;* two o'clock in the afternoon. *Nijo dibabishkodjigan sisibâkwad,* two pounds of sugar.
Nijo-anamiegijigad. A fortnight.
Nijobanênindj. Twice a handful.—*Nijobanénindj eta mandaminan nin gi-ashamig ;* he gave me only twice a handful of corn.
Nijôbidonon, (*nin*). I tie two together ; p. *nâj..dod.* — *Nin*

nijôbidonan onow mitigonsan ; I tie two of these sticks together.

Nijôbina, (*nin*). I catch two fishes in a net, (or in several nets ;) p. *najobinad.*—S. *Bina.*

Nijôbinag, (*nin*). I tie two together ; p. *naj..nad.*

Nijôbisomin, (*nin*). We are two tied together ; p. *naj..sodjig.*

Nijobônikan. Twice both hands full.

Nijodé. Twin ; pl.-*iag.*

Nijôde. Two families.—*Nijôde aiawog,* they are two families. *Nijôde dagwishinog,* two families arrive.

Nijôdewisimin, (*nin*). We are two families ; p. *naj..sidjig.*—*Nin nijodewisimin eta, minik oma aiaiâng ;* we are only two families, all of us here.

Nijodêike, (*nin*). I am delivered of twins ; p. *naj..ked.*

Nijodêshkani. It has two horns ; p. *naj..nid.*

Nijogâde, (*nin*). I have two legs ; p. *naj..ded.*

Nijogamig. Two lodges or houses.—*Kawin batainassinon omâ wigiwâman, nijogamig eta atewan ;* there are not many lodges (or houses) here, there are only two.

Nijogamigisimin, (*nin*). We are in two lodges (or houses ;) p. *naj..sidjig.*

Nijogijig. Two days, (but only *one* night.)

Nijogijigad. Tuesday, (two days after Sunday.) S. *Nijogwanagad.*

Nijogijigad. It is Tuesday ; p. *naj..gak.*

Nijogisisswagad, It is two months since, two months ago ; p. *naj..gak.* — For the rest, as : *Nissogisisswagad,* etc., S. *Gisisswagad.*

Nijogisisswagis, (*nin*). I am two months old ; p. *naj..sid.*

Nijogwan, two days, (and two nights.) S. *Nijogijig.*

Nijogwanagad. There are two days, (and two nights ;) p. *naj..gak.*—But when they regard only the days, they will say, *Nijogijigad,* there are two days, (but not yet two nights.) For that reason they call Tuesday, "*Nijogijigad,*" because on Tuesday there are two *days* after Sunday, but yet two *nights,* beginning from Monday morning, where the workdays of the week begin.

Nijogwanagis, (*nin*). I am two days old ; p. *naj..sid.*

Nijogwanénd, (*nin*). I am absent two days, (going on a voyage, etc.) ; p. *naj..did.*

Nijôkâmawa, (*nin*) or *nin nijokawa.* I help or assist him ; *naj..wad.*

Nijôkâmin, (*nin*). We are two in a canoe or boat ; p. *najokangig.*

Nijôkwew, (*nin*). I have two wives, I am a bigamist ; p. *najôkwewid.*

Nijominag. Two round globular objects. *Nijominag eta kid ashamin mishiminag ;* I give thee only two apples.

Nijônag. Two canoes, boats, etc. *Nin wâbandanan tchimânan nijonag ;* I see two canoes.

Nijonijigan. Two pieces, (of fish, pork, meat, etc.)

Nijonik. Two fathoms.
Nijonindj. Two fingers, that is, two inches.
Nijonindjin, (*nin*). I join both hands together; p. *naj..nid.*
Nijonje, (*nin*). I have two children; p. *najonjed.*
Nijôshimag, (*nin*). I lay two together in one place; p. *naj ..mad.—Nin nijoshimag abinodjiiag;* I lay two children in one bed.
Nijôshinimin, (*nin*). We lie two together in one place; p. *najoshidjig.*
Nijoshk. Two breadths of stuff or cloth; also, relating to two shoes, two pieces of stovepipe, etc.
Nigoshkad ow pâshkisigan. This is a gun with two barrels, a double-barreled gun; p. *naj.. kak.*
Nijoshkigwâdan, (*nin*). I sew two breadths of stuff or cloth together; p. *naj..dang.*
Nijoshkigwade, or-*magad.* It is sewed in two breadths, two breadths are sewed together; p. *naj..deg,* or-*magak.*
Nijoshkin. Two bags full.—*Opinig nin gi-gishpinanag nijoshkin;* I bought two bags of potatoes.
Nijosid. Two feet, (24 inches.)
Nijossag. Two barrels full of s. th., or two wooden boxes full.
Nijossitchigadewan. Two objects are put or laid together; p. *naj..deg.*
Nijossitonan, (*nin*). I lay or put two together; p. *naj..tod.*
Nijtana, num. Twenty.
Nijtanâk, num. Twenty hundred, two thousand.
Nijtanâkosimin, num. We ar two thousand in number; p. *naj..sidjig.*
Nijtanakwadon, num. There are twenty hundred, (two thousand.)
Nijtanawemin, (*nin*), num. We are twenty; p. *naj..djig.*
Nijtanawêwan, num. There are twenty.
Nijtanowêwan, num. There are twenty pair of...
Nijwâbiginan, (*nin*). I put two together, (threads, cords, strings;) p. *naj...ang.*
Nijwâbik. Two objects of metal, stone, glass.—They use this word also to signify, "two dollars." Sometimes they add to it the word *joniia,* silver; as: *Nijwâbik nin gi-dibaamag;* he paid me two dollars; or, *nijwâbik joniian nin gi-dibaamag.*
Nijwaiagad. It is double, it is in two manners, it is in two kinds or sorts, there are two kinds of it; p. *naj..gak.*
Nijwaiagisimin, (*nin*). We are of two kinds or classes; p. *naj..sidjig.*
Nijwâk, num. Two hundred.
Nijwâkosimin, (*nin*), num. We are two hundred; p. *naj..djig.*
Nijwakwadon, num. There are two hundred.
Nijwakwêwan, num. There are two hundred pair.—*Nijwakwewan makisinan, nijwakwewan gaie mandjikawanag;* two hundred pair moccasins, and two hundred pair mittens.
Nijwâkwoagan. Two spans, (as measurement.)
Nijwassimidana, num. Seventy

Nijwassimidanâk, num. Seventy hundred, seven thousand.
Nijwassimiganâkosimin, (*nin*), num. We are seven thousand in number; p. *naj..sidjig.*
Nijwâssimidanâkwadon, num. There are seven thousand.
Nijwâssimidanawemin, (*nin*), num. We are seventy; p. *naj..wedjig.*
Nijwâssimidanawêwan. There are seventy.
Nijwâssimidanawéwan, num. There are seventy pair of...
Nijwâsso, num. Seven, (before substantives denoting MEASURE, of time or any other thing.) S. *Nijo.*
Nijwâsswi, num. Seven.
Nijwâtchimin, (*nin*), num. We are seven; p. *najwâtchidjig.*
Nijwâtching, num. Seven times.
Nijwâtching midasswâk. Seven thousand.
Nijwâtchinon, num. There are seven; p. *najwatchingin.*
Nijwâtig. Two objects of wood, —*Nijwâtig missan pindigadon;* bring in two sticks, or two pieces of wood for fuel. *Nijwâtig gaie gijikag pindigaj;* bring in also two pieces of cedar.
Nijweg. Two objects of cloth or stuff, or two sheets of paper, tin, iron, etc.— *Nijweg môshweg, nijweg dash nibaganigi-non;* two handkerchiefs and two bedsheets.
Nijwêwân. Two pair of.... *Nijwêwan pijikiwog*, two pair of oxen; *nijwéwan mojwaganan*, two pair of scissors.
Nik. Arm. This word is always connected with a possessive pronoun; as; *Ninik*, my arm; *kinik*, thy arm; *onik*, his arm. *Kinikân*, thy arms, etc.
Nika. A kind of wild goose; (C. outarde;) pl. *nikag.*
Nikâbandam, (*nin*). I faint and have a vision in my fainting; p. *nek..ang.*
Nikâd. My leg; pl.-*an.*
Nikâdigan. My shinbone, the bone of my leg; *kikâdigan*, thy shinbone; *okâdigan*, his shinbone.
Nibagwindjin, (*nin*). S. *Nikibishin.*
Nikan. My bone; pl.-*an.*
Nikanab, (*nin*). I remain in a place over night, I don't start but the following day; p. *nek..bid.* — *Nikanabi na kishime?* Will your brother remain here over night? (Will he not start before to-morrow?)
Nikanend, (*nin*). I am absent for a night, I don't come back before to-morrow; p. *nek.. did.*
Nikâniss. My friend; my brother, (in friendship;) pl.-*ag.*
Nikéwaam, (*nin*). I pass round a point in a canoe, boat, etc.; p. *nek..ang.*
Nikibi, (*nin*). I am overflowed, submerged, under water; p. *nekibid.*
Nikibi, or-*magad.* It is overflowed, it is under water; p. *nekibig*, or-*magad.* (S. *Bajidebi.*)
Nikibishin, (*nin*). I disappear under the water; p. *nek..ing.*
Nikibiwin. Inundation, flood.
Nikim, (*nin*). I grumble like a dog; p. *nakimod.*

Nikimotawa, (*nin*). I grumble at him like a dog; p. *nak..wad.—Animosh nin nikimotâg;* the dog grumbles at me.
Nikinikesse, (*nin*). I put my whole arm in; p. *nek..sed.*
Nikiwigad. It is twilight; p. *nek..gak.*
Nikonâss. My blanket, (which I cover myself with in going somewhere.) *Kikonâss, okonass;* thy blanket, his blanket.
Nikwan, (pr. *nikon.*) My liver. —*Okwan*, (*okôn*,) his liver.
Nikwégan. My neck.—*Okwegan*, his neck.
Nim, (*nin*). I dance; p. *namid.*
Nimaa, (*nin*). I carry some obj. on s. th.; *namaad.*
Nimaan, (*nin*). I carry it on s. th.; (or a bird carrying s. th. in his bill or beak;) p. *namaang.*
Nimaigan. Ornament of a snowshoe; pl.-*an.*
Nimaige bineshi. The bird carries s. th. in his beak; p. *nâmaiged.*
Nimâkonigan. Hand-barrow to carry s. th. on it; pl.-*an.*
Nimakonige, (*nin*). I am carrying on a hand-barrow, or on a pole or stick; p. *nam..ged.*
Nimâkona, (*nin*). I carry some obj., (with some other person,) on a hand-barrow, pole, or stick; p. *nam..ad.*
Nimâkonan, (*nin*). I carry it, (with some other person,) on a hand-barrow, on a pole or stick; p. *nam..ang.*
Nimâkwaan, (*nin*). I put it to the end of a stick; p. *nam..ang.*
Nimâma. My eyebrow; pl. *nimâmag.— Omâman*, his eyebrow, or, his eyebrows.
Nimama, (*nin*). I carry some obj. in my mouth; p. *nam..ad.*
Nimandan, (*nin*). I carry it in my mouth; p. *nam..ang.*
Nimandjige, (*nin*). I carry s. th. in my mouth; p. *nam..ged.*
Nimâshkaigan. Feathers, as an ornament of the head, plume of feathers; also, a bayonet; pl.-*ag.*
Nimâshkaige, (*nin*). I have a plume of feathers on my head; p. *nam..ged.*
Nimia, (*nin*). I make him dance, I cause him to dance; p. *namiad.*
Nimibâgan. Water-pot, water-pail, bucket; pl.-*an.*
Nimidana, num. Forty.
Nimidanâk, num. Forty hundred, four thousand.
Nimidanakosimin, (*nin*), num. We are four thousand in number, or forty hundred; p. *nem..sidjig.*
Niminâgan. Place of crossing over a bay, a lake, etc., traverse; pl.-*an.*
Niminam, (*nin*). I cross over a bay, lake, river, etc., in a canoe or boat; p. *neminang.*
Niminawâ, (*nin*). I put out into the lake or sea; (F. je gagne au large;) p. *nem..od.*
Niminawaam, (*nin*). S. *Niminawâ.*
Niminawekinigade, or-*magad.* There is a wharf made; p. *nem..deg*, or-*magak.*
Niminawekinigan, Wharf, (an

object stretching out in the lake;) pl.-*an*.

Niminawekiniganike, (*nin*). I am building a wharf; p. *nem ..ked.*

Niminawenan, (*nin*). I launch it in the water gently; p. *nem ..ang.*

Niminaweshka, (*nin*). I push my canoe or boat from the shore, I go out into the lake; p. *nem..ad.*

Niminaweshka, or-*magad tchimân*. The canoe goes out into the lake; p. *nem..kag*, or-*magak*.

Niminawewebinan, (*nin*). I push it into the water; p. *nem..ang.*

Nimishk, (*nin*). I like too much dancing; p. *nam..kid.*

Nimishkiwin. Habit of dancing.

Nimishôme. My uncle, my FATHER's brother; also, my step-father; pl.-*iag*.—S. *Nijishe*.

Nimishômiss. My grand-father; pl.-*ag*.—*Kimishomiss*, *omishomissan*; thy grand-father, his grand-father.

Nimiskama, (*nin*). I insult him, by certain signs with the hand; (great insult among the Indians.) (C. je lui pousse des nasardes;) p. *nem..mad.*

Nimiskandan, (*nin*). I insult it, by certain signs with the hand; p. *nem..ang.*

Nimiskandimin, (*nin*). We insult each other, by certain signs with the hand; p. *nem ..didjig.*

Nimiskandjige, (*nin*). I insult, by signs with the hand; p. *nem..ged.*

Nimissab, (*nin*). I squat, I sit squat, I sit cowering; p. *nam ..bid.*

Nimissad. My belly; *kimissad*, thy belly.

Nimisse. My sister, (older than I;) pl.-*iag*.

Nimitamaam, (*nin*). I paddle in the foremost part of the canoe; p. *nem..ang.*

Nimitawa, (*nin*). I dance for him, to make him pleasure; p. *nem..wad.*

Nimiwin. Dancing, the act of dancing.

Nin, pron. I, me, my, mine; we, us, our.

Ninagask. My palate. *Onagaskon*, his palate.

Ninamabikad. It is weak, (metal;) p. *nan..kak.*

Ninamabikisi. It is weak, (metal); p. *nan..sid.*—*Ninamabikisi kid akik;* thy kettle is weak.

Ninamad. It is weak, frail; p. *nanamak*. Freq. *Naninamad*.

Ninamadin. The ice is weak; p. *nan..ing.*

Ninamadis, (*nin*). I am weak, I am unable to walk or to work; p. *nan..sid.*

Ninamakwad. It is weak, (wood); p. *nan..wak.*

Ninamakosi. It is weak, (wood); p. *nan..sid.*

Ninamendan, (*nin*). I think it is weak; p. *nan..ang.*

Ninamenima, (*nin*). I think he is weak; p. *nan..mad.*

Ninamis, (*nin*). I am weak; p. *nanâmisid*. Freq. *nin naninamis*.

Ninamissagad. It is weak (wood,); p. *nan..gak.*

Ninamissagisi nabagissag. The

board or plank is weak; p. *nan..sid.*

Ninân. The calf of my leg; pl. *ninânag.*—*Kinân, onânan.*

Ninanagâkisid. The sole of my foot; pl.-*an.* *Kinanagâkisid, onanagâkisid.*

Ninasid. The fleshy part of my leg.—*Kinâsid, onâsid.*

Ninawind, pron. We, us, ours.

Ninbimébigwadai. My side, my flank; pl.-*ag.*— *Obimébigwadaian,* his flank.

Nind, pron. S. *Nin.*

Nindâa, (*nin*). I send him s. th.; p. *nendaad.*

Nindäi. My dog; pl.-*ag.*

Nindaiwe, (*nin*) or, *nin nindaige.* I send s. th. to some person; p. *nen..wed.*

Nindaiwe-masinaigan. Paper sent to somebody, that is, a letter.

Nindaiwen, (*nin*). I send it; p. *nen..wed.*

Nindaiwenan, (*nin*). I send some obj. to some person; p. *nen..wed.* (V. Conj.)

Nindâmikan. My jaw.—*Odâmikan,* his jaw.

Nindamikanabid. My grinder, (large tooth;) *Kidamikanabid, odamikanabid;* thy, his grinder.—S. *Gitabid.*

Nindâmikigan. My jawbone.—*Odamikigan,* his jawbone.

Nindâmikigegan. S. *Nindâmikigan.*

Nindân. My daughter. This word is not used in the first and second person, but only in the third, *odanan,* his daughter, (grown up.) S. *Nindâniss.*

Nindângoshe. My cousin; pl.-*iag.*—Only a *female* speaking to her he-cousin, or of her, will use this expression. A *male* will say: *Ninimoshe,* or, *nitâwiss;* which see.

Nindângwe. My sister-in-law; my friend, my companion.—Only a *female* will say so, speaking to a female or of a female. A *male* will say: *Ninim,* my sister-in-law; *Nidji,* or *nidjikiwesi,* my friend, my comrade.

Nind ânike nimishomiss. My great grand-father; (F. mon bisaïeul.)

Nind anike nokomiss. My great grand-mother; (F. ma bisaïeule.)

Nindâniss. My daughter; pl.-*ag.* This word, in the first and second person, is used to express both a small and an adult daughter. But in the third person, *odanissan,* it signifies only a small young daughter.—S. *Nindân.*

Nindânissikâwin. My god-daughter; (F. ma filleule;) also, my adopted daughter; pl.-*ag.*—*Kidânissikâwin,* thy god-daughter; *odânissikâwinan,* his god-daughter.

Nindatissiwag. My nerve, my sinew, with the flesh on it; pl.-*og.* *Odatissiwagon,* his nerve.

Nindawâtch, nindawa, enâbigis, adv. well, well then, rather; and so.—*Nindawâtch ijada;* well then, let us go. *Nind anijitam nindawâtch;* I give up rather.

Nindé. My heart, *kidé, odé;* thy heart, his heart.

Nindengwai. My face; *kidengwai,* thy face; *odengwai,* his face.

Nindenigom. The side of my nose; pl.-*ag. Kidenigom. Odenigoman.*

Nindibogan. Ot. The bone of my head, my skull.

Nindigo, adv. As it were, it seems like.

Nind ijinikasowin nind aton. I sign, I subscribe my name.

Nindindawa. The father or the mother of my son-in-law or daughter-in-law; pl.-*g.*

Nindinigan. My shoulder-blade; pl.-*ag.*— *Kidinigan. Odiniganan.*

Nindinimangan. My shoulder; pl.-*an.*— *Kidinimangan. Odinimangan.*

Nindiss. My navel; *kidiss,* thy navel; *odiss,* his navel.

Nindj. Hand. This word is never used so, but always connected with a possessive pronoun; as: *Ninindj,* my hand; *kinindj,* thy hand; *onindj,* his hand.

Nindjanj. My nose; *kidjanj,* thy nose; *odjanj,* his nose.

Nindjitad. My sinew; pl.-*an.*; *kidjitad,* thy sinew; *odjitad,* his sinew.

Nindonâgan. Ontonagan, Lake Superior. The proper meaning of this word is, " My dish." — *Nindonagâning,* at Ontonagan, from or to Ontonagan.—An Indian tradition says, that a squaw once came to the river, now called " Ontonagan," to fetch water with an Indian earthen dish; but unfortunately the dish escaped from her hand and went to the bottom of the river; whereupon the poor squaw began to lament: *Niâ nind onâgan, nind onâgan!* Ah. my dish, my dish!—And the river was ever since called after this exclamation.

Ninga. My mother. *Kiga, ogin.*

Ninga, or-*magad.* It melts, or, it is melted; p. *nengag,* or-*magak.*

Ningabâwadon, (*nin*). I dilute it, I make it thin, (liquid); p. *nen..dod.*

Ningabâwana, (*nin*). I dilute some obj.; p. *nen..nad;* imp. *ningabawaj.*

Ningabian. West, occident.

Ningabianakwad. Cloud coming from the west.

Ningabianibissa. The rain comes from the west; p. *nen..sag.*

Ningabiani-nodin. Westwind.

*Ningabikide,*or-*magad.* It melts, or, it is melted, (only metal;) p. *nen..deg,* or-*magad.*

Ningabikisan, (*nin*). I melt it, or smelt it, (only metal); p. *nen..ang.*

Ningabikisigan. Smelting-furnace; pl.-*an.*

Ningabikiso. It melts, (metal;) p. *nen..sod.*

Ningabikiswa, (*nin*). I melt it, or smelt it, (only metal;) p. *nen..wad;* imp. *ningabikiswi.*

Ningakamate aki. The earth or ground thaws; p. *nen..teg.*

Ningakamigishka, or-*magad.* The ground thaws in spring; p. *nen..kag,* or-*magak.*

Ninganema, (*nin*). I let melt in

my mouth some obj., (*mikwam*, ice;) p. *nen..mad.*

Ninganendan, (*nin*). I let it melt in my mouth, (*sisibâkwad*, sugar, etc.); p. *nen..ang.*

Ningâpon, (*nin*). I am gathering and eating berries; p. *nen..nod.*

Ningâponag, (*nin*). I am gathering them, (berries; *miskwiminag*, etc.)

Ningâponan, (*nin*). I am gathering them, (berries; *minan*, *odéiminân*, etc.)

Ningashi. *Ot.* My mother.

Ningashkobissige, (*nin*). I melt snow to have water; p. *nen..ged.*

Ningâssimonon. Sail; pl.-*an.*

Ningâssimononak. Mast; pl.-*og.*

Ningâssimononâtig. Mast; pl.-*on.*

Ningâssimononeiâb. Sail-rope, a rope or cord to hoist the sail; pl.-*in.*

Ningâssimononigin. Sail cloth, canvass.

Ninge! voc. Mother!

Ningé! or *n'ge!* (interjection used only by females,) ha! aha!

Ningide, or-*magad*. It melts; p. *nengideg*, or-*magak.*

Ningidig. My knee; pl.-*ag.*—*Ogidigwan*, his knee, or his knees.

Ningikide, or-*magad*. It thaws; (F. il *dégèle*;) p. *nen..deg*, or-*magak.*

Ningikosan, (*nin*). I melt it; p. *nen..ang.*

Ningikosigan. Melting-pot made of clay, crucible; smelting-furnace; pl.-*an.*

Ningigosige, (*nin*). I am smelting, (metal, ore, etc.); p. *nen..ged.*

Ningikosigêwigamig. Smelting-house, foundry, casting-house; pl.-*an.*

Niagikosigewinini. Smelter, founder; pl.-*wag.*

Ningikoso. It melts; p. *nen.sod.*

Ningikoswa, (*nin*). I am melting or smelting some obj; p. *nen..wad*; imp. *ningikoswi.*

Ningim, adv. Quickly, immediately.

Ningiskode, or-*magad*. It is thawing, it is thaw-weather; p. *nen..deg*, or-*magak.*

Ningiskos, (*nin*). The thaw-weather comes during my voyage, before I reach home; p. *nen..sod.*

Ningiso gon. The snow is melting; p. *nengisod.*

Ningitawamo mikana. See the *freq.* verb of it, which is more frequently used: *Naningitawamo.*

Ningitâwitigweia sibi. The river divides or splits in two or more branches; p. *nen..iag.*

Ningitawitigweiâg. Place where a river divides.

Ningô! interj. of females, ah! ha! aha!

Ningo, num. One, (before substantives denoting MEASURE, of time or other things.) — *Ningo dibaigan*, one hour, one mile, etc. *Ningo dibâbishkodjigan*, one pound.

Ningo-anamiegijigad. A week.

Ningobimogigin. A plant is covered over or choked by other plants or herbs; p. *nen..ging.*

Ningobiminik. One cubit.

Ningogisisswagad. It is a month since ; p. *nen..gak*
Ningogisisswagis, (*nin*). I am a month old ; p. *nen..sid.*
Ningo-nâwakwé. A forenoon, half a day.
Ningo-passangwâbiwin. One moment, the twinkling of an eye.
Ningot, adv. Something ; one.—*Kawin ningot,* nothing.
Ningot-abwewin. A panful.
Ningotano, adv. Something.
Ningotâwassidog, adv. Happy.
Ningotchi, adv. Somewhere.—*Kawin ningotchi,* nowhere.
Ningotchi bakân, adv. Elsewhere.
Ningot-emikwân. A spoonful.
Ningoteshkani. It has only one horn, it is one-horned ; p. *nengoteshkanid,* unicorn.
Ningoting, adv. Once, at one time.
Ningotobanénindj. A handful.
Ningotobônikan. Both hands full ; (F. une jointée.)
Ningotôde. One family, one household.
Ningotodon. A mouthful ; also, one word.
Ningotogamig. One house ; also, all the inhabitants of a house ; (F. une maisonnée.)
Ningotogwane, (*nin*) (pron. *nin ningotogone ;*) I fast one day ; p. *nen..ned.*
Ningotonâgan. A dishful.
Ningotonendjigan. A mouthful ; (F. une bouchée.)
Ningotonjigan. A piece, (cut off from s. th.), a piece of meat, of fish, etc.
Ningotonik. A fathom.
Ningotonindj. One inch.
Ningotonjân. All the children of a family.
Ningotônsibide. A skein or hank; also, a sheaf of wheat, etc.
Ningotopwâgan. A pipe full ; also, the period of time in which a pipe of tobacco is commonly smoked.
Ningotôshkin. A bag full of...
Ningotosid. One foot, (twelve inches.)
Ningotossag. A barrel full of...
Ningotowan. A sack full of...
Ningotwâk, num. A hundred.
Ningotwâk dassing. A hundred times ; hundredfold.
Ningotwâssimidana, num. Sixty.
Ningotwâssimidanak, num. Sixty hundred, six thousand.
Ningotwâsso. Six, (before substantives denoting MEASURE, of time or of other things.)
Ningotwassobanénindj.
Ningotwasswi, num. Six.
Ningotwatchimin, (*nin*) num. We are six; p. *nen..djig.*
Ningotwâtching, num. Six times.
Ningotwâtching midasswâk. Six thousand.
Ningotwewanagisiwin. A pair, a couple, a set.
Ningwaabwe, (*nin*). I bake s. th. burying it in hot ashes ; p. *nen..wed.*
Ningwaabwen, (*nin*). I bake it in hot ashes ; p. *nen..wed.*
Ningwaabwenan, (*nin*). I bake some obj. in hot ashes ; p. *nen..wed.* (V. Conj.)
Ningwaakadan, (*nin*). S. *Ningwaan.*
Ningwaakan. Place where s. th. is buried ; pl.-*an.*

Ningaakana, (*nin*). S. *Ningwâwa.*

Ningwaan, (*nin*). I bury it; p. *nengwaang.*

Ningwakwad. It is very cloudy, (the sky is buried in clouds;) p. *nen..wak.*

Ningwanapakwâdân, (*nin*) (pr. *nin ningonapakwadan.*) I cover it with bark, (a lodge;) p. *nen..ang.*

Ningwanapakwe, (*nin*). I am covering with bark, (a lodge;) p. *nen..wed.*

Ningwaniss, (*nin*). I fetch venison or fish; p. *nen..sod.*

Ningwano, (*nin*). I am covered with snow; p. *nen..nod.*

Ningwano, or-*magad.* It is covered with snow; p. *nen..nog,* or-*magak,*

Ningwatchaân, (*nin*). I hoe or hill it; p. *nen..ang.*

Ningwatchaige, (*nin*). I hoe, I hill; p. *nen..ged.*

Ningwatchâwa, (*nin*). I hoe or hill some obj.; p. *nen..wad;* imp. *ningwatchâ.*

Ningwatchawag opinig, (*nin*). I hoe or hill potatoes.

Ningwawa, (*nin*). I bury him. (a person or any other obj.); p. *nengwawad;* imp. *ningwa.*

Ningwigan. Wing; pl.-*an.*

Ningwiss, or *ningwississ.* My son; pl.-*ag,* or *ningosis.*

Ningwissikâwin. My godson; (F. mon filleul;) also, my adopted son; pl.-*ag.*—*Kigwissikawin,* thy godson; *ogwissikawinan,* his godson, etc.

Ninidjâniss. My child; pl.-*ag.*

Ninidjânissikawin. My godchild; also, my adopted child; pl.-*ag.*—*Kinidjânissikawin,* thy godchild; *Onidjanissikawinan,* his godchild; etc.

Ninigiigog. My parents, my father and mother.

Ninik. My arm; pl.-*an. Kinik, onik;* thy arm, his arm.

Ninikinassabi, (*nin*). I visit my net, (to see whether any fishes are caught in it;) p. *nen..bid.*

Ninikwai. The skin of my scull.

Ninim. My brother-in-law, (a *female* speaking;) my sister-in-law, (a *male* speaking;) pl. *ninimog.*— *Kinim, winimon,* etc.

Ninimoshé. My cousin, (he-cousin or she-cousin.) *Kinimoshé, winimoshéian.*

Ninindib. My brain. *Kinindib, winindib;* thy, his brain.

Ninindj. My hand; pl.-*in.*— *Kinindj, onindj;* thy hand, his hand.

Niningadj, (*nin*). I am very cold, I tremble with cold, I shiver; p. *nen..id.*

Niningadjiwin. Shivering with cold.

Niningakamigishka aki. The earth quakes, there is an earthquake; p. *nen..kag.*

Niningapine, (*nin*). I have the shaking fever; p. *nen..ned.*

Niningapinewin. Shaking fever.

Niningassin, or *niningana shkassin.* It is shaken by the wind; p. *nen..ing.*

Niningibinig, (*nin*). I tremble, I shake; p. *nen..god.*

Niningidee, (*nin*). I have pain in my heart, my heart trembles, shakes; p. *nen..ed.*

Niningim, adv. S. *Naningim.*

Nininginike, (*nin*). My arm shakes; p. *nen..ked.*

Nininginindj, (*nin*). My hand shakes; p. *nen..id.*

Niningisegis, (*nin*). I tremble with fear; p. *nen..sid.*

Niningishka, (*nin*). I shake, I tremble; p. *nen..kad.*

Niningishka, or-*magad.* It shakes, it quakes; p. *nen..kag*, or-*magak.*

Niningishkâwapine, (*nin*). S. *Niningapine.*

Niningishkawapinewin. S. *Niningapinewin.*

Niningisse, or-*magad.* It is weak, it shakes; p. *nen..seg*, or-*magak.*

Niningwan. My son-in-law; pl.-*ag.*—*Oningwanan*, his son-in-law, or his sons-in-law.

Niningwaniss. My nephew; pl.-*ag.* — *Oningwanissan*, his nephew, or his nephews.

Niningwi. My armpit, arm-hole;—*Kiningwi*, thy armpit; *oningwi*, his armpit.

Ninishk. My gland; pl.-*wag.* —*Onîshkwan*, his gland.

Ninisiss. My hair, (one only;) pl. *ninisissan*, my hair. *Winisissan*, his hair.

Niniskigomân. S. *Niskigomân.*

Ninitam. I in my turn, I now. —*Nin wi-tchime dash ninitam;* I will paddle now in my turn.

Ninitamiwind. We in our turn, we now; (the person or persons spoken to, not included.) S. *Kinitamiwind.*

Ninjagaâi. My skin.—*Kijagaâi*, thy skin; *ojagaâian*, his skin.

Ninôgan. My hip; pl.-*an.* *Onogan*, his hip.

Ninoshe, or *ninwishe.* My aunt, (my *mother's* sister;) also, my step-mother; pl.-*iag.* S. *Ninsigoss.*

Ninow. My cheek; pl. *ninowag.* — *Kinow*, thy cheek; *onowan*, his cheek or cheeks.

Ninsigoss. My aunt, (my *father's* sister;) pl.-*ag.* *Osigossan*, his (her) aunt.

Ninsigosiss. My mother-in-law; pl.-*ag.*— *Kisigosiss*, thy mother-in-law; *osigosissan*, his (her) mother-in-law.

Ninsiniss. My father-in-law; pl.-*ag.*— *Osinissan*, his (her) father-in-law.

Nin tchingwan. The upper part of my leg, up from the knee, my thigh.—*Ki tchingwan*, *o tchingwan;* thy thigh, his thigh.

Nin tchingwanigan. The bone of my thigh, my thigh-bone; pl.-*an.*—*O tchingwanigan*, his thigh-bone.

Nin tchishibodâgan. The bone of my hip; *ki tchishibodâgan*, *o tchishibodâgan;* the bone of thy, his hip.

Nio, num. Four, (before substantives denoting MEASURE of time or other things.)

Niogijigad. Thursday, (four days after Sunday).—S. *Nijogijigad.* *Nijogwanagad.*

Niogijigad. It is Thursday; p. *naogijigak.*

Nipan. My lungs. — *Kipan*, *opan;* thy lungs, his lungs.

Nipigegan. My rib; pl.-*an.*— *Opigegan*, his rib.

Nisaiendagos, (*nin*). I am considered dangerous, I am feared, mistrusted; p. *nes..sid.*

Nisaiendagwad. It is considered dangerous, it is feared, mistrusted; p. *nes..wak.*

Nisaiendam, (*nin*). I fear, I am fearful, easy to be scared; p. *nes..ang.*

Nisaiendamowin. Fear, mistrust.

Nisaiendân, (*nin*). I fear it, I am afraid of it, I mistrust it; p. *nes..ang.*

Nisaienima, (*nin*). I fear him, I mistrust him; p. *nes..mad.*

Nisakosi. Ear of Indian corn; pl.-*g.*

Nishangâdis, (*nin*). I am tender, not used to hardship; p. *nesh..sid.*

Nishangigia, (*nin*). I bring him up tenderly, softly; p. *nesh..ad.*

Nishi, (*nin*). I come down sliding; p. *nashid.*

Nishi, (*nin*). I come to a premature or abortive birth; p. *neshid.*

Nishibanikam, (*nin*). I run after persons of the other sex; p. *nesh..ang.*

Nishibapinodage, (*nin*). I scorn, I mock, I waste; p. *nesh..ged.*

Nishibapinodan, (*nin*). I scorn it, I mock and ridicule it; I squander it, waste it; p. *nesh..ang.*

Nisibapinodawa, (*nin*). I scorn or mock him, I ridicule him; I squander or waste some obj.; p. *nesh..wad.*

Nishibon, (*nin*). I go down a rapid in a canoe or boat; p. *nashibonod.*

Nishibona, (*nin*). I take him down the stream in a canoe; p. *nashibonad.*

Nishigiwanis, (*nin*). I riot, I cause disturbance; p. *nesh..sid.*

Nishigiwanisiwin. Riot, disturbance.

Nishimagad. It comes down, it slides down, it descends; p. *nash..gak.*

Nishime. My brother or my sister, (younger than I;) pl.-*iag.*

Nishimiss. My niece; pl. *ag.*—S. Otch. Gram., Chap. II.

Nishi pikiji. The cow has a calf untimely, abortively; p. *neshid.*

Nishiwanâdad. It spoils, it perishes, it is ruined; p. *nesh..dak.*

Nishiwanâdakamigad. There is trouble, dissension; p. *nesh..gak.*

Nishiwanâdakamigis, (*nin*). I make trouble, I cause disturbance; p. *nesh..sid.*

Nishiwanâdakamigisiwin. Disturbance, noise, trouble.

Nishiwanâdendam, (*nin*). I am disturbed in my thoughts, I have trouble in my mind; p. *nesh..ang.*

Nishiwanâdendamia, (*nin*). I cause him trouble of mind, to be disturbed in his thoughts; p. *nesh..ad.*

Nishiwanâdendamowin. Disturbed and troubled mind or thought.

Nishiwanâdis, (*nin*). I become spoiled, wicked, ruined; p. *nesh..sid.*

Nishiwanadjia, (*nin*). I spoil him, I seduce him, ruin him, I make him wicked, unhappy, I waste, squander or spend foolishly some obj.; p. *nesh..ad.*

Nishiwanâsoma, (*nin*). I trouble him with words ; I despise him ; p. *nesh..mad.*

Nishiwé, (*nin*). I kill, I murder ; p. *neshiwed.*

Nishiwewin. Killing, murder.

Nishiwin. Premature abortive birth, abortion, miscarriage.

Nishkâb, (*nin*). I look with anger, I cast angry looks ; p. *neshkâbid.*

Nishbâbama, (*nin*). I look at him with anger ; p. *nesh..mad.*

Nishkâbandan, (*nin*) I look at it with anger ; p. *nesh..ang.*

Nishkâdéndam, (*nin*). I have angry thoughts ; p. *nesh..ang.*

Nishkâdendamowin. Angry thinking, angry thought ; pl. *-an.*

Nishkâdis, (*nin*). I am angry, wrathful ; p. *nesh..sid.*

Nishkâdjingwe, (*nin*) or, *nin nishkadjingweshka.* I have an angry face, I look angry ; p. *nesh..wed*, or *nesh..kad.*

Nishkanigan. My gum ; (F. ma gencive ;) pl.-*an.* — *Kishkanigan*, thy gum ; *oshkanigan*, his gum.

Nishkânj. My nail, (on a finger or toe ;) also, claw or hoof; pl.-*ig.*—*Oshkanjin*, his nail (claw, hoof.)

Nishkâsitagos, (*nin*). I speak in a passion, angry ; p. *nesh..sid.*

Nishkâsitawa, (*nin*). I hear him speak angry ; p. *nesh..wad.*

Nishkâsoma, (*nin*). I speak to him angry ; p. *nesh..mad.*

Nishkêndjige, (*nin*). I am in anger, I keep anger or rancor, I am rancorous ; p. *nesh..ged.*

Nishkênima, (*nin*). I have angry thoughts against him, I am angry with him, I keep rancor towards him ; p. *nesh..mad.*

Nishkendan, (*nin*). I have angry thoughts against it ; p. *nesh..ang.*

Nishkia, (*nin*). I offend him, I make him angry, I irritate him ; p. *neshkiad.*

Nishkidee, (*nin*). My heart is angry ; p. *nesh..ed.*

Nishkideewin. Anger in the heart.

Nishkima, (*nin*). I make him angry with my *words ;* p. *neshkimad.*

Nishkinawa, (*nin*). I treat him ill ; p. *nesh..wad.*

Nishkinjig. My eye ; my face ; pl.-*on.*—*Kishkinjig*, *oshkinjig;* thy eye, his eye.

Nishtigwân. My head.—*Kishtigwân*, *oshtigwân ;* thy head, his head.

Nishwâsso, num. Eight (before substantives denoting MEASURE, of time or other things.)

Nishwâtchimin, (*nin*), num. We are eight of us ; p. *nesh..djig.*

Nishwâtching, num. Eight times.

Nishwâtchinon, num. There are eight (objects.)

Nisid. My foot ; pl.-*an.*

Niskâbiden, (*nin*). I gnash, I collide the teeth in anger ; p. *nes..nid.*

Niskâbidetawa, (*nin*). I gnash at him in anger ; p. *nes..wad.*

Niskâdad. It is bad weather ; p. *neskadak.*

Niskadendam, (*nin*). I think it is too bad weather to go somewhere; p. *nes..ang.*

Niskanagwetchigan. Ruffle; pl. *-an.*

Niskasika, (*nin*). I walk or travel in bad weather; p. *nes ..kag.*

Niskasoma, (*nin*). I disturb him with my words in his sleep, or in any state of tranquillity; p. *nas..mad.*

Niskia, (*nin*). I encumber him with a heavy pack; or with much work or care; p. *naskiad.*

Niskigoman. Snot.—This word is always preceded by a possessive pronoun, which remains attached to it; as: *Niniskigoman, winiskigamonan*, etc.

Niskiigon, (*nin*). It encumbers me in my walking or traveling; p. *nas..god.*

Niskikâge, (*nin*). I encumber people; p. *nas..ged.*

Niskikâgon, (*nin*). It encumbers me, (not on a voyage;) p. *nas..gôd.*

Niskikân, (*nin*). I encumber it; p. *nas..ang.*

Niskikawa, (*nin*). I encumber him, (not on a voyage;) p. *nas..wad.*

Niskimamawe, (*nin*). My eyebrows are bristled up; p. *nas ..wed.*

Niskiminensikadân, (*nin*). I embroider or trim it with small glass-beads; p. *nas.. ang.*

Niskingwen, (*nin*). I make faces, grimaces; p. *nas..nid.*

Niskitchigade, or-*magad.* It is ornamented with lace or ruffles; p. *nas..deg.*, or-*magak.*

Niskitchigan. Lace, ruffle.

Niskitchige, (*nin*). I ornament with lace; p. *nas..ged.*

Niskitenimangânedjigan. Epaulet, a military ornament worn on the shoulder; pl.*an.*

Niskonje, (*nin*). I have a large family, many children; p. *naskonjed.*

Nissâ, (*nin*). I kill him, I murder him; p. *néssad;* imp. *nishi.*

Nissâbawadon, (*nin*). I wet it, I moisten it; p. *nes..dod.*

Nissabawana, (*nin*). I wet some obj.; p. *nes..nad;* imp. *nissabawaj.*

Nissabawas, (*nin*). I get wet; p. *nes..sod.*

Nissabawe, (*nin*). I get wet, I am wet also, I am drowned; p. *nes..wed.*

Nissâbawe or-*magad.* It gets wet, it is wet or damp; p. *nes ..weg*, or-*magak.*

Nissâbigina, (*nin*). I let him down on a rope; p. *nas..nad.*

Nissâbon, (*nin*). I go down the stream with the current, in a canoe or boat; p. *nas..nod.*

Nissâdjiwan, adv. Down, below, (respecting the course of a river or of rivers.) *Nissâdjiwan nin wi-ija sigwang.* I intend to go below next spring. S. *Osidâdjiwan.*

Nissâdjiwe, (*nin*). S. *Nisâkiwe.*

Nissaie. My brother, (older than I;) pl.*-iag.*

Nissâii, adv. Below, down.

Nissâki, adv. At the foot of a hill or mountain, below.

Nissâkiwe, (*nin*). I descend a hill or mountain p. *nas..wed.*

Nissakiwebato, (*nin*). S. *Gadadjiwebato.*

Nissâkobidon, (*nin*). I break it down; p. *nas..dod.*

Nissâkonamawa, (*nin*). *Ot.* S. *Nassâkonamawa.*

Nissâkonan, (*nin*). *Ot.* S. *Nassâkonan.*

Nissâkoshka, (*nin*). I fall down; p. *nas..kad.*

Nissakoshka, or-*magad.* It falls down; it opens; p. *nas..kag,* or--*magak.*

Nissâkoshkan, (*nin*). I let it fall down; p. *nas..âng.*

Nissâkôshkawa, (*nin*). I let it fall down, also, I hurt him in falling upon him; p. *nas..wad.*

Nissâkosse, (*nin*). I slide down; p. *nas..sed.*

Nissâkosse, or-*magad.* It slides down; it opens, it is thrown open; p. *nas..seg,* or-*magak.* —*Tchibegamigon gi-nissâkossewan api ga-nibod Jesus ajitteyâtigong*; the graves were opened when Jesus died on the cross.

Nissândawaa, (*nin*). I take him down or carry him down; p. *nas..ad.*

Nissândawaton, (*nin*). I take it or carry it down; p. *nas..tod.*

Nissândawe, (*nin*). I descend, I go down or come down on a ladder, or stairs, or from a tree, etc.; p. *nas..wed.*

Nissândawébato, (*nin*). I run down stairs or down a ladder; p. *nes..tod.*

Nissandawénajâwa, (*nin*). I send him down stairs. I bid him go down; p. *nas..wad;* imp. *nis..najâ.*

Nissanêndagwad. It is sad, lonesome; p. *nas..wak.*

Nissânendam, (*nin*). I am sad, sorrowful, lonesome; p. *nas.. ang.*

Nissâtakoki, (*nin*). I put my foot down, I descend a step; p. *nas..kid.*

Nissâwaii, adv. In the middle.

Nissâwaiiwan. It is the middle, between two other objects; p. *nes..ang.*

Nissean, (*nin*). I stir s. th. in a vessel, (sugar, etc.;) p. *nessêang.*

Nisséigan. Maple-sugar, (loose, not in solid cakes;) (F. cassonade.)

Nisséige, (*nin*). I stir, (especially sugar in sugar-making;) p. *nes..kag.*

Nissi, num. He is three, three in one.

Nissibidjigade, or-*magad.* It is pulled down; p. *nas..deg,* or-*magak.*

Nissibidon, (*nin*). I pull it down, I make it fall down; p. *nas..dod.*

Nissidimîn, (*nin*). We kill one another; p. *nessididjig.*

Nissidiwin. Killing of several persons, massacre, carnage, slaughter.

Nissîgon, (*nin*). It kills me; p. *nessigod.*

Nissigwashkon, (*nin*) or *nin nissigwashkwan.* I leap down, jump down; p. *nas..id.*

Nissim. My daughter-in-law; pl.-*ig.*

Nissimidana, num. Thirty.

Nissimidanâk, num. Thirty hundred, three thousand.

Nissimidanâkosimin,(*nin*). num. We are three thousand in number ; p. *nes..sidjig.*
Nissimidanawemin, (nin), num. We are thirty ; *nes..wedjig.*
Nissimidanawewan, num. There are thirty (objects.)
Nissimin, (nin), num. We are three ; p. *nessidjig.*
Nissina, (nin). I put him down ; p. *nassinad.*
Nissinan, (nin). I put it down ; p. *nassinang.*
Nissing, num. Three times.
Nissingwâm, (nin). I sleep profoundly ; p. *nes..ang.*
Nissinon, num. There are three.
Nissitâ, adv. Right, well, exactly.
Nissitâ-dodam, (nin). I act right, I do it prudently, exactly ; p. *nes..âng.*
Nissitawâb, (nin). I discern, I recognize ; p. *nes..bid.*
Nissitawâbama, (nin). I discern him, I recognize him ; p. *nes.. mad.*
Nissitawâbandân, (nin). I discern it, recognize it ; p. *ness.. ang.*
Nissitawendam, (nin). I understand, I conceive ; *nes..ang.*
Nissitawendân, (nin). I recognize it, (in thoughts ;) I comprehend it, conceive it ; p. *nes..ang.*
Nissitawenima, (nin). I recognize him, (in thoughts ;) p. *nes..mad.*
Nissitawinâge, (nin). I recognize people ; p. *nes..ged.*
Nissitawinâgos, (nin). I look known, I am easy to be known, to be recognized ; p. *nes..sid.*
Nissitawinâgwad. It looks known, it can be recognized, it is easy to be known ; p. *nes ..wak.*
Nissitawinan, (nin). I recognize it ; I know it ; p. *nes..ang.*
Nissitawinân masinaigan, (nin). I can read.
Nissitawinawa, (nin). I know him ; I recognize him ; p. *nes ..wad.*
Nissitchibina, (nin). I spoil it by tasting it often in my hands, by handling it too often ; p. *ness..nad ;* imp. *nissitchibij.*
Nissitchibinân, (nin). I spoil it by taking it often in my hands, by handling it too often ; p. *nes..ang.*
Nissitôpidân, (nin). I know what it is, by taking it, I know it by the taste ; p. *nes.. dang.*
Nissitôpidjige, (nin). I know s. th. by the taste ; p. *nes.. ged.*
Nissitôpwa, (nin). I know some obj. by the taste ; p. *nes..wad ;* imp. *nissitopwi.*
Nissitotâdimin, (nin). We understand each other ; p. *nes.. didjig.*
Nissitotâgos, (nin). I speak distinctly ; I am easily understood ; p. *nes..sid.*
Nissitotâgosiwin. Distinct plain speaking.
Nissitotâgwad. It is intelligible, plain, comprehensible, easy to understand ; p. *nes..wak.*
Nissitotam, (nin). I understand what is said, what I hear ; p. *nes..ang.*
Nissitotân, (nin). I understand

it, I conceive it, comprehend it; p. *nes..ang.*

Nissitotawa, (*nin*). I understand him; p. *nes..wad.*

Nissiwebina, (*nin*). I throw him down, (any obj.); p. *nas..nad.*

Nissô, num. Three (before substantives denoting MEASURE, of time or other things.)

Nisso-bejigo Kije-Manito. God is one in three persons. *Nesso-bejigod K. M.*, the Blessed Trinity.

Nisswi, num. Three.

Nita. My brother-in-law, (a *male* speaking. A *female* will say, *Ninim*, my brother-in-law); pl.-*g.* *Kita*, thy brother-in-law; *witan*, his brother-in-law.

Nitâ, or, *nitta* This word is always connected with another word in the sentence; commonly with a verb, and in some instances with a substantive. It marks a custom or *habit* in doing s. th., or a *faculty* and power to do s. th. (Examples in many of the following words.)

Nitâ-âgonwetam, (*nin*). I use to contradict or gainsay, I don't often believe sayings and reports; I am incredulous; I am disobedient; p. *net..ang.*

Nitâ-âkos, (*nin*). I am often sick, I am sickly; p. *net..sid.*

Nita-âkosiwin. Poor health, infirmity.

Nitaam, (*nin*). I go up the stream in a canoe or boat, on a river, I go up against the current; p. *netaang.*

Nitâ-anoki, (*nin*). I am industrious, active, diligent, I use to work always; p. *net..id.*

Nitâ-anokiwin. Industry, assiduous working.

Nitâ-bâwâdjige, (*nin*). I am a dreamer, I dream often; p. *net..ged.*

Nitâgan. Person killed in a massacre; pl.-*ag.*

Nitagânakwad. Black cloud, mourning cloud; pl.-*on.*

Nitâge, (*nin*). I kill, (hunting or butchering;) p. *netâged.*

Nitâge, (*nin*). I am in mourning, I wear a mourning-dress; (F. je porte le deuil;) p. *netaged.*

Nitageowin. Sackcloth, mourner's dress, penitent's dress.

Nitagewaiân. Crape.

Nitagewin. Mourning; (F. deuil.) Also killing of animals, butchering.

Nitagewinini. A man that kills animals, a butcher; good hunter; pl.-*wag.*

Nitâ-gikadj, (*nin*). I soon feel cold; (F. je suis frileux;) p. *net..id.*

Nitâ-gikâwidam, (*nin*). I am quarrelsome, I am a quarreler; p. *net..ang.*

Nitam, adv. and adj. First, the first.

Nitamab, (*nin*). I am in the first place; p. *net..bid.*

Nitamabikishin aw assin. This stone is placed first, (it is the corner-stone); p. *net..ing.*

Nitamage, (*nin*). I kill animals, or I butcher, for people; p. *net..ged.*

Nitamas, (*nin*). I kill animals, or I butcher, for myself; p. *net..sod.*

Nitamâson, (*nin*). I kill it for

myself; p. *net..sod.*—*Nin nitamason gego.* I kill s. th. for my own use.

Nitamasonan, (*nin*). I kill some obj. for myself; p. *net..sod.*—*Makwa nin gi nitamâsonan ;* I killed a bear for me.

Nitamawa, (*nin*). I kill it for him or to him; p. *net..wad.*

Nitamenima, (*nin*). I consider him to be the first; p. *net.. mad.*

Nitamigâbaw, (*nin*). I am standing in the first place, (in a range;) p.*net..wid.*

Nitamige, (*nin*). I live in the first house or lodge of a village or camp; p. *net..ged.*—S. *Ishkwege.*

Nitaminig, (*nin*). I am the first-born; p. *net..gid.*

Nitâmissin. It is the first, the foremost; p. *nêtamissing.*

Nitamanagong. In the foremost part of a canoe, boat, etc.

Nitamonjân. The first-born child; pl.-*ag.*

Nitaôna, (*nin*). I take him up the stream in a canoe or boat, I convey him up against the current; p. *net..nad.*

Nitâonje, (*nin*). I am often delivered, (of a child;) p. *nêtâonjed.*

Nitâosse, (*nin*), or, *nin nita-bimosse.* I walk well, I am used to walking; p. *netâossed,* a good walker.

Nitawadaga, (*nin*). I can swim; I swim well; p. *netâwadagad,* a good swimmer.

Nitawag. My ear; pl.-*an.*—*Kitawag, otawag;* thy ear, his ear.

Nitâwagimosse, (*nin*). I walk well with snowshoes; p. *netâwagimossed,* a good snowshoe-walker.

Nitâwâkamîgwe, (*nin*). I can go everywhere without a trail; p. *net..wed.*

Nitâwandan, (*nin*). I like to eat it, I am fond of it; p. *net.. ang.*

Nitâ-wânendam, (*nin*). I forget easily, I am forgetful; p. *net ..ang.*

Nitâwe, (*nin*). I can speak; I am eloquent; p. *netâwed.*

Nitâwia, (*nin*). I know how to make it, I can make it, I use to make it; p. *netawind.*— *Ki nitawia na dibaigisisswân ?* Canst thou make a watch?

Nitawigia, (*nin*). I bring him up, I raise him, (a child, etc.) I raise or produce any vegetable; p. *net..ad.* — *Opinig, mandaminag gaie nin nitawigiag ;* I raise potatoes and corn.

Nitâwiss. My cousin, (a *male* speaking. A *female* will say: *Ninimoshê,* my cousin. — S. Otch. Grammar, Chap. II.) Pl. *nitawissag.*

Nitâwiton, (*nin*). I can make it; p. *net..tod.*

Nitômis, (*nin*). I am pensive; I am solitary, I like to be alone, I don't like company; p. *netomisid.*

Niton, (*nin*). I kill it, destroy it; p. *nétod.*—*Nin niton niyaw,* I kill myself.

Niwaj. My load, my pack, my bundle; pl.-*an.*— *Kiwaj, wiwaj ;* thy pack, his pack.

Niwakwewan, num. There are four hundred pair of....

Niwakwoagan. Four spans, (as measurement.)

Niwanawa, (*nin*). I kill him, I knock him down dead ; p. *naw..wad ;* imp. *niwanâ.*

Niwanje ishkote. The fire decreases, it goes out ; p. *newanjeg.*

Niwaog, (*nin*). My swelling decreases, abates ; p. *nawaogod.*

Niwatenan, (*nin*). I unbend it, (the lock of a gun ;) p. *naw..âng.*

Niwin, num. Four.

Niwing, num. Four times.

Niwing inakakeia wendânimak. From the four winds ; (from the four principal winds, north, south, east, west.)

Niwinon, num. There are four, (objects.)

Niwish, (seldom used.) My wife. —*Kiwish,* thy wife ; *wiwishan,* or *wiwan,* his wife. *Wiwan* is generally used.—They also say : *Nin mindimoiêmish, ki mindimoiemish, wiwan ;* my wife, thy wife, his wife.—The most polite term for "wife" is *Widigémagan,* (which also signifies "husband.") *Nin widigemagan,* my wife ; (or, my husband.) *Ki widigemagan,* thy wife, (or thy husband.) *O widigemaganan,* his wife, (or, her husband) ; *my* partner, the one with whom I cohabit.

Nôdab, (*nin*). I watch, I sit up at night ; p. *nwadabid.*

Nôdabiwin. Watching, sitting up at night.

Nôdâjashkwe, (*nin*). I am hunting or trapping muskrats ; p. *nwâd..wed.*

Nôdâmikwe, (*nin*). I am hunting or trapping beavers ; p. *nwad..wed.*

Nôdikwewe, (*nin*). I frequent bad women, I am a libertine, a licentious lascivious man ; p. *nwad..wed.*

Nôdikwewewin. Licentiousness, lasciviousness.

Nôdin. Wind.

Nôdin. It is windy, it blows ; p. *nwâding.*

Nôdinish, (*nin*) or *nin nodinoshka.* I have wind (on my voyage ;) p. *nwadinishid,* or *nwa..kad.*

Nôdjia, (*nin*). I acquire some object, I procure it by labor for food, (hunting or fishing ;) p. *nwadjiad.* — *Gigôiag nin nodjiag, nimisse dash wâboson o nodjiân.* I procure fishes, and my sister procures rabbits, (for our living) ; too, I put him in trouble, I tease him.

Nodjidikome, (*nin*). I search lice, I clean myself of lice ; p. p. *nwa..med.*

Nôdjim, (*nin*). I recover from a sickness, I am cured, healed ; p. *nwâdjimod.*

Nodjimoa, (*nin*). I cure or heal him ; I deliver him, save him, I restore or repair some obj. ; p. *nwa..ad.*

Nôdjimoiwe, (*nin*). I heal, cure, restore health ; p. *nwa..wed.*

Nôdjimôiwemagad. It cures ; p. *nwa..gak.*—*Mandan mashkiki kitchi nodjimoiwemagad* ; this medicine cures well, (is very wholesome.)

Nôdjimoiwewin. The act of healing or curing a sick person.

Nôdjimotawa, (*nin*). I heal, cure, or save, s. th. relating to him; p. *nwa..wad.*

Nôjimoton, (*nin*). I cure it, I restore it, repair it, mend it; p. *nwa..tôd.—Eniwek na ki gi-nôdjimotân nin tchimân?* Hast thou mended a little my canoe?

Nôdjimowin. Recovery from sickness.

Nôdjishibe, (*nin*). I am hunting ducks; p. *nwad..bed.*

Nôdjiton, (*nin*). I acquire or procure it by labor for food, hunting or fishing; p. *nwa-jitod.*

Nôgendan, (*nin*). I desist from it, I drop it; p. *nwagendang.*

Nôgenima, (*nin*). I desist from him, I drop what I intended to say to him, or to do him; p: *nwa..mad.*

Nôgi, (*nin*). I stop; I give up; p. *nwagid.*

Nôgibato, (*nin*). I stop running; p. *nwa..tod.*

Nôgigâbaw, (*nin*). I stop walking, I stand still; p. *nwa..wid.*

Nôgina, (*nin*). I stop him; p. *nwaginad.*

Nôgishka, or-*magad.* It stops, (a machine or engine;) p. *nwa ..kad,* or-*magak.*

Nôgishkan, (*nin*). I stop it, (a machinery, etc.); p. *nwagish-kang.*

Nojê, or *nojé-aiaa.* The female of an animal; pl.-*g.*

Nojéiag. A she-porcupine, female porcupine; pl.-*wog.*

Nojéiakig. A female otter; pl.-*wog.*

Nojêk. She-bear, pl.-*wog.*

Nojékwaiân. Skin of a female bear; pl.-*ag.*

Nojémeg. A female fish; pl.-*wog.*

Nojêmik. A she-beaver; pl.-*og.*

Nojes. A hind, the female of the deer-kind, as of a moose, stag, roe-buck, raindeer; also, a mare; pl.-*og.*

Najésse. The female of a bird; pl.-*g.*

Nojéssim. A bitch; pl.-*og.*

Nojêwaiân. The skin of a female quadruped, not very large, not larger than a deer; pl.-*ag.*

Nojêwegin. The skin of a female quadruped of the largest kind, as, buffalo, moose, stag; pl.-*on.*

Nojishé. My grand-child, (grand-son, or grand-daughter;) pl.-*iag.*

Nôka, or-*magad.* It is soft, tender, weak; p. *nwakag,* or-*magak.*

Nokabigad. It is soft, weak, (string, cord, etc.)

Nokabigisi. It is weak, tender, (silk, ribbon;) p. *nwa..sid.*

Nokâbikad. It is weak, it is soft, not hard, (metal, glass;) p. *nwa..kak.*

Nokâbikisan, (*nin*). I make it weak, I make it soft or softer, by heat, (metal;) p. *nwa..ang.*

Nokâbikisi. It is soft, weak; (silver, stone;) p. *nwa..sid.*

Nokâbikiswa, (*nin*). I make it weak or soft, by heat, (metal;) p. *nwak..wad;* imp. *nok..wi.*

Nôkâdad. It is soft, mild; p. *nwa..dak.*

Nôkâdis, (*nin*). I am meek, mild, gentle; p. *nwa..sid.*

Nôkâdisitawa, (*nin*) or, *nin no-kadisitamawa.* I am meek, gentle, patient towards him; p. *nwa..wad.*

Nokâdisiwin. Meekness, mildness.

Nôkâganaga, or-*wagad.* The snow is soft; p. *nwa..gag,* or-*magak.*

Nôkaje, (*nin*). My skin is soft, tender; p. *nwakajed.*

Nôkan. It is soft, tender, weak, feeble; p. *nwakang.*

Nôkendagos, (*nin*). I am considered mild; weak; p. *nwa.. sid.*

Nôkendagwad. It is considered soft, it is soft, it is weak; p. *nwa..wak.*

Nôkia, (*nin*). I make some obj. soft, tender, I soften it; p. *nwakiad.*

Nôkibidon, (*nin*). I soften it, I make it tender; p. *nwa..dod.*

Nôkibina, (*nin*). I soften some obj.; p. *nwa..nad;* imp. *nokibij.*

Nôkide, or-*magad.* It is well done, well cooked, it is tender, (meat, etc.); p. *nwakideg,* or-*magak.*

Nôkidee, (*nin*). My heart is soft; it is weak, fickle; p. *nwa..ed.*

Nôkis, (*nin*). I am tender, delicate, weak, not inured to hardship; p. *nwakisid.*

Nôkisan, (*nin*). I cook it well, tender, soft, (meat, etc.); p. *nwa..ang.*

Nôkisi. It is soft, tender, weak, not strong; p. *nwakisid.* — *Osâm nokisi wâwashkeshiwaiân;* the deer-skin is too soft, too weak.

Nôkiso. It is well done, well cooked, tender; p. *nwakisod.* —*Gigo nokiso, opinig gaie nôkisowog;* the fish is well cooked, and the potatoes are well cooked.

Nôkiswa, (*nin*). I cook it well or tender; v. *nwa..wad.*

Nôko! voc. My grand-mother!

Nôkomiss. My grand-mother; pl.-*ag.*

Nôkwésan, (*nin*). I perfume it; p. *nwa..ang.*

Nokwêsigan. Herb that smells good; (F. foin de senteur;) perfume; frankincense.

Nokwêsige, (*nin*). I perfume, I burn s. th. to give a good odor; p. *nwa..ged.*

Nokwesigen, (*nin*). I burn it as a perfume, to make a good odor; p. *nwa..ged.*

Nokwesigenan, (*nin*). I burn some obj. as a perfume, to make a good odor; p. *nwa.. ged.*

Nokwéswa, (*nin*). I perfume him, I make him inhale the odor of s. th. I burn; p. *nwa.. wad;* imp. *nokweswi.*

Nômâbikina, (*nin*). I oint or grease some obj. of stone or metal; p. *nwa..nad.*

Nômâbikinan, (*nin*). I oint or grease some obj. of metal; p. *nwa..ang.*

Nômag, adv. A certain length of time, pretty long.

Nômageb, (*nin*). I am sitting a certain length of time, pretty long; p. *nwa..bid.*

Nômagewis, (*nin*). I don't like to give s. th., I am begged a certain length of time for it before I give it; p. *nwa..sid.*

Nômaia, adv. Not long ago, recently, lately.

Nomakona, (*nin*). I grease or

oint some object of wood; p. *nwa..nad.*

Nomikwen, (*nin*). I nod with the head, as a sign of affirmation, approbation or salutation; p. *nwa..nid.*

Nominikwêtan, (*nin*). I salute it, I make salutes or inclinations towards it; p. *nwa..ang.*

Nôminikwêtawa, (*nin*). I salute him, I make salutations or compliments towards him; also, I give him signs of affirmation or approbation, nodding with the head; p. *nwa..wad.*

Nôminâ, (*nin*). I grease him, I oint him, I anoint him; p. *nwaminad.*

Nôminan, (*nin*). I grease it; I oint it; p. *nwâ..ang.*

Nôminigan. Grease, ointment, balsam.

Non, (*nin*). I suck; p. *nwanid.*

Nona, (*nin*). I make him suck, I give him suck, I suckle him; p. *nwanad;* imp. *noj.*

Nônâwass, (*nin*). I give suck, I suckle; p. *nwa..sod.*

Nond, adv. Before the end, before the due time, before all is over.

Nôndâgos, (*nin*). I am heard; p. *nwa..sid.*

Nôndâgwad. It is heard; p. *nwa..wak.*

Nondam, (*nin*). I hear something, a saying, a voice, a noise, etc.; p. *nwandang.*

Nondâss, adv. Less, deficiently.

Nondawa, (*nin*). I hear him; p. *nwa..wad.*

Nôndé.—This word has the same signification as *nond;* it signifies *giving up, letting off,* or *going away,* before all is over or done, *deficiency.* (Examples in many of the following words.)

Nôndebininike, (*nin*). I miscarry, I come to a premature abortive delivery or childbirth; p. *nwa..ked.*

Nondéiâbanish, (*nin*). I don't survive the winter, I die before spring; p. *nwan..id.*—See the contrary, *Nin wâbanish.*

Nondêiabas, (*nin*). I don't survive the night, (a sick person,) I die before daylight; p. *nwan..sod.* — The contrary, *Nin wâbas.*

Nondê-nigiâwass, (*nin*). I am delivered of a child before my time; p. *nwa..sod.*

Nôndéoki, (*nin*). I have not enough to give to all; or, to give them a full share; (in a distribution;) p. *nwa..id.*

Nondéona, (*nin*). I don't give him enough, (in a distribution;) or, I have not enough to give to him; p. *nwa..nad.*

Nôndes, (*nin*). I am deficient, I cannot do it, cannot afford it; p. *nwandesid.*

Nôndêshima, (*nin*). I cannot put it, it is too short, as *nabagissag,* a board;) p. *nwa..mad.*

Nôndéshima, (*nin*). I leave him behind, he is unable to walk with me; p. *nwa..mad.*

Nôndêshin, (*nin*). I become weak, unable to walk any further, (on a voyage;) p. *nwa..ing.*

Nôndéshkawa, (*nin*). I don't come to him, I don't reach him; p. *nwa..wad.*

Nôndésse, (*nin*). I cannot afford it, my time (or my strength) is not sufficient to do the work ; there is not enough of some obj., it runs out before the right time ; p. *nwa..sed.*

Nôndéssiton, (*nin*). I cannot put it, it is too short ; p. *nwa ..tod.*

Nondétibikishka, (*nin*). The night overtakes me before I reach a certain place, I am benighted ; p. *nwa..kad.*

Nongom, adv. Now, at present, actually ; to-day ; now-a-days.

Nonokasse. Wren, honey-bird, (small bird ;) pl.-*g.*

Nôpiming, adv. In the woods, in the inland ; any distance from the lake-shore.—*Nopiming nawatch aton ki tchimân ;* put thy canoe a little further from the shore.

Nopinadan, (*nin*). I follow it, I walk behind it ; p. *nwa..ang.*

Nôpinaki, (*nin*). I follow (some person or persons going somewhere ;) (L. sequor ;) p. *nwa.. kid.*

Nôpinana, (*nin*). I follow him; I walk after him going somewhere ; p. *nwapinanad* ; imp. *noginaj.*

Noshkâna, (*nin*). I van it, (some produce, as *mandaminag,* Indian corn ;) p. *nwe..nad.*

Noshkatchigan, or *noshkatchinagan.* Van for vanning, cleansing wild rice, or other produce ; pl.-*an.*

Noshkâtchige, (*nin*). I am vanning, cleansing grain ; p. *nwe ..ged.*

Noshkaton, (*nin*). I van it, cleanse it ; p. *nwe..tod.*

Nôskwâdam, (*nin*). I lick ; (F. je lèche ;) p. *nwa..ang.*

Nôshwâdamawa, (*nin*). I lick s. th. belonging or relating to him ; p. *nwa..wad.*

Nôskwâdan, (*nin*). I lick it ; p. *nwa..ang.*

Nôskwâdjige, (*nin*). I am licking ; p. *nwa..ged.*

Nôskwâna, (*nin*). I lick him (with the tongue) ; p. *nwaskwanad ;* imp. *noskwaj.*

Noskwâs, (*nin*). I eat the interior bark of a tree containing the sap or vital juice ; p. *nwa sod.*

N'oss. My father.—*K'ôss, ossan;* thy father, his father ; pl.-*n'ossag.*

N'osse! voc. Father!

Nôsswâadon, (*nin*). S. *Madaadon.*

Nôsswaana, (*nin*). I follow his track ; p. *nwas..nad ;* imp. *nosswâaj.*

Nôsswanêwa, (*nin*), (pron. *nossonewa.*) I pursue him, I go after him ; p. *nwa..wad ;* imp. *nosswanê.*

Nôw. Cheek.—This word is always connected with a possessive pronoun ; as : *Ninow,* my cheek ; *kinow,* thy cheek ; *onowan,* his cheek, etc.

O

Some words that might be supposed to be under O, *are to be found under* Wa, *as the syllable* wa *is often pronounced like* o; *as:* Wanagek, *is often pronounced,* Onagek, *etc.*

O.—This vowel is always pronounced in Otchipwe like *o* in the English word *bone*.

O, before a consonant, and *od,* before a vowel, signifies, his, her, its or their, when preceding a substantive; and it signifies, him, her, it or them, when before a verb.

O! interj. Well! ay, ay! — To express approbation, consent or thanks, as: *O! O! O! migwetch!* great thanks!

Obijashkissi. A kind of gray wild goose; pl.-*wog.*

Obiwai. Its hair or fur, (of an animal;) pl.-*an.*

Obiwaiâshkina. Reed; (F. roseau; L. arundo;) pl.-*g.*

Obodashkwanishi. Dragon-fly; musketo-eater; pl.-*iag.*

Obwâm. His thigh; pl.-*an.*—*Nibwâm, kibwâm,* my, thy thigh.

Obwâmima. Thigh.

Obwâmens. That part of the gun-lock where the flint sticks in, the cock of a gun; pl.-*an.*

Odâbâdân, (*nind*). I draw or drag it after me, I carry or convey it in a carriage; p. *wed..ang.*

Odâbân. Sled, sleigh, carriage, any vehicle on which s. th. is drawn; pl.-*ag.*

Odâbanâ, (*nind*). I draw or drag him after me, I convey him in a carriage; p. *wâd..nad;* imp. *odâbaj.*

Odabanâk; pl.-*ak.* S. *Odabân.*

Odâbânigo, (*nind*). I ride in a sleigh or carriage; p. *nin wedâbânigoiân, win wedâbânind,* etc.

Odâbanike, (*nind*). I make a sleigh, (or any other vehicle;) p. *wed..ked.*

Odâbi, (*nind*). I draw or drag; p. *wedabid.*

Odâbia, (*nind*). I make him draw or drag s. th.; p. *wed..ad.*

Odâbi-pijki. Draught-ox; pl.-*wog.*

Odâbiwin. Drawing, dragging, carrying in a sleigh.

Odâdjigakan. Fishing-line with a hook, to catch fish; pl.-*an.*

Odadjigoke, (*nind*). I am fishing with a hook; p. *wed..ked.*

Odâdjisingwesse, (*nind*). I lie in ashes; p. *wed..sed.*

Odâgim, (*nind*). I walk with snow-shoes; p. *wedâgimid.*

Odaiaaman. His property; pl.-*odaiaaman.—Nindaiaam,* my property; *kidaiaam,* thy property.

Odaian. His dog, or his dogs. —*Nindai,* my dog; *kidai,* thy dog.

Odaiim. His property; pl.-*odaiiman.— Nindaiim, kidaiim*; my property, thy property.

Odajawameg, or *ajawameg.* Salmon-trout; pl.-*wog.* (*Majamégoss.*)

Odâkan. Rudder, helm; also, the place where the steersman stands or sits, the stern of a ship, boat, canoe, etc.; pl.-*an.*

Odâke, (*nind*). I steer a canoe, boat, vessel, etc.; p. *wedaked.*

Odâke-abwi. Steering-paddle, a long and strong paddle to steer with; pl.-*n.*

Odâkéekawa, (*nind*). I assist him in steering; p. *wed..wad.*

Odâken, (*nind*). I steer it; p. *wedaked.*

Odâkeshkage, (*nind*). I succeed, I am the successor of somebody; p. *wed..ged.*

Odâkeshkam, (*nind*). S. *Odakeshkage.*

Odâkeshkawa, (*nind*). I succeed in his place, I take his charge, his office, I am his successor; p. *wed..wad.*

Odâkewin. Steering, the act or the art of steering.

Odakêwinini. Steersman, wheelsman; pl.-*wog.*

Odamâganak, or *odamaganâtig;* pl.-*on.* S. *Okidj.*

Odamaweshi. A small white bird that appears in spring and fall; pl.-*iag.*

Odâmikan. His jaw.—*Nindâmikan; kidâmikan.*

Odâmikanabid. His grinder, large tooth; pl.-*an.—Nindamikanabid,* my grinder.

Odâmikigan. S. *Odâmikigegan.*

Odâmikiganima. Jawbone.

Odâmikigegan. His jawbone.—*Windamikigegan,* my jawbone.

Odamin, (*nind*). I play, (like children;) p. *wedaminod.*

Odaminowâgan. Plaything for children; pl.-*an.*

Odaminowin. Children's play, playing.

Odanâmissakadoweshi. A small bird that remains always near the ground, under fallen trees, a kind of wren; (F. roitelet); pl.-*iag.*

Odanendan, (*nind*), or, *nind odanamonotan.* I sip it, I draw it in my mouth; p. *wed ..ang.*

Odâniss, (*nind*). I have a daughter; p. *wedânissid.*

Odânissikonan, (*nind*). I have her for a goddaughter, she is my goddaughter; also, my adopted daughter; p. *wed.. kad.* (V. Conj.)

Odânissima, (*nind*). I have her for a daughter; p. *wed..mad.*

Odanissimig, (*nind*). I am his daughter; p. *wedanissimid,* he whose daughter I am.

Odânissimigo, (*nind*). I am a daughter; p. *odânissima; nin wedanissimigoiân; win wedanissimind,* etc.

Odânissinan, (*nind*). I have her for a daughter, she is my daughter; p. *wedanissid.* (V. Conj.)

Odâpibidon, (*nind*). S. *Odâpibinan.*

Odâpibina, (*nind*) (*nind odapina.* I take him; *nin wikobina*, I draw him to me;) I take some obj. drawing it to me; p. *wed..nad;* imp. *odâpibij.*

Odâpibinan, (*nind*). I take it, drawing it to me; p. *wed..ang.*

Odâpina, (*nind*). I take him, I accept, receive, admit him; p. *wedapinad;* imp. *odâpin.*

Odâpinamâdis, (*nind*). I take it on me, for me, to me; p. *wed..sod.*

Odapinamawa, (*nin*). I accept it from him, I take or accept s. th. belonging or relating to him; p. *wed..wad.*

Odâpinan, (*nind*). I take it, I accept it, receive it; p. *wedapinang.*

Odâpinan anamiewin, (*nind*). I take religion, I become a Christian.

Odâpinan Jawendagosiwin, (*nind*) or *nind odapinan K. Eukaristiwin.* I receive Communion, I receive the Holy Eucharist.

Odâpinigade, or-*magad.* It is taken, accepted, received; p. *wed..deg*, or-*magak.*

Odâpinigas, (*nind*). I am accepted, received; p. *wed..sôd.*

Odâpinige, (*nind*). I take; p. *wed..ged.*

Odaski, or-*magad nibi.* The water falls, lowers, the *ebbing* tide; p. *wedaskig*, or-*magak.* —S. *Moshkâgami.*

Odatagâgomin. A kind of mulberry.

Odatagâgominagawanj. A kind of mulberry-shrub; pl.-*ig.*

Odatissiwagoma. Nerve, sinew.

Odé. His heart. *Nindé, kidé;* my heart, thy heart.

Odéima. Heart.

Odéimin. Strawberry; (F. fraise) (heart-berry;) pl.-*an.*

Odeimini-gisiss. The moon of strawberries, the month of June.

Odem; nind odem. My Indian family-mark; as: *Makwa*, bear; *amik*, beaver; *migisi*, eagle, etc.—*Kid odem, od odeman;* thy family-mark, his family-mark. — S. *Ododeminan.*

Odêna. Village, town, city; pl.-*wan.*

Odenaniwama. Tongue.

Odênawan. It is, or there is, a village, a town, a city; p. *wed ..ang.*

Odênawens. Hamlet, little village, little town; pl.-*an.*

Odengwai. Alg. S. *Oshkinjig.*

Odetomin, (*nind*). We form a village, we live together in a village; pl. *wedetodjig.*

Odikom, (*nind*). I have lice; p. *wedikomid.*

Odikwan. S. *Wadikwan.*

Odinimanganima. Shoulder.

Odishiwe, (*nind*). I arrive; I am a new comer; p. *wed..wed.*

Odishkwagami. Algonquin Indian; pl.-*g.*

Odishkwagamikwe. Algonquin squaw; pl.-*g.*

Odiskinakam, (*nind*). I have eggs of lice (nits) in my clothes, or on my head; p. *wed..mid.*

Odiss. His navel.—*Nindiss*, my navel; *kidiss, odiss;* thy, his, navel.

Odissâ, (*nind*). I come to him, I visit him; p. *wedissad*; imp. *odishi*.

Odissaa niniskigomân, (*nind*). I draw back my snot; p. *wed..ad*.

Odissâbama, (*nind*). I arrive to the point or moment of seeing him; p. *wed..mad*.

Odissâbandan, (*nind*). I arrive to the moment of seeing it; p. *wed..ang*.—*Nin kitchi minwendam odissâbândamân anamikodading*; I am very glad to arrive to the moment of seeing new-year's day again.

Odissigon, (*nind*). It comes to me, it reaches me; p. *wed..god*.

Odissikâgon, (*nind*). S. *Odissigon*.

Oditamadis, (*nind*) (or, *nind oditamadison*.) I cause it to myself, I am the cause that it reaches me, I incur it; p. *wed..sod*.

Oditan, (*nind*). I come to it or into it, I reach it; p. *weditang*.

Oditaowe, (*nind*). I arrive in a canoe to a certain place; p. *wed..wed*.

Odjânimakamigad. There is noise, trouble, excitement; p. *wed..gak*.

Odjânimakwaamog (*animikig*). It thunders frightfully, with great noise.

Odjânimendam, (*nind*). I am troubled in my thoughts; p. *wed..ang*.

Odjânimendamowin. Trouble, troubled thoughts.

Odjânimia, (*nind*). I trouble him, molest him, plague him; p. *wed..ad*.

Odjanj. His nose. — *Nindjanj*, my nose; *kidjanj*, thy nose.

Odji. Fly; pl. *odjig*.

Odjigaden, (*nind*). I draw back my leg; p. *wed..nid*.

Odjima, (*nind*). I kiss him; p. *wedjimad*.

Odji-mashkiki. Blister, visicatory.

Odjimenima, (*nind*). I forgive him in my thoughts; p. *wed..mad*.

Odjindamawa, (*nind*). I kiss s. th. belonging or relating to him; p. *wed..wad*.

Odjindan, (*nind*). I kiss it; p. *wed..ang*.

Odjindimin, (*nind*). We kiss one another; p. *wed..didjig*.

Odjindiwin. Kiss, kissing.

Odjikdiwini-gijigad. Kissing-day, that is, new-year's day.

Odjina, (*nind*). I feel him, I grope him, I search him by feeling in the dark; p. *wedjinad*.

Odjinan, (*nind*). I grope it, I search it by feeling in the dark; p. *wed..ang*.

Odjinige, (*nind*). I feel in the dark, I grope, I search by feeling in the dark; p. *wed..ged*.

Odjiniken, (*nind*). I draw back my arm; p. *wed..nid*.

Odjishig, (*nind*). I have a scar; p. *wed..gid*.

Odjishidjane, (*nind*). I have a scar on the nose; p. *wed..ned*.

Odjishîgade, (*nind*). I have a scar on the leg; p. *wed..ded*.

Odjishindibe, (*nind*). I have a

scar on the head ; p. *wed..bed.*

Odjishingwe, (nind). I have a scar on the face; p. *wed..wed.*

Odjishinike, (nind). I have a scar on the arm; p. *wed..ked.*

Odjishinindji, (nind). I have a scar on the hand; p. *wed..id.*

Odjishiside, (nind). I have a scar on the foot; p. *wed..ded.*

Odjishiwin. Scar.

Odjissikagon, (nind). S. *Odissikagon.*

Odjitchia, (nind). I appease him; p. *wed..ad.*

Odjitchisse, or-*magad.* It arrives (a certain time, a certain day,) it comes to pass; p. *weg..seg.* or-*magak.*

Odôdeminan, (nind). I have him (her, it) for my family-mark; p. *wedodemid.—Makwâ nind ododeminan ;* the bear is my family-mark. *Migisiwan od ododeminan ;* the eagle is his family-mark.

Odôn. His mouth.—*Nindôn, kidôn ;* my mouth, thy mouth.

Odon, at the end of some verbs, alludes to the conveying of s. th. in a *canoe* or *boat* to some place; as: *Nind ajawaodon,* I cross it, or take it to the opposite shore, in a canoe or boat. *Nin giweodon ;* I take or convey it back again in a canoe or boat; etc.—S. *Ona.*

Odôndan. His heel; pl.-*an.*—*Nindondan,* my heel; *kidondan,* thy heel.

Odônima. Mouth.

Odôskwanawa, (nind). I strike him with the elbow; p. *wed..wâd ;* imp. *odoskwanâ.*

Odoskwanishin, (nind). I lean on my elbows; p. *wad..ing.*

Ogâ. Pickerel, (fish ;) pl.-*wog ;* (C. doré.)

Ogâns. Young pickerel.

Ogebwamij. S. *Pagânimij.*

Ogejagim. Worm, (in the body of a person ;) pl.-*ag.*

Ogejagim, (nind). I have worms, (in my body ;) p. *weg..mid.*

Ogejagimi-mashkiki. Worm-medicine, medicine to destroy worms, vermifuge.

Ogi, (nind). I have a mother; p. *wégid.*

Ogidâbik, adv., or *ogidâbikang.* On a rock, upon a rock.

Ogidâbikissin. There is stone upon stone, one stone upon another ; p. *wed..ing.*

Ogidadjiw, adv. On a mountain.

Ogidâdjiwan, adv. Up, upwards, (respecting the course of a river or of rivers,) in the upper country.—S. *Nissâdjiwan.*

Ogidâdjiwe, (nind).—S. *Ogidakiwe.*

Ogidagimod. The second stomach of a ruminating animal.

Ogidakamig, adv. On earth, on the surface of the earth.—S. *Anâmakamig.*

Ogidaki, adv. On the hill or mountain ; p. *weg..wed.*

Ogidakiwebato, (nind). I run up on a hill or mountain ; p. *weg ..tod.*

Ogidibig, adv. On the water, on the surface of the water.—*Jesus ogidibig gi-bimosse ;* Jesus walked on the water.

Ogidigamig, adv. On the top of a lodge or house.

Ogidjaii, or *odgidj',* adv. On, upon.

Ogidjidon, adv. On the lips, with the lips only, (without the heart.)
Ogidjina, adv. Above, on the surface; on the outside, outwardly, superficially.
Ogikadanangwe. Lizard; pl.-*g*.
Ogikanan, (*nind*). I have her for an adopted mother; she is my adopted mother; also, my godmother; p. *wegikad*.
Ogikawin. S. *Mamaikawin*.
Ogima, (*nind*). I have her for a mother, she is my mother; p. *wegimad*. *Kid ogimin*, thou art my mother. *Kin wegiminân*, thou who art my mother. *Kin wegimigoian*, thou who art our mother.
Ogimâ. Chief, chieftain; superior, agent; officer; pl.-*ag*. *Kitchi ogima*, king, emperor.
Ogima-gijigad. Day of the Kings, Epiphany.
Ogimâkadage, (*nind*) or, *nind ogimakandamage*. I am chief or superior over people; I reign; p. *weg..ged*.
Ogimâkangamagemagad. It reigns, it has power over people; p. *weg..gak*.
Ogimâkandan, (*nind*). I am at the head of it, I am chief over it, I have power over it, it is under my command; p. *weg..ang*.
Ogimâkandawa, (*nind*). I am his chief, his master, his superior; his king; p. *weg..wad*.
Ogimâkandawe, (*nind*). I command, I reign; p. *weg..wed*.
Ogimâkaniw, (*nind*). S. *Ogimaw*.
Ogimâkwe. The wife of a chief; a female chief; pl.-*g*. *Kitchi-ogimâkwe*, queen, empress.
Ogimâkwew, (*nind*). I am the wife of a chief; I am a queen, an empress; p. *weg..wid*.
Ogimâkwewia, (*nind*). I make her a queen, I crown her; p. *weg..ad*.
Ogimaw, (*nind*). I am chief, I command, I reign; p. *weg..wid*.
Ogimâwâdis, (*nind*). I live like a chief, or I act like a chief, or king; p. *weg..sid*.
Ogimâwia, (*nind*). I make him a chief, I make him a king, I crown him; p. *weg..ad*.
Ogimâwigamig. The chief's lodge or house; palace, the king's house; pl.-*on*.
Ogimâ-wiwakwân. The chief's hat; crown; pl.-*an*.
Ogimâwiwin. Chieftainship, the dignity and authority of a chief or king; kingdom, empire; pl.-*an*.
Ogimigo, (*nind*). I am a mother, (I am had for a mother;) p. *wegimigoiân; wegimigoian, wegimind*, etc.
Ogin. His mother. *Ningâ, kigâ;* my mother, thy mother.
Ogin. Rose; pl.-*ig*.
Oginan, (*nind*). I have her for a mother, she is my mother; p. *wegid*. (V. Conj.)
Oginiminagawanj. Rose-tree, rose-bush; pl.-*ig*.
Oginiwâbigon. Rose-flower; pl.-*in*.
Oginiwabigoning inand. It is rose colored.
Oginiwâbigoning inanso. He is rose colored.
Ogishkimanissi. Kingfisher, (bird;) pl.-*g*.

Ogitchida. A brave warrior, a brave, a hero; pl.-*g.*
Ogitchida, (*nind*). I am a hero, a brave; p. *weg..wid.*
Ogôw, pron. These, these here.
Ogowêssi. Bed-bug; pl.-*wog.*
Ogwiss, (*nind*). I have a son; p. *wêgwissid*, (which is often pronounced *wêgossid.*)
Ogwissikânan, (*nind*). He is my godson; he is my adopted son; p. *weg..kad.* (V. Conj.)
Ogwissikâwin. Godson. — This word is always preceded by a possessive pronoun; as: *Nind ogwissikâwin*, my godson; *od ogwissikawinan*, his godson, etc.
Ogwissima, (*nind*). I have him for a son, he is my son; p. *wegwissimad*, (which is often pronounced *wégossimâd.*)
Ogwissimân. Pumpkin; (F. citrouille;) pl.-*an.*
Ogwissimânishigwân. Gourd-bottle with some shot in, used as a rattle at the Indian Grand Medicine. Pl.-*an.*
Ogwissimigo, (*nind*). I am a son, (I am had for a son;) p. *wegwissimigoiân, wegwissimigoian, wegwissimind*, (often pronounced *wegossimind.*)
Ogwissinan, (*nind*). I have him for a son, he is my son; p. *wegwissid*, (which is often pronounced *wégossid.*) V. Conj.
Ojakwess. A kind of small shell; pl.-*ag.*
Ojâsha, or-*magad.* It is slippery; p. *wejashag*, or-*magak.*
Ojashabikishin, (*nind*). I slide and fall on a *stone;* p. *wej.. ing.*
Ojashagoneshin, (*nin*). I slide and fall on the *snow;* p. *wej.. ing.*
Ojashakamigishin, (*nind*). I slide and fall on the *ground;* p. *wej..ing.*
Ojashakon. Tripe de roche.
Ojâshigob. A kind of elm-tree; (C. orme gras;) pl.-*ig.*
Ojâshikwishin, (*nind*). I slide and fall on the *ice;* p. *wej.. ing.*
Ojashishin, (*nind*). I slide or slip and fall; p. *wej..ing.*
Ojawanashkwakone, or-*magad.* There is a blue flame; p. *wes ..neg*, or-*magak.*
Ojâwano. A kind of blue bird; pl.-*g.*
Ojâwashkos, (*nind*). I am green; p. *wej..sid.*
Ojâwashkwa, or-*magad.* It is green; p. *wej..wag*, or-*magak.*
Ojawashkwabaga, or-*magad*, (pron. *ojawashkobaga.*) There are green leaves, the leaves on the trees are green; p. *wej.. gag*, or-*magak.*
Ojawashkwadissan, (*nind*) or, *nind ojawashkwansan.* I dye it green; p. *wej..ang.*
Ojawashkwadissige, (*nind*) or, *nind ojawashkwansige.* I dye green; p. *wej..ged.*
Ojawashkwadisso, or, *ojawashkwanso.* He is dyed green; *senibâ*, ribbon; *moshwe*, handkerchief; p. *wej..sod.*
Ojawashkwaaisswa, (*nind*) or, *nind ojawashkanswa.* I dye him green; p. *wej..wad;* imp. *oj..wi.*
Ojawashkwadite, or-*magad* or, *ojawashkwande*, or-*magad.* It

is dyed green ; p. *wej..eg*, or-*magak*.
Ojawashkwa-ginebig. Green serpent ; pl.-*og*.
Ojawashkwanaie, (*nind*). I am dressed in green, I have a green dress on ; p. *wej..ied*.
Ojawashkwanigade, or-*magad*, (pron. *ojawashkonigade*). It is painted green ; p. *wej..deg*, or-*magak*.
Ojawashkwanigaso, (*ojawashkonigaso*.) He is painted green ; p. *wej..sod*.
Ojawashkwashka, or-*magad*. It greens, the grass begins to grow ; p. *wej..kag*, or-*magak*.
Ojawashkwasigwa, or-*magad*. It is green, (ice, etc.) ; p. *wej..wag*, or-*magak*.
Ojawashkwassaginigade, or-*magad*, (pron. *ojawashkosssaginigade*.) It is painted green, (wood) ; p. *wej..deg*, or-*magak*.
Ojawashkwassaginigaso, (*ojawashkossaginigaso*.) He is painted green, (wood.)
Ojawashkwawegad. It is green, (stuff) ; p. *wej..gak*.
Ojawashkwawegisi. It is green, (stuff) ; p. *wej..sid*.
Ojia, (*nind*). I make some obj. ; p. *wêjiad*.
Ojibiamawa, (*nind*). I write him or to him ; p. *wej..wad*.
Ojibian, (*nind*). I write upon it, I make marks on it ; I describe it ; p. *wej..ang*.
Ojibiigade, or-*magad*. It is written, described ; there are marks upon it ; p. *wej..deg*, or-*magak*.—S. *Ijibiigade*.
Ojibiigan. Writing, writ, document ; pl.-*an*.
Ojibiiganâbik. Steel-pen ; pl.-*on*.
Ojibiiganâbo. Ink.
Ojibiigan-assin. Slate ; pl.-*ig*.
Ojibiiganâtig. Pencil ; pl.-*on*.
Ojibiigas, (*nin*). I am written, I am described ; p. *wej..sod*.—S. *Ijibiigas*.
Ojibiige, (*nin*). I write, I mark ; p. *wej..ged*.—S. *Ijibiige*.
Ojibiigêwigamig. Writing-house, office ; pl.-*on*.
Ojibiigewin. Writing, the act or art of writing.
Ojibiigewinini. Writing man, writer, clerk ; scribe, (in the Bible ;) pl.-*wog*.
Ojibiwa, (*nind*). I write or mark on some obj. ; I describe some obj. ; p. *wej..wad* ; imp. *ojibi*.
Ojig, (*nind*). I am formed ; p. *wejigid*.
Ojigaigan. Notch or incision in a maple-tree in making sugar ; pl.-*an*.
Ojigaige, (*nind*). I make incisions in maple-trees, to let the sap run out, in making sugar ; p. *wej..ged*.
Ojige, (*nind*). I make or build a lodge, or a house ; p. *wejiged*.
Ojigêwin. The act of building a lodge ; also, carpenter's trade or work, carpentry.
Ojigéwinini. Builder of houses, carpenter ; pl.-*wag*.
Ojigi abinodji (*ogin wiiawining*.) The child is formed, (in its mother's womb.)
Ojigi mandamin, *ojikiwog mandaminag*. The corn is formed into ears.
Ojigi ôpin, *ojigiwog opinig* (*akikang*). The potato is formed,

the potatoes are formed, (in the ground.)

Ojigin. It is formed ; p. *wejiging.—Ojigin mashkossiw,* an herb is formed. *Ojiginon mashkossiwan* (*mashkodeng ;*) the grass is formed, (in the meadow.)

Ojigondagan, (*nind*). I have a fine voice; p. *wej..ang.*

Ojigwan. His tail, (of a fish.)

Ojiiawes, (*nind*). I have a fine looking appearance; p. *wej.. sid.*

Ojim, (*nind*). I fly for safety, I flee, I run away; I escape; I take refuge; p. *wejimod.*

Ojima, (*nind*). I fly, or run away, from him; I avoid him, shun him; p. *wejimad.*

Ojimôa, (*nind*). I save him by flight, I cause him to flee, to escape; p. *wej..ad.*

Ojimotan, (*nind*). S. *Ojindan.*

Ojimotawa, (*nind*). S. *Ojima.*

Ojimowin. Flight, escape.

Ojindan, (*nind*). I fly from it; I avoid it, I shun it; p. *wej.. ang.*

Ojingibiss, (*nind*). I have a whitlow; p. *wej..id.*—S. *Jingibiss.*

Ojinindam, (*nin*). S. *Naangab.*

Ojishima, (*nind*). I put him right, I prepare him; p. *wej..mad.*

Ojissaga, or-*magad.* The floor is even p. *wej..gag,* or-*magak.*

Ojissagisi nabagissag. The board is even; p. *wej..sid.*

Ojissin. It is made, prepared, ready; p. *wejissing.*

Ojissitamawa, (*nind*). I make or prepare it for him; p. *wej.. wad.*

Ojissiton, (*nind*). I construct it, prepare it; I put it right, I establish it; p. *wej..tod.*

Ojita, (*nind*). I am getting myself ready, I am preparing, (especially for a voyage;) p. *wejitad.*

Ojitâa, (*nind*). I cause him to get ready, to prepare; p. *wejitaad.*

Ojitaidis, (*nin*). I prepare myself, I am getting myself ready; p. *wej..sôd.*

Ojitamadis, (*nind*) or, *nind ojitamas.* I make it to myself, or for myself; p. *wej..sod.*

Ojitamawa, (*nind*). I make it for him, or to him; p. *wej.. wad.*

Ojitawa, (*nind*). S. *Ojitamawa.*

Ojitâwin. Getting ready, preparing, preparation.

Ojitchigade, or-*magad.* It is made, constructed, done; p. *wej..deg,* or-*magak.*

Ojitchigas, (*nind*). I am made; p. *wej..sod.*

Ojitchishkiwagina, (*nin*). I knead it, (dough, clay, etc.); p. *wej..nad.*

Ojitchishkiwaginan, (*nind*). I knead it; p. *wej..ang.*

Ojiton, (*nind*). I make it, I do it, I construct it; p. *wejitod.*

Okâd. His leg; pl. *okâdan.*

Okâdakik. Kettle with legs, broth-pot; pl.-*og.*

Okadâkons. Radish; pl.-*on.*

Okadèiâb. A platted cord or string; (F. corde nattée;) p. -*in.*

Okadenamawa, (*nind*). I plat it for him or to him; p. *wek., wad.*

Okadenag minessagawanjig, (*nind*). I plat thorns together.
Okâdenan, (*nind*). I plat it; p. *wek..ang*.
Okadenige, (*nind*). I am platting, I plat; p. *wek..ged*.
Okâdetchigade, or-*magad*. It has legs, (a table, a stool, etc.)
Okâdetchigan. Leg of a chair, table, etc.; pl.-*an*.
Okâdigan. Shin-bone; pl.-*an*.
Okâdiginebig. A kind of serpent with four short legs; pl.-*og*.
Okâdima. Leg; pl.-*n*.
Okakiganama. Breast.—S. *Kakigan*.
Okan. His bone; pl. *okanan*.
Okanâk. The core of an ear of Indian corn; pl.-*wog*.
Okandikan. Buoy, (to mark the place where a net is set;) pl.-*ag*.
Okandikan bekodjikosod. A kind of big round buoy, fisher's buoy.
Okanima. Bone; pl.-*n*.
Okanisse. A kind of gray bird; pl.-*g*.
Okaw, (*nind*). There are my footsteps, my footsteps or tracks are visible, (where I walked in the snow, in mud, in sand, etc.); p. *wekawid*.
Okawamo mikana, or-*magad*. There are tracks on the trail, the trail is visible, it shows; p. *wek..mog*, or-*magak*.
Okâwanj. Juniper-bush; pl.-*ig*.
Okâmanjimin. Juniper-berry; pl.-*an*.
Okawia, (*nind*). I see his track where he walked; p. *wekawiad*.
Okawinade, or-*magad*. There are tracks or footsteps, (of persons or animals;) p. *wek..deg*, or-*magak*.
Okawissin ojibiiganâbo. The ink is black, (the track of the pen is very visible;) p. *wek..ing*.
Okawiton mikana, (*nind*). I see the trail; p. *wek..tod*.
Okawiwin. Track, trace, footstep.
Okiwiss. Herring; pl.-*ag*.
Okiwissab. Net with small meshes, for catching herrings; pl.-*ig*.
Okidj. Pipe-stem; p.-*in*.
Okikândag. Cypress-tree; pl. -*og*.
Okikiwishin, (*nind*). I lie squat; p. *wek..ing*.
Okishkimonisse. Fisher, (bird;) pl.-*g*.
Okitchigadima. The right leg, in general, without alluding to any person.
Okitchinikama. The right arm, in general, without a report to a person.
Okitchinikamang nakakeia. On the right hand, or to the right.
Okitchinindjima. The right hand, in general.—S. Example at *Onamandjinindjiwa*.
Okitchinowama. The right cheek, in general, without regard to a person.
Okitchishkinjigoma. The right eye, in general.
Okitebago-wassakwane. A kind of yellow flower growing in the water; pl.-*n*.
Okoj. His bill, his beak, (of a bird.)
Okonâss. His blanket, his cov-

ering ; peel, paring ; pl.-*an*.

Okonima. Liver.

Okwanim, (pron. *okonim*.) Beaver's dam, or any dam ; pl.-*in*.

Okwanimikâte, or-*magad*. There is a dam made ; p. *wek..deg*, or-*magak*.

Okwanimike, (*nind*). I am making a dam ; p. *wek..ked*.

Okwe. Worm coming out of a fly's egg ; pl. *okweg*.

Okwegissin. It is wrapped together ; p. *wek..sing*.

Okwêmij. Cherry-tree ; pl.-*ig*.

Okwémin. Cherry ; pl.-*an*.

Okwik. The cross-stick in a snow-shoe ; pl.-*in*.

Okwinomin, (*nind*). We are many together in one band, one flock, one heap ; p. *wekwinodjig*. — *Manisktanishag wekwinodjig*, a whole flock of sheep.

Okwishimâk, (*nind*). I put them together in a heap or pile ; p. *wek..mad*.

Okwishinog. They are together in a heap or pile ; p. *wekwishidjig*.

Okwissinon. They are together in a heap or pile (*inan*); p. *wekwissingin*.

Okwissitonan, (*nind*). I put them together in a heap or pile ; p. *wek..tod*.

Omâ, adv. Here, hither.

Omakaki Toad ; pl.-*g*.

Omamakis, (*nind*). I have the small pox ; p. *wem..sid*.

Omashkôs. Stag; pl.-*og*.

Omashkoswano, (proper name of some Indians.) The tail of a stag.

Omashkoswegin. The hide of a stag ; pl.-*on*.

Omashkosweshkan. Stag's horn, hart's horn ; pl.-*ag*.

Ombaan dassonagan, (*nind*). I set a trap ; p. *wembaang*.

Ombâbate. The smoke ascends ; p. *wem..teg*.

Ombâbigina, (*nind*). I lift him up, I hoist him up ; p. *wem..nad*.

Ombâbiginan, (*nind*). I hoist or lift it up ; p. *wem..ang*.

Ombabiginigan. Pulley ; windlass ; pl.-*an*.

Ombabiginige, (*nind*). I lift up, I hoist, I work at a windlass or pulley ; p. *wem..ged*.

Ombajeiakis, (*nind*). My skin is puffed up by a burning ; p. *wem..sod*.

Ombâjis, (*nin*). I play the buffoon, I droll, I jest ; p. *wem..sid*.

Ombâjisiwin. Buffoonery, drollery.

Ombâkamigis, (*nind*). I make noise, I play or divert myself in a noisy manner ; p. *wem..sid*.

Ombâkamigisishk, (*nind*). I use or like to make noise, to divert myself in a noisy manner : p. *wem..kid*.

Ombâkamigisishkiwin. Habit of indulging in noisy amusements.

Ombâkamigisiwin. Noise, noisy play or amusement.

Ombâkobidjige, (*nind*). I hoist the sail ; p. *wem..ged*.

Ombâkobidon, (*nind*). I lift it up, I hoist it ; p. *wem..dod*.

Ombakobina, (*nind*). I lift up or hoist some object ; p. *wem..nad*.

Ombâkona, (*nind*). I raise or

lift up some object (of wood especially ;) p. *wem..nad.*

Ombâkonan, (*nind*). I raise it up, (especially the mast in a canoe, with the sail tied to it ;) I lift it up, I make it stand ; p. *wem..ang.*

Ombakonige, (*nind*). I lift up, I hoïst ; p. *mem..ged.*

Ombâkwaigan. Lever ; pl.-*an.*

Ombâkwaige, (*nind*). I am lifting, raising up, (especially with a lever ;) p. *wem..ged.*

Ombânite, or-*magad.* There are optical appearances of land on the surface of a lake or sea, called "mirages" by voyagers. P. *wem..teg*, or-*magak* ; (F. il y a des mirages.)

Ombânitewin. Mirage ; (F. mirage ;) pl.-*an.*

Ombaog, (*nind*). I swell up ; p. *wem..god.*

Ombâsh, (*nind*). I am lifted up by the wind ; p. *wembâshid.*

Ombâsoma, (*nind*). I stir him up, I excite him ; p. *wem..mad.*

Ombâsondimin, (*nind*). We stir up each other, we excite each other to sedition or riot ; p. *wem..didjig.*

Ombâsondiwin. Stir, tumult, sedition, riot.

Ombâsonge, (*nin*). I stir up people, I cause a riot ; p. *wem..ged.*

Ombâssin. It is lifted up by the wind ; p. *wembassing.*

Ombia, (*nind*). I raise him, I incite him to some bad action or mischief ; I cause him to disobey, to revolt ; p. *wembiad.*

Ombibide, or-*magad.* It flies up in the air ; p. *wem..deg*, or-*magak.*

Ombibisigan. S. ***Ombisigan.***

Ombigamide, or-*magad.* It rises up boiling ; p. *wem..deg*, or-*magak.*

Ombigamisige, (*nind*). I make boil maple-syrup to make sugar ; p. *wem..ged.*

Ombigia, (*nind*). I make him cry, I cause him to make noise ; p. *wem..ad.*

Ombigis, (*nind*). I make noise ; also, I speak imprudently ; p. *wem..sid.*

Ombigisiwin. Noise ; imprudent language.

Ombigwemagad. It makes noise ; p. *wem..gak.*

Ombima, (*nind*). S. ***Ombia.***

Ombina, (*nind*). I lift or raise him up, (a person or any other obj.) ; p. *wembinad.*

Ombinan, (*nind*). I lift or raise it up ; p. *wem..ang.*

Ombiniken, (*nind*). I lift up my arm ; p. *wem..nid.*

Ombishin pakwejigan. The bread rises up ; p. *wem..ing.*

Ombishka, (*nind*). I rise on high ; p. *wem..kad.*

Ombishkamagad. It rises, it is lifted up ; p. *wem..gak.*

Ombisiden, (*nind*). I lift up my foot ; p. *wem..nid.*

Ombisigan, or *ombibisigan.* S. *Odji-mashkiki.*

Ombisse, (*nind*). I fly up in the air ; p. *wem..sed.*

Ombissitchigan. Leaven, yeast.

Ombissitchigaso pakwejigan. There is leaven or yeast in the bread, the bread is leavened ; p. *wem..sod.*—Leavened bread, *wembissitchigasod pakweji-*

gan. — *Wembissitchigâsossig pakwejigan*, unleavened bread.

Ombiwidon, (*nind*). I lift it up and carry it away; p. *wem..dod.*

Ombiwina, (*nind*). I lift him up and carry him away, (a person or any other obj.); p. *wem..nad.*

Ombândaa, (*nind*). I lay s. th. on him to carry; p. *wem..ad.*

Ombwêan, (*nind*). I stir it up, lifting it; p. *wem..ang.*

Ombwêtogibidon, (*nind*). I pluck or pull it out, (thread, etc.); p. *od..om....*

Ombwêwebinige, (*nind*). I overthrew, I put in disorder and confusion; p. *wem..ged.*

Omigi, (*nind*). I am scabby; p. *wemigid.*— *Nin kitchi omigi*, I am a leper, I have the leprosy.

Omigiwin. Scab; (F. gale.) *Kitchi omigiwin*, leprosy.

Omimi. Pigeon, wild pigeon; turtle-dove; pl.-*g*. *Omimins*, young wild pigeon; pl.-*ag.*

Omimi-sibi. Pigeon River, Lake Superior.

Omiskossi. A poisonous insect that runs on the surface of the water; pl.-*g.*

Omissadâma. Belly.

Omissandamo. A kind of water serpent; pl.-*g.*

Omissandamowaiân. The skin of the water-serpent; pl.-*ag.*

Omôdai. Bottle, flagon, flask; pl.-*an.*

Omôdai. Crop of a fowl.

Omôdens. Vial, small bottle.

Omonsom. Trail of animals in the woods; deer-trail; pl.-*in.*

Ona, at the end of some verbs, alludes to the conveying of some body in a *canoe* or *boat* to some place; as: *Nind âjawaona*, I take or convey him to the opposite shore, in a canoe or boat. *Nin giwêona*, I take or convey him back again in a canoe or boat, etc. S. *Odon.*

Onâbama, (*nind*). I choose him, I select him; p. *wen..mad.*

Onâbanad. There is a hard crust on the snow, the snow is hard, a person can walk on it without breaking through or sinking in; p. *wen..nak.*

Onâbandamowin. Choice, selection.

Onâbandan, (*nind*). I select it, choose it; p. *wen..ang.*

Onâbandjigade, or-*magad*. It is selected, chosen out of others; p. *wen..deg*, or-*magak.*

Onâbandjigan. A thing selected or chosen out of others; pl.-*ag.*

Onâbandjigas, (*nind*). I am chosen; p. *wen..sod.*

Onâbandjige, (*nind*). I choose, I select; p. *wen..ged.*

Onâbani-gisiss. The moon of the crust on the snow, the month of March, or, *niskikisis*, the wild gooses month.

Onâbem, (*nind*). I have a husband, I am a married woman; p. *wenabemid.*

Onâbemima. Husband; pl.-*g.*

Onâbide, (*nind*). I have fine even teeth; p. *wen..ded.*

Onâbikad. It is even, flat, (metal;) p. *wen..kak.*

Onabikamagad. It is even; (F. c'est uni;) p. *wen..gak.*

Onâbikisi. It is even, *joniiâ*,

silver; *assin*, stone; p. *wen.. sid.*

Onâdaan, (*nin*). I press it down, (in a box, etc.); p. *wen ..ang.*

Onâdaan biwâbik, (*nind*). I hammer iron, (I beat it down flat); p. *wen..ang.*

Onadaigade biwâbik, or-*magad.* The iron is hammered, (not cast;) p. *wen..deg*, or-*makak.*

Onâdamoton mikana, (*nind*). I make a road well or even; p. *wen..tod.*

Onâdina pakwejigan, (*nind*). I knead bread; p. *wen..nad.*

Onâdinige, (*nind*). I am pressing down; I am kneading bread; p. *wen..ged.*

Onâgan. Dish; pl.-*an.*

Onâganike, (*nind*). I make a dish or dishes, (especially of wood;) p. *wen..ked.*

Onâganikewin. The act, or art, of making dishes.

Onâganikewinini. A man that uses to make dishes, (especially of wood;) pl.-*wog.*

Onâgans. Little dish; cup; saucer; bowl; pl.-*an.*

Onagaskon. His palate.—*Ninagask, kinagask;* my palate, thy palate.

Onagaskwawai. Fine elegant embroidery with porcupine-quills; pl.-*an.*

Onagaskwawaie, (*nind*). I embroider with porcupine-quills, (Indian embroidery;) p. *wen.. ied.*

Onagek. S. *Wanagek.*

Onagij. Bowels; pl.-*in.*

Onagima, (*nind*). I put a price on some obj.; also, I judge him; p. *wen..mad.*

Onagindamawa, (*nind*). I make a price for him or to him; p. *wen..wad.*

Onagindan, (*nind*). I put a price on it; p. *wen..ang.*

Onâgosh. Evening.

Onâgoshi, or-*magad.* It is evening, it is late in the afternoon, towards evening; p. *wen..ig*, or-*magak.*

Onâgoshi-anamiang. Evening prayer, Vespers.

Onâgoshi-wissiniwin. Evening meal, supper.

Onâgwanaga, or-*magad.* There is an even snowshoe-trail; p. *wen..gag*, or-*magak.*

Onakakwaan, (*nind*). I put it on the spit, I spit it; p. *wen.. ang.*

Onakâkwâwa, (*nind*). I put him on a spit, I spit him; p. *wen.. wad;* imp. *on..kwâ.*

Onâkamiga, or-*magad.* There is a plain, even, level ground; p. *wen..gag*, or-*magak.*

Onakamigaan, (*nind*). I make it even, I level it, (ground;) p. *wen..ang.*

Onâkamigaigade, or-*magad.* It is made even, level, (ground;) p. *wen..deg*, or-*magak.*

Onâkamigamo mikana. The trail or road is even, is level; p. *wen..mog.*

Onâkamigissitchigan. The foundation of a house.

Onâkona, (*nind*). I appoint him, (to some place or office;) p. *wen..nad.*—S. *Inakona.*

Onâkonamawa, (*nind*). I make a regulation or law for him, or in regard to him; p. *wen..wad.*

Onâkonige, (*nind*). I make appointments, laws, regulations;

p. *wen..ged.*—S. *Inakonige.*

Onâkosi mitig. The tree is straight; p. *wen..sid.*

Onâkossidon, (*nind*). I haft it, I put a handle, haft or crank to it; p. *wen..dod.*—S. *Nabâkossidon.*

Onâman. Red clay, (for painting;) vermillion.

Onamandjigadima. The left leg, in general, without regard or report to a person.—S. Example at *Onamandjinindjima.*

Onamandjinikama. Left arm in general.

Onamandjinikamang nakakeia. On the left hand, or to the left.

Onamandjinindjima. The left hand, in general, without alluding to a person.—*Sanagadakosing onamandjinindjima, awashime dash sanagad okitchinindjima âkosing.* It is hard to have a sore left hand, but it is harder yet to have a sore right hand.

Onamandjinowama. The left cheek, in general.

Onamandjishkijigoma. The left eye, in general.

Onamandjisidama. The left foot, generally, without report to a person.

Onâmanines, (*nind*). I have the herpes, (a cutaneous inflammation;) p. *wen..sid.*

Onâmaninesiwan. Herpes, erysipelas, (an eruption of a hot acrid humor;) (F. erysipèle.)

Onamani-sâgaigan. Vermillion Lake.

Onanan. The calf of his leg. *Ninan, kinan,* etc.

Onandewegin. Dyed cloth; scarlet.

Onânigos, (*nin*). I rejoice; p. *wen..sid.*

Onânigosiwin. Joy, rejoicing.

Onânigoton, (*nind*), (*nind onanigwiton.*) I make it joyful, I make it rejoice; p. *wen..tod.*—*Nin gad onanigoton kidê;* I will make your heart joyful.

Onanigwendam, (*nind*). I have joyful thoughts, I rejoice; p. *wen..ang.*

Onanigwendamowin. Joyful thought, joy; pl.-*an.*

Onanigwia, (*nind*). I make him joyful; p. *wen..âd.*

Onansigan. Dye, color; pl.-*an.*

Onânsige, (*nind*). I am dyeing, coloring, I am a dyer; p. *wen..ged.*

Onansigéwigamig. Dye-house; pl.-*on.*

Onansigéwin. Dyer's business or trade.

Onansigéwinini. Dyer; pl.-*wog.*

Onapina, (*nind*). I harness him, (a horse or dog;) p. *wan..nad;* imp. *onapij.*

Onapis, (*nind*). I am harnessed; p. *wan..sod.*

Onapisowin. Harness; pl.-*an.*

Onashkinaa opwâgan, (*nind*). I fill a pipe; p. *wen..ad.*

Onashkinadass, (*nind*). I am putting my things in a trunk, box, etc.; I decamp, move off; (F. je plie bagage;) p. *wen..sod.*

Onashkinade pâshkisigan. The gun is loaded; p. *wen..deg.*

Onashkinadon pâshkisigan, (*nind*). I load a gun; p. *wen dod.*

Onaskwêia, or-*madad*. It is even, (*wigwáss*, bark); p. *wen ag*, or-*magak*.
Onassa, (*nind*). I put conveniently some obj.; p. *wenassad*.
Onâssigan. Smoked meat.
Onâssige, (*nind*). I smoke meat; p. *wen..ged*.
Onatâwanga, or-*magad*. The beach is even; p. *wen..gag*, or-*magak*.
Onâte, or-*magad*. There is soot; p. *wenâteg*, or-*magak*.
Onâton, (*nind*). I put it well, conveniently; p. *wenatod*.
Ond, *ondj*, in compositions, alludes to the *reason* or *origin* of s. th.; to the *place* from which, or out of which, some object comes or is obtained. (Examples in some of the following words.)
Ondâbate, or-*magad*. The smoke comes from..., or out of...; p. *wen..teg*, or-*magak*.
Ondâdad. It comes from...; p. *wendadak*.
Ondadém, (*nind*). I weep or cry for a certain reason, (pain, loss, sadness, fear, anger, joy;) p. *wen..mod*.
Ondadêmon, (*nind*). I bewail it; p. *wen..mod*.
Ondadémonan, (*nind*). I bewail some object; p. *wen..mod*. (V. Conj.)
Ondâdis, (*nind*). I am born, I descend from... I come from...; p. *wen..sid*.
Ondâdisia, (*nind*). I give him birth, I bring him forth; p. *wen..ad*.
Ondadisike, (*nind*). I bring forth, (a child,) I give birth, I am delivered, (of a child); p. *wen..ked*.—S. *Nigiâwass*.
Ondadisikewin. Child-birth, birth-giving.
Ondâdisiton, (*nind*). I bring it forth, I bring it into existence; p. *wen..tod*.
Ondâdisiwin. Birth.
Ondadisiwini-gijigad. Birthday.
Ondagodjin, (*nind*). I tumble down; p. *wen..ing*.
Ondâibân. Place from which water is obtained, a well; pl.-*an*.
Ondaibi, (*nind*). I obtain water from...; p. *wen..bid*.—*Mi oma wendâibiiân*; I obtain water from this place; (or, I fetch my water here.)
Ondam, alludes to *occupation*, having no time to spare; or to the *losing* of time. (Examples in some of the following words.)
Ondamakamigis, (*nin*). I am busy; p. *wen..sid*.
Ondamendam, (*nind*). I am distracted in my thoughts, I am occupied by other thoughts; p. *wen..ang*.
Ondamendan, (*nind*). It occupies my mind, I cannot leave it, I cannot cease to think on it; p. *wen..ang*.
Ondamenima, (*nind*). He occupies me in my thoughts, I cannot leave him, (a sick person, etc.); p. *wen..mad*.
Ondamia, (*nind*). I occupy him; also, I keep him back from his work, I make him lose his work-time; p. *wen..ad*.
Ondamibi, (*nind*). I am losing

my time by drinking liquor; p. *wen..bid.*

Ondamibiige, (*nind*). I am occupied in writing, all my time is taken up by writing ; p. *wen..ged.*

Ondamiiwe, (*nin*). I occupy people ; also, I make people lose their time, I keep them back from work; p. *wen..wed.*

Ondamima, (*nind*). I make him lose his work-time by talking to him; p. *wen..mad.*

Ondamis, (*nind*). S. *Ondamita.*

Ondamishka, (*nind*). I am absent from home, occupied elsewhere; p. *wen..kad.*

Ondamisiwin. Occupation.

Ondamita, (*nind*). I am busy, I am occupied, I have no time; p. *wen..tad.*

Ondamitagos, (*nind*). I occupy people by my speaking; p. *wen..sid.*

Ondamitakas, (*nind*). Feign. I make vain excuses of having no time, I dissimulate occupation ; p. *wen..sod.*

Ondamitchige, (*nind*). I am busy in doing this or that; p. *wen.. ged.*

Ondamonje, (*nin*). I am occupied or busy in nursing my child, it takes me all my time to take care of my child, (or children ;) p. *wen..jed.*

Ondanam, (*nind*). I run myself breathless after it, to reach it, to have it ; p. *wen..mod.*

Ondanândan, (*nind*). I starve, in order to have it; p. *wen.. ang.*

Ondâshân. Come here, come this way.

Ondâshime, adv. This way, nearer to this place here.

Ondâss. Come here.

Ondâssagâm, adv. On this side of a river, bay, lake, etc. S. *Awâssagâm.*

Ondâss inakakéia, adv. On this side, this way, here, towards this place.

Ondâssônag, adv. On this side of the canoe, boat, etc.

Ondê, or-*magad.* It boils ; p. *wendeg,* or-*magak.*

Ondénd, (*nind*). I am absent from home for such a reason; p. *wendendid.*

Ondênima, (*nind*). I have had feelings, revengeful thoughts, against him, for a certain reason; p. *wen..mad.*

Ondenindimin, (*nind*). We have bad feelings against each other, for a certain reason ; p. *wen..didjig.*

Ondenindiwin. Anger for such a reason, cause of anger; cause or title of condemnation.

Ondib. Ot. S. *Oshtigwân.*

Ondina, (*nind*). I get some obj. from..., or out of... ; p. *wendinad* ; imp. *ondin.*—*Atawéwigamigong nind ondina kokosh;* I get pork out of the store.

Ondinamage, (*nind*). I furnish people s. th., I let them have, I procure them; p. *wen..gek.*

Ondinamas, (*nind*) or, *nind ondinamadis.* I procure to myself s. th., I earn, I acquire ; p. *wen..sod.*

Ondinamason, (*nind*) or, *nind ondinamadison.* I procure it to myself, I earn it; p. *wen.. sod.*

Ondinamasonan, (*nind*) or, *nind ondinamadisonan*. I procure to myself some obj.; p. *wen.. sod.* (V. Conj.)

Ondinamawa, (*nind*). I let him have s. th., I furnish him, procure him s. th.; p. *wen.. wad.*

Ondinan, (*nind*). I get it from..., or out of...; p. *wen..ang.*— *Masinaiganing nind gi-ondinan nin kikendâsowin;* I got my knowledge from books, (or out of books.)

Ondinigade, or-*magad*. It is got or obtained of..., from...; p. *wen..deg*, or-*magak.*

Ondinige, (*nind*). I get things from..., of...; p. *wen..ged.*

Ondinimanganima. Shoulder; pl.-*n*.

Ondis, (*nind*). S. *Ondinige*.

Ondisin. It is profitable, it brings profit; p. *wendising.*

Ondisin, (*nind*). I have the profit of it; p. *wendisid.*

Ondisinan, (*nind*). I have the profit of some obj.; p. *wendisid.*

Ondj. Because, for, on account of, for the sake of..., in regard to...; *wendj*. S. Otch. Gram. Ch. VI. No. III.

Ondj. Through; as: *Bodâwâning gi-ondji-pindige, wassetçhiganing dash gi-ondji-sâgaam.* He came in through the chimney, and went out through the window.

Ondji, (*nind*). I come from..., out of...; p. *wendjid.*— *Wâssa wendjidjid*, those that come from far.

Ondji, or-*magad*. It comes from..., out of...; p. *wendjig*, or-*magak.*

Ondjia, (*nind*). I hinder him or forbid him to do s. th. or to go somewhere; p. *wendjiâd.*

Ondjiba, (*nind*). I come from...; p. *wendjibad.*

Ondjibamagad. It comes from..; p. *wen..gak.*

Ondjibide, or-*magad*. It comes flying from..., it flies from...; p. *wen..deg*, or-*magak.*

Ondjigo, or-*magad*. It leaks, (the water, etc., runs out of it, or into it;) p. *wendjigag*, or-*magak.*

Ondjigawiion, (*nin*). I make it run out of it, (liquid;) p. *wen ..tod.*

Ondjigidas, (*nind*). I get angry, on account of...; p. *wen..sod.*

Ondjiiwe, (*nind*). I hinder people to go somewhere, or to do s. th.; p. *wen..med.*

Ondjine, (*nind*). I die for such a reason, on account of...; p. *wendjined.*

Ondjinana, (*nind*). I kill him for the sake of...; p. *wen..ad;* imp. *ondjinaj.*

Ondjishkaosse, (*nind*). I walk against the wind; p. *wen..sed.*

Ondjishkawaam, (*nind*). I have head-wind, contrary wind, (traveling in a canoe, boat, etc.); p. *wen..ang.*

Ondjishkawaanigwad. The wind is ahead, contrary; p. *wen.. ak.*

Ondjissin. It comes from..., it results from...; p. *wendjissing.*

Ondjitâ, adv. Purposely, on

purpose; much, very; thanks, thank you.

Ondandanama. Heel, in general, without report to a person.

Ondonje, (*nind*). I have a child from...; p. *wendonjed.*

Ondwéwe, or-*magad.* A voice or noise comes out of..., or from... ; p. *wen..weg,* or-*magak.* — *Wadjiwing ondwéwemagad,* the noise comes from the mountain.

Ondwéwidam, (*nind*). I speak out of such a place; I speak for such a reason; p. *wen.. ang.*

Onendan, (*nind*). I judge it, privately, in thoughts; p. *wen ..ang.*

Onenima, (*nind*). I judge him, privately, in thoughts ; p. *wen..mad.*

Oniamawa, (*nind*). I set him a trap or snare, to catch him ; p. *wen..wad.—Amik nind oniamawa, wâbijeshiwog gaie nind oniamawag;* I set a beaver-trap, and a marten-trap, (I set traps to a beaver and to martens.)

Onidjâni. The female of an animal, of a quadruped, (not bird ;) pl.-*wog.*—S. *Nojésse.*

Onidjâniss, (*nind*). I have a child, or children; p. *wen..sid.*

Onidjanissikanan, (*nind*). He is my godchild; also, I adopt him for my child ; p. *wen.. kad.* (V. Conj.)

Onidjânissikawinan. S. *Ninidjânissikâwin.*

Onidjanissima. Child; pl.-*g.*

Onidjanissimig, (*nind*). I am his child, he has me for a child.

Onidjanissimigo, (*nind*). I am child; I am had for a child; p. *nin wenidjanissimigoiân ; win wenidjanissimind.*

Onidjanissinan, (*nind*). I have him for a child, he is my child; p. *wen..sid.* (V. Conj.)

Onidjanissindan, (*nind*). I have it for a child, I am its father; p. *wen..ang.* — *Wenidjânissindang gaginawishkiwin ;* he who has the lie for his child, (" the father of lies.")

Onidjâniwaiân. The skin of a female animal; pl.-*ag.*

Onigadan, (*nind*). I carry it on my shoulder; p. *wen..ang.*

Onigam. Portage; pl.-*in.*—*Kitchi-Onigaming,* at Grand Portage. *Watjaskonigaming,* at Rat-Portage.

Onigana, (*nind*). I carry him on my shoulder; p. *weniganad.*

Oniganâtig. Hand-barrow, to carry s. th. on it; pl.-*on.*

Onige, (*nind*). I make portage, I carry over a portage ; p. *weniged.*

Onigiigoma. Parent; pl.-*g.*

Oniige, (*nind*). I make traps in the woods, to catch little animals, as martens, minks, etc.; p. *weniiged.*

Onijan, (*nind*). I cut it, (a coat, etc.); p. *wenijang.*

Onijige, (*nind*). I cut, (a coat, etc.); p. *wen..ged.*

Onijigan. Shred; (F. retaille ;) pl.-*an.*

Onijish, (*nind*). I am fair, beautiful, fine; good, (a person or any other obj.); p. *wenijishid.*

Onijishabaminagos, (*nind*). I have a fine appearance ; p. *wen..sid.*

Onijishabaminagwad. It has a fine appearance, it looks beautiful ; p. *wen..wak*.
Onijishendam, (*nind*). I have fair thoughts, good thoughts ; p. *wen..ang*.
Onijishia, (*nind*). I embellish or adorn somebody ; p. *wen.. ad*.
Onijishin. It is fair, fine, beautiful ; it is good, useful ; it is agreeable ; p. *wen..ing*.
Onijishiton, (*nind*). I embellish it, adorn it; I make it good, useful, agreeable ; p. *wen..tod*.
Onijishiwin. Beauty, usefulness.
Onika, (*nind*). I have arms ; p. *wenikad*.
Onikama. Arm ; pl.-*n*.
Onimik. Bud ; browse, sprout ; pl.-*on*.
Onimakoke pijiki. The ox (or cow) eats little branches and shrubs, it browses ; p. *wen.. ked*.
Onina, adv. S. *Wanina*.
Oninassabi, (*nind*). I am getting a net ready for setting ; p. *wen..bid*.
Onindji, (*nind*). I have hands ; p. *wen..id*.
Onindjigan. Its fin, (of a fish ;) pl.-*an*.
Onindjima. Hand, or finger ; pl.-*n*.
Oningwi. His armpit, his armhole ; pl.-*n*.
Oningwigan. His wing ; pl.-*an*.
Oningwigana, (*nin*). I have wings ; p. *wen..nad*.
Onishka, (*nind*). I rise up, (when lying, not sitting ;) p. *wen..kad*.—S. *Pasigwi*.
Onishka, or-*magad*. It rises up, it comes up ; p. *wen..kag*, or-*magak*.
Onishkabato, (*nind*). I rise up quickly, briskly ; p. *wen..tod*.
Onishkâbina, (*nind*). I raise him up, lift him up ; p. *wen.. nad*.
Onishkâbinân, (*nind*). I raise it up, lift it up ; p. *wen..ang*.
Onishkwan. His gland.—S. *Ninishk*.
Onishkwêa, (*nind*). S. *Wanishkwea*, and the NOTE to it. N. B.—Sometimes the above words meaning "rising" are more pronounced with the root *We* than *O*.
Onotâgan. Employed person ; pl.-*ag*.
Onôw, pron. These, these here.
Onowan. His cheek, or his cheeks.—S. *Now*.
Onsâb, (*nind*). I look from a certain place, from a certain distance ; p. *wensâbid*.
Onsâbama, (*nind*). I see him from a certain distance ; p. *wen..mad*.
Onsâbandan, (*nind*). I see it from a certain distance ; p. *wen..ang*.
Onsâm, adv. S. *Osâm*.
Onsan, (*nin*). I boil it ; p. *wensang*.
Onsekwe, (*nind*). I boil s. th., I make boil ; p. *wen..wed*.
Onsibân. Sap, vital juice of plants and trees ; (F. sève.)
Onsika, (*nind*). I come for some reason ; p. *wensikad*.—*Wegonen ba-onsikâian ?* What is the reason of thy coming here? —S. *Bêsinika*.
Onsika, or-*magad*. It comes

from..., out of... ; p. *wen..kag*, or-*magak*.

Onsitagos, (*nind*). I am heard out of a certain place ; p. *wen ..sid.—Tchibegamigong gi- onsitagosi;* he was heard out of the grave; (a man that was buried before he was really dead.)

Onsitagwad. It is heard out of a certain place, out of s. th. ; p. *wen..wak—Gigitowin anakwadong gi bi-onsitagwad ;* a speaking was heard out of the cloud.

Onsitan, (*nind*). I hear a voice or noise coming out of some place ; p. *wensitang*.

Onsitawa, (*nind*). I hear him out of some place; p. *wen.. wad*.

Onso akik. The kettle boils ; p. *wensod*.

Onsoma, (*nind*). I reproach him, I scold him for s. th., or in regard to... ; p. *wen..mâd*.

Onsomâwass, (*nind*). I scold or reproach, in regard to my children ; p. *wen..sod*.

Onsonge, (*nind*). I reproach, I scold, for such a reason, in regard to... ; p. *wen..ged*.

Onswa, (*nind*). I boil some obj. ; p. *wenswad ;* imp. *onswi*.

Onwâs, (*nind*). I am lucky ; p. *wenwâsid*.

Onwâsiwin. Good luck, chance.

Onwâtawa, (*nind*). I have a foreboding of him, or in regard to him ; I augur or foretell of him ; p. *wen..wad*.

Onwâtchige, (*nind*). I have a foreboding by some mark, a presentiment ; I foretell by that presentiment, or from certain signs, I augur ; p. *wen..ged*.

Onwâtchigewin. Presentiment, foreboding, prognostic, augu- foretelling from signs.

Onwâtchigewinini. A man that has presentiments or forebodings by certain marks, and foretells future events accordingly, an augur, foreteller.

Onwâwe, (*nind*). I have the hiccough or hickup.

Onwâwewin. Hiccough, hickup.

Oôjishima, (*nind*). He is my grandchild ; p. *weo..man*.

Oôss, (*nind*). I have a father ; p. *weossid*.

Oossikanan, (*nind*). I have him for my adopted father, he is my adopted father ; my godfather ; p. *weo..kad*. (V. Conj.)

Oôssima, (*nind*). I have him for a father, he is my father ; p. *weossimad*.

Oôssimigo, (*nind*). I am had for a father, I am father ; p. *nin weôssimigoiân, win weôssimind*.

Oôssinan, (*nind*). I have him for a father, he is my father ; p. *weossid*. (V. Conj.)

Opâma, (*nind*). I hinder him to sleep, by talking or making noise ; p. *wepamad*.

Opâwe, (*nind*). I hinder people to sleep ; p. *wepawed*.

Opigêgan. His rib ; pl..*an.— Nipigêgan, kipigégan ;* my rib, thy rib.

Opikominân. Stone or kernel in fruits ; pl.-*an*.

Opikwad. Gut; pl.-*ag*.

Opikwadj. Air-bladder of a fish ; pl.-*in*.

Opikwan. S. *Pikwan*.

Opikwanâma. Back.
Opimeaii, adv. By, apart, aside, by the side of... ; obliquely.
Opimékana, adv. By the way-side.
Opimêna, adv. In the side of the body.
Opimêshima, (*nind*). I make him lie on his side, (not on the back ;) I lay him on his side ; p. *wep..mad.*
Opimêshin, I lie on my side, (not on the back ;) p. *wep..ing.*
Opimêsse, (*nind*). I fall on my side ; p. *wep..ed.*
Opimessidon, (*nind*). I lay it on the side ; p. *wep..dod.*
Opimessin. It lies on the side ; p. *wep..ing.*
Opin. Potato ; pl. *opinig.*
Opini-okonâss. Potato-paring ; pl.-*an.*
Opiniwigamig. Root-house ; pl.-*on.*
Opitchi. Thrush, robin ; (F. grive ;) pl.-*wag.*
Opwâgan. Pipe, (smoking-pipe ;) pl.-*ag.*
Opwâgan-assin. Pipe-stone, (soft white, black or red stone, fit to make a pipe out of it ;) pl.-*ig.*
Osâgi. Sack Indian ; pl.-*g.*
Osâgikwe. Sack squaw ; pl.-*g.*
Osâgim, (*nind*). I speak the Sack language, (the language of the Sack Indians ;) p. *wesâgimod.*
Osâgimowin. Sack language.
Osagin. His shoulder, (of an animal,) the fourth part of an animal.
Osâm, adv. Too ; too much ; very much.
Osâmakide, or-*magad.* It is too much burnt ; p. *wes..keg*, or-*magak.*
Osâmendam, (*nind*). I have too much care ; p. *wes..ang.*
Osâmendamowin. Too much care, trouble.
Osâmenim, (*nind*). I am very glad ; p. *wes..mod.*
Osâmia, (*nind*). I treat him too badly ; p. *wesamiad.*
Osâmidon, (*nind*). I speak too much, I am talkative, I prattle, chatter ; p. *wes..dod.*
Osamidonowin. Prattling, talkativeness, loquacity.
Osâmigidas, (*nind*). I am too angry ; p. *wes..sod.*
Osâminad. There is very much of it ; (there is too much of it ;) p. *wes..nak.*
Osâmine, (*nind*). I am very sick, (too much sick,) I have very much pain, (too much ;) p. *wês..ned.*
Osâminewin. A very great sickness ; pl.-*an.*
Osâmingwâm, (*nind*). I sleep too much, too long, I rise too late ; p. *wes..ang.*
Osâminimin, (*nind*) or, *nind osâminomin.* We are very many, too many ; p. *wes..djig.*
Osâminowe, (*nind*). S. *Osamidon.*
Osâmis, (*nind*). I am extravagant, exorbitant ; I am too bad, too noisy, too frivolous ; p. *wes..sid.*
Osâmisiwin. Extravagancy ; excess in making noise, in being frivolous, etc.
Osâmitchige, (*nind*). I act or behave too badly ; I do many things which I ought not to do ; p. *wes..ged.*

Osâmiwane, (*nind*). I carry too heavy a load; p. *wes..wed.*

Osâm nibiwa nind ani ikkit. I say too much of it, I exaggerate.

Osâm nin wewibita. I precipitate, I act too much in a hurry.

Osâmodama, (*nind*). I speak too much of him; p. *wes..mad.*

Osânaman. Vermillion, red paint or rouge, to paint the cheeks; (F. fard.)

Osânamani, (*nind*). I paint my cheeks red; p. *wes..niod.*

Osawa, or-*magad.* It is yellow; p. *wesawag*, or-*magak.*

Osâwâbân. Bile; (F. bile.)

Osâwâbi, (*nind*). I am bilious, I have much bile in me; p. *wes ..bid.*

Osawâbigin. Yellow flannel.

Osawâbik. Yellow metal, brass; also, copper.

Osawâbiko-nâbikawagan. Collar of brass-wire, worn by pagan Indians; pl.-*an.*

Osawâbikons. A cent, copper-cent. — *Nij osawâbikonsan*, two cents. *Nisswi osawâbikonsan*, three cents, etc.

Osâwâdissan, (*nind*),*osâwânsan*, (*nind*).

Osawadissige, (*nind*), *osawansige*, (*nind*).

Osawadisso, *osawanso.*

Osawadisswa, (*nind*),*osawanswa*, (*nind*).

Osawadite, *osawande.*—S. *Ojawashkwakissan*; *ojawashkwansan*, etc.; changing in the English signification *green* into *yellow.*

Osâwag wâwan, or *osâwawan* The yolk of an egg.

Osâwaje, (*nind*). I have a yellow skin; p. *wesâwajed.*

Osâwa-joniia. Gold, (yellow silver.)

Osawa-joniiakadan, (*nind*). I gild it; p. *wes..ang.*

Osawa-joniiakade, or-*magad.* It is gilt; p. *wes...deg*, or-*magak.*

Osawa-joniiakâso. It is gilt; p. *wes..sod.*

Osawa..joniiakana, (*nind*). I gild some obj.; p. *wes..nad.*

Osawâkadakons. Carrot; pl.-*an.*

Osawanashko-minikan. Mustard seed; pl.-*an.*

Osawegin. Yellow cloth or other yellow stuff; pl.-*on.*

Osawegisan, (*nin*). I make it yellow by smoke, (stuff;) p. *wes..ang.*

Osawegisige, (*nind*). I make yellow by smoke; p. *wes..ged.*

Osâwegiswa, (*nind*) (*an.*). I make it yellow and soft by smoke, (a deer skin;) p. *wes..wad;* imp. *osawegiswi.*

Osâwi ginebig. Yellow serpent; pl.-*og.*

Osâwi-makate. Brimstone, sulphur.

Osâwindibe, (*nind*). My head is yellow, I have yellow hair, flaxen hair; p. *wes..bed.*

Osâwines, (*nind*). I have the jaundice; p. *wes..sid.*

Osâwinesiwin. Jaundice; (F. jaunisse.)

Osawinigade, or-*magad.* It is painted yellow; p. *wes..deg*, or-*magak.*

Osawinigaso. It is painted yellow; p. *wes..sod.*

Osâwis, (*nind*). I am yellow; p. *wesawisid.*

Osawissaginigade, or-*magad*. It is painted yellow, (wood); p. *wes..deg*, or-*magak*.
Osawissaginigaso. He is painted yellow.
Osawitchiss, Rutabaga, yellow turnip; (F. chou de Siam); pl.-*an*.
Oshaiawigan, (*nind*). I have a sharp back, (I am extremely lean, poor;) p. *wesh..ang*.
Oshâkawa, (*nind*) or, *nind oshawa*. I scare him, I frighten him away, I màke him fly; p. *wesh..wad*.
Oshédina, or-*magad*. There is a long narrow ridge of a mountain; (F. il y a une crête de collines;) p. *wesh..nag*, or-*magak*.
Oshimêindimin, (*nind*). We are brothers together; p. *wesh.. didjig*.
Oshkabewiss. Waiter or attendant of an Indian Chief; pl.-*ag*.
Oshkâkaan. New field, newly broken land; (F. terre neuve.)
Oshkâkamigaigade, or-*magad*. There is a new field made, new land broken up; p. *wesh ..deg*, or-*magak*.
Oshkakamigaige, (*nind*). I sow or plant in a new field, I make a new field; p. *wêsh..ged*.
Oshkanjikadjigan. Horse-shoe; pl.-*an*.
Oshkânjima. Finger-nail; pl.-*g*.
Oshkânjin. His finger-nail; his hoof; his claw.— *Nishkânj*, *kishkanj*; my finger-nail, thy finger-nail.—In compositions the *k* is softened into *g*; as: *Bebejigoganj*, one hoofed animal. *Pijikiwiganj*, claw of an ox or cow.
Oshkassim. Young dog; pl.-*og*.
Oshki, adj. New, recent, fresh, young, first.
Oshki-abinodji. New-born child, infant, babe, baby; pl.-*iag*.
Oshki-aiaa. A new or young obj.; pl.-*g*.
Oshki-aiaans. A young animal or bird; pl.-*ag*.
Oshki-aii. A new obj.; pl.-*n*.
Oshki-aiiwan. It is new, (not yet used, or not much need;) p. *wesh..ang*.
Oshki-bimâdis, (*nind*). I am young, I begin to live; p. *wesh..sid*.
Oshki-bimâdisiwin. Youth.
Oshkigaigan. Fresh notch or incision in a maple-tree, in a sugar-making; pl.-*an*.
Oshkigin. Young shoot; (F. rejeton;) pl.-*on*.
Oshkigin. It is a young shoot; p. *weshkiging*.
Oshki ijitwâwin. The New Testament.
Oshkikwanaie, (*nind*) or, *nind oshkigwaje*. I have a new dress on; p. *wesh..ed*.
Oshkinagosi. He seems new, he looks like new; p. *wesh..sid*.
Oshkinagwad. He seems new, he looks like new; p. *wesh..wak*.
Oshkinawe. Young man, youth, lad, chap; pl.-*g*.
Oshkinawew, (*nind*). I am a young man; p. *wesh..wid*.
Oshkinig, (*nind*). I am newly born, that is, I am young; I am single, not married; p. *wesh..gid*.
Oshkinigikwe. Grown-up girl, young woman, (not married,) maid, virgin; pl.-*g*.
Oshkinigikwew, (*nind*). I am a

young woman, a maid, a virgin ; p. *wesh..wid.*

Oshkinigiwin. Youth, young age; single state.

Oshkinj. Its snout, its muzzle.

Oshkinjig. His eye ; his face ; pl. *oshkinjigon,* his eyes. — *Nishkinjig, kishkinjig ;* my eye, or face ; thy eye, or face.

Oshkinjig, (*nind*). I have eyes ; p. *wesh..god.*

Oshkinjigokade, or-*magad.* It is made like an eye ; p. *wesh.. deg,* or-*magak.*

Oshkinjigokâdjigan. Spectacles; pl.-*an.*

Oshkinjigoma. Eye ; pl.-*n.*

Oshkinjigones, (*nind*). I have sore eyes ; p. *wesh..sid.*

Oshkisagis, (*nind*). I have the monthly flowings for the first time ; p. *wesh..sid.*

Oshkitibikad. It is the beginning of the night ; p. *wesh.. kak.*

Oshtigwân. His head. — *Nishtigwân, kishtigwân ;* my head, thy head.

Oshtigwânigegan. Skull, (the bone of the head.)

Oshtigwânima. Head.

Oshtigwân-jâbonigan. Pin, (needle with a head ;) pl.-*an.*

Osidâkwâtig. Handle (of an axe, hoe, etc.) ; pl.-*on.*

Osidama. Foot; pl.-*n.*

Osigingwe, (*nind*). I have a wrinkled face, (from old age ;) p. *wes..wed.*

Osigwakomin. Pear ; pl.-*ag.*

Osigwâkominagawanj. Pear-tree ; pl.-*ig.*

Osissigobimij. Willow-tree ; pl. -*in.*

Oskanabewis, (*nind*) or, *nind oskanis.* I am lean, poor, thin ; p. *wesk..sid.*

Oskwan. The foremost part of the arm, (from the fingers up to the elbow).—There is always a possessive pronoun prefixed to this word ; as : *Nind oskwan,* my elbow ; *kid oskwan,* thy elbow ; *od oskwan,* his elbow, etc.

Oskweiâb. Vein, pulse ; pl.-*in.* —There is always a possessive pronoun prefixed to this word ; as : *Nind oskweiâb,* my vein ; *od oskweiâb,* his vein, etc.

Osow. His tail ; particularly the *bone* of the tail.

Ossikawin. S. *Babaikawin.*

Ossitawendam. S. *Wassitawendam.*

Ossossodam, (*nind*). I cough ; p. *wes..dang.*

Osossodamowin. Cough.

Ostiwin. Host.

Otawa. Otawa Indian, (or Ottowa Indian ;) pl.-*g.*

Otawag. Ear ; powder-pan of a gun ; pl.-*an.* — *Nitawag,* my ear ; *kitawag,* thy ear, etc.

Otawaga, (*nind*). I have ears ; p. *wetawagad.*

Otawagama. Ear ; pl.-*n.*

Otawagameg. A kind of lizard ; pl.-*mag.*

Otawakwe. Otawa squaw, (or Ottowa squaw ; pl.-*g.*

Otawam, (*nind*). I speak the Ottowa language ; p. *wet..mod.*

Otawamowin. Ottowa language.

Otawâwissiton, (*nind*). I translate it in the Ottowa language ; p. *wet..tod.*

Otawâwissin. It is in the Ottowa language; p. *wet..sing.*
Otchibik. Root; pl.-*an.*
Otchibikawi mitig. The tree has roots; p. *wet..wid.*
Otchideepinig, (nind). I have spasms, or cramps, at the heart; p. *wet..god.*
Otchig. Fisher, (animal ;) (C. pécan ;) pl.-*ag.*
Otchigadepinig, (nind). I have cramps in a leg or in the legs; p. *wet..god.*
Otchiganang. The constellation called "the great bear."
Otchingwan. S. *Nin tchigwan.*
Otchingwanigan. S. *Nin tchingwanigan.*
Otchinikepinig, (nind). I have cramps, or spasms, in my arms; p. *wet..god.*
Otchinindjipinig, (nind). I have cramps in my hand; p. *wet..god.*
Otchipinig, (nind). I have cramps, spasms, convulsions; p. *wet..god.*
Otchipinigowin. Cramps, spasms, convulsions.
Otchipwe. Chippewa Indian; pl.-*g.*
Otchipwê-kitchigami. The great water or sea of the Chippewa Indians, that is, Lake Superior.
Otchipwekwe. Chippewa squaw; pl.-*g.*
Otchipwem, (nind). I speak the Chippewa language; p. *wet..mod.*
Otchipwemowin. The Chippewa language.
Otchipwew, (nind). I am a Chippewa Indian; p. *wet..wid.*
Otchipwewibiigan. A writing in the Chippewa language; pl.-*an.*
Otchipwewibiige, (nind). I write in Chippewa; p. *wetch..ged.*
Otchipwewissitchigade, or-*magad.* It is translated in the Chippewa language; p. *wetch..deg,* or-*magak.*
Otchipwewissiton, (nind). I translate it in the Chippewa language; p. *wet..tod.*
Otchishibodagan. The bone of his hip.
Otchisidepinig, (nind). I have cramps in my foot or feet; p. *wet..ged.*
Otchitchâg, (nind). I have a soul; p. *wet..ged.*
Otchitchâgoma. Soul; pl.-*g.*
Otchitchingwanab, (nind). I kneel; p. *wet..bid.*
Otchitchingwanigabaw, (nind). I stand on my knees, I am kneeling; p. *wet..wid.*
Otchitchingwanigabawitan, (nind). I am kneeling before it; p. *wet..ang.*
Otchitchingwanidabawitawa, (nind). I stand on my knees before him, I am kneeling before him; p. *wet..wad.*
Otchitchingwanisse, (nind). I fall down on my knees; p. *wet..sed.*
Otchitchingwanita, (nind). I kneel down; p. *wed..tad.*
Otchitchingwanitan, (nind). I kneel down before it; p. *wet..ang.*
Otchitchingwanitawa, (nind). I kneel down before him, (any obj.); p. *wet..wad.*
Otchitchingwanitawin. Genuflection.
Otetêgwan. His ear, (of a fish.)

Otig, *otigwag*. Roe, eggs of fish.

Ow, pron. This, this here.

Ow! Here! here it is.

Owassamigonan, (*nind*). I illuminate it, I light it; p. *wew.. ang*.

Owibida, (*nind*). I have teeth; p. *wewibitad*.

Owidjikiwéima, (*nind*). I have him for a brother, he is my brother, my friend; p. *wew.. mad*.

Owidjikiweindimin, (*nin*). We are brothers together; or friends; p. *wew..didiig*.

Owigiwâm, (*nind*). I have a house; p. *wewigiwâmid*, the proprietor of a house, or of the house, the landlord.

Owiiâss, (*nind*). I have flesh; v. *wewiiasid*. — *E owiiâssing*, as one has flesh; (L. secundum carnem.)

Owiiaw, (*nind*). I have a body; p. *wewiiawid*.

Owiitawinodan, (*nind*). I have it in my body, I have it in me, it is incorporated to me, it is natural to me; p. *weg..ang*.

Owikanissima, (*nind*). I have him for a friend, brother, he is my brother, my friend; p. *wew..mad*.

Owikanissindimin, (*nind*). We are brothers or friends together; p. *wew..didjig*

Owinge, adv. S. *Wâwinge*.

Owinges, (*nind*). S. *Wâwinges*.

Owingesiwin. S. *Wâwingesiwin*.

P

Some words which are not found under P, *may be looked for under* B.

Pabig. Flea ; pl.-*wag.*

Pâbige, adv. Forthwith, immediately.

Păbigos, (*nin*). I have fleas ; p. *peb..sid.* — *Pabigosi animosh,* the dog is full of fleas.

Padagwaboéigan. Cover of a kettle ; pl.-*an.*

Padagwanaan, (*nin*). I cover it ; p. *ped..ang.*

Padagwanaigade, or-*magad.* It is covered over with s. th.; p. *ped..deg,* or-*magak.*

Padagwanaigas, (*nin*). I am covered over with s. th.: p. *ped..sod.*

Padagwanâwa, (*nin*). I cover him, (a person or any other obj.) ; p. *ped..wad ;* imp. *padagwanâ.*

Padagwanishkagon. (*nin*). It covers me ; p. *ped..god.*

Padagwanishkan, (*nin*). I cover him with my body ; p. *ped..ang.*

Padagwanishkawa, (*nin*). I cover some obj. with my body ; p. *ped..wad.*

Padagwawagishkam pakaakwe, bineshi. The hen, the bird, is hatching, covering her eggs; p. *ped..ang.*

Padashkaanji. Woodcock, snipe ; pl.-*g.*

Pagaadowan; pl.-*ag.* S. *Pagaadowânak.*

Pagaâdowanak. Indian crosier, to play with ; pl.-*on.*

Pagaadowe, (*nin*). I play with crosier and ball, I am playing ball ; p. *paia..wed.*

Pâgaadowewin. Indian ball-play, playing with crosier and ball.

Pâgaakokwan. Drum-stick ; pl.-*an.*

Pagakâban. It is broad daylight ; p. *peg..ang.*

Pagakigin. S. *Miskwegin.*

Pagakissin. It shows plainly, it is plainly visible ; p. *peg..ing.*

Pagakissidon nin gigitowin, (*nin*). I express plainly my speaking, to be easily understood ; p. *peg..dod.*

Pagakitagos, (*nin*). I speak plainly, so as to be well heard, I am well heard ; p. *peg..sid.*

Pagakitawa, (*nin*). I understand him plainly, I hear him well ; p. *peg..wad.*

Pagakowe, (*nin*). I speak plainly ; p. *peg..wed.*

Pagakwaige, (*nin*). I knock with s. th. ; p. *peg..ged.*

Pagamâdis, (*nin*). I arrive somewhere ; p. *peg..sid.*

Pagamâgan. Club, cudgel; war-club; pl.-*an.*

Pagamakosse, (*nin*). I get hurt in falling; p. *peg..sed.*

Pagamâmadjiwe, (*nin*). I arrive at the summit of a hill or mountain; p. *peg..wed.*

Pagamanimad. The wind rises, a strong wind comes on; p. *peg..mak.*

Pagamâsh, (*nin*). I arrive sailing; p. *peg..id.*

Pagamâssin. It comes or arrives driven by the wind; p. *peg..ing.*—*Nâbikwân gi-pagamâssin;* a vessel arrived, (driven by the wind.)

Pagami. In the beginning of some verbs, alludes to *arriving, coming on.* (Examples in some of the following words.)

Pagami-aiamagad. It comes to pass, it happens, it arrives; p. *peg..gak.*

Pagamibato, (*nin*). I arrive running; p. *peg..tod.*

Pagamibissa. The rain is coming; p. *peg..ssag.*

Pagamishka, (*nin*). I arrive (on foot or in a canoe, by land or by water;) p. *peg..kad.*

Pagamishka, or-*magad.* It comes on, it arrives; p. *peg..kag,* or-*magak.*

Pagamishkagon, (*nin*). It comes upon me, it happens to me; p. *peg..god.*

Pagamishkawa, (*nin*). I come upon him; p. *peg..wad.*

Pagân. Nut, walnut, hazelnut; pl.-*ag.*

Paganak; pl.-*wag.* S. *Pagân.*

Paganakomij. A kind of walnut-tree; (C. noyer tendre;) pl.-*in.*

Paganakomin; pl.-*ag.* S. *Pagân.*

Pagândis, (*nin*). I do nothing, I am good for nothing, I can make nothing, I know no work; p. *peg..sid.*

Pagândjikwe. A woman that knows no work and does not work; pl.-*g.*

Pagândjinini. A good for nothing fellow, who knows no works and does nothing; pl.-*wog.*

Pagânimij. Hazel; pl.-*in.*

Pagaskajêwa, (*nin*). I strike him on the bare skin; p. *peg wad;* imp. *pagaskajê.*

Pagéssan. Plum; pl.-*ag.*

Pagéssanimin. S. *Pagéssan.*

Pagessaniminagawanj. Plum-tree; pl.-*ig.*

Pagésse, (*nin*). I play the dish game, (Indian game;) (C. je joue au plat;) p. *pegessed.*

Pagessewin. Dish game.

Pagidabân. Line with many hooks on to catch fish; pl.-*an.*

Pagidâbi, (*nin*). I set a line with hooks, to catch fish; p. *peg..bid.*

Pagidânam, (*nin*). I breathe, I take respiration; I sigh; p. *peg..mod.*

Pagidanamowin. Breath, respiration, sigh.

Sagidandjige, (*nin*). I abstain from eating, I fast; p. *peg..ged.*

Pagidandjigewin. Privation of eating, abstinence, fasting.

Pagidawa, (*nin*). I set a net or nets, to catch fish; p. *peg..wad.*

Pagidawa assâb, (*nin*). I set a net; p. *pegidawad assabin.*

Pagidawéwin. Fishing-ground; (F. endroit de pêche;) pl.-*an.*

Pagidawéwinini. A man that sets nets, fisherman; pl.-*wag.*

Pagidéndagos, (*nin*). I am considered free, I am released; p. *peg..sid.*

Pagidéndamawa, (*nin*). I give it to him; I bring him a sacrifice; p. *peg..wad.*

Pagidéndamowin. Giving, sacrifice; renunciatton; burial, funeral.

Pagidéndan, (*nin*). I give it away, I sacrifice it, offer it, I renounce to it, cede it, reject it, I let it go; p. *peg..ang.*

Pagidênima, (*nin*). I give him away, I sacrifice him, offer him, I renounce him, I cede him, reject him; I bury him; p. *peg..mad.*

Pagidênindis, (*nin*). I sacrifice myself; I give myself up to somebody, or for some purpose, I put myself in the power of....; p. *peg..sod.*

Pagidina, (*nin*). I let him go, release him, I permit him to do s. th., or to go somewhere; I betray him; also, I sow it, I plant it; p. *peg..nad.*

Pagidinamawa, (*nin*). I give or deliver it to him, I cede it to him; I permit it to him; p. *peg..wad.*

Pagidinan, (*nin*). I let it go (from my hands,) I release it, I give it up, I desist from it; also, I sow it; p. *peg..ang.*

Pagidina tchî dibénindisod, (*nin*). I give him liberty, I emancipate him.

Pagidinigan. Gift; sacrifice, offering; pl.-*an.*

Pagidinigé, (*nin*). I give, I sacrifice, I bring or make an offering, a sacrifice, I immolate; also, I sow, I plant; p. *peg..ged.*

Pagidinigê-adopowin. Altar.

Pagidinigéwin. Sacrificing, sacrifice, offering, immolation.

Pagidinigéwinikan. Place where a sacrifice is made, altar, sacrificing altar, in the Old Testament.

Pagidinigéwinini. A man that performs sacrifices, sacrificer; jewish priest in the Old Testament; pl.-*wog.*

Pagidinissan. The quantity of wood that is put in the fire at one time.—*Ningo pagidinissan, nijo pagidinissan, nisso pagidinissan,* etc.; wood enough to put in the fire once, twice, three times, etc.

Pagidinisse, (*nin*). I put wood in the fire to keep up the fire; p. *peg..sed.*

Pagidjia, (*nin*). S. *Pagidina.*

Pagidji-aia, (*nin*). I am free, I am loose, released; p. *peg..iad.* — *Bebejigoganji pagidji-aia,* the horse is loose, not tied.

Pagidjigan. S. *Pagidinigan.*

Pagidjigé adopowin. S. *Pagidinigé adopowin.*

Pagidjigewin. S. *Pagidinigewin.*

Pagidjigewinikan. S. *Pagidinigewinikan.*

Pagidjigewinini. S. *Pagidinigewinini.*

Pagidjinige, (*nind*). I put down

a load I carried on my shoulder; p. *ped..ged.*

Pagidjinindjitawa, (*nin*) or *nin paginindjitawa. Alg.* I lay my hand or hands upon him; p. *peg..wad.*

Pagidjinodawa, (*nin*). I come upon him: p. *peg..wad.*

Pagidjiwanan. Stopping or resting-place in a portage, where the pack is put down; pl.-*an.*

Pagidjiwane, (*nin*). I put down a pack I carried on my back; p. *peg..ned.*

Pagidjwebina, (*nin*). I let him go suddenly; p. *geg..nad.*

Pagidjwebinan, (*nin*). I let it go suddenly; p. *peg..ang.*

Pagidoma, (*nin*). I put him down, (carrying on my back;) p. *peg..mad.*

Pagidôndan, (*nin*). I put my pack down (from my back;) p. *peg..ang.*

Pagis, (*nin*). I bathe; p. *pegisod.*

Pagisikawa, (*nin*). I let him go, I let him come up, (when I had kept him down;) p. *peg ..wad.*

Pagisswigamig. Bathing-house, bath; pl.-*on.*

Pagisowimakak. Bathing-tub; pl.-*on.*

Pagisowin. Bathing.

Pagissab, (*nin*). S. *Ishkatawab.*

Pagossâbama, (*nin*). I look at him with the hope that he will give me something, (when he is eating, counting money, etc.); p. *peg..mad.*

Pagossêndam, (*nin*). I ask with hope, I hope; p. *pég..ang.*

Pagossêndamowin. Asking, request, petition, hope.

Pagossêndân, (*nin*). I ask or pray for it; I hope for it; p. *peg..ang.*

Pagossêndjige, (*nin*). I beg, pray, ask; hope; p. *peg..ged.*

Pagossénim, (*nin*). S. *Pagossendam.*

Pagossênima, (*nin*). I ask him for s. th. with confidence, with hope; p. *peg..mad.*

Pagwâdakamig, adv. In the desert, in the wilderness.

Pagwâdakamigawan. There is a wilderness, a desert; p. *peg ..wang.*

Pagwâdassim. Wild dog, a dog that remains rather in the woods than about houses; pl.-*og.*

Pagwâdj, adv. Somewhere in a desert wild place, far from human habitations.

Pagwâdj-aiaâ. Wild animal, not tamed; or any obj. in a wild natural state; as, a wild fruit-tree, a wild potato, etc.; pl.-*g.*

Pagwâdj-aii. Any obj. in a wild natural state; as, herbs and plants, etc.; pl.-*n.*

Pagwâdji-bebejigoganji. Wild horse; pl.-*g.*

Pagwâdji-bimiskodissi. Wild small snail; pl.-*g.*

Pagwana, adv. By heart; at random, in a guessing manner; without knowing or seeing.

Pagwana nin debwetam. I believe without seeing.

Pagwana nind ikkit. I say it without knowing it well.

Pagwana nin wâwindân. I guess, I conjecture.

Pagwanawis, (*nin*). I am uneducated, I am ignorant, I am in a wild natural state, untutored; p. *peg..sid.*

Pagwanawisiwin, pagwanawâdisiwin. Ignorance, wild natural state, savage life.

Pagwanawiton, (*nin*). I don't know how to make it, or how to do; p. *peg..tod.*

Pagwanean, (*nin*). I pierce it, I bore it through, I make a hole in it; p. *peg..ang.*

Pagwanêbidon, (*nin*). I pierce it with my finger; p. *peg..dod.*

Pagwanêbitchige, (*nin*). I bore, I make a hole; p. *peg..ged.*

Pagwanégaigan. S. *Pagwanêigan.*

Pagwanêgaige, (*nin*). S. *Pagwanêige.*

Pagwanéia, or-*magad.* It is perforated, there is a hole in; p. *peg..iag,* or-*magak.*

Pagwanéiabika, or-*magad.* There is a hole in a rock; p. *peg..kag,* or-*magak.*

Pagwanéiakiswa, (*nin*). I burn a hole in some obj.; p. *peg..wad.*

Pagwanéigan. A tool to make a hole or mortise with, a chisel; pl.-*an.*

Pagwanéige, (*nin*). I make a hole, a mortise; p. *peg..ged.*

Pagwané-jagigamiwan. There are holes or openings in the ice on the lake; p. *peg..wang.*

Pagwanés, (*nin*). I have a hole or holes in some limb or limbs of my body; p. *peg..sid.*

Pagwanêshkawa, (*nin*). I wear out, I pierce or perforate, some obj.; p. *peg..wad.*

Pagwanéssidon, (*nin*). S. *Pagwanéshkan.*

Pagwanéssin. S. *Pagwanéshka.*

Pagwanéwa, (*nin*). I pierce or perforate some obj.; p. *peg..wad;* imp. *pagwané.*

Pagwanoma, (*nin*). I speak of him in his absence, I speak ill of him, I backbite him; p. *peg..mad.*

Pagwanondan, (*nin*). I speak of s. th. when absent from it, I backbite it; p. *peg..ang.*

Pagwanonge, (*nin*). I backbite: p. *peg..ged.*

Pagwanoskkan, (*nin*). I notch it, I cut small hollows in; p. *peg..ang.*

Pagwanoshkawa, (*nin*). I notch some obj.; p. *peg..wad.*

Pagwanotam, (*nin*). I listen stealthy, unperceived; p. *peg ..ang.*

Pagwanotawa, (*nin*). I hear him stealthy, unperceived by him, I overhear him; p. *peg..wad.*

Pagwishia, (*nin*) (pron. *nin pagoshia.*) I beg him for s. th. to eat, or for other things; p. *peg..ad.*

Pagwishiiwe, (*nin*) (pron. *nin pagoshiiwe.*) I beg s. th. to eat, or other things; p. *peg..wed.*

Pagwishiiweshk, (*nin*). I am in the habit of begging s. th. to eat, etc., I act the parasite, I am a parasite; p. *peg..kid.*

Pagwishiweshkiwin. The habit of asking for s. th. to eat, the practice of a parasite.

Pagwishiiwéwin. Begging for s. th. to eat, etc.

Pagwishiton, (*nin*). I use it, (I require it to give me s. th.) I have the profit of it; p. *peg..tod.—Nin pagwishiton iw kitigan;* I have a good profit of that field.

Pâjidji, adv. Above, over; (over another person or thing.)

Pâjidji-gwâshkwanodan, (*nin*). I jump over it; p. *paiaj..ang.*

Pâjidji-gwaskkwanodawa, (*nin*). I jump over somebody; p. *paiaj..wad.*

Pâjigwadendam, (*nin*). I persist upon my opinion or thought; also, I intend to make haste; p. *paiaj..ang.*

Pâjigwadis, (*nin*). I persist, I persevere; also, I make haste, I am diligent; p. *paiaj..sid.*

Pak. Easter. *Pak-kijigad*, Easter-Sunday.

Pâkaakwawâwan. Hen's egg; pl.-*on.*

Pâkaâkwê. Cock, hen; pl.-*iag.*

Pâkaâkwens. Young chicken; pl.-*ag.*

Pâkaâkwe-wâwan. Hen's egg; pl.-*on.*

Pâkabâgwe, (*nin*). I suffer thirst; p. *paia..wed.*

Pâkagwajena, (*nin*). I uncover him; p. *paia..nad.*

Pâkajawe, (*nin*). I clean or dress fish; p. *pek..wed.*

Pakajwa gigo, (*nin*). I clean and wash a fish; p. *pek..wad;* imp. *pakajwi.*

Pâkâkâb, (*nin*). My eyes are open; p. *paia..bid.*

Pakäkados, (*nin*). I am lean, poor; p. *pek..sod.*

Pakâkadosowin. Leanness.

Pakâkadwabewis, (*nin*). I am extremely lean, poor, I have nothing but the bones; p. *pek..sid.*

Pakâkadwengwe, (*nin*). I have a lean face; p. *pek..wed.*

Pâkâkendam, (*nin*). I am sure, I know plainly; p. *paia..ang.*

Pâkakendân, (*nin*). I am sure, I know it for certain, (it is open before me;) p. *paia..ang.*

Pâkakonamawa, (*nin*). I open it to him, (especially a door;) p. *paia..wad.*

Pâkâkomigan. The latch of a door; pl.-*an.*

Pâkakoshkan, (*nin*). I open it, (especially a door;) p. *paia..ang.*

Pâkâkossin. It is open; p. *paia..ing.*

Pâkakwaan. Shield, buckler; pl.-*an.*

Pâkatawâb, (*nin*). I open my eyes; p. *paia..bid.*

Pâkatch, adv. Absolutely, resolvedly, expressly, once.

Pâkawan. The fog disappears; p. *paiâkawang.*

Pâkêsiwin. Limb; (F. membre;) pl.-*an.*

Pakibidon, (*nin*). I tear it, break it, (a string, cord, etc.;) p. *pek..dod.*— The freq. v. of it is: *Nin papakibidon*, I tear it to *pieces.*

Pakibina, (*nin*). I tear some obj. (*senibâ*, ribbon;) p. *pek..nad.* —The *freq.* v. of it is: *Nin papakibina*, I tear it to pieces.

Pakibinindjibina, (*nin*). I dislocate or sprain his hand by pulling.

Pakibode, or-*magad*. It breaks by rubbing, (thread, cord, etc.); p. *pek..deg*, or-*magak.*

Pakibodon, (*nin*). I tear or

break it by rubbing, I rub it through, (cord, string, etc.;) p. *pek..dod.*

Pakibona, (*nin*). I tear or break some stuff by rubbing, (*seniba*, ribbon, silk;) p. *pek..nad.*

Pakiboso. It breaks by rubbing, (*seniba*, ribbon, *moshwe*, handkerchief;) p. *pek..sod.*

Pakidadjiwe, (*nin*). I pass a mountain, I am over it on the other side; p. *pek..wed.*

Pâkidonemagad. It opens its mouth; p. *paia..gak.*—*Aki gi-pâkidonemagad*, the earth opened its mouth.

Pâkidonen, (*nin*). I open my mouth; p. *paia..nid.*

Pâkidonena, (*nin*). I open his mouth; p. *paia..nad.*

Pâkidonetawa, (*nin*). I open my mouth to him; p. *paia..wad.* —*O kinawa Korinthing endanakiieg, ki-pâkidonetâgom!* O ye Corinthians, our mouth is open unto you!

Pâkigadebina, (*nin*). I dislocate his leg by pulling; p. *paia..nad.*

Pâkiginan masinaigan, (*nin*). I open a book, a letter, or any other folded paper; p. *paia..ang.*

Pakinâge, (*nin*). I surpass people, I excel, I gain the advantage over others; p. *pekinaged.*

Pâkinamawa, (*nin*). I open it to him; p. *paia..wad.*

Pâkinan, (*nin*). I open it; p. *paiâkinang.*

Pakinassabi, (*nin*). I break or tear a net; p. *pek..bid.*

Pakinawa, (*nin*). I surpass him, I beat him; p. *pek..wad.*

Pâkindenan, (*nin*). I open or lift the door of a lodge; p. *paia..ang.*

Pâkingwen, (*nin*). My face is uncovered; p. *paia..nid.*

Pâkisse, or-*magad*. It breaks open; p. *paiak..seg*, or-*magak.*

Pâkissin. It is open, it opens; p. *paiâkissing.*

Pâkissitamawa, (*nin*). I open or uncover it to him; p. *paia ..wad.*

Pâkissiton, (*nin*). I open it; I uncover it; p. *paia..tod.*

Pakitéakoshima, (*nin*). I throw down some obj. on a *rock* or *log;* I knock him down, throw him down; p. *pek.. mad.*

Pakiteoshimigon, (*nin*). It throws me down; p. *pek..god.* —*Akosiwin nin gi-pakiteoshimigon;* a sickness threw me down.

Pakitean, (*nin*). I strike it; p. *pekiteang.*

Pakitéianimad. There is a sudden squall of wind; p. *pek.. mak.*

Pakitêiâssin. The wind strikes something; *pek..ing.*

Pakitéigade, or-*magad*. It is beaten, it is hammered; p. *pek..deg*, or-*magak.*

Pakitéigan. Hammer; pl.-*an.*

Pakitêigas, ((*nin*). I am beaten; p. *pek..sod.*

Pakiteige, (*nin*). I strike, beat, knock; p. *pek..ged.*

Pakiteigewin. Striking, knocking.

Pakitêodis, (*nin*). I strike myself; p. *pek..sod.*

Pakitéoman, (*nin*). I strike some obj. belonging or relating to him ; p. *pek..mad.*—*Nin gi-pakitêoman onidjanissan ;* I struck his child.

Pakiteoshima, (*nin*). I throw him down, I knock him down; p. *pek..mad.*

Pakiteossidon, (*nin*). I throw it down, knock it down ; p. *pek ..dod.*

Pakitêshima, (*nin*). I make him fall ; p. *pek..mad.*

Pakitêshin, (*nin*). I fall hard, I tumble ; p. *pek..ing.*

Pakitêshkawa, (*nin*). I knock him with my shoulder ; p. *pêk..wad.*

Pakitêwa, (*nin*). I strike him; p. *pek..wad ;* imp. *pakitê.*

Pakojishib. A dock when it becomes so fat that it cannot fly ; pl.-*ag.*

Pakona, (*nin*). I flay or skin him ; p. *pekonad ;* imp. *pakôn.*

Pakonige, (*nin*). I flay, I skin ; p. *pekoniged.*

Pakwanagemak. Red pine ; pl.-*og.*

Pakwândibejwa, (*nin*). I scalp him, I take off his pericranium ; p. *pek..wad ;* imp. *pakwandibejwi.*

Pakwandj. A tree with its roots, (thrown down by the wind ;) pl.-*in.*

Pakwâni mitig. The bark of the tree can be taken off ; p. *pekwânid.*

Pakwâsika, or-*magad,* (pron. *pakoshka.*) It unglues; p. *pek..kag,* or-*magak.*

Pakwéamo. A kind of woodpecker ; pl.-*g.*

Pakwêbidon, (*nin*). I break off a piece ; p. *pek..dod.*

Pakwebigad. It is turbid, (any liquid) ; p. *pek..gak.*

Pakwebigami nibi. The water is turbid, not clear ; p. *pek..mig.*

Pakwêbina, (*nin*). I break off a piece of some obj. ; p. *pek.-nad.*—The *freq.* verb of it, *nin papakwebina,* signifies, I break it in several pieces.

Pakwêgaan mitig, (*nin*). I break off a piece of that wood; p. *pek..ang.*

Pakwêgawa mitig, (*nin*). I break off a piece of that wood ; p. *pek..wad ;* imp. *pakwegâ.*

Pakwêjan, (*nin*). I cut it, I cut a piece off from it ; p. *pek.. ang.*

Pakwêjigan. Bread, flour.—When the Indians first saw white people cutting pieces off from a loaf of bread, they called the bread *pakwêjigan,* that is to say, *a thing from which pieces are cut off.* S. *Pakwêjige.*

Pakwêjiganâbo. Flour-pap ; (F. bouillie.)

Pakwêjiganashk. Straw, or stalk of wheat; also, wheat, (improperly ;) pl.-*on.*—S. *Pakwêjiganimin.*

Pakwêjiganikan. Oven for baking bread ; pl.-*an.*

Pakwêjiganike, (*nin*). I bake, I make bread, cakes, etc. ; p. *pek..ked.*

Pakwejiganimin. A grain of wheat ; pl. *pakwejiganiminag,* wheat.—This word is often used in the diminutive, *pakwêjiganiminens ;* pl.-*ag.*

Pakwejiganiwaj. Flour-bag ; pl.-*an.*

Pakwêjigans. A small bread,

biscuit, cake, cracker; pl.-*ag*.

Pakwéjige, (*nin*). I cut off a piece, or pieces; p. *pek..ged.* —From this word is derived *pakwêjigan*, bread.

Pakwêjodiwin. Circumcision; also, castration.

Pakwejwa, (*nin*). I cut off a piece from some obj.; I circumcise him; also, I geld him, castrate him; p. *pek..wad;* imp. *pakwejwi*.

Pakwekotchigan. Potato-germ, potato-bud; pl.-*ag*.

Pakwéma, (*nin*). I bite off a piece from some obj.; p. *pek..mad.*—*Pakwejigan nin pakwema; assemân o pakwemân.* I bite off a piece of bread; he bites off a piece of tobacco.

Pakwéndan, (*nin*). I bite off a piece from it; p. *pek..ang*.

Pakwêndjige, (*nin*). I bite off; p. *pek..ged.*

Pakwêne. There is smoke; p. *pekwéneg*.

Pakwenessaton, (*nin*). I cense it, or incense it; p. *pek..tod.*

Pakwenessatawa, (*nin*). I cense him, or incense him; p. *pek..wad.*

Pakwenessatchigan. Censer, incensory; pl.-*an*.

Pakwenessatchige, (*nin*). I incense with a censer; p. *pek..ged.*

Pakwénibi (*nin*). I am choked by swallowing water; p. *pek..bid.*

Pakwênishkag, (*nin*). I am choked by eating s. th.; p. *pek..god.*

Pakwénishkodon, (*nin*). I choke it, I suffocate it; p. *pek..dod.*

Pakwénishkona, (*nin*). I choke him, by giving him s. th. to eat or to drink, (a child;) p. *pek..nad.*

Pakweshka onagek. The cedar-bark can be taken off from the tree; p. *pek..kad.*

Pakweshka, or-*magad*. It breaks off, falls off; p. *pek..kag*, or-*magak*.

Pakwesideshin, (*nin*). I hurt my foot in walking; p. *pek..ing*.

Pak-wissiniwin. The Passover.

Pama, adv. S. *Pânima*.

Panadjâ. Young chicken; young bird; pl.-*iag*.

Pangaân miskweiâb, or *oskweiâb*. The pulse is beating; p. *pengaang*.

Pangaân nind oskweiâb. My pulse is beating; p. *pangaanini od iskweiâb*.

Pangaog, (*nin*). My pulse is beating; p. *pen..god.*

Pangi, adv. A little.

Pangigag. Drop; (F. goutte.) *Abiding pangigag*, one drop; *nijing, nissing, midâtching pangigag*; two, three, ten drops. *Midâtching ashi nijing pangigag*, twelve drops. *Nijtana dassing pangigag*, twenty drops.

Pângigawisibingwe, (*nin*). I shed a tear; p. *paia..wed.*—*Nin papângigâwisibingwe*, freq. I shed tears, my tears are falling in drops; p. *pepang..wed.*

Pangi nind âkos. I am unwell, indisposed.

Pangishé, adv. Very little.

Pangishéwagad. There is very little of it; p. *pen..gak*.

Pangishéwagisi. There is very little of him ; p. *pen..sid.*

Pangishewagisimin, (*nin*). We are very little, in a very small number ; p. *pen..sidjig.*

Pangishima, (*nin*). I let him fall to the ground, I drop him, lose him, (a person or any other obj.) ; p. *pen..mad.*—*Pangi joniia nin gi-pangishima pitchinâgo ;* I dropped some money yesterday, (I lost it.)

Pangishimo gisiss. The sun sets ; p. *pengishimod.*

Pangishin, (*nin*). I fall ; p. *panjishing.*

Pangishkones, (*nin*). I fall sick suddenly ; p. *pèng..sid.*

Pangissin. It falls ; p. *pengissing.*

Pangissiton, (*nin*). I let it fall to the ground, I drop it, I lose it ; p. *pen..tod.*

Panibigaan, (*nin*). I make a hole in it, or through it, with a chisel ; p. *pen..ang.*

Panibigaigan. Chisel ; pl.-*an.*

Panigâwa, (*nin*). I make a hole in it, or through it, with a chisel ; p. *pen..ad ;* imp. *panigâ.*

Pânima, adv. By and by, later afterwards, not before a certain time or a certain event.

Pânima, nind ikkit mojag. I say always, by and by, that is, I delay always, I postpone, (in *words.*)

Pânima nind inendam mojag. I think always, by and by, that is, I delay always, I postpone, (in *thoughts.*)

Panossim. Sea-dog ; (F. chien marin) ; pl.-*og.*

Pantkot, or *Pantkot-gijigad.* Pentecost or Whit-Sunday.

Pâpagaan ishkwandem, (*nin*). I knock at a door ; p. *paia..ang.*

Pâpagâbidewadj, (*nin*). I chatter with the teeth being cold ; p. *pep..djid.*

Pâpagakwaan, (*nin*). S. *Papagaan.*

Pâpagakwaige, (*nin*). I knock (at a door) ; p. *paia..ged.*

Papâgimak. A kind of ash-tree ; pl.-*wog.*

Papâgiwaiân. Cotton, shirt ; pl.-*an.*

Papâgiwaiânegamig. House of cotton, a tent ; pl.-*on.*

Papâgiwaianeshkimod. Bag made of cotton ; pl.-*an.*

Papagiwaiânigin. S. *Papâgiwaian.*

Pâpagwash, adv. Always, continually, incessantly.

Papâkanje, or-*magad.* The sparks fly up ; p. *pep..jeg,* or-*magak.*

Papâkine. Cricket ; grass-hopper ; pl.-*g.*

Papâkine, or-*magad ishkote.* The fire crackles ; p. *pep..neg,* or-*magak.*

Papâkwaam, (*nin*). I come out of the woods ; p. *pep..ang.*

Papakwânadji. Bat, flitter-mouse ; pl.-*iag.*

Papângibissa. It begins to rain, drops of rain are falling here and there ; p. *pep..sag.*

Papâshkigiw. Pitch of the firtree, balsam.

Papâshkisiganak. Elder-tree ; pl.-*on.*

Papashkojan, (*nin*). I shear it

thoroughly, I take all off; p. *pep..ang.*

Papashkojwa, (*nin*). I shear him thoroughly, close to the skin; p. *pep..wad;* imp. *papashkoj.*

Papashwâkamiga, or-*magad.* There is clear ground, a clearing, (the trees have been cut down and taken away); p. *pep..gag,* or-*magak.*

Papashkwâkondibe, (*nin*). I am bald, bald-headed; p. *pep..bed.*

Papassâkamigadin. The ground splits from cold; p. *pep..ing.*

Papâssangwâb, (*nin*), or, *nin papassangâanâb.* I blink with the eyes; p. *pep..bid.*

Papâsse. A kind of small woodpecker; pl.-*g.*

Papikwakamiga, or-*magad.* There is a rough, hilly ground, not even; p. *pep..gag,* or-*magak.*

Pasagôbidon, (*nin*). I scratch it; p. *pes..dod.*

Passagôbijiwe, (*nin*). I scratch; p. *pes..wed.*

Passagôbina, (*nin*). I scratch him; p. *pes..nad;* imp. *passagôbij.*

Pasagwâmiton, (*nin*). I make it thick, (some liquid;) p. *pes..tod.*

Pashagishkanakwad. Dark cloud; pl.-*on.*

Pashagishkibikad. It is a dark night; it is very dark; p. *pesh..kak.*

Pashagishkinam, (*nin*). I am in darkness, I cannot see immediately, coming in a house from sunshine, I am dazzled; p. *pesh..mod.*

Pâshkâb, (*nin*). I am blind on one eye, I am one-eyed; p. *paiâshkâbid.*

Pâshkâbawa, (*nin*). I make him one-eyed, I knock him an eye out; p. *paia..wad.*

Pâshkâbide, (*nin*). My teeth are distant from each other; p. *pesh..ded.*

Pâshkabide-binâkwân. Large dressing-comb; pl.-*an.*

Pâshkâbideia, or-*magad.* Its teeth are distant from each other, (rake, harrow, etc.); p. *pesh..iag,* or-*magak.*

Pâshkâbidjin, (*nin*). I burst one of my eyes; p. *paia..ing.*

Pâshkâbis, (*nin*). My eyes are spoiled (or lost) by too much smoke; p. *paia..sod.*

Pâshkâkwadin. It bursts by freezing; p. *paia..ing. Gi-pâshâkkwadin omodai;* the bottle burst, (by the freezing of the water that was in.)

Pâshkâkwadji mitig. The tree cracks or splits by extremely cold; p. *paia..djid.*

Pashkandamo. A kind of bird; pl.-*g.*

Pâshkâp, (*nin*). I burst into laughter; p. *paiashkâpid.*—S. *Nanissap.*

Pâshkâweo panadjâ. The small young bird or chicken comes out of the egg, is hatched out; p. *paia..od.*

Pâshkide, or-*magad.* It bursts by extreme heat; p. *paiashkideg,* or-*magak.*

Pâshkikawog tigowog. The waves on the lake (or sea) are white, they flourish; p. *paia..djig.*

Pâshkikwaamog (*animikig*). It

thunders with a great crash, there are great peals of thunder.

Pâshkiminassanan, (*nin*). I make them burst; I confect them, I make sweetmeats or preserves of them, (of berries); p. *paia..ang.*

Pâshkiminassigan. Sweetmeats, preserves; (F. confitures.)

Pâshkiminassige, (*nin*). I confect, I make preserves; p. *paia..ged.*

Pâshkiminasswag, (*nin*). I make them burst; I confect them, I make preserves of them, (of berries); p. *paia..wad.*

Pâshkisan, (*nin*). I shoot at it, I shoot it; p. *paia..ang.*

Pâshkisi assâb. The net has large meshes; p. *paia..sid.*

Pâshkisigan. Gun, rifle, musket; pl.*-an.*—*Kitchi-pâshkisigan*, cannon.

Pâshkisiganâtig. The stock of a gun; pl.*-on.*

Pâshkisigans. Pistol; pl.*-an.*

Pâshkisigans nessoshkak, naoshkak, nanoshkak, nengotwâssoshkak. Revolver with 3, 4, 5, 6 barrels.

Pâshkisige, (*nin*). I shoot, I am shooting; p. *paia..ged.*

Pâshkisigewin. The act of shooting with a gun, etc.; also, powder and shot, or either of these articles, ammunition.

Pâshkiswa, (*nin*). I shoot him; p. *paiâshkiswad;* imp. *pâshkis.*

Pâshkobidjigaso bineshi. The bird is picked, its feathers are plucked out; p. *paia..sod.*

Pâshkobidon, (*nin*). I pluck it out, I weed a field; p. *paia..dod.*

Pâshkobina, (*nin*). I pick him, (a bird,) I strip a bird of his feathers; p. *paia..nad;* imp. *pâshkobij.*

Pashkodon, (*nin*). I have no beard; p. *péshkodong.*

Pashkodonebina, (*nin*). I pull his beard out; p. *pesh..nad;* imp. *pash..bij.*

Paskkosi aw bineshi, or *papashkosi*. That bird is naked, has no feathers; p. *pesh..sid.*

Pashkwadashi. A kind of wolf almost without hair, prairie-wolf; (F. loup de prairie;) pl.*-wog.*

Pashkwadikwebigisi aw awessi. That animal has no hair or fur; p. *pesh..sid.*

Pashkwakobidon, (*nin*). I pull it out, I weed; p. *pesh..dod.*

Pashkwashkijan, (*nin*). I mow it; I reap it; p. *pesh..ang.*

Pashkwashkijigan. Scythe or sithe; sickle; pl.*-an.*

Pashkwashkijige, (*nin*). I mow, I reap; p. *pesh..ged.*

Pashkwégin. Leather.

Pashkwegino-babisikawâgan. Coat made of leather; pl.*-an.*

Pashkwegino-midâss. Legging made of leather; pl.*-an.*

Pashkwegin-omôdai. Leather-bottle; pl.*-an.*

Pasigwao bineshi. The bird starts, flies away; p. *pes..ed.*

Pasigwi, (*nin*). I rise up, I stand up; (F. je me mets debout;) p. *pesigwid.*

Pasigwia, (*nin*). I make him rise up, stand up; I rouse him; p. *pes..ad.*

Pasigwiton, (*nin*). I make it stand up; p. *pes..tod.*

Pâssaan, (*nin*). I break it, (a plate, glass, etc.); p. *paiassaang.*

Passâbika, or-*magad.* There is a cleft, gap or fissure in a rock; there is a steep rock; p. *pes..kag*, or-*magak.*

Passadina, or-*magad.* There is a low place between two mountains, a valley; p. *pes..nag*, or-*magak.*

Pâssadin makakossag, omodai, etc., the barrel, the bottle, etc., bursts by cold; p. *paia.. ing.*

Passâginiken, (*nin*). I stretch out my arm; p. *pes..nid.*

Passaginikena, (*nin*). I stretch out his arm; p. *pes..nad.*

Passâginindjin, (*nin*). I open my hand; p. *pes..nid.*

Passagita, (*nin*). I erect myself, I stand upright; p. *pessagitod.*

Passaige, (*nin*). I cut and split cedar-wood, to make a canoe; p. *pes..ged;* also, I square wood.

Passâkadem, (*nin*). *Alg.* I sigh; p. *pes..mod.*

Passâkamiga, or-*magad.* There is narrow hollow valley, a ravine; p. *pes..gag*, or-*magak.*

Passakonandawa, (*nin*). I fillip him; p. *pes..wad.*

Passängaanâb, (*nin*). I twinkle or blink, (once); p. *pes..bid.*—See the *freq.* v. of it, *nin papassangaanâb.*

Passângaanâbiwin. Twinkling, the twinkling of an eye, a moment.

Passangwâb, (*nin*). I shut my eyes, I keep my eyes shut; p. *pes..bid.*

Passangwâbishka, (*nin*). My eyes shut against my will, I am sleepy, I am drowsy; p. *pes..kad.*

Passanikadan, (*nin*). I make a ditch in it or through it; p. *pes..ang.*

Passanikade, or, *passanikaigade*, or-*magad.* There is a ditch made; p. *pes..deg*, or-*magak.*

Passanikan, or *passanikaigan.* Ditch, trench; pl.-*an.*

Passanike, (*nin*) or, *nin passanikaige.* I am digging a ditch or trench; p. *pes..ed.*

Passanowêwa, (*nin*). I strike him on the cheek, I buffet him; p. *pes..wad;* imp. *passanowe.*

Passâtawanga, or-*magad.* There is a small valley of sand; p. *pes..gak*, or-*magak.*

Pâssâwa, (*nin*). I break some obj.; p. *paia..wad;* imp. *passâ.*

Passekânak. A kind of frog; pl.-*wag.*

Pâssibidon, (*nin*). I break it to pieces with my hands; p. *paia..dod.*

Pâssibina, (*nin*). I break some obj. to pieces with my hands; p. *paia..nad.*

Passidon, (*nin*). My lip is cloven; split; p. *passidong.*

Passidonéganama, (*nin*). I give him a *violent* blow on the mouth; p. *pes..mad.*

Passidonêwa, (*nin*). I strike him on the mouth; p. *pes.. wad;* imp. *passidoné.*

Pâssigaigan. Iron cleaver used especially by shingle-makers to split pine blocks into shingles; pl.-*an*.

Pâssigaige, (*nin*). I am splitting with a cleaver; p. *paia..ged*.

Pâssika, or-*magad*. It breaks, it splits, rends; p. *paia..kag*, or-*magak*.

Pâssikan, (*nin*). I break, (split it); p. *paia..ang*.—*Nin pâpassikan*, freq., I break it into several pieces.

Passikawan; pl.-*ag*; or *passikawanak*; pl.-*on*. The stick or rod used by the squaws in playing their play.

Passikawe, (*nin*), (*nin papassikawe*, freq. v.) I am playing the Indian women's play; p. *pes..wed*.

Pâssikwad. S. *Tashkikwad*.

Passikwébodjigan. Sling; pl.-*an*.

Passikwébodjige, (*nin*). I am throwing with a sling; p. p. *pess..ged*.

Pâssiton, (*nin*). I break it, (split it); p. *paia..tod*.—*Nin papassiton*, freq. v., I break it in several pieces.

Passwéwe, or-*magad*. It re-echoes, it resounds; p. *pess..weg*, or-*magak*.

Passwéweshin, (*nin*). I create echo, I make resound my voice; p. *pess..ing*.

Passwéweton, (*nin*). I make it re-echo, resound; p. *pess..tod*.

Patabinan masinaigan, (*nin*). I close a book *slightly*; p. *pet..ang*.

Patabiwebinan masinaigan, (*nin*). S. *Patakowebinan*.

Patagwakonindjin, (*nin*). I close my hand; p. *pet..nid*.

Patakaan, (*nin*). I close my hand; p. *pet..nid*.

Patakaan, (*nin*). I sting it, I prick it, I pick it up with something pointed; p. *pet..ang*.

Patakaigan. Fork, table-fork; pl.-*an*.

Patakâige, (*nin*). I pick it up with a fork; p. *pet..ged*.

Patakâkamigissidon, (*nin*). I stick it in the ground; p. *pet..dod*.

Patakâkodjin, (*nin*). I am stung by it, I have it sticking in me; p. *pet..ing*.—*Nin patakakodjin minessagawanj nishtigwâning*; I have a thorn sticking in my head. (III. Conj.)

Patakashkaigan. Hay-fork; pl. *an*.

Patakâwa, (*nin*). I sting some obj., I pick it up or take it up with a pointed object; p. *pet..wad*; imp. *patakâ*. — *Opin nin patakawa*; I sting and pick up a potato.

Patakibidjigan. Harpoon; iron hook for catching sturgeon; pl.-*an*.

Patakibidjige, (*nin*). I am harpooning; I am hooking with an iron hook; p. *pet..ged*.

Patakibidon, (*nin*). I harpoon it, or hook it and draw it to me; p. *pet..dod*.

Patakibina, (*nin*). I hook him and draw him to me, I hook and grapple him; p. *pet..nad*; imp. *patakibij*.

Patakibinweon. Plume of feathers, head-ornament of feathers; pl.-*an*.

Patakide, or-*magad*. It sticks in s. th., it is erected, it stands up; p. *pet..deg*, or-*magak.*

Patakidjin, (*nin*). S. *Patakakodjin.*

Patakina, (*nin*). I stick some obj. in s. th., I put up, I erect some obj.; p. *pet..nad;* imp. *patakij.*

Patakinindjidjin. I have it sticking in my hand, it sticks in my hand; p. *pet..ing.*

Patakishima, (*nin*). I stick or thrust some obj. in s. th.; p. *pet..mad.*

Patakishin. Some obj. sticks in s. th.; it stands up in s. th.; p. *pet..ing.*

Patakisidedjin, (*nin*). I have it sticking in my foot, it sticks in my foot; p. *pet..ing.*

Patakiso. S. *Patakishin.*

Patakissidon, (*nin*). I stick or thrust it in s. th; p. *pet..dod.*

Patakissin. S. *Patakide.*

Patakiwebina, (*nin*). I stick it in s. th. throwing it, I make it stand up with force; p. *pet..nad.*

Patakiwebinan, (*nin*). I stick or thrust it in by throwing, or with force; p. *pet..ang.*

Patakowebinan masinaigan, (*nin*). I close a book somewhat briskly; p. *pet..ang.*

Patashkanje. Long billed curlew, (water fowl;) pl.-*wog.*

Patchishkabikad. It is pointed, (metal); p. *pet..kak.*

Patchishkabikisi. It is pointed, (stone, silver;) p. *pet..sid.*

Patchishkan, (*nin*). I sting it, pierce it; p. *pet..ang.*

Patchishkawa, (*nin*). I prick him, sting him, pierce him; p. *pet..wad.*

Patchishkibodon, (*nin*). I cut it pointed; p. *pet..dod.*

Patchiskibona, (*nin*). I cut some obj. pointed; p. *pet..nad;* imp. *patchishkiboj.*

Patchishkigaan, (*nin*). I cut it pointed with an axe; p. *pet..ang.*

Patchishkigad. It is cut pointed, (wood,) it is pointed; p. *pet..gak.*

Patchishkigad. It is cut pointed, (stuff;) p. *pet..gak.*

Patchishkigâwa, (*nin*). I cut it pointed with an axe; p. *pet..wad;* imp. *patchishkigâ.*

Patchishkigisi. It is cut pointed, (stuff;) p. *pet..sid.*

Patchishkigisi. It is cut pointed, it is pointed, (wood;) p. *pet..sid.*

Patchishkigan, (*nin*). I cut it pointed; p. *pet..ang.*

Patchishkijwa, (*nin*). I cut it pointed; p. *pet..wad.*

Patchishkikodan, (*nin*). I cut it pointed with a knife; p. *pet..ang.*

Patchishkikona, (*nin*). I cut some obj. pointed with a knife; p. *pet..nad;* imp. *patchishkikoj.*

Patchishkiwine gisiss. The moon has pointed horns, (first or last quarter;) p. *pet..ned.*

Pawengwai, adv. Asleep, in sleep, sleeping.

Pawengwai nin bimosse. I walk in sleep.

Pawengwai nin gigit. I speak in sleep.

Pawindeige, (*nin*). I sweep a chimney; p. *pew..ged.*

Pekwawigang. He that is hump-backed; camel; pl.-*ig.*

Pepeshodis, (*nin*). I scarify myself, in order to bleed; p. *paie ..sod.*
Pepeshowewin. Scarification of the skin, for letting blood.
Pepeshwa, (*nin*). I bleed him, by scarifying, by incisions of the skin; p. *paie..wad;* imp. *pepeshwi.*
Pepigwed. Player on the flute, flute-player; pl.-*jig.*
Pêshkwe. A kind of owl; pl.-*g.*
Pigidgissag. Rotten wood.
Pigidjissagad. It is rotten, (stick, pole, or any wooden obj.); p. *peg..gak.*
Pigidjissagisi nabagissag. The board is rotten; p. *peg..sid.*
Pigikâdân, (*nin*). I pitch it; I tar it; I putty it; p. *peg..ang.*
Pigikâna, (*nin*). I pitch or tar some obj.; p. *peg..nad;* imp. *pigikaj.*
Pigike, (*nin*). I pitch, I tar, I putty; p. *pegiked.*
Pigikêwanissag. Firebrand used in pitching a canoe; pl.-*on.*
Pigishkanad. It is rotten; putrefied, corrupted; p. *peg..nak.*
Pigishkanan, (*nin*). I am rotten, putrefied, I mortify; p. *peg..nid.*
Pigishkibidon, (*nin*). I break it off by small pieces; p. *peg.. dod.*
Pigisakibina assema, (*nin*). I break off tobacco by small bits; p. *peg..nad.*
Pigishkishin, (*nin*). I fracture my body by falling from a certain height; p. *peg..ing.*
Pigishkissin. It breaks to pieces, falling from a height; p. *peg.. ing.*
Pigiw. Pitch.
Pigiwisigan. Maple sugar made to resemble pitch; (C. sucre en gomme.)
Pigongweigan. Hoe; pl.-*an.* S. *Bimidjiwagakwad.*
Pigonekwe. A kind of small frog; pl.-*g.*
Pigwâwe aw animosh. This dog has long hair,(poodle-dog); p. *pag..wed.*
Pijiki. Ox, bull; cow; buffalo; pl.-*wog.* *Nâbé-pijiki*, bull. *Ikwê-pijiki*, cow. *Mashkodê-pijiki*, buffalo. *Odâbi-pijiki*, draught-ox.
Pijikimasitagosi. The ox (or cow) bellows; p. *mes..sid.*
Pijikins. Calf; pl.-*ag.*
Pijikiwanow. The tail of an ox or cow; pl.-*an.*
Pijikiwegin. Ox-hide, cow-hide, buffalo-robe; pl.-*on.*
Pijikiwigamig. Stable; pl.-*on.*
Pijikiwiganj. The claw of an ox or a cow; pl.-*ig.*
Pijikiwimo. Dung.
Pijikiwitotosim. The udder of a cow; pl.-*ag.*
Pijikiwiiâss. Beef.
Pijikiwi-wissiniwâgan. Manger; pl.-*an.*
Pijishig, adv. Alone, only; without a load, empty.
Pijishigônagaam, (*nin*). I have nothing in my canoe; p. *pej ..ang.*
Pijishigowis, (*nin*). I am alone, I have no wife; I have no husband; p. *pej..sid.*
Pikikiwe, (*nin*). S. *Pikikiweta.*
Pikikiwepogosi. It has the taste of an animal that was tired out before it was killed; p. *pek..sid.*

Pikissanagokan. Partition in a house; pl.-*an.*
Pikiséanagoke, (*nin*). I make a partition in a house; p. *pek ..ked.*
Pikissânagong. In the closet.
Pikodjân. A ball of thread; pl.-*an.*
Pikodjane, (*nin*). I have a knob on my nose; p. *pek..ned.*
Pikodjanoadon, (*nin*). I wind it on a ball, (thread, cord, etc.); p. *pek..dod.*
Pikodji, (*nin*). I have a big fat belly; p. *pekodjid.*
Pikonâgiji, (*nin*). S. *Pikodji.*
Pikoganân, or *pikwakoganân.* Ankle-bone; pl.-*an.*
Pikwabikisse, or-*magad.* It tumbles; (F. il s'écroule;) p. *pek ..seg,* or-*magak.*
Pikwadinâ. S. *Papikwadina.*
Pikwadj. Fish-bladder; pl.-*in.*
Pikwadjish. A kind of mushroom; pl.-*an.*
Pikwagondagan. Big throat.
Pikwajeshka, (*nin*), *nin papikwajeshka,* freq. v. I have pimples or pustules on my skin; p. *pek..kad.*
Pikwâk. Arrow, made of wood only; pl.-*on.* S. *Assawan.*
Pikwakamiga, or-*magad.* It is a hilly ground, there are small hills; p. *peg..gag,* or-*magak.*
Pikwakokweweshi. Jay, (bird;) (F. geai;) pl.-*iag.*
Pikwakonindj. Fist; pl.-*in.*
Pikwakonindjitawa, (*nin*). I cuff him, I strike him with the fist; p. *pek..wad.*
Pikwâkoshib. A kind of wild duck, an autumn-duck; pl.-*ag.*
Pikwâkôssagidiie, (*nin*). I have a large rump, large buttocks; p. *pek..ied.*
Pikwâkwad. Knob on a tree; play-ball; pl.-*on.*
Pikwâkwado-pagamâgan. Indian war-club, with a big knob on the end; pl.-*an.*
Pikwan. Back.— There is always a possessive pronoun prefixed to this word; as: *Nin pikwan,* my back; *o pikwan,* his back, etc.
Pikwanénindj. The back of the hand.—There is always a possessive pronoun before this word: as: *Nin pikwanenindj, ki pikwanenindj, o pikwanenindj;* the back of my, thy, his hand.
Pikwanénindjitawa, (*nin*). I strike him with the back of my hand; p. *pek..wad.*
Pikwâwigan. Humpback.
Pikwâwigan, (*nin*). I am humpbacked; p. *pek..ang.*
Pinaamawa, (*nin*). I put or thrust it in for him; p. *pan.. wad.*
Pinaan, (*nin*). I put or thrust it in; I take it down; p. *panâang.*
Pinawa, (*nin*). I put or thrust somebody in some vessel; I take him down; p. *panawad;* imp. *pinâ.*
Pinawe aw awéssi. That animal is shedding its hair, it is moulting; p. *penawed.* — S. *Pinigwane.*
Pinaweshka. S. *Pinawe.*
Pindaadon, (*nin*). I catch it in a net; p. *pan..dod.*
Pindaam, (*nin*). I catch in my net or nets; p. *pandaang.*

Pindaana, (*nin*). I catch in a net or in nets; p. *pan..nad.*

Pindaas, (*nin*). I am caught in a net; p. *pan..sod.—Nibiwa gigoiag pindaasowog;* many fishes are caught in the net.

Pindâbawadjigan. Clyster-pipe; pl.-*an.*

Pindâbawadjigan. Injection, (given to a sick person,) clyster; (F. lavement.)

Pindâbawadjige, (*nin*). I am giving an injection; p. *pan..ged.*

Pindabawana, (*nin*). I give him an injection; p. *pan..nad;* imp. *pindabawaj.*

Pindâgan. S. *Mashkimod.*

Pindâganiwe, (*nin*). I put in a bag; p. *pan..wed.*

Pindâganwen, (*nin*). I put it in a bag; p. *pan..wed.*

Pindâganiwenan, (*nin*). I put some obj. in a bag; p. *pan..wed.*

Pindakatewân. Powder-horn; pl.-*ag.*

Pindakatewe, (*nin*). I am filling my powder-horn; p. *pan..wed.*

Pindakodjane, (*nin*). I take snuff; p. *pan..ned.*

Pindâkoshima, (*nin*). I put him in a mortise, etc.; p. *pan..mad.*

Pindakossiton, (*nin*). I put it in a mortise, etc.; p. *pan..tod.*

Pindâkwe, (*nin*). I snuff, I take snuff, (the same as, *nin pindakodjane;*) p. *pan..wed.*

Pindâkwewin. The act, or habit of taking snuff; snuff; (F. tabac en poudre.)

Pindanikanisse, (*nin*). I fall or slide in a hole, or in a ditch, or in any hollow place; p. *pan..sed.*

Pindanona, (*nin*) or, *nin pindanobina.* I put my finger (or hand) in his mouth, (or in a trap or snare;) p. *pan..nad.*

Pindanonikadjigan. Case; scabbard; pl.-*an.*

Pindanwân. Quiver, case for arrows; pl.-*ag.*

Pindaode, or-*magad.* It is in a case, cover or scabbard; p. *pan..deg*, or-*magak.*

Pindaodjigan. Cover or scabbard of a gun, etc.; pl.-*an.*

Pindaodon, (*nin*). I put it in a scabbard or cover, (a gun, etc.); p. *pan..dod.*

Pindashkwadan, (*nin*). I stuff it; (F. je le bourre;) p. *pan..ang.*

Pindashkwana, (*nin*). I stuff him; p. *pan..nad;* imp. *pindashkwaj.*

Pindashkwe, (*nin*). I stuff; p. *pan..wed.*

Pindassa. A bar in a canoe or boat; pl.-*ag.*

Pindassinan, or *pindassinadjigan.* Shot-pouch; pl.-*an.*

Pinde, or-*magad.* It is in s. th.; p. *pandeg*, or-*magak.*

Pindigadon, (*nin*). I bring it in, I carry it in, I enter it; p. *pan..dod.*

Pindig. Inside.

Pindigamig, adv. In the lodge or house.

Pindigana, (*nin*). I bring him in, I carry him in, I lead or conduct him in; p. *pan..nad;* imp. *pindigaj.—Endaiân nin pindigana;* I take him to my house, (I take him in.)

Pindigawa, (*nin*). I come to his

house, to his dwelling, I visit him ; *fig.* I enter into him, in his heart, in his mind ; p. *pan..wad ;* imp. *pindigaw.*

Pindigé, (*nin*). I go in, I come in, I enter ; p. *pandiged.*

Pindikomân. Knife-sheath, scabbard for a knife ; pl.-*an.*

Pindj', or *pindji*, adv. In, inside. (Always connected with a substantive.)

Pindjâii, adv. Inside, within, interiorly.

Pindjibide, or-*magad.* It flies in ; p. *pan..deg*, or-*magak.—Biwigaigan gi-pindjibide ;* a chip flew in.

Pindjidawamagad sibi. The river has an entrance, a mouth ; p. *pan..gak.*

Pindjidawaam, (*nin*). I go in, or I come in, in a canoe or boat ; p. *pan..ang.*

Pindjideeshkâgon, (*nin*). It comes in my heart ; p. *pan..god.*

Pindjideeshkawa, (*nin*). I come in his heart ; p. *pan..wad.*

Pindjidikibina, (*nin*). I put s. th. in his wound ; p. *pan..nad;* imp. *pindjidikibij.—Pindjidikibijishin kinindj oma gainaganamigoiân ;* put thy hand here where I was wounded.

Pindjidjanj. Inside the nose, nostril.

Pindjidon. Inside the mouth.

Pindjinaweshkawa, (*nin*). I come into him, I enter into him, I abide in him ; p. *pan..wad.— Matchi manitog o gi-pindjinaweshkawâwân kôkoshan*, the evil spirits entered into the swine.

Pindjinindjin, (*nin*). I put my finger in..., (or my hand ;) p. *pan..nid.*

Pindjisideshin, (*nin*). I put my foot in.. . ; p. *pan..ing.*

Pindjisidesse, (*nin*). I slide in, or fall in, with one foot ; p. *pan..sed.*

Pindjisse, (*nin*). I slide or fall in... ; p. *panjissed.*

Pindomowin. Bosom. — *Abraham o pindomowining*, in Abraham's bosom.

Pindonag, adv. In a canoe, boat, etc.

Pindônag nâbikwâning. In the hold of the vessel.

Pingewewem, (*nin*). I am tired of weeping ; p. *pan..mod.*

Pingosh. A kind of stinging fly, sandfly ; (C. moustique ;) pl.-*ag.*

Pingoshens. A very small stinging fly ; (C. brûlot ;) pl.-*ag.*

Pingwâbik. Sand-stone ; pl.-*og.*

Pingwâbo. Lie, (ash-water.)

Pingwâwa, (*nin*). I throw ashes on him ; p. *pen..wad ;* imp. *pingwâ.*

Pingweombassin. The dust is raised and driven by the wind ; p. *pen..ing.*

Pingwi. Ashes ; fine white sand.

Pingwi-gijigad. Ash-Wednesday.

Pingwi-kisibigaigan. Liquid soap ; (C. potasse.)

Pingwiwina, (*nin*). I powder him ; also, I put ashes on him, (as on Ash-Wednesday in the Church ;) p. *pen..nad ;* imp. *pingwiwin.*

Pinigwane aw bineshi. That bird is shedding its feathers ;

it is moulting; p. *pen..ned.*—S. *Pibawe.*

Pinishi, adv. S. *Anisha.*

Pinomon, (*nin*). I put it in my bosom; p. *panomod.*

Pins, (*nin*). I am in s. th.; p. *pansod.*—*Anindi kissaie?*—*Ningotchi sa pinso.* Where is thy brother?—He is in some place, (or house.)

Pinsab, (*nin*). I peep out from under s. th. (from under a blanket, etc.); p. *pansabid.*

Pinsibadjigan. Funnel; (F. entonnoir;) pl.-*an.*

Pipigwis. S. *Migisananissi.*

Pipigwan. Flute, fife, flageolet; pl.-*an.*

Pipigwe, (*nin*). I play on the flute, etc.; p. *pep..wed.*

Pipigwewanashk. Elder-shrub; pl.-*on.* (Properly, flute-reed.)

Pipiwige. A kind of sparrow-hawk; pl.-*g.*

Pisikan, (*nin*). I hit it, (not purposely;) p. *pesikang.*

Pisikawa, (*nin*). I hit him, (accidentally;) p. *pes..wad.*

Pitawashka, or-*magad.* There is a shallow place in the lake where the waves break; p. *pet..kag,* or-*magak.*

Pitâwigan. Shed at the entrance-door; pl.-*an.*

Pitchâ, or-*magad.* It is long; it is distant, far; p. *petchag,* or-*magak.*

Pitcha, or-*magad gijigad.* The day is long, (in summer.)

Pitcha, or-*magad mikana.* The road is long, (a far distance to walk.)

Pitcha, or-*magad sigwan.* The spring is long, (the warm summer-season comes late this year.)

Pitcha, or-*magad tibikad.* The night is long, (in winter.)

Pitchi, or *Pit.*—This word gives to the verb or substantive that follows it, the signification of *mistake, accident, involuntary action.* (Examples in some of the following words.)

Pitchib, (*nin*). I poison myself, I eat or drink poison in my food; p. *petchibod.*

Pitchibajiwe, (*nin*). I administer poison, I give poison to people in their food; p. *pet..wed*

Pitchibona, (*nin*). I give him poison, I poison him; p. pe...*nad;* imp. *pitchiboj.*

Pitchibowin. Poison. S. *Matchimashkiki.*

Pitchi-dodam, (*nin*). I do it by mistake, not purposely; p. *pet..ang.*

Pitchidon, (*nin*). I say s. th. by mistake, or by want of attention; p. *petchidong.*

Pitchi-ikkit, (*nin*). I say s. th. by mistake, I did not mean to say that; p. *pet..tod.*

Pitchi-ikkitowin. Unvoluntary word, mistake in speaking, blunder; pl.-*an.*

Pitchinag, adv. Now only, not before this time; soon; by and by.

Pitchinâgo. Yesterday.

Pitijodis, (*nin*). I cut myself accidentally; p. *pet..sod.*

Podjishema, (*nin*). I speak very close to his ear; p. *pwad..mad.*

Podjidiie, (*nin*). I commit sodomy; p. *pwa..ied.*

Podjidiiewin. Sodomy.

Potch, or *potchige,* or *poshke,* adv. Still, yet; notwithstanding; at all events, at any rate.

Potch gaie kin. As thou pleasest.

Potch gaie kinawa. As you please.

S

Sa, or *isa;* particle used in answers. It signifies nothing in itself, nor is it absolutely necessary in answers, but usual. (It sometimes signifies, *because,* or, *for;* as: *Kitchi kashkendam aw ikwe, gi-nibowan sa onidjânissan;* this woman is very much afflicted, because her child is dead.) It follows immediately the first verb of the answer; and when that verb ends in a consonant, a euphonical *i* is ordinarily (although not necessarily) prefixed to this syllable; as: *Ki nondaw ina?—Ki nondon isa.* Dost thou hear me?—I hear thee. This remark has also report to the interrogation-particle *na,* or *ina.*)

Sâbâdis, (*nin*). I am strong; p. *saia..sid.*

Sâbâdisiwin. Strength.

Sâbendân, (*nin*). S. *Babamendan.*

Sâbenima, (*nin*). S. *Babamenima.*

Sâbigané, (*nin*). I have strong bones, I have much strength in my bones; p. *saia..ned.*

Sagaâkwaam, (*nin*). S. *Papâkwaam.*

Sâgaam, (*nin*). I go out; p. *saiagaang.*

Sâgaamomagad. It goes out; p. *saia..gak.*

Sâgâbide, (*nin*). My teeth begin to come forth; p. *saia..ded.*

Sâgâbigina, (*nin*). I lead him or conduct him away, on a string or cord; p. *saia..nad.*

Sâgabiginigan. Handle of a pot, kettle, etc.; pl.-*an.*

Sâgadina, or-*magad.* There is a group of mountains or hills, of which the summits only are seen; p. *saia..nag,* or-*magak.*

Sâgadinang. A mountain, or a certain spot on a mountain, from where such a place can be seen.

Sâgadjiwe, (*nin*). I arrive to the summit of a mountain, or to some other spct on the mountain, from where I can see a certain place; p. *saia..wed.*

Sâgagwinde, or-*magad.* It is half in the water and half out of the water; p. *saiâ..deg,* or-*magak.*

Sâgaigadeg biwâbik. Cast iron. —S. *Wenadaigadeg.*

Sâgaigan. Inland lake; pl.-*an.*

Sagaigan. Nail; pl.-*an. Kitchi sagaigan,* large nail, spike.
Sagâiganike, (*nind*). I make nails, I am a nail-maker; p. *seg..bed.*
Sagakâmis, (*nin*). I am careful and orderly about my things, keeping them in good order; p. *seg..sid.*
Sagakâmisiwin. Carefulness, good order.
Sagakâtch, adv. Orderly, put in good order, orderly together.
Sâgaki, or-*magad.* It comes out of the ground, it grows; p. *saia..gakig,* or-*magak.*
Sagâkomân. Berry growing on the weed used for smoking; pl.-*an.*
Sagâkominagawanj. A kind of weed used by the Indians to smoke with tobacco.
Sagakwaigade, or-*magad.* It is pegged; p. *seg..deg,* or-*magak.*
Sagâkwaigan. Peg, large wooden pin; (F. cheville;) pl.-*an.*
Sagâkwaon, or *sagâkwaonens.* Pin; pl.-*an.*
Sagânikamabis, (*nin*). I tie my blanket under my chin, (Indian fashion;)p. *seg..sod.*
Sagânikwena, (*nin*). I take him by the hair; p. *seg..nad.*
Sâganimikwi mitig. The tree begins to bud; p. *saia..wid.*
Sâgânwi. Germ; bud; pl.-*n.*
Sâgânwi. It sprouts, it germinates; p. *saiaganwid.* — *Jaigwa opinig sâgânwiwog,* the potatoes sprout already.
Sâgânwi, or-*magad.* It sprouts or germinates; p. *saia..wig,* or-*magak.*—*Jaigwa tchiss sâgânwimagad;* the turnip sprouts already.
Sâgânwia, (*nin*). I make it sprout or germinate; p. *saia ..ad.*
Sâgâshka, or-*magad.* The grass begins to grow; p. *saia..kag,* or-*magak.*
Sagaskwadjime. Leech; pl.-*g.*
Sagassanojebison. String to hold up the leggings; pl.-*an.*
Sâgassige gisiss. The sun comes out of the clouds; p. *saiagas ..siged.*
Sagasswâ, (*nin*). I smoke tobacco; p. *segasswad.*
Sagasswâwin. Smoking, the act or habit of smoking tobacco.
Sagassweidimin, (*nin*). We smoke together; p. *seg..did-jig.*
Sagassweidiwin. Smoking of several persons together, that is, an Indian assembly or council, where every Indian present lights his pipe and smokes; (C. fumerie.)
Sagatâgan. Tinder, destined to catch fire from a spark falling on it by striking a flint.
Sagatâganishib. Teal, (a kind of wild duck; pl.-*ag.*
Sâgâte gisiss. The sun (or moon) shines; p. *saiagated.*
Sâgâte, or-*magad.* It shines, it gives light, (the sun or the moon;) p. *saiagateg,* or-*magak.*
Sâgi. The mouth of a river. *Sâging,* at the mouth of a river.
Sâgia, (*nin*). I love him, I am attached to him; p. *saiâgiad.*

Sagibâdan, (*nin*). I sew it a little; p. *seg..ang.*

Sagibâdjige, (*nin*). I sew a little, I make a few stitches; p. *seg ..ged.*

Sâgibaga, or-*magad*. The leaves come forth, (in spring ;) p. *saia..gag*, or-*magak.*

Sâgibagisi mitig. The tree is getting new leaves; p. *saia.. sid.*

Sagibâna, (*nin*). I sew it a little; p. *seg..nad.*

Sâgibi, (*nin*). I am partly out of the water, (and partly in it;) p. *saiâgibid.*

Sagibidjigan. String or cord to tie with; pl.-*an.*

Sagibidon, (*nin*). I tie it, bind it; p. *seg..dod.*

Sâgibimagisi mitig. The tree has young shoots; p. *saiag.. sid.*

Sagibina, (*nin*). I tie him, I bind him, (a person or any other obj.); p. *seg..nad;* imp. *sagibij.*

Sâgida. The place in the lake round the mouth of a river.

Sâgidawidjiwan. The current of a river comes out or in the lake; p. *saia..ang.*

Sâgidenaniwen, (*nin*). I show my tongue; p. *saia..nid.*

Sâgidenaniwetawa, (*nin*). I show him the tongue,(through contempt;) p. *saia..wad.*

Sâgigikwanagisi mitig. The tree has branches; p. *saia.. sid.*—Figuratively, *Nin sâgidikwanagis*, signifies, I have children. (*Wâdikwan*, branch of a tree.)

Sâgidina, (*nin*). I carry him out of doors; I turn him out; p. *saia..nad.*

Sâgidjideeshkawa, (*nin*). I go out of his heart, I leave his heart; p. *saia..wad.*— *Wenijishid Manito o sagidjideeshkawân baiata - ijiwebisinidjin;* the Holy Ghost abandons the heart of the sinner, (he goes out of it.)

Sâgidjidjiwan sibi oma. Here the river flows out, (here is the mouth of the river.)

Sâgidjinajawa, (*nin*). I send him out of doors, I bid him go out; p. *saia..wad;* imp. *sagidjanaja.*

Sâgidjinaweshkagon, (*nin*). It goes out of me, it leaves me; p. *saia..god.*—*Apitchi nongom âkosiwin nin gi sâgidjinaweskkagon* ; the sickness is now perfectly gone out of me.

Sâgidjinaweshkan, (*nin*). I go out of it; p. *saia..ang.*

Sâgidjinaweshkawa, (*nin*). I go out of him; p. *saia..wad.* —*Matchi manito o gi sâgidjinaweshkawan iniw ininiwan ;* the evil spirit went out of that man.

Sâgidjiwebina, (*nin*). I throw him out, I turn him out; p. *saia..nad.*

Sâgidjiwidon, (*nin*). I carry it out; p. *saia..dod.* — *Nin bisagidjiwidon*, I bring it out.

Sâgidjiwina, (*nin*). I lead or conduct him out; p. *saia..nad.*

Sâgidode, (*nin*). I leave home, I go from my family, I leave my father and mother, etc.; also, I move, I go out of one house and move into another; p. *saiâgidodeod.*

Sâgidode, (nin). I creep out, (*nin bimôde,* I creep, I cannot walk ;) p. *saiâ..od.*

Sâgidonebidjigan. Bridle; pl.-*an.*

Sâgidonebidjigâso bebejigoganji. The horse has a bridle on; p. *saia..sod.*

Sâgidwewidam, (nin). I walk out talking; p. *saia..ang.*

Sâgienima, (nin). I love him in my thoughts, with affection ; p. *saia..mad.*

Sâgiganagisi aw gigo. This fish is full of bones ; p. *saia..sid.*

Sâgiganeshin, (nin). A bone comes out of me, (out of some part of my body ;) p. *saia..ing.*

Sâgigin. It comes forth from..., it grows from.... ; p. *saia..ing.* —*Wadikwan sâgigin mitigong ;* a branch grows out from the tree.

Sâgigondaganena, (nin). I take him by the throat; p. *saia..nad;* imp. *sag..nen.*

Sâgikwegôm, (nin). My head only is out of the water, (the rest of my body is in the water ;) p. *saia..mod.*

Sâgikwen, (nin). My head only is out of s. th., (the rest of my body is in ;) p. *saia..nid.*—*Nin sasâgikwen,* freq. v. I reach out my head from time to time, and draw it back again; for instance, through a window.—*Wâwâbigonodji bi-sasâgikweni oma;* a mouse comes here from time to time, and shows her head only, (reaches only her head out.)

Sâgima. An Indian not belonging to the Grand Medicine, yet knowing well medicines; pl.-*g.*—S. *Midê.*

Saginâ, (nin). I keep some obj. slightly with my fingers; p. *seginad;* imp. *sagin.*

Saginan, (nin). I keep it slightly with my fingers; p. *seginang.*

Saginéshkawa, (nin). I make him pleasure with my arrival; p. *seg..wad.*

Sâginiken, (nin). I stretch out my arm; I show forth my arm; p. *saia..nid.*—*Nibikang gi pangishin kwiwisens, sâginikeni dash,* a boy fell in the water, but he stretches his arm out of the water.

Sâginikena, (nin). I take him by the arm; p. *saia..nad;* imp. *saginiken.*

Sâginindjin, (nin). I reach forth my hand; p. *saia..nid.*

Sâginindjina, (nin). I reach him my hand ; I shake hands with him. I take him by the hand; p. *saia..nad.*

Sâgisia, (nin). I carry him out, I lead or take him out; p. *saia..ad.*

Sâgisidabâdan, (nin). I drag it out of doors; p. *saia..ang.*

Sâgisidabâna, (nin). I drag him out of doors; p. *saia..nad.*

Sâgiwan nibi. The water comes out of a vessel ; p. *saiâgiwang.*

Sâgiwan sibi oma. The river runs into the lake here, here is its mouth.

Sâgiwia, (nin). I sacrifice some obj., (according to pagan rites ;) p. *saia..ad.*

Sâgiwitawa, (nin) or, *nin sâgiwitamawa.* I make him an offering, I offer him a sacrifice, (a pagan sacrifice ;) p. *saia..wad.*

Sakaân, (*nin*).* I light it, I kindle it, I set it on fire ; p. *sekaang.*

Sakâigade, or-*magad.* It is lit or lighted, fire is set to it; p. *sek..deg*, or-*magak.*

Sakâige, (*nin*). I set on fire, I am an incendiary ; p. *sek..ged.*

Sakâigewin. The act of setting on fire ; the work of an incendiary.

Sakaipwâgane, (*nin*). I light my pipe ; p. *sek..ned.*

Sakaôn. Cane, walking-stick ; pl.-*an.*

Sakaôn, (*nin*). I use it as a cane, as a walking-stick ; p. *sekaod.*

Sakâwa, (*nin*). I set him on fire, I make him burn ; also, I set his house on fire ; p. *sekawad ;* imp. *sakâ.*

Sakide, or-*magad.* It catches fire ; p. *sekideg*, or-*magak.*

Sakis, (*nin*). I catch fire, I begin to burn ; also, my lodge or house begins to burn, it is on fire ; p. *sekisod.*— *Kotaging sakisowag ;* the house of our neighbors is on fire. *Ki sagikosimin gosha ;* our house is on fire.

Sakramâ. Sacrament ; pl.-*ian.*

Sanagad. It is difficult, disagreeable, painful, inconvenient, troublesome, hard ; it is dear, high, costly, precious ; p. *senegak.*

Sanagagindass, (*nin*). I sell at high prices ; p. *sen..sod.*

* NOTE. — This root ought to be pronounced by two *k* instead of one, i.e. *nin sakkaân*, and the other words of the same root.

Sanagêndam, (*nin*). I have thoughts of difficulty ; p. *sen ..ang.*

Sanagendamowin. Difficulty and trouble in thoughts.

Sanagendân, (*nin*). I find it difficult.

Sanagénima, (*nin*). I find him difficult, I think he is difficult, intractable, not easy to be dealt with, severe, strict ; p. *sen..mad.*

Sanagis, (*nin*). I am difficult, particular, severe, strict, exact ; I am intractacle, not easy to be dealt with, of ill humor, troublesome, insupportable ; also, I have difficulties, I am in a difficult awkward situation ; p. *sen.. sid.*

Sanagishka, (*nin*) or, *nin bisanagishka.* I come to tell s. th. difficult, painful, disagreeable ; p. *sen..kad.*

Sanagishkawa, (*nin*) or, *nin bisanagishkawa.* I come to tell him s. th. painful, etc. ; p. *sen..wad.*

Sanagisia, (*nin*). I cause him difficulties, trouble, pain ; p. *sen..ad.*

Sanagisiwin. Intractableness, ill humor, difficult disposition of mind ; also, difficulty, awkward situation.

Sanagitâgos, (*nin*). I am telling difficult things, what I say, or recommend, is difficult ; p. *sen..sid.*

Sanagitawa, (*nin*). I listen to him with the impression that what he is saying, or recommending, is difficult ; p. *sen.. wad.*

Sanagwe, (*nin*). I speak a difficult language; p. *senagwed.*

Sângwewe, or-*mâgad*, or *sangwewessin.* It sounds, (metal, being moved or struck;) p. *saia..weg*, or-*magak.*

Saninind pijiki. Milch-cow; pl.-*saninindjig pijikiwog.*

Sasaga, or-*magad.* It is full of brushwood, of underwood, (a place in the woods;) p. *sesagag*, or-*magak.*

Sasâgakwane, or-*magak.* The flame is ascending high; p. *ses..neg*, or-*magak.*

Sasâgis, (*nin*). I am avaricious; p. *ses..sid.*

Sasâgisibingwe, (*nin*). I have tears in my eyes, tears come out of my eyes; p. *ses..wed.*

Sasâgisibingweiakas, (*nin*). Tears come out of my eyes by smoke; p. *ses..sod.*

Sasâgisiwin. Avarice.

Sasagiwinigowin. The gift received in a sacrifice, or, as a sacrifice.

Sasâgiwina, (*nin*). I give it to him in a sacrifice, or as a sacrifice; p. *ses..nad.*

Sasâgiwitchigan. Pagan offering, sacrifice for the preservation of life; pl.-*an.*

Sasâgiwitchige, (*nin*). I give s. th. or contribute towards a sacrifice for the preservation of life; p. *ses..ged.*

Sasâgwana, adv. Often, frequently, repeatedly.

Sasâssagibina assâb, (*nin*). I fix a net to set it, I tie the stones and the floats to the net; p. *ses..nad*; imp. *sa..bij.*

Saségâ, or-*magad.* It is fair, it is ornamented, splendid; p. *sesegag*, or-*magak.*

Sasega-babissikawâgan. A fine splendid coat; pl.-*an.*

Sasegakwanaie, (*nin*). I am dressed vainly, with many ornaments, I dress splendidly; p. *ses..sed.*

Sasega-misisse. Pea-cock; pl.-*g.*

Sasegana, (*nin*). I adorn it, I ornament or embellish it; p. *ses..nad.*

Sasegatchigan. Ornament, embellishment, adornment, decoration; pl.-*an.*

Sasegawendan niiaw, (*nin*). I am proud, I am self-conceited.

Sasegawenima, (*nin*). I think he is fair, (a person or any other obj.); p. *ses..mad.*

Sasegawenindis, (*nin*). S. *Sasegawendan niiaw.*

Sasegawenindisowin. Pride, self-conceit.

Sasikis, (*nin*). I am older, I am the oldest; I am the first-born; p. *sesikisid.*

Sasikisiwin. Greater age; also, primogeniture of first-birth.

Sasina. A kind of nightingale; pl.-*g.*

Sâssabikona, (*nin*). I make his head perspire, in order to cure him, to deliver him from head-ache; p. *saia..nad.*

Sâssabikwan. A medical root which the Indians use to burn on coal, to cure head-ache; pl.-*an.*

Sâssabikwe, (*nin*). I make my head perspire for a cure; p. *saio..wed.*

Sâssabis, (*nin*). I am dazzled by it, I cannot look on it, (sun, etc.;) p. *saia..sod.*

Sassagâkwaan, (*nin*). I nail it to s. th., I nail it down; p. *ses..ang.*

Sassagâkwâwa, (*nin*). I nail him to s. th.; p. *sés..wad;* imp. *sass..kwâ.*

Sassagibidon, (*nin*), freq. I tie it in different places; p. *ses.. dod.*

Sassâgôdis, (*nin*). I am a magician; p. *ses..sid.*

Sassagôdisiwin. Indian magic.

Sassâkâb, (*nin*). I feel a burning pain in my eyes; p. *ses.. bid.*

Sassâkingwe, (*nin*). I have sore eyes, I am snow-blind, (from walking on snow in sunshine;) p. *ses..wed.*

Sassâkingwewin. Snow-blindness; (C. mal de neige.)

Sassakisibingweiâbâs, (*nin*). I feel a burning pain in my eyes from much smoke; p. *ses.. sod.*

Sâssakokwadan, (*nin*). I fry it; p. *saias..ang.*

Sâssakokwana, (*nin*). I fry some obj.; p. *saias..nad.*

Sâssakokwe, (*nin*). I fry; p. *saias..wed.*

Sassâkwe, (*nin*). I shout with joy; p. *ses..wed.*

Sassâkwewin. Joyful shooting.

Sassâssabis, (*nin*). S. *Sassabis;* p. *ses..sod.*

Saswébigaandan, (*nin*). I sprinkle or water it, I asperse it; p. *ses..ang.*

Saswebigaandawa, (*nin*). I sprinkle or water some obj.; I asperse him; p. *ses..wad.*

Saswébigaandjigan. Watering-pot, watering-cart; sprinkling-pot and brush.

Sasweshkamagad. It is scattered about, dispersed; p. *ses.. gak.*

Sasweshkan, (*nin*) or, *nin saswénan*. I scatter it, I disperse it, squander it; p. *ses.. ang.*

Saswêshkawa, (*nin*) or, *nin saswéna*. I scatter about or disperse some body; p. *ses..wad.* —*Ondjita ki sasweshkawa joniia;* thou scatterest money about purposely.—*Maingan o sasweshkawan manishtanishan;* the wolf scatters the sheep.

Saswêwebina, (*nin*). I throw about some body; p. *ses..nad.*

Saswéwebinan, (*nin*). I throw it about; p. *ses..nag.*

Saswéwebinige, (*nin*). I am throwing about; p. *ses..ged.*

Sâtênagosi. It looks rancid; p. *saiat..sid.*—*Sâtenagosi aw kokosh;* this pork looks rancid.

Sâténagwad. It looks rancid; p. *saia..wak.*

Sâtêpogosi. He tastes rancid; p. *saia..sid.*

Sâtépogwad. It tastes rancid; p. *saia..wak.*

Sâtéshin. It is rancid; p. *saiateshin.*

Sê! interj. Shame!

Ségêndagos, (*nin*). I am dreadful, fearful, to be feared; p. *saie..sid.*

Sêgéndagwad. It is fearful, dreadful, it is to be feared; p. *saieg..wak.*

Ségéndam, (*nin*). I fear, I have fearful thoughts; p. *saie..ang.*

Ségéndamowin. Fear, (especially in thoughts,) apprehension.

Ségia, (*nin*). I frighten him, I intimidate him by my threats. I alarm him; p. *saiëgiad*.
Ségibanwa, (*nin*). I wear a cue, (a tuft of hair;) p. *saieg..wad*.
Segibanwân, (pron. *segibanon*). Cue, tuft of hair; pl.-*an*.
Segibanwanishi. A kind of small black bird; (C. récollet;) pl.-*iag*.
Sêgima, (*nin*). S. *Segia*.
Séginagos, (*nin*). I look frightened; p. *saié..sid*.
Sêgis, (*nin*). I fear, I am afraid; p. *saiégisid*.
Sêgisiwin. Fear.
Sêgitagos, (*nin*). I speak so as to excite fear, to make somebody afraid of me; p. *saie..sid*.
Sêgitawa, (*nin*). I listen to him with fear, he excites fear in me by his speaking; p. *saie..wad*.
Sekwadjiged. A spitter; pl.-*jig*.
Senibâ. Silk, silk-stuff; ribbon, riband; pl.-*iag*.
Senibawassabâb. Sewing-silk.
Senibawegin. Silk, silk-stuff.
Sesagisid. He that is avaricious, avaricious person, miser; pl.-*jig*.
Sésika, adv. Suddenly, unforeseen, instantly, in a moment, in an instant.
Sesika-nibowin. Sudden death.
Sesika nin nishkâdis. I am passionate, irascible, choleric, of a quick temper.
Sésikisid. The oldest; the first born of a family; pl.-*jig*.
Sességan. Little hail.
Sességandag. White spruce; (C. épinette blanche;) pl.-*og*.
Sêsségidee, (*nin*). My heart beats violently; p. *saie..ed*.
Sességideewin. Violent beating of the heart; (F. battement de cœur.)
Sessessakis, (*nin*). I burn and weep; p. *saie..sod*.
Sessessima, (*nin*). I insult him and make him weep; p. *saie..mad*.
Siamo. A kind of wild duck which alights sometimes on a tree, what other ducks never do; wood-duck; (C. canard branchu;) pl.-*g*.
Sibi. River, stream; pl.-*wan*.
Sibingwai. Tear; pl.-*ag*.—There is always a possessive pronoun prefixed to this word; as: *Nin sibingwai*, my tear; *nin sibingwaiag*, my tears. *O sibingwaian*, his tear or his tears.
Sibiskâdis, (*nin*). I am not well, I am indisposed; p. *sab..sid*.
Sibiskadisiwin. Indisposition, little sickness.
Sibiskadj, adv. Slowly, slightly.
Sibiskâgad. It is flexible, it does not break when bent; p. *sab..kag*.
Sibiskan. It is viscous, tenacious; p. *sabiskang*.
Sibiskanamowin. Phlegm.
Sibiskendam, (*nin*). I suffer a long time; p. *sab..ang*.
Sibiskendamôwin. Long suffering, continued sorrow and affliction.
Sibiwassâb. River-net, small net, fit to be set in a river; pl.-*ig*.
Sibwâgan. Corn-stalk; sugar-cane; pl.-*ag*.
Sibwâganâbo. Molasses; (mo-

lasses of the sugar-cane, not maple-sugar molasses; for which see *Jiwâgamisigan.*)

Sibwâgani-sisibâkwat. Cane-sugar, brown sugar, Havannah sugar.

Sibwâgans. Sprout or bud of the corn-stalk; pl.-*ag.*

Sidogawishkode, or-*magad.* It is ballasted; p. *sad..deg*, or-*magak.*

Sidogawishkodjigan. Ballast.—*Nind agwâssiton sidogawishkodjigan*, I take out the ballast.

Sigaabowe, (*nin*). I mould, I cast; p. *sag..wed.*

Sigaan, (*nin*). I mould it, cast it; p. *sagaany.*

Sigaandâdiwin. Baptism, by pouring water on the person to be christened.

Sigaandage, (*nin*). I pour water on s. body; I baptize, I christen; p. *sag..ged.*

Sigaandagewin. The act of baptizing or christening, baptism *given.*

Sigaandagowin. Baptism *received.*

Sigaandan, (*nin*). I pour water on it; also, I bless it, sprinkling it with holy water; p. *sagaandang.*

Sigaandas, (*nin*). I am baptized; p. *sagaandasod.*

Sigaandasôwin. S. *Sigaandagowin.*

Sigaandawa, (*nin*). I pour water on him; I baptize him, I christen him; p. *sag..wad.*—This word also signifies, I bless somebody, sprinkling him at the same time with holy water.

Sigaandjigade, or-*magad.* It is blessed, (and sprinkled with holy water;) p. *sag..deg*, or-*magak.*

Sigaandjigâso. He is blessed; p. *sag..sod.*—*Ajittéaiâtigons sigaandjigâso; anamieminag sigaandjigâsowog.* The little cross is blessed; the beads are blessed.

Sigaanowa, (*nin*). I pour him s. th. in the mouth; p. *sag..wad;* imp. *sigano.*

Sigaigade, or-*magad.* It is moulded or cast; p. *sag..deg*, or-*magak.*

Sigaigan. Maple-sugar cake, moulded in s. th.; or any thing moulded, cast; pl.-*an.*

Sigaiganâtig. Wooden mould for casting maple-sugar cakes; pl.-*on.*

Sigaigaso. It is moulded or cast; p. *sag..sod.*

Sigaige, (*nin*). I mould or cast; p. *sag..ged.*

Sigaog, (*nin*). The waves leap in my canoe, or boat; p. *segaogod.*

Sigashkinadon, (*nin*). I fill it so that it runs over; p. *sag..dod.*

Sigashkine, or-*magad.* It is so full that it runs over, it is overrunning, (a vessel or measure;) p. *sag..neg*, or-*magak.*

Sigâwa opwâgan, (*nin*). I lead or plumb a pipe, I ornament it with lead; p. *sagawad;* imp. *sigâ.*

Sigibadon, (*nin*). I make it so full (with a liquid) that it runs over, (a vessel;) p. *sag..dod.*

Sigigamide, or-*magad.* It overflows in boiling; p. *sag..deg,* or-*magak.*

Siginamawa, (*nin*). I shed it or pour it out to him or for him; also, I syringe him, I give an injection, a clyster; p. *sag..wad.*

Siginan, (*nin*). I pour it out, I shed it, spill it; p. *saginang.*

Siginige, (*nin*). I pour out, I shed; I keep tavern, or a dram-shop; I deal in liquor; p. *saginiged.*

Siginigé-masinaigan. License for selling liquor; pl.-*an.*

Siginigêwigamig. A house where liquor is poured out, (sold,) tavern, dram-shop, liquor-house; pl.-*on.*

Sigiskwena, (*nin*). I shed his blood; p. *sag..nad;* imp. *sigiskwen.*

Sigisse, or-*magad.* It is overflowing, it runs over; it is shed; p. *sagisseg,* or-*magak.*

Sigwan. It is spring; p. *sagwang.* — *Sigwang,* in spring. *Sâgwangin,* when it is spring, or every time when it is spring, every spring. *Sigwanong,* last spring.

Sigwaningwewadj, (*nin*). I am brown, (of a brown complexion, by the warm air of the spring;) p. *sag..djid.*

Sigwanish, (*nin*). I spend the spring in such a place, or in such a manner; p. *sag..id.*— *Ki kitchi mino sigwanishimin nongom;* we spent this spring in a very good and comfortable manner. *Wâssa nin gisigwanish;* I spent my spring far away.

Sigwebina (*nin*). I pour out some obj., I make it fall out of a vessel; p. *o sig..n.* — *Joniia nin sigwebina; mandaminag nin sigwebinag;* I pour out money (of some vessel or bag;) I pour out corn.

Sik, (*nin*). I spit; p. *sekod.*

Sikapidan, (*nin*). I drink it all up; p. *sak..ang.*

Sikawidjane, (*nin*) or, *nin sikawiniskigome.* The snot is running from my nose, I snivel; p. *sak..ed.*

Sikawidon, (*nin*). The spittle is running out of my mouth; p. *sak..ong.*

Sikawiniskigomewadj, (*nin*). The snot is running from my nose by *cold;* p. *sak..djid.*

Sikobigagode, or-*magad.* It is hung up to let the water drop out; p. *sak..deg,* or-*magak.*

Sikobigagodjin. It is hung up to let the water drop out of it; p. *sak..ing.*

Sikobigina, (*nin*). I hung it up, to let the water drop out; p. *sak..nad;* imp. *sikobigin.*

Sikôwâgan. Spittle.

Sikowin. Spitting.

Sikowini-makak. Spit-box; pl.-*on.*

Sikwâdan, (*nin*). I spit it; p. *sek..ang.*—*Miskwi nin sikwadan;* I spit blood.

Sikwâna, (*nin*). I spit upon him; p. *sek..nad.*

Sikwâningwéwa, (*nin*). I spit in his face; p. *sek..wad;* imp. *sik..gwé.*

Simingwash, (*nin*). I have not slept enough, I am yet very sleepy; p. *sam..id.*

Simis, (*nin*). I feel sick; p. *samisid.*

Sinakode, or-*magad mishi*. A piece of wood whistles in the fire; p. *san..deg*, or-*magak*.
Sindaagan. A kind of press; (F. serre;) pl.-*an*.
Sindabiginan, (*nin*). I contract it, make it tighter, (a cord, string, etc.); p. *san..ang*.
Sindagaan, (*nin*). I press it together, I compress it; p. *san ..ang*.
Sindagawa, (*nin*). I press it together, I compress it; p. *san way;* imp. *sindaga*.
Sindâigaso. He is pressed together; p. *san..sod*.
Sindaige, (*nin*) or *nin sindakwaige*. I press together, compress; p. *san..ged*.
Sindakwaigan. S. *Sindaagan*.
Sindapis, (*nin*). I gird myself very strongly; p. *san..sod*.
Sindji, (*nin*). I overstrain myself, I make too violent efforts; p. *sandjid*.
Sindjia, (*nin*). I overstrain him, I cause him to make too violent efforts; p. *sandjiad*.
Sindjigabawimin, (*nin*). We stand close together, we are crowded, standing somewhere; p. *san..djig*.
Sindjishimimin, (*nin*). We are lying close together, crowded; p. *san..gig*.
Singa. *Ot.;* p. *sengag*. S. *Neiashiwan*.
Sinigogadebina, (*nin*). I rub his leg (with some medicine); p. *sen..nad*.
Sinigona, (*nin*). I rub him with s. th.; p. *sen..nad*.
Sinigonamawa. I rub him some part of the body, (with some medicine or ointment;) p. *sen ..wad*.
Sinigonikebina, (*nin*). I rub his arm, (with some medicine, etc.); p. *sen..nad*.
Sinigonindjama, (*nin*). I rub him, (with my hand only); p. *sen..mad*.
Sinigonindjibina, (*nin*). I rub his hand, (with some medicine, etc.); p. *sen..nad*.
Sinigoshkinjigwena, (*nin*). I rub his eyes, (with some medicine); p. *sen..nad*.
Sinigosidebina, (*nin*). I rub his foot, (with some medicine, etc.); p. *sen..nad*.
Sinigwaan, (*nin*). I rub it with s. th.; p. *sen..ang*.
Sinina pijiki, (*nin*). I milk a cow; p. *saninad*.
Siniskigomân. Snot.
Siniskigomân, (*nin*). I am snotty; p. *sen..nid*.
Siniskigome, (*nin*). I blow my nose; p. *sen..med*.
Sinsigabawimin, (*nin*). S. *Sindjigabawimin*.
Sinsigawiskigome, (*nin*) .S. *Sikawiniskigome*.
Sinsikan, (*nin*). I press upon it; also, I fill it too much (with my body), it is too narrow for me, two small, (some vestment, or shoes, etc.); p. *sansikang.—Nin sinsikan ow babisikawâgan, onow gaie makisinan nin sinkikânan;* this coat is too narrow (too small) for me, and these shoes (or moccasins) are too small for me.
Sinsikawa, (*nin*). I press upon him; also, it is too small for me; p. *san..wad.—Nin sinsi-*

kawag nin mindjikawanag; my mittens are too small for me, (for my hands.)

Sinsikodadimin, (nin). We press upon each, we are crowded, we throng; p. *san..didjig*.

Sinsiningwama, (nin). I hold under my arm, or I carry under my arm, some obj.; p. *san..mad*.

Sinsobina, (nin). I dress his wound, I tie him up; p. *sen..nad*; imp. *sinsobij*.

Sinsôbis, (nin). My wound is dressed, tied up; p. *sen..sod*.

Sinsobisowin. Bandage of a wound; pl.-*an*.

Sinsokwebina, (nin). I tie up his head, (in head-ache;) p. *sen..nad*.

Sinsokwebis, (nin). I tie up my head, (in head-ache;) p. *sen..sod*.

Sisibâkwat. Sugar.

Sisibâkwatâbo. Sugar-water, sap from maple-trees.

Sisibâkwatokân. Place where sugar is made, sugar-camp, sugar-bush; (C. sucrerie;) pl.-*an*.

Sisibâkwatoke, (nin). I make sugar; p. *ses..ked*.

Sisibâkwatôkewin. Sugar-making.

Sisibâkwatonsan. Confectionary articles; (F. dragée).

Sissâwêmin. A kind of wild cherry; (C. cerise à grappe;) pl.-*an*.

Sissâwéminagawanj. Wild cherry shrub; pl.-*ig*.

Sissibodjigan, or, *biwâbiko-sissibodjigan*. File, rash; pl.-*an*.

Sissibodjige, (nin). I file, I rasp, I sharpen; p. *ses..ged*.

Sissibodon, (nin). I file it; I rasp it; I sharpen it; p. *sis..dod*.

Sissibona, (nin). I file some obj.; p. *ses..nad*; imp. *sissiboj*.

Sissigaan, (nin). I make a clearing in the woods, I clear it, (a place in the woods;) p. *ses..ang*.

Sisswama, (nin). I spit cold water on him, (as the Indians do to persons that faint;) p. *ses..mad*.

Sisiwamingwena, (nin). I spit cold water in his face; p. *ses..nad*.

Siwakwadan, (nin). I suck it out; p. *saw..ang*.

Siwakwana, (nin). I suck some obj.; p. *saw..nad*.

Siwakwe, (nin). I am sucking the sap or juice of s. th.; p. *saw..wed*.

Sobama, (nin). I lick and suck some obj.; p. *swabamad*.

Sôbandan, (nin). I lick and suck it; p. *swab..ang*.

Sogipo, or-*magad*. It snows; p. *swagipog*, or-*magak*.

Sôngâdis. I am strong, stout, robust; p. *swa..sid*.

Sôngan, adv. Strongly, firmly. —*Songan nin debwetân*, I believe it firmly.

Sôngan. It is strong, durable; it is hard, firm, solid, steady; p. *swangang*.

Sônganamia, (nin). I pray strongly, that is, I am a good staunch Christian, I am religious, devout, pious; p. *swan..ad*.

Songanamiawin. Devotion, piety.

Songaona, (nin). I give him a

good large share, (in a distribution;) p. *swan..nad ;* imp. *songaoj*.

Songaonidis, (*nin*). I take a good large share for myself, (in a distribution which I make ;) p. *swang..sod*.

Sôngendagos, (*nin*). I am considered strong, I am strong, firm; p. *swang..sid*.

Sôngendagwad. It is considered strong, it is strong; p. *swan..wak*.

Songendam, (*nin*). I have strong thoughts, I am firmly resolved ; I am constant; p. *swan.. ang*.

Songendamia, (*nin*). I make him have strong thoughts, a firm resolution, I fortify his mind ; p. *swang..ad*.

Songendamowin. Strong thought, firm resolution, constancy.

Songendân, (*nin*). I think it is strong ; also, I think on it strongly ; I resolve it firmly ; p. *swan..ang*.

Songenima (*nin*). I think he is strong ; also, I think firmly on him; p. *swan..mad*.

Songidee, (*nin*). I am strong-hearted, I am brave, courageous, fearless, intrepid, audacious, daring ; p. *swan..ed*.

Songideeshkage, (*nin*). I make the heart of somebody strong; I give fortitude, courage, strength of mind, I comfort, I console; p. *swan..ged*.

Songideeshkagewin. Fortification of the heart, giving strength of mind ; the Sacrament of Confirmation. *Nin migiwe Songideeshkagewin*, I give Confirmation, I confirm. *Nin mina Songideeshkagewin*, I confirm him. *Nin minigo Songideeshkagewin*, I receive Confirmation.

Songideeshkawa, (*nin*). I make his heart strong, I fortify his heart, his mind ; I comfort him ; p. *swang..wad*.

Songideeshkawenima, (*nin*). I give him strong thoughts, a firm resolution in his heart, a firm will; p. *swang..mad*.

Songideewin. Fortitude of heart, courage, bravery, fearlessness, intrepidity, audacity.

Songigawishka, or-*magad*. It is sure, not rolling, (a canoe or boat). S. *Kitagwinde*.

Songigi, (*nin*). I grow stronger, I increase in size and strength; p. *swangigid*.

Songigondagan, (*nin*). I have a strong brave voice ; p. *swan.. ang*.

Songigwadan, (*nin*). I sew it strong ; p. *swan..ang*.

Songigwana, (*nin*). I sew some obj. strong ; p. *swan..nad*.

Songigwâss. I sew strongly ; p. *swan..sod*.

Songinâgos, (*nin*). I look strong, I have the appearance of a strong man ; p. *swan..sid*.

Songinâgwad. It looks strong, durable, lasting ; p. *swan.. wak*.

Songingwâm, (*nin*). I sleep strongly, I am not easy to awaken ; p. *swan..ang*.

Sôngis, (*nin*). I am strong ; p. *swangisid*.

Sôngishin. He is placed solidly, assuredly ; p. *swan..ing*.

Sôngisia, (*nin*). I make him

strong, I strengthen him, fortify him; p. *swan..ad.*

Sôngissin. It is placed strongly, solidly, assuredly; p. *swan..ing.*

Sôngiton, (*nin*). I make it strong; I strengthen it, I fortify, confirm, ratify it; p. *swangitod.*

Ssag, ssaga, at the end of some substantives and verbs, alludes to *wood;* as: *Ininâtigossag,* maple-wood; *mitigomijissag,* oak-wood; *nabagissag,* a flat piece of wood, (a board;) *binissaga,* the floor is clean, etc.

Sse, as end-syllable of some verbs, denotes *flying;* as: *Bineshi bimisse, kijisse, nanjisse,* etc.; the bird flies, flies quick, flies down, etc.

Swanganamiad. Strong good Christian, firm in his religion; pl.*-jig.*

Swangideed. He that has a strong heart, a brave, courageous person, or audacious person; pl.*-jig.*

Swangideeshkawed. He who makes the heart strong; a comforter, consoler; pl.*-jig.*—*Swangideeshkawed Wenijishid-Manito,* the Comforter, the Holy Ghost.

T

Some words which are not found under T, *may be looked for under* D.

Ta.— This particle marks the third person of the future tense. (S. the Conj. in Otchipwe Gram.)

Tabas, (*nin*). I lower myself, to avoid a blow, or some other thing that is flying towards me; p. *tebasod.*

Tabashish, adv. Below, low.

Tabassâ, or-*magad.* It is low; p. *tebassag,* or-*magak.*

Tabassabid. Undertooth, a tooth of the under jawbone; pl.-*an.*

Tabassadina, or-*magad.* S. *Tabassakamiga.*

Tabassâdis, (*nin*). I am low, abject, mean, humiliated; p. *teb..sid.*

Tabassâkamiga, or-*magad.* There is a low ground; p. *teb..gag,* or-*magak.*

Tabassakwa, or-*magad.* There is a low forest, low trees; p. *teb..wag,* or-*magak.*

Tabassâkwaamog (*animikig*). It thunders low; a low thunderstorm, (thunders make noise low.)

Tabassansika, or-*magad.* It is low, thin, (a book, etc.); p. *teb..kag,* or-*magak.*

Tabassashkad. It is narrow, (stuff, cloth, mat;) p. *teb..kad.*

Tabassendâgos, (*nin*). I am esteemed low, mean, I am despisable, despicable, I am despised; p. *teb..sid.*

Tabassendân, (*nin*). I esteem it low, I despise it; p. *teb..ang.*

Tabassénim, (*nin*). I have humble thoughts of myself, I humble myself; p. *teb..mod.*

Tabassenimowin. Humble conceit of one's self.

Tabassênima, (*nin*). I esteem him low, I think little of him, I despise him; p. *teb..mad.*

Tabassénindis, (*nin*). I esteem or think myself low, I humble myself, I am humble; p. *teb..sod.*

Tabassénindisowin. Humility.

Tabassia, (*nin*). I lower or abase some obj. I put him lower; p. *teb..ad.*

Tabassigabawi aw awessi. This animal stands low, that is, it is short-legged; p. *teb..wid.*

Tabassina, (*nin*). S. *Tabassia.*

Tabassinan, (*nin*). I put it lower, I lower it; p. *teb..ang.*

Tabassipagidendan, (*nin*) or, *nin tabassipagidinan.* I humbly submit it, I subject it; p. *teb..ang.*

Tabassipagidenima, (*nin*). I humhly submit him, I subject him; p. *teb..mad.*

Tabassipagidenindis, (*nin*). I humbly submit myself, I subject myself; p. *teb..sod.*

Tabassipagidenindisowin. Humble submission, subjection.

Tabassisé aw bineshi. That bird flies lcw, near the ground; p. *tebassissed.*

Tabassiton, (*nin*). I lower or abase it, I put it lower; p. *tebassitod.*

Tabassônagad. It is low, (canoe, boat, vessel;) p. *teb..gak.*

Tabassowe, (*nin*). I speak with a big thick voice; p. *teb..wed.* —S. *Ishpowe.*

Tabasswêweton, (*nin*). I sing it low; p. *teb..tod.*

Tabinoige, (*nin*). I make a shelter or shade against the wind, or the sun; p. *teb..ged.*

Tabinôon. Shelter against the wind, or the heat of the sun; pl.-*an.*

Tabinôshimon, (*nin*). I shelter myself, I am behind a shelter against the wind, or under a shade against the sun; p. *teb..nod.*

Tâbishkotch, adv. Likewise, equally.

Tagâ! or *taga taga!* interj. Well! halloo! let me see!

Tâgokomân. S. *Mojwâgan.*

Tâgos, at the end of some neuter verbs, alludes to *being heard;* and the first part of the verb denotes the *manner* in which one is heard; as: *Nin jingitâgos*, they ate to hear me, I am heard with displeasure, with disgust. *Nin nibwakatâgos*, I am heard speaking prudent words, I speak wisely. *Nin minotâgos.* I am heard with pleasure.—S. *Tawa.*

Tagosideshkawa, (*nin*) or, *nin tagwasideshkawa.* I tread on his toes; p. *teg..wad.*

Tagwaadonenak. Mallet used in making a canoe; pl.-*on.*

Tagwaanâbo. Corn-soup, Indian corn-soup.

Tagwâgi. Fall, the fall of the year, autumn.

Tagwâgi. It is fall, it is the fall of the year; p. *tegwâgig.* — *Tegwâgigin*, in fall; *dassing tegwâgigin*, every fall. *Tagwâgong*, last fall.

Tagwagish, (*nin*). I spend the fall of the year in such a place, or in such a manner; p. *teg..id.*—*Moniang nin witagwâgish;* I intend to spend the fall at Montreal.

Tagwakonindjishkos, (*nin*). My hand (or finger) is caught between the door, in shutting it; p. *teg..sod.*

Tagwakonindjiwa, (*nin*). I catch or crush his hand (or finger) between the door, in shutting it; p. *teg..wad.*

Tagwâwâg mandaminag, (*nin*). I stamp or crush Indian corn with a stone; p. *teg..wad.*

Taiâ! interj. S. *Ataiâ!*

Taiashkibodjiged. He that saws, a sawyer; pl.-*jig.*

Taiatagâdisid. He who is lazy, a lazy person: pl.-*jig.*

Tajwâbikinan, (*nin*). I make it straight, (metal,) I straighten it; p. *tej..ang.*

Tajwâkogâbaw, (*nin*). I stand up straight; p. *tej..wid.*
Tajwakota, (*nin*). I straighten up, and stand upright; p. *tej ..tad.*
Takâbâwadon, (*nin*). I wet it with cold water, cooling it by wetting it; p. *tek..dod.*
Takâbâwana, (*nin*). I wet him with cold water, I cool him by wetting him; p. *tek..nad.*
Takâbikad. It is cold, (metal;) p. *tek..kak.*
Takâbikisi. It is cold, (metal); p. *teb..sid.*
Takâgami, or-*magad.* It is cool or cold, (some liquid;) p. *tek.. mig*, or-*magak.*
Takâgamishkodon, (*nin*). S. *Takibadon.*
Takâia, or-*magad.* It is cool; p. *tekaiag*, or-*magak.*
Takamadasi, (*nin*) or, *nin takamagasi.* I wade through a river, I ford it; p. *tek..sid.*
Takânimad. There is a cold wind; p. *tek..mak.*
Takâsh, (*nin*). I catch cold; p. *tckashid.*
Takâshima, (*nin*). I make him catch cold, I expose him to cold; p. *tek..mad.*
Takâssin. It is cold by the wind; p. *tek..ing.*
Takâtê or-*magad.* It is cold, (in a building;) p. *tekâteg*, or-*magak.*
Takénis, (*nin*). I feel cold in my whole body; p. *tek..sid.*
Takib. A spring of cold water; pl.-*in.*
Takibadon, (*nin*). I cool it pouring cool water in; p. *tek..dod.*
Takibissa. The rain is cold; p. *teb..sag.*
Takidee, (*nin*). My heart is cold; p. *tek..ed.*
Takideeiabawana, (*nin*). I cool his heart, by giving him cold water to drink; p. *tek..nad.*
Takideeiabawanidis, (*nin*). I refresh my heart, by drinking cold water; p. *tek..sod.*
Takidjane, (*nin*). My nose is cold; p. *tek..ned.*
Takigâde, (*nin*). My leg is cold, (or my legs are cold;) p. *tek.. ded.*
Takigami. Cold spring-water.
Takijeiabawanidis, (*nin*). I cool my skin with cold water; p. *tek..sod.*
Takinibin. It is a cool summer; p. *tek..ing.*
Takis, (*nin*). I am cold, my body is cold; p. *tekisod.*
Takishima, (*nin*). I cool some obj.; p *tek..mad.*
Takiside, (*nin*). My foot is cold, (or my feet are cold;) p. *tek.. ded.*
Takissin. It is cold; p. *tekissing.*—*Takissin nin midjim;* my meat is cold.
Takôbidawa, (*nin*) or, *nin takobidamawa.* I tie s. th. to him or for him, or s. th. relating to him; I tie some remedy to his wound or on his wound; p. *tek..wad.*
Takôbide, or-*magad.* It is tied, it is bound up; p. *tek..deg*, or-*magak.*
Takobideg (*mashkossiwan*). Bundle (of hay.) *Abiding takobideg, nissing takobideg, nâning takobideg*, etc. One bundle, three bundles, five bundles, etc.
Takobidjigan. Tying-string, any

thing to tie with, a cord, a string, pack-thread, etc.; pl.-*an*.

Takobidjigan, or *makakossag-takôbidjigan*. Hoop, barrel-hoop; pl.-*an*.

Takobidjigâs, (*nin*) or, *nin takobiigâs*. I am tied, I am bound; p. *tek..sod*.

Takôbidjige, (*nin*). I tie, I bind; p. *tek..ged*.

Takôbina, (*nin*). I tie him, I bind him; I swathe him, (a child;) p. *tek..nad; imp. takobij*.

Takobinigewin, or *takôbidjigewin*. Tying, binding.

Takobinigowin. Tie, being tied; bond.—*Sanagad nin takôbinigowin; minotch nin wi-ganawendân*. My bond (obligation) is difficult; but still I will keep it.

Takobis, (*nin*). I am tied, I am tied up in a cradle, (a child;) p. *tekobisod*.

Takobona, (*nin*). I shorten some obj. by sawing a piece off; p. *tek..nad*.

Takokâdan, (*nin*). I tread on it; I trample it; p. *tek..ang*.

Takokâdjigade, or-*magad*. It is trodden upon; p. *tek..deg*, or-*magak*.

Takokâdjigas, (*nin*). I am trodden upon, I am trampled; p. *tek..sod*.

Takokâna, (*nin*). I tread upon him; I trample him (any obj.); p. *tek..nad*.

Takoki, (*nin*). I tread, I step; p. *tekokid*.

Takokiwin. Step, pace.

Takona, (*nin*). I hold him; I seize him, I take him up, I arrest him; I make him a prisoner; also, I am his sponsor at baptism, his godfather or godmother; p. *tekonad*.

Takônagad. It is short, (canoe, boat, vessel, etc.); p. *tek..gak*.

Takonan, (*nin*). I hold it, I seize it, I distrain it; p. *tek..ang*.

Takonâwâss, (*nin*). I hold a child in my arms; also, I am a sponsor at baptism, godfather or godmother.

Takonde, or-*magad*. It is short, (a building;) p. *tekondeg*, or-*magak*.

Takonidiwin. Seizure, arrest, distraint.

Takonigade, or-*magad*. It is seized, arrested, distrained; p. *tek..deg*, or-*magak*.

Takonigâs, (*nin*). I am taken up, seized, arrested, I am made a prisoner; p. *tek..sod*.

Takôs, (*nin*). I am short, I am small; p. *tekosid*.

Takwabâwis, (*nin*). I am short and thick; (F. courtaud;) p. *tek..sid*.

Takwâbigade. It is short, (thread, string, etc.;) p. *tek..gak*.

Takwâbigisi. It is short, (some stuff, *seniba*, etc.); p. *tek..sid*.

Takwâbikad. It is short, (metal, glass;) p. *tek..kak*.

Takwâbikisi. He is short; p. *tek..sid*.

Takwâganama, (*nin*). I strike him too much; p. *tek..mad*.

Takwâkinindjiwadj, (*nin*). My hands are very cold, benumbed with cold; p. *tek..id*.

Takwâkisideiâbâwe, (*nin*). My feet are cold being wet; p. *tek..wed*.

Takwâkisidewadj, (*nin*). My feet

are extremely cold, benumbed with cold ; p. *tek..id.*

Takwâkosi. It is short, (a board, etc. ;) p. *tek..sid.*

Takwâkwaan, (*nin*). I shorten it by cutting off a piece with an axe ; p. *tek..ang.*

Takwâkwad. It is short, (a wooden object ;) p. *tek..wak.*

Takwâkwawa, (*nin*). I shorten some obj. by cutting off a piece with an axe; p. *tek.. wad ;* imp. *takwâkwa.*

Takwama, (*nin*). I bite him ; p. *tek..mad.*

Takwâmbis, (*nin*). I wear a short petticoat or frock, (a woman ;) also, I tie or gird up high my blanket ; p. *tek..sod.*

Takwamig, (*nin*) *;* p. *tek..god.*— S. *Miniwapine.*

Takwanâm, (*nin*). I have a short respiration, short breath; p. *tek..mod.*

Takwandân, (*nin*). I bite it ; p. *tek..ang.*

Takwândjigan. Tongs ; (F. tenaille ;) pl.-*an.*

Takwandjigans. Pincers, nippers ; pl.-*an.*

Takwangê, (*nin*). I bite ; p. *tek.. ged.*

Takwangéshk, (*nin*). I am in a habit of biting ; p. *tek..kid.*

Takwânikwe, (*nin*). I have short hair ; p. *tek..wed.*

Takwânowe aw animosh. That dog has a short tail ; p. *tek.. wed.*

Takwâton, (*nin*). I shorten it ; p. *tek..tod.*

Takwéndam, (*nin*). I keep in memory ; p. *tek..ang.*

Takwéndamowin. Memory, keeping in memory.

Takwêndân, (*nin*). I keep it in memory, I think on it ; p. *tek ..ang.*

Takwêgad. It is short, (stuff, vestment, etc.) ; p. *tek..gak.*

Takwêgisi. It is short, (stuff, *seniba,* etc. ;) p. *tek..sid.*

Takwénima, (*nin*). I keep him in memory, I think on him ; p. *tek..mad.*

Takwindima. S. *Ginwindima.*

Tân. This end-syllable of some verbs, is the *inanimate* of *tawa,* which see for an explanation. —*Nin jingitân,* I hate to hear it; *nin minotân,* I like to hear it, etc.

Tânapi ? adv. *Ot.* when ?

Tanâssag, adv. Like..., like as..., I may say...

Tândi ? adv. Where ?

Tangagwindjima, (*nin*). I dip him a little in water, I touch the water with him, (a person, or some other obj. ;) p. *taian.. mad.*

Tângama, (*nin*). I taste it, I eat a little of it ; p. *taia..mad.*

Tângandan, (*nin*). I taste it, I eat a little of it ; p. *taia..ang.*

Tângina, (*nin*). I touch him ; (L. tango ;) p. *taia..nad.*

Tânginamawa, (*nin*). I touch s. th. belonging or relating to him ; p. *taian..wad.*

Tânginan, (*nin*). I touch it; p. *taia..ang.*

Tânginidis, (*nin*). I touch myself ; p. *taia..sod.*

Tangishkâge, (*nin*). I kick ; p. *ten..ged.*

Tangishkâge bebejigoganji. The horse kicks ; p. *ten..ged.*

Tangishkân, (*nin*). I kick it ; p. *ten..ang.*

Tangishkawâ, (*nin*). I kick him; p. *ten..wad.*

Tangishkige, (*nin*). I kick, I am kicking; I stamp with the foot; p. *ten..ged.* (The same as *tangishkage.*)

Tângissiton, (*nin*). I make it touch s. th., I bring it in contact with s. th.; p. *taian..tod.*

Tani? adv. *Ot.* how? what?

Tanish? (or, *tani dash?*) adv. *Ot.* but how? how?

Tapâb, (*nin*). I peep in, look in, (through the door or window;) p. *tepâbid.*

Tâpi? adv. *Ot.* when?

Tapikwen, (*nin*). I stretch my head through a window or other opening, to see s. th.; p. *tep..nid.*

Tapikweshin, (*nin*). I peep in a house or lodge through a window or door; p. *ep..ing.*

Tâshkaan, (*nin*). S. *Tashkinan.*

Tâshkâbikad. It is cracked or split, (rock or metal;) p. *taia ..kak.*

Tâshkâbikishka, or-*magad.* There is a fissure or gap in a rock; p. *taia..kag*, or-*magak.*

Tâshkabikisi. He is cracked or split, (rock or metal;) p. *taia ..sid.*

Tâshkâbikisse, or-*magad.* It rends, splits, cracks, (metal, rock;) p. *taia..seg*, or-*magak.*

Tâshkama, (*nin*). I split some *an.* obj. with the teeth; p. *taia.. mad.*

Tâshkanashkidieweian. Coat, overcoat, overall; (F. Pardessus;) p.-*an.*

Tâshkandan, (*nin*). I split it with the teeth, I bite it through; p. *taia..ang.*

Tâshkatawangibidjige, (*nin*). I plough in a sandy ground; p. *taia..ged.*

Tâshkibodjigan. Splitting-saw, split-saw; pl.-*an.*

Tâshkibodjigan, or *tashkigibodjigan.* Saw-mill; pl.-*ag.*—*Ishkote-tâshkibodjigan*, steam saw-mill.

Tâshkibodjige, (*nin*) or, *nin tâshkigibodjige.* I saw with a whip-saw or splitting-saw; I saw in a saw-mill; p. *taia.. ged.*—S. *Kishkibodjige.*

Tâshkibodjigewin. Sawing (along, not across); saw-mill business, occupation or work of a sawyer.

Tâshkibodjigewinini. Sawyer; sawyer in a saw-mill, also, proprietor of a saw-mill; pl.-*wag.*

Tâshkibodon, (*nin*) or *nin tâshkigibodon.* I saw it (along); p. *taia..dod.*

Tâshkibona, (*nin*) or, *nin tâshkigibona.* I saw some obj. (along); p. *taia..nad*; imp. *tâshkiboj.*

Tâshkigaigan. Wedge to cleave with, frower; pl.-*an.*

Tâshkigaige, (*nin*). I cleave, I split; p. *taia..ged.*

Tâshkigaisse, (*nin*). I split wood for fuel; p. *taia..sed.*

Tâshkigân, (*nin*). I split it; p. *taia..ang.*

Tâshkigawa, (*nin*). I split some obj.; p. *taia..wad*; imp. *tâshkiga.*

Tâshkigishka. It is split or rent; p. *taia..kad.*

Tâshkigisse, or-*magad.* It splits or rends; p. *taia..seg* or-*magak.*

Tâshkijan, (*nin*). I split it or divide it in two, cutting it; p. *taia..ang.*

Tâshkijwa, (*nin*). I split or divide in two some *an.* obj., cutting it; p. *taia..wad*; imp. *tashkijwi.*

Tâshkika, or-*magad.* It is split or rent; p. *taia..kag* or-*magak.*

Tâshkikamigibidjigan. A thing to rend the ground with, that is, a plough; pl.-*an.*

Tâshkikamigibidjige, (*nin*). I rend or tear the ground, that is, I plough; p. *taia..ged.*

Tâshkikwad. There is a fissure or crevice in the ice; p. *taia..wak.*

Tâshkikwadin. The ice splits, rends, opens; p. *taia..ing.*

Tâshkina, (*nin*). I split some obj. in the middle, I divide it in two; p. *taiashkinad.*

Tâshkinan, (*nin*). I split it in the middle, I divide it in two; p. *taia..ang.*

Tâtagâdis, (*nin*). I am inactive, not working, sluggish, indolent, lazy; p. *taia..sid.*

Tâtagâdisiwin, or-*tâtagâdjiwin.* Sluggishness, inactivity, indolence.

Tatagâgwan. Backbone, spine. —There is always a possessive pronoun prefixed to this word; as: *Nin tatagâgwan, ki tatagâgwan, o tatagâgwan*; my, thy, his backbone.

Tatagonindjiodis, (*nin*). I bruise my hand, (or finger,); p. *taiat..sod.*

Tatagoganjiodis, (*nin*). I bruise my nail, (on hand or foot;) p. *taiat..sod.*

Tatagagomin. S. *Odatagagomin.*

Tatagosideodis, (*nin*). I bruise my foot; p. *taia..sod.*

Tatagwa, or-*magad.* S. *Jingakamiga.*

Tawa, at the end of some verbs, signifies *hearing;* and the first part of the verb denotes the *manner* in which one hears somebody; as: *Nin gimitawa*, I hear him in a stealthy manner, I overhear him. *Nin minotawa*, I hear him with pleasure, etc. S. *Tâgos.*

Tawa, imp. verb. There is room.

Tawâbide, (*nin*) or, *nin tatawabide.* I lost several teeth, I have gaps or vacant places in the rows of my teeth; p. *tew..ded.*

Tawâbika, or-*magad.* There is a crevice or opening in a rock, through from one side to the other; p. *tew..kag*, or-*magak.*

Tawâbikad. It is cracked through, (metal;) p. *tew..kak.*

Tawabitawa, (*nin*). I make room for him to sit down; p. *tew..wad.*

Tawadina. There is a low place between mountains, a valley; p. *tew..nag.*

Tâwân, (*nin*). I open my mouth; p. *taiâwanid.*

Tâwanobidon dassônagan, (*nin*). I open an iron trap, I set it; p. *taia..dod.*

Tâwanona, (*nin*). I open his mouth; p. *taia..nad*; imp. *tawanon.*

Tâwanongwâm, (*nin*). I sleep with my mouth open; p. *taia..ang.*

Tâwigâbaw, (*nin*). I make room in standing aside; p. *tew..wid.*

Tâwishkâde, or-*magad.* There is

room, (in a lodge, house, etc.); p. *tew..deg*, or-*magak.*

Tâwissaga, or-*magad.* There is a crack or opening in a piece of wood, in a floor, etc.; p. *tew..gag*, or-*magak.*

Tâwissin. There is room; p. *tewissing.*

Tchâg, or *tchâgi*, in composition, alludes to *consuming*, *spending.* (Examples in some of the following words.)

Tchâgaé, (*nin*). My provisions, ammunition, etc. are at an end, are gone; p. *tchaiâgaed.*

Tchâgakatewishin, (*nin*). My powder is all gone; p. *tchaia..ing.*

Tchâgakide, or-*magad.* It is consumed by fire, it burns up entirely; p. *tchaia..ded*, or-*magak.*

Tchâgakis, (*nin*). The fire consumes me, I burn all up; p. *tchaia..sod.*

Tchâgakisama, (*nin*). I burn up all my wood; p. *tchaia..mad.* (I Conj.)

Tchâgakisan, (*nin*). I burn it entirely; p. *tchaia..ang.*

Tahâgakiswa, (*nin*). I burn some obj. entirely; p. *tchaia..wad*; imp. *tchagakiswi.*

Tchâganwissin, (*nin*). My shot and balls are all gone; p. *tchaia ..ing.*

Tchâgidabadan, (*nin*). I have drawn all of it, I have nothing more to draw, (on a sleigh); p. *tchaia..ang.*

Tchâgidabana, (*nin*). I have drawn, or fetched on a sleigh, all of it; p. *tchaia..nad.*

Tcnâgide, or-*magad.* It burns; p. *tchaiâgideg*, or-*magak.*

Tchâgidjiwan. It runs out entirely, (liquid;) p. *tchaia..ang.*

Tchâgimodima, (*nin*). I steal all his things from him; p. *tchaia ..mad.*

Tchâgina, (*nin*). I spend or consume all of him, I exterminate some obj.; p. *tchaiâginad.*

Tchâginago, (*nin*). I lose all, in gaming; p. *tchaiaginawind.*

Tchâginan, (*nin*). I spend it all, I consume or use up all of it; p. *tchai..ang.*

Tchâginemin, (*nin*).. We die all away; p. *tchaiâginedjig.*

Tchâginige, (*nin*). I spend all, I consume all; p. *tchai..ged.*

Tchâginigeshk, (*nin*). I am in a habit of spending too much, I waste, I am a spendthrift; p. *tchai..kid.*

Tchâginigeshkiwin. Extravagant spending, squandering, waste.

Tchâgis, (*nin*). I burn; p. *tchaiâgisod.*

Tchâgisan, (*nin*). I burn it; p. *tchaia..ang.*

Tchâgishkan, (*nin*). I wear it out entirely, (clothing, shoes, etc.); p. *tchaia..ang.*

Tchâgishkawa, (*nin*). I wear out entirely some obj., (as *moshwe*, etc.); p. *tchaia..wad.*

Tchâgisige, (*nin*). I burn s. th.; p. *tchaia..ged.*

Tchâgisige-pagidinigewin. Burnt sacrifice, burnt-offering, holocaust; pl.-*an.*

Tchâgisowin. A burn; a hurt caused by scalding or burning; pl.-*an.*

Tchâgisse. It is used up, all is gone; p. *tchaiâgissed.*

Tchâgisse, or-*magad*. It is used up, all spent, all gone.
Tchâgiswa, (*nin*). I burn him, I scald him; p. *tchai..wad;* imp. *tchagiswi*.
Tchâins. A kind of prey-bird; pl.-*ag*.
Tchâkiwi, (*nin*). I hurt myself by working too hard, or by lifting up some heavy object; p. *tchaiakiwid*.
Tchâmâniked. He that makes a canoe or canoes, or boats, canoe-maker, boat-maker, boat builder; pl.-*jig*.
Tchâtchâm, (*nin*). I sneeze; p. *tchaiatchang*.
Tchatchangakoshkamadimin, (*nin*). We play see-sawing; pl.-*tche..didjig*.
Tchatchangakoshkamadiwin. S. See-sawing.
Tchatchingwakamiga, or-*magad*, freq. There is a shaking of the earth from a cause above ground, in different parts, or at different times; p. *tche..gag*, or-*magak*.
Tchêkagamina, (*nin*). I dip him in water, etc.; p. *tchaie..nad;* imp. *tche..min*.
Tchékagaminan, (*nin*). I dip it in water or some other liquid; p. *tchaie..ang*.
Tchékâsh, (*nin*). I run aground with a canoe or boat, *sailing;* p. *tchaiekashid*.
Tchékibidon, (*nin*). I draw it a little out of the water, not entirely; p. *tchaie..dod*.
Tchékibina, (*nin*). I draw some one a little out of the water, not entirely; p. *tchaie..ad*.
Tchekisse, (*nin*). I run aground with a canoe or boat, *paddling;* also, I arrive briskly to the shore; p. *tchaiékissed*.
Tchéssakid. He who performs jugglery, Indian juggler; pl.-*jig*.
Tchêtchatchibân, adv. Dispersedly, in different directions, in different places or to different places.
Tchi, conj. That, to, in order to.
Tchibai. Corpse, dead person; ghost, spectre, phantom; pl. *ag*.
Tchibaiâtig. Wood of the dead, wood to be placed on a grave, that is, a cross; pl.-*og;* or more used: *âjitteiâtik*.
Tchibaiâtigonamawa, (*nin*). I make the sign of the cross upon him, or over him; p. *tchab..wad*, or, *ajittéiatigonamawa*.
Tchibaiâtigonige, (*nin*). I make the sign of the cross with my arm, I bless myself; p. *tchab..ged*. or, *ajitteiatigonige*.
Tchaibaigan. Dead person's bone; pl.-*an*.
Tchibaigijigad. The day of the Dead, All Souls day; (L. Comm. Omn. Fid. Def.)
Tchibai-makak. Box of the dead, that is, a coffin; pl.-*on*.
Tchibai-oniganâtig. Hand-barrow of the dead, that is, a bier; pl.-*on*.
Tchibâkwas, (*nin*). I cook for myself, I cook my own meals; p. *tcha..sod*.
Tchibâkwâwa, (*nin*). I cook for him; p. *tcha..wad;* imp. *tchibakwâ*.
Tchibâkwe, (*nin*). I cook; p. *tchâkakwed*.

Tchibakwéwikwe. Woman that cooks, cook, cook-maid ; pl.-*g.*
Tchibâkwe-kijâbikisigan. Cook-stove, cooking-stove ; pl.-*an.*
Tchibakwéwigamig. Cook-house kitchen ; pl.-*on.*
Tchibakwewin. Cookery, cooking, occupation or art of a cook.
Tchibakwewinini. A man that cooks, cook ; pl.-*wag.*
Tchibatâko, in composition, signifies *stiff.* (Examples in some of the following words.)
Tchibatakogade, (*nin*). I have a stiff leg, or legs ; p. *tchab..ded.*
Tchibatchigisi. It is stiff, (silk-stuff ;) p. *tchab..sid.*
Tchibêgamig. House of the dead, grave ; graveyard, cemetery ; pl.-*on.*
Tchibêkana. Road of the dead, that is, the Milky Way, (according to Indian notions.)
Tchibenake, (*nin*). I make a feast of the dead, (according to the Indian superstition ;) p. *tchab ..ked.*
Tchibenakewin. Indian feast of the dead.
Tchibingwén, (*nin*). I wink or twinkle with the eyes ; p. *tchab..nid.*
Tchibingwenowin. A wink, a twinkle of the eyes ; pl.-*an.*
Tchibingwétawa, (*nin*). I wink him with the eyes ; p. *tcha.. wad.*
Tchi bwâ wâbang. Before day-light.—S. *Wâban.*
Tchig', or *tchigâii.* Near, close by, nigh, by, at.
Tchigaana gigô, (*nin*). I take the scales of the fish off, I scale it ; p. *tchag..ad.*
Tchigaawe, (*nin*). I scale ; p. *tcha..wed.*
Tchigâdjiwan, adv. Along the rapid of a river.
Tchigaêmikwân. A kind of hollow chisel for making wooden spoons ; pl.-*an.*
Tchigagâm, adv. On the lake near the shore.
Tchigaii. S. *Tchig',* etc.
Tchigâkwa, adv. Near the wood, the forest.
Tchiganagekwaan, (*nin*). I take it off, (the bark of a tree ;) p. *tchag..ang.* — *Wigwâss nin tchiganagekwaan ;* I take off the bark of a birch-tree.
Tchiganagekwawa, (*nin*). I take it off, (bark ;) p. *tchag..wad ;* imp. *tchig..kwa.*—*Nin tchiganagekwawa wanagek ;* I take off the bark of a cedar-tree.
Tchigandâweige, (*nin*). I cut down branches from trees ; p. *tchag..ged.*
Tchigandawéwa mitig, (*nin*). I cut down the branches of a tree ; p. *tchag..wad ;* imp. *tchig..wê.*
Tchigapidan, (*nin*). *Alg.* S. *Wébikodan.*
Tckigapijwa, (*nin*). *Alg.* S. *Wébikona.*
Tchigataan, (*nin*). I sweep it ; p. *tcha..ang.*
Tchigataigade, or-*magad.* It is swept ; p. *tchag..deg,* or-*magak.*
Tchigataigan. Broom ; pl.-*an.*
Tchigataiganak, or *tchigataiganatig.* Broomstick ; pl.-*on.*
Tchigataige, (*nin*). I sweep ; p. *tchag..ged.*
Tchigâtig, adv. Near a piece of wood.

Tchigewaam, (*nin*). *Ot.* S. *Jijodewaam.*

Tchigibig, adv. On the beach, on the lake shore, near the lake on the shore.

Tchigigaan, (*nin*). I square it ; p. *tchag..ang.*

Tchigigaigan. Axe for squaring timber, broad axe, squaring-axe ; pl.-*an.*

Tchigigaige, (*nin*). I hew timber, I cut it square ; p. *tchag..ged.*

Tchigigaigewin. Squaring timber cutting it square.

Tchigigâwa mitig, (*nin*). I square a log ; p. *tchag..wad ;* imp. *tchigiga.*

Tchégikana, adv. By the wayside.

Tchigikitchigami, adv. Along the great lake, or, the sea.

Tchigwakamigissin. It falls to the ground *hard ;* p. *tchag..ing.*

Tchimaâgan. Large draw-net ; (F. seine) ; pl.-*ag.*

Tchimân. Canoe ; pl.-*an.*

Tchimânijig. Canoe-bark, birch-bark for a canoe, to make a bark canoe ; pl.-*on.*

Tchimânike, (*nin*). I make a canoe, or canoes ; p. *tcha..ked.*

Tchimânikewin. Canoe-making, work or art of a canoe-maker.

Tchimaa, (*nin*). I am fishing with a large draw-net ; (F. je seine ;) p. *tchamaad.*

Tchime, (*nin*). I paddle ; p. *tchamed.*

Tchimemagad. It paddles, (the wheel of a steamboat ;) p. *tcham..gak.*

Tchingidaabowe, (*nin*). I tumble over head, playing ; p. *tchan..wed.*—S. *Abodjigwanisse.*

Tchingidjisse, (*nin*). I fall on my face ; p. *tchan..sed.*

Tchingwakamiga. There is a shaking of the earth from a cause above ground, thunder, etc. ; p. *tchan..gag.*

Tchingwamagad. The ground shakes, trembles ; p. *tchan..gak.*

Tchingwan. Meteor ; pl.-*an.*

Tchingwan. Thigh, the upper part of the leg, up from the knee. This word is always preceded by a possessive pronoun ; as : *Nin tchingwan,* my thigh ; *ki tchingwan,* thy thigh, etc.

Tchingwanigan. Thigh-bone. There is always a possessive pronoun prefixed to this word ; as : *Nin tchingwanigan,* my thigh-bone, etc.

Tchishajeshka, or-*magad.* The skin goes off by scalding ; p. *tcha..kag,* or-*magak.*

Tchishakwaan, (*nin*). I scrape it, (a skin, *pijikiwegin,* ox-hide ;) p. *tcha..ang.*

Tchishakwaigan. Scraper ; pl.-*an.*

Tchishakwaige, (*nin*). I scrape, (a skin ;) p. *tcha..ged.*

Tchishakwawa, (*nin*). I scrape it ; (a skin, *wawashkéshiwaiân,* deer-skin ;) p. *tcha..wad ;* imp. *tchi..kwâ.*

Tchisse. Turnip ; pl.-*an.*

Tchissakan. Juggler's lodge ; pl-*an.*

Tchissaki, (*nin*). I perform the Indian jugglery, in order to know the future, or to know events that happened at a distance; p. *tchassakid.*

Tchissakiwin. Indian jugglery, to know the future, or distant events.

Tchissakiwinini. Juggler; pl.-*wag.*

Tchissibina, (*nin*). I pinch him; p. *tcha..ad;* imp. *tchis-sibij.*

Tchissiga, or-*magad.* The water drops out of s. th.; p. *tchassigag,* or-*magad.*

Tchissigabaw, (*nin*). I stand on tiptoe; p. *tchas..wid.*

Tchissigawisibingwe, (*nin*). I am blear-eyed; p. *tchass..wed.*

Tchissigawisibingwewin. Blearedness.

Tchissikawa, (*nin*). I surprise him by my coming, I arrive unexpectedly to him; p. *tcha..wad.*

Tchissi-minikan. Turnip-seed; pl-*an.*

Tchitanendagos, (*nin*). I am considered serious, grave, I am grave; p. *tchat..sid.*

Tchitchâg. Soul. This word is always preceded by a possessive pronoun; as: *Nin tchitchâg, ki tchitchâg, o tchitchâgwan,* etc.; my, thy, his soul, etc.

Tchitchibakona, (*nin*). I rock him, (a child); p. *tche..nad;* imp. *tchitchibakon.*

Tchitchibakonagan. Cradle; pl. -*an.*

Tchitchibi, in compositions, alludes to *convulsion.* (Examples in some of the following words.)

Tchitchibigadeshka,(*nin*). I have convulsions in my leg; p. *tchatch..kad.*

Tchitchibinikeshka, (*nin*). I have convulsions in my arm; p. *tcha..kad.*

Tchitchibinindjishka, (*nin*). I have convulsions in my hand, or in my fingers; p. *tcha..kad.*

Tchitchibishka, (*nin*). I have convulsions in my body; p. *tcha..kad.*

Tchitchibishkawin. Convulsion, the state of being convulsed in any part of the body.

Tchitchibisideshka, (*nin*). I have convulsions in my foot; p. *tcha..kad.*

Tchitchibiwebinan, (*nin*). I shake it together; p. *tcha..ang.*

Tchitchiboan, (*nin*). S. *Tchitchibogwadan.*

Tchitchibogwadan, (*nin*). I sew it slightly, with wide stitches; p. *tcha..ang.*

Tchitchibogwade, or-*magad.* It is sewed slightly; p. *tcha..deg,* or-*magak.*

Tchitchibogwana, (*nin*). I sew slightly some obj.; p. *tcha..nad,* imp. *tchi..gwaj.*

Tchitchibogwâss, (*nin*). I sew slightly with wide stitches; p. *tcha..sod.*

Tchitchigi, (*nin*). I scratch myself slightly with my nails; p. *tchatchigid.*

Tchitchigibina, (*nin*). I scratch him slightly; p. *tcha..nad;* imp. *tchitchigibij.*

Tchitchigom. Wart; (F. verrue); pl.-*ag.*

Tchitchikinjean, ishkote, (*nin*). I stir the fire; p. *tcha..ang.*

Tchitchikinjeigan. Poker to stir the fire; pl.-*an.*

Tchitchikinjeige, (*nin*). I am stirring a fire; p. *tcha..ged.*

Tchitchwiskiwé. Plover, (bird); pl.-*iag*.
Tebinâk, adv. Negligently, badly; at least.
Tekassing. Something cool or cooling, peppermint.
Tekobisod abinodji. An infant yet in the cradle. — *Takobis*.
Tekoniwed. He that takes up, seizes, arrests, that is, a constable; pl.-*jig*.
Tekosid. He that is short, a small person; pl.-*jig*.
Ténde. Very big toad; pl.-*g*.
Téssab, (*nin*). I am sitting on a bench; also I am on horseback, sitting in the saddle; p. *taiéssabid*.
Téssâbân. Shelf, a board fixed so that things may be put upon it, cupboard; pl.-*an*.
Téssabadan, *nin*). I put it on a shelf or cupboarp; p. *taies..ang*.
Téssabana, (*nin*). I put some *an*. obj. on a shelf or cupboard; p. *taie..nad*; imp. *tessabaj*.
Téssâbik. Flat stone; pl.-*on*.— *Nij tessâbikon*, two tables of stone, (the two Tables of the Covenant).
Téssâbikad. It is flat, (metal, stone); p. *taie..kak*.
Téssâkonigan. Hand-barrow; pl.-*an*.
Téssâkwaigan. Scaffold to put s. th. on it, to preserve it from damage by water, by wild beasts, etc.; pl.-*an*.
Téssanakwe. Virgin, maid, unacquainted with man; pl.-*g*.
Téssanaw, (*nin*). I am in a virginal state, (a male speaking,) unacquainted with woman; p. *taie..wid*.
Téssigina, (*nin*). I spread out somewhere some *an*. stuff; p. *taie..nad*; imp. *tessigin*.
Téssinâgan. Plate, (F. assiette); pl.-*an*.— *Ningo tessinâgan*, a plate full; *nijo tessinâgan*, *nisso tessinâgan*, etc.; twice a plate full, three times a plate full, etc.
Téssinan, (*nin*). I spread it out; p. *taie..ang*.
Téssinawa, (*nin*) or, *nin tessina*. I take too much care of him, I spoil him, (especially a child); p. *taie..ad*.
Téssinindj. The flat hand. *Nin téssinindj*, *ki tessinindj*, *o tessinindj*; my, thy, his flat hand.
Téssinindjin, (*nin*). I open my hand, I spread it out flat; p. *taie..nid*.
Téssinindjitawa, (*nin*). I stretch my open flat hand towards him, or over him; p. *taie..wad*.
Téssitchigade, or-*magad*. There is a porch made; p. *taiê..deg*, or-*magak*.
Téssitchigan. Porch, (F. portail); pl.-*an*.
Téssiton, (*nin*). I make it flat, I flatten it; p. *taie..tod*.
Téssiwakwân. Flat low hat, or flat cap; pl.-*an*.
Tetebaagwinde, or-*magad*. It is floating about; p. *taiete..deg*, or-*magak*.
Tetebaagwindjin, (*nin*). I am floating about on the surface of the water; p. *taie..ing*.
Tetebikinâk. A kind of tortoise with a soft shell; pl-*wok*.
Tetibibaginigasod assema. Tobacco in rolled leaves, cigar. S. *Titibibaginigaso*.
Tetissanimad. There is a light

wind, raising no sea, a smooth wind; p. *taie..mak.*

Tewéigan. Drum; tambarine; tabouret, tabret; pl.-*ag.*

Téwéige, (*nin*). I beat the drum, I drum; p. *taie..ged.*

Teweigéwinini. Drummer, tabourer, tabrer; pl-*wag.*

Tibi, adv. This adverb cannot be given in English with a corresponding adverb. It signifies, "I don't know where." *Anindi k'oss? — Tibi.* Where is thy father? — I don't know where he is. *Tibi ge dapinewânen;* I don't know where I shall die.

Tibijigan. Pattern for cutting a coat or any other vestment; pl.-*an.*

Tibik. Night.

Tibikabâminagosi gisiss. The sun is darkened; p. *teb..sid.*

Tibikabâminagwad. It is twilight, it is crepusculous; p. *teb..wak.*

Tibikâdis, (*nin*). I am benighted, I live in darkness, I am ignorant; p. *teb..sid.*

Tibikgisiss, or *tibikigisiss.* Night-sun, that is, the moon; which is also called *gisiss;* only for a distinction from the sun, they will call the moon *tibikgisiss,* when a distinction becomes necessary.

Tibikinam, (*nin*). I have dim eyes, I cannot see distinctly; p. *tebikinang.*

Tibikong. Last night, or last evening.

Tibinawe, adv. Self; properly, as a property.

Tibinawewiidis, (*nin*). I make myself master or proprietor of s. th.; p. *teb..sod.*

Tibinawewisiwin. Property.

Tibishka, (*nin*). I come to my anniversary; p. *tebishkad.*

Tibiska abinodji. The child comes to the same time in the year at which it was born last year, to its anniversary, it is just one year old. P. *tebishkad.* — *Nijing tibishka, nissing tibishka,* etc.; he comes to his second, to his third anniversary, etc.

Tibishkamagad. It comes to the same time in the year, to its anniversary; also, it is fulfilled, accomplished; p. *teb..gak.*

Tibishkô, adv. and prp. Likewise, just so, equally; equivalent, tantamount; opposite, (F. vis-à-vis); p. *teb..ang.*

Tibishkokawa, (*nin*). I am equal to him, I equal him; p. *teb..wad.*

Tibishkosse, or-*magad.* It arrives again, (a certain periodical time or event;) or a foretold event comes to pass; p. *teb..seg,* or-*magak.*

Tibishkossitchigade, or-*magad.* It is fulfilled; it is made or put equal; what was lost is regained; p. *teb..deg,* or-*magak.*

Tibishkossiton, (*nin*). I fulfill or accomplish it, I put or make it equal; I regain what I had lost; p. *teb..tod.*

Tibishkowendagos, (*nin*). I am considered equal to somebody; p. *teb..sid.*

Tibishkowendagwad. It is esteemed equal to s. th., or compared with s. th.; p. *teb..wak.*

Tibissaton, (*nin*), or *nin tibissiton.* I fulfil it, (a promise, a vow); p. *teb..tod.*

Tigôw. Wave, billow; pl.-*og.*

Tigweia. At the end of some unipersonal verbs, alludes to a *river;* as: *Waiekwâtigweia,* it is the end of the river. *Manëtigweia,* there is scarcity of rivers, (in a country). *Giwitatigweia,* the river turns round (or back again) in its course.

Tikinâgan. Indian cradle; pl.-*an.*

Tipa, or-*magad.* It is much damp, it is moistened; p. *tepag,* or-*magak.*

Tipabaga, or-*magad.* The leaves of a tree or shrub are damp, wet, (from dew or rain); p. *tep..gag,* or-*magak.*

Tipabagisi aw assema. This tobacco is fresh, (not too dry); p. *tep..sid.*

Tipabawadon, (*nin*). I moisten it; p. *tep..dod.*

Tipabawana, (*nin*). I moisten some *an.* obj.; p. *tep..nad;* imp. *tipabawaj.*

Tipashka, or-*magad.* The grass is wet (from dew or rain); p. *tep..kag,* or-*magak.*

Titibâbissidon, (*nin*). I twist it around s. th.; p. *tet..dod.*

Titibakossatchigan. Roller; pl. -*an.*

Titibakossatchige, (*nin*). I roll; p. *tet..ged.*

Titibakossatwadan, (*nin*). I roll it, I move it on rollers; p. *tet..ang.*

Titibakossatwana, (*nin*). I roll some *an.* obj. on rollers; p. *tet..nad;* imp. *tit..waj.*

Titibakwaan, (*nin*). I twist it up, I curl it; p. *tet..ang.—Nin titibakwaanan ninisissan;* I twist or curl my hair. — S. *Babisigakwaan.*

Titibanowe. It has a curled or twisted tail; p. *tet..wed.*

Titibaode, or-*magad.* It is twisted; p. *tet..deg,* or-*magak.*

Titibaodjigan. Reel; pl.-*an.*

Titibaodjige, (*nin*). I wind up (thread or twine, etc.); p. *tet..ged.*

Titibaodon, (*nin*). I wind it up, (on a ball); p. *tet..dod.*

Titibaona, (*nin*). I wind it up, (*an.* obj., *seniba,* etc.); p. *tet..nad;* imp. *titibaoj.*

Titibâshka, or-*magad.* The surf or swell of the sea beats against the shore and returns; p. *tet..kag,* or-*magak.*

Titibashkwemaginan, (*nin*). I roll it up, I roll it together, (birch-bark, paper, etc.); p. *tet..ang.*

Titibew, adv. *Ot.* S. *Jijodew.*

Titibewaam, (*nin*). *Ot.* S. *Jijodewaam.*

Titibewe, (*nin*). *Ot.* S. *Jijodewe.*

Titibibagina, (*nin*). I roll together a leaf or leaves, (*bag,* alludes to leaves,) tobaccō leaves, *an.;* p. *tet..nad.*

Titibibaginan, (*nin*). I roll together a leaf or leaves, *in.;* p. *tet..ang.*

Titibidâbân. Wagon, cart, coach, carriage; pl.-*ag.*

Titibigina, (*nin*). I roll together some *an.* stuff. (*seniba,* etc.) I wind it up; p. *tet..nad;* imp. *titibigin.*

Titibigwadan, (*nin*). I sew it all round, that is, I hem it; p. *tet..ang.*

Titibigwade, or-*mogad.* It is hemmed; p. *tet..deg,* or-*magak.*

Titibigwana, (*nin*). I sew all round some *an.* stuff, I hem it; p. *tet..nad;* imp. *titibigwaj.*

Titibigwâso. It is hemmed, (*an.* stuff, *seniba, moshwe*); p. *tet.. sod.*

Titibigwâss, (*nin*). I sew all round, I hem s. th.; p. *tet..sod.*

Titibina, (*nin*). I roll some *an.* obj. (a person or any other *an.* obj.); p. *tet..nad;* imp. *titibij.*

Titibinamawa, (*nin*). I roll some object belonging to him, or relating to him, I roll it for him; p. *tet..wad.*

Titibingwebina, (*nin*). I wrap up his face in s. th.; I cover his eyes with s. th.; p. *tet..nad;* imp. *titibingwebij.*

Titibishaweon nind agwiwin, (*nin*). I wrap or cast around me my garment or vestment; p. *tet..od.*

Titibishimon, (*nin*). I roll about lying, I wallow in s. th.; p. *tet..nod.*

Titibishkan, (*nin*). I made it roll or fall down, with my *body,* (touching or pushing it); p. *tet..ang.*

Titibishkawa, (*nin*). I make roll down some *an.* obj., with my *body;* p. *tet..wad.*

Titibisse, (*nin*). I roll down, I roll off; p. *tet..sed.*

Titibisse, or-*magad.* It rolls off; p. *tet..seg,* or-*magak.*

Titibisse-odâbân. S. *Titibidâbân,* etc.

Titibita, (*nin*). I roll or turn from one side to the other, lying; p. *tet..dad.*

Titibitchipina, (*nin*). I wrap him up, I swathe him, (a child); p. *tet..nad;* imp. *titibitchipij.*

Titibitchipis,(*nin*). I am wrapped up in s. th., I am swathed, (a child); p. *tet..sod.*

Titissawe aw awessi. The hair or fur of this animal is short; p. *tet..wed.*

Tiwé! interj. Used by males only to express admiration, astonishing; reprimand; pain, sorrow. (The females say, *nià!*)

Toskâb, (*nin*). I look with scarcely opened eyes, with almost closed eyes; also, I aim at s. th. (with a gun, etc.); p. *twâskabid.*

Toskâbama, (*nin*). I look at him with only a little opened eyes, with almost closed eyes; I aim at him; p. *twas..mad.*

Toskâbandan, (*nin*). I look at it with only a little opened eyes; I aim at it; p. *twas..ang.*

Totôgan. A trembling piece of ground, in a marsh or swamp; pl.-*on.*

Totôganowan. There is a trembling piece of ground; p. *twet.. ang.*

Totokwewessin kitotâgan. The bell tolls, it is struck only on one side; p. *twet..ing.*

Totokwewessiton kitotâgan,(*nin.*) I am striking the bell only on one side; (F. je tinte); p. *twet.. tod.*

Totosh. Woman's breast, dug; also, the udder or dugs of a cow, or other quadruped; pl. -*ag.*

Totoshâbo. Milk.

Totoshâbo-bimide. Butter, (milk-grease).

Totoshâbôwigamig. Milk-house, dairy; pl.-*on.*

Totoshike, (*nin*). I suck; p. *twet..ked.*

Towêigan. A top whirling about, (boy's plaything); pl.-*ag.*

Towêige, (*nin*). I play with a top, I make it whirl round; p. *tweweîged.*

Totowesi. Moth; pl.-*wok.*

Twâan, (*nin*). I make a hole in it; p. *twaiâang.*

Twâibân. A hole in the ice for water; pl.-*an.*

Twâibi, (*nin*). I make a hole in the ice to have water; p. *twaiâbid.*

Twâige, (*nin*). I make a hole in the ice; p. *twaiâiged.*

Twâwa mikwam, (*nin*). I cut the ice through, I make a hole in it; p. *twaiâwad;* imp. *twâh.*

Twâshin, (*nin*). I break through the ice, walking on it; p. *twaiâshing.*

Twâtwâskobidinam, (*nin*). I walk in the water on the ice; p. *twaiat..ang.*

W

Some words that might be supposed to be under Wa, *are to be found under* O, *as the syllable* wa *is often pronounced like* o, *and* o *like* wa.

Wa? adv. What?

Wa–, the *Change* of *wi–*, which see.

Waaw, pron. *an.* this one, this here.

Wâb, (*nin*). I see; p. *waiâbid.**

Wâbabigan. White clay; lime.

Wâbabiganige, (*nin*). I whitewash; p. *waiâb..ged.*

Wâbabiganikan. Place where lime is made; limekiln; pl.*-an.*

Wâbabiganike,(*nin*).I burn lime; p. *waiab..ked.*

Wâbabiganikewin. Business or trade of a lime-burner.

Wâbabiganikewinini. Lime-burner; pl.*-wag.*

Wâbabik. Tin, (white-iron).

Wâbadjidjak. White crane; pl. *-wag.*

Wâbado. Rhubarb.

Wâbagamishkinjigwan. The white of the eye.

Wâbajashki. White mud; white clay for dishes and plates.

Wâbakik, or *wâbâbikwakik.* White kettle, that is, a kettle made of tin, tin kettle; pl.*-og.*

* Note.—From this word to *wâbo* on page 393, all the words belong to the root *wâb*, white.

Wâbakosi mitig. The tree is whitish; p. *waia..sid.*

Wâbakwa, or*-magad.* The forest has a white appearance; p. *waia..wag,* or*-magak.*

Wâbama, (*nin*). I see him; p. *waiâbamad.*

Wâbamegoshin gigô. The fish looks whitish, (spoiled); p. *waia..ing.*

Wâbaminagos, (*nin*). I am visible, I appear; p. *waia..sid.*

Wâbaminagosiwin. Visibility.

Wâbaminagwad. It is visible, it shows, it appears; p. *waia..wak.*

Wâbaminagwiidis, (*nin*). I make myself visible, I appear; p. *waia..sod.*

Wâban. East, orient.

Wâban. It is twilight, (in the morning); p. *waiabang.*—*Biwâban,* daylight is approaching.

Wâbânakwad. East-cloud, cloud coming from the east; pl.*-on.*

Wâbanang. Morning-star.

Wâbandaa, (*nin*). I let him see s. th., I show him s. th.; p. *waia..ad.*

Wâbandaan, (*nin*). I show it; p. *waia..ang.*
Wâbandaiwe, (*nin*). I show, I let see; I manifest; I prove; p. *waia..wed.*
Wâbandaiwen, (*nin*). I show it, I manifest it; I prove it; p. *waia..wed.*
Wâbandaiwenan, (*nin*). I show him, I bring him to light, (any *an.* obj.); p. *waia..wed.*
Wâbandaiwewin. Showing, show; manifestation; proving, proof; pl.-*an.*
Wâbandaiwewini-pakwejigan. Show-bread, (in the Old Testament).
Wâbandama, (*nin*). I am in my monthly flowings, (a woman); p. *waia..mad.*
Wâbandamadis, (*nin*). I see s. th. belonging or relating to me; I see myself, I cast immodest looks upon myself; p. *waia..sod.*
Wâbandamawa, (*nin*). I see s. th. belonging or relating to him; p. *waia..wad.*
Wâbandan, (*nin*). I see it, I perceive it; p. *waia..ang.* — *Nin wâbandan masinaigan,* I read, I am reading.
Wâbandis, (*nin*). I see myself (in a looking-glass, in the water, etc.); p. *waia..sod.*
Wâbandjigade, or-*magad.* It is seen; p. *waia..deg,* or-*magak.*
Wâbandjigâs, (*nin*). I am seen, (any *an.* obj.); p. *waia..sod.*
Wâbandjige, (*nin*). I see (some obj.); p. *waia..ged.*
Wâbang, adv. To-morrow. *Wâbang kigijeb,* to-morrow morning; *wâbang onâgoshig,* to-morrow night, (evening).
Wâbange, (*nin*). I look on, I am a spectator; p. *waiâbanged.*
Wâbanibissa. The rain comes from the east, or, it rains in the east, east-rain; p. *waia..sag.*
Wâbaningosi. Snow-bird; pl.-*g.*
Wâbaninodin. Eastwind.
Wâbanish, (*nin*). I pass the winter, I survive the winter, I am spared to see the spring again; p. *waia..shid.* S. *Nondéiabanish.*
Wâbanomin. Rice.
Wâbanong. In the east; from the east.
Wâbanow, (*nin*). I am a sorcerer, (after the Indian notion); p. *waia..wid.*
Wâbanowiwin. Indian sorcery.
Wâbanowiwinini. Indian sorcerer; pl.-*wag.*
Wâbanowe. It has a white tail; p. *waia..wed.*
Wâbansig. A kind of white duck; pl.-*wag.*
Wâbas, (*nin*). I survive the night, I see the day once more, (a sick person); p. *waia..sod.* S. *Nondéiâbâs.*
Wâbashkad mashkossiw. The herb is whitish; p. *waia..kak.*
Wâbashkiki. Swamp, marsh, morass, bog; pl.-*wan.*
Wâbashkikomân. Pewter; (F. étain).
Wâbassim. A white dog; pl.-*og.*
Wâbassin. White stone; alabaster.
Wâbassini-makak. Alabaster-box.
Wâbâwan. The white of the egg.
Wâbia, (*nin*). I make him see, I open his eyes; p. *waiâbiad.*
Wâbide, or-*magad.* It is ripe;

p. *waiabideg*, or-*magak*.—*Manomin wâbidemagad*; the wild rice is ripe. — S. *Wâbiso.*

Wâbidwi. Long potatoe-sprout; pl.-*ian.*

Wâbidwi. It sprouts (in long sprouts); p. *waiabidwid.*

Wâbidwimagad. It sprouts; p. *waia..gak.*

Wâbigad ojigaigan. The incision in the maple-tree is whitish, (the running of the sugar-sap is near its end). P. *waiabigak.*

Wâbigama, or-*magad.* There are straits between two lakes; p. *waia..mag*, or-*magak.*

Wâbigan. Clay; (F. terre-glaise).

Wâbigaige, (*nin*). I plaster with clay, I put clay on; p. *waia..ged.*

Wâbigaigewin. Plastering with clay, clay-plastering.

Wâbigan-minikwâdjigan. Earthern pitcher; pl.-*an.*

Wâbigan- omodai. Jar, jug; pl. *an.*

Wâbigan-onâgan. Earthern plate or dish; pl.-*an.*

Wâbigan - onaganike, (*nin*). I make earthern plates and dishes, I am a potter; p. *waia..ked.*

Wâbigan - onaganikewinini. A man that makes earthern dishes, a potter; pl.-*wag.*

Wâbigin. Flannel.

Wâbigin bebigwatagak. Soft flannel, swanskin; (F. molleton).

Wâbigon. Flower, bloom, blossom; pl.-*in.*

Wâbigini-gijigad. Day of flowers, (the holiday of Corpus Christi.)

Wâbigoni-gisiss, or *wâbigon-gisiss.* The moon of flowers and blooms, the month of May.

Wâbigonike, (*nin*). I make flowers, (artificial flowers); p. *waia..ked.*

Wâbigonikewikwe. A woman making artificial flowers; pl. *-g.*

Wâbigoniwimitig. The tree is blooming, is flourishing; p. *waia..wid.*

Wâbigwan. White feather; pl. *-ag.*

Wâbijakwe. A kind of eagle, with a white head and a white tail; pl.-*g.*

Wâbijéshi. Marten; pl.-*wog.*

Wâbijêshiwaiân. Martenskin; pl.-*ag.*

Wâbijêshiwatchâb. Ivy; (F. lierre.)

Wâbikadin, or *wâbikamigadin.* S. *Nigigwakamigadin.*

Wâbikwanaie, (*nin*). S. *Wâbishkikwanaie.*

Wâbikwe, (*nin*). I have white hair, (a white head), I am gray-headed; p. *waiabikwed.*

Wâbikwewin. Gray head, gray age; (L. canities).

Wâbinagos, (*nin*). I look pale; white; p. *waia..sid.*

Wâbinéwadengwe, (*nin*). My face is pale, wan; p. *waia..wed.*

Wâbinewis, (*nin*). I am pale; p. *waia..sid.*

Wâbinewisiwin. Paleness.

Wâbinigade, or-*magad.* It is painted white; p. *waiag..deg*, or-*magak.*

Wâbinigaso. It is painted white, (*an.* obj.); p. *waia..sod.*

Wâbininishib. A kind of large white duck; pl.-*ag.*

Wâbipapasse. A kind of white wood-pecker; pl.-*g.*
Wâbishka, or-*magad.* It is white, p. *waia..keg,* or-*magak.*— *Wâbishkamagad nishtigwân;* my head is white, gray.
Wâbishkaan, (*nin*). I whiten it; I make it white; p. *waia..ang.*
Wâbishkabigibidon, (*nin*). I make it white, (a string, cord, etc.); p. *waia..dod.*
Wâbishkâgami. A whitish liquid or weak liquid; p. *waia..mig.*
Wâbishkag wawan. S. *Wâbawan.*
Wâbishkaigan. Whitewashing-brush; pl.-*an.*
Wâbishkaje, (*nin*). I have a white skin; p. *waia..jed.*
Wâbishkawa, (*nin*). I whiten him, make him white; p. *waiabishkawad.*
Wâbishkia, (*nin*). I make him white, in making him, (*an.* obj.); p. *waia..ad.*
Wâbishkibejibiigan. Chalk, Spanish white.
Wâbishkibeshaigan. S. *Wâbishkibejibiigan.*
Wâbishkigin. White cotton or linen.
Wâbiskigiton, (*nin*). I make it white, (stuff), I bleach it; p. *waia..tod.*
Wâbishki-papagiwaiân. S. *Wâbishkigin.*
Wâbishkwanaie, (*nin*). I am dressed in white; p. *waia..ied.*
Wâbishkingwe, (*nin*). I have a white face, I am wan, I am pale-faced; p. *waia..wed.*
Wâbishkis, (*nin*). I am white; p. *waiabishkisid.*
Wâbishkisigwa, or-*magad.* It is white; p. *waia..wag,* or-*magak.*
Wâbishkitchiss. Turnip, (white turnip); pl.-*an.*—S. *Miskotchis. Osawitchiss.*
Wâbishkiton, (*nin*). I make it white, in making it; p. *waia..tod.*
Wâbishkiwe, (*nin*). I am a white person, (not an Indian or negro); p. *waia..wed.*
Wâbisi. Swan; pl.-*g.* *Wâbisins.* A young swan; pl.-*ag.*
Wâbisipin. *An.* swan's potato, (an eatable root growing in the water); pl.-*ig.*
Wâbiso. It is ripe, (*an.* obj.); p. *waiâbisod.* — *Pakwejiganiminag wâbisowog,* the wheat is ripe. —S. *Wâbide.*
Wâbissaginigade, or-*magad.* It is painted white, (wood, *in.*); p. *waia..deg,* or-*magak.*
Wâbissaginigan. A white wall, or any thing whitened; pl.-*an.*
Wâbissaginigaso. He is painted white, (wood, *an.*).
Wâbitchiia, or-*magad.* It becomes whitish, it fades, (stuff); p. *waia..iag,* or-*magak.*
Wâbitchiiâbâwe, or-*magad.* It fades or becomes whitish, in *washing;* p. *waia..wag,* or-*magak.*
Wâbitchiiate, or-*magad.* It fades or becomes whitish by the *sun;* p. *waia..teg,* or-*magak.*
Wâbmimi. White turtle-dove, that is, a dove, a domestic pigeon; pl.-*g.* — (*Omimi,* wild pigeon.) *Wâbmimins.* Young pigeon; pl.-*ag.*
Wâbmotchitchagwan. Looking-glass, mirror; pl.-*an.*
Wâbo. At the end of some compound substantives, denotes *liquid, fluid;* where the preceding part of the compound

word ends in a *vowel;* as: *Anamiewâbo*, holy water; *mashkikiwâbo*, liquid medicine; *ishkotewâbo*, firewater, ardent liquor; etc. —S. *Abo*.

Wâboiakisin, (*wâboiân*, blanket, *makisin*, shoe.) A shoe made of a piece of blanket, blanket-moccasin; pl.-*an*.

Wâboiakisine, (*nin*). I wear moccasins made of a piece of blanket; p. *waia..wed.*

Wâboiân, or, *wâboweiân*. Blanket; pl.-*an*.

Wâbomini. S. *Wâbmimi*.

Wâbôs. Rabbit; pl.-*og*. *Wâbosons*. Young rabbit; pl.-*ag*.

Wâbosanaman. Hair-powder.

Wâbôsomin. Rabbit's berry; black berry; pl.-*an*.

Wâbosowaiân. Rabbitskin; pl. -*ag*.

Wâboswekon. Coat made of rabbitskins; pl.-*an*.

Wâboswekonike, (*nin*). I make a coat of rabbitskins; p. *waia ..ked*.

Wâbwewe. A white goose; pl.-*g*.

Wâdema, (*nin*). I put it in my belly, in my stomach, (I eat it up), I have it in my belly, *an*. obj.; p. *wed..ad*. — *Anindi kokosh ga-aiad oma?* — *Nin gi-wadema*. Where is the pork that was here? — I put it in my belly, (I ate it up).

Wâdendan, (*nin*). I put it in my belly, (I eat it up), I have it in my belly; *in*. obj.; p. *wed..ang*.

Wadi, *wadibi*, adv. *Ot*. S. *Wedi*.

Wâdiged ikwe. Married woman, wife; pl. *wâdigedjig ikwewog*.

Wâdiged inini. Married man, husband; pl. *wâdigedjig ininiwog*.

Wadigessig inini. Bachelor; pl. *wadigessigog ininiwog*.

Wadikwan, (often pronounced, *Odikwan*), branch of a tree; pl.-*an*.

Wadikwani mitig. The tree has branches or boughs; p. *wed.. nid*.

Wadjépadis, (*nin*), or *nin wadjêpi*. I am nimble, light, flexible; p. *wed..id*.

Wâdji–, is the *Change* of *widji*–; which see.

Wadjiw. Mountain; pl-*an*.

Wadjiwan. There is a mountain; p. *wedjiwang*.

Wadô. Coagulated blood.

Wadokasod. Helper, assistant; pl.-*jig*.

Wadôp. Alder-tree; pl.-*in*.

Wadopika, or-*magad*. There are alder-trees; p. *wed..kag*, or-*magak*.

Wadopikang. In a place where there are alder-trees.

Wadôpiki. A forest of alder-trees, alder-forest; pl.-*wan*.

Wâgâkosi mitig. The tree is crooked; p. *waia..sid*.

Wâgâkwad. Axe; pl.-*on*.*

Wâgâkwadons. Hatchet, tomahawk; pl.-*an*.

Wâganabitawanan, (*nin*). We are sitting around him in a *semicircle;* p. *waiag..wadjig*. —S. *Giwitabitawanan* or, *Wâganagabawitawanan*, (*nin*). We are standing around him in a *semicircle;* p. *waia..wadjig*—S. *Giwitagabawitawanan*.

Wâgânakibitchigan. A kind of crooked war-club, on which

---

* Note.—It is crooked, a stick, because when first the Indians saw an axe they saw it with a crooked handle.

the Indian warriors hang the scalps of their slain enemies; pl.-*an*.

Wâgânakisi aw mitig. The top or head of that tree is crooked or bent; p. *waiâ..sid.*

Wâgashkawa, (nin). I remain about him, in walking; p. *waia..wad.*

Wâgênis, (nin). I am bent forward, inclined; p. *waia..sid.*

Wâgidjane, (nin). I have a crooked nose, an aquiline nose; p. *waia..ned.*

Wâgigika, (nin). I am bent forward, by age; p. *waia..kad.*

Wâgikomân. Crooked knife; pl. -*an*.

Wâgina. Rib of a canoe, etc.; (F. varangue); pl.-*g*.

Wâgina, (nin). I bend it, I make it crooked, (*an.* obj.); p. *waiaginad.*

Wâginan, (nin). I bend it, I bow it; (*in.* obj.); p. *waia..ang.*

Wâginige, (nin). I bend; p. *waia..ged.*

Wâginindji, (nin). I have crooked fingers; *fig.* I am a thief; p. *waia..id.*

Wâginogân. Round Indian lodge; pl.-*an*. S. *Nassawâogan.*

Wâginoge, (nin). I build a round lodge; or, I live in a round lodge; p. *waia..ged.* S. *Nassawâoge.*

Wâgishka, (nin). I am bent, bowed; p. *waia..kad.*

Wâgishkamagad. It is bent or bowed; p. *waio..gak.*

Wâgisi. Indian silver ornament in the shape of a half moon; pl.-*iag*.

Wâgitchibik. Crooked root, rib of a boat or barge; (C. courbe); pl.-*on*.

Wâgiwine. It has crooked or bent horns; p. *waia..ned.*

Wâgosh. Fox; pl.-*ag*. *Wâgoshens.* Young fox; pl.-*ag*.

Waiâbaminagosissig. He that is not visible, the invisible; pl. -*og*.

Waiâbaminagwassinog. Invisible *in.* object; pl.-*in*.

Waiâbanged. He that looks on, a spectator; pl.-*jig*.

Waiâbandang masinaigan. He that looks in the paper, a reader; pl.-*ig*.

Waiâbishkag masinaigan. White paper, not written upon. (Or, *wejibiigadessinog masinaigan.*)

Waiâbishkisigwag mashkiki. Alum. — S. *Jiwâbik.*

Waiâbishkiwed. A white, a white man or a white woman; pl. *waiâbishkiwedjig*, white people, the whites.

Waiân. Skin. This word is never used alone, but is always attached to the name of an animal, to signify its skin; as: *Wawashkeshiwaiân*, deer-skin; *makwawaiân*, bear-skin; *wâbijheshiwaiân*, marten-skin; etc. Pl.-*ag*. S. *Wégin.*

Waiânag. Basin of water; pl. -*in*. S. *Wâna.*

Waiânag kakâbikawang. A basin of water where there is a water-fall over steep rocks, that is, Niagara Falls.

Waiâwanendagos, (nin). I am considered imperfect, I am imperfect, wicked; p. *weia..sid.*

Waiawanendagwad. It is esteemed imperfect, it is imperfect, bad, good for nothing; p. *waia ..wak.*

Waiba, or *waiêba*, adv. Soon, shortly.

Waiba nin nishkâdis. I am soon angry, I am passionate, choleric.

Waiêbinang od anamiewin. He who rejects his religion, an apostate, renegado.

Waiêjima, (*nin*). I cheat him, I defraud him; I deceive him; I seduce him; p. *weiêjimad.*

Waiêjindan, (*nin*). I cheat, deceive it; p. *wei..ang.*—*Ki giwaiêjindan ninde;* thou hast deceived my heart.

Waiêjindis, (*nin*). I deceive myself; p. *wei..sod.*

Waiêjindisowin. Self-deceit, illusion.

Waiêjinge, (*nin*). I cheat, deceive, seduce; I swindle, I defraud, I embezzle; p. *wei.. ged.*

Waiejinge—, in compositions, signifies *false, deceiving;* as: *Waiejinge-Kristag*, false Christs; *waiejinge-niganadjimowininiwok*, false prophets; *waiejinge-gâgikwewin*, false deceiving preaching; etc.

Waiejingeshk, (*nin*). I am in a habit of cheating, etc., (as above under *Waiejinge*); p. *wei..kid.*

Waiêjingewin. Cheating, deceit, shuffling, cheat, fraud, imposture; swindling, embezzlement, trick; seduction.

Waiêjitagos, (*nin*). I deceive or seduce with my words; p. *wei ..sid.*

Waiêkwa, in compositions, alludes to the *end* of s. th.. (Examples in some of the following words.)

Waiekwâ akiwan. It is the end of the world; p. *weiek..ang.*

Waiekwâ-akiwang. At the end of the world.

Waiêkwagâm, adv. At the end of a lake.

Waiêkwaia, or-*magad.* It has an end, or there is an end; p. *weiê..ing*, or-*magad.* S. *Waiêkwaiassinog.*

Waiekwaiabiki-assin. Cornerstone; (L. lapis angularis); pl. *-ig.*

Waiêkwaiaii, adv. At the end.

Waiekwaiendagwad. It is considered the end of it; p. *weiek ..wak.*

Waiekwaiendan, (*nin*). I think it is the end of it; p. *weiek.. ang.*

Waiekwâkamiga. It is the end of the earth, of the ground; p. *weie..gag.*

Waiekwâkitchigami. The end of the great lake, (C. Fond du Lac.)

Waiêkwaminiss. The end of the island.

Waiêkwashkan, (*nin*). I arrive to the end of it; p. *weiê..ang.*

Waiêkwasse, or-*magad.* It comes to an end, it arrives to its end; p. *weie..seg*, or-*magak.*

Waiêkwassiton, (*nin*). I bring it to an end, I finish it; p. *weie.. tod.*

Waiêkwatigweia sibi. It is the end of the river; p. *weiek..iag.*

Waiekwaton, (*nin*). S. *Waiekwassiton.*

Waiêshkat, adv. In the beginning, at first.

Waj. Den, abode or hole of a wild animal; pl.-*an*.
Watjashk. Musk-rat; pl.-*wag*.
Watjashkobiwai, pl.-*an*. The fur of a musk-rat.
Watjashkonigam. Rat-Portage.
Watjashkwaiân. Musk-rat's skin; pl.-*ag*.
Watjashkwaj. Hole (not lodge) of a musk-rat; pl.-*an*.
Wajashkwêdo. Mushroom growing on a tree, or on the ground; cork; pl.-*wag*.
Wajashkwêdo - gibâkwaigan. Cork-stopper to a bottle, etc.
Waje. S. *Aje*.
Wajibiia. Pond, pool; pl.-*n*.
Wajibiians, a little pond or pool; pl.-*an*.
Wak. Spawn, roe, (eggs of a fish or frog); pl. *wâkwog*.
Wâkabitawanan, (*nin*). We are sitting around him; p. *waiak..djig*.
Wâkaigan. Fort, fortress, redoubt; house.
Wâkaiganâtig. Log for a house; pl.-*on*.
Wâkaige, (*nin*). I build a log-house, or a frame-house; also, I live in a house, (not in a lodge); p. *waiakaiged*.
Wâkaigewin. Building, carpenter's work or trade, carpentry.
Wâkâikawa, (*nin*). I remain about him or around him; p. *waiâ..wad*.
Wâkâkina, (*nin*). I fence him in, I put him in an enclosure or park; p. *waiak..ad*.
Wâkâkinan, (*nin*). I fence it in, I enclose it; p. *waia..ang*.
Wâkami, or-*magad*. The water is clean, clear; p. *waia..mig*, or-*magak*.
Wakamissiton, (*nin*). I make it clear or clean, (liquid), I let it settle; p. *waia..tod*.
Wakê–,* in compositions, signifies *often*, *habitually*; *weakness*. (Examples in some of the following words.)
Waké-dodom, (*nin*). I do s. th. often, habitually.
Wakéiawishib. A kind of small duck, very difficult to shoot, and therefore called *shot-eater*; (C. mangeur de plomb); pl.-*ag*.
Waké-ijiwebis, (*nin*). I use to be so, or to do so....
Waké-mamikaw, (*nin*). I think always on home and on my relations, when abroad; p. *wek..wid*.
Waké - mamikwendan, (*nin*). I think always on it when abroad; p. *wek..ang*.
Wakê - mamikwenima, (*nin*). I think always on him when abroad; p. *wek..mad*.
Waké-panghishin, (*nin*). I fall often.
Wâkeshka, or-*magad*. It is shining; p. *waia..kag*, or-*magak*.
Wakêwadj, (*nin*). I feel soon cold, I cannot endure much cold; p. *wek..id*.
Wakéwakis, (*nin*). I feel soon warm, I cannot endure much heat; p. *wek..sod*.
Wakêwan. It is weak, easily torn, (stuff); p. *wekêwang*.
Wakêwanâmos, (*nin*). I cannot endure much smoke; p. *wek..sod*.

* Note. This root is perhaps better pronounced *wokke*.

Wakéwine, (*nin*). I am of a weak constitution, delicate health; p. *wek..ned.*

Wakêwis, (*nin*). I am weak, delicate, I cannot endure hardship; p. *wekewisid.*

Wakéwissin. It is weak, it is not durable; p. *wek..ing.*

Wâkomind. He who is invited to a meal, a guest; p.-*jig.*

Wâkon. Moss of cedar, and some other trees. (It is eaten by the Indians). Pl.-*ag.*

Wakwâgami nibi. The sap of the maple-trees is whitish, is spoiled; p. *wek..mig.*

Wakwi. Ot. Paradise, heaven. *Wakwing,* in heaven, or to heaven, or from heaven.

Wâna, or-*magad.* It is hollow, deep; also, there is a basin of water; p. *waiânag,* or-*magak.*

Wanâadjige, (*nin*). I lose the track or trace; p. *wen..ged.*

Wanâadon mikana, (*nin*). I lose the trail; p. *wen..dod.*

Wanaam, (*nin*). I mistake or commit a blunder in singing; p. *wenaang.*

Wanâamowin. Mistake in singing.

Wanadeshkodjigan. Model of a canoe or boat, etc. (F. gabari); pl.-*ag.*

Wânadina. The mountain is hollow, there is a cavern in the mountain; p. *waia..nag.*

Wânâdis, (*nin*). I am wealthy, rich; p. *waia..sid.*

Wânâdisia, (*nin*), or *nin wânâdisiwia.* I make him rich; p. *waia..ad.*

Wânâdisiwin. Wealth, riches.

Wanâdjim, (*nin*). I mistake in telling or relating s. th.; p. *wen..mod.*

Wânadjissaga, or-*magad.* There is plenty of wood; p. *waia..gag,* or-*magak.*

Wanagâai. Fish-scale; pl.-*ag.*

Wanagâkisid. The sole of the foot; pl.-*an.*

Wanagêk, (often pronounced and written, *onagêk.*) Cedar-bark; pl.-*wag.*— *Wanagek mekwanagekosid,* cinnamon.

Wanagêkogamig. Bark-lodge, lodge made of cedar-bark; pl. -*on.*

Wanagima, (*nin*). I mistake in counting some *an.* obj. as, *joniia,* money; p. *wen..mad.*

Wânaki, (*nin*). I inhabit a place in peace, undisturbed, I live somewhere in peace; p. *waiânakid.*

Wânakia, (*nin*). I make him live in peace, I procure him peace and tranquillity; p. *waia..ad.*

Wânakiwendam, (*nin*). I am appeased in my thoughts, in my mind, I am out of danger, out of trouble; p. *waia..ang.*

Wânakiwidee, (*nin*). My heart is in peace, it is contented; p. *waia..ed.*

Wânakiwideewin. Peace of the heart, tranquillanimity.

Wânakiwin. Peace, tranquillity; quiet inhabitation of a place.

Wanakodjaonag. The foremost part of a canoe; (C. pince du canot); pl.-*on.*

Wanakong. At the top or head of a tree.

Wanâkosid. The point or extremity of the foot; pl.-*an.*

Wanakowin. Top, extremity, summit, pinnacle.

Wanakowiwan. There is a top, a summit; p. *wen..ang.*— *Wanakowiwang anamiewigamig;* there where the temple has its summit, (on the pinnacle of the temple).

Wanakwâtig. The end of a tree or log; pl.-*on.*

Wanashkid. The tail of a bird; pl.-*in.*

Wanashkobia, or-*magad.* There is a reservoir or basin of water; p. *waia..ag,* or-*magak.*

Wanatan. There is a whirlpool, where the water turns round; p. *waia..ang.*

Wanendagos, (*nin*). I am forgotten, neglected; p. *wen..sid.*

Wanendagwad. It is forgotten, as well as forgotten, obliterated; p. *wen..wak.*

Wanendam, (*nin*). I forget; p. *wenendang.*

Wanêndama, (*nin.*) I lose my senses, I faint; p. *wen..mad.*

Wanêndamowin. Forgetting, forgetfulness.

Wanêndan, (*nin*). I forget it; p. *wenendang.*

Wanênima, (*nin*). I forget him, I forget his name; I neglect him; p. *wen..mad.*

Wanênindis, (*nin*). I forget myself, I neglect myself, omit myself; p. *wen..sod.*

Wângawia, (*nin*). I tame him, I break him, (a horse, an ox, etc.) I subdue him; p. *waia.. ad.*

Wangawima, (*nin*). I appease him, I pacify him with good soft *words;* p. *waia..mad.*

Wângawina, (*nin*). I appease him, or make him quiet, caressing him with my *hand;* p. *waia..nad.*

Wângawisi, or *wawangawisi, aw bekejigoganji.* This horse is well broken, is gentle; p. *waia..sid.*

Wângawitchigaso aw awessi. This animal is tamed; p. *waian ..sod.*

Wângawiton, (*nin*). I tame it, I subdue it; p. *waia..tod.*— *Kawin awiia o da gashkitossin tchi wangawitod o denaniw;* nobody can tame his tongue.

Wangoma, (*nin*). I adopt him or her, (for a father, mother, child, brother, sister); I take him (her) to me; p. *waiângomad.*

Wângondân, (*nin*). I adopt it, I take it for me; p. *waia..ang.*

Wani, (*nin*). I disguise myself; p. *weniod.*

Wani–, in compositions, signifies *mistake, error.* (Examples in some of the following words.)

Wanià, (*nin*). I lose him; I miss him, I perceive or notice his absence; p. *weniad.*

Wanibiigan. Mistake, blunder or error in a writing; pl.-*an.*

Wanibiige, (*nin*). I make a mistake in writing; p. *wen..ged.*

Wanibiigewin. Blunder in writing; the act of making a blunder or mistake.

Wanidodam, (*nin*). I do s. th. through mistake; p. *wen..dang.*

Wanidodamowin. Mistake or error in action; pl.-*an.*

Wanigijwe, (*nin*). I make a mistake or blunder in speaking; p. *wen..wed.*

Wanigijwewin. Blunder in speaking; pl.-*an.*

Wanigika, (*nin*). I speak nonsense, (through old age); p. *wen..kad.*

Waniidis, (*nin*). I seduce myself in error; I lose myself; p. *wen..sod.*

Wânikân. A hole in the ground, a grave, etc.; pl.-*an.*

Wânike, (*nin*). I dig a hole in the ground, I dig a grave, etc.; p. *waiâniked.*

Wanike, (*nin*). I forget to take s. th. along with me, I leave s. th. somewhere by mistake, or forgetting; p. *weniked.*

Waniken, (*nin*). I forget it some where, I leave it behind, forgetting; p. *weniked.* — *Nin giwanikenag nin mindjikawanag gabeshiwining;* I forgot my mittens in the camp.

Wanimik. S. *Onimik.*

Wanimikaw, (*nin*). I faint, I swoon away; p. *wen..wid.*

Wanimikawiwin. Swoon, fainting.

Wanimod. Indian sack made of the inner part of the elm-bark; pl.-*an.*

Wanina, adv. Much, strongly.

Waninawéan. I stir it, I mix it; p. *wen..ang.*

Waningwash, (*nin*). I walk round in sleep, (somnambule); p. *wen..id.*

Waninishka, (*nin*). I follow a circuitous route; I go round; p. *waiâ..kad.*

Wanishima, (*nin*). I lead him astray; I pervert him, seduce him; p. *wen..mad.*

Wanishin, (*nin*). I go astray, I get lost; p. *wenishing.*

Wanishindis, (*nin*). I cause myself to go astray, to get lost; p. *wen..sod.*

Wanishkwea, * (*nin*), or *nin wanishkwema.* I disturb and trouble him in his doings, or in his speech, lecture or prayer, by my speaking or laughing, I cause him to make mistakes; p. *wen..ad.*

Wanishkweiendam, (*nin*). I am troubled in my thoughts; p. *wen..ang.*

Wanishkweiendamowin. Troubled thoughts, trouble of mind.

Wanishkwekamigad. There is trouble, noise, disturbance; p. *wen..gak.*

Wanishkwês, (*nin*). I am disquiet, troublesome, frivolous, wild, never quiet and still; p. *wen..sid.*

Wanishkwêsiwin. Disquietness, turbulence, troublesome disposition or behavior.

Wanishkwetagos, (*nin*). I am noisy and turbulent in my speaking, I cause trouble with my words; p. *wen..sod.*

Wanishkwetawa, (*nin*). He causes me trouble with his words, I hear him or listen to him with a troubled mind; p. *wen..wad.*

Wanishkweton, (*nin*). I disturb it, (an assembly, etc.); p. *wen ..tod.*

---

* Note. This and the eight following words, are more conveniently placed here under *Wani,* than under *Oni,* (although the pronunciation remains the same,) because *Wani..,* alludes to *mistake, trouble,* etc.

Wânisid ikwe. Dirty woman, slut.

Wânisid manito. Unclean spirit, evil spirit, devil.

Wanisse, (*nin*). I mistake, I commit a blunder; p. *wenissed.*

Wanissin. It gets lost; p. *wenissing.*

Wanitagos, (*nin*). I am not well understood in my speaking, I am misunderstood; p. *wen..sid.*

Wanitawa, (*nin*), or *nin wanitamawa.* I lose s. th. belonging to him, or any way relating to him; p. *wen..wad.*

Wanitawa, (*nin*). I mistake in hearing him, that is, I misunderstand him; p. *wen..wad.*

Wanitchige, (*nin*). I act by mistake; p. *wen..ged.*

Wanitchigewin. S. *Wanidodamowin.*

Waniton, (*nin*). I lose it; I miss it; p. *wenitod.*

Wano. At the end of some substantives, signifies the *tail* of an animal, and more especially the *hair* of the tail; as: *Bebejigoganjiwano,* the tail of a horse; *pijikiwano,* the tail of an ox or cow; *kâgwano,* the tail of a porcupine, (so dangerous to hunting dogs, because the porcupine, when persuit, will shoot the quills of its tail in the head of the dog, and injure, or even destroy the dog). — S. *Osôw.*

Wanowe, (*nin*). S. *Wanigijwe.*

Wanowewin. S. *Wanigijwewin.*

Wapagakindibe, (*nin*). My head is half bald; p. *wep..bed.*

Wapagessi. A kind of large carp, (fish); (C. carpe de France); pl.-*wag.*

Wâpidassâbi, (*nin*). I mend a net; p. *waia..bid.*

Wâshkeiâbikishkan, (*nin*). I make it bright, I make it shine, by walking often over it, (metal); p. *waia..ang.*

Wâshkobitchigasod pakwejigan. Sweet bread, sweet cake; ginger-bread.

Wa-sigaândasod. He that is to be baptized, a catechumen, a person receiving religious instruction, and preparing for baptism; pl.-*jig.*

Wasisswan, or, *wasisôn.* Bird's nest; pl.-*an.*

Wasisswanike bineshi. The bird builds its nest; p. *wes..ked.*

Wass. S. *Awass.* At the end of some neuter verbs, etc.

Wâssa, adv. Far, afar off, a great way off, distant.

Wâssaakwakwa, or-*magad.* The wood, or forest, is far.

Wâssakodewan wigwâssan. The birch-trees are white.

Wâssakone, or *wassakwane.* Bloom or flower of a pumpkin; pl.-*n.*

Wâssakwaam. Lightning. (*Wassakwamog animikig,* there are lightnings.)

Wâssâkwaigan. Blaze on a tree to indicate the right road in the woods; pl.-*an.*

Wâssâkwaigaso mitig. The tree is blazed; p. *waiâ..sod.*

Wâssâkwaige, (*nin*). I blaze trees to indicate the right road or trail through the woods; p. *waiâs..ged.*

Wâssakwaneamawa, (*nin*). I

light it for him, or to him, or in regard to him ; p. *waia..wad.*

Wâssakwanean, (*nin*). I light it, I make it light, (for instance a house, by lighting a candle, or building a fire in the chimney) ; *waia..ang.*

Wâssakwanendamawa, (*nin*). I enlighten his mind, his thoughts ; p. *waia..wad.*

Wâssakwanendjigan. Candle, lamp ; lantern ; also a lighthouse ; pl.-*an.*

Wâssakwanendjiganâbik. Candle-stick of iron, brass, etc. ; pl.-*on.*

Wâssakwanendjiganâtig. A candlestick made of wood ; pl. -*on.*

Wâssakwanendjigan - bimide. Lamp-oil.

Wâssakwanendjiganeiâb. Wick ; (F. mèche.)

Wâssakwanendjigen, (*nin*). I use it for a light, I burn it ; p. *waia..ged.*—*Gigobimide nin wassakwanendjigen* ; I burn fish-oil. *Ka gego nin wâssakwanendjigessi*, I have no light, no candles or oil.

Wâssamowog animikig. It lightens.

Wâssamowin. Lightning, thunderbolt ; pl.-*an.*

Wâssa nin takoki. I make a long step. *Wawassa nin takoki*, or, *wâssa nin tatakoki*, I make long steps in walking. — S. *Besho nin takoki.*

Wâssâshka, or-*magad.* There are foaming billows or waves on the lake, the lake is white ; p. *waia..kag*, or-*magak.*

Wâssawad. It is far, far off, distant ; p. *waia..wak.*

Wâssawekamig, adv. Far off.

Wâssawendam, (*nin*). I think it is far ; p. *waia..ang.* — *Pabige ki wassawendam, kishpin ningotchi ininajaogoian* ; thou thinkest immediately, it is far, when thou art sent somewhere.

Wâssawendan, (*nin*). I find it far, I think it far, (the distance from one place to another, in walking, sailing, etc.) ; p. *waia ..ang.*

Wâssêia. Light.

Wâssêia, or-*magad.* It is light ; p. *waiasséiag*, or-*magak.*

Wâssêiadis, (*nin*). I am in the light, I am not in darkness ; p. *waia..sid.*

Wâssêiâb, (*nin*). I see clearly, plainly ; p. *waia..bid.*

Wâssêias, (*nin*). I am resplendent, I shine ; p. *waia..sid.*

Wâsseiâsiwin. Light, splendor, shine, brightness.

Wâsseiâssige gisiss. The sun or moon shines ; p. *waia..ged.*

Wâssêiendamia, (*nin*). I enlighten his understanding, his thoughts ; p. *waia..ad.*

Wâssêingwe, (*nin*). My face is resplendent, shining, radiant ; p. *waiâ..wed.*

Wâssênangoshka anâng. The star is bright, shining much ; p. *waia..kad.*

Wâssênamawa, (*nin*). I enlighten him ; p. *waia..wad.*

Wâssenamowin. Light.

Wâsseshkawa, (*nin*). I make some *an.* obj. light, I enlighten some person, I cause him to be enlightened ; p. *waia..wad.*

Wâssesi gisiss. The sun is brilliant ; p. *waiassesid.*

Wâssêtchigan. Window ; pl.-*an.*

Wâssêtchiganâbik. Window-glass, pane; pl.-*on.*
Wâssétchiganâtig. Window-frame, sash; shutter; pl.-*on.*
Wâssétchigan-pigiw. Putty, (window-pitch.)
Wâssidjiwan. There is a strong foaming current in a river; p. *waia..ang.*
Wâssikogamissin. The water is calm like a mirror; p. *waia..ing.*
Wâssikogide, or -*magad.* It shines, (rotten wood); p. *waia..deg,* or-*magak.*
Wâssikwâbikaan, (nin). I make it shine, I make it bright, (metal); p. *waia..ang.*
Wâssikwâbikad. It is shining, it is bright, (metal); p. *waia..kak.*
Wâssikwabikaigan. Any thing to polish metal with, to make it bright; also, black lead for polishing stoves.
Wâssikwabikawa, (nin). I make it shine, I make it bright, *(an.* obj., *joniia,* silver); p. *waia..wad.*
Wâssikwabikisi. It is shining, bright, (metal, *an.*); p. *waia..sid.*
Wâssikwade, or-*magad,* (pr. *wâssikode.*) It shines, it is polished, (a polished table, etc.); p. *waia..deg,* or-*magak.*
Wâssikwadewaigan, (pr. *wâssikodewaigan.*) Black-lead for polishing stoves.
Wâssikwâdjigan, (*makisin*-). Shoe-brush; pl.-*an.*
Wâssikwâdjige, (nin). I polish, I make shine, I give lustre to s. th.; p. *waia..ged.*
Wâssikwâdon, (nin). I polish it, I make it shine; p. *waia..dod.*
Wâssikwêgaan, (nin). I make it shine, I give it a lustre, (stuff); p. *waia..ang.*
Wâssikwêgad. It has a lustre, (stuff); p. *waia..gak.*
Wâssikwegawa, (nin). I make it shine, I give it a lustre, (stuff, *an.*); p. *waiâ..wad;* imp. *was..ga.*
Wassitâ, (often pronounced *ossita,*) alludes to *grief, sorrow, affliction.* (Examples in some of the following words.)
Wassitâwendam, (nin). I am sad, I am sorrowful, mournful, afflicted; p. *wess..ang.*
Wassitâwendamia, (nin). I make him sad, I cause him grief and sorrow, I afflict him; p. *wess..ad.*
Wassitawendamowin. Sadness, grief, affliction, chagrin, sorrow.
Wassitâwendan, (nin). I feel sad against it, I feel antipathy against it; p. *wess..ang.*
Wassitâwenima, (nin). I feel sad against him, I have antipathy against him; p. *wess..mad.*
Wassitâwidee, (nin). My heart is afflicted, is sorrowful; p. *wess..ed.*
Wassitâwideewin. Sorrow or affliction of heart.
Wassitâwitagos, (nin). I speak in a manner as to cause sorrow and affliction, I am heard with sadness, with grief; p. *wess..sid.*
Wassitâwitawa, (nin). I listen to him with grief and sorrow; p. *wes..wad.*
Wâsswa, (nin). I am spearing

fish at night by the light of a torch ; p. *waiâsswad.*

Wâsswâgan. Torch, flambeau ; pl.-*an.*

Wasswâganak. Torch-stick, a stick or pole to fasten a torch to one end of it ; pl.-*on.*

Watab. The root of small trees of the fir-kind or pine-kind, used to sew a bark-canoe with.

Watabimakak. Basket.

Watapin. A small eatable root ; pl.-*ig.*

Wâtebaga, or-*magad.* The leaves of the trees become yellow, (in the fall of the year) ; p. *waia..gag,* or-*magak.*

Watig. S. *Atig.*

Wâtikwaamawa, (*nin*). I nod him, as a sign of affirmation or approbation ; also, I beckon him, I wink him, I make him a sign to come to me ; p. *waia wad.*

Wâtikwaige, (*nin*). I nod, I beckon, I wink ; p. *waia..ged.*

Watikwan, etc. S. *Wadikwan,* etc.

Wawabijagakwaigan. S. *Wassakwaigan.*

Wawâbigonodji. Mouse ; pl.-*iag.*

Wawabishkabide, (*nin*). I have white teeth ; p. *wew..ded.*

Wawagaami, (*nin*). I walk with my toes turned inside ; p. *wew ..mid.* — S. *Jajashagaami.*

Wawaiba, adv. (the frequentative of *waiba.*) Soon one after another, in quick succession. — *Wawaiba ginibowog nossiban, ningiban gaie ;* my father and my mother died soon one after another.

Wâwan. Egg ; pl.-*on. Wâwanons.* Small egg. *Wawanosk.* Spoiled egg.

Wawânendam, (*nin*). I am embarrassed in my thoughts, I don't know what to think ; p. *wew..ang.*

Wawânendamia, (*nin*). I cause him to be embarrassed in his thoughts, I embarrass him ; p. *wew..ad.*

Wawangawisi. S. *Wangawisi.*

Wawâni-dodam, (*nin*). I am at a loss to do s. th. ; p. *wew..ang.*

Wawanima, (*nin*). I embarrass him wtih my words, he cannot answer, I silence him ; p. *wew ..mad.*

Wawânimotawa, (*nin*). I beg his aid or assistance, I embarrass him by my request ; p. *wew..wad.*

Wawânis, (*nin*). I am in want of..., I am at lost for..., I want badly s. th. ; p. *wew..sid.*

Wâwan onagaawang. Shell of an egg.

Wâwâshkeshi. Deer ; pl.-*wog.*

Wâwâshkeshiwaiân. Deerskin ; pl.-*ag.*

Wâwâshkeshiwano. Tail of a deer.

Wâwâshkeshiwigan. Bone of a deer ; pl.-*an.*

Wawatessi. Glow-worm ; pl.-*wog.*

Wawéiendam, (*nin*). I think it is so ; p. *wew..ang.*

Wawejaaton nin tchimân, (*nin*). I mend and fix my canoe ; p. *wew..nod.*

Wawéji, (*nin*). I dress elegantly, I adorn myself; I paint my face ; p. *wewejiod.*

Wawéjia, (*nin*). I dress and adorn him well, nicely ; p. *wew..ad.*

Wawêjikama, (*nin*). I take s. th.

without permission; p. *wew..mad.*

Wawejinige, (*nin*). I use ornaments, I adorn myself; I paint myself; p. *wew..ged.*

Wawejindawa, (*nin*). I prepare and adorn myself for him, (to receive or meet him, etc.); p. *wew..wad.*

Wawéjissiton, (*nin*). I prepare it, I fix it; I adorn or dress it nicely; p. *wew..tod.*

Wawéjita, (*nin*). I make myself ready, I prepare myself; p. *wew..tad.*

Wawéjitawin. Preparing, getting ready.

Wawejiton, (*nin*). S. *Wawejissiton.*

Wawekwadan, (*nin*). I fix, I repair it, sewing; p. *wew..ang.*

Wawekana, (*nin*). I fix some *an.* obj. sewing; p. *wew..nad.*

Wawekwâss, (*nin*). I fix or repair sewing; p. *wew..sod.*

Wawénab, (*nin*). I sit down; p. *wewenabid.*

Wawénabama,* (*nin*). I choose him amongst many others, I select him; p. *wew..mad.*

Wawénabandan, (*nin*). I choose it amongst many other objects, I select it, I pick it out; p. *wew..ang.*

Wawenabandamomin. Selection, choice amongst many objects; election.

Wawenadamoton mikana, (*nin*). I repair a road or trail; p. *wew..tod.*

Wawênadan, (*nin*). I settle it, determine it; p. *wew..ang.*

* NOTE. This and some of the following verbs are rather *frequentative;* the *simple* verbs occur under *Onabama*, etc.

Wawenapidamawa wiwaj, (*nin*). I fix better his pack, I tie it over again, I tie it well; p. *wew..wad.*

Wawenapidon, (*nin*). I bind or tie it again, I tie it well; p. *wew..dod.*

Wawenapina, (*nin*). I tie him over again, I tie him well, (a child, etc.); p. *wew..nad;* imp. *wawenapij.*

Wawenendam, (*nin*). I reflect, consider; choose; p. *wew..ang.*

Wawenendam, (*nin*). I think it over again, I reflect upon it; p. *wew..ang.*

Wawépina, (*nin*). I put him his clothes on, I dress him; p. *wew..nad;* imp. *wawepij.*

Wawêpis, (*nin*). I put my clothes on; p. *wewepisod.*

Wa-widiged. A person that intends to get married, bridegroom; bride; pl.*-jig.*

Wawiiadendagos, (*nin*). I am considered droll, curious, I am droll; p. *wew..sid.*

Wawiiadendagwad, (*nin*). It is droll, curious, considered droll; p. *wew..wak.*

Wawiiadendân, (*nin*). I think it curious or droll; p. *wew..ang.*

Wawiiadenima, (*nin*). I think him curious, droll, (a person or some other *an.* obj.); p. *wew..mad.*

Wawiiadis, (*nin*). I wrong myself, I cause to myself s. th. disagreeable; p. *wew..sid.*

Wâwiiag gego. Several things, all kinds of things.

Wâwiiagim, (*nin*). I say what I ought not to say, it is not my business to say that; p. *waiaw mod.*

Wâwiiagis, (nin). I do (or say) what is not my business; p. *waiaw..sid.*

Wawiiaj, adv. Curiously. *Wawiiaj nind ijiwebis,* I act or do curiously.

Wawiiajitagos, (nin). I speak curiously, I make drolleries in speaking, jokes; p. *wew..sid.*

Wawiiatan. The city of Detroit.

Wawiiatanong. In or at Detroit, to or from Detroit.

Wawiiawama. Wawiiawe, etc. *Ot.* S. *Mamoiawama. Mamoiawe,* etc.

Wawiiebiigan. Compass, the instrument with which circles are drawn; pl.*-an.*

Wâwiiéia, or*-magad.* It is round or *circular;* p. *waiâwiiéiag,* or*-magak.*

Wâwiiékodân, (nin). I cut it round, in a circular or semicircular form; p. *waiaw..ang.*

Wâwiiékona, (nin). I cut some *an.* obj. in a circular or semicircular form; p. *waia..nad.*— *Pakwejigan nin wawiiekona;* I cut a piece of bread round.

Wawiiemigan. A kind of seashell; pl.*-ag.*

Wâwiiêminagad. It is round or *globular;* p. *waiaw..gak.*

Wâwiieminagisi mishimin. The apple is round.

Wâwiiendagan. S. *Makakossag.*

Wâwiiês, (nin). I am round, of a round shape; p. *waiâwiiêsid.*

Wâwiieton, (nin). I make it round; p. *waia..tod.*

Wâwij, adv. S. *Memindage.*

Wawijendam, (nin). I rejoice, I am glad, I am proud of joy; p. *wew..ang.*

Wawijendamia, (nin). I make him rejoice; *wew..ad.*

Wawijendamowin. Joy, rejoicing.

Wawijenian, (nin). S. *Wawijendam.*

Wawijenima, (nin). I praise him *in thoughts;* p. *wew..mad.*

Wawijia, (nin). I please him, I say what pleases him; p. *wewijiad.*

Wawijim, (nin). I glory, I boast, I praise myself; p. *wew..od.*

Wawijindiwin. Praise, flattery.

Wawika, adv. (the frequentative of *wika*). Seldom, very seldom, once in a long time.

Wawikawind. An Indian to whom a woman is given to marry her, nolens volens; pl. *-jig.*— S. *Wiwikawa.*

Wâwikweia, or*-magad.* There is a corner; p. *waiâ..iag,* or*-magak.*

Wâwina, (nin). I name him often, I call upon his name, I mention him frequently; p. *waiâwinad;* imp. *wawij.*— *Wina.*

Wawinâke, (nin). I am a good archer or bowman; p. *wew..ked.*

Wawinawea, (nin). I approve him; p. *waia..ad.*

Wâwindaganes, (nin). I am much named, I am renowned, celebrated, famous; p. *waia..sid.*

Wawindaganesiwin. Renown, fame, celebrity.

Wâwindamadimin, (nin). We promise each other; p. *waiâw..didjig.*

Wâwindamadiwin. Mutual promise, or promise made to several persons ; pl.-*an.*

Wawinge, adv. (often pronounced, *Owinge,*) Well, perfectly, thouroughly, exactly, entirely. fully, precisely.

Wawingeikan, (*nin*). I do it well ; p. *wew..ang.*

Wawinges, (*nin*). I do s. th. to perfection, I am skilful, precise, able, I am a master, I am perfect in doing or saying s. th. ; p. *wew..sid.*

Wawingesiwin. Precision in working or speaking, skill, skilfulness, ability, perfection, exactness.

Wawingetchige, (*nin*). I act with precision, exactness, skill ; p. *wew..ged.*

Wawingeton, (*nin*). I fix it well, I make it sure, I arrange it exactly ; p. *wew..tod.*

Wawinikâb, (*nin*). I have hollow eyes ; p. *wen..bid.*

Wâwon, (*nin*). I howl, (like a dog or wolf) ; p. *waiawonod.*

Wâwonowin. Repeated howling. — S. *Wonowin.*

Webabog, (*nin*). I am carried away by the current of a river ; p. *waieb..god.*

Wébagodjin, (*nin*). S. *Pakiteshin. Gawisse.*

Wébâsh, (*nin*). I am carried away by the wind ; p. *waiébashid.*

Wébâssin. It is carried away by the wind ; p. *waié..ing.*

Wébendam, (*nin*). I made up my mind, I am resolved ; p. *waiê.. ang.*

Webi–, Ot. S. *Mâdji–.*

Webigaan, (*nin*). I cut off with an *axe,* what is spoiled or rotten ; p. *waiê..ang.*

Wêbigawa, (*nin*). I cut off with an axe, from some *an.* obj., what is spoiled or rotten ; p. *waie..wad.*

Wêbijan, (*nin*). I cut off with a *knife,* what is spoiled or rotten ; p. *waiebijang.*

Wébijwa, (*nin*). I cut off with a knife, from some *an.* obj., what is spoiled or rotten ; p. *waié..wad ;* imp. *webijwi.*

Wêbina, (*nin*). I throw him away, I reject him, abandon him ; p. *waiébinad.*

Wébinamagowini - jawendagosiwin. Indulgence ; pl.-*an.*

Wébinamawa, (*nin*). I throw away s. th. belonging or relating to him ; also, I forgive him, I pardon him ; p. *waiê..wad.*

Wébinan, (*nin*). I throw it away, I cast it off ; I abandon it, reject it ; I wean myself of a habit or practice ; p. *waiébinang.*

Webinan nind anamiewin, (*nin*). I apostatize, (I reject my religion).

Wêbinidimin, (*nin*). We reject or abandon each other, we separate ; p. *waie..didjig.*

Webinidiwi-masinaigan, or *webinidiwi-ojibiigan.* Bill of divorce ; pl.-*an.*

Webinidiwin. Separation (of persons that lived together), mutual rejection ; divorce.

Wébinigan. Abandoned or rejected person ; or any other *an.* obj. thrown away, rejected or abandoned ; pl.-*ag.*

Wébinigâs, (*nin*). I am rejected,

cast off, abandoned ; p. *waie.. sod.*

Wébinige, (*nin*). I throw away, I reject; also, I confess my sins ; p. *waie..ged*, or, *tipâdjindiso.*

Wébinigewin. The act of throwing away ; also, confession, or, *tipâdjindisowin.*

Wébishima, (*nin*). I throw him down to the ground ; p. *waié.. mad.*

Wébissiton, (*nin*). I make it fall down, or fall off; p. *waie..tod.*

Wedâbâniked. He that makes a sleigh, a cart, a wagon, etc., cartwright ; pl.*-jig.*

Wedâbiad bebejigoganjin. He that makes horses draw, coachman, cartman, driver ; pl.*-jig beb....*

Wedâbiad pijikiwan. He that makes oxen draw, oxen-driver ; pl.*-jig pij....*

Wedâked. He that steers, steersman, pilot ; pl.*-jig.*

Wedapinang anamiewin. He that takes religion, a convert ; pl.*-ig ana....*

Wedapinang jawendagosiwin. He that takes in communion, communicant ; pl.*-ig*

Wédi, adv. There.

Wedi nakekana, adv. On that side of the road.

Wégin. Skin, hide. This word is never used alone ; it always occurs attached to the name of some *large* quadruped, and signifies its hide or skin ; as : *Pijikiwegin*, oxhide, cowhide ; buffalo-robe. *Monswegin*, the hide of a moose. *Omaskkoswegin*, the hide or skin of a stag or hind. Pl.*-on*. — S. *Waiân.*

Wegingin. Like one's own mother. — *Wegingin nind iji sâgia aw ikwe ;* I love that woman like my own mother.

Wégonen ? pron. What ? how ?

Wegonen wendji-.... ? Why ? — *Wegonen wendji-ikkitoian iw ?* Why dost thou say that ?

Wêgotogwen. I don't know what. - *Wegotogwen ged-ikkitogwen ;* I don't know what he will say.

Wegotogwen wendji-.... I don't know why.— *Wegotogwen wendji - nishkâdisigwen ;* I don't know why he is angry.

Wegotogwenish. Any *an.* object a little respected, considered as a trifle; pl.*-ag.* — *Wegotogwenishing nin dodawa ;* I trifle with him, I make light of him, I respect him little.

Wegotogwenish. Any *in.* object little considered, trifle ; pl.*-an.* — *Wegotogwenishing nin dodan ;* I treat it as a trifle, as a worthless thing.

Wegwâgi ! interj. Lo ! see ! *Wegwâgi badâssamosse !* See, he is coming !

Wegwissimind, (pron. *wegossimind*). He that is a son, a son ; pl.*-jig.*

Weiejingeshkid. He that is cheating habitually, cheater, swindler, embezzler ; deceiver, impostor, seducer ; pl.*-jig.*

Weiekwaiassinog ; p. *neg.* That which has no end, endless, eternal.

Wejawashkwasigwag mashkiki. Green medicine, vitriol.

Wejina, (*nin*). I paint some *an.* obj. ; p. *waiejinad.*

Wejinan, (*nin*). I paint it; p. *waie..ang.*
Wejinigan. Paint; pl.-*an.*
Wejinige, (*nin*). I paint; p. *waiejiniged.*
Wembissitchigasossig pakwejigan. Unleavened bread; (F. azyme).
Wemigid. He that has the scab, scabious, mangy; leper; pl.-*jig.*
Wémitigoji. Frenchman; Canadian; pl.-*wok.*
Wémitigoji-anamia, (*nin*). I pray French, that is, I profess the Roman Catholic religion; p. *waiem..ad.*
Wêmitigoji - anamiewigamig. French church, that is, a Catholic church; pl.-*on.*
Wémitigoji - anamiewin. The Roman Catholic religion. — The Indians call it so from the circumstance that the Canadians, whom they saw first and whom they call *Wemitigojiwok*, (Frenchmen), are all Catholics with very rare exceptions.
Wemitigojikwe. Frenchwoman; pl.-*g.*
Wemitigojikwens. A young French girl; pl.-*ag.*
Wêmitigojim, (*nin*). I speak French; p. *waie..mod.*
Wemitigoji masinaigan. A French book, or letter.
Wemitigogi - mekatewikwanaie. Catholic priest; pl.-*g.*
Wemitigojimowin. French language.
Wemitigojiwaki. France, (land of the French). *Wemitigojiwaking*, in France, to or from France.
Wemitigojiwissin. It is written (or printed) in French; p. *waiem..ing.*
Wemitigojiwissitchigade, or-*magad.* It is translated into French; p. *waiem..deg*, or-*magak.*
Wemitigojiwissiton, (*nin*). I translate it into French; p. *waie..top.*
Wenadaigadeg biwâbik. Hammered iron, (not cast iron), wrought iron.
Wenâganiked. A maker of wooden dishes; pl.-*jig.*
Wéndad. It is easy; it is cheap, low; p. *waiéndak.*
Wéndeg nibi. Boiling water.
Wendis, (*nin*). I sell cheap; p. *waiéndisid.*
Wêndisi. It is cheap, low, (any *an.* obj.); p. *waiendisid.*— *Wendisi kokosh, wendisiwog opinig;* pork is cheap, potatoes are cheap.
Wendji–, the *Change* of *ondji;* which see.
Wendji-mokaang. Where the sun rises, east, orient.
Wendjita! Wendjita! Very well! thanks! thank you!
Wendjita. Properly, proper, simple. — *Wendjita anamiegijigad*, properly Sunday, (not a holiday).
Wéndwe, (*nin*). S. *Wendis.*
Weni, pron. *Ot.* Who?
Wéniban! Gone! disappeared! — *Anindi nin mokomân gaateg oma?* - *Weniban! Kawin nin mikansin.* Where is my knife that was here? - It is gone! I cannot find it.
Wênibik, adv. A short time, a moment.
Wenidjânissingid. Like one's

own child or children. — *Wenidjânissingin nind iji sagia;* I love him like my own child. *Wenidjânissingin ki dodagonan Kije-Manito;* God treats us like his own children.

Wenijishid. S. *Onijish.*

Wenijishid-Manito. Holy Ghost.

Wenijishing. S. *Onijishin.*

Wénipaj, or *wênipanaj,* adv. Easily, without much labor or cost; for nothing.

Wénipanad. It is easy; it is cheap; p. *waiê..nak.*

Wênipanendam, (*nin*). I think s. th. is easy; p. *waié..ang.* — *Osâm ki wenipanendam iko;* thou thinkest all things to be easy.

Wénipanenima, (*nin*). I think it is cheap, I find it cheap, (*an.* obj.); p. *waiê..mad.*

Wénipanis, (*nin*). I am cheap; p. *waié..sid.*

Wenish! Ot. (abridged from *weni dash?*) Who?

Weossimind. He that is a father, a father; pl.*-jig.*

Wêossingin. Like one's own father. — *Weossingin babamitaw aw inini;* be obedient to that man like to thy own father.

Wesâwag degwandaming. The yellow thing that is eaten with other things, mustard.

Weshki-anamiad. He that prays of late, a new convert to religion, a new Christian, a neophyte; pl.*-jig.*

Weshkiging mitigons. Pound shoot. (The same as *oshkigin.*)

Weshkinigid. He that is born of late, a young person, a young man, a lad, a youth; or a young woman, a maid, a grown girl. Pl. *weshkinigidjig,* young folks.

Weshki-tibikak. In the beginning of the night.

Wéshowâb, (*nin*). I keep prepared, (for death, etc.); p. *waiéshowabid.*

Wéshowinidis, (*nin*). I prepare myself; p. *waié..sod.*

Wêshowissiton, (*nin*). I prepare it; p. *waié..tod.*

Wéshowita, (*nin*). S. *Weshowinidis.*

Wessean. There are trees blown down by the wind; p. *waiesseang.*

Wêwe. Goose; pl. *weweg.*

Wewêbanaban, or *wewebanabagan.* Implement necessary for fishing with a hook.

Wewébanabanak. The stick or rod on which the line with the fishing hook is fastened; pl.*-on.*

Wêwêbanabi, (*nin*). I am fishing with a hook; p. *waie..bid.*

Wéwêbanoweni animosh. The dog wags his tail; p. *waiew..nid.*

Wêwébikwen, (*nin*). I wag my head to signify, *no!* p. *waiew nid.*

Wewebikwetawa, (*nin*). I wag my head to him, in sign of negation; p. *waiew..wad.*

Wewebina, (*nin*). I swing him, I rock him on a rocking-chair; p. *waie..nad;* imp. *wewebij.*

Wewebis, (*nin*). I swing or rock myself; p. *waie..sod.*

Wewebison. A swing; pl.*-an.*

Wewebisoni-apabiwin. Rocking-chair; pl.*-an.*

Wewendjigano. Great horned owl; pl.-*g.*

Weweni, adv. Well, right, just, exactly, diligently.

Wewepotawa, (*nin*). *Ot.* S. *Pakitewa.*

Wewesseidis, (*nin*). I move the air with a fan to cool myself, I fan myself; p. *waie..sod.*

Wewesseigan, or *wewesseowin.* Fan; pl.-*an.*

Wewesseige, (*nin*). I move the air with a fan, I fan; p. *waie..ged.*

Wewesséwa, (*nin*). I fan him, I cool him with a fan; p. *waie wad;* imp. *wewessé.*

Wewib, adv. Immediately, quickly, soon.

Wewibendam, (*nin*). I am in a hurry to return home; p. *waie ..ang.*

Wewibendamowin. Hurry to return home.

Wewibia, (*nin*) or, *nin wewibima.* I hurry him; p. *waiewibiad.*

Wewibiidis, (*nin*). I hurry myself, I make haste; p. *waie..sod.*

Wewibingangwe. Teal, a kind of wild duck; (F. sarcelle); pl.-*g.*

Wewibis, (*nin*). I am in a hurry; p. *waiewibisid.*

Wewibishka, (*nin*). I make haste to go somewhere, or to return home, (travelling by land or by water); p. *waie..kad.*

Wewibisiwin. Hurry, haste.

Wewibita, (*nin*). I make haste in *doing* s. th; p. *waie..tad.*

Wewibitawin. Hurry or haste in *doing* s. th.

Wewigiwâmid. He who owes a house, the proprietor of a house, or of the house, the landlord; pl.-*jig.*

Wi-. Particle denoting will, desire, intention, resolution; p. *wa-.* — *Nind ija,* I go; *nin wi-ija,* I intend to go. *Wa-ijad,* he who intends to go; (L. iturus).

Wibéma, (*nin*). I sleep with him; p. *wabemad.* (*Wibemâgan,* bed-fellow.)

Wibendimin, (*nin*). We sleep together in the same bed; p. *wab..didjig.*

Wibid. His tooth; pl.-*an.* — *Nibid, kibid,* my tooth, thy tooth; pl.-*an.*

Wibidâma. Tooth; pl.-*n.* — *Sanagad wibidaman âkosing;* it is hard (painful) to have tooth-ache.

Wibidâ-mashkiki. Medicine for tooth-ache, anodyne drops for tooth-ache.

Wibidekadjigan. Lace, (F. dentelle).

Wibona, (*nin*). I make him narrower, I straighten him, (*an.* obj.); p. *wabonad.*

Wibonan, (*nin*). I make it narrower, (*in.* obj.); p. *wab..ang.*

Wibwamagad. It is made narrower, it is straightened; p. *wab..gak.*

Wid, widj, widji, in compositions, signifies *association, accompanying, co-operation.* (Examples in some of the following words.)

Widabima, (*nin*). I am sitting with him, or by his side; p. *wadabimad.*

Widakamigisima, (*nin*). I play

or amuse myself together with him; p. *wad..mad.*

Widam. At the end of verbs, alludes to *speaking;* as: *Nind inâpinéwidam,* I use bad language, offensive words, in a certain manner. — *Nind ajidewidam,* I gainsay. *Nind anwewidam,* I speak in such a place.

Wi-débwe, (nin). I will say the truth, that is, I persist upon what I say, I obstinately maintain it, I urge it, I want to have it believed, or done; p. *wa-debwed.*

Widige, (nin). I cohabit, I live together in the same room with another, or with others; also, I am married; p. *wadiged.*

Widigema, (nin). I live with her (him) in the same room; also, I am married to her, (him); p. *wad..mad.*

Widigêmâgan. Cohabitant, a person that lives together with another, or with others; also, husband, wife.— This word is always preceded by a possessive pronoun, *nin widigêmagan, ki widigémagan, o widigémaganan,* etc. — S. *Niwish.*

Widigendaa, (nin). I join him (her) in marriage with another person, I marry him (her) to some person; p. *wad..ad.*

Widigendimin, (nin). We cohabit, we live together in the same room; we are married together; p. *wad..didjig.*

Widigendiwin. Cohabitation; marriage, wedding; married state. —*Anamie-widigendiwin,* Christian marriage.

Widigendiwini-titibinindjipison. Wedding-ring, nuptial-ring; pl.-*an.*

Widigendiwini-wikondiwin. Wedding-feast, nuptials; pl.-*an.*

Widigewin. Cohabitation, or marriage, in regard to *one* of the parties; (in regard to *both* parties it is *widigendiwin*). *Minwendagwad nin widigewin;* my cohabitation (or marriage) is agreeable. *Minwendagwad nin widigendiwininân;* our marriage is agreeable.

Widigewini-agwiwin, or, *widigendiwini-agwiwin,* or, *widigendiwini - bâbisikawâgan.* Wedding-garment, nuptial robe; pl.-*an.*

Widj' or *widji–.* Is the third person of *nidj'* or *nidji–;* which see. — (*Widj ikwewan,* a woman like herself. *Widj' anokitagewininiwan,* his fellow-servant. *Widji-kwiwisensan,* his fellow-boy.)

Widjaiawa, (nin). I have him with me, or, I am with him; p. *wad..wad.*

Widjanimisima, (nin). I suffer with him; p. *wad..mad.*

Widj'anishinaben. His fellow-man, his neighbor.

Widjanokima, (nin). I work with him; p. *wad..mad.*

Widjanokimagan. Fellow-laborer; pl.-*ag.* — This word is always preceded by a possessive pronoun; as: *Nin widjanokimagan,* my fellow-laborer; *o widjanokimaganan,* his fellow-laborer, etc.

Widjibibonishima, (nin). I spend the winter with him, I winter with him; p. *wad..mad.* (*Widjibibonishimagan*, fellow-winterer.)

Widjibima, (*nin*). I drink together with him; p. *wad..mad.* (*Widjibimagan*, compotator.)

Widji-bimadisin. His fellow-liver, his neighbor.

Widjibindimin, (*nin*). We are drinking together; p. *wad..didjig.*

Widjibindiwin. Compotation.

Widjidakiwema, (*nin*). I live with him (her) in the same country or place; he is my countryman, (she is my countrywoman), I am a native of the same country or place as he (she) is; p. *wad..mad.* (*Widjidakiwemagan*, countryman; fellow-citizen.)

Widjideêma, (*nin*). I have the same heart with him, I love him from all my heart, and he loves me, we have but one heart together; p. *wad..mad.*

Widjidonama, (*nin*). I accompany him with my mouth, I converse with him; p. *wad..mad.*

Widjigabawitawa, (*nin*). I am standing with him, or by his side; p. *wad..wad.*

Widjigwabaamawa, (*nin*). I dip my hand in the same vessel with him, to draw s. th. out of it; p. *wad..wad.*

Widjiiwe, (*nin*). I accompany, I keep company; p. *wâdjiiwed.*

Widjiiwemagad. It accompanies, it goes with....; p. *wad..gak.*

Widjiiwewin. Keeping company, accompaniment.

Widj'ijinikasoma, (*nin*). I have the same name as he; he is my namesake, (my patron-saint); p. *wad..mad.*

Widjikiwéian. His brother; his comrade. — S. *Nidjikiwé.*

Widjindaa, (*nin*). I send him along with somebody, I make him go with somebody; p. *wad..ad.*

Widjindan, (*nin*). I make it come with me, I come with it; p. *wad..ang.* — *Jesus ta-bi-dagwishin ishpiming anakwadong, o ga-bi-widjindan gashkiewisiwin, kitchi kitchitwawisiwin gaie;* Jesus shall come in the clouds of heaven with power and great glory.

Widjindimagad. It goes together, it has communication with s. th., it agrees well; p. *wad..gak.*

Widjindimin, (*nin*). We go together somewhere; we help or assist each other; we are in company together; p. *wad..didjig.*

Widjindinowagan. Companion; pl.-*og.* — There is always a possessive pronoun before this word; as: *Nin widjindinowagan*, my companion, etc.

Widjindiwin. Mutual accompaniment.

Widjinibishima, (*nin*). I spend the summer with him; p. *wad..mad.* — (*Widjinibishimagan*, fellow-summerer. S. *Widjanokimagan.*)

Widjiniboma, (*nin*). I die with him; p. *wad..mad.* — (*Widjinibomagan.*)

Widjipasigwima, (*nin*). I rise up with him; p. *wad..mad.*

Widjiwa, (*nin*). I am with him, I accompany him, I go with him somewhere; or he goes with me, I take him along with me; p. *wadjiwâd.*

Widjiwagan. Companion, associate, partner; husband; wife; comrade; pl.-*ag.* — This word is always preceded by a possessive pronoun, as: *Nin widjiwagan, o widjiwaganan,* etc.

Widjiwikongema, (*nin*). I feast together with him; p. *wad..mad.*

Widjogima, (*nin*). I have the same mother as he has; p. *wad..mad.*

Widjogindiwin, (*nin*). We have all of us the same mother; p. *wad..didjig.*

Widjonwatoma, (*nin*). I rejoice with him; p. *wad..mad.*

Widjoossewa, (*nin*). I have the same father as he has; p. *wad..mad.*

Widjoossendimin, (*nin*). We have the same father, all of us; p. *wad..didjig.*

Widokage, (*nin*). I help somebody, I take party; p. *wad..ged.*

Widokagewin. Help, single help, (not mutual).

Widokamadimin, (*nin*). We help each other; we are in company; p. *wad..didjig.*

Widokamawa, (*nin*). S. *Widokawa.*

Widokâs, (*nin*). I help, I keep company, I do or say as others do; p. *wad..sod.*

Widokawa, (*nin*). I help him; assist him. I take his party; p. *wad..wad.*

Widokawenima, (*nin*). I assist his thoughts, his mind; p. *wad..mad.* — *Debendjiged ki widokawinimigonan;* the Lord assists our mind (with his grace).

Widokodadimin, (*nin*). We help each other, we are associated, allied; p. *wad..didjig.*

Widokodadiwin. Mutual help, association, alliance.—*Ketchitwawendagosidjig o widokadadiwiniwa,* the Communion of Saints.

Widopama, (*nin*). I eat with him, at the same table or out of the same plate or dish; p. *wad..mad.*

Widossema, (*nin*). I walk with him; p. *wad..mad.*

Wigimagan. Husband; wife. — There is always a possessive pronoun before this word; as: *Nin wigimagan, ki wigimagan,* etc. (*Widigémagan* is more commonly used for "husband" or "wife," than *wigimagan.*)

Wigiwâm. Lodge; house; pl.-*an.*

Wigob. The bark of a linden-tree; bass-wood; pl.-*in.*

Wigobimij. Large linden-tree; bass-wood; pl.-*in.*

Wigwâss. Birch-tree; pl.-*ag.*

Wigwâss. The bark of a birch-tree, birch-bark; pl.-*an.*

Wigwâssapakwei. Several large pieces of birch-bark sewed together in one long piece, for the construction of a lodge; pl.-*ag.*

Wigwâssika, or-*magad.* There are birch-trees, or, there is birch-bark in abundance; p. *weg..keg,* or-*magak.*

Wigwâssikang. In a place where there are birch-trees.

Wigwâssike, (*nin*). I am taking off the bark from the birch-trees; p. *weg..ked.*
Wigwâssi-makak. Box made of birch-bark, a mawkawk; (C. casseau); pl.-*on.*
Wigwassiwigamig. Lodge of birch-bark; pl.-*on.*
Wigwâss-onâgan. Dish made of birch-bark; pl.-*an.*
Wigwâss-tchimân. Bark-canoe; pl.-*an.*
Wiiagad. It is a pity; p. *waiagak.*
Wiiagassiian. Dust.
Wiiagassiiman. Rags, tatters; trifles.
Wiiagi. Several, of different kinds, of all kinds. — *Wiiagi bineshiiag*, different kind of birds. — *Wiiagi awessiag*, all kinds of beasts.
Wiiagia, (*nin*). I defile him, I injure him; I spoil or damage some *an.* obj.; p. *waia..giad.*
Wiiagiaii, adv. All kinds of things; (L. quodlibet).
Wiiagiidis, (*nin*). I defile, injure, damage myself; p. *waia..sod.*
Wiiagiminan. Different kinds of fruit.
Wiiagishkawa, (*nin*). I defile, stain, pollute him; p. *waia..wad.*
Wiiagishkendagos, (*nin*). I am troublesome, noisy, plaguy; p. *waiag..sid.*
Wiiagishkendagosiwin, troublesomeness, importunity, vexation.
Wiiagiskima, (*nin*). S. *Migoshkasoma.*
Wiiagiton, (*nin*). I defile it, I injure it, I spoil it, damage it; p. *waiagitod.*
Wiiagweweto bineshi. The bird sings, warbles; p. *waia..tod.*
Wiiâs. Meat, his flesh. — *Niiâs, kiiâss, wiiâss*; my, thy, his flesh.
Wiiâssâbo. Water in which meat was boiled, broth.
Wiiâssike, (*nin*). I make meat, that is, I procure meat by hunting, and preserve it by drying and smoking; p. *waiâssiked.*
Wiiâssima. Flesh, in general, without regard to a person or animal.
Wiiâssiw, (*nin*). I am flesh; p. *wiiassiwid.*
Wiiassiwiidis, (*nin*). I make myself flesh, I incarnate myself; p. *waias..sod.*
Wiiassiwiidisowin. Incarnation. — *Manito - wiiâssiwiidisowin*, divine Incarnation.
Wiiaw. His body; himself. *Niiaw*, my body; *kiiaw*, thy body.
Wiiaweeian. His namesake. S. *Niiawee.*
Wiiawima. Body.
Wijâma, (*nin*), or *wisâma.* I persuade him to go with me somewhere, I request, invite or excite him to go with me; p. *wajamad.*
Wijigan. Skull. (His skull, *o wijigan.*)
Wijiganikan. Place where there are skulls, Calvary; (F. Calvaire.)
Wijina. Beaver's kidney; pl.-*g.*
Wijinawassema. Roll of tobacco.
Wika, adv. Seldom; late. *Wika go*, very seldom; *ka wika*, or *kawin wika*, never.

Wika nin dagwishin. I tarry, I come late.

Wike. Angelica-root, a medical root; (F. belle-angélique).

Wikobidon, (*nin*). I draw it to me, I pull it, haul it; p. *wak.. dod.*

Wikobina, (*nin*). I draw or pull him to me, I attract him; p. *wak..nad.*

Wikodenima, (*nin*). I wish he would come, I long after him; p. *wak..mad.*

Wikoma, (*nin*). I invite him to a meal, or to a feast; p. *wakomad.*

Wikondiwin. A feast of several persons together; pl.-*an.*

Wikondiwini-agwiwin. Feast-garment.

Wikonge, (*nin*). I make a feast; also, I invite to a feast; p. *wak..ged.*

Wikongewin. Feast; inviting to a feast, invitation.

Wikoshka, (*nin*). It attracts me, it draws me; p. *wakoshkad.*

Wikotawagebina, (*nin*). I pull him by the ear; p. *wak..nad;* imp. *wik..bij.*

Wikwabigina, (*nin*) or, *nin wikwabigibina.* I draw him up to me on a rope, chain, etc.; p. *wak..nad;* imp. *wikwabigin.*

Wikwabiginan, (*nin*) or, *nin wikwabigibidon.* I draw it up to me on a rope, etc.; p. *wak.. ang.*

Wikwâkwaan bonakadjigan, (*nin*). I lift the anchor; p. *wak..ang.*

Wikwam, (*nin*). I draw s. th. in my mouth, sucking; p. *wakwamod.*

Wikwama, (*nin*). I suck him, (her), I draw in my mouth s. th. out of him, (her); p. *wak.. mad.* — *Nin wikwama aw aiakosid inini,* I suck some blood out of this sick man. *Abino dji o wikwaman ogin,* the child sucks its mother, (it draws into his mouth some milk out of its mother).

Wikwandan, (*nin*). I draw it in my mouth, I suck it in; also, I draw it out with the teeth; p. *wak..ang.*

Wikwandjigan. Indian sucking-horn, to suck the blood out, in bleeding a sick person; pl. -*an.*

Wikwandjige, (*nin*). I am sucking out, (especially the blood of a sick person); p. *wak..ged.*

Wikwasoma, (*nin*). I entice him, allure him, I entreat him or urge him to follow me, I try to gain him over; p. *wak..mad.*

Wikwasondimin, (*nin*). We entreat or entice each other to some action or enterprise; p. *wak..didjig.*

Wikwasondiwin. Persuasion, entreating to some action, enticing, allurement.

Wikwasonge, (*nin*). I entice, allure, I try to gain over somebody; *wak..ged.*

Wikwasongewin. Enticing, allurement; (in regard only to the person enticing; *wikwasondiwin,* in regard to the person enticing, and the person enticed.)

Wikwatchi, (*nin*). I try, I endeavor, (especially to go over or through s. th. or to get out of s. th.); p. *wak..od.*

Wikwatchia, (*nin*). I endeavor

to prevail upon him, to gain him, (in any thing, good or evil), I solicit him; p. *wak..ad.*

Wikwatchitamas, (*nin*). I earn or gain s. th.; I deserve, I cause s. th. to myself; p. *wak sod.*

Wikwatchitamasowin. Earning; merit, desert, deserving.

Wikwatchito, (*nin*). I endeavor, I try, I strive, I make efforts; p. *wakwatchitod.*

Wikwatchiton, (*nin*). I try it, I essay it, I endeavor to effect it; p. *wak..tod.*

Wikwatchiwikwandamawa, (*nin*). I try to draw him out s. th. with the teeth, (a thorn, etc.); p. *wak..wad.*

Wikwatchiwina, (*nin*). I endeavor to lead him away, I try to make him go with me; p. *wak..nad.*

Wikwatendam, (*nin*). I try or strive in my thoughts; p. *wak ..ang.*

Wikwatenima, (*nin*). I endeavor to get some *an.* obj.; p. *wak.. mad.*

Wikwatendan, (*nin*). I endeavor to get it, to obtain it; p. *wak.. ang.*

Wikwed. Bay; (F. anse). *Wikwedong,* in a bay.

Wikwéia, or-*magad.* It forms a bay, there is a bay; p. *wak.. iag,* or-*magak.*

Wikwekamigag aki. In a corner of the earth.

Wikwessagag. In a corner of the room.

Wikwikwassimwe, (*nin*). I am calling a dog; p. *wak..wed.*

Wikwingodee, (*nin*). My heart is beating much; p. *wak..ed.*

Wimbabika, or-*magad.* There is a hollow in a rock, cave, cavern, grotto; p. *wam..kag,* or-*magak.*

Wimbabikaan ajibik, (*nin*). I make a hollow in a rock; p. *wam..ang.*

Wimbagodjin mikwam. The ice on the ground is hollow, (there is no water under it); p. *wam ..ing.*

Wimbakamiga, or-*magad.* There is a hollow or opening in the ground; p. *wam..gag,* or-*magak.*

Wimbashk. (Hollow-herb), reed; (F. roseau); pl.-*on.*

Wimbashkad. It is hollow, (herb, plant); p. *wam..kak.*

Wimbigaan mitig, (*nin*). I make a hole in a piece of wood, a mortise; p. *wam..ang.*

Wimbinikisi mitig. The tree is hollow; p. *wam..sid.*

Wimbissagashk. S. *Pipigwewanashk.*

Wimbwewe, or-*magad.* It gives a hollow sound; p. *wam..weg,* or-*magak.*

Wîn. Marrow; (in the bones of the body), pith.

Win, pron. He, she. *Nin win,* I for my part.

Win, or *wini.* In compositions, signifies *unclean, impure.*

Wina, (*nin*). I name him, I pronounce his name; p. *wanad;* imp. *wij.*

Winab, (*nin*). I am in dirt, in filth, it is dirty where I am, or live; p. *wanabid.*

Winad. It is dirty, filthly; impure; p. *wânak.*

Winâdis, (*nin*). I behave unchastely, my conduct is impure; p. *wan..sid.*

Winâdisiwin. Impure life, unchaste conduct.

Winâdjim, (*nin*). I tell a dirty story, my discourse is filthy, indecent; p. *wan..mod.*

Winâdjimowin. Filthy story, indecent narration or discourse; pl.-*an.*

Winâgami, or-*magad.* It is unclean, dirty, (liquid); p. *wan.. mig*, or-*magak.*

Winange. A kind of vulture with a naked head; pl.-*g.*

Winashâgandibân. The filth of the head.

Winâssag. The paunch of an animal.

Winawa, pron. They.

Windamagen, (*nin*). I announce it, I tell or relate it, I communicate it, I make it known, I publish it, (with words only); p. *wan..ged.*

Windamagewin. Information *given*, telling, announcing, publication, (by words, not by writing), communication; warning.

Windamagowin. Information *received.*

Windamagowis, (*nin*). I receive a supernatural warning or communication; p. *wan..sid.*

Windamagosiwin. Supernatural warning or communication.

Windamawa, (*nin*). I tell him, I announce, communicate, explain, declare it to him; I inform him; I warn him; p. *wan..wad.*

Windamawewis, (*nin*). I understand, I am informed by words or signs; p. *wan..sid.*

Windamawewisiwin. Information; communication, obtained by words or signs.

Windan, (*nin*). I name it, I tell its name; p. *wandang.*

Windibegan. Scull, or his scull, brainpan.

Windigo. Fabulous giant that lives on human flesh; a man that eats human flesh, cannibal; pl.-*g.*

Windigobineshi. Giant's bird, (a blue bird); pl.-*iag.*

Windigokwe. Fabulous giantess living on human flesh; pl.-*g.*

Windigowakon. A large kind of "tripes de roche," or moss, which the Indians eat when they are starving; pl.-*ag.*

Win dowan. One like himself. S. *Dowa.*

Winéndan, (*nin*). I think it is impure; dirty, filthy; p. *wan ..ang.*

Winenima, (*nin*). I think he is impure, or unclean; p. *wan.. mad.*

Winéwis, (*nin*). I am in my monthly flowings, (a female); p. *wanewisid.*

Winewishkote. Impure fire, (the fire of a pagan Indian woman which she is obliged to make out of doors, during her monthly flowings, and where she cooks her meals.)

Winéwisiwin. Monthly flowings of a female, catamenia.

Wingâgamandjige, (*nin*). I like liquor; p. *wen..ged.*

Wingâgami, or-*magad.* It is an excellent liquid; p. *wen..mig*, or-*magak.*

Wingashk. Aromatic herb; pl. *-on.*

Winges, (*nin*). S. the freq. *Wawinges.*

Wingesininapijiki, (*nin*). I milk a cow thoroughly, leaving no milk in her; p. *wan..nad.*

Wingipogosi. It has an excellent taste, (*an.* obj.); p. *wan..sid.*

Wingipogwad. It has an excellent taste, (*in.* obj.); p. *wan..wak.*

Wingogane, (*nin*). S. *Nibashk.*

Wingoganewin. S. *Nibashkiwin.*

Wingosh. Drowsiness, inclination to sleep, sleepiness. *Wingoshan o badagoshkagon;* sleepiness oppresses him, he is overwhelmed with sleep.

Wingwai. S. *Wingosh.*

Winia, (*nin*). I make him dirty; I defile him; p. *waniad.*

Wi-niba, (*nin*). I want to sleep, I am drowsy, sleepy; p. *wanibad.*

Winibassige gisiss. The sun (or moon) has a circle; p. *wani..ged.*

Winidee, (*nin*). I have an unclean, impure heart; p. *wanideed.*

Winideewin. The state of having an impure heart, uncleanness of the heart.

Winidenigome, (*nin*). I have an unclean nose, a sniveling nose; p. *wan..med.*

Winidimagad. It is named often; p. *wan..gak.*

Winidis, (*nin*). I name myself, I call myself so....; p. *wanidisod.*

Winidjishkiwaga, or *-magad.* There is mire; p. *wan..gag,* or *-magak.*

Winidon, (*nin*). I have an unclean mouth; also, I speak dirty words; p. *wanidong.*

Winigan. Marrow-bone, a bone full of marrow; pl.*-an.*

Winigijwe, (*nin*). I speak impurely, unchastely, indecently; p. *wan..wed.*

Winigijwewin. Unchaste, impure speaking, indecent, filthy language.

Winiidis, (*nin*). I make myself unclean, I defile myself; p. *wan..sod.*

Winiigon, (*nin*). It makes me unclean, it defiles me; p. *wan god.*

Winiiwe, (*nin*). I make dirty or unclean somebody; p. *waniiiwed.*

Winikwai. The skin of the skull.

Winima, (*nin*). I speak to him bad impure words; p. *waniwad.*

Winin. Fat, the fat part of meat.

Winin, (*nin*). I am fat; p. *waninod.*

Winindib. His brain. *Ninindib, kinindib.*

Winindibegan. His skull. S. *Windibegan.*

Winingwe, (*nin*). I have a dirty face; p. *wan..wed.*

Winindji, (*nin*). I have dirty hands; p. *wan..id.*

Wininoa, (*nin*). I fatten him; p. *waninoad.*

Wininodjigas, (*nin*). I am fattened; p. *wan..sod.*

Wininwingwe, (*nin*). I have a fat full face; p. *wan..wed.*

Winis, (*nin*). I am dirty, filthy, unclean, sluttish, nasty; indecent, unchaste, impure; p.

wanisid. — *Wanisid manito,* the unclean spirit.

Winishkawa, (*nin*). I make dirty some *an.* obj.; p. *wan..wad.*

Winisik. Wild cherry-tree; pl. *-an.*

Winisikensibag. A certain leaf used for tea and for medicine; pl.*-on.*

Winisiss. His hair of the head; pl.*-an.* — *Ninisiss,* my hair; *kinisiss,* thy hair; etc.

Winisiwin. Uncleanness, dirtiness, sluttishness; impurity, unchastity.

Winiskigomanan. His snot.

Winissaga, or*-magad.* The floor is dirty; p. *wanissagag,* or*-magak.*

Winissagisi nabagissag. The board is dirty; p. *wan..sid.*

Winissibag. A kind of Indian tea, wintergreen; pl.*-on.*

Winissimin. A kind of small red berry, the fruit of wintergreen; pl.*-an.*

Winitam. He now, now he in his turn. S. *Ninitam.*

Winitamawa. They now in their turn. — *Winitamawa ta-manissewok,* let them now chop in their turn.

Winiwi paganens. The hazelnut begins to ripen; p. *waniwid.*

Winjide. Soot, (in a chimney or stove-pipe).

Winjide, or*-magad.* There is soot, or it is sooty; (a chimney or stove-pipe); p. *wandjiged,* or*-magak.*

Winomasoma, (*nin*). I speak to or of him impurely, unchastely; p. *wan..mad.*

Wins, (*nin*). I am called; p. *wansod.*

Winsop. Gall, his gall. — *Ninsop,* my gall; *kinsop,* thy gall. — S. *Osawâbân.*

Wish. Lodge of a beaver or musk-rat; pl.*-an.*

Wishagomagos, (*nin*). I smell bad from much perspiration; p. *wash..sid.*

Wishagoningwi, (*nin*). I smell bad from perspiration in the arm-pit; p. *wash..wid.*

Wishagwagami. The liquid swells the sweat; p. *wash..mig.*

Wishdanakima, (*nin*) or, *nin wishdanakiwema.* I inhabit the same country or the same place with him; p. *wash..mad.*

Wishdanakiwemagan. Cohabitant of the same country or place, fellow-citizen; pl.*-ag.*— That word is always preceded by a possessive pronoun, *nin, ki, o.*

Wishkobad. It is sweet; p. *washkobak.*

Wishkobagami, or*-magad.* It is sweet, (liquid); p. *wash..mig,* or*-magak.*

Wishkobimin. Sweet corn; pl.*-ag.*

Wishkobipogosi. It has a sweet taste, (*an.* obj.); p. *wash..sid.*

Wishkobipogwad. It has a sweet taste; p *wash..wak.*

Wishkobisi pakwejigan. The bread is sweet; p. *wash..sid.* — *Washkobisid pakwejigan,* sweet-cake.

Wishkobiwagad wiiâss. The meat is sweet; p. *wash..gak.*

Wishkobiwe makwa, or *wishkobiwagisi.* Bear-meat is sweet; p. *wash..wed.*

Wishkons. Wisconsin. — *Wishkonsing,* in Wisconsin, from or to Wisconsin. (The small lodge of a beaver or muskrat.)

Wishkonsi-sibi. Wisconsin river.

Wishkibina, (*nin*). S. *Tchissibina.*

Wiss. Spleen, milt.

Wissaga, or-*magad.* It is bitter; p. *wassagag,* or-*magak.*

Wissagagami, or-*magad.* It is bitter, (liquid); p. *wass..mig,* or-*magak.*

Wissagaganama, (*nin*). I cause him much suffering by striking him; p. *was..mad.*

Wissagaje, (*nin*). I feel pain on my skin; p. *was..jed.*

Wissagak. Ash-tree; (C. frêne gras); pl.-*wag.*

Wissagakis, (*nin*). I suffer bitterly from burning, I burn; p. *was..sod.*

Wissagakiswa, (*nin*). I make him suffer bitterly by burning him, I burn him; p. *was..wad;* imp. *wissagakiswi.*

Wissagan. It is bitter; p. *wassagang.*

Wissagate, or-*magad.* It is extremely hot weather; p. *was..teg,* or-*magak.*

Wissagatewin. Exceeding heat of weather.

Wissagendam, (*nin*). I suffer bitterly; p. *wass..ang.*

Wissagendamia. I make him suffer much; p. *was..ad.*

Wissagendamiton, (*nin*). I make it suffer severely; p. *was..tod.*

Wissagendamowin. Great bitter suffering.

Wissagendagwad. It is considered very painful, it is very hard, painful, bitter; p. *was..wak.*

Wissagendan, (*nin*). I find it painful, bitter, I think it is painful; p. *was..ang.*

Wissagibag. It is bitter (a leaf or leaves); p. *was..bak.*

Wissagines, (*nin*). S. *Wissagakis.*

Wissagipogosi. It has a bitter taste, (*an.* obj.); p. *was..sid.*

Wissagipogwad. It has a bitter taste, (*in.* obj.); p. *was..wak.*

Wissagishin, (*nin*). I hurt myself in falling, I fall hard; p. *was..ing.*

Wissagisi. It is bitter, (*an.* obj.); p. *wassagisid.* — *Pakwejigan kitchi wissagisi;* the bread is very bitter.

Wissagisiwin. Bitterness.

Wissâkode. Burnt forest, or part of a forest burnt, trees burnt partly or entirely; (C. un brûlé); *Wissâkodeng,* in a burnt forest.

Wissâkodewan. There is a burnt forest, or part of a forest burnt; p. *was..deg,* or-*magak.*

Wissâkodewikwe. Half-breed woman, (or half white and half Indian origin); half-burnt-wood-woman; pl.-*g.*

Wissâkodéwinini. Half-breed man, half whiteman and half Indian, (from a white father and an Indian mother, or vice versa); half-burnt-wood-man; pl.-*wog.* — They call the half-breeds so, because they are half-dark, half-white, like a half-burnt piece of wood, burnt black on one end, and left white on the other.

Wissin, (*nin*). I eat, I am eating; p. *wassinid*.
Wissiniwâgan. Manger, trough; pl.-*an*.
Wissiniwigamig. Eating-house, boarding-house, hotel; pl.-*on*.
Wissiniwin. Eating, boarding; food.
Wissôkan, (*nin*). I keep up company with it, I like it, I frequent it, I use it frequently; p. *wassokang*. — *Osâm o wissokan ishkotéwâbo, siginigéwigamig gaie*; he likes too much ardent liquor, and frequents too much the tavern.
Wissokawa, (*nin*). I keep up company with him, I am frequently with him; I like him; p. *wass..wad*.
Wissoke, (*nin*). I frequent; p. *wassoked*.
Wiw, (*nin*). I have a wife; p. *wâwid*.
Wiwaj. His pack carried on a portage-strap; pl.-*an*.
Wiwajima. Pack; pl.-*n*.
Wiwakwân, and, *wiwokwân*. Hat, cap; bonnet, hood; capuchin; pl.-*an*.
Wiwakwenindibis, (*nin*). S. *Wiwindibebis*.
Wiwakwéwa, (*nin*). I cover his head; p. *waw..wad*; imp. *wiwakwê*.
Wiwan. His wife; or *wiwishan*, which is seldom used.
Wiwegina, (*nin*). I swathe him; p. *waw..nad*.
Wiweginan, (*nin*). I wrap it up; p. *waw..ang*.
Wiwegishin, (*nin*). I am lying wrapped up; p. *waw..ing*.
Wiwikawa, (*nin*). I give him a wife, I let him have a wife; p. *waw..wad*.
Wiwikodadis, (*nin*). I give to myself a wife, I marry; p. *waw ..sod*.
Wiwima. Wife; pl.-*g*.
Wiwima, (*nin*). I take her for a wife, I marry her; p. *wawimad*.
Wiwindan, (*nin*). I guess it; (F. je le devine); p. *waw..ang*.
Wiwishan, (not much used). His wife. *Niwish*, *kiwish*; my wife, thy wife.
Won, (*nin*). S. the frequentative, *Nin wawon*.
Wonongwâm, (*nin*). I howl in sleep, dreaming; p. *wen..ang*.
Wonowin, or *wawonowin*. Howling.